STATE OF NEW YORK
MESSAGES FROM THE
GOVERNORS

STATE OF NEW YORK
MESSAGES FROM THE
GOVERNORS

COMPRISING

Executive Communications to the Legislature
and other Papers Relating to Legislation from the
Organization of the First Colonial Assembly in
1683 to and Including the Year 1906

WITH NOTES

Edited By
CHARLES Z. LINCOLN

VOLUME XI
1683-1906
TABLES AND INDEXES

Published by

Gyan Publishing House
5, Ansari Road
Daryaganj, New Delhi-110002
Phone: 011-47034999, 9811692060
E-mail: books@gyanbooks.com

Distribution Network
gyanbooks.com
India, USA, Canada, UK, Australia, France

ISBN: 978-81-212-9851-3 (Set)
978-81-212-9840-7 (PB)
First Published, 1909

2nd Impression 2023

Printed at: Gyan Press, Delhi.

STATE OF NEW YORK
MESSAGES FROM THE GOVERNORS (VOL. XI)
Edited by: CHARLES Z. LINCOLN

STATE OF NEW YORK

MESSAGES FROM THE GOVERNORS

COMPRISING

Executive Communications to the Legislature and Other
Papers Relating to Legislation from the Organization
of the First Colonial Assembly in 1683 to
and Including the Year 1906

WITH NOTES

EDITED BY CHARLES Z. LINCOLN

PUBLISHED BY AUTHORITY OF THE STATE

VOLUME XI

1683–1906

TABLES AND INDEXES

ALBANY
J. B. LYON COMPANY, STATE PRINTERS
1909

PREFACE.

Volume XI contains a table of cases cited in previous volumes, a table of constitutional references, memorandums on approval of bills, an index of vetoes, and a general index of the entire work. In the messages and other documents persons are often mentioned only by their surnames, but, with a few exceptions, the editor has been able to identify the persons so described and give the full name in the index.

CONTENTS OF VOLUME XI.

Table of cases 1
Table of constitutional references............................... 19
Memorandums on approval of bills............................. 49
Index of vetoes 55
General index 169

[v]

TABLE OF CASES.

Alexander v. Bennett, 60 N. Y. 205, X, 678.

Allen v. Northville, 39 Hun, 240, VI, 120.

Allison v. Welde, 172 N. Y. 421, IX, 512; X, 195, 679.

Amsterdam, Re, 126 N. Y. 158, VII, 1014; VIII, 92.

Anonymous, Re, 1 N. Y. Code Rep. 49, IV, 414.

Answer of Justices to House of Representatives, 148 Mass. 623, VIII, 1048, 1049.

Apgar v. Hayward, 110 N. Y. 225, VII, 1006.

Astor v. Arcade R. Co., 113 N. Y. 93, VIII, 270.

Atkin v. Kansas, 191 U. S. 207, X, 915.

Austin v. Searing, 16 N. Y. 112, X, 680.

Ballston Spa v. Markham, 58 Hun, 238, VI, 120.

Bank of Chenango v. Brown, 26 N. Y. 467, IV, 380.

Bank of Rome v. Rome, 18 N. Y. 38, VI, 503.

Bank for Savings v. Grace, 102 N. Y. 313, VIII, 162, 187.

Barker v. Jackson, 1 Paine, 559, Fed. Cas. No. 989, II, 405.

Bartemeyer v. Iowa, 18 Wall. 129, X, 781.

Barto v. Himrod, 8 N. Y. 483, IV, 475, 551; VI, 437, 484; VII, 217, 250.

Beardsley v. Bridgeport, 53 Conn. 489, IX, 638.

Beecher v. Allen, 5 Barb. 169, IV, 365.

Beekman v. Saratoga & S. R. Co., 3 Paige, 73, VII, 244.

Behan v. People, 17 N. Y. 516, V, 94.

Bell v. Niewahner, 54 App. Div. 530, IX, 680.

Belles v. Burr, 75 Mich. 1, IX, 96.

Benedict v. Goit, 3 Barb. 459, IV, 379.

Berridge v. Shults, 32 Misc. 444, VIII, 1029.

Billings v. New York, 68 N. Y. 413, VI, 520.

Blake v. McClung, 172 U. S. 239, II, 613.

Blauvelt v. Nyack, 9 Hun, 153, IV, 380.

Board of Excise v. Merchant, 103 N. Y. 143, V, 20; VIII, 361.

Bohmer v. Haffen, 161 N. Y. 390, IX, 102.

Boston & A. R. Co., Re, 64 App. Div. 257, aff'd 170 N. Y. 619, VIII, 1029; IX, 744.

Boyd v. Stewart, 30 Abb. N. C. 127, VII, 1125; VIII, 36.

Brady v. Mayor, etc., of New York, 20 N. Y. 312, V, 248.

Brenner, Re, 170 N. Y. 185, IX, 514, X, 195.

Brewster v. Rogers Co., 169 N. Y. 73, X, 458.

Bronson v. Kinzie, 17 Pet. 28, IV, 349.

Budd v. New York, 143 U. S. 517, aff'g. 117 N. Y. 1, 621, VIII, 606.

Buffalo v. Buffalo Gas Co., 81 App. Div. 505, VIII, 1029.

Buffalo Gas Co. v. Volz, 31 Misc. 160, X, 71.

Buffalo & N. Y. C. R. Co. v. Brainard, 9 N. Y. 100, IV, 496.

Bullard v. Van Tassel, 3 How Pr. 402, IV, 365.

Burger, Re, 21 Misc. 370, IX, 704.

Burlington v. Beasley, 94 U. S. 310, VII, 245.

Burnham v. Acton, 35 How. Pr. 48, V, 768.

Bush v. Board of Supervisors, Orange Co., 159 N. Y. 212, X, 264, 909.

Butter v. Penns., 10 How. (U. S.) 416, VII, 379.

Cancellation of Names, Re, 5 Misc. 375, IX, 94.

Carboy, Re, 27 Hun, 82, VIII, 85.

Cashman v. Johnson, 4 Abb. Pr. 256, X, 675.

Cayuga County v. State, 153 N. Y. 279, VII, 87.

Chapman, Re, 168 N. Y. 80, X, 942.

Chenango Bridge Co. v. Paige, 83 N. Y. 178, VIII, 381.

Chicago, etc., R. R. Co. v. Day, 35 Fed. Rep. 879, IX, 501.

Chicago, etc., R. R. Co. v. Minn., 134 U. S. 455, IX, 501.

Chittenden v. Wurster, 152 N. Y. 345, VII, 838.

Chrystal v. New York, 63 App. Div. 93, IX, 451.

Church, Re, 92 N. Y. 1, VI, 676, 822; IX, 510.

Clark v. New York, 111 N. Y. 621, VII, 1006.

Clark v. State, 142 N. Y. 101, X, 915.

Clarke v. Rochester, 28 N. Y. 605, VI, 503.

Close v. Noye, 58 N. Y. S. R. 115; 147 N. Y. 597, IX, 138.

Coe v. Schultz, 47 Barb. 64, V, 702.

Cohen v. Virginia, 6 Wheat. 264, II, 1125.

Cole v. Rose, 65 How. Pr. 520, VII, 1054.

Cole v. State, 102 N. Y. 48, VII, 1048.

Colon v. Lisk, 153 N. Y. 188, X, 456.

Commercial Bank v. Sparrow, 2 Denio, 97, III, 634.

Commissioners of Excise v. Merchant, 103 N. Y. 143, V, 20; VIII, 361.

Commissioners of Excise, Tompkins County v. Taylor, 21 N. Y. 173, VI, 569.

Commonwealth v. Interstate Consol. St. R. Co., 187 Mass. 436, X, 883.

Conkey v. Hart, 14 N. Y. 22, IV, 242.

Conner v. Mayor, New York, 5 N. Y. 285, VII, 379.

Connolly v. Van Wyck, 35 Misc. 746, VI, 521; IX, 753.

Cooper v. Schultz, 32 How. Pr. 107, V, 702.

Corning v. Greene, 23 Barb. 33, III, 10; VI, 503.

County of Ulster v. State of New York, 177 N. Y. 189, X, 782.

Crossman v. Lurman, 57 App. Div. 393; 171 N. Y. 392; 192 U. S. 189, V, 863; VIII, 175; IX, 206.

Cullinan, Re (Kray Certificate), 82 App. Div. 445; 97 App. Div. 122, IX, 667.

Cullum, Re, 145 N. Y. 593, IX, 349.

Cunningham v. Bucklin, 8 Cow. 178, X, 670.

Daggett v. Hudson, 43 Ohio St. 548, VIII, 567.

Danolds v. New York, 89 N. Y. 36, VII, 375.

Dartmouth College Case, 4 Wheat. 518, III, 1024.

Davies, Re, 168 N. Y. 102, X, 675, 680.

Deansville Cemetery Assoc., Re, 66 N. Y. 569, VI, 163, 607; VII, 245.

De Bow v. People, 1 Denio, 9, III, 656.

De Camp, Re, 151 N. Y. 557, VI, 271; VIII, 1029.

De Hart v. Hatch, 3 Hun, 375, X, 678.

Delano, Re, 176 N. Y. 486, VIII, 929; IX, 680.

Dells v. Kennedy, 49 Wisc. 555, VIII, 567.

Demarest v. New York, 74 N. Y. 161, VI, 520.

Demarest v. Wickham, 67 Barb. 312; 63 N. Y. 320, VI, 520.

Devlin v. New York, 63 N. Y. 8, V, 221.

Devoy v. New York, 36 N. Y. 449, V, 28.

Doolittle v. Supervisors of Broome County, 18 N. Y. 155, VI, 731.

Doyle v. New York, 58 App. Div. 588, VIII, 1029.

Drake v. Hudson River R. Co., 7 Barb. 508, X, 693.

Drake v. Mayor, etc., New York, 7 Lansing, 340, VI, 565.

Duanesburgh v. Jenkins, 57 N. Y. 177, VII, 453.

Dudley v. Flushing Jockey Club, 14 Misc. 58, IX, 548.

Duffghe v. Met. St. Ry. Co., 109 App. Div. 603, VI, 521.

Dutch Church v. Mott, 7 Paige, 77, II, 468.

Eadie v. Slimmon, 26 N. Y. 9, VII, 80.

East River Bridge Co., Re, 75 Hun, 119, IX, 510.

Edmonds v. Barbury, 28 Iowa, 267, VIII, 567.

Eichhorn, Re, 74 Hun, 58, IX, 510.

Eilenbecker v. District Court, 134 U. S. 35, VII, 613.

Elmira Sav. Bank v. Davis, 142 N. Y. 590, VIII, 7; IX, 137, 472.

Excise Commissioners v. Merchant, 103 N. Y. 143, V, 20; VIII, 361.

Excise Commissioners, Tompkins County v. Taylor, 21 N. Y. 173, VI, 569.

Ferguson v. Ross, 126 N. Y. 459, IX, 511.
Fire Department v. Stanton, 159 N. Y. 225, VI, 520.
First National Bank v. Fancher, 48 N. Y. 524, V, 588.
Fitzgerald v. Green, 134 U. S. 379, VII, 33.
Fletcher v. Peck, 6 Cranch, 87, III, 1023.
Fobes v. Rome, Watertown & O. R. R. Co., 121 N. Y. 505, X, 693.
Forster v. Scott, 136 N. Y. 577, VI, 521.
Fort George Realty Co., Re, 179 N. Y. 49, X, 720, 722.
Frees v. Ford, 6 N. Y. 176, IV, 365, 562.
French v. Merrill, 27 App. Div. 612, X, 680.
Frost v. Brisbin, 19 Wend. 11, III, 345.
Fuller, Re, 62 App. Div. 428, VIII, 929; IX, 680.

Gagan, Re, 47 N. Y. S. R. 444, IX, 44.
Gage, Re, 141 N. Y. 112, VII, 77; IX, 94.
Germania Sav. Bank v. Suspension Bridge, 159 N. Y. 362, IV, 536.
Gerould v. Wilson, 81 N. Y. 573, VII, 1094.
Getman v. New York, 66 Hun, 236, VI, 520, 521.
Gibbons v. Ogden, 9 Wheat. 1, II, 1025.
Gibson, Re, 21 N. Y. 9, aff'd Sherman v. Smith, 1 Black, 587, III, 656.
Gifford v. Livingston, 2 Denio, 380, III, 656.
Gilbert Elev. R. Co. v. Kobbe, 70 N. Y. 361, VII, 592.
Gilroy, Re, 11 App. Div. 65, X, 679.
Gilroy, Re, 32 App. Div. 216, VII, 901.
Gloversville v. Howell, 70 N. Y. 287, VI, 503.
Gmaehle v. Rosenberg, 83 App. Div. 339, X, 365.
Goodsell v. Hartford & N. H. R. Co., 33 Conn. 55, VII, 245.
Gordon v. Cornes, 47 N. Y. 608, V, 695.
Green, Re, 134 U. S. 379, VII, 33.
Green v. Biddle, 8 Wheat. 1, 84, III, 1024; IV, 349.
Green v. Shumway, 39 N. Y. 418, V, 749; VIII, 912.
Griswold v. Sheldon, 4 N. Y. 581, IV, 365.
Grobe v. Erie County Mut. Ins. Co., 39 App. Div. 183, IX, 138.
Guild v. Rogers, 8 Barb. 502, IV, 242.
Guilford v. Supervisors of Chenango County, 13 N. Y. 143, VII, 452.

Harbeck v. New York, 10 Bosw. 366, V, 28.
Hargraves Mills v. Harden, 25 Misc. 665, IX, 138.
Harrison v. Clark, 87 N. Y. 572, VII, 1094.
Hartung v. People, 22 N. Y. 95, II, 635; V, 172, 264, 265.
Hartung v. People, 26 N. Y. 167, V, 172, 264, 265.
Hathaway, Re, 71 N. Y. 239, IV, 365; X, 677, 679.
Hayner v. James, 17 N. Y. 316, X, 675.

Hawker v. New York, 170 U. S. 189, aff'g 152 N. Y. 234, VIII, 175; IX, 206.

Healey v. Dudley, 5 Lansing, 115, VI, 124.

Health Department v. Trinity Church, 145 N. Y. 32, VI, 520; VIII, 317; X, 456.

Heckman v. Pickney, 81 N. Y. 211, VII, 1053.

Heerwagen v. Crosstown St. R. Co., 90 App. Div. 275, X, 486.

Henderson v. Wickham, Mayor, etc., New York, 92 U. S. 259, IV, 441; VI, 997, 1001; VII, 14, 163, 309, 433.

Herdic v. Roessler, 109 N. Y. 127, VI, 334.

Hill v. Supervisors, 12 N. Y. 52, VIII, 384.

Hill v. Thompson, 16 Jones & S. 481, VI, 520.

Hinckley v. Schwarzschild & Co., 107 App. Div. 470, IX, 137.

Hirshfeld v. Bopp, 145 N. Y. 84, VIII, 7; IX, 137.

Hogle v. Stewart, 8 Johns. 104, II, 784.

Holmes, Ex parte (1840), 12 Vt. 631.

Holmes v. Jenison (1840), 14 Pet. 540.

Houston & Texas Cent. R. Co. v. Mayes, 201 U. S. 321, X, 927.

Howard, Re, 54 Hun, 305, VIII, 1139.

Hubbard v. Sadler, 104 N. Y. 223, VI, 676, 822.

Hurlburt v. Banks, 52 How. Pr. 196, aff'd 1 Abb. N. C. 172, VI, 429.

Inman SS. Co. v. Tinker, 94 U. S. 238, V, 381; VII, 122, 436, 531, 714, 834, 969, 1049.

Inspectors of Election, Re, 25 N. Y. Supp. 1063, IX, 94.

Irving v. Britton, 8 Misc. 201, VIII, 436.

Irwin v. Met. St. R. Co., 38 App. Div. 253, VI, 520; IX, 753.

Jack v. Martin, 12 Wend. 312; 14 Wend. 507, IV, 8.

Jackson ex dem. Montgomery v. Chapin, 5 Cow. 485, X, 670.

Jackson v. Dominick, 14 Johns. 443, X, 670.

Jackson ex dem. Ten Eyck v. Frost, 5 Cow. 346, IV, 534.

Jackson ex dem. Lepper v. Griswold, 5 Johns. 139, II, 405.

Jackson v. Groat, 7 Cow. 285, IV, 361.

Jackson ex dem. Hart v. Lamphire, 3 Pet. 280, II, 405.

Jackson ex dem. Hopkins v. Leek, 12 Wend. 105, X, 670.

Jackson ex dem. McCloughry v. Lyon, 9 Cow. 664, V, 653.

Jackson v. Schultz, 18 Johns. 174, IV, 360, 361.

Jackson v. Silvernail, 15 Johns. 277, IV, 360.

Jacobs, Re, 98 N. Y. 110, X, 457.

Jachne v. New York, 128 U. S. 189, aff'g 35 Fed. 357, VI, 521.

John & C. Streets, Re, 19 Wend. 659, V, 653.

Johnston v. Spicer, 107 N. Y. 185, VIII, 614.

Jones v. Chamberlain, 109 N. Y. 100, V, 455.
Jorgensen v. Squires, 144 N. Y. 280, VI, 520.
Joy v. Berdell, 25 Ill. 540, VII, 245.
Justices to the House of Representatives, Answer of, 148 Mass. 623, VIII, 1048, 1049.

Kane v. McClellan, 110 App. Div. 44, VI, 521; X, 206.
Kantro v. Armstrong, 44 App. Div. 506, VI, 520; IX, 753.
Kelley v. New York, 89 Hun, 246, IX, 226.
Kelly v. Van Wyck, 35 Misc. 210, VI, 521, IX, 753.
Kelsey v. Forsyth, 21 How. (U. S.) 85, X, 680.
Kenny, Re, 23 Misc. 9, aff'd 30 App. Div. 624, VI, 521; IX, 753.
Keymer, Re, 148 N. Y. 219, IX, 561.
Kinne v. Syracuse, 3 Keyes, 110, VIII, 289.
Kinney v. Roberts, 26 Hun, 166, X, 676.
Kirkwood v. Newbury, 122 N. Y. 571, VI, 676, 822.
Koch v. New York, 152 N. Y. 72, IX, 530.
Kresser v. Lyman, 74 Fed. 765, IX, 667.
Kuekler v. People, 5 Park. Crim. Rep. 212, II, 635; V, 172.
Kundolf v. Thalheimer, 12 N. Y. 593, IV, 365, 562.

Lake Shore & M. S. R. Co v. Smith, 173 U. S. 684, X, 882.
Lanning v. Carpenter, 20 N. Y. 447, V, 229; VIII, 289.
Lansing v. Smith, 8 Cow. 146, aff'd 4 Wend. 9, III, 10.
Lawton v. Steele, 51 Hun, 643; 6. N. Y. Supp. 15, aff'd 119 N. Y. 226; 152 U. S. 133, VIII, 627, 628.
Le Couteulx v. Erie County, 7 Barb. 249, IV, 244.
Lee, Oliver & Co.'s Bank, Re, 21 N. Y. 9, aff'd 1 Black, 587, IV, 442.
Leich, Re, 31 Misc. 671, VI, 521; IX, 753.
Lemmon v. People, 20 N. Y. 562, IV, 811, 860.
Livingston, Re, 24 App. Div. 51, IX, 667.
Livingston v. Bank of New York, 26 Barb. 304, V, 44.
Livingston v. Hollenbeck, 4 Barb. 9, IV, 244.
Livingston v. Stickels, 8 Paige, 398, IV, 361.
Livingston v. Van Inneg, 9 Johns. 507, II, 1025.
Lochner v. New York, 198 U. S. 45, rev'g 177 N. Y. 145, VIII, 317; IX, 743.
Long v. New York, 81 N. Y. 425, VI, 129.
Lord v. Thomas, 64 N. Y. 107, VII, 378.
Lucy, The, 8 Wall. 307, X, 680.
Ludington v. Dudley, 61 N. Y. S. R. 115, VIII, 436.
Lyman, Re, 46 App. Div. 387, aff'd 163 N. Y. 552, IX, 667.

McCafferty v. Guyer, 59 Pa. St. 109, IX, 95.

McCollum, Ex parte, 1 Cow. 550, VI, 327.

McConologue v. McCaffrey, 29 Misc. 139, VI, 521; IX, 753.

McCulloch v. Maryland, 4 Wheat. 316, X, 67.

McGrath v. Grout, 171 N. Y. 7, X, 25, 152, 208.

McKee v. United States, 97 U. S. 233, VII, 380.

McKoan v. Devries, 3 Barb. 196, IV, 365.

McLaughlin v. Kipp, 82 App. Div. 413, IX, 827.

McMaster v. State of New York, 108 N. Y. 542, IX, 277.

McPherson, Re, 104 N. Y. 306, VIII, 102.

Magowan v. Sinclair, 5 Daly, 63, X, 682.

Mahon v. Board of Supervisors, 171 N. Y. 263, VII, 257, 550.

Malone Waterworks Co., Re, 38 N. Y. S. R. 95, VI, 504.

Mangam v. Brooklyn, 98 N. Y. 585, VII, 251, 257, 550.

March v. New York, 69 App. Div. 1, VIII, 1144.

Mayer v. Hazard, 49 Hun, 227, IX, 140.

Mechanicsville v. Stillwater & M. St. R. Co., 35 Misc. 513, IX, 137.

Meigs v. Roberts, 162 N. Y. 571, X, 263.

Menges v. Albany, 47 How. Pr. 244, aff'd 56 N. Y. 374, X, 678.

Mercer v. Floyd, 24 Misc. 164, VI, 334; VII, 753; X, 275.

Metropolitan Board of Health v. Heister, 37 N. Y. 661, V, 702.

Monroe v. Collins, 17 Ohio St. 666, VIII, 567.

Morgan v. Hedstrom, 164 N. Y. 224, X, 185.

Morley v. Lake Shore & M. S. R. Co., 146 U. S. 162, aff'g 95 N. Y. 428, 667, III, 88; VII, 404.

Mugler v. Kansas, 123 U. S. 623, X, 781.

Munn v. Illinois, 94 U. S. 113, VII, 245; VIII, 604.

Mussen v. Ausable Granite Works, 63 Hun, 367, VI, 521.

Nash v. People, 36 N. Y. 607, X, 675.

Negus v. Brooklyn, 62 How. Pr. 291, VII, 592.

Newell v. People, 7 N. Y. 9, IV, 549, 602, 633, 670.

New Rochelle Water Co., Re, 46 Hun, 525, VI, 287, 504.

New York, Re, 135 N. Y. 253, VI, 520.

New York v. Broadway & S. Ave. R. Co., 12 Hun, 571, VI, 521.

New York v. Compagnie General Transatlantique, 107 U. S. 59, VII, 712.

New York ex rel. Cutler v. Dibble, 21 How. 336, aff'g 16 N. Y. 203. II, 695, 1076; V, 202.

New York v. Emigration Commissioners, 36 N. Y. S. R. 721, VII, 713.

New York v. Gorman, 26 App. Div. 191, VIII, 1025.

New York v. Herdje, 68 App. Div. 370, X, 206, 746.

New York v. Roberts, 171 U. S. 658, aff'g 149 N. Y. 608; 91 Hun, 158, VII, 454.

New York v. Tax & A. Commissioners, 94 U. S. 415, V, 588.
New York v. Wright, 34 N. Y. S. R. 904, VII, 901.
New York Cable Co., Re, 40 Hun, 1, VII, 894.
New York Central & H. R. R., Re, 64 N. Y. 60, X, 678.
New York Elev. R. Co., Re, 70 N. Y. 327, VII, 592, 854; IX, 511.
New York, L. & W. R. Co. v. Roll, 32 Misc. 321, X, 71.
New York, N. H. & H. R. Co. v. New York, 105 U. S. 628, aff'g 142
   N. Y. 646, VII, 732.
New York Rubber Co. v. Rothery, 112 N. Y. 592, IX, 391.
New York Sanitary Utilization Co. v. Health Department, 61 App. Div.
   106, VI, 521; IX, 753; X, 58, 457.
North River S. B. Co. v. Livingston, 3 Cow. 713, II, 1025.

Oakley v. Aspinwall, 3 N. Y. 547, IV, 365.
Oliver Lee & Co.'s Bank, Re, 21 N. Y. 9, aff'd 1 Black, 587, IV, 442.
Orient Ins. Co. v. Daggs, 172 U. S. 561, II, 613.
Orr v. Gilman, 183 U. S. 278, aff'g 167 N. Y. 227, VIII, 929; IX, 680.
Oviatt v. Hopkins, 20 App. Div. 168, IX, 680.

Page v. Allen, 58 Pa. St. 338, VIII, 567.
Page v. Shainwald, 52 App. Div. 349, X, 369.
Parker v. Willard State Hospital, 50 App. Div. 622, VIII, 485; IX, 680.
Parsons, The Robert W., 191 U. S. 20, III, 78; V, 720.
Parsons v. Van Wyck, 56 App. Div. 329, VII, 846.
Paterson v. Tash, 2 Strange Rep. 1178, III, 88.
Payne v. O'Brien, 188 N. Y. 185, X, 852.
Peck v. State, 137 N. Y. 372, IX, 370, 600.
Pelham Manor v. New Rochelle Water Co., 67 Hun, 98, aff'd 143 N. Y.
   532, X, 541.
Pelletreau v. Greene Consol. Gold Min. Co., 49 Misc. 233, VIII, 1029.
Pendleton v. O'Brien, 188 N. Y. 185, X, 852.
People v. A. Booth & Co., 105 App. Div. 184, X, 102, 346.
People v. Adirondack R. Co., 160 N. Y. 225, IX, 752.
People ex rel. Bolton v. Albertson, 55 N. Y. 56, VII, 108; X, 677.
People v. Allen, 42 N. Y. 378, VIII, 381.
People ex rel. Killeen v. Angle, 109 N. Y. 564, VII, 838; IX, 549; X, 678.
People v. Arensberg, 105 N. Y. 123, VIII, 34; IX, 320.
People ex rel. Washington Park v. Banks, 67 N. Y. 574, VII, 630;
   VIII, 387.
People v. Barber, 48 Hun, 198, IX, 96.
People ex rel. Bijur v. Barker, 155 N. Y. 330, IX, 94.
People v. Batchelor, 22 N. Y. 128, VI, 1029.

People v. Beattie, 96 App. Div. 383, IX, 743.

People ex rel. Warren v. Beck, 10 Misc. 77; 144 N. Y. 225, VII, 1103; VIII, 1030.

People v. Biesecker, 169 N. Y. 53, IX, 175; X, 120.

People v. Bishopp, 106 App. Div. 266, IX, 175.

People ex rel. Munro v. Board of Canvassers, 129 N. Y. 468, IX, 33.

People ex rel. Nichols v. Board of Canvassers, 129 N. Y. 395, VIII, 670; IX, 33.

People ex rel. Sherwood v. Board of Canvassers, 129 N. Y. 360, IX, 33.

Poeple ex rel. N. Y. C. & H. R. Co. v. Board of Health, 58 Hun, 595, V, 863.

People v. Bowen, 21 N. Y. 517, IV, 524; VII, 670.

People v. Brooklyn, F. & C. I. R. Co., 89 N. Y. 75, VII, 397.

People ex rel. Bull v. Buffalo, 52 App. Div. 157, aff'd 166 N. Y. 604, VII, 1103; VIII, 1030.

People ex rel. Fowler v. Bull, 46 N. Y. 57, VII, 45; X, 913.

People v. Burleigh, 1 N. Y. Crim. Rep. 522, V, 20.

People ex rel. Dunkirk, A. Valley & P. R. Co. v. Campbell, 74 Hun, 210, VII, 454.

People ex rel. Strough v. Canvassers, 143 N. Y. 84, IX, 365.

People ex rel. Scott v. Chenango, 8 N. Y. 317, IV, 557.

People ex rel. Bassett v. City Prison, 6 App. Div. 520, IX, 667.

People ex rel. Furman v. Clute, 50 N. Y. 451, VI, 424.

People ex rel. Lentilhon v. Coler, 61 App. Div. 223, VIII, 317.

People ex rel. Rodgers v. Coler, 166 N. Y. 1, VIII, 317; X, 7, 909, 915.

People ex rel. Treat v. Coler, 166 N. Y. 144, IX, 743.

People ex rel. McSpedon v. Comptroller, New York, 34 Barb. 69, V, 222.

People v. Cook, 8 N. Y. 68, VIII, 571.

People ex rel. Percival v. Cram, 164 N. Y. 166, X, 211.

People ex rel. Lord v. Crooks, 53 N. Y. 648, VII, 45.

People ex rel. Pub. Char. Comrs. v. Cullen, 153 N. Y. 629, IX, 580.

People ex rel. Underwood v. Daniell, 50 N. Y. 274, VI, 113.

People v. Davis, 78 App. Div. 570, VI, 521; X, 206.

People ex rel. Williams v. Dayton, 55 N. Y. 367, VI, 107; VII, 453.

People v. Devlin, 33 N. Y. 269, IV, 752.

People v. Dooley, 171 N. Y. 74, VI, 521; IX, 753; X, 206.

People ex rel. Wood v. Draper, 15 N. Y. 532, V, 28; VI, 30, 128; VII, 108; IX, 512.

People ex rel. Taylor v. Dunlap, 66 N. Y. 162, VI, 520.

People ex rel. Kemmler v. Durston, 119 N. Y. 569; 136 U. S. 436, VIII, 37, 484.

People ex rel. Travis v. Durston, 3 N. Y. Supp. 522, IX, 549.

People ex rel. Morris v. Edmonds, 15 Barb. 529, IV, 615.

People v. Edye, 11 Daly, 132, VII, 712.

People v. English, 29 N. E. Rep. 678, IX, 95.

People v. Equitable Trust Co., 96 N. Y. 387, VII, 454.

People ex rel. Howard v. Erie County, 42 App. Div. 510; 160 N. Y. 687, VII, 1103.

People ex rel. Lawrence v. Fallon, 152 N. Y. 12, IX, 548.

People ex rel. Sturgis v. Fallon, 152 N. Y. 1, IX, 548.

People ex rel. Demarest v. Farley, 1 How. Pr. (N. S.) 71, VI, 520.

People v. Fields, 53 N. Y. 491, VI, 727, 732.

People v. Fitch, 148 N. Y. 71, IX, 651.

People ex rel. Follett v. Fitch, 145 N. Y. 261, VI, 520.

People ex rel. Kehoe v. Fitchie, 76 Hun, 80, IX, 224.

People v. Fitzgerald, 180 N. Y. 269, VI, 521; X, 206.

People ex rel. Kenny v. Folks, 89 App. Div. 171, X, 420.

People ex rel. Leroy v. Foley, 148 N. Y. 677, X, 913.

People ex rel. Abrams v. Fox, 77 App. Div. 245, VI, 521; X, 206.

People v. Gold & S. Teleg. Co., 98 N. Y. 67, VII, 454; IX, 279.

People v. Granite State Provident Association, 161 N. Y. 492, VIII, 7; IX, 137.

People ex rel. Cossey v. Grout, 179 N. Y. 417, VIII, 317; X, 916.

People ex rel. Richmond Hook and Ladder Co. No. 4 v. Grout, 79 App. Div. 61, VI, 521; X, 206.

People ex rel. Thornton v. Hagan, 14 Misc. 481, IX, 580.

People v. Hall, 169 N. Y. 184, IX, 514; X, 679.

People v. Hatch, 33 Ill. 9, VII, 670, 673.

People ex rel. Eckerson v. Haverstraw, 151 N. Y. 75, VI, 120, 217.

People v. Hawkins, 85 Hun, 43, IX, 329.

People v. Hawkins, 157 N. Y. 1, X, 9.

People ex rel. Mitchell v. Haws, 32 Barb. 207, IV, 615.

People v. Hill, 44 Hun, 472, VIII, 34.

People ex rel. Leo v. Hill, 126 N. Y. 497, VII, 429.

People v. Hills, 64 App. Div. 584, IX, 175; X, 120.

People ex rel. Smith v. Hoffman, 166 N. Y. 462, X, 350.

People v. Home Ins. Co., 92 N. Y. 328, aff'd 119 U. S. 129, VII, 454.

People v. Horn Silver Min. Co., 105 N. Y. 76, aff'd 143 U. S. 305, VII, 454.

People ex rel. Bush v. Houghton, 182 N. Y. 301, VIII, 175; IX, 206.

People ex rel. Burby v. Howland, 155 N. Y. 275, VI, 327; X, 673, 676, 677.

People v. Hurlbutt, 44 Barb. 126, IV, 365; X, 675.

People ex rel. Cochran v. Hyatt, 172 N. Y. 177, aff'd 188 U. S. 691, III, 604.

People v. Ingersoll, 58 N. Y. 1, VI, 727, 732.

People v. Keeler, 17 N. Y. 370, IV, 433.

People ex rel. McDonald v. Keeler, 99 N. Y. 463, IV, 534; IX, 61.

People ex rel. Consol. Ginseng Co. v. Kelsey, 105 App. Div. 175, aff'd 182 N. Y. 526, X, 837.

People ex rel. Angerstein v. Kenney, 96 N. Y. 294, VI, 461, 521; VIII, 281.

People v. Kerr, 27 N. Y. 188, V, 242.

People ex rel. Zeiser v. Kessell, 21 Hun, 277; 81 N. Y. 638, VII, 651.

People v. Kibler, 106 N. Y. 321, VIII, 34.

People ex rel. Hopkins v. Kings County, 52 N. Y. 556, V, 817; IX, 282.

People ex rel. Holmes v. Lane, 53 App. Div. 531, VI, 327.

People ex rel. Met. Board of Health v. Lane, 55 Barb. 168, IV, 442.

People ex rel. Griffin v. Lathrop, 142 N. Y. 113, VIII, 679, 815.

People v. Learned, 5 Hun, 626, VI, 809.

People ex rel. Healy v. Leask, 67 N. Y. 521, VII, 47, 451.

People v. Levy, 24 Misc. 469, VI, 521; IX, 753.

People ex rel. Harvey v. Loew, 102 N. Y. 471, VIII, 127, 1161; IX, 142.

People v. Long Island R. Co., 134 N. Y. 506, VII, 732.

People v. Lyon, 27 Hun, 180, V, 20.

People ex rel. Williamson v. McKinney, 52 N. Y. 374, VII, 45; IX, 399; X, 913.

People v. Maine, 20 N. Y. 434, X, 676.

People v. Marx, 99 N. Y. 377, VIII, 34; X, 456.

People v. Maxwell, 83 Hun, 157, VIII, 643; IX, 106.

People v. Meach, 14 Abb. Pr. (N. S.) 429, VIII, 385.

People ex rel. Balcom v. Mosher, 163 N. Y. 32, VII, 838; X, 20, 678.

People ex rel. Einsfeld v. Murray, 149 N. Y. 367, VIII, 436; IX, 667, X, 854.

People v. National Fire Ins. Co., 27 Hun, 188, VII, 454.

People v. New York, 20 How. Pr. 144, V, 242.

People ex rel. American Bible Soc. v. New York, 142 N. Y. 348, VIII, 732; IX, 232.

People ex rel. Mut. L. Ins. Co. v. New York, 16 N. Y. 424, IX, 61.

People v. N. Y. Floating Dry Dock Co., 92 N. Y. 487, VII, 454.

People v. N. Y., N. H. & H. R. Co., 55 Hun, 409, aff'd 123 N. Y. 635, VII, 732.

People ex rel. Mayor, etc. v. Nichols, 79 N. Y. 589, X, 678.

People v. O'Brien, 111 N. Y. 1, VIII, 205.

People ex rel. Board of Commissioners v. Oneida County Supervisors, 170 N. Y. 105, X, 768.

People v. O'Neil, 109 N. Y. 251, VI, 520, 521.

People ex rel. Burrows v. Orange County, 17 N. Y. 235, IV, 782.

People v. Orange County Road Const. Co., 175 N. Y. 84, VIII, 317; X, 915.

People ex rel. Weed-Parsons Printing Co. v. Palmer, 18 Misc. 103, IX, 690.

People v. Pease, 27 N. Y. 45, VIII, 587.

People v. Pierson, 176 N. Y. 201, II, 577.

People ex rel. McCune v. Police Board, 19 N. Y. 188, V, 28.

People v. Quant, 12 How. Pr. 83, IV, 802.

People ex rel. Hatch v. Reardon, 184 N. Y. 431, aff'g 110 App. Div. 821, X, 490, 836, 886.

People ex rel. Carter v. Rice, 135 N. Y. 473, VIII, 156, 1057; IX, 155.

People ex rel. Daley v. Rice, 129 N. Y. 449, IX, 33.

People ex rel. Derby v. Rice, 129 N. Y. 461, IX, 33.

People ex rel. Sherwood v. Rice, 129 N. Y. 391, IX, 33.

People ex rel. A. Klipstein & Co. v. Roberts, 36 App. Div. 597, aff'd 167 N. Y. 617, VIII, 929; IX, 680.

People ex rel. Eisman v. Ronner, 185 N. Y. 285, X, 836.

People ex rel. Cunningham v. Roper, 35 N. Y. 629, IV, 727; V, 613.

People v. Rouse, 39 N. Y. S. R. 656, VIII, 607.

People ex rel. Detroit & Howell R. Co. v. Salem, 20 Mich. 452, VII, 246.

People v. Santa Clara Lumber Co., 55 Mich. 507, X, 187.

People ex rel. Ward v. Scheu, 167 N. Y. 292, VII, 1103; VIII, 1030.

People ex rel. Cisco v. School Board, 161 N. Y. 598, IX, 328.

People ex rel. Underhill v. Skinner, 74 App. Div. 58, IX, 328.

People v. Smith, 69 N. Y. 175, VII, 164.

People ex rel. Cox v. Special Sessions Justices, 7 Hun, 214, 520.

People ex rel. N. Y. Elec. Lines Co. v. Squire, 107 N. Y. 593, IX, 511.

People ex rel. Nichols v. St. Board of Canvassers, 129 N. Y. 395, IX, 33.

People ex rel. Sherwood v. St. Board of Canvassers, 129 N. Y. 360, IX, 33.

People ex rel. Brooklyn City R. Co. v. St. Tax Commissioners, 174 N. Y. 417, aff'd 199 U. S. 48, X, 71.

People ex rel. Met. St. R. Co. v. St. Tax Commissioners, 174 N. Y. 417, aff'd 199 U. S. 1, X, 71.

People v. Stout, 23 Barb. 349, VI, 503.

People ex rel. McSpedon v. Supervisors, New York, 21 How. Pr. 288, aff'g 10 Abb. Pr. 233, V, 222.

People ex rel. Board of Commissioners v. Supervisors, Oneida County, 170 N. Y. 105, X, 763.

People ex rel. Rice v. Supervisors, Orleans County, 98 App. Div. 390, VIII, 1029.

People v. Supervisors, Westchester County, 4 Barb. 70, VI, 158, 488.

People ex rel. Hanford v. Thayer, 88 Hun, 136, VIII, 1029.

People ex rel. Atkinson v. Tompkins, 64 N. Y. 53, VIII, 385.

People ex rel. Eckerson v. Trustees, 151 N. Y. 84, X, 678.

People v. Tweed, 58 N. Y. 1, VI, 732.

People v. Tweed, 63 N. Y. 202, VI, 727.

People ex rel. Weaver v. Van De Car, 150 N. Y. 439, IX, 548.

People v. Van Rensselaer, 9 N. Y. 291, IV, 413, 614, 654.

People ex rel. Moscowitz v. Voorhis, 41 Misc. 360, X, 612.

People v. Walker, 17 N. Y. 502, VII, 1006.

People v. Warren, 77 Hun, 120, VII, 1103; VIII, 1030.

People v. Waterbury, 44 Hun, 493, VIII, 34.

People ex rel. Decker v. Waters, 4 Misc. 1, VIII, 643; IX, 106; X, 679.

People ex rel. Simpson v. Wells, 181 N. Y. 252, VI, 521; X, 206.

People ex rel. Hamilton Park Co. v. Wemple, 67 Hun, 495, rev'd 139 N. Y. 240, IX, 220.

People ex rel. Platt v. Wemple, 117 N. Y. 136, VII, 454.

People ex rel. Southern Cotton Oil Co. v. Wemple, 131 N. Y. 64, VII, 454.

People ex rel. Howard v. Wende, 25 Misc. 330, VII, 1103; VIII, 1030.

People v. West, 106 N. Y. 293, VIII, 34.

People ex rel. Henderson v. Westchester County, 147 N. Y. 1, VIII, 289; X, 850.

People ex rel. Cassidy v. Whalen, 189 N. Y. 534, X, 852.

People v. Williams, 51 Misc. 383, VIII, 317; IX, 743.

People v. Windholz, 92 App. Div. 569, IX, 175.

People ex rel. Price v. Woodbury, 38 Misc. 189, VI, 521; IX, 753; X, 206.

People v. Young, 18 App. Div. 162, IX, 547.

Perrine v. Striker, 7 Paige, 598, III, 632.

Persons v. Gardner, 42 App. Div. 490, VIII, 7; IX, 741.

Phillips x. Schumacher, 10 Hun, 405, VI, 676, 822.

Pierson v. Ward, 27 Misc. 793, VI, 521; IX, 753.

Pocantico Waterworks Co. v. Bird, 130 N. Y. 249, VI, 287, 504.

Polinsky v. People, 73 N. Y. 65, VI, 520.

Power v. Village of Athens, 99 N. Y. 592, VIII, 411.

Powers v. Bergen, 6 N. Y. 358, V, 653.

Powers v. Shepard, 48 N. Y. 540, V, 610.

Pratt Inst. v. City of New York, 183 N. Y. 151, VIII, 929.

Prigg v. Pennsylvania, 16 Pet. 539, III, 1028, 1037; IV, 8; V, 301.

Prospect Park & C. I. R. Co., Re, 85 N. Y. 489, IV, 496.

Prospect Park & C. I. R. Co. v. Williamson, 91 N. Y. 552, IX, 508.

Provident Sav. Life Assurance Society, Re, 179 N. Y. 227, X, 720, 722.

Purdy v. People, 4 Hill, 384, III, 1013.

Quackenbush, Ex parte, 2 Hill, 369, IV, 685.
Queen v. Helson & Brand, Law Magazine, London, Vol. 23, p. 222, VI, 771.
Quinn, Re, 152 N. Y. 89, IX, 580.

Rapid Transit R. Commissioners, Re, 65 Hun, 63, VIII, 1144.
Rathbone v. Wirth, 150 N. Y. 459, VIII, 84; IX, 589.
Reciprocity Bank, Re, 29 Barb. 369, aff'd 22 N. Y. 9; IV, 442.
Reed v. Schmit, 39 Hun, 223, VII, 775, 878.
Reilly v. Gray, 77 Hun, 402, VIII, 436.
Renard v. Hargous, 13 N. Y. 259, X, 675.
Reynolds v. Schultz, 34 How. Pr. 147, V, 702.
Richardson v. Thurber, 104 N. Y. 606, VIII, 37.
Richter v. New York, 24 Misc. 613, VI, 120.
Ricketts v. New York, 12 Daly, 504, VI, 520.
Rieser v. Charles F. Parker & Co., 27 Misc. 205, VI, 521; IX, 753.
Riggs v. Shannon, 44 N. Y. S. R. 365; 27 Abb. N. C. 456, VII, 1125; VIII, 36.
Robert W. Parsons, The, 191 U. S. 20, III, 78; V, 720.
Roberts v. State, 160 N. Y. 217, IX, 250.
Rochester Water Commissioners, Re, 66 N. Y. 413, VII, 1101; IX, 508.
Rodman v. Munson, 13 Barb. 188, IV, 549.
Rogers v. Buffalo, 123 N. Y. 173, VII, 838.
Rogers v. Jacob, Mayor, etc., 88 Ky. L. Rep. 502, VIII, 912.
Rogers v. Rochester H. & P. R. Co., 21 Hun, 44, VI, 429.
Roosevelt v. Draper, 23 N. Y. 318, VI, 731.
Roosevelt v. Godard, 52 Barb. 533, V, 381.
Routenberg v. Schweitzer, 165 N. Y. 175, VI, 521; IX, 753.
Rumsey v. People, 19 N. Y. 41, VIII, 156.
Rupp, Re, 28 Misc. 703, aff'd 45 App. Div. 631, VIII, 1030.
Ryan v. New York, 177 N. Y. 271, IX, 743; X, 7, 915.
Ryan v. People, 78 App. Div. 134, VIII, 317.

Salters v. Tobias, 3 Paige, 338, IX, 61.
Saranac Land & Timber Co. v. Roberts, 177 U. S. 318, X, 263.
Saunders v. N. Y. C. & H. R. Co., 144 N. Y. 75, IV, 496.
Sbarboro v. Health Department, 26 App. Div. 177, VI, 520.
Schillinger Fireproof Cement & Asphalt Co. v. Arnott, 152 N. Y. 584, VII, 1125; VIII, 36.
Schultes, Re, 33 App. Div. 524, VI, 520; IX, 753.
Scofield v. Churchill, 72 N. Y. 565, VII, 1095.
Scott v. Sandford, 19 How. 393, IV, 813; V, 31, 34.
Seeley v. Stevens, 190 N. Y. 158, VII, 838; X, 20.

Seneca Nation v. Hammond, 6 T. & C. 595, VII, 74, 384.
Senton v. Steele, 119 N. Y. 226, X, 456.
Seymour v. Mercer, 13 How. 564, X, 676.
Shepherd v. People, 25 N. Y. 406, II, 635; V, 172. .
Sherman v. Smith, 1 Black, 587, aff'g Re Gibson, 21 N. Y. 9, III, 656;
    IV, 442.
Sherrill v. O'Brien, 188 N. Y. 185, X, 852.
Signell v. Wallace, 35 Misc. 656, X, 206.
Sill v. Village of Corning, 15 N. Y. 300, X, 677.
Silvey v. Lindsay, 107 N. Y. 55, VIII, 500.
Sixth Ave. R. Co. v. Kerr, 72 N. Y. 330, V, 242.
Smith v. Levinus, 8 N. Y. 472, IV, 433.
Smith v. Turner, 7 How. (U. S.) 283, IV, 273.
Spencer v. State, 135 N. Y. 619, IX, 429.
Soldiers Voting Bill, 45 N. H. 607, VII, 670.
Stamford Water Co. v. Stanley, 39 Hun, 424, VI, 287, 504.
Standfast v. Crotty, 37 N. Y. S. R. 673, X, 678.
State v. Baker, 38 Misc. 71, VIII, 567.
State v. Cones, 15 Neb. 44, IX, 96.
State v. Conner, 24 Pac. 723, VIII, 567.
State v. Kings Co., 125 N. Y. 312, VI, 630.
State ex rel. Hovey v. Noble, 118 Ind. 350, X, 678.
State Reservation, Re, 37 Hun, 537; 102 N. Y. 734, VII, 301.
Steck v. Colorado Fuel & Iron Co., 142 N. Y. 236, X, 682.
Steinway, Re, 159 N. Y. 256, X, 671.
Stenson v. Koch, 152 N. Y. 87, IX, 580.
Stocking v. Hunt, 3 Denio, 274, IV, 242.
Story v. New York El. R. Co., 11 Abb. N. C. 236, VI, 717.
Stryker v. Churchill, 39 Misc. 578, VIII, 672.
Stutzbach v. Coler, 168 N. Y. 416, VII, 833; X, 20.
Sugden v. Partridge, 174 N. Y. 87, VI, 521; X, 206.
Sun Printing & Publishing Association v. New York, 152 N. Y. 257,
    VIII, 1144; IX, 504.
Supreme Lodge K. of P. v. Meyer, 198 U. S. 508, IX, 44.
Swan v. Mutual Reserve Fund Life Association, 155 N. Y. 9, IX, 138.
Sweet v. Hulbert, 51 Barb. 312, VI, 194.
Sweet v. Syracuse, 129 N. Y. 316, VIII, 1015.
Swift v. New York, 89 N. Y. 52, VII, 373.
Syracuse v. Hubbard, 64 App. Div. 587; 168 N. Y. 668, X, 289.

Tappan v. Gray, 9 Paige, 509, IV, 773.
Taylor v. Porter, 4 Hill, 140, IV, 761.

Tenement House Department v. Moeschen, 179 N. Y. 325, X, 206, 746.
Thirty-fourth St. R. Co., Re, 102 N. Y. 343, VII, 894.
Thirty-second Election District, Re, 18 N. Y. S. R. 785, VI, 520.
Thrasher v. Bentley, 1 Abb. N. C. 39; 59 N. Y. 649, X, 676.
Tillinghast v. Merrill, 151 N. Y. 135, X, 275.
Tinken v. Stillwagon, 1 N. Y. City Ct. Rep. 390, V, 381.
Tinkham v. Tapscott, 17 N. Y. 141, V, 187.
Tobias v. Perry, 25 Misc. 74, VIII, 562.
Tompkins v. Hodgson, 2 Hun, 146, VII, 847.
Townsend, Re, 39 N. Y. 171, VII, 245.
Townsend v. New York, 77 N. Y. 542, VI, 520; VII, 309.
Truesdale v. Rochester, 33 Hun, 574, VII, 257.
Tuthill, Re, 163 N. Y. 133, VI, 189; IX, 550.
Tyroler v. Gummersbach, 28 Misc. 151, VI, 521; IX, 753.

Ulster County v. State of New York, 177 N. Y. 189, X, 782.
Union College, Re, 41 N. Y. S. R. 640; 129 N. Y. 308, IX, 59.
Union Ferry Co., Re, 98 N. Y. 151, VIII, 411, 463.
United States, Re, 96 N. Y. 227, VI, 520.
United States v. Anthony, 11 Blatchf. 200, IX, 96.
U. S. Illuminating Co. v. Grant, 55 Hun, 222, VIII, 451.
United States Trust Co. v. U. S. F. Ins. Co., 18 N. Y. 199, IV, 442.

Van Allen v. Assessors, 3 Wall. 573, V, 588; VI, 280.
Van Rensselaer v. Snyder, 13 N. Y. 299, IV, 242.
Viemeister v. White, 179 N. Y. 235, V, 189; VIII, 175; IX, 206.

Wager v. Troy Union R. Co., 25 N. Y. 526, V, 802.
Walker, Re, 57 App. Div. 1, VIII, 485; IX, 680.
Wallace, Re, 71 App. Div. 284, VIII, 929.
Wallace v. International Paper Co., 84 App. Div. 88, VIII, 929; IX, 680.
Walters, Re, 84 Hun, 457, VIII, 175; IX, 206.
Warner v. Palmer, 66 App. Div. 127, IX, 680.
Warner v. People, 2 Denio, 272, IV, 625; VII, 108.
Waterbury v. Egan, 3 Misc. 355, VIII, 34.
Weismer v. Douglas, 64 N. Y. 92, VI, 180.
Wheaton v. Gates, 18 N. Y. 395, V, 150.
Wheeler v. Brady, 15 Kans. 26, IX, 96.
Wheelock v. Young, 4 Wend. 648, II, 902.
White v. County, 10 Pac. 484, VIII, 567.
White v. Miller, 71 N. Y. 118, IX, 277.
White v. Miller, 78 N. Y. 393, IX, 277.

Whitmore v. Mayor, N. Y., 67 N. Y. 21, VII, 47, 451.

Willard v. Tayloe, 8 Wall. 557, VI, 166.

Willcox et al, v. Consolidated Gas Co., 212 U. S. 19.

Williams v. Stein, 38 Ind. 89, VIII, 586, 1007.

Wilson v. United Traction Co., 72 App. Div. 233, X, 884.

Woods, Re, 5 Misc. 575, IX, 94.

Worthington v. London Guarantee & Accident Co., 164 N. Y. 81, VI, 521; IX, 753.

Wright v. Hart, 182 N. Y. 330, X, 929.

Wright v. Stranahan, 61 Hun, 264; 83 Hun, 615; 149 N. Y. 495, IX, 141.

Wynehamer v. People, 13 N. Y. 378, IV, 771, 802, 859; V, 19; VIII, 367, 371.

Yates Co. National Bank v. Carpenter, 119 N. Y. 550, IX, 113.

Zborowski, Re, 68 N. Y. 88, VI, 129.

TABLE OF CONSTITUTIONAL REFERENCES.

UNITED STATES CONSTITUTION.

PREAMBLE.

Purpose of Constitution, IV, 680; V, 321.

ARTICLE 1.

Section 2, clause 1:

Qualifications of voters for representatives in Congress, VI, 38; VII, 306.

Section 2, clause 2:

Qualifications of representatives, III, 883.

Section 2, clause 3:

Apportionment of representation and direct taxes, II, 546; III, 94, 622; IV, 85; V, 317, 356, 391.

Census, V, 295.

Congressional reapportionment, VII, 725; VIII, 135.

Section 3, clause 1:

Election of senators, II, 303.

Section 3, clause 2:

Appointment of senator to fill vacancy, II, 537.

Section 3, clause 3:

Qualifications of senators, III, 883.

Section 4, clause 1:

Congressional elections, IV, 5; VI, 38.

Section 5, clause 1:

Congress to determine qualifications and elections of members, VIII, 983, 985.

Section 6, clause 2:
Senators and representatives not to hold certain offices, II, 1062.

Section 7, clause 2:
President's veto power, III, 977; IX, 406.

Section 8, clause 1:
Duties and taxes, III, 331, 433, 898; IV, 616.

Section 8, clause 3:
Commerce, III, 234, 420, 462; IV, 393, 616.

Section 8, clause 4:
Bankruptcy, III, 842, 876; IV, 5.

Section 8, clause 5:
Coining money, III, 630; VI, 134, 142; VII, 310.
Weights and measures, III, 101.

Section 8, clause 8:
Patents, VII, 571.

Section 8, clause 11:
Congress, power to declare war, IV, 417.

Section 8, clause 16:
Militia, II, 853; III, 345, 405; IV, 493; V, 393, 541.

Section 8, clause 17:
District of Columbia, III, 138, 588, 645, 906, 907.
Lands ceded by State, VIII, 1115.

Section 18, clause 18:
Congress to enact needed laws to carry Constitution into effect, III, 234, 357.

Section 9, clause 1:
Importation of slaves, III, 94; V, 30.

Section 9, clause 2:
Suspending writ of habeas corpus, V, 500; VII, 504.

Section 9, clause 3:

Congress not to pass *ex post facto* law, II, 215, 582; V, 264.

Section 9, clause 4:

Apportionment of taxes, II, 546.

Section 9, clause 5:

No tax on exportations, IV, 667.

Section 9, clause 7:

Title of nobility. Proposed amendment to, II, 679. Not approved.

Section 10, clause 1:

State not to pass *ex post facto* law, II, 215.
Obligation of contracts, II, 354, 427, 594, 704, 1082, 1112; III, 188,
   1023; IV, 6, 240, 347, 350; VI, 518, 668; VII, 96, 333, 356, 375,
   397, 595, 856; VIII, 100, 752; IX, 453, 500.
Vested rights, II, 582; VIII, 361.

Section 10, clause 2:

State not to keep troops without consent of Congress, VII, 763.

ARTICLE 2.

Section 1, clause 2:

Presidential elector, who not eligible, II, 1062.

Section 1, clauses 2 and 3:

Presidential electors. See also Twelfth Amendment, II, 545; VII, 35.

Section 1, clause 5:

Qualifications of President, III, 883.

Section 2, clause 2:

Nominations by President, II, 500; V, 480.
Senate's power of confirmation, VII, 559.
Treaties, III, 689; IV, 417; V, 480.

ARTICLE 3.

Section 2, clause 1.

Federal judicial authority, III, 359, 364, 1026; VII, 575.

Section 2, clause 3:
   Trial, where held, VII, 613.

Section 3, clause 1:
   Treason, V, 306, 319.

ARTICLE 4.

Section 2, clause 1:
   Privileges and immunities of citizens. See also Fourteenth Amendment, II, 613, 1026, 1041; III, 844, 981; V, 309, 325.

Section 2, clause 2:
   Fugitives from justice, III, 350, 584, 594, 596, 777, 778, 852, 869, 915, 917, 922, 1030; IV, 8.

Section 2, clause 3:
   Fugitive slaves, III, 574, 917, 922; IV, 7, 569, 810, 828; V, 302, 317, 355, 356.

Section 3, clause 1:
   Erecting new States, III, 390; V, 30.

Section 3, clause 2:
   Claims of States, III, 985.
   Territories, IV, 828; V, 29, 32.

Section 4:
   'State entitled to republican form of government, V, 616.

ARTICLE 5.

Section 1:
   Method of amending Constitution, II, 546; III, 574.
   Constitutional Convention, V, 325, 328, 329, 356, 464.

ARTICLE 6.

Section 2:
   Supreme law, III, 364, 432.

Section 3:
   Official oath, V, 859.

ARTICLE 7.

ection 1:

When Constitution deemed established, V, 464.

FIRST TEN AMENDMENTS.
General provisions, IV, 750.

FIRST AMENDMENT.
Religious freedom, IV, 750.
Free speech and free press, III, 589, 645; IV, 750; V, 483.
Right of people to assemble, VI, 375.
Right of petition, IV, 750; V, 483.

SECOND AMENDMENT.
Right of people to keep and bear arms, IV, 726, 750; V, 281.

FOURTH AMENDMENT.
Unreasonable searches and seizures, IV, 750, 755; V, 471.

FIFTH AMENDMENT.
Indictment by grand jury, V, 471.
Witness against himself, IV, 310.
Due process of law. See also Fourteenth Amendment, II, 522, 585,
    603, 646, 663, 820; III, 574; IV, 48; V, 471; IX, 351, 500; X,
    884.

SIXTH AMENDMENT.
Trial by jury, IV, 750; VII, 613.

EIGHTH AMENDMENT.
Cruel and unusual punishments, VIII, 588.

NINTH AMENDMENT.
Reserved rights, IV, 618, 750; VI, 395, 831.

TENTH AMENDMENT.
Reserved powers, III, 234, 582, 590; IV, 618, 750; VI, 395, 831.

ELEVENTH AMENDMENT.

Suability of State, II, 335; III, 1026; VII, 250.

TWELFTH AMENDMENT.

Presidential elections, II, 537, 546; III, 30, 608; VII, 34, 37, 40.
Presidential electors. See also article 2, § 1, clauses 2 and 3, II, 545; VII, 34, 37.

THIRTEENTH AMENDMENT.

Slavery prohibited, III, 574; IV, 382; V, 616, 623, 858; VI, 768.

FOURTEENTH AMENDMENT.

General, V, 744, 790, 858; VI, 768.
Privileges and immunities of citizens. See also United States Constitution, article 4, § 2, clause 1, II, 1041; III, 844, 981; V, 309, 325; VIII, 367.
Due process of law. See also Fifth Amendment, II, 594; VII, 760; VIII, 367; X, 884, 902.
Equal protection of the laws, II, 687; VII, 591; VIII, 367; X, 882.
Apportionment of representatives, IV, 85; VII, 725; VIII, 135.

FIFTEENTH AMENDMENT.

Right of suffrage protected, VI, 50, 255, 768.

CONSTITUTION OF 1777.

Section 1:
  . People the source of authority, II, 27.

Section 3:
  Council of revision, II, 4, 495, 741; III, 2.

Section 8:
  Voter's oath of allegiance, II, 38.

Section 18:
  Prorogation of Legislature, II, 708.

Section 23 (see am. 1801):
  Council of Appointment, II, 3, 247, 314, 361, 403, 468, 473, 479, 489, 497, 564, 1020, 1054; III, 2, 17, 92, 1001; VI, 832; VIII, 1053.

Section 24:

Appointment of judges, II, 740; X, 671.
Tenure of military officers, II, 403, 564.

Section 25:

County judge not to hold other office, II, 1053.

Section 36:

Appointment of municipal officers, II, 499.

Section 40:

Magazines of warlike stores, II, 360, 510, 524, 600, 911.

Section 41:

New courts, II. 61, 71, 85, 205, 216, 235, 250, 257, 269.

CONSTITUTION OF 1821.

ARTICLE 1.

Section 2 (Const. 1777, §§ 10, 17; abolished, am. 1845):
Property qualifications of Senators. 1845, IV, 109, 137.

Section 15:

First election of Governor, Lieutenant-Governor and members of
Legislature, III, 1.

ARTICLE 3.

Section 2 (Const. 1777, §§ 10, 17; abolished, am. 1845):
Property qualifications of Governor. 1845, IV, 109, 137; VII, 324.

ARTICLE 4.

Section 7:

Appointment of judges, III, 1012.

Section 12:

Masters, examiners and registers, X, 672.

ARTICLE 5.

Judiciary, III, 719; IV, 53.

Section 5:

Judicial circuits, III, 6, 210, 444; IV, 136; X, 671.

ARTICLE 7.

Section 4 (Const. 1777, § 39):

Clergymen not eligible to office, III, 103.

Section 10 (Am. 1833; am. 1835; Const. 1846; art. 7, §§ 1, 2, 3; am. 1854):

Canal fund, 1821, III, 164, 348, 384, 413, 477, 505, 544, 547, 552, 619, 808; IV, 88, 97, 107.

1833, III, 330, 384, 385, 413, 477, 505, 544, 619; IV, 53.

1835, III, 414, 505, 544, 552, 619; IV, 53.

CONSTITUTION OF 1846.

ARTICLE 1.

Section 17:

Codification, IV, 488; V, 596; VII, 182, 183, 348, 794; IX, 28.

ARTICLE 3.

Section 6 (Const. 1821, art. 1, § 9):

Length of legislative session, 1846, V, 251; VI, 400.

ARTICLE 5.

Section 4 (am. 1876):

State prison inspectors.

1846, IV, 777; V, 77, 268, 437, 758.

1876, V, 78, 437.

ARTICLE 6.

(Am. 1869.)

Judiciary. 1846, V, 746; 1869, VI, 124.

Section 3 (Judiciary Art., 1869, § 6; am. 1888):

Court of Appeals, second division. 1888, VIII, 486; X, 373.

Judiciary Art., 1869, § 12; (abrogated 1894):

Local city courts, appointments to fill vacancies. 1869, VIII, 487.

Section 23:

Tribunals of conciliation, IV, 443, 480, 856.

Section 24:

Commission to revise procedure, IV, 366, 654; V, 596; VII, 182, 183.

Section 25:

Court of Appeals to be organized, X, 673.

Judiciary Art., 1869, § 28; (added 1882):

Additional general term. 1882, VII, 728, 837.

ARTICLE 7.

Canals and finance, IV, 599, 660, 784; VI, 887.

Sections 1, 2, 3 (am. 1854; am. 1874):

Canal sinking fund.

> 1846, IV, 371, 422, 472, 473, 540, 596, 602, 661, 668, 679, 781; V, 3, 4, 49, 65, 151, 208, 253, 255, 360, 363, 368, 590, 705, 706, 783, 828; VI, 10, 11, 12, 14, 103, 349, 384, 629, 658; VII, 4, 6, 230, 422, 685.
>
> 1854, IV, 678, 736, 781, 783, 784, 831, 833, 834; V, 3, 4, 5, 6, 65, 67, 151, 159, 208, 209, 253, 255, 360, 363, 590, 592, 705, 783, 828; VI, 10, 11, 12, 14, 103, 349, 615, 629, 658, 799; VII, 6, 280, 422, 576.
>
> 1874, VI, 540, 799, 1010; VII, 422, 576.

Section 3 (See am. 1854; am. 1874):

Completion of canals.

> 1846, IV, 369, 375, 387, 546, 549, 587, 599, 600, 628, 661, 741, 742.
>
> 1854, IV, 678, 736, 781, 783, 784, 831, 833, 834; V, 3, 5, 6, 65, 67, 152, 208, 209, 253, 255, 360, 363, 590, 592, 705, 783, 828; VI, 10, 11, 12, 14, 103, 349, 615, 629, 658, 799; VII, 6, 280, 422, 576.
>
> 1874, VI, 540, 799, 1010; VII, 422, 576.

Section 5 (am. 1882; abrogated, 1894):

Loans on credit of sinking fund. 1846, IV, 473; VI, 792.
Taxation for canal debt. 1882, VII, 685.

Section 6 (am. 1874; abrogated in 1882):

Canal expenditures. 1874, VII, 6, 359, 684.

Section 7 (1821, art. 7, § 10; abrogated in 1894):
  Salt springs not to be sold.
       1821, III, 148.
       1846, VI, 822, 824; VII, 386; IX, 274, 550.

ARTICLE 10.

Section 1 (1777, § 26; 1821, art. 4, § 11):
  Coroner (omitted in 1894). 1846, VI, 171; IX, 704.

ARTICLE 14.

Section 1:
  First election of members of Legislature, IV, 363.

Section 2:
  First election of Governor, IV, 363.

Section 4:
  First election of judges, IV, 363.

Section 6:
  Disposing of pending judicial business, IV, 363.

Section 8:
  Certain courts abolished, IV, 655.
  Office of Supreme Court commissioner abolished, X, 670.
  Offices of master and examiner in chancery abolished, IV, 414.

CONSTITUTION OF 1894.
ARTICLE 1.

Section 1 (1777, § 13; 1821, art. 7, § 1; 1846, art. 1, § 1):
  Rights of citizens.
       1777, II, 40, 60, 223, 234, 235, 237, 239, 250, 284, 288, 373,
          388, 418, 466, 522, 582, 594, 603, 646, 663, 687, 921.
       1821, II, 40, 60; III, 262.
       1846, II, 40, 60; VIII, 367.
       1894, II, 40, 60, 522, 603, 646, 663.

Section 2 (1777, § 41; 1821, art. 7, § 2; 1846, art. 1, § 2):
  Trial by jury. 1777, II, 71, 85, 205, 223, 235, 249, 250, 269, 284, 757.

Section 3 (1777, § 38; 1821, art. 7, § 3; 1846, art. 1, § 3):
Religious freedom.
1777, II, 921, 948.
1846, VII, 597; VIII, 23, 178, 302, 479.

Section 4 (1821, art. 7, § 6; 1846, art. 1, § 4):
Habeas corpus. 1846, VIII, 504.

Section 5 (1846, art. 1, § 5):
Cruel and unusual punishments. 1846, V, 268; VII, 611, 641; VIII, 588.

Section 6 (1777, § 13; 1821, art. 7, § 7; 1846, art. 1, § 6):
Twice in jeopardy. 1846, VII, 755.
Witness against himself. 1846, IV, 310, 764.
Due process of law.
1777, II, 60, 234, 522, 585, 603, 646, 663.
1846, IV, 759; V, 653; VII, 760, 801; VIII, 367, 874, 1120; IX, 60, 351, 500, 520.
1894, II, 60, 234, 522, 585, 603, 646, 663; X, 534, 777, 884.
Taking private property for public use.
1821, IV, 347.
1846, IV, 496; V, 512, 517, 653; VI, 286, 504, 605, 642; VII, 241, 243, 866, 1015; VIII, 730; IX, 513.
1894, X, 305, 761.

Section 7 (1846, art. 1, § 7):
Eminent domain, compensation for property taken. 1846, IV, 694; V, 880; VI, 90, 97, 217; VII, 775, 1108.
Drainage of agricultural lands, VI, 189; IX, 550, 558.

Section 8 (1821, art. 7, § 8; 1846, art. 1, § 8):
Free speech and free press. 1846, IV, 581; VIII, 573.

Section 9 (1821, art. 7, § 11; 1846, art. 1, § 10):
Right of people to assemble. 1846, VI, 375; VIII, 578.
Lotteries.
1821, II, 1127; III, 526, 567; IV, 807; VII, 715.
1846, IV, 307; VII, 532, 625, 715.
1894, IX, 548.
Pool selling and bookmaking. 1894, IX, 548, 602; X, 982.

Section 11 (1846, art. 1, § 12):
> Feudal tenures. 1846, IV, 409, 559.

Section 13 (1846, art. 1, § 14):
> Limitation of agricultural leases.
> 1846, IV, 245, 409, 559, 653.
> 1894, IV, 245.

Section 14 (1846, art. 1, § 15):
> 'Quarter 'sales 'abolished. 1846, IV, 653.

Section 15 (1777, § 37; 1821, art. 7, § 12; 1846, art. 1, § 16):
> Indian contracts.
> 1777, II, 224, 302, 695.
> 1821, IV, 295.

Section 16 (1777, § 35; 1821, art. 7, § 13; 1846, art. 1, § 17):
> Colonial laws continued.
> 1777, II, 219, 255, 740; X, 681.
> 1821, X, 681.
> 1846, X, 681.
> 1894, X, 681.

Section 17 (1777, § 36; 1821, art. 7, § 14; 1846, art. 1, § 18):
> Royal grants. 1777, II, 610.

Section 18:
> Damages for injuries causing death, VIII, 318.

ARTICLE 2.

Section 1 (1777, § 7; 1821, art. 2, § 1; am. 1826; 1846, art. 2, § 1; am.
> 1864; am. 1874):
> Qualifications of voters.
> 1777, II, 35, 685.
> 1821, III, 58, 158, 772; IV, 133.
> 1826, III, 58, 59, 135, 158; IV, 52.
> 1846, IV, 825, 826; V, 605, 749; VI, 77, 389, 461, 471.
> 1874, VI, 725; VII, 78, 136, 306; VIII, 566, 580, 910, 911, 955,
> 959, 1008, 1117; IX, 95, 97, 195, 395.
> 1894, IX, 555; X, 421.

Section 1 (1846, art. 2, § 1; am. 1864; am. 1874):
  Soldier vote.
      1846, V, 509.
      1864, V, 512, 516.
      1894, IX, 877.

Section 2 (1821, art. 2, § 2; 1846, art. 2, § 2; am. 1874):
  Exclusion from right of suffrage.
      1846, IV, 825; VI, 264, 389.
      1874, VI, 725; VII, 32, 724; VIII, 1093.

Section 2 (1821, art. 2, § 2; 1846, art. 2, § 2; am. 1874):
  Bribery at elections.
      1846, IV, 829.
      1874, VI, 725; VII, 32, 724; VIII, 566, 1093.

Section 3 (1846, art. 2, § 3):
  Voting residence.   1846, VIII, 499, 500.

Section 4 (1821, art. 2, § 3; 1846, art. 2, § 4):
  Registration of voters.
      1821, III, 9.
      1846, IV, 825; V, 92, 195, 605; VII, 306; VIII, 566, 580.
      1894, IX, 309, 555; X, 257.

Section 5 (1777, § 6; 1821, art. 2, § 4; 1846, art. 2, § 5):
  Method of voting.
      1777, VIII, 778, 913.
      1821, VIII, 778, 912, 913.
      1846, VIII, 573, 584, 670; 778, 912, 914, 952, 957; IX, 247.

Section 6:
  Bi-partisan election boards, VIII, 575; 959; IX, 102, 309, 556, 539,
      883.

ARTICLE 3.

Section 1 (1777, § 2; 1821, art. 1, § 1; 1846, art. 3, § 1):
  Legislative power.
      1777, II, 26, 42, 113, 315, 317.
      1821, III, 788, 1021; X, 671.
      1846, IV, 475, 709; VI, 437; VII, 217.

Section 2 (1777, §§ 5, 12; am. 1801; 1821, art. 1, § 2; 1846, art. 3, § 2):
Number of members of Senate and Assembly.
>1777, II, 463; IX, 644.
>1821, IX, 644.
>1846, V, 224.
>1894, IX, 644.

Section 2 (1777, §§ 4, 11; 1821, art. 1, § 2; 1846, art. 3, § 2):
Official term of Senators and Members of Assembly.
>1821, III, 1.
>1846, III, 729.

Section 3 (1846, art. 3, § 3):
Senators to be chosen by single districts. 1846, IV, 363.

Section 4 (1777, § 5; 1821, art. 1, § 6; 1846, art. 3, § 4):
Enumeration of inhabitants.
>1777, II, 305, 651.
>1821, II, 1047; III, 65; IV, 247.
>1846, IV, 857; V, 601; VI, 723; VIII, 40, 59, 66, 84, 133, 135,
>141, 155, 298, 397, 491, 676, 892, 1055; IX, 154.
>1894, X, 722, 868.

Sections 4 and 5 (1777, §§ 4, 12; am. 1801, § 4; 1821, art. 1, §§ 5, 6, 7;
1846, art. 3, §§ 4, 5; am. 1874):
Legislative reapportionment.
>1777, II, 653.
>1801, II, 651, 849.
>1821, II, 1047; III, 567; IV, 250.
>1846, IV, 383, 857; V, 126, 224; VII, 100, 164, 303, 401; VIII,
>157, 397, 677, 741, 1055; IX, 5, 154.
>1894, X, 851.

Section 5 (1777, § 12; 1821, art. 1, § 7; 1846, art. 3, § 5; am. 1874):
Erecting or dividing counties.
>1821, V, 228.
>1846, V, 228; VIII, 289.

Section 6 (1821, art. 1, § 9; 1846, art. 3, § 6; am. 1874):
Compensation of members of the Legislature.
>1846, V, 37, 41, 42; VI, 400, 550.
>1874, VI, 400, 550, 726; VIII, 228.

Section 7 (1821, art. 1, § 10; 1846, art. 3, § 7; am. 1874):
  Members of Legislature not to receive certain civil appointments.
  1821, III, 1001.
  1846, VII, 322.
  1894, X, 46.

Section 8 (1821, art. 1, § 11; 1846, art. 3, § 8; am. 1874):
  Member of Legislature, who not eligible.
  1821, II, 1062.
  1846, II, 1062.
  1894, II, 1062.

Section 10 (1777, §§ 9, 12; 1821, art. 1, § 3; 1846, art. 3, § 10):
  Quorum of Legislature. 1846, IV, 578.
  Legislature to determine qualifications and election of members.
  1777, VIII, 985.
  1846, VIII, 983, 986.
  Legislature to choose its own officers. 1846, V, 486.

Section 11 (1777, § 15; 1821, art. 1, § 4; 1846, art. 3, § 11):
  Legislative journals. 1821, III, 975.

Section 14 (1777, § 31; 1846, art. 3, § 14):
  Enacting clause. 1846, VIII, 143.

Section 15 (1846, art. 3, § 15):
  Manner of passing bills.
  1846, IV, 578; VII, 185, 675.
  1894, VI, 400; VII, 43; IX, 618, 676; X, 145.

Section 16 (1846, art. 3, § 16):
  Private or local bills limited to one subject.
  1846, IV, 517, 524, 774; V, 219, 387, 797; VI, 60, 80, 90, 91,
    174, 190, 271, 326, 328, 331, 506, 508, 509, 596, 693, 702,
    705, 706, 715, 1030, 1032; VII, 326, 334, 758, 768, 775,
    1088, 1098, 1099, 1100, 1120; VIII, 386, 390, 407, 408, 458,
    460, 614, 1122; IX, 75, 211, 271.
  1894, X, 898.
  Local bill must have title. 1846, VIII, 617, 618.
    XI — 3

Section 17 (am. 1874):
    Existing laws not applicable by reference. 1874; VI, 90; IX, 431.

Section 18 (am. 1874; am. 1901):
    Private and local laws.
        1874, VI, 402, 550, 662, 726; VII, 65, 69, 157, 159, 446, 535, 565,
            600, 628, 729, 763, 939; VIII, 52, 101, 343, 1099.
        1894, X, 747, 864.
        1901, VII, 159; VIII, 732; X, 864.
    Changing names. 1874, VI, 813; VII, 748.
    Highways.
        1874, VII, 63, 91, 208, 215, 222, 320, 337, 358, 440, 630, 887;
            VIII, 387, 615, 616, 879, 1086; IX, 134.
        1894, X, 235.
    Draining swamps and lowlands. 1874, VI, 189; VII, 369, 630; VIII,
        614.
    Villages.
        1874, VI, 683, 825; VII, 159, 214, 390, 645, 775, 878, 879, 1123;
            VIII, 330, 1115, 1131, 1155; IX, 258.
        1894, X, 233.
        1901, VII, 159.
    Supervisors. 1874, VII, 769, 843, 860; IX, 224.
    Jurors. 1874, IX, 516.
    Elections. 1874, VII, 263, 370.
    Fees and allowances. 1874, VI, 877; VII, 251, 259, 260, 497, 540,
        549, 604, 753, 777, 1055, 1098, 1115, 1121; VII, 412.
    Exclusive privilege.
        1874, VI, 662, 691, 814, 949, 1034; VII, 336, 845; VIII, 411,
            463, 880.
        1894, X, 305, 399, 467.
    Railroads.
        1874, VII, 395, 592, 895, 900, 1063; VIII, 615; IX, 271, 509.
        1894, X, 542.
    Tax exemptions. 1901, VIII, 732; IX, 232.
    Bridges.
        1874, VII, 208, 383, 578, 589, 909.
        1894, X, 874.
    Street railroads.
        1874, VII, 896, 900, 1037, 1040, 1064, 1068.
        1894, X, 574, 624.

Section 19 (am. 1874):

Private claims not to be audited by Legislature.
1874, VI, 875; VII, 81, 83, 86, 88, 158, 227, 230, 463, 485, 492,
495, 525, 779, 782, 785, 792, 850, 922, 929, 1055; IX, 142.
1894, IX, 717.

Section 20 (1821, art. 7, § 9; 1846, art. 1, § 9):

Two-thirds bills.
1821, III, 15, 36, 37, 91, 533, 592, 655; IV, 56, 193.
1846, IV, 578, 693; V, 139, 245, 351, 352, 440, 442, 443; VI,
212, 331, 332, 579, 678, 690, 692, 707; VII, 48; VIII, 381,
463.
1894, IX, 618; X, 778.

Section 21 (1846, art. 7, § 8):

No money paid from treasury except by appropriation. 1846, IV,
378; V, 72, 816; VI, 588, 863, 947; VII, 82, 220, 799, 912; VIII,
246, 420, 547.
When appropriations expire. 1846, VI, 947; VII, 1026.

Section 22:

Riders in appropriation bills. 1894, VII, 26, 159, 1085; IX, 276,
403.

Section 24 (1846, art. 7, § 13):

Tax Law to state object of tax. 1846, V, 817; VI, 584; VII, 772;
IX, 60.

Section 25 (1846, art. 7, § 14):

Three-fifth bills.
1846, IV, 578.
1894, IX, 618.

Section 26 (am. 1874, art. 3, § 22; am. 1899):

Boards of supervisors established.
1874, VII, 65, 70, 136, 848, 939; VIII, 517; IX, 224.
1894, IX, 585, 706, 753.
1899, IX, 706, 753.

Section 27 (1846, art. 3, § 17; am. 1874, art. 3, § 23):

    Powers of boards of supervisors.
        1846, IV, 434, 496, 575.
        1874, VI, 402; VII, 65, 70, 729, 757, 848, 939; VIII, 509, 517.

Section 28 (am. 1874):

    Extra compensation prohibited.
        1874, VI, 403; VII, 49, 158, 223, 259, 260, 261, 262, 372, 374,
            499, 539, 540, 550, 753, 773, 777, 791, 1055, 1115; VIII,
            228.
        1894, X, 243.

Section 29:

    Prison labor. 1894, IX, 181, 549, 559, 653, 659, 668, 683, 739; X,
        166.

ARTICLE 4.

Section 1 (1777, § 17; 1821, art. 3, § 1; 1846, art. 4, § 1; am. 1874):

    Executive power.
        1777, II, 114.
        1821, III, 1021; X, 671.
    Official term of Governor and Lieutenant-Governor.
        1777, VI, 398.
        1821, III, 1, VI, 398.
        1846, VI, 398.
        1874, VI, 398.

Section 4 (1777, § 18; 1821, art. 3, § 4; 1846, art. 4, § 4; am. 1874):

    Governor, general powers and duties. 1846, IX, 1.
    Commander-in-chief.
        1821, III, 833.
        1894, IX, 640.
    Extraordinary sessions.
        1777, II, 251.
        1821, III, 40.
        1846, IV, 579, 694, 734; VII, 122; VIII, 132, 133, 135, 643; IX,
            154.
        1894, X, 695, 820, 821.

Message to Legislature.
    1821, III, 1.
    1846, VI, 719; VIII, 2.
Condition of State, recommendations.
    1777, II, 2, 1014.
    1821, III, 1003.
    1846, V, 458, 582, 789; VI, 4, 644, 719, 751; VII, 728; VIII, 2, 80, 784.
    1894, IX, 537, 578; X, 832.
Governor to see that laws are executed.
    1821, III, 222, 1002, 1031; IV, 149.
    1846, IV, 729, 778; V, 105, 466.
Compensation. 1874, VIII, 228.
Section 5 (1777, § 18; 1821, art. 3, § 5; 1846, art. 4, § 5):
  Reprieves. 1777, II, 576, 621, 922.
  Commutations.
    1821, III, 33.
    1846, IV, 405.
  Pardons.
    1777, II, 68, 599, 855.
    1821, III, 1, 284.
    1846, IV, 405, 427, 435; V, 93, 116, 171, 266, 758; VI, 268, 426; VII, 199, 345, 707, 994; IX, 1.

Section 6 (1777, § 20; 1821, art. 3, § 6; 1846, art. 4, § 6):
  When Governor may act as commander-in-chief out of State. 1777, II, 271.

Sections 6 and 7 (1777, § 20; 1821, art. 3, §§ 6, 7; 1846, art. 4, §§ 6, 7):
  Gubernatorial succession.
    1777, II, 674, 887.
    1821, III, 221, 269.
    1846, IV, 433; VIII, 1.
    1894, IV, 433.

Section 8 (1846, art. 4, § 8; am. 1874):
  Lieutenant-Governor's compensation. 1874, VIII, 228.

Section 9 (1777, § 3; 1821, art. 1, § 12; 1846, art. 4, § 9; am. 1874):
  Executive consideration of bills.
    1846, VIII, 434; IX, 1.
    1894, IX, 537; X, 832.

Veto.
> 1821, III, 2; IV, 251.
> 1846, IV, 769; VII, 668.
> 1874, IX, 404.
> 1894, X, 832.

Passage of bill over veto.
> 1821, III, 531, 1003; IV, 252.
> 1846, VI, 117, 1003.
> 1874, VII, 672, 675.

Ten-day period. 1874, VII, 242, 338, 400, 667, 668, 673, 802, 891, 998; VIII, 429, 1003.

Thirty-day period. 1874, IV, 524; VI, 642, 852, 884, 909; VII, 169, 940.

Veto of items in appropriation bills.
> 1874, V, 263; VI, 369, 403, 642, 852, 864, 883, 924; VIII, 867; IX, 404.
> 1894, I, 7; X, 935.

ARTICLE 5.

Section 1 (1777, § 23; 1821, art. 4, § 6; 1846, art. 5, §§ 1, 2):
State officers. 1821, III, 1004.
State Engineer and Surveyor. 1846, VIII, 74, 175; IX, 425.

Section 3 (am. 1876):
Superintendent of Public Works. Am. 1876. VI, 397, 934; VII, 11, 50, 143, 235, 358, 365, 423, 1024; VIII, 487, 710.
Suspension of Superintendent.
> 1876, VIII, 488.
> 1894, IX, 549.

Section 4 (am. 1876):
Superintendent of Prisons.
> 1876, V, 78, 373, 437; VI, 109, 233, 355, 397, 398, 942, 984; VII, 9, 11, 424, 519, 963; VIII, 487.
> 1894, IX, 549.

Section 5 (1846, art. 5, § 5):
Commissioners of the Land Office. 1846, VIII, 53, 726, 735; IX, 425.
Canal board. 1846, VI, 106.

Section 6 (1846, art. 5, § 6):
Powers and duties of State boards and officers. 1894, X, 187.

Section 7 (1846, art. 5, § 7):
Suspension of State Treasurer. 1846, VI, 633; VIII, 488.

Section 8 (1846, art. 5, § 8):
Commercial inspections abolished. 1846, III, 722; VI, 282; VII, 659, 751; IX, 522.

Section 9:
Civil service, VII, 838; VIII, 151; IX, 549, 560, 663, 749, 760, 840; X, 18, 419, 470, 741.

ARTICLE 6.

Section 1 (1821, art. 5, § 4; 1846, art. 6, § 3; Judiciary Art., § 6; am. 1905):
Supreme Court.
  1821, IV, 136; X, 672.
  1846, IV, 366; X, 672.
  1869, VII, 80, 238, 615, 798.
  1894, X, 375, 675.
Judicial districts.
  1821, III, 6.
  1846, IV, 857; X, 673.
  1905, X, 337.
Reorganization of judicial districts.
  1846, IV, 857.
  1905, IV, 857; IX, 547; X, 337.
Increase of judges according to population.
  1846, IV, 615.
  1905, X, 337, 516, 849, 936.

Section 2 (1846, art. 6, § 6; 1869, § 7; am. 1899; am. 1905):
Appellate Division.
  1894, IX, 545, 546; X, 373.
  1899, X, 373.
  1905, X, 373, 849.
Judicial departments. 1894, IX, 545, 546.
Supreme Court reporter. 1894, X, 679.

Section 3 (1846, art. 6, § 5; Judiciary Art. 1869, § 8):
Testimony in equity cases. 1846, IV, 367, 368.
Legislative regulation of judicial proceedings. 1846, IV, 367.

Section 4 (1821, art. 4, § 7; 1846, art. 6, § 13; Judiciary Art. 1869, § 9):
Supremè Court, appointments to fill vacancies. 1869, VIII, 487.

Section 5 (Judiciary Art. 1869, § 12; am. 1880):
Certain local courts abolished. 1894, IX, 545.

Section 6:
Oyer and terminer and circuit courts abolished. 1894, IX, 545.

Section 7 (1846, art. 6, § 2; Judiciary Art. 1869, § 2; am. 1899):
Court of Appeals, continued.
    1846, X, 672.
    1894, X, 674.
Court of Appeals, additional judges. 1899, X, 373.

Sections 7, 19 (1777, § 27; 1821, art. 4, §§ 9, 13, 14; 1846, art. 6, § 19; Judiciary Art. 1869, §§ 2, 19):
Court clerks. 1777, II, 243, 500.

Section 8 (1821, art. 4, § 7; 1846, art. 6, § 13; Judiciary Art. 1869, § 3):
Court of Appeals, appointments to fill vacancies.
    1869, VIII, 487.
    1894, X, 674.

Section 9:
Jurisdiction of Court of Appeals. 1894, VIII, 181, 230; IX, 545; X, 344, 674.

Section 10 (1777, § 25; 1821, art. 5. § 7; 1846, art. 6, § 8; Judiciary Art. 1869, § 10):
Judges not to hold other office. 1777, II, 325, 647, 1053; X, 671, 679.
    1821, III, 6; X, 672, 679.
    1846, X, 679.
    1869, IX, 515.
    1894, X, 679.

Section 11 (1821, art. 1, § 13; art. 6, § 6; am. 1845; 1846, art. 6, § 11; Judiciary Art. 1869, § 11):
Removal of judicial officers.
    1821, X, 672.

1845, IV, 109, 137.
1846, V, 723.
1869, VI, 440; VII, 533, 534; VIII, 935.
1894, VII, 534; X, 830.

Section 12 (1777, § 24; 1821, art. 5, § 3; 1846, art. 6, § 7; Judiciary Art.
§§ 13, 14; am. 1880):
Compensation of judges.
1846, VII, 259.
1869, VII, 259, 260, 262.
Judicial age limit.
1777, II, 362, 461, 622.
1821, III, 85; X, 671.
Judicial pensions. 1880, II, 363.

Section 13 (1777, §§ 32, 33; 1821, art. 5, § 2; 1846, art. 6, § 1; Judiciary
Art. 1869, § 1):
Court for the trial of impeachments.
1777, X, 671.
1894, X, 674.

Section 14 (1777, § 24; 1821, art. 5, § 6; 1846, art. 6, § 14; Judiciary
Art. 1869, § 15):
Jurisdiction of County Court.
1869, IV, 562; VII, 614.
1894, IV, 562.
County Judge.
1821, III, 1012.
1846, IV, 625, 626; X, 673.
When to act as surrogate. 1869, VII, 615.
Holding court in other county.
1869, IV, 627.
1894, IV, 627.

Section 15 (1777, § 24; 1821, art. 5, § 6; 1846, art. 6, § 14; Judiciary
Art. 1869, § 15):
Surrogates.
1869, IX, 124.
1894, IX, 122.

Section 16 (1846, art. 6, § 15; Judiciary Art. 1869, § 16):
Special county judge and surrogate.
     1846, IV, 626; X, 675.
     1894, X, 676.

Section 17 (1777, § 23; 1821, art. 4, § 7; Am. 1826; 1846, art. 6, § 17;
     Judiciary Art. 1869, § 18):
Justices of the peace, election and tenure of office.
     1777, III, 161.
     1821, III, 17, 57, 161, 1012.
     1826, III, 17, 57, 135, 161; IV, 52; X, 673.
     1846, 1V, 684; VI, 74, 208, 327, 480.
     1869, VI, 327, 480, 512, 517; VII, 44.
     1894, III, 57.
Removal of justices of the peace. 1846, VI, 49.
City judicial officers. 1894, X, 675.

Section 18 (1777, § 24; 1821, art. 5, § 6; 1846, art. 6, § 14; Judiciary Art.,
     § 19):
Inferior local courts.
     1846, V, 138; VI, 937; X, 673.
     1894, X, 674, 675.

Section 19 (1821, art. 4, § 9; 1846, art. 6, § 19; Judiciary Art. 1869,
     § 20):
Supreme Court clerks. 1869, VI, 266, VII, 356.
Clerk of Appellate Division. 1894, X, 679.

Section 20 (1846, art. 6, § 20; Judiciary Art. 1869, § 21):
Judicial officers, who may not receive fees.
     1846, IV, 684, 686, 777.
     1869, IX, 481.

ARTICLE 7.
Section 1 (1846, art. 7, § 9):
No State credit to private enterprise. 1846, V, 138, 245, 443; VI,
     177, 178, 346, 384.

Section 2 (1846, art. 7, § 10):
Emergency debts. 1846, VI, 473; V, 253, 360, 590, 705, 783; VI,
     890, 923; VII, 400.

Section 4 (1846, art 7, § 12; am. 1905):

Limiting State debts.

    1846, IV, 56, 262, 546, 549, 587, 631, 668, 670, 677, 678, 744,
        833; V, 68, 153, 253, 360, 590, 705, 708, 783, 817, 828;
        VI, 11, 12, 72, 178, 346, 349, 384, 629, 658, 838, 890, 909;
        VII, 399; VIII, 926.

    1894, IV, 56; X, 246, 495, 496, 577, 600, 781.

    1905, IV, 883; V, 7; IX, 305; X, 246, 496, 577, 731, 781, 848.

Section 5 (am. 1874):

Sinking funds. 1874, VI, 540.

Section 6 (am. 1874):

Claims barred by Statute of Limitations. 1874, VI, 540; VII, 599,
    602, 606, 644, 773, 781, 801, 1120, 1121, 1124; VIII, 1125; IX,
    66, 119, 370, 429, 452; X, 255, 268.

Section 7:

Forest Preserve. 1894, IX, 187, 300, 569, 835; X, 263, 339, 458,
    753, 756.

Section 8 (1846, art. 7, § 6; am. 1874; am. 1882):

Canals not to be sold.

    1846, V, 158, 208; VI, 106, 239.

    1874, VI, 540, 749, 796; VII, 280.

    1882, VII, 685.

    1894, X, 731.

Sale of lateral canals.

    1874, VI, 540, 749, 796.

    1882, VII, 685.

Section 9 (1821, art. 7, § 10; 1846, art. 7, § 3; am. 1854, 1874, 1882):

No tolls on canals.

    1821, III, 169, 462.

    1882, VII, 685, 818; VIII, 13.

Annual tax for canals. 1882, VII, 685, 818.

Canal contracts.

    1854, V, 712; VII, 369.

    1874, VI, 540; VII, 369.

    1882, VII, 685, 818.

No extra compensation to canal contractors.

    1874, VI, 540; VIII, 626.

    1882, VIII, 626; IX, 431.

Section 10:
> Canal improvement. 1894, IX, 305, 549.

Section 11 (added 1905):
> State debts, sinking funds. 1905, IX, 305; X, 577, 601, 731, 848, 923.

Section 12 (added 1905):
> Improvement of highways. 1905, VIII, 1043; X, 214, 513, 732, 833, 850, 909.

ARTICLE 8.

Section 1 (1821, art. 7, § 9; 1846, art. 8, § 1):
> Corporations.
> 1821, III, 521, 539, 655.
> 1846, IX, 379, 513, 522, 526, 531, 574, 593, 633, 636, 638, 639,
> 823; V, 129, 133, 147, 191, 231, 645, 655, 658, 711, 848;
> VI, 168, 246, 353, 640; VII, 202, 233, 241, 336, 357, 371,
> 546, 565, 745, 845, 857, 868, 939; VIII, 52, 197, 297; IX, 93.
> 1894, X, 865.

Section 2 (1846, art. 8, § 2):
> Dues from corporations. 1846, IV, 401, 402, 824; V, 644.

Section 4 (1846, art. 8, § 4; am. 1874):
> Savings banks charters.
> 1846, VI, 315; VIII, 231.
> 1874, VI, 725; VIII, 232.

Section 6 (1846, art. 8, § 6):
> Redemption of bills and notes. 1846, IV, 380, 394.

Section 7 (1846, art. 8, § 7):
> Liability of bank stockholders. 1846, IV, 402, 441.

Section 9 (am. 1874):
> State aid restricted. 1874, VII, 90, 91, 206, 915, 1033; VIII, 250,
> 253, 254, 405; IX, 107.

Section 10 (am. 1874, art. 8, § 11; am. 1884, 1899, 1905, 1907):

Limiting municipal indebtedness.

1874, IV, 806; VI, 402, 917; VII, 47, 569, 617, 652, 661, 727, 754, 846, 867, 1018, 1047, 1088, 1107; VIII, 239.

1884, VII, 728; VIII, 27, 161, 162, 184, 189, 239, 529, 880, 996; IX, 142, 512.

1894, IV, 806; VIII, 29.

1899, VIII, 29; X, 243, 264, 275, 343, 453, 535, 777, 804.

1905, VIII, 28; X, 851, 908, 942.

1907, VIII, 29.

Section 11:

State Board of Charities. 1894, V, 761; VIII, 173; IX, 550; X, 157, 190.

State Commission in Lunacy. 1894, VI, 629; VIII, 173, 485; IX, 191, 550.

Prison Commission. 1894, IX, 550, 654; X, 191.

Section 12:

Commissions, how appointed. 1894, IX, 550.

Section 13:

Existing laws continued. 1894, IX, 550; X, 157.

Section 14:

General provisions, institutions and inmates. 1894, IX, 550, 551, 568.

State Board of Charities, rules regulating admissions to institutions. 1894, V, 761.

Section 15:

Commissioners continued; additional powers. 1894, IX, 550; X, 405.

ARTICLE 9.

Section 1:

Common schools 1894, II, 729; VI, 617; VIII, 171; IX, 549, 616.

Section 2:

University. 1894, VIII, 171; X, 113.

Section 3 (1821, art. 7, § 10; 1846, art. 9, § 1):
    Education funds.
        1821, III, 8, 411; IV, 65, 88, 112.
        1846, IV, 377, 396, 550, 782; V, 230; VIII, 148; IX, 69.

Section 4:
    Sectarian aid prohibited. 1894, IX, 549.

ARTICLE 10.

Section 1 (1777, §§ 26, 28; 1821, art. 4, § 8; 1846, art. 10, § 1):
    County officers.
        1846, VI, 734, 833.
        1894, IX, 704.
    Sheriff. 1821, VI, 734.
    District attorney.
        1846, VI, 491, 833; IX, 410.
        1894, X, 392.
    Governor's power of removal.
        1821, III, 133.
        1894, X, 230.

Section 2 (1777, §§ 22, 29; 1821, art. 4, §§ 10, 15; am. 1833, 1839; 1846,
    art. 10, § 2):
    Home rule, local officers.
        1777, II, 41.
        1821, II, 41; VI, 832.
        1833, III, 212; IV, 52.
        1839, IV, 53.
        1846, II, 41; IV, 684; VI, 30, 75, 77, 128, 216, 425, 496, 497,
            504, 507, 517, 734, 1019, 1029, 1031, 1032, 1033; VII, 106,
            107, 218, 357, 746, 1098; VIII, 85, 86, 1143; IX, 29, 96, 97,
            337.
        1894, II, 42; IX, 591; X, 210, 288, 541, 750, 913.
    Appointment by Legislature. 1846, VII, 126, 179, 208, 216, 317, 327,
        901; VIII, 519, 594, 635, 880, 995; IX, 371, 399, 411, 497, 511.
    Meaning of term " authority."
        1846, VIII, 85, 86.
        1894, IX, 584.

Section 3 (1777, § 28; 1821, art. 4, § 16; 1846, art. 10, § 3):
    Duration of office. 1777, II, 500.

Section 5 (1846, art. 10, § 5):

Vacancies in office. 1846, IV, 433; VI, 75, 497, 989; VII, 44, 179; IX, 224.

Section 6 (1777, § 2; 1821, art. 1, § 14; 1846, art. 10, § 6):
Annual meeting of Legislature.
    1777, II, 252.
    1821, II, 960.
    1846, II, 960; V, 251; VII, 729.
    1894, II, 960.

Section 7 (1846, art. 10, § 7):
Removal of officers, 1846, VI, 806.

Section 8 (1846, art. 10, § 8):
Legislature may determine vacancies. 1846, VI, 497.

Section 9 (am. 1874):
Compensation of State officers. 1874, VIII, 228.

ARTICLE 11.

Militia, general. 1894, IX, 743, 827.

Section 1 (1777, § 24; 1821, art. 7, § 5; 1846, art. 11, § 1):
Military service; exemptions.
    1821, III, 880.
    1846, V, 456.
    1894, X, 510.

Section 3 (1777, § 40; 1821, art. 7, § 5; 1846, art. 11, § 1):
Militia to be maintained.
    1777, II, 399, 600, 853, 911; X, 456.
    1821, III, 85.
    1846, IV, 726; V, 392.
    1894, X, 15.
Naval militia. 1894, VIII, 829.

Section 4 (1777, § 21; 1821, art. 4, § 2; 1846, art. 11, § 3):
Appointment of militia officers. 1846, V, 608; VIII, 487.

Section 5 (1777, § 25; 1821, art. 4, § 3; 1846, art. 11, §§ 4, 6):
Militia elections. 1846, VII, 797.

ARTICLE 12.

Municipal government. 1894, VII, 136.

Section 1 (1846, art. 8, § 9; am. 1905):

Cities and villages, restricting taxation and indebtedness. 1846, IV, 563, 701, 730; V, 849; VI, 825; VII, 31, 637.
Protection of employees. 1905, VIII, 317; X, 190, 850, 916.

Section 2 (am. 1907):

Special city laws.
1894, IX, 339, 547, 617, 621, 650, 677, 696, 709, 715; X, 152, 153, 208, 355, 541, 574, 624, 683, 685.
1907, IX, 678.

Section 3:

City elections. 1894, VIII, 17; IX, 704, 705; X, 911.

ARTICLE 13.

Section 1 (1821, art. 6, § 1; 1846, art. 12, § 1; am. 1874):
Official oath.
1821, III, 209.
1846, V, 38, 445; VI, 1; VII, 45.
1874, VII, 32, 44, 45; VIII, 583, 892.
1894, III, 209.

Section 2 (am. 1874, art. 15, § 1):
Bribery of public officers. 1874, VI, 725.

Section 3 (am. 1874, art. 15, § 2):
Bribery, how punished. 1874, VI, 725.

ARTICLE 14.

Section 1 (1821, art. 8, § 1; 1846, art. 13, § 1):
Constitutional amendments.
1821, IV, 52, 103, 677.
1846, IV, 547; V, 597; VI, 394; VII, 161; VIII, 921, 1060, 1062.

Section 2 (1846, art. 13, § 2):
Constitutional Conventions.
1846, V, 597, 708, 744; VIII, 177, 308, 394, 471, 484.
1894, VIII, 474.

MEMORANDUMS ON APPROVAL OF BILLS.

ADIRONDACK PARK. Established, IX, 145.

ALBANY. Hawk street bridge, VIII, 612; paving certain streets, 790; public market, 447.

ALBANY AND BATH-ON-THE-HUDSON BRIDGE CO. Charter, IX, 715.

ALBANY BURGESS CORPS. Arms for, VII, 248.

AMSTERDAM. City charter, VIII, 88.

APPORTIONMENT ACT. 1879, VII, 401.

APPROPRIATION BILL. 1905, X, 781; 1906, X, 930.

ASSEMBLY CHAMBER. Repairs to ceiling, VIII, 608.

ATTORNEY-GENERAL. Appearance before grand juries, IX, 409.

AUBURN. Increasing salaries, VIII, 825.

BALDWINSVILLE. Legalizing water bonds, VIII, 1026.

BALLOT REFORM ACT. 1890, VIII, 1005.

BANKS. Suspension act, III, 645.

BENSONHURST PARK. Amending act, VIII, 1157.

BOARD OF CLAIMS. Awards, VIII, 100; Peck & Co., Linus Jones, IX, 600.

BOYS TRAINING SCHOOL. Establishing, X, 518.

BROCKPORT. Legalizing special election for establishment of sewer system, X, 518.

BROOKLYN. Bedford and Remsen avenues, improvement, X, 155; elevated railroad bill, VII, 129; gas, regulating price, 431; health department, VII, 455; Lee and Nostrand avenues, VIII, 559; street improvements, 1021; unpaid taxes and assessments, VII, 502.

BUCKET SHOPS. Regulating, VIII, 815.

BUFFALO. Firemen, disabled, half pay, VIII, 561.

CANAL DEBT. Interest, X, 922.

CANAL DEBT SINKING FUNDS. Appropriation, X, 922.

CANALS. Cayuga and Seneca, repairing wall, VI, 858.

Clark and Skinner, docking, VI, 861.

Erie. Black Rock harbor, dredging and excavating, VI, 860; Buffalo basin, deepening, 860; Buffalo, Black Rock improvements, 858, deepening near Macedon locks, 859; Jordan level and Weedsport, repairs, 856; Medina improvements, 858; Pittsford, rebuilding wall, 862; Pittsford and Brighton, damages, 861; Port Byron, rebuilding wall, 857; Port Gibson, repairs, 860; Rochester, road bridge, Averill and Munger streets, 859; State dam on

XI — 4

CANALS — (*Continued*).
  Erie — (*Continued*).
        Scajaquady creek, removal, 861; towing path, repairs, Utica
            and other points, 854.
    Fort Edward feeder, completing bridge, VI, 855.
    Genesee Valley, Genesee river bridge, Mount Morris, VI, 862.
    Glens Falls feeder, rebuilding lock, VI, 855.
    Improvements, VIII, 561.
    Oneida lake, completion of, VI, 858.
    Oswego, various repairs, VI, 857; Syracuse, bridge, North Salina
        street, X, 929.
    Rochester, swing bridge, Buffalo street, VI, 852.
    Rocky Rift feeder dam, completion of, VI, 853.
    Watervliet bridge, completion, VI, 854.
CHARITABLE INSTITUTIONS AND REFORMATORIES. Monthly estimates in
    certain cases, IX, 436.
CIVIL SERVICE. Two examinations act, 1897, IX, 756; veterans, preference
    and removals, X, 419.
COLLATERAL INHERITANCES. Graduated tax, VIII, 1150.
COMMERCIAL TRAVELERS' HOME ASSOCIATION OF AMERICA. Charter. IX,
    87.
CONVICT LABOR. Act of 1888, VIII, 658; 1889, VIII, 814.
CORONERS. Kings county, term of office, IX, 704.
CORPORATIONS. Tax act of 1880, VII, 454.
CORRUPT PRACTICES ACT. 1890, VIII, 1001.
COUNTY CLERK. Chautauqua, salaried office, VIII, 1025; Monroe, salary,
    VIII, 260.
COUNTY TREASURER. Queens county, appointment of deputy, VIII, 998.
COURT OF CLAIMS. Deltry, Draper and Borgersrud, submission of claims,
    X, 286.

DOG TAX, VIII, 823.
DUTCHESS COUNTY. Water rights, X, 691.

EAST AURORA. Legalizing bonds, X, 284.
EAST RIVER. Bulk-head line, VIII, 834.
EAST RIVER BRIDGE CO. Charter, IX, 90.
ELEVATED RAILROADS. New York, rates of fare, IX, 500.
ELEVATORS. Grain, regulating charges, VIII, 603.
EMIGRATION COMMISSIONERS. Appropriation, VII, 802.
ESCHEAT. General act, VIII, 1014.
EXCISE. Five gallon sales, VIII, 440; laws, revision, 1892, IX, 105.

FOREIGN INSURANCE COMPANIES. Canceling authority, IX, 691.
FOREST PRESERVE. Purchase of lands, VIII, 999.
FREE SCHOOL FUND. Apportionment, X, 941.

GAME AND FISH PROTECTORS, VIII, 607.
GAME LAW. Fishing in Lake Ontario, VIII, 432.
GAS. Illuminating, regulating price in certain cities, VIII, 1021.
GENERAL ELECTRIC COMPANY. Charter, IX, 99.
GENERAL LAWS. Corporations, towns and highways, VIII, 1027.
GENESEO NORMAL SCHOOL. New buildings, IX, 593.
GREATER NEW YORK. Charter commission, IX, 705.
GUARANTORS AND SURETIES. Bonds of foreign insurance companies, IX, 596.

HANCOCK. Compromising railroad indebtedness, VIII, 128.
HEMPSTEAD. Free school, amending act, VIII, 1156.
HIGHWAYS. Amending act of 1898, X, 909; improvement bonds, 909; improvement debt interest, 922; improvement fund, appropriation, 922; streams as public, condemnation proceedings, 457.
HORSE-RACING. State Racing Commission, IX, 601.

ICE. Hudson river, rights of riparian owner, X, 689.
INSANE. State care, IX, 226.
INSANE ASYLUMS. Buffalo and Hudson River, appropriation, VII, 123.
INSANITY LAW. State hospitals, boards of managers abolished, X, 404.
INSURANCE LAW. Amendments, X, 906.
INTEREST. Reducing rate of, VII, 404.
INTERNATIONAL PRISON CONGRESS. Delegate to, VIII, 127.
ISABELLA HEIMATH, THE. Charter, VIII, 789.

JAMAICA BAY. Protection of fish in, VIII, 1025.
JOHNSON ESTATE. Amending act, X, 283.
JOHNSON MANSION AND BLOCKHOUSE, JOHNSTOWN. Acquisition, X, 941.

KINGS COUNTY. Brooklyn supervisors, filling vacancies, IX, 223; interpreters, compensation, X, 158; sheriff, county clerk and register, making office salaried (3 bills) 290.
KINGSTON. Consolidation of school districts, X, 437.

LABOR. Hours and wages, X, 914; regulating hours of, X, 48.
LACONA. Legalizing sale of bonds, X, 285.
LEGISLATURE. Persons appearing before committees, notice of employment, X, 904.
LIBRARIES. Free, encouraging growth of, VIII, 290.
LIQUOR TAX LAW. Act of 1896, IX, 696; amendments, X, 290 inspection of hotels, 902; inspection of hotels, revocation of certificate, 780 (2 bills); sales by pharmacists, 542.
LITTLE FALLS. Highway commissioners, legalizing acts of, VIII, 1156.
LOCKPORT. Sewer, VIII, 562; water supply, X, 418.

MADISON FORKS OBITUARY SOCIETY. Changing name, acquiring land, VIII, 1163.

MEDICAL EXAMINERS. Examination of certain candidates, VIII, 1152.

MIDDLETOWN. City charter, VIII, 564.

MILO. Failure to make assessment, new authorized, VIII, 257.

MORTGAGES. Tax act, 1905, X, 800; recording tax, 1906, 920.

MOUNT VERNON. Schools, licensing teachers, IX, 598.

MUTUAL LIFE INSURANCE COMPANIES. Election of directors, X, 899.

NAVAL MILITIA. Established, VIII, 829.

NEW CAPITOL. Advisory board created, appropriation, VIII, 31, 93; appropriation, 1879, VII, 403; 1892, IX, 89; appropriation, new commission created, VIII, 1017; continuing work, 1880, VII, 453; 1888, VIII, 610; 1891, 1149; 1893, IX, 223; liability of commissioners, liquidation, VII, 399.

NEW CAPITOL AND INSANE ASYLUMS. Appropriations, VII, 123.

NEW YORK. Board of electrical control, extending duration, VIII, 1163; comptroller and fire insurance, 433; consolidation act, 1882, VII, 802; Croton aqueduct, new commission, VIII, 656; district courts, relief of clerks and assistants, VII, 451; dock commissioners, VIII, 832; elections, III, 851; election boards, IX, 102; electrical subways, VIII, 450; gas, eighty cent bill, X, 900; gas companies, limiting price of gas, VIII, 241; gas companies, organization, VIII, 240; high school, additional evening, 261; mayor, appointments without confirmation, VII, 1056; normal college, incorporation and maintenance, VIII, 607; park commissioners, extending jurisdiction, 430; police justices, increasing number, 794; public health, act relative to, 430; railroads in annexed district, IX, 99; rapid transit, VIII, 1142, IX, 90, 504; register, act relative to, VII, 1072; registry law, repeal, III, 988; steam railroads, terminating use of certain streets, X, 897; tax bill, 1872, VI, 415; teachers' retirement fund, IX, 411; teachers' salaries, X, 154; water supply, increasing, VII, 900, VIII, 270; water supply, sanitary protection, IX, 225; using for generation of electricity, X, 804.

NEW YORK ARCADE RAILWAY CO. Relative to, VIII, 261.

NEW YORK AND BROOKLYN BRIDGE. Completion and opening, VII, 450.

NEW YORK HISTORICAL SOCIETY. Changing site, VIII, 824.

NEW YORK HOSPITAL. Changing site, continuing exemption from taxation, VIII, 824.

NORTHERN NEW YORK INSTITUTION FOR DEAF-MUTES. Appropriation, VIII, 835, X, 289.

OGDENSBURG. Changing date of election; school officers, X, 910; sewers, VIII, 96.

OSWEGO. County jail, changing site, VIII, 429; creating office of city chamberlain, reducing number of aldermen, 427.

OSWEGO & MIDLAND RAILROAD CO. Aiding construction, V, 813.

Palisades. Extending park, X, 940.

Penal Code. Original act, VII, 663.

Penn Yan. Water supply, IX, 411.

Perjury. Presumption, outside contradictory statements, X, 905.

Pipe Line Companies. General act, VII, 241.

Police Matrons. Appointment required in certain cities, VIII, 1147.

Police Patrolmen. Pay in certain cities, IX, 498.

Political Enrollment. In towns, X, 417.

Pool-Selling. Prescribing periods of racing on grounds of incorporated associations, VIII, 434.

Poughkeepsie Bridge. Extending time for completion, VIII, 443.

Printing. Legislative legalized, Bloomingdale Asylum investigation, VIII, 793.

Public Instruction. Increasing salary of deputy superintendent, VIII, 565.

Quarantine. Amending act, VIII, 557.

Queens County. Court attendants, X, 151.

Railroads. Incorporation and powers, amending general act, X, 799; injuries to employees, 924; inspection of locomotive boilers, 772; limiting hours of service, IX, 145.

Rapid Transit. Harvey experiments, VIII, 125.

Receivers. Moneyed institutions, repeal, III, 973.

Rochester. Streets and water pipes, X, 540; wards, increase of, IX, 85.

Rochester Athenaeum. Changing name and number of directors, VIII, 1162.

Savings Banks. Investments, Buffalo Creek railroad, X, 576; Los Angeles bonds, X, 454.

Schools. Temperance instruction, IX, 612.

Sheriff. New York, salaried office, VII, 1023, IX, 413.

Smithtown. Relief of, IX, 703.

Soldiers and Sailors' Home. Supervision by State Board of Charities X, 156.

Southern Central Railroad Company. Aiding construction, V, 813.

State. Laborers, regulating pay, VIII, 1003; paying debt, preserving credit, III, 1008.

State Hospital. Northeastern part of State, reappropriation, X, 794.

State Survey. Appropriation, VII, 248.

Statutory Revision Bills. 1892, IX, 135.

Stenographers. First judicial department, salaries, X, 152.

Stock Transfers. Taxation of, X, 769.

Street Railroads. Operation and extension, VII, 1063; operation in cities and villages, VIII, 200.

SUFFOLK COUNTY. Annexation of Lloyd's Neck, VIII, 289.

SUNDAY MERCURY. Relief, VIII, 128.

SUPPLY BILL. 1868, V, 881; various appropriations to be expended by
Superintendent of Public Works, VIII, 559.

SUPREME COURT. Additional justices in certain districts, X, 936; increasing number of justices, VII, 890; submitting constitutional
amendment increasing number of justices, IX, 97.

SURROGATE. New York, additional, IX, 122; Rensselaer, increasing salary, 224.

SYRACUSE. Claims against, audit, X, 288; water act, VIII, 1015; water
department, 258.

TAXATION. Collateral inheritance tax, VIII, 102; restricting deduction of
debts, IX, 93.

TAXES. Extending time for collection, V, 119.

TAX RATE. 1890, VIII, 1026; 1891, 1164; 1892, IX, 122; 1902, X, 459;
1903, 577; 1904, 683.

TEACHERS. Classes, transfer from Regents to Department of Public
Instruction, VIII, 791.

TENEMENT-HOUSES. Regulating construction, X, 286.

TIOGA COUNTY. Railroad strike, expense of National Guard, IX, 594.

TROY. Police, VIII, 84.

TUBERCULOSIS HOSPITALS, X, 575.

UNITED LIFE AND ACCIDENT INSURANCE ASSOCIATION. Changing name,
VIII, 1144.

UNITED STATES DEPOSIT FUND. Reducing rate of interest, VIII, 1149;
Steuben county, local custody of fund, 429.

UTICA. Additional engine-house, VIII, 1003; Central Advanced School
bonds, legalizing, X, 285; courthouse, 768; Mary street school bonds,
legalizing, 285; river improvement, VIII, 1145.

WARWICK UNION FREE SCHOOL DISTRICT. Legalizing bonds, X, 283.

WATERLOO. Amending charter, VII, 775.

WATERVLIET. Police justice, amending act, IX, 87.

WATKINS GLEN. Acquisition, X, 940.

WAYNE COUNTY. Legalizing contracts, County Agricultural Society
and town of Galen, VIII, 1148.

WEST TROY. Police, IX, 589.

WOMEN. Authorized to vote for school commissioners, IX, 94.

WORLD'S FAIR. Bill relative to, 1890, VIII, 996.

YONKERS RAILROAD. Extending time for completion, IX, 270.

YOUNG WOMEN'S CHRISTIAN ASSOCIATION. State executive committee,
charter, IX, 86.

INDEX OF VETOES.

NOTE.— The general index contains a record of vetoes under the names of persons, places or topics to which they relate, but it is believed that the reader will find this separate table a convenience in examining the history of a particular subject.

VETOES DURING COLONIAL PERIOD

BY CROWN. Charter of Liberties, I, 10; Assembly, triennial elections, 267, 278, 279, 292; Cumberland county, erection, 722; Indian goods, prohibiting sale of, to French, 236, 237; partition bill, 231; prosecutions by information, 236; tariff act, 198, 211; township division bill, 231; troops, support of, 710, 716, 722.

BY COLONIAL GOVERNORS. Deserters, I, 56; duty on slaves, 171; duty on tonnage of vessels, 171; frontier supplies, 54; levy money, 59; money bills, 121; present to Governor, 56; salaries, 172.

VETOES BY COUNCIL OF REVISION

ACTIONS. Small causes, II, 274; amendatory, 594.

ALBANY. Lamps and night watch, II, 396.

ALIENISM. Of certain persons, II, 202.

APPROPRIATION ACT. Including Senate apportionment, II, 849.

ARREST. On justice's warrant, II, 210.

BANK OF NIAGARA. Charter, II, 871.

BIGAMY. Restraining, II, 780.

CANAJOHARIE AND PALATINE BRIDGE CO. Rebuilding bridge, II, 638.

CHARLOTTE COUNTY. Military exemptions, II, 123.

COLUMBIA COLLEGE. Relative to, II, 610.

COLUMBIA COUNTY. Courthouse and jail, II, 419.

COMMISSIONERS OF LAND OFFICE. Powers, II, 287.

CONSPIRACIES. Prevention, II, 81.

CONSTITUTIONAL CONVENTION, 1820. Bill for, II, 1055.

CONVEYANCES. Curing defects in II, 245.

COUNCIL OF SAFETY. Ratifying acts of, II, 113.

COUNTY CLERK. Honeywood, practicing as attorney, II, 395.

COURT OF CHANCERY. Proceedings in, II, 1053.

COURT OF OYER AND TERMINER AND GENERAL SESSIONS. Relative to, II, 1002.

CRIMES. Relative to, II, 589, 623 (2 bills); punishment of, 602.

DEATH PENALTY. Imposed for escape, II, 583.

DEBEAVOIS, JOOST. Sale of real estate, II, 222.

DEBTS DUE TO COLONY AND STATE. Payment, II, 240.

DEBTS DUE PERSONS WITHIN ENEMY'S LINE. Amending act, II, 204.

DEEDS AND CONVEYANCES. Proof, II, 486.

DELAWARE COUNTY. Courthouse and jail, II, 417.

DESERTERS. Arrest, II, 819.

DISORDERLY PERSONS. Arrest and punishment, II, 284.

DIVORCE. Trial in action for, II, 272.

DONNELLY, TERENCE. Stage route along Hudson river, II, 638.

DOWER. In land of person attainted, II, 581.

ELECTIONS. Authorizing minors to vote for members of Assembly, II, 685; colored voters, 686; general act, 34.

EMBARGO. General act, II, 125.

ESCAPES. Relative to, II, 84.

ESTATES. Decedents, wills and administrations, II, 257, 267 (2 bills); forfeited, limitation of actions, 783; sale of, 94, 112; forfeited and confiscated, sale, 214; entails and joint tenants, 239.

EVIDENCE. Commission to obtain, II, 227; perpetuation, 1083.

FEES. Court officers, II, 275.

FERRY. Hudson river, Mount Pleasant to Clarkstown, II, 476.

FINANCE ACTS. Suspension, II, 128.

FITCH, JOHN. Steamboat privilege, repeal, II, 415.

FLOUR, MEAL AND GRAIN. Exportation, II, 26.

FORFEITURES AND CONFISCATIONS. General act, II, 70.

GERMAN SOCIETY FOR PROMOTING EMIGRATION. Charter, II, 243.

GRIST MILLS. Marshall and Brown, II, 485.

HARLEM BRIDGE COMPANY. Amending charter, II, 782.

HARLEM. Common lands, II, 1110.

HART, PHEBE B., AND OTHERS. Estate, authorizing conveyance, II, 713.

HERKIMER COUNTY. Courthouse and jail, II, 388.

HIGHWAYS. In certain counties, II, 348; streams in Steuben and Chenango counties, 521; Westchester county, 592.

HOLLENBECK, JOHN R. Free road, II, 591.

HORSE RACING AND THEATRICAL PERFORMANCES. Prevention, II, 85.

HUDSON. City charter, II, 246; night watch, 395.

IMMORALITY. Suppression, II, 416.

IMPORTS. Explanatory act, II, 236.

INDIANS. Oneidas, Onondagas and Cayugas, better support of, II, 356.

INSOLVENT DEBTORS. Relief of certain, II, 190.

JOINT TENANTS. Tenants in tail, abolishing entails, II, 779.

JUSTICES' COURTS. Jurisdiction, II, 170.

LAND. Forfeited and unappropriated, II, 603; waste and unappropriated, sale, 213.

LIBELS. Candidates for office, II, 551.

LIMITATION OF ACTIONS. Claims by State, II, 441.

LOCK NAVIGATIONS. Amending act, II, 329.

LOTTERY. Insuring tickets, II, 613.

MAGISTRATES. Power as to seamen in foreign service, II, 459.

MARRIED WOMEN. Estates of, II, 703.

MARVIN, ANTHONY. Estate of, II, 716.

MASTERS IN CHANCERY. Appointment of guardians, II, 488.

MECHANICS AND TRADESMEN. New York. Charter, II, 228.

MILITIA. Amendments, 1781, II, 131; 1798, 403.

MILITARY BOUNTY LANDS. Amending act, II, 309.

MILITARY TRACT. Survey, II, 664.

MORTGAGES. Proof of execution, II, 486.

NEWBURGH AQUEDUCT ASSOCIATION. Charter, II, 584.

NEW YORK. Actions for small debts, II, 532; Canal street, 646; elections, 544; license of carriages, 315; streets and highways, 331; surveys, 661; tax bill 1784, 211; 1791, 316; 1796, 373; taxes, support of poor, 247; taxes, petit larceny and disorderly persons, 222.

NEW YORK AND BROOKLYN. Relief of, II, 665.

NEW YORK MARINE HOSPITAL. Charter, II, 565.

NORTON, PHILO. Carding machines, exclusive privilege, II, 534.

OFFICIAL OATHS. Act requiring, II, 21.

OFFICERS. Staying suits against, II, 173.

PAPER. Use in legal proceedings, II, 409.

PATENTS. Land, relief from; II, 354.

PROUDFIT TRUST FUND. Charter, II, 717.

PROVISIONS. Supplying enemy, II, 129.

PUBLIC ACCOUNTS. Settlement, II, 288.

QUEENS COUNTY. Courthouse and jail, II, 417.

REFORMED DUTCH CHURCH OF GERMAN FLATTS. Relief of, II, 671.

REFORMED DUTCH CHURCH OF NEW UTRECHT. Sale of lands, II, 645.

RELIEF. Breadbake, II, 406; Chapman, 920, 946 (2 bills); Devoe, 662; Fairchild, 716; Ford, 688; Gilchrist, 249; Hardenburgh and others, 663; Henry, 309; Jones, estate, 685; Philips, estate, 688; Reynolds, 582; Schultz, estate, 714; Shaler, 563; Trotter, 343; Vanderlocht, 287.

RENSSELAER COUNTY. Courthouse and jail, II, 417.

REPRESENTATIVES IN CONGRESS. Election, II, 325.

ROMAN CATHOLIC BENEVOLENT SOCIETY, NEW YORK. Relative to, II, 1036.

ST. ANN'S CHURCH, BROOKLYN. Sale of property, II, 56.

SALARIES. Public officers, 1785, II, 249; 1800, 460.
SCHOHARIE COUNTY. Courthouse and jail, II, 417.
SCHOHARIE TURNPIKE ROAD. Relative to, II, 776.
SENATE DISTRICTS. Equalizing, II, 651.
SENATORS. United States, election of, II, 303.
SEQUESTRATION. Powers of commissioners, II, 191.
SEQUESTRATIONS AND FORFEITURES. Indemnification of commissioners,
    . II, 233.
SLAVERY. Abolition of, II, 237.
SMALLPOX. Inoculation, II, 225.
SMITH, ZILPHA. Conveyance by, II, 580.
STATE. Freedom and independence of, II, 215.
SUPREME COURT. Where to be held, II, 242; clerks, 756; judges, 740.
TAX ACT. 1778, II, 39; 1784, 213.
TAX. In specie and paper currency, II, 134.   .
TAXES. Collection of, II, 234; raising additional amount, 59; support
    of poor, contingent expenses, 95.
TAXES AND PUBLIC ACCOUNTS. Relative to, II, 172.
TEEPLE, GEORGE. Estate of, II, 708.
TOLL BRIDGE. Saugerties, II, 1081.
TROOPS. Raising, II, 41.
TROY AND LANSINGBURGH. Municipal powers, II, 402.
TURNPIKES. Inspectors, II, 593.
VAN CORTLANDT, WILLIAM R. Vesting estate in trustees, II, 248.
VESSELS. At New York, removal, powers of city, II, 819.

VETOES BY GOVERNORS OF STATE.

ACCOUNTANTS. Amending Code, X. 808 om.
ACCOUNTS. Between States and counties, adjustment of, VIII, 640 om.
ACKNOWLEDGMENTS. Instruments in Cuba and other islands, X, 63 om;
    conveyances of real property, 444 om; proof of, and effect as evi-
    dence, IX, 266.
ACTIONS. Continuance of certain, VII, 413 om; continuing against
    estate of deceased party, VIII, 131 om; preferred, VII, 1093, X,
    173; railway construction, damages, limitation of time, IX, 260;
    settlement without consent of attorneys, X, 150; speedy disposition
    of, IV, 510; on undertaking on chamber order, VIII, 629.
ADAMS. Aiding Hungerford Collegiate Institute, VI, 77.
ADIRONDACK PARK. Amending general act, X, 310 om; extending bound-
    aries, 379; restocking with wild moose, 563.
ADIRONDACK PARK AND FOREST PRESERVE. Acquisition of land, extension
    of boundaries, X, 291.

ADIRONDACK REGION. Restocking with wild moose, X, 814 om.

ADIRONDACK SURVEY. Continuing work, VII, 373, VIII, 74; public records, VIII, 551.

ADMINISTRATORS. Bonds, VIII, 468 om; letters, grant of, IX, 860 om.

ADMINISTRATORS, GUARDIANS, ETC. Proceedings against, VII, 1094.

AGENT TO INVESTIGATE CHARITABLE INSTITUTIONS. Compensation, VII, 779.

AGRICULTURAL EXPERIMENT STATION, GENEVA. Electric light and power plant, X, 546; fence, 547; poultry-house extension, 547; storage building, 546.

AGRICULTURAL EXPERIMENT STATION, LONG ISLAND. Establishing, IX, 232.

AGRICULTURAL LAW. Various amendments, X, 809 om; appraisers of condemned animals, 592 om; condensed milk, 776; violations and penalties, 583 om.

AGRICULTURAL MUSEUM. Arranging collection of fowls, IX, 83.

AGRICULTURAL SOCIETIES. Distribution of money to, VIII, 875.

AGRICULTURAL AND GEOLOGICAL HALL. Repairs and improvements, X, 300.

AGRICULTURAL AND HORTICULTURAL SOCIETIES. Protection of property, appointment of policemen, VIII, 378.

AGRICULTURE. Amending general law, IX, 800 om; compensation of agent to examine yellows or black knot in peach trees, 354; concentrated commercial feeding stuffs, sale, license fee, X, 447, 588 (2 bills); sale and analysis, 699 om; dairy products, preventing deception, VIII, 1037 om; encouragement of, IX, 109; premiums, butter, cheese and hops, VII, 1078; promotion of, 90.

ALBANY. Amending charter, VIII, 640 om; assessments, confirmation, IX, 632 om; assessors, VII, 805; Beaver creek sewer, VI, 1036 om; care and improvement of streets, V, 650; cession to United States, public buildings, VI, 449; charter revision, VII, 805 om; City Court, IX, 792 om; — jurisdiction and jury list, X, 321, 635 om (2 bills); elections, registration, VII, 263; fire department, reorganizing, VI, 331; Hudson avenue, repaving, VII, 264 om; justices' courts, IX, 630 om; Knox street viaduct, 729 om; land under water, VI, 210; lanes and alleys, VII, 935 om; official papers, increasing number, 1121; paving assessments, 1107; Pine avenue assessments, IX, 734 om; police, VI, 445; police department, reorganization, IX, 489; printing and advertising, paying debts for, 869 om; school funds, using for other purposes, VII, 755; street extensions, assessments for, IX, 729 om; street improvements, VII, 1012; streets, repairs, VI, 1031; taxes, annexed territory, VII, 412 om; tax on manufactories, VIII, 468 om; Washington Park bonds, VI, 693; water commissioners, IX, 420; water supply, 420 om, 729 (2 bills).

ALBANY COUNTY. Commitments, support of prisoners, compensation of sheriff and others, IX, 730 om.

ALBION. Relative to, VII, 807 om; schools and school district, X, 948 om.

ALIENS. Taking and holding real estate, VII, 662 om; IX, 725.

ALLEGANY INDIAN RESERVATION. Highways and bridges, VI, 690; new schoolhouse, VII, 909; State road improvement, VIII, 847.

ALLEGANY AND CATTARAUGUS INDIAN RESERVATIONS. Repair of highways, appropriation, X, 429.

AMERICAN MUSEUM OF NATURAL HISTORY, NEW YORK. Appropriation, 1898, IX, 868 om; instruction of teachers, 84.

AMSTERDAM. Revising village charter, V, 512; city charter, VII, 1014; legalizing assessments, IX, 374; official newspapers, VIII, 943 om, 1039; water works, payment of claims, VII, 1107.

AMSTERDAM AND FLORIDA. Towns, relief of, V, 725.

AMUSEMENTS. New York, public dancing within half mile of cathedral in process of erection, X, 456; places of, regulating management, VII, 804 om; regulating sale of tickets, 804 om.

ANDES. Fire department, VII, 65.

ANIMALS. Contagious abortion in cows, investigation, IX, 857 om; cruelty to, IX, 793 om, 812 om; Erie county, 869 om; glanders, affected with, destruction of, VIII, 1166; infectious and contagious diseases, 730.

APPEALS. Amending Code, VIII, 1038 om; consent of General Term, VII, 1093; to County Court, VIII, 406; to Court of Appeals from New York Marine Court, VII, 1092; criminal cases, proceedings against fugitives from justice, IX, 793 om; criminal cases, from order denying motion for a new trial, X, 927 (2 bills); decision on, 587 om; defendant on judgment overruling demurrer to indictment, 705 om; exceptions and case, IX, 283, 390; from General Term, VIII, 718; joining issue, VII, 931 om; from justices' courts, VIII, 468 om; notice of, VII, 932 om; from orders, IX, 152 om; by people in criminal cases, VIII, 981; from special sessions, stay of execution, IX, 45; practice on, amending Criminal Code, 792 om; stay, judgment for real property, VII, 265 om; Surrogate's Court, VII, 1109.

APPELLATE DIVISION. Designation of justices, X, 808 om; first department, special deputy clerk, 717 om.

APPLE BARRELS. Relative to, VII, 508 om.

APPRAISERS. Decedents' estates, fees, X, 61 om.

APPROPRIATION BILL, 1894, IX, 403.

APPROPRIATIONS. Deficiency, 1856, V, 36; unexpended balances, reappropriation, X, 585 om.

ARBOR DAY. Observance, appropriation, IX, 291; printing circulars, programmes, X, 423.

ARCHITECTURE. Regulating practice of, om, IX, 150, 624; X, 313, 704.

ARDSLEY. Village relief, X, 62 om.

ARMORERS. In cities, compensation, VII, 417 om.

ARMORIES.

Control of, amending Military Code, X, 707 om; control and use of, 385; purchase of land, VIII, 886, 1038 om; magazines and flagging, VII, 479; maintenance, limiting State expenses, VIII, 292 om; use by veteran associations, 873.

Albany, local assessments, VII, 927.

Brooklyn, relative to, 804 om; acquiring site, IX, 783 om; 23d Regiment, completion, 778 om.

Buffalo, 74th Regiment, IX, 607.

Catskill, completion, IX, 263.

Cortland, appropriation, VIII, 887 om.

Flushing, 17th Separate Company, VII, 482, 778.

Geneva, erection, VIII, 887 om.

Glens Falls, erection, VIII, 887 om.

Hudson, acquiring site, erection, IV, 626 om.

Kings county, 47th Regiment, repairs and enlargement, IX, 777 om; site for, VII, 541; reappropriation, 795.

Malone, erection, VIII, 886 om.

Medina, acquiring site, erection, IX, 777 om.

Middletown, Orange county, erection, VIII, 455.

Mohawk, appropriation, VIII, 294 om.

Newburgh, deficiency appropriation, VII, 482; repairs and improvements, reappropriation, IX, 857 om.

New York, erection, VI, 911, VII, 933 om; drillrooms, payment for, VI, 910 om; supplies, X, 580.

Niagara county, appropriation, VIII, 293 om.

Niagara Falls, erection, VIII, 887 om.

Ogdensburgh, 40th Separate Company, appropriation, IX, 571.

Olean, erection, VIII, 455; completion of, IX, 147 om.

Oneonta, assessment for local improvement, appropriation, X, 788.

Oswego, addition, VII, 482; indoor rifle range, IX, 604; repairing street and sidewalk, VII, 927.

Penn Yan, erection, VIII, 886 om.

Poughkeepsie, erection, VII, 481.

Rochester, acquiring site, erection, X, 586 om.

Saratoga Springs, erection, VIII, 291 om.

Sing Sing, erection, IX, 625 om.

Syracuse, replacing property destroyed by fire, VI, 875.

Tonawanda, payment for labor and materials, X, 587; relief of contractors on construction, X, 383; settlement of claims, X, 703 om.

ARMORIES — (*Continued*).

   Troy, acquiring site, erection, VII, 776.

   Walton, repairs and improvements, IX, 245.

   Watertown, repairs, X, 319 om.

   Whitehall, erection, IX, 575; Williams and Manogue claim, X, 650.

ARREST. On civil process, deposit in lieu of bail, X, 317, 388 om.

ARSENALS. Buffalo, local assessments, VII, 927; Rochester, local assessment, 1878, VII, 927; 1882, 927; acquiring site, IX, 788 om.

ARSENALS, ARMORIES AND STATE CAMP. Repairs and improvements, appropriation, IX, 76.

ASHFORD. Transfer from third to first school commissioner district, X, 948 om.

ASSEMBLY. Filling vacancies, VI, 347; cartage of documents, VIII, 106; ceiling and staircase, examination by experts, 839; clerk, additional clerical service, VII, 461; advances by Comptroller for contingent expenses, X, 796; extra services, wrapping department, VII, 906; clerk's manual, appendix, 223; committee, National Camp G. A. R., expenses, 463; examination of stone arch vaults, VIII, 840; financial clerk, appropriation for 1896, IX, 604; Harris, doorkeeper, compensation, VII, 1078; index to bills not printed, 225, 460; index to laws, 224, 460; index to papers, 224, 459; index to printed bills, 225, 460; insurance investigating committee, clerk, compensation, 783; judiciary committee, codes and statutes, VIII, 858; railroad investigating committee, expenses, deficiency, VII, 463; resolutions, engrossing, IX, 773; safe for financial clerk, VIII, 858; select committee to investigate condition of Indians, 1888, attorney and stenographer, appropriation, VIII, 842; tontine insurance investigating committee, legal services, 247.

ASSEMBLY CHAMBER. Ceiling investigation, appropriation, VIII, 547; examination as to alleged defects of ceiling, 421.

ASSESSMENTS. Local improvements, review, X, 316 om.

ASSESSORS. Qualifications, IX, 865 om; Malone, compensation, VI, 210; Rotterdam, fixing compensation, X, 439.

ASSIGNEES AND RECEIVERS. Lands conveyed to, VI, 562.

ASYLUMS. Admission of persons not paupers, VII, 505 om.

ATTACHMENT. Amending Code, X, 310 om; claim of property, how tried, 807 om; judgments on, VII, 1093; liens on real property, IX, 474; undertakings on discharge, om, X, 441, 534; undertaking for restitution, 706 om.

ATTACHMENTS AND EXECUTIONS. Indemnity bonds on claim of property, IX, 150 om.

ATTORNEY-GENERAL. Action by, VII, 934 om; additional employee, X, 784; assistant, additional salary, 784; attorneys, counsel and com-

ATTORNEY-GENERAL — (*Continued*).

missioners, compensation, 297, 559; Burr claim, counsel for Dike, sheriff of Kings county, 559; counsel and other persons, investigation of forest preserve trespasses, 796; Court of Claims deputy, expenses, 785; Dudley claim, legal services, German Bank matter, 784; McHale claim, legal services, Consolidated Gas Company case, 785; powers and duties, IX, 724 om; special counsel, VII, 582.

ATTORNEYS. Admission to examination, X, 311 om; Block and Sullivan, admission to examination, 63 om; Browne, admission to examination, 311 om; compensation, enforcing lien, IX, 523; lien, VIII, 293 om; MacKenzie, admission to practice, X, 262; Queens county justices' courts, laymen not to practice in, IX, 373; wearing gowns, X, 37.

AUBURN. Acquiring land for cemetery, VI, 602; enlarging boundaries, 304; new grammar school, enlarging high school, X, 717 om; police and street lighting expenses, VII, 770; establishing public park, IX, 783 om; public schools, X, 478 om; railroad aid bonds, VIII, 504; refunding assessments on State property, VI, 869.

AUBURN ASYLUM FOR INSANE CONVICTS. Chapel, enlarging and furnishing, VII, 914; fire protection, 914; heating apparatus, fire protection, enlarging chapel, 784; steam heating and cooking apparatus, 914; various repairs and improvements, 485.

AUBURN PRISON. Electric light plant, VIII, 851; gas for cells, VII, 484; library, 484; medical services, audit of claims, 666 om; repairing roofs, 484; repairing and refurnishing chapel and officers' quarters, 484; shops, apparatus for heating and extinguishing fires, 484; rebuilding and enlarging, 484; stone warehouse, IX, 80; Strong, keeper, injuries, appropriation, VII, 465; wings, ventilation, 484.

AUCTIONEERS. Bonds in certain cities, IX, 859 om; examinations, expenses of agent, VII, 904, VIII, 114; New York, license, X, 957 om.

AUSABLE CHASM. Acquiring for State park, X, 317 om.

AUSABLE RIVER. Improvement, VI, 597.

AUTOMOBILES. On streets, highways and public places, X, 441 om.

BABYLON. Repairing State dock, X, 935.

BADGES. Unauthorized wearing of, X, 807 om.

BAIL. Forfeiture, VIII, 886 om; procedure, VII, 1091.

BALDWINSVILLE. Relative to, VII, 415 om.

BANK COMMISSIONERS. Appointment, III, 1000.

BANKING ASSOCIATIONS. Liability of stockholders, VII, 413 om.

BANKS. Amending general act, IV, 700, 739; VII, 804 om; om, IX, 152, 800 (2 bills); conferring trust company powers on certain moneyed corporations, IX, 366; banking department, incidental expenses, X, 552; deficits in capital, making good, VII, 508 om;

BANKS — (*Continued*).

directors, election, IX, 800 om; final closing, V, 665; first class cities, bonds for security of certain depositors, IX, 791 om; insolvent, receiving deposits, VIII, 890 om; liability of stockholders, VII, 268 om; private, first class cities, security for deposits, IX, 867 om; redemption of circulating notes, VII, 508 om; securities for redemption of circulation, 412 om; taxation, 936 om; Westchester county, VI, 599.

BANKS AND TRUST COMPANIES. Relative to, VII, 1097.

BARGE CANAL, 1903. Appraisal of lands, structures, etc., X, 706 om; amending general act, locks and channel, 813 om.

BARRELS. Size for fruits and vegetables, VI, 188; X, 317 om.

BATAVIA. Place of holding elections and town meetings, VIII, 698.

BATAVIA INSTITUTION FOR THE BLIND. Appliances for object teaching, IX, 79; boiler and power house plant, X, 547; improvements, VII, 488; laundry, power house, smoke stack, and coal pockets, X, 547; repairs and equipment, 654; sewerage, VIII, 854; water supply, VII, 229.

BATH-ON-THE-HUDSON. Amending village charter, VI, 1035 om; VIII, 620.

BEDFORD REFORMATORY FOR WOMEN. Relative to, X, 448 om; two cottages, grading, electric light unit, 656.

BEER. Adulteration, X, 55.

BENDER & Co. Rebinding law books for attorney-general's office, X, 796.

BENEVOLENT AND CHARITABLE CORPORATIONS. Amending act, VI, 907; VII, 414 om; dissolution, 1020; establishing cemeteries, IX, 442; extending act to literary societies, VII, 132 om.

BENEVOLENT INSTITUTIONS. Reporting appointments or commitments, repeal, IX, 534 om.

BENEVOLENT ORDERS. Amending general act, IX, 800 om; powers of joint corporations, X, 593 om; power of trustees to issue bonds, 812 om.

BICYCLES. Regulating use of, IX, 866 om.

BIG CHAZY RIVER. Improving navigation, VIII, 848.

BINGHAMTON. Changing fiscal year, VIII, 873; enlarging corporate limits, 468 om, 753; judgment, payment, submitting question to people, VII, 1017; mayor, member of board, repeal, 46; police, 752, 806 om; schools, VI, 504.

BINGHAMTON INSANE ASYLUM. Amending act, VII, 414 om; additional assistants, VIII, 132 om; apple and pear trees, VII, 912, 1080; appropriation, 785; blacksmith's tools, carpenter's tools, 1080; cows, purchase of, farm and buildings, 912; farm and garden utensils, 1080; fencing, 912; fertilizer, 1080; furnishing buildings, 912;

BINGHAMTON INSANE ASYLUM — *(Continued)*.

general repairs, 912, 1080; harness, increased accommodations for patients, 1080; laundry machinery, 912; loss of horse and wagon; lumber wagons, 1080; maintenance, 912; meat room and ice house, medical books and surgical instruments, new boiler, new detached building, furniture, 1080; painting and piping, 912; plumbing and steam fitting tools, 1080; repairs and improvements, 487; smoke house, 1080; tools, using unexpended balances, 912; vegetable cellar, 1080; wagons and harness, 912; ward windows, weighing machine, waterworks engineer's tools, 1080.

BINGHAMTON STATE HOSPITAL. Cottage for engineer, covering for steam pipe, IX, 79; electric light, 78; entertainment hall, 295; hot water generators, 79; new roof, main building, pointing up main building, 934; sewer extension, 295; shed for dry lumber, 79; steam road machines, 295.

BLACK, FRANK S. Counsel for Senate committee on investigation of election frauds, IX, 533.

BLACK CREEK. Cleaning and deepening, IX, 81; improving channel, X, 301.

BLACK LAKE. Draining adjoining land, VI, 1036 om; overflowed land, drainage, 1036 om; drainage, repealing act, VII, 268 om.

BLACK RIVER. Castorland dyke, repairing and improving, also dyke road in Croghan, X, 570, 644; raising bank, Denmark and Croghan, 300.

BLIND. See also Batavia Institution for the Blind. Adult in cities, relative to, IX, 791, 866; permanent commission appointment, X, 696.

BLISS, THALES S. Contested election Assembly, New York, expenses, VII, 918.

BOARD OF AUDIT. Applications for legislation, VIII, 470 om. See also Board of Claims and Court of Claims.

BOARD OF CLAIMS.

Appeals to, Court of Appeals in certain cases, VIII, 56; appropriation, undetermined awards, IX, 49; auctioneers, 720 om; awards, VIII, 885; interest on, IX, 140, 238; corporation taxes unlawfully collected, claims for, 278; general awards, 1893, 275; jurisdiction, escheats, 524; report, publication and distribution, VIII, 857.

HEARINGS. Bassler, IX, 66; Bensen, VIII, 1039 om; Benway, VIII, 890 om; IX, 270; Best, VIII, 1039 om; Birge, 626; Boyd, 639 om; Bray, Auburn Prison keeper, injured by convict, IX, 452; Brock and Wiener, national guard uniforms, IX, 237; Brown, VIII, 888, 1033 om; Burhans, IX, 50; Cayuga county, Auburn Prison case, VII, 932 om; Chemung county, Elmira Reformatory

XI — 5

BOARD OF CLAIMS — (*Continued*).

   HEARINGS — (*Continued*).

      case, 931 om; Clinton county, prison case, 887; Conkling, 884; Costello and Curtis, 1124; county insane asylums, IX, 265; Crouse and Fyler, 428; Davies, VIII, 1041 om; Drury and Van Arnum, IX, 430; Dudley, VIII, 291, 408; Featherstone VII, 1120; Fingar, VIII, 1124; Frazee, 887 om; Gilgan, IX, 797 om; Hall, id.; Hanus, VIII, 1039 om; Hasbrouck, 1128; Hendricks, 888 om; Holdridge, VIII, 1041 om; IX, 285; Humphrey and others, VIII, 1166; Hutchinson, om, 888, 1037; Jarvis, IX, 429; Johnson, VIII, 1040 om; Kennedy, auction agent, 247; Kowalski, 626, 727; Lawlor, VII, 1121; Leet, VIII, 1039; Lockman and Devery, IX, 473; Lynch, 797 om; McGowan, VIII, 639, 886; McIntyre, 887 om, IX, 152 om, 451; McKinstry, om, 149, 269; McMaster, 797 om; Milliete, VIII, 1125; IX, 66; Moore, 430; Morgan, 66, 268; Morhous, 797 om; Myers, VIII, 976, 1120; National Guard uniforms, IX, 452; O'Brien, VIII, 886; Parks, IX, 797 om; Peck & Co., 369; Pilon, VIII, 839 om; Powell and others, IX, 119; Putnam, VIII, 889 om; IX, 269, 353; Ray, VIII, 626; Steuben county, Redding trial, 888 om; Risely, 1038 om; Roberts, Abner L. 1040 om; Roberts, John, IX, 250; Rochester, 154 om, 290; amending submission act, om, 719, 797; Ross and Sanford, 237, 721 om; Ruso, 623 om; Sadler, 721 om; Silversmith's Company, om, 627, 717; Smith, VIII, 1040 om, 1129; Strohm, IX, 149 om; Tanner, VIII, 292 om; Tuttle, 886 om; Turner, 1041 om; Weed-Parsons & Co., 1167.

BOARD OF SUPERVISORS. Amending act, VIII, 460, 1154; Broome county, legalizing proceedings, IX, 795 om; compensation, VII, 131 om (2 bills); confirming audits of accounts, VIII, 886 om; county schools of agriculture and domestic economy, establishing, X, 440 om; courthouses and jails, changing location, VII, 412 om; election districts, 388; fire districts in unincorporated villages, VIII, 872; Fulton county, equalizing representation, VII, 769, 860; licenses to peddlers, IX, 372; members, increasing compensation, VIII, 640 om; Oneida, legalizing audits of accounts, IX, 231; powers, amending general act, VII, 506 om; extending, VI, 593; St. Lawrence, appointing purchasing committee, X, 175; streets in territory adjoining cities, VII, 416 om.

BOTTLES, BOXES, SYPHONS AND KEGS. Used in connection with certain drinks, IX, 267.

BOUNTIES. Legalizing act, V, 673.

BRADY, BENJAMIN F. Preparing Wagner memorials, VII, 777, 928.

BREED, O. C. Services, Phoenix dam investigation, X, 933.

BRIBERY. At elections, VIII, 598.

BRIDGE COMPANIES. Amending act,VIII, 598.

BRIDGES. Broken by heavy loads, when town not liable, IX, 274; on county lines, 587; inspection by State Engineer and Surveyor, 801 om; joint, apportionment of expense, 525; Oneida county, 525; Addison, borrowing money for, VI, 52; Albany Railway, over Hudson river, X, 52; Allegany, over Allegany river, V, 345; Allegany Indian Reservation, Onoville, VIII, 845; Red House, VII, 587; Vandalia, VI, 707; Ausable and Chesterfield, 556; Big Flats Chemung river, VII, 578; Binghamton, accepting foot-bridge, 415 om; preservation of, VI, 149; Black river, Lewis county, VIII, 292 om; Cairo, Catskill creek, 383; Carrol, erection, VI, 96; Cattaraugus Indian Reservation, Clear creek, VII, 908 (2 bills), X, 429; repairing State bridges, VII, 383; Crooked Lake, over outlet, VIII, 849; Cuyler, over Tioughnioga river, VI, 78; Drake's drawbridge, Wappingers creek, maintenance, operation and repair, IX, 712; Elko, Allegany river, X, 698; Ellisburgh, relative to, VI, 98; Erie and Niagara counties, Tonawanda creek, VI, 696; Fall Creek, Havana, 327; Fort Covington, amending act, 46; Glenville, purchasing bridge, amending act, VII, 1102; Grass river, Russell, 474; over Great Sodus bay, VI, 212; Hudson and other rivers, VII, 808 om; Long Lake, IX, 255; Lyonsdale, reimbursement for bridge over Moose river, VIII, 552; Marbletown, Rondout creek, VI, 585; free-bridge, Ulster county's contribution, IX, 817 om; Minisceongo creek, penny bridge, declaring jurisdiction of, IX, 264; Newburgh and New Windsor, relative to, 818 om; Newtown creek, free public drawbridge, 778 om; New York-Harlem drawbridge, 631 om; Harlem river bridges, VIII, 1035 om; Harlem river bridge, 145th street, IX, 897 om; Jerome Park Reservoir, X, 176, 326 om; Mott Haven canal, IX, 633 om; Niagara river, Grand Island, X, 63 om, 703 om, 774; Onondaga Reservation, bridge over Onondaga creek, VII, 476; repair, 909; Oswego county, VI, 212; Otisco lake, bridge over inlet, IX, 777 om; Pelham, purchase of bridge, VIII, 889 om; Phoenix, protection of, VI, 147; Sacandaga river bridge, VII, 474; Seneca river, Salina and Lysander, X, 697; Sherburne, raising money for new, VIII, 336; Sullivan (town) reimbursement for bridge over Douglass State ditch, IX, 818 om; Syracuse, Onondaga creek, West Water street, 790 om; Tompkins, Delaware river, X, 873; Tonawanda creek, bridge, VII, 805 om; Tonawanda Indian Reservation, bridge over Tonawanda creek, VII, 477, IX, 348; Wellsville, tax for, VI, 311.

BRIGHT, GEORGE. Estate, relative to, VII, 508 om.

BRIGHTON. Assessors, compensation, IX, 371.

BRISTOL, WHEELER H. Claim, VI, 875.

BRONX BOROUGH. Exempt Firemen's Benevolent Fund Association, headquarters, X, 581 om; Pelham avenue, legalizing opening, 326 om; White Plains avenue improvement, apportionment of expense, 477 om; White Plains road improvement, 712 om.

BROOKLYN. Amending charter, VI, 911; VII, 128 (2 bills), 267, 804; aldermen,— election by wards, IX, 347; — holding federal offices, VII, 321; — appointment, VI, 517; arrears, IX, 630 om; Ashland place, railroads, X, 176, 324 om; assessors, VIII, 638 om; Atlantic avenue, railroads on, VII, 394, X, 175 om; repavement, VII, 664 om; Avenue M, reducing width, IX, 779 om; Banker street, improvement, VI, 193; Bedford avenue, railroads in, om, IX, 779, 780; Belmont avenue and Crystal street improvements, 778 om; Board of Aldermen, VIII, 470 om; method of electing, 739; Board of Audit, powers, IX, 630 om; Board of Excise, VI, 489; Board of Health, extending jurisdiction, 517; Board of Police Commissioners, establishment, VII, 417 om; booths and stands, permits for, IX, 779 om; bridge over Mill pond, 31st and 32d wards, X, 59 om; buildings department, IX, 729 om; Bushwick, altering map, VI, 695; cemetery, 32d ward, trustees, mayor to appoint, IX, 780 om; charitable institutions, free water, VII, 804 om; payments to, VIII, 1036 om; city clerk, IX, 626, 733 om; city marshals, powers and compensation, 780 om; city works, dividing department, 626 om; Clinton avenue, om, 868, X, 451; Clymer street, closing portion, IX, 263; commissioners' map, altering, VIII, 1102; Kent avenue, IX, 729; common council, election of messenger, VII, 509 om; constables, 439; Crospey avenue, railroads in, IX, 781, X, 322 om; Cumberland street and others, railroads in, IX, 781 om; department of assessment, VIII, 1036 om; department of city works and health, VII, 415 om; disorderly persons, VI, 333; dispensaries, increasing number, VIII, 969; drainage in 29th and 32d wards, X, 322 om; drains and sewers in certain wards, VIII, 635; East 18th street, railroads on, IX, 780, 874 om; East 14th street, railroad on, 874 om; East 19th street, railroad on, 874 om; East river bulkhead and pier line, VIII, 470 om; 8th ward improvements, IX, 263; elections, counting ballots and facilitating trial of actions, VII, 370; elevated railroads, preventing construction in certain streets, VIII, 291 om; Enfield street, railroads on, IX, 781 om; fire department, insurance fund, 475; legalizing appointments, 874 om; salaries, IX, 262; fire limits, om, 734, 876; excise licenses in concert buildings, VIII, 462; firemen, confirming appointment, IX, 779 om; Flatbush, payment of services, 876 om; fire, police and excise departments, supplies, 364; Flatbush, Prospect avenue opening, 874 om;

BROOKLYN — (*Continued*).

4th street improvement, VI, 192; gaslight companies, use of electricity, VIII, 132 om; government of, VII, 126, 134 om; Grand street improvement, 413 om; Gravesend, taxes, arrearages, settlement, IX, 782 om; Hall street and St. James place, railroads on, 778 om; Hancock street improvement, 780 om; Heyward street, closing portion of, 263; high school, establishment, VII, 134 om; Hooper street, railroads on, 778 om; indebtedness, deficiency, consolidation of, VII, 416 om; inferior courts, increasing number, VIII, 887 om; police justices, how chosen, VI, 512; interest on assessments, X, 176 om; Irving and Sedgwick streets, VIII, 469 om; Jewel street closing, 463 om; Johnson avenue improvement, VII, 804 om; Johnston avenue, repairing, VIII, 468 om; justices' courts, additional number, IX, 476; justices of the peace, election, VII, 415 om; increasing number, 1119; reducing number, 804 om; Kingsley and Keeney claim, construction of storage reservoir, 617; land for streets, 16th ward, IX, 148 om; Lewis avenue, 626 om; lighting streets, 26th ward, VIII, 638 om; Livingston street improvement, X, 326 om; local improvements, duplicate bill, IX, 434; Lorraine street, grading, VII, 572; Manhattan avenue, relative to, VIII, 468 om; extension and improvement, 636; map, alteration, VI, 335; Pratt street, 186; municipal building, increasing office accommodations, VIII, 1036 om; municipal court, X, 59 om; New Lots, annexation, VII, 936 om; 9th and Garnet streets, grading, 665 om; Norman avenue and other streets, relative to, IX, 779 om; North Second street, improvement, VI, 92; Ocean avenue improvement, IX, 876 om; offensive trades, X, 57, 60 om; officers, fees, IX, 778 om; tenure 521; Old Clove road, closing, 779 om; Old road, 31st ward, closing, 781 om; park commissioners, extending term, VI, 531, VII, 762; park department, om, VIII, 468, X, 477; park improvement, IX, 779 om; park lands, duplicate bill, 434; park police pension fund, 733 om; parks, protection, VIII, 131 om; 31st ward, IX, 632 om; parkway and driveway, 782 om; Penn street, etc., railroads in, 782 om; pier, 8th ward, IX, 779 om; near Navy Yard, 438; North 7th street, 448; police courts, police force, VIII, 1036 om; police patrolmen, 887 om; police station, 14th precinct, VIII, 294 om; police and excise, relative to, IX, 151, 152 om; departments, relative to, 633 om; engineer, qualifications, 119; Prospect avenue, improvement, X, 324 om; Prospect park, VII, 804 om; Prospect park reservoir, payment of award, VI, 911 om; Prospect place, railroads on, IX, 780 om; public driveway and parkway, 720 om; public parks, acquiring land for, VIII, 1036 om; public schools, protection of life and property, VII, 27; public works, wages of

BROOKLYN — (*Continued*).

employes, IX, 733 om; repaving certain avenues, VIII, 638 om; Robinson, Jeremiah P., authorized to build and maintain bulkhead, 12th ward, IX, 873 om; Sackett street contract, payment of balance, VII, 605; St. Mark's place, etc., railroads in, IX, 782 om; school funds, changing custody of, VII, 750; schools, free books and supplies, 626; Second avenue, etc., railroads in, IX, 782 om; sewers and drainage, om, VII, 804, 932 936; soldier's monument, VIII, 527; special sessions, IX, 634 om; street cleaning department, 476; streets and avenues, use of certain, VIII, 890 om; streets, avenues and highways, completing proceedings commenced before annexation to New York, IX, 872 om; streets and highways improvement, 780 om; street improvements, VII, 932; discontinuance 30th ward, X, 322 om; streets, opening certain, VIII, 638 om; Surf avenue extension, IX, 780 om; taxation of stocks and bonds, 148 om; theater exits, VII, 804 om; Third avenue sewer, 413 om; Throop avenue and other places, railroads in, IX, 781 om; truant reform school, om, VII, 133; VIII, 293; 12th street and others, railroads in, IX, 780 om; unpaid taxes, VII, 771; Van Brunt Street and Erie Basin Railroad Company, relief, VI, 518; Vermont avenue, relative to, IX, 781 om; Wallabout improvement, VI, 579, IX, 873 om; Wallabout market, improvement, 781 om; — lands, relative to, 783 om; wards, increasing number, 121; Waterbury street improvement, 781 om; water companies, acquiring property of in 30th ward, 779 om; water front, 262; Water street, railroads on, VII, 446; Wayside Home, commitment of female delinquents to, IX, 733 om; West 17th street, completing grading contract, 876 om.

BROOKLYN BOROUGH. Atlantic avenue, Long Island railroad on, X, 582 om; buildings and improvements, 807 om; children's court, clerk's salary, 711 om; Donlon Contracting Company, claim for cleaning sewers, 959 om; Hoff estate, relative to, 584 om; Prospect avenue improvement, 716 om; releasing city interest in land, 807 om; Remsen avenue improvement, 582 om; Sisters of Mercy, relief from assessments, 716 om; zoological garden in Prospect park, 476 om.

BRUTUS. Fixing northern boundary, VII, 806 om.

BUCKET SHOPS. Business prohibited, VII, 1090; taxation of, VIII, 445.

BUFFALO. Amending charter, V, 734, VII, 505 om, 666 om (2 bills), 933, 934 om, 1103, IX, 626 om, 633 om, 726 om (3 bills), 784 om; Albany street, release to adjoining owners, X, 316 om; assessments, om, IX, 730, X, 686; board of health, proceedings, VII, 414 om; bonds, redemption of outstanding, IX, 372; Busti terrace, use of by Mechanic's Institute, VII, 804 om; Carrol street, paving, VIII, 639 om; Cazenovia creek and Buffalo river improvement, IX, 783 om;

BUFFALO — (Continued).

charter revision, VII, 804 om (3 bills), VIII, 1030; charter, supplemental act, VII, 131 om; city hall and jail, construction and custody of, VII, 316; Clark and Skinner canal, abating nuisances, X, 634 om; county taxes, collection, VII, 356; drainage and sewerage, contracts with adjoining municipalities, X, 960 om; Fillmore avenue extension, VI, 851; fire department, relative to, VII, 413 om, 870, VIII, 889 om; holidays, IX, 51; storekeeper, X, 776; firemen, vacations and leaves of absence, IX, 869 om; floating debt, IV, 524; forestry department, X, 713 om; funds, local, 474 om; grade crossings, damages, 474 om; Guilford street, legalizing excavation, audit of Gisel claim, VIII, 1038 om; hostlers and van drivers, X, 583 om; inferior criminal courts, IX, 784 om; labor organizations, no discrimination against, 869 om; Leng claim, X, 806 om; local court, VII, 666 om; Louisiana street, railroad on, IX, 783 om; Main street road improvement, 356, 795 om; Municipal Court, 784 om; nuisance, VII, 507 om; offices, elective, filling vacancies, X, 685 om; park improvement, 11th ward, 712 om; Parkside avenue, extension, IX, 268; police act, amending, VII, 266 om; police department, om, VIII, 886, 1038, X, 713, 805; police, relative to, 583 om; police and parks, VII, 413 om; public improvements, IX, 723 om; pumping station tunnel, settling claims relative to, 869 om; quarantine hospital, purchasing land for, X, 475 om; Scajaquada creek, dredging, 319 om; school department, VIII, 639 om; school taxes, 292 om; sea wall highway, use of, IX, 783; State property, local assessment, 784 om; street improvements, legalizing, VI, 221; taxes, relative to, IX, 784 om;— and assessments, om, X, 685, 686;—unpaid, VII, 804 om;—unpaid and assessments, collectors, X, 476; union railroad station commission, 777; water commissioners, increasing salary, VIII, 1106; water supply, IX, 784 om; water works bonds, X, 685 om; water works company, subscribing to stock, IV, 517.

BUFFALO INSANE ASYLUM. Administration building, completing, VII, 786; appropriation of unexpended balances not specified, 913; bakery, 584; chapel, finishing and furnishing, 786; drain about foundation walls, 786; electric light, VIII, 852; exercise grounds, VII, 786; farm stock and improvements, 785; furniture for administration buildings, 584, 913; furniture for wards, 584; garden improvements, 436; improvements, 88; laundry apparatus, 584; legal expenses in mandamus proceedings, VIII, 852; maintenance fund, reimbursement, VII, 913; mortuary rooms, 913; office furniture and fixtures, 786; sewerage, 384; storm windows, 786; storm windows and cistern, 913; water storage system, 786.

BUFFALO STATE HOSPITAL. Electric light plant, VIII, 1137; new buildings, IX, 77.

BUILDING AND LOAN ASSOCIATIONS. Amending general act, VII, 132 om.

BULKHEAD LINES. Establishing, appropriation, VII, 874.

BUREAU OF MILITARY RECORD. Deficiency appropriation, IX, 774.

BUSINESS CORPORATIONS. Formation, amending act, X, 451 om; organization and regulation, VII, 507 om; mortgage of property, 1114; mortgaging real estate, VIII, 457.

BUTTER. Deception in sales of, VII, 571.

BUTTER AND CHEESE FACTORIES. Protection of patrons, VII, 805 om.

CAMDEN. Amending village charter, VI, 1036 om; legalizing proceedings for electric light system, X, 708 om.

" CAMPBELL LEASES." Tenants, protecting rights under, VI, 584.

CANAJOHARIE. Revising village charter, VI, 683, 824.

CANAL APPRAISERS. Salaries and expenses, VII, 774.

CANAL AUDITOR. Increasing compensation, VI, 877; suit against, services and expenses of counsel, VII, 904.

CANAL BOARD AND APPRAISERS. Defining jurisdiction, VII, 266 om.

CANAL BOATS. Liens on, VI, 510; Tyrell, John and James, loss of, VIII, 599, 805 om.

CANAL BRIDGES. Erie, eastern division, superstructures, VI, 953; middle division, iron superstructures, 857; western division, iron bridge superstructures, 860; lift and swing bridges, compulsory operation by State IX, 444; Albany, Water street, repayment of expenditures, om, IX, 730, 777; Amsterdam, Erie, Minaville street, X, 698; Brewerton, Oneida river, VII, 366, 473, 576; Brighton, Erie, lift bridge, VI, 1005, VII, 96, 117; Brockport, Erie, bridge, VI, 1004, VII, 116, 931 om; Brutus, approach, culvert under, VIII, 294 om; Buffalo, Clark and Skinner, Ohio street, VI, 861; — Scott street, 1036; Erie, Austin street, VII, 114; — Hudson street, VIII, 293 om; Carthage, Black River, VII, 362; Cohoes,—Champlain, Ship street, 115, 249, 361; — removal, Champlain, 554; Fort Ann, Champlain (Dewey) 577; Fort Edward,— Champlain, VI, 448; — Exchange bridge, VIII, 234; — Main street, VII, 115; Fultonville, Erie, VI, 1007, VII, 508 om, VIII, 453; Geddes, Erie, Magnolia street, VII, 361, 576; Glens Falls feeder, Champlain, VI, 504, 1007; — Glen street, VII, 361; Green Island Mohawk basin, Arch street, 115; Greenwich to Northumberland, Champlain, X, 699; Hamilton and Madison, Erie, VIII, 453; Lockport,—Erie, lift bridge, Exchange street, VI, 1005, VII, 115;— Mill street, 363;— Prospect street, VI, 1007; Lyons, Erie, Water street, X, 314 om; Mechanicville,— Champlain, Burke avenue and Francis street, 434, 547;— lift bridge, VIII, 130 om;—North street, IX, 285; Medina, Erie, Prospect street, VII, 577; Minden, Erie, X, 314 om; Mud Lock, Erie, foot bridge, VI, 1007, VII, 95; Newark,

CANAL BRIDGES — *(Continued)*.

Erie, 1099; VIII, 131, 887 om; North Tonawanda, State ditch, Oliver and Foundry streets, VII, 363; Norwich, VI, 588; Oneida river, draw-bridge, VII, 94, 232; Onondaga county, Erie, Willis avenue and Van Vleck road, X, 569; Palmyra,— Erie, Earle and Kent streets, VII, 116; — lift bridge, VI, 1005; Phoenix, Oswego, Bridge street, IX, 216; Portville, Genesee Valley, VI, 709; Rochester,— Erie, approaches, Averill street, 1008;— Brown and Smith streets, VII, 324; — Lyell avenue, X, 929; Lyell street, VII, 362, 589;— Monroe avenue, IX, 59; Rocky Rift feeder, farm, VI, 854; Rome, Erie, George street, om, VIII, 294, IX, 628; Sandy Hill, Champlain, Glens Falls feeder, 755; Saratoga, farm bridge, VI, 504; Schenectady, Erie, Church street, VIII, 890 om; Syracuse,— Erie, VI, 324; — Bridge street, IX, 870 om;— Catherine street, VII, 364;— Clinton street, VIII, 886 om;— Crouse avenue, 885 om;— Crouse avenue or Beach street, IX, 245;— foot bridge, Franklin street, VI, 857; Oswego, North Salina street, X, 327 om;— Oswego, lift bridge, Salina and Bridge streets, VII, 95, 232, 366, 456;— Oswego, swing bridge, Salina street, VI, 1005;— Westcott street, IX, 870 om; Tonawanda,— Erie, VI, 1007, VII, 505 om, 665 om, X, 319 om;—foot bridge, Kohler street, VII, 232;— Main and Delaware streets, 233, 361, 577;— North Niagara street, X, 314 om, 435;— State ditch, three bridges, VI, 1007; State ditch, Delaware and Fletcher streets, VII, 95;— Marion, Oliver and Van Vort streets, 96;— Tonawanda creek, VI, 859; Utica,— Erie, Genesee street, VI, 854; VII, 506 om; VIII, 206; — Genesee street, removal, IX, 732 om; Waterford, Champlain, VII, 116, 361; Waterloo, Cayuga and Seneca, 115; West Troy, Erie, lift bridge, Genesee street, VI, 1005; Whitehall, Champlain, 154, 584;— farm bridge, 689;— farm bridge, Brown, 1007;— farm bridge, Rathbun crossing, IX, 139.

CANAL COMMISSIONERS. Payment of drafts and certificates, V, 143.

CANALS. Relative to, IV, 194; abandoned, drainage of, VII, 412 om; agent for defense of State, services and expenses, IX, 856; appraisers, hearing certain claims for damages, VII, 417 om; AWARDS,— Reappropriation, VI, 1027; — Jenkins, VII, 456; — Mesereau, 774: — Miser, payment, 666 om; Rodman, 774; — Schoelkoff, 1072; — Simson, 1072; blind drains, section III, VI, 855; Board of Claims, surveys and maps, VIII, 868; certificates, payment of, VII, 131 om; CLAIMS,— Private bill, waiving statutes, X, 775; — appraisal, amending act, VII, 415 om; — against State, VI, 580; collectors of tolls, VII, 131 om; commerce on, improvements for promoting, IX, 110; contractors, refunding, VII, 588; electrical communications,

CANALS — (Continued).

reappropriation, X, 465; electrical conductors, repeal, IX, 453; electricity as motive power, experiment, X, 572; extraordinary repairs, completion of contracts, unexpended balances reappropriated, VII, 265 om; general act, 1878, 234; McAlpin certificate, appropriation, 231; oaths, administration of, 1115; Seeley claim, settlement, VI, 592, 696; sinking fund, tax for, VI, 1010; subordinates and employees, appropriation, 1896 (55 bills), IX, 716; taxes, 1881, reappropriation, VII, 930; time of opening, X, 61 om; towage, improved methods, Baker, VII, 266 om; — testing Stevenson system, 266 om; weigh-locks, abolition of, 412 om; work on, general act, VI, 884.

BARGE, see BARGE CANAL.

BLACK RIVER. Improving navigation, dams, Beaver and Independence rivers, VII, 457; temporary administration, 118; Stillwater reservoir, VIII, 849.

CAYUGA INLET. Dredging, VI, 876.

CAYUGA LAKE OUTLET. Improvement, certificate, payment, VII, 466, 924.

CAYUGA AND SENECA. Berme bank, repairs, Geneva, IX, 329; sewer under, Waterloo, VI, 339, VIII, 413.

CHAMPLAIN. Enlargement, VI, 584; Fort Ann, repairing road bed, VII, 114, 457; Fort Edward, cleaning Bond's creek, 473; damage to highways, VIII, 453; steam motive power, VII, 508 om.

CHEMUNG. Abating nuisance, cleaning Catherine creek, X, 789; Catherine creek, improving channels, 946 om; Corning, berme bank, repairs, 430; dam at Horseheads, VII, 268 om; temporary administration, 117.

CHENANGO. Relative to, VII, 265 om; Baldwin's Creek Junction cut-off, X, 644, 791; damages from extension, claims, VII, 1120; settling claims, VI, 508; temporary administration, VII, 118.

CROOKED LAKE. Temporary operation, VII, 117.

ERIE. Amherst, cleaning ditches, VII, 365; basin,— Buffalo, deepening, X, 814 om;— improvement, Buffalo, 652;— dredging, VII, 456;— dredging Black Rock Harbor, IX, 58; Brockport, culvert, VII, 456; Buffalo,— sewerage, Black Rock, 365, 457;— towing path wall, Austin street, IX, 449; Buffalo harbor, Bird Island pier, VI, 1008; Canajoharie, repairs, 852; Cazenovia dam, reappropriation, VII, 119; constructing walls, VI, 347; culvert under, Utica, VIII, 1132; Dead creek improvement, 452; drainage, providing for, Somerset and Hartland, X, 645; Durhamville steel trunk aqueduct, 573, 790; East Frankfort, repairs, VI, 856; Eighteen Mile creek, improvement, VII, 363;— enlarging

CANALS — (*Continued*).

ERIE — (*Continued*).

west branch, 449; Herkimer, completing vertical wall, VIII, 1112; Ilion vertical wall, 521; Jordan ditch, VII, 456; leakage ditch,—Kirkville, VIII, 850;—Manlius, 849; lengthening lock 46, VII, 933 om; Lockport, lifting locks, IX, 606; locks, western division, VI, 347; Macedon, rebuilding walls, 860; Murray, draining lands of Isaac U. Cole, VII, 457; Newark, rebuilding vertical wall, VI, 860; Oak Orchard creek and canal feeder, improvement, IX, 55; Oneida feeder, culvert under, X, 935; Rome, —canal feeder wall, IX, 239;—canal wall, reappropriation, VIII, 890 om;—retaining wall, Whitesboro street, VII, 586; Royalton,—cleaning out Eighteen Mile creek, 456;—drainage of flooded lands, X, 437;—vertical wall, VIII, 887 om, IX, 48; Schenectady, fence on berme bank, VII, 364; settling claim for work, VI, 698; Skaneateles feeder, repairs, X, 314 om; Spencerport waste gates, VII, 1100; State sewer, Canastota, arch over creek, X, 313 om; Syracuse,—raceway wall, VI, 868;—rebuilding walls, VI, 855; Tonawanda,—fence on berme bank, VII, 364;—dam and feeder, 457; Tonawanda feeder, improvement, 358; Utica,—pipe under, 938 om;—sewer Andes avenue, VIII, 454;—sewer or culvert under canal, 710; Verona, wall, IX, 469; wall branches and slop walls, VI, 855; Watervliet, retaining wall, X, 646; Wayne county, ditch for drainage, VII, 908; Whitestown, culvert, VIII, 453.

ERIE AND CHAMPLAIN. State ditches, cleaning, X, 569.

GENESEE RIVER FEEDER. Rochester, stop gate, VII, 233, 362.

GENESEE VALLEY. Extending time for sale of, VII, 216, 267 om; release to adjoining owners, VIII, 463.

GENEVA HARBOR. State piers, repairs, VI, 857.

GLENS FALLS FEEDER. Repairs, X, 427, 434.

GRIFFIN CREEK FEEDER. VII, 805 om.

HUDSON RIVER. Dock, Lansingburgh, VII, 366.

MAIN AND HAMBURG. Buffalo, repairing dock, VI, 1007.

MOOSE RIVER. Dam, VII, 118, 364.

OHIO BASIN. Buffalo, dredging, VII, 455, IX, 256.

ONEIDA LAKE. Completing reconstruction, VII, 325; navigation of, V, 730.

ORVILLE FEEDER. Repairs, Dewitt, X, 426, 645.

OSWEGO. Dam on Oswego river, VII, 365; dredging Baldwinsville branch, X, 426.

SAWYERS' CREEK. Deepening and improving channel, X, 300, 427.

SHINNECOCK TO GREAT SOUTH BAY. Reappropriation, X, 302.

CANALS — (*Continued*).

STATE DITCHES. Cleaning, X, 644; Erie, Salina, removing obstructions, IX, 150 om; Tonawanda, cleaning, VII, 456; Mentz, VIII, 413; Murray, removing obstructions, 539; Oswego, Onondaga county, 377; Salina, 867.

SYRACUSE. Filling mill-race and side-cuts, X, 569, 643.

TONAWANDA CREEK. Tonawanda, leakage, VII, 363.

WOODHULL. State reservoir, Herkimer county, cleaning and deepening, X, 320 om.

CANANDAIGUA. Legalizing acts, VII, 569; sewers and drains, VIII, 348.

CANASTOTA. Amending village charter, VI, 187.

CANCER LABORATORY. Buffalo, deficiency appropriation, X, 934.

CANISTEO COUNTY. Erection, V, 223.

CARLTON. First Methodist Episcopal Burial Ground, prohibiting interments in, VI, 1035 om, VII, 120.

CARTHAGE. Amending village charter, VII, 78; excise license, 1047.

CASSIDY, OWEN. Counsel to Senate Committee, investigation of State Board of Health, IX, 401.

CATSKILL. Fixing boundaries, IX, 818 om; purchasing stone crusher, X, 380.

CATSKILL CREEK. Dredging and cleaning, VIII, 248.

CATTARAUGUS COUNTY. South Valley, division of, legalizing action of board of supervisors, VIII, 1089.

CATTLE. Distraint, VII, 509 om; examinations for tuberculosis, IX, 773.

CAYUGA COUNTY. Auburn prison claim, submission to State Board of Audit, VII, 801; expenses of criminal trials, Auburn prison, VI, 876, VII, 87, 226, 471, 781.

CAYUGA CREEK. Improving channel, VIII, 868.

CAYUGA INDIANS. Land Commissioners to hear memorial, X, 955 om.

CAYUGA LAKE. Dredging inlet, repairing State pier, X, 570, 644; lamps for lighting east shore and for lighthouse, X, 791; outlet — dredging, VII, 496;— removal of obstructions, reappropriation, VI, 100, VII, 405;— removal of obstructions, deficiency, VI, 1001.

CEMETERY ASSOCIATIONS. Family cemetery corporations, X, 591 om; rural,— relative to, VII, 509 om;— amending general act, VIII, 619, 874, IX, 624 om;— exempting Mount Pleasant, X, 446 om.

CEMETERIES.

Bethpage, Oyster Bay, sale of lots, improvement fund, VII, 1122; Cherry Creek, taking charge of public burying ground, VI, 332; cities, removal and reinterment of bodies, moving and resetting monuments, etc., X, 448 om; Hornell, Hornellsville, removal of remains, IX, 352; Lockport Episcopal, removing bodies from, VIII, 887 om; Lyons, taxing lots, VI, 191; Norwood, removal of bodies,

CEMETERIES — Continued).
1035; Owego, school district number 35, 697; Perry reinterments, VII, 870; Port Byron, relative to, VI, 1035 om; sale of unoccupied lots, disposal of proceeds, X, 591 om; Saratoga Springs, — regulating burials, VI, 591;—Nelson street, removing dead, VII, 121; Scriba, Old Burt cemetery, removal of remains, VIII, 1118; taxing lots, X, 61 om; Worcester Congregational Society, removing remains, IX, 57.

Rural, acquiring property by eminent domain, Jefferson and Cayuga counties, VI, 162 id. Oneida county, 208; funds for permanent care of lots, deposit with county treasurer, X, 947 om.

CENSUS. General act, VIII, 66, 134.

CENTRAL ISLIP STATE HOSPITAL. Relative to, X, 704 om.

CENTRAL NEW YORK INSTITUTION FOR DEAF-MUTES, ROME. Appropriation for payment of debt, paving street in front of, X, 949 om; new building, VII, 90; deficiency appropriation, 470.

CHAPELS AND CREMATORIES. Endowment, X, 700 om.

CHARITABLE, BENEVOLENT AND BENEFICIARY CORPORATIONS. Exempting from life insurance laws, VII, 543.

CHARITABLE INSTITUTIONS. Appointments by Boards of Managers, X, 592 om; women as trustees or managers, VII, 761.

CHARITABLE AND BENEVOLENT INSTITUTIONS. Trustees and directors to receive compensation in certain cases, IX, 439.

CHARLOTTE. Police office and lock-up, VI, 193.

CHATEAUGAY. Village charter, VI, 76.

CHATEAUGAY LAKES. Upper and lower, Clinton county, cleaning channel, X, 814 om.

CHATFIELD, BYRON. Loss of public funds, Elbridge, relief, X, 275.

CHATHAM. Amending charter, VIII, 469 om.

CHAUTAUQUA COUNTY. Legalizing acts of board of supervisors, fishing in Lake Erie, VIII, 79; soldiers and sailors' monument, VII, 845; taxes, VI, 331.

CHAUTAUQUA LAKE OUTLET. Deepening, VIII, 890 om; removing obstructions, VII, 331, 473, 1095, VIII, 114.

CHEESE. Promoting consumption of, IX, 287.

CHEMUNG RIVER. Corning, extension of dyke, X, 315 om; Elmira, constructing dyke, 645.

CHENANGO COUNTY. Special county judge and district attorney, VI, 692.

CHILDREN. Custody of, IX, 860 om; Ella Deming, legalizing adoption, VI, 559; employment by contract in public institutions, VII, 764; guardians, appointment in certain cases, VIII, 631; illegitimate, right of inheritance, VII, 1126; legitimizing birth of Robert J. Ehlers, 633;

CHILDREN — (*Continued*).

    placing out, regulations by State Board of Charities, IX, 812 om; protection, VII, 804 om.

CIGARETTES. Preventing sale to children, VII, 1108; prohibiting sale to minors, VIII, 131 om; cigars and tobacco, preventing sale to children, 663.

CITIES. First class, railroads, right of way, use of, IX, 791 om; policemen, district telegraph companies, VII, 268; public burdens, 252; second class, general charter, IX, 791 om; second and third classes, reports of financial conditions, X, 816 om; third class, contracts for lighting streets, IX, 869 om.

CITIZENS. Claims against other States, VII, 250.

CIVIL CODE. Establishing, VII, 348, 794.

CIVIL LIST. Printing and distribution, VIII, 1038 om.

CIVIL SERVICE. Cities, assistant attorney or corporation counsel, exemption from examination, IX, 715; claims of persons employed in violation of law, X, 773; examinations, qualifications of applicants, 520, 812 om, 952 om; examinations, residence of candidates, IX, 816 om; exempting physicians from examinations for municipal appointments, 230; exemptions, X, 309; law department, IX, 724 om; preference, persons holding life saving medals, IX, 353; veterans, om, X, 592, 710, 714, 805.

CIVIL SERVICE COMMISSION. General office expenses, deficiency, X, 562.

CIVIL WAR. Enlistments, expenditures, VII, 478.

CLIFTON. Aiding railroad, VI, 190.

CLIFTON SPRINGS. Legalizing village election, VIII, 1122.

CLINTON, GENERAL JAMES. Monument, X, 697.

CLINTON COUNTY. Expenses of criminal trial, Clinton prison, VII, 782; fishing in waters of, VI, 906.

CLINTON PRISON ASYLUM FOR INSANE CRIMINALS. Dining room wing, X, 588.

CLINTON PRISON. Completing yard wall, VIII, 250, 291 om, 855; extra guards, hose, iron water pipe, VII, 484; library, 484, 920; new guard posts, new ovens, repairing buildings, repairing pickets, 484; repairing plank-road to Dannemora station, VIII, 862; repairing road through State lands, VII, 920; repairing roofs, sewers, steam heating apparatus, switch and track from railroad to prison yard, 484; water works, sale to Dannemora, X, 440 om.

CLYDE. Borrowing money, VI, 706; village, sale of land for non-payment of taxes, 217.

COAL. Anthracite, regulating grade and sale of, IX, 272; protection of purchasers in certain cities, 522.

CODE OF CIVIL PROCEDURE. Amendments, VII, 262, 805 om (8 bills), VIII, 890 om, IX, 148 om, 718 om; supplemental act, VII, 182, 337, 665 om.

CODE OF CRIMINAL PROCEDURE. Relative to, VII, 417 om, 504, 509 om; printing, 508 om. '

CODE OF EVIDENCE. Establishing, om, VIII, 292, 890; publication of, 890 om.

CODE OF PROCEDURE. General amendments, VI, 343, 708, 912 om.

CODE OF PUBLIC INSTRUCTION. Distribution to school districts, VIII, 422; publication, VII, 220, 469.

CODE OF REMEDIAL JUSTICE. Amendments, om, VII, 134, 169.

COHOCTON. Water commissioners, abolishing board, IX, 722 om.

COHOES. Amending charter, VI, 197, VII, 265 om, VIII, 886 om, 1041 om, IX, 784; liability for damages, VII, 412 om; powers of recorder, 327; bonds for taxes, IX, 120; election inspectors and poll clerks, 64; legalizing construction of sewers, VI, 192; legalizing State and county taxes, 1035 om; Schuyler street extension, IX, 51; water supply, VII, 1124.

COLLATERAL INHERITANCE TAX. Amending act, VIII, 293 om, IX, 118 om; Howard estate, restitution of tax, VIII, 1139; New York, fees of county treasurer and comptroller, 412.

COLLECTORS. Taxes, fees, X, 171; New Hartford, reimbursing, VI, 701.

COLLEGE POINT. Amending charter, IX, 628 om; conveying real estate to school district, Flushing, 819 om; school taxes, 818 om.

COLONIAL HISTORY. Printing and binding 15th volume, VIII, 424; printing volume 15, deficiency, 866.

COLONIE. Relative to eastern boundary, X, 702 om.

COLTON. Lock-up, VIII, 229.

COLUMBIA COUNTY. Equalizing assessments, VI, 95.

COMAN, HENRY B. Counsel for Comptroller, Tonawanda case, appro-.priation, X, 933.

COMMISSION ON CLASSIFICATION OF SALARIES. Allowance for expenses, X, 792.

COMMISSIONER OF AGRICULTURE. Expenses, made necessary by amendments to law, X, 786.

COMMISSIONERS OF DEEDS.
    New York,— additional number, VII, 206;— powers, X, 61 om; Yonkers, additional number, 437.
    LEGALIZING ACTS. O'Toole, X, 943 om; Prime, IX, 368; Reevs, VIII, 518; Simon, X, 958 om; Swikehard, IX, 150 om.

COMMISSIONERS OF EXCISE. McCollum and McCleary, legalizing acts of, VIII, 354.

COMMISSIONER OF LABOR. Additional officers and employees, salaries, enforcement of L. 1902, chap. 454, X, 554, 564; Buffalo, free employment bureau, id.; cataloguing library, 564; deputies and other subordinate officers, expenses, deficiency appropriation, 640; expenses, deficiency appropriation, 641; expenses, reappropriation, 564.

COMMON SCHOOLS. General amendments, IX, 800 om; apportionment of moneys, VII, 109, VIII, 291 om; apportionment of moneys, examination of teachers, IX, 622 om; collectors' notice to taxpayers, X, 439 om; district officers, election, VIII, 129 om; election of officers in certain districts, VII, 508 om; flags, amending general act, VIII, 1038 om; free school fund, apportionment, union schools, appropriation, X, 949 om; music, study of, IX, 116; Palmyra, permitting supervisors to hold school office, VIII, 47; officers, election, 470 om; Richmond county, amending general act, IX, 718 om; State school moneys, apportionment, X, 956 om.

COMPTROLLER. Accountant, examination of county treasurers' accounts, compensation, X, 558; annual report, amending Revised Statutes, VIII, 208; clerical services on tax sales, deficiency appropriation, 110; corporation tax bureau, New York office, temporary clerks and stenographers, X, 557; John W. Ennis, confidential inspector in the Bureau of Charitable Institutions, compensation, 558; examination of public institutions, 295, 422; expenses of legislative committees, compensation of witnesses, VII, 779; expenses of legislative committees, reception of Massachusetts delegates, 779; expenses incurred by legislative committee and officers of State government, 586; Hamilton county, repayment to, office expenses, reappropriation, X, 558; public statement of warrants, VIII, 129 om; special counsel, deficiency appropriation, X, 557; transfer tax and land bureaus, furniture, 296.

COMPULSORY EDUCATION. General act, VIII, 817.

CONDEMNATION LAW. Amending Code, X, 761; possession of property on giving security, 808 om.

CONEWANGO CREEK. Improvement, IX, 106.

CONEY ISLAND. Concourse lands, improvement, IX, 152 om.

CONGDON, BENJAMIN F. Claim, payment, VII, 1109.

CONGREGATIONAL CHURCHES. Extinct or disbanded, relative to property of, X, 813 om.

CONGRESSIONAL APPORTIONMENT, VI, 493.

CONHOCTON COUNTY. Erection, V, 249.

CONNECTICUT BOUNDARY. Act creating commission, VII, 172, 268 om.

CONSTABLES. Game and fish, auditing accounts, VIII, 469 om; Scio, appointment, VII, 218.

CONSTITUTIONAL CONVENTION. Bill providing for, VIII, 393; contested elections, fees of judicial officers, IX, 481; submission of amendments, 480; 1894, additional copies of debates, X, 301.

CONTRACTS. State, notice of, VIII, 130 om.

CONTRACTORS WITH STATE. Hearing of certain claims, VII, 666 om.

CONVERSION. Demand before action, VIII, 469 om.

CONVICTS. Commutation, VII, 508 om; commutation for good behavior, increasing rate, VI, 89; Elmira Reformatory, imprisonment, VII, 666 om; maintenance in penitentiaries, deficiency appropriation, 462, 584, 792, VIII, 118.

COOK AND CLARY. Counsel to Assembly committee on privileges and elections, appropriation, X, 796.

CO-OPERATIVE INSURANCE COMPANIES. Town and county — amending acts, IX, 152 om; — classification of risks, VII, 293 om; — extending powers, 881.

CO-OPERATIVE SAVINGS AND LOAN ASSOCIATIONS. General amendments, IX, 472; profits and losses; security for loans, X, 810 om.

COPENHAGEN. Village, commissioners to ascertain street damages, VI, 217.

CORNELL UNIVERSITY. College land scrip fund, loan to State, IX, 357.

CORNING. City charter, VIII, 562; amending charter, IX, 238, 869, X, 583 om; bonds, payment of, VII, 334; excise moneys, payment to St. Joseph's Orphan Asylum, VIII, 465.

CORNING LIBRARY. Acquiring property, fixing annual election, VI, 691.

CORONERS. Relative to, VIII, 292 om; acting as sheriff, 292 om; abolishing juries, IX, 860 om; Boughton, Wyoming county, X, 813 om; Erie county,— relative to, VI, 170; — fees on post mortem examinations, VIII, 1153; — fixing term, election of successor, IX, 861 om; Kings county — clerk, VIII, 638 om; physician, eastern district, IX, 434; New York — abolishing, medical examiner, X, 712 om; — duties and compensation, VII, 129 om; — inquests, expenses, VI, 844; — stenographers for, 910 om; Rensselaer county, compensation, proceedings, VIII, 62.

CORPORATIONS.

Act concerning certain, IX, 794, 861 om; amending tax act of 1880, 153 om; acquisition of property without State, X, 521; annual reports to Comptroller, VIII, 293 om; assessments for taxation, VII, 502; bankrupt receivers, VIII, 129 om; buildings, erection of, 1041 om; changing names, X, 705 om; credit, guaranty and indemnity companies, amending act, VIII, 459; directors, IX, 864 om; directors, definition, X, 311 om; evading taxation, expense of inquiry, VIII, 418; extension of business, IX, 865 om; extending existence, VII, 1103; franchise tax, X, 706 om;

XI — 6

CORPORATIONS — (*Continued*).

— equalization of, VIII, 640 om; indictment against, 640 om; loans on personal property, IX, 534 om; medical and benevolent, legalizing certain charters, VII, 937 om; mortgages, consents of stockholders, VIII, 888 om; names, prohibiting use by other corporations, IX, 625 om; New York, affording facilities for transaction of business by officers and employees, 719 om; organized under general laws, relief, VII, 1114; pneumatic tubes, franchise tax, IX, 794 om; receivers,— action against corporations, X, 309 om; commissions, compensation of counsel, 960 om; relief of, VIII, 470 om; stockholders voting per capita, 469 om; taxation of, IV, 775; taxation,— exempting agricultural and horticultural societies, VIII, 619; amending tax law, VII, 807 om, 1096; voluntary dissolution, X, 808 om; Young Men's Christian Associations, amending general act, VIII, 974.

ORIGINAL CHARTERS: — Accounting Guarantee Company, IX, 794 om; Albany Loan and Trust Company, VI, 342; Allemania Savings Bank, Brooklyn, 589; American Chronological and Autographical Society, VII, 412 om; American Exploring and Mining Company, V, 726; American Geographical and Statistical Society, IV, 633; American Jersey Cattle Club, VII, 202; American Mutual Benevolent Association, New York, VI, 187; American Order of United Workmen, Grand Legion of Select Knights, VII, 546; American Title Insurance and Trust Company, IX, 718 om; Anglo-American Loan and Trust Company, VI, 342; Association of the Bar of the City of New York, 192; Atlantic Base Ball Club, V, 645; Auburn City Hospital, VII, 241; Ausable Valley Masonic Hall and Library Association, VI, 697; Bachelor Club, New York, VII, 507 om; Bankers Loan and Trust Company, New York, VI, 342; Barnes Corners Burial Association, 186; Barryville and Shehola Delaware Bridge Company, IV, 521; Battalion Independent des Gardes Lafayette Francais, VI, 598; Bayard Homeopathic College Hospital and Dispensary, IX, 233; Baywood Land Improvement Company, VI, 329; Bethelehem Mutual Insurance Association, 90, 910 om; Binghamton Masonic Board of Trustees, VIII, 460; Boys' Industrial Home, IX, 246; Brewer Fire Company, Monsey, VII, 268 om; Brooklyn Elevated Silent Safety Railway Company, VI, 595; Brooklyn Retail Grocers Association, VIII, 198; Buffalo Light Battery, VII, 763; Buffalo Pipe Line Company, 133 om; Buffalo and New York Oil Tankage and Transportation Company, VI, 502; Canton Lodge No. 558, Independent Order

CORPORATIONS — (*Continued*).

ORIGINAL CHARTERS — (*Continued*).

of Good Templars, 187; Cascade Association, Little Falls, 277; Cascade Fire Company No. 1, Little Falls, 187; Catholic Union, New York, 676; Catskill Mountain National Camp Meeting Association of the Methodist Episcopal Church, New York Conference, VII, 867; Chautauqua County Police, IX, 795 om; Chemung and Tioga Bridge Company, VI, 221; Children's Aid Society, Rochester, IX, 450; Chinese Society, New York, VIII, 637; Clarkson Cemetery, VI, 325; Clyde Waterworks Company, 95; Cohoes Hotel Company, 579; Commercial Credit Guaranty Company, New York, 191; Commercial Travelers Association, New York, 340; Commercial Trust and Banking Company, New York, 342; Continental Loan and Trust Company, 341; Co-operative Savings and Loan Association, VI, 339, IX, 148 om; Cornell Hose Company No. 2, Kingston, VII, 600; Corn Exchange Warehouse Company, VI, 215; Dairymen's Manufacturing Association, Perth, 501; Darwin R. Barker Library Association, Fredonia, VII, 845; Eagle Hose Company No. 2, Buffalo, VI, 196; Eagle Trust Company, New York, 342; Eastern New York Fanciers' Association, VII, 371; Eastern Star Hall and Home Association, X, 311 om; Edgewater Fire Department, VIII, 616; Edgewater Fire Department, Richmond Borough, X, 473 om; Eighth Ward Savings Bank, New York, VI, 213; Emerald Beneficial Association, Supreme Council, VIII, 876; Empire Yacht Club, VII, 509 om; Equitable Loan and Trust Company, VI, 341; Erie County Pipe Line Company, VII, 133 om; Excelsior Hose Company, Warwick, 507 om; Excelsior Temple of Honor No. 23, Albany, VI, 55; Expressmen's Savings Bank, New York, 326; Farmers and Mechanics' Savings Bank, New York, 342; Farmers and Mechanics' Savings Banks, Schenectady County, 214; Father Mathew Total Abstinence Benefit Society No. 6, New York, V, 654; Female Academy of the Sacred Heart, New York, IV, 531; Fifth Avenue Savings Bank, New York, VI, 97; Firemen's Benevolent Fund Association, Mount Vernon, IX, 469; Flatlands Fire Department, VIII, 1097; Franklin Bridge Company, IV, 694; Free School District No. 12, Newtown, VIII, 338; Frewsburg Cemetery Association, VI, 186; Frontier Gas-Light Company, Watertown, 215; Fulton Savings Bank, New York, 322; German-American Colonization Society, V, 643; German Association Erheiterung Association, Staten Island, 643; German Missionary Church, Buffalo, IV, 633; Germania, The, Brooklyn, VIII, 704; Gladiator Benevolent

CORPORATIONS — (*Continued*).

ORIGINAL CHARTERS — (*Continued*).

Association, New York, V, 644; Gleneida Savings Bank, VI, 310; Gloversville Savings Bank, 333; Gouverneur Fire Company, VII, 327; Governor's Guard, 506 om; Grand Street Savings Bank, Brooklyn, VI, 342; Granite Lake Company, 270; Grocers' Trust Company, New York, VIII, 292 om; Guilderland Center Turnpike Company, VI, 339; Harlem Hospital, New York, 323; Harlem Yacht Club, 90; Haverstraw Savings Bank, 186; Hebrew Free Loan Association, X, 813 om; Heffley Collegiate Institute, 709 om; Highland Fire Engine and Hose Company No. 3, Florida, VIII, 462; Hill Land Horticultural Society of Southern Central New York, 876; Homeopathic Medical College, Buffalo, VII, 266 om; Howland College for the Education of Young Women, VI, 671; Idlewild Temperance Association, Cornwall, 309; Immaculate Conception Total Abstinence Beneficial Society, Yonkers, 325; Inebriates' Home, New York, X, 323 om; International Employment Guaranty and Deposit Company, VI, 341; International Fraternal Alliance, Grand Assembly, IX, 150' om; International Improvement and Loan Company, VI, 343; International Loan, Trust and Guarantee Company, VIII, 463; International Trust and Banking Company, VI, 342; Ione Yacht Club, 195; Island City Trust Company, 342; Ithaca Company, 700; Jamestown Savings Bank, 333; Jefferson Medical University, 339; Johnstown Loan and Trust Company, 342; Journeymen's Pork Butchers Union Benevolent Society, New York, 330; Knickerbocker Gas Company, V, 673; Knickerbocker Loan and Trust Company, New York, VI, 305; Knights of Honor, Grand Lodge, VII, 509 om; Knights of Maccabees of the World, 506 om; Lake George Baptist Association, VI, 333; Lenox Farmers and Mechanics' Association, 451; Life Saving Benevolent Association, Buffalo, VII, 414 om; Little Equinunk Bridge Company, VIII, 874; Little Valley Waterworks Company, VI, 284; Long Island City Savings Bank, 342; Madison Association, IV, 592; Mamaroneck and New Rochelle Steam Navigation Company, V, 133; Manhattan Indemnity and Loan Company, New York, VI, 342; Manhattan Loan and Trust Company, New York, 503; Maritime Association, New York, 585; Masonic Hall Association, Buffalo, VIII, 464; Masonville Turnpike Road Company, III, 758; Mechanics' Savings Bank, Troy, VI, 342; Mechanicville Bridge Company, 333; Mental and Moral Improvement Society, Irvington, 196; Merchants' Exchange Salesroom, VII, 417 om; Mer-

CORPORATIONS — (Continued).
ORIGINAL CHARTERS — (Continued).

chants' Loan Company, VI, 587; Merchants' Trust Company, New York, VIII, 292 om; Metropolis Finance Company, New York, IX, 379; Metropolitan Nautical Institute, New York, VI, 328; Metropolitan Post-Graduate School of Medicine, IX, 623 om; Minstrel Fund Association, V, 231; Monhagen Hose Company No. 1, Middletown, VI, 341; Monticello Academy, IV, 574; Mount McGregor Memorial Association, VIII, 625; Mutual Aid Society of the East German Conference, Methodist Episcopal Church, VI, 588; Mutual Loan and Depositors Institution, New York, 219; Mutual Trust Institution, New York, 342; Nassau Loan and Security Company, id.; Nassau Savings Bank, Brooklyn, 220; Nassau Trust Company, VIII, 291 om; National Book Exchange, New York, VI, 328; National Glee Club, New York, V, 645; National Guard Mutual Relief Association, VII, 506 om; National Improvement Company, New York, VI, 340; National Mutual Benefit Association, Buffalo, 172; National Security and Trust Company, 341; National Tent of the National Order of the Independent Rechabites of North America, VII, 415 om; New Baltimore Chestnut Lawn Cemetery Association, VI, 501; New York Advertising Company, 191; New York Annuity Company, 208; New York Arcade Railway, 197; New York and Brooklyn Tunnel Company, VIII, 888, 1135; New York Club, VI, 661; New York Coal Exchange, 337; New York College of Medicine and Surgery, VIII, 100; New York Conference of the African Methodist Episcopal Church, 1101; New York Exporting Company, IV, 639; New York Finance Company, IX, 256; New York Financial Association, VI, 340; New York Fruit and Spice Exchange, VII, 804 om; New York Investment Company, VIII, 376; New York Jewelers' Association, VII, 415 om; New York Juvenile Asylum, IV, 526; New York Life Policy Guaranty Loan and Trust Company, VI, 343; New York Musical Instrument Saving and Loan Society, 289; New York Mutual Title Insurance Company, IX, 861 om; New York Pipe Line, VII, 133 om; New York Rapid Transit Company, 1873, VI, 585; 1874, 694; New York Real Estate Banking Company, 315; New York Realty Bond and Exchange Company, IX, 794 om; New York State Trust Company, VII, 935 om; New York Stock Exchange, VI, 343; New York Towage Company, 598; New York Transit Company, VII, 1104; New York Warehouse and Railway Company, VI, 684; Nyack Waterworks Company, 504; Oatka Hose

CORPORATIONS — (*Continued*).

ORIGINAL CHARTERS — (*Continued*).

Company, Le Roy, VII, 806, 877 om; Oneida River Road Company, VI, 211; Oneonta Fire Department, VII, 415 om; Order Germania, 508 om; Oriental Lodge No. 267, Independent Order of Good Templars, VI, 578; Oswego Dry Dock and Marine Railway Company, IV, 525; Oswego Pier and Dock Company, VI, 84; Ours Hose Company No. 4, Elmira, 56; Patriotic Tract Society, VIII, 131 om; Peabody Mutual Benefit Company, New York, VI, 171; People's Mutual Benefit Association, 326; Personal Property Loan Company, om, X, 594, 708; Philomathian Society, Sherburne, V, 129; Phœnix Trust Company, New York, VI, 342; Pneumatic Railway and Express Company, V, 670; Polytechnic Institute, Brooklyn, VIII, 708; Port Morris Warehouse and Elevator Company, VI, 328; Presbyterian Society of Stephentown, IV, 633; Progress Health Insurance Company, New York, VI, 332; Protection Hose Company No. 3, Binghamton, 179; Protestant Episcopal Church Fund for Aged and Infirm Clergymen, New York, IV, 637; Provident Industrial Insurance Company, VIII, 414; Quincy Rural Cemetery Association, Ripley, VI, 501; Real Estate and Progress Board, Buffalo, VIII, 293 om; Red House Driving Park Agricultural Society, VII, 506 om; Red Men, Improved Order of, Delaware Tribe No. 44, Eldred, VIII, 877; Republic Life Insurance and Trust Company, New York, VI, 336; Rescue Hook and Ladder Company No. 1, Bath, 55; Rescue Hook and Ladder Company, Tonawanda, 825; Retail Grocers Union, New York, VIII, 197; Rochester Electro-Medical Institute, VII, 416, 506; Rome Street Railroad Company, 806 om; Royal Arcanum, Grand Council, 507 om; Royal Templars of Temperance, Grand Council, 417 om; Royal Templars of Temperance, Grand Council, New York, 240; Safe Deposit and Trust Company, Buffalo, VI, 503; Safety Elevator Insurance Company, New York, VII, 1113; St. Ann's Total Abstinence and Benevolent Society, Hornellsville, VI, 672; St. John's College, Brooklyn, 339; St. Joseph's College, Buffalo, 691; St. Patrick's Benevolent Society, Dansville, 592; Security Bank, Brooklyn, 210; Seth N. Hedges Post No 216, G. A. R., Dansville, VIII, 462; 17th Ward Savings Bank, New York, VI, 342; Sing Sing Branch of the American Society for the Prevention of Cruelty to Animals, VII, 744; Sixpenny Savings Bank, Albany, VI, 342; Society of St. Vincent de Paul, Yonkers, VII, 805 om; Sons of Liberty, Grand Lodge, VIII, 737; South Brooklyn Loan and Trust Company, VI, 342;

CORPORATIONS — (*Continued*).

ORIGINAL CHARTERS — (*Continued*).

South Hill Waterworks Company, Ithaca, 320; State Loan and Trust Company, New York, VII, 1096; Staten Island Bridge Company, VI, 91, Staten Island North Side Railroad Company, 323; Stock Exchange, New York, 221; Tau Chapter of the Delta Kappa Epsilon Fraternity, Clinton, 592; Teachers' Mutual Benefit Association, New York, VIII, 336; Teutonia Singing Society, Winfield, VI, 341; Thistle Benevolent Association, New York, IV, 531; Tonawanda Gas Company, VII, 807 om; Tompkins County New York Patrons Mutual Fire Relief Association, 133 om; Tornado Hook and Ladder Company No. 1, Union, 233; Troy Public Library, 336; Troy and Colonie Bridge Company, X, 585 om; Troy and Green Island Bridge Company, IX, 153 om; Tyrian Hall Association of East New York, New Lots, VI, 590; Ulster County Loan and Trust Company, Kingston, VIII, 230; Uniformed Veterans 23d Regiment, VII, 1108; United States Commission and Storage Company, VI, 325; United States Mutual Benefit Company, New York, 167; United States Trade Mark Association, VII, 355; Utica Corn Hill Benefit Association, Utica, X, 320 om; Veteran Association Coreoran Irish Legion, VI, 341; Veteran Association, 71st Regiment, National Guard, VII, 1106, VIII, 404; Veteran Reserve of the National Guard, VII, 1111; Volunteer Firemen's Benevolent Association, Richmond Hill, X, 472 om; Ward's Island Bridge Company, om, IX, 725, 793; Washington Park Association, VI, 501; Washington Rifles, VII, 412 om; Washington Savings Bank, Brooklyn, VI, 342; Webbs' Academy and Home for Shipbuilders, VIII, 623; Westchester Trust Company, 469 om; Western Mortgage Debenture Company, X, 439 om; Williamsburgh Firemen, IV, 531; Wolf Island Bridge Company, IX, 248; Workingmen's Friendly Society of America, VI, 326; Yorkshire Rural Cemetery Association, 596; Young Men's Christian Association, Ogdensburgh, VIII, 379; Young Men's Father Mathew Total Abstinence Benefit Society No. 1, V, 654.

CHANGING NAMES: — American Female Guardian Society, VIII, 337; American Loan Company, VII, 267 om; Association for the Benefit of Colored Orphans, New York, 1006; Bankers' Life Insurance and Trust Company, New York, 567; Black River Insurance Company, Watertown, VI, 813; Brooklyn Guaranty and Indemnity Company, VIII, 617; Brooklyn Nursery, 876; Brooks Locomotive Works, VI, 699; Buffalo Association for the

CORPORATIONS — (*Continued*).

CHANGING NAMES —(*Continued*).

Relief of the Poor, VIII, 1038 om; Buffalo, Corry and Pittsburgh Railroad Company, extending road, VI, 508; Central Throat Hospital Polyclinic Dispensary, Brooklyn, IX, 793 om; Citizens' Loan Agency and Guarantee Company, VIII, 981; Davenport Institution for Female Orphan Children, IX, 356; Elmira Female College, VII, 506 om, VIII, 62; First Baptist Church, Greenpoint, IX, 348; First Congregational Church, Poughkeepsie, VI, 433; First Congregational Society, Byron, VIII, 205; Foundling Asylum of the Sisters of Charity, New York, 876; Garfield Memorial Home, VII, 931 om; German Social Turn-Verein of Rochester, IX, 348; Gooderson Fire Engine Company No. 2, Winfield, VII, 748; Groton Cemetery Association, VIII, 974; Hamburg Cemetery Association, legalizing conveyance, X, 256; Knox Railway Clamp Company, VI, 189; Lutheran League, Rochester, om, IX, 793, 794; Methodist Episcopal Church, Tompkinsville, VI, 270; New York Orthopœdic Dispensary, 693; New York Real Estate Guaranty Company, defining powers, VIII, 617; Niagara Fire Insurance Company of Erie County, X, 242; Ninth Baptist Church, Syracuse, 377; North Protestant Dutch Church, Gowanus, V, 127; Orphan Asylum of the Society of the Reformed Churches, Brooklyn, X, 253; Pittsburg, Lackawanna and Northwestern Railroad Company, VIII, 327; Protestant Reformed Dutch Church, Duanesburgh, V, 125; Purcell Company, C. J., IX, 794; Reformed Low Dutch Church, Taghkaniek, VII, 807 om; Reformed Protestant Dutch Church of Cattsbane, IX, 37; Rochester and Charlotte Turnpike Road Company, VII, 933 om; Rochester and Pine Creek Railway Company, VI, 1034; Sacred Heart Academy, X, 813 om; St. George's Methodist Episcopal Church, North Haverstraw, VIII, 617; St. Luke's Home, Utica, 326; Schenectady Free Dispensary, 617; Society for the Relief of Orphan and Destitute Children, Albany, enlarging property limit, IX, 56; Spring Supply Water Company, Oneida, VII, 1000; Troy Young Men's Association, X, 235; Union Literary Society, Ellisburgh, VIII, 980; United Presbyterian Church, North Hamden, 1096; Washington Hook and Ladder Company No. 1, Lawrence and Cedarhurst, additional powers, X, 261.

CHARTERS AMENDED: American Mortgage and Trust Company, New York, VIII, 630; American Popular Life Insurance Company, VI, 189; Associated Hotel Company, 335; Brooklyn Institute of Arts and Science, IX, 838 om; Brooklyn Library

CORPORATIONS — (*Continued*).

CHARTERS AMENDED — (*Continued*).

Building Fund Association, Eastern District, VII, 96; Buffalo Association for the Relief of the Poor, VIII, 886 om; Buffalo Merchants Exchange, X, 318 om; Buffalo Young Men's Christian Association, VIII, 618; Buffalo and Williamsville McAdam Road Company, VI, 218; Catholic Mutual Benefit Association, Supreme Council, IX, 57; Catholic Protectory Juvenile Delinquents, VII, 914; Central Savings Bank, New York, VI, 308; Central Association, VIII, 709; Citizens' Loan Agency and Guarantee Company, IX, 257; City Loan and Trust Company, New York, VI, 336; Clinton Hall Association, IX, 147 om; Fireproof Warehouse Company, VI, 328; Flatbush Fire Company, VIII, 728; Franklin Loan and Trust Company, New York, 630, 890 om; Genesee Annual Conference, VI, 92; Hamilton Savings Bank, 187; Industrial Exhibition Company, 331, 482; Inebriates' Home, X, 586 om; Insurers' Indemnity Company, New York, VI, 340; Liberty Normal Institute, om, VII, 935, VIII, 130; Lordville and Equinunk Bridge Company, VIII, 1041 om; Lutheran Cemetery, Middle Village, VI, 595; Machpelah Cemetery Association, Le Roy, 585; Manhattan Loan and Trust Company, New York, VIII, 293 om; Methodist Episcopal Hospital, Brooklyn, 464; Mutual Fire Insurance Company, VI, 319; New York Bridge Company, 586; New York Building and Improvement Company, VIII, 1036 om; New York Post-Graduate Medical School and Hospital, 707; New York State Loan and Trust Company, VI, 337; New York and Canada Bridge Company, VIII, 469 om; New York and Harlem Railroad Company, V, 63; New York and Long Island Bridge Company, VI, 91, VIII, 1037; New York and Queens County Bridge Company, VI, 582; New York and Shawangunk Mining Company, IV, 823; Niagara, Lockport and Ontario Power Company, X, 686; Onondaga Historical Association, IX, 217; Oswego Fire Department, VIII, 1040 om; Patent and Copyright Protective Association, New York, X, 312 om; Peekskill Academy, VI, 1035 om; People's Water Transit Company, 703; Port Byron and Conquest Turnpike Road and Bridge Company, V, 146; Portchester Savings Bank, VI, 441; Port Morris Land and Improvement Company, 593; Protectives Number One, Rochester, 329; Public Exchange, 593; Rochester Atheneum, 671; Safe Deposit Company, Rochester, 503; Safety Fund Mutual Insurance Company, VII, 1121; St. Lawrence University and Theological Seminary, VIII, 703; Saratoga County Mutual

CORPORATIONS — (*Continued*).

CHARTERS AMENDED — (*Continued*).

Fire Insurance Company, VI, 197; Society for the Protection of Destitute Roman Catholic Children, VII, 415 om; Society of the War of 1812, X, 947 om; Southern Tier Savings Bank, Elmira, VI, 324; Southside Sportsmen's Club, Long Island, IX, 217; State Women's Hospital, VIII, 458; Tidal Waterway Company, X, 175; Ulster Female Seminary, VI, 693; United States Mortgage Company, 580; West Side German Dispensary, New York, IX, 534 om; Young Men's Catholic Association, Rochester, VI, 683.

EXEMPTION FROM TAXATION, ETC. Bedford Reformed Dutch Church, continuing, VIII, 465; Beth Israel Hospital Association, om, IX, 806, 810; Catholic Union, Albany, VIII, 623; Ebenezer Baptist Church, New York, VII, 931 om; Gallaudet Home, VIII, 623; House of Good Shepherd, IX, 868 om; House of Good Shepherd, Rockland County, VII, 266 om; International Fire Association, 413 om; Ladies Deborah Nursery and Child's Protectory, IX, 232; Larchmont Manor Park Society, 431; Masonic Association, Utica, 791; Missionary Society of the Most Holy Redeemer, New York, X, 176 om; German-American School Society, VIII, 460; New York Hospital, VI, 703; New York University, X, 179 om; Pythian Association, Amsterdam, IX, 449; Poughkeepsie Associated Fire Department, VIII, 878, 972; Rochester Homeopathic Hospital, IX, 235; St. John's Armenian Apostolic Church, X, 326 om; St. Joseph's Asylum, New York, om, 176, 179; St. Vincent's Retreat for the Insane, IX, 253; Sanitarium for Hebrew Children, VIII, 1036 om; Sanitarium for Hebrew Children, New York, IX, 152 om; Spalding Literary Union, New York, 810 om; Supreme Grange Life Association, exemption from payment before commencing business, 802 om; University Settlement Society, New York, Educational Alliance, 794; Young Men's Association, Buffalo, membership, exemption from collateral inheritance tax, VIII, 732; Young Men's Hebrew Association, om, X, 179, 869; Young Women's Association, Troy, VIII, 332.

EXTENSIONS. Batavia and Northern Railroad Company, time to begin construction, X, 700 om; Broadway Underground Railway Company, rights, powers and duties, VII, 1031; Brooklyn City Railroad, road, VI, 695; Delhi and Hudson River Railroad Company, charter, repealing act, VIII, 1039 om; Dry Dock and East Broadway and Battery Railroad Company, road and use by another company, V, 646; East Hamburg Turnpike Road

CORPORATIONS — (*Continued*).

EXTENSIONS —(*Continued*).

Company, charter, VI, 162; East River Gas Company, powers, X, 657; Erie and New York City Railroad Company, time for completion, VII, 807 om; Forty-second Street and Grand Street Ferry Railroad Company, tracks, VI, 335; Little Falls, Van Hornesville and Otsego Lake Narrow Gauge Railroad Company, time to begin construction, X, 258, 959 om; Middletown and Wurtsboro Turnpike Company, charter, VII, 265 om; Milford Center Cemetery Association, powers, VIII, 712; New York Arcade Railway Company, powers, 102; New York Canadian Pacific Railway, time for completion, X, 949; New York Elevated Railroad Company, road, VI, 715; Point Chautauqua Association, powers, VIII, 294; Schoharie Central Bridge Company, IV, 513, 637; Schoharie Valley Railroad, road, VI, 90; Second Avenue Railroad Company, tracks, V, 667; Staten Island and Elizabethport Ferry Company, time, VI, 595; Ulster and Delaware Plank Road Company, VII, 565; Unadilla Bridge Company, charter, IV, 636; Utica, Chenango and Cortland Railroad, road, VI, 433; Utica Ice Company, Limited, time for payment of stock, VII, 869; Webster Plank Road Company, charter, VI, 163; White's Corners and Buffalo Plank Road Company, charter, 161.

RELIEF. Attica and Arcade Railroad Company, VII, 416 om; Beth Israel Bikur Cholim Congregation, New York, IX, 808 om; Beth Israel Hospital Association, New York, taxes and water rents, X, 326 om; Church of the Resurrection, New York, assessments, VI, 711; Eagle Avenue German Baptist Church, New York, Evangelical Lutheran Church of· St. James, New York, First Methodist Episcopal Church, New York, X, 60 om; First Universalist Society, Mount Vernon, assessments, 254; Fulton, Wall and Cortland Street Ferry Railroad Company, VIII, 1119; German Hospital and Dispensary, New York, X, 449 om; Hopkinton Manufacturing Company, VI, 169; Locomotive Engineers Mutual Benefit Association, VII, 414 om; Lutheran Cemetery, Newtown, 268 om; Manhattan East Side Mission, X, 59 om; Mount Sinai Hospital, New York, IX, 861 om; Mount Vernon Young Men's Christian Association, X, 806 om;· St. Luke's Church, New York, assessment, IX, 809 om; Second Baptist Church, Harlem, assessment for street improvement, VI, 710; West Side Street Railway Company, Buffalo, certain obligations, VIII, 1117.

CORPORATIONS — (*Continued*).

MISCELLANEOUS. Adirondack Railroad Company, facilitating construction, VI, 172; Albany and Susquehanna Railroad, aiding construction, V, 138, 242, 350; — facilitating construction and extending time, 439; — providing for completion, 737; American and Foreign Bible Society, consolidating with American Baptist Publication Society, VI, 327; Baptist Church Society, Hoosick, removing dead from burying ground, VII, 76; Beth Israel Hospital Association, relative to, X, 59 om; Black River and St. Lawrence Railroad Company, town aid to, VI, 348; Brooklyn Elevated Railroad Company, annulling agreement with railroad commissioners, VIII, 293 om; Brooklyn Equity Gaslight Company, relative to, 469 om; Buffalo Cemetery Association, additional land and office building, VII, 760, 933 om; Buffalo Law School, relative to, VIII, 1038 om; Buffalo and Green Island Ferry Company, increasing capital stock, VI, 1036 om; Buffalo Plank Road, improvement, 195; Buffalo and Washington Railroad Company, facilitating construction, 172; Carthage, Watertown and Sacketts Harbor Railroad Company, facilitating construction, 172; Cattaraugus Railway, facilitating construction, id.; Chautauqua Lake Camp Meeting Association, taxing property, 850; Clyde and Rose Plank Road Company,— repealing charter, VII, 97; — abandonment, 267 om; College of the City of New York, acquiring new site, IX, 381; Colored Home, New York, relative to, VII, 267 om; Cortland Opera House Company, mortgage for indebtedness, VIII, 381; Delaware and Susquehanna Plank Road Company, assessments, V, 233; Edison Electric Illuminating Company, Brooklyn, right to use streets, 591; Elmira Firemen's Association, relative to, VII, 806 om; Eureka Basin Warehouse and Manufacturing Company, Long Island, powers and privileges, repeal, 766; Evans Mills Cemetery Association, raising money for fences, VI, 184; First Congregational and First Baptist Church, Kendall, sale and division of property, VII, 881; First Congregational Church and Society of Cambria, sale of parsonage property, V, 150; First German Methodist Episcopal Church, New York, land for cemetery purposes, IX, 254; First Methodist Episcopal Society, Watkins, relative to, VII, 121; First National Bank, Buffalo, settlement of claims against sureties, 874; First Presbyterian Church, Batchellerville, legalizing acts of trustees, 1106; First Presbyterian Church of Perry, sale of real estate, VI, 45; First Universalist Society, Mount Vernon, relative to, IX, 59 om; First Wesleyan Methodist Church, Chazy, confirming reorganization, VII, 357; Five Points

CORPORATIONS — (*Continued*).
  MISCELLANEOUS —(*Continued*).
    House of Industry, New York, powers of, 334; Flatbush Fire
Company, aid to, VI, 183; Fulton Market Fishmongers Asso-
ciation, relative to, X, 177 om; General Electric Company, refunding franchise tax, IX, 713; Genesee Camp Ground Associa-
tion, supplemental act, trustees, VII, 1019; German Looking
Glass Plate Company, refunding franchise tax, IX, 713; Green
Point Ferry Company, boats on East river, VI, 336; Gypsum
Cemetery Association, revival, VII, 412 om; Harpersville Ceme-
tery Association, granting certain powers, 98; Highland and
Modena Turnpike Road Company, tolls chargeable by, VIII,
1112; Hillside Cemetery Association, Madison county, control
of certain lands, VII, 807 om; Hillside Cemetery Association,
Middletown, raising money for improvements, IX, 794 om; Hope
Savings Bank, Albany, dissolution, VIII, 469 om; Hudson River
Telephone Company, renewal of Senate telephone, 245; Jewish
Theological Seminary, New York, relative to, X, 60 om; Johns-
burgh Electric Light, Heating and Power Company, dam across
Hudson river, om, X, 445, 453; Ladies Deborah Nursery and
Child Protectory, New York, relative to, VII, 267 om; Le Cou-
teulx St. Mary's Institution, deficiency appropriation, 470; Le
Couteulx St. Mary's Institution for the Improved Instruction
of Deaf-Mutes, Buffalo, new buildings, VIII, 888 om; Lockport
Home for the Friendless, care of poor children, VI, 503; Long
Island Historical Society, relative to, IX, 794 om; Lowell Ceme-
tery Association, reducing number of trustees, VIII, 52; Malone
Waterworks Company, sale of water, 941; Manhattan Gas Com-
pany, increasing price of gas, V, 671; Manhattan Loan and
Trust Company, New York, supplemental act, VI, 911 om;
Methodist Episcopal Church, Northville, sale of property, 437;
Methodist Episcopal Church Home, New York, relative to, VII,
509 om; Metropolitan Railroad Company, tunnel under Broad-
way, V, 669; Metropolitan Transit Company,— relative to, VII,
415 om;— supplemental act, 592; Mill Brook Log Company,
improving Mill brook, VI, 97; Mishkan Israel Anshe Suwalker
Congregation, New York, relative to, IX, 868 om; Missionary
Society of the Most Holy Redeemer, release from existing assessments, om, IX, 868, X, 175; Mohawk and Ilion Horse Railroad
Company, using bank of canal, VI, 581; Mountain View Cemetery Association, relative to, VII, 807 om; Municipal Loan
Company, organization tax, VIII, 638 om; National Conservatory of Music, contracts with pupils for instruction, X, 63 om;

CORPORATIONS — (*Continued*).

MISCELLANEOUS —(*Continued*).

National Life Insurance Company, distribution of funds, VII, 267 om; National Trust Company, investigation of Receiver Best, counsel fees, VII, 906; New Baltimore and Rensselaerville Turnpike Road Company, authorizing sale of road, 132 om; Newburgh and Cochecton Turnpike Road, relative to, IX, 793 om; Newark and Rosendale Lime and Cement Manufacturing Company, purchasing land, IV, 827; New York Building and Improvement Company, increasing or diminishing capital stock, VIII, 1101; New York Central Railroad Company, increasing fares, V, 659, 802; New York Central and Hudson River Railraod Company, taxes in Mentz, application of, VII, 207; New York and Oswego Midland Railroad, bonds, postponing taxes, 415 om; New York River Road Company, constructing roads, VI, 98, 419; New York and Harlem Railroad, motive power and terminal facilities, New York, X, 466; New York and London Trust Company, purchase of stocks and issue of debentures, 586 om; New York and New Jersey Bridge Company, elevated railroad, West street, New York, 303; New York and Oswego Midland Railroad Company, facilitating construction, VI, 172; Niagara Street Railroad Company, Niagara Falls, changing route, VIII, 1132; Orange County Mutual Insurance Company, relative to, VII, 412 om; Oswego County Agricultural Society, mortgage for indebtedness, VIII, 341; Otisville and Wurtsboro Turnpike Road Company, rates of toll, VI, 216; Otsego County Agricultural Society, mortgaging property, VIII, 388; Panama Railroad Company, refunding taxes erroneously paid, IX, 605; Pawling and Beekman Turnpike Company, surrender of part of road, VI, 215; Poppenhusen Institution at College Point, taxation, X, 700 om; Potsdam and Watertown Railroad, discharging judgment against, IV, 693; Queen City Gaslight Company, Buffalo, supplying city with gas, repeal, IX, 723 om; Quincy Rural Cemetery Association, acquiring additional land, VI, 501; Red Men, Improved Order of, taking and holding property, VIII, 877; Reformed Church of Helderberg, sale of property, VI, 209; Richmond County Storage and Business Company, increasing capital stock, 815; Roman Catholic Orphan Asylum, New York, reappropriation, 587; Rome, Watertown, Ogdensburgh Railroad Company, purchasing bridge company stock, VIII, 1130; Round Lake Association, water supply, right to condemn property, IX, 794 om; St. Joseph's Institution for the Improved Instruction of Deaf-Mutes, deficiency appropriation,

CORPORATIONS — *(Continued)*.

MISCELLANEOUS —*(Continued)*.

VII, 470; — relative to, 806 om; St. Joseph's Seminary, New York, relative to real estate, IX, 808 om; St. Paul's Methodist Episcopal Church, Onondaga Valley, legalizing title to land, VII, 1100; St. Paul's Reformed Episcopal Church, Bronx borough, relative to, X, 806 om; St. Peter's Church, Cortland, Westchester county, regulating interments, 563 om; Salina and Central Square Plank Road Company, rates of toll, statement of receipts and disbursements, IX, 795 om; Salisbury and Manheim Plank Road Company, renewing charter, VII, 1106; Saratoga Agricultural Society, improvement of grounds, VI, 181; Sennett and Auburn Plank Road Company, assessment of stockholders, V, 119; Smith and Parmelee Gold Company, issuing preferred stock, VI, 96; Society for the Preservation of Scenic and Historic Places and Objects, trustees of, changing name and extending powers, X, 241; Society for the Protection of Destitute Roman Catholic Children, relative to, VII, 505 om; Sodus Point and Southern Railroad Company, tickets, VI, 690; Susquehanna Turnpike Company, abandoning part of road, VIII, 539; Susquehanna Valley Orphans' Home, Binghamton, improvements, VII, 90; Syracuse, Chenango and New York Railroad Company, using Chenango canal towing path, 268 om; Syracuse Water Company, supplying adjacent villages, VII, 1100; Syracuse Waterworks Company, sale of property, VIII, 469 om; Temple Adas Jeshurun Society, holding land for cemetery purposes, VI, 588; Title Guaranty Company, securities, X, 955 om; Troy Female Seminary, trustees, increasing number, method of appointment, IX, 373; Union Literary Society, Ellisburgh, changing name, enlarging income limit, 56; Union Methodist Episcopal Church, New York, releasing taxes, 1894, 794 om; Union Mission Chapel Association, Brooklyn, trusts, legacies and donations, VIII, 1127; Union Veteran Protective Association, annual meetings, IX, 793 om; United States Harvey Way and Construction Company, VIII, 639 om; University of Buffalo, cancer investigation, IX, 772; Utica and Black River Railroad, aid by certain towns, VI, 92; Vassar College, right to hold additional property, VIII, 728; Venice Town Insurance Company, changing location of business office, VII, 1013; Warren County Electric Light, Heat and Power Company, dam across Hudson river, om, X, 446, 453; Western New York Agricultural Society,— regulating voting, VI, 1036 om; sale of real estate, id.; Westfield Academy, donation of fossils to, VII, 417 om; Whitehall and

CORPORATIONS — (*Continued*).

  MISCELLANEOUS —(*Continued*).

  Plattsburg Railroad, facilitating construction, V, 737, 864, VI, 68, 172; Williamsville Academy, sale of property, VI, 336; Yates County Agricultural Society, selling part of real estate, VII, 1103.

CORTLAND. (City) Contracts, powers of common council, sidewalks, X, 593 om.

CORTLAND. Westchester county. Highway tax in Croton-on-Hudson, payment to village, IX, 867 om; reducing town expenses, salaries of justices of the peace and overseers of the poor, 722 om.

COSTS. Amending Code, IX, 860 om; relative to, VII, 665 om; in actions, X, 179 om, 880, 916; judgments against State, payment of, VIII, 546.

COTTMAN, THOMAS. Proof of claim, VII, 552.

COUNSEL IN CRIMINAL CASES. Allowances, X, 942.

COUNTIES. Amending general act, IX, 624 om; certain exempted from act of 1872, chap. 733, VII, 506 om; claims against State, adjustment, VIII, 755; Genesee, Erie and Niagara, boundaries between, 1102; institutions in certain counties, purchasing supplies for, X, 700 om; officers, report of financial transactions, VII, 609; Oneida, abolishing fee system, IX, 124; railroad commissioners, VI, 911 om; St. Lawrence and Franklin, changing boundaries, X, 320 om.

COUNTY AUDITOR. Saratoga, creating office, X, 450 om.

COUNTY CLERK.

  Acknowledgments, taking authorized, IX, 722 om; authentications by, X, 171; criminal statistics, IX, 861 om; fees, including sheriff's fees, 150 om; fees in certain counties, X, 445 om; fees in relation to notaries public, IX, 346; fees for searches in certain counties, X, 381; office hours in certain counties, IX, 462; offices, records and indexes, VI, 911 om; office hours, IX, 863 om; recording and indexing notices of pendency in certain counties, VIII, 70; Paddon, Oneida county, expenses notaries public, VII, 83.

  Albany. Fees, VII, 604, 805 om; — filing with assessors certificates of sale of property, 888; — office hours, VII, 757.

  Cattaraugus and Columbia counties. Recording notices of pendency of actions, VIII, 705.

  Cayuga. Salaried office, VIII, 1103, IX, 124.

  Columbia. Office hours, repeal, IX, 625 om.

  Erie. Salaried office, IX, 272.

  Herkimer. Special deputies, X, 811 om.

COUNTY CLERKS — (*Continued*).

Kings. Employees, X, 584 om; expenses, notaries public, VII, 83; index clerks and custodians, compensation, X, 711 om; management of office, id.; office fees, 588 om; salaried office, VIII, 124, X, 179 om; salary, 594 om.

Monroe. Assistants and special deputies, VI, 266.

New York. Duties and compensation, VII, 413 om.

Oneida and Columbia. Recording notices of pendency, VIII, 63.

Onondaga. Index and abstract clerks, X, 388; recording papers, VII, 806 om; records and indexes, VI, 821.

Richmond. Recording certain papers, VII, 497, 506 om.

St. Lawrence. Ferris, expenses notaries public, VII, 83.

Seneca. Transcribing certain records, IX, 39.

COUNTY DETECTIVES. Creating office, IX, 153 om; amending act, duplicate, X, 173; Kings county, salaries, 955 om.

COUNTY JUDGE. Compensation in certain counties, X, 439 om; exchanging terms, IV, 625; Greene, repealing salary law, VII, 807 om; Rockland, compensation, 507 om; Westchester, designation of constables, 1092.

COUNTY JUDGE AND SURROGATE. Special, term of office in certain counties, X, 700 om.

COUNTY LAW. General amendments, IX, 259, 289.

COUNTY ROADS. Repayment for maintenance, X, 639.

COUNTY TREASURERS. Amending Revised Statutes, VIII, 291 om; salaries, VII, 807 om; excepting certain counties from provisions of act, 265 om; excepting Fulton, 1010; fees, excepting Oneida and Schoharie, VI, 151; Kings county, relative to, VII, 266; Monroe and Seneca, amending act, 71; Oswego, 266 om; Rensselaer, relative to, VI, 333, X, 583 om; Ulster, fees, VI, 508.

COURT OF APPEALS. Clerk's messenger, salary, VIII, 72; jurisdiction, 131 om, 229; law clerk, appropriation, X, 574; relief, IV, 532, 772; reports, VII, 892.

COURT OF CLAIMS.

Canals, damages under $9,000,000 act 1895, X, 172; counties,— insane asylums, IX, 858 om; — railroad aid bonds, X, 945 om; expenses and disbursements, appropriation, 556; judges, salaries and expenses, additional appropriation, 933; jurisdiction, om, 703, 709; militia, counsel fees, 945 om; national guard uniforms, IX, 858 om; railroad aid, amending act, X, 315 om.

HEARINGS. See also BOARD OF CLAIMS. Abeel, X, 943 om; American Glucose Company, IX, 797 om; Androvic, X, 946 om; Angel,

XI — 7

COURT OF CLAIMS — (*Continued*).

    HEARINGS — (*Continued*).

Auburn prison, 702 om; Argus Company, 944 om; Auburn, local assessment, State property, om, 585, 634; Bailey, Auburn prison, 702 om; Baker, damages, destruction of animals, 593 om; Bawden, chaplain, Rochester Industrial School, 707 om; Bernard, E. J. & Co., 61 om; Brandow Printing Company, om, 315, 444; Brown, 945 om; Bulson and Polock, bridge tenders, Watervliet, 593 om; Burgard, 441 om; Cane, McCaffrey and Company, 702 om; Cleever, 707 om; Commercial Construction Company, 589 om; Considine, 170; Conway adm. Hendy, 944 om; Cragin, om, IX, 798, 857; Cusick, X, 944 om; Devitt, Mulheron, Manville and Wood, 945 om; Dibble Company, 945 om; Dinehart, injuries received on canal, 255; Dunn, 703 om; Dutton Pneumatic Lock and Engineering Company, 449 om; Evans, 708 om; Fleeck, 165, Frankfort, claims of residents, 706 om; Frost, IX, 721 om; Galvin, injuries received while at work on capitol, X, 267; Gard, Auburn prison, 702 om; Gibier estate, 591 om; Gordon, 165; Hall, Amos C., 441 om; Hall, James, IX, 858 om; Hamill, injuries received in Clinton prison, X, 259; Hess and Company, om, 315, 588; Horseheads and Elmira, Newtown creek, improvement, om, 588, 708; Indian lake, service of fire wardens, 946 om; Kineally escheat, 310 om; Leith, 236; Levy, 309 om; Linkie, Carrie and Charles E., 165; Marningham, Hudson River State Hospital, 704 om; Mathews escheat, 312 om; McDough, injuries received at Sing Sing prison, 699 om; McMaster, 64 om; Monahan and others, 165; Moriarity, 945 om; Moore, 308 om; Myers, 447 om; Nagle, X, 944 om; New York, Park avenue improvement, claims for damages, 589 om; Niewenhous, New York Park avenue improvement, 699 om; O'Keefe, 165, 240, 584, 944; Onondaga Pottery Company, IX, 797 om; Oswego dam, claims for damages, X, 311 om; Parker and Company, om, 703, 944; Payne, 591 om; Pfeiffer, 701 om; Pierce, 442 om; Riseley and Love, 709 om; Roth, 944 om; Schlaefer, 442 om; Smith, Annie M., 443 om; Smith, John T., 701 om; Smith, Thomas H., 445 om; Snyder, 707 om; Stockbridge Indians, 703 om; Storms, etc., 445 om; Stuart, 442 om; Turzkowska, injuries received at Niagara reservation, 707 om; Tyron and others, 61 om; Van Gorder, 165; Van Slyke and others, om, IX, 858, X, 449; Wallace, 943 om; Watts, 709 om; Weishem, 946 om; White and Coughlin, Soldiers and Sailors' Home damages and extra work, 377; Whitney, 443 om; Windholz, 946 om.

COURT OF SPECIAL SESSIONS.
Jurisdiction, IX, 260; jury, method of selecting, 129; trial, method of, defendant's right to elect, 139.

Albany, relative to, VIII, 639 om; New York — appeals, disorderly persons, neglect to support family, IX, 526; — appeals, disorderly persons, neglect to support family, when judgment of special sessions final, 526.

CRAIG COLONY FOR EPILEPTICS. See also EPILEPTIC COLONY. Heating plant, X, 656; repairs and equipment, id.; roads, walks and grading, 546.

CRANBERRY LAKE RESERVOIR. Removing dead and floating timber from shores and waters, X, 427.

CRENEY, MARY F. Widow of James Creney, Assistant Commissary-General, claim for compensation, VII, 917.

CRIMES. Against public peace, X, 807 om.

CRIMINAL CASES. Services in, VII, 414 om.

CRIMINAL LAW. Certificates of conviction, VIII, 129 om; new trials in capital cases, VII, 1091.

CRIMINAL STATISTICS. Amending Criminal Code, om, VIII, 1040, IX, 153.

CUSTODIAL ASYLUM FOR FEEBLE-MINDED WOMEN, NEWARK. Relative to, X, 812 om; additional property, IX, 79; Cottage H, X, 653; electric light unit, 544, 653; inspector's salary, 544; new cottages, IX, 296; water supply, X, 653.

CYCLES. Uniform ordinances regulating use of, IX, 811 om.

DADY, MICHAEL J. Purchase of property for Long Island Hospital, IX, 773 om.

DANFORTH. Contract with Syracuse Water Company, VII, 1105.

DANOLDS, CHARLES A. Contractor, Elmira Reformatory, compensation, VII, 375, 787.

DANSVILLE. Extending boundaries, VI, 702.

DARLING, GRISWOLD & COMPANY. Furnishing accommodations to Senate committee, VII, 86.

DAVENPORT, JOHN I. Counsel to Senate committee, VII, 85.

DEAF-MUTES. Amending act, VIII, 872; care and education, 129 om, 1166; instruction, amending School Law, X, 447 om.

DEAN, ELIZABETH. Estate of, IX, 393.

DEATH. Damages for causing by negligence, IX, 792 om.

DEBTORS. Imprisonment, facilitating discharge of, VII, 265 om (2 bills).

DECEDENTS. Estates, action against executor, VIII, 1092; inventory of estate, X, 62 om; payment of creditors and legatees, VIII, 890 om; sale of real estate, VII, 414 om.

DEER RIVER. Water supply, VII, 505 om.

DELAWARE RIVER. Dykes and barriers, Cochecton, X, 814 om; dykes, — Hancock, 788; — Highland, 935; — Port Jervis, 946 om; improvement of, VIII, 407; improvement, Cochecton, 886 om.

DEMING, HORACE E. Counsel, investigation of charges against New York district attorney, X, 297.

DEMURRER. Amendments after decision, IX, 791 om.

DENTISTS. Students, admission to examination, X, 265; displaying professional signs, IX, 803 om; examination and practice, X, 942 (2 bills); relief of certain students, 174.

DERRICK, RICHARD A. Contested election, Assembly, Rensselaer county, expenses, VII, 917.

DE RUYTER. Village, extending boundaries, VI, 189.

DISORDERLY PERSONS. Relative to, VIII, 458.

DISPENSARY. Regulating incorporation, licenses, etc., IX, 816 om.

DISTRICT ATTORNEY. Amending County Law, X, 444 om; assistants, IX, 801 om; compensation, retaining taxable costs, VIII, 404; employment of counsel, IX, 863 om; Erie county, assistants, 800 om; filing stenographic notes, VII, 265 om; special, appointment of, X, 699 om; special, appointment in certain cases, 591 om; Washington county, assistant, VI, 143.

DISTRICT TELEGRAPH COMPANIES. Appointment of policemen, VII, 268 om, 416.

DIVORCE. Advertising business of procuring, prohibited, VIII, 534; foreign judgment, enforcement in this State, X, 594 om; when action may be maintained, 758.

DOCUMENTS. Recording, amending act, VII, 806 om.

DODD, CHARLES J. Counsel fees, expenses, Assembly contested election, Waite Case, Kings county, X, 795.

DOGS. Running at large, Rockland county, VI, 92; tax on, Tonawanda reservation, IX, 725 om.

DONOVAN, JOHN J. Claim against State, X, 63 om.

DOWER. Procedure, VI, 502.

DRAINAGE. Amending act of 1869, VI, 509, VII, 412 om; amending Revised Statutes, VI, 190, VIII, 130 om, X, 812 om; Amherst, Clarence, 698; Black lake, VIII, 614; Cato, swamp lands adjacent to Otter lake and Parker's pond, 613; Cicero and Clay, VI, 189; commissioners, evidence of indebtedness, VII, 413 om; Conewango creek, X, 315 om (2 bills); Orange county, VII, 508 om.

DRUGS. Offenses connected with sale of, X, 592 om.

DUNKIRK. Amending charter, VI, 587, VII, 79; purchasing steam fire engine, VI, 334; revising charter, VIII, 881; water supply, om, IX, 730, 785.

EASTCHESTER CREEK. Changing name, VIII, 469 om.

EASTERN NEW YORK REFORMATORY. Relative to, IX, 245; continuing construction, X, 697; buildings and expenses, IX, 776 om; cells, access to, duplicate bill, X, 293; claim of John R. Thomas, architect, 296; dining-room, kitchen and bakery, 566.

EAST RIVER BRIDGE. Relative to, L. 1895, chap. 789, IX, 873 om.

EATON; JAMES W. Superintendent of new capitol, counsel fees, VII, 83; expense of experts, 84; stenographer's services, id.

EDGEWATER. Changing boundaries, VIII, 639 om.

EDYE AND VOLCKENS. Judgment against people for costs, payment, VII, 926.

EDYMOIN, FRANCIS B. *Habeas Corpus*, payment of expenses, VI, 678.

ELECTION DISTRICTS. Sodus, relative to, VI, 58; West Turin — legalizing division into, IX, 818 om; — repealing act, X, 441 om.

ELECTIONS. Amending general act, om, IX, 724, 801, 863 (3 bills), X, 955; ballots, VIII, 762, 949, IX, 150; ballots, prescribing size, weight and appearance, VII, 412 om; Davis voting machine, authorizing use of, in towns and cities, IX, 626 om; districts — creating and altering, X, 960 om; — amending general law, IX, 863 om,' independence of voters, secrecy of ballot, VIII, 566; inspectors, — amending Revised Statutes, VII, 130 om; — method of appointment, VII, 203; New York — commissioners of election, term, X, 716 om; — notices, VIII, 638 om; nominations, filling vacancies, X, 705 om; notices of, VII, 129 om; officers, — compensation, IX, 463; — compensation in certain counties, 722 om; official ballot, pasters, 477; poll clerks, VII, 333; registration, forms of, X, 808 om; registration and enrollment books, consolidation, 279; towns, places of registry and voting, IX, 863 om.

ELECTRICAL SUBWAYS. Amending act, VIII, 871.

ELECTRICITY. Regulating price in certain cities, X, 585 om.

ELECTRIC LIGHT. Meters and wires, unlawful interference with, X, 311 om.

ELECTRIC LIGHT COMPANIES. In towns and villages, acquiring real estate, X, 159.

ELEVATED RAILROADS. Harvey claim, IX, 141; percentage tax receipts, VIII, 1160; regulating travel on, IX, 626 om.

ELEVATED RAILWAY INCOME PERCENTAGE SPECIAL TAX RECEIPTS. Custody and disbursement of, Harvey claim, VIII, 886 om.

ELEVATORS. Mercantile establishments, regulating use of, X, 594 om; steam, protection of openings, VII, 268 om.

ELMIRA. Amending charter, VII, 807, 934, VIII, 1041, IX, 785, X, 583; common council, legalizing acts, VI, 845; damages for defective streets, VII, 843; fire department building bonds, IX, 734 om; political primaries and conventions, VIII, 386; revising charter, new ward, 64.

102 MESSAGES FROM THE GOVERNORS.

ELMIRA REFORMATORY. Revising act, X, 62 om; sentences, 917; transportation facilities, IX, 135, 244; boiler-house, VII, 783; domestic building, X, 548; electric plant, repairs, 548; engines and dynamos, 295; hospital, VII, 783; industrial fund, 486; pumphouse, 783; piping and connections, X, 295; trade school building, 548; water supply and fire protection, VII, 784; Worthington, contractor, claims, 381, 788.

EMIGRATION COMMISSIONERS. Creating board, VI, 511; interest on Ward's Island mortgage, VIII, 112; rebuilding landing wharf at Castle Garden, 113.

EMINENT DOMAIN. Incomplete proceedings, restoring land to owner, X, 260.

EPILEPTIC COLONY. Establishing, IX, 240. See CRAIG COLONY.

ERIE COUNTY. Bureau of elections, X, 451 om; Cayuga Creek road improvement, VII, 265 om; compensation of court officers, 538; county auditor, election of, IX, 861 om; election notices, 153 om; fishing in Niagara river, VI, 906; refunding unexpended balance of money raised for Tonawanda armory site, IX, 795 om; support of poor, VI, 509, VII, 441; public buildings and grounds, Buffalo, 354; publication of legal notices in German newspapers, 390.

ESCHEAT. Various bills, names not given, X, 778; Baldwin, VI, 483; Bashford, 157; Beattie, VIII, 405; Booth estate, X, 635 om; Brunn, VIII, 723; Bruno, 980; Cass, X, 273; Chamberlain, VI, 158; Coddington, X, 706 om; Corbett, VII, 805 om; De Groat, 642; Dennison, 1116; Dickson, IX, 384; Faenger, VI, 692; Feller, VIII, 882; Froelich estate, X, 312 om; Frost, IX, 284; Geib, X, 451 om; Gibson, 952 om; Grady, 704 om; Greene, VIII, 882; Harvey, VII, 550; Hohenholz, 548; Hurford and Barnett, VIII, 882; Hyne and Kilgour, IX, 428; Joyce, heirs, VII, 805 om; Kleindinst, IX, 815 om; Lang and others, X, 588 om; Marvin, VII, 1107; McGee, 805 om; McLoughlin, 748; McKenna, VIII, 725; Meyer, VII, 749; Neusch, VII, 805 om; Pax, id.; Peters, IX, 816 om, X, 266, 376; Pierce, VIII, 630; Porter, heirs of Hoenig, VII, 549; Power, X, 958 om; Racka, VIII, 722; Reilly, IX, 467; Riley, X, 446 om; Roebuck, 953 om; Scherer, VIII, 882; Schroeder, VII, 1116; Schuyler, X, 252; Shriver, heirs of, VII, 805 om; Smith, IX, 403; Spicer, VIII, 882, 1036; Steche, VII, 805 om; Stewart, 619; Stierle, X, 273; Straack, VIII, 734; Sullivan, IX, 370; Thebaud, VIII, 731; Theiss, 890 om; Tracy, X, 954 om; Turner, VIII, 1040 om; Wakeman, VII, 935 om; Washington, VIII, 755; Watters and Fleming, X, 958 om; Winship, IX, 285; Wyoming County Agricultural Society, VI, 708.

ESSEX COUNTY. Newcomb, repealing act, VI, 699.

EVIDENCE. Relative to, VIII, 1167; in action against deceased party, 292 om; confidential communications, IX, 44; depositions, om, 792, X, 313; deposition, application for, VIII, 469 om; documentary, IX, 860 om; handwriting, proof of, X, 444 om; notary's certificate of protest, VIII, 293 om; physicians, 639 om; record of ancient deeds, X, 386; transcripts of testimony, fees, IX, 722 om; weather records, New York, X, 955 om; of wife to disprove adultery, VII, 1093.

EXCISE. Amending general act of 1857, VI, 94; amending act of 1870, 505; boards of, amending act of 1874, VIII, 973; commissioners, VII, 412 om; — Bath, legalizing acts of, 178; — compensation, IX, 275; exempting Soldiers and Sailors' Home from general act of 1892, 625 om; licenses, terminating May 1, VII, 265 om; local option, VI, 506, 568; New York, relative to, VII, 803 om; New York and Brooklyn, VIII, 355; Ontario county, habitual drunkards, VII, 266 om; prohibiting sales of liquor, Allegany and Cattaraugus reservations, VI, 97; prohibiting sale of liquor on State property, VIII, 291 om, 351; regulating sale of intoxicating liquors, 540; revision bill, 1889, 801; sale of liquor on election days, X, 162; tax on beverages, VIII, 797; tax on sales, 436.

EXECUTIONS. Relative to, VIII, 1040 om; claim of property by third person, how tried, X, 807 om.

EXECUTIVE LAW. Amendments, IX, 218.

EXECUTORS. Accounting, X, 282.

EXECUTORS AND ADMINISTRATORS. Amending Revised Statutes, IX, 272; judicial settlement of accounts, 283.

EXTRADITION. William R. Foster, X, 59 om.

FACTORY INSPECTOR. Deputy, labor on public works, IX, 864 om; female deputies, VIII, 885; reports of accidents, 1039 om.

FALSE LABELS. Relative to, VIII, 632.

FALSE PRETENCES. Evidence, IX, 259.

FAR ROCKAWAY. Claim of Eureka Fire Hose Company, X, 324 om; claim of Gamewell Fire Alarm Telegraph Company, id.

FAYETTEVILLE. Purchasing fire apparatus, VII, 848.

FELONY. Trial, second offense, VI, 849.

FERRIS, ROBERT M. Deceased, bounties to heirs, VI, 324.

FERRY. Conesus lake, Long Point to McPherson Point, VIII, 1098; Genesee river, Rochester, VII, 417 om; Great South bay, fees, VIII, 639 om; Hudson river, Chadeayne, VII, 664 om; Philipstown, VI, 813; Tarrytown and Nyack, VIII, 880; Troy and West Troy, VI, 705; Lake Champlain, Barber's Point, VIII, 410; Crown Point, 463; Essex county, X, 953 om; Ticonderoga, VIII, 1099; New York and Brooklyn, VI, 697; Niagara river, Youngstown, VI, 593; Sammis, David, S. S., Babylon to Fire Island Beach, VII, 936 om; Seneca lake, extending Goodwin franchise, IX, 372; Lodi Landing, VI, 1033.

FERRY AND EXCURSION BOATS. Life saving crews, X, 807 om.

FERTILIZER. Preventing fraud in manufacture and sale, VII, 130.

FINES. Remission of, IX, 793 om.

FIRE DISTRICTS. Amending County Law, IX, 622 om.

FIRE ESCAPES. Erection of, VII, 267 om; school buildings, IX, 355.

FIRE INSURANCE. Amending general law, VII, 507 om; policies, construction of, 332.

FIRE INSURANCE COMPANIES. Amending Insurance Law, X, 533 om; preventing false and deceptive statements, VII, 267 om, 322; securities, investments, 891.

FIRE AND FIRE INLAND NAVIGATION COMPANIES. Reports, VII, 416 om.

FIREMEN. Volunteer, death from injuries received while on duty, payment to estate, IX, 815 om; volunteer, peddler's license, IX, 866 om.

FIRST NEW YORK VOLUNTEERS. Relative to, VII, 804 om.

FIRST REGIMENT MEXICAN VOLUNTEERS. Relief, VII, 882.

FISCAL SUPERVISOR. Office expenses, services of examiner of accounts of institutions, X, 554.

FISH.

    Bass,— not to be fished for in certain waters, IX, 623 om; — in St. Lawrence county, X, 61 om; — striped in Hudson river, 392; black bass,— in Brant lake, VIII, 975; — close season, om, X, 308, 313; — Crystal lake, close season, IX, 799 om; catching in certain waters, X, 61 om; eel-weirs in Chemung river, IX, 721 om; giving free access to private streams and ponds stocked by State, 444; Esopus creek, protection, VII, 234; fisheries, New Utrecht, V, 123.

    Fishing,— destruction of illegal devices, X, 448 om; with certain devices prohibited, IX, 717 om; with set lines, X, 312 om; — Honeoye lake, 64 om; in Canadaigua and Honeoye lakes, 173; in Chautauqua lake, 174; in Fall creek, Ithaca, IX, 798 om; Lake Erie, X, 61 om; Ouleout creek, 161; Orange county, om, 319, 320; Skaneateles lake, 174; Tonawanda creek, Wyoming county, VI, 906; in certain waters in Seneca county, X, 168; through ice, IX, 446; — id., in certain lakes, 721 om; — id., in certain waters, om, 798, X, 954; — id., Lake Neahtahwanta, 954; — id., Washington county, om, 309, 313; Hudson river, pound and purse nets, VIII, 627; Kings county, preservation of, VII, 264 om; Lake Erie, preservation, VIII, 457; Lake George, 888 om; Lake Ontario and other waters, IX, 798 om; — protection of, VIII, 627; Loon lake, certain fish not to be taken, VII, 204 om; method of taking, VIII, 131 om; Monroe county, preservation and protection, VII, 264, 507 om; nets,— use of, IX, 799 om; id., in Hudson and Delaware rivers, X, 443 om;

FISH — (*Continued*).

id., Jamaica bay, IX, 798 om; net and set lines, X, 445 om; replenishing lakes and rivers, VII, 458; replenishing waters with, VIII, 75; St. Lawrence river, VI, 911 om; salmon, close season, IX, 799 om; Salmon river, preservation of, VII, 807 om; seines and spawning beds, south of Croton Point, IX, 470; shad and game fish, protection, Delaware river, VIII, 888 om; shellfish,— protection in certain waters, VII, 415 om; — taking by nonresidents, X, 448 om; snares and nets, use of, VIII, 976; spawning, Hudson river, protection, VII, 264 om; spearing in Lake Ontario, X, 954 om; spearing suckers and eels, Long pond, 440 om; Steuben county, Loon lake, 446 om; sturgeon,— Lake Ontario, IX, 800 om; method of taking, Thousand Islands, om, 798, 863; taking by drawing off water from ponds and reservoirs, 798 om; transportation of, X, 590 om; trespasses on private ponds, IX, 233; trout,— lake, taking or possession of, X, 445 om; — season, Keuka lake, 443 om; — Owasco lake, prohibition against taking, VII, 69; — sale of, X, 708 om; — Ulster county, protection in certain waters, VII, 131 om; Wallkill river, taking fish from, 506 om.

FISH CREEK. Cleaning and deepening, IX, 81.

FISH HATCHERY. Caledonia, VII, 902; — purchase of additional land, VIII, 249; Catskill, Middletown, rearing ponds, X, 562; Cold Spring, VII, 902; Ellington, trout, X, 787; Jefferson county, VII, 632, VIII, 249; Oneida county, Watkins creek, IX, 221; Palenville VII, 902; Schroon, IV, 777 om; shad hatching car, equipment, VIII, 1136; southern tier, IX, 43; Sullivan County, 38.

FISHWAYS. Relative to, VII, 805 om; Cattaraugus creek, VIII, 890 om; Chenango Forks, 880 om; Chenango river, Fort Dickinson, X, 787; Chittenango creek, VIII, 713; Delaware river, dam at Deposit, X, 787; Ogdensburgh dam, IX, 80; Oswego and Seneca rivers, VIII, 888 om; Rossie dam, IX, 80; State dams, Oswego, Oneida and Seneca rivers, VII, 61.

FLAGS. Battle flags, permitting use of, in Oswego county old home week, X, 919; desecration of, 62 om; foreign, preventing display on public buildings, IX, 527; national or State, improper use of, 860 om.

FLANAGAN, JOHN. Interest on judgments, VII, 230; judgments for costs, id.

FLATBUSH. Increasing policemen and salaries of officers, VIII, 1110; licensing public hacks, etc., VII, 1111; lighting streets, VIII, 1036 om; Parkville, streets and avenues, 615; police department,— captain, increasing salary, IX, 117; — increasing salaries, 107; Prospect

FLATBUSH — (*Continued*).
    avenue,— assessments, X, 177 om; refunding assessments, 325 om; street and sewer commissioners, 29th ward, transferring powers and duties to Brooklyn commissioner of city works, IX, 720 om.

FLATLANDS. Amending annexation act, IX, 634 om; public hacks and amusements, licensing, VIII, 975.

FLATLANDS AND FLATBUSH. Remsen avenue improvement, IX, 275.

FLOOD, MICHAEL. Land devised by, relative to, IX, 811 om.

FLUSHING. Bond for arrears of taxes, IX, 819 om; correcting assessment maps, VII, 413 om; free shools, increasing tax rate, IX, 718 om; street improvements, VIII, 724; surplus on certain bonds, authorizing use for other purposes, IX, 819 om.

FOOD AND DRUGS. Adulteration, VII, 1113.

FOOD. Horse flesh, prohibiting sale of, IX, 793 om.

FOREIGN CORPORATION. Certificate of authority, IX, 864 om.

FOREIGN FIRE INSURANCE COMPANIES. Agent's authority, om, IX, 721, 802; tax on, Jamaica and Flushing, om, 817.

FOREIGN LIFE INSURANCE COMPANIES. Taxation of, X, 590 om.

FOREIGN INSURANCE COMPANIES. Preventing removal of causes, VII, 265 om; removal of actions to Federal courts, 573.

FOREIGN MUTUAL INSURANCE COMPANIES. Tobacco, authorizing business in this State, VII, 934 om.

FOREST, FISH AND GAME COMMISSION. General expenses, forest preserve improvement, X, 786; office, mezzanine gallery and filing cases, 563; office expenses, IX, 768; reforesting burned and barren lands, publication and distribution of forest information, X, 562; stenographer and clerk, salary, 421.

FOREST COMMISSION. Act to create, VII, 1110; reimbursing maintenance fund, IX, 76.

FOREST PRESERVE. Commission to investigate titles, X, 814 om; map of, in certain counties, IX, 776; preventing waste of timber killed by forest fires, X, 706 om.

FORESTS. Assistant superintendent of forest, salary, X, 421, 424, 553, 563; classifying and describing, 640; park preserves, hunting grounds, VII, 412 om; replanting, promotion of, 932 om; St. Lawrence county, appointing commissioner, 933 om.

FORT BREWSTER. Acquiring site of, X, 435.

FORT COVINGTON. Annual school meeting, VIII, 130 om; town house, VI, 910 om.

FORT DEFIANCE. Perpetuating memory of defenders, appropriation, VIII, 886 om.

FORT EDWARD. Board of education, contract with Fort Edward Collegiate Institute, VII, 205.

FRANCHISE. Amending act of 1899, X, 171; taxation as real property, 63 om.

FRANKFORT. Better administration of justice, IX, 867 om; payment of certain indebtedness, X, 815 om.

FRAUD. Transfers, prevention of, IX, 376.

FREDONIA. Amending charter, VIII, 457.

FRENCH, EDWARD H. Canal contract, appropriation, VI, 1008.

FULTON. Amending city charter, X, 583 om; sidewalks and paving, 715 om.

FULTON COUNTY. Relief of poor, VIII, 130 om.

GALLIEN, ELIZA M. Widow of Henry Gallien, former Deputy Comptroller, salary, appropriation, VII, 1081, VIII, 109.

GAME AND FISH PROTECTORS. Amending act, IX, 151 om; compensation, X, 810 om; powers, 319 om; protectors and foresters, IX, 862 om; — compensation, 768; Jamaica bay and adjacent waters, om, X, 815, 949; right of search, IX, 798 om.

GAME LAW. See also FISH. Amendments, VI, 505, 906 (5 bills); VII, 264 om (5 bills); 507 om, 508 om, 611, 938 om; IX, 233, 258, 717 om, 798 om, 863 om, X, 448 om (2 bills); board of supervisors, powers, IX, 234; Adirondack Park, X, 317 om; bird skins, sale of, IX, 799 om; Cattaraugus county, hunting with ferret, X, 587 om; close season, VI, 274; deer, hounding, in certain towns in Washington county, IX, 723 om; digging worms on shores of Queens and Suffolk counties, 799 om; disseminating knowledge of birds and wild animals, 798 om; elk, protection of, 799 om; protection of ducks and fish, VIII, 979; fire wardens,— compensation, IX, 768; — in Jefferson county, X, 954 om; — and assistants, Sullivan county, IX, 799 om; fish culturist, salary, X, 421, 553; forest fires, services at, X, 161; fur-bearing animals, IX, 722 om; game, places of refuge for, X, 309 om; grey squirrels, 700 om; grouse and other birds, IX, 798 om; grouse, close season, X, 311 om; grouse, 442 om; hares and rabbits, close season, 954 om; — Orange county, id.; hounds running at large where deer inhabit, IX, 798 om; killing wild fowl and fish, VIII, 130 om; Jefferson and Oswego counties, releasing certain waters from operation of, VII, 442; Kayutah lake, X, 954 om; Oneida county, protection of game, VIII, 716; Orange county, close season, X, 954 om; pigeons, Antwerp or homing, interference with, 309 om; pollution of streams, 810 om; preservation of game, VII, 1095; preservation of certain animals, VII, 264 om; private parks, protection of, id.; publication and distribution, IX, 798 om; recoveries in actions by people, disposal of, 799 om; Rockland county, taking game in, X, 444 om; special game constables, VII, 263; squirrels, black and gray, close season, X, 444 om; squirrels, hares and rabbits, IX, 798 om;

GAME LAW — (*Continued*).

    Sullivan county, hunting and fishing on Sunday, X, 539 om; Sunday observance, VI, 505; supervisors, powers in certain counties, X, 441 om; supplemental act, VII, 264 om; venison, possession of, IX, 799 om; wild fowl, 721 om; — taking in Black river bay, X, 700 om; woodcock, close season, 382; woodcock and grouse, close season, 439 om; woodcock on Long Island, close season, 440 om.

GAS. Auburn, regulating price, X, 907; inspectors of meters, IX, 722 om; Seneca Falls and Waterloo, regulating price, X, 907.

GAS COMPANIES. Preventing extortion by, VI, 589.

GASLIGHT COMPANIES. Amending act, VII, 808 om; use of electricity, 864.

GAS METERS. Inspection, VI, 282.

GEDDES. Relative to, VII, 806 om.

GENERAL LAWS. Correcting manifest errors, IX, 447.

GENESEE COUNTY. Authorizing annual appropriation to corporations for prevention of cruelty, X, 812 om.

GENESEE RIVER. Removing obstructions, Allegany county, VIII, 847; State dam, IX, 609.

GENESEO. Public building, X, 960 om.

GENEVA. Assessment on State property, X, 649; depositaries of city funds, 583 om; finances, sinking and highway funds, 716 om; Indian Mound, purchase of, VIII, 887 om; railroads, VII, 1105; street improvements, sewer extension, X, 806 om.

GENEVA COLLEGE. Appointing delegate to State Medical Society, III, 593.

GEOLOGICAL MAP. Publication, VIII, 113; printing and distributing, 252.

GEOLOGICAL SURVEY. Map, Catskill region, VII, 469.

GERMAN FLATS. Board of alms, VII, 215.

GETTYSBURG. Battlefield, marking positions of New York troops, and defensive works, VII, 1083; battlefield monuments, VIII, 253; battle of, repulse of Longstreet, Walker's painting, purchase of, IX, 291.

GETTYSBURG AND CHATTANOOGA BATTLEFIELD COMMISSION. Publishing and distributing report, X, 302.

GILDED WARE. Preventing deception in manufacture and sale of, IX, 47.

GLEN CREEK. Improvement, VIII, 1123; repairing and reconstructing banks and channels, X, 314 om, 435.

GLENVILLE. School district fire department, VI, 1035 om.

GLIDDEN, HENRY A. Index to legislative documents, VII, 225, 461.

GLOBES. Purchase for Executive Chamber, legislative libraries and State Library, VIII, 108.

GLOVERSVILLE. Fire department, term of service, VIII, 409; gas supply, VI, 329.

GOLD. Articles made of, stamping, X, 705 om.

GOSHEN. Water supply, X, 232.

GOVERNOR. Expenses of confidential investigations, X, 422; investigation of State officers, appropriation, IX, 712; removal of officers, expenses of investigations, appropriation, 75; messages, printing in German, VIII, 251.

GRADE CROSSINGS. Brooklyn borough, abolishing, X, 714 om.

GRAND ARMY OF THE REPUBLIC. Badges, prohibiting wearing of, VII, 1108; badges or buttons, relative to, X, 62 om; posts, exempting property from taxation, IX, 470; preservation of records, VIII, 528; Sherman Post No. 401, Rose, use of room in town hall, id.; unincorporated posts, taking and holding property, 878.

GRAND JURY. Madison county, clerk, X, 61 om; New York, selection of, 634 om; preparation of list, IX, 148 om; who may be present at sessions of, X, 392.

GRANTS. English, relative to, X, 450 om.

GRASS RIVER. Improvement, VI, 575; improving navigation, VIII, 846.

GRAVESEND. Common lands, om, VII, 665, 804, IX, 729; common lands fund, X, 714 om; common lands, Senate investigation, counsel fees, VII, 905; local improvement bonds, relative to, IX, 872 om; preservation of peace, VIII, 1037 om; police department, authorizing increase of expenditures for, 1111; sewer property, sale of, 1036 om.

GREAT CHAZY RIVER. Dam at Chazy lake, X, 789.

GREENBURGH. Assessment, when to be made, compensation of assessors, IX, 817 om.

GREENBUSH. Amending charter, VII, 806 om.

GREENPORT. Relative to, VII, 805 om.

GREENWICH. Aiding railroad, VI, 164.

GREENWOOD. Fire district, water works, bonds, X, 704 om.

GUARDIANS. In socage, real property sold to, X, 62 om.

GUNPOWDER. Keeping or unauthorized use, IX, 289.

HABEAS CORPUS AND CERTIORARI. Amending Revised Statutes, VII, 197.

HABITUAL DRUNKARDS. New York, relative to, X, 806 om.

HAGAR, LAWRENCE. Damages, death of son, appropriation, VII, 466.

HAMILTON, ALEXANDER. Statue of, X, 586 om.

HAMILTON COUNTY. Cleaning Brown's Tract inlet and other streams, X, 320 om; publication of legal notices, V, 508.

HARBOR MASTER. Albany, relative to, VII, 121; Port Chester, creating office, X, 590.

HARLEM RIVER BRIDGE. Commissioners, closing affairs of, IX, 154 om.

HART, JAMES I. Senate assistant sergeant-at-arms and postmaster, expenses attending Abbott funeral, VII, 586.

HARTFORD. Southern Central Railroad, school taxes, distribution, VI, 1035 om.

Harts Falls. Changing name, VI, 341.
Hastings-on-the-Hudson. Changing boundaries, X, 233.
Hector. Railroad aid, VI, 187.
Hempstead. Personal property of, relative to, IX, 817 om; unpaid taxes, VII, 415 om.
Herkimer, Nicholas. Monument, IX, 240.
Higgins, Ann. Damages, death of son, VII, 464.
Highland. Appropriation of certain moneys, VI, 592.
Highland Trans-Hudson Railroad Company. Bridge across Hudson river, VII, 937 om.
Highways.
    Amending general act, om, IX, 624, 628, X, 317, 445, 446; amending Revised Statutes, VI, 695; abandonment, qualified, X, 948 om; Alden, legalizing election of commissioner, VI, 1034; alteration and discontinuance, compensation of commissioners, IX, 801 om; altering, discontinuing or laying out, 625 om; boulevard, Buffalo to Niagara Falls, VIII, 639 om, 879; Camden and Annsville, assessment for highway labor, VII, 130 om; Canandaigua, relative to, IV, 771; Cattaraugus Indian reservation, repairs, VII, 221, 475, VIII, 845; Clinton county, exempting from certain provisions relative to commissioners for laying out, IX, 861 om; Colonie, collection and disbursement of money, X, 589 om; commissioners in certain towns, 590 om; commissioners to assess damages, compensation, VIII, 459; connecting, construction of, X, 439; construction of, between towns divided by navigable tidal stream, VIII, 388 om; county roads, IX, 864 om; Croghan, break-water, Black river, X, 791; deposits of ashes and rubbish in, VII, 646; Dewitt, special system of working, X, 234; discontinuance, amending Revised Statutes, VII, 201; Eastchester, — relative to, 130 om; — number of commissioners, VIII, 461, 616; Easton, election of commissioners, VII, 932 om; Elliott, improvement of roads and bridges, VI, 47; Florence, establishing, 182; Fowler,— over certain lands, 188; — repairs, appropriation, X, 428; — along Oswegatchie river, 791; Franklin county,— facilitating travel, VII, 650; — special, road district, VI, 481; Goshen, opening, 213; Great Valley, encroachments, 160; Greenburgh, election of commissioners, VIII, 54; Hamilton county — relative to, VI, 82; — Johnsburgh to Long Lake, VII, 133 om; 320; — Totten and Crossfield's Purchase, exemption from taxes, VI, 701; Haverstraw, amending charter, VIII, 1040 om; Herman, repairs, appropriation, X, 428; Heuvelton to Depeyster town line, repairs, appropriation, id.; improvement, VII, 807 om; improvement,— acquisition of materials, X, 384; — act of

HIGHWAYS — (*Continued*).

1898, appropriation, 572; — act of 1898, Rome included in, 522; — repairs and maintenance, 946 om; Irondequoit, Hudson avenue improvement, reimbursement, 785; Irving, widening and raising embankment, 789; in two or more towns in same county, amending act, 316 om; instruction in methods, good roads school, 793; Jay, separate road district, VI, 332; labor, VII, 325; labor, commutations, IX, 524, 864 om; laying out and altering, VII, 367, 372, 509 om; laying out,— commissioner's notice of meeting, om, IX, 864, X, 809; — damages, compensation of commissioners, IX, 864 om; — decision of commissioners denying application, X, 809 om; — limitation on, id.; Lewis county, VI, 193; Lewis county, No. 4 to Stillwater reservoir, VIII, 851; Livonia, road two rods wide, VI, 707; Lowville, commissioners, borrowing money, VI, 318; Madison, repair, X, 645; Middleburgh, separate road district, amending act, VII, 414 om, 440; money system, IX, 524; Mount Pleasant, opening, VI, 330; New Baltimore, consolidation and repairs, VIII, 387; Newtown,— construction, VI, 195; — opening, 330; New Utrecht, relative to, VIII, 1134, IX, 264; non-resident taxes, Essex and Hamilton counties, VI, 338; Northfield, separate road district, VII, 1099; North Tonawanda, improvement, VIII, 1155; noxious weeds, X, 450 om; obstructions by snow, VII, 1108; Olive, protection from overflow of Bush creek, IX, 768; Onondaga county, VIII, 617; Onondaga Indian reservation, VII, 92, 223, 384, 474, 587; VIII, 116, 845, IX, 80, X, 426; opening in one town on application of freeholders in another town, VII, 885; Orange county roads, IX, 862 om; orchards and vineyards, excepting Pultney, VII, 1098; overseers,— appointment, X, 594 om; — annual report, IX, 801 om; — Hamburgh, fixing bail, VI, 91; Owasco lake,— protection of highway along outlet, IX, 141; — highway on west shore, protection, 239, X, 646; Philipstown, opening, VI, 326; Piercefield, repairs, appropriation, X, 428; Plattsburg, stone crusher, IX, 433; plowing, digging and cropping, X, 276; poll tax,— Suffolk and Westchester, 955 om; — in towns under money system, 956 om; Portland, special act, VIII, 879; Port Richmond, improving road to New Springville, VI, 330; private roads, X, 809 om; public,— Gouverneur, John street, VI, 76.

PUBLIC STREAMS AS. Black creek, VII, 358; Bonaparte creek, 934 om; Deer river, VIII, 454, X, 444; Fulton Chain of lakes, IX, 531; Indian river, extending act, VI, 327; Sacandaga river, amending act, VIII, 621; Salmon and Mad rivers, repealing act,

HIGHWAYS — (*Continued*).

   PUBLIC STREAMS AS — (*Continued*).

   IX, 121; South Sandy'creek, X, 444 om; Queens county, labor, VIII, 1154; railroads, highway labor assessments, IX, 801 om; rebate of taxes for wide tire wagons, exempting Franklin and Oswego counties, X, 393; referees' fees, VIII, 470 om; Richmond county, Middletown, separate road district, VII, 497, 507 om; road from Carthage to Lake Champlain, VI, 315; road commissioner, Fishkill, creating office, VIII, 388; road implements, 873; Rockland lake, improvement, VI, 338; Rome, outside of tax district, om, X, 438, 446; Rossville, road extension, VI, 340; St. Lawrence county improvement, X, 439 om; St. Regis Indian reservation, VII, 91, 475, 909, VII, 850, X, 427; Scarsdale and Greenburgh, improvement, VI, 328; Schenectady county, Glenville assessments, 701; separate district, certain towns in Herkimer county, IX, 250; side-paths,— amending general act, X, 594 om; — Chemung county, IX, 729 om; — Monroe county, 731 om; — Niagara county, 629 om; — Oneida county, 726 om; snow, removal of, om, X, 594, 707; South Hampton, discontinuing road, VI, 333.

   SPECIAL.   Albany county, VI, 670; Fulton county, 598; Hamilton county, 502, VII, 215, 932 om; Kings county, IX, 130; Washington county, VII, 886; Westchester county, IX, 722 om; State aid, X, 952 om; — appropriation, 796; — to towns, 585 om; system of repairs, VII, 69; tax, amending Revised Statutes, VIII, 1106; taxes, Hamilton and Warren counties, VI, 442; Thurman, non-resident taxes, VII, 268 om; traction engine on, damages, VIII, 1156; Ulster and Delaware Road No. 16, Shandaken, X, 696; use of, IX, 150 om; Virgil, opening, extending time, VIII, 1086; Warren county, opening road, VI, 93; Washington county, near Fort Miller bridge, VII, 805 om; water, free flow in rivers and streams, IX, 801 om; weeds and brush, VII, 1095; Westchester county,— exemption from poll tax, X, 952 om; — public roads in certain towns, VI, 589; — Westchester, town,— bonds for highway purposes, VIII, 292 om; borrowing money for highway improvement, VII, 1023; Westchester and Richmond counties, labor, VI, 336; Westerlo, Chesterville separate road district, VIII, 615; Wilmington to North Elba, repair, VII, 1099; Yates county improvement, X, 703 om; Yonkers and Eastchester, VI, 512.

HOGAN, CATHERINE.   Damages, death of husband, VII, 464, 910.

HOLIDAYS.   General act, VI, 679; amending act, VIII, 291 om; adding Columbus day, X, 584 om; Saturday half-holiday provision, VIII, 535; closing sheriffs and county clerks' offices, VI, 287.

HOMEOPATHIC INSANE ASYLUM, MIDDLETOWN. Fund in aid of, VI, 333; addition to pavilion, VII, 1081; furniture, new wards, 913; gymnasium and workshop, 786, 913; house for gardener, VIII, 853; ice-house, addition, VII, 786; improving exercise grounds, drainage of land, 1081; improvements, 583; medical library and surgical appliances, 786; medical library, 913; officers, salaries, id.; renovating heating apparatus, 786; tile floor, 786, 913; water closets, water supply, 786.

HOMER. Aiding Cortland academy, VI, 94.

HOOSICK. Board of education, additional powers, VII, 934 om.

HOP BOXES. Regulating size of, VIII, 1040 om.

HORNELLSVILLE. Amending village charter, VII, 935 om; elections and officers, X, 819 om; excise money, payment to St. James Mercy Hospital, IX, 723 om; establishing manufacture of machinery, VI, 180; sewerage system, VIII, 880.

HORSEHEADS. Amending village charter, regulating sales of goods, VIII, 622.

HORSE-SHOEING. Regulating practice in certain cities, IX, 622 om.

HORSE STEALING. Societies for prevention of, VIII, 1039 om.

HORTICULTURE. Instruction, investigations, and experiments, appropriation, X, 552.

HOTCHKISS, LEMAN. Contested election, Wayne county, expenses, VII, 917.

HOTELS. Fire escapes, om, X, 701, 709.

HOTELS, STEAMERS AND RAILROADS. Soliciting patronage for, VII, 415 om.

HOUGH'S CLASSIFIED ABSTRACT OF LAWS. Purchase of, VII, 469.

HOUSES OF REFUGE. Amending Penal Code, IX, 718 om.

HOUSEHOLD FURNITURE AND SEWING MACHINES. Sale on instalment plan, VII, 758.

HUDSON, HENDRICK. Statue of, IX, 222.

HUDSON. Amending city charter, om, VII, 935, VIII, 889; public schools, legalizing official acts, 978; removal of poles and wires from certain streets, X, 805 om; water system, commissioner of public works, 583 om.

HUDSON HOUSE OF REFUGE FOR WOMEN. Administration building, reconstruction, X, 545; coal pockets and driveway, 654; electric light plant, 647; new buildings, IX, 143; nursery cottage, VIII, 1137; repairs and equipment, X, 654; prison, reconstruction, 545.

HUDSON RIVER. Dam, Warren county, North Creek, X, 705 om; dyke at Albany, IX, 606.

HUDSON RIVER ASYLUM FOR THE INSANE. Contracts, deficiency appropriations, VII, 487; improvements, 89; repairs and improvements, 487; various buildings, VIII, 853.

XI — 8

HUDSON RIVER STATE HOSPITAL.   Coal sheds, VII, 785; electric light
    plant, IX, 78; extending water main, X, 934; fire protection, IX, 78;
    house for night nurses, IX, 294; limiting use of maintenance fund,
    VII, 785; purchase of land, VIII, 1138; refunding maintenance
    account, VII, 785; roadway under railroad, id.; State care cottages,
    IX, 295.
HUDSON RIVER AND CATSKILL CREEK.   Improving navigation, VI, 908.
HUMMEL, LOUIS.   Dock on Jamaica bay, VI, 705.
HUMO, BENNETT A.   Damages, Hudson River Hospital, VII, 910.
HUNTER AND JEWETT.   Bonding, VI, 328.
HUSBAND AND WIFE.   Liabilities and remedies, IX, 148 om; partition
    of land held by, VII, 416 om.

ICE.   Preventing deception in sale of, VIII, 633.
ICHTHYOLOGICAL SOCIETIES.   Incorporation, VIII, 787, 1039 om.
IDIOTS.   Care of estates, VII, 415 om.
IDIOT ASYLUM.   Cottages, farm buildings, VII, 914; farmhouse furni-
    ture, farm stock and tools, 913; plumbing and furniture, VIII, 853.
ILION.   Amending charter, IX, 148 om.
IMPRISONMENT.   Hard labor, VII, 805 om.
INDEPENDENCE RIVER.   Relative to, VII, 507 om.
INDIANS.   Actions against, on contract, X, 590 om; Six Nations, Sullivan's
    expedition against, publication of records, VII, 934 om, 1084;
    undertaking given by, prosecution of, X, 169; welfare, providing for,
    VIII, 1037 om.
INDIAN RESERVATIONS.   Felonies committed on, expense of trials and
    proceedings, X, 164.
INDIAN RIVER.   Improvement, IX, 80; reclaiming overflowed lands in
    Jefferson and St. Lawrence counties, VII, 1115.
INEBRIATES.   Institution for, establishing, IX, 246.
INFANTS.   Mortgaging property, X, 808 om.
INFANTS, LUNATICS, IDIOTS, HABITUAL DRUNKARDS.   Sale of property,
    VIII, 1041 om, IX, 283.
INJUNCTIONS.   Amending Code, IX, 791 om.
INSANE.   Care and custody, om, VII, 413, 506; care and custody, county
    charges, VIII, 132 om; criminals, confined in asylums, X, 317 om;
    custody and discharge, regulation of, VIII, 891 om; Genesee county,
    support, VI, 1035 om; Saratoga county, removal from State asylums
    to poorhouse, 182.
INSANE AND IDIOTS.   New York, relative to, VI, 324.
INSANITY LAW.   General amendments, X, 538.
INSOLVENT DEBTORS.   Relative to, V, 292; assignments, om, VIII, 130,
    X, 315; assignments, cost in actions for fraud, IX, 139; to mature
    debts, 866 om.

INSPECTORS OF ELECTIONS AND POLL CLERKS. Queens county, fixing compensation, VIII, 340.

INSURANCE. Amending general act, IX, 625 om; fire, policies, construction of, X, 441 om; limitations of risks, 312 om; minors, 320 om; policy, fixing amount to be paid on, VII, 506 om; policy not to be forfeited without notice, IX, 864 om; steam boilers, VII, 507 om.

INSURANCE COMPANIES. Credit guaranty, relative to, IX, 802 om; foreign, VI, 221; fraternal, beneficiary societies, X, 812 om; life, health and casualty,—incorporation, IX, 802 om; — amending act, VIII, 1040 om.

INSURANCE DEPARTMENT. Amending act, VII, 126, 134 om.

INSURANCE LAW. General provisions, limiting application, IX, 802 om; investments by insurance companies, VII, 266 om; superintendent's examinations, id.

INTEMPERANCE. Act to suppress, IV, 752.

INTERPRETER. Court, first and second judicial districts, classification of, IX, 812 om.

ITALY. Dividing town, V, 126.

ITHACA. Amending charter, IX, 719 om; police department, VIII, 256; school system, VII, 1105.

JAIL LIBERTIES. Relative to, VIII, 632; Orange county, VII, 234; Ulster county, extending, 265 om.

JAMAICA. Amending charter, VI, 90, VIII, 469 om.

JAMESTOWN. Acting police justice, salary; overseer of the poor, X, 717 om; police, care of indigent sick, 472; public schools, maintenance and government, IX, 858 om; schools, designating special holidays, X, 173; water supply, IX, 785; — acquiring property, 858 om.

JAMESTOWN TER-CENTENNIAL EXPOSITION. New York's participation in, appropriation, X, 815 om.

JEFFERSON AND ST. LAWRENCE COUNTIES. Assessments for railroad purposes, VII, 807 om.

JEWELL, GUSTAVUS, AND OTHERS. Erection of dam, III, 37.

JOHNSON, EDWARD M. Preparing appendix to Clerk's Manual, appropriation, VII, 459.

JOHNSON, JAMES F. Laborer, injuries, appropriation, VII, 465.

JOHNSON, RUSSELL S. Assembly, 1891, election contest, appropriation, VIII, 1142.

JOHNSTOWN. Amending charter, om, IX, 785, 870; officers, method of voting for, VIII, 1041 om; streets, opening, X, 327 om; consolidating school districts and establishing graded school, VI, 86; voting by ballot on bridge appropriation, VIII, 1087.

JORDAN ACADEMY AND FREE SCHOOL DISTRICT No. 4, ELBRIDGE. Relative to, VI, 81.

JUDGMENT. Application for, X, 707 om; docket, 814 om; entry, IX, 624 om; unknown owners, om, VII, 266, 508; United States courts, docketing in county clerk's office, VIII, 1039 om.

JUDGMENT CREDITORS. Actions by, IX, 792 om.

JUDICIARY. Amending act of 1847, VIII, 470 om, 621; relative to, VII, 414 om.

JURORS. In certain counties, IX, 791 om; commissioners — in certain counties, om, 811, 866, X, 440; — in certain counties, general regulations concerning lists of jurors, qualifications, etc., IX, 514; — compensation of judges, X, 710 om; — Albany county, 44; — notice server, 532; — qualifications and exemptions of jurors, 587 om; — powers of, exemptions, 701 om; — salary, 450 om; — Richmond county, creating office, IX, 796 om; compensation, 726 om; exemptions, om, X, 808, 953; fees, om, IX, 792, X, 62, 947; Kings county,— certificate of attendance, VII, 938 om; commissioner and special commissioner, abolishing office, X, 178 om; New York, exemptions, IX, 631 om; peremptory challenges in criminal cases, X, 956 om.

JURY. Kings county, exemptions, VIII, 1037 om; notices, service of, IX, 792.

JUSTICES' COURTS. Attachment, service of papers, VII, 1094; attorneys in, IX, 792 om; Brooklyn, Doolittle, assistant clerk, claim, 779 om; executions, VII, 1094; jurors in, VIII, 1166; jurors' fees, IX, 427; summons, service on corporations, VII, 1094; verifications of pleadings, 506 om; where not to be held, IX, 860 om.

JUSTICES OF THE PEACE. Relative to, IX, 534 om; additional,— Deer Park, VI, 208, 276; — Yorkshire, VIII, 338; criminal docket, IX, 722 om; definition and meaning of term, om, X, 704, 808; fees, IX, 375; Guilderland, appointment in first district, 816 om; jurisdiction, 792 om, X, 704, 808 (2 bills); Lowville, vacancies in office, VI, 48; Owasco, appointing special officers, IX, 623; vacancies in office, VI, 74; Verona, additional, 326.

LEGALIZING ACTS. General, om, VIII, 639, X, 163; taking oath and filing bond, VIII, 323; Orange, Rockland and Sullivan, acts of, X, 62 om; Bagg, filing oath and bond, IX, 725 om; Curtis, 369; Guion, VII, 44; Hale and Reid, IX, 725 om; Horton, VII, 413 om; Howe, VIII, 943; McCormick, X, 813 om; Noyes, VII, 412 om; Richardson, X, 63 om; Seymour, VI, 479; Sherman, IX, 346; Steele, X, 62 om; Tibbitt, 948 om; Weller, VII, 413 om; Williams, 507 om.

JUSTICES OF SESSIONS. Kings county, compensation, VII, 1090.

KEENAN, PETER MAJOR. Monument to, X, 163.

KENMORE. Frontage tax for water purposes, X, 812 om.

KENNEDY, BARBARA. Damages, death of husband, appropriation, VII, 466.

KEUKA LAKE. Lighthouse and breakwater, IX, 713.

KIDNAPPING. Punishment, X, 699 om.

KINGS COUNTY. Board of charities, VI, 1018; board of health, establishment of, 518; charities commission, reorganization, IX, 583; charities and corrections, board of, reorganization, 440; clerks of board of supervisors and courthouse engineers, VII, 440; commissioner of charities, ousting incumbent, Kessel case, 651; County Court, clerks, relief, X, 59 om; County Court and Court of Sessions, clerks and records, IX, 795 om; court officers, appointment and dismissal, VII, 804 om; Court of General Sessions, deputy clerk, VI, 506; courthouse property, 510; Cunningham, commissioner of charities, reimbursement for local expenses, VII, 544, VIII, 294 om; farm commissioners, 1037 om; farm at St. Johnland, changing supervision of, 594; gaslight companies, VII, 1119; Hall of Records, keeper, IX, 861 om; map, closing part of East 92d street, repealing act, X, 815 om; new inferior court, IX, 873 om; New Lots, Bushwick avenue, VII, 63; poor and insane, farm, VIII, 292 om; public administrator, IX, 792 om; public buildings, inspector, duties, 861 om; register, VIII, 124; register and clerk's office, transcribing records, compensation, X, 710 om; religious societies, relief of, VIII, 468 om; roads and streets, commissioner's map, alteration, IX, 628 om; sale of drugs, medicines and poisons, VII, 936 om; Sherman street, closing part of, IX, 872 om; soldiers and sailors' memorial arch, legalizing acts relative to, 211; Supreme and County Courts, messengers, doorkeepers and attendants, VI, 341.

KINGS COUNTY PENITENTIARY. Sentences, VI, 512.

KINGS PARK STATE HOSPITAL. Building for industries, X, 935.

KINGSTON. City Court, jurisdiction and powers, IX, 785 om; officers, relative to, VII, 416 om.

KIRKHAM, HENRY P. Repairs to hospital ships, VII, 792, 929.

KNOX, JAMES AND WILLIAM. Releasing interest in securities, IV, 693.

LABOR. Free public employment bureaus, IX, 630 om; hours in State service, 724 om; employees, safety appliances, X, 52; employer's liability, 305; mediation and arbitration, 439 om; New York and Brooklyn, protection of female employees, VII, 509; protection of persons employed on buildings in cities, X, 760; preference on public works, 424; servile, amending Penal Code, IX, 793 om.

LABOR DEPARTMENT. Expert examiner of machinery, compensation, X, 787.

LABORERS. Actions for wages and materials, IX, 726 om; Brooklyn, fixing rate of wages, 448; employed on buildings in cities, protection of, X, 62 om.

LAKE GEORGE. Battle of, acquiring land to commemorate, reappropriation, X, 423; islands, preservation of trees and shrubbery, VII, 655.

LAMONT, MRS. Providing for payment to, VII, 805 om.

LANCASTER. Amending charter, VII, 416 om.

LAND. Defining, amending Revised Statutes, VII, 506 om; persons dying seized, relative to, 413 om.

LANSINGBURGH. Eligibility to office, VII, 323; new wards, sidewalks, repairs, VIII, 991.

LARCENY. By false pretense, IX, 860 om.

LAW LIBRARY.
    Binghamton, appropriation, IX, 83.
    Canton, VII, 82.
    Court of Appeals: Albany, X, 549; judges, VII, 902, VIII, 856; Rochester,— librarian, X, 952 om; — purchase of books, VIII, 856; Syracuse, purchase of books, 856, X, 550.
    Delhi, appropriation, VII, 219; books and rebinding, X, 556; purchase of Justice Murray's library for, VIII, 539.
    Eighth Judicial District, VII, 220.
    Elmira, books and rebinding, X, 556.
    Fifth Judicial District, Oswego, IX, 130; purchase of books, VIII, 856.
    First Department, Appellate Division and trial courts, appropriation, IX, 770.
    Fourth Judicial District, VII, 218.
    Judicial districts, appropriation, VII, 81, 220.
    Kingston, relative to, IX, 776; rebinding books, X, 556.
    Newburgh, relative to, IX, 769.
    New York: Court of General Sessions, X, 475 om; — custodian, 390.
    Seventh Judical District, Rochester, VII, 220.
    Sixth Judicial District: Use of books, VII, 807 om; Binghamton, 220; Elmira, establishing, IX, 45; — appropriation, 769; Judge Follett, X, 784.
    Supreme Court, Newburgh, VIII, 856.
    Utica, books and rebinding, X, 556; librarian, increasing compensation, 519.

LAWRENCE, THOMAS J. Corporal 22d Regiment, National Guard, damages for permanent injury, VII, 465, 910.

LAW SCHOOLS. Harvard university and Yale college, graduates, relative to, VII, 416 om.

LAWS. Enforcement of, VII, 807 om.

LEGISLATIVE COMMITTEES. Compensation of, V, 41 (2 bills).

LEGISLATIVE RECORD. Printing and distributing, VIII, 891 om.

LEGISLATURE. Cartage of documents, VII, 901; clerks,—advances, purchase of file boards, VIII, 857;—books, stationery, printing, etc., X, 793;—deficiency, VII, 581; Clerk's Manual, printing, VIII, 118; committees, deficiency, counsel and stenographers, printing testimony, contingent expenses prior to 1887, 550. (2 bills); committees, deficiency, counsel and stenographers, printing testimony, contingent expenses, 1888, 549; compensation of certain officers after adjournment, VII, 1078, VIII, 106; contingent expenses, VII, 903, VIII, 1037 om, X, 933; employees, om, VII, 806, VIII, 639;—compensation, VII, 372; employees and investigating committees, VII, 133 om;—deficiency appropriation, VIII, 107; furniture for clerk's rooms, 841; investigating committees,—composing and printing testimony, VII, 1079;—expenses, VIII, 419, 420;—services of counsel, VII, 647;—traveling and incidental expenses, 1890, VIII, 989; journals, VII, 264 om; officers and employees, compensation, IX, 802 om; parliamentary rules and precedents, revision, X, 795; printing, continuing appropriation of 1885, VIII, 252.

LENOX. Reimbursement for bridge over Douglass State ditch, IX, 817 om.

LE ROY. Village trustees, additional powers, VII, 337.

LEWIS AND CLARK CENTENNIAL EXPOSITION. Expenses of commission, X, 799.

LEWIS AND HERKIMER COUNTIES. Establishing boundaries, VII, 783.

LIBRARIES.

Orange County Reference Law Library, VII, 1025.

Senate: Arrangement and classification, VII, 906; books and binding, IX, 773.

Senate and Assembly: Promoting usefulness of, IX, 153 om; removal to new capitol, VII, 581.

LICENSES. Itinerant vendors of goods, IX, 465.

LIENS. Conditional contracts, goods and chattels, IX, 865 om; filing notice of, IX, 865 om, X, 310 om; hotels, boarding and lodging-house keepers, 593 om; livery stable keepers, IX, 866 om; personal property, sale to satisfy, 865 om (2 bills).

LIFE INSURANCE COMPANIES. Forfeitures of policies, VI, 601; reserves and transfers, 506; suicide as defense, VII, 1098.

LIFE SAVING STATIONS. Buildings for, VI, 502.

LIMA. Amending village charter, VIII, 621.

LIMITATION OF ACTIONS. Cause of action arising in another State, X, 703 om; person dying within State, VII, 665 om.

LINDSAY, DAVID. Contested election, Assembly, Kings county, expenses, VII, 918.

LIQUOR TAX LAW. Amending, om, IX, 865, X, 948; buildings for hotel purposes, consents, IX, 802 om; rebates, payment of, om, X, 590, 638; refund on certificates, 553; sale within prohibited distance of a church, Gotham hotel, 779; sale within 200 feet of a church or school, 959 om.

LITERATURE FUND. Increasing, VIII, 291 om.

LITTLE FALLS. Amending charter, om, VII, 416, VIII, 1040, IX, 785, X, 714; annual tax levy, 686 om; election inspectors, IX, 458; public buildings, 785 om.

LIVERY STABLE KEEPERS. Liens, amending act, VIII, 457.

LIVINGSTON, ROBERT R. Statue of, appropriation, VII, 382, 469.

LIVINGSTON COUNTY. Legalizing election, VII, 415 om.

LIVONIA. Auditing claim of Reed and others, VIII, 889 om.

LOAN ASSOCIATIONS. Personal property, amending act, X, 317 om.

LOAN. On personal credit, IX, 534 om.

LOCKPORT. Electric light system, om, IX, 730, 786; hose carriage, purchase of, VII, 267 om; lighting contracts, X, 636 om; poor fund, maintenance of provident woodyard, IX, 785 om; salary and lift bridge funds, X, 583 om; trading stamps, licenses for, 636 om; wages, preference of laborers, IX, 719 om.

LOGS. Floating on rivers, VII, 506 om.

LONG ISLAND CITY. Amending charter, om, VIII, 1033, IX, 629, 786; aldermen, salary, VII, 641; Astoria, certain streets and avenues, 369; Bach claim, audit of, IX, 786 om; East River Gas Company, relative to, X, 582 om; expenses of government, IX, 786 om; Fiesel, claim for services, board of education, X, 950 om; fire department improvement, IX, 786 om; Flushing avenue improvement, VII, 368; Grand avenue and Main street, improvement, IX, 254, 786 om; Greenpoint avenue improvement, VII, 635; improvement commission, IX, 786 om; intersection of certain avenues, VII, 417 om; Jackson avenue improvement, 603, 862; legalizing certain claims, IX, 468; closing Ninth street, VII, 609; parks and parade ground, om, VIII, 888, IX, 726; Pender's claim, work and materials for board of education, X, 322 om; police patrolmen, salaries, IX, 141; reducing expenses, repealing part of act, VIII, 130 om; overseer of the poor, 886 om; relative to certain streets in, VII, 266 om; rent of buildings for educational purposes, IX, 253, 468; schools, additional accommodations, 786 om; Second avenue, 734 om; sick poor, medical and surgical aid, 253; Steinway avenue improvement, VII, 353; street improvements, om, IX, 633, 731; Thompson avenue, making part of county road system, 786 om; treasurer, moneys received by, 730 om; unpaid taxes, collection, VII, 265 om; unpaid taxes assessments, water rates and rents, VIII, 120, IX, 726 om; water supply, additional, IX, 726 om.

LORRAINE. Borrowing money for vault, VIII, 639 om.

LOTTERIES. Amending Penal Code, IX, 534 om; tickets, sale of, III, 186.

LOW, HENRY R. Claim against State, Middletown Homeopathic Asylum, VII, 665 om.

LUDDEN, WILLIAM J. Counsel for Senate committee, investigation of election frauds, IX, 533.

LUMBER, LOGS AND TIMBER. Floating on streams, om, VII, 415, VIII, 1041, IX, 815.

LUNACY COMMISSIONER. Expenses, visiting institutions, VII, 923; traveling and incidental expenses, VIII, 867.

LYONS. Revising charter, VII, 878.

MACGUIRE, DAVID. Dock on Hudson river, VI, 705.

MALICIOUS DESTRUCTION OF PROPERTY. Relative to, VIII, 890 om.

MAMAKATING. Railroad commissioners, bonds to retire outstanding bonds, X, 235.

MANHATTAN STATE HOSPITAL. Establishment, IX, 617; Kimball, treasurer, reimbursement for premium on bonds, X, 642 om.

MANLIUS. Soldiers' monument, changing location, IX, 817.

MANUFACTURES. Branding prison-made goods from other States, IX, 465.

MANUFACTURING CORPORATIONS. Amending act, VI, 708, VII, 414 om, 806 om, VIII, 132 om, 1038 om; relative to, 130 om; floating dock, VII, 569; Herkimer county, facilitating dissolution, 59; mercantile and commercial business, 1871, VI, 335; 1872, 501; patent rights, extending powers, VII, 621; mortgages, VI, 582; payment of capital stock, 179; extending act, 580, 910 om (2 bills); relief of, IX, 794 om; uniform standard of time, central clock, VII, 1027.

MANUFACTURING ESTABLISHMENTS. Women and children, employment in, VIII, 837, IX, 477.

MARINE INSURANCE COMPANIES. Regulating charges, VII, 804 om.

MARINERS' FAMILY ASYLUM. Insurance and general improvements, VII, 490; new buildings, id.

MARRIAGE. Licenses for, VIII, 470 om.

MARRIED WOMEN. Contracts, VII, 331; dower rights, release of, VI, 597, 820; insuring husband's life, VII, 80.

MARTINUS, GEORGE A. Senate messenger, appropriation, VII, 459.

MATHER, FREDERICK G. Preparation of papers, war of 1812, appropriation, X, 784.

MATTEAWAN. Village, lighting streets, VI, 704.

MATTEAWAN STATE HOSPITAL FOR INSANE CRIMINALS. Additional buildings, plumbing and water supply, IX, 295; propagating and greenhouse, X, 299; reception and maintenance of patients, 591 om; vegetable and fruit cellar, IX, 295; walks and driveways, 296,

MATTHEWS, THOMAS F. Counsel fees and expenses, Assembly contested election, Palmer case, Kings county, X, 795.

MCAVOY, THOMAS. Damages, injuries, new capitol, VII, 910.

MCCAUGHEL, GEORGE. Escheat, IV, 693.

MCDONALD, WILLIAM J. Substitute for Senate journal clerk, compensation, VII, 907.

MCKINLEY MEMORIAL. Printing and distributing, X, 430.

MCMILLEN, DUNCAN C. Stenographer, appropriation, VII, 81.

MCNAMARA, ROGERS. Estate of, sale, VIII, 1090.

MECHANICS. Protection of, om, IX, 624, 724.

MECHANIC'S LIEN. Amending act, om, VIII, 1040, IX, 259; cities, om, VII, 665, 666; claims against contractors, notice to owner, IX, 128; dredging and improving low lands, 127; extending act, VII, 417 om; New York, VI, 213;—repealing part of consolidation act, IX, 872 om; revising acts, VII, 1125; stone cutters, etc., IX, 623 om.

MECHANICVILLE. Fire commissioners, VIII, 621; purchasing fire apparatus, VII, 849.

MEDICAL COLLEGES. Corpses to be delivered to, in certain cases, IX, 627 om.

MEDICAL SCIENCE. Promotion of, amending act, VII, 353, 415 om, 806 om, IX, 117.

MEDICAL SOCIETIES. County, amount of property, VII, 412 om.

MEDICINE. Charles E. Abbott, admission to examination, X, 313 om; regulating practice, degrees, VI, 337; practice,— admission to examinations, IX, 803 om;—authorizing by certain persons, X, 63 om; — elevating standard, VI, 194; licenses, VI, 512, IX, 803 om; proscriptions and remedies, VI, 325; students, preliminary education, VIII, 131 om.

MEDINA. Police department, X, 440 om.

MEISNER, CARL. Battery G, 7th Division, National Guard, damages, permanent injury, appropriation, VII, 466, 910.

MEMBERSHIP CORPORATIONS. Amending general law, IX, 802 om; directors, quorum, annual reports, X, 432; drawing juries on exhibition grounds, 450 om; managers and trustees, election, 946 om.

MEMORIAL. Kingston, organization of State government, VII, 85.

MEMORIAL HALL. White Plains, IX, 221.

MEMPHIS. Village charter, VI, 341.

MERCHANDISE. Fraud in sale or exchange of, VII, 388; weighing in New York, III, 528.

METROPOLITAN ELECTION DISTRICT. Salaries of deputy superintendents, X, 429.

METROPOLITAN POLICE. Inspecting steam boilers, VI, 96.

METROPOLITAN POLICE BOARD. Temporary president, VI, 50.

METROPOLITAN SANITARY DISTRICT. Amending act, Newtown, VII, 267 om; repeal as to Queens county, 113.

MIDDLEPORT. Repairing drain into culvert under Erie canal, X, 798.

MIDDLETOWN (Orange county). City charter, VIII, 470 om; extending boundaries, IX, 787 om; payment of village bonds, VII, 131 om; village hall, 1042, VIII, 61.

MIDDLETOWN STATE HOMEOPATHIC HOSPITAL. Cement walk, completing, X, 934; fence on Monhagen avenue, id.

MIDWIFERY. Regulating practice,— Montgomery county, IX, 862 om; — New York city, X, 172.

MILITIA. Certificates of service, 1812, VI, 902; revision of laws, VII, 411.

MILITARY CODE. Amendments, om, VII, 416, VIII, 891; revision, VII, 796.

MILK. Adulteration, VI, 710, 904, VII, 416 om; cans, unlawful detention, X, 447 om; pasteurized or clarified, encouraging formation of companies to supply, 813 om; seizure and destruction, VIII, 1037 om; skimmed, regulating sale in certain cities, id.

MILTON. School bonds, payment of, VII, 391.

MINING COMPANIES. Reports, VII, 589.

MINK, DAVID F. Claim, VII, 805 om.

MINORS. Adoption, VI, 816; protection of, III, 845, VI, 210.

MISDEMEANORS. Cazenovia lake, cutting ice, failure to guard openings. VIII, 461.

MISCELLANEOUS REPORTER. Office expenses, clerks, obtaining copies of opinions, X, 555.

MOHAWK. Village, amending charter, VI, 327; village cemetery, revising act, VIII, 391.

MONROE COUNTY. Enrollment of political parties, X, 257.

MONTEZUMA. Amending charter, VII, 934 om, 1104.

MONTEZUMA TURNPIKE. Repairs, X, 646 om; across Montezuma marsh, repairs, 814 om.

MONTGOMERY COUNTY. Borrowing money, VII, 841.

MONUMENT. Battle of Saratoga, appropriation, VII, 84; Battle of White Plains, commemorating, X, 698; Fort Green, Brooklyn, prison ship martyrs, VII, 85; Sanford and Deposit, 806 om; Tall-Chief, Seneca Indian Chief, VIII, 110.

MOORE, EDWARD M. Claim, State Board of Audit, VII, 849.

MORRISTOWN. Legalizing town bonding proceedings, VI, 583.

MORTGAGES. Chattel, where to be filed, X, 63 om; compelling assignments of, VIII, 469 om; foreclosure, VI, 678; foreclosure by advertisement, VI, 707; — legalizing, VIII, 1039 om; — surplus moneys, VI, 92; foreclosure costs, IX, 153 om; taxation of, X, 809 om, 885.

MORTGAGE AND LOAN COMPANIES. Investments by, VIII, 891 om.

MOUNT PLEASANT. Railroad avenue improvement, VI, 335.

MOUNT VERNON. Amending charter, om, VII, 936, IX, 629, 734, 787, X, 318; relative to, om, VII, 806, 807; city officers, X, 583 om; comptroller, om, IX, 787; fire engines and apparatus, om, 629; grade crossing, Harlem Railroad, Mount Vernon avenue and Oak street, cost of changing, X, 454; grade crossing over New York and Harlem Railroad, 590 om; official newspapers, 583 om; police department, IX, 787 om; sinking fund commission, id.; street paving bonds, X, 59 om; tax on annexed territory, VIII, 456; taxes and budget, 1902, X, 471; water supply, IX, 734 om.

MUD CREEK. Straightening, VII, 414 om.

MULLIN, LYDIA. Widow of Judge Mullin, residue of salary, VII, 805 om, 916.

MUNICIPAL CORPORATIONS. Actions against, in certain cases, X, 451 om; assessments for local improvements, recovery of, 710 om; leasing buildings to G. A. R. posts, 585 om; negligence, limiting time to commence action, 709 om; railroad aid bonds, VII, 937 om.

MUNN, STEPHEN B. Land conveyed to trustee, sale of, X, 312 om.

MUTUAL INSURANCE COMPANIES. Albany and Greene counties, VII, 1097; Catskill and Athens, VI, 595, VII, 132 om.

NAMES. Business, continuing use of, VII, 415 om.

NASSAU COUNTY. Assessments in certain towns, om, X, 444, 450; towns, preservation of records, 243.

NATIONAL GUARD. Armory, 71st Regiment, fire at, reimbursement for private property lost, X, 566; commission to examine small arms, VIII, 455; 54th Regiment, replacing uniforms and equipments, VII, 481; Hollingworth, service medal, X, 173; military storehouse, Binghamton, addition, VII, 928; 9th Regiment, replacing uniforms and equipments, 480; pay and allowance, X, 961 om; Remington rifles, altering sights, VII, 478; separate companies, funds for, 478; 7th Separate Company, infantry, commutation for rations, 496; 74th Regiment, replacing uniforms and equipments, 480; Shaffer claim, authorizing settlement, X, 592 om; 65th Regiment, replacing uniforms, VII, 479; 12th Separate Company, replacing uniforms and equipments, 480; 27th Regiment, equipments, purchase of, 479.

NATURAL HISTORY. Free instruction, continuing, VIII, 1037 om; purchase of Wolcott collection, VII, 467.

NAUTICAL SCHOOL. Establishing, IX, 256, 380, 627 om.

NAVAL MILITIA. Chartering vessel for, IX, 777 om.

NAVIGATION. Inspection of vessels on certain lakes, VIII, 1121.

NEWARK. Public hall, VI, 210; revising charter, VII, 1122.

NEWARK VALLEY. Legalizing water bonds, X, 702 om.

NEW BRIGHTON. Amending village charter, VI, 592; fire department, VIII, 532; regulating use of dock, VI, 907.

NEWBURGH. Amending charter, om, VIII, 1040, IX, 719, 787 (2 bills); boundaries, VII, 1099; increasing tax for contingent expenses, VIII, 76; amending free school act, VI, 507; alteration of map, VIII, 697; land purchased at tax sales, X, 633 om; legalizing Water street paving bonds, IX, 719 om; St. Luke's Home and Hospital, poor in, payments for, 723 om; sewer, 787 om.

NEW CAPITOL. Additional accommodations, finishing room and corridor on fifth floor for Department of Education, X, 643; additional office facilities, 642; Agricultural Department, repairs and furniture, 299; Board of Commissioners of Construction, VIII, 213; change of lighting appliances, 422; Department of Education, additional accommodations, X, 643; Eidlitz, Richardson & Company, advances, VII, 903; former Adirondack survey rooms, fitting and furnishing, X, 788; general appropriation, VII, 92; O'Keefe, damages, 910; Senate Chamber, rearranging lighting system, X, 51; Sullivan, claim for work, VII, 498, 788; Taylor, claim for damages, 911; unappropriated tax, VI, 1002; ventilation, reappropriation, X, 425; water supply, VII, 903; work on, new commission, VIII, 869; work on exterior walls, VII, 652; Young, damages, 911.

NEW HARTFORD. Village charter, VI, 183; legalizing aid to Bridgewater Turnpike, X, 811 om.

NEW LOTS. Annexing to Brooklyn, VII, 1110; Atlantic avenue, grading, X, 177 om; police commissioners, VII, 804 om; register, 413 om; sidewalks and street improvements, 936 om.

NEW ROCHELLE. Bonds for public improvements, legalizing previous issues, X, 636 om; city charter, IX, 858 om; amending charter, X, 318 om; drainage, VII, 392, 414 om; election of comptroller, etc., X, 312 om; retirement of teachers, 478; schools, sites and buildings, 717 om; sewer, Residence park, 313 om.

NEWTOWN. Local government, VI, 449, 558; election districts, 193; road improvement, VIII, 469 om.

NEWTOWN CREEK (Chemung county). Restoration and protection of former work, X, 301.

NEWTOWN CREEK (Long Island). Nuisances, abatement, IX, 778 om; widening bulkhead lines, 725 om.

NEW UTRECHT. Board of improvement, powers, IX, 133; fire hydrants, water supply, 151 om; Franklin and Eighteenth avenues, VIII, 468 om; Franklin avenue, alteration of, 615; local improvements, IX, 522.

NEW YORK. Amending charter, VII, 936 om, IX, 520, 628 om, 867 om, 875 om, X, 473 om; abandonment proceedings, undertaking on

NEW YORK — (*Continued*).

appeal, X, 178 om; actions against, VIII, 292 om; action by Isidor Ball, granting permission, IX, 727 om; administration, securing better, VII, 125; Alger, acting supervisor of truancy, compensation, X, 473 om; ambulances, 178 om; amusement, places of, 475 om; animals, diseased, destruction of, compensation, repeal, om, IX, 810, 870; annual instalment payments, X, 581 om; application of Gerichten and Brown, police commissioners to reconsider, 62 om; aqueduct act, amending, VIII, 1035 om; aqueduct commission, additional member, VII, 1118, VIII, 45; aqueduct extension and improvement, 636; assessments for local improvements, om, 293, X, 713, 715, 716; — cancellation, IX, 872 om; — by boards of assessors, X, 475 om; attendants in several courts, compensation, IX, 727 om; Avenue C, railroad extension, VI, 74; Bailey claim, VII, 1089; banks — assessment of shares, correction, X, 475 om; — repayment of penalties to certain, id.; Bartholdi statue fund, contribution, VII, 1088; Beardslee, counsel to board of education, settlement of claim, IX, 805 om; bi-partisan park commission, VIII, 758; bi-partisan police commissioners, 756; Bleakley claim, VII, 1089; Bloomingdale road, VI, 692; boards of aldermen and estimate and apportionment, powers, X, 816 om; board of estimate and apportionment, om, 715, 818; board of police, granting new trials, VI, 848; board of revision of assessments, V, 724; board of taxes and assessments, compensation, X, 581 om; borough presidents — powers, 959 om; — salaries, 580 om; Boston and Third avenues, paving, VII, 129 om; Bronx borough, changing grade of streets and avenues, damages, IX, 870 om; Brooklyn — confirming certain appointments by fire commissioners, X, 59 om; — firemen, confirming appointment, 806 om; maps, Strom claim, settlement, IX, 874 om; Brooklyn Free Library, transfer of land to, 867 om; Brooklyn Public Library, transferring property to, 873 om; Brown claim, X, 806 om; Brown and Fleming Contracting Company, Queens borough, highway department, materials, 950 om; buildings,— VI, 590, IX, 809 om, 873 om, X, 175 om; — elevators in, IX, 445, 461; — erection of, VII, 1117; — height of, X, 807 om; building department, filing plans with, IX, 633 om; cable railroad, VIII, 1035 om; Campbell, patrolman, X, 806 om; captain of the port and harbor masters, compensation, VII, 1048; Carpenter, Municipal Court clerk, Brooklyn, services, X, 950 om; Carrigan, patrolman, reinstatement, 949 om; Cedar park, VIII, 129 om; Central park — altering map, VI, 93; parade ground, VIII, 467; — railways in transverse roads, 1035 om; — refreshment house, VII, 578; — zoological collection, VIII, 449; — North and East River Railroad Company, claim against, settlement, 1035 om; charter,—

NEW YORK — (*Continued*).

1872, VI, 453, VII, 1061; — supplemental act, 99; charter election, VI, 495; charitable institutions, water supply, IX, 805 om; City College, site and buildings, X, 176 om; City Court,—om, 313, 635; — assistant clerks, IX, 732 om; — establishment of, VII, 129 om; — justices' clerks, X, 956 om; city magistrates,—method of selection, 178 om; — qualifications, 582 om; city prison,— third district, city magistrate's court and county jail, 179 om; — compensation of keepers, VII, 597; — keepers, increasing compensation, 772; claims, — settlement of, VI, 518; — arising under contests of certain judgments, X, 307; Clarke claim, VIII, 883; clerks and employees, legalizing transfer and assignment from consolidated municipalities, IX, 874 om; Cohen, appointed policeman, X, 176 om; Collins claim, department of education, 691, 818 om; commissioner of jurors, VII, 129 om, 251, 803 om; commissioner of street improvements, 23d and 24th wards, IX, 151 om; — increasing compensation, 727 om; commitments to Bedford Reformatory, X, 633 om; commitment of females, 709 om; common council — legalizing proceedings, VII, 509 om; — powers of, IX, 149 om; — powers and duties, 631 om; common schools, VII, 933 om; condemnation proceedings,— commissioners, X, 807 om; — pay of commissioners, 179 om; confirming ordinance, Third Avenue Railroad Company, V, 667; amending Consolidation Act, VI, 508, VII, 938 om, IX, 150 om; contagious diseases, prevention of, VI, 325; construction of conveyances, contracts and instruments, relative to assessment, X, 177 om; contracts for filling certain lots, V, 728; convicts and paupers, employment of, VI, 982; Cooper Union, release from assessments, X, 178 om; corporations, taxation of, VII, 777; court attendants, X, 176 om; — compensation, 716 om; court buildings and jail, 582 om; court officers, salaries, VIII, 132 om; courts,— clerks and interpreters, IX, 875 om; — officers and attendants, 807 om; Court of General Sessions, X, 176 om; Coyle, subpœna clerk special sessions, compensation, 313 om; Crane estate, release, 712 om; criminal court building, VIII, 638 om; — authorizing acceptance of, and completion, IX, 808 om; criminal courts, repeal, III, 1009; Cross claim, audit, IX, 805 om; Croton aqueduct, settlement of claims, VIII, 1035 om; Croton water,— amending act, IV, 773, VI, 596; — arrears of rent and charges, VII, 509 om; Daly, dock department, superintendent of sections, compensation, X, 691, 957 om; damages, awards, payment, 634 om; Davenport, judge Thirteenth Civil District Court, legalizing appointment of attendants and employees, IX, 809 om; debt, payment of, VII, 209; Deering claim, settlement, IX, 872 om; department heads, appointment and removal, 415; department of correction, X,

NEW YORK — (*Continued*).

474 om; department of education, services in, compensation, 477 om;
Devlin, roundsman, reinstatement, 951 om; Diamond claim, school
department, om, 326, 636; Diegan, Municipal Court attendant, compensation, 473 om; Dillon, policeman, rehearing charges, 817 om;
Dismore claim, VIII, 884; district courts,— additional clerk, VI, 281;
— clerks, 1029, VII, 47, 451; — increasing jurisdiction, 1045; —
janitors, 326, 804 om, 933 om; — justices, legalizing acts, compensation, IX, 872 om; — revision of laws, VII, 129 om; dock board,
leasing land for boathouse services, IX, 875 om; dock commissioners,
salaries, VIII, 889 om; dock department, om, VII, 416, VIII, 403,
IX, 235, 286; docks, VII, 622, VIII, 293 om; docks and ferries,
om, X, 325, 475; docks, wharves, piers and bulk-heads, management,
VII, 129 om; dock masters,— claims, X, 818 om; — defining duties,
VIII, 456; — Powers claim, X, 321 om; — reinstatement, om, 472,
477; — White claim, 308 om; Dolan and Loutrel claim, VIII, 883;
Donnelly claim, 131 om; Douglass, services in water department, X,
949 om; Dowling claim, 310 om; Duggan, patrolman, 806 om;
duplicate docket books, VI, 507; Eastern boulevard, amending map,
695; East 100th street, widening, VII, 666 om; East river bridge,
Blackwell's island, X, 176 om; East river, piers, slips and wharves,
regulating use of, IX, 873 om; East river park,— legalizing laying
out, refunding assessments, 808 om; — refunding assessments, om,
X, 715, 806; Eighty-sixth street improvement, VI, 599; election
advertisements, VIII, 1036 om; election districts, VI, 596; — advertising boundaries, IX, 151 om; election officers, compensation,
om, 859, X, 474; elections,— 1872, VI, 479; — separate department,
om, X, 59, 178; electrical conductors, right to construct, compensation
for, VIII, 887 om; electrical subways, repealing act of 1897, IX, 875
om; elevated railroads, fares, VII, 850; Ellett and Miller, secretary
and watchman, Richmond county park commissioners, X, 959 om;
employment agencies, 308 om; engineers,— relative to, 60 om; —
powers and duties, VI, 715; evening high school,— relative to, IX,
74, 216; — for males, 19th ward, VIII, 638 om; — for males, 22d
ward, 637 om; excise,— commissioners, 273; — moneys, disposition
of, 467; excursion boats and barges, fire protection, X, 805 om;
Feely claim, assistant expert accountant, 690; Fellows, district attorney, payment of unearned salary to widow, IX, 805 om; Fifth
avenue, repavement, VII, 1090; finance department,— relative to,
IX, 733 om; — city magistrate's court, claims for services, X, 172;
— city magistrate's court, clerk's compensation, 176 om; — division
of notification, IX, 806 om; — Wernberg claim, X, 817 om; fires,—
prevention and extinguishment of, VI, 911 om; explosives and

NEW YORK — (*Continued*).

combustible materials, prevention of, X, 313 om; fire boat captains, retirement, 474 om; fire commissioners,—Brooklyn and Long Island City, legalizing appointments, 178 om; — not to be candidates for other office, IX, 521; — powers of, om, 733, X, 582, 806; fire department,— relative to, IX, 728 om, 805; — assignments and promotions, X, 634 om; — chaplains, compensation, 581 om; — claims for labor, services and materials, 633 om; — deputy chief, Brooklyn and Queens boroughs, 818 om; — employees, appointment to uniformed force, om, IX, 732, X, 580, 806; — employees, relative to, 583 om; — life insurance fund, deposit, X, 321 om; — pension roll, claims of chiefs of battalions to be placed thereon, IX, 808 om; — Reilly reinstatement, IX, 804 om; — reinstatements, X, 713 om; — relief fund, 176 om; — sites for buildings, IX, 235; — Sweeney reappointment, X, 818 om; — uniformed, compensation of officers, IX, 727 om; — volunteers, preference, om, X, 580, 717 om; — marshals, om, 715, 816; firemen's association veteran volunteers, exemptions, Queens and Richmond boroughs, 323 om; firemen,— exempt Westchester annexed district, VIII, 1036 am; — volunteer associations in certain former towns, X, 472 om; — volunteer, Queens and Richmond, om, 60, 715; — volunteer, Westchester annexed district, services after annexation, compensation, IX, 871 om; — fire and police departments, uniforms, IX, 732 om; firemen and policemen, reinstatements (19 bills), X, 53; Foley, supervisor, salary, VII, 643, 933 om; foreclosure sales, publication of notice, 267 om; foreign insurance companies, taxes, X, 177 om; free college, Brooklyn, establishing, 956 om; Fulton market, rebuilding, VII, 507 om; Garvey claim, charities department, X, 169, 311 om; gas companies, VIII, 240; gas meters, inspection, X, 60 om; gas supply, VI, 180; Gavin claim, extra work, X, 323 om; general sessions,— attendants, salary, 582 om; — clerks and stenographers, compensation, 953 om; — record clerks, salaries, 953 om; — stenographer's compensation, VII, 768; grade crossings, abolition of, X, 176 om; Grand boulevard and Concourse, refunding assessments, 807 om; Gravesend, Surf avenue, relative to, om, IX, 872, X, 476; hackney coaches and carriages, VII, 415 om; Hall claim, audit of, VIII, 467; Ham claim, 131 om, IX, 468; Hamilton grange, acquiring and maintaining, X, 324 om; Hamilton park, om, 60, 473; harbor and port, VII, 507 om; harbor, — bulk-head lines, Staten Island, VIII, 1037 om; — pier and bulk-head lines, Newtown creek, VII, 111; Hart's island, annexation of, VIII, 1035 om; Head, dock department engineer, rehearing charges, X, 951 om; health, protection of, VI, 324; health department,— antitoxin accountant, compensation, X, 160; Hell Gate pilots, om,

XI — 9

NEW YORK — (*Continued*).

IX, 728, X, 316; High bridge park, VIII, 294 om; hospital upper part of city, VII, 1086; Hottenroth claim, VIII, 883; House of Good Shepherd, cancellation of assessments, X, 179 om; Hudson claim, 59 om; Hudson street; premises on, receiving testimony concerning, VIII, 889 om; Hughes, patrolman, reinstatement, X, 950 om; hydrants, VIII, 1035 om; inspectors of elections and poll clerks, IX, 151 om; illegal voting, IV, 825; improvements, VII, 417; improvement of streets, avenues and public places, VI, 220; improvements, Eighth avenue and 155th street, amending act, VII, 664 om; indictments, transcribing, IX, 732 om; inferior criminal courts, om, 859, X, 959; inspectors of buildings, deputy, VIII, 130 om; interest on unpaid assessments, X, 476 om; Jamaica and Brooklyn plank road, adjustments, 178 om; janitors of public schools, 319 om; Jewish Protectory and Aid Society, authorizing appropriation for, 475 om; jury servers, fixing salary, IX, 807 om; justices of special sessions and city magistrates, qualifications, 859 om; Kelly, coroner's clerk, Queens borough, X, 956 om; Kings county penitentiary, removal, 177 om; Krenkel claim, VIII, 132 om; land, acquisition by board of estimate and apportionment, X, 580 om; land for public use,— acquisition of, IX, 236;— in certain cases, 627 om; law department, Juergen's claims, om, X, 816, 957; legalizing act, V, 246; legal proceedings and notices, publication, VI, 591; legislative department, X, 46; Lexington avenue, opening, canceling assessment on certain property, IX, 809 om; liens, discharge of, 520; livery stables, VII, 416 om; local boards of improvement, meetings, X, 582 om; local government, VI, 499, 1029; — better administration, VII, 129 om; — expenses, 129 om; local improvements,— assessments, VIII, 638 om; — expenses, VI, 519; Long Island City claims, X, 60 om; lunacy examiners, board of, id.; Lyons, fireman, reinstatement, 950 om; McCullen, fireman, reinstatement, 951 om; magistrates, additional, police clerk, 582 om; Manhattan street opening, compensation of commissioners, 326 om; manure,— deposits of, VI, 323;— facilitating removal of, VII, 553; map,— alteration of, VI, 220, 590;— College avenue, VIII, 130 om; — Lewis street, VI, 705;— Morris avenue, VII, 1088;— 23d and 24th wards, IX, 809 om;— providing for, X, 713 om; marine court, jurisdiction, VII, 1116, VIII, 711; markets, relative to, VII, 450;— 13th ward, VI, 209;— 21st ward, 93; marshals, om, VII, 509, X, 175; mayor, aldermen, comptroller and president of the board of aldermen, election, terms of office and powers, VIII, 278; McCabe claim, 884; McGee, policeman, X, 807 om; McGowan, refund taxes, 806 om; McNeil, coroner's clerk, Kings county, compensation, 957 om; Melrose avenue, alteration, VIII, 467; Memorial Day celebration,

NEW YORK — (Continued).

Richmond borough, X, 762; Methodist Episcopal Church Home, releasing from assessments, 175 om; Metropolitan Museum of Art, Ward claim, IX, 873 om; Metropolitan Transit Company, discontinuing part of line, changing Harlem river bridge, VIII, 132 om; Monaghan claim, 883; Montefiore Home, amending Consolidation Act, 638 om; Montefiore Home for Invalids and canal boat pier in East river, amending Consolidation Act, 131 om; mortgages on lands under water, VI, 611; Mott avenue, widening portion of, IX, 810 om; municipal clubhouses for boys, X, 712 om; Municipal Court,— amending charter, om, IX, 859, 860, X, 580, 713, 714; — additional justices, 473 om; — attendants, claims, 165; — attendants, relative to, 806 om; — clerks and assistants, 60 om; — employees, payment for services, 177 om; enforcement of judgments, 308 om; — interpreter and attendants, compensation, 474 om; — interpreters' salaries, 714 om; — judges, designation and rotation, 818 om; — justices, om, 176, 717; — justice's clerk, 819 om; — justices' salaries, om, 178, 581; — Manhattan borough, maintenance claims, 817 om; — marshals, additional number, 635 om; — officers and marshals, om, 588, 633, 816; — revision commission, 177 om; — salaries, 712 om; — summons, proof of service, 312 om; newspapers for advertising corporate notices, designation, om, IX, 875, X, 59, 177; newspaper claims, VI, 607; Newtown creek bridge, damages to owners of land abutting on Vernon avenue, X, 957 om; Newtown creek, nuisances, repeal, 176 om; New York Produce Exchange, claim, Foster extradition case, 473 om; Nineteenth street, repaving, VIII, 389; Ninth avenue, relative to, IX, 807 om; normal college, 871 om; northwest section, laying out and improving, VII, 664 om; notification of assessments, X, 389; O'Connor claim, VIII, 131 om, 884; old armory building, 889 om; 111th street,— relative to, VII, 506 om; — closing a portion of, VIII, 738; 135th street improvement, X, 324 om; 126th and 127th streets, opening, VII, 507 om; O'Neil claim, Municipal Court, assistant clerk, Brooklyn, X, 691; Ophthalmic Institute, amending Consolidation Act, VIII, 638 om; ordinances,— code of, X, 580 om; — powers of common council, IX, 806 om; oyer and terminer, stenographic notes, VI, 330; park commissioners,— appointment, IX, 434; — alteration of map, Spuyten Duyvil road, VII, 629; — powers, X, 179 om; park department,— relative to, VII, 1075, 1118; — extending jurisdiction, VIII, 714; — jurisdiction over certain streets and places, om, 293, IX, 727, X, 323; — altering map, 24th ward, VIII, 350; altering map, 23d ward, 350; Parker claim, fire department, relief of minor daughter, X, 818 om; park keepers,— relative to, VII, 934 om; — removal, 1086; park police, VIII, 638 om, IX, 52, 630 om; parks,

NEW YORK — (*Continued*).

— relative to, X, 178 om; — acquiring site, IX, 806 om; — additional, X, 582 om; — compensation of laborers and employees, IX, 393; — 4th ward, X, 60 om; — park openings, fund for, 635 om; — protection of, IX, 517, 727 om; — St. Nicholas, X, 60 om; — St. Nicholas, proceedings, rehearing by Supreme Count, 713 om; — Silver Lake park, Richmond county, 715 om; — 12th ward, 176 om; — West End avenue, IX, 262; patrolmen,— acting as precinct detectives, salaries, VIII, 889 om; — appointment, X, 806 om; — qualifications, 176 om; — and firemen, qualifications, om, 476, 580, 581; Patterson, release of land owned by city in Putnam county, IX, 806 om; pavements, repair, VIII, 887 om; Pelham avenue, Bronx, X, 807 om; pharmacists and druggists, regulating prescriptions, IX, 871 om; Phillips, coroner's clerk, Brooklyn, X, 951 om; piers,— North river, VII, 1119; — for recreation, om, X, 580, 581, 582; Pier 37, use of, VII, 935 om; pilotage, VI, 911 om; Pinkley, appointment as policeman, X, 817 om; places of amusement, exempting certain hall from license fee, VII, 1086; playgrounds, acquisition of, om, X, 582, 635; police, — additional patrolmen, VII, 1087; — captains, increasing salaries, VIII, 211; — clerks, X, 807 om; — qualifications, 713 om; — salaries, amending Consolidation Act, section 287, VII, 935 om; — sergeants and detective sergeants, salaries, VIII, 524; — surgeons and doormen, compensation, IX, 632 om; police courts, assistant clerks, V, 149; police department,— relative to, om, VII, 414, IX, 632, X, 176, 325; — reinstatements, 713 om; — reorganization, IX, 490; police justice, VI, 897; police and district court janitors, 598; police and fire commissioners, VIII, 636; police and fire departments,— promotion for bravery, X, 580 om; — salaries, VII, 803 om; poor, adult blind, appropriations and relief, om, VIII, 889, 1036; port, regulations, VII, 414 om; prison ship martyrs, monument to, IX, 874 om; public administration, VII, 252; public bath, 551, 804 om, 873, IX, 807 om; public buildings, commissioners, costs, X, 582 om; — 12th ward, Manhattan borough, 323 om; public driveway, 60 om; public exchange, VII, 507 om; public exhibitions, license fee, payment to Actors' Fund of America, IX, 872 om; public health, summons, service in actions for penalties, VII, 1117; public hospital, X, 806 om; public instruction, VII, 127, 128; public market, VIII, 292 om; public officers, official terms, VII, 1074, 1118; public place, 24th ward, X, 60 om; public schools, Queens and Richmond, id.; public works,— assessments for improvements, VIII, 1035 om; — department, Senate investigation, counsel fees, VII, 905; Queens Borough Electric Light and Power Company, payment for lighting, X, 308 om; railroads,— in certain streets, V, 517; —

NEW YORK — (*Continued*).

Avenue D, 238; — Broadway and other streets, 809; — Christopher and other streets, 796; — 14th street, 238; — 125th street, 871, VI, 62; — 7th avenue, V, 238; — South West street, 238; — 10th avenue, 238; rapid transit, relative to, X, 60 om; rapid transit railways, commissioners, costs, 582 om; real estate, 23d and 24th wards, recording documents, IX, 460; recorder, city judge and general sessions judges, fixing compensation, X, 321 om; records, preservation, om, VII, 268, 804; registry of voters, publication, 579; Rehwinke, fireman, charges against, hearing, X, 63 om; Reilly, fireman, reinstatement, IX, 727 om; religious corporations, exemption from assessments, X, 583 om; removal of garbage and night soil, 177 om; removal of officers, procedure, VII, 413 om; removal of refuse matter, 268 om; repealing certain acts, 509 om, 1118; reservoirs, etc., assessment and taxation, X, 308 om; retirement fund, om, 714, 806; revenue bonds, special, 635 om; Riverside drive, extension, damages, 325 om; Riverside park improvement, VII, 655; Roberts claim, VIII, 884; Russell claim, om, X, 476, 690, 817; St. Joseph's asylum, releasing assessments, 473 om; Savage, patrolman, rehearing charges, om, 817, 950; schools, — relative to, 177 om; — lectures for working men and women, IX, 807 om; — trustees, 19th ward, actions against, legal services and expenses, 871 om; sealers of weights and measures, salaries, X, 308 om; sewers, — Bronx district, IX, 805 om; — Brooklyn and Queens, construction and maintenance, X, 474 om; — 22d street, reconsidering assessments, IX, 236; Westchester annexed district, 871 om; sheriff's jury, VII, 595; sheriffs, deputies, appointment and compensation, IX, 459; Shill, claim of, audit, 807 om; sidewalks, removing snow and ice, X, 60 om; — sinking fund, improving condition of, VII, 1087, VIII, 99; 6th ward, opening street, X, 582 om; Smith, legal services, settlement of claim, IX, 806 om; snow and ice, removal from streets, 459; soldiers and sailors' memorial arch or monument, VIII, 1029, 1160; stable refuse, removal, VII, 935 om; stables, — near churches, IX, 520; — near churches and hospitals, X, 807 om; stands in streets, permits for, VIII, 467; station house, 30th precinct, VII, 128 om; Stemmler, justice, district court salary, VIII, 294 om, 884; stoop lines, X, 59 om; streets, — changing grades, VII, 657; — changing grade, claim for damages, Bronx borough, X, 323 om; — change of grade, damages, 23d and 24th wards, 713 om; — closing, changing grade, VI, 583; — cleaning, VII, 803 om, IX, 474, 631 om, 724 om; — encroachments, ordinances, relative to, om, 634, 728; — improvements, VI, 326, X, 63 om; — improvement, damages, 23d and 24th wards, om, X, 712, 807;

NEW YORK — (*Continued*).
—improvements, 23d and 24th wards, om, VII, 129-X, 712; —near schools, hospitals, etc., asphalting, 177 om; — opening, VII, 665 om, opening, 6th ward, X, 715 om; — projections on, 323 om; — permanent exterior, VII, 1087; — removal of incumbrances, 23d and 24th wards, IX, 732 om; — repairs south of 14th street, VII, 129 om; — through Cypress Hill cemetery, X, 325; summary proceedings, om, VII, 413, 417, X, 159, 175; superintendent of buildings, IX, 806 om; — appeals from, X, 475 om; supplies for departments, purchase of, 635 om; surrogate, official term, expenses of proceedings, VII, 804 om; Surrogate's Court, proceedings, 417 om; taxes,— 1860, V, 221; — assessments and water rates, Greenfield · property, cancellation, X, 325 om; — 120th street, settlement, VIII, 1036 om; — sales, notice to unknown owners, 467; Taylor claim, X, 806 om; teachers,— salaries, IX, 854, 859 om; — supply of, X, 172; telegraph, public use of, VI, 706; tenement-houses, relative to,' VIII, 886 om, IX, 67; tenements and lodging-houses, IX, 868 om; 10th avenue and 93d street, improvement, VI, 597; 10th avenue and 145th street, improvements, VII, 665 om; third police judicial court, salary of assistant clerk, VI, 564; Tompkins square, improvement, 698; trees and vegetation, cultivation of, X, 60 om; trees in streets, cultivation, 178 om; tuberculosis hospital, 178 om; tunnel under Washington park · prohibited, VII, 999; tunnel railroads, franchise, X, 471; Turner claim, finance department, 310 om; 23d ward, altering certain streets, VIII, 467; 23d and 24th wards, alteration of map, IX, 805 om; Uvalde Asphalt Paving Company, labor and · materials, Brooklyn, X, 951 om; vagrants, VI, 330; Van Cortland park, vaults and burial plots, VIII, 889 om; Vogel claim, 884; volunteer fire department benevolent fund, VI, 1028; Ward's Island, water rights, X, 176 om; Washington market, lease of, VI, 594; Waterbury claims, counsel fees, retaxation, om, VIII, 1035, X, 807; water front improvement, corporate stock for, 176 om; water rents, apportionment, 475 om; water supply,— relative to, VII, 593, 635; — 23d and 24th wards, 129 om; — department, Wydler claim for reinstatement, X, 815 om; weights and measures, inspectors, VIII, 131 om; Weise, fireman, reinstatement, X, 950 om; Westchester annexation act, amendment, VI, 911 om; Westchester annexed · district,— claims against municipalities, IX, 732 om; — public building. in, 808 om; West Farms and Morrisania, amending act, VII, 417 om; Westfield, Richmond county, claims for · school supplies, X, 320 om; West Side German · Dispensary, exempting from taxation, licenses, · VIII, 294 om; West street, widening, V, 878, VI, 93; wharf · property, X, 175

NEW YORK — (*Continued*).

om; Williamsburgh Volunteer Firemen's. Association, headquarters for, 175. om; Wilson, policeman, relief, 61 om; wooden buildings, construction prohibited, VII, 444, VIII, 467; Woodside. Water Company,—relief, X, 175 om;—claim, 326 om.

NEW YORK AND BROOKLYN. Fire department, appointments to uniformed force, IX, 809 om; protection of female employees, VII, 509, om; public buildings, exemption from taxation, VII, 267 om.

NEW YORK AND BROOKLYN BRIDGE. Completion, control and management, VIII, 123; elevator at, IX, 806 om; lighting during fogs, 733 om; maintenance and government, VIII, 637; policemen, compensation, 992; reports of commissioners, amending act of 1895, X, 477 om; running cars, regulations, IX, 733 om; trustees, legislating out of office, 441.

NEW YORK HOUSE OF REFUGE. Apparatus for extinguishing fires, IX, 771; coal building, deficiency appropriation, current expenses, dormitory for employees, VII, 489; electric light plant, IX, 770; fire-escapes, 771; galleries in chapel, VII, 489; instruction shops and equipment, laundry, IX, 770; lavatory equipments, 771; plumbing, 770; printing plant, 771; repairs and improvements, VII, 584; school furniture, IX, 770; steam heating, 771.

NEW YORK AND KINGS COUNTIES. Closing certain offices on Saturdays, VII, 757.

NEW YORK PRISON ASSOCIATION. Compilation of criminal statistics, VIII, 122.

NEW YORK STATE REFORMATORY FOR WOMEN AT BEDFORD. See BEDFORD REFORMATORY.

NEW YORK STATE WOMEN'S RELIEF CORPS HOME. See WOMEN'S RELIEF CORPS HOME.

NEW YORK AND ROCHESTER HOUSES OF REFUGE. Commitments, X, 705 om.

NIAGARA. School trustees, VI, 188.

NIAGARA COUNTY. Board of equalization of taxes VIII, 737; claim of Roswell Park, authorizing reconsideration of, X, 268.

NIAGARA FALLS. Amending charter, om, IX, 633, 731; 788; board of public works, powers and contracts, X, 478 om; Liefer claim against board of education, 716 om; Pierce avenue extension, IX, 534 om; terms of officers, X, 322 om.

NIAGARA FALLS RESERVATION. Labor saving machinery, X, 788; roads, 568.

NIAGARA RIVER. Limiting use of water, X, 918; power experiments, Mather plan, 54, 629 om, 813 om.

NORMAL SCHOOLS. Free privileges of, VIII, 506; secretary of board, right to salary, 407.

Albany,—repairs, furniture and books, VII, 469; scientific apparatus, repairs, expense, 926.

Brockport,— additions and repairs, VII, 468; repairs and improvements, VIII, 865; sewer system, X, 315 om.

Cortland,— heating apparatus, VIII, 863; repairs and improvements, VII, 468, IX, 106; salaries of teachers removed and restored, VII, 927.

Fairfield,— establishing, VIII, 888 om.

Fredonia,— rooms for school societies, X, 649; repairs and improvements, VII, 468, VIII, 863, 1138.

Geneseo,— building for school of practice, VIII, 116.

Jamaica,— establishing, VIII, 888 om, IX, 134, 627 om.

Millerton,— establishing, IX, 622 om.

New Paltz,— repairs and improvements, VIII, 864.

Oneonta,— grading and repairing grounds, repairs and improvements, VIII, 864.

Oswego,— industrial department, VIII, 865.

Oswego Training School, instruction of kindergarten teachers, VII, 792.

Plattsburg,— reducing number of managers, IX, 433.

Potsdam,— insurance, repairs and improvements, VIII, 864.

Ramapo,— establishing, IX, 711.

Saratoga Springs, establishing, VIII, 888 om.

Watkins,— establishing, VIII, 888 om.

White Plains,— establishing, VIII, 888 om.

Whitesboro,— establishing, VIII, 888 om.

NORTHEASTERN DISPENSARY, NEW YORK. Lease for, VI, 706.

NORTHERN NEW YORK INSTITUTION FOR DEAF-MUTES. General improvements, VIII, 531; reappropriation unexpended balance, IX, 771.

NORTHFIELD. Board of education, VIII, 1039 om; macadamizing certain roads, VII, 132 om.

NORTH HEMPSTEAD. Support of patients in Nassau Association Hospital, IX, 818 om.

NORWICH. Revised charter, IX, 289.

NOTARIAL CLERKS. Amending Executive Law, X, 442 om; in certain counties, compensation, VIII, 1131.

NOTARIES PUBLIC. Additional number, VII, 54, 415 om, 443, 863, VIII, 130 om; county clerks' fees, 1038 om; in certain counties,— relative to, VI, 1036 om; — powers of, VII, 131 om; Erie county, increasing number, 1095; Monroe and Onondaga counties, additional number, VIII, 43; preventing traffic in office of, X, 948 om.

NOTARIES PUBLIC — (*Continued*).

LEGALIZING ACTS:— General, VIII, 334, X, 813 om; Cantwell, IX, 365; Cornell, VII, 507 om; Gilbert, VI, 690; Green, IX, 720 om; Larkin, 812 om; McCormick, X, 813 om; Stier, VIII, 387; Wells, 291 om; Whitney, VII, 507 om.

NOTICES AND CITATIONS. Publication of, VI, 509.

NOTICES OF PENDENCY. Cancellation, om, IX, 624, 627; directing record of certain, VIII, 887 om.

NUISANCE. Spencerport, VII, 805 om; trials in certain cases, 416 om.

OAK ORCHARD CREEK. Deepening and straightening, X, 313 om.

OBSCENE LITERATURE. Relative to, VIII, 293 om.

OFFICERS. Chosen at certain elections, VII, 506 om.

OGDENSBURGH. Amending charter, X, 584 om; board of public works, VIII, 993; street openings, X, 806 om.

O'HARA, JOHN H. Member of Assembly, death of, unearned salary, appropriation, VIII, 114.

OILS AND FLUIDS. Illuminating, regulating standards, VII, 659, 751; dangerous, preventing manufacture and use of, 924.

OLEAN. Amending village charter, VIII, 1133; acquiring land for Buffalo and Washington Railroad Company, VI, 91; commitments to Erie county penitentiary, X, 806 om; mayor, powers of, 478 om.

OLEOMARGARINE. Regulating manufacture and sale, VII, 590; regulating sale, 803 om.

OLIVE. Bushkill creek, improvement bonds for, IX, 818 om.

ONEIDA. Amending charter, X, 583 om; refunding bonded indebtedness, IX, 432.

ONEIDA COUNTY. Extending time for collection of taxes, V, 343; fines, VI, 696; reservoir, completion of, VIII, 640 om.

ONEIDA LAKE. Construction of dock, VI, 156.

ONEONTA. Prohibiting new cemeteries, VIII, 327.

ONONDAGA COUNTY. Disposing of old clerk's office and lot, VII, 866; Harbor brook and Onondaga lake, X, 321 om; penitentiary property, sale of, VIII, 945.

ONONDAGA COUNTY PENITENTIARY. Amending act, V, 336.

ONONDAGA COURTHOUSE AND JAIL. Relative to, III, 190.

ONONDAGA CREEK. Draining and filling up, IX, 735 om.

ONONDAGA INDIAN RESERVATION. New schoolhouse, VII, 909; road, reimbursing Onondaga for expense, 588.

ONONDAGA INDIANS. Annuities, VII, 417 om.

ONTARIO COUNTY. Excise moneys, disposal of, IX, 267.

ORANGE COUNTY. Ninety-first Regiment funds, transfer, VI, 691.

ORDINANCES. Relative to buildings, X, 702 om.

ORLEANS. Railroad bonds, VII, 412 om.

ORLEANS COUNTY. Auditing claims for construction of power-house, VII, 1046; lock-up at Medina, VI, 273.

ORPHAN ASYLUMS. Instruction in, VI, 518.

ORTHOPEDIC HOSPITAL. Pavilion for contagious diseases, X, 294.

OSSINING. Fire department, X, 443; revising charter, extending boundaries, 812 om.

OSWEGATCHIE. Assessment-rolls, VI, 88, 288.

OSWEGATCHIE RIVER. Breakwater, VI, 331; improving navigation, VIII, 848; repairing State works, VI, 94.

OSWEGO. Amending charter, X, 59 om; contracts, method of letting, VIII, 1158; electrical college for appointment of officers, IX, 360, 432; fixing value of certain lots, VI, 215; nonpartisan boards, VIII, 624; police department, 469 om; water supply, VII, 1100, VIII, 98.

OSWEGO FALLS. Amending village charter, VII, 861.

OSWEGO RIVER. Improvement, VIII, 292 om; restoring channel, VI, 96.

OWEGO. Amending charter, VI, 79, VII, 935 om; electric light, VIII, 129 om; railroad in certain streets, VI, 330.

OX CREEK. Improvement, VIII, 292 om.

OXFORD. Amending village charter, IV, 684.

OYER AND TERMINER. Removal of causes to, VII, 1090; trial of special causes, VI, 490.

OYSTER BAY. School moneys, VII, 807 om.

PALATINE BRIDGE. Amending village charter, VI, 195.

PALISADES INTERSTATE PARK COMMISSION. Extending jurisdiction, X, 451.

PAN-AMERICAN EXPOSITION. Report, printing and distribution, X, 571.

PARDONS. Applications for, expenses of witnesses and sheriffs, VIII, 861.

PARIS. Election of railroad commissioners, VI, 194.

PARIS GREEN. Sale of, preventing fraud, om, IX, 815, X, 318

PARISHVILLE. Lock-up, VIII, 1039 om.

PARKER'S POND, CATO. Cleaning obstructions from outlet, X, 810 om.

PARTITION. Actions for, VIII, 1039 om; funds, unknown owners, withdrawal, 629.

PARTNERSHIPS. Amending general act, X, 585 om; fictitious firm names, preventing use of, VIII, 131 om; limited, amending Revised Statutes, IX, 718 om.

PATENT RIGHTS. Frauds in sale, VI, 334, 502.

PATRIOTISM. Encouragement of, VIII, 1040 om.

PAWNBROKERS. Regulation of, om, VII, 803, VIII, 889.

PEACH TREES. Preventing spread of yellows, VII, 416 om, VIII, 376.

PECONIC RIVER. Completing channel, VIII, 846.

PEEKSKILL. Additional water bonds, X, 443 om; building commissioner, creating office, 961 om.

PELHAM. Town, relative to, VII, 807 om.

PENAL CODE. Enactment, VII, 417 om; general amendments, IX, 282.

PENAL AND CRIMINAL CODES. Printing, VII, 416 om.

PENAL INSTITUTIONS. Boiler plant, building for illiterates, grading, X, 655; manufactures in, branding and marking, IX, 138; steel cells, X, 655.

PENITENTIARIES. Confinement of convicts, VI, 711; medical treatment of persons convicted of intoxication, IX, 252.

PENATAQUIT CREEK. Improving navigation, VIII, 848.

PENN YAN. Amending charter, IX, 249; changing boundary, 63.

PENSIONS.

Albany, police pension fund, amending act, IX, 632.

Brooklyn,— fire department, VIII, 131; police, VII, 413, VIII, 523; Dalley, 638; park police, IX, 733; police pensions, time of payment, 781.

Buffalo,— police, X, 276, 958; Dowd case, 875.

Jamestown, police, X, 322.

New Rochelle, teachers, tax for, X, 435.

New York,— teachers, VII, 804, 931, X, 477; police, VII, 937, VIII, 891, 1129, X, 580; fire department,— Nunn and Wilson, VII, 1083; — Hudson claim, IX, 728; police pension fund, 728, X, 60, 474; fire department, Mahoney claim, IX, 732; health department, 804; fire department, pension roll, claims of chiefs of battalions to be placed thereon, 808; firemen, Bowen case, X, 321; fire department, 582; firemen, 717; Mahon, 807; Murphy, fire department, 816.

Retirement of teachers, New York and Brooklyn, VII, 606; for retiring veterans, X, 924.

Rochester, paid fire department pension fund, IX, 249; act passed 1894, 249; teachers' retirement fund, 788; fire department, X, 713, 714; police pension fund, 714.

Syracuse, police pension fund, amending act, IX, 790.

Teachers, conditional compensation after twenty-five years' service in towns, IX, 463.

Utica, polic pensions, IX, 790; firemen's pension fund, X, 476.

PERJURY. Extending definition of, VII, 413 om.

PERRY. Railroad aid, using funds for general town purposes, VIII, 1105.

PERSONAL PROPERTY. Conditional sales, IX, 287; transfers of goods in bulk, X, 929; title, relative to, VII, 508 om.

PHARMACISTS AND DRUGGISTS. Regulating hours, X, 56.

PHARMACY. Amending Public Health Law, X, 956 om; practice of, IX, 532.

PHELPS, W. L. M. Preparing railroad report, appropriation, VII, 778.

PHOENIX. Amending charter, VII, 1123.

PIERMONT. Macadamizing highways, VII, 509 om.

PIERSON, CATHERINE D. Widow of William W. Pierson, Senate journal clerk, appropriation for residue of salary, VII, 917, 1082, VIII, 109.

PIGEONS. Homing and fancy, protection of, VIII, 633.

PIKE. Sale of portion of schoolhouse site, VII, 111.

PILOTS. Hell Gate, reducing fees, VII, 568.

PINE HILLS. Tunnel, VI, 172.

PLANK ROADS. Albany county, tolls, VI, 209; Ulster county, inspector, exemption, VII, 414 om.

PLANK ROAD COMPANIES. Repealing certain acts, VI, 596.

PLANK ROAD AND TURNPIKE CORPORATIONS. Amending act, VII, 267 om; additional tolls, V, 656.

PLATE GLASS INSURANCE COMPANIES. Deposit of securities, VII, 55.

PLATTSBURG. Amending charter, IV, 592; bonds for public improvements, X, 440 om; elections, IX, 819 om; fire department, VII, 64; free public library, charter, om, X, 713, 717; street improvement, borrowing money for, IX, 723 om; taxes,— collection of, om, VII, 130, 265; — sales, redemptions, applying general Village Law, IX, 819 om.

PLUMBERS. Registration, New York and Brooklyn, VII, 933 om; registration and supervision,— amending act, om, IX, 631, 729; — in cities, 810 om.

PNEUMATIC TUBES. Amending act, VI, 289; supplemental act, 485.

POISON. Liquids, preparation and sale of, IX, 447; regulating sale, VI, 710; sales on prescription, IX, 860 om.

POLICE. False impersonation of, VII, 573.

POLICE JUSTICES. Legalizing acts, Bellis, Penn Yan, IX, 258; Dansville, 471; Geneva, appointment, VI, 216; Greene county, repealing act, 1035 om; Herkimer, VIII, 330; Northville, relative to, VII, 932 om; Tonawanda, repealing act, 415 om; villages, relative to, 131 om; Wolcott, 389; Waterford, amending act, IX, 867 om; Watervliet, VI, 1032; Wellsville, legalizing acts of, VIII, 132 om.

POLICE MATRONS. Relative to, VII, 804 om; amending act, VIII, 890 om; compulsory appointment, 1034.

POLICE POWER. Regulation, exhibiting pictures of suspected and convicted persons, X, 585 om.

POLITICAL DIVISIONS. General act, IX, 272.

POOL SELLING. Amending act, exempting certain associations, VIII, 631.

POOR. Clinton, Niagara and Orleans counties, support of, VII, 367; children, exempting certain counties from act relative to, 413 om; compilation of law, 1124; Greenbush, relief, VIII, 699; Indian poor persons, support of, IX, 802 om; Jefferson county, amending act, VIII, 1121; Niagara and Orleans counties, expenses, VII, 328; nonresidents, care of, IX, 68; officers giving orders on places where liquors are sold, VIII, 633; overseers,— compensation, 130 om; — Ontario county, compensation in certain towns, 696; relief and support, om, VIII, 1040, X, 61; Rensselaer county, support of, VI, 339; Westchester county, outdoor relief, X, 272.

POOR LAW. Revision and consolidation, VII, 505 om.

POPE'S DAM. Purchase of, IX, 80.

PORT CHESTER. Amending village charter, VIII, 621; legalizing sewer bonds, 942.

PORT JERVIS. Public building, IX, 371.

PORT WARDENS. Expenses, IX, 68; office expenses, 83; services, assisting board of alienists, appropriation, X, 793.

POUGHKEEPSIE. Amending charter, om, IX, 633, 634, 788 (3 bills); bonding commissioners, transferring duties, VII, 509 om; employees, term of service, VIII, 751; purchasing steam fire engine, V, 338; street railroads, VII, 73; — changing motive power, VIII, 729.

PRATTSBURGH. Village, relative to, VII, 806 om.

PREVILLE, OLIVER. Claim, VII, 805 om.

PRIMARY ELECTIONS. Amending act, VIII, 890 om; general amendments, X, 420, 442; ballots, written consent of citizens to use of name, 709 om; enrollment books, publishing list of electors, 700 om; oaths, town clerks to administer, 161; political parties, enrollment lists in towns, filing with county clerk, 705 om.

PRINTING.

Forest, Fish and Game Commission, 7th report, appendix, X, 797; legalizing legislative resolutions, IX, 814 om; legislative, VIII, 255, 891 om, 1037 om; nature study and extension bulletins, X, 797; public or legislative, defining, VII, 1120; report, "Birds of New York," X, 797; public,— relative to, III, 1021; — legislative, 1899, settlement of balance, X, 315 om; water storage commission report, publication and distribution, 651; report Louisiana Purchase Exposition, 796; report, State Dairymen's Association, extra copies, VIII, 860; Sheridan memorial, 875; State,— office and superintendent, IX, 70; legislative, reappropriating unexpended balance not specified, X, 933; — messages and reports, 952 om; University Convocation, 1884, proceedings, VIII, 119.

PRINTING— (*Continued*).

    VAN BENTHUYSEN & SONS. Claims — Brooklyn bridge investigation, election case, Trowbridge against Tighe, printing testimony, VII, 491; insurance reports, 490; Kingston election case, printing testimony; Natural History, Paleontology, volume 5; roster of volunteers, Civil War, 491.

    WEED, PARSONS & COMPANY. Adirondack survey,— report of, VII, 493; seventh annual report, 495; Assembly Committee on Commerce and Navigation, 494; Assembly Committee on General Laws, Assembly special committee on normal schools, report, 492; Assembly special committee on railroads, 494; books for Senate, 492; Clerk's Manual for Assembly clerk, 494; committee on railroads, minority report, 493; department of public instruction, 494; election case, Assembly, Carman against Duryea, printing testimony, 492; election case, Assembly, Liddle against Lynes, printing testimony, 493; geological survey, Catskills, map and documents, 495; legislative file boards for Assembly clerk, 494; legislative bill file boards for State officers, 493; legislative proceedings on removal from old to new capitol, 492; natural history, State cabinet,— reports, printing and lithographing, 493; Natural History, State Museum, printing and binding for, 494; New York Civil List, furnishing copies of, Senate Committee on Code Revision, Senate Committee on Revision of Statutes, 493; Senate Judiciary Committee, printing for, 494; State Assessors, report, printing, 495; Statutory Revision Commissioners,— printing for, 231; — Clerk's Manual, 494; University Convocation, proceedings, printing and binding, University, Regents Manual, 1880, printing and binding, 494.

PRISON LABOR. On highways near Sing Sing prison, IX, 775; prohibiting manufacture of certain articles in penal institutions, 464; road building, 814 om.

PRISONERS. Civil, maintenance in certain counties, VI, 596, 706.

PROCEDURE. Compulsory accountings in equity actions, X, 443 om; condemnation proceedings, answer, 442 om; judgment, notice of application, 444 om; orders of publication, papers for, 443 om; pleadings, copartnership, denying allegations, 309 om; substituted service, publication, 952 om; trial,— exceptions, IX, 625 om; — requests to find, X, 587 om; — in certain counties, 709 om.

PROCESSIONS AND PARADES. Cities, regulation of, VII, 335.

PROPERTY, PRIVATE. Protection of, VII, 640.

PROTESTANT EPISCOPAL CHURCH. Incorporation of churches connected with, vestrymen and church wardens, annual election of, VIII, 618.

PUBLIC ACCOUNTANTS. Exemption from examinations, X, 239.

PUBLIC ADMINISTRATOR. Amending Revised Statutes, VI, 583; New York, regulating bureau of, 584.

PUBLIC BUILDINGS. Control of repairs, additions and alterations, X, 586 om; employees and furniture, appropriation, 573; repairs and improvements, IX, 768.

PUBLIC HEALTH. Adulteration of drugs, chemicals, etc., X, 447 om; cities and villages, IX, 151 om; Corning, waters of Chemung river, 719 om; depositing refuse matter in waters about New York, repeal, 384; local boards, amending general act, 720 om; penalties, collection, 504; amending Penal Code, X, 63 om; reclaiming overflowed lands, Jefferson and St. Lawrence counties, VII, 934 om; sanitary inspection of steamboats, railroad stations and cars; State sanitary commissioner, IX, 234; special agent, VII, 582; vital statistics, registration, IX, 238.

PUBLIC INSTRUCTION. Amending general act, om, VII, 507, VIII, 293; amending act of 1864, delinquent taxes, VII, 442; department, deputy superintendent's salary, VIII, 72.

PUBLIC OFFICERS. Relative to, VIII, 889 om; security on bonds, VII, 508 om.

PUBLIC RECORDS. State, preservation of, VIII, 666 om.

PULASKI. Fire limits, VII, 806 om.

PUTNAM COUNTY. Town business, Phillipstown and Carmel, VI, 674.

QUARANTINE. Appleton contract, Southfield land, appropriation, VII, 929; appliances in boiler house, X, 549; artesian wells on Swinburne and Hoffman islands, IX, 292; boiler house,— addition, X, 294; — new, 549; buildings for cabin passengers, equipment, 549; care of establishment, VIII, 252; commissioners,— completing contract for Southfield lands, VII, 385; — method of appointment, VIII, 555; dock repairs, dredging, VII, 791; entering grounds or vessels without leave, X, 317 om; general improvements, IX, 83; grading, X, 294; health officer,— gas apparatus, heating apparatus, 792; — land at Clifton station, 567; — mason work, plumbing, repairs to steamers, 792; — residence and other adjacent buildings, repairs, VII, 1085; — residence, painting and repairs, VIII, 425; Hoffman Island,— continuing sea-wall, repairs, 426; — docks and dredging, VII, 588; — enlargement, IX, 292; — general repairs, VII, 588; — repairs at, 1085; hospital ship Illinois, repairs, 791, VIII, 425; lighting plant, X, 294; maintenance account, deficiencies in salaries, appropriation, 568; new boarding tug, VII, 1084; The N. K. Hopkins, repairs, 791; painting buildings, Swinburne and Hoffman islands, IX, 292; plumbing, X, 294; repair of buildings, VII, 473; repairing dock at upper boarding station, VIII, 426; roadway, upper boarding station, VII,

QUARANTINE — (*Continued*).

791; Swift, contractor, claim, 373; Swinburne island,— buildings on, IX, 777 om; — dock, general repairs, X, 549; Swinburne and Hoffman islands, repairs, 792; warehouse company,— revival, VII, 588; — existence continued, 1085.

QUEENS COUNTY. Court attendants, compensation, X, 711 om; new indices, VI, 310; personal property, apportionment under Nassau county act, X, 62 om; unpaid taxes, sales of land, VII, 415 om; Woodbine street, IX, 778 om.

RACING ASSOCIATIONS. Annual tax on gross receipts, X, 891; examiner, furnishing office for, rent of office for, 422; examining books, compensation of experts, IX, 856.

RACKET RIVER. Improving navigation, VI, 348, 599.

RAILROAD AID. Amending act, VI, 190, VIII, 459; Berlin railroad commissioner, abolishing office, IX, 232; relief of certain towns, VIII, 371; town bonds in certain counties, 639 om.

RAILROAD COMMISSION. Clerk, preparing index maps and report, VII, 921; grade crossings, reappropriation, X, 647, 653; railroad maps from State Engineer's office, reports, additional copies, VII, 921.

RAILROAD COMMISSIONERS. Abolition of office, VII, 509 om; defining duties, 1096; increasing number, IX, 761.

RAILROADS. Amending general act, VI, 326, VII, 266 om, 806 om (2 bills), 1096, IX, 803 om, 865 om; aiding construction, V, 814; Allegany and other counties, aid to, VI, 95; cars and engines, preventing intrusions on, VII, 417 om; commission to ascertain damages, VIII, 619; condemnation, right of, X, 710 om; consents for construction, 574; consolidation of certain companies, VI, 814; construction and operation, VII, 806 om; corporations in foreign counties, 1097; county act, VIII, 470 om; electric light and power companies becoming railroad companies, IX, 246; elevated, construction outside New York, VIII, 889 om; extending time for completion of, 237; extortion, prevention of, 1128; freight transportation, X, 926; grade crossings, om, VIII, 1037, X, 568, 591; Jefferson and St. Lawrence counties, stocks, relief from existing burdens, VII, 847; local authorities, definition, IX, 462; between Long Wharf and Matteawan, VI, 211; in hands of receivers, limiting time for construction, X, 959 om; mail, III, 592; mountain,— operation of, VIII, 293 om; — rates of fare, 291 om; municipal aid, VI, 214; passenger cars, lighting, VIII, 889 om; receipts for freights, IX, 472; reports, X, 699 om; school taxes, exempting Cattaraugus county, VII, 1095; street surface and elevated, hours of labor, IX, 626 om; terminal facilities, first class cities, X, 466; town sinking funds, VII, 268 om; tunnel

RAILROADS — (*Continued*).

roads, IX, 803 om; unfinished, aiding, VI, 345; using tracks of other companies, VIII, 889 om; White Plains to Connecticut line, 615.

RAPID TRANSIT. General act, VI, 905; condemnation, procedure, X, 446 om; presentation of claims, 806 om.

RAQUETTE POND. Removing dead and floating timber from, X, 428.

REAL PROPERTY. Actions to recover, om, IX, 791, 792; levy after ten years, VIII, 468 om; life estates, sale of, unknown remaindermen, X, 592 om; maps, division of lots, abandonment, IX, 623 om; penalty for using long forms of covenants, repeal, 803 om; sale on execution, application of certain sections of Code, VIII, 470 om.

RECEIVERS. Moneyed corporations, VII, 416 om; and trustees, commissions and bonds, X, 589 om.

RECORDER. Norwich, creating office, IX, 75; Oswego, amending charter, X, 806 om; Utica, increasing salary, VI, 427; Watervliet, appointment, X, 434.

REFEREES. Appointment in first judicial department, X, 318 om; investigating charges against attorneys, compensation, VII, 266 om; to sell real property, appointment, VIII, 632.

REGENTS. Assistant secretary's salary, VIII, 72; objects of natural history, purchase of, VII, 410; evening examinations, X, 432; examinations in academies and academic departments, deficiency appropriation, VII, 467; purchase of Revolutionary letters, 409; purchase of Tompkins papers, 922; secretary's salary, VIII, 71; Woolworth, honorary secretary, compensation, VII, 467.

REGISTER.

Kings county,— additional subordinates, appointment, salaries, X, 770; employees, 592 om; management of office, 711 om; salaried office, 179 om; salaries of clerks, 449 om; salary, 594 om.

New York,— additional deputy, X, 956 om; compensation of copyists, 712 om; duties and compensation, VII, 412 om.

REGISTRATION OF VOTERS. Fishkill, VIII, 719; requiring personal appearance of voter, 415.

RELIEF. Albro, III, 262; Andreus and Kent, VII, 805 om; Anthony, Backer, VI, 185; Baldwin, VI, 684; Ballou, om, VII, 416, 506; Barker, X, 770; Barlow, VII, 666 om; Barrett, X, 178 om, 581; Bates, IX, 630 om; Becker, Benson, Bissell, Blood, VI, 185; Bohan, Bolles, X, 178 om; Boody, 582 om; Bradley, 581 om; Buck, VI, 680; Burrows, 185; Calrow, 219; Carney, 185; Cassidy, X, 177 om; Chappell and Currell, VIII, 1100; Chiesa, extending time to sue for personal injuries, X, 473 om; Christian church, Tonawanda, VI, 185; Church, V, 149; Clark, VI, 185; Clifford, X, 177 om; Clifford, Sachs and Foster, 176 om; Cohen, 581 om; Cole and others.

XI — 10

Relief — (*Continued*).

IX, 152 om; Cole and Meeham, X, 582 om; Collins, 581 om; Cotter, VI, 185; Cratz, X, 178 om; Crook, om, VII, 132, 267; Curley, X, 178 om; Cutler, VI, 185; Darcy, X, 178 om; Davis, Guy, VI, 185; Davis, Richard, volunteer fireman, X, 817 om; De Graff and others, VI, 306; Devlin, X, 582 om; Dillon, 177 om; Dourigan, 176 om; Dubois, om, 63, 179; Enright, 178 om; Fitzgibbons, James, 177 om; Fitzgibbon, John, id.; Fitzpatrick, VI, 159; Flood, Charles, X, 176 om; Flood, Jeremiah, VI, 185; Frantz, 312; Fraser, 185; Galway, 573; Gavin, X, 60 om; Ginley, 63 om; Grattan and others, VI, 213; Gray, VII, 507 om; Green, VI, 185; Griffin, X, 177 om; Guiman, 176 om; Hall, heirs, VI, 589; Hamlin, VIII, 292 om; Harris, VI, 698; Hart, X, 581 om; Hatzel, VII, 616; Hegaman, X, 177 om; Heimath, 59 om; Hendricks, VI, 185; Howard, 503; Hubbard, 185; Humphrey, 215; Jackson, 185; Jacobs, X, 177 om; Jewish Theological Seminary Association, IX, 628 om; Kehr, Kellner and Ott, VII, 601; Kenehan, X, 581 om; Kennedy, 177 om; Krenkel, om, VIII, 291, 1036; Linehan, X, 581 om; Loutrel, VI, 573; Loveland, 185; Lynch, X, 177 om; McCann, om, 176, 179; McCarthy, 176 om; McDowell, 581; McGrath, 177 om; McGraw, 179 om; McGuire, VI, 185; McVeany, VII, 507 om; Meagher, Mitchell, X, 178 om; Monaghan, VIII, 636; Morton, VII, 508 om; Munson, X, 178 om; Murphy, Matthew T., 177 om; Murphy, Thomas F, 581 om; Newsam, Newschaffer, 177 om; New York Tunnel Company, VI, 343, 507; O'Connor, X, 175 om; Palladino, om, 324, 581; Palmer, 582 om; Parks, IX, 721 om; Peck, III, 36; Pinkley, X, 581 om; Piser, VII, 509 om, 1089; Quinn, X, 178 om; Quirk and others, VI, 595; Ramsey, 692; Reynolds, 185; Robinson, 334; Ryan, X, 582 om; Sackett and Gage, VI, 344; St. John and others, 591; Schaub, 334, 591; Scholes, X, 178 om; Seymore, VI, 673; Seymour, 185; Shenandoah, 184; Smith, Charles, 185, X, 176 om; Smith, Charles C., VI, 185; Snook, 183; Stemmler, VII, 508 om, 661; Storen, VI, 185; Strauss, Striebel, X, 178 om; Syracuse, VI, 185; Taylor, Richard E., and William A., X, 581 om; Thirty-fourth street ferry and Eleventh Avenue Railroad, VIII, 1119; Thompson, X, 176 om; Townsend, VI, 438; Turner and Mac-Donald, X, 581 om; Underwood, III, 15; Vandervoort, IX, 451, 727 om; Van de Water, VII, 507 om; Van Slyck, VI, 697; Vogel, VIII, 638 om; Waller, VII, 267 om; Walsh, X, 582 om; Wasserman, 175 om; Weyburn, heirs, III, 37; Wheeler, Dunn and Flannagan, X, 178 om; White, VI, 185; Wilkinson, Schuh and Cox, VIII, 630; Williams, VI, 185; Williamson, X, 316 om; Wilson, Thomas P., 177 om; Wilson, William, VI, 698; Wilson, William H., VII, 803 om; Wright, Luther, VI, 185; Wright and Hubbard, 343; Wynn, William S. and James C., IX, 809 om; Yard, VII, 1089.

RELIGIOUS CAMP MEETINGS. Preventing disturbance of, IX, 811 om, X, 170.

RELIGIOUS CORPORATIONS. Amending general act, VII, 132 om; African Methodist Episcopal Church, special provisions, VIII, 1095; appointment of constables, VII, 508 om; burial plots, taking in trust, 935 om; changing names, om, 133, X, 700; extinct churches, VII, 265 om; grounds, buildings and property, powers of trustees, VII, 931 om; Methodist Episcopal church, transfers and conveyances, X, 704 om; supplemental act, VI, 583, 684.

RELIGIOUS AND CHARITABLE CORPORATIONS. Devises to, limiting amount of, VII, 266 om.

RELIGIOUS MEETINGS. Disturbance of, VII, 1043.

RELIGIOUS TOLERATION. Freedom of worship, institutions for care of poor, VII, 596.

RENSSELAER. Police, members and compensation, X, 715 om.

RENSSELAER COUNTY. Contracting board, bill to create, X, 63 om; House of Industry, Board of Governors, VI, 1032; publication of session laws, VII, 267 om.

REPLEVIN. Possession of property on giving security, X, 590 om.

RESTLESS, THE. United States steamship, repairing and equipping, X, 299.

REVISED STATUTES. Amending (3 bills), VII, 805 om; Birdseye's edition, purchase and distribution, X, 430; ninth edition, appropriation, for distribution, IX, 767.

RICHFORD. Public square, VII, 807 om.

RICHMOND BOROUGH. High school, changing site, erecting buildings, X, 447 om.

RICHMOND COUNTY. Assessors, establishing board, VII, 1114; changing site of court house and clerk's office, 250; construction of certain avenues, VI, 196; courts, where to be held, IX, 868 om; judicial sales of land, VII, 933 om; laying out Central park, VI, 191; police department, reorganization, IX, 490; police force, VI, 511, VII, 130 om; recording notices of pendency and discharges of mortgages, VI, 323, 331; survey, water supply, 503.

RIFLE RANGE. Bath-on-the-Hudson, additional land, IX, 244; Creedmoor, —additional land, X, 319 om; — repairs, IX, 76.

RIVER IMPROVEMENT COMMISSION. Appropriation, X, 793; assessments on property benefited, 955 om.

ROCHESTER. Amending charter, VI, 587, VII, 134, VIII, 468 om; X, 583 om, 635 om, 705 om; boundaries, VII, 267 om; bridge tenders, 1024; Brighton, enrollments, etc., X, 806 om; city hall, remodeling, IX, 731 om; free academy, bonds, redemption of, IX, 731 om; indorsements of ballots, shade trees, repeal, 723 om; market, III, 531; parks, om, IX, 724, 727; park boulevards, 731 om; police, vacations,

ROCHESTER — (*Continued*).

120; police department, reorganization, X, 469; salaries for members of board of education, VIII, 882; State property, assessment, appropriation, X, 321 om, 640; streets, restricting right to lay out, repeal, IX, 217; waterworks bonds, 731 om.

ROCHESTER STATE HOSPITAL. Local assessment, X, 697.

ROCKTON. Amending village charter, VII, 120, 330.

ROME. Amending charter, VII, 265 om; borrowing money for school buildings, VIII, 874; board of education, 130 om; city officers, powers and duties, X, 472 om; defining boundary, VIII, 408; fire commissioners, extending jurisdiction over police department, 390; increasing salaries, VI, 503; sewer system, refunding assessments, IX, 788 om.

ROME STATE CUSTODIAL ASYLUM. Approach to stable, X, 295; cottage for employees, 548, 656; cylinder locks for buildings B and E, 295; floors in electric light building, 549; grading, 295, 549; graveling ice pond, 549; increasing stable facilities, 656; vegetable store-house, 295.

ROWLEY, FRANCIS E. Suit against, counsel fees, appropriation, VII, 905.

RUTHERFORD, ALLEN. Supplies for Ninth Regiment, appropriation, VII, 500.

SAG HARBOR. Fire apparatus and water supply, VII, 68.

ST. LAWRENCE RESERVATION. Repairing docks, pavilions, etc., X, 934.

ST. LAWRENCE STATE HOSPITAL. Bridge over Tibbitt's brook ravine, X, 432; building for employees, roads and grading, IX, 294.

ST. REGIS INDIANS. Amending Indian Law, IX, 801 om; Franklin county, removing intruders, VIII, 115; regulating occupation of land, 1120; relief, VII, 414 om.

ST. REGIS RIVER. Improvement of West and East branches, VI, 579; preventing obstruction of, VIII, 619; West branch improvement, 423; West branch and Stony Brook, improvement, 115.

SALAMANCA. Village charter, VI, 704.

SALARIES. Loans on, X, 700 om.

SALEM. Electric light plant, IX, 819 om.

SALINA. Salt act, amending, III, 147.

SALMON RIVER. Protection of banks, VIII, 380.

SALT. Reducing duty on, VII, 930 om.

SALT SPRINGS. Amending act, VIII, 886 om; current expenses, VI, 1002; donation to Onondaga Historical Association, VII, 932 om; experimental well, 787, 907; lots, Onondaga, 385, renewing leases, IX, 274; sale of lots, purchase of other lands, VII, 393; sale and exchange of lots, VI, 822, VII, 935; repairs and improvements, VI, 866.

SANDY HILL. Regulating speed of railroad trains, VII, 936 om; trustees, borrowing money, legalizing proceedings, X, 960 om.

SARANAC LAKE. Village charter, IX, 258.

SARANAC LAKE AND OSEETAH LAKE. Cleaning and removing timber from, X, 792.

SARANAC RIVER. Cleaning between Lake Flower and State dam, X, 570; dredging, 427; improvement, IX, 62; protection of, 816 om; removing obstructions, VII, 382.

SARATOGA COUNTY. Clerk hire, authorizing oyer and terminer to direct payment of, VII, 207.

SARATOGA SPRINGS. Board of Health, VII, 1098; cemeteries, confirming purchase of land for, 391; clerk of fire commissioners, Congress street, VIII, 292 om; fire department,— VII, 413 om; — hose, 1102; floating debt, 130 om; hack stands, 1112; police department, VIII, 292 om; receiver of taxes, surety, X, 591 om; sewage,— VII, 1102; — disposal of, IX, 819 om; sewers—in Church street, VIII, 331; sewer, water and street commissioners, X, 811 om; street improvements, om, VII, 930, VIII, 873.

SAUGERTIES. Certain town officers, compensation, VII, 130 om; harbor and creek, improving navigation, VIII, 249, 293 om; town clerk and highway commissioner, salaries, X, 810 om.

SAVANNAH. Engine house and fire department, VIII, 410.

SAVINGS BANKS. Deposits, publishing statements of, IX, 425; enlarging scope of investments, VII, 893; insolvent, reducing deposits, 934 om; investments, X, 710 om.

SAVINGS BANKS, TRUST, LOAN AND INSURANCE COMPANIES. Insolvent, settlement of affairs, VII, 797.

SCHENECTADY. Additional policemen, Union College, VI, 1032; assessments, X, 262; diverting fourth of July appropriation to San Francisco relief, 908; lease of armory to Union University, VI, 709; Mill creek, filling up, damages, om, VII, 804, 937; pest house, X, 806 om; police, relative to, VI, 698; sewers, VII, 806 om; sewer bonds, IX, 789 om; street on canal land, om, 788, 789.

SCHIFF, B. BENJAMIN. Regent's certificate, clerk of Court of Appeals to file nunc pro tunc, X, 174.

SCHOHARIE CREEK. Improvements at Fort Hunter, VIII, 886 om.

SCHOOL COMMISSIONER DISTRICTS. Amending act, om, VIII, 470, IX, 625; Cattaraugus county, increasing number, VIII, 713; formation in certain counties, IX, 365; Yonkers, creating, VI, 708.

SCHOOL COMMISSIONERS. Increasing number, VIII, 639 om.

SCHOOL DISTRICTS. Alteration, IX, 800 om; boards of education, election in certain districts, X, 439 om; bonded indebtedness, alteration in case of, 812 om; election of officers, VII, 664 om; Benton No.

SCHOOL DISTRICTS — (*Continued*).

11, tax for new schoolhouse, VI, 337; Castleton, No. 4, borrowing money, 262; Half Moon and Stillwater, No. 10, regulating elections, IX, 817 om; Huntington, No. 4, sale of schoolhouse, VI, 506; Lyons, No. 6, additional accommodations, VIII, 702; Mentz,— consolidating districts, amending act of 1857, IX, 252; — relative to, VII, 938 om; North Hempstead, refunding bonds, X, 961 om; Mount Morris, consolidating, IX, 73, 817; Owego, consolidating, VII, 935 om; Oyster Bay, No. 5 new schoolhouse, VIII, 977; Smithtown, No. 5, relief, X, 449 om; White Plains, consolidation, VI, 183.

SCHOOLS. Military instruction in, IX, 628 om; public, preventing nuisances near, VI, 95.

SCHUYLER COUNTY. Borrowing money, county buildings, VII, 859; special tax for benefit of State, IX, 796 om.

SCHUYLERVILLE. Battlefield monument, VIII, 253.

SEA BATHING PLACES. Protection of persons and property, VII, 130 om.

SEA CLIFF. Village charter, VII, 936 om.

SEAMEN'S RETREAT HOSPITAL. General improvements, appropriation, VII, 490; cemetery repairs, line fence around hospital property, reimbursing hospital fund for miscellaneous expenses, repairs to building, sewer repairs, steam heating apparatus, 585.

SEARCH WARRANTS. Relative to, VII, 1092.

SECOND CLASS CITIES. Amending general act, X, 164 (2 bills), 447 om, 448 om, 450 om; clerk, chief of police, 444 om; official newspapers, designation, 589 om; police courts, 586 om; police justice, jurisdiction, 593 om.

SECRETARY OF STATE. Allowance for expenses, X, 637; carpets and office furniture, VII, 463; disposing of certain papers, IX, 811 om; expense of preparing for census, 1885, VIII, 111; first deputy, allowance for expenses, X, 639; gallery and book cases in corporation department, 557, 639; labor statistics, collection of, VII, 409; office expenses, temporary services, reappropriation, X, 557.

SENATE. Cartage of documents, VIII, 106, 851; clerk,— additional clerical service, VII, 462; — services to Committee on General Laws, VIII, 860; Committee on Cities,— investigation, Jack, janitor's compensation; — Kane, attendant, compensation, 1140; — sergeant-at-arms, compensation, 1141; — Tate, accountant, compensation, 1140; — Thornton, stenographer, compensation, 1141, X, 570, 647; Committee on General Laws, investigation of trusts, appropriation for attorney, VIII, 843; Committee on Public Health, counsel fees, appropriation, 841; Committee on Taxation and Retrenchment, counsel, appropriation, 439, 548, 842; electrical investigation, printing testi-

SENATE — (*Continued*).

mony, 1033 om; gas investigating committee, printing testimony,
119, 251; health office investigating committee, clerk, compensation,
VII, 783; index to record,— Ellis trial, 226, 461;— Smyth trial,
226, 461; indexing legislative documents, appropriation, VIII, 860;
insurance investigating committee, clerk, compensation, VII, 783; investigating committee, New York police department, expenses, IX,
484; library,— furnishing various books for, VIII, 859;— removing
and rearranging books, stairs and bookcases, 422; messenger to
Finance Committee, compensation, VII, 782; New York investigating
committee, expenses, 462; superintendent of wrapping department,
compensation, VIII, 859.

SENECA COUNTY. Draining Gorman swamp, X, 698, 797; id., cleaning
Black brook, 651.

SENECA FALLS. Board of education, appointment of assessors, VII, 60;
bonds for bridge and cemetery addition, X, 278; revising charter,
VII, 935 om; school of anatomy, dissections, IX, 264.

SENECA INDIANS. Amending act, VI, 910 om; leases, ratification, 336;
oil pipe line, Allegany reservation, VII, 73.

SENECA LAKE. Breakwater repairs, X, 798.

SHARPE, MARILA I. Widow of Rev. Ichabod B. Sharpe, damages for
husband's death, VII, 88; extending time to file canal claim, 773.

SHEEP. Killed by dogs, amending Revised Statutes, VIII, 469 om.

SHERIDAN, THOMAS J. Contested election, Assembly, Kings county, expenses, VII, 918.

SHERIFF. Increasing fees, V, 875; office hours, om, IX, 801, 863.

Albany,— fees and compensation, VII, 1121.

Cattaraugus,— boarding United States prisoners, X, 706 om.

Dutchess,— legalizing audit of account, X, 956 om.

Erie,— relative to, X, 61 om; additional subordinates, purchase of
supplies, 380; compensation of deputies, 318 om.

Essex,— Chinese prisoners, om, X, 701, 708; making office salaried
in part, 316 om.

Kings,— additional subordinates, X, 770; assistant deputies, om 710,
711; salaried office, 179 om.

Livingston,— compensation, under-sheriff, jailer and attendants, X,
811 om.

Nassau,— reimbursement for services and expenses after expiration
of term, X, 242.

New York,— amending title to act, also amending act, X, 960 om;
amending act, om 581, 706; allowance for expenses after expiration of term, om 321, 594, 716; salaries, om 711, 772, 948;
Tamsen, investigation, expenses, IX, 777 om.

Sheriff — (*Continued*).

Rensselaer,— fixing compensation, VII, 1115.

Richmond,— deputy attending court, compensation, X, 961 om.

Shinnecock Bay. Dredging channel connecting with Moriches bay, X, 645.

Shore Inspectors. Increasing number, VII, 1124.

Sidewalks. Rochester, exemption from damages for injuries from defective, VIII, 629; Unadilla, VI, 195; Waterford, injuries from defects, notice, IX, 54.

Sidney Plains. Village, separate road district, VI, 684.

Silver Creek. Straightening Walnut creek, VIII, 129 om.

Simon, Charles. Assembly, contested election, appropriation, VI, 866.

Sing Sing Prison. Bloomer claim, marble quarry, VI, 589; Brandow, keeper, appropriation for injury, VII, 464; drains and sewers, completion of, 483; female prison, new roof, id.; flagging and grading walks, id.; gates in fence on river front, id.; general repairs and supplies, id.; guardhouse, altering and repairing, id.;—rebuilding, id.; icehouse, id.; iron fence, survey and plans, id.; iron gate near main building, id.; iron gate and fence, south wall entrance, id.; library, id.; prison hall, key room, gun racks, id.; repairing roofs, id.; sidewalks and gutters in front of, 920; stable, relaying floors and building stalls, 483; two new guardhouses, id.; wall, building and repairing, id.; waterworks, completion, id.

Skaneateles. Amending charter, VII, 1008; engine house, 97; revising charter, 933 om.

Slot Machines. Trials for keeping, X, 162.

Slung Shot. Preventing use of, VI, 507.

Social Clubs. Amending act, VI, 501, VIII, 809 om; trustees, changing number, VII, 1112.

Societies and Clubs. Amending act, VII, 664 om, VIII, 625, 890 om; maximum amount of property, 1119.

Society for the Reformation of Juvenile Delinquents, New York. See also New York House of Refuge. Relative to, IV, 518; relief fund, V, 219.

Society for the Reformation of Juvenile Delinquents, Randall's Island. Repairing wall, restocking greenhouse, X, 298; cottage for florist and gardener, 545; window sash and casings, id.

Soldier's Monument. St. Lawrence county, VI, 162; corporations, relative to, X, 810 om; authorizing incorporation of associations for erection of, 63 om; Sweden, 703 om.

Soldiers. Relief, G. A. R., X, 809 om; relief from Union Veteran Legion, IX, 803 om.

SOLDIERS' HOME. Lands of, taking for railroad purposes, VII, 808 om.

SOLDIERS AND SAILORS. Absent voters, V, 513; honorably discharged, certificates of, VII, 1110; relief, amending act, VIII, 626, 872; relief, amending Poor Law, om, X, 808, 947.

SOLDIERS AND SAILORS' HOME, BATH. Bakery building, X, 546; cement walks, 293; chapel, VII, 478; engineer's department, repairs and improvements, X, 546; hospital, VII, 478; house of detention and lock-up, X, 546; improvements, VII, 478; officers, local rank of, IX, 815 om.

SONS OF VETERANS. Issuing arms to, X, 61 om; parading with firearms, IX, 398.

SPAULDING, W. M. Counsel, Assembly Committee on Privileges and Elections, 1903, appropriation, X, 571.

SPRINGFIELD CENTER. Separate road district, VIII, 1039 om.

S. R. SMITH INFIRMARY. Exempting property from taxation, VIII, 538.

STAGE AND OMNIBUS COMPANIES. Incorporating, VII, 807 om.

STANCHFIELD, JOHN B. Counsel for Assemblyman Vacheron, appropriation, IX, 775.

STATE. Claims against, relative to, VII, 805 om; public records, preservation, 666.

STATE AGENT FOR DISCHARGED CONVICTS. Amending act, VII, 264 om; bill to abolish office, VIII, 870.

STATE ARCHITECT. Consulting experts, reappropriation, X, 561; engineers and stenographer, 552; office expenses, deficiency appropriation, 561; office expenses, 552; office salaries, reappropriation, 424; stenographers, deficiency appropriation, 561.

STATE ASSESSORS. Powers of, VII, 133 om.

STATE ASYLUM FOR INSANE CRIMINALS, MATTEAWAN. Acquiring land for sewer, IX, 74; supplies and improvements, 77.

STATE BOARD OF AUDIT. Defining powers of, VII, 509 om; appeals from, 412 om; Lawlor and quarantine improvement claims, 938 om; Rider claim, 936 om.

STATE BOARD OF CHARITIES. Current expenses, deficiency appropriation, VII, 471; State paupers, deficiency appropriation, id.

STATE BOARD OF EMBALMERS. Authorizing receipt of application of Burke for license, X, 818 om.

STATE BOARD OF HEALTH. Adulteration of food and drugs, VII, 924; deficiency appropriation, VIII, 856; office supplies, 112; printing mortality bulletins, 111; rules and regulations, IX, 367; sanitary inspectors, deficiency appropriation, VIII, 111; sanitary work, 254.

STATE BOARD OF MEDICAL EXAMINERS. Deficiency appropriation, IX, 76.

STATE BOARD OF PHARMACY. Amending act, VIII, 622.

STATE BOARD OF UNDERTAKERS. Establishing, IX, 265.

STATE BOTANIST. Charles H. Peck, expenses, VII, 582, 779.

STATE CAMP GROUND, PEEKSKILL. Lighting, VIII, 855; military road to Highland station, IX, 290; road to, repairs, VIII, 1136.

STATE CHARITIES LAW. Transfer to penitentiaries and reformatories, X, 312 om.

STATE COLLEGE OF AGRICULTURE. Free winter courses for farmers' sons and daughters, X, 935.

STATE COLLEGE OF FORESTRY. Appropriation, X, 555.

STATE COMMISSION IN LUNACY. Office expenses, reappropriation, X, 565.

STATE COMMISSIONER OF EXCISE. Secretary, allowance for expenses, X, 424.

STATE CONTRACTS. Public notice of, VIII, 1040 om.

STATE DAIRYMEN'S ASSOCIATION. Extending dairy knowledge, appropriation, VII, 907, VIII, 246; report and expenses of annual meeting, appropriation, IX, 772.

STATE DAIRY COMMISSIONER. Attorney for, Senate investigation, appropriation, VIII, 840.

STATE DAM. Black river, waste gates, IX, 244; Erie county, drainage of land overflowed by, X, 790; Genesee river, Mount Morris, VII, 908; Grasse river, repairs, X, 739; Mamakating, cleaning, 791; Port Byron, enlargement, VIII, 452.

STATE DEPARTMENT OF HEALTH. Epidemic and contagious officers, appropriation, X, 787; special equipment, expenses, id.

STATE ENGINEER AND SURVEYOR. Balconies in office, X, 560; clerk, preparing railroad report, VII, 922; carpet, oil cloth and letterhead die, 463; chief bridge designer and assistants, compensation, X, 560; dredging channel between Great South bay and Shinnecock bay, 786; engineers,— compensation, 550; salaries and expenses, 637 om; furniture and repairs for, 299; monuments on State boundaries, 559, 786; new blue line maps, Erie, Champlain and Oswego canals, 297, 423; Phœnix dam investigation, Breed claim, 786; surveys for Forest Commission, forest preserve, 560; survey of canal from Hempstead bay to Jamaica bay, 649; United States geological survey, — appropriation, 785; — hydrographic work, water supply, id.

STATE ENTOMOLOGIST. Office expenses, VII, 778, 906.

STATE EXPERIMENT STATION. Buildings for chief chemist and others, IX, 291; building on State fair grounds, id.

STATE FAIR. Changing railroad tracks, X, 544; Elmira, reconstruction of buildings, VII, 90; poultry building, repairs, X, 544.

STATE FINANCE LAW. Receipts and expenditures, X, 812 om.

STATE FLAG. Amending act relative to, IX, 622 om.

STATE GEOLOGIST. Printing and distributing paleontology, volume 8, part 2, IX, 402.

STATE HISTORIAN. Translation of ecclesiastical documents, X, 298, 563.

STATE HOSPITALS. Autopsies, IX, 534 om; employees, additional compensation, X, 650; general maintenance, 425; — deficiency appropriation, 642; inmates, letters by or to, regulations concerning, IX, 118; officers and employees, salaries, X, 954 om; treasurers, clerical assistants, appropriation, 641.

STATE INDUSTRIAL SCHOOL. Establishing, VII, 631.

STATE INDUSTRIAL SCHOOL, ROCHESTER. Repairs and improvements, VIII, 853; appropriation, X, 319 om.

STATE INEBRIATE ASYLUM, BINGHAMTON. Finishing basement and first story, VII, 230.

STATE INSPECTOR OF GAS METERS. Office expenses and seals, X, 934.

STATE INSTITUTIONS. Printing reports, VIII, 129 om.

STATE LABORERS. Regulating payment of, VIII, 1041 om.

STATE LANDS. Deed, effect on rights of others, IX, 623 om; sale, V, 235; Franklin county, conveyance to Robert Schroeder, VIII, 131 om; trespasses, procedure, IX, 530; under water,— Tonawanda, conveyance to Nicholas Munch, 284; — Yonkers, conveyance of, VIII, 53.

STATE LIBRARY. Additional assistant librarian, VIII, 113; books, binding, etc., 862; Clinton papers, arrangement of, 247; frame for portrait of Abraham Lincoln, VII, 86; purchase of " Public Service of New York," 920; temporary services, appropriation, X, 551; transfer to new rooms, expenses, VIII, 861.

STATE MEDICAL LIBRARY. Books and binding, IX, 69, 84.

STATE MUSEUM OF NATURAL HISTORY. Expenses, X, 552; printing and binding, VII, 494; publication of palaeontology, VIII, 553; purchase of Hurst collection of zoological specimens, 108; labels, books and binding, appropriation, VII, 1082.

STATE OF NEW YORK, THE. Tug, new boiler, IX, 292.

STATE PRISONS. Amending acts, VI, 582, IX, 814 om, 816 om; accounts of purchases and sales, VI, 507; additional instruction, IX, 80; additional religious instruction for convicts, VII, 919; Bertillon method of identifying criminals, X, 707 om; clerk of prison, IX, 428; commutations, insane criminals, X, 309 om; convict labor investigating commission, extending time, VII, 1001; convicts, confinement of, Sing Sing, additional cells, 937 om; convict-made goods, labeling, repealing certain acts, IX, 813 om; — sales and license fees, id.; double chloride of gold treatment authorized, 622 om; electrocution apparatus, purchase of patent rights, X, 567; Gilson claim, VI, 703; investigating commission, IV, 777; labor in, manufacture of school furniture, X, 165; new, removal from Sing Sing, VI, 600; parole of prisoners, om, X, 585, 812; plant for publication of literature for blind, 293; reducing force, VI, 507; religious instruction, VII, 784; repealing part of act, VI, 334; superintendent,— Bruyn, assignee materials for Sing Sing prison, VII, 485; — counsel fees,

State Prisons — (*Continued*).

Auburn railroad investigation, id.; counsel fees, Dannemora railroad investigation, id.; — furniture, carpets and shelving, id.; — office rent, id.; — safe, id.; — Sing Sing dock, 785.

State Prisons and Penitentiaries. Relative to, VI, 899.

State Property. Appraisal and inventory, IX, 775.

State Road. Forestport to Woodhull, VIII, 850, 1138; Piercefield, repairs, X, 645.

State School Moneys. Monroe and Seneca counties, VII, 412 om.

State Survey. Appropriation, VII, 1077, IX, 423; boundary between Lewis and Herkimer counties, 856; commissioners, relative to, VII, 806 om; continuance, 372, VIII, 452; deficiency, VII, 464; expenses of completion, VIII, 423; oil and gas regions, IX, 774; publishing and distributing report, VIII, 551; topographic map, 73.

State Tax Commissioners. Expenses under mortgage tax law, X, 798; experts, 554.

State Treasurer. Additional clerks, VIII, 891 om; deposit of funds, IX, 57; office expenses, deficiency appropriation, VIII, 861; removing books and records to new capitol, 249.

Statuary. Marble group "Struggle for Liberty," proposed purchase of, IX, 812 om.

Statutes. Chronological table, VIII, 293 om; index, 1886–1897, IX, 774; publication of, X, 704 om; publication, designation of newspapers, IX, 813 om; publication in newspapers, VIII, 130 om; purchase and distribution of, IX, 776 om; repealing act, VII, 129 om.

Statutory Construction Law. Amendments, X, 319 om.

Staves and Heading. Cullers of, Rensselaer, III, 438.

Steamboats. Frauds on owners and managers, IX, 793 om; inspection in certain counties, VIII, 469 om; inspectors, traveling expenses, X, 465.

Steele's Creek. Cleaning channel, X, 301.

Stenographers. Amending Code, X, 587 om; amending Code of Criminal Procedure, VI, 209; Assembly Committee to prepare rules, appropriation, VIII, 844; Buffalo Superior Court, 291 om; compensation, 639 om; duties of, criminal cases, 890 om; eighth judicial district, additional, IX, 286; grand jury,— compensation, om, VIII, 468, IX, 725, 811; — Westchester county, X, 387; Kings county — coroners, VIII, 890 om; — court, X, 808 om; Lee, Assembly Committee, 1899, VIII, 839; Moynahan, New York, service in Supreme Court, criminal term, X, 950 om; New York City Court, 805 om; — additional, 816 om; Onondaga County Court, VI, 326; O'Sullivan, New York Municipal Court, compensation, X, 310 om; Richmond County Surrogate and County Court, 259; second judicial district,— deficiency appropriation, VII, 583; — Kings county, appointment

STENOGRAPHERS — (*Continued*).

and removal, 769; — excepting Kings county, deficiency appropriation, 780; Senate Committee on Privileges and Elections, appropriation, VIII, 547; Senate Committee on Taxation and Retrenchment, appropriation, Bloomingdale Asylum investigation, 844; Senate special railroad investigating committee, compensation, VII, 780; Senate and Assembly, preparing records for publication, VIII, 854; services, VII, 808 om; Supreme Court, third judicial district, salaries, VIII, 699; Supreme Court, trial terms, X, 699 om; Surrogates' Courts,— second and third districts, VI, 317; — New York, increasing salary, VIII, 82;— transcribing notes, IX, 115.

STEUBEN, FREDERICK WILLIAM. Baron, statue to, IX, 427.

STEUBEN COUNTY. Increasing school commissioner districts, VIII, 402; jury districts, courthouse in Hornellsville, 880.

STILLWATER. Amending charter, VIII, 889 om.

STOCK CORPORATIONS. Amending general act, om, IX, 625, 627; borrowing money and mortgaging property, X, 810 om; foreign, licensing, IX, 529; increasing or reducing capital stock, X, 446 om; issue of debenture bond stock, 321 om; issue and transfer of stock, 62 om; mortgages, consents of stockholders, 590 om; reduction of capital, id.

STOCKPORT. Legalizing settlement of Haynes claim, X, 814 om.

STOCK TRANSFER TAX. Amending act, X, 958 om.

STREET RAILROADS. Amending general act, X, 448 om; abandoning part of road, IX, 443; acquisition of property, X, 310 om; Brooklyn and Flatbush, VI, 597; cities, regulating hours of drivers and conductors on horse cars, VII, 1109; consents, VIII, 1037 om; consents and percentages, 887 om; fares,— in Brooklyn borough, X, 882; — Erie, Albany and Rensselaer counties, V, 656; — Queensborough, X, 882; — rates in villages and third class cities on certain grades, IX, 866 om; hours of labor,— relative to, 144; — in certain cities, 266; maintenance and operation in cities, towns and villages, VII, 793, 894; New York, Wall street ferry to North river, VI, 601; percentages payable by, VIII, 1037 om, 1124; Queens and Nassau counties, X, 316 om, 431;— exempting certain highways, 587 om; rate of fare, IX, 150 om; villages in Nassau county, X, 145.

SUFFRAGE, RIGHT OF. Crimes against, X, 162.

SUGAR. Bounty for, IX, 725 om.

SUGARS, SYRUPS, MOLASSES AND HONEY. Fraud in manufacture and sale of, VII, 648.

SULLIVAN, THOMAS. Claim for capture of Hardy, an escaped convict, X, 62 om.

SULLIVAN COUNTY. Poorhouse keepers, exempting from act, VII, 508 om; town officers, compensation, repealing act, 507 om, 540.

SUMMARY PROCEEDINGS. New York, service of precept, om, X, 714, 717, 805, 806; petition, 450 om; rents and taxes, VII, 1094; restitution, New York district courts, VIII, 469 om.

SUNDAY. Barbering on, amending act, IX, 804 om; sale and delivery of uncooked flesh food, X, 292; trades and mechanical employments on, IX, 623 om.

SUPERINTENDENT OF CANAL REPAIRS. Abolishing office, VI, 344.

SUPERINTENDENT OF THE POOR. Appeals, om, VIII, 130, 190; and county treasurers, election, 1038 om; Albany county, VI, 504; Clinton county, keeper of poorhouse, VIII, 537; Clute, Schenectady, legalizing election, VI, 424; Columbia county, relative to, VII, 508 om; Fulton county, election, 930 om; Lewis county, reducing to one, VIII, 461; Westchester county, VII, 508 om.

SUPERINTENDENT OF PUBLIC INSTRUCTION. Chief of statistical bureau, salary, deficiency appropriation, X, 561; clerk hire, deficiency, VIII, 866; contract with American Museum of Natural History, X, 638 om; establishing department for instruction of teachers in anatomy and kindred subjects, VII, 923; furniture, books and office expenses, deficiency, VIII, 866; inspector, traveling expenses, X, 637, om; inspector of various schools, compensation, X, 637 om; law books, VIII, 246; legal expenses in Waters case, X, 561; Manual of Patriotism, publication of, 297; six inspectors, compensation, 637.

SUPERINTENDENT OF PUBLIC WORKS. Relative to, VII, 49; authorizing return of certain certificates of deposit, 545; clerks, expenses of collectors and inspectors, X, 422.

SUPERINTENDENT OF WEIGHTS AND MEASURES. Salary, VII, 907.

SUPPLEMENTARY PROCEEDINGS. Amending Code, new section, IX, 792 om.

SUPERVISORS. Compensation, VII, 883; preservation of records, 268 om.
Albany county, terms and salary, VI, 165.
Chautauqua county, compensation in certain towns, VI, 588.
Denmark, conveyance of certain land, VII, 1105.
Erie county, relative to, VII, 266 om.
Monroe and Orleans counties, compensation, VIII, 129 om.
Monroe, Orleans and Broome counties, fixing compensation, VII, 1115.
Oneida, compensation, VI, 327.
Onondaga, salary, VII, 806 om.
Sangerfield, bond, refunding surety for payment on, VII, 753.

SUPREME COURT. Appellate Division justices designated to, expenses, IX, 628 om; Balcom, justice, payment of salary, VII, 931 om; clerk, Erie county, 356; commissioners, bill to establish, X, 662; constitutional amendment, increasing number of justices, submission, VIII, 1033; fifth judicial district, justices, clerks to, IX, 812 om; first judicial district, additional justices, X, 947 om; fourth judicial district, additional justice, id.; justices, appointment of trustees, 450 om;

SUPREME COURT — (*Continued*).

Kings county,— amending order transferring employees from Brooklyn City Court. to Supreme Court, IX, 795 om; messengers and attendants, VI, 512; reporter, furnishing papers to, IX, 791 om; second judicial department, 446; — expenses of justices outside Kings county, 815 om; — justices, additional compensation, VII, 780; sixth judicial district,— additional justices, X, 947 om; — justices' clerks, IX, 816 om; third judicial district,— additional justices, X, 947 om; —justices' salaries, VII, 257.

SURROGATES. Clerks, compensation, VII, 649; Niagara, compensation, VIII, 1038 om; Oneida, new seal, 1096; Queens, salary, X, 711 om; Rensselaer, increasing compensation, IX, 108.

SURROGATE AND COUNTY JUDGE. Albany, fixing salary, IX, 624 om; Clinton, relative to, VII, 614; Monroe, increasing salary, 414 om; Queens, compensation, om, IX, 800, X, 584; Rensselaer, increasing compensation, IX, 107; Seneca, compensation, VII, 549; Suffolk, salary, IX, 369; Washington, special, IV, 776, VII, 551.

SURROGATE'S COURT. Additional allowance on settlement of accounts, X, 254; appearance in proceedings, 253; costs, VI, 340, IX, 625 om; costs and allowances, X, 955 om; final accountings, VII, 414 om; proceedings in, 79; Erie, relative to, 113; New York,— preservation of records, X, 536 om; — referees, law assistants, 712 om.

SUSQUEHANNA RIVER DAM. Relative to, V, 652.

SYRACUSE. Amending charter, om, VII, 267, IX, 628, 631, 633, 727, 789, 790 (4 bills); assessments on State property, VII, 86, 228; — paving Salina street, 472, 585, 928; — sewer, Leavenworth avenue and Clark street, 472; assessments for local improvements, X, 815 om; department of assessment and taxation, supplemental act, id.; electric light plant, establishing, om, 327, 474; exempting bonds from taxation, IX, 450; culvert under Harbor brook, 731 om; fire department, VII, 1098, IX, 789 om; — support of, 790 om; high school, new site and building, 731 om; legalizing local assessments, om, X, 634, 705; light and heat supply, investigation of sources, 59 om; Municipal Court, practice and fees of jurors, 441 om; officers, relative to, IX, 790 om; Onondaga creek and Harbor brook, 734 om; penitentiary, maintenance of convicts, VI, 587; police justices, warrants, bonds and fines, IX, 790 om; police and fire commissioners, VII, 317; repealing certain acts, X, 960 om; subways, municipal ownership, IX, 789 om.

SYRACUSE INSTITUTION FOR FEEBLE-MINDED CHILDREN. Electric light plant, VIII, 1138; laundry machinery, X, 294; sidewalks, id.

TARRYTOWN AND NORTH TARRYTOWN. Construction of sewers, VIII, 462.

TAX. State, equalizing among counties, VI, 332.

Taxation. Amending general law, IX, 803 om; assessments — amending Revised Statutes, VIII, 1038 om; — regulating and equalizing, VII, 1109; — when to be made in certain towns, X, 590 om; clergymen, exemptions, IX, 722 om; colleges and universities, exemptions, X, 947 om; Erie county, equalizing real estate, VIII, 752; exempt property assessments for local improvements, X, 595 om; illegal assessments, review of, costs, VIII, 466; pension money, property purchased with, exemption, repeal, IX, 113; personal property of nonresidents, X, 876; property liable to, VIII, 890 om; Queens borough, X, 177 om; Queens and Nassau counties, id.; real property,— divided by tax district line, IX, 803 om; — report on exemptions, X, 439 om; relief in certain counties, extending act, VI, 278; savings banks, X, 451 om; State lands in Dannemora and Altona, 953 om.

Taxes. Assessments,— collection, VII, 110; — reassessments for illegal, IX, 724 om; — review, railroad and telegraph companies, 132; Binghamton, extending time for collection, VII, 412 om; cancellation,— Cozine case, X, 263; — Doherty, 592 om; — Dreyer, 953 om; — Jones, 960 om; — Leech and Lord, 317 om; — Mittnacht, comptroller to hear, IX, 815 om; — Moriarity, X, 590 om; — Osgood, 701 om; — Ostrander, om. 446, 588; — Walker, 589 om; — Warren, 448 om; — Wheeler, 447 om; Chautauqua and Cattaraugus counties, collection, VIII, 967; cities, receivers of, proceedings by, X, 272; Clinton county, collection, IX, 282; Cohoes,— legalizing, VII, 133 om; — arrears, collection, X, 436; collection, IX, 722 om; collector's notice to nonresidents, X, 386; collectors, receipts by, VIII, 1040 om; collectors and receivers, VII, 62; corporations, State fees, X, 433; delinquent, statements by county treasurers, VIII, 749; Elmwood, enforcement of, IX, 723 om; equalizing assessments, VII, 666 om; equalization of, IX, 627 om; Essex county, assessment, VI, 188; extending time for collection, 1859, V, 116; — 1860, 215; First National Bank, Ballston Spa., refund, X, 452; foreign capital, VII, 445; Gilmour, application for cancellation, Flatbush, comptroller to hear, IX, 810 om; Hamilton county, redemption, Robinson, X, 953 om; Herkimer and Lewis counties, rejected, reassessment, VII, 664 om; Hornellsville, extending time for collection, 878; Hudson, extending time for collection, 199; Jefferson county,— collection of, VIII, 706, 1039 om; — enforcement of, VII, 805 om; land sold for, conveying State's interest, 656; Monroe county,— collection, IX, 148 om; — collection by treasurer, VI, 1035 om; Morehouse relief, X, 274; Morrisania and West Farms, collection, VI, 589; New York,— levy and collection, X, 472 om; — McCaddin property, settlement of, IX, 238; — 12th ward, discharge of, VIII, 638 om; — Westchester annexed district, cancellation, IX, 870 om; nonresidents, sales for nonpayment, 282; Oneida county,— collection, X, 447 om; — redemption, VIII, 1126;

TAXES — (*Continued*).

property, assessments where made, IX, 626 om.; Queens borough, equalizing, X, 322 om; Queens county,—arrearages, settlement, IX, 796 om;—sales, 862 om; redemption from sale of 1877, VII, 414 om; revision commission, 407; Richmond county,—collection, IX, 399; — extending time for collection, VII, 866; Rockland county, collection, VIII, 878, IX, 282; Rockland and Delaware counties, sales for non-payment, VI, 1035 om; Rye, receiver, bond and deputy, X, 442 om; sales, amending general act, IX, 865 om; school districts, railroad, telephone, telegraph and pipe line companies, apportionment, X, 439 om; statement and payment of, 445 om; Suffolk county,—collection, VIII, 807 om;—collectors' notices, om, X, 310, 441; supplementary proceedings for collection of, 592 om; unpaid,—in certain counties, sales for non-payment, IX, 804; — Binghamton, sale for, VIII, 392; — Clinton county, sales, om, X, 440, 595; — Erie county, VII, 937 om; — Madison county, sale for, VIII, 411; — Monroe county, sales for, VII, 208; — Mount Vernon, bonds for, IX, 450; — New York, unpaid, Long Island City, Jamaica, Flushing and Hempstead, X, 62 om; Newtown, Flushing, Jamaica and Hempstead, 322 om; Oswego county, sales for, assignments of land, IX, 796 om; — Queens county, county treasurer's list and notice of sale, id.; Richmond borough, sale, X, 806 om; Steuben county, sales for, VII, 506 om; Utica, legalizing, om, X, 806, 819; Wayne county, collection of, VIII, 754; Wostergron Company, reimbursement, X, 784; York, confirming and levying assessments, IX, 59.

TAX LAW. Notice of assessment and grievance day, X, 809 om.

TAXPAYER. Action against public officers, IX, 364; protection of, VI, 429.

TEACHERS. Common school, instruction of, VI, 1035 om; instruction of, VII, 495; licenses, VIII, 448; professional training, promotion of, 1037 om, IX, 482 om; State certificates, examinations, deficiency, VIII, 865; uniform examinations, deficiency, id.; wages, payment of, 240.

TEACHERS' INSTITUTES. Deficiency appropriation, VIII, 1141; time spent at, 291 om.

TELEGRAPH COMPANIES. Relative to, VII, 507 om.

TELEGRAPH, TELEPHONE AND ELECTRIC LIGHT LINES. Assessments, VII, 934 om.

TENEMENT HOUSES. License to manufacture in, X, 37.

THEATRES. Tickets, regulating sale, X, 51.

THOMAS ASYLUM FOR ORPHAN AND DESTITUTE INDIAN CHILDREN. Boiler house and heating apparatus, VIII, 853; changing nursery to laundry, X, 295; electric lighting, id.; equipments and betterments, id.; laundry

XI—11

THOMAS ASYLUM FOR ORPHAN, ETC.— (*Continued*).
and apparatus, 544; new boilers, etc., 295; Dr. W. C. Phelps' claim
for surgical services, 798; power house and electric light plant, 544;
power house, chimney stack and connecting subways, 295; repairs
and improvements, VII, 489; tanks and fittings, X, 295.

TIDAL STREAMS. Bridges and highways over, VII, 640 om.

TOBACCO. Leaf, regulating sale in New York, VI, 480.

TOLL ROADS AND BRIDGES. Abolition of, X, 813 om.

TONAWANDA. Amending charter, VII, 805 om; taxes, collection, IX, 718
om; Delaware road, refunding indebtedness for, X, 63 om; sewers,
VIII, 876.

TONAWANDA CREEK. Breakwater at Wendellville, VIII, 888 om.

TONAWANDA INDIANS. Manual labor school, VII, 477.

TONAWANDA INDIAN RESERVATION. Manual labor school, VII, 132 om;
repair of highways, X, 429.

TOWN AUDITORS. Amending act, VIII, 872, 1039 om; exempting Chemung and Greene counties, VII, 554; exempting Coeymans, 622;
Hornellsville, creating board, VIII, 48; Lenox, VI, 435; Moravia,
relative to, VII, 413 om; raising money for roads and bridges, VI,
329; Wappinger, VIII, 616; Westchester county,—relative to, VII,
807 om; — repealing act, 806 om.

TOWN HALL AND TOWN HOUSE. Providing for,—Fort Covington, VI,
910; Harrietstown, VIII, 508; Hopkinton, tax for, VI, 309; Long
lake, VIII, 1041 om; Mexico, rebuilding, VII, 71; Parishville, relative to, VIII, 516.

TOWN INSURANCE COMPANIES. Amending act, VI, 153, 509, VIII, 131 om;
amending repealed act, VII, 1097; formation of, 130 om; general act,
249, 387; Parma, relative to, VI, 592.

TOWN MEETINGS. Amending general law, X, 62 om; Albany and Onondaga counties, fixing time, IX, 718 om; Barre, by election districts,
VI, 674, 690; Bath, time and place of holding, IX, 117; continuance
and adjournment of, repeal, 392; Goshen, biennial on general election day, 816 om; Hancock, voting in three places, 817 om; Hector,
fixing time of, VII, 842; Hurley, by election districts, VI, 674, 690;
Montgomery county, X, 449 om; Mount Pleasant, by election districts,
VI, 674, 707; North Collins, election districts, VIII, 886 om; Ontario,
legalizing proceedings, VI, 1031; Oswegatchie, legalizing. proceedings,
VIII, 885 om; Oyster Bay, legalizing elections, IX, 818 om; Pelham,
restricting powers, VIII, 721; Phelps, legalizing, 887 om; Putnam
county, IX, 862 om; Shawangunk, legalizing resolution fixing place,
VI, 581; special, Hempstead, 97; tax propositions, VII, 1106; tax
propositions, voting by ballot, VIII, 470 om; time of transacting
business, VII, 387; voting by ballot on money proposition, 807 om.

TOWNS. Amending general law, IX, 804 om; balloting outside incorporated villages, 439; clerk and collector, official term, 149 om; division ditches, 286, 522; division fences,— relative to, X, 440 om; — compelling erection of, IX, 401; excise moneys in, VIII, 469 om; G. A. R., renting rooms for, X, 535; highway commissioners,— compensation, IX, 462; — number of, VIII, 461; liability for damages, defective highways, VII, 767; lighting districts, IX, 814 om; Memorial Day, money for observance of, 813 om; officers, compensation, om, 147, 309; officers,— Nassau county, compensation, X, 533; — reducing number, VIII, 887 om; reducing expenses, VI, 329.

TRADE MARKS. Relative to, VIII, 632.

TRAMPS. Punishment, om, VII, 413, IX, 867; vagrants, Columbia county, regulating commitment and discharge, VIII, 891 om.

TRANSFER TAX. Amending general act, X, 586 om; appraisers, increasing compensation, IX, 447; appraisers and stenographers, X, 586 om; appraisers and surrogate's assistants, 770; experts, appointment, 550; graduated, IX, 762; Kings county, appointment of special officer, 275; New York, salaries, 273; release of tax on Cullum legacy to United States, 349; surrogate's transfer tax clerk, fees, 273.

TRAVELERS. Protection, powers of conductors, VII, 414 om.

TREES. Fruit,— preventing disease, X, 809 om; — to prevent poisoning while in blossom, IX, 811 om; shade, encouraging planting of, VII, 266 om.

TRIALS. Capital cases, giving defense right to make closing address, VII, 754; postponing, IX, 791 om; preferred causes (2 bills), X, 159.

TROY. Amending charter, IX, 149 om; board of school commissioners, VI, 508; claims of Riley and others, school janitors, X, 634 om; commissioner of education, X, 151; excise, violations, VII, 1101; increasing salaries, 776; inferior local courts, IX, 630 om; inspector of elections, 343; Jacob and North Third streets, assessment for improvements, VII, 1022; lands, disposition of, X, 583 om; parks and park commission, IX, 633 om; police, appointment of chief detective, VII, 1041; police commissioners, 132 om; police department, reorganization, IX, 489; sewers, expense, how assessed, VIII, 399; street improvemnt, IX, 629 om; waterworks, X, 583 om.

TRUST COMPANIES. Amending general act, X, 810 om; directors, quorum, 586 om; organization in villages, VIII, 507; powers in certain counties, amending act, om X, 318, 320.

TRUSTEES, COMMITTEES AND GUARDIANS. Relief of sureties, VII, 508 om.

TRUST FUNDS. Investment of, VIII, 1040 om.

TRUSTS. Amending Revised Statutes, VI, 708; for charitable purposes, VII, 868; establishing for humane, charitable and religious purposes, IX, 725 om.

Tunnel. Under Newtown creek, IX, 474.

Turnpikes, Plankroads and Bridges. Counties to acquire title, amending act, X, 952 om.

Ulster. Amending village charter, duplicate bill, IX, 432.

Ulster County. Bonds to pay former bonds, VII, 994; insane asylum, purchase by State, IX, 243.

Union College. Taxes, adjustment of, IX, 534 om.

Union Schools. Academic departments, use of academies, IX, 364; Carthage, new school building, VIII, 117; Cortland, amending act, 888 om; Deer Park, examination of teachers, VI, 337; Hempstead, amending act, VIII, 701; Lyons, clerk of trustees, IX, 431; Ontario, District No. 6, bonds for new schoolhouse site and building, 470; Palmyra, additional building, X, 752; Saratoga Springs, consolidating districts, VI, 182; Weedsport, amending act, VII, 933, VIII, 717.

Union School Districts. Powers except in cities and villages, VIII, 889 om; Baldwinsville, borrowing money, VII, 1013; Clarence, No. 1, teachers employment fund, VI, 484; Cortland No. 7, establishing boundary, IX, 816 om; Lenox, extending boundaries, VIII, 130 om; Luzerne and Hadley No. 1, legalizing proceedings relative to new site and school building, X, 811 om; Lysander and Van Buren, relative to, VII, 1106; Madrid No. 1, borrowing money, VI, 325; Orangetown No. 4, date of annual meeting, VIII, 334; Pomfret, establishing, 82; Port Byron, relief, VII, 265 om; Tyrone and Wayne, relative to, id.; Walton, refunding bonds, IX, 812 om; Wawarsing, boundary, VII, 806 om.

United States. Acquiring jurisdiction over Harlem river and Spuyten Duyvil creek, VII, 406; cession of land in Brooklyn, 932 om; cession of land in Queens county, VIII, 1113.

United States Deposit Fund. Jefferson county, VI, 511; loan commissioners,— Delaware county, sale of judgment, VII, 877; — increasing fees, IX, 115; — Ontario county, transferring funds to, VIII, 401.

University Extension. Appropriation, IX, 82.

University Law. Amending, IX, 804 om (2 bills).

University of New York. Amending charter, VII, 266 om; general appropriation, X, 551; college and high school department, temporary service, appropriation, id.; grants to academic schools, id.; home education department, temporary service, id.; temporary service in administrative department, id.; veterinary examinations, id.

Uses and Trusts. Amending Revised Statutes, VIII, 131 om.

Usury. On personal credit security, X, 171.

UTICA. Amending charter, IX, 732 om; assessment on State property, VII, 229; — sewers, 472; board of assessors, 131 om; board of park commissioners, VIII, 880; drainage, extending system, X, 717 om; police and fire commissioners, VIII, 889 om; town expenses, X, 686 om; water supply, VII, 1101.

UTICA INSANE ASYLUM. Appropriation of surplus, VII, 912; fire apparatus, 787; land for asylum, 89; purchase of additional land, VIII, 852; repairs, deficiency appropriation, 851; ward repairs, VII, 786.

UTICA STATE HOSPITAL. Extending Hickory street through lands of, X, 957 om; printing press and equipments, IX, 294; repairs, id.; barn at Graycroft and silos, X, 934; purchase of farm land, VIII, 1137.

VACANCIES IN OFFICE. Amending Revised Statutes, IV, 772.

VAGRANTS. Commitment, om, VII, 932, X, 312; sentences, hard labor in jail, VIII, 132 om; relative to, V, 383.

VALATIE. Public hall, borrowing money for, VII, 265 om.

VESSELS. Demands against, collection of, IX, 813 om.

VETERANS. Peddler's license to, IX, 811 om.

VETERINARY MEDICINE AND SURGERY. Admission to examinations, X, 317 om; practitioners, legalizing acts, IX, 376; practicing without license, penalty, X, 438 om; regulating practice, om, IX, 153, X, 169.

VIENNA. Police regulations, VIII, 534, 1131; real estate assessments, VI, 1033.

VIENNA AND CONSTANTIA. Railroad bonds, VII, 267 om.

VILLAGES.. See also names of villages. Amending general act, VI, 341, VII, 130, 131 om (2 bills); VIII, 640 om; — Akron, VI, 502; — Clayton, VII, 664 om; — Corning, VI, 693; — Dresden, VII, 644; — Mount Vernon, VIII, 891 om; — New Rochelle, 942; — Niagara City, VII, 75; — Niagara Falls, 98; — Northville, 214; — Tonawanda, special powers, VIII, 1115; borrowing money, X, 814 om; crosswalks, assessment on property benefited, IX, 252; changing boundaries, om, X, 449, 523; election notices, publication of, 62 om; electric light companies, contracts with, IX, 126, 623 om; extending limits for health purposes, VII, 416 om; fence viewers, X, 812 om; general act, VII, 933 om; incorporation,— relative to, 509 om; — requisite population, IX, 866 om; — requisite territory and population, X, 591 om; in two or more towns, withdrawal of part, 441 om; jurisdiction of town constables, VII, 265 om; licensing temporary or transient business, IX, 350; lighting companies, contract with, 814 om; local improvements, assessments, VIII, 888 om; Myers' automatic ballot machine, authorizing use of, IX, 247; oath of office, VIII, 1041 om; ordinary expenditures, amending act of 1870, IX, 131; peddler's license, X, 163; poll tax, actions to recover,

VILLAGES — (*Continued*).

IX, 62; relief of certain, X, 309 om; streets, opening or altering, damages, IX, 622 om; superintendent of buildings, VIII, 639 om; taxation for water, qualifications of voters on proposition, VIII, 406; taxes, nonresident, report to county treasurer, IX, 523; trustees, confirming elections, VII, 132 om; water,— furnishing to other municipalities, IX, 866 om; — rates, 627 om — supply, VIII, 130; water supply,— commissioners, 1040 om; — contract with water companies, IX, 810 om; water system, extending outside corporate limits, 813 om.

VINEGAR. Adulteration, VII, 572; adulterated, preventing sale, 507 om; cider, relative to, IX, 863 om; sales, deception in, 148 om.

VINEYARDS. Opening roads through, exempting certain towns, VII, 806 om.

WAGES. Judgments for, IX, 246; prevailing rate, how determined, 864 om.

WALTS, CHARLES H. Referee's fees, Armour case, X, 648.

WAR OF 1812. Documents, compiling and arranging, X, 572.

WAR WITH SPAIN. New York city employees serving in, compensation, amending act, X, 264; State employees in military or naval service, compensation while absent, appropriation, 314 om.

WAREHOUSES. Regulating business relative to, X, 319 om.

WARREN COUNTY. State loan to, VI, 194.

WARSAW. Amending charter, IX, 718 om.

WASHINGTON COUNTY. Convictions for crimes less than felony, charging expense on towns, IX, 796 om.

WASHINGTON'S HEADQUARTERS. Tappan, purchase of, VII, 410; purchase of additional land, VIII, 855; care of, VI, 581.

WATER. Investigating sources of supply and systems of sewerage, X, 650; surface, obstructing flow of, IX, 247, 473.

WATER COMPANIES. Amending Transportation Corporations Law, IX, 804 om.

WATERFORD. North Side Water Company, sprinkling streets, X, 593 om.

WATERLOO. Amending charter, X, 174.

WATERS OF THE STATE. Protection of life and property in certain cases, IX, 720 om.

WATER SUPPLY. Towns and villages, VI, 591.

WATERTOWN. Amending charter, VI, 509, 581, IX, 870 om; commissioners of education, X, 713 om; election inspectors, IX, 453; legalizing local assessments, duplicate bill, 451; sidewalks, VIII, 1041 om.

WATERVILLE. Open air concerts, IX, 718 om.

WATERVLIET. Annexing territory to Green Island, X, 179 om; restoring territory to Green Island, id.; election of town officers, VII, 64; public peace, 1101.

WATERWORKS COMPANIES. Cities and villages, VII, 807 om; relative to, VIII, 640 om.

WATKINS. Amending charter, X, 61 om; water supply, 161.

WAYNE COUNTY. Highways and bridges, VI, 332.

WEATHERWAX, DELIA. Widow of James H. Weatherwax, State assessor, appropriation for residue of salary, VII, 917.

WEEDSPORT. Amending charter, VIII, 620.

WEIGHTS AND MEASURES. Amending act, VI, 912 om; potatoes, VII, 414 om; reappropriation, VIII, 246.

WESTBROOK, JULIA A. Widow of Justice Westbrook, appropriation for salary, VIII, 250.

WESTBROOK, THEODORIC R. Justice of Supreme Court, investigation, counsel fees, VII, 924.

WESTCHESTER COUNTY. Bronx river sewer commission, X, 713 om; county jail, addition to, VII, 130 om; Historical Society, books and records to be delivered to, IX, 862 om; indexing records, id.; indigent children, care of, VIII, 1159; keeping open certain offices, VII, 201, 412 om; lighting highways, public places, etc., in towns, X, 948 om; Mamaroneck avenue, repayment of money, VI, 488; Morrisania,— changing grade of certain streets, 590;—107th street, 566; payment to Westchester County Society for the Prevention of Cruelty to Children, X, 311 om.

WESTCHESTER AND WEST FARMS. Avenues in, amending act, VI, 158, 505.

WESTERN HOUSE OF REFUGE. Amending act, VI, 599; compensation for loss of earnings, VII, 1082; deficiency appropriation, repairs and improvements, 489; female department, VI, 875; local assessment, VII, 927; new barn, 489; new department for boys, id.; school of technology, 1082; steam heating apparatus, 916.

WESTERN HOUSE OF REFUGE FOR WOMEN, ALBION. Additional accommodations, IX, 293; chapel, assembly hall, gymnasium, X, 655; commitments, IX, 525; electric light and power, X, 547; farm buildings, IX, 293; horses and carriage, X, 547.

WEST FARMS. Relief of board of education, VI, 718.

WESTFIELD. Establishing water department, VIII, 518.

WEST SENECA. Assessments for local improvements, collection, om, X, 811, 952.

WEST TROY. Board of fire commissioners, VI, 911 om; contract with West Troy Waterworks Company, water for sewers, VIII, 382; electric light commission, 1117; fire commissioners, VII, 805 om.

WHEAT. Adulterated, preventing sale of, VIII, 837 om.

WHITE PLAINS. Amending charter, IX, 248, 819 om; bonded indebtedness, VII, 265 om; repealing acts as to part of village in Green-

WHITE PLAINS — (*Continued*).
burgh, 931 om; sidewalks and curbs, compelling lot owners to repair, X, 61 om; water system, fire protection tax, 592 om.

WHITESBOROUGH. Fixing village boundaries, IX, 862 om.

WILLARD ASYLUM FOR INSANE. Additional buildings, VI, 870; bridge and railroad extension, VII, 486; completion of laundry floor, id.; furniture for new group, id.; new buildings, 88, 583; prohibiting sale of liquor within half a mile, VIII, 340.

WILLARD STATE HOSPITAL. Addition to barn, IX, 294; clergymen for, appropriation, X, 565, 783; furniture, IX, 294; new floors and ceilings and other repairs, id.

WILLS. Construction of, X, 316 om; Cunningham estate, 585 om; decedents' estates, VI, 505; devise to charitable and religious corporations, limiting effect of, IX, 623 om; devises and bequests, preventing lapse, VII, 266 om; foreign, relative to, 665 om; Power, execution of certain provisions, X, 391; probate, effect of, IX, 131; proof of, VI, 684; revocation of probate, jury trial, X, 318 om; and letters of administration, foreign certification, 585 om.

WITNESSES. Agents, informers and spies, testimony, VII, 624; conditional examination, IX, 718 om; in criminal cases, VIII, 468 om; fees, IX, 446; fees in criminal cases, 860 om.

WOMEN. Election as school officers, VII, 76; imputing unchastity to, VI, 901; judgments for wages, VIII, 293 om; reformatory for, 819.

WOMEN'S RELIEF CORPS HOME. Additional buildings, IX, 777 om; construction, equipment and repairs, 772; electric light and power machinery, X, 545; electric light unit, 654; vegetable cellar, 546.

WORCESTER. Separate road district, VI, 196.

WYOMING COUNTY. Refunding moneys paid to State, VI, 867.

YONKERS. Amending charter, VI, 683, VII, 509 om, IX, 858 om; board of police to borrow money, 870 om; bonded debt, consolidation of, VI, 712; bonds for election purposes, IX, 61; City Court, 791 om; — removal of cause to Supreme Court, repeal, X, 819 om; — supplementary proceedings, 522; election inspectors, IX, 458; electric light wires and appurtenances, supervision and inspection, X, 433; police, VII, 807 om; revising charter, X, 62 om; wards, erection of, VII, 664 om; water rents, X, 60 om; water supply, VIII, 887 om.

VETOES. PRESIDENT.

LEXINGTON AND MAYSVILLE ROAD (JACKSON), III, 319, 391, 464.

PUBLIC IMPROVEMENTS IN WISCONSIN (POLK), IV, 393.

RIVER AND HARBOR BILL (POLK), IV, 392.

GENERAL INDEX.

A.

ABBOTT, CHARLES E. Admission to medical examination, veto, X, 313.

ABBOTT, CHAUNCEY O. Senate committee clerk, death of, expenses of committee attending funeral, veto, VII, 586.

ABBOTT'S DIGEST. Cited, powers of Supreme Court commissioners, X, 670.

ABDUCTION. William Morgan, III, 184 (see that name); Atticus, a slave, 748 (see that name); of citizens for alleged political offenses, V, 466.

ABEEL, JAMES. Damages to lands, Little Falls, Court of Claims, veto, X, 943.

ABEEL, JOHN. Smith for Seneca Indians, I, 389.

ABERCROMBIE, JAMES, MAJOR-GENERAL. Appointed commander-in-chief of American forces, I, 619; letter from, embargo, 622; sends force to Mohawk valley, 625; posts troops on western frontier, 626.

ABERDEEN, LORD. Secretary of State, interview with Edward Everett, colonial history, III, 1014; IV, 175; correspondence with Edward Everett, III, 1016, 1020; IV, 175; grants permission to examine documents, 181.

ABERT, JAMES WM., LIEUTENANT-COLONEL. Report, value of lake commerce, IV, 391.

ABINGDON SQUARE SAVINGS BANK. Alleged violation of charter, VII, 66.

ABSCONDING DEBTORS. Revision of laws relating to, II, 554.

ABSENTEES. Required to return to colony, I, 16, 17; proclamation requiring, 22; claims to land, II, 218.

ACADEMIES. Aid to, II, 321, 904; limitation of usefulness, 350; Governor Lewis comments on, 557; operation only partial, 719; trustees, act relating to, 877; female at Waterford, 972, 1018; Wesleyan Seminary in New York, 972; female seminary at Catskill, 1018; number and patronage of, 1820, 1049; estimate of State's share in national domain, 1101; students in, III, 61, 653; instruction of teachers, 159, 454, 499, 538, 613, 652; IV, 552, 647; statistics, III, 456, 539, 653, 740, 857; IV, 795; number reporting, III, 500; VII, 688, 947; deserve public support, III, 539; aid from United States deposit fund, 613; IV, 118; V, 174; VI, 22; proposed change of supervision, III, 614; regents, supervision of, 617; libraries in, 654; used as normal schools, importance of visitation, 743; endowments, 946; when entitled to share in literature

Academies—(*Continued*).

    fund, IV, 117; should be sustained, 119, 397; special appropriations, effect of new Constitution, 378; text-books and apparatus for, 552; advantages afforded by, general act for incorporation of, 648; State scholarships, 716; should be more closely associated with educational system, 799; more supervision needed, 840; prosperous condition of, V, 274; VII, 157; military training in, V, 375; enlistments from, 522; teachers' classes, IV, 647; V, 523, 604, 695, 779, 852; increasing attendance, 605; adoption by school district, VI, 87; when not public schools, 95; good results of higher requirements, 618; Governor Robinson opposes taxation for, VII, 21, 295; comparative statement, 1905, X, 738.

    Vetoes. Female Academy of the Sacred Heart, New York, charter, IV, 531; Monticello Academy, charter, 574; Cortland, aid to, VI, 94; Williamsville, sale of property, 336; Peekskill, amending charter, 1035; Westfield, donation of fossils to, VII, 417; regents, examinations, deficiency appropriation, 467; instruction of teachers, appropriation, 495; use as academic departments of union schools, IX, 364, new act passed; Rochester, free academy bonds, redemption, 731; Heffley Collegiate Institute, charter, X, 709.

Academy of Medicine, New York. Report of committee on quarantine establishment, VIII, 527.

Accessory. Trial of, VI, 126.

Accomplice. Turning State's evidence, duty of government, II, 997.

Accountant Guarantee Company. Charter, veto, IX, 794.

Accountants. Amending Code, veto, X, 808.

Accounts, see Public Accounts.

Accoutrements. States to supply, II, 43; lost in service, compensation for, 92; provided at public expense, 337; ruinous condition of, 524.

Ackerson, Garret. Seizing forfeited cattle, II, 250.

Acknowledgments. Commissioners to take outside of State, III, 770; taken in foreign countries, authentication of, 821; V, 212; foreign, communications, relative to, V, 111.

    Vetoes. Proof of and effect as evidence, IX, 266; by county clerks, 722; of instruments in Cuba and other islands, X, 63; conveyances of real property, 444.

Actions. In which people are interested, expenses in, II, 431; limitation of, 441, 783; for small amounts, 450; for slander and assault and battery, costs, III, 219; on New Jersey boundary, 312, 356; Astor claim, 312, 389; to test validity of Van Rensselaer titles, IV, 412; criminal, challenges and exceptions, 489, 490; procedure, further revision needed, 655; damages, sale of intoxicating liquor,

ACTIONS—(*Continued*).

765; by Attorney-General against public officers, VI, 732; for canal frauds, 980; against public officers, no reimbursement of defendant for expenses, VII, 544; against railroads by employees for personal injuries, X, 96; divorce, decision and entry of judgment, 224.

VETOES. For small causes, II, 274, 594; in New York for small debts, 532; speedy disposition of, IV, 510; continuance of certain, VII, 413; criminal, services in, 414; by Attorney-General, 934; preferred causes, increasing number, 1093; penalties for violation of New York Health Law, method of service, 1117; death of party, continuing suit against estate, veto, VIII, 131; conversion, prior demand, 469; railway construction, damages, limitation of time, IX, 260; to recover real property, 791, 792; by judgment creditors, 792; settlement without consent of attorneys, X, 150; preference, 173; costs in, 179, 880, 916; equity, compulsory accountings in, 443; against municipal corporations in certain cases, 451; Chiesa case, New York, extending time to sue, 473; against Indians on their contracts, 590; limitation, cause arising in another State, 703; against certain municipal corporations for negligence, limiting time, 709; divorce, when may be maintained, 758.

ACTORS' FUND OF AMERICA. Amusement license fees payable to, veto, IX, 872.

ADAMS. Village, aiding Hungerford Collegiate Institute, veto, VI, 77.

ADAMS, AMOS. Albany under-sheriff, resistance to process, III, 824, 827; affidavit by, 829.

ADAMS, CAMPBELL W. State Engineer and Surveyor, communication from recommending canal investigation, 1898, IX, 850; commission created, 849; report and action thereon, 850; statements connected with canal investigation, 1898, X, 41; complaints against, 77; exonerated by special investigating commission, 78.

ADAMS, DANIEL. Paymaster of militia, funds received by, II, 765.

ADAMS, JOHN. President of United States, reply to Legislature's address on relations with France, II, 446; communication to Congress, death of Washington, 461; report on weights and measures, III, 101; death of, 178; as life Senator, possible length of service, VIII, 693.

ADAMS, JOHN QUINCY. Secretary of State and President-Elect, notice of special meeting of Senate, III, 104; chosen President, 199; as life Senator, possible length of service, VIII, 694.

ADDISON. Town, borrowing money for bridges, veto, VI, 52.

ADDRESS TO CROWN. By colonial Legislature, I, 19, 22, 29, 59, 69, 78 101, 104, 131, 153 157, 174, 180, 205, 228, 258, 269, 304, 512, 662, 671, 710.

ADDRESS TO GOVERNOR.

  COLONY

    To Governor Hunter, I, 161, 182, 186, 189.

    To Governor Burnet, I, 195, 221.

    To Lieutenant-Governor Clarke, I, 266, 294, 298.

    To Governor Clinton, I, 329, 402, 406, 462, 475, 484, 492, 508, 514, 518, 524.

    To Lieutenant-Governor Delancey, I, 535, 541, 551, 559, 622, 624, 627.

    To Governor Hardy, I, 586, 604, 607, 611, 612.

    To President Colden, I, 651.

    To Lieutenant-Governor Colden, I, 661, 678, 682, 766.

    To Governor Moore, I, 702, 710, 716, 726.

    To Governor Dunmore, I, 739.

  STATE. To Governor Clinton, II, 11, 14, 51, 292.

    To Governor Jay, II, 442, 444.

    To Governor Lewis, II, 587.

    From Seneca chiefs, II, 941.

ADIRONDACK PARK. Established, 1892, VIII, 938, 1081; IX, 145; should be self-sustaining, 146; use of property by private owners, 185, 298; general act, 1893, 187; revision, 1895, 569; John Brown farm transferred to State, 669; private preserves in, 1897, devastations should be stopped, 751; Forest Preserve Board established, 752; purchase of land, appropriation for, 1898, 838; State debt, X, 180, 327, 718, 832; purchase of lands and expenses, 1900, 182; description amended, 607.

  VETOES. Acquisition of land, X, 291; amending general act, 310, 317; extending boundaries, 379.

ADIRONDACK RAILROAD COMPANY.

  VETOES. Facilitating construction, VI, 172; aid from Clifton, 190; aiding completion, 345.

ADIRONDACK REGION. Large sales for taxes, VII, 657; value as a health resort, 721; VIII, 22; losses by fires, State land should not be sold, park commission of 1872, VII, 722; lands in, sale prohibited, 983; forests should be preserved, 984; forest preserve established, VIII, 23; description of, IX, 147; should be kept as public park, X, 100; restocking with wild moose, reappropriation, veto, 563, 814. .

ADIRONDACK SURVEY. Discontinuance recommended, VII, 373; progress of work, 720; appropriation for, 721; total expense of, 1883, 876; heavy expenditures, 986; deposit of maps and outlines recommended, 987; methods and expenditures disapproved, VIII, 176; statement of expense, 1872-1884, IX, 424.

ADIRONDACK SURVEY — (Continued).

VETOES. Continuance, VII, 373; VIII, 74; report, furnishing copies of, VII, 493, 495; expense of completion, VIII, 423; publishing records, 551; appropriation, 1894, IX, 423.

ADJUTANT-GENERAL, English. Expected visit from, I, 286.

ADJUTANT-GENERAL, New York. Report, II, 369, 439, 459, 707, 1029, 1081, 1122; III, 96, 143, 183, 218, 259, 315, 354, 389, 431, 482, 527, 637, 680, 747, 820, 907, 972; IV, 45, 83, 153, 283, 287, 381, 419, 452, 506, 573, 624, 681, 751, 817; V, 11, 41, 62, 132, 219, 306, 413, 486, 564, 617, 717, 862; VI, 142, 260, 414, 554, 769; VII, 42, 316; VIII, 195, 325, 500, 941, 1091; IX, 35, 210, 339, 570, 682, 754, 851; X, 142, 371, 628, 866; report on brevet appointments in militia, II, 992; report on artillery and cavalry, 1037; return of militia inspection, III, 14, 34; difficulties attending transaction of business, 19; to issue military commissions, 189; correspondence with Secretary of War, militia claims, 692; consultation with, anti-rent troubles, 829, 833; operations in anti-rent troubles, 839; report on movements of militia, 840; IV, 148, 236; visits Delaware county, 237; report on new militia system, V, 393; Civil War, number of troops from New York, 404; transcribing military records, 576; communication from, quotas under call for troops, 618; to adjust war claims, 1812, VI, 358; member of Military Code Revision Commission, VII, 428; department rooms in new capitol, 694; duty under statute providing for examination of arms for National Guard, IX, 636; exchanges Remington rifles for Springfield rifles supplied by Federal government, 643; under Federal Militia Act of 1903 appointed for each State, X, 16; report, 1905, arms and equipments furnished by United States for local militia, 16; Nelson H. Henry, State, Henry C. Corbin, United States, accompany Prince Henry at Assembly reception, 480.

VETOES. Remington rifles, altering sights, VII, 478; separate companies, funds for, 478; roster of Civil War volunteers, printing report, 491; various appropriations for local assessments, armories, 927; furnishing daily rations of cheese to National Guard, at State Camp, IX, 287; service medal for George T. Hollingworth, X, 173; repairing and equipping the "Restless," 299; settlement of Shaffer claim, 592; battleflags, permitting use at Old Home Week, Oswego county, 919.

ADMINISTRATORS. Powers of, II, 986; public, in New York, III, 216.

VETOES. Amending act, VI, 505; bonds, VIII, 468; amending Revised Statutes, IX, 272; judicial settlement of accounts, 283; letters, grant of, 860; inventory, fees of appraisers, X, 61.

ADMIRALTY. See COURT OF ADMIRALTY.

ADOPTION. Of children, see Deming case, VI, 559; proposed regulation of, veto, VII, 350.

ADULTERATION. Food and drugs, general act, VII, 649; acts relative to, VIII, 320, 477.
>   VETOES. Food and drugs, VII, 924, 1113; wheat, preventing sale of, VIII, 887; drugs, chemicals, etc., X, 447.

ADULTERY. Made a crime, II, 780.

ADULTS. Authorized to convey land, I, 11.

ADVERSE POSSESSION. Defined, IV, 353; under manorial leases, 411.

ADVICE AND CONSENT. Meaning of, II, 497.

AFRICA. Liberia, negro colonization in, IV, 621; slave trade, suppression of, 622.

AFRICAN METHODIST EPISCOPAL CHURCHES.
>   VETOES. Incorporation, amending general act, VIII, 1095; New York Conference Methodist Episcopal Church, charter, 1101.

AGAN, PATRICK. Member of Adirondack Park Commission, 1872, VII, 722.

AGE LIMIT. Under first Constitution, II, 362, 622.

AGENT. For Onondaga Indians, office created, II, 684; to procure and transcribe colonial documents, III, 752, 935, 1008, 1013; to explore mineral districts, 1034; for care of soldiers, V, 577; military, see Military Agencies.
>   VETOES. Testimony in certain cases, VII, 624; to investigate charitable institutions, compensation, 779; foreign fire insurance companies, authority of, IX, 721, 802; for defense of State, canals, appropriation, 856.

AGENT FOR CARE OF SOLDIERS. Act providing for, V, 577; report, 578; services of, 681.

AGENT FOR COLONY. Fletcher shows need of, I, 57, 72; William Nicolls appointed, 58, 59; letters from, 73; act for appointment of, 175; letters from Ambrose Philips, 181, 183; communication from, relative to Tariff Act, 198; importance of maintenance, 208, 292, 297, 321, 333; action of, relative to New York collector's district, 213; withdrawal of, 215; claims of, to be paid, 218, 222; communication from, relative to Eastern Indians, 219; new act relative to, 222; services in matter of French at Niagara, 227; Le Heup reappointed, 233; Assembly recommends continuance of, 267; appointment of, urged, 270, 313; petitions sent to, 687, 730; method of appointing, 732.

AGENT, INDIAN. See INDIAN AGENT.

AGRICULTURAL COLLEGES. Distribution of national public land for establishment of, II, 1080; commission to consider plan of, IV, 433; report of commission, 477, 553; State recommended, 432, 552, 603. See STATE AGRICULTURAL COLLEGE.

AGRICULTURAL EXPERIMENT STATION. At Geneva, see State Agricultural Experiment Station, Geneva; established at Cornell University, IX, 179; annual report, 343, 570, 754; establishing at Long Island, veto, 232.

AGRICULTURAL LAW. Enacted, 1893, IX, 175.

VETOES. Violations and penalties, X, 583; — appraisers of condemned animals, 592; — condensed milk, 776; — various amendments, 809.

AGRICULTURAL LEASES. Limiting term of, IV, 244; constitutional provision, 245, 409, 559, 653.

-AGRICULTURAL MUSEUM. Arranging collection of fowls, appropriation, veto, IX, 83.

AGRICULTURAL SCHOOL. In Oneida county, III, 298; recommended, IV, 432, 552, 603.

AGRICULTURAL SOCIETIES. County, appropriation for, II, 970, 1005; State society incorporated, III, 386; local societies dissolved, 386, 421; suggested organization of, 745, 878; appropriation for, 878; organization of, 945; benefits resulting from, IV, 37; V, 177; general act, IV, 648; general act amended, mortgages authorized, VIII, 388; Wayne County Agricultural Society, legalizing Borck contract, 1148.

VETOES. Wyoming County Agricultural Society, escheat, VI, 708; Oswego County Agricultural Society, mortgage for indebtedness, VIII, 341; protection of property, appointment of policemen, 378; Otsego County Agricultural Society, mortgage of property, 388; exempting from taxation, 619; distribution of money to, 875.

AGRICULTURAL AND GEOLOGICAL HALL. Repairs and improvements, veto, X, 300.

AGRICULTURE. Encouragement of, I, 506; II, 292, 897, 1005; pursuit of, 254; prosperous condition of, 313, 1089; III, 23; V, 384, 595; experiments at Botanic Garden, II, 579; Legislature should encourage, 597; general references, V, 595, 693, 777; VI, 4; VIII, 32; effect of embargo, II, 632; extension of, 658; report on, general note, 955; in English, history of, 956; various plans proposed by committee, 957; Governor Clinton's views on, 969; III, 63, 125; appropriation for promotion of, II, 970, 1005; dependence on home market, 1047; agricultural department proposed, III, 64; progress of, 298; school in Oneida county, id.; instruction in common schools, 337; fairs recommended, 386; State Agricultural Society, see that title; importance of, 420; Governor Marcy's comments on, 421, 457; Senate's report on agricultural instruction, 458; expected benefits from geological

AGRICULTURE—(*Continued*).

    survey, 568; benefits from United States deposit fund, 624; increasing results of, 745; board of, suggested, id.; treatise on, recommended for school libraries, id.; Rensselaerwyck leases, 776; does not receive proper legislative attention, 877; appropriation for agricultural societies, 878; books on, included in school library, id.; importation of foreign grain, IV, 37; statement of productions, 42; increasing interest in, 80; State Fair, see that title; promotion of, act extended, 139; lease, limiting term, 244, 356, 409; census statistics, 248; American Agricultural Association incorporated, 284; effect of leasehold tenures, 334; products, foreign markets for, 398; schools for instruction, 404, 552, 603; national department established, 505; instruction in normal schools suggested, 843; State should aid development of, 853; no aid needed, V, 84; results of aid to, 177; People's College, IV, 648; V, 178, see that title; influence on national prosperity, 290; Cornell University, see that title; improvement of implements, 693; general improvement in, 777; acreage under improvement, value of farms, 1865, 820; products in State not sufficient for local consumption, VI, 104; seriously affected by tariff, 131; drainage, constitutional provisions, see DRAINAGE; underlies all other industries, VII, 312; experiment station established, 697, see STATE AGRICULTURAL EXPERIMENT STATION; dairy products, regulating manufacture and sale, VIII, 33; State Dairy Commissioner, office created, 34; extending dairy knowledge and science, appropriation, id.; needed reduction of taxation, 1063; Farmer's Institutes, cost of, 1891, IX, 11; proportion of population engaged in, 171; X, 29; various plans for improvement of, IX, 171; proposed bureau of, 172; high rank of State, 174; State department established, 1893, 175, 318; Cornell University, agricultural instruction at, 175; dairy husbandry, promotion at Cornell University, 179; New York's leadership, 319; imitation dairy products transported from other State made subject to its police regulations, 321; expert instruction, id.; harvest holiday recommended, 322; Drainage Act of 1895, 550, 558; act unconstitutional in part, 550; penalties for watering milk, X, 120; adulterated milk and cream, sale of, id.; encouragement of Farmers' Institutes, 121; State Agricultural College, Cornell University, 627, see that title; proper functions of State, 739; improvement needed, 861.

VETOES. Promotion of, appropriation, VII, 90; peach trees, preventing spread of yellows, 416; Red House Driving Park Agricultural Society, charter, 506; butter, deception in sales, 571;

AGRICULTURE, VETOES — (Continued).

oleomargarine, regulating manufacture and sale, 590; State Dairymen's Association, extending dairy knowledge, appropriation, 907; VIII, 246; premiums, butter, cheese and hops, VII, 1078; dairy products, preventing deception, VIII, 1037; hop boxes, regulating size of, 1040; Agricultural Museum, arranging collection of fowls, IX, 83; encouragement of, 109, 172; Agricultural Experiment Station on Long Island, establishing, 232; promoting consumption of cheese, 287; compensation of agent to examine yellows or black knot in peach trees, 354; amending general law, 800; county schools of agriculture and domestic economy, establishing, X, 440; concentrated commercial feeding stuffs, sale, license fee, 447, 588, 699; horticultural instruction, investigations and experiments, appropriation, 552; printing nature study and extension bulletins, appropriation, 797; fruit trees, preventing disease, 809; free winter course for farmers' sons and daughters, State Agricultural College, 935.

AIDE-DE-CAMP. To Governor Tompkins, gratuitous services of, II, 810.

AIKMAN, WILLIAM H. New York Municipal Court attendant, claim, veto, X, 168.

AINSWORTH, DANFORTH E. Member of Educational Unification Commission, 1899, X, 114.

AIX-LA-CHAPELLE. Treaty of peace at, I, 471, 481.

AKRON. Village, extending boundaries, veto, VI, 502.

ALABAMA. Disapproves Ohio proposition relative to abolition of slavery, III, 183; disapproves New Jersey proposition relative to colonization of colored persons, 184; protests against protective tariff policy, and recommends constitutional convention, 438; requisition for extradition, Williams case, 583, 594; resolutions relative to anti-slavery agitation, 588; recommends annexation of Texas, 683, 975; stocks of, securities in New York banks, 725; IV, 36; resolutions protesting against protective tariff, III, 907; sustains Georgia's claim for surrender of abductors of Atticus, 908; exchanging judicial decisions with New York, id.; refuses to receive proceeds of public lands, 974; opposes repudiation and sustains Virginia against New York, IV, 48; recommends temporary suspension of tariff on railroad bars, 864; seizure of national forts and property, V, 306; resolutions, continuing postal arrangements, 318; secession ordinance, 396; retail liquor licenses, 1892, IX, 666; Employer's Liablity Law, X, 190.

ALABAMA, THE. Consequences of possible entry into New York harbor, V, 549.

ALBANY. (COLONY.) Garrison I, 19, 26, 52, 131; Major Ingoldesby visits, 26; Governor Fletcher urges defense of, 28; trade with Indians, 30; Legislature urges defense of town, id.; fort to be built, 33, 35, 93; additional legislation for defense recommended, 34, 99; Governor Fletcher's proposed visit, 35; fusileers, 36, 43; aid from Crown, 41; aid not expected from Boston, 49; Fletcher visits, 65, 68, 69, 70; address from magistrates of, 67, 68; barrier to New York and other provinces, 70; Governor recommends barracks, 70, 602; townhouse and jail recommended, 89; defense of, 23, 25, 27, 37, 44, 45, 48, 49, 103, 105, 113, 114, 117, 125, 128, 137, 138, 160, 166, 315, 548; weakness of, 109; Colonel Redknap visits, 130; post to Westfield and Boston, 136; repairs of fort, 143, 147, 157, 179; bounties for volunteers, Canadian expedition, 151; condition at, 154; Governor Hunter visits, 155, 156; justices of the peace ask for law against sale of liquor to Indians, 161; act for better watching and guarding, 161; stockades, 196; Indians trading at, 197; gunner at, claim for arrears, 202; houses for Indian service, id.; estimated expenses of repairing fort, 203; regulating Indian trade, 223; jail, petition of justices, relative to, 234; new stone fort, 238, 239; blockhouses, 239; memorial from, relative to defense of, 244; new fort, 247, 249, 390, 460; petition for dissolution of Assembly, 252; petition from, for appointment of Kerr as surgeon at Oswego, 258; letter from, relative to French designs on northern settlements, 271; supplies for Indians, 300; act for completing fortifications in, 318; conference with Indians at, 319; dangerous situation resulting from destruction of Saratoga, 361; King's troops sent to, 363; town major of, proposed allowance to, 377; military arrangements, 383; troops at, 398, 416, 441; rich men in, charged with opposing war, 399; dangerous condition of, 406; location of, with reference to neighboring towns, 407; number of able-bodied men in, 408; troops should be stationed at, 409, 418; rendezvous for Crown Point expedition, 419; rangers at, 439; retaining troops at, 453; removing cannon from Saratoga, 460; troops disbanded at, 477; breaking open storehouse, 497; mayor, recorder and aldermen to be commissioners of excise, 529; defenseless condition of, 547, 563; sale of rum to Indians prohibited, 549; French scheme to attack, 550; convention at, forms plan of union, id.; strengthening fortifications, 553; bedding for troops, 555; letter from corporation, Indian affairs, 563, 751; agents of colonies for Indian service, 572; plan of fortifications, id.; Colonel Dunbar's forces, 575, 591; Governor Hardy visits, 583; barracks sufficient for quartering soldiers, 703; disturbances near, payment for losses suffered by, 713.

ALBANY. (STATE.) Letter from common council, scarcity of provisions, II, 54; first meeting of Legislature at, 87; IX, 688; Legislature meets at, II, 114, 289, 301, 332, 386; ammunition to be deposited at, 122; prison proposed at, 336; expense in preventing spread of infectious disease, 336, 440; State prison at, 364, 387; epidemic in, 364, 366, 372; southern terminus of proposed Hudson river improvement, 365; becomes State capital, 397; arsenal at, 401, 436, 437; appointment of charter officers, 499; sanitary regulations, 537, 542; dangers from deposit of powder in, 683; powder magazine, id.; militia from, 1812, 744; road to St. Lawrence river, report of commission, 756, 795; deposit of arms, 798; sale of arsenal, 828; arsenal to be leased, 871; condition of arsenal, 878, 896; improvement of Hudson river, 900, 954; action of common council, relative to first capitol, 934, 935; share of expense in erecting capitol, 936; arsenal, lease of unoccupied land, 1076; justices in, III, 7; aldermen *ex officio* judges, 161; railroad to Schenectady, 328; authorized to invest in stock of Albany and West Stockbridge Railroad Company, 750; uniform corps called out to aid sheriff, anti-rent troubles, 830; act relating to, 1029; public inconvenience resulting from unfinished canal bridges, IV, 16; convention to consider question of holding constitutional convention, 84; provides building for normal school, 265; reimbursed for construction of canal basin, 426, 474; idiot asylum, 555; university organized, 603; immigrant passengers, protection of, 793; Dudley Observatory, V, 17; memorial, board of trade, obstructions in Hudson river, 40; new arsenal at, 88, 175, 642; rendezvous of troops, Civil War, 400; barracks for soldiers' Hospital, 488; services and observances on death of President Lincoln, 679; Ira Harris Hospital, use of, 684; military agency at, id.; Soldiers' Home, transfer of inmates, id.; offers site of building for military records and trophies, 689; furnishes site for new capitol, 722, 759; temporary soldiers' home, 774, 835; bonds, damages from Albany basin improvement, VI, 44; riots of 1877, VII, 152; ladies granted use of old Assembly chamber, 315; police board, method of appointment unconstitutional, VIII, 84; new capitol patronage, 224; large number of special acts, 347; number of excise licenses, 1887, 359; public market, 447; Hawk street bridge, act for, 612, 1146; excise license fees, 1889, 685; filtration plant, acts of 1897 and 1905, IX, 420; a city of the second class, 678; centennial anniversary of establishment of capital, 688; conveyance to, of land under water of Albany basin, X, 897.

ALBANY—(*Continued*)

VETOES. Smallpox, inoculation for, II, 225; lamps and night watch, 396; care and improvement of streets, V, 650, 655; Excelsior Temple of Honor, No. 23, charter, VI, 55; land under water, 210; reorganizing fire department, 231; police, 445, passed over veto; cession to United States, public buildings, 449; Washington park bonds, 693; street repairs, 1031; Beaver creek sewer, 1036; harbor master, VII, 121; elections, registration, 263; repaving Hudson avenue, 264; taxes, annexed territory, 412; school funds, using for other purposes, 755; charter revision, 805; assessors, 805; armory, local assessments, 927; lanes and alleys, 935; street improvements, 1012; paving assessments, 1107; official papers, increasing number, 1121; tax on manufacturers, VIII, 468; Hope Savings Bank, dissolution, 469; Catholic Union, exempting property from taxation, 623; special sessions, 639; amending charter, 640; paving certain streets, 790; Society for the Relief of Orphan and Destitute Children, changing name, increasing property limit, IX, 56; water supply, 420, 729; water commissioners, 420; police department, reorganization, 489; dyke at Albany, 606; justices' courts, 630; assessments, confirmation, 632; police pension fund, 632; street extensions, assessments for, 729; Knox street viaduct, 729; Water street, canal bridge, repayment of expenditures, 730, 777; Pine avenue assessments, 734; City Court, 792; printing and advertising, paying debts for, 869; McGraw relief, X, 179; City Court and jury list, 321, 635; statue to Alexander Hamilton, 586.

"ALBANY," THE. Used for quarantine purposes, VI, 360; returned to Federal government, 533.

ALBANY ARGUS. Federal statutes published in, II, 1068.

ALBANY BASIN. Act providing for, III, 10; usefulness of, IV, 426; city reimbursed for construction of, 426, 474; act for improvement of, VI, 44; conveyance of land under water to Albany, X, 897.

ALBANY AND BATH-ON-THE-HUDSON BRIDGE COMPANY. Charter granted, IX, 715.

ALBANY BURGESS CORPS. Arms for, VII, 248.

ALBANY CITY BANK. Trustee of securities for Farmers' Bank of Orleans, IV, 36.

ALBANY COMMERCIAL BANK. Funds deposited in, geological survey, III, 996; advances funds for Civil War bounties, V, 454; reimbursement, 455.

ALBANY CONVENTION. (Colonial Union). Meeting, I, 550, 577; primary object, 578; forms plan of union, 578; proceedings and plan transmitted to Lords of Trade, 581; plan not approved, 582.

ALBANY COUNTY. (COLONY.) Representation in first Assembly, I, 9; persons prohibited from leaving without Leisler's consent, 16; sale of liquor to Indians in, prohibited, 157; proceedings to recover fines and forfeitures in, 233; petition for removal of Fort Hunter garrison to Carrying place, 258; ordnance for forts in, 295; new fort near Crown Point, 324; additional force to be maintained in, 325; detachment for Canadian expedition, 374; rangers for, 377, 393, 395, 439; dangerous conditions in, 406; ammunition for forts in, 460; certain inhabitants prisoners in Canada, 476; sale of rum to Indians prohibited, 549; levies in, 570; draft for northern garrisons, 588; long marches of militia, 596; militia ordered into service, 614; line between it and Ulster county, survey recommended, 672; riots in, expenses of suppressing, 717; disturbances in northeastern part of, 764; Philip Livingston, Assembly, favors Colonial union, 767.

ALBANY COUNTY. (STATE.) Indian ravages on western frontier, II, 50; King's district, memorial from, 55; condition on northern frontier, 101; included part of New Hampshire grants, 103; condition of jail, 392; share of expense of erecting capitol, 936; tread mill in jail, III, 10; resistance to process, anti-rent troubles, 774, 822; sheriff applies for military aid, 774; *posse* summoned, anti-rent troubles, 827, 830; agricultural society in, 945; penitentiary established, IV, 74; tenants represented before Assembly committee on anti-rent troubles, 328; Van Rensselaer leases, description of, 329; memorial on anti-rent troubles, V, 792; average excise license fees, 1889, VIII, 686; highways, cost of labor system, 1892, IX, 199; insane, care of, county and State systems compared, 228.

VETOES. Smallpox, inoculation for, II, 225; highways in, relative to, 348; street railroads, fares on, V, 653; supervisors, terms and salaries, VI, 165; plankroad companies, tolls, 209; subjecting to Railroad Aid Act, 214; superintendent of the poor, 504; Watervliet, police justice, 1032; Watervliet, election of town officers, VII, 64; clerk, fees of, 604; exempting Coeymans from Town Auditor's Act, 622; clerk, office hours, 757; clerk, fee bill, 805; clerk, filing with assessors certificates of sale of property, 888; mutual insurance companies in certain towns, 1097; sheriff, fees and compensation, 1121; Westerlo, Chesterville, separate road district, VIII, 615; surrogate and county judge, fixing salary, IX, 624; town meetings, fixing time, 718; commitments, support of prisoners, compensation of sheriff and others, 730; commissioner of jurors, X, 44.

ALBANY GAZETTE. Cited, Thanksgiving proclamations after War of 1812, II, 824.

ALBANY LOAN AND TRUST COMPANY. Charter, veto, VI, 342.

ALBANY NORMAL SCHOOL. Established, IV, 67, 265; objections to, 115; appropriations, 117, 265, 267, 552; supervision of, 65, 265; successful work of, 266, 377, 429, 647, 716; V, 15; method of selecting State pupils, IV, 266; volunteer pupils, 268; experimental classes, 269; new building for, 395, 429, 476; instruction of Indian youth, 477; agricultural instruction suggested, 843; proposed removal of, 843; number of pupils, V, 15, 174, 523, 604, 695; appropriation for new buildings, X, 930.

VETOES. Repairs, furniture and books, VII, 469; scientific apparatus, repairs and expenses, 926.

ALBANY PENITENTIARY. Established, IV, 74; good management and condition of, 611, 724; superintendent opposes bill relating to confinement of convicts, VI, 712; discontinuance, to be used as jail, X, 629.

ALBANY PLAN OF UNION. Formed by convention of commissioners, I, 550, 551, 577; referred to as Constitution, 579; text of, where published, 579; synopsis of, 579; scheme of government, 579; proceedings and plan transmitted to Lords of Trade, 581; plan not approved, 582.

ALBANY RAILWAY COMPANY. Bridge over Hudson river, veto, X, 52.

ALBANY AND SCHENECTADY RAILROAD COMPANY. Consolidation with other companies authorized, V, 803.

ALBANY AND SUSQUEHANNA RAILROAD. New appropriation suggested, V, 194; State aid to, 531, 864; asks State aid, 866; VI, 70; bill to facilitate construction, veto, V, 138, 242, 350, 439, 737.

ALBANY AND WEST STOCKBRIDGE RAILROAD COMPANY. Aid to, route of, III, 750; completion of, 953.

ALBION. Western House of Refuge for Women at, IX, 293; vetoes,— village, relative to, VII, 807; — schools and school district, X, 948.

ALBION HOUSE OF REFUGE FOR WOMEN. Established, IX, 144. See WESTERN HOUSE OF REFUGE FOR WOMEN, ALBION.

ALBRO, REBECCA. Relief, veto, III, 262.

ALBRO, WAIT. Wife of, legacy to, relative to, veto, III, 262.

ALDEN. Town meeting, legalizing election of highway commissioner, veto, VI, 1034.

ALDERMEN. New York, petition of, relative to French prisoners, I, 166; New York and Albany, to be commissioners of excise, 529; Brooklyn, holding other office, veto, VII, 321.

ALDRICH, W. F. Bank examiner, charges against Superintendent Ellis, VII, 66.

ALDRICH, WILLIAM H. Commissioner, Allegany Reservation, Red House bridge, veto, VII, 587.

ALDRIDGE, GEORGE H. Superintendent of Public Works, communication from, recommending canal investigation, 1898, IX, 850; commission created, 849; report and action thereon, 850; suspended from office, 850; statements concerning canal investigation, 1898, X, 41; complaints against, 77; exonerated by special investigating commission, 78.

ALEHOUSES. Quartering soldiers in, I, 604.

ALEXANDER, WILLIAM. See STIRLING, LORD.

ALEXANDER, WILLIAM C. Member of New Jersey commission to procure Constitutional Convention, V, 325.

ALEXANDRIA, D. C. Lieutenant-Governor Delancey visits, to confer with General Braddock, I, 566, 568; retrocession to Virginia, III, 980.

ALEXANDRIA, N. Y. Town, aid to Utica and Black River Railroad Company, veto, VI, 92; relief from railroad burdens, veto, VII, 847, new bill passed.

ALGER (MRS.), MARY E. R. Acting supervisor of truancy, New York, compensation, veto, X, 473.

ALGIERS. War with, II, 852.

ALGRAVE. Defeat of French fleet on coast of, I, 640.

ALIEN AND SEDITION ACTS. Condemned by Virginia, II, 430.

ALIENS. Result of joining enemy, II, 202; claims to land, 218; right to take and hold property, III, 88, 771, 1039; V, 90, 191, 293, 386; VI, 365, 550; VII, 662; children of, schools for, III, 768, 947; wives and children, status of, 850; naturalization, 883; alleged improper naturalization, 928; passenger tax unconstitutional, IV, 273, 441, 485; number of arrivals, 644, 719, 793, 849; V, 188, 278, 377, 450, 535, 599, 842; VI, 28, 117, 238, 362, 534, 627; VII, 15, 309, 432, 530, 711, 831, 965; case of Venezuelan minister, V, 617; children of American women marrying foreigners, VI, 365; comparative statement of arrivals, 909; paupers returned to their homes, VII, 705, 830, 959; returned to their homes, 965; when included in militia, X, 15.

VETOES. Relative to, II, 202; right of alien father to custody of children, III, 846; Hoenig escheat, VII, 549; purchasing and holding real estate, 662; taking and holding real estate, IX, 725.

ALLDS, JOTHAM P. Assembly, member of Prince Henry reception committee, X, 479; escorts Prince Henry at his reception by the Assembly, 480; member of joint committee on taxation, 1899, 801.

ALLEGANY COUNTY. Arms and supplies for, II, 775; average excise license fees, 1889, VIII, 636; highways, cost of labor system, 1892, IX, 199; insane, care of, county and State systems compared, 228.

VETOES. Aiding railroads, VI, 95; Scio, constables, appointment, VII, 218; removing obstructions from Grass river, VIII, 847; Feller escheat, 882.

ALLEGANY INDIAN RESERVATION. Number of Indians on, 1819, II, 976; act relative to Seneca Indians, IV, 290; sale of land for taxes, release of, V, 36; ascertaining damages caused by trepassers, 863; villages, survey under act of Congress, VI, 704; compulsory education of Indian children, VII, 709; bridge over Allegany river, VIII, 560.

VETOES. Prohibiting sales of liquor on, VI, 97; highways and bridges, 690; bridge at Vandalia, 707; Senecas, amending act, 910; oil pipe line, contract for, VII, 73; Red House bridge, 587; new schoolhouse, 909; bridge at Onoville, VIII, 845; State road, improvement of, 847; repair of highways, X, 429.

ALLEGANY RIVER. Improvement of, II, 965; canal connection with Susquehanna and Genesee rivers, III, 70; proposed canal connection with Lake Erie via Chautauqua lake, 96; proposed canal connection with Erie canal, 104, 165.

VETOES. Bridges,— at Allegany, V, 345; — Vandalia, VI, 707; — Portville, 709; — Onoville, VIII, 845; — Elko, X, 698.

ALLEGANY. (TOWN.) Bridge over Allegany river, veto, V, 345.

ALLEMANIA SAVINGS BANK, BROOKLYN. Charter, veto, VI, 589.

ALLEN, EVERETT. Canal department, appropriation for services, veto, IX, 716.

ALLEN, IRA, COLONEL. Delivers letter from Governor Chittenden to Governor Clinton, II, 136; Vermont's agent before Congress, 176.

ALLEN, NATHANIEL, MAJOR. Appointed paymaster of militia, II, 764; funds received by, 765, 766.

ALLEN, PETER. Lieutenant-colonel 20th Regiment, II, 766.

ALLEN, STEPHEN. Member of prison investigating commission, III, 22.

ALLEN, WILLIAM F. Member of commission on readjustment of quotas, V, 537, 572; Comptroller, report, powers of canal commissioners, VI, 344; Buck case, 682.

ALLISON, COLONEL. Letter from, relative to New York prisoners of war, II, 101.

ALMSHOUSES. Good effect of, III, 176; New York, efficient administration of, IV, 606; site, how changed, VIII, 945.

ALSOP, JOHN. Delegate to Continental Congress, I, 768.

ALTONA. Taxation of State lands in, veto, X, 953.

ALVORD, THOMAS G. Speaker, delivers address at ceremonies on first occupation of Assembly Chamber, new capitol, VII, 271; Assembly, member of committee on first occupation of new Senate Chamber, 540; remarks at ceremonies, 540; candidate for Speaker, 1881, 676; Lieutenant-Governor, delivers address at Capital Centennial Celebration, 1897, IX, 690.

AMBASSADORS. Appointment of, II, 500.

AMENDMENTS TO CONSTITUTION. General. Proposed relative to capital punishment, III, 863; proposed judiciary article, 936; amendments, how made, IV, 52, 103, 547, 677; V, 597; VI, 394; VII, 161; VIII, 1060; Legislature, contested elections, transferring power to courts, amendment rejected, 1892, VIII, 982, 1076; method of submission under Election Law, 1033; Supreme Court, additional justices, rejected, 1892, 1033, 1062; IX, 97; prohibition amendment, 1891, VIII, 923, 1060; forest preserve, 1896, rejected, IX, 187, 569, 669; prison labor, 1895, not submitted, 550; biennial sessions, 1898, 847; forest preserve, 1902, X, 339; designating county judges for service in Supreme Court, 375; forest preserve, 1903, 512; abandonment of parts of canals, not adopted, 731.

1801. Powers of Council of Appointment, II, 3, 361, 468, 505, 1043.
   Reorganization of Legislature, II, 468, 511, 651, 849, 1043.
1826. Justices of the peace, how chosen, III, 17, 57, 135, 158, 161; IV, 52.
   Extending right of suffrage, III, 58, 59, 135, 158; IV, 52.
1833. Election of mayor, New York, III, 212; IV, 52.
   Duties on salt, III, 330, 384, 413, 477, 505, 544, 619.
1835. Salt and auction duties restored to general fund, III, 413, 414, 505, 544, 552, 619; IV, 53.
1838. Election of mayors by people, IV, 53.
1845. Removal of judicial officers, IV, 55, 109, 137.
   Property qualifications of officers abolished, IV, 109, 137; VII, 324.
1854. Completing canals, IV, 549, 678, 735, 781, 783, 784, 833, 834; V, 65, 152, 209, 590, 705; VI, 347.
   State stock, IV, 784.
   Canal contracts to be let to lowest bidder, IV, 735, 834; V, 712; VI, 347, 799.
1864. Soldier vote, V, 512.
1869. See JUDICIARY ARTICLE, 1869.
1874. Adoption of, VI, 657, 725.
   Art. 2. Bribery, persons guilty of, excluded from right of suffrage, VI, 725; VII, 724.
   Art. 3, § 6. Compensation of members of Legislature, VI, 400, 550, 726.
   Art. 3, § 18. Limiting private and local laws, VI, 402, 550, 726; VII, 69, 157, 535, 628, 729, 757, 763; VIII, 52, 101, 343.
      Bridges, VII, 383, 578, 589, 909.
      Changing names, VII, 748.
      Drainage, VI, 189; VII, 369, 406; VIII, 614.

AMENDMENTS — (*Continued*).

Elections, VII, 263, 370.

Exclusive privilege, VI, 662, 691, 814, 949, 1034; VII, 336, 845; VIII, 411, 463, 880.

Highways, special act prohibited, VII, 63, 91, 208, 215, 222, 320, 440, 630, 887; VIII, 387, 615, 616, 879, 1086.

Increasing or decreasing compensation of officers, VI, 877; VII, 251, 255, 259, 497, 540, 549, 604, 753, 777, 1055, 1098, 1115, 1121; VIII, 412.

Jurors, IX, 516.

Railroads, VII, 395, 592, 895, 1037, 1063; VIII, 615; IX, 271.

Supervisors, VII, 769, 843, 860.

Villages, special charters prohibited, VI, 120, 683, 825; VII, 214, 645, 879, 1123; VIII, 330; IX, 258.

Art. 3, § 19. Audit of claims against State, VI, 875; VII, 81, 83, 86, 88, 158, 227, 230, 462, 463, 495, 779, 782, 792, 850, 922, 929, 1055.

Art. 3, § 23. Boards of supervisors, powers conferred by general law, VI, 402; VII, 65, 757; VIII, 509, 517.

Art. 3, § 24. Extra compensation, VI, 403; VII, 49, 158, 223, 259, 372, 374, 499, 539, 540, 550, 753, 773, 777, 791, 1055, 1115.

Art. 4, § 1. Term of Governor, VI, 398.

Art. 4, § 9. Executive consideration of bills after adjournment of Legislature, IV, 524; VI, 642, 883.

Veto of separate items in appropriation bills, II, 460; V, 263; VI, 369, 403, 642, 852, 864, 883, 924; IX, 404.

Thirty-day period, VI, 852, 884; VII, 940.

Art. 7, § 3. Canal revenues, VI, 540; extra compensation, VI, 540; VIII, 626; canal contracts to be let to lowest bidder, VI, 799.

Art. 7, § 6. Sale of lateral canals, VI, 540, 749, 796; canals, expenditures cannot exceed revenues, VII, 6, 359, 684.

Art. 7, § 13. State sinking funds, VI, 540.

Art. 7, § 14. Limitation of claims against State, VI, 540; VII, 599, 602, 606, 644, 773, 781, 801, 1120, 1121, 1124; IX, 429, 452.

Art. 8, § 4. Savings banks, uniform charters, VI, 725; VIII, 232.

Art. 8, § 10. State aid to private enterprise, VII, 915, 1084.

Art. 8, § 11. Prohibiting municipal aid to private enterprise, IV, 806; VII, 206, 617, 652, 661, 848, 867, 1047, 1106;

AMENDMENTS — (*Continued*).

VIII, 239, 529; limiting municipal expenditures and indebtedness, VI, 402; VII, 47, 617, 754, 846, 1018, 1088, 1107.

Art. 12, § 1. Official oath, VII, 44.

Art. 15. Bribery, VI, 725.

1876. Superintendent of Prisons, V, 78, 373, 437; VI, 109, 233, 335, 938, 942, 984; VII, 11, 424, 519, 963; VIII, 487.

Superintendent of Public Works, VI, 397, 934; VII, 11, 50, 143, 235, 358, 423; VIII, 487; appointment of subordinate officers, VII, 1024.

1880. Judicial pensions, II, 363.

1882. Supreme Court, additional justices, General Term, VII, 728, 837.

Canal tolls abolished, VII, 818; VIII, 13.

1884. Municipal indebtedness, limitation of, VI, 917; VII, 727; VIII, 27, 161, 184, 239, 880.

1888. Second Division, Court of Appeals, VIII, 486; X, 373.

1899. Art. 3, § 26. Boards of supervisors, IX, 753.

Art. 6, § 7. Court of Appeals, temporary designations from Supreme Court, X, 373.

Art. 8, § 10. Municipal indebtedness, limitation of, VI, 917; VIII, 29.

1901. Taxation, special exemption laws prohibited, IX, 232.

1905. Art. 6, § 1. Supreme Court, increasing number of justices, X, 516, 849, 936; ninth judicial district, IV, 857; IX, 547; X, 337.

Art. 6, § 2. Appellate Division, members of, power to hold other courts, X, 849.

Art. 7, § 4. Extending term of credit on State debt, IV, 56, 833; V, 7; IX, 305; X, 214, 496, 577, 731, 848.

Art. 7, § 11. Sinking fund, any money in treasury may be used for general purposes, IX, 305; X, 577, 601, 731, 848, 923.

Art. 7, § 12. Highway improvements, State debt for, VIII, 1043; X, 214, 513, 732, 833, 850, 909.

Art. 8, § 10. Municipal indebtedness, limitation, VI, 917; VIII, 29; X, 851.

Art. 12, § 1. Labor interests, VIII, 317; X, 97, 190, 850, 916.

1907. Art. 8, § 10. Municipal indebtedness, second class cities, VI, 917; VIII, 29.

Art. 12, § 2. Reducing population limit of first class cities, IX, 678.

AMENDMENTS TO CONSTITUTION, UNITED STATES. Proposed by New York convention, II, 290; IV, 750, 757; proposed by Virginia, II, 294; adoption of first ten, 290, 304; IV, 750; VIII, 505; Arkansas slavery amendments, not to be altered except by unanimous consent of States, V, 356; subsequent to Civil War, acceptance of, VI, 768.

FIRST AMENDMENT. Freedom of speech and press, III, 589, 645; V, 483; right of petition, 483; VI, 375; right to assemble, 375.

SECOND AMENDMENT. Right of people to keep and bear arms, IV, 726; V, 281.

FOURTH AMENDMENT. Unreasonable searches and seizures, IV, 755; V, 471.

FIFTH AMENDMENT. Property taken for public use, II, 522, 585, 646, 663; due process of law, 603, 820; III, 574; IV, 48; V, 471; IX, 351, 500; witness against himself, IV, 310; indictment for infamous crime, V, 471.

SIXTH AMENDMENT. Crimes, right of accused to speedy and impartial trial by jury, VII, 613.

NINTH AMENDMENT. Reserved rights of States, IV, 618; VI, 831.

TENTH AMENDMENT. Reserved powers of States, III, 234, 582, 590; IV, 618; VI, 831.

ELEVENTH AMENDMENT. Adopted, II, 335, 347; tax on bank of United States for local business, 1077; not violated by act creating bank of United States, 1118; jurisdiction of Federal courts, III, 1026; State cannot be sued by citizens of another State, VII, 250.

TWELFTH AMENDMENT. Adopted, presidential elections, II, 537, 546, 608; cited, 545; presidential electors, III, 30; counting vote, VII, 34, 40.

THIRTEENTH AMENDMENT. Slavery abolished, III, 574; IV, 382, 449; V, 616, 623, 636; general purpose of, V, 858; rejected by Southern States, 858.

FOURTEENTH AMENDMENT. Equal protection of the laws, II, 594; V, 790; VII, 591; VIII, 367; X, 882; right of suffrage, II, 687; privileges and immunities of citizens, 1041; III, 844, 981; V, 309, 325, 790; VIII, 367; apportionment of representatives, IV, 85; V, 790; VIII, 135; description of, V, 742; ratified, 744, 790; rights of citizens, 790; due process of law, 790; VIII, 367; Senators and Representatives, who disqualified, V, 790; public debt confirmed, 791; general purpose of, 858; rejected by Southern States, 858.

FIFTEENTH AMENDMENT. Right of suffrage protected, VI, 50; Legislature of 1870 rescinds resolution of adoption, 50.

AMENDMENTS TO UNITED STATES CONSTITUTION PROPOSED BUT NOT ADOPTED. Governor Hoffman, popular election of Senators, VI. 377; Governor Hill, President and Vice-President, extending term to six years, ineligibility to re-election, VIII, 691.

ARKANSAS. Method of choosing President and Vice-President, V, 354; regulating slavery in territories, 354; when United States liable for loss of fugitive slaves, 355; excluding negroes from rights of citizenship, 355.

CONGRESS. Titles of nobility, II, 678; securing perpetuity of slavery, V, 349, 398.

CONNECTICUT. Eligibility of President and Vice-President, Senators and Representatives, II, 425; basis of representation and direct taxes, admission of new States, limiting duration of embargo, interdiction of commerce, limiting power to declare war, only native citizens entitled to hold office, ineligibility of President to re-election, II, 827, 828; limiting President's power of appointment, III, 747; ineligibility of President to second term, 972.

DELAWARE. Limiting eligibility of President to one term, III, 909.

GEORGIA. Reducing term of Senators, II, 827; prohibiting importation of colored persons into a State without its consent, III, 34; House of Representatives not to determine election of President, 182, 314.

KENTUCKY. Jurisdiction of Federal courts, II, 562; prohibiting increase of salary of Representatives during term, 919; limiting eligibility of President to one term, III, 909.

LOUISIANA. Extending term of President to six years, and making him ineligible to re-election, III, 281.

MAINE. Prohibiting House of Representatives from choosing President and the Senate from choosing a Vice-President, III, 591; ineligibility of President to second term, 972.

MARYLAND. Qualifications of Vice-President, Senators and Representatives, II, 434; election of presidential electors and Representatives by districts, 471; importation of slaves, 605.

MASSACHUSETTS. Foreign influence in national councils, II, 424; apportionment of Representatives, 546; importation of slaves from West Indies, 562; limiting duration of embargo, 665; basis of representation and direct taxes, admission of new States, limiting duration of embargo, interdiction of commerce, limiting power to declare war, only native citizens entitled to hold office, ineligibility of President to re-election, II, 827, 828; apportioning representatives according to free persons, excluding Indians not taxed, IV, 85.

AMENDMENTS — (*Continued*).

> NEW HAMPSHIRE. Qualifications of President, Vice-President, Senators and Representatives, II, 433.
>
> NEW JERSEY. Election of Representatives and presidential electors by districts, II, 919.
>
> NORTH CAROLINA. Choosing presidential electors by districts, II, 513; importation of slaves from West Indies, 552; election of Representatives and presidential electors by single districts, 750, 864.
>
> OHIO. Popular election of President and presidential electors, III, 184; prohibiting House of Representatives from choosing a President or the Senate from choosing a Vice-President, 589.
>
> PENNSYLVANIA. Tribunal for determining questions between Federal and State governments, II, 667; prohibiting national banking corporations except in District of Columbia, 1024.
>
> TENNESSEE. Importation of slaves, II, 589; reducing senatorial term from six years to four years, 795; prohibiting increase of salary of Representative during term, 930; election of President and Vice-President by popular vote, III, 137; perpetuation of slavery, V, 315.
>
> TEXAS. Federal officers, tenure should be fixed, VIII, 1091.
>
> VERMONT. Importation of slaves, II, 586; removal of Federal judges, 627; election of Representatives and presidential electors by districts, 990; ineligibility of President to second term, III, 907.
>
> VIRGINIA. Approval of treaty by House of Representatives; tribunal other than Senate for trial of impeachments; reorganizing Senate, Federal judge ineligible to other office, II, 366; qualifications of Senators, Representatives, judicial and executive officers, 439; removal of Senator, 631.

AMERICAN. Meaning of term, IX, 637.

AMERICAN ACADEMY OF FINE ARTS, NEW YORK. Act relating to, II, 877.

AMERICAN BANK. See BANK OF NORTH AMERICA.

AMERICAN AGRICULTURAL ASSOCIATION. Incorporated, IV, 284.

AMERICAN ANTIQUARIAN SOCIETY. Applies for copies of laws and legislative journals, II, 930, 994, 1114; applies for laws and judicial decisions, III, 749.

AMERICAN ATHENAEUM, PARIS. Requests copies of New York laws, IV, 46.

AMERICAN BAPTIST PUBLICATION SOCIETY. Consolidating with American and Foreign Bible Society, veto, VI, 327.

AMERICAN CHRONOLOGICAL AND AUTOGRAPHICAL SOCIETY. Charter, veto, VII, 412.

AMERICAN COLONIZATION SOCIETY. Memorial from, III, 144; objects of, IV, 621.

AMERICAN CYCLOPEDIA. Quoted, voting by ballot, VIII, 584.

AMERICAN DAIRYMEN'S ASSOCIATION. Protests against milk adulteration bill, VI, 710.

AMERICAN EXPLORING AND MINING COMPANY. Charter, veto, V, 726.

AMERICAN FEDERATION OF LABOR, NEW YORK BRANCH. Approves Governor Flower's recommendations concerning coal combinations, IX, 216.

AMERICAN FEMALE GUARDIAN SOCIETY. Changing name, veto, VIII, 337.

AMERICAN AND FOREIGN BIBLE SOCIETY. Consolidating with American Baptist Publication Society, veto, VI, 327.

AMERICAN FORESTRY CONGRESS. Memorial on forest preservation and cultivation, VII, 1001.

AMERICAN GEOGRAPHICAL AND STATISTICAL SOCIETY. Charter, veto, IV, 633.

AMERICAN GLUCOSE COMPANY. Court of Claims, veto, IX, 797.

AMERICAN INSTITUTE. Communication from, cultivation of silk and beet sugar, III, 821; required to report, IV, 80.

AMERICAN JERSEY CATTLE CLUB. Charter, veto, VII, 202.

AMERICAN LOAN COMPANY. Changing name, veto, VII, 267.

AMERICAN MORTGAGE AND TRUST COMPANY, NEW YORK. Amending charter, veto, VIII, 630.

AMERICAN MUSEUM OF NATURAL HISTORY, NEW YORK. Receives donations of natural history specimens, VI, 22.

VETOES. Instruction of teachers in anatomy and kindred subjects, VII, 923; instruction of teachers in natural history, IX, 84; appropriation, 1898, IX, 868; contract with Superintendent of Public Instruction, appropriation, X, 638.

AMERICAN MUTUAL BENEVOLENT ASSOCIATION, NEW YORK. Charter, veto, VI, 187.

AMERICAN ORDER OF UNITED WORKMEN. Grand Legion of Select Knights, charter, veto, VII, 546.

AMERICAN POPULAR LIFE INSURANCE COMPANY. Amending charter, veto, VI, 189.

AMERICAN SCENIC AND HISTORIC PRESERVATION SOCIETY. Succeeds Society for the Preservation of Scenic and Historic Places and Objects, X, 241.

AMERICAN SOCIETY FOR THE EXTENSION OF UNIVERSITY TEACHING. Extension movement, IX, 18; quoted, higher education not self-sustaining, 20.

AMERICAN TITLE INSURANCE AND TRUST COMPANY. Charter, veto, IX, 718.

AMHERST. VETOES. Cleaning canal ditches, VII, 336; drainage, X 698.

AMHERST, JEFFERY. Commands English forces in Louisburg campaign, I, 635; borrows money for campaign, 637, 695; care of troops, 639; partial payment of loan, 639; thanks Legislature for approving loan, 641; payment of loan, 646; conquest of Canada, 648; volunteers for frontier service, 57, 669; complimented by council, 658; offers bounties for volunteers, 664; campaign against Western Indians, 674, 676; letter from, Indian War, 678; plans of, approved, 679; return of money to colony, 709.

AMMUNITION. Crown furnishes for colony, I, 48; for forts in Albany county, 460; purchase from Indians prohibited, 467, 549; Indians receive from both French and English, 535; King to furnish, 620, 634, 644, 654, 663; scarcity of, II, 122, 360; supply needed, 148; provided at public expense, 337; collection and deposit of, 453; purchase of, 537, 569, 608, 619; for use on frontiers, 636; furnished by United States, 791.

AMORY, COLONEL J. Aide-de-camp, carries letter to Major-General Doughty, anti-rent trouble, III, 831.

AMSTERDAM, NETHERLANDS. Archives, colonial documents, IV, 172; early ecclesiastical documents, translation, veto, X, 298, 563.

AMSTERDAM, NEW YORK.
CITY. Incorporated, VII, 1014; VIII, 88; number of excise licenses, 1887, 359; excise license fees, 1889, 685.
VETOES. Charter, VII, 1014; official newspapers, VIII, 943, 1039; estate, sale, 1090; legalizing assessment, IX, 374; Pythian Association, exemption from taxation, 449; canal bridge, Minaville street, X, 698.

AMSTERDAM.
TOWN. Relief of, veto, V, 725.
VILLAGE. Revising charter, veto, V, 512; water works, payment of claim, veto, VII, 1107.

AMUSEMENTS. Places of, better protection in, VII, 29; places of, excise licenses in, VIII, 462; Horton Boxing Law, repeal, X, 104.
VETOES. Bill to restrict, V, 220; places of,—regulating sale of tickets, VII, 804; — regulating management of, 804; — New York, exempting certain hall from license fee, 1086; Flatlands, licenses, VIII, 975; New York, places of, license fees, payments to Actors' Fund, IX, 872; theater tickets, regulating sale, X, 51; public dancing within half mile of cathedral in process of erection, 456; New York, places of, 475; New York, recreation piers, 580, 581, 582; New York playgrounds, acquisition, 582, 635.

·ANDERSON, HENRY H. Opinion, unconstitutionality of ballot bill, 1888, VIII, 574, 580.

ANDERSON, ROBERT. Major, commands at Fort Sumter, V, 399.

ANDES, DELAWARE COUNTY. Anti-rent troubles in, IV, 299; village, fire department, veto, VII, 65.

ANDREUS, JOHN E. Relief, veto, VII, 805.

"ANDREW FLETCHER," THE. Quarantine vessel destroyed by fire, VI, 533.

ANDREWS, CHARLES. Court of Appeals, quoted, legislative power, grant of relief to individuals not limited to actionable cases, VII, 453; opinion, origin of office of town clerk, IX, 399.

ANDREWS, CHARLES B. Superintendent of Public Buildings, VIII, 501.

ANDREWS, GEORGE H. Senate, committee on adjustment of quotas, V, 634.

ANDREWS, T. P. Washington committee, lottery memorial, II, 1126.

ANDROS, SIR EDMUND. Governor, letters from Duke of York to, relative to Assembly, I, 3; effect of departure from colony without arranging for collection of duties, 4; appointed Governor of New England and New York, 14; imprisoned in Boston, 14; letters from, missing, IV, 184; official service, I, pref. ix.

ANDROVETT, PETER. Westfield, Richmond county school supplies, claim, veto, X, 320.

ANDROVIC, ANNA AND STANISLAUS. Court of Claims, veto, X, 946.

ANGEL, JAMES R. Court of Claims, injuries, Auburn prison, veto, X, 702.

ANGEL, WILKES. Senate, committee on alleged interference in speakership contest, V, 485.

ANGELIS, PASCAL C. I. D. Bond for return of arms, II, 774.

ANGLO-AMERICAN LOAN AND TRUST COMPANY. Charter, veto, VI, 342.

ANIMALS. Destruction of, rewards for, II, 1106, 1107; in New York, number and description of, III, 761, 993; diseased, slaughter authorized, claims for, VII, 990; as source of human disease, IX, 179; tuberculosis, report of special investigating committee, 1900, X, 120.

    VETOES. Sing Sing Society for Prevention of Cruelty to, VII, 745; infectious and contagious diseases, amending act, VIII, 730; affected with glanders, destruction of, 1166; fur-bearing, protection of, IX, 722; cruelty to, 793, 812; disseminating knowledge of birds and wild animals, 798; diseased, destruction of, repealing acts applicable to New York, 810, 870; contagious abortion in cows, investigation, 857; cruelty to, Erie county, 869; condemned, appraisers of, X, 592; destruction of, Baker case, claim for damages, 593.

ANNAPOLIS ROYAL. French attempt on, I, 331, 336, 347.

ANNE, QUEEN OF ENGLAND. Accession of, I, 98; appoints Lord Cornbury Governor, 98; success in campaign against French, 104; pro-

Anne, Queen of England — (*Continued*).

hibits presents to Governor, 106, 116, 143, 148; recommends repeal of Colonial act to quiet disorders, 109; act repealed, 110; correspondence with enemies prohibited, 118; Assembly authorized to appoint treasurer, 123, 168, 298; address to, relative to corruption of coin, 131; address to, 140, 153, 157; letter in behalf of Lady Lovelace, 145; forts and missionaries in Indian country, 156; instructions relative to use of public funds, 164; not pleased with Fourteenth Assembly, 167; death of, 174.

Annsville. Assessment for highway labor, veto, VII, 130.

Annual Message. Governor Yates, III, 2, 16; Governor De Witt Clinton, 53, 113, 153, 197; Governor Van Buren, 230; Lieutenant-Governor Throop, 282; Governor Throop, 318, 366; Governor Marcy, 399, 441, 493, 534, 605, 647; Governor Seward, 706, 762, 853, 934; Governor Bouck, IV, 1, 49; Governor Wright, 87, 230; Governor Young, 363, 385; Governor Fish, 421, 467; Governor Hunt, 538, 594; Governor Seymour, 640, 709; V, 445, 520; Governor Clark, IV, 780, 830; Governor King, V, I, 42; Governor Morgan, 64, 151, 249, 357; Governor Fenton, 582, 680, 741, 818; Governor Hoffman, VI, 1, 99, 225, 348; Governor Dix, 522, 613; Governor Tilden, 719, 912; Governor Robinson, VII, 1, 137, 271; Governor Cornell, 418, 510, 677; Governor Cleveland, 815, 938; Governor Hill, VIII, 1, 143, 294, 475, 662, 891, 1054; Governor Flower, IX, 1, 156, 296; Governor Morton, 536, 643; Governor Black, 738, 820; Governor Roosevelt, X, 1, 74; Governor Odell, 180, 327, 482, 595; Governor Higgins, 718, 831.

Annuities. To Indians, II, 311, 357, 381; for Oneida Indians, 608; advance to Indians on account of famine, 882; advance to Stockbridge Indians, 988; advance to New Stockbridge Indians, 1116; to Stockbridge Indians, III, 183; Senecas, changing method of payment, IV, 460; Onondaga Indians, veto, VII, 417.

Answer to Governor's Speech. Discontinued, II, 1014.

Anthon, William Henry. Judge-Advocate-General, communication from, pay of volunteers discharged on inspection, V, 421.

Anthony, Peter W. Relief, veto, VI, 185.

Antietam. Battle of, number of New York regiments in, IX, 341; regimental monuments at, 341; communication from Federal Antietam Board, War Department, 341.

Antietam National Cemetery. Burial of New York soldiers in, V, 636, 841; VI, 261; documents relative to, V, 725; appropriation for, 764; VI, 261; New York commission, report of, V, 791; report of New York commissioner, 840, 869; origin of, 840; national monument in, 841; list of New York soldiers buried in, 870; transferred by Maryland to United States, VII, 172.

ANTI-RENT TROUBLE. Application for military aid, III, 774; Governor Seward issues proclamation, 775; special message on, 822; inquiry into causes, 841; Governor Wright's review of, IV, 139, 232; in Columbia county, 147, 235; in Rensselaer county, 147; in Delaware county, 234, 235; in Schoharie county, 234; assault on Columbia deputy sheriff, 235; murder of Deputy Sheriff Steele, Delaware county, 235; proclamation declaring Delaware county in state of insurrection, 238, 246, 297; proclamation revoked, 238, 326; changing leases to tenures, 240; report of Assembly committee, 241, 328; distress for rent, 241; taxation of reserved rents, 242; expense of, Delaware county, 246; anti-rent associations in Delaware county, 297, 302; duty of tenants, 306; duty of landlords, 307; Governor Wright's letter to Delaware county sheriff, 309; number of persons convicted of Steele's murder, 323; estimated quantity of land under lease, 1848, 408; memorial from Albany and Rensselaer counties, V, 792.

ANTONETTI, CARDINAL. Letter from, transmitting gift from Pope, IV, 455.

ANTWERP, BELGIUM. International Exposition, 1894, IX, 317.

ANTWERP, NEW YORK. Town, aid to Utica and Black River Railroad Company, amending act, veto, VI, 92.

APGAR, EDGAR K., JR. Large per capita cost of construction of Hudson River and Middletown State Hospitals, X, 410.

APGAR, JAMES K. Stenographer, Assembly committee to prepare rules, appropriation, veto, VIII, 844.

APPEAL. Right of, should be preserved, II, 417; in militia cases, III, 524; limiting right of, 610; none after judgment rights become fixed, IV, 532; by taxpayers from town audit, VI, 436; in capital cases, VIII, 82, 302, 476; in criminal cases, power of Court of Appeals to affirm conviction notwithstanding improper testimony, 486; from Court of Claims, bill should permit, IX, 285; delay in capital cases, X, 344; capital cases, direct from Supreme Court to Court of Appeals, 344; prompt argument required, 345.

VETOES. From State Board of Audit, VII, 412; amending Code of Civil Procedure, 931, 932; from New York Marine Court to Court of Appeals, 1092; to Court of Appeals, consent of General Term, 1093; from Surrogates' Courts, 1109; from Board of Claims to Court of Appeals, VIII, 56; from superintendents of the poor, 130, 199; to County Court, 406; justices' courts, 468; from General Term, extending time, 718; by people in criminal cases, 981; Code of Civil Procedure, amending, 1038; from special sessions, stay of execution, IX, 45; from orders, 152; exceptions and case, 283, 390; practice on, amending Criminal Code, 792; in criminal cases, and proceed-

Appeal, Vetoes — (*Continued*).

> ings against fugitives from justice, 793; New York abandonment proceedings, undertaking on, X, 178; decision on, 587; by defendant on judgment overruling demurrer to judgment, X, 705; criminal cases, from order denying motion for a new trial, 927.

Appellate Division, Supreme Court. See Court, Appellate Division.

Apple. Size of barrels, veto, X, 317.

Appleton, John A. Sale of Southfield land for quarantine, appropriation, veto, VII, 385, 929.

Appomatox. Lee's army surrenders at, V, 676.

Apportionment.

> House of Representatives. Act for, II, 324, 511, 705; III, 387, 939, 1033; IV, 590; V, 388; extraordinary session called to consider, III, 393; census of 1850, IV, 577; census of 1860, V, 296; Fourteenth Amendment, 790; act of 1872, veto, VI, 493, passed over veto; act of 1883, VII, 725, 838; VIII, 157; constitutional provision, 135; inequalities in New York, 1892, IX, 6; act of 1892, 7; of 1901, X, 278, 281.

> Legislature. Act for, II, 312, 511; reconstruction of Senate districts, veto, 651; act for, cannot be amended, 651, 849; Senate, veto, 849; based on United States census, 1820, 1047; of 1826, III, 133; 1836, 567; 1846, IV, 250; Assembly districts in Niagara county, special act, 383; Governor Robinson's protest against delay in making, VII, 100, 164, 303; of 1879, 303, 401; VIII, 157; memorandum on, VII, 401; legislative power is a continuing one, VIII, 156; IX, 4; constitutional provision, VII, 100, 164; VIII, 157, 491, 677, 741, 1055; X, 851; inequalities under apportionment of 1879, VIII, 494; IX, 4; act of 1892, VIII, 1057; IX, 3, 154; at extraordinary session constitutional, 155; act of 1906 unconstitutional, X, 852.

Appraisers. Decedents' estates, fees, veto, X, 61.

Apprentice. Act relating to, I, 11; need of proposed subsidy for, 281; enlistments of, reimbursing masters, 599; prohibiting sale of liquor to, IV, 753; laws should be revised, VI, 123; decline of system, VIII, 322; duties of factory inspector, 323.

Appropriation Bill After 1874. See also Supply Bill. Action on, VIII, 71, 255, 439, 553, 989; IX, 68, 403; X, 421, 549, 637, 781, 783.

Appropriations.

> Colony. Support of government, I, 10, 11, 15, 16, 20, 23, 40, 81; reward to Captain Kidd, 21; defense of Albany, 37, 48, 160; presents to Indians, 44, 129, 173, 196, 200, 312; to rebuild chapel in fort, 51, 63; King's troops, 57; agent of colony, 58, 59; defense of frontiers, 62, 71, 93, 99, 105; relief of Indians, 65; additional militia, 66; fort in Indian country, 86, 89;

APPROPRIATIONS, COLONY — (Continued).

batteries at Narrows, 103; Peter Schuyler, visit to Indians, 125; repairs of guardhouse at Schenectady, 125; Colonel Peartree, 128; David Schuyler and Lawrence Claesen, 134; expedition against Canada, 135, 151; repair of fortifications and frontier defense, 155; British officers in Canadian expedition, 157; expenses of commissioners to Onondagas, 167; Hansen's claim, Indian service, 172; agent to Great Britain, 175; expenses in procuring royal assent to public debts bill, 180; encouraging Indian trade, 198; fortifications and Indian trade, 208; salaries of agents, 216; barracks at New York, 231; expense of Indian negotiations, 265; to be made annually, 267, 277, 285, 291, 303, 307, 312, 470, 472, 484, 556, 559, 584, 605; Oswego garrison, 290; expenses relating to triennial bill, 292; supplies for Indians at Albany, 300; State Constitution, 1846, 303; Governor's house, 314, 349, 673; defense of Oswego, 315; fortifications in Albany, 318; outscouts, 325, 346, 353, 462; to aid Massachusetts in Cape Breton expedition, 332, 349; rebuilding fort at Saratoga, 364; expense of commissioners, 370; Canadian expedition, 374, 388, 391, 393; to Governor for conference with Indians, 376; Albany rangers, 378; to reimburse Governor for repairs on fort at Albany, 390; Governor's expenses to Albany, 392; Vandenbergh and Hart, 394; Van Dam, subsistence of French prisoners, 445; salaries, 458; Stevens, Indian interpreter, 459; to Colonel Johnson for provisions, 420, 504, 522; scalps, 460, 468; frontier service, 468; de Joncourt, 478, 507; subsistence of prisoners, 478; method of applying, 482, 483, 488, 505, 534, 556; expense of exchanging prisoners, 507, 510; Bruning and Van Zandt, 511; Shuckburgh, 518; to aid Virginia against French, 536; fortifications, general act, 547, 741; general military purposes, 565; arms, 568; Philip Verplanck, 572; Connecticut men in Crown Point expedition, 576; permanent fund recommended for fixed charges, 584; Orange and Ulster rangers, 588; expedition against Indians, 594; by Parliament to aid colonies, 598, 645; allowance to militia, 603; various military purposes, 607, 608, 611, 616; Lieutenant-Governor's expenses, 626; Kingston blockhouses, 627; Canadian campaign, 636; Boston fire sufferers, 646; Sandy Hook lighthouse, 655; Attorney-General, 672, 729; unspiking cannon, 710; riot losses, 713; Lieutenant-Governor Colden's salary, 728; New York hospital, 743; Quebec boundary, 745, 747, 755, 757, 764; Governor, New York fire, 754; Pennsylvania boundary, 761; Root and Rood, services of, warrant, 762; master of rolls, 763.

APPROPRIATIONS.

STATE. Militia, II, 53; support of prisoners, 259; expenses under Indian treaties, 201; fortifications, 334, 360, 422; Mohawk delegates, 373; lazaretto, 382; entertainment of Indians, 408, 410; extra compensation of judicial and executive officers, 449; veto of separate items, 460; V, 263; VI, 369, 403, 642, 852, 864, 924; IX, 404; X, 794, 799, 935; cannot be made by concurrent resolution, II, 741; VIII, 547, 840; sufferers on western frontier, II, 787; promotion of agriculture and manufactures, 970; children of De Witt Clinton, III, 220; State Lunatic Asylum, 715, 766; IV, 78; New York Institution for the Blind, III, 716; McLeod case, 943; limiting legislative power over, IV, 54; Clinton prison, 125, 276, 278; militia, antirent trouble, 148; canal construction, 391; Western House of Refuge, 408; V, 180; canal damages, IV, 438; new buildings for New York House of Refuge, 557; general canal purposes, 678, 743; contracts not to be made in excess of, 744; idiot asylum, 792; New York harbor commissioners, 858; failure of appropriation and supply bills, 1856, V, 8; Kansas sufferers, 34, 345; rebuilding part of State Lunatic Asylum, 55; acts making, purpose and limitations of, 72, 107, 816; VI, 863; excise money for State Inebriate Asylum, V, 87; to reimburse Governor King for expenses in quarantine disturbance, 89; bills for, should be considered early in session, 94; VI, 246, 368; Governor in pardon cases, V, 172; protection of New York harbor, 185; general act and supply bill, 263; pilot commissioners, 284; People's College, 376; Civil War bounties, 454, 530, 571; Prison Association, 527; harbor and frontier defenses, 530; enlarging locks on Champlain canal, 533; extension of Chenango canal, 534; care of soldiers and their families, 577, 585; canal awards, 591; soldiers' cemeteries at Gettysburg and Antietam, 636; arsenals and armories, 642; care of soldiers, 684; National Guard, 686; new quarantine establishment, 701, 767; VI, 27; Hudson river improvement, V, 707, 789; new capitol, 759; VI, 24, 116, 229, 350; Institution for the Blind at Batavia, V, 762, 839; Antietam National Cemetery, 764; military agencies, 775; Lincoln monument, 795; Soldiers' Home, at Albany, 837; VI, 62; Willard and Hudson River Asylums, 838; preventing spread of infectious disease, 845; enlargement of Champlain canal, VI, 107; Elmira Reformatory, 110, 234; redemption of militia certificates, War of 1812, 113; redemption of State stock, 167; altering or exchanging arms, 236; should be accompanied by means of payment, 524; improvement of streams, views of Governor

APPROPRIATIONS, STATE — (*Continued*).

Dix, 576; continuing or reviving, amount to be stated, 588; VIII, 246; re-enactment after two years, 864, 947; VII, 1026; Governor's accountability for, VI, 925; riders, protest against, VII, 26, 159; must specify object, 82, 220, 912; VIII, 420; for widow of Chief Judge Church, VII, 449; no money paid from treasury except on appropriation by law, 799; VIII, 547; Niagara Falls reservation, VII, 989; good roads, VIII, 1043; expenses, Buffalo railroad strike, 1892, IX, 160; proper rule for consideration of, 739; comparative statement, 1893–4; 1901 –2, X, 462; comparative statement, 1903, 578,—1904, 684; highway improvement, 1904, 619; for charitable institutions included in one bill, 727; comparative statement, 1905, 781; expenses of Hooker trial, 820; California earthquake sufferers, 891; additional and unusual, 1906, 930.

VETOES. Bill including Senate apportionment, II, 849; deficiency bill, V, 36; unexpended balance not specified, VII, 912, 913; appropriation bill, 1894, IX, 403, new bill passed; unexpended balance, reappropriation, X, 585.

AQUEDUCTS. Needed in procuring water for cities, II, 1017; for Erie canal, over Genesee river, III, 552, 670; Croton water supply for New York, 1034.

ARBITRATION. Proposed for settlement of differences between capital and labor, VIII, 164; State and local boards created, 165, 321; State board, how functions invoked, 1072; compulsory, suggested, 1072; labor, special boards recommended, X, 365; labor disputes involving necessaries, courts should have power to interfere, 509.

ARBOR DAY.

VETOES. Observance, appropriation, IX, 291; printing circulars and programmes, X, 423.

ARCADE RAILWAY, NEW YORK. Charter, veto, VI, 197.

ARCHIEPISCOPAL LIBRARY. Lambeth, colonial documents in, IV, 183.

ARCHITECT. Deposit of maps and plans, III, 934; John R. Thomas, Eastern New York Reformatory, appropriation, veto, X, 296.

ARCHITECTURE. Regulating practice of, veto, IX, 150, 624; X, 313, 704.

ARCULARIUS, HENRY. Elected commissary-general, III, 430.

ARDSLEY. Village, relief, veto, X, 62.

ARGAL, CAPTAIN. Visits Manhattan island, III, 1017.

ARGENTINA. Participation in Cotton States Exposition, IX, 581.

ARGUS, FRANK. Board of Claims, veto, VIII, 1166.

ARGUS, JOHN. Board of Claims, VIII, 1166.

ARGUS COMPANY. Court of Claims, veto, X, 944.

ARKANSAS. Exchanges maps with New York, III, 225; resolution relative to public lands, 705; stocks of, securities in New York banks,

ARKANSAS — (*Continued*).

725; IV, 36; admitted as a slave State, 814; approves repeal of Missouri Compromise and condemns Ohio's action relative to slavery, 824; recites grievances of slave-holding States, V, 353; proposed amendments,—method of choosing President and Vice-President, 354; — regulating slavery in Territories, 354; — when United States liable for value of fugitive slaves, 355; — excluding negroes from rights of citizenship, 355; secession ordinance, 396.

ARKELL, JAMES. Nominated as railroad commissioner, withdrawn, VIII, 373.

ARMORERS. For Senecas, I, 323; for Watervliet arsenal, II, 477; cities, compensation, veto, III, 417.

ARMORIES. National, supplying arms to States, IV, 71; erected at several places, V, 175; for separate companies, policy not approved, VII, 482; established at New York, Brooklyn and Flushing, 953; Assembly committee to investigate expenses of repairs, 1008; several repair bills pending, 1895, IX, 571; bills for new armories, 1895, 573; 71st Regiment, fire at, reimbursement for private property lost, X, 566.

VETOES. Schenectady, lease to Union University, VI, 709; Syracuse, replacing property destroyed by fire, 875; New York, 911; VII, 933; armorers in cities, 417; magazines and flagging, 479; Poughkeepsie, erection of, 481; Oswego addition, 482; Flushing, 17th Separate Company, erection, 482, 778; Kings county, site for, 541; Troy, 776; Kings county, reappropriation, 795; Brooklyn, 804; Albany, local assessment, 927; Oswego, repairing street and sidewalk, 927; Saratoga Springs, VIII, 291; maintenance, limiting State expense, 292; Niagara county, appropriation, 293; Mohawk, appropriation, 294; Olean, 455; Middletown, 455; use by veteran associations, 873; Malone, 886; purchase of land, amending act, 886, 1038; Penn Yan, 886; Niagara Falls, 887; Geneva, 887; Glens Falls, 887; Cortland, 887; New York, old building, relative to, 889; repairs and improvements, IX, 76; Olean, completion of, 147; Walton, repairs and improvements, 245; Catskill, completion of, 263; Ogdensburg, 571; provided for, 1896, 571; Whitehall, 575; provided for, 1898, 575; Oswego, indoor rifle range, 604; Buffalo, 74th Regiment, 607; Sing Sing, 625; Hudson, 626; Medina, 777; Kings county, 47th Regiment, repairs and enlargement, 777; Brooklyn, 23d Regiment, completion, 778; Brooklyn, acquiring site, 783; Tonawanda, expense of site, refunding unexpended balance to Erie county, 795; Newburgh, repairs and improvements, reappro-

ARMORIES, VETOES — (Continued).

priation, 857; Watertown repairs, X, 319; Tonawanda, relief of contractors on construction, 383; control and use of, 385; New York, purchasing armory supplies, 580; Rochester, 586; Tona-wanda, payment for labor and materials, 587; Whitehall, Williams and Manogue claim, 650; Tonawanda, settlement of claims, 703; control of, amending Military Code, 707; Oneonta, assessment for local improvement, appropriation, 788.

ARMS. For colony, furnished by Crown, I, 36; New York ought to furnish for itself, 124; purchase from Indians prohibited, 467, 549; Indians receive from both French and English, 535; loan of, requested from Governor Dinwiddie, 567, 569; appropriation for, 568; inspection of, 617; King to furnish, 620, 634, 644, 654, 663; French, captured at Fort Frontenac, 625; for troops in Indian War, 679; lost in service, compensation for, II, 92; provided at public expense, 337; scarcity of, 360; report on, 371; manufacture of, recommended, 437, 458, 525; collection and deposit of, 453; importation, 458; preservation, 510; ruinous condition, 524; purchase, 537, 619, 680; Hamborough, report relative to, 561; for militia, State should furnish, 571; insufficient supply for militia, 600; loaned by United States, 609; for use on frontiers, 636; purchase of rifles, 647; manufacture provided for, 667; deposits of, 682; adequate supply of, 682; received from United States, distribution, 762, 798; distribution, 770; limited quantity owned by State, 910; proposed sale to State, 954; right of people to bear, 1016; IV, 726; V, 281; insufficient quantity, 1103; offer to furnish for State, 1113; not to be taken from arsenals by militia, 1120; received from United States, III, 21; repeating pistol, communication relative to, 105; use of, request from Hopkinton Cavalry Company, 180; unlawful seizures from arsenals, 683; supplying States from national armory, IV, 71; loan for local purposes, 150, 155, 288; quota from United States, 450; in certain counties to be sold, 495; proposed distribution of, 854; national government should furnish, V, 53; Enfield rifles, 392, 414, 769; for State, purchased in Europe, 402, 413; manufacture at Springfield, 415; foreign purchases discontinued, 416; appropriation for, 530; Springfield rifles, 769; substitution for breech loaders, VI, 113, 357; altering or exchanging, appropriation, 236; system of accounts, 620; for Albany Burgess Corps, VII, 248; for National Guard, new, needed, IX, 570; X, 14; National Guard, general note, IX, 634; X, 15; board of examiners created, 1895, IX, 634; Governor Morton's

Arms — (*Continued*).

    decision, 635; Savage military magazine rifle recommended by board, 635; used in Federal army, proposition to supply National Guard with, 639; National Guard supplied with Springfield rifles, 643; of national and State forces should be uniform, X, 14; defects of Springfield musket, 14; arms and accoutrements for State troops furnished by United States, 16, 97.

    Vetoes. Remington rifles, altering sights, VII, 478; commission to examine for National Guard, VIII, 455; issuing to Sons of Veterans, X, 61.

Arms of State. Inquiry concerning, VII, 725; adopted, note on, 726; act of 1882, 726; modified, act of 1896, 727; amending act relative to, veto, IX, 622.

Armour, Philip B. State's action against, referee's fees, veto, X, 648.

Armstrong, Captain. Engineer, report on New York fortifications, I, 467.

Armstrong, John, General. Commands troops, 1812, II, 747; leasehold estates, IV, 333; chosen Senator in Congress, II, 469; resignation of, 517; second election, 537; resigns to become Minister to France, 546; Secretary of War,— communication from, pensions, 760; — acquisition of land, 777.

Armstrong, John J. Queens county judge, Roberts pardon case, IX, 251.

Armstrong, William A. Nominated as railroad commissioner, withdrawn, VIII, 374.

Armstrong, William W. Senate, Chairman Insurance Investigating Committee, 1905, X, 825.

Army. For Canadian expedition, I, 620, 634, 644, 645; chaplain for, 623; Continental, establishment of, II, 44; scarcity of forage, 54, 56; clothing for, 55, 76; supplies for, 57, 66, 88, 89, 107, 111, 117, 150, 165, 169; consumption of wheat at White Plains, 73; more troops for, 77, 108; State quotas, 93; hospital nurses, 95; supplies, apportionment among States, 98; supplies for French, 108, 111; supply of flour, 114, 161; militia not suitable for permanent defense, 174; orderly conduct after disbandment, 197; act of Congress relative to, 264; regimental chaplains, act of Congress, 538; exemptions from military duty, 739; War of 1812, New York's quota, 742; State troops enlisted in Federal service, 1812, 744; organizing volunteer reserves, 758, 759; on Niagara frontier, supplies for, 791; organization of volunteers recommended, 787, 794; number and location of State troops, 1814, 809; deserters, relative to, veto, 819; United States tactics, militia to conform to, 951; Revolutionary,

ARMY — (*Continued*).

ascertaining survivors of, III, 979; Military Academy, resolutions favoring abolition of, IV, 45, 46, 83; United States, greater equality between officers and men, 381; dismissal of officer for alleged interference in elections, V, 515; Bureau of Military Statistics, 521; United States, should be increased, X, 13; militia defined, act of Congress, 1903, 15.

ARNAUD, ESTELLE N. Estate of, escheat, veto, VIII, 731.

ARNEY, W. F. M. General shipping agent, Kansas relief, letter from, V, 345.

ARNOLD, BENEDICT. Major-General, letter from, relative to court-martial, II, 102.

ARNOLD, STEPHEN. Convicted of murder, II, 575; punishment commuted to hard labor for life, 577.

ARNOT, STEPHEN T. Member of Elmira Reformatory Commission, VI, 233.

ARREST. On civil process, I, 11; frivolous, prevention of, 631; arbitrary, condemned by Governor Seymour, V, 465.

VETOES. On justice's warrant, II, 210; of deserters without warrant, 819; children, relative to, IV, 527; power of conductors, VII, 414; without warrant, Game Law, 613; power of, Lyons charter, 879; without process, vagrants, Amsterdam charter, 1016; on civil process, deposit in lieu of bail, X, 317, 388.

ARSENALS. Provision for, recommended, II, 220; act for one in New York, 401, 425; Governor authorized to provide for erection of, 424, 425; Watervliet, 453, 755; additional, proposed, 538; in New York, 618, 636, 642, 680, 751, 769; IV, 72; in Richmond county, II, 751, 758; in Genesee county, 758; in Franklin county, 758; Sag Harbor, 768; Plattsburg, 769; Elizabethtown, 769; Canandaigua, 775; Batavia, 775; Watertown, report on, 818; Albany (Colonie), sale of, 828; Albany, to be leased, 871; condition of Albany arsenal, 878, 896; in New York, street improvements about, 895, 953, 999, 1115; in Albany, lease of unoccupied land, 1076; Watervliet, cession of land for, III, 264; New York, attacked by mob, 524; Watertown, seizure of arms at, 683; Batavia, seizure of military stores, 683; Elizabethtown, seizure of arms, 684; guards needed, 685; repair of, 972; New York, condition of, IV, 71; in certain counties to be sold, 495; New York, proposed sale of, 854; new arsenals at several places, V, 88, 175; New York, damages caused by falling of roof, 88, 175; Brooklyn, condemned as unsafe, 282; transfer to counties, VI, 113; six sold, 620; Assembly committee to investigate repairs, VII, 1008.

Arsenals — (Continued).

   Vetoes. Buffalo, local assessments, VII, 927; Rochester, local assessment, 1878, 927; 1882, 927; repairs and improvements, IX, 76; Rochester, acquiring site, 788.

Arson. Improper classification of, II, 584; punishment of, 584, 590, 602, 635, 731; III, 285; V, 265, 371; two pardons for, II, 855; pardon, proposed constitutional amendment, III, 863; first degree, punishment and commutation for good behavior, veto, VI, 899.

Artesian Wells. On Swinburne and Hoffman islands, veto, IX, 292.

Arthur, Chester A. Vice-President, protests against appointment of William H. Robertson as collector of New York, VII, 557; becomes President on death of President Garfield, 678.

Articles of Capitulation.

   Colony. Guaranteed representative government, I, 3.

Articles of Confederation. See also Confederation. Compared with Albany plan of union, I, 579; first use of term, 582; ratified by Legislature, II, 18; ratified by all States, 127; annual meeting of Congress, 146; census of white inhabitants, 164; when State not to be deprived of territory, 179; article 8 amended, 184, 276; hearing on Massachusetts claims, 217, 260; proposed convention for revision of, 270.

Artificers. Complain that slaves learn trades, I, 260; impressment of, 374; in military service, relief requested, II, 181.

Artillery. At New York, carriages need repair, I, 137; for Spanish War, 287; matrosses to be provided, 323; King supplies for Crown Point campaign, 598; King to furnish for Canadian expedition, 620, 634, 644; provided at public expense, II, 337; organization of, 339;. purchase of, 569, 629; increasing quantity of, 573, 609; additional regiment to be organized, 601; proposed erection of gunhouses, 630; flying or horse, treatise on, 639; field, adequate supply of, 682; powder and ball for practice, 954; statement relative to, 1037; horse or flying, brigade of, 1050; treatise on, 1050; care of, 1103; increase of, recommended, 1114; offer to furnish for State, 1116; insufficient supply of, III, 21, 99, 131, 176; theft of, 677, 686; in New York arsenal, not properly protected, IV, 71; instructors for, V, 53.

Assault. By convict on prison officers, punishment for, veto, II, 589.

Assault and Battery. Actions for, costs, III, 219.

Ashford. Transfer from third to first school commissioner district, Cattaraugus county, veto, X, 948.

Ashton, Rev. James W. Rector St. Stephen's Episcopal Church, Olean, offers prayer at Higgins memorial services, X, 964.

Aspinwall, Lloyd. Member of Yorktown Centennial Commission, VII, 734.

ASSEMBLY.

COLONY. Duke of York rejects propositions for, 1, 3; petition for, 4; letter from Werden to Brockholls relative to, 4; promised by Duke, 5; granted, 5; powers granted to First, 6; Governor's power in relation to bills, 7; Governor's power to adjourn and dissolve, 7.

First Assembly called, meeting of, I, 9, 688, 698; records lost, 9; compensation of members, 10; discontinued, 13.

Leisler issues writs for, 14, 18; Assembly meets, 15; legislation by, 15, 16.

Assembly revived, 18; meeting of, 19; provision for approving bills, 20; declines to express opinion as to Leisler's reprieve, 21; approves execution of Leisler and Milborne, 22.

First Assembly, second session, 23; third session, 24; fourth session, 25; status on death of Governor, 28; First Assembly dissolved, 31.

Second Assembly, I, 31, 34; dissolved, 39.

Third Assembly, I, 39; compensation of members, 43; dissolved, 43.

Fourth Assembly, I, 43, 47, 51; disagreements with Governor, 54; cannot interpret laws, 55; printing votes of, 55; dissolved, 56.

Fifth Assembly, I, 56, 57, 61, 64, 69; Fletcher recommends examination of local conditions, 60; members from Westchester absent themselves, 69; dissolved, 75.

Sixth Assembly, I, 74; elections of, abuses in, 77; withdrawal of certain members of, 78; dissolved, 79.

Seventh Assembly, I, 79, 85, 89, 90; Governor urges moderation in debate, 82; elections of members, act to regulate, 84; convoked by council, 91; adopts resolution confirming power to sit, 92; affirms power of Council, 92; dissolved, 93.

Eighth Assembly, I, 93, 96; dissolved, 98.

Ninth Assembly, I, 98, 101, 105, 107, 111; appoints chaplain, 101; sergeant-at-arms appointed, 101, 266; meets in Jamaica, 98; no control over royal funds furnished for colony, 109; controversy with Governor concerning legislative power, 110; dissolved, 113.

Tenth Assembly, I, 114, 118, 119, 122; power over money bills, 118, 123, 157, 159, 162, 166, 493; extraordinary session, validity of, 119, 120; authorized to appoint treasurer, 123; dissolved, 126.

Eleventh Assembly, I, 126; dissolved, 132.

Assembly, Colony — (*Continued*).

Twelfth Assembly, I, 132, 136, 140; protests against Newport Conference, 139; refuses appropriation, 140; expiration of Twelfth Assembly, I, 140.

Thirteenth Assembly, I, 141, 148; votes money for Governor Lovelace; requests information as to Governor's power to act out of colony, 150; denies power of Governor to act while out of colony, 150; dissolved, 150.

Fourteenth Assembly, I, 150, 154, 159, 163; views of, concerning congress of Governors, 158; royal complaint against conduct of, 166; dissolved, 167.

Fifteenth Assembly, I, 167, 171, 172; proposed frequent meetings with council, 169; dissolved, 174.

Sixteenth Assembly, 174; dissolved, 177.

Seventeenth Assembly, I, 177, 180, 181, 182, 183, 184, 186, 190, 195, 197, 201, 204, 207, 211, 216; action on memorial against colony, 182; Robert Livingston chosen Speaker, 183; adjourned by President of Council, 190; not to be dissolved for want of prorogation, 192; continued under succeeding Governors, 196, 197, 311; appointment of treasurer approved, 197; Auditor-General's fees, 197; recommends restriction of Canadian passes, 200; action relative to quotas of troops, 203; declines to aid Massachusetts in Indian war, 204; presents congratulatory address to King on deliverance from conspiracy, 205; admission of Stephen De Lancey, 214; dissolved, 220; longest colonial Assembly, 220.

Eighteenth Assembly, I, 220; address to Governor relative to revenue, 221; terminated by death of King, 225.

Nineteenth Assembly, I, 225; resolutions against Court of Chancery, 229; dissolved, 229.

Twentieth Assembly, I, 230, 232, 236, 238, 242, 244, 245, 250, 251, 254, 258; rights and liberties to be preserved, 231; action relative to Millington library, 235; memorial to King on Indian trade, 237; meets at house of Harmanus Rutgers, 239; transfer of session to city hall, 240; memorial against aid to sugar colonies, 240; action relative to French encroachments on Lake Cadaracqui, 241; adjourns because of smallpox, 242, 280; Governor requested to dissolve, but declines, 250; Albany petitions for dissolution, 252; Governor's relation to Legislature, general note, 253; King's prerogative to prorogue or dissolve, 254; prorogation instead of adjournment, 258; meets at Fort George, 258; dissolved, 262.

ASSEMBLY, COLONY — (*Continued*).

Twenty-first Assembly, I, 262, 268; free and frequent elections recommended, 266; act limiting term to three years, vetoed by King, 267, 271, 278, 279; adjournment after prorogation and without quorum does not dissolve, 268; instruction against uniting different subjects in same bill, 272; difference with Lieutenant-Governor as to revenue bills, 273; dissolved, 275.

Twenty-second Assembly, I, 275, 280, 285, 289, 292, 301, 305, 307, 309; declines to furnish garrison supplies, 282; approves expedition against West Indies, 289; insists on appointment of revenue officers, 294; denies inclinations toward independence, 294; requests royal aid in restoring public buildings destroyed by fire, 304; dissolved, 310, 311.

Twenty-third Assembly, I, 310, 311, 314, 317, 331; usually dissolved on accession of new Governor, 311; act for defense of colony, 318; declines to engage in negotiations for union of colonies, 320; suggests that prisoners of war be sent out of colony, 329, 624; differences with Governor Clinton, 344; dissolved, 344.

Twenty-fourth Assembly, I, 345, 367, 372, 381, 390, 413; meets at Greenwich, 367; declines to send troops to Louisburg, 370; pledges support in Canadian expedition, 374; declines to assume entire expense of transporting army to Canada, 379; consents to waive personal delivery of opening speech, 381; criticism relative to Canadian expedition, 387; Governor charges unwillingness to give adequate aid for carrying on war, 399; charged with disrespect to Governor, 399; address of, referred to home government, 402; agrees to make appropriations for joint war measures, 405; declines to furnish additional supplies, 411; agrees to furnish provisions for Saratoga garrison, 413; approves joint colonial report, relative to war measures, 414, 421, 432; asserts independence in Legislative action, 422; sits with door locked, 422, 430; sends remonstrance to Governor, which he refuses to receive, 422, 432; criticises Governor Clinton's administration, 423; authority to sit, 430; source of authority, 430; how communications to be presented to Governor, 432, 475, 484; committee of, not received by Governor, 445; orders remonstrance to be published in Gazette, 446; asserts liberty of members, 447; refuses credit for royal advances until action by Parliament, 453; charged with a desire to assume supreme military authority, 454; assumes right to nominate officers, 456; dissolved, 457.

Assembly, Colony — (*Continued*).

Twenty-fifth Assembly, I, 457, 469, 481; disapproves Massachusetts alterations in agreement for union, 462; right of access to Governor, 478, 479, 494; differences with Governor, 486, 494; dissolved, 503.

Twenty-sixth Assembly, I, 503, 512, 515; expresses opinion that Pennsylvania should, without assistance, secure fidelity of Ohio river Indians, 509; dissolved, 519.

Twenty-seventh Assembly, I, 520, 521, 526, 534, 545, 546, 583, 602, 609, 618, 624; proposed establishment of seminary, 521; convenes at Jamaica, 521; promises assistance to colonies invaded by hostile force, 531, 535, 539, 542, 549, 551; criticised by King, 532; settlements in townships and patents compared, 552; disclaims intention to encroach on prerogative, 559; suggestions concerning revenue, 586; resolutions relative to movement against Ticonderoga, 590; proposed joint expedition against Indians, 593; recommends a common colonial fund, 599; protests against maintenance of French prisoners, 604; conduct approved by King and Parliament, 607; adjourned by Lieutenant-Governor Delancey, 618; members expedite enlistments, 623; dissolved, 629.

Twenty-eighth Assembly, I, 630, 640, 647; joint committee on frontier settlements, 631; approves Amherst loan for war purposes, 638, 641; dissolved by death of George II, 649.

Twenty-ninth Assembly, I, 650, 656, 659, 662, 669, 673, 679, 681, 700, 706, 714, 717, 720; address on death of George II, 651; declines to enact new Draft Law, 656; resolutions relative to enlistments in Spanish War, 667; address to King, judicial tenures, 671; address to Lieutenant-Governor Colden, inquiry as to cause of Indian War, 678; address, termination of Indian War, 682; taxation only by consent, 683, 688, 729, 769, 772; memorandum relative to Indian land grants, 686; petitions to home government, 687, 729; resolutions, relations to home government, 704; protests against requisition for support of troops, 708, 716; provides for support of King's troops, 709, 719, 721; statement as to war expenses, 719; dissolved, 723.

Thirtieth Assembly, I, 723; Indian trade and boundary line, 724; asserts its loyalty, 726; asserts right of petition, 730; dissolved, 731.

Thirty-first Assembly, I, 731, 734, 736, 739, 746, 753, 759; not dissolved on Governor Tryon's appointment, 740; demands

ASSEMBLY, COLONY — (*Continued*).

home rule, 765; majority loyal to home government, 766; rejects patriotic resolutions, 768; refuses to send delegates to Continental Congress, 769; resolution declaring attitude toward home government, 769; statement of colonial grievances, 771; resolution against popular education, III, 946; asserts popular rights, IV, 711; dissolved by failure of prorogation, I, 765.

Address to Governor, I, 161, 182, 186, 189, 195, 221, 266, 294, 298, 329, 402, 462, 475, 484, 492, 508, 514, 518, 524, 535, 541, 551, 559, 586, 604, 607, 613, 622, 627, 651; announces policy of annual appropriations, I, 267, 303, 312, 472, 484, 559, 584, 605.

ASSEMBLY, STATE.

Continued from colonial period, II, 1; elects Council of Appointment, 3; members of, when to be chosen, 10; official term, beginning of, 10; sudden adjournment of, 15; qualifications of voters for members of, 35; observations on Vermont controversy, 51; Vermont controversy, Governor Clinton's message on, 143; does not favor appointment of additional judge, 295; recommends publication of proceedings of Council of Appointment, 314; address to Governor, relations with France, 444; number of members, 468; alleged attempted bribery of members, 710; address on resignation of Governor Tompkins, 884; committee recommends constitutional convention, 1021; institutes inquiry as to conduct of Judge Van Ness, 1031; requests information as to Federal interference in elections,.1060; official term under second Constitution, III, 1; vacancies, how filled, 133; VI, 242, 366; manuscript records relative to Morgan matter, III, 185; approves President's veto of public lands bill, 482; committee, abolition of capital punishment, 863; declines to recommend impeachment of Judge Inglis, 906; first election under Constitution, 1846, IV, 363; delay in organizing, 1856, 830; — 1858, V, 42; 1863, 445; journal, first meeting, 1780, presented to State, resolutions thereon, V, 132; favors reimposition of railroad tolls, 163; requests information as to pensions, 420; election of Speaker, 1863, alleged interference by mob, 485; to choose its own officers, 486; requests information from harbor defense commissioners, 564; delegation visits Washington on matters relating to quotas, 632; Governor Hoffman proposes abolition

XI—14

Assembly, State — (*Continued*).

    of single districts, VI, 401; judiciary committee, investigation of charges against Judge McCunn, 497; contested elections, see that title; clerk, compensation, VII, 223; occupies chamber in new capitol, 269; proceedings on Senate's occupation of new chamber, 539; speakership contest, 1881, 676; committee to investigate expenses of repairs of arsenals and armories, 1008; action on death of former Governor Seymour, VIII, 196; inequalities of representation under apportionment of 1879, 494; members, *viva voce* election under first Constitution, 913; select committee, 1887, employment of counsel, 976; vote on United States Senator, 1891, 1054; bill for canal investigation, 1891, 1118; under early Constitutions, IX, 644; increased to 150 members, Constitution of 1894, 644; Walter Livingston, first Speaker, 688; special committee on revision bills, 1900, X, 107; New York, thirty-first district, ratifying nominations, 130; select committee on revision, 1901, 223; forest preserve investigating commission, 1903, 512; members of joint committee to investigate life insurance companies, 825; judiciary committee investigates complaints against Justice Hooker, 827; right of members of judiciary committee to sit in Hooker case, challenge overruled, 830; members of joint committee on Higgins memorial services, 963.

    Reports. Committee on revision of criminal law, II, 336; on slavery, 692, 693; capital punishment, 729; Federal direct tax, 789; relative to Indian affairs, 976; committee on brevet appointments in militia, 992; commercial relations with Canada, III, 69; Fulton claim, 150; Morgan abduction, 184; search for coal, 205; monuments to Generals Herkimer and Woodhull, 226; banks, 245; care of insane, 379; railroads, 396; prison committee, 401; lotteries, 404; instruction of the blind, 516; canals, 735; monument to De Witt Clinton, 746; Virginia extradition case, 778; select committee on anti-rent trouble, IV, 241, 328; from Comptroller, taxation of reserved rents, 243; required population in new county, V, 230; select committee's report on veto of Constitutional Convention bill, 1887, VIII, 470.

    Resolutions. Protesting against Vermont's independence, II, 164; Council of Appointment, 361, 489, 503; disapproving Massachusetts plan of apportioning representatives in Congress, 546; disapproving North Carolina resolution on importation of slaves, 552; disapproving several amendments

ASSEMBLY, STATE. RESOLUTIONS — (*Continued*).

proposed by other States, 678; requesting information as to distribution of arms, 762; requesting information as to war expenses; disapproving amendments proposed by Georgia, Massachusetts and Connecticut, 827; Astor claim, 867; disapproving Georgia's proposition as to importation of colored persons, III, 34; disapproving Ohio's proposition as to gradual abolition of slavery, 34; on resignation of Governor Van Buren, 268; distribution of Federal revenues, 331, 986; public lands, 747; New Brunswick boundary question, 758; declining to receive proceeds of public lands, IV, 49; against special laws, V, 337; as to pay of rejected volunteers, 417; on death of Samuel F. B. Morse, VI, 444; recommending congressional action relative to coast defenses, VIII, 183; on Federal force bill, 1085; McMahon memorial on General Sherman's death, 1088; declaring in favor of municipal home rule, IX, 592; and committee on reception of Prince Henry, X, 478; investigation of bank department, 873, 879.

VETOES. Qualifications of voters for members of, minors, II, 685; election to fill vacancy, VI, 347; employees and investigating committees, VII, 133; Clerk's Manual appendix, 223; index to papers, 224, 459; index to laws, 224, 460; index to bills, 225, 460; journals, relative to, 264; index to printed bills, 460; clerk, additional clerical services, 461; railroad investigating committee, expenses, deficiency, 463; committee, National Camp, G. A. R., expenses, 463; election case, Trowbridge against Tighe, printing testimony, 492; election case, Carman against Duryea, printing testimony, 492; printing report special committee on normal schools, 492; committee on general laws, printing and material for, 492; election case, Liddle against Lynes, printing testimony, 493; clerk, file boards for, 494; committee on commerce and navigation, printing balance, 494; clerk, manuals for, 494; special committee on railroads, printing report, 494; clerk, deficiency appropriation, 581; removal of library to new capitol, appropriation, 581; insurance investigating committee, clerk, compensation, 783; cartage of documents, 901; VIII, 106; clerk, extra services, wrapping department, VII, 906; contested election,— Hotchkiss, Wayne county, expenses, 917; — Derrick, Rensselaer county, expenses, 917; — Lindsay, Eighth district, Kings county, expenses, 918; Sheridan, Kings county, expenses, 918; — Bliss, New York,

ASSEMBLY, STATE. VETOES — (*Continued*).

expenses, 918; Westbrook investigation, counsel fees, 924; compensation of certain officers after adjournment, 1078; VIII, 106; Harris, doorkeeper, compensaton, VII, 1078; library, purchase of standard geographic time globe for, VIII, 108; O'Hara, death of, unearned salary, appropriation, 114; printing Clerk's Manual, 118; tontine insurance investigating committee, legal services, 247; ceiling and staircase, examination by experts, appropriation, 839; examination of stone arch vault, appropriation, 840; clerk's room, furniture for, 841; select committee to investigate condition of Indians, attorney and stenographer, appropriation, 842; committee to prepare rules, stenographer, appropriation, 844; stenographers, 1889, preparing records for publication, 854; clerk, 1889, advances to, purchase of file boards, 857; safe for financial clerk, 858; judiciary committee, codes and statutes, appropriation, 858; Johnson contested election case, Oneida county, 1891, appropriation, 1142; library, promoting usefulness of, IX, 153; financial clerk, appropriation for 1896, 604; resolutions, engrossing, 773; committee on privileges and elections, 1903, appropriation for counsel, X, 571; contested election,— Waite against Dodd, counsel fees and expenses, 795; — Palmer against Matthews, counsel fees and expenses, 795; Cook and Clary, counsel to Assembly committee on privileges and elections, appropriation, 796; clerk, advances by Comptroller for contingent expenses, appropriation, 796.

ASSEMBLY CHAMBER. Old capitol,— President Lincoln's body lies in state in, V, 679; use of, granted to ladies of Albany, VII, 315. New capitol,— completion of, VII, 174; first occupation of, 269; defects in ceiling, 524, 696, 836; State arms to be hung on walls of, 727; defects in ceiling, communication from architects, VIII, 502; repairs to ceiling, act for, 608.

VETOES. Repairs to ceiling, appropriation, VII, 903; examination as to alleged defects of ceiling, appropriation, VIII, 421; ceiling investigation, appropriation, 547; examination by experts, appropriation, 839, 840.

ASSEMBLY DISTRICTS. Alteration of, V, 126, 224; VIII, 289; Governor Hoffman proposes representation by counties, VI, 401; criticism on apportionment of 1879, VII, 402; one student from each, at Cornell University, IX, 177.

ASSESSMENTS. Of States by Continental Congress, II, 85; on New York arsenal lot, 953, 999; real estate, Governor Bouck on, IV, 24;

ASSESSMENTS — (*Continued*).

personal property, 64; X, 620; inequality, IV, 564; large increase, 597; notice of hearing, V, 512; defective method of assessing personal property, 691; wide difference in various States, 825; personal property, returns by owners as basis of assessment, 826; real and personal property, inequality of assessment, VI, 553; VII, 942; reduction in assessments on personal property, 514; failure to make, new authorized, Milo, VIII, 257; personal property, Governor Flower, 1893, IX, 158; property where to be assessed, 626; local, suggested review by State Tax Commissioners, X, 343; of State lands in forest preserve, 607.

VETOES. Albany,— confirmation, IX, 632; — paving, VII, 1107; — Pine avenue, IX, 734; — street extensions, 729; Amsterdam, legalizing, 374; Albany armory, local, VII, 927; Oneonta armory, local, X, 788; Buffalo, arsenal, local, VII, 927; Rochester arsenal, local, 927; local improvements, review, X, 316; Auburn on State property, refunding, VI, 869; Brooklyn borough, Sisters of Mercy, relief from, X, 716; Buffalo,—relative to, 730; X, 686; — State property, IX, 784; — unpaid, X, 476; Central New York Institution for Deaf-Mutes, Rome, paving street, 949; Church of the Resurrection, New York, relief from, VI, 711; Columbia county, equalizing, VI, 95; Auburn, local, State property, X, 585, 634; Delaware and Susquehanna Plankroad Company, V, 233; Ebenezer Baptist Church, New York, exemption, VII, 931; Essex county, relative to, VI, 188; First Universalist Society, Mount Vernon, relief, X, 254; Flatbush, Prospect avenue, 177, 325; Geneva, Cayuga and Seneca canals, 648; Geneva, State property, 649; Greenburgh, when to be made, compensation of assessors, IX, 817; Camden and Annsville, highway labor, VII, 130; railroads, highway labor, IX, 801; Jefferson and St. Lawrence counties, railroad purposes, VII, 807; Missionary Society of the Most Holy Redeemer, release from, IX, 868; X, 175; municipal corporations, local improvements, recovery, 710; Nassau, in certain towns, 444, 450; New York, local improvements, VIII, 293, 638; X, 713, 715, 716; New York,— cancellation, IX, 872; — by boards of assessors, X, 472; construction of conveyance, contracts and instruments relative to, 177; — East River park, refunding, IX, 808; X, 715, 806; — Grand boulevard, refunding, 807; — House of Good Shepherd, cancellation, 179; — interest on unpaid, 476; — Jamaica and Brooklyn plankroad, adjusting, 178; — Lexington avenue opening, cancellation, IX, 809; —

ASSESSMENTS, VETOES — (*Continued*).
Methodist Episcopal Church Home, releasing from, X, 175; — notification of, 389; — public works, improvements, VIII, 1035; — bank errors, correction, X, 475; — religious corporations, exemption, 583; — reservoirs, 308; — St. Joseph's Asylum, releasing, 473; — Oswegatchie, rolls, relative to, VI, 88, 288; river improvement commission, assessments on property benefited, X, 955; Rochester,—on State property, 321, 640; — State hospital, local, 697; Rome, sewer system, refunding, IX, 788; St. Luke's Church, New York, relief, 809; Schenectady, relative to, X, 262; Schenectady county, Glenville, assessments, VI, 701; Second Avenue Baptist Church, Harlem, street improvements, relief, 710; Syracuse,—State property, VII, 86, 228, 472, 585, 928; — legalizing local, X, 634, 705, 815; taxation,—amending Revised Statutes, VIII, 1038; — regulating and equalizing, VII, 1109; — when to be made in certain towns, X, 590; of corporations, VII, 502; on exempt property for local improvements, X, 595; illegal, review, costs, VIII, 466; taxes, assessment and collection, VII, 110; reassessments for illegal, IX, 724; review, railroad and telegraph companies, 132; equalizing, VII, 666; taxes, Essex county, VI, 188; Herkimer and Lewis counties, rejected taxes, reassessments, VII, 664; telegraph, telephone and electric light lines, 934; Troy, local improvements, 1022; Troy, sewers, VIII, 399; Utica — on State property, VII, 229, 472; — legalizing, X, 819; villages,—crosswalks on property benefited, IX, 252; — local improvements, VIII, 888; Western House of Refuge, local, VII, 927; West Seneca, local improvements, collection, X, 811, 952; notice of grievance day, 809.

ASSESSORS. Act for election of, I, 16; right of people to choose, II, 41; not to determine amount of tax, 59; functions of, 62, 212; oath to assessment-roll, V, 175.

VETOES. Malone, compensation, VI, 210; Newtown, powers of, 450; Seneca Falls, board of education, appointment of, VII, 60; creating board of, Utica, 131; Flushing, correcting assessment maps, 413; Albany, 805; Albany county, filing certificates of sale with, 888; Richmond county, establishing board, 1114; Brooklyn, VIII, 638; exhibiting deeds to, before record, Dunkirk, 881; Brighton, compensation, IX, 371; Greenburgh, compensation, 817; qualifications, 865; Rotterdam, compensation, X, 439.

ASSIGNEES. Lands conveyed to, veto, VI, 562.

ASSIGNMENT FOR CREDITORS. Limiting preference, VIII, 36, 297, 476; vetoes,—amending act, 130; X, 815; cost in actions for fraud, IX, 139.

ASSIZES, COURT OF. See COURT OF ASSIZES.

ASSOCIATED HOTEL COMPANY. Amending charter, veto, VI, 335.

ASSOCIATION OF THE BAR OF THE CITY OF NEW YORK. Charges against Judge Curtis, VI, 498; resolution as to powers of sheriff, service of process, 898; approves New York Consolidation Act, VII, 802; recommends change in divorce proceedings, X, 365; represented by counsel at trial of Justice Hooker, 829; bill to incorporate, veto, VI, 192.

ASSOCIATION FOR THE BENEFIT OF COLORED ORPHANS, NEW YORK. Changing name to the Colored Orphans Asylum and Association for the Benefit of Colored Children, New York, veto, VII, 1006.

ASSOCIATION FOR THE EXHIBITION OF THE INDUSTRY OF ALL NATIONS. Incorporation and objects, IV, 657; erects Crystal Palace, 657.

ASTOR, JOHN J. Claim to land in Putnam county, II, 867, 940, 986, 990; investigation of claim, III, 132; proposition for settlement, 146; settlement of claim, 174, 196, 389; suit by, 312, 318, 349, 355, 389; State stock issued to, 413; bequest for public library, IV, 428.

ASTOR, WILLIAM W. Member of Yorktown Centennial Commission, VII, 734.

ASTOR LIBRARY. Established, IV, 428, 429.

ASYLUM FOR COLORED CHILDREN, NEW YORK. Destroyed in draft riot, V, 547.

ASYLUM FOR INSANE CONVICTS. At Auburn, V, 78, 166, 272; insane convicts transferred from Utica to Auburn, 272; number of convicts, 374; VII, 828, 958; transfer of insane from county jails, V, 374; investigation of, 423; Superintendent Pilsbury's report, 438; established at Matteawan, VIII, 822; at Auburn, to be used as prison for women, IX, 182; vetoes,—various repairs and improvements, VII, 485, 784;—various appropriations, 914.

ASYLUM FOR INSANE EMIGRANTS. Number of inmates, VII, 958.

ASYLUMS. Admission of persons not paupers, veto, VII, 505.

ATHENAEUM. Philadelphia, distribution of statutes to, II, 994; Boston, distribution of statutes to, 994; American, Paris, requests copies of New York laws, IV, 46.

ATHENS. Mutual insurance company, veto, VI, 595; VII, 132.

ATKINSON, FRANK H. Member of Elmira Reformatory commission, VI, 233.

ATLANTA, GEORGIA. Cotton States Exposition, 1895, IX, 581.

ATLANTIC AVENUE RAILROAD COMPANY. Succession to rights of Brooklyn and Jamaica Railroad Company, VII, 395.

ATLANTIC BASEBALL CLUB. Charter, veto, V, 645.

ATLANTIC DOCK COMPANY. Constructs canal basin in New York, IV, 426.

ATTACHMENTS. For contempt in anti-rent troubles, III, 830; against public officers for misappropriation of funds, VI, 730, 829.

VETOES. Relative to, II, 594; judgment, VII, 1093; justice's court, service of papers, 1094; indemnity bonds on claim of property, IX, 150; liens on real property, 474; amending Code, X, 310; personal property, undertakings on discharge, 441; undertaking on discharge, 534; undertaking for restitution, 706; claim of property, how tried, 807.

ATTAINDER. Act of, prohibited, II, 61, 71; of Latting Carpenter, 288; Wallace and White, 374; widows of attainted persons, 507, 581, 784; Roger Morris and wife, 940.

ATTICA AND ARCADE RAILROAD COMPANY. Relief, veto, VII, 416.

ATTICUS. A slave, alleged abduction of, III, 748, 822, 908.

ATTORNEY-GENERAL. COLONY. To draft bills for Assembly, I, 20; member of conference committee, 78; appointed, 90; Crown provides salary, 95; opinion as to status of Assembly, 177; complaint against, by Albany justices, 234; compensation, 672, 729.

ATTORNEY-GENERAL. ENGLAND. Opinion as to Governor's relation to Legislature, I, 253.

ATTORNEY-GENERAL. STATE. Letter from, II, 209; directed to take proceedings concerning the Francis Child's publication, 274; payment of Snedeker legacy, 288; observations on criminal law, 318, 336; report of, 318; assistant, office created, districts established, 363; to examine Mohawks' claims, 377; suit on Connecticut claim, 386; New York district altered, 399; authorized to repair State seal, 404; action under Connecticut's claim, 404, 406; communication from, suits in which people of State are interested, 431; member of commission to make cessions to United States, 825; member of canal board, 901; member of commission on Astor claim, 940, 986; forgery of records in Secretary's office, 952; report, land in military tract, 991; communication from, intrusions on Grand island, 995; communication from, counsel to assist district attorney, III, 146; New Jersey boundary case, 312, 349, 356; Astor case, 312, 318, 349, 355, 389; consultation with, anti-rent troubles, 829, 833; service in McLeod case, 933; how chosen, 1004; opinion, prison labor contracts, IV, 48; to investigate manorial titles, 413; to represent State in Lemmon case, 811, 860; report on Stockbridge Indian claims, 857; correspondence with Governor King, quarantine affairs, V, 99; attending criminal trials, 169; opinion, Canisteo county bill, 224; opinion, required population for new county, 229, 230; member of commission to organize militia, 281; opinion, jurisdiction over lower New York bay, 640; member of commission on normal schools, 695·

ATTORNEY-GENERAL, STATE — (*Continued*).

when to take charge of proceedings for removal of officers, 717; proceeding against New Jersey Central Railroad Company to prevent construction of docks in New York harbor, 846; proposed appointment by Governor, VI, 396; should have supervision of district attorneys, 396; opinion, legalizing acts of justices of the peace, 479; communication from, bill relative to assignees and receivers, 562; action on Buck case, 682; opposes Code amendments, 708; actions against public officers, 732; appropriations for canal actions and proceedings, 929, 996; opinion, vacancy in office, failure to take oath, VII, 45; proceedings to determine Connecticut boundary in Long Island sound, 172; member of Connecticut boundary commission, 172; opinion, bill extending time for sale of Genesee Valley canal, 217; opinion, pipe lines, eminent domain, 242; to examine Swift claim, 374; opinion, Danolds case, 377; member of commission on State's property rights, War of 1812, 601; opinion, status of Bankers' bill, ten-day period, 667; member of commission on administration of charitable institutions, 964; counsel to the Governor, VIII, 27; member of new capitol advisory board, 31; opinion, application of Civil Service Law to census enumerators, 60; opinion, enumeration bill at extraordinary session cannot include subjects not recommended by Governor, 136; *ex-officio* member State Board of Health, 175; recommends supervision of capitol construction by single architect, 222; opinion, excise bill, 1887, unconstitutional, 362, 365; opinion, unconstitutionality of ballot bill, 1890, 950; opinion, World's Fair bill constitutional, 996; opinion, constitutionality of laws authorizing women to vote at school meetings, IX, 94; appearance before grand juries, act for, 409; member of Greater New York Charter Commission, 553; opinion, meaning of American inventions, 637; requested to examine report of Canal Investigating Commission and take charge of criminal proceedings based thereon, 850; should do legal work of State hospitals, X, 22; opinion, Soldiers' Home Act, 1900, 156; powers only statutory, may be increased, diminished or modified by Legislature, 187; member of State Printing Board, 196; opinion, public dancing bill, 456; opinion, railroad bill, relative to consents for construction, 574; opinion, Supreme Court commissioners' bill, 663; opinion, extent of forest preserve restriction as to timber, 754; designation of counsel for State Tax Commissioners, 845.

VETOES. Special counsel, Sage case, VII, 582, 905; Rowley case, counsel fees, appropriation, 905; action by, 934; appointment of

ATTORNEY-GENERAL, STATE.   VETOES — (Continued).
counsel to various departments, IX, 403, 488; powers and duties,
amending Executive Law, 724; attorneys, counsel and commissioners, compensation, X, 297, 559; Burr claim, counsel for
Dike, sheriff of Kings county, compensation, 559; assistant,
employees and counsel, compensation, 784, 785; deputy for Court
of Claims, expenses, appropriation, 785; rebinding law books,
appropriation, 796; counsel and others, investigation of forest
preserve trespasses, 796.

ATTORNEYS. Act relating to, I, 59; improper conduct of, II, 918; liability for costs, 924; fees of, III, 774; admission, act relative
to, VI, 260; State Board of Law Examiners, VIII, 1100; admission of non-residents, 1100; examination, exemptions, 1153;
for State departments, abuse of system, X, 186; for State
hospitals, act amended, 187; employment by Forest, Fish and
Game Commission, 187; in forest department, Governor's approval of salaries and expenses, 194.

VETOES. Court clerks cannot practice, II, 395; investigation of
charges against, compensation of referees, VII, 266; liens, amending Code, VIII, 293; must be citizens, application for admission,
Chappell and Curell case, relief, 1100; Queens county, justices'
courts, laymen not to practice in, IX, 373; compensation, enforcing lien, 523; in justices' courts, 792; wearing gowns, X,
37; Block and Sullivan, admission to examination, 63; settling
actions without consent of, 150; Schiff case, filing Regent's
certificates nunc pro tunc, 174; MacKenzie, a foreigner, admission to practice, 262; employed by Attorney-General, compensation, 297, 555; Browne, admission to examination, 311; admission to examination, 311; appointed to attend before grand
jury, right to appear, 392.

ATTOWA INDIANS. Invited to join Indian conference, I, 354.

ATWATER, RUSSELL. Senate, arms and supplies delivered to, II, 772.

ATWOOD, WILLIAM. Chief justice, Governor transmits papers relative to,
I, 104.

AUBURN. Prison established at, II, 855; armory at, V, 175; number of
excise licenses, 1887, VIII, 359; excise license fees, 1889, 685;
salaries increased, 825, 993.

VETOES. City, enlarging boundaries, VI, 304; acquiring land for
cemetery, 602, 642; refunding assessments on State property,
869; police and street lighting expenses, VII, 770; railroad aid
bonds, VIII, 504; public park, establishing, IX, 783; public
schools, X, 478; Court of Claims, assessment on State property,
585, 634; new grammar school, enlarging high school, 717;
regulating price of illuminating gas, 907.

AUBURN CITY HOSPITAL. Charter, veto, VII, 241.

AUBURN PRISON. Established, II, 855; provision for completion of, 913; number of convicts, 983; III, 339, 402, 446, 514, 540, 764, 860; IV, 79, 122, 273, 609, 650, 721, 844; V, 77, 163, 271, 374, 525; VI, 941; VII, 8, 146, 828, 954; separate dormitories, II, 1015; solitary cells, 1051; III, 9; life prisoners, transfer to New York, II, 1103; Bibles for prisoners, 1121; III, 22; to receive convicts from certain counties, 22; female convicts at, 207, 379; separate buildings for women, 208; becomes self-supporting, 289, 340, 383, 447, 515, 764, 860; IV, 273, 786, 844; V, 600; arrangement of cells, III, 316; additional cells, 382, 402; additional land for, 448; female prison at, 515; manufacture of silk, 541, 945; raising mulberry trees, 542; change of management, 765; chaplain, 977; results of Prison Labor Act of 1842, IV, 48; transfer of convicts to Clinton prison, 276; statistics, 407; V, 525; VI, 616; VII, 281, 425, 520, 701, 827, 954; IX, 25; convicts under seventeen, transferred to Western House of Refuge, IV, 432; new buildings, 607; V, 78, 166; asylum for insane convicts, 78, 166, 272; insane convicts transferred from Utica asylum, 272; Superintendent Pilsbury's report on, 435; methods of punishment, 436; transfers from Elmira Reformatory, VII, 955; results of abolition of contract system, VIII, 10, 167, 646; loss by fire at, IX, 25; separate prison for women, 182; built in 1817, X, 28; unsanitary condition of, 204.

VETOES. Habeas corpus, Edymoin case, expenses, VI, 678; crimes committed in, trial of offenders, reimbursing Cayuga county, 876; VII, 87, 226, 471, 781, 932; Chapman S. Strong, keeper, injuries, appropriation, 465; various repairs and improvements, 484; warden, investigation and counsel fees, appropriation, 485; medical services, audit of claims, 666; Cayuga county claim, submission to State Board of Audit, 801; electric light plant, VIII, 851; stone warehouse, IX, 80; claim of Keeper Bray, injured by convict, 452; assessment for local improvement, X, 585, 634; Gard case, claim for injuries, 702; Angel case, claim for injuries, 702; Bailey case, claim for injuries, 702.

AUBURN AND SYRACUSE RAILROAD COMPANY. See also SYRACUSE AND AUBURN RAILROAD COMPANY. State aid to, IV, 831.

AUBURN AND ROCHESTER RAILROAD. Progress of construction, III, 866; State aid to, 887; IV, 10, 831; completion of, III, 953.

AUCHWICK. Minister at, complains against sale of rum to Indians, I, 569.

AUCTION. Act imposing duties on sales, II, 199; Federal tax on, 789; State tax on, 902, 907; income from, III, 245, 305, 334, 708, 763,

AUCTION — (*Continued*).

  855, 951, 1040; IV, 23; V, 72; sales, alleged to be monopolies, III, 246; duties restored to general fund, 414, 505, 544, 552, 619; IV, 53.

AUCTIONEERS. Appointment, II, 574, 575; regulating method of appointment, III, 7, 18; extension of privileges, 247.

  VETOES. Examinations, expenses of agents, VII, 904; VIII, 114; claims, Board of Claims, IX, 720; bonds in certain cities, 859; New York licenses, X, 957.

AUDITING BOARD OF ENLISTMENTS. Report, V, 577, 870; members of board, 870.

AUDITOR. See STATE AUDITOR.

AUDITOR OF CANAL DEPARTMENT. See CANAL AUDITOR.

AUDITOR-GENERAL. Assembly memorial relative to fees of, I, 197; English, statement of accounts, 202; functions of, 293, 299; when office established, 293.

AUDITORS OF MILITARY CLAIMS. Settlement of certain accounts, II, 150.

AUGUR, AMY. Pardoned for murder, II, 67, 68.

AURORA. Centennial celebration of Sullivan's campaign, VII, 1084.

AURORA MANUAL LABOR SEMINARY. Incorporated, III, 407.

AUSABLE. Bridges in, veto, VI, 556.

AUSABLE CHASM. Acquiring for State park, veto, X, 317.

AUSABLE RIVER. Improvement, veto, VI, 597.

AUSABLE VALLEY MASONIC HALL AND LIBRARY ASSOCIATION. Charter, veto, VI, 697.

AUSTRALIA. Ballot system, application in New York, VIII, 576, 777, 897; candidates' contribution for expenses, 668; suffrage not universal, 897; outline of Ballot Law, 898, 960.

AUSTRO-HUNGARY. Participation in Cotton States Exposition, IX, 581.

AUTHENTICATION. Of conveyances, II, 486; III, 175; instruments executed in other States and countries, 211, 770, 821; V, 111, 212; by county clerks, veto, X, 171.

AUTOMOBILES. On streets, highways and public places, veto, X, 441.

AUTOPSIES. In State hospitals, veto, IX, 534.

AVENUE C RAILROAD COMPANY, NEW YORK. Extension, veto, VI, 74.

AVERILL, LEWIS, BRIGADIER-GENERAL. Notice to, calling militia into service, anti-rent troubles, III, 831, 834, 836; arrives at Albany, 836.

AVERILL IRON ORE BED. Purchased for Clinton prison, IV, 608; settlement of claim, V, 168.

AVISO DERMONT D'URVILLE. French vessel, escort to French delegation to Yorktown Centennial Celebration, VII, 738.

AYLESWORTH, MARCUS. Pardoned, restoration to citizenship, IV, 294.

B.

BABCOCK, LODOWICK S. Captain volunteer cavalry, funds received by, II, 766.

BABCOCK, SAMUEL D. Member of Tax Revision Commission, 1881, VII, 538.

BABYLON. VETOES. Ferry at Fire Island beach, VII, 936; — repairing State dock, X, 935.

BACH, AMELIA L. A. Claim against Long Island City, audit of, veto, IX, 786.

BACHE, PROFESSOR A. D. Survey of New York harbor, V, 21; report of, 95, 109; correspondence with quarantine commissioners, 99.

BACHE, HARTMAN, MAJOR. Surveyor, railroad from Williamsport to Elmira, III, 528.

BACHELOR CLUB, NEW YORK. Charter, veto, VII, 507.

BACKER, ESTHER. Relief, veto, VI, 185.

BACKUS, SAMUEL D. Member of Connecticut Boundary Commission, V, 112.

BACON, FRANCIS. House of Commons, address on privileges, VIII, 984.

BADEAU, ADAM. Consul-General, London, appointment of successor, VII, 555.

BADGES. Unauthorized wearing of, veto, X, 807.

BAGG, E. MERRIAM. Justice of the peace, West Turin, legalizing acts, filing oath and bond, veto, IX, 725.

BAIL. Excessive, not to be required, II, 595; VII, 611; reducing number of magistrates authorized to take, III, 941.

> VETOES. On arrest, where taken, VII, 1091; amending Code of Criminal Procedure, VIII, 886; arrest on civil process, deposit in lieu of bail, X, 317, 388.

BAILEY, BENJAMIN. Assembly, member of select committee on anti-rent troubles, IV, 328.

BAILEY, CLARENCE. Injuries, Auburn prison, Court of Claims, veto, X, 702.

BAILEY, FRANK. Vice-president, Title Guaranty and Trust Company, New York, opinion, taxing mortgages, X, 802.

BAILEY, ROBERT T. New York, claim against city, veto, VII, 1089.

BAINBRIDGE. Town meeting, requests postponement of collection of United States deposit fund loan, IV, 47.

BAINBRIDGE, WILLIAM, COMMODORE. Gallant conduct of, commended by Legislature, II, 780; letter from Governor Tompkins, 781; reply, 781.

BAKER, GEORGE E. Editor of Seward's Works, quoted, III, 974, 977.

BAKER, HALSEY H. Canal towage, testing method, veto, VII, 266.

BAKER, ISAAC V. Sale of land to State for site of State hospital, X, 794.

BAKER, ISAAC V., JR. Nominated as railroad commissioner, VIII, 374.

BAKER, WILLIAM H. Damages, destruction of animals, Court of Claims, veto, X, 593.

BAKERS. Preventing frauds of, I, 302.

BALCOM, RANSOM. Justice of the Supreme Court, salary, payment, veto, VII, 931.

BALDWIN, JAMES, SR. Relief, veto, VI, 684.

BALDWIN, THOMAS. Appointed paymaster of militia, II, 764; funds received by, 765, 766.

BALDWIN, TIMOTHY. Escheat, veto, VI, 483.

BALDWIN'S CREEK. Restoring channel, veto, X, 644, 791.

BALDWINSVILLE. Legalizing water bonds, VIII, 1026.

VETOES. Village, relative to, VII, 415; union free school district, borrowing money, 1013.

BALDWINSVILLE CANAL. Tolls, V, 66, 154, 257, 361; financial statement, 1875, VI, 930.

BALL. (Shot). Colony to furnish, I, 295, 310; to be arranged for ready use, 323; for Crown Point expedition, 571; Connecticut's claim for, II, 100; procuring supply of, 609, 629; for artillery practice, 954.

BALL, ISIDOR. Action against New York, granting permission, veto, IX, 727.

BALLOT. Use at elections, II, 10; VIII, 573, 584, 670, 778, 912, 952, 957; IX, 247; secrecy, efforts to prevent, IV, 129; purity of, basis of free government, VII, 434; uniform, prescribed, 435; limiting voter's rights, VIII, 568; Australian system, application to New York, 576; furnishing at public expense, 577, 667, 765; defined, 584, 779, 912, 913; adopted in England, 585; ballot clerks, 669; improper distribution, 1891, result in twenty-fifth Senate district, 670; secrecy guaranteed by Constitution, 670; Massachusetts act of 1888, 670; official, exclusive, unconstitutional, 765, 953, 961; historical sketch, 778, 913; booths at elections, 763, 898, 900, 916, 962, 1010; system in use, 1890, 895; official and unofficial, act of 1890, 906; Massachusetts act, 908; method of voting under first Constitution, 913; Senate and Assembly, *viva voce* voting under first Constitution, 913; limitations of legislative power, 953; Ballot Reform Act, 1890, 1005; blanket ballot objectionable, 1010; reform act of 1890, judicial construction noted, IX, 33; voting machines authorized, 247; blanket ballot established, 308, 393, 554; blanket ballot, paster necessary, omission unconstitutional, 394; party emblems, 554; statutes need amendment, 1896, 664; use of Davis voting machine au-

BALLOT — (*Continued*).

thorized in cities and towns, 665; only one should be used, X, 370; large number of defective, 508, 613.

VETOES. Prescribing size, weight and appearance, VII, 412; town meetings, voting on money propositions, 807; town meetings, voting on tax propositions, VIII, 470; secrecy, bill to secure, 566, 763; reform bill, 1889, 762; elections, ballot bill, 1890, 949, new bill passed; for excise commissioners, indorsement, 973; Johnstown, bridge appropriation, voting by ballot, 1087; general act, 1890, amendments, IX, 150; official ballot, pasters, 477; at primary elections, written consent by citizens to use of name, X, 709.

BALLOT BOX. Provided for, II, 35; regulating use of, IV, 808.

BALLOT CLERK. Represent political parties, VIII, 570; provision for selection of, 669; bi-partisan election of, alleged unconstitutionality, 959; compensation in certain counties, veto, IX, 722.

BALLOU, THEODORE P. Relief, veto, VII, 416, 506.

BALLSTON SPA. Armory at, V, 175, 642.

BALTIMORE. British defeat at, II, 802; exportation of grain, IX, 557.

BAMFIELD, GEORGE. Memorial received from, relative to colonial affairs, I, 182; communication from, relative to Tariff Act, 198; withdraws as agent, 215.

BANK OF AMERICA. Proposed incorporation of, occasions prorogation of Legislature, II, 709; incorporation of, alleged conduct of Justice Van Ness relative to, 1031.

BANK OF CORNING. Holder of State securities, V, 257, 364.

BANK OF ENGLAND. Asks relief, V, 45; issues no small notes, VI, 647; regulation of bank note circulation not practicable, 755; charter of 1844, 963.

BANK OF FRANCE. Issues no small notes, VI, 647.

BANK OF LANSINGBURGH. Financial condition of, VII, 66.

BANK OF MONTREAL. Forgery of bills on, II, 1104.

BANK OF NEW YORK. Loan from, II, 436, 906; debt against State, 1098.

BANK OF NIAGARA. Charter, veto, II, 871.

BANK OF NORTH AMERICA. Incorporated, II, 164.

BANK FOR SAVINGS, NEW YORK. Incorporated, II, 981; investments by, 1016; report, 1119; III, 104, 144; communication from, publication of unclaimed dividends and deposits, 566.

BANK OF UNITED STATES. Paper, high character of, II, 699; capital of, investment in new bank, 710; suit against Ohio State Auditor, 1077; Massachusetts resolutions relative to, 1118; New Hampshire resolutions relative to, III, 434; renewal of charter, 476, 494, 516; reducing debt, 483, 489; transfer of funds from, 483; increasing loans,

BANK OF UNITED STATES — (*Continued*).

485; aggressive operations ineffectual, 496; New York branch, discontinuance of, 562; attitude toward national administration, 606; attitude toward resumption of specie payments, 703.

BANK OF WESTERN NEW YORK. Insolvent, situation of, IV, 35.

BANK COMMISSIONERS. Appointment, III, 245, 311, 475, 633; supervision of, 1003; salaries paid by banks, 1007; bill changing manner of appointment, veto, 1000; office abolished, IV, 37.

BANKERS, INDIVIDUAL. Examination of, VII, 949; prohibited from advertising as bank, VIII, 7, 476; supervision by Superintendent of Banks, 7.

BANKERS LOAN AND TRUST COMPANY, NEW YORK.

VETOES. Charter, VI, 342; changing name, VII, 567; veto not transmitted within ten-day period, 667.

BANKING CORPORATIONS LAW. Enacted, 1892, IX, 28, 135.

BANKRUPTS. Relief of creditors, I, 143; bill relating to, veto, II, 309; meeting to consider national law, III, 841; constitutional provision, 842, 876; IV, 5; New York favors enactment of law, 845, 876; Georgia opposes law, 977; difference between Bankrupt Law and Insolvent Law, IV, 5; repeal of law recommended, 45.

BANKS. See also NATIONAL BANKS, SAVINGS BANKS, and TRUST COMPANIES.

Large number of, II, 696, 917; speculative character of, 697; 917; IV, 703, 731; taxation of stock, II, 700; capital in New York, 1812, 710; discontinuing specie payments, 871; general statistics, IV, 657; V, 449, 527, 585, 692; VI, 19, 111, 231, 350, 529, 622, 951; VII, 427, 520, 689, 822, 947; VIII, 6; X, 732; cashier in New York, issuance of State loan certificates, II, 907; private, unauthorized banking prohibited, 916; excessive circulation of notes, 980; III, 171, 475; number and capital of, II, 981; IV, 69, 703, 729, 784; V, 8, 173, 274, 376, 450, 527, 585, 692; counterfeiting in Canada, II, 983; protection against embezzlements, 998; need of strict regulations, III, 172; Governor Van Buren on renewal of charters, 238, 259; State bank not approved, 240; protection of depositors and billholders, 243; safety fund, 245, 260, 475, 502, 654 (see that title); commissioners, 245, 311, 475, 633, 1000; origin of business, 272; repeal of certain provisions in Revised Statutes, 311; large number of applications for charters, 469, 522, 555; sale of franchise, 470, 632; interest on loans, 472; reducing circulation, 475, 519, 665; small bills, limiting circulation of, 476, 517, 519, 564, 633, 667, 723; State loan to, 481, 491, 496; deposits of government funds, 483; State bank suggested, 490; New York banks should

BANKS — (*Continued*).

be strengthened, 492; attack on New York banks, 495; excessive discounts, 520, 521; New York loan to, resulting from fire, 535, 584; extended speculation, 555, 557; original purpose of, 558; increase of capital, 562, 632; Bank of United States, discontinuance of, 562; unclaimed dividends and deposits, 566; restraints on deposits and discounts, 628, 630; authorized to subscribe to loan for lateral canals, 633; circulation limited according to capital 633; Suspension Act, 645, 661, 698, 723; Free Banking Law, 656, 724, 781, 784, 1005; suspension of payments, 659; results of panic of 1837, 663; specie reserve, 666, 667; resumption of specie payments, 667, 694; IV, 34; loans on canal stock, III, 702; location under Free Banking Law, 724; prohibition against circulation of foreign bills, 725; redemption of circulating notes, 784, 860, 939; IV, 380, 395, 837; institutions close, III, 938; receivers, 973; Pennsylvania, method of supervision, 1004; insolvent, loans due from, IV, 20, 62, 271; proper functions of, 32; inadequate supervision, 34; act relating to, 37; Oswego county, requests more bills, 48; bills and notes, registry of, 380; liability of stockholders, 403, 441; V, 75; investment of funds by Comptroller, IV, 479; sound circulating medium, 563; bank department established, 564; general condition, 612; city stocks not suitable as securities, 704, 731; State stocks available as securities, 731; amount of circulating notes, 784, 837; speculating in stocks, 838; failure of State Bank of Sackett's Harbor, V, 8; in New York suspend specie payments, 43; specie payments resumed, 44; Bank of England, condition of, 45; deposit of coin, 46; in New Orleans, condition of, 46; amount of trust securities, 172; aid national government, 359; authorized to hold State and Federal stocks, 376; national banking system, 528, 550, see NATIONAL BANKS; State, changing to national banks, act unconstitutional, 588; number changed to national banks, 692, 749; New York city, large increase of business, 819; organized as national, return to State system, VI, 20, 112; taxation of capital, 280; regulating powers of, 315; special charters prohibited, 315; failure, when State not liable to depositor, 334; taxation, plan of Tax Commission, 372; bank note described, 752; checks, 752; certificates, New York associated banks, 755; ineffective attempts to regulate circulation, 755; bank notes, relation to credit, 966; taxing surplus, VII, 25; charges against Superintendent Ellis, 56; taxation of, 515; certificates of deposit, advances on, not subject to usury laws, 719; examinations, 823,

BANKS — (*Continued*).

    949; more supervision needed, 949; name not to be used by
    individual bankers, VIII, 7; constitutional provision, 231; trust
    companies, general act, 234; various reforms suggested, 1894,
    IX, 333; increase in business, 1895, 561; capital stock to be
    paid in full before commencing business, 562; limiting powers
    of directors, 562; loans to officers, etc., restricted, 562; surplus
    to be accumulated, 562; loans on capital stock prohibited, 562;
    savings banks and discount banks not to be united in business,
    563; good record, 1896, 740; dissolution, action to be brought
    by receiver, 741; increase in business, 1897, 821; good condition
    of, X, 28; proposed tax on stock, 81; limiting right to use
    certain names, 104; department self-supporting, 119; capitali-
    zation, 1900, 199; proposed tax on capital, 199; resources,
    1900, 221; receivers, limiting expenses of administration, 352;
    taxation of shares of stock, 368; resources, 733; restricting
    loans, 734; periodical examinations required, 735; charges
    against Superintendent Kilburn, 872.

VETOES. Amending General Banking Act, IV, 700, 730; increasing
    capital, 776; final closing of, V, 665; amending act, West-
    chester county, VI, 599; liability of stockholders, VII, 268;
    securities for redemption of circulation, 412; banking asso-
    ciations, liability of stockholders, 413; receivers, 416; deficits
    in capital, making good, 508; redemption of circulating notes,
    508; amending general law, 804; IX, 152, 800; taxation, VII,
    936; relative to, 1097; holidays, amending Saturday half-
    holiday provision, VIII, 535; insolvent, receiving deposits,
    amending Penal Code, 890; conferring trust company powers on
    certain moneyed corporations, IX, 366; in first-class cities,
    bonds for security of certain depositors, 791; directors, elec-
    tion, 800; private, first-class cities, security for deposits, 867;
    New York,—repayment of penalties to certain, X, 475; assess-
    ment of bank shares, correction, 475.

BANQUETTE. At Copsey and Flatrock batteries, I, 323.

BANYER, GOLDSBROW. Leasehold estate, IV, 334.

BAPTIST CHURCH SOCIETY, HOOSICK. Removing dead from burying
    ground, veto, VII, 76.

BARBADOES. Lieutenant-Governor Nanfan visits, I, 93.

BARBERS. Doing business on Sunday, act regulating, amending, veto,
    IX, 804.

BARBER'S POINT. Ferry across Lake Champlain, veto, VIII, 410.

BARCLAY, ANNA DOROTHY. Claim of, I, 224.

BARCLAY, REV. HENRY. Missionary to Indians, I, 291; purchase of cer-
    tain lands for Mohawks, 553.

BARGE CANAL. Appropriation for, approved by people, X, 141, 252, 363, 496; Advisory Board established, 496; tenure of office, 596; special examiners, 597; methods of meeting cost, 598; proposed special tax on counties, 599; new revenues needed, 602; appraisal of land, structures, etc., veto, 706; progress of work, 730; amending general act, locks and channel, veto, 813; bonds authorized, 833; appropriation in lieu of tax, 833; appraisals of land taken for, 844.

BARKER, ADELIA QUEENIE. Illegitimate child, legitimizing birth, veto, X, 770.

BARKER, GEORGE BELL. Legitimizing illegitimate child, veto, X, 770.

BARKER, WILLIAM H. Preparing index to Assembly bills not printed, veto, VII, 460.

BARLOW, FRANCIS C. Secretary of State, communication from Governor, action on bills after adjournment, V, 814; Attorney-General, communication, bill relative to assignees and receivers, VI, 562; member of Yorktown Centennial Commission, VII, 734.

BARLOW, SAMUEL. Commissioner, highway, St. Regis reservation, veto, VII, 909.

BARLOW, WILLIAM H. Relief, veto, VII, 666.

BARNES CORNERS BURIAL ASSOCIATION. Charter, veto, VI, 186.

BARNES, ALFRED C. Member of Yorktown Centennial Commission, VII, 734.

BARNES, STEPHEN. Relief of, II, 209.

BARNETT, BESSIE P. Escheat, veto, VIII, 882.

BARR, WESTLEY. Court of Claims, veto, X, 449.

BARR, WILLIAM. Auburn prison convict, crime committed by, trial, reimbursing Cayuga county, veto, VII, 227, 472, 781.

BARRACKS. In Fort William Henry, repair of, I, 48; recommended for Albany, 70, 602; New York, 137; in Fort George, 222, 227, 231, 238, 244, 260, 265, 270, 277, 322, 608, 753; New York, destroyed by fire, 297, 302; rebuilt, 298; for Schenectady, 602; new, authorized in New York, 617; New York and Albany, sufficient for quartering soldiers, 703.

BARRATRY. Act to prohibit, I, 11.

BARRE. Town meetings by election districts, veto, VI, 674, 690.

BARRELS. Size of, for fruits and vegetables, veto, VI, 188; X, 317; apple, relative to, veto, VII, 508.

BARREN ISLAND. Temporary quarantine establishment on, V, 767, 845.

BARRETT, EDWARD J. Relief, veto, X, 178, 581.

BARRY, JOHN A. Complaint against Judge William Inglis, III, 906.

BARRYVILLE AND SHEHOLA DELAWARE BRIDGE COMPANY. Charter, veto, IV, 521.

BARTHOLDI STATUE FUND. New York authorized to contribute, veto, VII, 1088.

BARTLETT, CHARLES H. Canal department, appropriation for services, veto, IX, 716.

BASHFORD, GEORGIANA. Escheat, veto, VI, 157.

BASSLER, CHRISTIAN. Injuries while in National Guard service, Board of Claims, veto, IX, 66.

BATAVIA. Deposit of military stores at, II, 755; arsenal, arms and ammunition supplied from, 775, 793; abduction of William Morgan, III, 185; arsenal, seizure of military stores, 683; Holland Land Company's office at, close of, 755; institution for the blind at, V, 762; Asylum for Blind, water supply, veto, VII, 229; number of excise licenses, 1887, VIII, 360; place of holding elections and town meetings, veto, 698; new bill passed.

BATAVIA INSTITUTION FOR THE BLIND. Established, V, 762; temporarily located at Binghamton, 762, 839; appropriation for, 762, 839; additional land for, 839; report, IX, 754, 851; X, 31, 142; classed as an educational institution, 334; board of managers to visit, 336.

VETOES. Sewerage, VIII, 854; appliances for object teaching, IX, 79; general improvements, X, 547; repairs and equipments, 654.

BATAVIA AND NORTHERN RAILROAD COMPANY. Extending time to begin construction, veto, X, 700.

BATAVIA TIMES. Federal statutes, published in, II, 1068.

BATCHELLER, GEORGE S. Inspector-General, member of auditing board of enlistments, V, 870.

BATCHELLERVILLE. First Presbyterian church, legalizing acts of trustees, veto, VII, 1106.

BATES, MARY T. Relief, veto, IX, 630.

BATH. Postmaster at, suggested removal, II, 1070; Soldiers' Home, V, 490; VII, 289.

VETOES. Rescue Hook and Ladder Company No. 1, charter, VI, 56; excise commissioners, legalizing acts, VII, 178; town meetings, time and place of holding, IX, 117.

BATH-ON-THE-HUDSON. VETOES. Amending village charter, VI, 1035; VIII, 620; rifle range, additional land, IX, 244.

BATTALION INDEPENDENT DES GARDES LAFAYETTE FRANCAIS. Charter, veto, VI, 598.

BATTERY. Proposed for New York, I, 41; on each side of Narrows, 103; proposed at Whitehall (New York), 247, 249, 338; New York, 280, 283, 295, 322; floating, proposed construction of, 555; at Fort George, 748, 763; repair of, II, 262; at Narrows (Fort Richmond), 658; other batteries on Staten Island, 659; on North river, 712.

"BATTOES." Construction of, recommended, I, 153; impressment of, 374; building of, ordered, 568.

BAUDISSIN, FRIEDRICH A. CHL. H. VON. Accompanies Prince Henry to Assembly Chamber at his reception, X, 480.

BAUMAN, SEBASTIAN, COLONEL. Commissary of military stores, report, II, 332.

BAWDEN, S. D. Chaplain Rochester Industrial School, Court of Claims, veto, X, 707.

BAXTER, ARCHIE E. Clerk of the Assembly, announces entrance of Prince Henry at his reception by Assembly, X, 480.

BAYARD, NICHOLAS. Accounts of, I, 73.

BAYARD & Co. Proposition to sell arms to State, II, 954.

BAYARD HOMEOPATHIC COLLEGE, HOSPITAL AND DISPENSARY. Charter, veto, IX, 233.

BAYARD'S RESERVATION. Purchased by Oliver Phelps, II, 1030.

BAYWOOD LAND IMPROVEMENT COMPANY. Charter, veto, VI, 329.

BEACH, ALLEN C. Lieutenant-Governor, member of Centennial Celebration Committee, VI, 302; report, powers of canal commissioners, 344.

BEACH PNEUMATIC TRANSIT COMPANY. Incorporated, VI, 291; VII, 1033; name changed to Broadway Underground Railway Company, 1035.

BEACONS. At Narrows and Rockway, I, 151, 607; discharge of sentinels at, 155; on Staten Island, II, 586, 589; on islands in St. Lawrence river, IV, 381.

BEARDSLEE, RUFUS G. Counsel to New York Board of Education, settlement of claim, veto, IX, 805.

BEATTIE, MARY. Escheat, veto, VIII, 405.

BEAUHARNAIS, CHARLES MARQUIS DE. Governor of Canada, negotiations with Indians, I, 271.

BEAVER RIVER. Canal dam, veto, VII, 457.

BEAVER SKINS. In trade with Far Indians, I, 214; danger of French interference, 241.

BECK, AUGUST. Sheriff, Erie county, asks military aid, Buffalo railroad strike, 1892, IX, 160.

BECK, DR. LEWIS C. Geological survey, mineralogist, III, 638, 753, 991; report, 644, 682, 754; IV, 81.

BECKER, GEORGE. Relief, veto, VI, 185.

BEDDING. For royal troops, I, 202, 282; needed by troops at Albany, 555; for troops in New York, 608.

BEDFORD. Letter from Deputy Governor Treat, relative to, I, 73; defection of, 73; public roads in, veto, VI, 589; House of Refuge for Women, X, 144.

BEDFORD HOUSE OF REFUGE FOR WOMEN. Established, IX, 144; completion, X, 106; classed as a reformatory, 334.

BEDFORD HOUSE OF REFUGE — (*Continued*).
    VETOES. Relative to, 448; commitments from New York, 633; general improvements, 656.

BEDFORD REFORMED DUTCH CHURCH. Continuing exemption from taxation, veto, VIII, 465, 624, 733.

BEDLOW'S ISLAND. Fortifications on, II, 360; lazaretto, 382; deeded by New York city to State, 382, 386.

BEEBE, JOHN. Memorial from, II, 54.

BEEBE, J. M. Governor of Kansas, communication from, V, 345.

BEEBE, Z. LAWRENCE. Commissioner, Onondaga reservation road, veto, VII, 587.

BEEF. Frauds in, I, 530; inspection, 617, 749; II, 436, 439, 457, 513, 529; reports on inspection, 1113; improved inspection, III, 99; reduction of tolls, 505.

BEEKMAN, HENRY, COLONEL. Assembly, motion relative to Governor's alleged interference with courts, I, 468.

BEEKMAN, HENRY R. Member of Commission on Uniform Laws, VIII, 1068.

BEEKMAN, SAMUEL. Canal waste ditch along premises of, veto, VI, 852.

BEER. Adulteration, veto, X, 55.

BEERKILL. Ulster county, protection of trout in, veto, VII, 131.

BEET SUGAR. Cultivation of, communication from Kentucky, III, 821; bounty for, 1897, IX, 745: manufacture commended by Governor Black, 823; appropriation for bounties, 1901, X, 216; large product expected, 1901, 216.

BEEVE RIVER. French fort on, I, 549.

BELCHER, JONATHAN. Governor of Massachusetts, letter from, relative to New York boundary, I, 241, 283; letter from, bounties for Indian scalps, 595; Governor of New Jersey, communication from, relative to New York boundary, 540.

BELGIA. Ownership of American property, II, 1033.

BELGIUM. Canal development should keep pace with railroads, X, 135.

BELKNAP, WILLIAM W. Secretary of War, letter from, Brooklyn pier and bulkhead lines, VI, 452; action relative to Louisiana disturbances, 771; communication from, cession of land at West Point, 788.

BELL, JAMES A. Senate, resolution requesting information as to certain military expenditures, V, 487; committee on procuring readjustment of quotas, 537, 572, 634; canal auditor, report on Albany basin improvement, VI, 44.

BELL, JOSHUA F. Delegate from Kentucky to Washington Peace Convention, V, 329.

BELLAMY, F. P. Attorney, communication to Superintendent Ellis, relative to Mechanics and Traders' Savings Institution, VII, 57.

BELLEVUE. Female convicts at, III, 401, 448; female prisoners transferred to Mount Pleasant, 618.

BELLINGER, CHRISTOPHER P. Lieutenant-colonel, service at Sackett's Harbor, II, 746.

BELLINGER, PETER, COLONEL. Petition from, appointment of surgeon, II, 117.

BELLIS, DELOS. Police justice, Penn Yan, legalizing acts, veto, IX, 258.

BELLOMONT, EARL OF. Appointed Governor, I, 74; assumes office, 75; .dissolves Fifth Assembly, 75.

Opening speech, Sixth Assembly, I, 75; unhappy condition of colony, 75, 80; suppression of piracy, 76; revenue, support of government, 76, 80, 84, 86, 90; restoring public credit, 77, 81; frontier fortifications, 77; reconciliation of parties, 77, 79, 82, 85; abuses in Assembly elections, 77; loyalty to Crown, 77; address to Crown, 78; judiciary, 78; excise, 78; powers and privileges of Assembly, 78; dissolves Sixth Assembly, 78.

Opening speech, Seventh Assembly, first session, I, 79; independence of colony, 79; obedience to English laws, 80; irreligion in colony, 80; public accounts, 81, 89; royal aid to colony, 81; urges calmness in Assembly's deliberations, 82; Indians, 82, 83, 84, 85, 87, 88, 89, 90; smuggling at Oyster Bay, 83; thanks Assembly for address, 83; recommends erection of town house and jail, 83; new law for election of Assembly, 84; official fees, 84; payment of public debt, 84; relief of owner of "The Fortune," 84; Robert Livingston's claim, 84; announces appointment of Speaker Graham, as member of council, 84.

Opening speech, Seventh Assembly, second session, I, 85; Protestant ministers and fort for Indians, 86, 88, 89; conference with Indians at Albany, 87.

Opening speech, Seventh Assembly, third session, abstract of, I, 89; town house and jail at Albany, 89; announces appointment of chief justice and Attorney-General, 90; purchase of masts for navy, 93. Death of, I, 90, 93; official service, I pref., IX.

BELMONT, PA. Obtaining coal from, III, 168.

BENDER, JOHN. Sealer of weights and measures, New York, salary, veto, X, 308.

BENDER (MATTHEW) & CO. Rebinding law books for Attorney-General's office, appropriation, veto, X, 796.

BENEDICT, DR. N. D. Superintendent of State Lunatic Asylum, IV, 554.

BENEDICT, SPENCER S. Aide-de-camp, letter from, anti-rent troubles, III, 835.

BENEVOLENT AND CHARITABLE CORPORATIONS.

VETOES. Amending act, VI, 907; VII, 414; extending act to literary societies, 132; devises to, limiting amount of, 266; exempting from life insurance laws, 543; legalizing certain charters, 937; dissolution, 1020; trustees and directors to receive compensation in certain cases, IX, 439; establishing cemeteries, 442; report, appointments or commitments, repeal, 534.

BENEVOLENT ORDERS.

VETOES. Amending general act, IX, 800; powers of joint corporations, X, 593; power of trustees to issue bonds, 812.

BENHAM, H. W., CAPTAIN. United States engineer, report on quarantine station, V, 80, 104; letter of instruction from Governor King and others, quarantine affairs, 100; report, 100.

BENEFICIARY CORPORATIONS. Exempting from life insurance laws, veto, VII, 543.

BENNETT, ALPHA E. Commissioner, bridge, Tonawanda reservation, veto, VII, 477.

BENNETT, E. Engineer, cost of enlarging canals, V, 507.

BENNETT, EDWARD L. Judgment against Binghamton superintendent of streets, payment, submitting question to people, veto, VII, 1017.

BENNETT, S. S. Canal department, appropriation for services, veto, IX, 716.

BENNETT, THOMAS. Bond for return of arms, II, 772.

BENNINGTON. Battle of, II, 8, 11.

BENSEN, CHARLES B. Board of Claims, veto, VIII, 1039.

BENSON, BENJAMIN. Relief, veto, VI, 185.

BENSON, EGBERT. Commissioner to Hartford Convention, II, 107; Attorney-General, letter from, 209; commissioner on Massachusetts boundary, 217; commissioner to Commercial Convention, 260; judge, correspondence with Governor Jay, Council of Appointment, 483.

BENSONHURST PARK. Amending act to establish, VIII, 1157.

BENTON. Town, School District No. 11, tax for new schoolhouse, veto, VI, 337.

BENTON, NATHANIEL S. Canal auditor, estimated cost of enlarging canal locks, V, 506.

BENWAY, THOMAS. Board of Claims, veto, VIII, 890; IX, 270.

BERKSHIRE COUNTY, MASS. Agricultural Society, model proposed for New York, III, 878.

BERLIN. Decrees of, noted, II, 672, 690.

BERLIN, RENSSELAER COUNTY. Railroad commissioner, abolishing office, veto, IX, 232.

BERMUDA. Letter from Governor of, I, 160; monopolizes carrying trade, 246; opposes New York Tonnage Act, 271.

BERNARD, E. J., & Co. Court of Claims, veto, X, 61.

BERNE (BERN). Proceedings for collection of Van Rensselaer rent, III, 823; Van Rensselaer leases, description of, IV, 329; disturbance in, 705.

BERRY, GEORGE A. Pipe line lease, Allegany reservation, veto, VII, 73.

BETH ISRAEL BIKUR CHOLIM CONGREGATION, NEW YORK. Relief, veto, IX, 808.

BETH ISRAEL HOSPITAL ASSOCIATION.
  VETOES. Exemption from taxes and water rents, IX, 806, 810; relative to, X, 59; taxes and water rents, relief, 326.

BETHLEHEM. Van Rensselaer leases, description of, IV, 329; part annexed to Albany, taxes, veto, VII, 412.

BETHLEHEM MUTUAL INSURANCE ASSOCIATION. Bill to incorporate and ratify proceedings, veto, VI, 90, 910.

BETHPAGE CEMETERY, OYSTER BAY. Sale of lots, improvement fund, veto, VII, 1122.

BEST, WILLIAM J. Charges against Bank Superintendent Ellis, VII, 56; receiver National Trust Company, investigation, counsel fees, veto, 906; Board of Claims, veto, VIII, 1039.

BETTING. On elections, IV, 131; VII, 32; proposed disfranchisement for, IV, 132; act to prevent, 135.

BIBLE. Proposed for use of convicts, II, 612; reading in schools, 727; quoted, capital punishment, 729; for convicts in Auburn prison, 1121; III, 22.

BICYCLES. See also CYCLES. Regulating use of, veto, IX, 866.

BIDDLE, CLEMENT, COLONEL. Commissary of forage, letter from, II, 54.

BIENNIAL SESSIONS. Advocated by Governor Cornell, VII, 723; Governor Black's comment, 1897, IX, 753; 1898, 847; adoption by other States, 847; proposed constitutional amendments, 847; X, 21.

BIGAMY. Bill to restrain, veto, II, 780.

BIG CHAZY RIVER. Improving navigation of, veto, VIII, 848.

BIGELOW, JOHN. Member of Canal Investigating Commission, 1875, VI, 928.

BIG FLATS. Chemung river bridge, bonding for, veto, VII, 578.

BIG KETTLE. Seneca chief, joins in address to Governor, II, 943.

BIGLER, WILLIAM. Governor of Pennsylvania, communication relative to monument to commemorate Declaration of Independence, IV, 681.

BILL, ELIJAH. Refugee, claim of, II, 308.

BILLEY, CAPTAIN. Seneca chief, joins in address to Governor, II, 943.

BILLINGS, JOHN. Bond for return of arms, II, 774.

BILL OF RIGHTS. Power of taxation, II, 316.

BILLS. Assembly, by whom to be approved, I, 20; different subjects not to be joined in same bill, 272; executive consideration of, II, 4; IV, 769; VII, 668, 673; VIII, 1003; passage over veto, II, 4; III, 531, 1003; IV, 252; VII, 675; returned by Governor for amendment, IV, 700; V, 12, 131, 136, 137; V, 332, 512, 574; VII, 1028; recall from Governor, IV, 751; VI, 167; X, 33; for appropriations, should be considered early in session, V, 94; VI, 246, 368, 641; action after adjournment of Legislature, IV, 524; V, 517, 665, 813, 881; VI, 89, 179, 323, 499, 578, 674, see THIRTY-DAY PERIOD; proper method of indicating amendments, V, 575; large number recalled, VI, 399; three readings should be had, 400; reading and passage of, 400; X, 145; appropriations, vetoing separate items, II, 460; V, 263; VI, 369, 403, 642, 852, 864, 924; IX, 404; X, 794, 799, 935; errors in engrossing, VI, 418; thirty-day period, see that title; engrossed, imperfect condition of, VII, 42; printing of, 43; constitutional rule as to printing, 43; emergency certificates, 43; status after adjournment of Legislature, 169; method of passing, constitutional provision, 185; reading on final passage, 185; index to bills, veto, 225; status after ten days without Governor's action, 242; local, meaning of term, third judicial district, 260; ten-day period, 667; VIII, 434; meaning of term "Legislature" as applied to adjournment, VII, 669; passage, majority of Legislature necessary, 675; IX, 618; legislative counsel, VIII, 25, 125, 298, 351; drafting department established, 27; legislative discretion, when may not be reviewed by Governor, 85, 89; denying opponents an opportunity to be heard, 102; defective, responsibility for failure, 125; extraordinary session, limitation of subjects, 135; question of constitutionality, bill should have benefit of doubt, 263; proper rule by Governor in disposing of constitutional questions, 605; local, must have title, 617, 618; States in which judicial opinion may be required as to constitutionality of, 947, 1046; for cessions of land to United States, necessary provisions in, 1114; should not contain preamble, 1130; defective, drafted and engrossed, reform needed, IX, 209; duties of Statutory Revision Commission and bill drafting department, 210; certificates of necessity of passage, see that title; Governor's jurisdiction, 618; proposed revision by legislative counsel, 676; large number left for thirty-day period, 848; presented by Statutory Revision Commission, 1900, X, 222.

BILLS OF CREDIT. COLONY. On expedition to Canada, I, 140; for general purposes, 176; new, recommended, 181; counterfeiting, 188, 749; act to revive and continue, 198, 212; destruction of counterfeit, 244; new issue authorized, 264; deficiency in sinking fund, 269; foundation of value, 270; proposed, pending collection of tax, 370;

BILLS OF CREDIT. COLONY — (*Continued*).

to be canceled by excise money, 529; not to be legal tender, 558; results of excessive issue of, 560; high character of New York bills, 560; new act relating to, 606; large issues of, 628; for expenses of campaign, 636, 645; for Amherst loan, 638; necessity of, in colony, 694; revocation of instruction prohibiting issue of, 714, 715.

BILLS OF CREDIT. STATE. Under $1 to be canceled, II, 52; counterfeiting, 66; taxation as a means of supporting, 77; cancellation of defaced bills, 77; national, New York act for redemption of, 97, 111; rate of exchange between national and State, 97; new emission of State, 97.

BILLS OF LADING. Advances on, not subject to usury laws, VII, 719.

BINGHAMTON. Southern terminus of Chenango canal, III, 234, 419; advantages derived from internal improvements, 815; State Inebriate Asylum at, V, 86; Institution for the Blind temporarily located at, 762, 839; Inebriate Asylum abolished, Insane Asylum established, VII, 286; number of excise licenses, 1887, VIII, 359; excise license fees, 1889, 689; law library, IX, 46.

VETOES. Bridges at, preservation of, VI, 149; Protection Hose Company, No. 3, charter, 179; schools, 504; board of education, VII, 46; Susquehanna Valley Orphans' Home, improvements, appropriation, 90; law library, 220; IX, 83; State Inebriate Asylum, finishing basement and first story, VII, 230; extending time for collection of taxes, 412; accepting foot-bridge, 415; police force, 752, 806; military storehouse, addition, 928; payment of judgment, submitting question to people, 1017; unpaid taxes, sales for, VIII, 392; Masonic Board of Trustees, charter, 460; enlarging corporate limits, 468; enlarging boundaries, 753; changing fiscal year, 873.

BINGHAMTON INSANE ASYLUM. Established, VII, 286; succeeds State Inebriate Asylum, 286, 288, 431; charges against trustees; not removed, 443; use of, 706; number of inmates, 958.

VETOES. Amending act, VII, 414; repairs and improvements, appropriation, 487; appropriation, 785; various appropriations, 912. 1080; appropriation of unexpended balances, 912; additional assistants, VIII, 132.

BINGHAMTON MASONIC BOARD OF TRUSTEES. Charter, veto, VIII, 460.

BINGHAMTON STATE HOSPITAL. Number of visits of local managers, X, 415; decrease in number of recoveries, 1902, 498.

VETOES. Electric light, IX, 78; improvements, 79; entertainment hall, steam road machines, sewer extension, 295; new roof, main building, pointing up main building, appropriations, X, 934.

BI-PARTISAN BOARDS. Police, VI, 445; election officers, VII, 203; Troy police board, VIII, 86; Syracuse water board, 259; poll clerks, election of, alleged unconstitutionality, 959; at elections, required, Constitution 1894, 959; IX, 102, 309, 556; Buffalo, bi-partisan board of aldermen proposed, alleged unconstitutionality, VIII, 960; Constitutional Commission, 1890, 1034; election boards in New York, change of, IX, 102; elections, general act, 1894, 102, 309, 343; police, West Troy, 589; elections in cities, act of 1898, 877, 885; New York bi-partisan election board established, X, 213.

VETOES. Troy school commissioners, VI, 508; Kings county board of charities, 1018; Little Falls, commissioners of public grounds, VII, 330; poll clerks, 333; Oswego, amending charter, VIII, 624; New York police commission, 756; New York park commission, 757, 758; election boards in Yonkers, Watertown and Little Falls not bi-partisan, IX, 458.

BIRDSEYE, CLARENCE F. Table of Statutes prepared by, furnishing for Assembly Judiciary Committee, veto, VIII, 858; Revised Statutes, third edition, prepared by, purchase and distribution, veto, X, 430.

BIRDSEYE, VICTORY. Appointed special counsel in Morgan matter, III, 351; report, 365.

BIRGE, JOHN I. Board of Claims, veto, VIII, 626.

BIRTHS. Registration of, V, 863.

BISHOP, CHARLES F. Mayor, Buffalo, asks military aid, railroad strike, 1892, IX, 160.

BISHOP, KETCHEL. Bond for return of arms, II, 771.

BISSELL, EDWIN B. Relief, veto, VI, 185.

BISSELL, HERBERT P. Commissioner to examine Cayuga Indian claim, report, X, 31.

BLACK, FRANK S. Counsel for Senate Committee on Investigation of Election Frauds, 1894, appropriation, veto, IX, 533; appropriation, 1895, 533; Governor, portrait, IX, 738; presides at Capital Centennial Celebration, 1897, 689.

1897. Annual message, IX, 738; financial condition, 738; proper rule for consideration of appropriations, 739; prisons, 739; banking, 740; insurance, 741; labor, 741; women should receive same compensation as men for same work, 742; investigating relations between capital and labor by means of university extension, 742; National Guard, 743; naval militia training, 743; chief executive officer of National Guard should have more permanent tenure, 743; railroads, 743; grade crossings, 744; agriculture, 744; public highways, 745; new capitol should be completed, 745; canals,

BLACK, FRANK S., 1897 — (*Continued*).

746; insane, 747; public schools, 748; compulsory instruction, 748; excise laws, 748; civil service, 749; forests, 750; devastations in forest preserve should be stopped, 751; Greater New York, 752; biennial sessions, 753; various reports, 754, 755; pardon report, 755; certificates of necessity of immediate passage of bills, 1897, 755, 756.

MEMORANDUM OF APPROVAL. Civil service, two examinations, IX, 756.

VETOES. Champlain canal, bridge over Glens Falls feeder, Sandy Hill, IX, 755; railroad commissioners, increasing number, 761; transfer tax, graduated, 762; items in supply bill, 767; items in supplemental supply bill, 774; omnibus veto, 776.

1898. Annual message, IX, 820; finances, 820; banking, 821; insurance, 821; railroads, 822; grade crossings, 822; canals, 822; aggregate cost, 822; excise, 823; good effects of Liquor Tax Law, 823; agriculture, 823; beet sugar industry, 823; commerce, 824; commission to examine New York commerce, 826; completion of new capitol, 826; National Guard, 827; schools, 827; University of the State, 828; value of libraries in education, 829; traveling libraries, 829; efficiency of State library, 829; charities, 829; insane, 830; condition of asylums around New York city, 830; prisons, 831; new system of prison labor successful, 831; Elmira Reformatory, indeterminate sentences, 832; labor, 832; proposed application of university settlement to labor questions, 833; effect of immigration on labor troubles, 833; forests, 834; cutting trees on State lands, 835; pulp-mills absorb large number of trees, 836; scientific cultivation of forests in other States and countries, 836; purchase of land for experiments, 837; college of forestry, 837; civil service, 838; opposes indefinite tenure of officers, 839; enlarging powers and opportunities of Civil Service Commission, 843; good roads, 844; money system, 844; taxation laws inadequate, 845; public expenditures, 846; reform in public printing, 846; biennial sessions, 847; short and active session, 848; too many private and local laws, 848; communication from State Engineer and Surveyor and Superintendent of Public Works, recommending canal investigation, 849, 850; commission created, 849; action on report, 850; transmits various annual reports, 851, 852; pardon report, 852; certificates of necessity of immediate passage of bills, 1898, 852, 853, 854, 884, 885; aiding Federal government, Spanish War, 852.

BLACK, FRANK S., 1898 — (*Continued*).

    VETOES. New York, teachers' salary bill, IX, 854; items in supply bill, 856; omnibus veto, 857.

    Proclamation convening Legislature in extraordinary session, IX, 876; message, 876; appropriation for troops in War with Spain, 877; absent soldiers voting, 877; protection of voters, 877, 878; enlistments in Spanish War, 1898, 878; meaning of home rule, 880; appropriation for expenses of extraordinary session, 84; metropolitan elections district, State superintendent, 885; bi-partisan representation on local election boards, 885; nomination of State Superintendent of Metropolitan Elections District, 885; quoted, — extravagance in construction of State hospitals, X, 410; — revenue from State forests, 862; official service, I, pref. XIII.

BLACK HAWK, THE. Commodore Porter's flag-ship, V, 567.

BLACK, JAMES. State clothier, letter from, clothing for New York troops, II, 91, 100.

BLACK CREEK. VETOES. Public highway, VII, 358; cleaning and deepening, IX, 81; improving channel, X, 301.

BLACK LAKE. VETOES. Draining adjacent land, VI, 1036; overflowed land, drainage, 1036; VIII, 614; drainage, repealing act, VII, 268.

BLACK RIVER. Militia in service at, II, 743; connection with Erie canal, III, 70, 166; canal connection with St. Lawrence river, 166; principal feeder of Erie canal, VII, 983; source in Adirondack region, IX, 147.

    VETOES. Bridge, Carthage, VII, 362; bridge, Lewis county, VIII, 292; State dam waste gates, IX, 244; raising bank, Denmark and Croghan, X, 300; Castorland dyke, repairing and improving, raising dyke road, Croghan, 570, 644; Croghan breakwater, 791.

BLACK RIVER CANAL. Suggested, III, 70, 509; construction authorized, 510, 789; IV, 360; loan for, III, 620, 711, 816, 865; banks authorized to subscribe to loan, 633; work of construction, 669, 865, 887; debt, 736; IV, 252; payments for, III, 763; estimated cost, 790, 865, 963; suggested discontinuance of construction, 798; construction suspended, 959, 1009, 1043, 1049; IV, 13, 102; work should be resumed, IV, 18, 59; expense charged on canal fund, 205; construction resumed, 369, 390, 424, 586; suspension of work a mistake (Young), 389; appropriation for, 391, 425, 474, 678, 735, 743; length of, 425; progress of work, 474, 599; expense of completing, 544, 670; importance of early completion, 696; tools, V, 66, 154, 257, 361; relation to canal system, 789; financial statement, VI, 930; VII, 5, 145; commission to examine,

BLACK RIVER CANAL — (*Continued*).
VI, 933; retention recommended, VII, 8; sale prohibited, 685; tonnage, 1893, IX, 301; abandonment of part, X, 731.

VETOES. Appropriation for work on, IV, 195; temporary administration, VII, 118; improving navigation, dams, Beaver and Independence rivers, 457; Stillwater reservoir, enlarging capacity, VIII, 849; improvement, IX, 110.

BLACK RIVER INSURANCE COMPANY, WATERTOWN. Changing name, veto, VI, 813.

BLACK RIVER AND MORRISTOWN RAILROAD COMPANY. Town bonds, legalizing act, veto, VI, 583; consolidation with Utica and Black River Railroad Company, VII, 847.

BLACK RIVER AND ST. LAWRENCE RAILROAD COMPANY. Town aid to, veto, VI, 348.

BLACK ROCK. Military post at, II, 512, 513; ferry at, 526, 605, 1029; troops at, 1812, 743, 746; engagement at, inhuman conduct of British and Indians, 787; battle at, 793; statement of killed and wounded, 872; harbor, construction of, 1096; fortifications, cession for, III, 850, 945; village, act relating to, 1029; cession of land, at, IV, 46; sewerage under Erie canal, veto, VII, 365, 457.

BLACK ROCK HARBOR. Improvements, VI, 858; dredging and excavating, 860; dredging, veto, IX, 58.

BLACKSNAKE, GOVERNOR. Indian chief, method of election, IV, 504.

BLACKSTONE, SIR WILLIAM. Quoted, secret voting, VIII, 585.

BLACKSTONE'S COMMENTARIES. Cited, IV, 358.

BLACKWELL'S ISLAND. Hospital for indigent insane, IV, 77; number of inmates, 604, 641, 718; patients from marine hospital removed to, V, 184; commitments for intoxication, 285; smallpox patients, VI, 237; East river bridge, veto, X, 176.

BLAINE, EPHRAIM, COLONEL. Commissary-General, letter from, army supplies, II, 116.

BLAKE, JOHN, JR. Nominated sheriff of Orange county, proceedings of Council of Appointment, II, 475, 493.

BLAKESLEY. Naval successes, II, 802.

BLAW, WALDRON. Estate of, II, 288.

BLEAKLEY, MARY E. New York, claim, veto, VII, 1089.

BLEECKER, HARMANUS. American chargé d'affaires at The Hague, services in procuring transcription of colonial documents, IV, 169.

BLEEKER, JACOBUS. Indian interpreter, I, 459.

BLENHEIM PATENT. Description of, IV, 331.

BLIND. Instruction of, III, 452, 516; New York Institution for, 453, see that title; number to be ascertained, 526; industrial education, IV, 430; number of, V, 10; new institution located at Ba-

BLIND — (*Continued*).

tavia, 762; fiscal year established, VII, 297; adult, provision for instruction recommended, X, 728.

VETOES. Batavia asylum, water supply, VII, 229; poor adult, New York city, appropriation, VIII, 889;, poor adult, New York, relief, 1036; adult in cities, relative to, IX, 791, 866; installing plant in State prison for publication of literature, X, 293; adult, permanent commission, appointment, 696.

BLINN MEMORIAL METHODIST EPISCOPAL CHURCH, NEW YORK. Canceling assessment on opening portion of Lexington avenue, veto, IX, 809.

BLISS, ELIPHALET W. Member of Board of Examiners of arms for National Guard, IX, 635.

BLISS, GEORGE. Director Western Railroad Company, communication from, III, 750.

BLISS, GEORGE. Attorney, Senate Committee on General Laws, investigation of trusts, appropriation, veto, VIII, 843; opinion, voter's freedom of selection of candidate cannot be restricted by form of ballot, IX, 395, 479.

BLISS, GEORGE, JR. Governor Morgan's private secretary, communication from, appointment of foreign commissioner of deeds, V, 214.

BLISS, THALES S. Contested election, Assembly, New York, expenses, veto, VII, 918.

BLOCK, PHILIP. Admission to examination as attorney, veto, X, 63.

BLOCKHOUSES. At Albany, I, 239; at Fort Hunter, 256; in Mohawks' country, suggested use of one for chapel, 291; recommended for New York city, 340; for outscouts, 357; six on northern frontier, 368; at Schenectady, 368; in Ulster and Orange counties, 590, 616; in New York to be fitted up, 608; for protection of Kingston, 627; at Palmertown, II, 113; sea-fencibles in, 808, 810.

BLOOD, ISAIAH. Senator, death of, VI, 242, 365.

BLOOD, JOHN D. Relief, veto, VI, 185.

BLOODGOOD, MAJOR. Report, anti-rent troubles, III, 832, 836, 839; directions to, 838.

BLOOM, ELIZA. Estate of, veto, II, 713.

BLOOM, HENRY. Lieutenant-colonel, 19th Regiment, II, 766.

BLOOM, JANE. Estate of, veto, II, 713.

BLOOM, SALLY ANN. Estate of, veto, II, 713.

BLOOMER, ELISHA. Claim, Sing Sing prison, marble quarry, veto, VI, 589.

BLOOMFIELD, JOSEPH, GENERAL. Commands troops on northern frontier, II, 746.

BLOOMINGDALE ASYLUM. For insane, III, 379, 451; IV, 77; State aid to, 77, 127; number of inmates, 126, 278, 431; report, VI, 156; investigation, legislative printing legalized, VIII, 793.

BLOSSBURG, PA. Coal mines, railroad to Chemung canal, III, 786.

BLUNT, GEORGE W. Pilot commissioner, communication from, New York harbor encroachments, V, 796; communication from, obstructions in New York harbor and Hudson river, VI, 557.

BLYTH'S MANUAL OF PRACTICAL CHEMISTRY. Quoted, composition of vinegar, VIII, 354.

BOARD OF AGRICULTURE, ENGLAND. Established, II, 956.

BOARD OF AGRICULTURE. Suggested by Governor De Witt Clinton, II, 898, 969; recommended by legislative committee, 957; State board established, 970, 1005, 1046; suggested by Governor Seward, III, 745, 878.

BOARD OF ALMS. Creating, German Flats, veto, VII, 215.

BOARD OF BROKERS, NEW YORK. Fixes standard of value of public securities, IV, 806.

BOARD OF CLAIMS. Created, jurisdiction, VII, 821; name changed to Court of Claims, 821; VIII, 977; organization and work of, VII, 978; slaughter of diseased animals, claims for, 990; work of, VIII, 14; awards, Appropriation Act relating to, VIII, 1000; proper requisites of bill submitting claims to, 1128; cost of, 1891, IX, 11; bill should state reason for submitting claim, 67; bill submitting claim should authorize appeal by either party, 285.

VETOES. Appeals to Court of Appeals in certain cases, VIII, 56; auction agent, award, 247; report, publication and distribution, 857; canal surveys and maps, 868; awards, 885; appropriation, undetermined awards, IX, 49; awards, interest on, 140, 288; county insane asylums, 265; general awards bill, 1893, 275; corporation taxes, unlawfully collected, claims for, 278; jurisdiction, escheats, 524.

VETOES,— HEARINGS. Conkling, VII, 884; Clinton county prison case, 782, 887; Chemung county, Elmira Reformatory case, 931; Cayuga county, Auburn prison case, 932; Featherstone, 1120; Lawlor, 1121; Costello and Curtis, 1124; Dudley, VIII, 291, 408; Tanner, 292; Ray, 626; Kowalski, 626, 727; Birge, 626; Boyd, 639; McGowan, 639, 886; Tuttle, 886; O'Brien, 886; McIntyre, 887; IX, 152, 451; Frazee, VIII, 887; Charles M. Brown, 888, 1038; Hutchinson, 888, 1037; Steuben county, Redding trial, 888; Hendricks, 888; Putnam, 889; IX, 269, 353; Pilon, VIII, 889; Benway, 890; IX, 270; Myers, VIII, 976, 1120; Risely, 1038; Best, 1039; Bensen, 1039; Hanus, 1039; Leet, 1039; Roberts, 1040; James G. Johnson, 1040; David T. Smith, 1040, 1129; Turner, 1041; Holdridge, 1041; IX, 285; Davie, VIII, 1041; Fingar, 1124; Milliete, 1125; IX, 66; Has-

BOARD OF CLAIMS, VETOES — (*Continued*).

bronck, VIII, 1128; Humphrey and others, 1166; Weed, Parsons & Co., 1167; Burhans, IX, 50; Bassler, 66; Morgan, 66, 268; Powell and others, 119; McKinstry, 149, 269; Strohm, 149; Rochester, 154, 290, 797; Brock and Wiener, National Guard uniforms, 237, 452; Ross and Sanford, 237, 721; Roberts, 250; Linus Jones, Peck & Co., 369, 600, new bill, 1895; Crouse and Fyler, 428; Jarvis, 429; Drury and Van Arnum, 430; Moore, 430; Bray, Auburn prison keeper, injured by convict, 452; Lockman and Devery, 473; Ruso, 623; Silversmith's Company, 627, 717; Rochester, amending submission act, 719, 797; auctioneers, 720; Sadler, 721; Hall, 797; Lynch, 797; Gilgan, 797; Parks, 797; McMaster, 797; Morhous, 797. See VETOES, Vol. XI.

BOARD OF COMMISSIONERS OF WEST BANK QUARANTINE STATION. Report, VI, 43.

BOARD OF EDUCATION. Proposed, III, 744; in New York city, 951; recommended for towns, IV, 840.

BOARD OF ENGINEERS. New York harbor defense, V, 568.

BOARD OF EXAMINATION OF ARMS. Created, 1895, IX, 634; report, 635; Governor Morton's decision, 635; report transmitted to Legislature, 1897, 754, 755.

BOARD OF HEALTH. Act of 1850, IV, 470; New York, reorganized, VI, 627; New York, report of sanitary committee, 658; New York, resolution relative to cheap trains, 658; New York, protests against milk adulteration bill, 710; national, approves New York quarantine methods, VII, 433.

VETOES. Newtown, Flushing and Jamaica, 113; Buffalo, proceedings, 414.

BOARD OF IMMIGRATION. Created, VII, 832, 966.

BOARD OF INTERNAL IMPROVEMENTS. Proposed by Governor Seward, III, 712; probable advantages of, 797.

BOARD OF ORDNANCE (English). Letter to Lord Carteret, I, 202.

BOARD OF POLICE COMMISSIONERS (Metropolitan). Created, V, 27; report, 110, 198, 305, 413, 563, 598, 617, 699, 715, 791, 861; VI, 43, 142; communication from, pay of patrolmen, 44; temporary president, veto, 50.

BOARD OF PUBLIC IMPROVEMENTS. Proposed by Governor Clinton, II, 1097; III, 67; established in Pennsylvania, 171.

BOARD OF RAILROAD COMMISSIONERS. Established, IV, 805, 836; expenses paid by railroad companies, 836; act of 1882, VII, 732; increase of number, 732; superseded by Public Service Commissions, X, 855.

BOARD OF REGENTS. See REGENTS AND UNIVERSITY OF NEW YORK.

BOARDS OF RELIEF. For soldiers, in towns and cities, V, 490.

BOARD OF SAFETY. Proposed in New York charter, 1872, VI, 471, 479.

BOARD OF STATUTORY CONSOLIDATION. Created, VI, 118; X, 107, 224.

BOARD OF SUPERVISORS. Alleged violations of law, II, 465; Ulster county, appointment of courthouse commissioners, 945; appropriations for agricultural purposes, 1089; nomination of justices, III, 17; general functions of, 192; not body politic or corporate, 533; appointing power, eliminating association with county judges, 770, 872; when to appoint additional county superintendents of schools, IV, 23, 66; legislative powers, 434, 496, 575; V, 191, 294; may apply for election of special county judge and surrogate, IV, 626; contracts with penitentiaries, V, 337; may authorize erection of bridges by towns, 346, 385; VI, 53, 311; power to alter or erect towns, VI, 60; Columbia county, equalizing assessments, 95; enlarging powers of, 96, 118, 226; VIII, 509, 517; expenses in criminal cases, VI, 143; fixing salary of district attorney, 144; soldiers' monument, 162; turnpike tolls, 216; fixing bridge tolls, 221; indices of records, 310; power of taxation should not be transferred to Comptroller, 316; authorizing towns to borrow money for roads and bridges, 319; recording notices of pendency and discharges of mortgages, 323; land for cemetery, 501; extending village boundaries, 502; care of books and records, 822; power to enact game laws, 906; VII, 69, 234, 301, 446; power as to town elections, 64; changing county seat, 250; election districts, 389; Kings county, report on charitable and penal institutions, 537; New York, abolition, transfer of powers, 643; office hours, county offices, 757; power as to bridges, VIII, 383; county roads, 1042; power to direct transcription of county records, IX, 39; cannot fix surrogate's salary, 124; Kings county, abolished, 585; re-established in New York, 1897, 753; constitutional amendment, 1899, 753; town meetings, legalizing action fixing time of holding, X, 236; auditing claims, action final, 268; proposed regulation of local game laws, 504; proposed power to validate municipal bonds, 519.

VETOES. Acts and proceedings of, V, 385; conferring additional power on, 673; compulsory audit of claims, VI, 307; extending powers, 593; compensation, amending general act, VII, 131; Niagara and Orleans counties, poor expenses, 328; changing location of courthouses and jails, 412; streets in territory adjoining cities, 416; Kings county, appointment of clerks and messengers, 440; Erie county, support of poor, 441; powers, amending general act, 506; Erie county, compensation of court

BOARD OF SUPERVISORS, VETOES — (*Continued*).

officers, legalizing acts, 538; fixing compensation of surrogate's clerks, 649; Fulton county, equalizing representation, 769; Montgomery county, borrowing money, 841; Chautauqua county, soldiers and sailors' monuments, 845; Schuyler county, borrowing money, county buildings, 859; amending act, VIII, 460; members, increasing compensation, 640; fire districts in unincorporated villages, 872; confirming audit of accounts, 886; Oneida county, legalizing audit of accounts, IX, 231; powers under Game Law, 234; licenses to peddlers, 372; Broome county, legalizing proceedings, 795; St. Lawrence county, appointing purchasing committee, X, 175; Niagara county, reconsideration of claim of Roswell Park, 268; acquiring materials for highway construction, 384; county schools of agriculture and domestic economy, establishing, 440; powers under Game Law in certain counties, 441; acquiring title to turnpike, plankroads and bridges, amending act, 952.

BOARD OF TREASURY (United States). Certain accounts to be presented at, II, 33.

BOARD OF WAR (United States). Report from, Continental battalions, II, 33; letter from, clothing for troops, 80.

BOARDING-HOUSES. To furnish lists of boarders to State Excise Commissioner, X, 202; liens of, veto, 593.

BOARDMAN, TRUMAN. Assembly, member of committee, first occupation of new Senate chamber, VII, 540.

BOERUM, SIMON. Assembly, favors colonial union, I, 767; delegate to Continental Congress, 768.

BOGART, WILLIAM H. Committee on procuring adjustment of quotas, V, 537, 572.

BOGERT, JACOB S. Appointed Commissary-General, III, 430.

BOHAN, PATRICK. Relief, veto, X, 178.

BOILERS. Inspection of, V, 283.

BOLLAN, WILLIAM. Presents to Lord Dartmouth petition of Continental Congress, I, 770.

BOLIVIA. Participation in Cotton States Exposition, IX, 581.

BOLLER, ALFRED P. Requests approval of Harvey rapid transit bill, VIII, 125.

BOLLES, FRANK. Relief, veto, X, 178.

BOLT AND BAKE. Equal right to, granted by Leisler Assembly, I, 16; bolting to be encouraged, 246.

BOLTERS. Preventing frauds of, I, 302.

BOMFORD, GEORGE, MAJOR. Service in procuring cession of land, II, 778.

BONAPARTE CREEK. Public highway, veto, VII, 934.

BOND, EDWARD A. Chairman Canal Advisory Board, X, 629.

BOND STREET SAVINGS BANK, NEW YORK. Financial condition of, VII, 66.

BOODY, ALVIN. New York, relief, veto, X, 582.

BOOKMAKING. Prohibited, constitutional provision, IX, 548, 602; act of 1895, 601.

BOOTH, CHARLES. Estate of, escheat, veto, X, 635.

BORCK, FREDERICK. Act legalizing contract with Wayne County Agricultural Society, VIII, 1148.

BORGERSRUD, JULIA. Court of Claims, veto, X, 286.

BOSTON. See also MASSSACHUSETTS. Andros imprisoned in, I, 14; aid from, not expected for defense of Albany, 49; post to Westfield and Albany, 136; arrival of Canadian expedition fleet, 151; English prisoners brought to, 409; fire in, 646; act shutting up port of, protest against, 774; scarcity of wheat and flour in, II, 69; Continental agent directed to sell rum and sugar to New York, 84; convention at, relative to national affairs, 107; Athenaeum, distribution of statutes to, 994; railroads and canal connection with west, III, 953; truant officers, reports of, V, 108; relation of taxation to population and property, VI, 412; fire, 547; exportation of grain, IX, 557.

BOSTON CORNERS. Ceded to New York by Massachusetts, IV, 817.

BOSTWICK, ANDREW. Deputy Forage-Master-General, letter from, public contracts, II, 208.

BOTANIC GARDEN. At Elgin, purchase of, II, 579, 973.

BOTTLES. Used in connection with certain drinks, amending act, veto, IX, 267.

BOUCK, WILLIAM C. Governor, portrait, IV, 1.

1843. Annual message, IV, 1; first farmer Governor, 1; general duties of Legislature, 1; business depression, 3; Federal relations, 4; act of Congress relating to choice of representatives, 5; Bankrupt Law, 5; congressional Insolvent Law, 5; trial by jury in fugitive slave cases, 7; Virginia extradition case, 8, 47; internal improvements, 9; railroad companies in default, 10; suspension of public work, 13; policy of 1842, 15; canal construction should be resumed, 17; canal legislation, 18; State debt, 19; education 23; finances, 23; assessment of real estate, 24; quality of salt, 25; State prisons, 27; convict labor competition, 28; blind, deaf and dumb, 29; relief of seamen, 30; judiciary, 30; public printing, 31; reducing official fees, 32; banks, 32; system of supervision apparently inadequate, 34; agriculture, 37; militia, 37; exemptions from execution, 39; repudiation of State debt, 40; Federal census, 1840; statement of agricultural

BOUCK, WILLIAM C., 1843 — (*Continued*).

      productions, 42; State lunatic asylum, 43; colonial history, 44; refunding fine against General Jackson, 44, 82; Vermont, Connecticut, New Hampshire and Rhode Island resolutions, 45; memorial, New York Free Trade Association, repeal of inspection laws, 45; Maine, Georgia, Michigan resolutions, 46; cession of land at Black Rock, 46; American Athenæum requests copies of statutes, 46; collection of United States deposit fund loan, 47; proposition to establish Museum of Mechanic Arts, 47; New Jersey, Maine, Alabama resolutions, 48; resolutions on Convict Labor Act of 1842, 48; communication from Comptroller of the Treasury relative to public lands, 49, 162.

      1844. Annual message, IV, 49; general conditions, 50; stability of government, 51; no necessity for national convention to revise Constitution, 51; review of constitutional conventions and amendments, 51; judiciary, 53; limiting legislative power over appropriations, 54; judiciary amendments, 54; abrogation of power to aid private enterprise, 55; limitation of power to create State debt, 55; appropriations, two-thirds vote, 56; Court of Common Pleas, 56; internal improvements, 57; extravagant increase of State debt, 58; policy of 1842, 58; canals, 60; State debt, 62; education, 65; rate bills, 66; salt, 67; bounties, 69; banks, 69; militia, 70; loaning arms to uniform companies, 71; New York arsenal, 71; prison labor, 72; visits charitable institutions, 74; quarantine establishment and marine hospital, 75; passenger tax, 75; lunatic asylums, 77; State prisons, 78; criminal statistics, 80; agriculture, 80; State fair, 80; reducing rate of interest, 81; geological survey, 81; closing canal locks on Sunday, 81; colonial history, 82; Connecticut resolutions, 83; South Carolina, Connecticut, Maine and Massachusetts resolutions, 84; proceedings of Albany Convention relative to Constitutional Convention, 84; Massachusetts, New Hampshire, Virginia and Mississippi resolutions, 85; Kentucky, Rhode Island, Maryland, and Georgia resolutions, 86; calls out militia, anti-rent troubles, 147; appoints Senators in Congress, 154; arrangement of colonial documents, 191; official service, I, pref. XII.

BOUGHTON, LYMAN C. Coroner, Wyoming county, legalizing acts, veto, X, 813.

BOUGHTON, SEYMOUR. Lieutenant-colonel, claim of, War of 1812, II, 946.

BOULANGER, GEORGES ERNEST. Chief representative of French war department, report on Yorktown celebration, VII, 739.

BOUNDARIES. See also particular topics. Of colony in 1691, I, 29; of counties, action relative to, 672; of counties, settlement recommended, 715, 722; survey of part of Hudson river, 757; between Half Moon and Schenectady, church lands, II, 117; Dutch and English colonies, III, 1018; State, restoring and placing monuments, expenses, veto, X, 786.

BOUNTIES. COMMERCIAL. English, on hemp, I, 256; for cultivation of hemp, lottery established, 682; for encouragement of manufactures, II, 40; effect of, 658; manufacture of woolen cloth, 702; cultivation of hemp, III, 206, 253; for silk cocoons and domestic reeled silk, 879, 945; on salt, IV, 68; coal, 69; lead, 69; gypsum, 69; empty casks, 69; improving manufacture of butter and cheese, cultivation of hops, veto, VII, 1078; for manufacture of sugar, veto, IX, 725; for beet sugar, 745; X, 216.

BOUNTIES. MILITARY. For Canadian expedition, I, 151; disposal of, 156; proposed for Spanish War, 287, 668; expedition against Canada, 374, 386; offer of land for, 598; offered by General Amherst, 664; of unappropriated lands, II, 115, 148, 187, 305, 308; amount paid to New York levies, 180; Trotter case, 343; recommended, War of 1812, 748; Civil War, offered by State, V, 454; by localities, 455, 540, 576; appropriation for, 530, 571; communication from Paymaster-General, 578; local, change of law needed, 609; local, prohibited, State provided for, act approved, 609, 610; amount expended for, 689; Federal equalization bounty bill, 774; bounty debt, see BOUNTY DEBT.

VETOES. Relative to, II, 309; legalizing local, V, 673; Ferris, heirs, VI, 324.

BOUNTY. For heads, I, 71; Massachusetts offers, for scalps, 595; for destruction of wolves, II, 1107.

BOUNTY DEBT. Created, V, 610; VI, 660; statistics, VI, 7, 100, 229, 348, 526, 614, 720, 914, 915; VII, 3, 138, 275, 420, 513, 680; payable in currency, VI, 100; payment of, 883, 915, 1014; VII, 4, 141; Governor Tilden's comment on, VI, 915; debt paid, VII, 273.

BOUVIER'S LAW DICTIONARY. Quoted, definition of ballot, VIII, 584.

BOWDOIN, JAMES. Governor of Massachusetts, letter from, rebellion suppressed II, 269.

BOWEN, MARY. New York, firemen's pension fund, Peter Bowen, relief, veto, X, 321.

BOWEN, RYER. Smith for Onondaga Indians, I, 389.

BOWLS. For King's troops, Assembly declines to furnish, I, 282.

BOWMAN, JOHN. Appointed canal commissioner, III, 570.

Bowman, John. Convicted of murder, sentence commuted to life imprisonment, II, 738.

Boxes. Used in connection with certain drinks, amending act, veto, IX, 267.

Boyd, Mary K. Board of Claims, veto, VIII, 639.

Boyce on Referees. Cited, reference of causes for trial, X, 682.

Boys' Industrial Home. Establishing, veto, IX, 246.

Brackenridge, William A. Member Canal Advisory Board, X, 629.

Brackett, William H. Canal department, appropriation for services, IX, 716.

Braddock, Edward, General. Requested to send engineer to New York, I, 562; arrives in Virginia, 565; approves Governor Shirley's plan of defense, 566; defeat of, by French and Indians, 572.

Bradley, Dr. Prevents removal of postmaster at Bath, II, 1071.

Bradley, Andrew. New York, ex-policeman, relief, veto, X, 581.

Bradley, George B. Constitutional commission, 1872, proposition for compulsory voting, VIII, 676.

Bradley, Stephen R. Vermont's agent before Congress, II, 176.

Bradner, Alonzo. Member of Tax Revision Commission, 1881, VII, 538.

Bradstreet, John. Lieutenant-colonel, takes Fort Frontenac, I, 625, 627; claim of, 719.

Brady, Benjamin F. Preparing Wagner memorials, appropriation, veto, VII, 777, 928.

Brady, James B. New York contractor, relief, veto, V, 247.

Braithwaite & Erickson. Locomotive engine, speed of, III, 397.

Braman, Isaac G. Canal department, appropriation for services, veto, IX, 716.

Brandow, A. T. Keeper Sing Sing prison, injuries, appropriation, veto, VII, 464.

Brandow Printing Company. Court of Claims, veto, X, 315, 444.

Brandy. French furnish, to Indians, I, 248.

Brant Lake. Black bass in, close season, veto, VIII, 975.

Brat, Captain. Commander of outscouts, I, 124.

Braun, Conrad. Estate of, escheat, veto, X, 273.

Braun, Franciska. See Stierle, Franciska.

Bray, John. Auburn prison keeper, injured by convict, Board of Claims, veto, IX, 452.

Bread. Good reputation of, should be preserved, 1, 302; false taring of casks, 530; scarcity in Rhode Island, II, 68; scarcity of, for troops, 161.

Breadbake, Anna. Relief, veto, II, 406.

Breadbake, John. Estate of, escheat, II, 406.

BREED, O. C. Claim, Phœnix dam investigation, appropriation, veto, X, 786, 933.

BRENT, DANIEL. Consul at Paris, communication from, relative to authentication of instruments executed abroad, III, 821.

BRESLIN, JAMES H. Nominated as quarantine commissioner, VIII, 520.

BREWER, DAVID J. Supreme Court, United States, opinion, railroads, reducing rate of fare, IX, 501.

BREWER FIRE COMPANY, MONSEY. Charter, veto, VII, 268.

BREWERS. Act relating to qualifications of, I, 11.

BREWERTON. Draw-bridge at, veto, VII, 94, 232, 366, 473, 576.

BRIBERY. At elections, III, 158, 249, 313, 525, 726; IV, 563, 614; VI, 263; VII, 31, 724; VIII, 1093; IX, 197; disfranchisement as a consequence of, III, 882; proposed constitutional amendment, IV, 614, 744; VI, 264, 265; in New York, V, 25; general act, VI, 37; resolutions of 1853, 264; resolutions of 1871, 387, 391; persons convicted excluded from right of suffrage, 725; VIII, 1002; constitutional amendment, article 15, VI, 725; Seneca Indian officers, act to prevent, VII, 436; at elections, veto, VIII, 598; conviction, disqualification from voting or holding office, 599; presidential election, 1888, alleged use of money, 664; should be made more difficult, 666; by successful candidate, exclusion from office, 1079, 1092; of representative of labor organization a misdemeanor, X, 616.

BRIDGE COMPANIES.

VETOES. Amending act, VII, 509; stock of, authorizing Rome, Watertown and Ogdensburg Railroad Company to purchase, VIII, 1130; Albany and Bath-on-the-Hudson Bridge Company, charter, IX, 715; Ward's Island Bridge Company, charter, 725, 793; Troy and Colonie Bridge Company, charter, X, 585; counties acquiring title of, amending act, 952. See also BRIDGES.

BRIDGES. See also TOLL BRIDGE. Over canals, II, 1010; III, 72, 120; IV, 18; encouraging construction of, II, 1012; canal, unfinished, inconvenience resulting from, IV, 16, 59; bridge companies, general act, 514; over rivers, declared to be public highways, V, 148; in towns, when authorized by supervisors, 346, 385; VI, 46; borrowing money for, 55, 98, 319; penalty for fast driving, 147, 556; canals, evils of frequent changes, 853; power of board of supervisors, VIII, 383; Poughkeepsie, extending time for completion, 443; over Allegany river at Onoville, 560; Albany, Hawk street, act for, 612; Mather Power Bridge Company, Niagara river, act relative to, X, 54.

VETOES. Barryville and Shehola Delaware Bridge Company, charter, IV, 521; over Allegany river, V, 345; Franklin Bridge Company, charter, IV, 604; Carrol, erecting, VI, 96; Phœnix bridge,

Bridges, Vetoes — (*Continued*).

protection of, 147; Binghamton, preservation of, 149; over Champlain canal, Whitehall, 154, 584; Oswego county, 212; over Great Sodus bay, 212; Livingston county, relief, 306; Wellsville, tax for, 311; Lowville, borrowing money, 318; town auditors, raising money for, 329; Ausable and Chesterfield, 556; over Rondout creek, Marbletown, 585; Erie and Niagara counties, Tonawanda creek, 696; Allegany river at Vandalia, 707; Cattaraugus Indian reservation, special, VII, 383; Allegany reservation, Red House, 587; Hudson and other rivers, 808; injuries from defects, notice before accident, 843; Onondaga reservation, repair, VIII, 116; New York and Brooklyn, bill relative to, 123; over Harlem river, Metropolitan Transit Company, changing location, 132; Cairo, over Catskill creek, 383; over Moose river, Lyonsdale, reimbursing town, 552; over tidal streams, 640; over Allegany river at Onoville, 845; over Crooked lake outlet, 849; Pelham, purchase of, 889; Brooklyn, policemen, compensation, 992; Johnstown, voting by ballot on appropriation for, 1087; New Utrecht board of improvement, 1134; Onondaga reservation, IX, 80; Troy and Green Island Bridge Company, charter, 153; Harlem river bridge commissioners, closing affairs of, 154; Wolf Island Bridge Company, charter, 248; over Long lake, 255; Penny bridge, Minisceongo, declaring jurisdiction over, 264; highway, broken by heavy loads, when town not liable, 274; on Tonawanda reservation, 348; canals, lift and swing bridges, compulsory operation by State, 444; joint, apportionment of expense, 525; on county lines, 587; Harlem draw-bridge, amending act, 631; over Mott Haven canal, New York, 633; Drake's draw-bridge, maintenance, operation and repair, 712; over inlet to Otisco lake, 777; Newtown creek, free public draw-bridge, 778; inspection by State Engineer and Surveyor, 801; over Harlem river, New York, 145th street, 807; over Douglass State ditch, reimbursing town of Lenox for construction of, 817; Marbletown, free bridge, Ulster county to contribute to expense of, 817; Newburgh, New Windsor, relative to, 818; Syracuse, bridge over canal at Bridge street, 870; Syracuse, Westcott street canal bridge, 870; East River bridge, relative to, 873; over Hudson river, authorizing Albany Railway Company to construct, X, 52; Brooklyn, over Mill pond, 31st and 32d wards, 59; Niagara river at Grand Island, 63; East river, Blackwell's island, 176; New York, Jerome park reservoir, 176; Seneca Falls, bonds for, 278; over Clear creek, Cattaraugus reservation, 429; over Madison reser-

BRIDGES, VETOES — (*Continued*).

voir, repairs, 645; over Seneca river, Salina and Lysander, 697; Allegany river, at Elko, 698; Niagara river, Grand Island, 703, 774; Tompkins, bridge over Delaware river, 873; Newtown creek, damages to owners of land abutting on Vernon avenue, Queensborough, 957.

BRIDGE TENDERS. Canals, by whom appointed, VII, 1024.

BRIDGEWATER, DUKE OF. Canal, effect on price of coal, III, 204.

BRIGGS, JOHN E. Member of board of education, Ogdensburg, communication favoring school bill, X, 912.

BRIGHAM, DR. AMARIAH. Superintendent of State Lunatic Asylum, IV, 43; death of, 483.

BRIGHT, GEORGE. Estate, relative to, veto, VII, 508.

BRIGHTON. Commissioner of common schools to be trustee of Rochester Colored School, III, 378; payment for canal damages, VI, 861.
VETOES. Canal lift-bridge, 1005; VII, 96, 117; — assessors, compensation, IX, 371.

BRIMMER, GEORGE. Family attacked by Indians, son murdered, I, 571.

BRISTOL, WHEELER H. Claim, appropriation, veto, VI, 875.

BRITISH. Evacuate New York, I, 780; II, 195; movements in Highlands, 15, 18; take Fort Montgomery, 16; defeated on northern frontier, 18; peace commissioners, 45; occupy New York city, 50; surrender at Yorktown, 150; act to prevent illicit trade with, 164, 184; persist in war, ulterior designs against United States, 184; attempt to monopolize West India trade, 197; conduct of war condemned, 206; statutes continued by Constitution, revision, 219, 255; seamen at New York, alleged indignity to French flag, 246; retain western posts, 253, 334; conduct of garrison at Point A'fere, 318; attack the Chesapeake, 616; attack the frigate "President," 690; complain of New York pilot fees, 888; murder of General Woodhull, III, 227; provinces, commercial reciprocity with, IV, 656.

BRITISH MUSEUM. Records of, sources of American history, III, 162; IV, 166; library, 182.

BROADWAY SURFACE RAILROAD COMPANY. Charter annulled, VIII, 205.

BROADWAY UNDERGROUND RAILWAY COMPANY. Extending rights, powers and duties, veto, VII, 1031; VIII, 263; successor to Beach Pneumatic Transit Company, VII, 1035.

BROCK, LOUIS M. See BROCK AND WIENER.

BROCKENBROUGH, JOHN W. Delegate from Virginia to Washington Peace Convention, V, 311.

BROCKHOLLS, ANTHONY. Receives letter from Secretary Werden relative to Assembly, I, 4; letter from Duke promising Assembly, 5; member of first legislative council, 9.

Brockport. Normal school at, V, 695, 780; legalizing special election for establishment of sewer system, X, 518.

    Vetoes. Canal lift-bridge, VI, 1004; VII, 116; Erie canal culvert, 456; bridge, 931.

Brockport Normal School. Established, V, 695, 780, 852; appropriation of common school fund unconstitutional, 695; appropriation for repairs, 1895, IX, 593.

    Vetoes. Additions and repairs, VII, 468; repairs and improvements, VIII, 865; sewer system, X, 315.

Brook and Wiener. Claim, National Guard uniforms, veto, IX, 237.

Brodhead, Charles C. Commissioner on Indian migration, III, 636; compensation, 636.

Brodhead, John Romeyn. Agent to procure records for colonial history, communication from, III, 1013; statement of needed documents, 1017; IV, 176; progress of work, III, 1035; IV, 43; more funds needed, 44, 164; results of service, 82; final report, 164; account settled, 165; appropriation for, 192.

Bronson, Greene C. Corporation counsel, New York, opinion, compulsory payments of judgments against city, V, 237; delegate to Washington Peace Convention, 310.

Bronx Borough. See also New York.

    Vetoes. Changing grade of streets, claims for damages, X, 323; Pelham avenue, legalizing opening, 326; White Plains avenue, improvement, apportionment of expenses, 477; Exempt Firemen's Benevolent Fund Association, headquarters, 581; White Plains road improvement, 712; St. Paul's Reformed Episcopal church, relative to, 806; street improvements, 23d and 24th wards, damages, 807; Pelham avenue, laying out, 807.

Bronx River. Water supply for New York city, II, 1017; sewer commission, establishing, veto, X, 713.

Brook (Brooke) Chidley. Presents Council's communication to Assembly, I, 28; agent for colony, letters from, 73.

Brookland (Brooklyn). Assembly meets at, I, 367.

Brooklyn. Assembly meets at, I, 367; General Haight's brigade at, II, 809; navy yard, officers and employees, improper conduct at election, 1065; naval hospital, III, 181; new arsenal, V, 88, 175; park commission, report, 204; arsenal condemned as unsafe, 282; proportion of policemen to population, 283; Civil War, adjustment of quota, 574; mayor, member of commission on new quarantine establishment, 701; VI, 25; insufficient school accommodations, V, 854; act relating to public health, VI, 129; pier and bulkhead lines, 452; pneumatic tubes, 289, 485; health department, VII, 455; unpaid taxes and assessments,

BROOKLYN — (*Continued*).

502; expenses should be reduced, 532; too many officers, 532; gratifying result of legislation of 1881, 715; civil service established, 976; registration of naturalized citizens, production of papers, VIII, 20; elevated railroad bill, 129; defects in Registration Law, 181; number of excise licenses, 1887, 359; gas, regulating price, 431; excise license fees, 1889, 685; participation in centennial celebration of Washington's inauguration, 695; street improvements, acts of 1890, 1021; Flatlands annexed to, 1098; Flatbush annexed, 1111; Gravesend annexed, 1112; New Utrecht annexed, 1134; memorial arch, act for, 1160; law library, IX, 46; bi-partisan election boards, 102; sale of coal, ton defined, coal inspector, 184; supervisors, filling vacancies, act relative to, 223; act sustained, 224; consolidation with New York, 300; merged in Greater New York, 300; aldermen, election by wards, 347; mayor, member of Greater New York Charter Commission, 553; armory proposed at, 573; consolidated with Kings county, 1896, 585, 588; rejects Greater New York bill, 1896, 709; Garbage Disposal Act, 1900, X, 57; Bedford and Remsen avenues, improvement, 155.

VETOES. Relief of inhabitants, II, 665; improving North Second street, VI, 92; map, alteration of, Pratt street, 186; improving Fourth street, 192; improving Banker street, 193; Security Bank, charter, 210; Nassau Savings Bank, charter, 220; disorderly persons, 333; map, alteration, 335; board of excise, 489; inferior courts, 512; board of health, extending jurisdiction, 517; Van Brunt Street and Erie Basin Railroad Company, relief, 518; board of health, establishment of, 518; Wallabout improvement, 579; park commissioners, extending term, 581; Brooklyn Elevated Silent Safety Railway Company, rapid transit, 595; Flatbush Railroad, 597; Bushwick, altering map, 695; ferry to New York, 697; Prospect park reservoir, payment of award, 911; Fort Green, monument, prison ship martyrs, VII, 85; Library Fund Association, eastern district, amending charter, 96; government of, 126, 134; amending charter, VI, 911, 1026; VII, 128, 267, 321, 804; truant reform school, 133; high school, establishment, 134; public buildings, exemption from taxation, 267; aldermen, 321; elections, counting ballots and facilitating trial of actions, 370; Atlantic Avenue Railroad, 394; Third avenue sewer, 413; Grand street improvement, 413; police pension fund, amending act, 413; justice of the peace, election, 415; department of city works and health, amending charter, 415; consolidation of deficiency

BROOKLYN, VETOES — (*Continued*).

indebtedness, 416; board of police commissioners, establishment, 417; constables, 439; railroad on Water street, 446; common council, election of messenger, 509; protection of female employees, 509; grading Lorraine street, 572; retirement of teachers, 606; Kingsley and Keeney claim, construction of storage reservoir, 617; schools, free books and supplies, 626; public schools, protection of life and property, 627; Atlantic avenue, repavement, 664; Ninth and Garnet streets, grading, 665; escheat, McLoughlin, 748; changing custody of school funds, 750; park commissioners, extending term, 762; unpaid taxes, 771; charitable institutions, free water, 804; sewers, drainage, 804, 932, 936; theater exits, 804; justices of the peace, reducing number, 804; Johnson avenue improvement, 804; Prospect park, 804; armory, 804; street improvements, 932; cession of land to United States, 932; plumbers, registration, 933; New Lots, annexation, 936, 1110; new armory, 1883, 953; justices of the peace, increasing number, 1119; fire department pension fund, VIII, 131; parks, protection of, 131; gaslight companies, use of electricity, 132; Retail Grocers' Association, charter, 198; elevated railroads, preventing construction in certain streets, 291; elevated railroad company, annulling agreement with commissioners, 293; truant school, 293; police station, fourteenth precinct, 294; amending General Excise Law, 355; fire limits, excise licenses in concert buildings, 462; Methodist Episcopal Hospital, Brooklyn, 464; Manhattan avenue, 468; Jewell street, closing, 468; park department, 468; repairing Johnson avenue, 468; Irving and Sedgwick streets, 469; board of aldermen, 470; East river bulkhead and pier line, 470; police pension fund, amending act, 523; soldiers' monument, amending act, 527, new bill passed; Lee and Nostrand avenues, 559; drains and sewers in certain wards, 635; Manhattan, extension and improvement, 636; pension, Abraham Dalley, 638; assessors, 638; streets, opening certain, 638; lighting streets, 26th ward, 638; repaving certain avenues, 638; board of aldermen, changing method of electing, 739; inferior courts, increasing number, 887; police patrolmen, amending act, 887; streets and avenues, use of certain, 890; dispensaries, increasing number, 969; municipal building, increasing office accommodations, 1036; charitable institutions, payments to, 1036; police courts, 1036; department of assessment, 1036; police force, 1036; public parks, acquiring land for, 1036; altering commissioner's map, 1102; Union Mission Chapel Association, trusts, legacies and donations for

BROOKLYN, VETOES — (Continued)

poor, 1127; police and excise departments, engineer, qualifications, IX, 119; wards, increasing number, 121; taxation of stocks and bonds, 148; land for streets, 16th ward, 148; police and excise, amending charter, 151, 152; soldiers and sailors' memorial arch, legalizing acts, 211; fire department, salaries, 262; water front, 262; 8th ward improvements, 263; closing portion of Clymer street, 263; closing portion of Heyward street, 263; fire, police and excise departments, supplies, 364; Hyne and Kilgour, escheat, 428; park lands, duplicate bill, 434; local improvements, duplicate bill, 434; pier near Navy Yard, 438; laborers, fixing rate of wages, 448; pier, North Seventh street, 448; fire department, 475; justices' courts, additional number, 476; street cleaning department, 476; police justices and police courts, appointments, 502; officers, tenure, 521; Lewis avenue, relative to, 626; city clerk, appointment, 626; city works, dividing department, 626; arrears, 630; board of audit, powers, 630; park, 31st ward, 632; police and excise departments, 633; courts of special sessions, 634; Flatlands Annexation Act, amendment, 634; public driveway and parkway, 720; Flatbush, street and sewer commissioners, 29th ward, transferring powers and duties to commissioner of city works, 720; buildings department, 729; Gravesend common lands, 729; commissioner's map, alteration, Kent avenue, 729; Wayside Home, commitment of female delinquents to, 733; public works, wages of employees, 733; city clerk, 733; park police pension fund, 733; fire limits, 734; completing armory, 23d Regiment, 778; Newtown creek, nuisance, abatement, 778; officers, fees, 778; Hooper street, railroads, 778; Belmont avenue and Crystal street improvement, 778; Hall street and St. James place, railroads on, 778; water companies, acquiring property of, 30th ward, 779; Bedford avenue, railroads in, 779, 780; Doolittle, assistant clerk, justices' court, claim, 779; Norman avenue and other streets, relative to, 779; Avenue M, reducing width, 779; firemen, confirming appointment, 779; Old Clove road, closing, 779; booths and stands, permits for, 779; park improvement, 779; pier, 8th ward, 779; Prospect place, railroads on, 780; East Eighteenth street, railroads on, 780; Twelfth street and others, railroads in, 780; Surf avenue extension, 780; Hancock street improvement, 780; city marshals, powers and compensation, 780; cemetery, 32d ward, trustees, mayor to appoint, 780; streets and highways, improvements, 780; Vermont avenue, relative to, 781; police pensions, time of payment, 781; Throop

BROOKLYN, VETOES — (Continued).

avenue and other places, railroads in, 781; Cumberland street
and others, railroads in, 781; Cropsey avenue, railroads in, 781;
Enfield street, railroads in, 781; Wallabout market improvement, 781; Waterbury street improvement, 781; Old road, 31st
ward, closing, 781; St. Mark's place, etc., railroads in, 782;
Gravesend, taxes, arrearages, settlement, 782; Second avenue,
etc., railroads in, 782; Penn street, etc., railroads in, 782; parkway and driveway, amending act, 782; Wallabout market lands,
relative to, 783; armory, acquiring site, 783; City Court, transferring employees to Supreme Court, 795; fire department, appointments to uniform force, 809; school lands, sales, proceeds,
868; Brooklyn Institute of Arts and Sciences, amending act, 968;
Clinton avenue, relative to, 868; streets, avenues and highways,
completing proceedings commenced before annexation to New
York, 872; Robinson, authorized to build and maintain bulkhead, 12th ward, 873; Wallabout lands, 873; Flatbush, Prospect avenue, opening, 874; East Eighteenth street, railroads on,
874; East Nineteenth street, railroads on, 874; East Fourteenth
street, railroad on, 874; fire department, legalizing appointments, 874; West Seventeenth street, completing grading contract, 876; firemen, Flatbush, payment for services, 876; fire
limits, 876; Ocean avenue improvement, 876; offensive trades,
X, 57, 60; confirming certain appointments by fire commissioners, 59; bridge over Mill pond, 31st and 32d wards,
59; Municipal Court, 59; Atlantic avenue, railroads on, 175;
Ashland place, railroads, 176; interest on assessments, 176;
grading Atlantic avenue, New Lots, 177; Flatbush, Prospect
avenue assessments, 177; fire commissioners, legalizing appointments, 178; drainage, 29th and 32d wards, 322; street improvements, discontinuance, 30th ward, 322; Cropsey avenue, railroads on, 322; Prospect avenue, improvement, 324; Ashland
place, railroads on, 324; Livingston street, improvement, 326;
Clinton avenue, relative to, 451; park department, 477.

BROOKLYN BOROUGH.

VETOES. Sewer in, X, 474; zoological garden, Prospect park, 476;
Remsen avenue improvement, 582; Atlantic avenue, Long Island
Railroad on, 582; Hoff estate, relative to, 584; children's court,
clerk's salary, 711; grade crossings, abolishing, 714; Prospect
avenue improvement, 716; Sisters of Mercy, relief from assessments, 716; firemen, confirming appointment, 806; releasing
city interest in land, 807; buildings and improvements, 807;
fire department, deputy chief, 818; street railroads, fares in,

BROOKLYN BOROUGH, VETOES — (*Continued*).
882; Uvalde Asphalt Paving Company, labor and materials, 951; free college, 956; Donlon Contracting Company, claim for cleaning sewers, 959.

BROOKLYN CITY BAR ASSOCIATION. Represented by counsel at trial of Justice Hooker, X, 829.

BROOKLYN CITY RAILROAD. Extending road, veto, VI, 695.

BROOKLYN EAGLE. Interview, 1883, aldermanic bill, VIII, 744, 745, 747.

BROOKLYN ELEVATED RAILROAD COMPANY. Annulling agreement with railroad commissioners, veto, VIII, 293.

BROOKLYN ELEVATED SILENT SAFETY RAILWAY COMPANY. Charter, veto, VI, 595.

BROOKLYN EQUITY GASLIGHT COMPANY. Relative to, veto, VIII, 469.

BROOKLYN FREE LIBRARY. Transfer of certain land to, veto, IX, 867.

BROOKLYN GUARANTY AND INDEMNITY COMPANY. Changing name, veto, VIII, 617.

BROOKLYN HEIGHTS RAILROAD COMPANY. Grade crossings in Brooklyn, X, 714.

BROOKLYN INSTITUTE OF ARTS AND SCIENCES. Amending act, veto, IX, 868.

BROOKLYN AND JAMAICA RAILROAD COMPANY. Transfer of rights to Atlantic Avenue Railroad Company, VII, 395.

BROOKLYN LIBRARY BUILDING FUND ASSOCIATION, EASTERN DISTRICT. Amending charter, veto, VII, 96.

BROOKLYN NAVY YARD. Officers and employees, improper conduct at election, II, 1065; hospital at, III, 181; cession of land for, IV, 465, 506, 512, 573; additional land asked for, 728, 794, 862; authorities object to Brooklyn pier bill, IX, 438.

BROOKLYN NURSERY. Changing name, veto, VIII, 876.

BROOKLYN PUBLIC LIBRARY. Transfer of property from New York for use of free library, veto, IX, 873.

BROOKLYN RETAIL GROCERS' ASSOCIATION. Charter, veto, VIII, 198.

BROOKLYN UNION ELEVATED RAILROAD COMPANY. Grade crossing in Brooklyn, X, 714.

BROOKS, D. Indian claims, II, 514.

BROOKS, ERASTUS. Assembly, member of committee on arrangements, opening of new capitol, VII, 270; delivers historical address at ceremonies on first occupation of Assembly chamber, new capitol, 271; remarks on opening new Senate chamber, 540; delivers address on former Governor Seymour at legislative memorial services, VIII, 196.

BROOKS LOCOMOTIVE WORKS. Changing name, relief, veto, VI, 699.

BROOM, CHARLES. Proposed purchase of Revolutionary letters from, veto, VII, 409.

BROOME. Scott patent includes part of, IV, 331.

BROOME COUNTY. Convicts to be sent to Sing Sing prison, III, 316; average excise license fees, 1889, VIII, 686; highways, cost of labor system, 1892, IX, 199; insane, care of, county and State systems compared, 228.

    VETOES. Colesville, Harpersville Cemetery Association, VII, 98; Union, Tornado Hook and Ladder Company No. 1, charter, 233; Sanford, monument, 806; Mountain View Cemetery Association, relative to, 807; supervisors, fixing compensation, 1115; Binghamton, sales for unpaid taxes, VIII, 392; board of supervisors, legalizing acts, IX, 795.

BROOME, JOHN. President of Senate, communication to, relative to Williams murder case, II, 627; signs cession to United States, III, 140; Lieutenant-Governor, death of, II, 674.

BROTHERTOWN. Indian lands at, act relating to, II, 364.

BROTHERTOWN INDIANS. Survey of lands, II, 306; Peters murder case, 514; report of intrusions, 939; superintendent, report, 991, 1027, 1060, 1115; III, 96, 182, 218; attorney for, II, 1076; trespasses on lands of, III, 183.

BROUGHAM, LORD. England, favors use of ballot at elections, VIII, 585.

BROWARD, NAPOLEON B. Governor of Florida, proclamation, proposed Isthmian Exposition, X, 866.

BROWN, MR. Postmaster at Hartford, removal of, II, 1069.

BROWN, ANDREW, CAPTAIN. Artillery, funds received by, II, 766.

BROWN, ARON. Grant of Oneida lands, II, 894.

BROWN, CHARLES M. Board of Claims, veto, VIII, 888, 1038.

BROWN, ELON R. Senate, 1900, calls to order joint session of Senate and Assembly at services in memory of former Governor Flower, IX, 535; member of Prince Henry reception committee, X, 479.

BROWN, GILBERT. Act authorizing erection of grist mill, II, 485.

BROWN, HURLBURT E. Member of commission on Tall-Chief monument, VIII, 110.

BROWN, ISAAC. Bond for return of arms, II, 772.

BROWN, JACOB, GENERAL. Commands troops at Sackett's Harbor, II, 744, 746; funds received by, 765; success in Niagara campaign, 802; movement of force, 806; thanked by Legislature and presented with sword, 832; letter from Governor Tompkins, reply, 834; recommends Gardner's Compend, 996.

BROWN, JERRY. Whitehall, farm bridge, veto, VI, 1007.

BROWN, JOHN. Farm, Adirondacks, transferred to State, IX, 669.

BROWN, JOHN, TRACT (John Brown Tract). Value of, V, 24.

BROWN, JOSEPH E. Governor of Georgia, seizes Fort Pulaski, V, 314.

BROWN, MANHEIM. Claim against New York city, veto, X, 806; Court of Claims, veto, 944.

BROWNE, IRVING. Member of Commission on Uniform Laws, VIII, 1068.

BROWNE, JOHN W. Admission to attorney examination, veto, X, 311.

BROWN AND FLEMING CONTRACTING COMPANY. Claim, Queensborough, highway department, materials, veto, X, 950.

BROWNSON, WILLARD HERBERT. Commander of the "Yankee," Spanish War, X, 17.

BROWNSTOWN. Noted, War of 1812, II, 737.

BROWN'S TRACT INLET. Cleaning and clearing shores, veto, X, 320.

BROWN UNIVERSITY. Extension movement, IX, 18.

BROWNVILLE. Arms and supplies for, II, 774; aid to Utica and Black River Railroad Company, amending act, veto, VI, 92.

BRUCE, M. LINN. Lieutenant-Governor, presides at trial of Justice Hooker, X, 829.

BRUNING, JOSEPH. Medical services, French prisoners, I, 511.

BRUNN, ARMIN E. Escheat, veto, VIII, 723.

BRUNO, RICHARD M. Escheat, veto, VIII, 980.

BRUCH, CHARLES B. Examination of Assembly ceiling and staircase, appropriation, veto, VIII, 839.

BRUTUS.

    VETOES. Fixing northern boundary, VII, 806; canal bridge, approach, culvert under, VIII, 294.

BRUYN, CHARLES D. Assignee of Thomas Hamilton, materials for Sing Sing prison, veto, VII, 485.

BRUZUAL, BLAS. Minister from Venezuela, requests permission to acquire and hold property in New York, V, 617.

BUCHANAN, JAMES. President, criticised for attitude toward Kansas, V, 60; special message on secession movement, 306; reply to New York resolutions, 307; measures ineffective to prevent rebellion, 396; special message on preservation of the Union, 397.

BUCK, HIRAM. Relief, veto, VI, 630.

BUCKBEE, JAMES A. Nominated as railroad commissioner, withdrawn, VIII, 374.

BUCKET SHOPS. Proposed taxation of business, VIII, 305, 445; act of 1889, 815; business prohibited, veto, VII, 1090; taxation of, veto, VIII, 445.

BUEL, JESSE. Appointed regent, III, 142; quartermaster, report of, anti-rent troubles, 832.

BUELL AND ERHARDT. Attorneys, appropriation for, VI, 421.

BUELL, ROSWELL. Contract with Chatfield, II, 580.

BUENZ, K. German Consul-General, New York, letter to Governor relative to Prince Henry's visit, X, 376.

BUFFALO. Militia in service at, II, 736, 746; burned by British, 792; statement of killed and wounded, 872; alleged Federal interference in elections, 1067; tax for extinguishment of fires, twothirds bill, III, 532; advantages derived from internal improvements, 815; cessions for fortifications at, IV, 294; canal basins in, 426; State fair at, 431; pier at, Erie canal, 571; immigrant passengers, protection, 793; new arsenal, V, 88, 175, 642; normal school, 695; insane asylum, established at, VI, 115; Erie canal improvements, 858; Clark and Skinner canal, Ohio street, bridge, 861; riots, 1877, VII, 152; Canisius College incorporated at, 947; charter of 1891, 1103; VIII, 1030; number of excise licenses, 1887, VIII, 359; disabled firemen, half pay, 561; excise license fees, 1889, 685; salaries increased, 828; law library, IX, 46; railroad switchmen's strike, 1892, 159; armory, 573, 607; city employees to receive compensation while in national military service, Spanish War, X, 13; development of iron industry, 136; McKinley monument, 394.

VETOES. Subscription to stock of Buffalo Waterworks Company, IV, 517; funding floating debt, 524; German Missionary church, charter, 633; Eagle Hose Company No. 2, charter, VI, 196; legalizing street improvements, 221; Safe Deposit and Trust Company, charter, 503; St. Joseph's College, charter, 691; Fillmore avenue, extension, 851; Main and Hamburg canal, repairing dock, 1007; Clark and Skinner canal, bridge at Scott street, 1036; VII, 95; Erie canal bridge, Austin street, 114; charter supplemental act, 131; amending Police Act, 266; Homeopathic Medical College, charter, 266; city hall and jail, construction and custody of, 316, 354; public buildings and grounds, 354; county taxes, collection, 356; Erie canal, sewerage under, Black Rock, 365, 457; sewerage from insane asylum, 384; police and parks, 413; fire department, 413, 870; VIII, 889; Life Saving Benevolent Association, charter, VII, 414; board of health, proceedings, 414; dredging Ohio basin, 455; dredging Erie basin, 456; amending charter, V, 734; VII, 505, 666, 804, 933, 934, 1103; IX, 626, 633, 726, 784; abating nuisances, VII, 507; local court, 666; Busti terrace, use of, by Mechanic's Institute, 804; unpaid taxes, 804; settlement of claims against sureties of First National Bank, 874; arsenal, local assessments, 927; cemetery association, acquiring land, 933; school taxes, VIII, 292; real estate and broker's board, charter, 293; canal bridge, Hudson street, 293;

GENERAL INDEX. **261**

BUFFALO, VETOES — (Continued).

Masonic Hall Association, charter, 464; school department, 639; paving Carroll street, old assessment-roll, 639; boulevard to Niagara Falls, 639, 879; Young Men's Association, membership, exemption from collateral inheritance tax, 732; Straack escheat bill, 734; police department, 886, 1038; X, 713, 805; Le Couteulx St. Mary's Institution for the Improved Instruction of Deaf-Mutes, new buildings, appropriation, VIII, 888; revised charter, 1890, 1030; legalizing Guilford street excavation, audit of Gisel claim, 1038; water commissioners, increasing salary, 1106; Parkside avenue extension, IX, 268; Winship escheat bill, 285; Main street road improvement, 356, 795; redemption of outstanding bonds, 372; canal towing path wall, Austin street, 449; West Side Street Railway, relief from certain obligations, VIII, 1117; fire department, holidays, IX, 51; Erie canal, dredging Ohio basin, 256; armory, 74th Regiment, 607; Niagara river power experiments, Mather plan, 629, 813; X, 54; public improvements, IX, 723; Queen City Gas-Light Company, supplying city with gas, repeal, 723; assessments, 730; Louisiana street, railroad on, 783; Cazenovia creek and Buffalo river, improvement, 783; sea wall highway, use of, 783; State property, local assessment, 784; inferior criminal courts, 784; taxes amending charter, 784; water supply, amending act, 784; Municipal Court, 784; pumping station tunnel, settling claims, relative to, 869; firemen, vacations and leaves of absence, 869; labor organizations, no discrimination against, 869; police pensions, X, 276; Albany street, release to adjoining owners, 316; Scajaquada creek, dredging, 319; local funds, 474; grade crossings, damages, 474; quarantine hospital, purchasing land for, 475; unpaid taxes and assessments, collectors, 476; free employment bureau, 554, 564; police force, 583; hostlers and van drivers, 583; Clark and Skinner canal, abating nuisances, 634; Erie basin improvement, 652; offices, elective, filling vacancies, 685; taxes and assessments, 685, 686; waterworks bonds, 685; annual assessment-rolls, 686; park improvement, 11th ward, 712; department of forestry, 713; fire department storekeeper, 776; Union Railroad Station Commission, 777; Leng claim, 806; Erie basin, deepening, 814; pension fund, Dowd case, 875; drainage and sewerage, contracts with adjoining municipalities, 960.

BUFFALO ASSOCIATION FOR THE RELIEF OF THE POOR.

VETOES. Amending charter, VIII, 886; changing name, 1038.

BUFFALO ASYLUM FOR INSANE. See also BUFFALO STATE HOSPITAL.
Established, VI, 115; estimates and expenditures, 650; statement
of appropriations, 872, 939; appropriations for, VII, 123;
expense of construction, 283; completion of, 285; number of
inmates, 958.

VETOES. Improvements, VII, 88, new appropriation passed;
sewerage, 384; garden improvements, 436; improvements, appropriation, 584, 786; various appropriations, 913; appropriation of unexpended balances, 913; electric light, VIII, 852;
legal expenses, mandamus proceedings, 852.

BUFFALO BASIN. Erie canal, construction of, IV, 426; V, 71; claim
against United States, 71; deepening, VI, 860.

BUFFALO CEMETERY ASSOCIATION. Additional land and office building,
veto, VII, 760, 933.

BUFFALO CITY BANK. Redemption of bills, III, 860.

BUFFALO, CORNING AND PITTSBURGH RAILROAD COMPANY. Asks State
aid, VI, 70.

BUFFALO, CORRY AND PITTSBURGH RAILROAD COMPANY. Asks State
aid, V, 866; extending road, changing name, veto, VI, 508.

BUFFALO CREEK. Indians at, visit from, II, 344, 346; land of Senecas
at, purchase of, 477; outlet, harbor at, 986, 991.

BUFFALO CREEK RAILROAD. Bonds of, savings banks authorized to invest in, X, 576.

BUFFALO AND GREEN ISLAND FERRY COMPANY. Increasing capital stock,
veto, VI, 1036.

BUFFALO HARBOR. Improvement of, II, 986, 991, 1011, 1095; deepening Erie basin, VI, 860; Bird island pier, continuing work on, veto,
1008.

BUFFALO LAW SCHOOL. Relative to, veto, VIII, 1038.

BUFFALO LIGHT BATTERY. Charter, veto, VII, 763.

BUFFALO AND LOCKPORT RAILROAD COMPANY. Consolidation with other
companies authorized, V, 803.

BUFFALO MERCHANTS' EXCHANGE. Amending charter, veto, X, 318.

BUFFALO AND NEW YORK OIL TANKAGE AND TRANSPORTATION COMPANY.
Charter, veto, VI, 502.

BUFFALO NORMAL SCHOOL. Established, V, 695, 852.

BUFFALO PIPE LINE COMPANY. Charter, veto, VII, 133.

BUFFALO PLANK ROAD. Improvement, veto, VI, 195.

BUFFALO RESERVATION. Number of Indians on, 1819, II, 976.

BUFFALO RIVER. Improvement of, veto, IX, 783.

BUFFALO AND ROCHESTER RAILROAD COMPANY. Consolidation with other
companies authorized, V, 803.

BUFFALO STATE HOSPITAL. See also BUFFALO ASYLUM FOR INSANE. Excessive cost per capita, X, 410; number of visits of local managers, 415.
VETOES. Electric light plant, VIII, 1137; new building, IX, 77.
BUFFALO AND WASHINGTON RAILROAD COMPANY. Asks State aid, V, 866; VI, 70.
VETOES. Acquiring land in Olean, 91; facilitating construction, 172.
BUFFALO AND WILLIAMSVILLE MCADAM ROAD COMPANY. Amending charter, veto, VI, 218.
BUFFALO YOUNG MEN'S CHRISTIAN ASSOCIATION. Amending charter, veto, VIII, 618.
BUFFALO WATERWORKS COMPANY. Authorizing city to subscribe to stock, veto, IV, 517.
BUILDING CORPORATIONS. Amending act, veto, VIII, 1041.
BUILDING AND LOAN ASSOCIATIONS. Statutes need revision, X, 102; surplus required, 369; subject to supervision of bank department, 369.
BUILDING, MUTUAL LOAN AND ACCUMULATING FUND ASSOCIATIONS. Amending general act, veto, VII, 132; general condition, 1896, IX, 741.
BULKHEADS. Establishing lines, appropriation, veto, VII, 874.
BULL RUN. Battle of, V, 402.
BULSON, ABRAM. Bridge tender, Watervliet, Court of Claims, veto, X, 593.
BUNDY, PHILO. Canal department, appropriation for services, veto, IX, 716.
BUNKER HILL. Battle of, I, 765.
BURCHARD, NATHAN. Attorney for Oneida Indians, payment of salary, III, 909.
BUREAU OF LABOR STATISTICS. Established, VII, 409, 977; cost of, 1891, IX, 11; service should be efficient, X, 10; appropriation, 1900, 188; abolished, 1901, 189.
BUREAU OF MILITARY RECORD. Succeeds Bureau of Military Statistics, V, 608; importance of, 689; name changed to Bureau of Military Statistics, 689, see that title; deficiency appropriation, IX, 774.
BUREAU OF MILITARY STATISTICS. Work of, V, 521; objects, 522, 771; report, 564, 794, 864; collections, 608, 834; named changed to Bureau of Military Record, 608, see that title; name restored, 689; room in new capitol, 772, 835.
BURGARD, HENRY P. Court of Claims, veto, X, 441.
BURGLARY. Punishment of, III, 173, 285.
BURHANS, HATTIE L. Board of Claims, veto, IX, 50; new bill passed, 1893, 50.

BURHANS, HIRAM. Mentz, overseer of highways, appointment, veto, VII, 208.

BURIALS. Act to regulate, I, 11; Saratoga Springs, regulating, veto, VI, 591.

BURK, THOMAS. Convicted of murder, pardoned, II, 856.

BURKE, EDMUND. Agent of colony, I, 768.

BURKE, JOHN. Troy school janitor, claim, veto, X, 634.

BURKE, PATRICK. Application for license as embalmer, Manhattan borough, authority to receive, veto, X, 818.

BURKE, THOMAS. Convicted of murder, pardoned, II, 998.

BURKE, THOMAS M. A. Roman Catholic bishop of Albany, offers prayer at Capital Centennial Celebration, 1897, IX, 689; pronounces benediction at Higgins memorial services, X, 964.

BURLEIGH, BRACKETT W. Ferry, Lake Champlain, at Ticonderoga, veto, VIII, 1099.

BURLEIGH, HENRY G. Assembly, canal committee, opinion, Erie canal improvement, VI, 1010; ferry, Lake Champlain, at Ticonderoga, veto, VIII. 1099.

BURLINGTON, NEW JERSEY. Governor Cornbury at, dissolves New York Assembly, I, 126; Governor Hunter at, prorogues New York Assembly, 149.

BURNET, WILLIAM. Becomes Governor of New York and New Jersey, I, 190.

     OPENING SPEECH. Seventeenth Assembly, eighth session, 190; compliments Governor Hunter, 191; acts for support of government, 191; Assembly not to be dissolved for want of prorogation, 192; frontier conditions, 192; French advances, 192; French at Niagara, 193; militia, 193; Indian trade, 193; English Revolution, 194; Indian presents, 194; thanks Assembly for address, 195; matter of Deputy Weighmaster Heath, 195.

     OPENING SPEECH. Seventeenth Assembly, ninth session, 195; continuance of Assembly, 196, 197; frontier defense, 196, 197; French aggressions, Indian presents, 196; approves appointment of treasurer, 197; fees of Auditor-General, 197; Indians at Albany, 197.

     OPENING SPEECH. Seventeenth Assembly, tenth session, I, 197; encouraging Indian trade, 198; tariff on European imports rejected by Crown, 198, 211; bills of credit, 198; examination of public accounts, 199; powder magazine in New York, 199; transmitting various papers, 200; trade with Canada, 200; Secretary Livingston's petition for payment of salary, 200; proposed conference with Indians, 200; Indian negotiations, 201.

BURNET, WILLIAM — (*Continued*).

OPENING SPEECH. Seventeenth Assembly, eleventh session; transmits various papers, I, 202; sends to Assembly copies of instructions relative to quotas of troops, 203; examination of statutes, 204, 211, 219.

OPENING SPEECH. Seventeenth Assembly, twelfth session, I, 204; address to King on deliverance from conspiracy, 205; new Revenue Act, 206; communication from Interpreter Claesen, 206; Connecticut boundary matter, 206.

OPENING SPEECH. Seventeenth Assembly, thirteenth session, I, 207; peace in Europe, 207; recommends repair of fort at New York, 208, 210, 213; new Revenue Act, 208; royal assent to Connecticut Boundary Act, 208; importance of maintaining agent in London, 208; restricting trade with Canada, 209, 212; instruction relative to private laws, 210; Connecticut boundary, 210, 215, 218, 219, 224; communication from Interpreter Claesen, 211.

OPENING SPEECH. Seventeenth Assembly, fourteenth session, I, 211; Canadian trade regulations, 212; growing trade with Indians, 212; agents for Senecas and Onondagas, 212; revenue, 212; protection of government officers, 213; restoring part of Long Island to New York collector's district, 213; approves choice of Speaker, 214; doubt as to eligibility of De Lancey, member of Assembly, 214; statement by Livingston as to Indian trade, 214; support of government, 215; acts passed, 216.

OPENING SPEECH. Seventeenth Assembly, fifteenth session, I, 216; relations between King and colony, 216; new Revenue Act, 217; recent trade laws not well executed, 217; Indian trade, 217; agents at London, 218; repairs of Fort George, 218, 221, 222; Massachusetts urges King to require New York to aid in Indian war, 219; importation of salt, 219; denies private use of public funds, 219; dissolves Seventeenth Assembly, 220.

OPENING SPEECH. Eighteenth Assembly, first session, I, 220; discussion with Assembly concerning revenue, 221; colonial agent, 222; conference with Six Nations, 222; relations with Indians, 222; regulating Indian trade, 223; death of George I, accession of George II, 225.

OPENING SPEECH. Nineteenth Assembly, first session, I, 225; means used to secure Five Nations, 225; Canadian Governor demands abandonment of Oswego, 225; reimbursed for expenses in frontier service, 226; need of ascertaining boundaries of colonies, 226; Massachusetts boundary, 226; repairs at Fort George, 227; New Jersey boundary, 227; French at Niagara, 227; transmits

BURNET, WILLIAM — (*Continued*).

   various papers, 228; Assembly resolutions against Court of
   Chancery, 229; dissolves Nineteenth Assembly, 229; calls new
   Assembly, 229; succeeded by Governor Montgomerie, 229; ac-
   counts for expenses to Oswego, 231; support of government
   under, acts in force five years, 470; claim against colony, 592;
   official service, I, pref. IX.
BURNETT, JONATHAN. Assembly, resolutions requesting information con-
   cerning Lawrence matter, IV, 705.
BURNETT, WARD B. Colonel, 1st Regiment, New York Volunteers,
   Mexican War, IV, 415; VII, 882.
BURNETT, WILLIAM, BRIGADIER-GENERAL. Calls out militia, II, 796.
BURNETT'S FIELD. French incursion on, I, 410.
BURNETT'S KEY, EAST RIVER. Tax for use of, I, 247; battery at, 322.
BURNS, THOMAS. Convicted of murder, not pardoned, II, 790.
BURNS, WILLIAM T. Grant of land under water by Land Board, X,
   266.
BURR, AARON. Letter from, declining appointment as puisne judge, II,
   327.
BURR, DAVID H. State map, purchase and distribution of, III, 162, 225,
   391.
BURR, JOSEPH A. Counsel for Dike, sheriff of Kings county, compen-
   sation, veto, X, 559.
BURRELL, WILLIAM (JAMES), CAPTAIN. Claim of, II, 167.
BURRILL, JOHN E. Opinion, unconstitutionality of ballot bill, 1888,
   VIII, 574, 591.
BURROWS, ROSWELL S. Relief, veto, VI, 185.
BUSH CREEK. Ulster county, protecting highways from overflow of,
   veto, IX, 768.
BUSHWICK. Brooklyn, amending map, veto, VI, 695.
BUSINESS CORPORATIONS. Amending act, power to mortgage property,
      VIII, 381; general law, 1890, 1027; revision, 1892, IX, 28, 135.
   VETOES. Organization and regulation, VII, 507; mortgages, 1114;
      mortgaging real estate, VIII, 457; formation, amending act,
      X, 451.
BUSTI. Town, compensation of supervisor, special services, veto, VI, 588.
BURT, HATHORN. Member of commission on Tall-Chief monument, VIII,
   110.
BURT, SILAS. Chief examiner, State Civil Service Commission, VII, 976.
BURTON, L. G. Canal department, appropriation for services, veto, IX,
   716.
BURZYNSKI, FRANK S. Assembly, member of joint legislative com-
   mittee on services in memory of former Governor Higgins, X, 963.

BUTLER, BENJAMIN F. Appointed statutory revision commissioner, III, 18; commissioner on New Jersey boundary, VI, 779.

BUTLER, F. M., CAPTAIN. Agent to settle claims against United States, VI, 357.

BUTLER, HELEN C. Communication to Governor, relative to appointment of William Church Osborn as State commissioner in lunacy, X, 43.

BUTLER, WALTER. Letter from, I, 338; letter from, Six Nations visit Canada, 355; letter noted, Cherry Valley massacre, VII, 812.

BUTLER, WILLIAM O. Delegate from Kentucky to Washington Peace Convention, V, 329.

BUTTER. Inspection of, recommended, I, 617; reduction of tolls on, III, 505; protection needed, VII, 699; imitations to be marked, 700; high quality of New York products, IX, 318; imitations, act of 1902, X, 395.

    VETOES. Deception in sales of, VII, 571, 699; factories, protection of patrons, 805; premium for improved manufacture, 1078.

BUTTERFIELD, DANIEL, COLONEL. 12th Regiment, supplies from Union Defense Committee, VII, 501.

BUTTERINE. Coloring and sale as food, prohibited, VII, 699; purchases prohibited for certain institutions, IX, 215.

BUTTERNUTS AND UNADILLA HEMP MANUFACTURING COMPANY. Incorporated, III, 253.

BYERLY, THOMAS. Collector of New York, report, I, 109.

BYRNE, JAMES. Communication to Governor relative to appointment of William Church Osborn as State commissioner in lunacy, X, 42.

BYRON. First Congregational Society, changing name, veto, VIII, 205.

C.

CABLE, FREDERICK O. Trustee Binghamton Insane Asylum, charges against, not removed, VII, 443.

CABLE RAILROAD. New York, veto, VIII, 1035.

CABLE TOWAGE. On canals, VI, 242.

CADARACQUI. Defense of, I, 52; French occupation of, 57, 88; French defeat at, 625; New York troops at, 627.

CADETS. Proposed organization of, II, 812, 814, 865.

CAESAR, JULIUS. Invasion of England, condition of people, II, 956.

CAGHNAWAGA INDIANS. Information received from, 1, 355.

CAIRO. Town, bridge over Catskill creek, veto, VIII, 383.

CALDERWOOD, ROBERT. Canal department, appropriation for services, veto, IX, 716.

CALDWELL. Postmaster at, removal of, II, 1069.

CALCUTTA. Vessels from, exempt from quarantine, III, 87.

CALEDONIA.

> VETOES. Fish hatchery, VII, 902; fish hatchery, purchase of addi-
> tional land, VIII, 249.

CALENDAR. Time, change of, IV, 192; of colonial documents, IV, 192.

CALHOUN, JOHN C. Secretary of War, correspondence relative to Staten
Island fortifications, II, 1081; Senate bill relative to cession of
public lands, III, 705; death of, action of Legislature, IV, 516.

CALIFORNIA. Militia regiments sent to, IV, 415; New York resolution
protesting against slavery in, 448; status of slavery, 497, 501;
Constitution prohibits slavery, 501; admitted to Union, 565; gold
from, 729; provision for agricultural instruction, IX, 178; International Exposition, 1894, 317; New York's appropriation for earthquake sufferers, X, 890.

CALORIC. Proposed use as motive power on canals, VI, 242, 539.

CALROW, RICHARD, JR. Relief, veto, VI, 219.

CAMBRIDGE UNIVERSITY. Extension movement, IX, 17.

CAMDEN.

> VETOES. Amending village charter, VI, 1036; assessment for high-
> way labor, VII, 130; legalizing proceedings for electric light
> system, X, 708.

CAMDEN, LORD. Opinion, against general warrants, IV, 756.

CAMERON, JAMES, COLONEL. 79th Regiment, supplies from Union Defense Committee, VII, 501.

CAMPBELL, ALLAN. Member of Board of Engineers, New York harbor
defense, V, 568; comptroller, New York city, opinion, cost of new
aqueduct, VII, 635.

CAMPBELL, THOMAS F. New York patrolman, veto, X, 806.

CAMPBELL, WILLIAM. Chosen Surveyor-General, III, 527.

CAMPBELL LEASES. Tenants, protecting rights under, veto, VI, 584.

CAMPS OF INSTRUCTION. National Guard, provision for, VII, 747, 826,
952; VIII, 14; usefulness of, VII, 953; under act of Congress,
1903, X, 16; benefits of, 217.

> VETOES. Peekskill,— lighting, 1889, VIII, 855; — road to, repairs,
> appropriation, 1136; repairs and improvements, IX, 76; mili-
> tary road to Highland station, 290.

CAMP MEETINGS. General act providing for, VII, 867.

CANADA. Major Schuyler's expedition to, I, 24; French of, attempt
on frontiers, 35, 137; Indians make peace with, 47; Governor of,
marches into Indian country, 65; expedition against, 135, 136, 137;
expedition abandoned, 140; new expedition proposed, 147, 151;
commissioners to furnish supplies, 152; transports exempted from
tonnage duty, 153; failure of expedition, 154; forces disbanded, 156;

CANADA — (*Continued*).

request that trade with, be stopped, 183; letter from Governor of, 196; clandestine trade with French prohibited, 200; New York residents in, required to return, 202; restricting trade with, 209; merchants oppose trade regulations with, 212; trade laws not well executed, 217; Governor of, demands abandonment of Oswego, 225; letters from Governor of, 228; Governor Beauharnais, negotiations with Indians, 271; Indians in, break neutrality treaty with Six Nations, 352, 356, 358; Indians from, attack New England settlements, 353, 356; Six Nations visit Governor of, 353; Mohawks visit, 355; Governor of, urges Six Nations to join in war against English, 355; expedition against, 373, 378, 379, 385, 420; Governor of, alleged negotiations with Albany merchants, 400; English prisoners brought from, 409; Indians sent against, 425; Governor of, Indians receive belts from, 425; expedition against, abandoned, 441; letter from Governor of, relative to, exchange of prisoners, 467, 470; Governor of, designs to alienate Indians, 486; Mohawks refuse to send deputies to, 487; Governor of, invites meeting of Six Nations at Montreal, 570; more French troops sent to, 591; projected invasion of, 619; Quebec taken, 640; completing reduction of, 643; expedition against Montreal, 643; conquered by English, 648, 691; chiefs of Seven Villages claim land in New York, II, 328, 343; Seven Nations of, treaty with, 368, 380, 381, 386, 390; New York and Vermont boundary, correcting alleged error, 606, see QUEBEC BOUNDARY; refugees from, War of 1812, 787; lower, act against counterfeiting, 983; Smith extradition case, 1104; commercial intercourse with United States, complaints relative to, III, 23, 68, 69; epidemic in, 394; improved navigation of St. Lawrence river, 510; action in extradition matter, 599; invasion of State from, 678, 683, 759; upper, communication from secretary relative to disturbances in northeastern New York, 761; Governor, correspondence with, McLeod case, 933; canals, 959; New York citizens aiding, imprisonment of, 1039; historical records as source of colonial history, IV, 166, 185; Parliamentary library, gifts from New York, 573; remonstrance against interruption of navigation between Missisquoi bay and Richelieu river, 574; canals, use of, by northwestern States, V, 505; does not offer adequate outlet to western products, 709; canal projects, VI, 240, 635; reciprocity in use of canals, 363; tax exemptions, 371; commercial relations with New York, 539; ship canal connecting St. Lawrence river and Lake Champlain, 539; canals, completion of, rivalry with New York, VII, 516, 685; IX, 557; efforts to secure lake traffic through canals, 303; expert instruction in agriculture, 321; Cayuga Indians, claim against New York, X, 31, 127; canals, competition with New York, 136.

Canada, Tite. French steamer, brings delegates to Yorktown Centennial Celebration, VII, 738.

Canadian Refugees. War of 1812, relief of, II, 787.

Canajoharie. Rangers at, I, 439; Indian treaty at, 554; Indian land grants claimed to be fraudulent, 601, 606, 611; asylum for instruction of deaf and dumb, III, 83, 97; revising village charter, veto, VI, 683, 824.

Canajoharie Falls. Proposed canal around, I, 728.

Canajoharie and Palatine Bridge Company. Rebuilding bridge, veto, II, 638.

Canal Advisory Board. Under Barge Canal Act, X, 496; civil service principles applicable in appointments to, 596; tenure of office, 596; names of members, 629.

Canal Appraisers. Additional, appointment of, II, 1046; III, 121; act relating to, 73, 121; to appraise damages for diversion of Tonawanda creek, 182; annual report, V, 276; jurisdiction to hear and determine claims, VI, 119, 226; work of, VII, 524, 685, 819; office abolished, 821, 978.

Vetoes. Filing claims with, VI, 580; jurisdiction, Seymore case, 673; Ramsey case, 692; Van Slyck case, 697; Harris case, 698; Wilson case, 698; defining jurisdiction, VII, 266; hearing certain claims for damages, 417; Tyrrell claim, loss of canal boat, 599; Sharpe claim, extending time to file, 773; salaries and expenses, 774; Mesereau and Rodman, awards, 774.

Canal Auditor. Report on canal finances, IV, 819; report, railroad tolls, V, 209; official term, 261; estimated cost of enlarging canal locks, 506; report, claims against State, 591; report, State debt, VI, 13; report, bond for Albany basin improvement, 44.

Vetoes. Increasing compensation, 877; — suit against, services and expenses of counsel, VII, 904.   Office abolished, VII, 820.

Canal Board. Established, II, 901; regulation of canal tolls, III, 169; delegation of power to, questioned, 788; to resume work on Erie enlargement, IV, 61; resolutions relative to Federal fees on canal boats, V, 721; extending powers, VI, 106; Frantz claim, 312; settlement of Seeley claim, veto, 592, 696; to report on disposal of lateral canals, 750; act enlarging powers, judicial functions imposed, 996; defining jurisdiction, veto, VII, 266.

Canal Boats. Number of, 425, 673; increased size of, 671, 686, 737; description of, 687; towed to New York, V, 453; Federal fees on, 721; "Major Anderson," claim for loss of, veto, VI, 312; State does not insure, 312; VII, 599; liens on, veto, VI, 510; change of form needed, 538; Ramsey case, veto, 692; lake boats not available, 739; rate of speed, 739; large number in use, 788; coming from

CANAL BOATS — (*Continued*).

Pennsylvania, protest against wharfage tax, 981; boatmen partners of State, VII, 7; exempt from tolls, 7; Tyrrell, loss of, claim, veto, 599; speed by horse, mule, steam or electrical power, IX, 456; estimated speed, State Engineer's report, 1901, X, 248.

CANAL BRIDGES. See also VETOES, CANALS AND CANAL BRIDGES. Use by street railroads, act of 1902, X, 363; limiting appropriations for supervision by Superintendent of Public Works, 364; authorized, Fort Edward feeder, completing, VI, 855; Mount Morris, Genesee river, 862; Rochester,— Averill and Munger streets, 859; — Buffalo street, 852; Syracuse, North Salina street, X, 929; Watervliet, VI, 854.

CANAL COMMISSION. Appointed, II, 675; report, 675, 706; new commission appointed, 854.

CANAL COMMISSIONERS. See also CANAL BOARD. Authorized to employ convict labor in constructing Erie canal, II, 875; powers of, 964; VI, 344; action relative to Buffalo harbor, II, 986; navigate part of Erie canal, 1007; additional commissioner provided for, 1046; various duties incident to canal construction, 1095, 1096; lease surplus water of canals, III, 67; to survey Hudson river ship canal route, 464; loans to general fund, 544; loaning canal stock to banks, 702; proposed limitation of term, 711; to be elected by people, IV, 61; statements under act of 1842, 255; charges against John C. Mather, 695; quoted, condition of canals, 737; to enlarge certain canals, 743; use of steam dredging machine, VI, 540; to consider disposal of lateral canals, 750; independent action of each, 805; resolution, Smith case, 546; office abolished, 50.

VETOES. Payment of drafts and certificates, V, 143; bridge over Champlain canal, Whitehall, VI, 154; settling claims, Chenango canal, 508; settling claim for work, 698; certificates, payment of, VII, 131.

CANAL CONTRACTORS. Claims under Canal Suspension Act of 1842, IV, 17, 18, 63, 260, 437; take State stocks to apply on claims, 665; relief of, 733, 744, 780; legislation for relief, objections to, V, 711; extra compensation prohibited, VIII, 626; IX, 431.

VETOES. Relief, Champlain canal, VI, 213; F. C. Smith, return of certificate of deposit, VII, 545; refunding appropriation, 588.

CANAL DEBT. Amount, 1825, III, 73; 1826, 119; 1827, 164; 1828, 233; 1829, 304; 1830, 333; 1831, 369; 1833, 479; 1834, 502; 1838, 736; 1844, IV, 96; 1845, 252; 1847, 386; 1848, 422; 1849, 470; 1850, 540; 1851, 595; 1856, V, 3; 1858, 64; 1859, 151; 1860, 252; 1861, 360; 1862, 451; 1864, 590; 1865, 705; 1866, 783; 1867, 828; 1868, VI,

CANAL DEBT — (*Continued*).

7; 1872, 526; 1873, 614; 1874, 720; 1875, 914; 1876, VII, 3; 1877, 139; 1878, 275; 1879, 420; 1880, 513; 1881, 680; 1882, 815; 1885, VIII, 145; 1886, 303; 1887, 496; 1888, 663; 1889, 934; 1890, 1082; 1891, IX, 7; 1892, 157; 1900, X, 180; 1901, 327; 1904, 718; 1905, 832; justification of, III, 416; Governor Seward's statement, 791; provision for redemption, IV, 95; payment of, constitutional provision, 107, 661; V, 3; sinking fund, IV, 207; VII, 944; X, 832; stock, amount of, IV, 212; loan for interest on canal certificates and Oswego loan, 700; tax for, V, 50; redemption of, 451; interest, payment of, 491; probable early payment of, 706, 787; act for payment, rejected by people, VI, 107; situation considered by Governor Tilden, 891; certificates of indebtedness, 891; sinking fund, annual contribution, X, 766; provisions for interest and sinking fund, 1906, 922.

CANAL FEEDERS.

VETOES. Glens Falls, bridge over, VI, 504, 1007; VII, 361; IX, 755; Oak Orchard improvement, 55; Oneida, culvert under, X, 935; Rome, repairing wall, IX, 239; Skaneateles, repairs, X, 314; Tonawanda, relative to, VII, 357, 457; Genesee river, stop-gate, 233, 362; Glens Falls, repairs, X, 427, 434; Griffin creek, VII, 805; Orville, De Witt, repairs, X, 426, 645; Rocky Rift, farm bridge, VI, 857.

CANAL FUND. General statistics, V, 451, 531, 589, 704, 782, 827; VI, 1, 102; created, II, 901, 1010; income of, 1097; III, 119, 232, 305, 334, 370, 410, 479, 709; IV, 88; V, 257, 531; sources of, II, 1099; III, 10, 73, 245; not to be diverted, 164, 307, 348, 547, 808; IV, 89, 97, 107, 200; loans to general fund, III, 544; investments from United States deposit fund, 674; due from general fund, 707; appropriation from, veto, IV, 194, 251, 257; meaning of, 199; charges against, 199; reimbursement of loans for bounties, V, 530; sinking fund, 1904, X, 718.

CANAL INVESTIGATING COMMISSION. Created, 1875, VI, 809, 928; report, 928; members of, 928; special message relative to, 978; 1898, new commission, IX, 849; scope of investigation, 849; report and action thereon, 850; X, 4, 34; new commission, 1899, 75; report, 1900, 75, 131, 134, 215.

CANAL REVENUES. Statement, IV, 371, 472, 540, 549, 587, 596, 600, 661, 668, 742, 781, 782, 832; V, 4, 49, 65, 209, 253, 257, 360, 361, 363, 531, 589, 704, 782, 827; VI, 9, 102; VII, 143, 279; loans to be paid from, IV, 781; special message by Governor Clark, 818, 832; diversion for payment of State debts, 819; increasing, Governor Morgan's special message, V, 204; inadequate for required constitu-

CANAL REVENUES — (*Continued*).

tional purposes, 211; repayments to general fund, VI, 792; extra-ordinary repairs, 887; expenditures limited by, VII, 6, 359, 684; cannot be used for new bridges, 576.

CANALS. General statistics, V, 451, 531, 589, 704, 782, 827; VI, 8, 102, 239, 362, 535, 930; VII, 5, 278, 422, 515, 683, 817, 944; IX, 301; at Canajoharie falls recommended, I, 728; at Languedoc, 728; from Fort Stanwix to Wood creek, II, 312, 320; from Hudson river to Wood creek, 312, 320; aid to navigation companies, 321, 335, 365, 511; commission appointed, 675; report of commission, 675, 706; preliminary act passed, 675; application for national aid, 675, 706; III, 806; general act relating to, II, 706; connecting Hudson river with northern and western lakes, 854; convict labor on, 875, 1110; Ohio offers aid in constructing Erie canal, 891; progress of construction, 901, 962, 1007, 1044, 1094; III, 10, 24; expected benefits of, II, 901, 902, 1007, 1046, 1050, 1098; III, 74; Seneca lake canal, II, 902; Pennsylvania Act, canal connecting Tioga river and Seneca lake, 902, 903; tolls, 908, see CANAL TOLLS; proposed canal connecting Seneca lake and Susquehanna river, 918; expected reduction of cost of transportation, 964; connection with Mississippi river, 966; Buffalo harbor, 986; opposition to construction of, 1008; general regulations, 1010; tax on contiguous territory, 1012; boats, speed of, 1096; III, 74; proposed board of public improvements, II, 1097; III, 67; historical sketch, 25; improvement of Oswego river, 26; Grand Island, sale of, use of proceeds, 26; projected along Hudson river, 26; jurisdiction of United States, 49, 78; tonnage duties, claim of United States, 50, 76, 154; plan of administration, 66; surplus water, lease of, 67, 202; extension of system, 67, 70, 121, 165, 201, 235, 327, 467, 787; Oswego canal, see that title; Chenango canal, see that title; Black River canal, see that title; Delaware and Hudson Canal Company, aid to, 70; bridges, plan of, 72; appraisers appointed, 73; proposed canal from Lake Erie to Allegany river, 96; report of Pennsylvania commissioners on canal between Tioga river and Seneca lake, 98; completion and opening of, 118; expense of construction, 118, 200, 465; bridges too low, 120; loss of life at celebration of completion, 120; in other States, 122, 123, 171, 235, 902; IV, 61; ship canal along Hudson river, III, 124, 464; expectations realized, 164, 200, 272, 327, 372, 417, 734; projected in southern counties, 166; Orange and Sussex Canal Company, 167; Tonawanda feeder, 182; revenue not chief object of construction, 199, 804; VI,

CANALS — (Continued).

241; proposed period of navigation, 202; exchanges of stock, 336; railroad competition, 374; IV, 674, 739; V, 156, 208, see that title; railroad tolls, III, 376, 787; allowance to contractors, 411; unequal benefits from, 414; principles on which extension of system should be based, 416, 509; extensive commerce of, 560; enlargement, 461, 506, 552, 622, 670, 671, 709, 729, 787, 793, 816, 864, 887, 955; list of, 465; aggregate length of, 465, 620, 953, 1041; V, 6; income from, III, 502, 952; IV, 20, 373, 386, 423, 471, 540, 598, 782, 832; V, 4; deficiency of revenues, III, 507; ship canal from Lake Ontario to Hudson river, 509, 816; ship canal around Niagara falls, 509; reservoirs, 669; stock loaned to banks, 702; general expenses, 712; compared with railroads, 732; new routes surveyed on upper Hudson, 733; proposed connection with North Branch canal of Pennsylvania, 759; action of Convention of 1821, 807; summary of canal construction, 811; results derived from construction of, 813; purchase of Oneida Lake and Junction canals, 816; deposit of maps and plans, 934; suspension of work, 959, 1009; IV, 225; outside connections, III, 1042; unfinished bridges, inconvenience resulting from, IV, 16, 18, 59; contractors, damages resulting from suspension of construction, 17, 18, 63, 260, see CANAL CONTRACTORS; officers not to be interested in contracts, 18; new project should not be based on indiscriminate taxation, 57; canal commissioners to be chosen by people, 61; closing locks on Sabbath, 81; constructed on credit, 96; discussion of policies, 99; taxation necessary, 101; sinking fund, 207, 474; V, 159; land damages, IV, 260; completion of, constitutional provision, 369, 546, 599, 661; V, 8; political patronage, IV, 376; boats, number of, 425; basins needed, 426; damages under act of 1842, 437; scarcity of water, 542; benefits resulting from canals, 542, 582; certificates of indebtedness, 545, 598, 669, 700; pledging revenue, 546, 549, 598, 631, 669; Loan Act unconstitutional, 549; importance of western commerce, 584; enlarging Oswego canal, 588; no real conflict with railroads, 590; act of 1851 unconstitutional, 602, 633, 668, 742; validity of revenue certificates considered by Governor Hunt, 631; appointment of counsel for State, 633; statistics by Convention of 1846, 660; defective financial policy, 663; purposes of system, 674; description of boats, 687; relief of contractors, 733, 744, 780; constitutional amendment, completing canals, 735, 833; contracts to lowest bidders, 735, 834; diversion of commerce, 736; results of economy, 740; embarrassments of commerce, 783; enlargement

CANALS — (*Continued*).

contracts, 783; loan for enlargement, 783; effect of railroad competition, 822; extending Genesee Valley canal, 835; not to be sold, V, 7, 158, 208; VI, 106, 239; X, 731; steam navigation on, V, 69; loan for, approved, 70, 152; rent of surplus water, 154, 258, 362, 531; report of Auditor, railroad tolls, 209; notices of contracts, publication of, 365; to be used for national defense, 367, 503; commerce on, 452, 532; Indiana memorial, relative to use of, 493; proposed new locks for use of national government, 502, 533; extension of Chenango canal, 533; permanent basis of revenue, 595; Detroit Convention resolution on enlargement of canal locks, 707; western products, no adequate outlet through Canada, 709; canal boats, Federal fees on, 721; Federal admiralty jurisdiction, 720; needed for transportation of western products, 735; steam power on, 736; beneficial results of, 788; VI, 103; should be kept in good repair, 16; Federal control, Governor protests against, 16; projected in Europe, 104; should be made free as soon as practicable, 105; contract system abolished, 105; act for payment of debt rejected by people, 107; steam towing on, 107, 242, 744; enlargement of Champlain canal, 107; canal appraisers, power to hear and determine claims, 119; caloric as motive power, 242; cable towage, 242; Frantz claim, 312; State does not insure boats, 312; proposed reciprocity with Canada in use of, 363; Superintendent of Public Works, office created, 397, 934; people should retain control, 536; rapid transit on, 537; Canadian projects, 538; amendments of 1874, 540; proceedings of New York Produce Exchange, 564; transportation problem, 634, 736; no cooperation with Federal government, 636; "a trust for the million," 737, 926; duties of the State, 738; increasing income, 747; general inefficiency of system, 749; petition from forwarders and boatmen, 788; partnership between State and boatmen, 788; VII, 7; taxation, comparative statement, VI, 791; character of expenditures, 793; laterals should be sold, 796; contracts, evasion of constitutional provision, 800; unbalanced bids, 800; regulation of estimates, 807; investigating committee, 809; investigating commission, 809, 928; Rochester swing-bridge, Buffalo street, 852; various appropriation items, action on, 852, 1004; large number of bridges, 853; awards, appropriation for, 863; unconstitutional extraordinary repairs, 887; expenditures exceed appropriations, 892; purpose and scope of canal construction, 926; actions and prosecutions, appropriations for Attorney-General, 929; commission on lateral canals, 933;

CANALS — (*Continued*).

    development of graft, 934; extravagant expenditures, 979; extraordinary repairs, statement of contracts, 991; Canal Board, powers enlarged, 996; comparative statement, 1876, 1015; expenditures cannot exceed revenues, VII, 6; Governor's responsibility resulting from amendment of 1876, 50; business and revenues of 1878, 142; proposed constitutional amendment, 1879, 280; State ditch, see that title; possible rivalry of Canadian canals, 516, 685; competition with other commercial routes, 685; tolls abolished, amendment of 1882, 685, 818; abolition of tolls, consequent taxation for expenses, 818; legislation of 1883, 819; improvements, act for, 1888, VIII, 561; laborers on, regulating pay of, 1003; proposed investigation, 1891, 1117; dead lock in Legislature, 1117; decrease in tonnage, 1891, IX, 33; tonnage, comparative statement, 1892, 112; tonnage, 1892, 167; 1893, 301; rapid transit, 168; electricity as motive power, VI, 242; IX, 168, 305, 453, 660; towage, experiments authorized, 169; navigation, when State not liable for damages resulting from, 270; general improvements, 1893, 302; increased capacities needed; constitutional provision, 1894, 305, 549; enlargement, acts of 1895, 1903, 305, 549, 556; amendments of 1905, 305; electrical conductors, repeal, 453; Cataract General Electric Company, contract for experiments with electrical conductors, 454; Improvement Act of 1895, 660; nine million appropriation of 1895 insufficient for purposes intended, 822, 850; X, 133; aggregate cost of, 1898, IX, 822; investigation of certain matters by Fox and Mac Farlane, X, 39; new canal commission, 1899, 75; contracts under Nine-Million Dollar Act, proceedings for termination of, 79; blanket appropriation for repairs and bridges, 126; report of New York Commerce Commission, 1900, 131; in Europe, different systems considered, 135; Canadian competition with New York, 136; enlargement needed, 137; transportation companies, unlimited capital, 132, 140, 204, 359; mechanical motive power, 141; civil service, 141; contracts, method of letting, revision of laws, 141; Barge Canal Act, 1903, 141, 252, 363, 496; expenditures, 1900, 132; repairs and improvements, 1900, 203; decline in tonnage, 203, 492; enlargement, survey for, 1900, 141, 215; improvement, State Engineer's special report, 1901, 244; estimated speed of boats, 1901, 248; problems and possibilities, 1901, 249; effect on New York commerce, 359; improvement of locks, 361; use of bridges by street

CANALS — (*Continued*).

railroad, 363; comparative statement of appropriations, 1893–4; 1901–2, 464; advisory board under Barge Canal Act, 496; constitutional amendment, 1905, extending debt period, 496; consulting engineers, tenure of office, 596; special examiners, barge canal, office created, 597; barge, proposed imposition of special tax on counties, 599; general conditions, 1906, 842.

VETOES. Lock navigation, II, 329; relative to, IV, 194, 251, 257; transportation of liquor, 768; payment of drafts and certificates, V, 143; Oneida Lake canal, navigation of, 730; bridge over Champlain canal at Whitehall, VI, 154, 584; Fitzpatrick relief, new act passed, 159; bridge at Syracuse, 324; bridge at Havana, 327; Cayuga and Seneca canal, sewer, Waterloo, 339; superintendent of canal repairs, abolishing office, 344; Erie canal, locks, western division, 347; Champlain, bridge at Fort Edward, 448; Champlain, farm bridge, Saratoga, 504; bridge over Glens Falls feeder, 504; Chenango canal, settling claims, 508; canal boat liens, 510; claims against State, filing with appraisers, 580; railroad using berme bank, 581; swing-bridge, Norwich, 588; Seeley claim, settlement of, 592; farm bridge, Whitehall, 689; bridge over Tonawanda creek, 696; Erie canal, settling claim for work, 698; Genesee Valley, bridge at Portville, 709; Cayuga inlet, dredging, 876; work on, general act, 884, 920; Cayuga lake outlet, removal of obstructions, 1001; French, contractor, appropriation, 1008; sinking fund, tax for, 1010; awards, reappropriation, 1027; Oneida river, draw-bridge, VII, 94, 232; administration bill, veto of items, 114, 249, 358, 576; Mohawk basin, Green Island, iron bridge, Arch street, 115; Moose river dam, 118; awards, counsel fees, certificates, appropriation, 119; certificates, payment of, 131; collectors of tolls, 131; local assessment, Utica, 229; McAlpine certificate, 231; general act, 1878, 234; extraordinary repairs, completion of contracts, unexpended balance, 265; improved method of towage, 266; weigh-locks, abolition of, 412; abandoned, drainage of, 412; claims, appraisal, amending act, 415; Jenkins award, 456; Cayuga lake outlet, improvements, certificates, payment, 466; steam motive power, Champlain canal, 508; contractors, refunding, 588; Miser award, payment, 666; Sharpe claim, extending time to file, 773; awards, Mesereau and Rodman, 774; Griffin creek feeder, relative to, 805; taxes, 1881, reappropriation, 930; oaths, administration, 1115; Brutus, canal bridge approach, culvert under, VIII, 294; State dam,

CANALS, VETOES — (*Continued*).

Port Byron, enlargement, 452; Board of Claims, surveys and maps, 868; commerce on, improvements for promoting, IX, 110; lift and swing-bridges, compulsory operation by State, 444; Mott Haven, New York, bridge over, 633; subordinates and employees, appropriation, 1896, 716; agent for defense of State, services and expenses, appropriation, 856; time of opening, X, 61; damages under Nine-Million Dollar Act of 1895, 172; damages for injuries received on towpath, Dinehart case, 255; Sawyer's creek, deepening and improving channel, 300; Black river, raising bank, Denmark and Croghan, 301; Black creek, improving channel, 301; Woodhull State reservoir, cleaning and deepening, 320; blue line maps, appropriation, 423; Orville feeder, repairs Dewitt, 426; electrical communications, reappropriation, 465; Syracuse, filling mill race and side cuts, 569, 643; electricity as motive power, experiments, 573; bridge tenders, Watervliet, claim, Court of Claims, 593; State ditches, cleaning, 644; barge, appraisal of lands, structures, etc., 706; claims, private bills, waiving statutes, 775.

CANAL TOLLS. Expected benefits of, II, 908; established, 964; probable effect on Federal tonnage duties, III, 77; should be reduced, 169; minimum limit of, 169; income from, 233, 305, 334, 370, 462, 551, 621, 668, 709, 763, 856, 889, 952, 1039; IV, 23, 60, 259, 373, 387, 424, 832; V, 4, 65, 153, 257, 361, 452, 531, 589, 704, 782, 827; VI, 9; VII, 143, 515, 683, 817; modification of, III, 307, 374, 462, 505; probable increase of, 794; on salt, coal and lead, IV, 18; reduction of, 541, 601, 662; V, 156, 708; VI, 107, 239, 636; VII, 280; reduced on flour and wheat, IV, 598, 666; pledging surplus, 600; large amount received from, 666, 741; Governor Seymour urges further reduction, 667; increase recommended, V, 157, 259; increased, 366; Indiana memorial, 493; suggested abolition on western canal products, 533; reduced on iron ore on Champlain canal, 707; reducing, Governor Hoffman's views, VI, 105, 363; should be limited to maintenance and debt, 241; reduced on several articles, 242; reduction, New York Chamber of Commerce memorial, 276; on wheat and corn, 744; comparative statement, 790; remission of tolls, 882; general reduction, boats exempted, VII, 7; collectors, appointment of, veto, 131; cannot be used for new bridges, 576; abolished, 1882, 685, 818; VIII, 13; collectors and weighmasters and assistant, offices abolished, 819; good results of abolition, 945; reimposition of, X, 495.

CANANDAIGUA. Arsenal, arms and ammunition supplied from, II, 775, 793; abduction of William Morgan, III, 185.

VETOES. Village highway bill, IV, 771; legalizing action of town meeting, VII, 569; sewers and drains, VIII, 348, new bill passed.

CANANDAIGUA LAKE. Connection with other lakes and Erie canal, III, 70; fishing in, amending Game Law, veto, X, 173.

CANASTOTA. Village, amending charter, veto, VI, 187.

CANASTOTA CREEK. Arch over, Canastota, veto, X, 313.

CANAWAGO INDIANS. See ST. REGIS INDIANS.

CANBY, EDWARD N. S. Brigadier-general, communication from, relative to military situation at Elmira, V, 562.

CANCER. Proposed investigation as to causes, etc., veto, IX, 772; appropriations for investigation, 1899, 1900, 772; report of New York Pathological Laboratory, University of Buffalo, X, 142.

CANCER LABORATORY, BUFFALO. Deficiency, appropriation, veto, X, 934.

CANDIDATES FOR OFFICE. See also OFFICERS. Proper limits of criticism, II, 551; limiting expenses of, III, 250, 313, 525; IV, 134; report of financial transactions, veto, VII, 609; conviction of bribery, forfeiture of office, IX, 198.

CANDLES. For garrisons, I, 131, 138, 608; manufacture of, license for, II, 382.

CANE, McCAFFREY & COMPANY. Breach of contract, Court of Claims, veto, X, 702.

CANFIELD, GEORGE F. Communication to Governor, relative to appointment of William Church Osborn as State commissioner in lunacy, X, 43.

CANFIELD, JOHN M. Superintendent of Lake Ontario lighthouses, communication from, lighthouse at mouth of Genesee river, II, 1113.

CANISIUS COLLEGE, BUFFALO. Incorporated, VII, 947.

CANISTEO COUNTY. Bill to erect, veto, V, 223.

CANNESTAGAYUNE. See also CONNESTAGUIOENA. Troops at, I, 397.

CANNON. See also ORDNANCE. For Oswego and other frontier garrisons, I, 315, 316, 318; distribution in New York, 322; sent to Boston for Cape Breton expedition, 332; for Canadian expedition, 379; removing from Saratoga to Albany, 460; for Crown Point expedition, 571; expense of unspiking, payment of, 710; purchase authorized, 751; Connecticut's claim for, II, 100; expense of collecting, 262; loan to United States, 416; preservation of, 510; foundry proposed, 813, 814.

CANOES. Number used in Indian trade, I, 214.

CANTERBURY, ARCHBISHOP. Grants permission to examine library, IV, 183.

CANTINE, JOHN. Indian claims, II, 514.

CANTINE, MOSES. Impressments for army service, II, 99.

CANTON, CHINA. Vessels from, exempt from quarantine, III, 87.

CANTON, NEW YORK. Home of Silas Wright, IV, 383; law library, veto, VII, 82.

CANTON LODGE, No. 558, INDEPENDENT ORDER OF GOOD TEMPLARS. Charter, veto, VI, 187.

CANTWELL, THOMAS. Notary public, legalizing acts, veto, IX, 365.

CAPE BRETON. Garrison at, I, 179; expedition against, 332, 340, 346, 349, 350; transports from Virginia, 371; reduction of, 624.

CAPE HENLOPEN. Southern limit of privateer service, I, 333.

CAPE MAY. Breakwater at, New Jersey resolutions, IV, 866.

CAPE VINCENT. Troops stationed at, II, 745, 746.

CAPITAL. Established at Albany, II, 397; centennial anniversary of establishment, IX, 688.

CAPITAL PUNISHMENT. See also DEATH PENALTY. Assembly recommends abolition of, except for treason and murder, II, 336; observations on, 548, 702; report of Assembly committee on, 729, 863; basis of right of, 730; proper limitation of, 731; reducing number of crimes subject to, III, 383; proposed constitutional amendment, 863; discussion by Governor Seward, 940; proposed review of convictions by Supreme Court, IV, 610; act of 1860, unconstitutional, V, 264; repealed, 371; electrocution, VIII, 37, 484; unreasonable delay in inflicting, after conviction, 80, 180; proposed separate building for confinement of condemned persons and execution of sentence, IX, 658; X, 111.

CAPITAL POLICE DISTRICT. Report of commissioners, V, 715, 862; VI, 43, 142.

CAPITAL. See also NEW CAPITOL. Governor Clinton's message relative to erection and use of, II, 934; expense of erection, 936; assignment of rooms in, 936; illuminated in honor of Union victories, V, 439; draped in mourning after President Lincoln's death, 678; project for new building, 721; Albany furnishes site for, 722; transfer to new capitol, VII, 175; Assembly chamber, use of, granted to ladies of Albany, 315; printing legislative proceedings on removal to new capitol, veto, VII, 492; demolition of, 524, 696, 980; illustration of Old Capitol, VII, 268.

CAPITOL COMMISSIONER. Duties, office changed to State Architect, VI, 653; office established, 1897, IX, 746.

CAPTAIN OF THE PORT OF NEW YORK. Office created, V, 188; acts relating to, revised, 381; VII, 1049; report, VI, 43, 143, 775, 977; VII, 178, 439; new act passed, 835, 969, 1049; abolition of office recommended, 996; New York, compensation, veto, 1048; duties assumed by dock department, 1051; claims for services submitted to Board of Claims, 1048.

CARBONDALE, PENNSYLVANIA. Coal mines, railroad connection with, III, 237.

CARLETON, SIR DUDLEY. Negotiations with States-General relative to Virginia, III, 1019.

CARLETON, SIR GUY. Correspondence with, II, 202.

CARLETON ISLAND. Justice of the peace to reside on, II, 1121.

CARLTON. First Methodist Episcopal burial ground, prohibiting interments in, veto, VI, 1035; VII, 120.

CARMAN, GEORGE F. Assembly contested election, VII, 492.

CARMEL. Town business, veto, VI, 674.

CARNATION, THE. British vessel, engagement with American vessel at Fayal, II, 859.

CARNEY, JAMES. Relief, veto, VI, 185.

CAROGA. Highway to Johnstown, veto, VI, 598.

CAROLINE, QUEEN. Death of, I, 269.

CAROLINE, THE. Seized and burned by Canadians, III, 678, 687; arrest of Alexander McLeod, 933.

CARPENTER, B. & J. Board of Claims, veto, VIII, 1166.

CARPENTER, FRANK B. Artist, portrait of Abraham Lincoln, VII, 769.

CARPENTER, JOHN W. Clerk, New York Municipal Court, claim, veto, X, 950.

CARPENTER, LATTING. Attainder of, II, 288.

CARPENTERS. Ship, proposition to encourage, I, 246; high wages of, 251; proposed subsidy for apprentices, 281; impressment of, 374.

CARR, JOSEPH B. Secretary of State, communication from Attorney-General, Bankers bill, VII, 667; communication from Governor Cornell, veto of ten-day bills, 671.

CARR, LEWIS E. Counsel for Justice Hooker, X, 829.

CARRIAGES. Rates on impressment, I, 596, 631; impressment of, recommended, 671; impressment, II, 67, 99, 109; licensing in New York, veto, 315; passing on highways, 554; Federal tax on, 789.

CARRIGAN, HARRY A. New York patrolman, reinstatement, veto, X, 949.

CARROL. Town, erecting bridge, veto, VI, 96.

CARROLL, CHARLES. Last surviving signer of Declaration of Independence, death of, III, 424.

CARROLL BROTHERS. Board of Claims, veto, VIII, 1166.

CARROLL AND COOK. Contract for printing and binding geological survey, IV, 162.

CARROLLTON. State road, Allegany reservation, improvement, veto, VIII, 347.

CARRYING PLACE. Above Saratoga, French at, I, 241; in Mohawk valley, proposed fort at, 256, 260; proposed removal of Fort Hunter garrison to, 258, 260; fort at, 362, 364, 423, 584; forts and magazines at, 392; fortified camp at, 396, 497; provision for, 498; council of war at, 575; proposed canal around, 728; between Lakes Erie and Ontario, II, 526.

CARTEL. None with Canada for exchange of prisoners, I, 467, 470.

CARTER, JAMES C. Opinion, voter's freedom of selection of candidate cannot be restricted by form of ballot, IX, 395, 479; member of Tilden Commission on Municipal Reform, 417.

CARTER, JOHN. Agent, letter from, supplies for French fleet and army, II, 111.

CARTER, JULIAN. Dock on Oneida lake, veto, VI, 156.

CARTERET, LORD. Secretary of State, letter from, I, 200; memorial from Kennedy, supplies for troops, 202; letter from board of ordnance, 202; letter to Governor, relative to supplies for troops, 202; letter to Governor, relative to Captain Holland's claim, 202.

CARTILAGE.

    VETOES. Road to Lake Champlain, VI, 315; amending village charter, VII, 78; bridge, Black river, 362; excise licenses, 1047; new union school building, appropriation, VIII, 117.

CARTHAGE, WATERTOWN AND SACKETT'S HARBOR RAILROAD COMPANY. Facilitating construction, veto, VI, 172.

CARTOUCH BOXES. Ordered by Lieutenant-Governor De Lancey, I, 567.

CASCADE ASSOCIATION, LITTLE FALLS. Charter, veto, VI, 277.

CASCADE FIRE COMPANY NO. 1, LITTLE FALLS. Charter, veto, VI, 187.

CASEY, WILLIAM R. Surveys railroad route, Essex county, III, 984.

CASKS. Frauds in use of, I, 302; false taring of, 530; empty, bounty on, IV, 69.

CASS, JOHN. Escheat, veto, X, 273.

CASS, LEWIS. Minister to France, procures leave to examine French colonial documents, IV, 185; Secretary of State, communication from, foreign acknowledgments, V, 111.

CASSIDY, OWEN. Counsel to Senate committee, investigation of State Board of Health, veto, IX, 401, new bill passed.

CASSIDY, THOMAS. Relief, veto, X, 53, 177.

CASTLE GARDEN. Designation as emigrant depot, IV, 851; V, 23; improvements at, 843; labor exchange, VI, 28; under supervision of emigrant commissioners, 534; arrivals at, VII, 432, 530, 711, 831, 965; employment bureau, 432; landing wharf, rebuilding, veto, VIII, 113.

CASTLEREAGH, LORD. Communication from, relative to war, II, 785.

CASTLES, INDIAN. Destruction of, by French, I, 65; of Senecas, to be removed, 323; church at Canajoharie, 554.

CASTLETON (RICHMOND COUNTY). School district No. 4, borrowing money, veto, VI, 262.

CASTORLAND. Dike at, repairing and improving, veto, X, 570, 644.

CASUALTY INSURANCE COMPANIES. Statistics, VII, 824, 950.

VETOES. Amending act, VIII, 1040; amending general law, IX, 802.

CATARACT GENERAL ELECTRIC COMPANY. Permit to experiment with electrical conductors on canals, IX, 454.

CATHCART, LORD. Commands North American forces, I, 300.

CATHERINE CREEK. Cleaning out, abating Chemung canal nuisance, veto, X, 789; improving channel, veto, 946.

CATHOLIC MUTUAL BENEFIT ASSOCIATION, SUPREME COUNCIL. Amending charter, veto, IX, 57.

CATHOLIC UNION, ALBANY. Exempting property from taxation, veto, VIII, 623, 733.

CATHOLIC UNION, NEW YORK. Charter, veto, VI, 676.

CAT ISLAND. Terminus of Oswegatchie reservation, II, 553.

CATO.

VETOES. Town, draining swamp lands, VIII, 613; cleaning Parker's pond, X, 810.

CATSKILL. Female seminary at, II, 1018; number of excise licenses, 1887, VIII, 360.

VETOES. Mutual insurance company, VI, 595; VII, 132; armory, completion, IX, 263; fixing boundaries, 818; purchasing stone crusher, X, 380.

CATSKILL AND CANAJOHARIE RAILROAD. State aid to, III, 887; IV, 10; default in payment of interest on State loan, III, 952; sold at auction, IV, 10; continuing construction of, 12.

CATSKILL CREEK. Not a navigable stream, VIII, 384.

VETOES. Improving navigation, VI, 908; dredging and cleaning, VIII, 248; bridge in town of Cairo, 383.

CATSKILL MOUNTAIN NATIONAL CAMP MEETING ASSOCIATION OF THE METHODIST EPISCOPAL CHURCH, NEW YORK CONFERENCE. Charter, veto, VII, 867.

CATSKILL MOUNTAINS. Geological survey, map, appropriation, veto, VII, 469, 495; public park in, X, 100.

CATSKILL PARK. Act describing, X, 607.

CATTARAUGUS COUNTY. Militia from, 1812, II, 743; entitled to share in appropriation for agriculture, 1006; exploration of ancient mounds, V, 720; average excise license fees, 1889, VIII, 686; unpaid taxes, sales under special act, 749; highways, cost of labor system, 1892, IX, 199; insane, care of, county and State systems compared, 228; district attorney protests against bill relating to trials for felonies committed on Indian reservations, X, 164.

CATTARAUGUS COUNTY.— (*Continued*).

    VETOES. Aiding railroads, VI, 95; credit for highways and bridges on Allegany reservation, 690; Salamanca, village charter, 704; Allegany reservation, bridge at Vandalia, 707; Portville, bridge over canal and Allegany river, 709; railroad school taxes, exempting from general act, VII, 1095; Yorkshire, additional justice of the peace, VIII, 338; county clerk, recording notices of pendency of actions, 705; school commissioner districts, increasing number, 713; taxes, collection, amending act, 967; South Valley, division of, legalizing action of board of supervisors, 1089, new bill passed; sheriff, boarding United States prisoners, X, 706; Ashford, transfer from third to first school commissioner district, 948.

CATTARAUGUS CREEK. Bridges over, Indian reservation, VIII, 560; fishways, veto, 890.

CATTARAUGUS INDIAN RESERVATION. Number of Indians on, 1819, II, 976; ferry privileges of Indians, 1030; act relative to Senecas, IV, 290; Seneca Constitutional Convention, 457; sale of land for taxes, release, V, 36; ascertaining damages caused by trespassers, 863; prohibiting sales of liquor on, VI, 97; villages, survey under act of Congress, 704; compulsory education of children, VII, 710; roads and bridges, VIII, 560.

    VETOES. Senecas, amending act, VI, 910; repairing highway, Gowanda to Perrysburgh, VII, 221, 475; repairing State bridges, 383; bridges over Clear creek, 908; X, 429; highways, repairs, VIII, 845; X, 429.

CATTARAUGUS RAILWAY COMPANY. Facilitating construction, veto, VI, 172.

CATTLE. Act relating to, I, 11; supply to British, act to prevent, II, 88; supplied to British by disaffected inhabitants of Westchester county, 90; number of, IV, 42; VI, 27; Texas cattle disease, 27; prevention of infectious diseases, 28; commission on, report of, 143; rinderpest, 245; diseases of, investigating committee of 1878, report, VII, 438; pleuro-pneumonia, movement for suppression of, 537; destroyed, when State liable, IX, 270; preventing spread of tuberculosis, 1893, 327.

    VETOES. Jersey Improvement, charter, VII, 202; distraining, 509; improving breed of, bill to promote, IX, 109; examination for tuberculosis, 773.

CAUGHDENIA REEF. Wing dam at, III, 37.

CAVALRY. Organization of, II, 339; statement relative to, 1037; Hopkinton, request for arms, III, 180; instructors for, V, 53.

CAYUGA. Smith to reside at, I, 306.

CAYUGA COUNTY. David Williams convicted of murder, II, 578; militia from, 1812, 743; canal celebration, loss of life at, III, 120; gypsum, market for, 815; agricultural society in, 945; silk culture in, 945; average excise license fees, 1889, VIII, 686; unpaid taxes, sales under special act, 749; highways, cost of labor system, 1892, IX, 199; insane, care of, county and State systems compared, 228.

VETOES. Rural cemetery associations, acquiring land, VI, 162; reimbursing for expenses of criminal trials, Auburn prison, 876; VII, 87, 226, 471, 781; reimbursement for foregoing expenses, 87; Auburn prison claim, submission to State Board of Audit, 801; Brutus, fixing northern boundary, 806; Auburn prison claim, submission to State Board of Claims, 932; Cato, draining swamp lands, VIII, 613; fish in Lake Ontario, protection of, 627; clerk, salaried office, 1103; IX, 124; special county judge and surrogate, term of office, X, 701.

CAYUGA CREEK. Improving channel, veto, VIII, 868.

CAYUGA CREEK ROAD. Erie county, improvement, veto, VII, 265.

CAYUGA INDIANS. French attack on, I, 66; smith for, 306, 419; Senecas' castles to be placed near, 323; treaty with, II, 296, 302; annuities to, 311; intrusions on land of, 319; memorial from chiefs, relative to leases, 328; act relating to lands of, 329; conference with, 338, 340, 343, 344, 346, 347; support of, act to provide for, 356, 364; visit of delegates, 393; purchase of land, 435; offer to sell land, 477, 518; claim of, 514; trespasses on lands of, 553; lands at Cayuga lake, sale proposed, 605, 607; claim of Canadian branch against State, X, 31, 127; alleged assistance to Great Britain in War of 1812, 32; land commissioners to hear memorial, veto, 955.

CAYUGA INLET. Tolls, V, 66, 154, 258, 361; dredging, veto, VI, 876; financial statement, 1875, 930.

CAYUGA LAKE. Connection with other lakes and Erie canal, III, 70; State road to Hudson river, 80.

VETOES. Outlet, removal of obstructions, VI, 1001; VII, 405, 496; outlet, improvement, certificates, payment, 467, 924; dredging inlet, repairing State pier, X, 570, 644; lamps for lighting east shore and for lighthouse, 791.

CAYUGA MARSHES. Drainage of, II, 1011; III, 81.

CAYUGA AND SENECA CANAL. Amount of debt, III, 304, 334, 736; IV, 252; receipts, III, 335, 370; deficiency, 410, 710; completion of, 465, 549; not self-supporting, 506; expenses exceed income, 549, 553; should not be abandoned, 799; length of, 811; appropriation for, charged on canal fund, IV, 199; appropriation

Cayuga and Seneca Canal — (*Continued*).

    for, 678, 735, 743; enlargement, 692, 743; V, 68; tolls, 65, 153, 257, 361; proposed new locks, 502; relation to canal system, 789; comparative financial statement, VI, 746; repairing wall near Montezuma, 858; financial statement, 930; VII, 5; tonnage, 1893, IX, 301.

    Vetoes. Sewer, Waterloo, VI, 339; Waterloo bridge, VII, 115; sewer under, Waterloo, VIII, 413; improvement, IX, 110; berme bank, repairs, Geneva, 239; assessment for local improvements, Geneva, X, 648.

Cazenovia. Number of excise licenses, 1887, VIII, 360.

Cazenovia Creek. Buffalo, improvement of, veto, IX, 783.

Cazenovia Dam. Reappropriation, veto, VII, 119.

Cazenovia Lake. Cutting ice, failure to guard openings, misdemeanor, veto, VIII, 461.

Cement. Discovery of, importance of, II, 1048; accumulations of, III, 1036.

Cemeteries. Taxing lots for improvements, VI, 184, 585; national, West Point and Cypress Hill, 558; Cypress Hills National Cemetery, cession of land for, VII, 998; control of, when Legislature cannot transfer to private association, VIII, 712; large number in Newtown, IX, 254.

    Vetoes. Cherry Creek, taking charge of public cemetery, VI, 332; Temple Adas Jeshurun Society, right to hold land, 588; Auburn, public cemetery, acquiring land for, 602, 642; Owego, school district No. 35, 697; Port Byron, 1035; Norwood, removal of bodies, 1035; Carlton First M. E. burial ground, prohibiting interments in, 1035; VII, 120; Baptist Society, Hoosick, removing dead from burying ground, 76; Saratoga Springs, Nelson street cemetery, removing dead, 121; Newtown, Lutheran, relief, 268; Saratoga Springs, confirming purchase of land for, 391; Gypsum Association, Ontario county, revival, 412; Perry, reinterments, 870; religious corporations, holding burial plots in trust, 935; Oneonta, prohibiting new, VIII, 327; Mohawk, revising act, 391; Lockport Episcopal cemetery, removing bodies from, 887; Scriba, Old Burt cemetery, removal of remains, 1118; Congregational Society, Worcester, removing remains from, IX, 57; First German Methodist Episcopal church, holding land for, 254; Hornell cemetery, Hornellsville, removal of remains, 352; permitting benevolent and charitable institutions to establish, 442; rural, amending act of 1847, 624; 32d ward, Brooklyn, trustees, mayor to appoint, 780; taxing lots, X, 61; Seneca Falls, bonds for addition, 278; Cypress Hill,

CEMETERIES, VETOES — (*Continued*).

New York, street through, 325; cities, removal and reinterment of bodies, moving and resetting monuments, etc., 448; sale of unoccupied lots, disposition of proceeds, 591; St. Peter's church, Cortland, regulating interments, 593; rural, funds for permanent care of lots, deposit with county treasurer, 947.

CEMETERY ASSOCIATIONS. Taxing lots for improvements, VI, 184, 186, 191; acquiring additional land, 501; reducing number of trustees, general act, VIII, 53; Greenwood, charges against management, report of investigating commission, 70; Madison Forks Obituary Society, changing name, acquiring land, act for, 1163.

VETOES. Rural, acquiring land by eminent domain, VI, 162, 208, 607; Frewsburg Association, 186; Barnes Corner's Burial Association, 186; Quincy Rural Cemetery Association, Ripley, 501; New Baltimore Chestnut Lawn Cemetery Association, 501; creditors, right to vote, 595; Yorkshire Rural Cemetery Association, charter, 596; rural, relative to, VII, 509; Mountain View, Broome county, relative to, 807; Hillside Cemetery Association, Madison county, control of certain lands, 807; Buffalo, acquiring land, office building, 933; Bethpage cemetery, Oyster Bay, sale of lots, improvement fund, 1122; Lowell Cemetery Association, reducing trustees, VIII, 52; rural, amending general act, 619, 874; Milford Center Cemetery Association, extending powers, 712; Groton Cemetery Association, changing name, 974; Hillside Cemetery Association, Middletown, raising money for improvements, IX, 794; Hamburg Cemetery Association, changing name, legalizing conveyance, X, 256; rural, exempting Mount Pleasant, 446; family cemetery corporations, 591.

CENSUS. In New York city, 1771, I, 743; of white inhabitants, II, 164; of electors, 305, 510, 1047; as basis of apportionment, 652, 1047; of 1821, 1047; United States, 1820, basis of State apportionment, 1047; State, 1825, statistical information required, III, 65; enumeration of defectives, 84; State, 1835, information required, 526; Federal, 1840, IV, 42; State, 1845, 247; of Indians, 248, 289; United States, 1850, 577, 590, 592; State, 1855, 856; V, 9; statistics, 1855, V, 9; Eighth Federal, 1860, 296; State, 1865, 601, 775; State, 1875, VI, 723, 950; tabulation of, 950; 1885, executive and legislative action relative to, VIII, 40, 43, 83, 132; statistical information, omission recommended, 41, 59, 66; X, 723; earlier completion of, recommended, VIII, 42; enumerators, method of appointment, 42; bills passed and vetoed, 43, 66, 134, 155, 492; enumeration of 1892, 43, 1057; IX, 2; 1885, expenses of Secretary of State preparing for, veto, VIII, 111; legislative power is continuing one, 156, 741;

CENSUS — (*Continued*).

    constitutional provision, 298, 397, 491, 676, 892, 1054; X, 722, 868; extraordinary session, 1888, legislation recommended, VIII, 652; Federal, 1890, alleged defects in, 1056; IX, 2; 1892, industrial classification, 326; of cities, certificate of population to be filed, 678; act of 1905, X, 723, 868; statistics required, tabulation recommended, 868.

CENTENNIAL CELEBRATION. Philadelphia, 1876, VI, 302; general committee, 302; board of managers, 655, 724; State centennial board created, 725, 951; communication from director-general, 785; historical memorial volume, proposition for, 809; benefits resulting from, VII, 718.

CENTENNIAL EXPOSITION. Tennessee Exposition, 1897, New York commission to, IX, 852.

CENTRAL ASYLUM FOR THE INSTRUCTION OF DEAF AND DUMB, CANAJOHARIE. Incorporated, III, 83; report of, 97, 137; State pupils in, 97, 292, 450; Senate recommends discontinuance of, 409; discontinued and consolidated with New York Institution, 543.

CENTRAL ISLIP STATE HOSPITAL. Relative to, veto, X, 704.

CENTRAL NEW YORK AGRICULTURAL, HORTICULTURAL AND MECHANICAL ASSOCIATION, UTICA. Distribution of premiums for improving manufacture of butter and cheese and cultivation of hops, veto, VII, 1078.

CENTRAL NEW YORK INSTITUTION FOR DEAF-MUTES, ROME.

    VETOES. New building, appropriation, VII, 90; deficiency appropriation, 470; appropriation for payment of debt, paving street in front of, X, 949.

CENTRAL PARK, NEW YORK. Established, V, 183; report of commissioners, 286; board reorganized, 286; museum established in, 381; improvement fund created, 598; cost of, VI, 407.

    VETOES. Altering map, VI, 93; laying gas pipes, 180; refreshment house, VII, 578; accommodations for zoological collection, VIII, 449; parade grounds, 467; relative to railways in transverse roads, 1035; projections on, legalizing certain permits, X, 323.

CENTRAL PARK, NORTH AND EAST RIVER RAILROAD COMPANY. New York, claim against, settlement, VIII, 1035.

CENTRAL SAVINGS BANK, NEW YORK. Amending charter, veto, VI, 308.

CENTRAL THROAT HOSPITAL POLYCLINIC DISPENSARY, BROOKLYN. Changing name, veto, IX, 793.

CENTRAL UNDERGROUND RAILROAD COMPANY. Incorporated, VI, 207.

CENTREPORT HARBOR. Protection of shellfish in, veto, VII, 415.

CENTURY ASSOCIATION. Amending charter, veto, VIII, 709.

CENTURY DICTIONARY. Quoted, definitions of inspect and visit, X, 157.

CERTIFICATE. Of purchasing officers to be received in payment of taxes, II, 100, 126; by loan office, use of, 158; loan, use of, 214; counterfeiting, prohibited, 224; loan office, Federal requisition to be paid in, 264; State loan, cashier appointed to issue, 907.

CERTIFICATES OF DEPOSIT. Advances on, not subject to usury laws, VII, 719.

CERTIFICATES OF NECESSITY OF IMMEDIATE PASSAGE OF BILLS. Legislative custom as to reading certificates, X, 145, 631.

1895. Kings county and Brooklyn, consolidation, IX, 588; supply bill, 588; civil service amendments, 588; tax rate, 588.

1896. Election Law, IX, 690; Capital Centennial Celebration, 691; tax rate, care of insane, 691; supplemental supply bill, 691; general tax rate, 691.

1897. Liquor Tax Law, amendments, IX, 755; Grant monument, New York, 755; supply bill, 755, 756; New York, financial bill, 756; tax rate, 756; care of insane, 756.

1898. Primary Election Law, IX, 852; supply bill, 852, 854; Spanish War, appropriation, 853, 884; care of insane, 854; supplemental supply bill, 854; tax rate bill, 854; metropolitan elections district, 885; extraordinary session, 1898, appropriation for expenses, 885; election officers in cities, 885; soldier vote, 885.

1899. Notary public, commissions, X, 33; civil service, revision, 42; supply bill, 44, 47; rapid transit, 45; elections, 45; New York, department of elections, 45; primary elections, 45; franchise tax, 45, 47, 72; second-class cities, 46; Brooklyn, offensive trades, 47; supplemental supply bill, 47; tax rate, 47; State Tax Commission, compensation, 72; Dewey reception, appropriation, 72; amending State Finance Law, payment of fees into State Treasury, 73; expenses of extraordinary session, 74.

1900. New York, Thirty-first Assembly district, ratifying nominations, X, 130; rapid transit, amending Greater New York charter, 130; New York Charter Commission, 144; New York, law department, 144; New York, water supply, powers of commissioner, 144; New York, teachers' salaries, 144; New York, separate department of elections, 145; State fair, 145; colored children, equal educational rights, 145; supply bill, 148; Statutory Revision Commmission, abolition of, 148; quarantine improvements, 148; Syracuse, city funds, deficiencies, 148; New York, investigations, appropriation, 149; Public Health Law, repealing section 65, 149; State tuberculosis hospital, Adiron-

XI—19

CERTIFICATES OF NECESSITY OF IMMEDIATE PASSAGE OF BILLS.— (Continued).

dacks, 149; primary elections in presidential years, 149; State Charities Law, amendments, 149; Agricultural Law, watering milk, 149; supplemental supply bill, 149, 150; tax rate, 150.

1901. Town meetings, legalizing action of boards of supervisors, changing time, X, 236; Election Law, amendments, 240; Oneida city charter, 244, 267; transfer tax amendments, 256, 281; Banking Law, building and loan associations, 267; tenement-houses, first-class cities, 267; Greater New York charter, general amendments, 267; Tax Law, foreign and domestic corporations, 275; congressional apportionment, 278, 281; supply bill, 278, 281; Church Insurance Association, amending charter, 278; appropriation bill, 279; Kings county, district attorney's chief clerk, compensation, 279; veterans' rights, 279; New York, department of education, 280; New York, board of city record, 280; New York, docks and ferries (3 bills), 280; New York, police department, 280; Sunday, sale and delivery of uncooked flesh foods, 280; New York, teachers' licenses, 281; Watervliet fire commissioners, 281; reappropriation of unexpended balances, 281; Tenement-House Act, amendments, 281; supplemental supply bill, 282; tax rate bill, 282.

1902. Second-class cities, X, 375; second-class cities, salaries, etc., 375; Oswego charter amendments, 378; Lockport charter amendments, 385; supply bill, 394, 403; rapid transit, amending act, 394; United States Marine Hospital, Erie county, cession, 394; transfer tax, appointment of appraisers, stenographers, etc., 394; McKinley monument, Buffalo, 394; Buffalo, amending charter, tax sales, redemption notices, 394; rapid transit, amending act, tunnel roads, 395; Tenement-House Act, amendments, 395; amending Agricultural Law, imitations of butter, 395; Kings county, commissioner of jurors, 395; tax rate, 403; supplemental supply bill, 403; county supervision of highways, 404; assignment of Supreme Court justices for service in other districts, 404.

1903. Liquor Tax Law, amendments, X, 524; appropriation bill, 535, 537; Game Law, amendments, 536; supply bill, 537, 539; State hospitals, general appropriations, 539; Common School Law, general amendments, 539; schools, academic department, free tuition, 539; Surrogates' Courts, compensation, 539; Clinton county, unpaid taxes, 540; Liquor Tax Law, amendments, 540; tax rate, 540.

CERTIFICATES OF NECESSITY OF IMMEDIATE PASSAGE OF BILLS — (*Continued*).

1904. Educational unification bill, X, 628; election officers in cities, 629; Albany penitentiary, 629; Elmira, amending charter, 630; rapid transit amendments, 630; railroads in certain cities, 630; game of policy, payment of fines, penalties and forfeitures, 630; Oneida, amending charter, 630, 632; New York, inspection of illuminating gas, 631; New York, Municipal Court, 631, 632; New York, health department, bureau of medical examiners, 631; supply bill, 631; sales of merchandise in bulk, 631; tenement-houses, first-class cities, 631; width of tires, 632; Binghamton, amending charter, 632; New York, City Court, 632; highways, removal of obstructions caused by snow, 632; tax rate bill, 632; Painted Post, protection of persons and property, 632; New York, classification of criminals and misdemeanants, 633; supplemental supply bill, 633.

1905. Elmira Reformatory, appropriation, X, 759; Enumeration Act, amendments, 759; New York water supply, 759; New York, street cleaning department, 763; taxing mortgages, 763; New York, electric power, sale to private consumers, 763, 765; New York, price of electric current sold to cities, 763, 765; New York, illuminating gas, sale to private consumers, 763, 765, 766; New York, illuminating gas, inspection and tests, 763, 765; New York, price of illuminating gas to city, 764; New York, manufacture of electricity, 764; Taxation Commission, 764; Liquor Tax Law, local option, 764, 765; Commission of Gas and Electricity, 764; mortgage tax, 764; municipal corporations, tabulation of accounts and expenses, 764; liquor tax, inspection of hotels, revocation of certificates, 765; canal debt sinking fund, annual contribution, 766; supplemental supply bill, 766; Election Law, campaign contributions, 767; appropriation for expenses of extraordinary session, 821.

1906. Syracuse, department of assessment and taxation, X, 876; Liquor Tax Law, amendments, 879; free employment bureau, act limiting to first-class cities, 880, 885; Insurance Law, amendments, 890; California relief bill, 891; second-class cities, revised charter, 892; Cobleskill, legalizing election for public improvements, 892; State Training School for Boys, amending act, 893; increasing number of justices of Supreme Court in first, second and ninth districts, 893; highways, reports to State Engineer, 893; supply bill, 893; apportionment bill, 893, 896; crimes against elective franchise, 894; new prison in place of Sing Sing prison, 895; mutual life insurance companies, elec-

CERTIFICATES OF NECESSITY OF IMMEDIATE PASSAGE OF BILLS — (Continued).

tion of directors, 1906, 895, 897; primary elections in second-class cities, 895; canal debt appropriation, 895; highway improvement, interest on debt, 896; canal debt interest, 896; highway improvement fund, appropriation, 896; canal debt sinking, fund appropriation, 896; authorizing conveyance to Albany of lands under water of Albany basin, 897.

CERTIORARI. Amending Revised Statutes, veto, VII, 197.

CESSIONS TO UNITED STATES. Extending powers of commissioners, II, 620, 825, 878; struck juries in proceedings to acquire land, 753, 777, 878; officers authorized to make, 825, 878; III, 140; provision requisite in bills for, VIII, 1114; general act, 1896, 1113; land for Sandy Hook lighthouse, II, 304; Eaton's Neck lighthouse, 415; lands about New York harbor, 457; land for military post at Black Rock, 513; lighthouse, Great Gull and Little Gull islands, 530; beacon, Staten Island, 586, 589; Watch Point lighthouse, 641; military academy on Staten Island, 677; military academy at West Point, 677; III, 141; Greenbush, magazine, II, 714; island at Rouse's Point, 878; land in Refugee tract, 878, 879; Island Point, 919; lighthouse, Genesee river, 1054, 1113; lighthouse, Oswego river, 1055; at New Utrecht Point, III, 47, 48, 138; lighthouse, Prince's bay, 178; for naval hospital, Brooklyn, 181; for Watervliet arsenal, 264, 314; of land on Staten Island, 570; ship canal around Niagara falls, 816; Lake Champlain outlet, Fort Niagara, 850; Black Rock, 850, 944; IV. 46; fortifications on northwestern frontier, 293, 294; land at Sackett's Harbor, 381; for Brooklyn Navy Yard, 465, 506, 512, 573; property for custom house in New York, V, 642; David's island, 861; Lake Champlain, Clinton county, lighthouse-keeper's dwelling, VI, 414; public buildings at Albany, veto, 449; land at West Point, 558; 788; land at Willet's Point, 774; lighthouse, Cold Harbor, VII, 393; land in Brooklyn, veto, 932; land for Cypress Hills national cemetery, 998; Chickamauga battlefield, Georgia cedes to United States, VIII, 1076; Missionary ridge and Lookout mountain, roads on ceded by Tennessee to United States, 1076; land in Queens county, veto, 1113; Old Orchard shoal, land at, IX, 211; palisades, 735; Iona island, X, 143; marine hospital, Erie county, 394.

CHADEAYNE, HENRY F. Ferry, Hudson river, veto, VII, 664.

CHAIN. For obstruction of Hudson river, II, 8, 19.

CHAMBERLAIN, MR. Postmaster at Oxford, removal of, II, 1070, 1071.

CHAMBERLAIN, WILLIAM. Escheat, veto, VI, 158.

CHAMPERTY AND MAINTENANCE. Act to prohibit, I, 11.

CHAMPION. Deposit of arms and ammunition at, II, 636; arms and supplies for, 774.

CHAMPLAIN. Communication from citizens to Assemblyman North, III, 760; aid to Utica and Black River Railroad Company, amending act, veto, VI, 92.

CHAMPLAIN, MARSHALL B. Attorney-General, report, powers of canal commissioners, VI, 344; Buck case, 682.

CHAMPLAIN CANAL. Progress of construction, II, 962, 1007, 1045, 1095; III, 24; proceeds from sale of Grand island, II, 1010; tax on contiguous territory, 1012; feeder to be made navigable, 1096; limiting speed of boats, 1096; completion of, III, 72, 469; Glens Falls feeder, 120; cost per mile, 200; debt, 304, 333, 479, 552, 736; IV, 252; redemption of stock, III, 372; income, 410; construction debt paid, 619, 888; length of, 811; stock, when redeemable, IV, 201; appropriation for, 678, 735; tolls, V, 65, 153, 257, 361; proposed new locks, 502; enlargement of locks, 533; reduction of tolls on iron ore, 707; relation to canal system, 789; improvement of, 829; enlargement of, VI, 107; comparative financial statement, 746; financial statement, 930; VII, 5, 145; extraordinary repairs, sum needed to settle contracts; new work, VI, 992; deepening, general appropriation, VI, 994; tonnage, 1893, IX, 301; enlargement, acts of 1895 and 1903, 305; enlargement, survey for, 1900, X, 141, 215; improvement, State Engineer's special report, 1901, 244; improvement act, 1903, 252, 363, 496.

VETOES. Bridge at Whitehall, VI, 154, 584; contractors, relief bill, 213; bridge at Fort Edward, 448; farm bridge, Saratoga, 504; enlargement, 584; Seeley claim, settlement of, 592; farm bridge, Whitehall, 689; Whitehall, farm bridge, Brown, 1007; Fort Ann, raising roadbed, VII, 114, 457; Cohoes, bridge, Ship street, 115, 249, 361; Fort Edward, bridge, Main street, 115; Waterford, bridge, 116, 361; cleaning Pond's creek, Fort Edward, 473; steam motive power, 508; Cohoes, removal of canal bridge, 554; Fort Ann, Dewey's bridge, 577; Mechanicville, lift-bridge, VIII, 130; Exchange bridge, Fort Edward, 234; damage to highways, 453; improvement, IX, 110; Whitehall, bridge, Rathbun crossing, 139; Mechanicville, bridge, North street, 285; bridge over Glens Falls feeder, Sandy Hill, 755; new blue line maps, X, 297, 423; Mechanicville, bridge, Burke avenue and Francis street, 434, 547; State ditches, cleaning, 569, 644; bridge, Greenwich to Northumberland, 699.

CHAMPLAIN FRONTIER. Military movements on, 1812, II, 743, 744; barracks destroyed by fire, 770; deemed secure, 807.

CHAMPLIN, GEORGE G. Assistant reference librarian, State Library, acknowledgments to, I, pref., XV.

CHAMPLIN, JOHN. Suit of, papers in, II, 950.

CHANCELLOR. Member of Council of Revision, II, 4; when not to hold other office, exception, "special occasion," 83; not to hold other office, 325; III, 6; salary, II, 362; III, 5, 256, 498; extra compensation, II, 460; tenure of office, 461; Governor's letter to, Council of Appointment, 479; reply, 481; communication from, court fees, 542, 702; communication from, transcribing records of court, 609, 754; communication from, reforms in court, 631; may authorize sales by religious societies, 645; member of commission to make cessions to United States, 825; communication from, Albro case, III, 263; to devise bill of foreclosure, 722; large accumulation of business, 772; additional chancellors recommended, 773; IV, 135; authority to determine custody of children of alien parents, veto, III, 848; office abolished, IV, 363; title of proposed head of State Department of Education, X, 129.

CHANDLER, ADONIRAM. Commissary-General, correspondence relative to disturbances in northeastern part of State, III, 762.

CHANDLER, CHARLES F. Communication to Governor relative to appointment of William Church Osborn as commissioner in lunacy, X, 43.

CHAPEL. In fort, repair proposed, I, 41, 44, 50; to be rebuilt, 51, 63; in forts in Indian country, 156; in Fort George, 222; for Mohawks, 290; at New York, destroyed by fire, 297, 302; rebuilding of, recommended, 306; endowment, veto, X, 700.

CHAPIN, ALFRED C. Comptroller, recommends abolition of common school fund, VIII, 147.

CHAPIN, CYRENUS, COLONEL. Communication from, intrusions on Grand island, II, 995.

CHAPIN, ISRAEL. Letters from, Indian affairs, II, 328, 344; visit of, 346; communication from, Mohawk delegates, 378; various Indian claims, 514.

CHAPLAIN. Assembly, appointed, I, 101; for army, 623; regimental, act of Congress, II, 538; for militia, III, 103; in State prisons, 289, 977; payments by Prison Discipline Society, 977.

VETOES. For Willard Asylum, appropriation, X, 565; for New York fire department, compensation, 581; State Industrial School, Court of Claims, 707.

CHAPMAN, EDWIN J. Contests Assemblyman Morgan's seat, 1903, X, 571.

CHAPMAN, EUNICE. Relief, veto, II, 920; second veto, 946.

CHAPMAN, FRANK. Ogdensburg, member of board of education, opposes school bill, X, 912.

CHAPMAN, JAMES. Act relative to marriage of, II, 920.

CHAPMAN, JOHN S. Court of Claims, veto, X, 165.

CHAPPELL, ROBERT STEPHENSON. Applicant for admission as attorney, relief, veto, VIII, 1100.

CHARITABLE INSTITUTIONS. Successful work of, IV, 641; appointments should not be subject to political influence, 722; supervision needed, 849; V, 287, 382, 760; need public support, 19; additional, 699; State Board of Charities, 761, see that title; Institution for the Blind at Batavia, 762, see that title; Hudson River Asylum for the Insane, 763, see that title; supervision of private lunatic asylums, VI, 367; religious instruction in, 468; unwise system of construction, 870, 938; reports, uniformity needed, VII, 297; fiscal year established, 297; legislation should not prescribe arbitrary payments by municipalities, 335; property held by, 526; Kings county, report of board of supervisors, 538; expenditures, 703, 829; sources of revenue, 704, 829; frequent examinations needed, 831; statistics, 958; powers of local boards, 960; agent to investigate condition, report, 962; superintendents should give more efficient supervision, 964; commission to prepare new plan of administration, 964; State should select part of managers, VIII, 480; investment in State hospitals, IX, 32; Custodial Asylum for Feeble-Minded Women, Newark, IX, 79, see that title; visited by Governor Flower, 1892, 156; property exempt from taxation, 232; Craig Colony for Epileptics, Sonyea, 240, see that title; report of Comptroller's agent for examination of, 339; monthly estimates of expenses by certain institutions, 436, 651; inspection, Constitution 1894, 550; payments by municipal corporations, 551; payments, regulations by State Board of Charities, 568; number of inmates, 1897, 829; importance of interests involved in, X, 116; expenditures, 1900, 182; unreasonable demands for repairs and improvements, 333; classification, 1902, 334; feeble-minded, comparative expense per capita, 335; visiting committees recommended, 335; office of Fiscal Supervisor created, 336; boards of managers required to visit, 336; increase in number of inmates, 1894–1902, 463; increase in appropriations for certain institutions, 1903, 578; increased accommodations, 608; Eastern New York State Custodial Asylum, provision for establishing, 726; committee on purchase of supplies, 727; appropriations included in one bill, 727; transfer of inmates from one institution to another, 723.

CHARITABLE INSTITUTIONS — (*Continued*).

VETOES. Devises to, limiting amount of, VII, 266; exempting from life insurance laws, 543; freedom of worship in, 596; women as trustees or managers, 761; agent to investigate condition, compensation, 779; Brooklyn, free water, 804; Brooklyn, payments to, VIII, 1036; Bayard Homeopathic College, Hospital and Dispensary, charter, IX, 233; directors and trustees to receive compensation in certain cases, 439; establishing cemeteries, 442; Children's Aid Society, Rochester, charter, 450; devises to, limiting effect of, 623; trusts for, 725; appointments by boards of managers, X, 592.

CHARITIES. Administration of, wisdom needed, II, 915; New York Hospital for Insane, 974; House of Refuge, New York, III, 82, 163; orphan asylum, New York, 83; deaf and dumb, instruction of, 83; beneficent character of institutions, 290, 453; care of the blind, 452; Governor Bouck visits New York institutions, IV, 74; appropriations not diminished by financial depression, 129; charitable institutions, effect of third Constitution, 378; idiots, 484, see that title; public, beneficent character of, 604; State supervision needed, 849; V, 287, 760; increase of benevolent institutions, 382; general references, 582, 698, 760, 837; VI, 24, 234, 355; VII, 703, 828, 957; additional institutions, V, 699; extension of system, 837; private, large appropriations for, VI, 525; property held for charitable purposes, VII, 526, 957; beneficiaries, 526; comparative statement of appropriations, 1893–4, 1901–2, X, 464; annual expenditures for, 856.

VETOES. Limiting amount of, II, 717; Kings county board of, VI, 1018; Kings County Charities Commission, reorganization, IX, 583; trusts for, VII, 868.

CHARLES I. Fatal consequences of usurpation, VI, 773.

CHARLES II. Grants patent of New York to Duke of York, I, 2; requires English subjects to leave France, 5; act confirming mortgages made before restoration, 11; Auditor-General's office established under, 293; supervision of colonial affairs, IV, 178; act abolishing feudal system, 358; death of, I, 12, 14.

CHARLESTON (New York). Leasehold estates in, IV, 331.

CHARLESTON CONVENTION. 1860, disruption of, V, 299.

CHARLOTTE. Village, police office and lockup, veto, VI, 193.

CHARLOTTE COUNTY. Disturbances in, I, 764; contingent expenses, veto, II, 95; included part of New Hampshire grants, 103; military exemptions, veto, 128.

CHARTER. Of Livingston manor, I, 612; of New York Hospital, 743; legislative interference with, II, 611; extension equivalent to new, IV, 514, 637, 824; V, 147; cities, uniform, not practicable, VI, 402; New York, judicial construction, 519; cities, early methods of preparation, 841.

CHARTER OF LIBERTIES AND PRIVILEGES. First enactment of, I, 10; approved, but afterward rejected, 10.

CHASE, S. G. Statement, condition of canal business, V, 507.

CHASE, SALMON P. Chief justice, United States Supreme Court, death of, legislative action thereon, VI, 566.

CHATEAUGAY. Village charter, veto, VI, 76; new act passed, 77.

CHATEAUGAY LAKES. Upper and lower, Clinton county, cleaning channel, veto, X, 814.

CHATFIELD, ANDREW G. Assembly, member of select committee on anti-rent troubles, IV, 328.

CHATFIELD, BYRON. Loss of public funds, town of Elbridge, relief, veto, X, 275.

CHATFIELD, CORNELIUS. Estate of, relative to, veto, II, 580.

CHATHAM. Amending village charter, veto, VIII, 469.

CHATTANOOGA. Battle of, New York troops in, monuments, VIII, 1076; commission to mark position of troops, 1076; monuments for New York soldiers, IX, 324, 577; battle, New York troops in, 576.

CHAUTAUQUA COUNTY. Militia from, 1812, II, 743; access to New York market, III, 815; exploration of ancient mounds, V, 720; average excise license fees, 1889, VIII, 686; unpaid taxes, sales under special act, 749; county clerk, salaried office, 1025, 1103; highways, cost of labor system, 1892, IX, 199; insane, care of, county and State systems compared, 228.

VETOES. Taxes, VI, 331; compensation of supervisors of certain towns, 588; soldiers and sailors' monument, VII, 845; legalizing acts of board of supervisors, fishing in Lake Erie, VIII, 79; Portland, special highway, 879; taxes, collection, amending act, 967; county police charter, IX, 795; draining Conewango creek, X, 315; special county judge and surrogate, term of office, veto, 701.

CHAUTAUQUA COUNTY POLICE. Charter, veto, IX, 795.

CHAUTAUQUA LAKE. Proposed canal between Lake Erie and Allegany river by way of, III, 96.

VETOES. Outlet, removing obstructions, VII, 381, 473, 1095; VIII, 114; outlet, deepening, 890; fishing in, X, 174.

CHAUTAUQUA LAKE CAMP MEETING ASSOCIATION OF THE ERIE CONFERENCE OF THE METHODIST EPISCOPAL CHURCH. Taxing property, veto, VI, 850.

CHAUTAUQUA (Town). Arms and supplies for, II, 775; compensation of supervisors, special services, veto, VI, 588.

CHAZY. First Wesleyan Methodist church, confirming reorganization, veto, VII, 357.

CHAZY LAKE. Great Chazy river dam, veto, X, 789.

CHECKS. Use in commercial transactions, VI, 753.

CHEESE. Reduction of tolls on, III, 505; adulterated, coloring and sale as food prohibited, VII, 699; high quality of New York products, IX, 318.

    VETOES. Factories, protection of patrons, VII, 805; lard, regulating sale of, 808; premium for improving manufacture, 1078; promoting consumption of, IX, 287.

CHEEVER, SAMUEL. President State Agricultural College, V, 16.

CHEMUNG CANAL. Transportation of coal on, III, 204, 865; construction authorized, 308; debt, 334, 736; IV, 252; expenditures, III, 410; completion of, 465; not self-supporting, 466, 506, 710; expense exceeds income, 549, 553; proposed connection with North Branch canal, Pennsylvania, 759; railroad connection with Blossburg coal mines, 786; should not be abandoned, 799; length of, 812; new locks on, 864; extension to Seneca lake, 865; usefulness of, 953; tolls, V, 66, 154, 257, 361; relation to canal system, 789; financial statement, VI, 930; VII, 5; sale recommended, 8; drainage, 517; abandonment, nuisance resulting from, 575.

    VETOES. Administration expenses, VII, 117; dam at Horseheads, 268; Corning, berme bank, repairs, X, 430; abating nuisance, cleaning Catherine creek, 789; improving channel, 946.

CHEMUNG COUNTY. Lumber from, finds market in New York, III, 815; average excise license fees, 1889, VIII, 686; authorized to make appropriation for law library at Elmira, IX, 45; highways, cost of labor system, 1892, 199; insane, care of, county and State systems compared, 228.

    VETOES. Exempting from Town Auditor's Act, VII, 554; VIII, 49; sidepaths, IX, 729.

CHEMUNG POINT. Indian treaty at, II, 328.

CHEMUNG RIVER. Canal connection with Seneca lake, III, 98.

    VETOES. Bridge over, Big Flats, VII, 578; waters at Corning, public health, IX, 719; eel-weirs in, 721; extension of dyke, Corning, X, 315; constructing dyke, Elmira, 645.

CHEMUNG AND TIOGA BRIDGE COMPANY. Charter, veto, VI, 221.

CHENANGO CANAL. Suggested, III, 70; construction recommended, 168; transportation of coal on, 204; construction provided for, 234, 303, 419, 465; progress of construction, 506; expense of, 549, 621; slow construction of, 553; completion of, 620, 669; not self-supporting, 621, 710; banks authorized to subscribe to loan for, 633; use of reservoirs for, 609; debt, 736; IV, 252; should not be abandoned, 799; length of, 812; appropriation for, charged on canal fund, IV, 200; water for Utica Lunatic Asylum, 281; tolls, V, 66, 154, 257, 361; extension, 71, 84, 533, 830; extension, resident engineer, 707; relation to canal system, 789; financial statement, VI, 930; VII, 5; commission to examine, VI, 933; sale recommended, VII, 8.

VETOES. Settling claims, VI, 508; temporary administration, appropriation, VII, 118; relative to, 265; towing path, authorizing use by Syracuse, Chenango and New York Railroad Company, 268; De Groat escheat bill, 642; damages from extension, claims, 1120; Baldwin's creek junction, cut-off, X, 644, 791.

CHENANGO COUNTY. Certain streams in, declared public highways, II, 521; Hill murder case, 635; convicts to be sent to Sing Sing prison, III, 316; refunding illegal taxes, VI, 278; Judge Prindle, charges against, 440; special county judge and district attorney, jurisdiction, veto, 692; two towns exempted from Auditor's Act, VIII, 49; average excise license fees, 1889, 686; unpaid taxes, sales under special act, 749; highways, cost of labor system, 1892, IX, 199; insane, care of, county and State systems compared, 228.

CHENANGO RIVER. Canal connection with Seneca lake, II, 902; Binghamton, supervision of bridges, VI, 150.

VETOES. Fishways at Chenango Forks, VIII, 838; fishway at Fort Dickinson, X, 787.

CHENEY, A. C. Approves Harvey claim against New York city, VIII, 1162.

CHENEY, T. APOLEON. Memorial, exploration of ancient mounds, V, 720.

CHERRY CREEK CEMETERY. Taking charge of public cemetery, veto, VI, 332.

CHESAPEAKE, THE. Attacked by British vessel, II, 616, 656; British tender of reparation, 690.

CHESAPEAKE BAY. Canal connection with Delaware river, III, 171.

CHESTER, ALBERT H. Examination of Assembly ceiling and staircase, appropriation, veto, VIII, 839.

CHESTERFIELD.
VETOES. Bridges in, VI, 556; A. P. Richardson, justice of the peace, legalizing acts, X, 63.

CHICAGO. Advantages derived from internal improvements, III, 815; fire of 1871, losses by New York insurance companies, VI, 355, 547; law library burned, New York's gift of books, 364; relation of taxation to population and property, 412; suggested selection as site of World's Fair, 1892, VIII, 931; World's Columbian Exposition located at, 933, 1077.

CHICKAMAUGA. Battlefield, Congress provides for purchase of, VIII, 1076; commission to mark position of troops, 1076.

CHICKAMAUGA AND CHATTANOOGA NATIONAL MILITARY PARK. Dedication of, IX, 575; appropriation for expenses of New York representation at dedication, 577; legislative committee, appropriation for expenses, 582.

CHIEF OF ENGINEERS, UNITED STATES ARMY. Member of board on Brooklyn pier and bulkhead lines, VI, 452.

CHIEF JUSTICE. Appointed for colony, I, 90; Crown provides salary of, 95; Atwood, relative to, 104; opinion in De Lancey's case, 214; Benjamin Pratt appointed, 662; inquiry as to destruction of property, II, 162; letter from, State Treasurer, 458; Governor Jay's letter to, Council of Appointment, 479; reply, 480; member of commission to make cessions to United States, 825.

CHIEF OF ORDNANCE. Member of Military Code Revision Commission, VII, 428.

CHIEF WARRIOR. Seneca chief, joins in address to Governor, II, 943.

CHIESA, JOHN. Relief, extending time to sue for personal injuries, veto, X, 473.

CHILDREN. When entitled to father's bounty land, I, 598; instruction in forms of government, III, 299; of foreigners, schools for, 768, 947; father natural guardian of, 845; in charitable institutions, large percentage foreign born, 834; New York House of Refuge, only reform school for girls, IV, 789; large number not in school, 795, 839; V, 13; colored, education of, communication from New York Society, 108; in public schools, vaccination of, 189; of American women marrying foreigners, status of, VI, 365; adoption, Deming case, 559; labor, compulsory education, 617; in poorhouses, investigation of condition, 724; limiting commitments to poorhouses, 724; vested rights, insurance of father's life, VII, 80; entitled to common school education, 295; of Indians, provision for education, 709; in certain institutions, employment by contract prohibited, 957; child labor, regulation of, VIII, 163, 477; employment, act regulating, 163; IX, 163; orphan, care of, VIII, 465; compulsory education, right of State, IX, 828; not to be employed in certain manufactories, X, 7; colored, equal educational rights,

CHILDREN — *(Continued).*

act of 1900, 145; laws need reform, 515; employment acts of 1903, 515; 1905, 738; commitment of girls to Randall's Island and Rochester Industrial School discontinued, 726; State Training School for Girls at Hudson, 726; State Training School for Boys, provision for, 726, 863; employed in factories, ascertaining age, 738; under certain age not to sell newspapers, 739; limiting hours of labor, 860; when not to be employed in mines or quarries, 860.

VETOES. Rights of, interference with, IX, 528; adoption, amending act, VI, 816; adoption, regulation, VII, 350; legitimizing birth, Ehlers case, 633; employment by contract in public institutions, 764; protection of, 804; preventing sale of cigarettes to, 1108; VIII, 131, 633; illegitimate, right of inheritance, VII, 1126; truants, school for, Brooklyn, VIII, 293; guardians, appointment in certain cases, 631; restricting labor of, compulsory education, 819; employment in manufacturing establishments, 837; indigent, Westchester county, care of, 1159; Boy's Industrial Home, establishing, IX, 246; employment in brickyards, 477; placing out, regulations by State Board of Charities, 812; custody of, amending Code, 860; Poppenhusen Institution at College Point, relative to, X, 700; boys' municipal clubhouses, New York, 712; special rate of fare on street railroads, 882.

CHILDREN'S AID SOCIETY. Industrial school established by, share in common school fund, 382.

CHILDREN'S AID SOCIETY, ROCHESTER. Charter, veto, IX, 450.

CHILDS, FRANCIS. Alleged improper publication by, II, 274.

CHILDS, J. MORRIS. Assignee of patent of Savage magazine rifle, IX, 637.

CHILDS, O. W. Member of Board of Engineers, New York harbor defense, V, 568.

CHILI. Participation in Cotton States Exposition, IX, 581.

CHINA. Silk culture in, III, 946; Chinese prisoners, Essex county, veto, X, 701, 708.

CHINESE SOCIETY, NEW YORK. Charter, veto, VIII, 637.

CHITTENANGO. Polytechnic school at, III, 298.

CHITTENANGO CREEK. Fishway in, amending act, veto, VIII, 713; new act passed.

CHITTENDEN, ELI. Claim, Averill iron ore bed, V, 168.

CHITTENDEN, THOMAS. Governor of Vermont, letter from, relative to new State government, II, 135, 142; letter to Congress, 136; papers from, 313.

CHOATE, JOSEPH H. Opinion, voter's freedom of selection of candidate cannot be restricted by form of ballot, IX, 395, 479; communication to Governor relative to appointment of William Church Osborn as State commissioner in lunacy, X, 42.

CHOLERA. Expected epidemic of, III, 394; epidemic in 1832, 399; at Mount Pleasant prison, 401; prevalence of, IV, 452; Asiatic epidemic, 468; no statistics, 506; on emigrant ships, 719; classed as a quarantine disease, V, 418; appearance in New York, 700, 717, 765; patients in floating hospital, 700; prevention of, Legislature asks Federal aid, 701; cold weather does not prevent, 766; expected visitation of, 863; report, 1872, VI, 359; 1873, 626; epidemic, 1892, IX, 204, 293; inefficient measures of prevention by consuls at foreign ports, 208; animals dying from, when State not liable, 270; preventive measures, 1893, 327.

CHONONDADO INDIANS. Invited to join Indian conference, I, 354.

CHRISTIAN CHURCH, TONAWANDA. Relief, veto, VI, 185.

CHRISTIAN COMMISSION. Aid to soldiers, V, 685.

CHRISTMAS. A public holiday, VI, 679.

CHURCH, ANN. Widow of Chief Judge Church, appropriation for, VII, 449.

CHURCH, CHAPMAN. Relief of estate, veto, V, 149.

CHURCH, SANFORD E. Comptroller, joins in instructions to Captain Benham, quarantine affairs, V, 100; chief judge, Court of Appeals, letter to Governor on taxpayer's bill, VI, 431; VIII, 1050; death of, VII, 447; legislative action, appropriation for widow, 449; law library, relative to, veto, 902.

CHURCH OF ENGLAND. In colony, I, 38, 55, 115.

CHURCHES. In colony mostly built by volunteer subscription, I, 291; for Mohawks at Canajoharie, 554; congregation at Hopewell request grant of land, II, 82; stealing from, death penalty, 363; for St. Regis Indians, 520; for Oneida Indians, 894, 930, 951, 976; number and value of, V, 11; should be exempt from taxation, VII, 25.

VETOES. Appropriations from sale of Harlem common lands, II, 1111; declaring certain churches extinct, VII, 265; Methodist Episcopal Home, New York, relative to, 509; New York, erection of stables near, IX, 520; X, 807; translation of early ecclesiastical documents, 298; Methodist Episcopal, transfers and conveyances, 704.

CHURCH INSURANCE ASSOCIATION. Amending charter, X, 278.

CHURCH OF THE RESURRECTION, NEW YORK. Relief from assessments, veto, VI, 711.

CHURCH WARDENS. Power to call dissenting minister, I, 55.

CICERO. Draining certain lands, veto, VI, 189.

CIDER. Definition of, VIII, 354.

CIGARETTES. Preventing sale to children, veto, VII, 1108; VIII, 131, 633.

CIGARS. Preventing sale to children, veto, VIII, 633.

CINCINNATI. Relation of taxation to population and property, VI, 412.

CIRCUIT. Judicial, under second Constitution, III, 5; established, 5.

CIRCUIT JUDGE. Office created, III, 5; IV, 136; vested with chancery jurisdiction, III, 5; compensation, 5, 256; powers, 6; proposition to abolish office, 493, 719, 872.

CITATIONS. Publication of, veto, VI, 509.

CITIES. Inherent qualities of growth, III, 75; limiting financial operations, IV, 563, 615, 701, 730; V, 849; VI, 825; VII, 31, 637; stocks not suitable for bank securities, IV, 704, 731; inferior courts recommended in, 856; judicial officers, how chosen, V, 138; bounties for volunteers, 455; board of relief for soldiers, 490; concentration of population in, 776; right of local government, VI, 29, 31; no taxation without representation, 33; executive responsibility in, 34, 129; minority representation in local government, 34; fire, hook and ladder and hose companies, 56; boards of excise, 127; charters need revision, 129; eminent domain, waterworks, 285; street processions, 374; charters should be permanent, 383; uniform charters not practicable, 402; report of indebtedness, 826; essential conditions of home rule, 835; New York charters, historical sketch, 837; early method of preparing charters, 841; commission on municipal reform, 844, 951; large indebtedness, 917; limiting indebtedness, constitutional provisions, 917; proposed constitutional amendment, VII, 134; elections, separation from State and national, 134; minority representation, proposed amendment, 136; separate companies of National Guard, 155; Legislature should not prescribe arbitrary payments to charitable institutions, 335; registration of voters, 435; property held for charitable purposes, 526; proposed constitutional amendment, 1882, not adopted, 728; street railroads, operation and extension, act relative to, 1063; elections, constitutional provision, VIII, 17; civil service regulations, 18, 148; indebtedness limited, amendment, 1884, 27, 161, 184; General Building Law recommended, 36; civil service, good effect in local administration, 148; home rule recommended, 160; street railroads, act relative to, 200; franchise, sale at auction, 200; tenement-houses, regulating construction and supervision, 317; general statutes needed, 346; statement of excise licenses, 1887, 359; uniform

CITIES — (*Continued*).

laws recommended, 449; excise license fees, 1889, 685; illuminating gas, regulating price, 1021; not included in county road
system, 1042; police matrons, act of 1891, 1147; home rule,
necessary in municipal reform, IX, 29; large number of people
living in, 29; schools, instruction in music, 116; consolidation
of New York and Brooklyn, 300; special city laws, hearings,
constitutional provision, 1894, 339, 547, 677, 696; special laws,
hearings, 547, 617; divided into three classes, 547; payments
to charitable institutions, 551; registration of voters, 555;
standard of teachers' qualifications, 564; use of Davis voting
machine authorized, 665; large number of laws relating to,
1895, 677; second and third classes, commissions on general
laws for, 677; second-class, general act, 1898, 678; first-class,
population limit reduced, 1907, 678; enumeration, certificate of
population to be filed by Secretary of State, 678; liquor tax
under act of 1896, 700; local option, 701; X, 355; bi-partisan
election boards, act of 1898, IX, 877; proposed uniform system of accounting, X, 25; should be considered a unit in
equalizing assessments, 262; local option, proposed extension
to, 736, 854.

VETOES. Bounties, legalizing, V, 673; local option, VI, 568; to
provide for rapid transit, 905; public burdens, VII, 252; policemen and district telegraph companies, 268; processions and
parades, music, 335; streets in adjoining territory, 416;
armorers in, 417; mechanic's lien, amending act, 665, 666;
street railroads, maintenance and operation, 793, 894; waterworks companies, 807; Amsterdam charter, 1014; horse cars,
regulating hours of conductors and drivers, 1109; electrical
subways, amending act, VIII, 871; Senate investigation, 1890,
various services to committee, 1140; public health and nuisances, IX, 151; hours of labor on street railroads, 266;
teachers' training classes, 482; coal, protection of purchasers,
amending act, 522; regulating horseshoeing in certain, 622;
Davis voting machine, authorizing use of, 626; free public
employment bureaus, establishing, 630; plumbers, registration
and supervision, amending act, 631, 729, 810; civil service,
assistant city attorney, or corporation counsel, exemption from
examination, 715; uniform fire department in certain, compensation of officers, 727; streets and highways in certain,
improvement, 780; second-class, general charter, 791; adult
blind, relative to, 791, 866; first-class, railroads, right of way,
use of, 791; first-class, banks in, bonds for security of certain

CITIES, VETOES — (*Continued*).

depositors, 791; street railroads, percentages payable by, 865; third-class, contracts for lighting streets, 869; laborers on buildings in, protection of, X, 62; receivers of taxes, proceedings by, 272; railroad aid claims, hearing by Court of Claims, amending act, 315; cemeteries, removal and reinterment of bodies, moving and resetting monuments, etc., 448; regulating price of electricity in certain, 585; lease of buildings to G. A. R. posts, 585; negligence, limiting time to commence action, 709; labor, protection of persons employed on buildings, 760, new bill passed; second and third classes, reports of financial conditions, amending act, 816.

CITIZENS. Roman, privileges of, not accorded to colonists, I, 491; rights of, II, 40, 60, 250, 284, 316; V, 471; State entitled to services of, II, 132; right of appeal to courts, 173; free, as basis of apportionment of public expenses, 184, 276; rights under tax laws, 212, 373, 388, 402, 418; rights, as result of war, 215; no right without a remedy, 235; freedmen, rights of, 237, 239; interference with judgments, 288; bill of rights, taxing power, 315; public funds, loan to, 320; eligibility to office, 438, 439; wills, 466; right of petition, 508; private property taken for public use, compensation, 522, 585, 646; detention of foreign vessels, 540; privileges and immunities, insurance, 613; corporations are not, 613; restrictions on right of suffrage, 686; presumed to be free, 687; arrest without warrant, 820; limiting to natives the right to hold office, proposed amendment, 828; right to marry, 921; religious toleration, Shakers, 921; husband's interest in legacy of wife, III, 262; legislative interference with rights of, 263; duty to sustain government, 432; State loan to, 481, 491, 496; pursuits of, Legislature should not interfere with, 554; duty to maintain neutral foreign relations, 690; term does not include negroes (Georgia), IV, 46; colored, unlawful imprisonment of (Maine), 48; duty to respond to sheriff's call for aid, 145; Tuscarora Indians protest against citizenship, 507; proposed amendment, excluding negroes from rights of, V, 355; duty to perform military service, 456; rights, how affected by Civil War, 466; abduction for political offenses, 466; fourteenth amendment, 790; naturalization of alien soldiers, VI, 40; need of education, VII, 20; duty to accept public office, 1123; naturalized, registration, production of papers, VIII, 20, 296; property in intoxicating liquors, 367; duty to vote, 674, 676; right to carry on business, IX, 351; duty to defend State, X,

XI—20

Citizens — (*Continued*).

    217, 510; preference in employment on public works, 424; written consent to use of name on ballots at primary elections, 709; should participate in making party nominations, 847.

Vetoes. Claims against other States, VII, 250; equal protection of the laws, oleomargarine, 591; patriotism, encouragement of, VIII, 1040; admission of foreigner to practice as attorney, X, 262; admission to bar examinations, 311.

Citizens Loan Agency and Guarantee Company.

    Vetoes. Changing name, VIII, 981; amending charter, IX, 257.

City Hall. In New York, act for erection of, I, 83; Assembly meets at, 240.

City Loan and Trust Company, New York. Amending charter, veto, VI, 336.

Civil Code. Proposed, submission to Legislature, V, 597; report of commission, VI, 29; adopted in Territories, 29; submitted to Statutory Revision Commission, 118; veto, VII, 348, 794; Senate Committee on Revision, printing for, veto, 493.

Civil Death. Described, II, 336; results from imprisonment for life, 399, 427; III, 863.

" Civil Liberty and Self-Government." (Lieber.) Quoted, supervision of elections, V, 514.

Civil List. Printing and distributing, veto, VIII, 1038.

Civil Service. See also Veterans. Proper qualifications of officers, III, 55; in prison administration, 290; patronage in canal department, IV, 376; penal and charitable institutions, appointments should not be subject to political influence, 722; appointment of military instructors, V, 53; examinations for military appointments, 403; method of selecting State prison inspectors, 437; prison management should be free from partisan influence, 697, 757; VI, 18, 234; State prisons, no appointments on ground of political partisanship, VII, 9; partisan appointments prohibited, 52; President Garfield's views, 561; Binghamton police, unlimited tenure, 753; State commission created, 838; constitutional provision, 838; VIII, 151; IX, 549, 560, 663, 840; X, 741; political assessments prohibited, VII, 838; judicial construction, 838; not applicable to department of public works, 838; status of veterans, 838; Silas W. Burt, chief examiner, 976; operation of new system, 976; in New York and Brooklyn, 976; veterans, preference of, 977; VIII, 19, 151; IX, 560; X, 20; new capitol, political tests in employment prohibited, VII, 982; extended to cities, VIII, 18; practical tests suggested, 19; orderlies and watchmen in new

CIVIL SERVICE — (*Continued*).

capitol, veterans preferred, 20; should apply to census enumerators, 42, 57, 68; classified, number of positions in, 148; good effects in cities, 148; New York leads in establishing system, VII, 976; VIII, 20, 149; principles of system, 150; appointments to be certified by commission, mandamus authorized, IX, 311; application in counties and villages, 663; protection of veterans, act of 1896, 664; principles on which examinations should be based, 749; merit and fitness, two examinations required, act of 1897, 750, 756, 838; X, 18, 118; New York, application of act of 1897, IX, 838; no office-holding class should be created, 839; new rules, 1897, 842; enlarging powers and opportunities of commission, 843; uniform system needed, X, 18; difficulty in administering the Double Examination Law of 1897, 18; revision of 1899, 20, 42; judicial construction, 20; new rules, 118; in cities, 118; should be applied to canals, 141; veterans, preference, removals, act of 1902, 419; limiting jurisdiction of courts, 517; application to appointments on Canal Advisory Board, 596; system should be extended to large counties, 742; should be extended to New York House of Refuge, 742.

VETOES. Canal department, appointment, complaints, VII, 238; exempting physicians from examinations for municipal appointments, IX, 230; preference, persons holding life saving medals, 353; cities, assistant attorney or corporation counsel, exemption from examination, 715; law department, amending act, 724; examinations, residence of candidates, 816; New York, anti-toxin accountant, compensation, X, 160, New York, Municipal Court attendants, compensation, 168, 474; New York, Garvey, superintendent of Bellevue Hospital Dispensary, compensation, 169; New York finance department, city magistrate's court, claims for services, 172; exemptions, 309; Rochester, police detectives, exemption from examination, 470; New York, Municipal Court attendant, compensation, 473; examinations, qualifications of applicants, 520, 812, 952; New York fire department, volunteers, preference, 580; veterans, amending act, 592, 710, 714; several New York bills, 690; claims of persons, employed in violation of law, 773; veterans, 805; pensions for retiring veterans, 924.

CLAESEN, LAWRENCE. Appropriation for, I, 134; letter from, 170; Indian interpreter, report from, 176; report of visit to Onondagas, 177; communication from, relative to Indian negotiations, 206; requests increase of salary, 211; offers to instruct Indian youth, 211.

Claims. State, against corporations, enforcement of, IV, 262.

    Vetoes. Citizens, claims against other States, VII, 250; Cottman, New York, proof of, 552.

Claims Against State. Of militia, payment of, II, 13, 96; general, 108; Governor Clinton, for personal expenses, 161; James Hamilton, commissary, 185; subsistence furnished by residents on frontiers, 189; by United States, act acceding to, 253; rapid payment of, 206; act for payment of, 312; Revolutionary, difficulties relating to, 539; militia service, War of 1812, 946; canal damages, IV, 437; how established, Governor's certificate, V, 292; canal awards, 591; 32d Regiment, 642; militia certificates, War of 1812, redemption of, VI, 113, 654; canals, powers of canal appraisers, 119; stale, when re-examination should not be permitted, 219; limitations, amendment, 1874, 540; VII, 599, 602, 606, 644, 773, 781, 801, 1120; IX, 66; must be audited, amendment of 1874, VI, 875; VII, 81, 83, 86, 88, 158, 227, 230, 462, 463, 479, 782, 792, 850, 922; printing public documents and reports, 495; limitation, Legislature cannot extend time, Sharpe claim, 773; State Board of Claims created, 821; limitation fixed at two years, VIII, 977; audit Harvey claim, IX, 142; Legislature cannot revive claim or waive limitation, 370.

    Vetoes. Payment, V, 41, passed over veto; floods in Mohawk river, 725; Auburn assessments, VI, 869; Syracuse armory, 875; Bristol, 875; Swift, contractor, quarantine buildings, VII, 373; Danolds, contractor, Elmira Reformatory, 375; Worthington, contractor, 381; Senate investigating committee, expenses, 462; Low, Middletown asylum, 665; contractors, hearing certain claims, 666; relative to, 805; animals slaughtered to prevent spread of disease, evidence, VIII, 730; counties, refunding certain taxes, 755, new bill passed; Steuben county, Redding trial, 888; by counties for value of insane asylums, Court of Claims, IX, 858; Donavan claim, X, 63.

    Audit. Preparing railroad report, VII, 778; State Botanist, expenses, 779; Kirkham, hospital ships, 929; captain of the port and harbormasters, New York, compensation, 1055; subordinates and employees in canal department, appropriation, 1896, IX, 716; personal injuries received on canal, Dinehart case, X, 255.

CLAIMS AGAINST STATE, VETOES — (*Continued*).

LIMITATION. Chenango canal, extension, VII, 1120; Featherstone claim, 1121; Costello and Curtis, 1124; Fingar, VIII, 1125; Milliete claim, 1125; IX, 66; Hasbrouck, VIII, 1128; Bassler claim, IX, 66; Powell and others, 119; Jarvis, 429; McIntyre, 452.

CLAIMS AGAINST UNITED STATES. Settlement of, recommended, II, 52, 201; act to provide for settlement of, 201; resolution relating to, 570; for fortifications, 667; War of 1812, 757, 789, 817, 867, 919, 986, 999, 1105, 1122; III, 14, 36, 106, 145, 177, 308, 349, 386, 978; V, 175, 457, 522; VI, 113, 358; correspondence relative to, II, 924, 1080; estimated amount of, III, 15; agent appointed, 106; report of agent, 145; Canadian disturbance, 691, 694; Hudson river improvement, V, 40, 56, 453; Buffalo basin, 71; Civil War, harbor defenses, 410; arms furnished by State, 415; soldiers after close of Civil War, 683, 684; Civil War, 702, 754, 773, 831; VI, 357, 621; commission appointed, V, 756; redemption of militia certificates, War of 1812, VI, 113, 903; payments on, 236, 621, 903; militia, certificates of service, 1812, veto, 902; States' property rights, War of 1812, commission created, VII, 601.

CLARENCE.

VETOES. Union School District No. 1, teachers' employment fund, VI, 484, amended bill passed; drainage, X, 698.

CLARENDON, EARL OF. Caveat against, bill for public debts, I, 175.

" CLARENDON STATE PAPERS." Quotation from preface, IV, 190.

CLARK, A. RALPH. Board of Claims, veto, VIII, 1166.

CLARK, ERSKINE G. Relief, veto, VI, 185.

CLARK, LOT. Suggested appointment as postmaster at Oxford, II, 1070.

CLARK, MYRON H. Governor, portrait, IV, 780.

1855. Annual message, IV, 780; finances, 780; canal revenues, 781; school funds, 782; canal income, 782; premium on canal enlargement loan, 783; canal contracts, 783; banking associations, 784; importance of penal institutions, 785; classification of offenses and criminals, 785; financial condition of prisons, 785; prison investigating commission, 786; Auburn prison self-supporting, 786; detention of witnesses, 787; commutation of sentences for good behavior, 787; procedure in pardon cases, 788; house of refuge, 789; State lunatic asylum, 789; additional asylum for insane recommended, 791; idiot asylum, 791; Institution for the Blind, 792; Institution for Instruction of the Deaf and Dumb, 792; emigration, 793; gifts to State Library, 793; public education, 794; amount expended for public schools, 795; number of children not attending schools,

CLARK, MYRON H., 1855 — (*Continued*).

795; rate bill, 796; supervision and visitation of common schools, 797; office of town superintendent abolished, 797; free academy in New York, 798; union schools, 799; revision of excise laws, 799; prohibition, 800; modification of usury laws, 802; extravagant bonding of railroads, 805; corporations not to plead usury, 805; railroads, 805; loans of municipal credit to railroad companies, 805; influence of New York board of brokers, 806; business of brokers, 806; time sales of securities, 807; use of ballot boxes, 808; Lemmon slave case, 809; proper tariff regulations, 812; repeal of Missouri Compromise, 813; Rhode Island resolutions, 817; Boston Corners ceded to New York, 817; Michigan resolutions, 817; canal revenues, 818; rapid increase of revenues, 819; diversion of canal revenues for payment of State debt, 819; effect of railroad competition on canal revenues, 820; railroad tolls abolished, 820; loans for interest condemned, 821; effect of railroad competition, 822; recommends reimposition of railroad tolls, 823; New Jersey resolutions, 823; Arkansas resolutions, 824; remonstrance against incorporation of Hellgate Navigation Company, 824; resolutions against extension of slavery, 827.

VETOES. New York and Shawangunk Mining Company, amending charter, IV, 823; illegal voting, New York city, 825; Newark and Rosendale Lime and Cement Manufacturing Company, purchasing land, 827.

1856. Annual message, IV, 830; finances, 830; general fund, 830; school funds, 831; sinking funds, 831; canal finances, 832; canal tolls, 832; recommends extension of term of credit on State debt, 833; loan for canal enlargement, 834; railroads, 835; Board of Railroad Commissioners, 836; banks, 836; amount of circulating notes, 837; amount of safety fund, 837; call loans upon stock securities, 838; common school statistics, 838; supervision of academies, 840; town boards of education, 840; high schools, 840; annual reports, 841; commissioners of school funds, 841; free schools, 842; repugnance to rate bill system, 842; agricultural department in normal schools, 843; suggests removal of Albany normal school, 843; State Library, 844; condition of State prisons, 844; commutation for good behavior, 844; county jails, 845; procedure in pardon cases, 845; graduation of penalties, 845; houses of refuge, 846; care of insane, 847; recommends new insane asylum, 848; instruction of deaf and dumb, 848; education of the blind, 848; asylum for idiots, 849; supervision of benevolent institutions receiving State aid, 849; emigration, 849; Castle Garden emi-

CLARK, MYRON H., 1856 — (*Continued*).

grant landing depot, 851; epidemic in Virginia, 852; quarantine, 852; State Agricultural College, 853; salt manufacture, 853; condition of militia, 854; sale of New York arsenal, 854; revision of criminal laws, 855; inferior courts for cities, 856; tribunals of conciliation, 856; census returns, 856; additional judicial district, 857; increasing number of justices in first judicial district, 857; claim of Stockbridge Indians, 857; encroachments on New York harbor, 857; Prohibitory Act of 1855, 858; Lemmon slave case, 860; organization of Kansas and Nebraska, 860; repeal of Missouri Compromise, 861; struggle in Kansas over slavery, 861; Connecticut boundary, 863; V, 112; letter from Governor of Kansas, IV, 863; Alabama resolutions, 864; Rhode Island resolutions, 865; Vermont resolutions, 865; New Jersey resolutions, 866; condition of quarantine buildings, 866; alien commutation fund, 866; commissioners of emigration ask aid from Legislature, 867; official service, I, pref., XIII.

CLARK, SIMEON. Member of commission on St. Regis river improvement, VIII, 115.

CLARK, THOMAS C. Requests approval of Harvey rapid transit bill, VIII, 125; examination of Assembly stone arch vault, appropriation, veto, 840.

CLARKE, A. B. Letter from, schools, V, 108.

CLARKE, JOHN J. Claim against New York, veto, VIII, 883.

CLARKE, GEORGE. President of council, assumes executive authority, I, 254; appointed Lieutenant-Governor, 255.

OPENING SPEECH. Twentieth Assembly, tenth session, I, 255; situation in colony, 255; deficiency in revenue, 255; ship building, 255; hemp cultivation, 255, 256; market for flour, 256; completion of fortifications, 256; condition of Fort Hunter, 256; new fort in Mohawk valley, 256, 258; Oswego tradinghouse, 257; smith and presents for Senecas, 257; Council's address to, as President, 257; petition for appointment of Kerr as surgeon at Oswego, 258; receives commission as Lieutenant-Governor, 255; address to Crown, 258; prorogues Assembly, 258.

OPENING SPEECH. Twentieth Assembly, eleventh session, I, 259; deficiency in revenue, 259; trade conditions, 259; hemp, ship building and iron, 260; frontier defense, 260; repairs at Fort George, 260; slaves learning trades, 260; encouraging manufactures, 260, 266; thanks Council for address, 261; dissolves Assembly, 262.

CLARKE, GEORGE — (*Continued*).

> OPENING SPEECH. Twenty-first Assembly, first session, I, 262; to
> meet Six Nations at Albany, 262, 265; to urge revocation of
> Seneca permit to Frenchmen for erecting building at Tieron-
> dequat, 262, 265; deficiency of revenue, 264; new act passed,
> 264; Oswego trading-house, 264; sergeant-at-arms for Assembly,
> 266; address to, 266; Assembly elections and terms of office,
> 266, 267, 271; vetoed by King, 267, 278, 279; agent at London,
> 267; new courts, 267; appropriations to be annual, 267; im-
> proved condition in colony, 267, 268; effect of failure to pro-
> rogue Assembly, 268.

> OPENING SPEECH. Twenty-first Assembly, second session, I, 269;
> death of Queen Caroline, 269; support of government, 269;
> bills of credit, 269; necessity of colonial agent at London, 270;
> completing fortifications, 270; payment of persons serving in
> Indian country, 270; Bermuda objects to Tonnage Act, 271;
> French encroachments on northern frontier, 271; proposes fort
> and settlements at Wood's creek, 272; danger of French aggres-
> sions, 272; urges acquisition of Tierondequat, 272; different
> subjects not to be united in same bill, 272; differences with
> Assembly as to revenue bills, 273; dissolves Assembly, 275.

> OPENING SPEECH. Twenty-second Assembly, first session, 275; birth
> of prince, 275; support of government, 277; repair of forti-
> fications, 277; proposed acquisition of land for fort at Tieronde-
> quat, 277, 548; proposed conference with Six Nations, 278, 286;
> proposed settlements north of Saratoga, 278; new Jury Law,
> 278; urges legislation conforming to English laws, 279.

> OPENING SPEECH. Twenty-second Assembly, second session, I, 280;
> completion of battery at New York, 280; urges revival of ship
> building, 280; Massachusetts boundary, 282, 283; supplies for
> garrisons, 282; estimated expense of battery at New York, 283;
> victuallers at Oswego, payment of, 283; recommends imitation
> of parliamentary financial methods, 283.

> OPENING SPEECH. Twenty-second Assembly, third session, I, 285;
> Revenue and Fortification Acts passed, 285; King approves Par-
> tition Act, 285; expected visit from English Adjutant-General,
> 286.

> OPENING SPEECH. Twenty-second Assembly, fourth session, I, 286;
> war against Spain, 286; expedition against West Indies, 287;
> military preparations, 287; instruction as to expedition against
> West Indies, 288.

CLARKE, GEORGE — (*Continued*).

OPENING SPEECH. Twenty-second Assembly, fifth session, I, 289; raising additional volunteers, 289, 290; defense of Oswego, 290; desertions from army and navy, 290; Mohawk chapel, 290; new Revenue Act, 291; prevention of illicit trade, 291; military stores, 292; royal approval of Oyster Bay Partition Act, 292.

OPENING SPEECH. Twenty-second Assembly, sixth session, I, 292; New York receives special royal favors, 292; royal prerogatives, 293; functions of revenue officers, 293; English jealousy of colony, 294; expected rupture with France, 295; urges preparations for defense of colony, 295; strengthening Oswego, 296; proposed conference with Six Nations, 296; employing Indians as spies, 296; reorganizing militia, 297; urges appointment of colonial agent, 297; fire destroys public buildings, 297; precautions against fires, 298; answer to Assembly's address, 298; Duke of Newcastle's instructions relative to recruits, 299; frontier affairs, 300.

OPENING SPEECH. Twenty-second Assembly, seventh session, I, 301; supplies for expedition, 301; English army in Cuba, 302; inspection of commodities, 302; military watches, 302; protests against revenue bills for one year only, 303; recommends doubling Oswego garrison, 304; relations with Indians, 304; troops for Spanish expedition, 304; declines to join in address to King requesting aid in rebuilding Governor's house, 304.

OPENING SPEECH. Twenty-second Assembly, eighth session, I, 305; preparing for defense of New York, 305; expense of transporting ordnance, 305; urges restoration of public buildings, 306; recruits for expedition, 306; smith for Indian tribes, 306; equalizing militia service, 306.

OPENING SPEECH. Twenty-second Assembly, ninth session, I, 307; Act for Support of Government, 307; support of Oswego garrison, 308; recruits for West Indies, 308; new Militia Act, 309.

OPENING SPEECH. Twenty-second Assembly, tenth session, I, 309; urges military preparations for defense, 309, 310; increasing provision for Indian presents, 310; succeeded by Governor Clinton, 310; patent of land, Montgomery county, IV, 331; official service, I, pref., X.

CLARKE, GEORGE. Title to land, investigation of, II, 883; suit of, papers in, 950.

CLARKE, GEORGE, JR. Secretary of province, communication from, relative to Tonnage Act, I, 271.

CLARKE, STEPHEN. Sells land to State for idiot asylum, IV, 555.

CLARK AND SKINNER CANAL, BUFFALO. Docking, VI, 861.

VETOES. Ohio street bridge, 861; bridge at Scott street, 1036; VII, 95; abating nuisance, X, 634.

CLARKSON, MATTHEW, GENERAL. Commissioner on New York fortifications, report, II, 370, 390; report on arms, 371.

CLARKSON, MATTHEW. Secretary of the colony, I, 20.

CLARKSON CEMETERY. Charter, veto, VI, 325.

CLARKSTOWN. Ferry to Mount Pleasant, veto, II, 476.

CLARKSVILLE. Resistance to process, Van Rensselaer rent, III, 828, 835.

CLARY, T. F. C. Counsel to Assembly Committee on Privileges and Elections, appropriation, veto, X, 796.

CLAY.

VETOES. Draining certain lands, VI, 189; straightening Mud creek, VII, 414.

CLAY, HENRY. Death of, IV, 641.

CLAY, JAMES B. Delegate from Kentucky to Washington Peace Convention, V, 329.

CLAYTON.

VETOES. Aid to Utica and Black River Railroad Company, amending act, VI, 92; amending Village Act of 1847, VII, 664.

CLEEVER, JOSEPH. Court of Claims, injuries while inmate of State Industrial School, veto, X, 707.

CLERGYMEN. See MINISTERS.

CLERK. Of Supreme Court, appointment of deputy, II, 243; of court, not to practice as attorney, 395; of courts, under first Constitution, appointment and removal, 500; Supreme Court, act relating to, 756; court and commission of appeals, VI, 124; of courts in certain counties, 268.

VETOES. New York courts, IX, 875; Kings County Court, relief, X, 59; New York Municipal Court, clerks and assistants, 60; grand jury, Madison county, 61; town, administering oath at primary elections, 161; Kings county, register's office, salaries, 449; special deputy, Appellate Division, first department, 717.

CLERK'S MANUAL.

VETOES. For Assembly clerk, VII, 494; for Statutory Revision Commission, 494; printing, VIII, 118.

CLEVELAND, GROVER. Governor, portrait, VII, 815.

1883. Annual message, VII, 815; finances, 815; receipts and expenditures, 816; revision of tax laws, 816; canals, 817; abolition of canal tolls, 818; tax for canal purposes, 818; canal appraisers and auditor, 819; State Board of Claims, 820; public education, 821; banks, 822; savings banks, 822; trust, loan and mortgage companies, 823; guaranty com-

CLEVELAND, GROVER, 1883 — (*Continued*).

panies, 823; supervision of banks, 823; insurance, 824; National Guard, 826; camp of instruction, 826; State prisons, 827; abolition of contract labor, 828; charitable institutions, 828; alien paupers returned to various countries of Europe, 830; insane, 830; frequent examination of charitable institutions, 831; immigration, 831; Federal Immigrant Tax Act, 832; quarantine and health officer, 833; harbor masters and captain of the port of New York, 834; port wardens and pilotage, 835; new capitol, 835; condition of Assembly chamber ceiling, 836; judicial amendment, 837; congressional apportionment, 837; reform in civil service, 838; municipal government, 839; primary elections, 839; special legislation, 839; urges confirmation of appointment of commissioner of immigration, 888.

MEMORANDUMS OF APPROVAL. Supreme Court, increasing number of justices, VII, 890; New York, increasing water supply, 900.

VETOES. Montgomery county, borrowing money, VII, 841; Hector, legalizing time of town meeting, 842; Elmira, damages for defective streets, 843; Darwin R. Barker Library Association, Fredonia, charter, 845; Chautauqua county, soldiers and sailors' monument, 845; railroads, Jefferson and St. Lawrence counties, stocks, relief from existing burdens, 847; Fayetteville, purchasing fire apparatus, 848; Mechanicville, purchasing fire apparatus, 849; Moore claim, State Board of Audit, 849; New York, elevated railroads, fares, 850; Schuyler county, borrowing money, county buildings, 859; Fulton county, board of supervisors, equalizing representation, 860; Oswego Falls, amending village charter, 861; Long Island City, Jackson avenue improvement, 862; notaries public, additional, 863; VIII, 44; gaslight companies, use of electricity, VII, 864; taxes, Richmond county, extending time for collection, 866; Onondaga county, disposing of old clerk's office and lot, 867; Catskill Mountain National Camp Meeting Association of the Methodist Episcopal Church, New York Conference, charter, 867; trusts for charitable purposes, 868; Utica Ice Company, limited, extending time for payment of capital stock, 869; Perry, cemeteries, reinterment of bodies, 870; Buffalo, fire department, 870; notes action as mayor of Buffalo, 871; New York, public baths, 873; First National Bank, Buffalo, settlement of claims against sureties, 874; item in appro-

CLEVELAND, GROVER, 1883, VETOES — (*Continued*).

    priation bill, establishing reference points, 874; Oatka Hose
Company, Leroy, charter, 877; United States deposit fund,
loan commissioners, Delaware county, sale of judgment,
877; taxes, Hornellsville, extending time for collection, 878;
Lyons, revising charter, 878; First Congregational and First
Baptist church, Kendall, sale and division of property,
881; 1st Regiment, Mexican volunteers, 882; supervisors,
compensation, 883; board of claims, Conkling, 884; highways, opening in one town on application of freeholders in
another town, 885; highways, Washington county, special,
886; board of claims, Clinton county, prison goods, 887;
Albany county clerk, filing with assessors certificates of sale
of property, 888; fire insurance companies, securities and
investments, 891; Code of Civil Procedure, Court of Appeals, reports, 892; savings banks, enlarging scope of investments, 893; street railroads, maintenance and operation
in cities, towns and villages, 894, 1065; items in supply
bill, 901; item in canal appropriation bill, 930; omnibus
veto, 930.

1884. Annual message, VII, 938; unnecessary legislative recesses,
939; too much special legislation, 939; finances, 940; reduction of taxes, 942; revision of tax laws, 942; inequality
of assessment of personal property and real estate, 942;
deduction of debts, 943; canals, 944; effect of abolition
of tolls, 945; public education, common school statistics,
946; colleges and academies, 947; banks, 947; loan, mortgage, guaranty and indemnity companies, 949; State supervision of banks, 949; insurance, 950; National Guard, 951;
uniforms for National Guard, 952; camp of instruction,
952; new armories, 953; amendments to Military Code,
953; State prisons, 954; indeterminate sentences, Elmira
Reformatory, 955; abolition of contract labor system, 957;
charitable institutions, 957; number of insane, 958; State
paupers, 959; supervision of charitable institutions, 959;
report of agent to investigate condition of charitable institutions, 962; commissioner to supervise and control
charitable institutions, 964; emigration, 965; commissioner
of emigration, 966; quarantine and health officer, 966; Senate
investigating committee, health officer, fees, 966; political
contributions by health officer, New York, 968; permanent
salary for health officer, 968; harbor masters, 969; pilotage

CLEVELAND, GROVER, 1884 — (*Continued*).

fees, 970; Railroad Commission, 971; railroad accidents, fatalities and injuries, 972; railroad grade crossings, 972; freight rates, 973; supervision of corporations, 974; civil service, 975; Bureau of Military Statistics, 977; Primary Election Law, 978; Board of Claims, 978; new capitol, 979; care of public buildings, 982; Adirondack wilderness, 983; sale of forest land, non-payment of taxes, 984; lands purchased by State for non-payment of taxes, 984; fires in Adirondack region, 985; Adirondack survey, 986; State survey, 987; proposes transfer of State survey to State Engineer's office, 988; Niagara Falls reservation, 989; State Board of Health, 989; pleuro-pneumonia, 990; summary of recent legislation, 991; De Tocqueville on American commercial supremacy, 992; pardon report, 994; annual report of Civil Service Commission, 996; Senate requests information concerning harbor masters and captain of the port of New York, 996; declines to furnish facts in response to Senate resolution, 998; cession of land on Long Island to United States, 998; communication from United States Agricultural Commissioner Loring, preservation of forests, 1000; examination of armories and arsenals, 1007; return of bills relating to register and surrogate in New York for amendment, 1028; resigns to become President, 1126; VIII, 1; I pref., XII; death of, VII, 1126; administration commended by Governor Hill, VIII, 5; presidential administration commended by Governor Hill, 692; QUOTED, — veto of New York aqueduct bill, 47; — veto of Gallien bill, 109; — method of conducting State survey, 177; — sale of franchise to highest bidder, 200; — veto of Veteran Association, 71st Regiment bill, 404; — provision for ex-Presidents, 694; — management of State hospitals, X, 409.

MEMORANDUMS OF APPROVAL. New York, mayor, appointments without confirmation, VII, 1056; street railroads, operation and extension, 1063; New York, register, 1072.

VETOES. Ulster county, bonds to pay former bonds, VII, 994; New York, railroads in certain parts, 999; Spring Supply Water Company, Oneida, changing name, 1000; State prisons, Convict Labor Investigating Commission, extending time, 1001; Association for the Benefit of Colored Orphans, New York, changing name, 1006; Skaneateles, amending charter, 1008; county treasurers, excepting Ful-

Cleveland, Grover, 1884, Vetoes — (*Continued*).

ton county, 1010; Albany, street improvements, 1012; Venice Town Insurance Company, changing location of business office, 1013; Baldwinsville union free school district, borrowing money, 1013; Amsterdam, charter, 1014; Binghamton, payment of judgment, submitting question to people, 1017; Genesee Camp Ground Association, supplemental act, trustees, 1019; benevolent and charitable corporations, amending act, dissolution, 1020; Troy, Jacob and North Third streets, assessment for improvements, 1022; Westchester, town, borrowing money for highway improvement, 1023; Rochester bridge-tenders, 1024; Orange County Reference Law Library, 1025; manufacturing corporations, uniform standard of time, 1027; Broadway Underground Railway Company, extending rights, powers and duties, 1031; Troy, police, appointment of chief detective, 1041; Middletown, village hall, 1042; VIII, 61; disturbance of religious meeting, VII, 1043; New York, district courts, increasing jurisdiction, 1045; Orleans county, auditing claims for construction of poorhouse, 1046; Carthage, excise licenses, 1047; New York, captain of the port and harbor masters, compensation, 1048; items in canal awards bill, 1072; New York, public officers, official terms, 1074; New York, park department, 1075; item in appropriation bill, 1077; items in supply bill, 1078; omnibus veto with brief reasons, 1086; official service, I, pref. XIII.

Clews, Henry and Lucy. Transfer John Brown farm to State, IX, 669.

Clifford, Michael J. Relief, veto, X, 177.

Clifford, Patrick. Auburn prison convict, crime committed by, trial, reimbursing Cayuga county, veto, VI, 876; VII, 87, 227, 471, 781.

Clifford, Robert. New York, relief, veto, X, 176.

Clift, Leonard. Canal department, appropriation for services, veto, IX, 716.

Clifton. Aiding Adirondack Railroad Company, veto, VI, 190.

Clifton Park. Patent, rights under, II, 354.

Clifton Springs. Legalizing village election, veto, VIII, 1122.

Clinton. Village, Tau Chapter of the Delta Kappa Epsilon Fraternity, charter, veto, VI, 592.

Clinton County. Erected, II, 272; arms and ammunition for, 636; militia from, 1812, 744; troops stationed in, 745, 746; militia called out, 807; communication from citizens relative to burning of Rouse's Point, III, 760; State prison in, IV, 124; arsenal and

CLINTON COUNTY — *(Continued)*.

equipment to be sold, 495; cession to United States for light-house-keeper's dwelling, VI, 414; land in, State park, 629; timbered lands, acquisition by State, VII, 722; four towns excepted from repeal of Town Auditor's Act, VIII, 50; average excise license fees, 1889, 686; highways, cost of labor system, 1892, IX, 199; insane, care of, county and State systems compared, 223.

VETOES. Bridges in, VI, 556; fishing in waters of, 906; Plattsburgh, collection of taxes, VII, 130; support of poor, 367; surrogate, powers of county judge conferred on, 614; Stewart escheat bill, 619; reimbursing for expenses of criminal trials, Clinton prison, 782; claim submitted to Board of Claims, 782; prison case, Board of Claims, 887; Wakeman escheat, 935; superintendent of the poor, keeper of poorhouse, VIII, 537; taxes, collection, IX, 282; exempting from certain provisions relative to commissioners for laying out highways, 861; Ausable Chasm, acquiring for State park, X, 317; taxes, unpaid, sales, 440, 595.

CLINTON, DE WITT. Council of Appointment, communication from, II, 490, 491; Senate, resolutions, Council of Appointment, 502, 503; appointed Senator in Congress, 517; State Senate, chairman, Committee on Coast Defense, 568; chosen Regent, 629; Senate, introduces bill for internal improvements, 675; visits Washington in behalf of New York canal project, 706; mayor of New York, letter from, proposed session of Legislature in that city, 805; elected Governor, 887; canal commissioner, letter to Governor of Ohio, 891, 893; Governor, portrait, 897.

1818. Opening speech, II, 897; agriculture, 897; Board of Agriculture, 898; manufactures, 899; internal communications, 899; improvement of Hudson river, 900, 954; turnpike companies, 900; canals, 901; Seneca Lake canal, 902; Pennsylvania Canal Act, 902; common schools, 903; colleges and academies, 904; medical colleges, 904; New York institution, 905; finances, 906; canal tolls, 908; frequency of wars, 909; militia, 910; prison system, 911; conditional pardons, 913; imprisonment for debt, 913; revision of poor laws, 914; migration of Indians, 915; banks, 916; canal connection between Seneca lake and Susquehanna river, 918; pilot fees on British vessels, 918; Island Point ceded to United States, 919; Kentucky, New Jersey and Connecticut resolutions, 919; claims against United States, 919; Chapman, relief bill, veto, 920, 946; Kesler murder case, 921; murder case of Linus and others, 923; communication from New York grand jury relative to poor debtors,

CLINTON, DE WITT, 1818 — (Continued).

   923; North Carolina resolutions, 924; settlement of accounts with United States, 924; church for Oneida Indians, 930, 951; Tennessee resolution, 930; American Antiquarian Society's application for laws and journals, 930; urges preservation of Indian documents, 931; report on Montauk Indians, 931; State capitol, 934; Vermont resolutions, 937; trustees for St. Regis Indians, 939; intrusions on Indian land, 939; Astor claim, 940; sale of Staten Island fortifications, 940; New Jersey boundary, 941; St. Regis and Seneca Indian affairs, 941; habeas corpus, 943; Ulster county courthouse commissioners, appointment, 944; transfer of insane criminals, 945; militia claims, War of 1812, 946; lotteries, 950; military tactics, 951, 953; privy seal, 952; State prison guard, 952; forgery of records in Secretary of State's office, 952; paymaster, compensation, 953; distribution of Revised Laws, 953; assessment on New York arsenal lot, 953; sale of arms to State, 954; powder and ball for artillery, 954; report on agriculture, general note, 955.

1819.   Opening speech, II, 961; condition of State, 961; internal communications, 962; effect of national dismemberment, 966; common schools, 967; lotteries, 968; agriculture, 969; poor quality of flour, 970; improvement of roads, 971; education, 972; colleges, 973; medical colleges, 973; New York Hospital for Insane, 974; New York Institution for the Instruction of the Deaf and Dumb, 974; migration of Indians, 975; Oneida Indian church, 976; proposes board of Indian commissioners, 977; negroes, 977; militia, 978; currency, 979; prisons, 981; counterfeiting, 983; separate dormitories in State prisons, 984; statement of convictions, 984; insurrection in New York prisons, 985; jurisdiction of court of sessions, 986; executors and administrators, 986; preference in payment of debts, 986; wills, 986; Buffalo harbor, 986, 991; Little Sodus bay and Great Sodus bay, harbor, 986; St. Regis village, 986; claims against United States, 986; General Montgomery's remains removed from Quebec to New York, 986, 999; removal of Stockbridge Indians, 987; marshals in military courts, 989; purchase of Stockbridge Indian land, 989; quarantine establishment, 990; Vermont resolution, 990; literature fund lottery, 990; Astor claim, 990; patents of land in military tract, 991; militia, brevet appointments, 992; removal of New York prison, 993; transmits resignation of Smith Thompson, as Regent, 993; conveyance to State of lands by Holland Land Company, 994;

CLINTON, DE WITT, 1819 — (*Continued*).

distribution of statutes, 994; books on military tactics, 994, 996; prison discipline, 995; Onondaga Indian agent, 995; intrusions on Grand Island, 995; protest against corporal punishment in prisons and convict labor on public works, 996; procedure in courts-martial, 996; Hodges and others, murder case, 996; defalcations in Merchants' Bank, 997, 998; Burke case, 998; Fish Creek reservation, 999; New York, arsenal assessments, 999; statement of expenses, removal of Montgomery's remains, 1000; veto, courts of oyer and terminer and general sessions, 1002.

1820. Opening speech, II, 1003; depressed condition of manufacturing interests, 1003; loan of public funds, 1004; agriculture, 1005; commerce, 1006; canals, 1007; salt, 1009; gypsum, 1009; limestone, 1010; coal, 1010; general canal suggestion, 1011; Hudson river improvement, 1011; tax on territory contiguous to canals, 1012; roads and bridges, 1012; reducing salaries of State officers, 1013; recommends omission of legislative answer to speech, 1014; judicial reform, 1014; prison administration, 1015; carrying concealed weapons, 1016; Bank of Savings, New York, 1016; militia, 1016; epidemic in New York, 1017; water supply, New York, 1017; education, 1018; revision of Constitution, 1018; Council of Appointment, 1019; Constitutional Convention, 1020; United States Senator, 1021; slavery, 1022; character of republican government, 1023; South Carolina resolution, 1024; Pennsylvania resolution, 1024; Connecticut resolution, 1025; Grand Island intrusions, 1026; distribution of statutes to Federal departments, 1026; lottery for literature fund, 1027; pensions for Revolutionary soldiers, 1027; transmits Regent Cochran's resignation, 1028; condition of Merchants' Bank, 1029; Ohio resolution, 1029; conference with Seneca Indians, 1029; Otsequette relief, 1030; Indiana resolution, 1030; inquiry concerning conduct of William W. Van Ness, 1031; purchasing Holland Land Company's property, 1031; Roman Catholic Benevolent Society, New York, charter, veto, 1036; Staten Island fortifications, 1037.

1821. Opening speech, II, 1038; comments on method of choosing presidential electors, 1039; United States Senator, 1040; national affairs, 1040; slavery, 1041; Federal interference in elections, 1042, 1054, 1059, 1060; Council of Appointment, 1043; Constitutional Convention, 1043; internal communications, 1044; agriculture, 1046; rate of interest, 1047; census, 1047; cement, 1048; coal, 1048; education, 1048; number of common

CLINTON, DE WITT, 1821 — (*Continued*).

schools, 1820, 1048; number of Lancastrian schools, 1820, 1048; teachers, 1049; academies, 1049; colleges, 1049; education of youth at public expense, 1049; militia, 1050; prison reform, 1051; lotteries, 1052, 1054; proceedings in Court of Chancery, veto, 1053; lighthouses, 1054; Constitutional Convention bill, veto, 1055; reply to Senate's criticism, 1059; Vermont resolutions, 1075; New Hampshire resolutions, 1076; lease of unoccupied land at Albany arsenal, 1076; Indian contracts, 1076; Seneca Indian attorney, 1076; Ohio resolutions, Bank of United States against State Auditor, 1077; quitrents, 1079; proceeds of public lands, 1079; Otsequette Relief Act, 1080; claims against United States, 1080; toll-bridge, Saugerties, veto, 1081; Illinois resolutions, 1082; perpetuation of evidence, veto, 1083.

1822. Opening speech, 1087; Constitutional Convention, 1087; agriculture, 1089; commerce, 1090; exports and imports, 1091; increasing price of wool, 1091; hemp and flax, 1092; iron, 1092; salt, 1092; manufacture of cotton cloth, 1092; trade with South American republics, 1093; pot and pearl ashes, 1093; coal, 1094; canals, 1094; Board of Public Improvements, 1097; III, 67; loans for canal construction, II, 1097; income of canal fund, 1097; canal revenue, 1098; public debt, 1098; finances, 1098; education, 1099; appropriating national domain for educational purposes, 1101; revision of militia laws, 1102; insufficient quantity of arms, 1103; Washington lottery, 1103, 1123; Smith extradition case, 1104; New Jersey boundary, 1105; claims against United States, 1105, 1122; escheats, 1106; Grand Island, 1106; use of oaths, 1106; rewards for destruction of wolves, 1107; migration of Indians, 1107; prison system, 1108; Harlem common lands, veto, 1110; Genesee river lighthouse, 1113; inspection reports, 1113; offer to furnish arms for State, 1113; Kentucky resolution, 1114; additional artillery, 1114, 1116; translation of Dutch records, 1115; Niagara courthouse and jail, 1117; Ohio resolutions, 1117; Onondaga Indian land, 1118; Massachusetts resolution, 1118, 1119; purchase of Stockbridge Indian land, 1119; criminal jurisdiction over Indian lands, 1119; purchase of New Stockbridge Indian lands, 1120; Konkapot claim, 1120; arms not to be taken from arsenals by militia, 1120; bibles for convicts in Auburn prison, 1121; magistrates on Carleton island, 1121; succeeded by Joseph C. Yates, III, 1; again chosen Governor, 53.

1825. Annual message, III, 53; military academy, 53; prosperous

CLINTON, DE WITT, 1825 — (*Continued*).

condition of State, 54; publication of Senate executive journals, 55, 107; method of choosing presidential electors, 52, 56; justices of the peace, 57; town courthouses, 58; elective franchise, 58; education, 60; limiting power of Regents to grant charters, 62; State Medical Society, 62; agriculture, 63; horticulture, 64; census, 65; rewards for inventions, 65; Mechanic and Scientific Institution, New York, 66; canals, 66; Canadian duties on American products, 68; various canal routes, 70; aid to Delaware and Hudson Canal Company, 70; coal on headwaters of Tioga river, 71; canal bridges, 72; Champlain canal, 72; iron, 72; sloop navigation, 72; canal appraisers, 73; canal debt, 73; speed of canal boats, 74; Ohio canal, 75; Federal tonnage duties on canal traffic, 76; Federal encroachments on rights of States, 78; Federal Senate proposed tribunal to settle controversies between State and national governments, 79; roads, 80; State road from Hudson river to Cayuga lake, 80; State road from Hudson river to Lake Erie, 81; drainage of Cayuga marshes, 81; salt works, 81; prison administration, 82; house of refuge, 82; orphan asylum, 83; lunatic asylum, 83; deaf and dumb, 83; enumeration of insane, 84; militia exemptions, 85; election of Senator in Congress, 85; reception of Lafayette, 85; New Jersey boundary, 86, 94, 107; quarantine laws, 87; water for cities, 87; aliens holding real estate, 88; reducing rate of interest, 88; rights and liabilities of factors, 89; revision of statutes relative to wills, 89; statutes should contain but one subject, 90; log-rolling, 91; resigns as Regent, 94; Georgia resolutions, 94; purchase of Stockbridge lands, 96; map of State, 96; proposed canal from Lake Erie to Allegany river, 96; Central Asylum for Instruction of Deaf and Dumb, 97; weights and measures, 98, 101; report of commissioners on canal between Tioga river and Seneca lake, 98; inspection of beef and pork, 99; New Jersey resolution, 99; field pieces, 99; investment of receipts of health office, 100; chaplains for militia, 103; special meeting of United States Senate, 104; Indiana resolutions, 104, 105; canal between Erie canal and Allegany river, 104; Mississippi resolutions, 105; agent for Onondaga Indians, 105; improvement in firearms, 105; resignation of justices of the peace, 106; claims against United States, 106; Missouri resolutions, 106; letter from Lafayette, 111.

1826. Annual message, III, 113; summary of State's condition, 113; education, 114; teachers, 116; colleges, 117; New York

CLINTON, DE WITT, 1826 — (*Continued*).

Historical Society, 118; canals, 118; celebration of completion of canals, loss of life, 120; extension of canal system, 121; canals in other States, 122, 123; Hudson river improvement, 124; New York harbor, 124; State roads, 124; agriculture, 125; instruction of mechanics, 127; coal, 127; classification of murder, 128; revision of Criminal Law, 129; condition of New York prison, 129; Sing Sing prison, 129; principles applied in granting pardons, 130; New York House of Refuge, 130; militia, 131; investigation of land titles in Putnam and Dutchess counties, 132, 146; election of United States Senator, 132; apportionment of Legislature, 133; vacancies in Assembly, 133; power of removal, 133; Lafayette's visit, 133; monument to Commodore Macdonough, 134; aid to heirs of Robert Fulton, 134, 150; rules of navigation, applicable to steamboats, 134; Indian affairs, 135; constitutional amendments, 135; Vermont, Illinois, Delaware and Connecticut resolutions, 136; Central Asylum for Instruction of Deaf and Dumb, 137; Tennessee resolutions, 137; cession to United States at New Utrecht Point, 138; cessions to United States, 138; as mayor of New York, signs cession to United States, 140; Governor, cession of land at West Point, 141; appointment of officers, 141; transmits resignation of Henry Rutgers as Regent, 142; destruction of weights and measures by fire, 142; Seneca Indians, 142; portrait of General Washington, 143; Kentucky resolutions, 143; purchase of Oneida Indian land, 143; Indiana resolutions, 144; Maine resolutions, 144; memorial from American Colonization Society, 144; Mississippi resolutions, 144; claims against United States, 145; Louisiana resolution, 145; counsel to assist district attorney, 145; expense of reception to Lafayette, 146; Salina salt act, amendment, veto, 147.

1827. Annual message, III, 153; cultivation of peace, 154; Federal tonnage duty on canals, 154; distribution of Federal revenues, 155; presidential electors, 156; New Jersey boundary, 156, 180; elective franchise, 157; improved methods in elections, 158; corrupt practices at elections, 158; education, 158; instruction of teachers, 159; library for common schools, 160; colleges, 160; justices of the peace, 161; New York Historical Society, 162; historical publications, 162; State map, 162; House of Refuge for Juvenile Delinquents, 162; Federal prisoners admitted to State prisons, 163; hospital at quarantine, 163; canals, 163; various canal projects, 165; bituminous coal in Pennsylvania, 168; Chenango canal, 168; coal, 168; canal tolls, 169;

CLINTON, DE WITT, 1827 — (*Continued*).

State road through southern tier of counties, 170; canals in other States, 171; banks, 172; revision of Criminal Code, 173; Putnam and Dutchess counties, land claims, 174, 196; proof of deeds, 175; vacancies in sheriffs and clerks' offices, 176; insufficient supply of artillery, 176; pauperism, 176; immigration, 177; claims against United States, 177; sale of Staten Island fortifications, 178; land ceded for lighthouse, Prince's bay, 178, 180; death of Adams and Jefferson, 178; pensions, 179; monument to General Herkimer, 179; petition for loan of arms, 180; Vermont resolutions, 181; navy hospital, 181; reports of inspectors, 182; Georgia resolution, 182; damages for diverting Tonawanda creek, 182; inspection of staves and heading, 183; treaty with Creek Indians, 183; Alabama resolution, 183; Ohio resolution, 184; Morgan abduction case, 184; Maine resolutions, 186; regulating sale of lottery tickets, veto, 186; militia commissions, 189; compensation of Horatio Jones, 189; Onondaga courthouse and jail, veto, 190; special session of Senate, 195.

1828. Annual message, III, 197; general prosperity, 197; malignant party spirit, 198; presidential electors, 198; canal revenues, 199; canal projects, 200; finances, 201; extension of canal system, 201; surplus canal waters, 202; proposed period of canal navigation, 202; coal, 203; plantation of forests, 203; transportation of coal, 203; cultivation of hemp and flax, 206; cultivation of tobacco, 206; prison system, 207; female prison, 207; duelling, 208; Revised Statutes, 210; judiciary, 210; commissioners to take proof of conveyances in other States, 210; municipal corporations, 211; New Jersey boundary, 212; education, 212; monitorial high school, 212; education of selected youth in colleges, 213; infant schools, 213; monuments to Generals Herkimer and Woodhull, 214; pensions, 214; standard of weights and measures, 215; public administrator, New York, 216; Seneca county clerk, 217; Vermont resolutions, 217; South Carolina resolutions, 218; Rensselaer school offered for instruction of teachers, 219; communication from Judge Irving, costs in actions for slander and assault and battery, 219; death of, 197, 219; I, pref. XII; legislative proceedings on death of, III, 220; gift to minor children, 220; quoted, distribution of Federal revenues, 330, 986; proposed monument for, 746, 905; Vice-President, New York Historical Society, memorial, publication of colonial documents, 751; IV, 166; quoted,— Federal interference at elections, VI, 258; — use of metallic money, 649; official service, I, pref. XII.

CLINTON, GEORGE. (Colony). Appointed Governor, I, 305, 310; receives address from colony requesting royal aid in rebuilding Governor's house, 305; letters from, relative to supplies and rebuilding Governor's house, 309; assumes office, 310; dissolves Twenty-second Assembly, 311; new Assembly called, 311.

OPENING SPEECH. Twenty-third Assembly, first session, I, 311; annual appropriations, 312; military supplies, 312; relations with Indians, 312; rebuilding Governor's house, 313; urges appointment of colonial agent, 313.

OPENING SPEECH. Twenty-third Assembly, second session, I, 314; supply of gunpowder, 314; new house for Governor, 314; announces naval engagement in Mediterranean, 314; fortifications, 315; provides for defense of Oswego, 315; increasing allowance to Indian commissioners, 315; small-pox in West Indies, 315; military supplies for frontier, 316; France declares war against England, 316; importance of preserving amicable relations with Indians, 316; additional appropriations needed, 317.

OPENING SPEECH. Twenty-third Assembly, third session, I, 317; war with France, 317, 318; act for defense of colony, 318; movements for frontier defense, 318; conference with Indians, 319; negotiations for union of colonies, 320, 330; naval preparations, 321; colonial agent, 321, 333; statement of needed military preparations, 322, 324; difficulties of situation at Oswego, 326; prisoners of war, 327, 328, 329, 330; address to, 329.

OPENING SPEECH. Twenty-third Assembly, fourth session, I, 331; Massachusetts movement against French, 331; sends cannon to Boston, 332; recommends province vessel, 332; two more forts on frontier, 333; troops sent to Oswego, 334; French prisoners sent to St. Domingo, 334; urges negotiations for colonial union, 335, 337; examination of Whitehall battery, 338, 339; sends information relative to affairs at Oswego, 338; repairs at Fort George, 339; expected French movement against British dominions in South America, 340; letter from Duke of Newcastle relative to colonial defense, 340; letter from Governor Shirley relative to Six Nations, 341; presents to Indians, 341; urges more effective measures for frontier defense, 341; complains of conduct of Assembly, 343; dissolves Assembly, 344.

CLINTON, GEORGE (Colony)—(*Continued*).

OPENING SPEECH. Twenty-fourth Assembly, first session, I, 345; fortifying New York, 345; urges new forts in Indian country, 346; negotiations with Indians, 346; urges assistance in Cape Breton expedition, 346; successes in expedition against Louisburg, 347; Governor Shirley's letter describing Cape Breton expedition, 350; Commodore Warren's letter relative to expedition against Louisburg, 351; storing powder in New York, 352; capture of Louisburg, 352; Canada Indians break neutrality treaty with Six Nations, 352, 356, 358; Canada Indians attack New England settlements, 353, 360; urges conference with Six Nations, 353; report among Indians of intended destruction of English and Dutch, 355; Indians visit Canada, 355; Orondax Indians on northern frontier, 355; murders by French Indians, 355; French Indians declare war against English; Six Nations invited to join, 355, 356; urges exclusion of French Indians from trading privileges, 356; Indians complain of lack of hospitality at Oswego, 357; blockhouses for outscouts, 357; powder duty, 357; conditions on frontier, 358; result of Indian conference, 359; new treaty with Six Nations, 359; urges more effective defense of frontier, 360; destruction of Saratoga, 361; sends militia to defend frontier, 361; French and Indians near Stockbridge, 363; King's troops sent to Albany, 363; rebuilding fort at Saratoga, 364; uniting with neighboring colonies in prosecution of war, 364; militia reform, 365; frontier defense, French intrigues, colonial union, 366.

TWENTY-FOURTH ASSEMBLY, second session, I, 367; Assembly meets at Greenwich, 367; blockhouses on frontier, 368; Indians refuse to engage in war, 368; defense of Oswego, 369; troops needed for Louisburg, 369, 371; commissioners appointed on colonial union, 370; declines to express opinion as to probable action on bill, 371; engineer for colony, 371; transports for Cape Breton, 371.

MESSAGE. Twenty-fourth Assembly, third session, I, 372; troops for Albany, 372; expedition against Canada, 373; French prisoners, 375; conference with Indians, 376; rangers for Albany county, 377; transportation of troops and supplies, 379; royal reimbursement of colonial war expenses, 379; Assembly waives personal delivery of opening speech, 381.

OPENING SPEECH. Twenty-fourth Assembly, fourth session, I, 381; Indians agree to join in war, 382; assumes command

CLINTON, GEORGE (Colony)—(*Continued*).

 of expedition, 382; military arrangements at Albany, 383; urges liberal appropriations, 384; probable postponement of expedition, 385; difficulties of administration, 387; Assembly's criticism, 387; assures Assembly that exact accounts will be rendered, 388; rewards for scalps, 389; smiths for Indians, 389; repairs fort at Albany, 390.

OPENING SPEECH. Twenty-fourth Assembly, fifth session, I, 390; frontier defense, 391; efforts to retain fidelity of Indians, 391; provisions for expedition, 391; negotiations with western Indians, 391; protection of northern frontier, 392; estimated expense of attack on Crown Point, 393; relief of Kinderhook, 394; review of recent military movements, 395; Assembly's alleged disrespectful treatment of, 399; charges against Albany merchants, 399; negro plot, 400; provisions for Albany rangers, 402; uses private fortune in public service, 403, 487; war measures in conjunction with neighboring colonies, 404; Indians loyal to English, 405; address from Council, 406; exchange of English prisoners, 409; declines to make further private contributions for war expenses, 409; provisions for Oswego, 410; movement against French near Saratoga, 410, 411; withdraws frontier garrisons because of Assembly's failure to furnish supplies, 411.

MESSAGE. Twenty-fourth Assembly, sixth session, I, 413; joint colonial report relative to war measures, 413, 419; strengthening Oswego, 416; protection of Albany, 416, 418; inviting assistance from neighboring colonies, 417, 420, 440; sachems visit New York, 418; Crown Point expedition, 419; condition of Indians, 421; Assembly asserts independence in legislative action, 422; refuses to receive Assembly's remonstrance, 423, 432; defends his administration against Assembly's criticism, 423; charges Assembly with improper motives in opposing his administration, 436; rangers on frontier, 439; Colonel Johnson's certificate as to French prisoners and scalps, 440, 441; Canadian expedition abandoned, 441; expense of retaining troops on frontiers, 443; refuses to receive communication from Assembly except from Speaker, 445; approves bill for frontier defense, 446; publication of Assembly remonstrance, 446; review of recent differences, 448; liberty of the press, 450; dissolves Assembly, 457.

CLINTON, GEORGE (Colony)—(*Continued*).

OPENING SPEECH. Twenty-fifth Assembly, first session, I, 457; agreement for colonial defense, 457; relations with Indians, 458, 462; Salaries Act, 459; Indian interpreter, 459; provisions for Oswego garrison, 459; smith at Oswego, 460, 462; fortifications at Albany, 460; rewards for scalps, 460; various war expenses, 460; commanding officer for new troops, 461; communications relative to agreement for union, 461; outscouts on frontiers, 462; address to, 462; Assembly disapproves Massachusetts alterations in agreement for union, 462; supplies for garrison at Fort Clinton, 462; troops from Connecticut, 463; projected movement against French, 464; alliance with Indians, 465, 466; restricting trade with Indians, 466; engineer's report on fortifications, 467; French privateers, 467; exchange of prisoners, 467, 470, 486; Colonel Johnson to command new levies, 468; volunteers from Connecticut, 468; alleged interference with courts, 468, 469.

OPENING SPEECH. Twenty-fifth Assembly, second session, I, 469; prospect of peace, 469; continuing protection of frontier, 470; urges five year appropriation acts, 470–472; Colonel Johnson's claim, 473, 490; frontier conditions, 474; answer to Assembly's address, 475; compensation of Indian interpreter, 478; subsistence of prisoners, 478; verification of accounts, 478; relations between Governor and Assembly, 479.

OPENING SPEECH. Twenty-fifth Assembly, third session, I, 481; treaty of peace, 481; method of applying appropriations, 482, 483, 505; regulations as to statutes, 484; refuses to receive address from Assembly, 484; French designs to alienate Indians, 486; difference with Assembly, 486; urges payment of public debt, 492; instruction as to method of passing bills, 493; controversy with Assembly continues, 494; Assembly neglects to pass proper laws, 497; Albany storehouse incident, 497; defends his official conduct, 501; dissolves Assembly, 503.

OPENING SPEECH. Twenty-sixth Assembly, first session, I, 503; maintaining Oswego garrison, 503; relations with Indians, 504; support of government, 505; encouraging manufactures, 506; exchanging prisoners, 507, 510; copper money, 507; letter from Governor Hamilton relative to uneasiness among Indians, 508, 511; address to, relative to Indians, 508; Indian affairs, 511; completion of buildings at Fort George, 511.

CLINTON, GEORGE (Colony)—(*Continued*).

OPENING SPEECH. Twenty-sixth Assembly, second session, I, 512; announces death of Prince of Wales, 512; Indian affairs, 513, 515; proposed joint colonial treaty with Indians, 514.

OPENING SPEECH. Twenty-sixth Assembly, third session, I, 515; support of government, 515; Indian negotiations, 517; dissolves Assembly, 519.

OPENING SPEECH. Twenty-seventh Assembly, first session, I, 520; Indian affairs, fortifications, 520; support of government, 520; report relating to Seneca Indians, 521.

OPENING SPEECH. Twenty-seventh Assembly, second session, I, 521; revision of colonial statutes, 521; smallpox in New York occasions meeting of Assembly in Jamaica, 522; repair of fortifications, 522; King's College established, 523; intrusions on royal and other lands, 523; inquiry into conduct of Mohawks, 524; New Jersey boundary, 525; succeeded by Governor Osborn, 526; official service, pref. X.

CLINTON, GEORGE (State). Assembly, favors colonial union, I, 767; chosen Governor, II, 6; enters New York city, I, 780; convenes Legislature, 780; establishes government, 780; portrait, II, 1; official oath, I, pref. X; II, 6; prorogues Legislature, 7.

1777. Opening speech, II, 7; British movements, 7; defeat of British on northern frontier, 8; battle of Bennington, 8; military movements, 8, 18; revision of militia laws, 9; finances, 9; organizing State government, 9; election law, 10, 34; one department should not encroach on another, 10, 12, 21, 246, 250, 278; conference on paper currency, 11; Assembly's address, 11; papers from Tryon county committee, 12, 13, 25; movements on frontier, 13; militia claims, 13; prisoners and arrests, 14; Council of Appointment, 14; Senate's address, 15; inquiry as to surrender of Ticonderoga and Mount Independence, 15; campaign in Highlands, 15, 16; letter from convention, 16; convenes Legislature at Poughkeepsie, 17, 43, 50, 105, 132, 146, 163, 182; Articles of Confederation, 18; letter from Washington, 18; Hudson river obstructions, 19, 31; papers relative to certain prisoners, 20; scarcity of iron, 20; presents various communications, 20; first veto, official oaths, 21; Vermont controversy, 24, 47, 67; fixing wages and prices, 25, 46; relief of soldiers' families, 25; treatment of prisoners, 25; Indian affairs, 26; exportation bill, veto, 26;

CLINTON, GEORGE (State), 1777 — (*Continued*).

improper duties imposed on, 30; defense of Hudson river, 31, 34; claims due United States, payment of, 32; recruiting Continental battalions, 33; exchange of prisoners, 33; removal of disaffected persons, 33, 34; tax bill, veto, 39; bill for raising troops, veto, 41; Captain Cregier's claim, 43; accoutrements for troops, 43; exemption of deserters and prisoners from military service, 43; establishment of Continental Army, 44; treaty with France, 44, 67; condemns British methods, 45; embargo on provisions, 46.

1778. Opening speech, II, 50; progress of war, 50; Indian ravages on western frontier, 50; disturbance in Vermont district, 51; depreciation of paper currency, 52; revision of statutes, 52; claims against United States, 52; militia expenses, 53; clothing and supplies for troops, 53, 55; army supplies, 54, 57, 66; Congress advances funds for State, 55; resolution of Congress, encouragement of religion and good morals, 56; militia payrolls, 57; obtaining goods from enemy under flags of truce, 57; tax bill, veto, 59; apportionment of Federal expenses, 65; sustaining paper currency, 65; Augur murder case, 67; scarcity of bread in Rhode Island, 68; scarcity of provisions in Boston, 69; requested by Congress to furnish supplies to Rhode Island, 69; account for expenses, 70; defense of western frontier, 70, 92; forfeitures and confiscations, veto, 70; visit of Massachusetts delegates, 72; convenes Legislature at Kingston, 75, 96, 186.

1779. Opening speech, II, 75; British invasion of Westchester county, 75; more tranquil condition on western frontier, 76; disorders diminishing, 76; Vermont controversy, 76, 82, 102; recruits and clothing, 76; supporting paper currency, 77; raising more troops, 77; Wood murder case, suspends execution, 78; completing Continental battalions, 78; scarcity of salt, 78, 84; various communications from Congress, 79, 80, 81; proclamation against plundering inhabitants of Long Island, 80; letter from James Wilkinson, Clothier-General, 80; outrages in Westchester county, 80; returns of militia, 81; prevention of conspiracies, veto, 81; presents various petitions, 81, 82; case of Thomas Cummings, convicted of treason, 82; recruiting Continental battalions, 82, 88; John Jay appointed minister to Spain, 83; regulation of prices, 83, 87; Congress offers to sell rum and sugar, 83; escapes, veto, 84; horse-racing and the-

CLINTON, GEORGE (State), 1779 — (*Continued*).

atrical performances, veto, 85; convenes Legislature at
Albany, 87, 114, 289, 301; witnesses before courts-martial,
87; army supplies, 88, 89, 90, 98, 101; militia, 89; British
losses, 89; proclamation authorized regulating dealings in
Westchester county, 90; privileges and immunities of French
subjects, 91; Massachusetts requests repeal of embargo
laws, 91; claim of Casper Stoudt, manufacturer of sulphur
and copperas, 92; militia losses, pensions, 92; quotas of
troops, 93; sale of forfeited estates, veto, 94; hospital
nurses, 95; tax for support of poor in certain counties,
veto, 95; militia claims, 96; Federal system of finance, 97;
relief of northern frontier, 99; transmits various communications, 99, 100; Connecticut's claim for cannon and
ball, 100; relief of New York prisoners of war, 101; communications from Congress, 101; Arnold court-martial, 102.

1780. Opening speech, II, 105; Vermont controversy, hearing
before Congress, 105; defense of western settlements, 106;
provisions becoming more abundant, 106; Hartford and
Providence conventions, 107, 108; progress of the war,
107; supplies for French fleet and army, 108, 111; relief
of distressed families in Tryon and Westchester counties,
109, 112; compensation of troops for depreciation in currency, 110; Connecticut repeals embargo laws, 110; Confederation of United States, 112; sale of forfeited estates,
amending act, veto, 112; Palmertown, blockhouse, 113;
conditions in Westchester county, 113; Council of Safety,
veto, 113; various communications from Congress, 114,
132; defense of State, 115; scarcity of clothing, 115;
remedy against delinquents, 115; relief of prisoners of war,
retaliation, 116; conditions in Tryon county, 116, 117;
transmits various papers, 117; enforcement of embargo,
118; imports on foreign merchandise, 120; conditions on
frontier, 121; threatens to prorogue Legislature, 123, 144;
letter from General Clinton, scarcity of provisions, 123;
correspondence with Washington, relative to frontier conditions, 123, 124; embargo, veto, 125; announces complete
ratification of Articles of Confederation, 127; Charlotte
county, military exemptions, veto, 128; suspension of finance acts, veto, 128; supplying provisions to enemy, veto,
129; amending Militia Act, veto, 131; completing New York
regiments, 133; accounts with United States for supplies,
134; pay of medical and hospital officers, 134; raising taxes

CLINTON, GEORGE (State), 1780 — (*Continued*).

in specie and in paper currency, veto, 134; letter from Governor Chittenden of Vermont, 135, 142; message to Assembly, Vermont controversy, 143.

1781. Opening speech, II, 146; Congress to meet annually, 146; currency questions, 147; improved conditions on frontier, 147; more troops, bounties for enlistments, 147, 148; aid from France, 148; army supplies, 148, 150; powder exhausted, 149; surrender of Lord Cornwallis, 150; report of State agent, 150; judge-advocate's claims, 150; situation at Saratoga, 151; service claims, 151; forage in Westchester county, 151, 165; Federal finances, letter from Robert Morris, 152; thanksgiving day, 152; account for personal expenses, 161; scarcity of bread, 161; destruction of property by British, 162; advances private funds for public purposes, 162; more troops, 163; alleged treasonable conduct of Vermont leaders, 163, 166; Bank of North America, 164; illicit trade with British, 164; census of white inhabitants, 164; wheat for army, 165; security of West Point, 165; protest against uniform scale of depreciation, 167; Captain Burrell's claim, 167; relief of certain families in Tryon county, 168; compensation of American prisoners, 168; subsistence of troops, 169; collection of forage, 169; fast day appointed, 170; justices' courts, jurisdiction of, veto, 170; taxes and public accounts, veto, 172; officers, staying suits against, veto, 173; defense of settlements on frontier, 174; Vermont controversy, 174; Federal finances, general note, 180.

1782. Opening speech, II, 182; Federal affairs, 182; birth of dauphin of France, 182; promotion of education, 183; revision of tax system, 183, 187; public accounts, 184; general financial matters, 184; forage for army, 185; appointment of receiver of Continental taxes, 185; James Hamilton's claim, 185; George Trimble's claim, 186; contribution for national expenses, 186; settlement of army claims, 187; troops for frontier, 188; disturbances in Cumberland county, 188; negotiations for peace, 188; treaty with Netherlands, 188; exchanging drafts for specie, 189; returns of State troops, 189; representation in Congress should be constant, 190; proposed Hartford Convention on taxation, 190; insolvent debtors, veto, 190; Provisional Treaty of Peace, 191, 192; Definitive Treaty of Peace, 191; powers of commissioners of sequestration, veto, 191; Fed-

CLINTON, GEORGE (State), 1782 — (*Continued*).

eral affairs, general note, 192; proposed convention to revise
system of government, 194; convenes Legislature at New
York, 195, 217, 251.

1784, January. Opening speech, II, 195; independence established, 195; condition of New York, 195; settlement of
militia arrears, 197; British attempt to monopolize
West India trade, 197; plans for commercial improvement, 198; disposition of public lands, 199; internal
duties and excise, 199; marine passes, auction duties,
199; naturalization, 199; compensation of officers, 199;
education, State university, 200; Council of Appointment, 200; delegates in Congress, 200; revision of
statutes, 200; militia, 200; claims against United States,
201; condition of posts on western frontier, 201; alienism of certain persons, veto, 202; debts due to persons
within enemy's line, veto, 204; treaty of peace ratified,
206; restitution of estates, 206, 207; settlement of
certain public contracts, 208; Massachusetts boundary,
208, 211; Barnes case, 209; disorders in Cumberland
county, 210; arrest on justice's warrant, veto, 210;
statement of receipts and expenditures, 211. VETOES.
New York tax bill, 211; general tax bill, 213; lands,
waste and unappropriated, sale of, 213; sale of forfeited and confiscated estates, 214; freedom and independence of State, 215.

1784, October. Opening speech, II, 217; Massachusetts territorial claim, 217; national debt, arrears of interest,
218; militia for western posts, 218; claims of absentees
and aliens, 218; ascertaining value of taxable property,
219; revenue, 219; revision of statutes, 219; university,
imposts, militia, 220; magazines and arsenals, 220;
Indian affairs, 220, 221; Debeavois bill, veto, 222; New
York city, taxes, petit larceny and disorderly persons,
veto, 222; alleged fraudulent contracts relating to
Indian lands, 224; revision of forgery laws, 224;
Surveyor-General, 224; burning of Dutchess county
courthouse and jail, 224; Pennsylvania boundary, 224,
225; John Jay becomes Secretary of State of United
States, 237; papers from commissioners of Indian
affairs, 239; claims of New York merchants, 241;
various communications from Congress, 245; Secretary
of Congress, 245; riot in New York harbor, 245.

CLINTON, GEORGE (State), 1784 — (*Continued*).

    VETOES. Inoculation for smallpox, 225; — evidence, commission to obtain, 227; — Mechanics and Trademen, charter, 228; — sequestration and forfeitures, indemnification of commissioners, 233; — taxes, collection of, 234; — imports, Explanatory Act, 236; — slavery, abolition of, 237; — estates, entails and joint tenants, 239; — debts due to colony and State, payment of, 240; — Supreme Court, where to be held, 242; German Society for Promoting Emigration, charter, 243; — curing defects in conveyances, 245; — Hudson, city charter, 246; — New York city, tax, support of poor, 247; — William R. Cortlandt, vesting estate in trustees, 248; — Gilchrist, relief, 249; — salaries of public officers, 249.

1786. Opening speech, II, 251; remarks on extraordinary sessions, 251; condition of State, 252; British still retain western posts, 253; claims against State, 253; agriculture, 254; commerce and manufactures, 254; trade with India, 254; iron and gunpowder, 254; militia, 255; revision of statutes, 255; commissioners of forfeitures, Surveyor-General, Merril memorial, 256; statement of Federal expenditures, 256; intestate estates, wills and administrations, veto, 257; revolutionary pensions, 259; Francis claim, 259; Commercial Convention, 259; Massachusetts boundary, 260, 261; Remsen claim, 261; Klock claim, 262; statement of expenses, 262.

1787. Opening speech, II, 263; requisition by Congress, 263; Army Act, Congress, 264; Federal revenue system, 264, 275; Massachusetts boundary established, 265; Pennsylvania boundary, 265; condition of militia, 266; insect ravages in wheat, 266; rapid payment of claims against State, 266; Indian lands, 267; intestates' estates, will and administrations, veto, 267; Shays' rebellion, 269, 271; Federal Constitutional Convention, 270, 271; authorized to leave State on military service, 271; proposes new county west of Lake Champlain, 271; divorce, trial in action for, veto, 272; Pennsylvania boundary, 272; Indian affairs, 273; complaint against Francis Childs, 274; actions, small causes, veto, 274; State laws inconsistent with treaty of peace, 274; fees of court officers, veto, 275; letter to President of Congress on Tariff Act, 278.

Clinton, George (State)—(*Continued*).

1788, January. Opening speech, II, 281; Federal affairs, 281;
Massachusetts and Pennsylvania boundaries established,
282; Federal Constitution submitted, 282; President of
convention to consider Federal Constitution, 283; encouragement of home manufactures, 283; disorderly persons,
arrest and punishment of, veto, 284; military tract, 286;
commissioners of the land office, powers of, veto, 287;
Vanderlocht relief, veto, 287; public accounts, settlement,
veto, 288.

1788, December. Opening speech, II, 289; transmits proceedings of convention to consider Federal Constitution, 289;
Indian treaties, 291, 296; national affairs, 291; reports of
State officers, 291; agriculture, 292; Senate's answer to
speech, 292; Governor's reply, 293; additional judge of
Supreme Court, 295; Federal government established,
general note, 296.

1789, July. Opening speech, II, 301; election of Senators in
Congress, 301; prospect of abundant harvest, 301; disturbance in Montgomery county, 302; election of United
States Senators, veto, 303; amendments to Federal Constitution, 304; United States prisoners in jails, 304; Sandy
Hook lighthouse, 304; State financial affairs, 304; State
census, 305; military bounties, 305; house in New York
for President, 305; Indian affairs, 306, 307; Massachusetts
boundary, 306; Brothertown Indians, 306; Vermont controversy, 307; Ossey claim, 307; Elijah Bill claim, 307;
modifying Governor's duties, 308; Henry relief, veto, 309;
military bounty lands, veto, 309; status of certain members of Legislature, 310.

1791. Opening speech, II, 311; militia, Indian affairs, 311;
internal communications, 311, 312; finances, 312; relief of
creditors, 312; legislative apportionment, 312; manufactures, 312; maple sugar, 313; publication of proceedings
of Council of Appointment, 314; New York city, license
of carriages, veto, 315; New York city, tax bill, 316;
College of Physicians and Surgeons, 317; Criminal Law,
318; conduct of British garrison at Point A'fere, 318.

1792, January. Opening speech, II, 319; murder of Columbia
county sheriff, 319, 322; intrusions on Indian lands, 319;
finances, 320; loan commissioners, 320; canals, 320; education, 321; presidential electors, 322, 323.

CLINTON, GEORGE (State)—(*Continued*).

1792, November. Opening speech, II, 323; congressional apportionment, 324; militia, 324; murder of Indian chief, 324; representatives in Congress, election of, veto, 325; Aaron Burr declines appointment of puisne judge, 327; Indian affairs, 328; lock navigation, veto, 329; Oswald case, 330, 335, 351; Vermont solicits · aid in establishing university, 330; New York city, streets and highways, veto, 331.

1794. Opening speech, II, 332; war in Europe, 332; defenseless condition of New York, 333; British retain possession of western posts, 334; suability of State, 334; eleventh amendment, 335, 347; canals, 335; revision of Criminal Code, 335; infectious disease, 336, 344; militia, 336, 339; Indian affairs, 338; conference with Indians, 338, 340, 341, 342, 343, 346, 347, 356; trustees for Indians, 339; objects to proposed appointment as Indian commissioner, 340, 347; Trotter relief, veto, 343; St. Regis Indians, 343, 345; visit of Indians at Buffalo creek, 344; Ryer case, 345; highways in certain counties, veto, 348.

1795. Sends message instead of making speech, 348; fortifications, 349; revision of Criminal Code, 349; common schools, 350; Legislature adjourns to New York, 351; Massachusetts boundary, 351; Indian claims, 351; conference with St. Regis Indians, 351; St. Domingo refugees, 353; land patents, relief from, veto, 354; Oneida, Onondaga and Cayuga Indians, relative to, veto, 356; succeeded by Governor Jay, 358; resumes office, succeeding Governor Jay, 506.

1802. Opening speech, II, 506; national prosperity, 506; finances, 506; fortifications, 507; revision of tax system, 507; estates of attainted persons, 507; prisons, 507; petitions, 508; slaves, 508; salt springs, 509; extra compensation to certain judges, fees for commissions and grants, 509; militia, 510; census, 510; apportionment of Legislature and House of Representatives, 510; vacancies, 511; internal communications, 511; turnpike companies, 511; common schools, 512; cession of Black Rock to United States, 512, 513; St. Regis Indians, 513; inspection of beef and pork, 513; North Carolina resolutions, 513; Massachusetts laws and maps, 514; Indian claims, 514; Peters murder case, 514; repairs to public building, removal of government house furniture, 515, 516; reply to Assembly's address, 516; resignation of Senator Armstrong, 517;

XI — 22

CLINTON, GEORGE (State), 1802 — (*Continued*).

    resignation of Rev. Benjamin Moore as Regent, 517; Oneida Indians, 517, 519; negotiations with Onondagas, 518; service in Land Board, 519; treaty with St. Regis Indians, 520; public health, 520; requests exemption from service on Land Board, 521; highways, streams in Steuben and Chenango counties, veto, 521.

    1803. Opening speech, II, 522; Spanish aggressions at New Orleans, 522; treaty with Senecas and Oneidas, 523; militia, 524, 525, 531; military stores, 524, 525; crimes diminishing, 525; finances, 526; Niagara river lands, 526; intrusions on public land, 527; Hudson river improvement, 527; turnpike companies, 527; common schools, 528; lighthouses on Long Island sound, 530; interchange of maps and statutes, 530; George murder case, 531; national militia system, 531; New York city, actions for small debts, veto, 532; Norton carding machine bill, veto, 534.

    1804. Opening speech, II, 535; Louisiana purchase, 535; fever epidemic, 536; appoints United States Senator, 537; twelfth amendment, 537; purchase of military stores, 537; militia, 538; unappropriated lands, 538; finances, 538; claims against State, 539; jurisdiction over New York harbor, 540; common schools, Hudson river improvement, 540; blessings of republican government, 541; Conklin murder case, 541; fees in Court of Chancery, 542; records of Provincial Congresses and Committee of Safety should be preserved, 542; New York city charter elections, veto, 544; succeeded by Governor Lewis, 544; Vice-President, communication from, defense of New York, 628; cited, common schools, V, 778; statue, United States capitol, VI, 435, 555; manuscripts and papers, purchasing and editing, VII, 688, 808; letter to Chancellor Livingston, 811; asks leave to resign command, 812; letters from Secretary Thompson and General Washington noted, 812; first Governor, IX, 688; official service, I, pref. XII.

CLINTON, GEORGE W. Editor of Clinton Papers, VII, 809; VIII, 247; report, VII, 809.

CLINTON, JAMES, COLONEL. Letter from, Indian incursions in Ulster county, I, 594; relief of northern frontier, II, 99; letter from, scarcity of provisions, 123; letter from, 131; letter to Walter Butler, Cherry Valley massacre, VII, 812; monument to, veto, X, 697.

CLINTON HALL ASSOCIATION. Amending charter, veto, IX, 147.

CLINTON MANUSCRIPTS. Purchase of, VII, 688, 808; report by trustees of State Library, 808; editor's report, 809; method of arrangement, 810; publication of, 814; arrangement, appropriation, veto, VIII, 247.

CLINTON PRISON. Provided for, IV, 74, 124, 406; appropriation for, 125, 276, 278, 381, 406; erection of, 273; transfer of convicts from other prisons, 276; description of buildings, 277; iron ore at, 277; convicts under seventeen years, transferred to Western House of Refuge, 482; neglect of iron manufacture, 607; purchase of ore bed, 608; V, 168; number of convicts, IV, 609, 650, 721, 844; V, 77, 163, 271, 374, 525; VI, 941; VII, 8, 146, 828, 954; decline in iron manufacture, IV, 651; V, 165; additional cells, 78; Governor Morgan's comment on location of, 165; enlargement of, 166; murder at, investigation of, 424; shoe contract, 426; iron contract, 426; discipline defective, 428; Superintendent Pilsbury's report, 425; manufacture of iron at, 601, 697; State work in, 842; purchase of woodlands, 882; statistics, VI, 616; VII, 281, 425, 520, 702, 827, 954; IX, 25; railroad to Lake Champlain, VII, 281; proposed enlargement of, 282; prisoners idle in consequence of failure of clothing company, VIII, 10; idleness of prisoners resulting from abolition of contract system, 646; appropriation for steel cells, 1892, IX, 24; loss by fire at, 25; employment of prisoners in road building, 181, 329; Asylum for Insane Criminal, 658; X, 343.

VETOES. Various repairs and improvements, VII, 484; expense of criminal trials, reimbursing Clinton county, 782; expense of trials, Board of Claims, 887; library, 920; repair of road through State lands, 920; completing iron wall, VIII, 250, 291, 855; repairing plank road to Dannemora station, 862; injuries received while operating machinery in, Hamill case, X, 259; waterworks, sale to Dannemora, 440; Asylum for Insane Criminals, dining-room wing, 588; appropriation for Asylum for Insane Convicts, 655.

CLOTH. Domestic woolen, bounty for, II, 702.

CLOTHIER-GENERAL. Letter from, II, 80.

CLOTHING. Purchase from Indians prohibited, I, 467, 549; for troops, II, 53, 76, 80, 88, 91, 100, 110; returns of, 55; scarcity of, 115; for certain Indians, 262, 394; for troops, Civil War, V, 401; number engaged in trade, New York, 1893, IX, 165.

CLUBS. VETOES. Social, amending act, VI, 501; VII, 664; social, trustees, changing number, 1112.

CLUTE, HARRISON. Schenectady, superintendent of poor, legalizing election, veto, VI, 424.

Clyde. Vetoes. Sale of land for nonpayment of taxes, VI, 217; borrowing money, 706.

Clyde Waterworks Company. Charter, veto, VI, 95.

Clyde and Rose Plankroad Company. Vetoes. Repealing charter, VII, 97; abandonment of road, 267.

Coach House. At Fort George, recommended, I, 306.

Coal. Search for, II, 1010, 1048, 1094; III, 127, 203; needed for various purposes, II, 1094; on head waters of Tioga river, III, 71; transportation on canals, 122; from Pennsylvania and Ohio, 127, 203; bituminous, in Pennsylvania, 168; indications of presence at Oxford, 168; supply from other States, 203; importance in manufactures, 205; transported by Delaware and Hudson Canal Company, 308; possible results of geological survey, 568; from Blossburg mines, additional facilities for obtaining, 786; transportation facilitated by canals, 815; transported on Chemung canal, 865, 953; from Ohio, reduction of tolls on, 871; not found in New York State, 1036; V, 83; canal tolls on, IV, 18; bounties on, 69; used as fuel in salt manufacture, V, 176; obtaining supplies from Pennsylvania, 533; alleged unlawful combination of producers, IX, 183; anthracite, chief deposits in Pennsylvania, 183; sale in certain cities, ton defined, 184; combination, Governor's recommendations approved by American Federation of Labor, 216.

Vetoes. Anthracite, regulating grade and sale of, IX, 272;—protection of purchasers in certain cities, 522.

Coast Defense. Recommended by Governor Lovelace, I, 133.

Coast Survey. Object of, V, 21; protection of signals and stations, VI, 991.

Coatsworth, Caleb J. Board of Claims, veto, VIII, 1166.

Cobden, Richard. England, favors use of ballot at elections, VIII, 585.

Cobleskill. Legalizing election for public improvements, X, 892.

Cochran, James. Resigns as Regent, II, 1028.

Cock, Townsend D. Assembly, member of committee on first occupation of new Senate chamber, VII, 540.

Cockburn, William. Preference of debt to, II, 583.

Cockerill, Thomas. Account for Indian service, I, 136.

Coddington, Charles E. Escheat, veto, X, 706.

Code of Civil Procedure. Homestead exemption, IV, 493; report of commission, VI, 29; adopted in other States, 29; submitted to Statutory Revision Commission, enacted, 118; extraordinary terms, 492; action by Attorney-General against public officers, 732; enactment, 1877, VII, 168; repeal proposed, 169, 196, 302; general amendments, 1895, IX, 546; new commission, 1895, 680.

CODE OF CIVIL PROCEDURE — (*Continued*).

VETOES. Supplemental act, VII, 182, 337; general amendments, 262; VIII, 890; IX, 148, 718; appeal to Court of Appeals from real property judgment, VII, 265; compensation of surrogate's clerk, 649; limitations, person dying within State, 665; costs, 665; amending supplemental act, 665; amendments (8 bills), 805; Court of Appeals, reports, 892; joining issues and appeals, 931; notice of appeal, 932; action by Attorney-General, 934; Kings county, attendance of jurors, certificate, 938; appeals to Court of Appeals from New York Marine Court, 1092; county judge, Westchester county, designation of constables, 1092; decedent's estate, action against executor, 1092; preferred causes, 1093; wife's testimony to disprove adultery, 1093; judgment on attachment, 1093; appeals, consent of General Term, 1093; summary proceedings, rents and taxes, 1094; administrators, guardians, etc., proceedings against, 1094; justices' courts, attachment, service of papers, 1094; justice's court, executions, 1094; justice's court, summons, service on corporation, 1094; New York Marine (city) Court, increasing jurisdiction, 1116; continuance of suit against estate of party deceased, VIII, 131; Court of Appeals, jurisdiction, 131, 229; testimony in action against deceased party, 292; coroner acting as sheriff, 292; protested notes, 293; women, judgments for wages, 293; attorney's lien, 293; appeal to County Court, 406; administrator's bond, 468; real property, levy after ten years, 468; appeals from justices' courts, 468; deposition, application for, 469; summary proceedings, restitution, New York district courts, 469; real property, sale on execution, application of certain sections, 470; chamber orders, action on undertaking, 629; partition actions, funds, unknown owners, withdrawal, 629; jail liberties, Onondaga county, 632; real property, appointment of referee to sell, 632; stenographers, compensation, 639; evidence of physicians, 639; corporations, indictment against, 640; New York Marine Court, jurisdiction, 711, new bill passed; General Term, appeals from, 718; payment of creditors and legatees, 890; jury, Kings county, exemptions, 1037; appeals, amending, 1038; partition actions, 1039; executions, 1040; trust funds, investment of, 1040; infants, lunatics, idiots, habitual drunkards, sale of property, 1041; juries in justices' courts, 1166; evidence, 1167; evidence, confidential communications, IX, 44; new bill passed; taxation, exemption of property purchased with pension money, repeal, 113; stenographers, Surrogate's Court, transcribing

CODE OF CIVIL PROCEDURE, VETOES — (*Continued*).

notes, 115; wills, probate, 131; fees, county clerks and sheriffs,
150; attachments and executions, indemnity bonds on claim of
property, 150; appeal from orders, 152; mortgages, foreclosure,
costs, 153; wages, judgments for, 246; acknowledgments, proof
of, and effect as evidence, 266; executors and administrators,
judicial settlement of accounts, 283; infants, lunatics and
habitual drunkards, sale of property, 283; appeals, exceptions
and case, 283, 390; taxpayer's action against public officer,
364; attorneys, justices' courts, Queens county, laymen not to
practice in, 373; justices of the peace, fees, 375; justices'
courts, jurors' fees, 427; witness' fees, 446; attachments, liens
on real property, 474; attorneys, compensation, 523; notices of
pendency, cancellation of, 624, 627; judgments, entry of, 624;
Surrogates' Courts, costs, 625; trial, exceptions, 625; wages,
actions for, 726; jurors, compensation, 726; juries in certain
counties, drawing, relative to, 791; injunctions, relative to, 791;
demurrer amendments after decision, 791; real property, action
to recover, 791, 792; Supreme Court reporter, furnishing
papers to, 691; trials, postponing, 791; jury notices, service of,
792; damages for causing death by negligence, 792; judgment
creditors, actions by, 792; Kings county, public administrator,
792; justices of the peace, jurisdiction in certain towns, 792;
justices' courts, attorneys in, 792; Albany, City Court, 792;
supplementary proceedings, new section, 792; jurors' fees,
792; X, 62; evidence, documentary, IX, 860; children, custody
of, 860; administrators, letters, 860; justices' courts, where not
to be held, 860; costs, 860; decedents, inventory of estate, X,
62; preferred causes, 159, 173; Surrogate's Court, appearance
in proceedings, 253; Surrogate's Court, additional allowance
on settlement of accounts, 254; pleadings, copartnership, denying allegations of, 309; attachments, 310; depositions, 313;
New York, City Court, 313; wills, construction of, 316;·
arrest on Civil process, deposit in lieu of bail, 317, 388;
wills, revocation of probate, jury trial, 318; attachments
on personal property, undertakings on discharge of, 441;
procedure, condemnation proceedings necessary, 442; compulsory accountings in equity actions, 443; papers for orders
of publication, 443; judgment, notice of application, 444;
proof of handwriting, 444; summary proceedings, petition,
450; attachment, undertaking on discharge, 534; foreign wills
and letters of administration, certification, 585; appeals,

CODE OF CIVIL PROCEDURE, VETOES — (*Continued*).
decision on, 587; stenographers, 587; receivers and trustees, commissions, bonds, 589; replevin, possession of property on giving security, 590; divorce, foreign judgment, enforcement in this State, 594; stenographers, Supreme Court, Trial Term, 699; jurors, powers of commissioners, exemptions, 701; Court of Claims, jurisdiction, 703, 709; limitation of actions, cause of action arising in another State, 703; justices of the peace, jurisdiction, 704; justices of the peace, defining term, 704; attachment, undertaking for restitution, 706; judgment, application for, 707; adding new section, providing for trials in cases of appointment of Supreme Court commissioners, 709; summary proceedings, service of precept, 717; when action may be maintained, 758; Condemnation Law, 761; claim of property, how tried, 807; execution, claim of property by third person, how tried, 807; Appellate Division, designation of justices, 808; accountants, 808; stenographers, Kings County Court, 808; jurors, exemptions, 808; justices of the peace, jurisdiction, 808; justices of the peace, meaning of term, 808; corporations, voluntary dissolution, 808; mortgaging property of infants, 808; possession of property on giving security, 808; judgment, docket of, 814; costs in action, 880, 916; jurors' fees, 947; procedure, substituted service, publication, 952; jurors' exemptions, 953; costs and allowances, Surrogate's Court, 955; evidence, weather records, New York, 955; deputy sheriff, Richmond county, attending court, compensation, 961.

CODE OF CRIMINAL PROCEDURE. Pardons, IV, 405, 435; counsel for defendants, V, 293; enacted, 597; report of commission, VI, 29; adopted in other States, 29; submitted to Statutory Revision Commission, enacted, 118; electrocution, VIII, 37; superseded acts repealed, 37; appeals in capital cases, 82, 181.

VETOES. Printing, VII, 416, 508; act relative to, 417, 509; Senate committee on, printing for, 493; act to establish, 504; vagrants, commitment, 932; oyer and terminer, removal of causes to, 1090; justices of sessions, Kings county, compensation, 1090; new trials in capital cases, 1091, authorized, 1091; bail, procedure, 1091; search warrants, 1092; certificates of conviction, VIII, 129; coroners, 292; disorderly persons, 458; witnesses in criminal cases, 468; Albany Special Sessions, 639; bail, 886; stenographer's duties, 890; appeals by people in criminal cases, 981; criminal statistics, 1040; IX, 153; appeal from Special Sessions, stay of execution, 45; jury in Special Sessions, 129; Special Sessions, jurisdiction, motions for new trial, 260; Court

COCHECTON. Delaware river dykes and barriers, veto, X, 814.

COHEN, SOLOMON. Policeman, New York, relief, veto, X, 176, 581.

COHOCTON. Water commissioners, abolishing board, veto, IX, 722.

COHOES. Number of excise licenses, 1887, VIII, 359; excise license fees, 1889, 685; new charter, 1892, IX, 51.

   VETOES. Legalizing construction of Canal street sewer, VI, 192; amending charter, 197; VII, 265; VIII, 886, 1041; IX, 784; Hotel Company, charter, VI, 579; legalizing State and county taxes, 1035; canal bridge, Ship street, VII, 115, 249, 361; taxes, legalizing, 133; powers of recorder, 327; liability for damages, 412; removal of canal bridge, 554; water supply, 1124; Schuyler street extension, IX, 51; election inspectors and poll clerks, 64; bonds for taxes, 120; taxes, arrears, collection of, X, 436.

COHOES FALLS. Proposed carriage around, I, 146.

COHOES HOTEL COMPANY. Charter, veto, VI, 579.

COIN. Clipping and defacing foreign, I, 116; act relating to corruption of, 131, 134; exportation of gold and silver prohibited, 133; rates of foreign, in colony, 134; copper, act relating to importation of, 507; power of Federal government in relation to, III, 630; proposed reserved deposits in banks, V, 46; used in paying State debt, 450; VI, 100, 166, 349, 526; appropriation for premium, interest on State debt, V, 493; should be restored to its proper place, VI, 137; payment of general fund debt, premium, 167; sold in Wall street, 249; amount received by United States treasury, 251; redemption of national obligations in, VII, 150; equivalent paper to be used in paying taxes, 170, 310.

COKE, LORD EDWARD. Quoted,— civil superior to martial law, V, 469; — death as result of martial law, when murder, VI, 772.

COKE'S INSTITUTES. Cited, IV, 358.

COKE'S LITTLETON. Cited, IV, 358.

COLDEN, CADWALLADER. Letter from, French intrigues with Six Nations, I, 366; provisions for Carrying Place, 498; President of Council assumes executive authority, 647.

   OPENING SPEECH. Twenty-eighth Assembly, third session, I, 647; conquest of Canada, 648; support of government, 649, 660, 681; Assembly dissolved by death of King, 649.

   OPENING SPEECH. Twenty-ninth Assembly, first session, I, 650; raising more troops, 651; military preparations, 653; military commissions, 653; Sandy Hook lighthouse, 655; appointed Lieutenant-Governor, 656.

   OPENING SPEECH. Twenty-ninth Assembly, second session, I, 656; volunteers for frontier service, 657; uneasiness among Indians

COLDEN, CADWALLADER — (*Continued*).

    in Ulster and Orange counties, 657, 658; succeeded by Governor Monckton, 659, 669; resumes executive authority during Governor's absence, 659.

OPENING SPEECH. Twenty-ninth Assembly, third session, I, 659; reform in legal proceedings, 660, 661; tippling houses, 660; authority of Legislature, 661; appointment of Chief Justice Pratt, 662; congratulatory address on King's marriage, 662.

OPENING SPEECH. Twenty-ninth Assembly, fourth session, I, 662; raising troops for general service, 663; recruits for King's regiments, 664; bounties for volunteers, 664; war against Spain, 666; Governor Monckton resumes executive office, 669; Governor Monckton goes to England, 673; Colden again resumes executive office, 673.

OPENING SPEECH. Twenty-ninth Assembly, sixth session, 673; peace, 673; western Indians attack frontier, 674; troops for Indian War, 675, 676; Assembly's inquiry as to cause of Indian War, 678.

OPENING SPEECH. Twenty-ninth Assembly, seventh session, I, 679; Indian affairs improving, 680; frontier defense, 680.

OPENING SPEECH. Twenty-ninth Assembly, eighth session, I, 681; peace with Indians, 681, 682; public debt, 681; cultivation of hemp, 682; address to, Indian War, 682; Assembly's observations on taxation, 683; English Sugar Act, 684; New Jersey boundary, 684; Massachusetts boundary, 685; annulment of certain Indian land grants, 685, 686; Assembly petitions to home government, 687; succeeded by Governor Moore, 700; letter from, opposition to Stamp Act, 711; mob destroys property of, 711; losses not paid, 713, 728; claims for salary and riot damages, 728; resumes executive office on death of Governor Moore, 734.

OPENING SPEECH. Thirty-first Assembly, first session, I, 734; expected repeal of objectionable duties, 734; Indian trade, 735; quartering troops, 735; repairs at Fort George, 736; succeeded by Governor Dunmore, 736; resumes executive office after Governor Tryon's departure, 759; prorogues Assembly, 759.

OPENING SPEECH. Thirty-first Assembly, seventh session, I, 759; support of government, 759; situation in colony, 760; Pennsylvania boundary, 761; claims of Root and Rood, 762; improvement of roads, 762; master of rolls, 763; secretary's office, 763; disturbance in Cumberland county, 764; Quebec boundary, 764; approves Assembly's address relative to colonial conditions, 767; official service, I, pref. X.

COLDEN, CADWALLADER (State). Prisoner, letter from, II, 20.

COLD HARBOR. Lighthouse, cession for, VII, 393.

COLD SPRING (Cattaraugus county). State road, Allegany reservation, improvement, veto, VIII, 847.

COLD SPRING. Fish hatchery, veto, VII, 902; fish hatchery established, IX, 192.

COLD SPRING HARBOR. Protection of shellfish in, veto, VII, 415.

COLE, CAPTAIN. Seneca chief, joins in address to Governor, II, 943.

COLE, CHESTER S. Captain of the port of New York, compensation, veto, VII, 1049; claim submitted to Board of Claims, act sustained, 1048.

COLE, DAN H. Senate, Canal Committee, canal appropriations, lift-bridges, VI, 1006.

COLE, EDWARD. Appointed sergeant-at-arms of Assembly, I, 101.

COLE, FREMONT. Speaker, trustee of public buildings, VIII, 501; member of New Capitol Commission, 1888, 650.

COLE, HUGH L. Opinion, voter's freedom of selection of candidate cannot be restricted by form of ballot, IX, 395, 479.

COLE, ISAAC U. Draining lands of, veto, VII, 457.

COLE, WILLIAM L. Relief, amending act, veto, IX, 152.

COLE, WILLIAM M. New York, relief, veto, X, 582.

COLE RIVER. Meeting of Quebec boundary commissioners at, I, 744.

COLESVILLE. Harpersville Cemetery Association, granting certain powers, veto, VII, 98.

COLLATERAL INHERITANCE TAX. See also TRANSFER TAX. Act relating to, VIII, 102; amount received from, 305, 1082; IX, 9, 158; Governor Hill's suggestions, 1890, VIII, 928; family exemption, 928, 1067; probate and succession tax, 1067; act of 1891, graduated tax, 1150.

VETOES. Amending act, VIII, 293; IX, 118; New York, fees of county treasurer and comptroller, VIII, 412; exempting Young Men's Association, Buffalo, 733; Howard estate, restitution of tax, 1139.

COLLECTOR OF THE PORT. Memorial from, I, 22; to receive weighhouse fees, 36, 38; Byerly's report, 109; New York district, restoring part of Long Island to, 213; seizure of gunpowder by, 532, 543, 552; William H. Robertson appointed, 1881, VII, 556.

COLLECTORS. Local, act for election of, I, 16; United States, under Revenue Act, II, 276; vacancies, how filled, V, 218; reimbursement for losses, Oneida county, unconstitutional, VII, 753; X, 275; canal tolls, office abolished, VII, 819.

VETOES. New Hartford, reimbursing collector, VI, 701; of taxes, VII, 62; receipts by, VIII, 1040; towns, official term, IX, 149;

COLLECTORS, VETOES — (*Continued*).

     Richmond county, bill to abolish, 399; of taxes, fees, X, 171; taxes, Suffolk county, notices, 310, 441; of taxes, notice to non-residents, 386; schools, notice to taxpayers, 439; taxes and assessments, unpaid, Buffalo, 476.

COLLEGE OF THE CITY OF NEW YORK. VETOES. Acquiring new site, IX, 381; site and buildings, X, 176.

COLLEGE POINT. VETOES. Amending village charter, IX, 628; school taxes, amending act, 818; conveying real estate to school district, Flushing, 819; Poppenhusen Institution at, relative to taxation, X, 700.

COLLEGES. Act to establish King's, I, 523; name changed to Columbia, II, 200; aid to Union, 453, 551; should be encouraged, 558; operation only partial, 719; aid to, 904; of physicians and surgeons, 317, 904, see particular colleges; number of students, 1049; III, 61; estimate of State's share in national domain, II, 1101; effect on subordinate institutions, III, 160; lotteries for, 187; endowment of, 296, 946; condition, 457, 501, 540, 857; United States deposit fund, 652; IV, 118; importance of visitation, III, 743; should be sustained, IV, 119, 397; special appropriations, effect of new Constitution, 378; for instruction in agriculture, 433; aiding new institutions, 552; advantages afforded by, 648; general act for incorporation, 648; State scholarships, 716; People's College at Havana, V, 178; military training in, 375; enlistments from, 522; increased attendance, 605; prosperous condition, VI, 618, 945; VII, 157; number, VI, 618; VII, 688, 947; Regents may incorporate, VI, 671; Governor Robinson opposes taxation for, VII, 21, 295; liberal endowments, 688; amount of property which may be held by, general act, 1889, VIII, 728; national military, instruction of State militia officers in, X, 16; comparative statement, 1905, 737.

VETOES. Homeopathic Medical College, Buffalo, charter, VII, 266; legalizing certain charters, 937; Vassar, right to hold additional property, VIII, 728; College of the City of New York, acquiring new site and buildings, IX, 381; exemption from taxation, X, 947; New York, establishing free college, Brooklyn, 956.

COLLIER, EDWARD L. Assembly, member of Committee on Taxation, 1899, X, 801.

COLLIER, JOHN A. Code commissioner, VII, 183.

COLLIN, CHARLES A. Revised prison administration laws, 1889, VIII, 814; prepares ninth edition of Revised Statutes, IX, 767.

COLLINS, CAPTAIN. Convoys transports to Cape Breton, I, 371.

COLLINS, EDWARD, MAJOR. Proposed allowance to, I, 377; service of rangers, 402; examined as to situation in Albany, 407.

COLLINS, JOHN. Claim, surveying Quebec boundary, I, 757; appropriation for completing survey, 757, 764.

COLLINS, LEVI. Bond for return of arms, II, 775.

COLLINS, VALENTINE M. VETOES. New York, relief, X, 581; department of education, claim, 691, 818.

COLMAN, ISAAC D. Relief, veto, VI, 595.

COLONIAL HISTORY. Proceedings for compilation of, III, 162, 751, 935, 1008, 1013; IV, 166; letter from J. R. Brodhead, agent, III, 1014; IV, 167; appropriations for, III, 1015; IV, 44, 165, 192; correspondence, Edward Everett and Lord Aberdeen, III, 1016, 1020; IV, 167; statement of needed documents, III, 1017; IV, 176; progress of work, III, 1035; IV, 43; volumes deposited in Secretary's office, 82; agent's final report, 164; Dutch West India Company records sold at auction, 172; arrangement of documents, 191.

VETOES. Printing and binding fifteenth volume, VIII, 424, 866; — translation of ecclesiastical documents, X, 298, 563.

COLONIAL LAWS. Printing, I, 11; IV, 488; IX, 681; distribution, 1897, 681.

COLONIE. Arsenal at, proposed sale to United States, II, 755; sale of, 828.

VETOES. Collection and disbursement of highway money, X, 589; — eastern boundary, relative to, 702.

COLONIES. See also UNION. Conference of Governors of, I, 137, 138, 140; importance of union, 320; should join in frontier defense, 324, 336, 337, 364; letter from Governor Shirley, 330; Governor Clinton urges negotiations for union, 335; defense of, by home government, 340; aiding in Cape Breton expedition, 351; Indian treaties with, 359; for mutual protection, 366, 368, 465; Massachusetts appoints commissioners for union of, 370; join in expedition against Canada, 373, 376, 404, 413; apportionment of expense of Canadian expedition, 392, 406; estimated expense of attack on Crown Point, 393; new war measures, estimated expense of, 404; agreement for colonial union, 419, 457, 461, 462; Crown Point expedition, 419, 440; difference between rights of colonists and of citizens, 491; joining in Indian treaty, 514; Crown urges union in opposing invasion, 531, 539, 565; meeting of commissioners at Albany, 541; general plan of union formed at Albany, 550, 577; township settlements compared with patents, 552; Governor Shirley's plan of defense approved, 566; apportionment for Crown Point

COLONIES —(Continued).

expedition, 571; agents for Indian service, 572; plan of union reported by Lords of Trade, 582; Albany plan not approved, 582; agreement relative to northern garrisons, 584; expense of northern garrisons, 585; receive King's financial aid, 598; common fund recommended, 599; joining in Indian War, 676; in North America, possibilities of, 690; alleged discriminations against, 690; extend British dominion and trade, 698; should join in support of King's troops, 709; duties on, protest against, 730; power of consultation with one another, 730; Indian trade regulations, 735, 739; New York's influence in promoting intercourse with England, 737; Congress meets in Philadelphia, 766; correspondence with, resolution relative to, 768; statement of grievances by New York Assembly, 771; not contemplated by English Constitution, 775; correspondence relative to colonial agreements, 777; Dutch and English, boundaries of, III, 1018; documents relating to; 1019.

COLONISTS. Not entitled to privileges of citizens, I, 491; extent of duty under acts of Parliaments, 704; no forfeiture of rights by emigration, 704, 772, 775.

COLONIZATION. Beginning of, in New York, I, 1.

COLONY. Early forms of government, I, 1; powers of States-General in, 1; Legislature established, 1; Governor and Council, powers of, 1; Twelve Men, 1; Eight Men, 2; Nine Men, 2; Duke of York becomes proprietor, 2; Dyer's case, 4; Governor's power in relation to bills, 7; change of government on accession of James II, 12; Assembly discontinued, 13; Leisler assumes executive authority, 14; Leisler Assembly, 15, 16; Assembly revived, 18; boundaries of, in 1691, 29; amount of debt, 1692, 34; aid from Crown, 36, 61, 132, 152, 217; heavy taxation in, 37; Crown furnishes troops for, 36, 49, 152; aid not expected from other provinces, 53, 67, 89; agent of, appointed, 58, 175; position of, protects neighboring colonies, 67, 70; recruits from Connecticut, 71; unhappy condition of colony, 75, 80, 98; relations to Crown, 80; irreligion and immorality in, 80; executive powers of Council, 91; President of Council vested with executive power, 94; grammar free school established in, 100; repeal of act to quiet disorders, 109, 110; expected French attempt on, 119; should furnish arms, 124; proposed settlement of Palatines in, 146; should have negative in confederacy, 158; Governor urges defense of, 205; relations with King, 213, 216; importation of salt, 219; proposed fixing of boundaries, 226; rights and liberties to be preserved, 231; Constitution described, 253, 283; more whites needed, 266; Assembly terms fixed at three years; King vetoes act, 267, 271, 278, 279;

COLONY—(*Continued*).

conditions improved, 266; importance of acquiring Tierondequat, 272; English troops in, 276; proposed settlements north of Saratoga, 278; supplies for expedition against West Indies, 288; receives special royal favors, 292; suggested movement for independence, 294; defense of, urged, 295; to furnish powder, ball and flags, 295; act for defense of, 318, 345; suggestion of union with other colonies, 320; expected invasion by French and Indians, 366; engineer appointed for, 371; proposed share of expense in French War, 406; must contribute to expense of war, 410, 412, 415; intrusions on land in, 523; heavy expenditures in Canadian expedition, 551; high character of New York bills of credit, 560; results if French should take Albany, 563; Governor Burnet's claim against, 592; troops of, not to serve outside North America, 598; heavy burdens of war, 599; King consents to annual appropriations, 605; reimbursement for military expenses, 627; extent of military service, 628; aid granted to other colonies, 629; frontier settlements, 631; foreign lotteries, sale of tickets prohibited, 641; share of parliamentary appropriation, 645, 647; recruits for King's regiments, 664; troops for Indian War, 676; English Sugar Act, mischiefs of, 684; Assembly petitions to home government, 687, 729; ruinous condition of colony, 692; trial by jury, 693; paper currency necessary, 694; burdens on, should be imposed by itself, 700; protest against parliamentary encroachments on rights of, 703; obedience to acts of Parliament, 704; authority of Parliament in, 712; Parliament prohibits legislation until grant of supplies for troops, 721, 730, 773; to regulate Indian trade, 723, 735, 738; consultation with other colonies, 730; influence in promoting intercourse between England and other colonies, 737; courts needed in remote parts of, 762; Assembly demands home rule, 765; committee of 51, 765; state of, Assembly resolution, 768; Assembly refuses to send delegates to Continental Congress, 769; grievances of, presented to home government, 771; Provincial Congresses, 778; martial law in, 765, 779; British evacuate New York, 780; State government established, 780.

COLORADO. Court to render opinion as to constitutionality of pending bills, VIII, 947; Employer's Liability Law, X, 190.

COLORED HOME, NEW YORK. Relative to, veto, VII, 267.

COLQUHOUN, FREDERICK. Petition from, IV, 84.

COLTON. Lockup, providing for, veto, VIII, 229.

COLUMBIA BANK. Failure, loss of bank stock, III, 300.

COLUMBIA COLLEGE. Formerly King's College, I, 523; II, 200; VIII, 168; aid to, II, 321, 375, 973; anatomical museum for, 389; petition of, 393; relative to, veto, 610; botanic garden for, 973; commended

Columbia College — (*Continued*).

by Governor Clinton, 1100; flourishing condition of, III, 296, 540, 739, 766, 857.

Columbia County. Governor Clinton visits, II, 273; murder of sheriff, 319, 322; courthouse and jail, 419; resistance to judicial authority, 451, 456; sealer of weights and measures, communication from, III, 98; agricultural society, 945; anti-rent troubles, IV, 147; assault on deputy sheriff, 235; tenants represented before Assembly Committee on Anti-Rent Troubles, 328; includes Livingston manor, 329; average excise license fees, 1889, VIII, 686; highways, cost of labor system, 1892, IX, 199; insane, care of, county and State systems compared, 228.

Vetoes. Equalizing assessments, VI, 95; excepting from provisions of County Treasurer's Act, VII, 264; superintendent of poor, relative to, 508; county clerk, recording notices of pendency, VIII, 63, 70, 705; tramps and vagrants, regulating commitment and discharge, 891; clerk's office hours, repeal, IX, 625; institutions, purchase of supplies for, X, 700.

Columbus, Christopher. Irving's life of, to be used in schools, III, 406; discovery of America, VIII, 931; 400th anniversary, celebration in New York, 933; IX, 24; soldiers and sailors' memorial arch, Brooklyn, veto, 211.

Columbus Day. Made a public holiday, 1909, X, 584.

Colve, Anthony. Dutch Governor, II, 1115.

Colvin, Andrew J. President of Senate, welcomes Abraham Lincoln, V, 334.

Colvin, Verplanck. Member of Adirondack Park Commission, 1872, VII, 722; Superintendent of State Land Survey, IX, 424, 425.

Coman, Henry B. Counsel for Legislature in trial of Justice Hooker, X, 829; counsel for Comptroller, Tonawanda case, appropriation, veto, 933.

Commander-in-Chief. Richard Ingoldesby becomes Acting Governor, I, 23.

Commerce. Act to encourage trade and navigation, I, 11; equal privileges of, granted by Leisler Assembly, 16; act to regulate transportation of property, 16; Governor Fletcher's suggestions concerning promotion of, 28; relations with neighboring colonies, 58; restrictions by Crown, 79; expected benefits from Spanish War, 287; danger from French privateers, 467; English on Great Lakes, French attempts to destroy, 486; interference with, by French intrigues among Indians, 504, 535; frauds in various commodities, 530; embargo on certain vessels, 622; ruinous condition of, 692; with West Indies, 692; with sugar colonies, 692; lumber and Irish linen; 693;

COMMERCE —(*Continued*).

extension of, 701; tax on, by Parliament, 706; with England should be free, 773; illicit, with British, act to prevent, II, 164; British attempt to monopolize, 197; plans for improvement of, 198; proposed treaty between United States and Great Britain, 236; encouragement of, 254; Virginia proposes commercial convention, 260; prosperous condition of, 313; French depredations on, 445; on Mississippi river, Kentucky protests against unlawful taxation of, 606; condition incident to approaching war, 622; effect of embargo, 632; effect of foreign war, 656; neutral, revocation of French decrees, 672, 690; interdiction of, by United States, proposed amendment, 827; to be maintained by war if necessary, 910; effect of canals, 966; internal should be encouraged, 1006, 1090; with South American republics, 1093; Federal tonnage duties on canals, III, 50, 76; powers of Congress, 234, 420, 462; IV, 394, 616; importance of, III, 420; on canals, 460; V, 452; a source of speculation, III, 486; threatened by abolition agitation, 571; excessive importations, effect of, 657; defined, promotion of, 779; wide area of, 814; Virginia attempts to restrict, with New York, 910, 925, 936, 980, 1028, 1037; South Carolina act for search of New York vessels, 980, 1028; colonial, documents relating to, 1019; canal, with western States, IV, 584; reciprocity with British provinces, 656; purpose of canal system, 674; diverted from canals, 736; too many officials at New York, V, 81; at New York, hindrances from quarantine regulations, 185; work of port wardens at New York, 187; free navigation of Mississippi river, 479; loss resulting from Civil War (Seymour), 534; increase resulting from Civil War (Fenton), 593; western products, no adequate outlet through Canada, 709; commercial union between New York and Mississippi river, 780; relation of Erie canal, VI, 14; conspiracies against, 121; restrictions should be abrogated, 553; at New York, neglect of, 685; natural course through New York, 736; importance of railroads, 748; origin and development of, 752; restrained by usury laws, VII, 719; advance on collateral securities, parties may fix rate, 719; American supremacy, opinion of De Tocqueville, 992; competition between railroads and canals, IX, 556; Governor Black's comments, 1898, 824; New York, commission of inquiry created, 1898, 826; X, 3; decrease at New York, 3; New York, report of special commission, 1900, 130; railroad discrimination against New York, 131, 136; New York, how affected by canals, 359; interstate, demurrage bill, veto, 926.

COMMERCIAL BANK, ALBANY. See ALBANY COMMERCIAL BANK.

COMMERCIAL CREDIT GUARANTY COMPANY, NEW YORK. Charter, veto, VI, 191.

COMMERCIAL CONSTRUCTION COMPANY. Court of Claims, Manhattan State Hospital, veto, X, 588.

COMMERCIAL TRAVELERS' ASSOCIATION, NEW YORK. Charter, veto, VI, 340.

COMMERCIAL TRAVELERS' HOME ASSOCIATION OF AMERICA. Incorporated, IX, 87.

COMMERCIAL TRUST AND BANKING COMPANY, NEW YORK. Charter, veto, VI, 342.

COMMISSARY. At Oswego, new, to be appointed, I, 245; on Massachusetts boundary, 718, 720, 747, 752, 754; James Hamilton, claim of, II, 185.

COMMISSARY OF FORAGE. Letter from, II, 54.

COMMISSARY OF MILITARY STORES. Report, II, 332, 433, 524, 560, 586, 605, 628, 647, 668, 682, 795, 816, 829, 866, 882, 939; compensation of deputy, 561; letter from, Staten Island beacon, 589; purchase of ball, 629.

COMMISSARY OF PRISONERS. Furnishing means for, II, 25.

COMMISSARY-GENERAL. Deputy, letter from, II, 20; letter from, 78; claim of, 79; compensation of officers of department, 793; to reside at Albany, 829; assistants provided for, 829; department, provision for, 831; to lease Albany arsenal, 871; communication from, filling Collect street, New York, 895; communication from, New York arsenal assessment, 953, 999; report, military stores, 987, 990; statement by, 1038, 1078; communication from, Albany arsenal, lease of unoccupied land, 1076; annual report, 1078, 1114; III, 13, 34, 97, 142, 183, 218, 261, 315, 355, 389, 482, 527, 587, 637, 680, 748, 869, 906, 972; IV, 45, 85, 154, 287, 381, 419, 450, 506, 573, 624, 681; V, 40, 199, 305, 486; communication from, additional artillery, II, 1114; III, 21, 99; repairs at Fort Richmond, 35; claims against United States, 36; artillery, 137, 145; persons chosen, 430; report, New York riot, 527; visits western frontier, 685; how chosen, 1004; location of gunhouses, IV, 452; to sell arsenals and arms in certain counties, 495; communication relative to arsenals and armories, V, 642; relative to arsenal at Dunkirk, 643.

COMMISSARY-GENERAL OF ORDNANCE. Report, II, 939, 1027; V, 570, 617, 719, 863; VI, 44, 143, 442, 554; VII, 200, 316.

COMMISSARY-GENERAL OF PURCHASES. Letters from assistant, scarcity of wheat and flour, II, 54, 82; letter from, supply of salt, 84; letter from deputy, 94.

COMMISSION, GOVERNOR. Extract from Governor Bellomont's, I, 91; extract from Governor Clinton's, 483, 505; powers conferred by, II, 2; extract from Governor Osborn's, 498.

COMMISSION ON ADMINISTRATION OF CHARITABLE INSTITUTIONS. Created, 1884, VII, 964.

COMMISSION OF APPEALS. Amendment to establish, not approved, V, 535, 597; provided, Judiciary Article, 1869, VI, 124.

COMMISSION ON CAPITAL CENTENNIAL CELEBRATION. Created, 1896, IX, 689; report, 1897, 690.

COMMISSION ON CHATTANOOGA BATTLEFIELD. Created, VIII, 1076; monument to New York troops, 1077; consolidated with Gettysburg Commission, 1077.

COMMISSION ON CLASSIFICATION OF SALARIES. Allowance for expenses, veto, X, 792.

COMMISSION ON COMMERCE OF NEW YORK. Created, IX, 826; time to report extended, 826; X, 3; report, 1900, IX, 826; X, 75, 130; supplemental report, proposed bills, 142.

COMMISSION ON CONVICT LABOR. Created, VI, 109, 234; report, 234; new commission, 1884, VII, 957; VIII, 9; extending time, veto, VII, 1001.

COMMISSION ON COTTON STATES EXPOSITION. Created, IX, 582.

COMMISSION ON EDUCATIONAL UNIFICATION. Created, X, 114; members of, 114; recommends department of education, 114; report, 128.

COMMISSION ON ELECTROCUTION. Created, VIII, 37.

COMMISSION ON ENLARGEMENT OF CLINTON PRISON. Created, VII, 282.

COMMISSION ON EXCISE LAWS. Created, VIII, 643; report, 688.

COMMISSION ON HERKIMER MONUMENT. Report, IX, 685, 754.

COMMISSION TO INVESTIGATE CHARGES AGAINST MANAGEMENT OF GREEN-WOOD CEMETERY. Report, VIII, 70.

COMMISSION TO INVESTIGATE FORESTS. Appointed by Comptroller, VIII, 23; report, 23.

COMMISSION TO INVESTIGATE JAILS, PENITENTIARIES AND REFORMATORIES. Created, VII, 287.

COMMISSION TO INVESTIGATE LUNATIC ASYLUMS. Report, VI, 554.

COMMISSION ON LATERAL CANALS. Appointment, VI, 750; report, 933; VII, 8; new commission created, VI, 933; appropriation for, VII, 9.

COMMISSION OF LAW'S DELAY. Appointed, 1902, X, 515, 620; report, 1904, 516, 621, 628; Supreme Court commissioner's bill, veto, 662.

COMMISSION ON LEGISLATIVE PROCEDURE. Created, 1895, IX, 676; report, 682.

COMMISSION ON LEWIS AND CLARK CENTENNIAL EXPOSITION. Expenses, appropriation, veto, X, 799.

COMMISSION ON LOCATION OF EASTERN NEW YORK STATE CUSTODIAL ASYLUM. Created, X, 726.

COMMISSION ON LOUISIANA PURCHASE EXPOSITION. Established, X, 350.

COMMISSION ON MUNICIPAL REFORM. Created, VI, 844, 1025; report, VII, 134; quoted, powers of mayor of New York, IX, 417.

COMMISSION ON NEW SITE FOR SING SING PRISON. Created, X, 863.

COMMISSION ON NIAGARA FALLS RESERVATION. Created, VII, 301.

COMMISSION ON NORMAL SCHOOLS. Created, V, 695, 780; report, 695, 780; resolution by, 781.

COMMISSION ON PALISADES. Created, IX, 670; report, 682.

COMMISSION ON PRISON BUILDINGS. Appointed, X, 863; report, 863.

COMMISSION ON PROBATION SYSTEM. Appointment, X, 863; report, 863.

COMMISSION ON PROCEDURE. Created, 1895, IX, 680; terminated, 1900, 681.

COMMISSION TO REVISE MILITARY CODE. Created, VII, 428; report, 429.

COMMISSION ON SECOND-CLASS CITIES. Created, IX, 677; report, 678.

COMMISSION ON STATE PENITENTIARY. Created, VI, 58; report, 110.

COMMISSION ON STATE'S PROPERTY RIGHTS, WAR OF 1812. Created, VII, 601.

COMMISSION ON TAX REVISION. See also COMMISSIONERS ON TAX REVISION. Created, 1898, IX, 846; 1906, X, 837.

COMMISSION ON TENNESSEE CENTENNIAL. Report, IX, 852.

COMMISSION ON THIRD-CLASS CITIES. Created, IX, 677; report, 678, 685.

COMMISSION ON TUBERCULOSIS IN CATTLE. Created, 1893, IX, 327.

COMMISSION ON UNIFORM LAWS. Created, VIII, 929, 1068; IX, 188; report, VIII, 930, 1068; National Conference on Uniform Legislation, 930; members of, 1068.

COMMISSION ON WAR CLAIMS AGAINST UNITED STATES. Created, V, 756, 832; VI, 903.

COMMISSION ON WATER STORAGE. Established, 1904, X, 743; report, publication and distribution, veto, 651.

COMMISSION ON WORLD'S FAIR. See WORLD'S FAIR COMMISSION.

COMMISSION ON YORKTOWN CENTENNIAL CELEBRATION. Appointment, VII, 734; appropriation for expenses, 735; report, 737; reception of German delegates, 741.

COMMISSIONERS. To visit Indians, I, 84; to examine public accounts, 89, 96, 100, 103; on supplies for Canadian expedition, 152; French, on exchange of prisoners, 510; Colonel Johnson appointed to confer with Indians, 526; to collect duties on Oswego trade, 540; proposed, for New Jersey boundary, 540; proposed, for Massachusetts boundary, 541; to Albany Convention, 550, 577; for Sandy Hook lighthouse, 655; on Massachusetts boundary, 718, 720, 752, 754; II, 211, 217, 260; for Indian trade regulations, I, 735, 739, 747; on Quebec boundary, 744; on preparation of currency plates, 749; to detect conspiracies, II, 20; British, peace overtures, 45; to superintend purchase of clothing, 110, 114; proposed, on Vermont controversy, 143; of public accounts, 172, 184, 437, 438; to Hartford Convention on system of taxation, 190; to Commercial Convention, 260, 270; to

COMMISSIONERS — (Continued).

make Indian treaties, 291, 295, 307; to arrange settlement with Vermont, 307; to explore canal routes, 312, 321; to settle Connecticut claim, 407; to purchase Oneida lands, 412; to settle Connecticut controversy, 449, 457; V, 286; on New Jersey boundary, II, 601; III, 157, 424; on revision of chancery procedure, II, 650; to investigate canal project, 675, 706; on common school system, 676, 702, 707, 717; to investigate title to salt lots, 695; on Astor claim, 867, 940, 986, 990; to investigate Montauk Indians, 931; Ulster county courthouse, 944; on change of New York prison, 993; Hudson river improvement, 1011, 1031; V, 453; investigate State prisons, III, 22; on State roads, 81; on new State prison, 82; on northeastern boundary, 389; to investigate convict labor, 514; to locate State lunatic asylum, 543, 617; to investigate judicial and equity system, 611, 648; on Indian migration, 636; to take proof of acknowledgments outside of State, 770; to examine conditions in Rensselaerwyck, 776, 863; to survey railroad from Ogdensburgh to Lake Champlain, 866; to devise plan of agricultural college, IV, 433; to prepare common school code, 603; to revise Military Code, 656, 726; to investigate prison affairs, veto, 723, 777, 786, passed over veto; on New York harbor encroachments, 857; on Connecticut boundary, 863; to select site for new quarantine hospital, V, 23; to take testimony, legislative investigations, 38; New York common schools, 62; to examine Kingsland claim, 167, 273; on services of militia in War of 1812, 175; on Brooklyn parks, 204; to ascertain damages resulting from destruction of quarantine building, 279; proposed international, on decimal system of weights, measures and currency, 323; on Kansas relief fund, 350; to investigate State prisons, 372; on defense of Narrows, 444; on harbor and frontier defense, 545, see that title; on normal schools, 695; proceedings for removal of officers, 716; on quarantine warehouses, 719; on new capitol, 722; on military affairs, 770; Antietam national cemetery, report, 791; Hudson River Insane Asylum, 791; International Penitentiary Congress, VI, 554; on new boarding station, quarantine, 776; on Tall Chief monument, VIII, 110; St. Regis river improvement, 115; Onondaga reservation, highways, 116.

COMMISSIONER OF ACCOUNTS. Appointed, II, 201.

COMMISSIONERS ON ADJUSTMENT OF QUOTAS. Appointment and report, V, 536, 572.

COMMISSIONER OF AGRICULTURE. Office created, IX, 175; State weather bureau, supervision of, 179; ex officio member of State Fair Commission, X, 120.

COMMISSIONER OF AGRICULTURE — (*Continued*).

VETOES. Counsel, appointment by Attorney-General, IX, 403; department in capitol, furniture and repairs, X, 299; expenses made necessary by amendments to law, appropriation, 786.

COMMISSIONERS OF THE CANAL FUND. Loan, arrearages to contractors, IV, 18, 260; loan, for land damages, 260.

COMMISSIONERS TO CENTENNIAL CELEBRATION. Appointment, VI, 656.

COMMISSIONERS OF CLAIMS (UNITED STATES). Presentation to, of accounts relating to prisoners, II, 33.

COMMISSIONERS ON COLONIAL UNION. Massachusetts appoints, I, 370; New York appoints, 370; apportionment of expenses of Canadian expedition, 392, 406; report, 413, 419, 457.

COMMISSIONERS ON CODIFICATION. Created, IV, 488; VII, 182; discontinued, IV, 489.

COMMISSIONERS ON COMMON SCHOOLS. In towns provided for, II, 967; in New York city, III, 951; office abolished, IV, 23.

COMMISSIONER OF DEEDS. Regulating method of appointment, III, 7, 719, 770; in towns, office abolished, 770, 873; to reside in Paris and Marseilles, V, 213.

VETOES. New York, additional number, VII, 206; Reevs, legalizing acts, VIII, 518; Swikehard, legalizing acts, IX, 150; Prime, legalizing acts, 368; New York, powers, X, 61; Yonkers, additional number, 437; O'Toole, legalizing acts, 948; Simon, legalizing acts, 958.

COMMISSIONERS ON DISEASES OF CATTLE. Report, VI, 143.

COMMISSIONER OF EDUCATION. Office created, IV, 716; X, 115, 605.

COMMISSIONERS OF ELMIRA REFORMATORY. Appointment of, VI, 233.

COMMISSIONERS OF EMIGRATION. Board organized, IV, 440; communication from, deficiencies in available funds, 452; report, 644, 793; V, 450; VIII, 1090; IX, 215; reforms in administration, IV, 850; Castle Garden designated as emigrant depot, 851; ask aid from Legislature, 866; expenditures of, V, 22, 188; loan to, 24; correspondence with Governor King, 99; receive no compensation, 278; new act relative to, 641; enlarging powers of, 844; board reorganized, VI, 117; New York city and Brooklyn, mayor, *ex officio* commissioner of emigration, 117; supervision of Castle Garden, 534; statement of business, 998; appropriation for, 1001; VII, 15; president of, protests against bill filling in channel between Ward's Island and Randall's Island, 46; statement of affairs and resources, 55; appropriation for, contracts with steamship companies, 712; appropriation, approval, 802; new commission created, 832, 966; special message urging confirmation of appointment of commissioner of emigration, 888; VIII, 489.

COMMISSIONERS OF EMIGRATION —(*Continued*).

VETOES. Creating board of, VI, 511; interest on Ward's Island mortgage, VIII, 112; rebuilding landing wharf at Castle Garden, 113.

COMMISSIONERS OF EXCISE. Office created, I, 529.

VETOES. McCollum and McCleary, legalizing acts of, VIII, 354; New York, charges against, stenographer's fees, 551; compensation, IX, 275.

COMMISSIONERS OF FISHERIES. VETOES. Stocking certain waters with fish, VIII, 75; repairs on State road, Forestport to Woodhull, 850; highway, Lewis county No. 4, to Stillwater reservoir, repairs, 851; counsel, appointment by Attorney-General, IX, 403.

COMMISSIONERS OF FORFEITURES. Act relating to, veto, II, 233; report, 256, 273.

COMMISSIONERS OF FORTIFICATIONS. Report from, New York fortifications, II, 413; appointment of, 418; report of, 712, 797, 813, 864, 883; communication from, 752, 822; communication from, redoubt on Signal Hill, 778; completion of fortifications, 830.

COMMISSIONERS ON HARBOR AND FRONTIER DEFENSE. Appointed, V, 545; report, 564.

COMMISSIONERS OF HEALTH OFFICE, NEW YORK. Report, II, 387, 529; communication from, 520; receipts by, investment of, III, 100; aid to Society for the Reformation of Juvenile Delinquents, 252.

COMMISSIONERS OF HIGHWAYS. Provided for, II, 385; erection of bridges, V, 347.

VETOES. Not to be superseded by special officers, VI, 211; liability for damages resulting from defective highways, VII, 767; Easton, election of, 932; Eastchester, number of, VIII, 461, 616; compensation, IX, 462; local authorities under Railroad Law, 462; in certain small towns, X, 590; Saugerties, salary, 810.

COMMISSIONERS OF INDIAN AFFAIRS. Reimbursing for advances, I, 130; report of, smith in Indian country, 145; report from, 161; French negotiations with Indians, 161; report relative to alliance between Tuscaroras and Five Nations, 170; relations between Flatheads and Five Nations, 170; report of French negotiations with Indians, 176, 177; more advanced settlements in Indian country, 181; Indian complaint as to prices of goods, 183; letter from, relative to clandestine trade with French, 200; communication from, relative to houses for Indian service at Albany, 202; communication from, Claesen, interpreter, 206; relative to Far Indians at Albany, 207; letter from, 214, 219; to pay Barclay claim, 224; communication from, transmitting various papers, 240; communication from, relative to French at Crown Point, 241; communication from, relative to defense of Albany, 244; smith and presents for Seneca Indians, 257; employing Indians as spies, 296; communication from, relative to affairs at

COMMISSIONERS OF INDIAN AFFAIRS — (*Continued*).

Albany, 300; communication from, relative to reclaiming Indians, 304; increasing allowance for Indian presents, 310; increasing allowance to, 315, 325; to deliver certain cannon and warlike stores, 316; frontier fortifications, 323; employment of outscouts, 325; French designs on Oswego, 328; defense of Oswego, 329; two more forts on frontier, 333; means for preserving friendship of Indians, 346; increasing allowance for expenses, 353, 369; visit of Mohawks to Canada, 355; Orondax hovering round frontier, 355; declaration of war by French Indians, 355; relative to destruction of Saratoga, 361; security of frontiers, 366; Indians refuse to engage in war, 368, 411; to invite Indians to attend conference with Governor, 376; rangers in Albany county, 377; letter from, 563; sends person to visit Indians, 570; of northern department, letter to, II, 26; papers from, 220, 221, 306; expenses of Indian visitors, 273; colony, papers missing, IV, 184.

COMMISSIONERS FOR THE INSPECTION OF TURNPIKE ROADS. Office created, II, 528.

COMMISSIONERS OF JURORS. New York, special commissioner, office abolished, X, 24; general act, 1899, 45; 1901, 24, 195; Kings county, 395.

  VETOES. New York, relative to, VII, 129, 251, 803; in certain counties, bill providing for, IX, 514, 811, 866; Richmond county, creating office, 796; Albany, act amended, X, 44; Kings county, commissioner and special commissioner, abolishing office, 178; in certain counties, amending act, 440; salaries, 450; notice server, amending act, 532; amending act of 1895, qualifications and exemptions of jurors in certain counties, 587; powers of, exemptions, 701; compensation of judges, 710.

COMMISSIONER OF LABOR. Office established, 1901, X, 189.

  VETOES. Enforcement of section 13, Labor Law, X, 424; additional officers and employees, salaries for enforcement of L. 1902, chap. 454, 554, 564; Buffalo, free employment bureau, appropriation, 554, 564; cataloging library, 564; expenses, reappropriation, 564; deputies and other subordinate officers, expenses, deficiency appropriation, 640; expenses, deficiency appropriation, 641.

COMMISSIONER OF LABOR STATISTICS. Office created, VII, 977; investigation of prison labor, 978.

COMMISSIONERS OF THE LAND OFFICE. Communication from, Remsen claim, II, 261; report on Ossey petition, 307; procedure of, modified, 309; report of, 330; report from, Mallory relief act, 387; to settle with St. Regis Indians, 457; ferries on Niagara river, 526; purchase of botanic garden, 579; to sell Squaw Island

COMMISSIONERS OF THE LAND OFFICE—(*Continued*).

to Jasper Parish, 857; patents of Oneida land, 895; to convey Indian land to John Sergeant, 989; to dispose of certain salt lands, 1010; conveyance of Stockbridge land, 1119; to sell Grand Island, III, 26; to sell to United States land on Staten Island for fortifications, 570; conveyance of land to United States for fortifications, 850; member of State Board of Equalization, IV, 25; V, 91; grants of land under water, VI, 156, 157, 690, 705; VIII, 53; constitutional provision relative to, VIII, 53, 726, 735; may survey State lands, 75; grant of escheated lands, 980; leases of land for oyster beds, IX, 194; leasing riparian lands, X, 117; grant of lands under water to Burns, Peter's case, 266.

VETOES. Powers of, II, 287; land sold for taxes, conveying State's interest, VII, 656; establishing boundary between Lewis and Herkimer counties, appropriation, 783; land in Franklin county, conveyance to Schroeder, VIII, 131; hearing memorial of Cayuga Indians, X, 955.

COMMISSIONERS FOR LOANING UNITED STATES DEPOSIT FUND. See LOAN COMMISSIONERS.

COMMISSIONER OF LUNACY. Office created, V, 448, 521; VI, 628; VIII, 172; department reorganized, VI, 628; expenses, visiting institutions, veto, 923; visitations and reports, 960; powers should be extended, 960; traveling and incidental expenses, veto, VIII, 867.

COMMISSIONERS ON MILITARY EQUIPMENT. Report of, II, 428.

COMMISSIONER OF NEW CAPITOL. Office created, powers and duties, VII, 836; VIII, 222; name changed to State Architect, VII, 837; political tests in employment prohibited, qualifications of deputies and employees, 982; bill abolishing office, veto, VIII, 213.

COMMISSIONERS ON NEW CAPITOL. Appointed, V, 722; new commission created, VI, 229; liquidating liabilities of, VII, 399; completion and supervision of portions of building, 430; claim of Eidlitz, Richardson & Co., architects, veto, 903; report, VIII, 195; new commission, 1888, 610, 650; 1895, IX, 545.

COMMISSIONERS OF PILOTS. Duties relative to New York harbor, V, 95; report, 111, 306, 380, 719, 861; VI, 43, 143, 263, 415; VII, 536; VIII, 195, 325, 503, 696, 935, 1085; IX, 35, 210, 339, 575, 682, 851; X, 31, 130, 371; expense not to be paid from State treasury, V, 185; ask to be relieved from certain duties, 223; efficient work of, 284; appropriation for, 284.

COMMISSIONERS ON PRACTICE AND PLEADINGS. Constitutional provision for, IV, 366, 654; VII, 182; report, IV, 654.

COMMISSIONERS OF PUBLIC ACCOUNTS. Report, V, 486, 571, 623, 724, 795, 862; VI, 47, 156; report, disbursements for military purposes, V, 863; VI, 61.

COMMISSIONERS OF PUBLIC CHARITIES AND CORRECTIONS. Department created, V, 284.

COMMISSIONERS ON PURCHASE OF EXECUTIVE RESIDENCE. Appointed, VII, 178; report, 178.

COMMISSIONERS OF QUARANTINE. Report various recommendations, V, 418; Governor recommends repeal of law creating board, 419; report, 487, 638, 717, 793, 861; VI, 27, 44, 143, 414, 415, 538, 746, 776, 848, 1006; VIII, 45, 197, 338, 717, 946, 1091; IX, 38, 216, 352, 575, 685, 754, 851; X, 31, 142; members of board on new quarantine establishment, V, 701; VI, 26; communication from, expected visitation of cholera, V, 863; communication from West Bank board, VI, 145; board, abolishing, 534; vacancies, nominations for, VIII, 520, 556.

VETOES. Completing purchase of Southfield land, VII, 385; Kirkham claim, 792, 929; care of establishment, appropriation, VIII, 252; proposed appointment by Legislature instead of Governor, 555.

COMMISSIONERS TO REVISE STATUTES. Appointed, II, 255, 675; III, 11, 18; colonial laws, IV, 488; 1870, consideration of various Codes, VI, 118; VII, 168, 184; acts of 1889 and 1904, VI, 118; 1870, names of, 238; report, 261, 318, 415; term extended, 661; quoted, submission of part of work, VII, 186.

COMMISSIONERS OF RINDERPEST. Report of, V, 791, 861; VI, 260; should be continued, 245.

COMMISSIONERS OF SEQUESTRATION. Powers of, II, 191; act relating to, veto, 233; Rush case, 250.

COMMISSIONERS ON STATE PRISONS. Report of, II, 434.

COMMISSIONERS ON STATE SURVEY. Office created, VII, 987; existence extended, 988.

COMMISSIONERS ON STATUES. Appointed, VI, 435.

COMMISSIONERS TO TAKE PROOF OF CONVEYANCES. Provided for, III, 210, 211, 770; in Great Britain and France, V, 212.

COMMISSIONERS ON TAX REVISION. See also COMMISSION ON TAX REVISION. Appointment, VI, 238; report, 238, 269, 370, 552; outline of plan, 371; correspondence between Governor Hoffman and Chairman Wells, 404; proposed Code, 428; new commission appointed, 1881, VII, 538; report on indirect taxation, 570.

COMMISSIONERS FOR TRADE AND PLANTATIONS. Memorial to, I, 72; sustain executive power of Council after Bellomont's death, 92; Assembly's power over money bills, 118, 123, 159, 162, 166; letter relative to colonial treasurer, 123; sustains Governor Cornbury's power to act while out of colony, 127; Palatine immigrants, 146; letter from, rela-

COMMISSIONERS FOR TRADE AND PLANTATIONS —(*Continued*).

tive to Governor's power to act out of colony, 150; more troops for colony, 179; trade and navigation laws, 184; objections to revenue and tonnage bills, 184; communication relative to pitch and tar, 188; communication relative to continuance of Assembly, 196, 197; recommend approval of New York act relative to Connecticut boundary, 208; Governor Burnet's letter to, relative to dissolution of Seventeenth Assembly, 220; letter to, relative to Assembly resolution against Court of Chancery, 229; letter to, relative to dissolution of Assembly, 229; inquiry from, relative to cultivation of naval stores and other products, 250; opinion as to Governor's relation to Legislature, 253; only colonial agent authorized to appear before, on bills, 270; recommend revision of colonial statutes, 521; letter to, relative to Governor Osborn's death, 526; letter from, resisting French invasion, 539; annual appropriations, 556; paper currency, 558; suggests union of colonies, 577; Albany agreement transmitted to, 581; plan presented to King, 581; report plan of colonial union, 582; letter from, proposed annulment of certain grants of Indian land, 600; King consents to annual appropriations, 605; recommend commissions on Massachusetts and New Jersey boundaries, 610; Governor Hardy's letter to, requesting permission to resign, 613; New Jersey boundary acts approved, 684; Indian trade, subject delegated to colony, 723; historical records, value and completeness of, III, 162; IV, 166, 185; records, examination of, III, 1015, 1019; board established, IV, 179; general powers and duties, 179; board dissolved, 179.

COMMISSIONERS OF THE TREASURY, ENGLAND. Letter from, I, 200; report of colonial expenditures, 202.

COMMISSIONS. Proposed for judges, V, 58.

COMMISSIONS (Governmental). For special purposes, too many appointed, IV, 778; list of, with appropriations, 1891, IX, 11; State, extravagant increase of, 543; reorganization recommended, X, 187, 208.

COMMISSIONS (Military). At large, declared invalid, I, 365; to be issued by Lieutenant-Governor De Lancey, 634, 643; to be issued by President Colden, 653; Adjutant-General to issue, III, 189.

COMMITTEE. County, district and precinct, power to continue denied, II, 28; legislative, compensation, expenses of, V, 36, 41; relief of sureties, VII, 508.

COMMITTEE OF 51. New York, Revolution, action on, I, 765; dissolved, 766.

COMMITTEE OF PUBLIC SAFETY. Revolutionary, journals and records to be transcribed, II, 543.

COMMITTEE OF 70. New York, propose charter, 1872, VI, 478.

Common Carrier. Bermudians become, for colony, I, 246.

Common Law. Continued by first Constitution, II, 740; Governor Tilden's appeal to, Louisiana case, VI, 772.

Common School Fund. Established, II, 551, 555, 560; IV, 112; investments for, II, 598; income of, 660; III, 232; increase and investment of, II, 660, 661; III, 411; distribution of, II, 676; apportionment of, 721; how composed, 722, 903, 967, 1099; III, 61; IV, 112, 782; receipts from quitrents, II, 968; under second Constitution, III, 8, 411; IV, 65, 89, 112; capital of, III, 295, 480, 501, 544, 618, 672, 711, 763, 857, 946; IV, 21, 63, 88, 112, 263, 377, 395, 426, 475, 549, 602, 645, 714, 782, 831; V, 2, 74; transfers to general fund, exchange of securities, III, 371; transfer of securities from general fund, 499; advances from United States deposit fund, 613; due from general fund, 707; importance of, IV, 114; increased by proceeds of sale of public lands, 117; unsold land, 263; revenue from United States deposit fund, 377, 396, 550; incorporated orphan asylums to share in, 476; not to be diverted, 782; V, 230; IX, 69; Children's Aid Society industrial school, share in, V, 482; appropriation for Brockport normal school unconstitutional, 695; proposed abolition of, VIII, 147.

Common Schools. General statistics, V, 522, 603, 694, 778, 851; VI, 22, 108, 235, 356, 528, 617, 945; VII, 19, 155, 296, 424, 518, 687, 821, 946; established, II, 350, 453; V, 778; Governor Clinton urges revival of, II, 512, 528, 540; Governor Lewis urges establishment of, 551, 557; common school fund, 555, 560, see that title; commission to report system of, 676, 702, 707, 717; proper scope of instruction in, 720; trustees, 721, 947; school age, 722; teachers, 725; books, 726; Bible in, 727; system permanently established, 729; New York city, law amended, 877; laws revised, 967; office of superintendent of common schools created, 967; number of, 1820, 1048; office of superintendent abolished, 1050; flourishing condition, 1100; V, 273; estimate of State's share in national domain, 1101; act for administration of, III, 8; good effects of, 33; in New York, free to become public, 115; number of children in, 61, 115, 159, 238, 296, 336, 377, 407, 456, 499, 538, 616, 653, 740, 857; IV, 22, 66, 112, 264, 377, 396, 428, 475, 549, 602, 645, 715, 795, 839; V, 13, 51, 82, 174, 375, 448, 523, 603, 779, 851; VI, 23, 108, 236, 356, 528, 617, 946; VII, 19, 155, 297, 424, 519, 687, 821, 946; IX, 14, 166, 328, 748, 828; proper subjects of study, III, 116, 296; qualifications of teachers, 116; library suggested, 160; usefulness of, 238, 336, 406; lack of suitable school books, 337; colored children in Rochester, 378; Irving's life of Columbus to be used in, 406; district libraries, 499, 538; Regents' report

COMMON SCHOOLS —(*Continued*).

on instruction of teachers, 499; United States deposit fund, 613, 652; average annual period of instruction, 653, 858; IV, 66, 112; system not adapted to cities and villages, III, 741; extending benefits of, 767; religious toleration in, 768; securing attendance at, 887; distribution of, 948; new system in New York city, 951; sectarian instruction prohibited, 951; town superintendents provided for, IV, 23, 66; county superintendents, 23, 66, 115, 429, 479, 840; rate bills, 66, 796; teachers' institutes, 269; free, act for, submission unconstitutional, 475, 551; incorporated orphan asylums to share in fund, 476; Free School Act, proposed repeal rejected, 550; property tax unequal, 550; Free School Act, 1851, 602, 794; school code, 603, 693; union free schools, 647; superintendent of common schools, office created, 716, see that title; large number of children not in schools, 795, 839; V, 13; supervision and visitation, 797; town superintendents abolished, 797, 843; general statement, 839; annual reports not satisfactory, 841; proposed new method of administering funds, 841; should be free, 842; cost per capita of population, V, 51; New York, commission to examine, 62, 108; changing school year, 83; truant officers, 108; vaccination of children, 189; Truant Law not properly enforced, 190, 294, 387; military training, 375; free tuition to children of deceased soldiers, 696; rate bill abolished, 780; insufficient accommodations, 854; academical departments in free schools, VI, 81; consolidation of districts, 86; property should not be mortgaged, 262; constitutional provision, 617; proposed constitutional amendment, compulsory maintenance of, 945; prohibiting sectarian aid, 945; taxes, comparative statement, 946; State certificates, 948; Sisterhood of Grey Nuns, graduates, teachers' certificates, 948; text-books, regulating changes, VII, 21, 22; officers, women eligible, 76, 423, 518, 761; should be the limit of general taxation, 157; Milton, school bonds, payment of, 391; meetings, qualifications of voters, 518; diminution of attendance, 1831, 686; Federal aid, Virginia resolutions, 744; guaranteed by Constitution, 1894, VIII, 171; IX, 549, 616; manual training in, VIII, 322, 483, 1081; Saturday holidays, 537; purchase of sites, general act, 977; Hempstead, increasing tax for school purposes, 1156; decline in attendance, 1851–1891, IX, 14; source of country's prosperity, 16; Consolidated Law, 1894, 16, 328, 364; efficiency of system, 563; flag to be displayed on schoolhouses, 564, 661; pictorial representations and lectures, 564; temperance instruction, act of 1895, 612; cen-

COMMON SCHOOLS —(*Continued*).

tennial celebration of establishment, 662; act of 1795, 662; New York, system reorganized, 1896, 687; revision of statutes, X, 27; consolidation with university, VIII, 171; X, 27, 114, 115, 537, 604, 628, 736; Rochester, new buildings, 34; unification commission, 1899, 114, 128; colored children, equal educational rights, 145; free school fund, modification of plan of distribution, 349; primary education defined, 603; comparative state-:nent, 1905, 736; statistical information included in census of 1905, 869; free school fund, apportionment, 1906, 941.

VETOES. Saratoga Springs, union school, consolidation of districts, VI, 182; White Plains, consolidation of districts, 183; Niagara, school trustees, 188; Benton, tax for schoolhouses, 337; teachers, examination by district trustees, 337; Newburgh, amending local act, 507; Owego, district No. 35, establishing cemetery, 697; Yonkers, creating commissioner districts, 708; board of education, relief, 718; teachers, instruction of, 1035; officers, election of women, VII, 76; apportionment of moneys, 109; Pike, sale of part of schoolhouse site, 111; New York, public instruction, 127, 128; Fort Edward, board of education, contract with Collegiate Institute, 205; Code of Public Instruction, publication, 220; Port Byron, free school district, relief, 265; Tyrone and Wayne, union free school district, relative to, 265; State moneys, Monroe and Seneca counties, 412; amending Consolidation Act of 1864, delinquent taxes, 442; instruction of teachers, appropriation, 495; election of officers in certain districts, 508; Brooklyn, free books and supplies, 626; Brooklyn, protection of life and property, 627; Albany, school funds, using for other purposes, 756; school moneys, Oyster Bay, 807; in New York, 933; railroad taxes, exempting Cattaraugus county, 1095; Ithaca, amending system, 1105; Palmyra, permitting supervisor to hold school office, VIII, 47; Pomfret, establishing union free school district, 82; Carthage union school, new school building, appropriation, 117; district officers, election, 129; Rome, board of education, amending act, 130; Fort Covington, annual school meeting, 130; Lenox, extending union school district boundaries, 130; payment of teachers' wages, 240; apportionment of moneys, 291; amending general act, 293; teachers' licenses, 448; officers, election, 470; Hempstead, free schools, 701; Rome, borrowing money for school buildings, 874; Oyster Bay, district No. 5, new schoolhouse, 977; flags, 1038; Northfield, board of education, 1039; Mount Morris, consolidation of districts, IX, 73; New York, evening high schools,

COMMON SCHOOLS, VETOES —(*Continued*).

74; music, study of, 116; Arbor day, observance, appropriation, 1893, 291; fire escapes on school buildings, 355; teachers' conditional compensation after twenty-five years' service in towns, 463; apportionment of money, examination of teachers, 622; Richmond county, amending general act, 718; Flushing, free schools, increasing tax rate, 718; Long Island City, additional accommodations, 786; general amendments, 1897, 800; taxes, unpaid, payment of, 800; College Point, school taxes, 818; New York, boroughs of Queens and Richmond, X, 60; Troy school bill, 1900, 151; Auburn, amending charter, 478; apportionment of free school fund, appropriation, 949; common schools, State school moneys, apportionment, 956.

COMMUTATIONS. (Crimes.) By Legislature,— in Arnold case, II, 577; — David Williams case, 578; — John Williams case, 621; —Bowman case, 738; — Sillick case, 894; by Governor Tompkins, convictions of arson, 855; of punishment for good behavior, 875; IV, 723, 787, 844; V, 374, 526, 842; VI, 18, 899; VII, 147, 708; by Governor, Kirby case, III, 32; number of, 341, 384, 862; persons convicted of murder of Deputy Sheriff Steele, IV, 237, 309; not applicable to indeterminate sentences, VII, 955.

VETOES. Increasing rate, VI, 89; relative to, VII, 508.

COMMUTATION TAX. Increased, IV, 645, 719.

COMPENSATION. Of member of Assembly, I, 43; of troops, 50; of British officers, 157; of public officers, II, 12; State officers in military service, 818; of judicial officers, 622; III, 5, 256, 444, 498; IV, 368; property taken for canals, III, 73; of receivers, 973; property taken for public use, II, 592; IV, 347, 694; V, 517, 653, 880; VI, 90, 97, 217; VII, 775, 1015, 1108; of members of Legislature, V, 37, 41, 42; VI, 400, 550; omnibus and stage lines superseded by railroads, V, 517; of district attorney, VI, 145; awards, review of, 271; extra, see EXTRA COMPENSATION; of public officers, when subject to legislative change, VII, 379.

VETOES. Supervisors, VII, 131; court officers, Erie county, 538; justices, second judicial district, additional, 780.

COMPTROLLER. See STATE COMPTROLLER.

COMPTROLLER OF THE TREASURY, UNITED STATES. Letter from, demanding tonnage duty on Erie canal, III, 49; communication from, public lands, IV, 49.

COMPULSORY EDUCATION. General act, VI, 617; VIII, 817; IX, 16, 167, 328, 661; of Indian children, VII, 710; relative to, 1889, veto, VIII, 819; compulsory institutions suggested, IX, 748; right of State, 828.

COMPULSORY VOTING. Recommended, V, 196; VIII, 674, 676, 930, 1078; early rule in Southampton, Long Island, 676; subject considered in convention of 1867, Constitutional Commission of 1872, Constitutional Convention of 1894, 676.

COMSTOCK, GEORGE F. Opinion, excise bill of 1887, unconstitutional, VIII, 362, 370.

CONCURRENT RESOLUTION. As substitute for bill, effect of veto power, II, 740; appropriation cannot be made by, 741; VIII, 547, 840; calling special election by, quære, 1061.

CONDEMNATION LAW. Enacted, IX, 26; Supreme Court commissioners, proposed powers of, X, 668.

VETOES. Railroads, power of, 710; Condemnation Law, amending Code, 761; possession of property on giving security, 808.

CONDITIONAL SALES. Contracts for, filing, amending, veto, IX, 287.

CONESUS LAKE. Ferry from Long Point to McPherson Point, veto, VIII, 1098.

CONESVILLE. Scott patent, includes part of, IV, 331.

CONEWANGO CREEK. Acts of 1898 and 1900, IX, 106.

VETOES. Improvement, 106; drainage, amending act, X, 315; drainage, appropriation, 315.

CONEY ISLAND. Quarantine establishment on, V, 767, 845; concourse lands, improvement, veto, IX, 152.

CONFEDERACY. Of colonies, New York should have negative in, I, 158.

CONFEDERATION. See also ARTICLES OF CONFEDERATION. Articles of, ratified, II, 18, 127; of United States, considered, 112; plan of, defective, 194; proposed convention to revise, 194, 270.

CONFERENCE. Of Governors at Newport proposed, I, 137, 138; at Rehoboth, 140; with Indians, 200; between Governor and Six Nations, 222, 224, 232, 262, 265, 278, 286, 296, 319, 353, 359, 376, 392, 466, 504, 512, 524, 531, 537; with Five Nations, 510; between Lieutenant-Governor DeLancey and General Braddock, 566; of Governors at Alexandria, 563; with Mohawks, relative to land grant, 686; of Massachusetts boundary commissioners, 754; between Governors Tryon and Hutchinson, 756; on paper currency, II, 11; with certain Indian troops, 338, 340, 341, 342, 343, 344, 356; with St. Regis Indians, 351.

CONFISCATIONS. Bill relative to, veto, II, 70; sale of confiscated estates, 199, 203; restitution of estates, 206, 207; claims against confiscated lands, 695.

CONGDON, BENJAMIN F. Claim of, payment, veto, VII, 1109.

CONGREGATIONAL CHURCHES. Extinct or disbanded, relative to property of, veto, X, 813.

CONGREGATIONAL SOCIETY, WORCESTER. Removing remains from cemetery, veto, IX, 57.

CONGRESS. Of Governors, Assembly's views on, I, 158; Continental, 583; meeting of, in Philadelphia, 766; first Provincial, 778.

CONGRESS (UNITED STATES). See also CONTINENTAL CONGRESS. Resolution relating to first meeting of, II, 297; distributing acts of, 302, 322, 409, 459, 530, 567; III, 226; Militia Act, II, 336; eleventh amendment, 335, 347; extraordinary session, 398; alien and sedition acts, 430; action on death of Washington, 462; to receive New York map and statutes, 543; power to declare war, limitation of, proposed amendment, 827; monument to General Montgomery, 1000; action as to Revolutionary pensions, 1028; lottery legislation, 1052; who ineligible to, 1062; requests New York statutes for Congressional Library, 1116; action relative to method of choosing presidential electors, III, 38; authority over lands ceded by State, 139; internal improvements, South Carolina denies power to make, 218; Georgia also denies power, 221; power to make internal improvements, 234; control of revenues and customs, 331; general powers of, 357; approves settlement of New York and New Jersey boundary, 422; VI, 780; no power as to slavery, III, 572; may abolish slavery in District of Columbia, 645; New Jersey denies power to exclude representatives properly certified by Governor, 820; power over District of Columbia, alleged abuse of, 906; act for distribution of proceeds of public lands, 974; act relating to choice of representatives, IV, 5; enacts Insolvent Law, 5; Rhode Island denies power to inquire into form of State government, 86; act relating to pilots, 157; power to declare war, 417; no power to authorize slavery in New Mexico and California, 501; power to determine status of slavery in Territories, V, 29; admission of new States, 30; Tennessee propositions, relative to powers concerning slavery, 316; special session, 1861, 399; partial representation caused by secession of States, 480; apportionment of representatives, fourteenth amendment, 790; small number of laws enacted, 849; should not interfere in local elections, VI, 38, 131; Centennial Celebration at Philadelphia, 1876, act for, 303; Expatriation Law, 1907, 365; Yorktown Centennial Celebration and monument, VII, 735; immigrant tax, 1882, 802, 832; each house judge of elections thereto, VIII, 983, 985; alleged improper seating of members, 987; elections, Federal control of, 1083; act refunding direct tax, 1107.

CONGRESS HALL, ALBANY. Demolition of, VII, 175.

CONGRESSIONAL LIBRARY. Destruction of, IV, 613.

CONHOCTON COUNTY. Bill to erect, veto, V, 228, 249.

CONKLIN, DAVID. Convicted of murder, pardoned, II, 997.

CONKLIN, WILLIAM. Convicted of murder, pardoned, II, 541.

CONKLING, ROSCOE. Resignation as United States Senator, VII, 555, 568; protests against appointment of William H. Robertson as collector of New York, 557.

CONKLING, VINCENT. Board of Claims, veto, VII, 884.

CONLEY, GEORGE B. Court of Claims, veto, X, 165.

CONNECTICUT. (Colony.) See also CONNECTICUT BOUNDARY. Governor Fletcher appointed to command militia of, I, 45; recruits from, 71; claim for extra Indian enlistments, 156; act relative to New York boundary, 206; letter from Governor of, boundary, 218, 219, 224, 234; Millington library, clergy to use, 234; commissioners confer with Indians at Albany, 319; joins in Cape Breton expedition, 350; murders in, by French Indians, 355; joins in Indian Conference, 359; colonial union, 366; asked to join in expense of engaging Indians in Canadian expedition, 376; joining other colonies in war measures, 404, 413, 584; presents to Indians, 417; agreement for colonial union, 419; share of expenses, Crown Point expedition, 419; approves joint agreement for colonial defense, 457, 461; furnishes troops to assist New York, 463; treaty with Indians, 466; offer of volunteers as outscouts, 468; enlistments for New York service, 567; raises large force for Crown Point expedition, 575, 594; represented in Albany convention, 578; distressed condition of forces at Fort William Henry, 597; financial aid from Crown, 599, 604; troops for Canadian expedition, 620, 634, 644, 654; aid granted by New York, 629; stamped paper for, destroyed, 706.

CONNECTICUT (State). Conference on paper currency, II, 11; called on for militia, 31; Governor of, requested by Congress to furnish supplies to Rhode Island, 69; Governor to issue proclamation to prevent plundering, 80; claim for cannon and ball, 100; repeals embargo laws, 110; action relative to army supplies, 111; Captain Burrell's claim, 167; papers from, Barnes case, 209; land claims in New York, 370, 371, 386, 404, 406, 441, 449; land released to New York, 407; resolution, amendment, eligibility of President, Vice-President, Senators and Representatives in Congress, 425; laws received, 530; residents of, requirements as to highways in this State, veto, 592; constitutional amendments, basis of representation and direct taxes, admission of new States, limiting duration of embargo, interdiction of commerce, limiting power to declare war, only native citizens to hold office, ineligibility of President to re-election, 827, 828; disapproves North Carolina proposition to elect representatives and presidential electors by districts, 919; protests against exclusion of vessels from New York waters, 1025; com-

CONNECTICUT (State)—(*Continued*).

munication from Governor, Van Ness case, 1030; approves Ohio proposition relative to abolition of slavery, III, 136; commissioners to authenticate instruments in other States, 211; disapproves Missouri proposition of direct election of President and depriving House of Representatives of power to determine presidential election, 353; asserts authority of Federal judiciary, 388; sustains protective tariff laws, 482; constitutional amendment, limiting President's power of appointment, 747; resolutions on public lands, 747; requested to enact legislation relative to depositions, 749; favors protective policy, 906, 972; resolutions on distribution of public lands, 907; constitutional amendment, limiting eligibility of President to one term, 972; resolution, public lands, protective tariff, repeal of Bankruptcy Law, IV, 45; resolutions, abolition of West Point Military Academy, 45, 83; French spoliation claims, 84; favors abolition of franking privilege and reduction of letter postage, 84; resolutions on slavery, 506; appoints commission on New York boundary, 863; V, 112; boundary question, 91; action on independence monument, 122; military to be subordinate to civil power, 470; usury laws repealed, VI, 552; communication from Secretary of State, Hell Gate pilotage, VII, 47; New York boundary, Long Island sound, 172; boundary established, 172; commission on New York boundary, 200, 536; memorial from, Hell Gate pilotage, 441; proposes transfer of Fisher's island from New York, 536; booths for voters, VIII, 902; State furnishes ballots at election, 963.

CONNECTICUT BOUNDARY. Commissions to establish, I, 176; letter from Governor Saltonstall relative to, 206; King approves New York act, 208; papers relating to, 210, 215, 218, 219, 224, 234; agreement, relative to, 226; new commissions appointed, IV, 863; V, 91, 112, 189; commissions disagree, 113, 190; New York commissioners directed to ascertain line, 190; report of commission, 286; through Long Island sound, VII, 172; bill creating commission, veto, 172, 268; boundary established, 172; Connecticut Commission, 200; boundary finally settled, 535, 536.

CONNECTICUT GORE. Controversy over, II, 407, 441, 449.

CONNECTICUT RIVER. Eastern terminus of Quebec boundary, I, 745; boundary between Vermont and New Hampshire, II, 141.

CONNESTAQUIOENA. See also CANNESTAGAYUNE. Garrison at, I, 26.

CONNOLLY, RICHARD B. Senate, committee on alleged interference in Speakership contest, V, 485.

CONRAD, TIMOTHY A. Geological survey, geologist, third district, III, 640; report of, 644, 993; appointed paleontologist, 681, 753, 991; report, 682, 754.

CONSIDINE, MARGARET C. Court of Claims, veto, X, 170.

CONSOLIDATED GAS COMPANY. Litigation with, legal services, appropriation, veto, X, 785.

CONSPIRACIES. Of slaves, act to prevent, I, 166; against King, deliverance from, 205; commissioners to detect, II, 20; act to prevent, veto, 81; unlawful combinations in Livingston, 411; against trade and commerce, VI, 121; efforts to increase wages, 122; laws amended, 225; labor meetings, statutes should be carefully framed, VIII, 318, 650.

CONSTABLE, WILLIAM. Estate, act relating to disposition of, II, 563.

CONSTABLES. Act for election of, I, 11.

VETOES. Scio, appointment by county judge, VII, 218; special game, 263; jurisdiction in villages, 265; Brooklyn, election, 439; appointment by religious corporations, 508; powers, vesting in agent of Society for Prevention of Cruelty to Animals, 746; Westchester county, designations to attend court, 1092; game and fish, audit of accounts, VIII, 469.

CONSTANTIA. Railroad bonds, veto, VII, 267.

CONSTITUTION, THE. Commodore Bainbridge captures British frigate Java, II, 781.

CONSTITUTION (General). Term applied to Albany plan of union, I, 579; elements of, II, 1; written, when needed, 1; Chancellor Kent's definition of, 1055; amendments, provisions relative to, collated, 1057, 1058; interpretation, common usage of words, VIII, 779; amendments, principles which should govern legislative consideration, 921; practice of courts in considering constitutional questions, 1045.

CONSTITUTION (Colony). Described, I, 253; based on English model, 233; commended, 293; Assembly charged with subverting, 294; need of adhering to principles of, 384; Assembly's right of access to Governor, 479; see Albany plan of union, 579; legislative power, 730; people entitled to all rights of British subjects, 772, 775; unwritten, but well understood, II, 1.

CONSTITUTION (English). Attempt to overturn, I, 205; to be maintained in colony, 231; model for that of colony, 283; method of issuing appropriations, 488, 505; colonial administration, 505; executive power lodged in Crown, 528; taxation without representation, inconsistent with, 691, 696; trial by jury, 693, 704; Parliament no power to grant colonial estates to Crown, 705; right of petition, 730; forms did not include colonies, 775; liberties of people, 776.

CONSTITUTION, STATE, GENERAL. First adopted, I, 779; II, 1, 5; amendments of 1801, 3; revision of, proposed, 1018; defects, VI, 392.

CONSTITUTION OF 1777. State government organized under, I, 779; II, 1, 5; duties of governor, 2; appointment of officers, 3, 247, 314, 361, 403, 473, 489, 495, 497, 564, 1020, 1054; III, 92, 1001; VI, 832; Council of Revision, II, 4, 495, 740, 1021; prorogation of Legislature, 7, 144, 708; did not authorize appointment of Council of Safety, 27; qualifications of voters for members of Assembly, 35, 685; oath of electors, 38; citizens' rights, 40, 60, 223, 234, 235, 237, 239, 250, 284, 288, 373, 383, 418, 466, 522, 582, 585, 594, 603, 646, 663, 687, 921; local officers, 41; legislative power, 42, 113; continuance of colonial laws, 52, 740; attainder, 61, 71; trial by jury, 61, 71, 85, 205, 223, 235, 249, 250, 268, 284, 757; new courts, 61, 71, 85, 205, 216, 235, 249, 250, 257, 269; pardoning power, 68, 599, 922; chancellor, when not to hold other office, exception "special occasion," application of, 83; executive power, 114; British and colonial statutes continued, 219, 255, 610; Indian contracts, 224, 302, 695; Supreme Court, appointment of clerks, 243; extraordinary session, 251; annual meeting of Legislature, 252; Governor authorized to leave State on military service, 271; census, 305; judges not to hold other office, 325, 647; magazine of warlike stores, 360, 510, 524, 600, 911; age limit of judges, 362, 622; militia, 399, 600, 853, 911; V, 456; appointment of militia officers, II, 403, 564; chancellor, tenure of office, 461; judges, tenure of office, 461, 740; number of Senators, 468; number of members of Assembly, 468; New York and Albany, appointment of charter officers, 499; removal of officers, 500; clerks of courts, appointment and removal of, 500; Court of Impeachments, 502; Governor's recommendations to Legislature, 506; reprieves, 576, 621, 922; Senate apportionment, 653; vacancy in office of Lieutenant-Governor, 674; common law continued, 740; commutations, 855; gubernatorial succession, 887; religious toleration, 921, 948; executive communications to Legislature, 1014; proposed revision of, 1018; no provision for amending, 1043; first judge of county, not to hold other office, 1053; tribute to framers of, III, 3; IV, 52; high character of, 712; term of Governor, VI, 398; a model for other States, VII, 813; elections by ballot, VIII, 778, 913; Legislature, each house judge of elections thereto, 985; Legislature, how composed, IX, 644; Supreme Court, X, 671; judges not to exercise other office or public trust, 679; statutes continued, 681.

AMENDMENTS OF 1801. Council of Appointment, II, 3, 361, 468, 505, 1043; IV, 52; reorganization of Legislature, II, 468, 511, 651, 849, 1043; IV, 52.

CONSTITUTION OF 1821. Citizens' rights, II, 40, 60, 262; local officers, 41; VI, 734; annual meeting of Legislature, II, 960; convention to prepare, 1044; submission of, 1087; adopted, 1044, 1127; III, 1; apportionment, II, 1047; III, 567; IV, 250; who not eligible to Legislature, II, 1062; lotteries prohibited, 1127; III, 526, 567; IV, 807; Governor's message, III, 1; pardoning power, 1, 284; veto power, 2; powers of circuit judges, 6, 210, 444; IV, 136; judicial districts, III, 6; judges not to hold other office, 6; common school fund, 8, 411; IV, 65, 88, 112; right of suffrage, III, 9; two-thirds bills, 15, 36, 37, 91, 531, 592, 655; IV, 56, 193; justices of the peace, how appointed, III, 17, 57, 135, 158, 161, 1012; extraordinary sessions, 40, 392; qualification of voters, 58, 158, 772; IV, 133; census, III, 65, 247; exemptions from militia service, 85, 880; clergymen ineligible to office, 103; removal of county officers, 133; salt springs not to be sold, 148; IV, 88; canal fund, III, 164, 307, 348, 547, 808; IV, 88, 97, 107, 200; canal tolls, III, 169, 462; IV, 88; official oath, III, 209; gubernatorial succession, 221, 269; Governor to see that laws are faithfully executed, 222, 833, 1002, 1031; IV, 149; duties on salt, III, 330, 384, 413, 477, 505, 544, 552, 619; IV, 88; auction sales, III, 413, 505, 544, 552, 619; IV, 88; appointment of Commissary-General, III, 430; corporations, 521, 531; judiciary, 719; IV, 53; passing bill over veto, vote required, III, 531, 1003; IV, 252; legislative power, III, 788, 1021; legislative journals, 975; when member of Legislature not eligible to civil appointment, 1001; Governor's recommendations to Legislature, 1003; State officers, how chosen, 1004; appointment of judicial officers, 1012; county judge, term of office, 1012; executive power, 1021; amendments, how made, IV, 52, 103; payment of canal debt, 107; Indian contracts, 295; property for public use, compensation, 347; new county, required population, V, 225; term of governor, VI, 398; elections by ballot, VIII, 778, 912, 913; Legislature, how composed, IX, 644; organization of departments, X, 671; judicial system, 671; judges not to exercise other office or public trust, 679; statutes continued, 681.

AMENDMENTS OF 1826. Justices of the peace, how chosen, III, 17, 57, 135, 158, 161; IV, 52; qualifications of voters, III, 58, 59, 135, 158; IV, 52.

AMENDMENTS OF 1833. Election of mayor, New York, III, 212; IV, 52; duties on salt, III, 330, 384, 413, 477, 505, 544, 619.

AMENDMENTS OF 1835. Auction and salt duties restored to general fund, III, 414, 505, 544, 552, 619; IV, 53.

CONSTITUTION OF 1821 — (*Continued*).

AMENDMENT OF 1838. Election of mayors by people, IV, 53.

AMENDMENTS OF 1845. Removal of judicial officers, IV, 55, 109, 137; abolishing property qualifications of officers, 109, 137.

CONSTITUTION OF 1846. Adopted, IV, 250, 363; biennial appropriation bills, I, 303; citizens' rights, II, 40, 60; VIII, 367; annual meeting of Legislature, II, 960; V, 251; VII, 729; who not eligible to Legislature, II, 1062; inspectors of merchandise, office abolished, III, 722; VI, 282; VII, 659, 751; IX, 522; limiting and approving State debt, IV, 56, 371, 546, 549, 587, 631, 668, 670, 677, 744, 833; V, 68, 153, 253, 360, 590, 705, 708, 783, 817, 828; VI, 11, 72, 107, 178, 346, 349, 384, 890; VII, 399, 430; VIII, 926; agricultural leases, IV, 245, 356, 409, 559, 653; claims against corporations, 262; witness against himself, 310, 764; judicial districts, 365, 857; commission on procedure, 366, 654; V, 596; VI, 29; VII, 182; Supreme Court, IV, 366; testimony in equity cases, 367; proceedings in law and equity, alterations of, 367; completion of canals, 369, 546, 599, 661; V, 8, 209, 828; VI, 10; canal revenues, IV, 371, 472, 540, 549, 587, 596, 600, 661, 668, 742, 781, 783; V, 49, 65, 209, 253, 360, 363, 590, 705, 783, 828; VI, 10, 103, 349, 540, 629, 887; VII, 4; canal sinking funds, IV, 371, 424, 473; V, 159, 590; VI, 10; VII, 818; general fund, sinking fund, IV, 371, 424, 661, 679; V, 3, 368, 590; VI, 10; common school fund, IV, 377, 396, 550; V, 230; appropriations for literary and charitable institutions, IV, 378; corporations, IV, 379, 513, 522, 526, 531, 574, 593, 633, 636, 638, 639, 823; V, 129, 133, 147, 191, 231, 645, 655, 658, 711, 848; VI, 168, 246, 353, 640; VII, 202, 233, 240, 241, 336, 357, 371, 546, 565, 745, 845, 868; VIII, 52, 197, 297; registry of bills and notes, IV, 380; dues from corporations 401, 824; V, 644; liability of bank stockholders, IV, 403, 441; reprieves, commutations and pardons, 405, 427, 435, 564; VI, 268; VII, 199, 707, 994; feudal tenures abolished, IV, 409, 559; masters and examiners in chancery, office abolished, 414; gubernatorial succession, 433; boards of supervisors, legislative power, 434, 496, 575; number of judges in New York, 443; tribunals of conciliation, 443, 480, 856; taxation for sinking funds, 473; loans for casual deficits, 473, 589; V, 152, 253, 360, 590, 705, 890, 923; VII, 399; legislative power, IV, 475, 709; codification, commission on, 488, 561; V, 596; VI, 29; VII, 182, 348, 794; property taken for public use, IV, 496; V, 517; VI, 286, 504, 605, 642; VII, 241, 775, 866, 1108; VIII, 730, 874; IX, 513; three-fifths bills, IV, 513, 578; private and local bills, only one subject in title, 517, 773; V, 219, 387, 797; VI, 60, 80, 90, 91, 174, 271, 326, 328, 331, 506, 508, 509, 596, 693, 702, 705, 706, 714,

CONSTITUTION OF 1846 — (*Continued*).

715, 1030, 1032; VII, 326,· 334, 631, 658, 758, 768, 1088, 1098, 1099, 1100, 1120; VIII, 386, 390, 407, 408, 458, 460, 617, 618, 1122; IX, 75, 211, 271; amendments, IV, 547, 677; V, 54, 597; VI, 394; VII, 161; VIII, 1060; judiciary article, 1869, see that title; quorum of Legislature, IV, 578; majority necessary to pass bills, 578; VII, 675; two-thirds, IV, 578, 694; V, 139, 245, 351, 442; VI, 212, 579, 678, 690, 692, 707; VII, 48; VIII, 381, 464; extraordinary session, IV, 579, 694, 734; VI, 331, 332; VII, 122, 728; VIII, 132, 135, 643; IX, 154; freedom of speech, IV, 581; VIII, 578; financial article, IV, 599, 600; increasing number of justices in first district, 615; county judge, 625; X, 673; special county judge and surrogate, IV, 626; X, 675; quarter sales, IV, 653; Court of Chancery abolished, 655; Court of Common Pleas, 655; canal amendment, 1854, 678; justices of the peace, 684; VI, 208, 480; VII, 44; X, 673; judicial officers' fees prohibited, IV, 684, 686, 777; local officers, how chosen, II, 41; IV, 684; VI, 30, 75, 77, 128, 216, 425, 496, 504, 507, 517, 734, 833, 1019, 1029, 1031, 1032, 1033; VII, 106, 107, 126, 179, 208, 216, 218, 317, 327, 357, 746, 901, 1098; VIII, 85, 86, 519, 594, 635, 880, 995, 1143; IX, 29, 96, 371, 399, 411, 511; property taken for public use, ascertaining damages, IV, 694; V, 880; VI, 90, 97, 217; VII, 1015, 1108; municipal corporations, restricting powers of, IV, 701, 730; V, 849; VI, 825; VII, 31, 569, 617, 637; militia, enrollment and discipline of, IV, 726; V, 392, 456; Governor to see that laws are faithfully executed, IV, 729, 778; V, 105, 466; due process of law, IV, 759; V, 512, 652; VII, 801; VIII, 367, 1120; IX, 60, 351, 500, 520; executive consideration of bills, IV, 769; VIII, 434, 1003; inspectors of State prisons, IV, 777; V, 77, 268, 437, 758; VI, 355; funds not to be diverted, article 9, section 1, IV, 782; lotteries prohibited, 807; VII, 532, 625, 715; qualifications of voters, IV, 825; V, 509, 605, 749; VI, 77, 389, 460; VII, 78; VIII, 566, 580, 910, 955, 1008; IX, 95; suffrage, right of, who may be excluded, IV, 825; VI, 264, 389; VIII, 566; registration of voters, IV, 825; V, 92, 195, 605; VII, 306; VIII, 566, 580; apportionment of Legislature, IV, 857; VII, 100, 164, 303, 401; VIII, 157, 491, 677, 741, 1055; IX, 154; education funds, IX, 69; canal debt, V, 3; compensation of members of Legislature, 37, 41, 42; official oath, 38, 145; VI, 1; VIII, 892; appropriations, frequency, purpose of, V, 72, 107, 816; VI, 803; pardoning power, V, 93, 116, 171, 266, 758; Assembly districts, alteration of, 126, 224; VIII, 289; judicial officers in cities and villages, V, 138; State aid to private enterprises prohibited, 138, 245, 443; VI, 178, 346; VII, 90; VIII, 254; IX, 107; canals not

CONSTITUTION OF 1846 — (*Continued*).

to be sold, V, 158, 208; VI, 106, 239, 540; duration of legislative session, 251; cruel and unusual punishments, 268; VII, 641; VIII, 588; Governor's communication to Legislature, V, 458, 582, 789; VI, 4, 644; VIII, 2, 80; Assembly to choose its own officers, V, 486; Constitutional Convention, 597, 708, 744; VIII, 177, 308, 471, 484; census, V, 601; VI, 723; VIII, 40, 59, 66, 84, 133, 135, 155, 298, 397, 491, 676, 892, 1054; appointment of military officers, V, 608; removal of judges, 723; VI, 440, 498; VIII, 935; Governor Fenton's comment on, V, 745; justices of the peace, removal, VI, 49; justices of the peace, how chosen, 74; vacancies in office, IV, 433; VI, 75, 989; VII, 44; existing laws, not applicable by reference, VI, 90; IX, 431; Canal Board, VI, 106; action of Legislature on vetoes, 117, 1003; villages, see amendment, 1874; coroners, 171; drainage, see amendment, 1874; Supreme Court, clerks of, VI, 266, see also JUDICIARY ARTICLE, 1869; bank charters, 315; right of people to assemble, 375; VIII, 573; term of Governor, VI, 398; limiting length of legislative session, 400; compensation of members of Legislature, amendment, 1874, 400, 726; limiting private and local laws, article 3, section 18, amendment of 1874, 402, 662, 683, 691, 726, 814, 825, 949, 1034; VII, 63, 69, 91, 157, 208, 214, 215, 222, 251, 255, 259, 263, 320, 336, 358, 369, 370, 383, 395, 406, 440, 497, 535, 540, 549, 578, 589, 592, 604, 628, 630, 645, 729, 748, 753, 757, 763, 769, 777, 843, 845, 860, 879, 887, 895, 909, 1037, 1055, 1063, 1098, 1115, 1121, 1123; VIII, 52, 101, 330, 343, 387, 411, 412, 463, 614, 615, 616, 879, 880, 1036, 1131, 1155; IX, 134, 224, 258, 271, 509, 516; boards of supervisors, powers conferred by general laws, amendment of 1874, VI, 402; VII, 65, 757; VIII, 509; extra compensation, amendment of 1874, VI, 403, 540; VII, 49, 158, 223, 259, 372, 374, 499, 540, 550, 753, 773, 777, 791, 1055, 1115; VIII, 626; IX, 431; term of Governor, amendment of 1874, VI, 398; executive consideration of bills, amendment, 1874, II, 460; IV, 524; V, 263; VI, 369, 403, 642, 852, 864, 883, 884, 924; VII, 169, 667, 668, 673, 891, 940; VIII, 434; municipal corporations, limiting expenditures and indebtedness, amendment of 1874, IV, 806; VI, 402; VII, 47, 206, 652, 661, 754, 846, 1018, 1047, 1088, 1107; VIII, 239; IX, 404, required residence in election district, VI, 471; district attorney, 491; IX, 410; State sinking funds, amendment of 1874, VI, 540; limitation of actions against State, amendment of 1874, VI, 540; VII, 599, 602, 606, 644, 773, 781, 801, 1120, 1121, 1124; VIII, 1124; IX, 66, 119, 370, 429, 452; Tax Law to state object, V, 817; VI, 584; VII, 220, 772; IX, 60; continuing or reviving appropriation, VI, 588, 947; removal of State Treasurer, 633; war debt, 660; bribery amend-

CONSTITUTION OF 1846 — (*Continued*).

ment, 1874, 725; VII, 724; savings banks, amendment of 1874, VI,
725; VIII, 232; disposal of lateral canals, VI, 749, 796; general
fund, repayment from canal revenues, 792; canal contracts to be let
to lowest bidder, 347; removal of officers, 806; salt springs, sale
prohibited, 822; audit of claims against State, amendment of 1874,
875; VII, 81, 83, 86, 88, 158, 227, 230, 462, 463, 495, 779, 782,
792, 850, 922, 929, 1055; IX, 142; limiting municipal indebtedness,
amendment of 1884, VI, 917; VII, 727; VIII, 27, 161, 184, 239;
IX, 142; Superintendent of Public Works, amendment of 1876, VI,
934; VII, 11, 50, 143, 235; VIII, 487; Superintendent of State
Prisons, amendment of 1876, VI, 842, 984; VII, 11; VIII, 487;
local judicial officers, how chosen, VI, 987; canal expenditures cannot
exceed revenue, amendment of 1874, VII, 6, 359, 684; official oath,
amendment of 1874, 44; appropriations must specify object, 82, 912;
VIII, 420; method of passing bills, VII, 185; bills becoming laws
after ten days without Governor's signature, 242; re-enactment of
appropriation bills after two years, VI, 864, 947; VII, 1026; compensation of judges, 259; members of Legislature cannot hold certain other offices, 322; salt springs, not to be sold, 386; expenses
not provided for, 400; *habeas corpus*, 504; religious toleration, 597;
VIII, 23, 178, 302, 479; Bill of Rights, VII, 611; veto objections
to be entered on legislative journals, 672; passage of bills over veto,
vote necessary, 675; legislative term, 729; twice in jeopardy, 755;
militia, changing method of appointment, 797; no appropriation
except by law, 799; canal tolls abolished, 818; VIII, 13; municipal corporations, aiding private enterprise, VII, 848, 867, 1106;
VIII, 529; IX, 512; State aid to private enterprise, amendment of
1875, VII, 915, 1084; VIII, 250, 253, 405; determining election
and qualifications of members of Legislature, VII, 918; VIII, 983,
986; canals, appointment of subordinate officers, amendment of
1876, VII, 1024; Lieutenant-Governor, when to assume the duties
of the office of Governor, VIII, 1; commissioners of land office,
53, 726, 735; State Engineer and Surveyor, 74, 175; IX, 425;
enacting clause, VIII, 143; amount of tax limited in certain counties and cities, 188; salary of Governor and Lieutenant-Governor,
227; salary of Temporary President and Speaker of Assembly, 228;
banks, 231; reappropriation must state amount, 246; second division, Court of Appeals, amendment of 1888, 486; militia appointments, confirmation by Senate, 487; voting residence, 499; elections
by ballot, 573, 584, 670, 778, 912, 913, 952, 957; IX, 247; no municipal expenditure, except for public purpose, VIII, 880, 996; voter's
right to vote for all officers, 959, 1117; bribery, 1093; judges not

CONSTITUTION OF 1846 — (*Continued*).

to hold other office, IX, 47; charters, Legislature may amend or repeal, 93, 501; vacancies, Legislature to provide for filling, 224; Supreme Court commissioners, etc., offices abolished, X, 670; judicial system, 672; Court of Appeals, 673; judges not to exercise other office or public trust, 679; statutes continued, 681.

CONSTITUTION OF 1894. Citizens' rights, II, 40, 60; due process of law, 234, 603; X, 534, 777, 884; judicial pensions abolished, II, 363; private property taken for public use, 522, 585, 646, 663; common schools, 729; VI, 617; VIII, 171; IX, 549, 616; annual meeting of Legislature, II, 960; who not eligible to Legislature, 1062; justice of the peace, election of, III, 57; official oath, 209; removal of judicial officers, IV, 55; VII, 534; X, 828; limiting State debt, IV, 56; agricultural leases, 245; powers of county judge, 627; prohibiting municipal aid to private enterprise, 806; X, 243, 264, 275, 453, 535, 777, 908, 942; gubernatorial succession, IV, 433; County Court, 562; State Board of Charities, V, 761; VIII, 173; IX, 568; X, 157, 190; drainage of agricultural lands, VI, 189; IX, 550, 558; reading and passage of bills, VI, 400; X, 145; census, VI, 723; X, 722, 868; municipal indebtedness, limitation of, VI, 917; VIII, 29; X, 343, 804, 851; riders on appropriation bills, VII, 26, 159, 1086; IX, 276, 403; printing bills, VII, 43; emergency certificates, 43; cities, 136; civil service, 838; VIII, 151; IX, 549, 560, 663, 840; X, 18, 470, 741; city elections, VIII, 17; appeals to Court of Appeals, capital cases, 82, 181; university, VIII, 171; X, 113; State Commission in Lunacy, VIII, 173, 485; IX, 191; Court of Appeals, jurisdiction, VIII, 230; labor interests, amendments of 1905, 317; X, 97, 190, 850, 916; damages for injuries resulting in death, limitation prohibited, VIII, 318; Constitutional Convention, 474; voting residence, 500; naval militia, 829; convention, new Constitution approved, 929; bi-partisan election boards, 959; IX, 102, 309, 556; Surrogate's Court, New York, 122; Legislature, membership increased, 155; State prisons, contract labor prohibited, 181, 549, 559, 653, 659, 739; X, 166; forest preserve, IX, 187, 300, 569, 835; X, 263, 458; X, 706, 753; taxation, special exemption laws prohibited, amendment of 1901, IX, 232; voting machines, 247; salt springs, prohibition against sale abrogated, 274, 550; canals, improvements, 305, 549; registration of voters, 309, 555; special city laws, 339, 547, 617, 677, 696, 715; X, 152, 153, 208, 574, 624, 657, 683, 685; Governor's messages, IX, 537, 578; executive consideration of bills, 537; judicial departments, 545; Appellate Division, 545; X, 373; various local courts abolished, IX, 545; bookmaking, poolselling, and

CONSTITUTION OF 1894 — (*Continued*).

gambling prohibited, 548, 602; X, 892; Superintendent of State Prisons, IX, 549; Superintendent of Public Works, 549; charitable institutions, State inspection, 550; voter, term of citizenship required, 555; local officers, II, 41; IX, 584, 591; X, 210, 288, 750, 913; board of supervisors, IX, 585, 753; bills, passage of, majority vote of Legislature required, 618; three-fifths bills, 618; two-thirds bills, 618; X, 778; military and naval forces, Governor, commander-in-chief, IX, 640; Legislature, how composed, 644; State Commission of Prisons, 654; X, 191; first-class cities, reducing population limit, amendment of 1907, IX, 678; coroner, office omitted, 704; county officers, New York and Kings, election in odd-numbered years, 705; audit of claims against State, 717; X, 255; boards of supervisors, amendment of 1899, 753; militia, classification, X, 15; Legislature, members not eligible to appointment, 46; Attorney-General, 187; extending term of credit on State debt, amendment of 1905, IV, 56, 833; V, 7; X, 214, 496, 577, 731, 848; county officers, Governor's power of removal, 230; limiting private and local laws, 233, 235, 399, 542, 574, 624, 864, 874; extra compensation to public officers prohibited, 243; State debt, term of bonds, 246, 577, 600; limitation of claims against State, 268; ninth judicial district, amendment of 1905, IV, 857; X, 337; appeals in capital cases, 344; Court of Appeals, temporary designations from Supreme Court, amendment of 1899, 373; district attorney, 392; Lunacy Commission, change of powers, 405; qualifications of voters, 421; militia, every citizen liable to duty, 510; highway improvement, State debt for, amendment of 1905, 214, 513, 732, 833, 850, 909; Supreme Court, increasing number of justices, amendment of 1905, 516, 849, 936; municipal self-government, 541; State debt, general fund, payments from, amendment of 1905, 577, 601, 731, 848, 923; franchises, local control of, 624; judicial system, 674; special county judge and surrogate, 676; circuit courts abolished, 676; judges not to exercise other office or public trust, 679; Supreme Court Reporter, 679; statutes continued, 681; canals not to be sold, 731; taking private property for public use, compensation, 761, 800; veto of separate items in appropriation bills, 794, 799, 935; extraordinary session, 820, 821; Governor's recommendations, 832; veto power, 832; power of members of Appellate Division to hold other courts, amendments of 1905, 849; apportionment of Legislature, 851; corporations organized under general laws, 865; private and local bills, article 3, section 16, 898; cities, when elections to be held, 911.

CONSTITUTION, UNITED STATES. Compared with Albany plan of union, I, 579; *ex post facto* laws, II, 215, 582; convention for framing, 270; Constitution submitted to States, 282, 298; New York convention for consideration of, 283; ratified by New York, 283, 299; VIII, 505; observations of New York Senate, II, 292; Federal government established, 296; election of President, 297, 299, 545; election of Senators, 303; ten amendments adopted, 290, 304; IV, 750; V, 471; eleventh amendment, II, 335, 347; VII, 250; obligation of contracts, II, 354, 427, 582, 594, 704, 1082, 1112; III, 188, 1023; IV, 6, 240, 347 350; VI, 518, 668; VII, 96, 333, 356, 375, 397, 595, 856; VIII, 100, 752; IX, 453, 500; national defense, II, 414; appointment of officers, 500; fifth amendment, 522, 585, 603, 646, 663, 820; III, 574; V, 471; IX, 351; Senate, appointment to fill vacancy, II, 537; twelfth amendment, 537, 545, 546, 608; privileges and immunities of citizens, 613, 1026, 1041; III, 844, 981; V, 309, 325; fourteenth amendment, II, 687; V, 744; VIII, 367; duty of State militia, II, 748; organization of militia, 853; III, 345, 405; IV, 493; V, 393, 541; Senators and Representatives ineligible to certain offices, II, 1062; presidential electors, III, 30; VII, 35; regulation of commerce, III, 76, 234, 420, 462; IV, 394, 616; slavery, III, 94; weights and measures, 101; District of Columbia, 138, 588, 645, 906, 907; tenth amendment, reserved powers of State, 234, 582, 590; IV, 618; VI, 831; revenues and customs, III, 331, 433, 893; IV, 616; fugitives from justice, III, 350, 534, 596, 777, 778, 852, 869, 915, 917, 922, 1030; IV, 8; Congress, general exercise of power, III, 357; controversies between States, 359; supreme law of the land, 364; judicial power, 364, 1026; President to see that laws are faithfully executed, 365; changing State boundaries, 390; not a compact between States, 435; fugitive slaves, 574, 917, 922, 937; IV, 7, 569, 810, 828; V, 302; amendments, procedure to obtain, III, 574; V, 329; thirteenth amendment, III, 574; first amendment, 589, 645; V, 483; direct taxes, III, 622; V, 391; coining money, III, 630; VI, 134, 142; foreign relations, III, 689; Bankrupt Law, 842, 876; IV, 5; qualifications of representatives, III, 883; qualifications of Senator, 883; qualifications of President, 883; veto power, 977; IX, 406; States' claim to territory, III, 985; representatives in Congress, election of, IV, 5; VI, 38; apportionment of Representatives, IV, 85; VII, 725; power to declare war, IV, 417; treaty-making power, 417; V, 480; general purpose of, IV, 617; V, 321; VI, 831; ninth amendment, States reserved rights, IV, 618; no tax on exports from State, 667; preamble, 680; second amendment, 726; V, 281; fourth amendment, unreasonable searches and seizures, IV, 755; V, 471; Territories, organization of, IV, 828;

CONSTITUTION OF UNITED STATES — (*Continued*).

V, 29, 32; new States, 30; restricting slave trade, 30; census, 295; treason, 306; Constitutional Convention, 325, 328, 343, 356, 464; number of States necessary for original ratification, 464; suspension of writ of *habeas corpus*, 500; republican form of government, V, 616; official oath, 859; qualifications of voters, VI, 38; VII, 306; fifteenth amendment ratified, VI, 50; how made, 394; severely tested by Civil War, 457; twelfth amendment, counting the vote, VII, 34; 40; *habeas corpus*, 504; patents, 571; powers of judiciary, 575; equal protection of the laws, 591; X, 882; sixth amendment, crimes, VII, 613; States not to keep troops in time of peace without consent of Congress, 763; congressional districts, VIII, 135; vested rights, 361; cruel and unusual punishments prohibited, 588; Congress, each house judge of elections thereto, 983, 985; jurisdiction over land ceded by States, 1115; executive consideration of bills, IX, 406; due process of law, X, 884.

CONSTITUTIONAL AMENDMENTS. See AMENDMENTS TO CONSTITUTION, BY YEARS.

CONSTITUTIONAL COMMISSION OF 1872. Suggested by Governor Hoffman, VI, 393; created, 394; meeting, report, result, 394; proposed amendment on prison administration, 109; State officers, how chosen, 397, 398; Superintendent of Public Works, 397; Superintendent of State Prisons, 398; Governor and Lieutenant-Governor, extension of term, 398; proposition as to reading and passage of bills, 400; Legislature, compensation of members, 400; Senate districts, 401; limiting municipal indebtedness, 402; limiting special laws, 402; boards of supervisors, 402; extra compensation, 403; appropriation bills, veto of separate items, 403; work of, comment by Governor Dix, 657; how composed, work substantially approved, VIII, 309; compulsory voting, 676.

CONSTITUTIONAL COMMISSION OF 1890. Created, VIII, 1034; recommendations not adopted, 1034; IX, 13.

CONSTITUTIONAL CONVENTION. See also CONVENTION. First, I, 778; adopts Constitution, 779; of 1801, II, 3; Governor Clinton recommends, 1020, 1043; bill for, veto, 1044, 1055; new act passed, 1044; recommended, III, 431, 438; no necessity for, IV, 51; State, proposition to call, 84, 228; Governor Wright opposes, 109; 1846, act for, 249; Seneca Indians, 457; how called, V, 597, 708, 744; VIII, 177, 308, 471, 484; 1887, legislative and executive action, relative to, 308, 393, 470; all political parties should be represented in, 310; Governor Hill suggests congressional district representation, 310, 397; minority representation, 310; IX, 195; should be fairly representative in membership, VIII, 396; IX, 196; Assembly, report of select

CONSTITUTIONAL CONVENTION — (*Continued*).

committee on veto, 1887, VIII, 470; legislative duty to provide for, is continuing, VIII, 484, 680; extraordinary session, 1888, legislation recommended, 652; act of 1892, 929, 1078; IX, 13; plan of choosing delegates, 13; act of 1893, 14; structure of convention, 14; proper method of submitting amendments, 481.

CONSTITUTIONAL CONVENTION OF 1776. Adopts Constitution, I, 779; IV, 51; institutes State government, II, 5, 6; included representatives from New Hampshire grants, 175; journals and records of, to be transcribed, 543; delegates, how chosen, VIII, 471.

CONSTITUTIONAL CONVENTION OF 1801. Amendment as to powers of Council of Appointment, II, 361, 468, 503, 505, 1043; IV, 52; re-organization of Legislature, II, 468, 511, 1043; IV, 52; IX, 644; Chancellor Kent's comment on, II, 1056; Governor Bouck's review of, IV, 52; delegates chosen at special election, VIII, 395; delegates, how chosen, 471.

CONSTITUTIONAL CONVENTION OF 1821. Act for, II, 1044; submitted to people, 1037; Constitution proposed by, approved, 1044; Governor Bouck on, IV, 52; how composed, VIII, 308; delegates chosen at special election, 395; delegates, how chosen, 471.

CONSTITUTIONAL CONVENTION OF 1846. Call for, IV, 110, 249; Constitution proposed by, 100, 250; apportionment of delegates, 250; general objects of, 916; how composed, VIII, 308; delegates chosen at special election, 395; delegates, how chosen, 471.

CONSTITUTIONAL CONVENTION OF 1867. Ordered by people, V, 744; questions needing consideration, 745; method of selecting delegates, 748; how composed, 748; VIII, 308; voter's oath of loyalty, if challenged, act unconstitutional, V, 749; meeting and proceedings of, 749; submission of Constitution, 749; work rejected except judiciary article, 749; VI, 391; VIII, 471; committee disapproves proposed bureau of pardons, V, 758; new capitol, 760; delegates chosen at special election, VIII, 395; delegates chosen by Senate districts, 398, 471; compulsory voting considered in, 676.

CONSTITUTIONAL CONVENTION OF 1894. Proposition for, approved in 1886, VIII, 178; compulsory voting, propositions for, 676; act creating, 929; IX, 14; appointment of delegates by Governor, constitutionality questioned, 195; act revised, 1893, 196; requires new legislation, 1895, 537; home rule for cities, 620.

VETOES. Submission of amendments, IX, 480; contested election of delegates, fees of judicial officers, 481; additional copies of debates, X, 301.

CONSTITUTIONAL CONVENTION, United States. Act of Congress providing for, II, 270; New York appoints delegates to, 271; submission
of Constitution, 282, 296; New York suggests new convention to consider amendments, 290, 293; Tennessee suggests convention to consider slavery amendments, V, 315; proposed by, New Jersey, 325;
— Kentucky, 328, 501; — Illinois, 343; — Indiana, 349; — Arkansas,
356; how called, 464.

CONSUL. French, at New York, letter from, alleged indignity to flag,
II, 245.

CONTEMPT. Attachments for, anti-rent troubles, III, 830.

CONTESTED ELECTIONS. Legislation needed, VII, 723; Governor Hill's
special message on change of method of determining, VIII, 982;
proposed amendment transferring power to courts rejected,
982, 1076; IX, 35; English history relative to, VIII, 983;
Governor Hill's annual message, 1891, 1074; Speaker Reed's
article on, 1075; Governor Hill's special message, 1891, 1091;
voluntary submission of questions to Court of Appeals, IX,
34.

VETOES. Assembly,— Simon, appropriation, VI, 866; — Trowbridge against Tighe, printing testimony, VII, 491; — Carman
against Duryea, printing testimony, 492; — Liddle against Lynes,
printing testimony, 493; — Hotchkiss, expenses, 917; — Derrick,
expenses, 917; — Lindsay, expenses, 918; — Sheridan, expenses,
918; — Bliss, expenses, 918; — Johnson, 1891, Oneida county,
appropriation, VIII, 1142; — Waite against Dodd, counsel fees
and expenses, X, 795; — Palmer against Matthews, counsel fees
and expenses, 795; Kingston case, printing testimony, VII, 491;
delegates to Constitutional Convention, 1894, fees of judicial
officers, IX, 481.

CONTINENTAL CONGRESS. Frames Declaration of Independence, I, 583;
meets in Philadelphia, 766, 768; proceedings of, motion relative to,
in New York Assembly, 768; New York Assembly rejects resolution
thanking delegates to, 768; New York Assembly refuses to send
delegates to, 768; petition of, presented to Lord Dartmouth, 770;
New York sends delegates to first, 778; raising national funds, II,
9; investigation as to surrender of Ticonderoga and Mount Independence, 15; submits Articles of Confederation to States, 18; act
to prevent treason, 20; regulations concerning prisoners of war, 25;
defending Hudson river, 31; collecting debts due to United States,
32; act of, recruiting battalions, 33; act of, exchange of prisoners,
33; resolution, accoutrements for troops, 43; exemption of deserters
and prisoners from military service, 43; establishing Continental
Army, 44; embargo on provisions, 46; action requested as to Vermont

CONTINENTAL CONGRESS — (*Continued*).

controversy, 47; delegates, election of, 52, 105, 146, 200; advances fund for use of State, 55; resolution, clothing for army, 55; resolution, encouragement of religion and good morals, 56; apportionment of Federal expenses, 65; letters from committee, supplies, 66; resolution, supplies for Rhode Island, Providence plantations, 69; resolutions, recruits, clothing, 76; act relating to recruits, 78; resolutions, claim of Commissary-General Trumbull, 79; resolutions, relative to Federal property, 79; to prevent plundering inhabitants of Long Island, 80; resolutions, embargo, 81; restricting inland trade, 81; clothing for troops, 81; circular letter from, 81; acts relative to Vermont controversy, 82, 103, 178; directing sale to New York of rum and sugar, 84; act of, assessment of States, 85; resolution recommending legislation to compel attendance of witnesses at courts-martial, 87; army supplies, 89, 98, 101; act relating to privileges and immunities to be conferred on French subjects, 91; State quotas of troops, 93; adopts system of finance, 97; certificates of purchasing officers to be received in payment of taxes, 100; concealment of deserters, 100; defects in powers of, 107, 194; act of, compensation of troops for depreciation in currency, 110; act of, relative to bills of credit, 111; delegates, compensation and expenses, 114; apportionment of expense among States, 115; relief of prisoners of war, 116; recommending retaliation in treatment of prisoners, 116; imports on foreign merchandise, 120, 121; Vermont controversy, letter from Governor Chittenden, 136; annual meeting, 146; settlement with judge-advocate and deputies, 150; appoints thanksgiving day, 152; more troops needed, 163; papers relating to American Bank, 164; act of, British goods found on land, 164; judicial remedies between French subjects and Americans, 164; census recommended, 164; papers from, 165, 196; staying suits against public officers, 170; appoints fast day, 170; limitation of power to admit Territory into union, 179; requests special session of Legislature, 182; authorized to settle New York proportion of expenses, 184; representation in, should be constant, 190; authority to regulate commerce, 198; garrisons on western frontier, 201; treaty of peace ratified, 206; restitution of estates, 206, 207; full representation needed, 209, 210; each State to have three delegates, 213; Massachusetts territorial claims, 217, 260; authorized by New York to establish Massachusetts boundary, 218; public debt, arrears of interest, 218; settlement of Indian accounts, 220; recommends revision of forgery laws, 224; claim of New York merchants, 241; northwestern frontier, Indian depredations, intrusion on land, 245; secretary, ordinance relative to, 245; revolutionary pensions, 259; proposed commercial convention,

CONTINENTAL CONGRESS — (*Continued*).

259; requisition on New York, 263; Army Act, 264; Federal revenue system, 264, 275; convention to revise Articles of Confederation, 270; resolutions, State action under treaty of peace, 274; resolutions, duties on imports, 276; recommends extraordinary session of New York Legislature on Tariff Act, 277, 280; submits Constitution for ratification, 282, 298; recommends monument to General Herkimer, III, 179, 229, 989.

CONTINENTAL LOAN AND TRUST COMPANY. Charter, veto, VI, 341.

CONTRACT. When State may not abrogate, III, 1022; canal, to be let to lowest bidder, IV, 735, 834; V, 712; VI, 347, 799; not to exceed available appropriations, IV, 744; for canal enlargement, 783; under act of 1857, V, 254; canals, publication of notices, 365; for military supplies, 406; prison labor, investigation of, 425; prison labor, objections to, 757; canals, system abolished, VI, 105; canals, evasion of constitutional requirement, 800; canals, abrogation, effect of, 994; construction, "dollars" means coin, VII, 170; when State may abrogate, liability to contractor, 375, 376; prospective profits, allowance of, 375, 376; performance, how affected by holidays, X, 369.

VETOES. State, notice of, VIII, 130; State, public notice of, 1040.

CONVENTION. See also CONSTITUTIONAL CONVENTION; ALBANY CONVENTION. For colonial union recommended, I, 582; first New York, 778; formed by Legislature, II, 16, 27, 38, 39, 42; letter to Governor Clinton, 16; meets at Poughkeepsie, 17; at New Haven, 24, 46; bills of credit issued by, defaced to be canceled, 77; proposed for regulating prices, 83, 84; at Boston, relative to national affairs, 107; at Hartford on national affairs, 108; at Providence, New York not to be represented, 108; at Hartford on taxation, 190; proposed Federal, to revise system of government, 194, 270; commercial, proposed by Virginia, 259, 270; to consider Federal Constitution, 283, 289; national, suggested for consideration of amendments, 290, 293; to consider structure of Legislature, and powers of Council of Appointment, 468, 503, 505, 511; to reconstruct Federal government, not favored, IV, 51; at Albany, to consider question of Constitutional Convention, 84; Seneca Indians, to adopt Constitution, 457; proposed, to consider rights of slave-holding States, 513; of original States, relative to independence monument, 681; Charleston, 1860, disruption of, V, 299; recommended by Virginia to adjust national difficulties, 309; proposed by Tennessee to consider amendments for perpetuation of slavery, 315; proposed for consideration of canal questions, 507; national, proposed for consideration of uniform laws, VIII, 930.

CONVEYANCES. Of real estate, curing defects in, veto, II, 245; proof of, 486; III, 175; commissioners to take proof of, in other States and countries, 211, 770, 821.

CONVICT LABOR. See also PRISON LABOR. Employed on public works, II, 875, 1110; new system inaugurated, 875; in New York prison, 913, 1015; on public roads, 983; protest against employment on public works, 996; in erection of Sing Sing prison, III, 129; in jails, 287; employment in State prisons, 288, 512; competition with outside labor, 512, 930, 940; IV, 28, 72, 123, 608; VII, 828; VIII, 166, 649, 679; IX, 659; report of investigating commission, III, 514; limiting instruction in mechanical trades, 514; in mines, 1034; IV, 29, 73; manufacture of iron, 74, 124; investigation of contracts, V, 425; in Clinton prison, 425; alternative methods authorized, VII, 9; by contract, abolition of, 828, 957; VIII, 9, 168, 295; investigating commission created, VII, 957, 1001; VIII, 9; employment of children by contract prohibited, VII, 957; historical sketch by Governor Hill, VIII, 8; future contracts prohibited, 9; employment on State account, 10, 165, 477, 646, 679; piece price plan authorized, 168, 679; permanent system needed, 295, 477; act of 1888, 295, 658; extraordinary session, 1888, 644; revision of system needed, 679; act of 1889, 679, 814.

CONVICTS. See also CONVICT LABOR. Importation of, should be discouragd, I, 248; bible proposed for, 612; pardons on condition of leaving State, 913; insane, transfer of, 945; transferred from State prison to house of refuge, III, 292; female, improved accommodations for, 339, 379; female, prison for, 403, 448, 515, 618; preventing importation of, 403; ratio of colored to white, 717; instruction of, 765; library books for, 861; reformation of, 874; women, proposed retreat for, 875; commutation for good behavior, IV, 723, 787, 844; V, 374, 525, 842; VI, 18, 899; VII, 147, 708; discharged, payments to, IV, 845; VI, 18; insane, asylum at Auburn, V, 78; expense of transportation, 168, 291, 386; women, sending to penitentiary instead of prisons, 293; financial aid on discharge, 374; female, insane to be sent to State prison, 583; women, where to be sent in certain districts, 599; expensive accommodations for, VI, 873; women, where to be imprisoned, VII, 10; discharged, State agent for employment of, 10; State prisons, comparative statement, 701; large number, 1883, 955; employment of State and county, in public roadmaking, IX, 668.

CONVICTS — (*Continued*).

VETOES. Assaults on prison officers, punishment for, II, 589; commutation, increasing rate, VI, 89; confinement in penitentiaries, 711; New York, employment of, 982; gratuity on discharge, VII, 264; maintenance in penitentiaries, deficiency appropriation, 462, 584, 792; VIII, 118; commutation, VII, 508; imprisonment in Elmira Reformatory, 666; State prisons, additional religious instruction for, 919; regulating confinement, 937.

CONWAY, HENRY SEYMOUR. English Secretary of State, letter from Colden, opposition to Stamp Act, I, 711.

CONWAY, JAMES. Relief, veto, VI, 306.

CONWAY, WILLIAM. Administrator, James Hendy, Court of Claims, veto, X, 944.

COOK, E. Counsel Assembly Committee on Privileges and Elections, appropriation, veto, X, 796.

COOK, HENRY R. M. New York, auditor of school department, statement concerning teachers' salaries, X, 154.

COOK, LEWIS. Trustee St. Regis Indians, II, 938; death of, 938.

COOK, WILLIAM B., JR. Assistant law librarian, acknowledgments to, I, pref. XV.

COOL, MARY. Convicted of murder, pardoned, II, 749.

COOLEY, JAMES S. Manager Jamaica normal school, Waters case, X, 561.

COOLEY'S CONSTITUTIONAL LIMITATIONS. Cited, eminent domain, VII, 244; public use, 246; license fee for revenue is taxation, VIII, 357; secret voting, 585; cruel and unusual punishments, 588; qualifications of voters, IX, 95.

COONEY, JAMES. New York Municipal Court, attendant, claim, veto, X, 168.

COOPER, CHARLES D. Secretary of State, communication from, occupancy, of rooms in capitol, II, 936.

COOPER, GEORGE. Bond for return of arms, II, 774.

CO-OPERATIVE LIFE INSURANCE COMPANIES. Act requiring annual reports, VII, 543; statistics, 825, 950; VIII, 7; operation of act of 1883, VII, 950.

VETOES. Exempting from insurance laws, VII, 543, 692; town and county, extending risks, VIII, 881; town and county, amending act, IX, 152.

CO-OPERATIVE SAVINGS AND LOAN ASSOCIATION. Charter, veto, VI, 339.

CO-OPERATIVE SAVINGS AND LOAN ASSOCIATIONS. VETOES. Amending Banking Law, IX, 472; — profits and losses, X, 810; — security for loans, 810.

COOPERSTOWN. Hurford and Barnett, escheat, veto, VIII, 882.

COOPER UNION FOR THE ADVANCEMENT OF SCIENCE AND ART. Report, V, 204, 313, 417, 487, 564, 634, 719, 793, 862; VI, 44, 143, 266, 427, 554, 661, 785, 981; VII, 43, 178, 316, 439, 537, 842, 996; VIII, 43, 195, 326, 500, 696, 938, 1085; IX, 37, 210, 340, 570, 685, 754, 851; X, 32, 130, 375, 875; release from assessment, veto, X, 178.

COOTE, RICHARD. See BELLOMONT, EARL OF.

COPENHAGEN. Village, commissioners to ascertain street damages, veto, VI, 217.

COPPER. Money, act relative to importation of, I, 507; deposits in New York, III, 1036.

COPPERAS. Manufacture of, claim relating to, II, 92.

COPSEY BATTERY. Protecting cannon at, I, 322; banquette at, 323; injured by storm, 528; repairs needed, 537.

COPYRIGHT. Patent and Copyright Protective Association, New York, amending charter, veto, X, 312.

CORBETT, MARY. Escheat, veto, VII, 805.

CORBIN, HENRY C. Adjutant-General, United States, accompanies Prince Henry to Assembly Chamber at his reception by the Assembly, X, 480.

CORCORAN, MICHAEL, COLONEL. Sixty-ninth Regiment, supplies from Union Defense Committee, VII, 501.

CORDWOOD. Act relative to sale of, I, 11.

COREY, WILLIAM. Bond for return of arms, II, 774.

CORLAR LAKE (Champlain). French at, I, 241.

CORONERS. To be member of militia reserves, I, 549; a county office, VI, 171; method of selection and removal, 833; investigation of fires, VIII, 690; Kings county, term of office, IX, 704; office omitted from Constitution, 1894, 704.

VETOES. Erie county, VI, 170; New York, inquests, expenses, 844; New York, stenographers for, 910; New York, duties and compensation, VII, 129; Rensselaer county, compensation, proceedings, VIII, 62; acting as sheriff, 292; duties, 292; Kings county, clerk, 638; Kings county, stenographer, 890; Erie county, fees, post mortem examinations, 1153; Kings county, physician, eastern district, IX, 434; relative to abolishing jury, 860; Erie county, fixing term, election of successor, 861; New York, abolishing office, X, 712; Boughton, Wyoming county, legalizing acts, 813; New York, services of clerk, 951, 956.

CORN. Blast upon, deemed Divine visitation, fast day recommended, I, 24; of Indians, destroyed by French, 65; exportation of, discouraged, 116; present of, to Indians, 570; proposed suspension of embargo on, II, 68; of certain Indian tribes, destruction of, 882; canal freight, 1881, VII, 683.

CORNBURY, LORD. Appointed Governor, I, 98; also Governor of New
    Jersey, 98; dissolves Eighth Assembly, 98.
    OPENING SPEECH. Ninth Assembly, first session, I, 98; unhappy
        condition of colony, 98; defense of New York, 99, 103, 104, 120,
        123, 125; defense of frontier, 99, 102, 103, 105, 107, 112, 113,
        114, 117, 118; militia, 99, 102, 109, 115, 121, 128; public schools,
        100; examination of public accounts, 100, 101, 102; civil and
        religious liberty, 100; address to Queen Anne, 101, 104; chaplain
        for Assembly, 101; announces appointment of Edward Cole,
        sergeant-at-arms of Assembly, 101; adjourns Assembly from
        Jamaica to New York, 101.
    OPENING SPEECH. Ninth Assembly, second session, I, 101; expected
        French attack on New York, 103; highways, 103; offensive
        trades in New York, 103; success of Queen Anne's naval move-
        ments, 104; charges against Chief Justice Atwood, 104; batteries
        at Narrows, 104, 120, 125; soliciting royal aid to province, 104;
        non-payment of claims against colony, 105, 116.
    OPENING SPEECH. Ninth Assembly, third session, I, 105; presents to
        Governor prohibited, 106, 116;   to visit Amboy, 106.
    OPENING SPEECH. Ninth Assembly, fourth session, I, 107; French
        and Indian successes in New England, 107; revenue, support of
        government, 108, 109, 112; repeal of part of act relating to
        disorders in colony, 109; thanks Assembly for address, 109;
        salaries of civil officers, 109; report of Collector Byerly, 109;
        protests against Assembly's action relative to militia, 109; As-
        sembly has no control of funds contributed by Crown, 109.
    OPENING SPEECH. Ninth Assembly, fifth session, I, 111; dissolves
        Ninth Assembly, 113.
    OPENING SPEECH. Tenth Assembly, first session, I, 114; Waghana
        Indians, 114; ministers, 115; duties on imports from other
        colonies, 115; exportation of corn and flour, 116; payment of
        public debts, 116; clipping and defacing foreign coin, 116;
        disorderly houses, 116; slaves, 116; expedition against French
        privateer, 117, 119; importation of naval stores from other
        colonies, 117; trade with France prohibited, 117; correspondence
        with Queen's enemies prohibited, 118; military stores, 118;
        amendment of money bills, 118, 123, 162.
    OPENING SPEECH. Tenth Assembly, second session, 118.
    OPENING SPEECH. Tenth Assembly, third session, I, 119; expected
        French attempt on colony, 119; Assembly declares validity of
        extraordinary session, 120; repair of fort in New York, 120,
        125; declines to approve money bills, 121, 123, 124.

CORNBURY, LORD —(*Continued*).

OPENING SPEECH. Tenth Assembly, fourth session, I, 122; fortifications bill, 123; colonial treasurer, 123; province ought to
furnish its own arms, 124; recommends new appropriation bill,
124; appropriations for military and other services, 124;
Schenectady guardhouse, 125; announces Captain Redknap's
appointment as colonial engineer, 125; defense of Albany, 125,
130; dissolves Tenth Assembly, 126; power to act out of colony,
126, 127, 149.

OPENING SPEECH. Eleventh Assembly, first session, I, 127; post-
office, 129; relations with Indians, 129; highways, 129; relief
of Richard Davis, 130; reimbursement of Indian commissioners,
130; amount for frontier defense, 130; reimbursing Colonel
Schuyler and Captain Norbury, 131; expedition against French
privateer, 131; address to Crown on act relative to corruption
of coin, 131; official service, I, pref. IX.

CORNELL, ALONZO B. Governor and portrait, VII, 418.

1880. Annual message, VII, 418; prosperous conditions, 418;
finances, 418, debt, 420; taxation, 421; revision of tax laws,
421; canals, 422; public education, 423; women eligible as
school officers, 423; common school statistics, 424; State
prisons, 424; insurance, 426; fire and insurance losses,
1878, 426; banks and savings banks, 427; trust companies,
428; national guard, 428; codification of military laws,
428; new capitol, 429; member of new capitol commission,
1868, 430; proposes loan for completion of new capitol,
430; insane asylums and charitable institutions, 430; county
jails and poorhouses, 431; emigration, 432; quarantine, 433;
railroad transportation, 433; election laws, 434; excise laws,
435; harbor masters, 435; pilotage, 436; Indians, 436;
local indebtedness, 437; municipal affairs, 437; first simultaneous election of executive officers and Legislature, 1879,
438; report of commission on diseases of animals, 438;
custodian of great seal, 439; Connecticut memorial, Hell
Gate pilotage, 441; charges against trustees of Binghamton Insane Asylum, 443; announces death of Sanford E.
Church, 447.

MEMORANDUMS ON APPROVAL. New York and Brooklyn bridge,
completion and opening, VII, 450; New York, district
courts, relief of clerks and assistants, 451; new capitol,
appropriation, 453; corporations, tax on, 454; Brooklyn,
health department, 455; Brooklyn, unpaid taxes and assessments, 502.

CORNELL, ALONZO B., 1880 — (*Continued*).

   VETOES. Brooklyn, constables, VII, 439; Middleburgh, separate
        road district, 440; Kings county, clerks of boards of su-
        pervisors and courthouse engineers, 440; Erie county, sup-
        port of poor, 441; public instruction, delinquent taxes,
        442; Game Law, Jefferson and Oswego counties, releas-
        ing certain waters from operation of, 442; notaries pub-
        lic, additional, 443; VIII, 44; New York, wooden buildings,
        construction prohibited, VII, 444; taxes, foreign capital,
        445; Game Law, Steuben county, fish, Loon lake, 446;
        Brooklyn, railroads on Water street, 446; Erie canal, en-
        larging west branch of Eighteen Mile creek, 449; New York
        markets, 450; items in canal appropriation bill, 455; items
        in supply bill, 458; Richmond county, clerk's office, record-
        ing certain papers, 497; Richmond county, Middletown, sep-
        arate road district, 497; items of awards by State Board
        of Audit, 498; taxation, assessment of corporations, 502;
        Code of Criminal Procedure, 504; omnibus veto, 505.

1881. Annual message, VII, 510; prosperous conditions, 510;
        finances, 511; debt, 512; taxation, 513; revision of tax
        laws, 514; canals, 515; possible rivalry of Canadian canals,
        516; enlargement of Erie canal, 517; abandoned canals
        detrimental to public health, 517; public education, 517;
        qualifications of voters at school meetings, 518; common
        school statistics, 518; State prisons, 519; banks, 520; con-
        dition of savings banks, 521; insurance, 521; life insurance
        reserves, rate of interest, 522; National Guard, 523; Mili-
        tary Code, 523; new capitol, 523; defect in Assembly cham-
        ber ceiling, 524; canal appraisers, 524; railroad transpor-
        tation, 525; charitable institutions, 526; number of insane
        persons, 527; Elmira Reformatory, 527; county jails and
        poorhouses, 528; reformatory for women, 528; State Board
        of Health, 529; emigration, 529; quarantine, 530; harbor mas-
        ters and port wardens, 531; revision of excise laws, 531;
        lottery laws, 532; municipal affairs, 532; removal of dis-
        abled judges, 533; imprisonment for debt, 534; local and
        special legislation, 534; Connecticut boundary, 535, 536;
        pardon report, 536; cattle diseases, pleuro-pneumonia, 537;
        Kings county, board of supervisors, report on charitable
        and penal institutions, 537; members of Tax Commission,
        538; Senate occupies new Senate Chamber, 539; petition
        for removal of Judge Sanford, 542; nuisances, New York
        and Brooklyn, 547; resignations of United States Senators

CORNELL, ALONZO B., 1881 — (*Continued*).

Conkling and Platt, 555; vacancies in United States Senate, 568; communication from Tax Revision Commission, indirect taxation, 570; Chemung canal nuisance, 575; War of 1812, State's property rights, commission recommended, 601; member of commission on State's property rights, War of 1812, 601; veto of ten day bills, general note, 667; communication to Secretary of State, veto of ten day bills, 671.

MEMORANDUM ON APPROVAL. Penal Code, VII, 663.

VETOES. Erie county, compensation of court officers, 538; Sullivan county, reducing pay of town officers, 540; Kings county, armory, site for, 541; charitable, benevolent and beneficiary corporations, exempting from life insurance laws, 543; Kings county, Cunningham, reimbursement, 544; Superintendent of Public Works, authorizing return of certain certificates of deposit, 545; Grand Legion of Select Knights of the American Order of United Workmen, charter, 546; Hohenholz escheat bill, 548; Porter escheat bill, 549; Seneca county, judge and surrogate, compensation, 549; Harvey escheat bill, 550; New York, public bath, 551; Washington county, special county judge and surrogate, 551; Cottman, proof of claim, 552; New York, manure, facilitating removal of, 553; Champlain canal, removal of bridge, Cohoes, 554; town auditors, exempting Chemung and Greene counties, 554; Ulster and Delaware Plankroad Company, extending charter, 565; Bankers' Life Insurance and Trust Company, New York, changing name, 567; pilots, Hell Gate, reducing fees, 568; Canandaigua, legalizing acts, 569; manufacturing corporations, floating dock, extending act, 569; butter, deception in sales of, 571; Brooklyn, grading Lorraine street, 572; vinegar, adulteration, 572; police, false impersonation of, 573; foreign insurance companies, removal of actions to Federal court, 573; items in canal administration act, 576; Chemung river, bridge over Big flats, 578; New York, Central park, refreshment house, 578; New York, registry of voters, publication, 579; items in supply bill, 581; Erie canal, Rochester, bridge, Lyell street, 589; mining companies, reports, 589; oleomargarine, regulating manufacture and sale, 590; Metropolitan Transit Company, supplemental act, 592; New

CORNELL, ALONZO B., 1881, VETOES — (*Continued*).

York, water supply, 593, 635; New York, sheriff's jury, 595; religious toleration, freedom of worship, institutions for care of poor, 596; New York, city prison, compensation of keepers, 597; Tyrrell, loss of canal boat, 599; Cornell Hose Company No. 2, Kingston, charter, 600; Kehr, Kellner and Ott, relief, 601; Long Island City, Jackson avenue improvement, 603; Albany, county clerk, fees, 604; Brooklyn, Sackett street contract, payment of balance, 605; teachers, retirement, New York and Brooklyn, 606; Long Island City, closing Ninth street, 609; county officers, report of financial transactions, 609; Game Law, amending general act, 611; Clinton county, surrogate, powers of county judge, 614; Hatzel relief bill, 616; Brooklyn, Kingsley and Keeney claim, construction of storage reservoir, 617; Stewart escheat, 619; manufacturing corporations, xtending powers, patent rights, 621; town auditors, exempting Coeymans, 622; New York, docks, 622; witnesses, agents, informers and spies, testimony, 624; Brooklyn, free books and supplies, 626; Brooklyn, public schools, protection of life and property, 627; New York, park commissioners, alteration of map, Spuyten Duyvil road, 629; State Industrial School, act to establish, 631; Game Law, Jefferson county fish hatchery, 632; Ehlers, legitimizing birth, 633; private property, protection, 640; Long Island City, salary of aldermen, 641; De Groat escheat, 642; New York, Foley, supervisor, salary, 643; villages, amending general act, Dresden, 644; highways, deposits of ashes and rubbish in, 646; Legislative investigating committee, services of counsel, 647; sugars, syrups, molasses and honey, fraud in manufacture and sale, 648; Code of Civil Procedure, compensation of surrogates' clerks, 649; highways, Franklin county, facilitating travel, 650; Kings county, commissioner of charities, ousting incumbent, Kessel case, 651; new capitol, work on exterior walls, 652; Lake George, islands, preservation of trees and shrubbery, 655; New York, Riverside park improvement, 655; taxes, land sold for, conveying State's interest, 656; New York, streets, changing grades, 657; oils and fluids, illuminating, regulating standard, 659; Stemmler relief, 661; aliens, purchasing and holding real estate, 662; omnibus veto, 664.

CORNELL, ALONZO B. — (*Continued*).

1882. Annual message, VII, 677; prosperity of State, 677; assassination of President Garfield, 677; finances, 678; receipts and expenditures, 679; debt, 680; taxation, 681; revision of tax laws, 681; special tax on corporations, 682; canals, 683; constitutional amendments, canal tolls, expenditures and debt, 685; canal appraisers, 685; public education, 686; diminution of attendance in common schools, 686; decline of school district libraries, 686; common school statistics, 687; colleges and academies, 688; purchase of Clinton manuscripts, 688; banks, 688; savings banks, 689; trust, loan and mortgage companies, 690; insurance, 690; co-operative insurance, 691; National Guard, 693; uniforms for National Guard, 694; progress of work on new capitol, 694; location of Court of Appeals in new capitol not satisfactory, 694; demolition of old capitol, 696; salt springs, 696; agricultural experiment station, 697; pleuro-pneumonia, 698; oleomargarine, 698; railroad transportation, 700; uniform freight charges, 700; State prisons self-sustaining, 701; Elmira Reformatory, 702; House of Refuge for Women, 703; charitable institutions, 703; alien paupers returned to homes, 705; number of insane persons. increasing, 705; county jails and poorhouses, 706; crime, 707; pardons, 707; commutations for good behavior, 708; imprisonment for debt, 708; Indians, 709; State Board of Health, 710; local boards of health needed, 710; sanitary construction of houses, 711; emigration, 711; tax on steamship companies, 712; quarantine, 713; harbor masters and port wardens, 713; excise laws, 714; lotteries, 715; municipal affairs, 715; New York, water supply, commission of inquiry recommended, 716; international exposition, 717; monetary disturbances, 718; modification of usury laws, 719; State boundary lines, 719; Adirondack survey, 720; northern wilderness, 721; State lands should not be sold, 722; Penal Code, 722; contested elections, 723; bribery at elections, 724; congressional representation, 725; arms of the State, 725; constitutional amendments, 727; biennial legislative session, 728; railroad accident, death of Webster Wagner, 730; prevention of railroad accidents, 731; report of commission for the reception of national guests, 733, 737; members of Centennial Commission, 734; Yorktown Centennial, 735; attends Yorktown Centennial Celebration, 736; reviews 1st Division National Guard, Yorktown Celebration, 739; portrait of

CORNELL, ALONZO B., 1882—(*Continued*).

Abraham Lincoln in new capitol, 743; Virginia resolutions, support of common schools, 744; camps of instruction for National Guard, 746; proposition to change portrait of Lincoln for smaller size, 769; purchase of Clinton Papers, note, 808; quoted, veto of bill exempting Chemung and Greene counties from Town Auditor's Act, VIII, 49; approves Poughkeepsie bridge extension, 444; quoted, need of excise revision, 513; general registration law for villages, 721; protests against riders in appropriation bills, IX, 405; official service, I, pref. XIII.

MEMORANDUMS ON APPROVAL. Waterloo, charter, VII, 775; New York, Consolidation Act, 802; emigration commissioners, appropriation, 802.

VETOES. Sing Sing Branch of the American Society for the Prevention of Cruelty to Animals, charter, VII, 744; Gooderson Fire Engine Company No. 2, Winfield, changing name, 748; McLoughlin escheat, 748; Meyer escheat, 749; Brooklyn, changing custody of school funds, 750; oils and fluids, illuminating, regulating standards, 751; Binghamton, police force, 752; West, refunding money paid as surety on supervisor's bond, Sangerfield, 753; trial, capital cases, giving defense right to make closing address, 754; Albany, school funds, using for other purposes, 755; Albany, county clerk, office hours, 757; New York and Kings counties, closing certain offices on Saturdays, 757; household furniture and sewing machines, sale on installment plan, 758; Buffalo Cemetery Association, additional land and office building, 760; charitable institutions, women as trustees or managers, 761; Brooklyn, park commissioners, extending term, 762; Buffalo Light Battery, charter, 763; children, employment by contract in public institutions, 764; Eureka Basin Warehouse and Manufacturing Company, Long Island, powers and privileges, repeal, 766; towns, liability for damages, defective highways, 767; New York, General Sessions, stenographer's compensation, 768; Fulton county, board of supervisors, equalizing representation, 769; stenographers, second judicial district, Kings county, appointment and removal, 769; Auburn, police and street lighting expenses, 770; Brooklyn, unpaid taxes, 771; New York, city prison keepers, increasing compensation, 772; Sharpe, extending time to file canal claim, 773; items in canal appropriation bill.

CORNELL, ALONZO B., 1882, VETOES —(*Continued*).

774; items in canal awards bill, 774; Troy, armory, 776; Troy, increasing salaries, 776; New York, corporations, taxation of, 777; items in supply bill, 777; street railroads, maintenance and operation in cities, towns and villages, 793; Civil Code, 794; Kings county, armory, 795; Military Code, 796; savings banks, trust, loan and insurance companies, insolvent, settlement of affairs, 797; Cayuga county, Auburn prison claim, submission to State Board of Audit, 801; omnibus veto, 803.

CORNELL, DANIEL P. Notary public, legalizing acts, veto, VII, 507.

CORNELL, EZRA. Endows Cornell University, V, 596, 693; gift to Genesee College, 596.

CORNELL HOSE COMPANY NO. 2, KINGSTON. Charter, veto, VII, 600.

CORNELL UNIVERSITY. Foundation of, II, 1080; V, 596; IX, 177; established at Ithaca, V, 596, 693; objects, endowment, 596; VI, 946; land scrip, Comptroller to fix price of, V, 694; development of, 854; opening of, VI, 22; agricultural instruction at, IX, 175; one free student from each Assembly district, 177; agricultural experiment station established at, 179, 319; appropriations for promotion of dairy husbandry, 179; experiment station, annual report, 215; College of Forestry, land furnished by State, 837; X, 605; College of Forestry, report, 1898, 32; proposed pedagogical department, 112; State Agricultural College established at, 627.

VETOES. College land scrip fund, loan to State, IX, 357; appropriation for College of Forestry, X, 555; agricultural college, good roads school, 793.

CORN EXCHANGE WAREHOUSE COMPANY. Charter, veto, VI, 215.

CORNFIELDS. Act relating to, I, 11.

CORNING. New arsenal at, V, 88, 175, 642; riots of 1877, VII, 152; number of excise licenses, 1887, VIII, 360; incorporated, 1890, 562; new charter, 1894, IX, 238.

VETOES. Amending Village Law, VI, 693; town boards, payment of, borrowing money for interest, VII, 334; excise moneys, payment to St. Joseph's Orphan Asylum, VIII, 465; city charter, 562; amending charter, IX, 238, 809; X, 583; public health, waters of Chemung river, IX, 719; extending dyke, Chemung river, X, 315.

CORNING, ERASTUS. Delegate to Washington Peace Convention, V, 310.

CORNING LIBRARY. Acquiring property, fixing annual election, veto, VI, 691.

CORNISH, GEORGE R. Canal department, appropriation for services, veto, IX, 716.

CORNITH. Northern terminus of proposed canal along North creek, III, 733.

CORNPLANTER. Indian Chief, method of election, IV, 504.

CORNWALL. Idlewild Temperance Association, veto, VI, 309.

CORNWALLIS, LORD. Surrenders at Yorktown, I, 779; II, 150.

CORNWALL LANDING. Ferry at, veto, VII, 664.

CORPORATIONS. See also particular corporations; should not be extended, II, 229, 246, 696; charters, publicity of passage recommended, 450; religious, act relating to, 467, 468; turnpike companies, 511, see that title; medical societies, see that title; charters, legislative interference with, 611; are not citizens, 613; forfeiture of stock, 638; when majority of corporators cannot control minority, 639; for charitable purposes, 717; manufacturing, 855, see that title; foreign, owning American land, 1033; power of Legislature to dissolve, 1082; railroads, see that title; power to create, III, 521, 531; charters should not interfere with individual enterprise, 554; banks, see that title; State aid to, IV, 10; State aid to, proposed abrogation of power, 55; State claims against, apportionment of, 262; general laws for, 379, 513, 522, 526, 531, 574, 593, 633, 636, 638, 639, 823; V, 129, 133, 147, 191, 231, 645, 655, 658, 711, 848; VI, 168, 246, 353, 640; VII, 202, 233, 240, 241, 336, 357, 371, 546, 565, 745, 845, 868; VIII, 52, 197, 297; X, 864; plankroad companies, IV, 379, see that title; villages, 379, see that title; dues from, constitutional provision, 401, 824; V, 644; personal liability of members, IV, 402; amending charters, 515; bridge companies, 514; academies, 575; benevolent, charitable, scientific and missionary, 635, 638; V, 131, 233; VI, 55; not to plead usury, IV, 805; foreign, see FOREIGN CORPORATIONS; frauds in organization of, 855; assessments against stockholders, V, 119, 233; objections against powers in perpetuity, 240; should not possess unrestricted powers, 807; liability of officers for improper use of funds, VI, 37; changing names, 119, 189, 1034; VII, 748, 931; VIII, 62, 205, 326, 327, 337, 617, 876, 974, 980, 981, 1144, 1162, 1163; IX, 56, 348, 356; X, 235; injunctions against, procedure, VI, 122; cemetery associations, see that title; taxing power, cemeteries, 184; limiting amount of property, 677; tax on, act of 1880; VII, 454, 682, 816, 941; VIII, 4, 145, 304, 1082; IX, 9, 158, 538, 647; X, 26, 181; interpretation, VII, 454; business, see BUSINESS CORPORATIONS; receiverships, payment of wages, VIII, 36; dissolutions, restricting power

CORPORATIONS — (*Continued*).

of, 39; issuing stock at less than par, 179; amount of bonds should be limited, 179, 303, 480, 680, 931; when Legislature may annul or dissolve, 204; organization tax, 305, 638, 1083; IX, 9, 158, 538, 647; X, 26, 181; bonds or other evidences of debt, taxation of, VIII, 306, 480; IX, 10; alleged contributions to campaign fund, 1888, VIII, 664; weekly payment of wages, 680, 930; limiting amount of property held by, 703, 709; general laws, 1890, 1027; IX, 26; organization in other States, 10, 99, 137; charters may be amended or repealed, 93, 501; should be encouraged to organize in New York, 10, 99; duty to employees, 163; when taxes should not be refunded, 281; to improve breed of horses, 548; large number paying taxes, 1895, 647; taxes, credit on resettlement, may assign claim to other corporations, 715; large increase of, X, 26; should bear larger share of taxation, 35; industrial conditions, Governor Roosevelt's discussion, 1900, 86; organized with improper titles, 103; limiting right to use certain names, 104; alphabetical list in office of Secretary of State, 110; laws should be more liberal, 184, 366; reports, failure to file, liability of directors, 185; organization tax reduced, 186; rights received from State, 197; taxation, statutes noted, 198; receivers, limiting expense of administration, 352; settling negligence cases, 372; franchise tax, New York's contribution, 1902, 483; taxing transfers of stock, 490; good results of liberal legislation, 621; protection on proceeding to change name, 622; capital employed in State, defined, 720, 722; political contributions prohibited, 842, 847; State's power to regulate use of property, 901.

VETOES. Enjoying special privileges, II, 229; assessment of stock, 777; transportation of liquor, IV, 768; taxation of, 775; forfeiture of stock, V, 120; changing name, 125; X, 705; Oswego Pier and Dock Company, extraordinary powers, VI, 85; converting common to preferred stock, 96; stockholders, hotel company, limiting liability, 335; power to issue attachments, 585; stockholders, relief from liability, 586; indefinite powers, 700; power of taxation, 850; moneyed, receivers, VII, 416; assessment of, 502; business, organization and regulation, 507; telegraph companies, relative to, 507; in New York, taxation, 777; amending Tax Law, 807, 1096; benevolent and charitable, dissolution, 1020; justice's court, service of summons, 1094; extending existence, 1103; organized under general laws, relief, 1114; bankrupt, receivers, VIII, 129; annual reports to Comptroller, 293; evading taxation, expenses of inquiry, 418; stockholders, voting per capita, 469; relief of, 470; taxation,

CORPORATIONS, VETOES —(Continued).

exempting agricultural and horticultural societies, 619; indictment against, appearance, 640; franchise tax, equalization, 640; mortgages, consents of stockholders, 888; buildings, erection of, 1041; amending Tax Act of 1880, IX, 153; taxes unlawfully collected, claims for, 278; loans on personal property, charter, 534; names, prohibiting use by other corporations, 625; New York, affording facilities for transaction of business by officers and employees, 719; concerning certain, 794, 861; pneumatic tubes, franchise tax, 794; foreign, certificate of authority, 864; directors, amending general laws, 864; extension of business, 865; for erection of soldiers' monument, authorizing formation of, X, 63; receivers, action against corporation, 309; director, definition, 311; State, fees and taxes, 433; acquisition of property without State, 521, new bill passed; franchise tax, 706; voluntary dissolution, 808; receivers, commissions, compensation of counsel, 960.

CORRECTIONAL INSTITUTIONS. Powers of local boards, VII, 960.

CORRUPT PRACTICES. (ELECTIONS.) Governor De Witt Clinton's protest against, III, 158; Governor Van Buren's comment on, 249; limiting candidates' expenses, 250, 313, 525; IV, 134; legitimate expenses of elections, 134; in New York, V, 25; at elections, VI, 36, 125; candidate's statement of expenses, VIII, 672, 918, 970, 1079, 1092; political committees, statement of election expenses, 918, 970, 1079; IX, 197, 310, 555; act relative to, 1890, VIII, 1001; candidates guilty of, exclusion from office, 1079, 1092; judicial candidates not to make political contributions, X, 123, 516; campaign contributions, act of 1906, 767; political contributions by corporations prohibited, 842, 847; reports of political committees, 847.

CORRY, WILLIAM. Receives patent of land, Montgomery county, IV, 331.

CORSS, ASHER N. Major-general, claim for services of infantry, III, 694.

CORTHELL, ELMER L. Member of Canal Advisory Board, X, 629.

CORTLAND. Normal school at, V, 695, 780; number of excise licenses, 1887, VIII, 360. VETOES. New armory, 887; union free school, 883; contracts, powers of common council, sidewalks, X, 593.

CORTLAND ACADEMY. Aid from town of Homer, veto, VI, 94.

CORTLAND COUNTY. Militia from, 1812, II, 743; agricultural society in, III, 945; average excise license fees, 1889, VIII, 686; Virgil, opening highway, extending time, veto, 1086; highways, cost of labor system, 1892, IX, 199; insane, care of, county and State systems compared, IX, 228.

CORTLAND NORMAL SCHOOL. Established, V, 695, 780, 852. VETOES. Repairs and improvements, appropriation, VII, 468; IX, 106; — salaries of teachers removed and restored, VII, 927; — heating apparatus, VIII, 863.

CORTLAND OPERA HOUSE COMPANY. Mortgage for indebtedness, veto, VIII, 381.

CORTLANDT, COLONEL. Regiment in national service, II, 18. See also VAN CORTLANDT.

CORTLANDT (Westchester County). Pierre Van Cortlandt, Assembly favors colonial union, I, 767. VETOES. Reducing town expenses, salaries for justices of the peace and overseers of the poor, IX, 722; union free school district No. 7, establishing boundaries, 816; highway tax in Croton-on-the-Hudson, payment to village, 867; St. Peter's church, regulating interments, X, 593.

COSBY, WILLIAM. Appointed Governor, I, 242.
OPENING SPEECH. Twentieth Assembly, fifth session, I, 242; new Revenue Act, 243; garrisons at Oswego and elsewhere, 243; defense of Albany, 244; destruction of counterfeit bills of credit, 244.
OPENING SPEECH. Twentieth Assembly, sixth session, I, 244; repairs at Fort George, 245; new commissary at Oswego, 245.
OPENING SPEECH. Twentieth Assembly, seventh session, I, 245; discussion of trade conditions, 245; tariff revision, 247; servants and slaves, 248; encouraging friendly relations with Six Nations, 248.
TWENTIETH ASSEMBLY, eighth session, inquiry from Lords of Trade, as to manufactures, I, 250; declines Assembly's request for dissolution, 250; approves Fortifications Act, 250.
OPENING SPEECH. Twentieth Assembly, ninth session, I, 251; renewal of covenant chain with Six Nations, 251; affairs at Oswego, 251; presents abstract of public accounts, 252; Albany petition for dissolution of Assembly, 252; dissolution refused, 252; Governor's relation to Legislature, 253; Van Dam prefers charges against Governor, 253; Lords of Trade defend Governor's status, 253; support of government under, acts in force five years, 470; death of, 254; official service, I, pref. X.

COSBY, CAPTAIN. To raise recruits for King's service, I, 306; reimbursed for expenses, 308.

COSTELLO, THOMAS M. Board of Claims, veto, VII, 1124.

COSTS. In Court of Chancery, II, 702; in actions for slander and assault and battery, III, 219; reducing amount of, 873; in New York district courts, VII, 1046.

COSTS — (*Continued*).

VETOES. Surrogate's Court, VI, 340; IX, 625; X, 955; amending Code, VII, 665; IX, 860; on review of illegal assessments, regulation of, VIII, 466; judgments against State, payment of, 546, new bill passed; in actions, X, 179, 880, 916.

COTTER, DANIEL. Relief of, veto, VI, 185.

COTTMAN, THOMAS. Proof of claim, veto, VII, 552.

COTTON. Manufactory, exempt from taxation, II, 876; abundance of raw material, 899; cloth, encouraging manufacture of, 1092; cultivation of, III, 386; manufactories, statistics of, IV, 42.

COTTONIAN COLLECTION. British Museum, IV, 183.

COTTON STATES EXPOSITION. Governor Morton's special message relative to, IX, 581; participation of foreign nations, 581; commission created, 582; legislative joint committee appointed, 582; appropriation for expenses, 582; transfer of buildings to Piedmont Driving Club, 582, 673; New York's success at, 672.

COUDERT, FREDERIC R. Opinion, unconstitutionality of ballot bill, 1888, VIII, 574, 589.

COUGHLIN, JOHN. Auburn prison convict, crime committed by, trial, reimbursing Cayuga county, veto, VI, 876; VII, 87, 227, 471, 781.

COUGHLIN, JOHN. Claim, damages and extra work, Soldiers and Sailors' Home, Court of Claims, veto, X, 377.

COUGHTRY, WILLIAM L. Assembly, member of Prince Henry reception committee, X, 479; escorts General von Plessin at reception, 480.

COULSON, FREDERICK D. State Law Librarian, acknowledgments to, I, pref. XV.

COUNCIL (Colony). Powers of, I, 1, 13; legislative, 6; freedom of debate in, 8; members of first legislative, 9; communications from, to be in writing, 20; assumes executive power on Governor Sloughter's death, 23; sustains validity of Assembly after Governor Sloughter's death, 28; communication from, relative to public affairs, 46; power to establish fees, 84; object to certain trade regulations, 86; assumes executive authority, 90; convokes Assembly, 91; power of, sustained by Assembly and Lords of Trade, 92; when President of Council to become acting Governor, 94; controversy with Assembly concerning legislative power, 110; claims right to amend money bills, 118, 123, 157, 159, 162, 166, 493; to establish fees, 144; proposes frequent meetings with Assembly, 169; recommends repair of New York custom house, 188; government transferred to President of, 190; papers relating to Treasurer, 200; proposed examination of recent statutes, 204; opinion as to Assembly's power over revenues, 221; action relative to importation of salt, 233; Rip Van Dam, President of, assumes executive authority, 238; meets

COUNCIL (Colony)—(*Continued*).

at Captain Kippen's house, 239; Governor's relation to Legislature, 253; Council sits in two capacities, 253; President Clarke becomes acting Governor, 254; address to President, 257; meets at Fort George, 258; approves expedition against West Indies, 289; joins with Assembly in address requesting royal aid in restoring public buildings destroyed by fire, 304; opinion as to care of prisoners of war, 328; address to Governor, 329, 406; advises sending prisoners of war out of colony, 330; certain members of, criticised by King, 532; address to Governor, money bills, 544; address to Governor, Massachusetts and New Jersey boundaries, 611; joint committee on frontier settlements, 631; Cadwallader Colden, President of, assumes executive authority, 647; compliments General Amherst, · 658; address on judicial proceedings, 661; decides to continue Assembly after Governor Tryon's appointment, 740; fire in Council Chamber, 753, 756, 758; declines to re-establish civil government during Revolution, 779; proceedings, documents relating to, III, 1018.

COUNCIL OF APPOINTMENT. Under first Constitution, II, 3; III, 1001; IV, 52; VI, 832; right of nomination in, II, 3; members of, appointed, 14, 52, 146, 200; suggests additional judge of the Supreme Court, 295; status of Philip Schuyler, a member of, 310; communication from, publication of proceedings, 314; appoints Aaron Burr, puisne judge, declines, 327; difference of opinion as to powers of, 360; convention to consider powers of, 468; IV, 52; Governor Jay's message relative to powers, II, 472; proceedings on various nominations, 474, 475; Governor Jay's letters to judicial members of, 479; chancellor and judges decline to give opinion on right of nomination, 482, 483; relations with Governor, 489 (general note); Assembly's views, 489, 503; Senate's views, 490, 502; communications from members of, 490; Governor Clinton's comment on, 1019, 1043; Assembly committee report on, 1021; limiting powers of, veto, 1054; abolished, III, 2, 92.

COUNCIL CHAMBER. Fire in, I, 753, 756, 758.

COUNCIL OF REVISION. See VETOES,— COUNCIL OF REVISION. Under first Constitution, II, 4; powers, 4, 740, 741; method of procedure, 5; first veto, 21; asks Legislature for certain information relative to Council of Safety, 42; requested to attend Legislature, 325; Secretary of State, *ex officio* clerk of, 369; appointment of doorkeeper, 369; extra allowance to judicial members of, 449; Governor Jay's correspondence with, on Council of Appointment, 479; status of Governor as member of, 495; jurisdiction over legislative

Council of Revision — (*Continued*).

    proceedings cannot be evaded by adopting concurrent resolution instead of passing a bill, 740; permanent character of jurisdiction, 741; Constitutional Convention to consider powers of, 1021; vetoes Constitutional Convention bill, 1055; rendering opinions as to constitutionality of bills, VIII, 948, 1046; abolished, III, 2.

Council of Safety. Created, powers of, II, 6; issues writs of election, 6; proclaims George Clinton Governor, 6; convenes Legislature at Kingston, 7; orders relative to military movements, 13; new, created, 16; meets at Hurley and Poughkeepsie, 17; veto of bill recognizing, 26; invalid under Constitution, 27; enactments of, become statutes, 29; persons denying authority of, deemed disloyal, 38, 39; legislative power of, denied, 42; proceedings of, request for, by Council of Revision, 42; of Connecticut, action relative to army supplies, 111; bill to create, veto, 113; General George Clinton asks leave to resign command, VII, 812.

Council of War. At Great Carrying Place, I, 575; Crown Point expedition, 591.

Counsel. For keeper of powder house, I, 532; Hamilton, Kent and Troup to examine dower cases, II, 374; to assist district attorney, communication from Attorney-General, III, 145, 146; in Morgan matter, 225, 251, 264, 350, 351; Victory Birdseye, special, Morgan matter, 351; C. R. Leland, letter from Seneca Indians, relative to elections, IV, 291; for State in canal cases, 633; for defendants, V, 292; Matthew Hale, Buck case, VI, 681; extravagant employment for investigating committees, VIII, 843; Assembly select committee, 1887, 976; special, for State hospitals should be abolished, X, 22; Austen G. Fox and Wallace MacFarlane, canal investigation, 40; Edwin Countryman, special, to examine report of Canal Investigating Commission, 1898, 41; appointment of special, to assist Attorney-General, 77; Governor's approval of, forest, fish and game commissioner, 194; John B. Stanchfield, Wallace MacFarlane, William B. Hoyt for Justice Hooker, 829; William B. Hurd, Brooklyn City Bar Association, Hooker trial, 829; Henry B. Coman, Legislature, Hooker trial, 829; Attorney-General, designation of, for State tax commissioners, 845; employment in special franchise tax cases, 845; for receivers, regulating fees, 845.

Vetoes. For James W. Eaton, superintendent, new capitol, fees, VII, 83; John I. Davenport, Senate committee, 85; Auburn prison, warden investigation, 485; Dannemora railroad investi-

COUNSEL, VETOES—(Continued).

gation, 485; legislative investigating committees, service, 647; Attorney-General, special, 582; services and expenses in suit against canal auditor, 904; Gravesend, common lands, investigation, fees, 905; New York public works department, fees, Senate investigation, 905; Rowley case, fees, appropriation, 905; fees, investigation of Receiver Best, 906; Justice Westbrook investigation, fees, 924; Senate Committee on Taxation and Retrenchment, appropriation, VIII, 548; employed by Legislature, compensation, 550; New York, Waterbury, fees, retaxation, 1035; X, 807; State dairy commissioner, Senate investigation, VIII, 840; Senate Committee on Public Health, fees, 841; Senate, trust investigation, appropriation, 843; Cassidy, Senate committee on investigation of State Board of Health, IX, 401; Attorney-General, appointment of counsel to departments, 403; Frank S. Black, Senate committee on election frauds, 533; William J. Ludden, Senate committee on investigation of election frauds, 533; John B. Stanchfield, for Assemblyman Vacheron, appropriation, 775; Beardsley, New York board of education, settlement of claim, 805; employment by district attorney, 863; Horace E. Deming, investigation of charges against New York district attorney, X, 297; appointed by Attorney-General, compensation, 297, 559; special, deficiency appropriation, 557; W. M. Spaulding, Assembly Committee on Privileges and Elections, appropriation, 571; Joseph G. Dudley, German Bank matter, appropriation, 784; Charles J. Dodd, Waite contested election case, 795; Attorney-General, investigation of forest preserve trespasses, 796; Cook and Clary, Assembly Committee on Privileges and Elections. appropriation, 796; Henry B. Coman for Comptroller, in Tonawanda case, 933; in criminal cases, allowance, 942; fees in militia cases, 945.

COUNSEL TO THE GOVERNOR. Office created, duties, VIII, 27; first appointment, 27.

COUNSEL TO THE LEGISLATURE. Recommended, VIII, 26, 125, 298, 351, 456, 459, 462, 478, 620; IX, 210, 505; duty of Statutory Revision Commission, VIII, 26, 478; duty of bill drafting department, 27; revision of bills, 676.

COUNTERFEITING. Bills of credit, I, 188; II, 66; currency, I, 749; II, 224; classification of, suggested, 550; aided by multiplicity of banks, 698; Canadian act against, 983; punishment of, III, 173.

COUNTIES. Erection and description of, I, 10; action relative to boundaries of, 672; settlement of boundaries recommended, 715, 722; committees of, power to continue, denied, II, 28; Clinton county erected, 272; superintendent of highways, office created, 385; regulating expenditures in, 464; New York harbor not included in, 540; agricultural societies in, 957; estimated apportionment of State agricultural fund, 959; appropriation for agricultural societies in, 970, 1005; distribution of United States deposit fund, III, 613, 623; proposed normal schools in, 652; equalizing assessments, IV, 25; superintendent of schools, 23, 66, 115; when may be declared in state of insurrection, 707, 728; insane asylums, V, 55; appropriations from excise money for State Inebriate Asylum, 87; liability for property destroyed by mob, 106; expense of transporting convicts, 168, 291, 386; sending girls to New York House of Refuge, 179; immigrant account, refund by commissioners, 188; new, required population, 225, 229; bounties for volunteers, 455; right of local government, VI, 29; transferring arsenals to, 113; boards of excise abolished, 127; chronic insane, care of, 235; court clerks, appointment of, 268; erection of lock-up (Orleans county), 273; State tax, equalizing, 332; laws should be uniform, 402; Legislature cannot extend jurisdiction of city officers over, 504; State tax, when payable, 630; care of books and records, 822; not liable for expense of trial for offenses committed in State prison, VII, 87; separate companies of National Guard, 154; heavy debt and taxation, 298; county insurance companies, 387; property held by, for charitable purposes, 526; reimbursement for maintenance of prisoners in penitentiaries, 462, 584, 792; indebtedness limited, amendment of 1884, VIII, 27, 184; inequalities of Assembly representation under apportionment of 1879, 494, 894, 1056; IX, 4; excise license fees, 1889, VIII, 686; unpaid taxes, special acts, list of, 749; system of State roads suggested by Governor Hill, 925; public buildings, changing site, 945; deputy county treasurers, 998; county roads, act to establish, 1041; IX, 203; seals for county officers, provision for, VIII, 1097; highway labor, cost of, 1892, IX, 199; insane, care of, county and State systems compared, 228; payments to charitable institutions, 551; civil service applicable to, 663; New York and Kings, officers to be elected in odd-numbered years, 705; board of supervisors, auditing claims, action final, X, 268; proposed imposition of special tax for barge canal, 599; proposed extension of Civil Service Law to, 742; tabulation of accounts and expenses, 763.

COUNTIES — (*Continued*).

VETOES. Canisteo county, bill to erect, V, 223; Conhocton county, bill to erect, 228, 249; bounties, legalizing, 673; reducing expenses, VI, 329; Cayuga county, reimbursement for expenses of trials for offenses committed in Auburn prison, 876; railroad commissioners, 911; clerk's office, records and indexes, 911; Rensselaer, house of industry, appointment of board of governors, 1033; treasurers' orders, receiving for taxes, VII, 62; offices, closing of, VI, 287; VII, 201; Richmond, changing site of courthouse and clerk's office, 250; medical societies, amount of property, 412; officers, report of financial transactions, 609; Chautauqua, soldiers and sailors' monument, 846; Schuyler, borrowing money, county buildings, 859; Monroe, compensation of supervisors, excepting from general act, 883; Orleans, poorhouse, auditing claims for construction, 1046; Chautauqua, legalizing acts of board of supervisors, fishing in Lake Erie, VIII, 79; statutes, publication in newspapers, 130; charges, care of insane, 132; Railroad Act, amending, 470; paying expenses of municipal elections, 575; Onondaga, amending Highway Act, 617; accounts with State, adjustment, 640; claims against State, adjustment, 755, new bill passed; Onondaga, sale of penitentiary, 945; boundaries, Erie, Genesee and Niagara counties, 1102; detective, creating office, IX, 153; Ulster, insane asylum, purchase by State, 243; claims for insane asylums, Board of Claims, 265; bridges on county lines, 587; fire districts, purchases for, 622; amending general act, 624; Chautauqua county police, charter, 795; insane asylums, claims against State, Court of Claims, 858; Erie, county auditor, election, 861; Kings, keeper, hall of records, 861; Queens, personal property, apportionment under Nassau County Act, X, 62; Rensselaer, creating contracting board, 63; railroad aid claims, Court of Claims, 315; highways in two or more towns, 316; St. Lawrence and Franklin, changing boundaries, 320; Saratoga, county auditor, creating office, 450; lease of buildings to G. A. R. posts, 585; repayments for county roads, 639; institutions in certain counties, purchasing supplies for, 700; Genesee, authorizing annual appropriation to corporations for prevention of cruelty, 812; allowance to counsel in criminal cases, 942; railroad aid bonds, Court of Claims, 945.

COUNTRYMAN, EDWIN. Special counsel to examine report of Canal Investigating Commission, 1898, X, 41.

COUNTY CLERK. Removal of, III, 133; appointments to fill vacancies, 176; when deputy to execute office, 176; to transmit to Governor testimony in criminal cases, V, 171; clerk of Supreme Court, VII, 356; Monroe, fixing salary, VIII, 260; New York, office not self-supporting, 1024; Chautauqua, salaried office, 1025; several offices become salaried, 1103; IX, 124; Kings, salaried office, X, 25, 208, 290.

VETOES. Practicing as attorney, II, 395; Monroe, assistant and special deputies, VI, 206; office, closing on holidays, 287; VII, 201; Onondaga, records and indexes, VI, 821; records and indexes, 911; Kings, expenses, notaries public, VII, 83; Oneida, expenses, notaries public, 83; St. Lawrence, expenses, notaries public, 83; offices, preservation of supervisors' records in, 208; New York, duties and compensation, 413; Richmond, recording certain papers, 497; Albany, fees, 604; Albany, office hours, 755; Albany, fee bill, 805; Onondaga, recording certain papers, 806; Onondaga, disposing of old office and lot, 867; Oneida and Columbia, recording notices of pendency, VIII, 63; recording and indexing notices of pendency in certain counties, 70; Kings, relative to, 124; Cattaraugus and Columbia, recording notices of pendency of actions, 705; fees, appointment of notaries, 1038; docketing judgments of United States courts, 1039; Cayuga, salaried office, 1103; IX, 124; Seneca, transcribing certain records, 39; fees, 150; Erie, salaried office, 272; fees in relation to notaries public, 346; office hours in certain counties, 462; Columbia, hours, repeal, 625; acknowledgments, taking, authorized, 722; criminal statistics, 861; authentications by, X, 171; Kings, salaried office, 179; fees for searches in certain counties, 381; Onondaga, index and abstract clerks, 388; fees in certain counties, 445; Kings, employees, 584; Kings,—office fees, 583; — salary, 594; — transcribing records, compensation, 710; — management of office, 711; — index clerks and custodians, compensation, 711; Herkimer, special deputies, 811.

COUNTY COURT. See COURT, COUNTY.

COUNTY DETECTIVE. VETOES. Creating office, IX, 153; amending act, X, 173; Kings, fixing salary, 955.

COUNTY INSURANCE COMPANIES. General act, VII, 387; laws amended, 692. VETOES. Co-operative,— classification of risks, VIII, 293; — extending powers, 881; — amending acts, IX, 152.

COUNTY JUDGE. Nomination of justices, III, 17; restricting appointing power, 770, 872; Madison, charges against, 928; term of office, 1012; first election under Constitution, 1846, IV, 363; jurisdiction limited to county, 625; special, when may be elected, 626;

COUNTY JUDGE — (*Continued*).

when may hold court in another county, 627; proposition to authorize veto of acts of boards of supervisors, V, 385; salary, act unconstitutional, VI, 124; proposed review of lunacy proceedings, 367; Chenango, charges against Judge Prindle, 440; method of removal, 833; powers, VII, 614; suggested temporary assignment to service in Supreme Court, X, 337, 373, 375; Constitution of 1846, 673; special, constitutional provision, 675.

VETOES. Powers in Court of Chancery, II, 1053; exchange of terms, IV, 625; special, Washington, 776; VII, 551; special, Chenango, jurisdiction, VI, 692; Allegany, appointment of constables, VII, 218; Monroe, increasing salary, 414; Rockland, compensation, 507; Seneca, compensation, 549; Clinton, powers conferred on surrogate, 614; Greene, repealing Salary Law, 807; Westchester, designation of constables, 1092; Rensselaer, increasing compensation, IX, 107; Suffolk, salary, 369; Albany, fixing salary, 624; Queens, compensation, 800; compensation in certain counties, X, 439; Queens, salary, 584; special, term of office in certain counties, 700.

COUNTY LAW. Care of books and records, VI, 822; changing county seats, VII, 250; enacted, 1892, IX, 28; amendments, veto, 259, 289.

COUNTY ROADS. Act to establish, VIII, 1041; IX, 308, 559; State aid, VIII, 1042; act of 1898, IX, 845; statement of miles constructed, X, 618.

VETOES. Orange county, amending act, IX, 862; amending Highway Law, 864; repayment for maintenance, X, 639.

COUNTY SEAT. How changed, VII, 250; VIII, 945.

COUNTY TREASURERS. Duties under Tax Law, II, 9; returns from, as to taxes, 147; to deliver wheat and rye for subsistence of troops, 169; method of appointment, III, 719, 770, 872; improper use of public money, VI, 630; should promptly pay taxes due State, VII, 72; Queens county, appointment of deputy, VIII, 998; deputies in certain counties, general act, 998; when to pay taxes to State Treasurer, IX, 542; transfer tax fees, X, 182.

VETOES. Fees, excepting Oneida and Schoharie from act relative to, VI, 151; Rensselaer, increasing fees, 333; fees, Ulster, 508; Monroe and Seneca, amending act, VII, 71; Monroe, sale of property for unpaid taxes, 208; excepting certain counties from provisions of act, 265; Kings, amending act, 266; Oswego, amending act, 266; excepting Fulton from provisions of act, 1010; amending Revised Statutes, VIII, 291; Broome, Binghamton, unpaid. taxes, sale for, 392; New York, fees, collateral in-

COUNTY TREASURERS, VETOES — (*Continued*).
    heritance tax, 412; partition actions, unknown owners, funds,
    withdrawal, 629; statements of delinquent taxes, 749; election,
    amending act, 1038; Richmond, deputies in towns, IX, 399;
    Rensselaer, relative to, X, 583; deposit of cemetery funds with,
    947.
COURTHOUSE. Herkimer county, repair, II, 388; Queens county, com-
    pletion, 417; Rensselaer county, repair, 417; Delaware county,
    building, 417; Schoharie county, building, 417; Columbia county,
    repairs, 419; proposed for towns, III, 58; Utica, expense of
    construction, increasing amount, X, 768.
    VETOES. Onondaga county, building, III, 190; Kings county, rela-
    tive to, VI, 510; Richmond county, changing site, VII, 250;
    Buffalo, city hall, construction and custody, 316; board of
    supervisors, changing location, 412; erection by Hornellsville for
    Steuben county, VIII, 880.
COURT (General). See also NEW COURTS, and particular courts. Settling
    courts of justice, I, 10; act requiring justices to attend, 11;
    compensation of judges, 11; act to provide for monthly, 12;
    act removing from Gravesend to Flatbush, 12; established,
    10, 11, 19, 20, 33; qualifications of jurors, 101; established
    for small causes, 267; new Jury Law proposed, 278;
    Governor Clinton's alleged interference with, 468, 499; offi-
    cers of, to be members of militia reserves, 549; delay in
    proceedings, 660, 661; clerk of oyer and terminer, compen-
    sation, 750; needed in remote parts of colony, 762; sup-
    pressing disorders, II, 76; right of appeal to, 173; limiting
    discretionary power of, 223; United States District, judge
    cannot hold seat in Legislature, 310; money paid into, care
    of, 427; fees in Court of Chancery, 542, 702; United States,
    proposed limitation of jurisdiction, 560; proposed tribunal
    for determining questions between Federal and State govern-
    ments, 667; inferior, reform in procedure, 1015; established
    under second Constitution, III, 16; criminal, number of,
    173; jurisdiction not given by consent, 362; exchange of
    decisions, 481; officers, fees, 720; fees of attorneys and
    solicitors, 774; new, proposed, 872; bills of exception, delay
    in criminal cases, IV, 490; inferior, recommended for
    cities, 856; injunctions extravagantly granted, V, 56; police,
    New York, assistant clerks, 149; commission of appeals,
    535; clerks in certain counties, VI, 268; examination of

COURT (General) — (*Continued*).

referee system, 365; Federal, Legislature cannot deprive of jurisdiction, VII, 574; State, practice in considering constitutional questions, VIII, 1045; New York, inferior, reorganization, IX, 578; New York city, magistrates, office created, 580; attendants, Queens county, X, 151; military courts of inquiry, judicial review of evidence, 350.

VETOES. Officers, fees, II, 275; relative to, 1002; recorder, Utica, increasing salary, VI, 427; inferior, Brooklyn, appointment of police justice, 512; officers, Erie county, compensation, VII, 538; inferior, Brooklyn, increasing number, VIII, 887; United States, docketing judgments in county clerk's office, 1039; Troy, inferior local, IX, 630; Buffalo, inferior criminal, 784; Buffalo, municipal, 784; City Court, Kingston, establishing, 785; New York, thirteenth civil district, legalizing appointment of attendants and employees, 809; Municipal Court, Greater New York, relative to, 859; New York, inferior criminal, 859; X, 959; Richmond county, where to be held, amending Laws 1897, chapter 541, 868; New York, district, justices, legalizing acts, compensation, 872; Kings county, new inferior, 873; New York, clerks and interpreters, 875; New York, court attendants, X, 176; city magistrates, method of selection, 178; children's, Brooklyn borough, clerk's salary, 711; children's court, New York, attendants, compensation, 716.

COURT OF ADMIRALTY. Gunpowder case in, I, 552; new acts limiting jury trial, 704, 769, 772.

COURT OF APPEALS. Suggested, to be composed of chancellor and associates, III, 610; first election of judges, IV, 363, 365; review of cases in abolished courts, 365; compensation of judges, 368; fixing terms, 443; quoted, Lemmon case, status of slaves brought from Virginia, 811; proposed amendment relative to, V, 193; proposed amendment for commission of appeals, 535, 597; organization, powers under Constitution of 1846, 746; resignation of judges, 747; reorganized under Judiciary Article of 1869, VI, 124; commission of appeals, 124; attorneys, rules for admission of, 260; VIII, 1100; X, 262; correspondence with Governor Hoffman on taxpayers' bill, VI, 431; judges attend ceremonies on first occupation of new capitol, VII, 270; location in new capitol not satisfactory, 694; authorized to select rooms, 695; State arms to be hung on walls of room, 727; com-

COURT (General), COURT OF APPEALS —(*Continued*).

    pletion of rooms for, 836, 979; new trials in capital cases, 1001; appeals in capital cases direct from oyer and terminer, VIII, 82, 181, 302, 476; jurisdiction, money limitation abolished, Constitution 1894, 230; affirmance of convictions in criminal cases, 486; second division, amendment providing for, 486; X, 373; work of, VIII, 486; constitutionality of ballot bill, 1890, Governor Hill suggests application to court for opinion, 948, 950, 1009, 1044; 1872, opinion as to possible act, 948, 950, 1050; general statement of powers, 1047; second division, jurisdiction, 1047; should not be asked for opinion on pending bills, 1050; State Board of Law Examiners, appointment of, 1100; second division, cost of, 1891, IX, 11; contested elections, voluntary submission to jurisdiction of court, 34; death of Chief Judge Ruger, 36; judges not to hold other office, 47, 515; capital cases, direct appeal from Supreme Court, X, 344; temporary designation from Supreme Court, 373; proposed enlargement to eleven members, 516; Constitution of 1846 and 1894, 673, 674; judges attend Higgins memorial services, 963.

    VETOES. Relief of, IV, 532, 772; stenographer for judge to be paid by Kings county, VII, 770; reports, contracts for publication, 892; appeals from Board of Claims, VIII, 56; clerk's messenger, salary, 72, new bill passed; jurisdiction, 131, 229; law library at Rochester, appropriation, 856; judges, law libraries, appropriation for, 856; clerk, filing Regents' certificate, *nunc pro tunc*, Schiff case, X, 174; Albany Law Library, appropriation, 549; law library, Syracuse, appropriation, 549; law clerk, appropriation, 574.

APPELLATE DIVISION. Established, Constitution of 1894, IX, 545; X, 373; number of justices in, IX, 645; first department, appointments under New York's special Jury Law, 1896, X, 195; proposed appointment of Supreme Court commissioners, 663; members of, power to hold other courts, 849.

    VETOES. Justices designated to, expenses, IX, 628; first department, attendants, compensation, 727; X, 716; first department, special deputy clerk, 717; designation of justices, amending Code, 808.

COURT OF ASSIZES. Petition to, for representative government, I, 2.

COURT (General) — (*Continued*).

COURT OF CHANCERY. Assembly resolutions against, I, 229; master of rolls, appointed, 763; jurisdiction of, in testamentary cases, II, 268; fees in, 542; should control disposition of estates.of minors, 563, 664, 685, 688, 708; Legislature should not interfere with powers of, 581, 583; records defective, 609; reforms in, 631; III, 609; proceedings in, for acquisition of Ellis island, II, 641; report of commissioners on procedure, 650; revision of fee system, 702; transcribing minutes of, 754; office of vice-chancellor created, III, 264, 720; proposed revision of procedure in, 648; trial by jury in, 649, 720; evidence in, 649; delays in, 718; IV, 30; division of powers, III, 719; fees of clerks and registers, 720; foreclosures in, procedure, 722; large accumulation of business, 772; IV, 54; proposed reorganization, III, 872; IV, 54, 135; patronage of, III, 973; abolished, IV, 55, 363.

VETOES. Masters, power to appoint guardians, II, 488; relative to, 1053; masters and examiners, mode of appointment, 1053.

CHILDREN'S. VETOES. Brooklyn borough, clerk's salary, X, 711; New York, attendants, compensation, 716.

CIRCUIT. Established by second Constitution, III, 5, 444; unsatisfactory structure of, 210; abolished, Constitution of 1894, IX, 545; X, 676.

CITY COURT. VETOES. Kingston, establishing, IX, 785; Yonkers, amending act, 791; Albany, amending Code, 792; Albany, jurisdiction and jury list, X, 321, 635; Yonkers, removal of causes to Supreme Court, repeal, 819.

CITY, BROOKLYN. Abolished, Constitution of 1894, IX, 545; transferring employees to Supreme Court, amending order, veto, 795.

CITY, NEW YORK. Suspension of Justice Pitshke, VIII, 935; appointment of James M. Fitzsimons, 935. VETOES. Appeals to Court of Appeals, VII, 1092; increasing jurisdiction, 1116; assistant clerks, IX, 732; amending Code, X, 313; judge, fixing compensation, 321; proposed enlargement of jurisdiction, 516; relative to, 635; attendants, compensation, 716; additional stenographers, 805, 816; justices' clerks, 956.

COURT OF CLAIMS. Established, successor to Board of Claims, VII, 821; VIII, 977; IX, 720; judges, official term, VII, 821; general law should be enacted for submission of claims, X, 626; jurisdiction defined, 775.

COURT (General), COURT OF CLAIMS—(*Continued*).

VETOES. Expenses and disbursements, appropriation, X, 556; jurisdiction, amending Code, 703, 709; judges' salaries and expenses, additional appropriations, 933. HEARINGS. Frost IX, 721; Onondaga Pottery Company, 797; American Glucose Company, 797; Cragin, 798, 857; National Guard uniforms, 858; Hall (James), 858; counties, insane asylums, 858; Van Slyke and others, 858; X, 449; Bernard, E. J., & Co., 61; Tyron and others, 61; Gordon, 165; Linkie, 165; Van Gorder, 165; Monahan and others, 165; O'Keefe, 165, 240, 584, 944; Fleeck, 165; canals, damages under Nine Million Dollar Act of 1895, 172; Leith, 236; Dinehart, injuries received on canal, 255; Hamill, injuries received in Clinton prison, 259; Galvin, injuries received while at work on capitol, 267; Deltry, Draper and Borgersrud, 286; Levy, 309; Kineally, escheat, 310; Oswego dam, claims for damages, 311; Mathews, escheat, 312; railroad aid, 315; Brandow Printing Company, 315, 444; Hess & Company, 315, 588; White and Coughlin, Soldiers and Sailors' Home, damages and extra work, 377; Hall, Amos C., 441; Burgard, 441; Stuart, 442; Schlaefer, 442; Pierce, 442; Whitney, 443; Smith (Annie M.), 443; Storms and others, 445; Smith, Thomas H., 445; Myers, Mamie, 447; Dutton Pneumatic Lock and Engineering Company, 449; Auburn, local assessments on State property, 585, 634; Horseheads and Elmira, Newtown creek improvement, 588, 708; Commercial Construction Company, 589; New York, Park avenue improvement, 589; Gibier estate, 591; Payne, 591; Bulson and Polock, bridge tenders, Watervliet, 593; Baker, destruction of animals, 593; McDough, injuries received at Sing Sing prison, 699; Niewenhous, New York, Park avenue improvement, 699; Pfeiffer, 701; John T. Smith, 701; Gard, Auburn prison, 702; Angel, Auburn prison, 702; Bailey, Auburn prison, 702; Cane, McCaffrey & Company, 702; Parker & Company, 703, 944; Stockbridge Indians, 703; Dunn, 703; Marningham, Hudson River State Hospital, 704; Frankfort, claims of residents, 706; Turzkowska, injuries received at Niagara reservation, 707; Snyder, 707; Bawden, chaplain Rochester Industrial School, 707; Cleever, State Industrial School, 707; Evans, 708; Watts, 709; Risley and Love, 709; Wallace, 943; Abeel, damages to lands, Little Falls, 943; Nagle, 944;

COURT (General), COURT OF CLAIMS, VETOES —(*Continued*).
Roth, 944; Cusick, 944; Conway, administrator Hendy, 944; Argus Company, 944; Manheim Brown, 945; Devitt, Mulheron, Manville and Wood, 945; counties, railroad aid bonds, 945; Moriarity, 945; militia, counsel fees, 945; Dibble Company, 945; Weishem, 946; Androvic, 946; Windholz, 946; Indian lake, service of fire wardens, 946.

COURT OF COMMON PLEAS. English, jurisdiction continued in Supreme Court, II, 740; first judge not to hold other office, 1053; jurisdiction defined, III, 5; communication from Judge Irving, costs, 219; inefficiency of, 718, 871; Superior Court proposed, 719; restricting appointing power, 719, 770; charges against Judge Inglis, 906; proposed improvement of, IV, 56; additional judges for, 124; abolished, Constitution 1894, IX, 545.

COURT FOR THE CORRECTION OF ERRORS. Accumulation of business, relief needed, IV, 55; abolished, 55, 365.

COUNTY. First judge not entitled to hold other office, II, 1053; first election of judges under Constitution of 1846, IV, 363; enlarging jurisdiction, 562; reorganized under Judiciary Article of 1869, VI, 124.

VETOES. Judges, exchanging terms, IV, 625; appeals to, VIII, 406; Kings, clerks and assistants, IX, 795; Kings, relief of clerks, X, 59; stenographer, Richmond, compensation, 259; Kings, stenographer, 808.

DISTRICT, UNITED STATES. Judge of, cannot hold seat in Legislature, II, 310.

ECCLESIASTICAL. Transfer of powers, II, 257, 268.

COURT OF EXCHEQUER. Jurisdiction under Tariff Act, II, 277; clerk of, letter from, 389; English, jurisdiction continued in Supreme Court, 740; new arrangement of, suggested, 913.

COURT OF GENERAL SESSIONS. Duties of assistant Attorney-General, II, 399; grand jury, communication from, relative to poor debtors, 923; jurisdiction defined, III, 5; Kirby murder case, 32; reform in, 1012.

VETOES. Relative to, II, 1002; stenographer's compensation, VII, 768; attendants, compensation, IX, 727; judges, fixing compensation, X, 321; NEW YORK,— amending Consolidation Act, X, 176; — law library custodian, 390; — law library, 475; — salary of attendants, 582; — attendants' compensation, 716; — record clerks, salaries, 953; — clerks and stenographers, compensation, 958.

COURT (General) — (*Continued*).

GENERAL TERM, SUPREME COURT. Organized, VI, 124; judges to
fix times and places of, 261; extraordinary terms, 492; additional term, amendment of 1882, VII, 728, 837; fifth department established, 837, 890; consent to appeal to Court of Appeals, veto, 1093; appeals from, veto, VIII, 718; fixing appropriations under New York Rapid Transit Act, *quaere,* IX, 513; abolished, Constitution 1894, 545.

COURT OF IMPEACHMENTS, STATE. How composed, II, 325, 502; proposed reorganization of, III, 648; trial of John C. Mather, canal commissioner, IV, 695.

COURT OF IMPEACHMENTS, UNITED STATES. New, proposed in place of Senate, II, 366.

COURT OF INQUIRY. Compelling attendance of witnesses at, II, 87.

COURT OF INQUIRY, MILITARY. Judicial review of findings, X, 350.

JUSTICES' COURTS. Jurisdiction, II, 170, 450; usually held in taverns, 170; oath of allegiance by parties, 171; in New York, reform in procedure, 599; enlarging jurisdiction, III, 773, 873.

VETOES. Verification of pleadings, VII, 505; attachments, service of papers, 1094; judgments, execution on, 1094; summons, service on corporation, 1094; appeals, amending Code, VIII, 468; jurors, amending Code, 1166; Queens county, laymen not to practice in, IX, 373; jurors' fees, amending Code, 427; Brooklyn, additional number, 476; Albany, amending charter, 630; Doolittle, assistant clerk, Brooklyn, claim, 779; attorneys in, 792; where not to be held, 860.

COURT OF KING'S BENCH. Jurisdiction continued in Supreme Court, II, 740.

MARINE. Justices for, III, 7; Judge Curtis, charges against, VI, 498; history of, 897; death of Judge Spaulding, 986; appointment of Judge Sinnott, 986.

VETOES. Abolition of, VII, 129; appeals to Court of Appeals, 1092; increasing jurisdiction, 1116; jurisdiction, VIII, 711.

COURTS-MARTIAL. Compelling attendance of witnesses, II, 87; Benedict Arnold, case of, 102; militia delinquents, veto, 131; need of reforms in, 692; IV, 38; compensation of marshal, II, 989; presidents, relief of, 996; large number of, III, 523; provision in Code of 1870 sustained, VI, 113.

COURT (General) — (*Continued*).

MUNICIPAL. New York, act of 1904, X, 632. VETOES. Brooklyn, X, 59; Greater New York, relative to, IX, 859, 860; X, 580, 713, 714. NEW YORK. Clerks and assistants, X, 60; — claims of attendants, 168, 474; — justices, 176; — Revision Commission, 177; — justices' salaries, 178, 581; — enforcement of judgments, 308; — O'Sullivan, stenographer, 310; — summons, proof of service, 312; — additional justices, 473; — Diegan, court attendant, claim, 473; — officers and marshals, 588, 633, 816; — additional marshals, 635; — O'Neil, assistant clerk, claim, 691; — salaries, 712; — interpreters' salaries, 714; — justices, 717; — attendants, 806; — Manhattan borough, maintenance claims, 817; — judges, designation and rotation, 818; — justice's clerk, 819; Syracuse, practice and fees of jurors, 441.

COURT OF NISI PRIUS. By whom held, III, 6.

COURT OF OYER AND TERMINER. Clerk, compensation, I, 750; Orange, conviction of Amy Augur, II, 67; Ulster, conviction of Thomas Cummings, treason, 82; Oneida, conviction of George Peters, 514; Ontario, conviction of Stiff-Armed George, 531; Otsego, conviction of Stephen Arnold, 575; New York, conviction of Francisco Son, 588; Chenango, conviction of Rufus Hill, 635; Ulster, conviction of Mary Cool, 749; Schoharie, conviction of Abraham Kesler, 921; Oneida, conviction of David Linus and others, 922; Orange, conviction of Jack Hodges and others, 997; by whom held, III, 6; powers defined, 5; extraordinary, Niagara county, to investigate Morgan matter, 314, 351, 352, 354; construes act relating to disguises, IV, 309; justices of sessions, appointments to fill vacancies, VI, 121; new trials, 126, 244, 366; appeals in capital cases direct to Court of Appeals, VIII, 82, 181, 302, 476; abolished, Constitution of 1894, IX, 545.

VETOES. Relative to, II, 1002; trial of special causes, VI, 490; payment of clerk hire, VII, 207; New York, stenographic notes, VI, 330; removal of causes to, VII, 1090.

COURT OF PROBATES. Origin of, II, 268; abolished, III, 7.

COURT OF SESSIONS. Westchester county, act relating to, I, 11; jurisdiction of, II, 986; Kings county, transfer of records, veto, IX, 795; abolished, 1894, 545.

COURT OF SPECIAL SESSIONS. VETOES. Appeal from judgments of, stay of execution, IX, 45; jury, method of selecting, 129; new act passed, 1893, 129; trial, method of, defendant's right to elect, 139; jurisdiction, 260; New York, appeals, disorderly

XI — 27

COURT (General), COURT OF SPECIAL SESSIONS —(*Continued*).
persons, neglect to support family, when judgment of special
sessions final, 526; Brooklyn, 634; New York, justices' qualifications, 859; New York, Coyle, subpœna clerk, compensation, X,
313; attendants, 716.

STATE SUPERIOR. Proposed, III, 498.

SUPERIOR, BUFFALO. Abolished, Constitution of 1894, IX, 545.
VETOES. Justices, appointment of trustees of public buildings,
VII, 354; stenographers, VIII, 291; appointment of commis-
sioners of jurors, IX, 515.

SUPERIOR, NEW YORK. Established, III, 210; increasing number of
judges, IV, 443; judges, appointing power, local authority, VI,
496; charges against Judge McCunn, 497; vacancies, how filled,
988; proposed removal of Judge Sanford for disability, VII,
533, 542; abolished, Constitution of 1894, IX, 545.

SUPREME (State). Created, I, 19; additional judge provided for,
641; judges of, members of Council of Revision, II, 4;
jurisdiction under Tariff Act, 277; additional justices suggested, 295; clerk, office to be kept in Albany, 397; source
of jurisdiction, 740; clerks, act relating to, 756; jurisdiction
over Indian lands, 1119; modified by second Constitution,
III, 5; reporter, 5; judges, compensation, 256, 498; additional justices proposed, 445, 498, 719; IV, 30, 54, 136;
unequal to opportunities, III, 718; fees of clerks, 720;
judges resign to become clerks, 720; under second Constitution, expectations not realized, 772; first election of judges
under Constitution of 1846, IV, 363, 365; proposed special
equity terms, 367, 414; compensation of justices, 368; proposed tax on suits, 368; justices vested with powers of
vice-chancellors, 443; proposed review of convictions in
capital cases, 610, 652; increasing number of justices in
first district, 615, 857; sale of church property, V, 150;
reorganized under Judiciary Article of 1869, IV, 124; departments, General Terms, 124; resolutions of justices on
admission of attorneys, 260; resolutions, payment of money
into court, 261; resolutions, fixing General Terms, 261; resolutions, appointment of reporter, 261; extraordinary terms,
492; justices, method of selection and removal, 833; justices,
powers cannot be abridged or annulled by Legislature, VII,
615; additional justices and General Term, amendment of
1882, 728, 857; jurisdiction, receivers of insolvent corporations, 798; increasing number of justices, act passed, 890;

COURT (General), SUPREME (State)—(*Continued*).

    judges not to hold other office, IX, 47, 515; General Term, fixing appropriations under New York Rapid Transit Act, 513; Appellate Division, see that title; justices, designations to Appellate Division, 546; reporter provided for, 546; number of justices, Constitution of 1894, 645; assigning judges to other districts, X, 337; suggested temporary assignment of county judges to service in, 337, 373, 375; additional judges, amendment of 1905, 337; appeal direct to Court of Appeals in capital cases, 344; first department, relief from large calendar, 371; designating justices for service in Court of Appeals, 373; first department, trial judges, suggested increase of hours of work, 374; assignment of justices to service in other districts, 404; increase in judges, 516; commissioners, proposition to establish, 516; colonial origin of, 671; constitutional provisions, 674; powers of justices to exercise administrative functions, 679; trial of Justice Hooker, 819; additional justices in certain districts, 936; justices assigned to appellate courts, 937; trial justices by districts, 937.

VETOES. Place of holding, II, 242; clerks of, appointment, 243; judges of, 740; appointment of village police justices, VI, 216; justices, assignments for special oyer and terminer, 490; Kings county, messengers and attendants, 512; jurisdiction, canal department, civil service, VII, 238; third judicial district, justices, salaries, 257; justices, chamber powers, vesting in Cohoes recorder, 327; Erie, county clerk, 356; justices, vesting chamber powers in Washington county special judge and surrogate, 551; second judicial district, justices, additional compensation, 780; Judge Mullin, retired, appropriation of residue of salary for widow, 916; Justice Westbrook, investigation, counsel fees, 924; Justice Balcom, salary, payment, 931; Justice Westbrook, death of, unearned salary, appropriation for widow, VIII, 250; guardians, appointment in certain cases, 631; stenographers, third judicial district, salaries, 699; General Term, appeals from, 718; law library, Newburgh, appropriation, 856; additional justices, submission of amendment, 1890, 1033; amendment submitted and rejected, 1892, 1033, 1062; IX, 97; second judicial department, IX, 446; justices, appointment of commissioners of jurors, 515; Appellate Division, justices designated to, expenses, 628; first department

COURT (General), SUPREME (State), VETOES — (*Continued*).

and district, attendants' compensation, 727; reporter, furnishing papers to, 791; Kings county, amending order, transferring employees from Brooklyn City Court to Supreme Court, 795; fifth judicial district, justices, clerks to, 812; second judicial district, expenses of justices outside Kings county, 815; sixth judicial district, justices' clerks, 816; first judicial department, appointment of referees, X, 318; justices, appointment of trustees, 450; commissioners, establishment, 662; stenographer, trial terms, 699; first judicial district, attendants, compensation, 716; third, fourth, sixth and first judicial districts, additional justices, 947.

SUPREME (United States). Oswald case against State, II, 330; removal of causes, 404; power to bind States, 1078; extent of authority, III, 79; controversies between States, 359; only tribunal for settlement of constitutional questions, 435; Dred Scott decision, New York protests against, V, 34; death of Chief Justice Chase, VI, 566.

SURROGATE'S. Established, III, 7; stenographers, general act, VI, 318; New York, two surrogates, IX, 122.

VETOES. Stenographers, second and third districts, VI, 317; amending act, 505; equity powers, VII, 79, 189; Erie, equity powers, 113; final accountings, 414; New York, relative to proceedings, 417; appeals, 1109; New York, stenographer, increasing salary, VIII, 82; stenographers, transcribing notes, IX, 115; costs, VI, 340; IX, 625; appearance in proceedings, X, 253; additional allowance on settlement of accounts, 254; stenographer, Richmond, compensation, 259; executors' accounting, 282; New York, preservation of records, 586; New York, referees and law assistants, 712; costs and allowances, 955.

COVENANT CHAIN. Alliance with Indians, I, 35; renewed with Five Nations, 65; renewal of, with Six Nations, 251; to be renewed, 262.

COX, JAMES. Relief, veto, VIII, 630.

COX, ROBERT LYNN. Assembly, member of insurance investigating committee, 1905, X, 825.

COXE, RICHARD. Bond for return of arms, II, 775.

COXSACKIE. Petition from inhabitants in behalf of John Cumming, II, 20; number of excise licenses, 1887, VIII, 360.

COYLE, CHARLES. Subpœna clerk, New York Court of Special Sessions, compensation, veto, X, 313.

COZINE, CHARLES C. Cancellation of tax sale, veto, X, 263, new act passed.

CRAGGS, JAMES. English Secretary of State, communication from, prorogation of Assembly, I, 192.

CRAGIN, IRVING F. Court of Claims, veto, IX, 798, 857.

CRAIG, OSCAR. Epileptic colony in honor of, IX, 240.

CRAIG, WASHINGTON. Residence, Wells, terminus of special highway, veto, VI, 443.

CRAIG COLONY FOR EPILEPTICS. Established, 1894, IX, 240; how classified, X, 334; additional accommodations, 857. VETOES. Roads, walks and grading, 546; general improvements, 656.

CRAMAHE, H. T. Lieutenant-Governor of Canada, appoints commissioners on Quebec boundary, I, 744; conference with Governor Tryon, 755.

CRAMER, HIRAM. Farm bridge, Champlain canal, veto, VI, 504.

CRAMER, MICHAEL J. Chargé d'affaires, Denmark, appointment of successor, VII, 555.

CRANBERRY LAKE RESERVOIR. Removing dead and floating timber from shores and waters, veto, X, 427.

CRANE, ANGELINA. New York, estate, release, veto, X, 712.

CRANE, J. B., LIEUTENANT-COLONEL. Letter to Governor Seward relative to disturbance on northeastern frontier, III, 761.

CRATZ, GEORGE T. New York, relief, veto, X, 178.

CRAWFORD, H. CLAY. Secretary of State, Florida, attests Governor's proclamation on Isthmian Canal Exposition, X, 867.

CRAWFORD, WILLIAM H. Secretary of War, letter from, military accounts with State, II, 868.

CREAM TARTAR. Manufacture of, nuisance, report of State Board of Health, VII, 547.

CREDIT, GUARANTY AND INDEMNITY COMPANIES. VETOES. Amending act, VIII, 459; relative to, IX, 802.

CREDITORS. Legislature cannot prefer, II, 583; public, preserving faith pledged to, III, 978.

CREEDMOOR. VETOES. Rifle range at, repairs, IX, 76; additional land, X, 319.

CREEK INDIANS. Defeat of, War of 1812, II, 786; treaty with, III, 183.

CREGIER, CAPTAIN. Claim for military expenses, II, 43.

CREMATORIES. Endowment, veto, X, 700.

CRENEY, JAMES. Assistant Commissary-General, death of, apprpriation for widow, veto, VII, 917.

CRENEY, MARY T. Widow of James Creney, Assistant Commissary-General, claim for compensation, veto, VII, 917.

CRIMES. See also FELONIES, MISDEMEANORS AND SPECIFIC OFFENSES.
Acts relating to perjury, I, 10; barratry, champerty and maintenance, 11; Sabbath breaking, 12; swearing and cursing, 12;
drunkenness, 12; privateers and pirates, 29; trials for, should
be held in colony, 770, 772; accused, right of speedy examination, II, 14; not to be created by retrospective laws, 38;
proposed extension of power of grand jury to other counties,
130; revision of laws relating to, 335, 349, 363, 399; punishment of felonies, 451; diminishing, 525; statutes need revision,
548; act relating to, 623; punishment of extraterritorial, 623,
624; trespass on Indian land, 695; statement of convictions,
984; carrying concealed weapons, 1016; extradition, 1104; by
Indians on Indian lands, 1119; large number of homicides, III,
128; included in Revised Statutes, 129; classification borrowed
from English system, 285; need of statistical information, 341,
383; what included under right of extradition, 777; State's
right to define felony, 929; stealing slaves, 937, 938; statistics, 940; IV, 28, 80; V, 171, 376; disguised persons, punishment of, IV, 150, 233, 245; reducing severity of punishment,
406, 434; vagrancy, 490; intemperance, a source of, 610;
better classification needed, 785; frauds in organizing corporations, 855; counsel for defendants, V, 292; infamous, must
be indictment for, 471; laxity in prosecutions, 759; laws should
be uniform, VI, 161; increase in New York, 545; trial by jury,
United States Constitution, VII, 613; results of intemperance,
707, 714.

VETOES. Relative to, II, 589, 602; bigamy, bill to restrain, 780;
felony, second offense, trial, VI, 849; perjury, extending definition, VII, 413; capital cases, trial, giving defense right to make
closing address, 754; exposing property for sale within two
miles of religious meeting, 1044; malicious destruction of property, VIII, 890; insolvent banks, receiving deposits, 890; horse
stealing, societies for prevention of, 1039; statistics, 1040; IX;
153; intoxication, persons convicted of, medical treatment in
penitentiaries, 252; false pretenses, evidence, 259; Washington
county, convictions less than felony, charging expense on town,
796; county clerk, criminal statistics, 861; against elective
franchise, X, 162; slot machines, trials for keeping, 162; suspected and convicted persons, regulating exhibition of pictures,
585; kidnapping, punishment, 699; against public peace, 807.

CRIMINAL CODE. Revision of, II, 335, 349, 363, 398, 548, 598, 1109;
III, 284; IV, 434, 480; need of revision, III, 173; challenges and ex-
ceptions, IV, 489, 490; counsel for defendants, V, 292; new trials,
VI, 126; accessory, trial of, 126.

CRITTENDEN, JOHN J. Senate, resolutions proposing amendment to Federal Constitution, V, 312, 324, 328.

CROGHAN. VETOES. Aiding Utica and Black River Railroad Company, amending act, VI, 92; dyke road in, repairing and improving, X, 570; breakwater, Black river, 791.

CROLY, THOMAS S. Canal department, appropriation for services, veto, IX, 716.

CROOK, ABEL. Relief, veto, VII, 132, 267.

CROOKED LAKE. Bridge over outlet, veto, VIII, 849.

CROOKED LAKE CANAL. Construction authorized, III, 308; allowance to contractors, 411; completion, 465; not self-supporting, 466, 506, 710; expense exceeds income, 549, 553; debt, 736; IV, 252; should not be abandoned, III, 799; length, 812; reconstruction of locks, veto, IV, 194; appropriation, 678, 735; tolls, V, 66, 154, 257, 361; VII, 118; relation to canal system, V, 789; financial statement, VI, 930; VII, 5; commission to examine, VI, 933; sale recommended, VII, 8; temporary operation, appropriation, veto, 117.

CROSS, ADAM A. Claim against New York city, audit, veto, IX, 805.

CROSSEN, JOHN. Troy, school janitor, claim, veto, X, 634.

CROSSTOWN RAILROAD COMPANY. Charter, veto, V, 796.

CROSWELL, CHARLES M. Governor of Michigan, communication from, lighthouse on Stannard's Rock, VII, 46; communication from, harbor of refuge, Lake Superior, 60.

CROSWELL'S MANUAL. Quoted, third reading of bills, VII, 185.

CROTON AQUEDUCT. Construction of, III, 1034; water for Mount Pleasant prison, IV, 276; importance of, VII, 594; changes in commission, VIII, 272; new commission created, 655, 656.

VETOES. Amending act, IV, 773; VI, 596; new, proposed, VII, 635, 716; commission, additional member, 1118; extending and improving system, New York, VIII, 636; settlement of claims for construction, 1035.

CROTON-ON-THE-HUDSON. Highway tax in, town to pay to village, veto, IX, 867.

CROTON RIVER. Used as water supply for New York, III, 1034.

CROUSE, JACOB. Board of Claims, veto, IX, 428.

CROWLEY, RODNEY R. Commissioner to ascertain damages by trespassers on Indian reservations, report, V, 863.

CROWN POINT. French occupation of, I, 241; new fort, 324; outscouts in vicinity, 325, 357; road to Albany opened, 361; estimated expense of attack on, 393; expedition against, 419, 440; procuring assistance of Indians in expedition against, 465, 466; fortifications at, 548; second projected expedition against, 568, 571, 583; forts to be erected at or near, 569; plan of operations, changes, 571; ap-

CROWN POINT —(*Continued*).
portionment of expenses, 571; raising troops for, 575, 588, 591, 594; council of war on, 591; French driven from, 640; lands at, ceded to Regents, resumption of, II, 376; ferry across Lake Champlain, veto, VIII, 463.

CRUEL AND UNUSUAL PUNISHMENTS. Arbitrary and excessive taxation, II, 61, 65; horse-racing, forfeiture by owner of horse, 85; by court-martial, 131; disorderly persons, 284; in State prisons, V, 268; elections, voters showing ballot, VIII, 588; Cooley's comment on, 588. VETOES. Game Law, penalties, VII, 611; posting notices in certain cases, 641.

CRUGER, HENRY. Commissioner on colonial union, I, 370.

CRUTCHLEY, JAMES H. Court of Claims, veto, X, 165.

CRYSTAL LAKE. Black bass, close season, veto, IX, 799.

CRYSTAL PALACE. New York, erection and purpose of, IV, 657; Governor and Legislature invited to attend opening, 708.

CUBA. English army in, I, 302; acknowledgment of instruments executed in, veto, X, 63; proposed illustration of social conditions at Pan-American Exposition, 125.

CULL, GEORGE D. Canal department, appropriation for services, IX, 716.

CULLUM, GEORGE W. Legacy to United States, release of transfer tax, veto, IX, 349.

CUMBERLAND COUNTY. Veto of bill erecting, I, 722; disturbances in, 764; II, 188, 210; aiding inhabitants, I, 764; included part of New Hampshire grants, II, 103.

CUMMING, JOHN. Prisoner, petition in behalf of, II, 20.

CUMMINGS, THOMAS. Convicted of treason, pardon of, II, 82.

CUMULATIVE VOTING. Proposed in New York charter, VI, 453; approved by Governor Dix, 544; Samuel J. Tilden opposes plan, VIII, 286; bill for, vetoed by Governor Hill, 278, 283; plan applied in Illinois, 286.

CUNNEEN, JOHN. Attorney-General, opinion, Supreme Court commissioners' bill, X, 663; opinion, scope of forest preserve restriction as to removal of timber, 754.

CUNNINGHAM, JOHN. Commissioner of charities, Kings county, reimbursement for legal expenses, veto, VII, 544; VIII, 294.

CUNNINGHAM, JOHN. Devise of land to widow, relative to, veto, X, 585.

CUNNINGHAM, MARY. Devise of land from husband, veto, X, 585.

CURELL, JOHN GIBSON. Applicant for admission as attorney, relief, veto, VIII, 1100.

CURLEY, DAVID J. Relief, veto, X, 178.

CURRENCY. See also MONEY, COIN AND BILLS OF CREDIT. Paper, use in colony, I, 558; bills of credit, not to be legal tender, 558; results of excessive issue, 560; bills of credit continued, 606; danger of depreciation of, 628; Amherst loan redeemable in, 638; paper, necessity of, in colony, 694; revocation of instruction prohibiting issue of bills of credit, 714, 715; scarcity of, 733; counterfeiting bills of credit, act to prevent, 749; restricting legal tender quality of, protest against, 773; paper, conference on, II, 11; depreciation of, 52; restricting further emissions of paper, 65; plans for supporting credit, 77; ratio between specie and continental money, 94; national bills of credit, New York act for redemption of, 97; compensation to troops for depreciation in, 110; exchanging old continental money for new, 147; equalizing values, 147; exchanging United States drafts for specie, 189; continental, depreciation of, 241; dangers from excessive circulation of bank notes, 917; paper, excessive issue of, 979, 1003; bank paper, Canadian act against counterfeiting, 983; paper, issued by banks, III, 272; small bills, limiting circulation, 476, 517, 519, 564, 633, 667, 723; panic of 1834, 483, 494; evils of irredeemable paper, 700; circulation of foreign bills prohibited, 725; mixed, coin and paper, advantages of, 780; bills and notes, registry of, IV, 380; too much expansion, 730; suspension of specie payments, V, 43; proposed international decimal system, 323; depreciation reduces pay of soldiers, 539; paper, large amount issued by national banks, 550; benefits of national banking system, 587; equalizing specie and paper, 752; fractional, bank notes and legal tenders, amount, 822; Governor Hoffman's comment on, VI, 133; redemption of legal tender notes, 134, 136; panic of 1869, 134; legal tenders, amount in circulation, 135, 251; treasury notes, 249; suspension of specie payments, unfortunate consequences, 645; production of gold and silver, 645; paper, must be supported by specie, 647; Governor Dix protests against inflation, 668; legislative protest against inflation, 670; increase cannot revive prosperity, 751; bank notes, 752; relation to prices, 754; certificates, New York associated banks, 755; legal tenders, inflation resulting from, 756; VII, 149; amount needed for business, VI, 762; legal tenders, influence on prices, 970; Governor Robinson's observations, VII, 27; inflation accompanying Civil War, 149.

VETOES. Tax payable in paper, II, 134; certificates of continental loans, depreciation of, 214; county orders as legal tender in payment of taxes, VII, 62.

CURRIE, MR. Letter from, army supplies, II, 57.

CURRY, ROBERT F. Extradition of, forgery, III, 910, 915; correspondence relative to, 915.

CURSING. Act to prevent, I, 12.

CURSON, SAMUEL. Letter from, seizure of gunpowder, II, 82, 91.

CURTENIUS, PETER. Brigadier-general, commands brigade at Greenwich, II, 810.

CURTENIUS, PETER T. Commissary, letter from, relative to clothing, II, 55.

CURTIN, ANDREW G. Governor of Pennsylvania, calls on New York for aid to repel Lee's invasion, V, 545.

CURTIS, CHARLES F. Justice of the peace, legalizing acts, veto, IX, 369.

CURTIS, CHARLES M. Board of Claims, veto, VII, 1124.

CURTIS, ELMER. Canal department, appropriation for services, veto, IX, 716.

CURTIS, GEORGE M. Judge, New York marine court, charges against, VI, 493; charges dismissed, 499.

CUSHMAN, JOSEPH B. Assembly clerk, information from, Harbor Defense Commission, V, 565; resolution requesting information from Governor, quotas, 618, 625.

CUSICK, LIZZIE B. Court of Claims, veto, X, 944.

CUSTODIAL ASYLUM FOR FEEBLE-MINDED WOMEN, NEWARK. New cottages, IX, 296; how classified, X, 334; additional accommodations provided, 726.

   VETOES. Additional property, IX, 79; duplicate electric light unit, X, 544; inspectors' salaries, 544; general improvements, 653; relative to, 812.

CUSTOM HOUSE. New York, repair of, I, 188; letter from, Staten Island beacon, II, 586; in New York, property acquired for, V, 642; Albany, cession for, veto, VI, 449.

CUSTOMS. Collection and control of, III, 331, 898; IV, 616; payable in coin, VI, 249.

CUTLER, STILLMAN. Relief, veto, VI, 185.

CUYLER. Bridge over Tioughnioga river, VI, 78.

CUYLER, CORNELIUS. Claim for expenses to Canada, I, 202.

CUYLER, GEORGE W. Member of Tax Revision Commission, VI, 238, 269, 370.

CUYLER, JACOB. Deputy Commissary-General of Purchases, letter from, II, 20, 94; account of, 124.

CUYLER, JOHANNIS. Examined as to situation in Albany, I, 407.

CYCLES. Act to prevent injuries to, IX, 668. VETOES. Taxation, use of funds, Niagara county, 629; side-paths, Oneida county, 726; Chemung county, 729; Monroe county, 731; uniform ordinances regulating use of, 811.

CYPRESS HILLS CEMETERY ASSOCIATION, LONG ISLAND. Sale of land to United States for national cemetery, VI, 558.

CYPRESS HILL CEMETERY, NEW YORK. Street through, veto, X, 325.

CYPRESS HILL NATIONAL CEMETERY. Cession of land for, VII, 998.

D.

DADY, MICHAEL J. Purchase of property for Long Island Hospital, veto, IX, 773.

DAIRYMEN'S MANUFACTURING ASSOCIATION, PERTH. Charter, veto, VI, 501.

DAIRY PRODUCTS. Adulteration of, VIII, 319; sale of, 320; preventing deception of, veto, 1037; oleomargarine and other imitations transported to other State made subject to its police regulations, IX, 321.

DAKER, GEORGE E. Dock on Oneida lake, veto, VI, 156.

DALIBY, MAJOR. See DALLIBA.

DALHOUSIE, EARL OF. Governor of Canada, Smith extradition case, II, 1104.

DALLEY, ABRAHAM. Pension, Brooklyn, veto, VIII, 638.

DALLIBA, JAMES, MAJOR. Settlement of accounts between New York and United States, II, 924.

DALMATIA, DUKE OF. See SOULT, MARSHAL.

DALTON, THOMAS. Court of Claims, veto, X, 165.

DALY, JAMES C. Section superintendent dock department, New York, claim, veto, X, 691, 957.

DALY, JOSEPH F. Member of Educational Unification Commission, 1899, X, 114.

DAMAGES. Canal, payment of, IV, 260; from sale of intoxicating liquor, 765; destruction of quarantine buildings, V, 280; river floods do not establish claim against State, 725; highways, vested right, VI, 158; for injuries resulting in death, limitation prohibited, VIII, 318, 481; for personal injuries in public buildings, right to recovery, quære, IX, 50; when State not liable for imprisonment, 251; resulting from navigation of canals, when State not liable, 270; when bill should state maximum limit to be recovered, 452.

VETOES. Injuries from defective highways, when notice necessary, VII, 843; injuries from defective sidewalks, Rochester, VIII, 629; causing death by negligence, IX, 792; injuries received on canal towpath, X, 255; injuries received while operating machinery in Clinton prison, 259; injuries received while at work on new capitol, X, 267; grade crossings, Buffalo, 474; New York, awards, payment, 634.

DANAHER, FRANKLIN M. Historical sketch, report of Capital Centennial Commission, 1897, IX, 690.

DANFORTH. Contract with Syracuse Water Company, veto, VII, 1105.

DANFORTH, GEORGE F. Late judge, Court of Appeals, opinion, constitutionality of Buffalo charter, bi-partisan board of aldermen, VIII, 960.

DANIELS, CHARLES. Supreme Court, opinion, assignments for creditors, IX, 140.

DANIELS, NATHAN. Contract with Chatfield, II, 580.

DANOLDS, CHARLES A. Contractor, Elmira Reformatory, compensation, veto, VII, 375, 787; claim sustained by Court of Appeals, 375; claim paid, 787.

DANNEMORA. Clinton prison established at, IV, 74, 124. VETOES. Purchase of Clinton prison waterworks, X, 440; taxation of State lands in, 953.

DANSVILLE. VETOES. St. Patrick's Benevolent Society, charter, VI, 592; extending boundaries, VI, 702; police justice, creating office, IX, 471.

DANUBE. Contains grave of General Herkimer, III, 228.

DARCY, STEPHEN. Relief, veto, X, 178.

DARLING, A. B. Approves Harvey claim against New York city, VIII, 1162.

DARLING, GRISWOLD & COMPANY. Furnishing accommodations to Senate committee, appropriation, veto, VII, 86.

DARTMOUTH, EARL OF. Letter from, expedition to Canada, I, 147; letter from, relative to military stores, 160; receives petition from Continental Congress, 770.

DARTMOUTH COLLEGE CASE. Cited, obligations of contracts, III, 1024,

DARWIN R. BARKER LIBRARY ASSOCIATION, FREDONIA. Charter, veto, VII, 845.

DAUPHIN OF FRANCE. Birth of, II, 182.

DAVENPORT, JAMES P. Judge, New York thirteenth civil district court, legalizing appointment of attendants and employees, veto, IX, 809.

DAVENPORT, JOHN I. Counsel to Senate committee, appropriation, veto, VII, 85.

DAVENPORT INSTITUTION FOR FEMALE ORPHAN CHILDREN. Changing name, veto, IX, 356.

DAVEZAC, M. French chief of archives, examination of American documents, IV, 187.

DAVID'S ISLAND. Ceded to United States, V, 861.

DAVIE, WILLIAM R. Presents Kosciusko's treatise on Horse Artillery to United States Philosophical Society, II, 639.

DAVIES, HENRY E. Court of Appeals, opinion, voter, when statement for whom he votes immaterial, VIII, 587.

DAVIES, JOHN C. Attorney-General, opinion, public dancing bill, X, 456.

DAVIES, JULIEN T. Counsel for Senate Committee on Taxation and Retrenchment, 1888, appropriation, veto, VIII, 842; Board of Claims, veto, 1041.

DAVIS, ALFRED. Son of General Daniel Davis, presented with sword by Legislature, letter from Governor Tompkins, II, 847.

DAVIS, C. H. Survey of New York harbor, V, 21.

DAVIS, DANIEL. Brigadier-General, killed at Fort Erie, son presented with sword by Legislature, II, 832.

DAVIS, MRS. DANIEL. Widow of Gen. Daniel Davis, letter from Governor Tompkins transmitting resolutions of Legislature, II, 847.

DAVIS, GUY. Relief, veto, VI, 185.

DAVIS, NOAH. Opposes excise commission bill, 1889, VIII, 805.

DAVIS, RICHARD. Relief of, I, 130.

DAVIS, RICHARD. Relief, volunteer fireman, veto, X, 817.

DAVISON, CHARLES A. Executor, Howard estate, restitution of collateral inheritance tax, veto, VIII, 1139.

DAVIS VOTING MACHINE. Authorizing use in towns and cities, veto, IX, 626; use authorized in cities and towns, 1896, 665.

DAY, LUKE. Arrest authorized, II, 269.

DEAD CREEK. Improvement, veto, VIII, 452.

DEAF AND DUMB. See also NEW YORK INSTITUTION FOR THE INSTRUCTION OF THE DEAF AND DUMB. Care of, II, 974; III, 83, 292, 542; census to include number of, 84; newspaper for, 715; number of, 900; V, 10; fiscal year established, VII, 297.
    VETOES. Central New York Institution for Deaf-Mutes, new building, VII, 90; Central Institution, deficiency appropriation, 470; Le Couteulx St. Mary's Institution, deficiency appropriation, 470; St. Joseph's Institution for the Improved Instruction of Deaf Mutes, deficiency appropriation, 470.

DEAF-MUTES. Northern New York Institution for Deaf-Mutes, appropriation, VIII, 835. VETOES. Care and education, VIII, 129, 872, 1166; instruction, amending School Law, X, 447; schools, inspectors of, compensation, 637; Northern New York Institution for Deaf-Mutes, appropriation for improvements, VIII, 531; appropriation, IX, 771.

DEAN, ELIZABETH. Estate, bill relative to, veto, IX, 393.

DEANE, JAMES. Letter from, Indian affairs, II, 26.

DEATH. See also DEATH PENALTY AND CIVIL DEATH. Of child, resulting from chastisement by parent, II, 576; registration of, V, 863; damages for injuries resulting in, VIII, 318, 481; damages for causing by negligence, veto, IX, 792.

DEATH PENALTY. Abolition except in certain cases, II, 363; imposed for escapes, veto, 583; for arson, 590; should not be frequently inflicted, 633; limited to treason and murder, III, 285; V, 172; act of 1860 unconstitutional, 264; method of inflicting, 265; electrocution, VIII, 37, 484; unreasonable delay in inflicting, after conviction, 80, 180; commission on method of inflicting, 484; proposed establishment of one plant and building for executions, IX, 23; proposed separate building for execution of, 658.

DEBT. Due State, collection of, II, 9, 574, 756; due persons within enemy's lines, veto, 204; Legislature cannot prefer creditors, 583; taxation of, when not double, IV, 340; evils of, VII, 299.

DEBTORS. Imprisonment, facilitating discharge of, veto, VII, 265.

DECATUR, STEPHEN. Commodore, gallant conduct commended by Legislature, II, 780; naval force defends New York, 810; alleged improper conduct in relation to elections, 1065.

DECEDENTS. VETOES. Sale of real estate, amending act, VII, 414; action against executor, 1092; estate, continuing suit against, after death of party, VIII, 131; estates, inventory, appraiser's fees, X, 61; inventory, amending Code, 62.

DECEITS. Act to prevent, I, 11.

DECENTRALIZATION. Governor Hoffman's comment on, VI, 403.

DECKER, CORNELIUS. Land conveyed to, veto, II, 288.

DECLARATION OF INDEPENDENCE. See also INDEPENDENCE. Early discussion of possible independence, I, 294; prepared by Continental Congress, 583; ratified by Fourth Provincial Congress, 778; effect of adoption of, II, 1; death of surviving signer, III, 424; quoted by Governor Seward, prevention of immigration, 803; quoted, equality of birth, 1030; proposed monument to commemorate, IV, 624, 681; V, 121; grievances, superiority of military over civil power, 469; quoted, consent of the governed, 605.

DECORATION DAY. See also MEMORIAL DAY. A public holiday, VI, 679.

DE CRANDCHAIN, MONS. Intendant of the army, letter from, II, 111.

DE DIESKAU, BARON. Defeat of, taken prisoner, I, 583.

DEED. From Indians, I, 727; of real estate, curing defects in, II, 245; proof of, 486; III, 175; commissioners to take proof of, in other States and countries, 211, 770; recording tax proposed, X, 490. VETOES. Exhibiting to assessors before record, VIII, 881; recorded before 1870, record as evidence, X, 386.

DEERFIELD. French and Indian attack on, I, 108.

DEERING, WILLIAM A. Claim against New York city, settlement, veto, IX, 872.

DEER PARK. Town, additional justice of the peace, veto, VI, 208, 276; union free school district No. 1, examination of teachers, veto, 337.

DEER RIVER. Water supply, veto, VII, 505; public highway, veto, VIII, 454, X, 444; made a public highway, 1891, VIII, 454.

DEER SKINS. In trade with Far Indians, I, 214.

DE FOREST, ROBERT W. Chairman Tenement House Commission, letter to Governor, X, 287.

DE GRAFF, SIMON. Relief of, veto, VI, 306.

DE GRASSE, COUNT. Courtesies to family, Yorktown Centennial, VII, 733, 736, 737.

DE GROAT, JOSEPH. Escheat, veto, VII, 642.

DE JONCOURT, PETER. Indian interpreter, appropriation for, I, 478; claim for translating documents, 507.

DE JONGE, YONKHEER, J. C. "Archivarius" Netherlands, custody of colonial documents, IV, 170.

DE KAY, DR. JAMES E. Geological survey, zoological department, III, 638, 753, 991; report, 644, 761, 993; IV, 81; letter on annual reports, III, 682.

DEKEY, THOMAS, COLONEL. Reports Indian incursions in northern Pennsylvania, I, 587; other Indian incursions, 589, 594.

DELAFIELD, JOHN. Services in establishing State agricultural college, V, 16.

DELAFIELD, RICHARD, MAJOR. Engineer, letter from, encroachments on New York harbor, IV, 704; consulting engineer with New York Harbor Defense Commission, V, 566.

DE LANCEY, JAMES. Lieutenant-Governor, letter from, relative to Governor Osborn's death, I, 526; becomes acting Governor, 527.

OPENING SPEECH. Twenty-seventh Assembly, third session, I, 527; comment on Governor Osborn, 528; instructions relative to forms and methods of legislation, 528, 532; revenue bills, 528; Indian affairs, 529; changing excise policy, 529; militia, 529; encouraging home products, 530; various instructions, 530; report of projected invasion by Indians and others, 531; conference with Indians, 531, 537; appoints counsel for keeper of powder-house, 532.

OPENING SPEECH. Twenty-seventh Assembly, fourth session, I, 534; French encroachments in western country, 534; Indian trade, 535; movements against French on Ohio frontier, 535; forts in Indian country, 536; strengthening Oswego, 537, 540; resisting French invasion, 539; New Jersey boundary, 540, 544, 554; Massachusetts boundary, 541, 544; reply to Assembly's address relative to French encroachments, 542; seizure of gunpowder by New York collector, 532, 543; address from Council, money bills, 544.

OPENING SPEECH. Twenty-seventh Assembly, fifth session, I, 545; re-enforcements for Oswego, 546.

DE LANCEY, JAMES — (*Continued*).

OPENING SPEECH. Twenty-seventh Assembly, sixth session, I, 546;
defeat of Washington on Ohio frontier, 546; aiding Virginia
and Pennsylvania in campaign against French, 547; frontier
fortifications, 547, 548; relations with Indians, 548; smiths for
Indians, 548; prohibiting sale of rum to Indians, 549, 569;
militia reform, 549; French movements on Ohio frontier, 549;
French schemes of conquest, 550; Albany plan of union, 550;
mutual assistance among colonies, 551; settlements in townships
compared with patents, 552; French Indians invade colony, 553;
creditors should be paid, 553; claims of Mohawks, 553; Indian
church at Canajoharie, 554; collection of quitrents, 554; floating
battery and naval stores, 555; new fort on Hudson river above
Albany, 555, 563; bedding for troops at Albany, 555; appropriation bills, 556; bills of credit, 559, 560; defense of colony,
561; fortifying New York, 562; defenseless condition of Albany,
563; French benefits from trade at Louisburg, 564; preparing
for war, 565; provisions for Oswego, 566; conference with
General Braddock, 566; application to Connecticut for volunteers, 567; application to Governor Dinwiddie for loan of arms,
567; new forts, 567; vessel for lake service, 567; plan of
campaign, 568; importance of strengthening Oswego, 568; arms
received from Virginia, 569; Crown Point expedition, 570; sends
present of corn to Indians, 570; progress of enlistments, 570;
French attack at Hoseck, 571; New York's apportionment for
Crown Point expedition, 571; Indian agents at Albany, 572;
plan of frontier fortifications, 572; Braddock's defeat, 572;
more troops needed, 573; proposed indirect taxes, 574; Colonel
Dunbar at Albany, 575; other colonies raising troops for expedition, 575; succeeded by Governor Hardy, 576; correspondence
with other Governors relative to colonial union, 578; transmits
proceedings of Albany convention to Lords of Trade, 581.

Resumes executive office on Governor Hardy's resignation,
613; orders militia to assistance of General Webb, 614; desertions at Fort Edward, 614; support of government, 616; Indian
raids, 616, 626, 631; New York barracks, 617; inspection of
farm products, 617; militia, 617; Stamp Act, excise on tea, 617;
indirect taxation, 618; adjourns Assembly, 618.

OPENING SPEECH. Twenty-seventh Assembly, tenth session, I, 618;
enlistment for campaigns, 619; General Abercrombie succeeds
Earl of Loudoun, 619; invasion of Canada, 619, 620; embargo
on certain vessels, 622; deserters, 622; payment of public debts,
623; pilots, 623, 630; chaplain for army, 623.

DE LANCEY, JAMES —(*Continued*).

OPENING SPEECH. Twenty-seventh Assembly, eleventh session, I, 624; military successes, 624; defeat at Ticonderoga, 624; situation in Mohawk valley, 625; capture of Fort Frontenac, 625; King's successes in Europe, 625; visits Albany, 625; Indians on western frontier, 626; protection of Kingston, 627; reimbursing New York for military expenses, 627; service and hardships of New York troops in Mohawk Valley campaign, 628; dissolves Assembly, 629.

OPENING SPEECH. Twenty-eighth Assembly, first session, I, 630; English success at Fort Duquesne, 630; impressments, 631; preventing frivolous arrests, 631; frontier settlements, 631; preparations for campaign, 632, 636; military commissions, 634, 643; reduction of Louisburg, 635; loan for war purposes, 637; continuing troops in service, 638.

OPENING SPEECH. Twenty-eighth Assembly, second session, I, 640; military successes, 640, 642; support of government, 641; stamps and excise, 641; foreign lotteries, 641; movement against Montreal, 643; appropriation by Parliament, 645, 647; Boston fire, 646; payment of public debt, 646; payment of Amherst loan, 646; death of, 647; succeeded by Cadwallader Colden, President of Council, 647; official service, I, pref. X.

DE LANCEY, JAMES. Assembly, resolution relating to petition to Parliament, I, 768.

DE LANCEY, STEPHEN. Member of Assembly, question as to qualifications, I, 214; takes oath as member, 214.

DELAWARE. Resolutions, II, 438; disapproves Vermont's amendment on removal of judges, 630; Constitution, procedure to amend, 1057; approves Ohio proposition relative to abolition of slavery, III, 136; disapproves Georgia's proposition relative to importation of negroes or colored persons, 137; approves tariff of 1828, 318, 388; approves distribution of Federal revenues and Revolutionary pensions, opposes extension of presidential term, also election of President by direct vote, 388; disapproves South Carolina nullification proceedings, 435; pledges support to government, protests against Constitutional Convention, 436; reorganization of militia, 437; favors distribution of proceeds of public lands, 908; constitutional amendment, limiting eligibility of President to one term, 909; sustains Virginia's demand for the extradition of Johnson and others, 972; action on independence monument, V, 122; military to be subordinate to civil power, 470; adheres to Union, 476; resolutions protesting against Federal interference in Louisiana, VI, 787.

"DELAWARE, THE." Used for quarantine purposes, VI, 360.

DELAWARE ACADEMY. Appropriation for, IV, 552.

DELAWARE COUNTY. Act for building courthouse and jail, II, 417; agricultural society in, III, 945; anti-rent disturbance in, IV, 234; murder of Deputy Sheriff Steele, 235; proclamation declaring it in state of insurrection, 236, 246, 297; commutation of sentences, Steele murder, 237, 309, 316; insurrection proclamation revoked, 238, 326; expenses incurred in anti-rent troubles, 246; anti-rent associations, 297; sheriff organizes armed guard, 299; proceedings against Moses Earl, 299; Governor Wright's letter to sheriff, 309; Steele murder trial, 312; tenants represented before Assembly committee on anti-rent troubles, 328; Clark patent, 332; Hunter and Overing's leases, 333; average excise license fees, 1889, VIII, 686; highways, cost of labor system, 1892, IX, 199; insane, care of, county and State systems compared, 228; extending forest preserve in, X, 22.

VETOES. Sidney Plains, village, separate road district, VI, 684; taxes, sales for non-payment, 1035; Andes, village fire department, VII, 65; Deposit, monument, 806; loan commissioner's judgment, Horton, sale of, 877; map of forest preserve in, IX, 776; Hancock, town meetings, voting in three places, 817; extending forest preserve in, X, 291.

DELAWARE AND HUDSON CANAL. Construction of, III, 70, 122, 165, 166, 167; transportation of coal on, 204; completion of, 237, 308; length of, 811.

DELAWARE AND HUDSON CANAL COMPANY. Aid to, III, 70; progress of work, 122, 165, 166; State aid to, 167, 237, 308, 348, 810, 953; IV, 10; projected railroad, III, 237; begins transportation of coal, 308; payment of interest on loan, 867; State stock, redemption of, IV, 261.

DELAWARE INDIANS. Movement against, I, 676; movement against, by Six Nations, 680; claim of, II, 514; land at White river, Indiana, ceded to United States, 987.

DELAWARE RIVER. New York and Pennsylvania boundary on, I, 761; West Branch road from, to Great Shandaken, II, 312; canal connection with Hudson river, III, 70, 165; canal connection with Chesapeake bay, 171; improvement at Cochecton, VIII, 886.

VETOES. Improvement, VIII, 407; shad and game fish, protection, 888; nets in, X, 443; fishway at Deposit dam, 787; dykes in town of Hancock, 788; dykes and barriers, Cochecton, 814; bridge over, Tompkins, 873; dykes in Highland, 935; dykes in Port Jervis, 946.

DELAWARE AND RARITAN CANAL. Experience as to long locks, VI, 745.

DELAWARE AND SUSQUEHANNA NAVIGATION COMPANY. Incorporated, III, 71.

DELAWARE AND SUSQUEHANNA PLANK ROAD COMPANY. Bill relative to assessments, veto, V, 233.

DELEGATION OF LEGISLATIVE POWER. Taxation, II, 61, 95; Council of Safety, 113; instructions to tax officers, 172; municipal taxation, 315, 317; canal tolls, III, 169; to Canal Board, 788; vote on Free School Law, IV, 475; eminent domain, municipal waterworks, VI, 285; submission of law to people, IV, 475; VI, 437, 484, 503; VII, 250; Regents, power to grant college charters, VIII, 708; escheats, 735; New York, rapid transit, municipal ownership, 1894, IX, 505, 512; Governor Odell opposes referendum as to sale of liquor on Sunday, X, 356.

VETOES. Construction of highways, VI, 196; separate boards of town auditors, 437; Chautauqua Lake Camp Meeting Association, taxing leased property, 850; Genesee Valley canal, extending time for sale of, VII, 217; levying taxes, local board, Brooklyn, 771.

DELEGATES IN CONGRESS. Election of, II, 52, 105, 146, 200; compensation and expenses, 114; letter from, 127, 211; requested to procure settlement of Vermont controversy, 145; communication from, Vermont controversy, 166; requested to protest against uniform scale of depreciation, 167; required to oppose recognition of independence of Vermont, 179; representation should be constant, 190; transmit provisional treaty of peace, 191; full representation needed, 209, 210; three from each State, 213; attendance of, 259; present New York resolutions for general convention, 270.

DELHI. Court held at, Steele murder case, IV, 312; law library, veto, VII, 219; law library at, IX, 46.

DELHI AND HUDSON RIVER RAILROAD COMPANY. Extending charter, repealing act, veto, VIII, 1039.

DELINQUENTS. Military service, remedy against, II, 115.

DE LOLBINIERE, MARQUIS DE CHARTIER. Claim of land on Lake Champlain, II, 295.

DELTRY, SUSAN J. Court of Claims, X, 286.

DEMING, ANN. See ELLA DEMING.

DEMING, ELLA. Legalizing adoption, veto, VI, 559.

DEMING, GEORGE W. See DEMING, ELLA.

DEMING, HORACE E. Counsel, investigation of charges against New York district attorney, appropriation, veto, X, 297.

DEMOCRACY IN AMERICA, DE TOCQUEVILLE. Quoted by Governor Cleveland, American commercial supremacy, VII, 992.

DE MUNNICK, MR. Keeper of Records, Amsterdam, Netherlands, IV, 172.

DENIO, HIRAM. Court of Appeals, quoted, compulsory tax on town, VII, 452; chief judge, opinion, secrecy of ballot, VIII, 587.

DENISE, MR. Farm, proposed purchase of, II, 778.

DENIZATION. Certification of Stephen De Lancey, I, 214.

DENMARK. Cumulative voting, VI, 544; illiteracy as compared with New York, X, 859.

DENMARK (NEW YORK). Supervisor, conveyance of certain land, veto, VII, 1105.

DENNEY, ABRAHAM. Grant of Oneida land, II, 894.

DENNEY, DOLLY. Grant of Oneida land, II, 894.

DENNEY, SALLY. Grant of Oneida land, II, 894.

DENNISON, HENRY D. Certificate, Cayuga lake outlet improvement, appropriation, veto, VII, 466.

DENNISON, J. STEWART. Escheat, veto, VII, 1116.

DENNISON, WILLIAM. Governor of Ohio, invited to visit Albany, V, 203; reply, 203.

DENNY, JOHN. Convicted of murder, pardoned, II, 923.

DENTIST. VETOES. Displaying professional signs, IX, 803; relief of certain students, X, 174; students, admission to examination, 265; examination and practice, 942.

DEPEW, CHAUNCEY M. Member of New Capitol Commission, VI, 229; Secretary of State, suggests earlier completion of State census, VIII, 42; delivers historical oration at Capital Centennial Celebration, 1897, IX, 690.

DE PEYSTER, MR. Dispute with Provoost, I, 156.

DE PEYSTER, ABRAHAM. Appointed to preside in Council, I, 91.

DE PETSTER, ABRAHAM, JR. Appointed treasurer, I, 196; papers relating to, 200.

DE PEYSTER, FREDERIC. President New York Historical Society, memorial on centennial volume, VI, 813.

DE PEYSTER, JOHN. Expenses in maintaining troops at Oswego, I, 251.

DE POINNIERRE, JOSEPH TOGUES. Petition from, exportation of provisions, II, 127.

DEPOSIT. Monument, veto, VII, 806.

DERRICK, RICHARD A. Contested election, Assembly, Rensselaer county, expenses, veto, VII, 917.

DE ROCHAMBEAU, MARQUIS. Courtesies to family, Yorktown centennial, VII, 733, 736, 737.

DE RONDE. Seizing forfeited cattle, II, 250.

DE RUYTER. Village, extending boundaries, veto, VI, 189.

DESBROSSES, JAMES. Leases in Greene and Sullivan counties, IV, 332.

DESERTERS. From militia, I, 48, 66; from royal troops and navy, 290; suits by, for pay, 469, 499; from army at Fort Edward, 614; able-bodied men leave home to avoid service, 622; exemption from military services, II, 43; concealing, punishment for, 100; large number of, 189.

VETOES. Act relating to, I, 56; relative to, II, 819.

DE SOELEN, BARON VERSTOLK. Minister of Foreign Affairs, Netherlands, applied to, for leave to transcribe colonial documents, IV, 170.

DETACHMENTS (Colony). Of militia, burdensome, I, 51; for service in Albany county, 325, 361, 372; for Oswego, 329, 334; for Albany and Schenectady, 366; from Albany for Canadian expedition, 374; a grievous method of procuring service, 444; militia for Indian service, 587; for northern garrisons, 588; Crown Point expedition, 588, 595; authorized if necessary to fill quota, 610, 621, 636, 645; Assembly declines to enact new law, 656.

DETACHMENTS (State). Of militia for frontier service, II, 13; of militia under act of Congress, 398; militia, War of 1812, 743.

DE TAILE, MONS. Intendant of the fleet, letter from, II, 111.

DETECTIVES. Private labor strikes, VIII, 1073.

DE TOCQUEVILLE. See TOCQUEVILLE.

DETROIT. Providing for company at, I, 675; successful resistance to Indian attack, 680; interpreter and smiths at, 733; conduct of militia at, II, 737.

DETROIT CONVENTION, 1865. Resolution on enlargement of New York canal locks, V, 707.

DEVEREUX, ALVIN. Trustee, Binghamton Insane Asylum, charges against, not removed, VII, 443.

DEVERY, CAREY. Board of Claims, veto, IX, 473.

DEVITT, GEORGE. Court of Claims, veto, X, 945.

DEVLIN, JOSEPH. VETOES. New York, relief, X, 582; roundsman, New York, reinstatement, 951.

DEVOE, WILLIAM H. Relief, veto, II, 662.

DEWEY, GEORGE. Admiral, reception to, X, 72; appropriation, 72.

DEWEY, MELVIN. Member of Educational Unification Commission, 1899, X, 114.

DEWITT. VETOES. Special system of working highways, X, 234; repairs, Orville feeder, 426, 645.

DE WITT, CHARLES. Assembly, favors colonial union, I, 767.

DE WITT, SIMEON. Commissioner on Massachusetts boundary, II, 218; Surveyor-General, letter from, 270; letter from, Pennsylvania boundary, 272; letter from, map of St. Regis lands, 454; report, Indian lands, 518; death of, Governor Marcy's eulogy, III, 526.

DE WOLF, DELOS. Member of New Capitol Commission, VI, 229.

DEY, J. OGDEN. Proposed new map of State, III, 96.

de ZWAAN, J. A. "Commis Chartermeester," Netherlands, IV, 171.

DIAMOND, M. A. Executrix of John Diamond, claim against New York city, veto, X, 326, 636.

DIANA. Aid to Black River and St. Lawrence Railroad Company, veto, VI, 348.

DIBBLE COMPANY, C. E. Court of Claims, veto, X, 945.

DICKINSON, DANIEL S. Chosen Senator in Congress, IV, 154.

DICKINSON, HENRI D. Engineer, examination of sanitary conditions in capitol, IX, 358.

DICKINSON, JOHN. Governor of Pennsylvania, letter from, boundary, II, 225.

DICKSON, LYDIA. Escheat, veto, IX, 384.

DIEGAN, JOHN G. New York, Municipal Court attendant, claim, veto, X, 168, 473.

DIETZ, JACOB I. Service of process on, Van Rensselaer rent, III, 825.

DIETZLER, GEORGE W. Secretary, Kansas Territory, communication from, expected invasion from Missouri, IV, 864.

DIKE, NORMAN S. Appointed sheriff of Kings county, counsel for, compensation, veto, X, 559.

DILLON, C. J. New York, clerk finance department, claim for services, veto, X, 172.

DILLON, JOHN F. Opinion, voter's freedom of selection of candidate cannot be restricted by form of ballot, IX, 395, 479.

DILLON, RICHARD. Relief, veto, X, 177.

DINEHART, WILLIAM. Injuries received on canal, Court of Claims, veto, X, 255.

DINWIDDIE, ROBERT. Lieutenant-Governor of Virginia, letter from, relative to French on Ohio frontier, I, 542; Governor, letter from, relative to affairs on the Ohio, 553; New York, requests loan of arms, 567; arms supplied, 569.

DIRECT TAX (United States). Federal, II, 788; basis of apportionment, proposed amendment, 827; amount paid by State, 906; how apportioned, III, 622; new method of apportionment (Massachusetts), IV, 85, 86; levied by Congress, 1861, V, 388; constitutional requirements, 391; adjustment of, 703; amount refunded to New York, VIII, 1107; how used, IX, 540.

DISMORE & COMPANY, S. P. Claim against New York, veto, VIII, 884.

DISSOWAY, GABRIEL. Westfield, Richmond county, school supplies, claim, veto, X, 320.

DISGUISES. Act to prevent, IV, 150, 233, 245, 303; act construed, 309.

DISORDERLY HOUSES. Suppression of, I, 116; sources of crime, III, 174.

DISORDERLY PERSONS. Combinations in town of Livingston, II, 411.
VETOES. Act relating to, II, 222; arrest and punishment of, 284; women, Brooklyn, VI, 333; amending Code of Criminal Procedure, VIII, 458; neglect to support family, appeals from conviction, procedure, IX, 526.

DISPENSARIES. New York, aid from passenger tax, IV, 75.
VETOES. Brooklyn, additional number, VIII, 969; Central Throat Hospital Polyclinic Dispensary, changing name, IX, 793; regulating incorporation, licenses, etc., 816.

DISTRESS FOR RENT. Abolished, IV, 241, 242, 338, 653; proceedings against Moses Earl, 299; report of Assembly committee, 343.

DISTRICT COMMITTEE. Power to continue denied, II, 28.

DISTRICT, LOCAL. Revision of statutes relating to, II, 219.

DISTRICT ATTORNEY. Office created, II, 363; to sue for penalties for intrusions on Indian land, 1076; appointments for temporary service, III, 17; employment of counsel to assist, 145; counsel to investigate Morgan matter to possess powers of, 225; to file minutes of testimony in criminal cases, V, 171; fees in criminal cases, 698; when to take charge of proceedings for removal of officers, 717; responsibility in criminal cases, 758; special, when may be appointed, VI, 144; compensation of, 145; should be subject to supervision of Attorney-General, 396; method of selection and removal, 833; Governor may remove, IX, 410; Cattaraugus county objects to bill regulating expense of trials for felonies committed on Indian reservations, X, 164; constitutional provision, 392.
VETOES. Assistant, Washington county, VI, 143; special, oyer and terminer, 490; Chenango county, jurisdiction, 692; Saratoga county, clerk, regulating payment of, VII, 207; filing stenographic notes, 265; compensation, retaining taxable costs, VIII, 404; Erie county, assistants, IX, 800; assistants, 801; New York, John R. Fellows, payment of unearned salary to widow, 805; employment of counsel, 863; New York, investigation, appropriation for counsel, X, 297; amending County Law, 444; special, appointment in certain cases, 591, 699.

DISTRICT ATTORNEY, UNITED STATES. Letter from, fees of New York pilots, II, 388.

DISTRICT OF COLUMBIA. Proposition to confine national banks to, II, 1025; lotteries in, 1052; lotteries prohibited in, 1127; cessions to constitute, III, 138; abolition of slavery, protest against, 582, 588; slavery in, Congress has power to abolish, 645; remonstrance from, abuses of power by Congress, 906; proceedings by Georgetown requesting retrocession to Maryland, 907; Alexandria retroceded to Virginia,

DISTRICT OF COLUMBIA — (*Continued*).
980; New York resolutions against slave trade in, IV, 448; New York urges abolition of slavery in, 502; abolition of slavery in, Maryland resolution, 513; status of slaves, Tennessee propositions, V, 316; tax exemptions, VI, 371.

DISTRICT TELEGRAPH COMPANIES. VETOES. Cities, policemen, VII, 268; appointment of policemen, 416.

DIVEN, ALEXANDER S., COLONEL. Enlistment of volunteers, V, 538; superintendent of volunteer recruiting service, 561.

DIVINE, JOSEPH. Bond for return of arms, II, 774.

DIVISION DITCHES. Requiring construction of, veto, IX, 286, 522.

DIVORCE. Ground of, joining Shakers, II, 920, 946; granted by Legislature, 947; conflict of laws in different States, VIII, 683, 929; decision and entry of judgment, X, 224, 366.

VETOES. Action for, mode of trial, II, 272; wife's testimony to disprove adultery, VII, 1093; advertising business of procuring, prohibited, VIII, 534; foreign judgment, enforcement in this State, 594; when action may be maintained, 758.

DIX, JOHN A. Chosen Senator in Congress, IV, 154; Secretary of the Treasury, communication from, national loan, V, 330; commands militia on northern frontier, 550; Governor, portrait, VI, 522.

1873. Annual message, VI, 522; presidential election, 522; Federal affairs, 523; finances, receipts and expenditures, 524; appropriations should be accompanied by means of payment, 524; giving Comptroller authority to increase tax levy, 525; large appropriations for private charities, 525; sectarian appropriations, 525; State debt, 526; redemption of State debt, 526; taxes, 527; salt springs, 527; common schools, 528; charities and asylums, 528; inquiry into condition of pauper children, 528; banks, 529; savings banks, 529; restricting investments of savings banks, limiting individual deposits, 530, 623; insurance department, 530; militia, 531; quarantine, 532; smallpox brought to New York in immigrant vessels, 532; quarantine structures at Hoffman's island, 533; steamboat for quarantine purposes, 533; boarding station for vessels from non-infected ports, 534; discontinuance of commissioners of quarantine as salaried officers, 534; power of removal of health officer, 534; emigration, 534; immigration property on Ward's island, 534; canals, 535; lateral canals not self-supporting, 535; value and importance of Erie canal, 536; canals should be retained, 536; rapid transit on canals, 537; steam power

DIX, JOHN A., 1873 — (*Continued*).

on canals, 537; change of canal boats, 538; Canadian enlargement of Welland and St. Lawrence canals, 538; Canadian ship canal from St. Lawrence to Lake Champlain, 539; funding State debt, 540; sinking fund should not be pledged for other purposes, 541; government of the city of New York, 542; extravagant salaries in New York city, 543; power of removal vested in mayor, 544; cumulative voting, 544; minority representation, 545; crime, 545; increase of murder in New York city, 545; raising standard of qualifications of juror, 546; protection against fire, 547; complaints against harbor masters, 548; constitutional commission, 549; limiting special laws, 550; compensation of members of Legislature, 550; aliens holding real estate, 550; repeal of usury laws, 551; tax revision, 552; removal of anti-commercial restrictions, 553; various annual reports, 554; statues for Hall of Representatives, 555; obstructions in New York harbor and Hudson river, 557; cession of land to United States at West Point, 558; land for national cemetery near Brooklyn, 558; report of board on exterior pier and bulkhead lines, New York harbor, 560; Maine resolutions, pilot fees passing Hell Gate, 560; Virginia resolutions, Federal assumption of State debts, 563; report of grand jury, usury laws, 564; proceedings, New York Produce Exchange, canals, 564; resignation of Regent Ottendorfer, 566; announces death of Chief Justice Chase, 566; report on condition of Hudson River Asylum and Elmira Reformatory, 567; improvement of streams, 576.

VETOES. Bridges, Clinton and Essex counties, VI, 556; Newtown, local government, 558; Deming, legalizing adoption of, 559; assignees and receivers, lands conveyed to, 562; New York, third police judicial court, salary of assistant clerk, 564; Westchester county, Morrisania, 167th street, 566; excise, local option, 568; Galway relief bill, 573; Loutrel relief bill, 573; Grass river improvement, 575; Oriental Lodge No. 267, Independent Order of Good Templars, charter, 578; Cohoes Hotel Company, charter, 579; St. Regis river improvement, 579; Brooklyn, Wallabout improvement, 579; canals, claims against State, 580; United States Mortgage Company, amending charter, 580; manufacturing corporations, extending act, 580; Watertown, amending charter, 580; Brooklyn, park commissioners, ex-

DIX, JOHN A., 1873, VETOES —(*Continued*).

    tending term, 581; Washington headquarters, care of, 581;
Shawangunk, legalizing resolution fixing place of town meeting, 581; Mohawk and Ilion Horse Railroad Company, 581;
State prisons, amending acts, 582; manufacturing corporations, mortgages, 582; New York and Queens County
Bridge Company, amending charter, 582; Morristown, legalizing town bonding proceedings, 583; New York, streets,
closing and changing grade, 583; religious corporations,
supplemental act, 583; public administrator, amending
Revised Statutes, 583; public administrator, New York,
regulating bureau of, 584; Champlain canal enlargement,
584; Campbell's leases, tenants' rights under, 584; canal
bridge at Whitehall, 584; Machpelah Cemetery Association, Leroy, amending charter, 585; New York Rapid
Transit Company, charter, 585; Marbletown, bridge over
Rondout creek, 585; Maritime Association, New York,
charter, 585; New York Bridge Company, amending charter,
586; Roman Catholic Orphan Asylum, New York, reappropriation, 587; Dunkirk, amending charter, 587; Rochester,
amending charter, 587; Syracuse, penitentiary, maintenance
of convicts, 587; Merchant's Loan Company, charter, 587;
canals, swing-bridge, Norwich, 588; Mutual Aid Society of
the East German Conference, Methodist Episcopal Church,
charter, 588; Chautauqua county supervisors, compensation
in certain towns, 588; Temple Adas Jeshurun Society, holding land for cemetery purposes, 588; relief of Hall heirs,
589; Allemania Savings Bank, Brooklyn, charter, 589; gas
companies, preventing extortion by, 589; Morrisania and
West Farms, collection of taxes, 589; Bloomer claim, Sing
Sing prison quarry, 589; Westchester county, public works
in certain towns, 589; New York, map, alteration of, 590;
Tyrian Hall Association of East New York, New Lots,
charter, 590; Westchester county, Morrisania, changing
grade of certain streets, 590; New York, buildings, amending act, 590; Saratoga Springs, regulating burials, 591; St.
John and others, relief, 591; Schaub, relief, 591; water
supply, towns and villages, 591; New York, legal
proceedings and notices, publication, 591; canals, Seeley
claim, settlement, 592; Parma, town insurance company,
592; Tau Chapter of the Delta Kappa Epsilon Fra-

DIX, JOHN A., 1873, VETOES — (*Continued*).

ternity, Clinton, charter, 592; Highland, appropriation of certain moneys, 592; St. Patrick's Benevolent Society, Dansville, charter, 592; New Brighton, amending village charter, 592; boards of supervisors, extending powers, 593; Niagara river, ferry at Youngstown, 593; public exchange, amending charter, 593; Port Morris Land and Improvement Company, amending charter, 593; New York, Washington market, lease of, 594; Mutual Insurance Company, Catskill and Athens, organization, 595; Quirk and others, relief, 595; Staten Island and Elizabethport Ferry Company, extending time, 595; Brooklyn Elevated Silent Safety Railway Company, charter, 595; Lutheran cemetery, Middle Village, amending charter, 595; civil prisoners, maintenance in certain counties, 596; plankroad companies, repealing certain acts, 596; New York city, Croton water, 596; Yorkshire Rural Cemetery Association, charter, 596; New York, election districts, amending act, 596; New York, Tenth avenue and Ninety-third street improvement, 597; Ausable river improvement, 597; married women, releasing dower in certain cases, 597; street railroads, Brooklyn and Flatbush, 597; Fulton county, special highway, 598; Battalion Independent des Gardes Lafayette Francais, charter, 598; New York, police and district court janitors, 598; New York Towage Company, charter, 598; Western House of Refuge, amending act, 599; New York, Eighty-sixth street improvement, 599; banks, Westchester county, 599; Racket river, improvement, 599; State prisons, new, removal of Sing Sing, 600; street railroads, New York, Wall street ferry to North river, 601; life insurance companies, forfeiture of policies, 601; Auburn, acquiring land for cemetery, 602; New York, newspaper claim, 607; New York, mortgages on lands under water, 611.

1874. Annual message, VI, 613; general condition of State, 613; receipts and expenditures, 614; State debt, 614; redemption of State debt, 615; taxes, 615; salt springs, 616; State prisons, 616; common schools, 617; colleges and academies, 618; State library, 619; militia, 619; sale of arsenals, 620; system of accounts for arms, etc., 620; improved inspection of National Guard, 621; payments on claims against United States, 621; trust companies, 621; banks,

DIX, JOHN A., 1874 —(*Continued*).

622; savings banks, 623; limitation of interest, savings banks, 623; savings bank officers, should not be officers in other banks, 624; insurance department, 624; quarantine, 625; board of health, New York city, 627; emigration, 627; insane, 628; State parks, 629; sinking fund, 629; payment of State taxes, 630; defalcation in State treasury, 632; canals, 634; cheapening transportation, 634; St. Lawrence canal, 635; reduction of canal tolls, 636; ship canal, connecting Hudson river with Lake Erie, 636; railroad companies, 636; embezzlement by public officers, 638; careless legislation, 639; supply bill, 641; eminent domain, 642; currency, 644; unfortunate consequence of suspension of specie payment, 645; coinage of gold and silver, 645; paper currency must be supported by specie, 647; how to resume, 648; public buildings, 650; State Architect, 652; certificates for service in War of 1812, 654; obstruction of New York harbor, 654; Centennial exhibition, 655; amendments to the Constitution, 656; various reports, 658; communication from Comptroller, sinking funds, 658; pardon report, 661; announces death of ex-President Fillmore, 662; investigation of Oneida Indian claims, 663; special message on currency, 668; protests against inflation of currency, 668.

VETOES. New York Club, charter, VI, 661; Albany county, special highway, 670; Rochester Atheneum, amending charter, 671; Howland College for the Education of Young Women, charter, 671; St. Ann's Total Abstinence and Benevolent Society, Hornellsville, charter, 672; Seymore, relief, 673; Putnam county, town business, Phillipstown and Carmel; Ulster county, Hurley, town meetings by election districts; Orleans county, Barre, town meetings, Mount Pleasant, 674; Catholic Union, New York, charter, 676; mortgages, foreclosure, 678; Edymoin, *habeas corpus*, payment of expenses, 678; holidays, general act, 679; Buck, relief, 680; Canajoharie, revising village charter, 683; Yonkers, amending charter, 683; Young Men's Catholic Association, Rochester, amending charter, 683; Sidney Plains, separate road district, 684; wills, proof of, 684; religious corporations, supplemental act, 684; Baldwin, relief, 684; New York Warehouse and Railway Company,

DIX, JOHN A., 1874, VETOES — (*Continued*).

charter, 684; canal farm bridge, Whitehall, 689; Allegany Indian reservation, highways and bridges, 690; Gilbert, notary, legalizing acts, 690; Sodus Point and Southern Railroad Company, docks, 690; St. Joseph's College, Buffalo, charter, 691; Orange county, 91st Regiment funds, transfer, 691; Corning library, acquiring property, fixing annual election, 691; Chenango county, special county judge and district attorney, 692; Faenger escheat, 692; New York, Bloomingdale road, 692; Ramsay, relief, 692; villages, amending general act, Corning, 693; Albany, Washington park bonds, 693; New York Orthopœdic Dispensary, changing name, 693; Ulster Female Seminary, amending charter, 693; New York Rapid Transit Company, charter, 694; New York, Eastern boulevard, amending map, 695; Brooklyn, Bushwick, altering map, 695; highways, amending Revised Statutes, 695; Brooklyn City Railroad, extending road, 695; Seeley claim, 696; bridges, Erie and Niagara counties, Tonawanda creek, 696; Oneida county, fines, 696; Van Slyck, relief, 697; Owego, school district No. 35, establishing cemetery, 697; New York and Brooklyn ferry, 697; Ausable Valley Masonic Hall and Library Association, charter, 697; Schenectady, police, amending act, 698; Harris, relief, 698; Wilson, relief, 698; Erie canal, settling claim for work, 698; New York, Tompkins square improvement, 698; Essex county, Newcomb, repealing act, 699; Brooks Locomotive Works, changing name, relief, 699; Ithaca Company, charter, 700; Schenectady county, Glenville, highway assessments, 701; Oneida county, New Hartford, reimbursing collector, 701; Hamilton county, Totten and Crossfield's purchase, exemption from highway taxes, 701; Dansville, extending boundaries, 702; People's Water Transit Company, amending charter, 703; New York hospital, exempting property from taxation, 703; State prisons, Gilson claim, 703; Matteawan, lighting streets, 704; Salamanca, charter, 704; MacGuire, dock on Hudson river, 705; Hummel, dock on Jamaica bay, 705; ferry, Troy and West Troy, 705; New York, alteration of map, Lewis street, 705; civil prisoners, maintenance of, 706; Northeastern dispensary, New York, lease for, 706; Clyde, borrowing money, 706; New York, telegraph, public use of, 706;

DIX, JOHN A., 1874, VETOES —(*Continued*).

  Allegany Indian reservation, bridge at Vandalia, 707; Livonia, two rod road, 707; mortgages, foreclosure by advertisement, 707; manufacturing corporations, amending act, 708; Code of Procedure, amendments, 708; Wyoming County Agricultural Society, escheat, 708; Yonkers, creating school commissioner districts, 708; trusts, amending Revised Statutes, 709; Schenectady, lease of armory to Union University, 709; Genesee Valley canal, bridge at Portville, 709; Second Baptist church, Harlem, relief from assessment for street improvement, 710; poisons, regulating sale, 710; milk adulteration, 710; Church of the Resurrection, relief from assessments, 711; penitentiaries, confinement of convicts, 711; Yonkers, bonded debt, consolidation of, 712; New York engineers, powers and duties, 715, New York Elevated Railroad Company, extending road, 715; West Farms, relief of board of education, 718.

 Death of, personal sketch, VII, 328; legislative action, 329; quoted,— special charters, VIII, 198; method of supervising construction of new capitol, 222, 1018; official service as Governor, I, pref. xiii.

DIX, JOHN D. New York agent, Curry extradition case, III, 915.

DIX ISLAND. Hospital, yellow fever patients at, VI, 626.

DOANE, WILLIAM CROSWELL. Protestant Episcopal Bishop of Albany, makes opening prayer at first occupation of Assembly chamber, opening new capitol, VII, 271; pronounces benediction at Capital Centennial Celebration, 1897, IX, 690.

DOBBIN, HUGH W., COLONEL. Commands 18th Regiment, II, 766.

DOBSON, THOMAS, & SON. Solicits purchase of Seybert's Statistics, II, 994.

DOCKSTEDDER, JACOB. Relief of, II, 433.

DOCUMENTS. Recording, amending act, veto, VII, 806.

DODD, CHARLES J. Counsel fees and expenses, Assembly contested election, Waite case, Kings county, veto, X, 795.

DODGE, EDWIN. Member of Tax Revision Commission, VI, 238, 269, 370.

DODGE, RICHARD, GENERAL. Commands troops on St. Lawrence frontier, II, 746; funds received by, 765.

DODGE, WILLIAM E. Delegate to Washington Peace Convention, V, 310.

DODSWORTH BAND. Accompanies 13th Regiment at Yorktown Centennial Celebration, VII, 736.

Dogs. Tax on, act relative to, VIII, 823. VETOES. Rockland county, running at large, VI, 92; killing sheep, amending Revised Statutes, VIII, 469; tax on, Tonawanda reservation, IX, 725; running at large where deer inhabit, 798.

DOHERTY, CHARLES. Cancellation of taxes, veto, X, 592.

DOLAN, MICHAEL. Claim against New York, veto, VIII, 883.

DOMESTIC ECONOMY. Proposed establishment of county schools, veto, X, 440.

DONGAN, THOMAS. Appointed Governor of New York, I, 5; sketch of, 5; instructions to, 6; calls Assembly, 9; Assembly organized, 10; Legislature provides for present to, 11.
Second Assembly, I, 12; receives letter from James II relative to change of government, 12; receives new commission, 13, pref., charter to East Hampton, II, 932; patent, 1685, confirmed, IV, 413; official service as Governor, I, pref.; ix.

DONGAN ASSEMBLY. First, organized, proceedings in, I, 9; second session, 11; records of, lost, 11; deemed dissolved by death of Charles II, 12; Second Assembly, first session, 12; records of, lost, 12.

DONLON CONTRACTING COMPANY. Claim for cleaning brick sewers, Brooklyn borough, veto, X, 959.

DONNELLY, JOHN. Claim against New York city, examination, veto, VIII, 131.

DONNELLY, TERENCE. Stage route along Hudson river, veto, II, 638.

DONOHUE, MICHAEL. Auburn prison convict, crime committed by, trial, reimbursing Cayuga county, veto, VI, 876; VII, 87, 471, 781.

DONOVAN, JOHN J. Claim against State, veto, X, 63.

DOOLITTLE, WARREN H. Brooklyn justice's court, assistant clerk, claim, veto, IX, 779.

DORN, ANDREW. Canal department, appropriation for services, veto, IX, 716.

DORR, THOMAS W. Rhode Island, treason judgment annulled by Legislature, IV, 817.

DORSHEIMER, WILLIAM. Lieutenant-Governor, communication from Governor on imperfect bills, VII, 42; president New Capitol Commission, delivers Assembly chamber to Assembly, 269; delivers address at ceremonies on first occupation of Assembly chamber, new capitol, 271.

DOTY, ALPHEUS. Postmaster in Sandy Hill, removal of, II, 1068.

DOTY, LOCKWOOD L. Secretary to Governor Morgan, letter to Commissioner Ruggles, V, 507.

DOUGHTY, GEORGE S., MAJOR-GENERAL. Letter to, calling militia into service, anti-rent troubles. III, 831.

DOUGLASS, ANTHONY C. Claim against Buffalo, settlement, veto, IX, 869.

DOUGLASS, DANIEL. Services in New York water department, claim, veto, X, 940.

DOURIGAN, JAMES A. Relief, veto, X, 53, 176.

DOWD, MICHAEL. Police pension, Buffalo, veto, X, 875.

DOWER. In land of person attainted, II, 374, 507, 581, 784; foundation of right, VII, 349. VETOES. Procedure, VI, 502; release in certain cases, 597, 820; proposed abolition of, VII, 349.

DOWLING, DAVID W. Claim against New York city, veto, X, 310.

DOWNING, BENJAMIN W. District attorney, Queens county, Roberts' pardon case, IX, 250.

DRAFT (Commercial). Exchanging for specie, II, 189.

DRAFT (Militia). See also DETACHMENTS. Ordered from militia, I, 372; Governor Clinton's comment on, 444; for Crown Point expedition, 570, 588; for service in Pennsylvania, 574; for northern garrisons, 588, 595; authorized if volunteers insufficient for quota, 610, 621, 636, 645; Assembly declines to enact new law, 656; for protection of Westchester, II, 8; Civil War, order for 300,000 men, V, 454; adjustment of quotas, 457, 536, 572; Governor Seymour's discussion of, 536; failure of, 539; riot in New York, 545; Governor Seymour's proclamation, 546; New York city declared in state of insurrection, 547; number killed and wounded in riots, 548.

DRAINAGE. Cayuga marshes, II, 1011; III, 81; lands in Orange county, V, 512; general act, 1869, VI, 189; lands in Onondaga county, 189; constitutional provisions, 189; VIII, 614; IX, 550, 558; Chemung and Genesee Valley canals, VII, 517; Conewango valley, act for, IX, 106.

VETOES. Amending Revised Statutes, VI, 190; VIII, 130; X, 812; amending general act, VI, 509; VII, 412; Black lake and adjoining land, VI, 1036; Black lake, repealing act, VII, 268; Long Island City, 369; New Rochelle, 392, 414; abandoned canals, 412; commissioners, evidence of indebtedness, 413; Orange county, 508; Cato, swamp lands adjacent to Otter lake and Parker's pond, VIII, 613; Black lake, 614; Brooklyn, certain wards, 635; Conewango creek, amending act, X, 315; Conewango creek, appropriation, 315; Brooklyn, 29th and 32d wards, 322; Royalton, lands flooded by canal feeder and dam, 437; Gorman swamp, Seneca county, 651, 797; Amherst and Clarence, 698; Utica, extending system, 717; Middleport, repairing drain into culvert under Erie canal, 798; Buffalo, contracts with adjoining municipalities, 960.

DRAKE, J. R. Congress, action on removal of postmaster, II, 1071.

DRAKE, SAMUEL, CAPTAIN. Funds received by, II, 766.

DRAKE'S DRAW-BRIDGE, WAPPINGER'S CREEK. Maintenance, operation and repair, veto, IX, 712.

DRAPER, EUGENE M. Court of Claims, X, 286.

DRESDEN. Amending General Village Law, veto, VII, 644.

DREXEL, JOSEPH W. Cottage in which General Grant died transferred to Mount McGregor Memorial Association, VIII, 625; death of, 625.

DREYER, ARTHUR. Cancellation of tax sale, veto, X, 953.

DRUGGISTS. Clerks, regulating hours of, act of 1900, X, 56, 96. VETOES. New York, regulating prescriptions, etc., IX, 871; regulating hours, X, 56.

DRUGS. VETOES. Adulteration, VII, 924, 1113; X, 447; sale in Kings county, VII, 934; offenses connected with sale of, X, 592.

DRUMMERS. Scarcity of, II, 572, 601.

DRUNKENNESS. Act to prevent, I, 12.

DRURY, WILLIAM. Board of Claims, veto, IX, 430.

DRY DOCK, EAST BROADWAY AND BATTERY RAILROAD COMPANY. Extending powers, veto, V, 646.

DUANE, JAMES. Commissioner on Massachusetts boundary, I, 721; II, 217; delegate to Continental Congress, I, 768; letter from, II, 100; commissioner to Commercial Convention, 260; seat in Senate declared vacant, 310.

DUANESBURGH. Milldam in, right to maintain, II, 662. VETOES. Taxes, extending time for collection, V, 116; — Protestant Reformed Dutch church, changing name, 125.

DUANESBURG TRACT. Location of, IV, 331.

DUBOIS, GEORGE CURTIS. · Relief, veto, X, 53, 63, 179.

DUDLEY, CHARLES E. Chosen Senator in Congress, III, 254.

DUDLEY, JAMES M. Board of Claims, veto, VIII, 291, 408.

DUDLEY, JOSEPH G. Claim, legal services, German bank matter, appropriation, veto, X, 784.

DUDLEY OBSERVATORY. Established, V, 17.

DUELLING. Governor Clinton urges suppression of, III, 208; act passed, 209.

DUE PROCESS OF LAW. Act relating to sequestrations and forfeitures, II, 234; Legislature exercising judicial power, 249; foreclosure of State mortgages by advertisement, 603; forfeiture of corporate stock, 638; arrest without warrant, 820; statute changing will, 1036; imprisonment of colored citizens, IV, 48; destruction of liquor, 759; meaning of, 761; martial law, V, 471; Amsterdam charter, 512; Susquehanna river dam, 652; Fourteenth Amendment, 790; preventing assignment of claim, VII, 801; destruction

XI—29

DUE PROCESS OF LAW. — (*Continued*).

of intoxicating liquors, VIII, 367; St. Regis Indian lands, trespasses, 1120; tax, notice of assessment, IX, 60; elevated railroads, reducing rates of fare, 500.

VETOES. Requiring license to transact ordinary mercantile business, IX, 351; prohibiting use of stables near churches in New York, 520; attachment, undertaking on discharge, X, 534; evidence on seizure and sale of prohibited articles of food, 777; reduced rates of fare for children on street railroads, 884.

DUFF, FRANCIS. Brooklyn, Sackett street contract, balance. veto, VII, 605.

DUFF, PATRICK. Administrator Francis Duff, Brooklyn, Sackett street contract, balance, veto, VII, 605.

DUFFERIN, LORD. Governor-General of Canada, suggests establishment of park at Niagara falls, VII, 299.

DUFFY, STEPHEN. Troy school janitor, claim, veto, X, 634.

DUGGAN, WILLIAM H. New York patrolman, claim, veto, X, 806.

DUKE OF NEWCASTLE. See NEWCASTLE, DUKE OF.

DUKE OF YORK. See YORK, DUKE OF.

DUKE'S LAWS. Promulgated, I, 2.

DUER, WILLIAM. Delegate in Congress, letter from, advance of funds, II, 55; chosen Regent, 1028.

DUER (WILLIAM) & COMPANY. Contractors, letter from, II, 165.

DUMB. See DEAF AND DUMB.

DUMOND, EGBERT. Impressments for army service, II, 99.

DUNBAR, DANIEL. Columbia county sealer of weights and measures, communication from, III, 98.

DUNBAR, THOMAS, COLONEL. Defeat of, by French and Indians, I, 572; forces march to Albany, 575, 591.

DUNKIRK. Armory at, V, 175, 642, 643; arsenal sold, refund from proceeds, VI, 620; number of excise licenses, 1887, VIII, 359; excise license fees, 1889, 685.

VETOES. Purchasing steam fire engine, VI, 334; amending charter, 587; VII, 79, new bill passed; establishing union free school district, VIII, 82; revising charter, exhibiting deeds to assessors, 881; water supply, IX, 730, 785.

DUNKIRK AND WARREN RAILROAD COMPANY. Asks State aid, V, 866.

DUNMORE, EARL OF. Appointed Governor, assumes office, I, 736.

OPENING SPEECH. Thirty-first Assembly, third session, I, 736; influence of colony in promoting intercourse between England and other colonies, 737; Spanish seizure of Fort Egmont, Falkland island, 737; quartering King's troops, 737; support of government, 737; declines salary voted by Assembly, 738; Indian trade,

DUNMORE, EARL OF — (*Continued*).

738, 739; repairs to Governor's house and additional barrack rooms, 739; Quebec boundary, 739, 744; succeeded by Governor Tryon, 739; official service, I, pref. x.

DUNN, WILLIAM. Court of Claims, veto, X, 703.

DUNN, WILLIAM J. Relief, veto, X, 178.

DUNNING, DAVID. Convicted of murder, not pardoned, II, 997.

DUPERRE, BARON. French Minister of the Marine, grants permission to examine colonial documents, IV, 185.

DURANT, EDWARD A. Nominated as railroad commissioner, no action, VIII, 373.

DURHAMVILLE. Erie canal, steel trunk aqueduct, veto, X, 573, 790.

DURKEE, HARVEY. Relief, II, 1120.

DURYEA, CHARLES T. Assembly contested election, VII, 492.

DUSTON, WILLIAM. Letter from, storm on Staten Island, effect on fortifications, II, 1038.

DUTCHER, SALEM, JR. Appropriation for compensation as claim agent, III, 145.

DUTCHER, SILAS B. Superintendent of Public Works, discretion in method of expending appropriations, VIII, 521.

DUTCHESS COUNTY. Courts in, Governor's alleged interference with, I, 468, 499; levies in, 570; draft for northern garrisons, 588; long marches of militia, 596; militia ordered into service, 614; riots in, expense of suppressing, 717; courthouse and jail destroyed by fire, provision for rebuilding, II, 224; nomination of sheriff, proceedings in Council of Appointment, 493; Jacob Van Ness, clerk, removal of, 1069; land titles, investigation of, III, 132, 146, 174; survey of Putnam boundary, 389; discontinuance of wheat raising in, 315; agricultural society in, 945; silk culture in, 945; citizens donate site for Hudson River Asylum, V, 763; authorized to borrow money to pay for asylum site, 763; average excise license fees, 1889, VIII, 686; unpaid taxes, sales under special act, 749; highways, cost of labor system, 1892, IX, 199; insane, care of, county and State systems compared, 228; included in ninth judicial district, 547, X, 850; estimated contribution to cost of barge canal, 602; water rights, act of 1904, 691.

VETOES. Contingent expenses, II, 95; smallpox, inoculation for, 225; highways in, relative to, 348; exempting from Highway Damage Act, VII, 767; Fishkill, road commissioner, creating office, VIII, 388; Millerton, Frost escheat bill, IX, 284; institutions, purchase of supplies for, X, 700; sheriff's account, legalizing audit, 956.

DUTCH RECORDS. Translation of, II, 1115; III, 162, 751.

DUTCH WEST INDIA COMPANY. Begins colonization in New York, I, 1; charter, powers of, 1; papers as source of colonial history, IV, 166, 172; records sold at auction, 172.

DUTIES. Imports from other colonies, I, 115; on European imports, 198, 211; arrears, 199; revision of, 247; none on vessels and stores intended for Canadian expedition, 420; Mohawk Indians complain against, 514; excise, collection and disposal of, 529; on trade with West Indies, 692; on colonies, protest against, 730; on importations from England, protest against, 773; act imposing, II, 199, 220; explanatory act, veto, 236; resolutions of Congress on, 276; payable in specie, 277; on salt, 902, 1010; III, 330; on steamboat passengers, II, 902; on auction sales, 902; under Federal Constitution, control of, III, 331, 898; IV, 616.

DUTTON PNEUMATIC LOCK AND ENGINEERING COMPANY. Court of Claims, veto, X, 449.

DWIGHT, EDMUND. Director Western Railroad Company, communication from, III, 750.

DWYER, MICHAEL. Convicted of murder, pardoned, II, 805.

DYER, WILLIAM. Collector, case of, I, 4; indicted for high treason, sent to England for trial, 4.

DYETT, PERRY. Legislative employee, compensation, veto, VII, 372.

DYKE. VETOES. On Hudson river at Albany, IX, 606; Delaware river, Hancock, X, 788; — Cochecton, 814; — Highland, 935; — Port Jervis, 946.

E.

EAGAN, PATRICK. Auburn prison convict, crime committed by, trial, reimbursing Cayuga county, veto, VI, 876; VII, 87, 227, 471, 781.

EAGLE AVENUE GERMAN BAPTIST CHURCH, NEW YORK. Relief, veto, X, 60.

EAGLE HOSE COMPANY NO. 2, BUFFALO. Charter, veto, VI, 196.

EAGLE TRUST COMPANY, NEW YORK. Charter, veto, VI, 342.

EARL, MOSES. Proceedings against, Delaware county, anti-rent troubles, IV, 299.

EARTHQUAKE. At San Francisco, appropriation for relief of sufferers, X, 890.

EAST AURORA. Legalizing bonds, X, 284.

EASTCHESTER. Part of, merged in Greater New York, IX, 300. VETOES. Completion of highways in, VI, 512; highways, VII, 130; number of highway commissioners, VIII, 461, 616; claims against, settlement, IX, 732.

EASTCHESTER CREEK. Changing name to Eastchester river, veto, VIII, 469.

EASTER. Assembly adjourns over, I, 219.

EASTERN INDIANS. Massachusetts declares war against, I, 203; Five Nations send commissioners to, 203; aid demanded of New York, 219.

EASTERN NEW YORK FANCIERS' ASSOCIATION. Charter, veto, VII, 371.

EASTERN NEW YORK REFORMATORY, NAPANOCH. Under supervision of prison department, X, 204; transfers from Elmira Reformatory, 501.

VETOES. Cells, access to, appropriation, X, 293; Thomas, architect, claim, 296; transfers to, amending State Charities Law, 312; dining-room, kitchen and bakery, appropriation, 566; parole of prisoners from, 585; appropriations for, 655; continuing construction, appropriation, 697.

EASTERN NEW YORK REFORMATORY, WAWARSING. VETOES. Relative to, IX, 245; buildings and expenses, appropriation, 776.

EASTERN NEW YORK STATE CUSTODIAL ASYLUM. Provision for establishing, X, 726.

EASTERN STAR HALL AND HOME ASSOCIATION. Charter, veto, X, 311.

EAST FRANKFORT. Canal repairs, veto, VI, 856.

EAST GREENBUSH. Excepting from Town Insurance Companies Act, veto, VI, 153.

EAST HAMBURGH TURNPIKE ROAD COMPANY. Extending charter, veto, VI, 162.

EAST HAMPTON. Charter, authority as to purchase of Indian lands, II, 932.

EAST INDIA COMPANY. Records examined, IV, 173.

EAST RIVER. Battery at Burnett's Key, I, 322; encroachments on, III, 28; bridge over, VI, 91; bulkhead line, establishment, VIII, 834; tunnel authorized, 1895, 1135; tunnel under, Pennsylvania Railroad, X, 396.

VETOES. Pneumatic tubes, amending act, VI, 289; Greenpoint ferry boats on, 336; New York and Queens County Bridge Company, amending charter, 582; New York Bridge Company, amending charter, 586; Pier 37, New York, use of, VII, 937; bulkhead and pier line, Brooklyn, relating to, VIII, 470; tunnel under, 1135; depositing refuse matters in waters of, repeal, IX, 384; regulating use of piers, slips and wharves, 873; bridge, relative to, Laws 1895, chapter 789, 873; bridge, Blackwell's island, X, 176.

EAST RIVER BRIDGE COMPANY. Charter, IX, 90; percentage tax on receipts, 92.

EAST RIVER GAS COMPANY. VETOES. In Long Island City, relative to, X, 582; extending powers, 657.

EASTON. Highway commissioner, election, veto, VII, 932.

EATJEN, J. H. New York, assistant clerk, city magistrate's court, claim for services, veto, X, 172.

EATON, AMOS. Relief of, geological survey, III, 591.

EATON, JAMES W. Contract with Timothy J. Sullivan, iron work, VII, 498. VETOES. Superintendent of new capitol, counsel fees, appropriation, VII, 83; expenses of experts, appropriation, 84; stenographers' services, appropriation, 84.

EATON'S NECK. Lighthouse at, II, 414, 415.

EBENEZER BAPTIST CHURCH. Exemption from assessments, veto, VII, 931.

ECCLESIASTICAL AFFAIRS. Documents relating to, III, 1018.

ECONOMICAL SCHOOL. Aid from auction duties, III, 246.

EDDY, GILBERT, GENERAL. At Plattsburgh, II, 807.

EDDY, THOMAS. Communication from, prison discipline, II, 995.

EDGERLY, A. J. Lieutenant, 4th New Hampshire Volunteers, dismissed for alleged interference in elections, V, 515.

EDGERTON, ERASTUS S. Constable, Delaware county, anti-rent troubles, IV, 300.

EDGEWATER. VETOES. Fire department, charter, VIII, 616; changing boundaries, 639.

EDGEWATER FIRE DEPARTMENT. Charter, veto, VIII, 616; X, 473.

EDISON ELECTRIC ILLUMINATING COMPANY, BROOKLYN. Right to use streets, veto, VIII, 591.

EDISON GENERAL ELECTRIC COMPANY. Price for power, IX, 456.

EDMUNDS, JOHN W. Justice Supreme Court, communication from, vagrants, IV, 505.

EDMUNDS, SAMUEL, MAJOR. Appointed paymaster of militia, II, 764; funds, received by, 765, 766; funds received from New York for sea fencibles, 816; statement of killed and wounded, 872; compensation of, 953.

EDUCATION. See also SCHOOLS and COMMON SCHOOLS. Grammar free school established, I, 100; proposed instruction of Indian youth in Mohawks' language, 211; proposed establishment of seminary, 521, 522; act to establish King's College, 523; Governor George Clinton urges promotion of, II, 183, 200; gospel and school lots, 291; appropriations for, 321, 1099; academies and common schools, 350; investment of certain funds, 528; using proceeds of State lands for, 556; report of joint legislative committee, 560; report of Commission on Common Schools, 717; acts relating to, 877; in agriculture, recommended, 898; III, 458, 745; for practice of medicine, 905; associations composing New York Institution, 905; literature fund, see that title; of selected youth at public expense, II, 1049; III,

EDUCATION — (*Continued*).

116, 213; national domain appropriated for, II, 1101; importance of, in a republic, III, 60, 114, 272, 454; progress of, 159, 212, 537; monitorial high school, 212; Rochester Institute of Practical Education, 378; industrial schools, 381; of American children, proposed appropriation of proceeds of public lands for, 391; expansion of system, 537; popular interest in, 615; aid from United States deposit fund, 650; relation to prosperity, 727; of immigrants, 729; department of, proposed, 744; children of foreigners, 768, 947; white illiterates in New York, 884; should reach all classes, 884; resolution of Colonial Assembly against, 946; conventions and associations, IV, 67; normal schools, see that title; State agricultural school, 80, 552; intimate connection of all schools, 647; New York's leadership, 713; State scholarships, 716; international exhibition in London, 752; general statistics, V, 602, 778, 850; VI, 22, 108, 235, 356; VII, 423, 686, 821, 946; not a charity but a right, IV, 796; People's College, Havana, 648; V, 178, see that title; people willingly pay taxes for, 273; opportunities neglected, 780; general policy, 850; compulsory, general act, VI, 617; all citizens should receive benefit of, VII, 21; text-books, regulation of changes, 22; principle of, proper taxation for, 156; in common schools, children entitled to, 295; public benefits of, 517; of Indian children, 710; university extension, IX, 17; higher, not self-sustaining, 20; Cornell University, one free student from each Assembly district, 177; agricultural, in several States, 178; pictorial representations and lectures, 564; military instruction in public schools, veto, 628; value of libraries, 829; Cornell University, College of Forestry, 837; revised law enacted, X, 27; unification of educational administration, 113, 128; State Department of Education, 129; expenditures, 1900, 182; comparative statement of appropriations, 1893–4; 1901–2, 464; free tuition in high schools, 514; primary and academic education defined, 603; joint legislative committee, 1903, 537, 604; illiteracy in State, 859.

EDUCATIONAL ALLIANCE, NEW YORK. Exempting from taxation, veto, IX, 794.

EDWARD III. England, status of House of Commons in time of, VIII, 983.

EDWARDS. Town, aid to Black River and St. Lawrence Railroad Company, veto, VI, 348.

EDYE, H. W. O. Judgment against people for costs, payment, veto, VII, 926.

EDYMOIN, FRANCIS B. *Habeas corpus*, payment of expenses, veto, VI, 678.

Ehlers, Robert John. Legitimizing birth, veto, VII, 633.

Eidlitz, Richardson & Company. New capitol architects, advances, veto, VII, 903; communications from, defects in Assembly chamber, VIII, 501.

Eigenbrod, William. Frœlich estate, escheat, veto, X, 312.

Eighteen Mile Creek. Vetoes. Royalton, improvement, VII, 364, 456; enlargement of west branch, 449.

Eighth Avenue Railroad, New York. Statement of receipts, VI, 66.

Eighth Judicial District. Additional justices for, VII, 837; X, 850, 936; included in fourth judicial department, IX, 546. Vetoes. Law library, VII, 220; additional stenographers for, IX, 286.

Eighth Ward Savings Bank, New York. Charter, veto, VI, 213.

Eight Men. Powers of, I, 2.

Eisendecher, Karl J. G. von. Accompanies Prince Henry to Assembly chamber at his reception, X, 480.

Ejectment. To test validity of Van Rensselaer titles, IV, 412; proposed Code provision, veto, VII, 187.

Elberon, New Jersey. President Garfield dies at, VII, 678.

Elbridge. Vetoes. Jordan academy and free school district No. 4, VI, 81; Chatfield, loss of public funds, relief, X, 275.

Eldred. Improved Order of Red Men, Delaware Tribe, No. 44, charter, veto, VIII, 877.

Election Day. Last Tuesday of April prescribed, II, 10; limited to one day, III, 771, 851; made a holiday, V, 196; sale of liquor on, amending Liquor Tax Law, veto, X, 162.

Election Districts (General). Required residence in, VI, 471; in cities, III, 881, 882; small districts required, VIII, 671, 919.
    Vetoes. Creating and altering, X, 960; amending general act, IX, 863; Newtown, relative to, VI, 193; Sodus, relative to, 58; West Turin, legalizing. division, repealing act, IX, 818; X, 441; New York, advertising boundaries, IX, 151.

Election Districts (Town Meetings). Town meetings, general act, VI, 676. Vetoes. Sodus, elections in, VI, 58; Newtown, elections in, 193; Philipstown and Carmel, 674; Hurley, Barre and Mount Pleasant, 674; amending Supervisor's Act, VII, 388; West Turin, legalizing division into, IX, 818.

Election Law. Vacancies in Senate and Assembly, how filled, VI, 242; enacted, 1892, IX, 28, 34.

Elections. Bellomont urges suppression of abuses in, I, 77; members of Assembly, act to regulate elections of, 84; free and frequent, recommended, 266; first Legislature, II, 6; ballot box, 35; poll list, 35; oath of electors, 38; under Freedom and Independence Act, 216; State, alleged interference by Federal officers, 1042,

ELECTIONS — (*Continued*).

1054, 1059, 1060; plurality of votes determines result, III, 56; among St. Regis Indians, 135; improved methods in, 158, 313; proposed separation of national, State and local, 248; VII, 134; VIII, 158, 279; of presidential electors, III, 248; bribery, see that title; limiting candidate's expenses, 250, 313, 525; IV, 134; general act, III, 726; registration, 771, 851; in Kings county, 771; "resident," meaning of term, suggested legislative definition, 772; election districts, cities, 881, 882; repeal of New York Registry Law, 988; riot in New York, 1034; secrecy, devices to prevent, IV, 130; betting, 131, 135; legitimate expense of, 134; frauds at, 808; in New York, corrupt practices at, V, 25; of judges, how determined, 58; polls at, 182; compulsory voting, 196; VIII, 676, 930; participation by absent soldiers and sailors, V, 513; alleged interference in, dismissal of army officer, 515; delegates to Constitutional Convention, 748; use of money at, VI, 36, 125; laws should apply equally to all citizens, 37; Federal control of, 37; qualifications of voters, United States Constitution, 38; election districts, town meetings, see that title; laws should be uniform, 125; in New York, act relating to, 125; representatives in Congress, Federal supervision, 255; militia at, dangerous to freedom, 258; frauds, registration not adequate protection against, 389; cumulative voting, proposed in New York charter, 453; minority representation, 460; majority should decide, 461; election districts, required residence in, 471; challenges, 725; contested, Legislature, see CONTESTED ELECTIONS, local judicial officers, 987; betting on results of, VII, 32; honest, promotion of, act of 1880, 435; primary, legislation needed, 839; primaries, regulation of, 978, see PRIMARY ELECTIONS; New York, spring elections recommended, VIII, 15; in cities, constitutional provision, 17; non-partisan board, New York, 159; Syracuse, issue of water bonds, 258; nominations, limiting rights of voter, 568; to be by ballot, constitutional provision, 573, 584, 952; reform needed in methods, 664; electioneering near polls should be prohibited, 666, 962; act of 1890, 666, 762, 900; coercion of workmen, 667; privileges of employees, 667, 673, 918, 1013; poll clerks, see that title; Twenty-fifth Senate district, 1891, use of irregular ballots, 670; small districts required, 671, 919; electioneering by pay envelopes prohibited, 671, 918, 1001; candidate's statement of expenses, 672, 918, 970, 1001, 1079, 1092; Massachusetts act of 1888, protection of employees, 672; booths for voters, 763, 898, 900, 916, 962, 1010; general statutory provisions, 1890, 895;

Elections — (*Continued*).

method of voting under first Constitution, 913; Senate and Assembly, *viva voce* under first Constitution, 913; political committees, statement of expenses, 918, 970, 1079; IX, 310; Ballot Reform Act, 1890, VIII, 1005; special power to call by concurrent resolution, *quære*, 1061; congressional, Federal ⸜control · of, 1083; Myers' automatic ballot cabinet, use authorized at town meetings, IX, 34; Penal Code, amendments, 34; Cohoes, inspectors and poll clerks, 64; New York city, changing election boards, 102; alleged interference by Federal officers in New York, 103; bi-partisan boards, general act and Constitution of 1894, 102, 309; use of money in, 196; blanket ballot, 308, 393, 554; registration, constitutional provisions, 1894, 309; act of 1895, party emblems, 554; Governor Morton suggests improvement in law, 664; general act of 1896, 665; use of Davis voting machine authorized in cities and towns, 665; frauds, prevention of, act of 1898, 877, 885; metropolitan elections district created, 1898, 885; New York, bi-partisan board established, X, 213; only one ballot should be used, 370; officers in cities, relative to, 629; new provisions relating to registration, 729; special in third-class cities, proposed extension of right to women, 730; campaign contributions, 767; direct nominations, 847; reports of political committees, 847.

Vetoes. General act, II, 10, 34; members of Congress, canvass of, 325; authorizing minors to vote for members of Assembly, 685; colored voters, 686; illegal voting, bill to prevent, IV, 825; non-resident voters, VI, 195; New York, 479; New York, special 495; notices of, VII, 120; inspectors, 130; inspectors, minority representation, 203; Albany, providing for, 203; poll clerks, bi-partisan, 333; Brooklyn, recanvassing result, special case, 370; ballots, prescribing size, weight and appearance, 412; cumulative voting, New York, VIII, 278, 283; inspectors and poll clerks, Queens county, compensation, 340; independence of voters, secrecy of ballot, 566; bribery at, 598; New York, notices, 638; Batavia, place of holding, repeal, 698; ballot bill, 1889, 762; ballot bill, 1890, 949, new bill passed; New York, election advertisements, 1036; Yonkers, bonds for expenses, IX, 61; Ballot Act, amendments, 150; districts, New York, advertising boundaries, 151; Erie county, publication of notices, 153; Myers' automatic ballot machine, authorizing use of, 247; inspectors, Troy, 343; officers, compensation, 463; official ballot, pasters, 477; Davis voting machine, authorizing use of, in towns and counties, 626; officers, compensation in certain counties, 722;

ELECTIONS, VETOES — (*Continued*).

amending act of 1892, 724; amending general law, 801, 863; X, 955; Plattsburgh, amending charter, IX, 819; election districts, amending general law, 863; towns, places of registry and voting, 863; New York, separate department, X, 59, 178; registration and enrollment books, consolidation, 279; West Turin, election districts, repeal, 441; bureau, Erie county, 451; nominations filling vacancies, 705; New York, commissioners of elections, term, 716; forms of registration, 808; districts, creating and altering, 960.

ELECTORAL COMMISSION. Created by Congress, VII, 33; result of action, 33.

ELECTORS. Census of, II, 305, 510.

ELECTRICAL SUBWAYS. Commission, cost of, 1891, IX, 11.

VETOES. Amending act, VIII, 871; New York, right to construct, compensation for, 887; New York, repealing act of 1897, IX, 875.

ELECTRICITY. Motive power on canals, VI, 242, 539; IX, 168, 305, 453, 600; wires, placing under ground, resolution of inquiry, VII, 865; use in inflicting death penalty, VIII, 37; State commission established, transfer of powers, 244, 312; electrical subways, New York, act relative to, 450; power created at Niagara Falls, IX, 307; Cataract General Electric Company, contract to experiment with electrical conductors on canals, 454; price for power, 456; New York, sale to city and to private consumers, X, 763; New York, manufacture of, 764, 804.

VETOES. Used by gaslight companies, VII, 864; Brooklyn, VIII, 132; New York, electrical conductors, right to construct, compensation, 887; investigation, Senate committee, 1890, printing testimony, 1038; electrical communications on canals, reappropriation, X, 465; as motive power on canals, experiments, 572; regulating price in certain cities, 585.

ELECTRIC LIGHT. VETOES. Owego, bill relative to, VIII, 129; at Auburn prison, 851; West Troy, establishing commission, 1117; Buffalo State Hospital, 1137; Syracuse Institution for Feeble-Minded Children, 1138; Hudson River State Hospital, IX, 78; Binghamton State Hospital, 78; Lockport, establishing system, 730, 786; New York House of Refuge, establishing system, 770; Salem, establishing system, 819; interference with meters and wires, X, 311; Syracuse, establishing plant, 327, 474; Yonkers, electric light wires and appurtenances, supervision and inspection, 433; Custodial Asylum for Feeble-Minded Women, Newark, duplicate unit, 544; Thomas Asylum for Indian Children, 544; State Agricultural Experiment

ELECTRIC LIGHT — (*Continued*).

    Station, 546; Lockport, lighting contracts, 636; Hudson House of Refuge, 647; Custodial Asylum for Women, Newark, 653; Woman's Relief Corps Home, 654; Bedford House of Refuge for Women, 656; Camden, legalizing proceedings for electric light system, 708.

ELECTRIC LIGHT COMPANIES. Supervising commission recommended, VIII, 1078; proposition to place under supervision of Railroad Commission, X, 220.

    VETOES. Assessment, VII, 934; Edison Electric Illuminating Company, Brooklyn, right to use streets, VIII, 591; contracts with villages, IX, 126, 623; becoming railroad corporations, 246; in towns and villages, acquiring real estate, X, 159.

ELECTROCUTION. Infliction of death penalty by, VIII, 37, 484; commission to examine subject, 37, 484; newspapers not to publish details of execution, IX, 22; prohibition repealed, 23; separate single building for all executions, 23; X, 614; Governor Morton recommends separate building for purposes of, IX, 658; apparatus, purchase of patent rights, veto, X, 567.

ELEVATED RAILROADS. New York, proposed, VI, 245; New York, act approved, 905; rapid transit needed in New York, VII, 857; Brooklyn, act relative to, VIII, 129; New York, rates of fare, IX, 500.

    VETOES. New York Rapid Transit Company, charter, VI, 585; New York Warehouse and Railway Company, charter, 686; extending road, 715; Brooklyn, Atlantic avenue, VII, 394; Brooklyn, Water street, 446; New York city, fares, 850; Brooklyn, preventing construction in certain streets, VIII, 291; Brooklyn Elevated Railroad Company, annulling agreement with railroad commissioners, 293; income percentage, special tax receipts, custody and disbursement, Harvey claim, 886; construction outside New York, 889; percentage tax receipts, Harvey, 1160; IX, 141; regulating travel on, 626; hours of labor, 626; New York, conferring power on New York and New Jersey Bridge Company, X, 303.

ELEVATORS. Grain, act regulating charges, VIII, 603. VETOES. Steam, protection of openings, VII, 208; in buildings in New York, IX, 445, 461; at Brooklyn bridge, 806; in mercantile establishments, regulating use of, X, 594.

ELEVENTH AVENUE RAILROAD COMPANY. Relief, veto, VIII, 1119.

ELFORD, CAPTAIN. Lands French prisoners at New York, I, 166.

ELGIN. Botanic garden at, purchase of, II, 579.

ELIZABETH, QUEEN. Privy Council records from time of, IV, 182; House of Commons, elections to, VIII, 984.

ELIZABETHTOWN. Deposit of arms at, II, 682; deposit of military stores at, 755, 769, 770; arsenal, seizure of arms, III, 684.

ELKO. Bridge over Allegany river, veto, X, 698.

ELLERY. Compensation of supervisor, special services, veto, VI, 588.

ELLETT, JAMES T. Secretary, Richmond county park commissioners, compensation, veto, X, 959.

ELLICOTT. VETOES. Improving roads and bridges, VI, 47; compensation of supervisor, special services, 588.

ELLICOTT, JOSEPH. Member of commission to distribute appropriation for Niagara frontier sufferers, II, 787.

ELLICOTT CREEK. Improvement of, III, 763.

ELLINGTON. Fish hatchery, veto, X, 787.

ELLIOT, ANDREW. Lieutenant-Governor and Acting-Governor, I, Pref. x.

ELLIS, DEWITT C. Bank Superintendent, charges against, VII, 56, 65, 122; removed, 58, 305; index to record of trial, veto, 226, 461.

ELLIS, SIR HENRY. Librarian, British Museum, aid to Mr. Brodhead, IV, 183.

ELLIS, JOHN, BRIGADIER-GENERAL. Detachment of militia, 1812, II, 743.

ELLISBURGH. VETOES. Bridges, VI, 98; Union Literary Society, changing name, VIII, 980; changing name, enlarging income limit, IX, 56.

ELLIS ISLAND. Acquisition of, II, 636, 641.

ELLISON, THOMAS, COLONEL. Letter from, Indian incursions in Ulster county, I, 594.

ELMIRA. Railroad to Williamsport, Pennsylvania, III, 527; advantages derived from internal improvements, 815; rendezvous of troops, Civil War, V, 400; rendezvous alleged to be overflowing, 562; reformatory at, VI, 58, see ELMIRA REFORMATORY; riots of 1877, VII, 152; battle of Newtown, Sullivan's campaign, celebration, 1084; number of excise licenses, 1887, VIII, 359; excise license fees, 1889, 685.

VETOES. Ours Hose Company No. 4, charter, VI, 56; Southern Tier Savings Bank, amending charter, 324; common council, legalizing acts, 845, new bill passed; State fair, reconstruction of buildings, VII, 90; Chemung river bridge, bonding for, 578; damages for defective streets, notice required, 843; revising charter, new ward, VIII, 64; political primaries and conventions, 386; amending charter, VII, 807, 934; VIII, 1041; IX, 785; X, 583; law library at, 1892; library established, 1895, IX, 45; fire department bonds, 734; law library, appropriation, 769; Newtown creek improvement, Court of Claims, X, 588, 708; dyke along Chemung river, 645.

ELMIRA FEMALE COLLEGE. Changing name, veto, VII, 506; VIII, 62.

ELMIRA FIREMEN'S ASSOCIATION. Relative to, veto, VII, 806.

ELMIRA REFORMATORY. Established, VI, 58, 110; contract labor prohibited, 110; appropriation for, 110, 234; VII, 11; commissioners appointed, VI, 233; architect's report on examination of, 568; estimates and expenditures, 650; statement of appropriations, 872, 939; completion and use of buildings, VII, 10, 147; age limit of prisoners, 11; fiscal year established, 297; system of labor in, 527; number of inmates, 702; not self-sustaining, 702; abolition of public account system of labor, substitution of piece plan, 764; indeterminate sentences, 955; IX, 330; transfers to State prisons, VII, 955; IX, 330, 389; investigation, 1893, 337; charges against managers, 388; terms of confinement should be fixed by court, 832; board of managers required to visit, X, 336; overcrowded, transfer of inmates, 501.

VETOES. Danolds claim, VII, 375, 787; industrial fund, 486; convicts, imprisonment, 666; various appropriations, 784; Worthington claim, 788; crime committed in, expenses of trial, submission to Board of Claims, 931; transportation facilities, IX, 135, 244; Revision Act, X, 62; repairs and improvements, 295; transfers to, amending State Charities Law, 312; domestic trade school buildings, electric plant repairs, 548; sentences to, 917.

ELMIRA (Town). Court of Claims, Newtown creek improvement, veto, X, 588, 708.

ELMWOOD. Taxes, enforcement of, veto, IX, 723.

EMANCIPATION. Of slaves in New York, II, 881; gradual, proposed, III, 34, 99; agitation intended to produce, 575; President's proclamation, V, 473; Kentucky protests against, 500; no claim for value of slaves, 791.

EMBALMERS. State Board established, IX, 265.

EMBARGO. Imposed on certain vessels, I, 622; of Council of Safety, II, 30; by Congress on provisions, 46; law, seizures under, 57, 58; proposed suspension as to flour and corn, 68; congressional resolution on, 81; inland, Massachusetts requests repeal of, 91; Connecticut, repeal of, 110; on flour, meal and wheat, 114, 120, 127; enforcement of, 118; act for, veto, 125; by Federal government, 617; effect of, 632; limiting duration of, proposed amendment, 665, 827.

EMBEZZLEMENTS. Protection of banks against, II, 998; by public officers, IV, 562, 615; VI, 727; fraudulently obtaining money for alleged charitable purposes, IV, 563; by public officers, punishment increased, VI, 638.

EMERALD BENEFICIARY ASSOCIATION. Supreme Council, charter, veto, VIII, 876.

EMERGENCY CERTIFICATES. Passage of bills, constitutional provision, VII, 43, see CERTIFICATES OF NECESSITY FOR IMMEDIATE PASSAGE OF BILL.

EMIGH, NICHOLAS, CAPTAIN. Funds received by, II, 766.

EMIGRATION. See also IMMIGRATION. From England and Holland, practical termination of, II, 955; commissioners of, see that title; statistics, IV, 485, 611; commutation fund, relief granted from, 644; foreign, an element of prosperity, 850; Indianapolis Convention, report of delegates, VI, 263; creating board of commissioners, veto, 511; passengers, indemnity bond, act unconstitutional, 997, 1001; VII, 14, 432; Federal legislation needed, 309; tax on steamship companies, inspection, unconstitutional, 712; Appropriation Act, 1882, approved, 802; new commission created, 832.

EMIGRANTS. To be encouraged, II, 232; support by State, 365; bond to indemnify against expense of, 384; frauds on, IV, 557, 720; aid to, 645; commutation tax, 645, 719, 849; cholera among, 719; Castle Garden, 851; care of sick and destitute, V, 22; Asylum for Insane, number of inmates, VII, 958.

EMINENT DOMAIN. Acquisition of property for quarantine purposes, V, 718; waterworks companies, VI, 285; taking private property for private use, 286, 605, 643; X, 458; mining companies, bill withdrawn, 606; principle not applicable to cemeteries, 643; subject of, discussed by Attorney-General, VII, 242; cemeteries, removing remains from private grounds, VIII, 1118; second taking, IX, 508; streams as public highways, condemnation proceedings, act of 1902, X, 457.

VETOES. Taking land for cemeteries, VI, 163, 208, 607; highway, special act, 188; Buffalo and New York Oil Tankage and Transportation Company, charter, 502; Nyack Waterworks Company, 504; Brooklyn Elevated Silent Safety Railway Company, charter, 595; New York Warehouse and Railway Company, 685; New York Rapid Transit Company, 694; pipe line companies, VII, 241; electric light poles and wires, 866; Round Lake Association, water supply, right to condemn property, IX, 794; New York, condemnation proceedings, pay of commissioners, X, 179; incomplete proceedings, restoring land to owner, 260; acquiring materials for highway construction, 384; condemnation, proceedings necessary, 442; New York, acquisition of land by board of estimate and apportionment, 580; railroads, power of condemnation, 710; amending Condemnation Law, 761.

EMMONS, EBENEZER. Geological survey, geologist, second district, III, 640, 754, 991; IV, 461; report of, III, 644, 683, 754; IV, 81.

EMMONS, EBENEZER, JR. Coloring plates for geological survey, IV, 463.

EMPIRE GAS COMPANY. Rights considered, X, 659.

EMPIRE YACHT CLUB. Charter, veto, VII, 509.

ENACTING CLAUSE. Statements in, controversy concerning, I, 110; instruction relative to, 493.

ENDICOTT, GEORGE. Lithographing illustrations, geological survey, III, 995, 998.

ENFIELD RIFLES. Use of, V, 392, 414, 769.

ENGINEER. To examine frontier fortifications, I, 77; to locate fort in Indian country, 88; Captain Redknap appointed for colony, 125; visits Albany, 130; for colony, appointed by home government, 371; report on New York fortifications, 467; to report as to New York fortifications, 562; deposit of maps and plans, III, 934; consulting, canals, tenure of office, X, 596.

  VETOES. New York, powers and duties, VI, 715; New York, relative to, X, 60; for State Architect, appropriation, 552.

ENGLAND. French set up impostor as King, I, 97; premium on exportation of manufactures, 198; frequent elections of members of Parliament, 267; maintains land force in colony, 276; war with Spain, 187, 286; jealous of New York, 294; France declares war against, 316; declares war against France, 602; declares war against Spain, 666; New York's influence in promoting intercourse with colonies, 737; disputes with colonies, 766; emigration from, practical termination of, II, 955; history of agriculture in, 956; railroad established in, III, 327; first mention of railroads, 396; obtaining historical records from, 751; silk culture in, 946; instruction of idiots, IV, 555; return to specie payments, VI, 135; cumulative voting, 544; right to hold real estate, equality of American citizens, 551; use of ballot at elections, VIII, 583, 777; suffrage not universal, 897; Corrupt Practices Act, 819, 1079, 1093; House of Commons, contested elections, historical sketch, 983, 1075; probate and succession tax, 1067; university extension, IX, 17; Central Lunacy Commission, 312; participation in Cotton State Exposition, 581; grants in New York colony, relative to, veto, X, 450; illiteracy as compared with New York, 859; railroads, liability for injuries to employees, 925.

ENGLISH CONQUEST. New York, I, 1; Articles of Capitulation, 3.

ENNIS, JOHN W. Confidential inspector, Bureau of Charitable Institutions, Comptroller's office, compensation, veto, X, 558.

ENRIGHT, JAMES N. Relief, veto, X, 53, 178.

ENTAILS. Abolition of, IV, 712. VETOES. Act relating to, II, 239; abolishing, 779.

ENUMERATION. See also CENSUS (STATE). What included in, VIII, 141.

ENUMERATORS. Under Census Act, V, 602; method of appointment, VIII, 42, 1057; suggested application of civil service rules to, 42, 57, 68.

EPIDEMIC. At Philadelphia, II, 336; at New York, 364, 366, 372, 382, 451, 570, 1017; III, 12; at Albany, II, 364, 366, 372; fever, 536; IV, 275; cholera, III, 394; ravages in 1832, 399; malignant fever at Mount Pleasant prison, IV, 275; yellow fever in Richmond county, 438; Asiatic cholera, 1849, 468; cholera on emigrant ships, 719; in Portsmouth and Norfolk, Virginia, 852; floating hospital in New York, V, 184; in Asia, westward movement, 699; yellow fever, historical sketch, VI, 782; typhoid fever, 1903, X, 623; investigation as to infectious and contagious diseases, 624; investigations by State Department of Health, appropriation, veto, 787.

EPILEPTIC COLONY. Craig Colony established, 1894, IX, 240; new asylum, X, 726; establishing, veto, IX, 240.

EQUAL PROTECTION OF THE LAWS. Turnpike companies, II, 594; Fourteenth Amendment, V, 790; VII, 591; X, 882; oleomargarine, use of coloring matter, veto, VII, 591.

EQUITABLE LOAN AND TRUST COMPANY. Charter, veto, VI, 341.

EQUITY. Testimony in, how taken, IV, 367; proceedings in, alteration of, 367; proposed Special Terms, 367, 414; use of injunctions, V, 56; application to proceedings against public officers, VI, 731; obligation of State, 893.

VETOES. Vesting powers of, in Surrogate's Court, VII, 79, 113, 189; actions, compulsory accountings in, X, 443.

ERIE CANAL. Employment of convict labor in construction of, II, 875; Ohio offers aid in construction of, 891; progress of construction, 901, 962, 1007, 1044, 1094; III, 10, 24; IV, 474; construction begun at Utica, II, 902; effect on western commerce, 966; connection with Buffalo harbor, 991; opposition to construction of, 1008; proceeds from sale of Grand Island, 1010; connection with Lake Ontario, 965, 1011; III, 68, 69, 166; tax on contiguous territory, II, 1012; limiting speed of boats, 1096; tonnage duties, claim of United States, III, 27, 50, 76, 154; longest in world, 66; extension to Black Rock, 67; canal connection with Susquehanna river, 70, 165; connection with Allegany river, 70, 104, 165; connection with Black river, 70, 166; completion and opening, 118, 465; lateral connections, 167, 329; cost per mile, 200; debt, 304, 333, 479, 552, 736; IV, 252; water for Watervliet arsenal, III, 335; redemption of stock, 372; income, 410; enlargement, 461, 506, 552, 622, 670, 671, 709, 729, 787, 793, 816, 864, 887, 955; IV, 388, 543, 663; extension at Buffalo, III, 554; construction debt paid, 619, 887; aqueduct over Genesee river at Rochester, 552, 670; feeder, payments for, 763; length of, 811; loan for, 671, 816, 865; locks, movement of boats through, 893; transportation of wheat and flour, 893; work of enlargement suspended, 959,

ERIE CANAL — *(Continued)*.

1009, 1043, 1049; IV, 13, 102; work should be resumed, 17, 59, 61; enlargement at Rome, use of, 61; stock, when redeemable, 201; enlargement debt, 252, 544; feeder, construction resumed, 369; work of enlargement resumed, 371, 390, 424, 586, 599; suspension of enlargement work a mistake (Young), 390; appropriation for enlargement, 391, 425, 475, 678, 735, 743; expense of completing enlargement, 544, 676, 735; V, 49, 68; pier at Buffalo, IV, 571; plan for early completion of enlargement, 623; sketch of, by Governor Seymour, 662; more water needed, 672; locks completed, 686; improvements needed, 690, 734; rapid increase of revenues, 819; tolls, V, 65, 153, 257, 361; steam navigation on, 69; enlargement completed, 255, 365; proposed new locks, 502, 787; tonnage, 1864, 594; subject to admiralty laws of Congress, 720; tonnage capacity, 785; average time from Buffalo to New York, 785; relations to commerce, VI, 14; trust for people, 14; neglect of repairs and improvements, 15; value and importance of, 536; use of steam dredging machine, 540; not to be abandoned, 738; enlarged locks and unenlarged waterway, 740; seventy-two locks, 741; comparative financial statement, 746; increasing capacity, 797; Watervliet bridge, completion of, approved, 854; repairs, towing path and slop walls, Utica and other points, approved, 854; repairs, Jordan level, Weedsport, appropriation for, approved, 856; Port Byron, rebuilding wall, 857; Buffalo and Black Rock, improvements, 858; Medina, improvements, 858; deepening near Macedon locks, 859; road bridge, Rochester, Averill and Munger streets, 859; Port Gibson, repairs, 860; Buffalo basin, deepening 860; Black Rock harbor, dredging and excavating, 860; State dam, Scajaquady creek, removal, 861; Pittsford and Brighton, damages, 861; Pittsford, rebuilding wall, 862; State policy concerning, 925; financial statement, 1875, 930; extraordinary repairs, sums needed to settle contracts, 992; deepening, general appropriation, 994; proposed enlargement, VII, 517; general improvements, 1894, VIII, 13; dependence on Adirondack water supply, IX, 147; tonnage, 1893, 301; Enlargement Acts of 1895 and 1903, 305; enlargement, survey for, 1900, X, 141, 215; improvement, State Engineer's special report, 1901; 244; problems and possibilities, 1901, 249; Improvement Act of 1903, 252, 363, 496.

VETOES. Appropriation for enlargement, IV, 194; locks, western division, VI, 347; constructing walls, 347; Mohawk and Ilion Horse Railroad Company, using berme bank, 581; settling claim for work, 698; Canajoharie, repairs, 852; eastern division, iron

ERIE CANAL, VETOES—(Continued).

bridge superstructures, 853; Rocky Rift feeder, farm-bridge, 854; Utica, Genesee Street bridge, 854; wall benches and slop walls, 855; blind drains, section 111, 855; Syracuse, rebuilding walls, 855; East Frankfort, repairs, 856; middle division, iron superstructures, 857; Syracuse, foot-bridge, Franklin street, 857; bridge over Tonawanda creek, 859; Macedon, rebuilding wall, 860; western division, iron bridge superstructures, 860; Newark, rebuilding vertical wall, 860; Syracuse, raceway wall, 868; Brockport, lift-bridge, 1004; VII, 116; Brighton, lift-bridge, VI, 1005; VII, 96, 117; West Troy, lift-bridge, Genesee street, VI, 1005; Lockport, lift-bridge, Exchange street, 1005; VII, 115; Palmyra, lift-bridge, VI, 1005; Fultonville, rebuilding bridge, 1007; Tonawanda, canal bridges, 1007; Tonawanda, State ditch, three bridges, 1007; VII, 95, 96; Mudlock, foot-bridge, VI, 1007; VII, 95; Lockport, iron bridge, Prospect street, VI, 1007; Rochester, approach to canal bridge, Averill street, 1008; VII, 117; Buffalo harbor, Bird Island pier, VI, 1008; Buffalo, bridge, Austin street, VII, 114; Palmyra, bridge, Earle and Kent streets, 116; Cazenovia dam, reappropriation, 119; Tonawanda, foot-bridge, Kohler street, 232; Tonawanda, bridge, Main and Delaware streets, 233, 361, 577; Rochester, bridge, Brown and Smith streets, 324; Tonawanda feeder, improvement, 358; Geddes, bridge, Magnolia street, 361, 576; Rochester, bridge, Lyell street, 362, 589; Lockport, bridge, Mill street, 363; North Tonawanda, State ditch, two bridges, 363; Eighteen Mile Creek, improvement, 363; Syracuse, bridge, Catherine street, 364; Schenectady, fence on berme bank, 364; Tonawanda, fence on berme bank, 364; Buffalo, sewerage Black Rock, 365, 457; Amherst, cleaning ditches, 365; enlarging west branch of Eighteen Mile creek, 449; dredging Ohio basin, Buffalo, 455; dredging Erie basin, Buffalo, 456; Brockport, culvert, 456; Royalton, cleaning out Eighteen Mile creek, 456; Jordan, ditch, 456; Tonawanda, State ditches, 456; Tonawanda dam and feeder, cleaning, 457; Murray, draining lands of Isaac U. Cole, 457; Tonawanda, canal bridge, 505, 665; Utica, bridge, Genesee street, 506; VIII, 206; IX, 732; Fultonville, enlarging bridge, VII, 508; Medina, bridge, Prospect street, 577; Rome, retaining wall, Whitesboro street, 586; Tyrrell claim, loss of boat, 599; Wayne county, ditch for drainage, 908; Brockport, bridge, 931; lengthening lock No. 46, 933; Utica, pipe under, 938; Rochester, bridge-tenders, 1024; Newark, bridge, 1099; VIII, 131, 887; Spencerport, waste gates, VII, 1100; Buffalo,

ERIE CANAL, VETOES —(*Continued*).

bridge, Hudson street, VIII, 293; Rome, bridge, George street, 294; IX, 628; improvement of Dead creek, 452; Hamilton and Madison, bridge, 453; Whitestown, culvert, enlargement, 453; Fultonville, bridge, 453; Utica, sewer, Andes avenue, 454; Ilion, vertical wall, 521; Utica, sewer or culvert under canal, 710; leakage ditch, Manlius, 849; leakage ditch, Kirkville, 850; Syracuse, bridge, Crouse avenue, 885; Syracuse, bridge, Clinton street, 886; Royalton, vertical wall, 887; IX, 48; Rome, canal wall, reappropriation, VIII, 890; Schenectady, bridge, Church street, 890; Herkimer, completing vertical wall, 1112; culvert under, Utica, 1132; Oak Orchard creek and canal feeder, improvement, IX, 55; basin, Black Rock harbor, dredging, 58; Rochester, bridge, Monroe avenue, 59; increase of lockage, 110; State ditch, Liverpool, removing obstructions, 150; Rome, canal feeder wall, 239; Syracuse, bridge, Crouse avenue and Beach street, 245; Buffalo, dredging Ohio basin, 256; Buffalo, towing-path wall, Austin street, 449; wall, Verona, 469; elevating locks, 606; Schenectady, street on canal land, 788, 789; new blue line maps, X, 297, 423; State sewer, Canastota, arch over creek, 313; Skaneateles feeder, repairs, 314; Lyons, bridge, Water street, 314; Minden, bridge, 314; Tonawanda, bridge, North Niagara street, 314, 435; Tonawanda, moving bridge, 319; Royalton, drainage of flooded lands in, 437; State ditches, cleaning, 569, 644; Onondaga county, bridge, Willis avenue and Van Vleck road, 569; Durhamville, steel trunk aqueduct, 573, 790; drainage, providing for, Somerset and Hartland, 645; Oneida feeder, culvert under, 935; Watervliet, retaining wall, 646; Erie basin, improvement, Buffalo, 652; Amsterdam, bridge, Minaville street, 698; Erie basin, deepening, 814; bridge, Rochester, Lyell avenue, 929.

ERIE COUNTY. Silk culture in, III, 945; includes part of Tonawanda reservation, V, 199; average excise license fees, 1889, VIII, 686; exempted from Dog Tax Law, 823; Genesee boundary, act relative to, 1102; county clerk, salaried office, 1103; sheriffs, salaried office, 1103; coroners, act of 1893, 1153; increase in population, IX, 3; sheriff calls for military aid, railroad strike, 1892, 160; expense of railroad strike, 161; State appropriation for, 161; highways, cost of labor system, 1892, 199; insane, care of, county and State systems compared, 228; Jury Act, 1895, 514; transfer tax assistant, X, 108; indirect taxes received from, 1902, 483; estimated contribution to cost of barge canal, 602.

ERIE COUNTY — (*Continued*).

VETOES. Street railroads, fares on, V, 653; coroners, VI, 170; Buffalo plankroad, improvement, 195; subjecting to Railroad Aid Act, 214; support of poor, 509; VII, 441; bridge over Tonawanda creek, VI, 696; fishing in Niagara river, 906; Alden, town meeting, legalizing election of highway commissioner, 1034; Surrogate's Court, equity powers, VII, 113; Cayuga Creek road, improvement, 265; supervisors, 266; public buildings and grounds, 354; taxes in Buffalo, collection, 356; Supreme Court clerk, 356; taxes, unpaid, 937; notaries public, increasing number, 1095; publication of legal notices in German newspaper, 390; compensation of court officers, 538; taxation, equalizing real estate, VIII, 752; protection of ducks and fish, 979; boundary, Genesee and Niagara counties, 1102; Tonawanda public parks and places, 1115; coroners, fees and post mortem examinations, 1153; election notices, amending act, IX, 153; county clerk, salaried office, amending act, 272; commissioner of jurors, 514, 516; refunding unexpended balance of money raised for Tonawanda armory site, 795; district attorney, assistants, 800; coroner, fixing term, election of successor, 861; county auditor, election of, 861; sheriff, relative to, X, 61; trust companies, powers, amending act, 318, 320; compensation of deputy sheriffs, 318; sheriff, additional subordinates, purchase of supplies, 380, new act passed; bureau of elections, 451; bridge over Niagara river, Grand Island, 703.

ERIE COUNTY PENITENTIARY. To receive female convicts from eighth district, V, 599.

ERIE COUNTY PIPE LINE COMPANY. Charter, veto, VII, 133.

ERIE COUNTY SOCIETY FOR THE PREVENTION OF CRUELTY TO ANIMALS. Relative to, veto, IX, 869.

ERIE INDIANS. Conquered and extirpated by Five Nations, I, 542.

ERIE AND NEW YORK CITY RAILROAD COMPANY. Extending time for completion, veto, VII, 807.

ERIE VALLEY RAILROAD COMPANY. Asks State aid, VI, 71.

ESCAPES. Reward for recapture, II, 393, 427; punishment for, 426, 478.
VETOES. Relative to, 84; death penalty imposed, 583.

ESCHEAT. Bill for, statements in, II, 406; proposed revenue from, 907; in military tract, relief of occupants, 991; valuable releases by State, 1106; general law needed, VIII, 723, 883; act of 1890, 723, 980, 1014; recall of Sullivan bill, X, 33; Board of Claims, general jurisdiction, veto, IX, 524.
VETOES. Knox, IV, 693; McCaughel, 693; Bashford, VI, 157; Chamberlain, 158; Baldwin, 483; Faenger, 692; Wyoming

ESCHEAT, VETOES —(*Continued*).

County Agricultural Society, 708; Hohenholz, VII, 548; Porter, heirs of Hoenig, 549; Harvey, 550; Stewart, 619; De Groat, 642; McLoughlin, personal estate, 748; Meyer, personal estate, 749; Shriver heirs, 805; Joyce heirs, 805; Neusch, 805; McGee, 805; Steche, 805; Pax, 805; Corbett, 805; Wakeman, 935; Marvin, 1107; Dennison, 1116; Schroeder, 1116; Beattie, VIII, 405; Pierce, 630; Racka, 722; Brunn, 723; McKenna, 725; Thebaud, 731; Straack, 734; Washington, 755; Hurford and Barnett, 882; Spicer, 882, 1036; Scherer, 882; Feller, 882; Greene, 882; Theiss, 890; Bruno, 980; Turner, 1040; Frost, IX, 284; Winship, 285; Sullivan, 370; Dickson, 384; Smith, (Elizabeth), 403; Hyne and Kilgour, 428; Reilly, 467; Kleindinst, 815; Peters, 816; X, 266, 376; Schuyler, X, 252; Cass, 273; Stierle, 273; Kineally, 310; Froelich, 312; Mathews, 312; Riley, 446; Geib, 451; Lang and others, 588; Booth estate, 635; Grady, 704; Coddington, 706; Gibson, 952; Roebuck, 953; Tracy, 954; Watters and Fleming, 958; Power, 958; various bills, names not given, 778.

ESOPUS. Representation in first Assembly, I, 9.

ESOPUS CREEK. VETOES. Toll-bridge across, II, 1081; fish, protection of, VII, 234.

ESSER, JOHN. Board of Claims, veto, VIII, 1166.

ESSEX COUNTY. Arms and ammunition for, II, 636; militia from, 1812, 744, 807; arms and supplies for, 770; survey of railroad route, III, 984; arsenal and equipments to be sold, IV, 495; land in, State park, VI, 629; boundaries relocated, VII, 720; timbered land, acquisition by State, 722; excepted from repeal of Town Auditor's Act, VIII, 50; average excise license fees, 1889, 686; highways, cost of labor system, 1892, IX, 199; insane, care of, county and State systems compared, 228.

VETOES. Levying taxes on certain lands, VI, 188; Jay, separate road district, 332; non-resident highway taxes, 338; bridges in, 556; Newcomb, repealing act, 699; Barber's Point, ferry across Lake Champlain, VIII, 410; Crown Point, ferry across Lake Champlain, 463; Saranac river improvement, IX, 62; fish hatchery at Schroon, 777; sheriff, making office salaried in part, X, 316; Ausable Chasm, acquiring for State park, 317; tax sale, cancellation, Doherty case, 592; sheriff, Chinese prisoners, 701, 708; ferry across Lake Champlain, 953.

ESTATES. Act relative to quieting, I, 11; certain forfeited, authorized to be sold, II, 199, 208; of decedents, distribution after conviction of crime punishable with death or life imprisonment, 336; of decedents, revision of statutes relative to, III, 89.

VETOES. Forfeited, sale of, II, 94, 112, 203; sale of confiscated and forfeited estates, 214; entails and joint tenants, 239, 779; of intestates, administration, relative to, 257, 267; forfeited, limitation of actions, 783.

EUREKA BASIN WAREHOUSE AND MANUFACTURING COMPANY, LONG ISLAND. Powers and privileges, repeal, veto, VII, 766.

EUREKA FIRE HOSE COMPANY. Claim against village of Far Rockaway, veto, X, 324.

EUROPE. Alliance with Roman Catholic princes, I, 622; English successes in, 625; war in, II, 332, 365; all nations of, represented in New York State, IV, 711; new canal projects, VI, 240.

EVANGELICAL LUTHERAN CHURCH OF ST. JAMES, NEW YORK. Relief, veto, X, 60.

EVANS, MARIE P. Court of Claims, veto, X, 708.

EVANS, ROBLEY D. Admiral, accompanies Prince Henry to Assembly chamber at his reception by Assembly, X, 480.

EVANS, W. W. Consulting engineer, Commission on Harbor Defense, V, 569.

EVANS MILLS CEMETERY ASSOCIATION. Raising money for fences, veto, VI, 184.

EVARTS, WILLIAM M. United States Senator, succeeded by Governor Hill, VIII, 1054; member of Tilden Municipal Reform Commission, 1875, IX, 417.

EVERS, WILLIAM H. Troy school janitor, claim, veto, X, 634.

EVERETT, EDWARD. Minister to Great Britian, interview with Lord Aberdeen, colonial history, III, 1014; IV, 175; correspondence with Lord Aberdeen, III, 1016, 1020; IV, 175.

EVIDENCE. Minutes of Court of Chancery, II, 754; by accomplice, 997; in Court of Chancery, how taken, III, 649, 720; deposition taken in this State to be used in other States, 749; statutes, when may be read in, IV, 32; title to land, 346; in equity cases, how taken, 367; sale of liquor, 758; in proceedings for removal of officers, V, 716; presumption, outside contradictory statements, X, 905.

VETOES. Commission to obtain, II, 227; of title to land in military tract, changing rule of, 664; bill for perpetuation of, 1083; agents, informers and spies, VII, 624; taken by legislative investigating committees, composing and printing, 1079; testimony in action against deceased party, VIII, 292; Code, establishing, 292, 890; notary's certificate of protest, 293; of physicians, 639;

EVIDENCE, VETOES—(*Continued*).
     claims for animals slaughtered to prevent spread of disease, 730;
     relative to certain premises in New York, authorizing reception
     of, 889; Code, publication of, 890; of party dying after trial,
     1167; physicians and surgeons, confidential communications, IX,
     44; false pretenses, 259; acknowledgments, proof and effect,
     266; transcripts of testimony, fees, 722; depositions, 792; X,
     313; documentary, IX, 860; record of ancient deeds, X, 386;
     handwriting, proof of, 444; seizure and sale of prohibited
     articles of food, 776; weather records, New York, 955.
EXAMINERS. In chancery, mode of appointment, veto, II, 1054; office
     abolished, IV, 414.
EXCELSIOR HOSE COMPANY, WARWICK. Charter, veto, VII, 507.
EXCELSIOR TEMPLE OF HONOR NO. 23, ALBANY. Charter, veto, VI, 55.
EXCEPTIONS. In criminal cases, delay caused by, IV, 490.
EXCHANGE, RATE OF. See RATE OF EXCHANGE.
EXCHANGE BUILDING, NEW YORK. Acquired by United States for custom
     house, V, 642.
EXCISE. Proceeds appropriated for public debt, I, 171; farmers of,
     bond, 188; act relating to farmers of, 194; new act passed, 240,
     641; farming out policy discontinued, 529; commissioners pro-
     vided, 529; State Department established, 529; excessive number
     of tippling-houses, 660; appropriation for New York Hospital,
     743; proposed for raising revenue, II, 199; restricting licenses,
     427; stills, Federal tax on, 789; licenses, proceeds for agricul-
     tural purposes, 958; laws inadequate, IV, 745; search warrants,
     754; Massachusetts law, 757; revision needed, 799; V, 386, 450;
     VII, 163, 310, 435, 531; new act passed, IV, 802; general act of
     1857, 802; V, 20, 94, 193; VIII, 1058; money appropriated
     for State Inebriate Asylum, V, 87; metropolitan police district,
     VI, 35; metropolitan district, repeal of act recommended, 126;
     laws should be uniform, 127; metropolitan district abolished,
     127; local boards established, 127, 226, 489; tax on sale of
     liquor, VII, 571; violations of law should be repressed, 714;
     alcoholic beverages, statement by Board of Health, VIII, 353;
     uniform laws recommended, election of Governor Tilden, 356;
     certain municipalities, licenses in 1887, 359, 360; prohibition
     versus high license, 362; sumptuary laws, 363, 684; tax should
     be uniform, 437; license fees should be for exclusive local benefit,
     438, 799, 1059; five-gallon sales, act relative to, 440, 798, 811;
     revision of laws, 509, 541, 681, 1058; high license, 356, 545, 684;
     Senate report of committee on general laws, 1888, 640; Re-

EXCISE — (*Continued*).

vision Commission created, 1888, 643; new act passed, 1892, 643, 929; home rule, 441, 683; license fees in force, 1889, 685; Governor Hill's sketch of recent legislation, 802; proposed amendment, 1890, 920; moneys from, distribution of, 1059; revision of 1892, IX, 105; exempting Soldiers and Sailors' Home from general act of 1892, 625; excessive number of saloons, 1895, 665, 698; retail licenses in several States, 1892, 666; Liquor Tax Law, 1896, 666, 696; State Department created, 666; high licenses not provided for by Liquor Tax Law of 1896, 700; local option, proposed extension to cities, X, 736.

VETOES. Amending general act of 1857, revoking licenses, VI, 94; prohibiting sale of liquor on Allegany and Cattaraugus Indian reservations, 97; Brooklyn, reorganizing board, 489; amending act of 1870, 505; local option, 506, 56C; Bath, commissioners, legalizing acts of, VII, 178; civil damages, proposed Code provisions, 190; licenses, terminating May 1, VII, 265; Ontario county, habitual drunkards, 266; amending act, New York, 803; licenses, Carthage, 1047; Troy, violations, amending act, 1101; New York, commissioners, appointment, VIII, 273, 656; prohibiting sale of liquor on State property, 291, 351; prohibiting sale of liquors within half a mile of Willard Insane Asylum, 340; McCollum and McCleary, commissioners, Salem, legalizing acts, 354; amending general act as to New York and Brooklyn, 355; tax on sales, 436, 797; Brooklyn, licenses in concert buildings, 462; Corning, license fees, payment to St. Joseph's Orphan Asylum, 465; New York, excise moneys, disposition of, 467; moneys in towns, 469; regulating sale of intoxicating liquors, 540; tax on beverages, 638, 797; high license bill, 1889, 688, 801; revision bill, 1889, 801; boards of, amending act of 1874, 973; Brooklyn, amending charter, IX, 151, 152; Ontario county, disposition of moneys, 267; commissioners, compensation, 275; Brooklyn, excise department, 633; Hornellsville, money, payment to St. James Mercy Hospital, 723; buildings for hotel purposes, consents, 802; sale of liquor on election days, X, 162.

EXECUTION. Exemptions, IV, 39, 492; exemption of homestead, 493, 558.

VETOES. Amending Code, VIII, 1040; indemnity bonds on execution, IX, 150; claim of property by third person, how tried, X, 807.

EXECUTORS. Powers of, 11, 986.

VETOES. Amending act, VI, 105; amending Revised Statutes, IX, 272; judicial settlement of accounts, 283; inventory, fees of

EXECUTORS, VETOES —(*Continued.*
    appraisers, X, 61; accountings, proceedings in Surrogate's Court,
    282.
EXECUTIVE CHAMBER. New capitol, completion of, VII, 430, 523; oc-
    cupation, 694; State arms to be hung on walls of, 727; purchase
    of standard geographic time globe, veto, VIII, 108.
EXECUTIVE LAW. Enacted, 1892, IX, 28; amending, veto, 218.
EXECUTIVE POWER. See also GOVERNOR and VETO. How exercised in
    early colonial period, I, 1; under Duke of York, 7; under State
    government, II, 2, 114; control of, 114; removal of officers, III,
    1021; defective under State Constitution, VI, 395; should not be
    distributed among large boards, 459.
EXECUTIVE RESIDENCE. Proposition to use part of new capitol, VI, 229;
    purchase of, VII, 178.
EXEMPT FIREMEN'S BENEVOLENT FUND ASSOCIATION, BRONX BOROUGH.
    Headquarters, veto, X, 581.
EXEMPTION. From involuntary taxes, I, 699; taxation, certain manufac-
    turing establishments, II, 876; from jury duty, of persons en-
    gaged in certain manufacturing establishments, 876; militia, of
    persons engaged in certain manufacturing establishments, 876;
    militia, from personal tax, suggested, 979; militia, Quakers,
    III, 85, 880; IV, 39; from executions, 39, 492; homesteads,
    493, 558; of militia from highway labor, 557, 727; of militia
    from jury duty, 557; from military service, V, 456, 613; taxa-
    tion, railroad aid bonds, 813; VIII, 128; from local taxation,
    VI, 78, 180, 215; tax, should be extended, 371; plan of Tax
    Commission, 372; taxation, New York Historical Society, chang-
    ing site, exemption continued, VIII, 824; taxation, historical
    societies, 824; New York Hospital, changing site, taxation
    exemption continued, 825; taxation,— hospitals, 824; — fire com-
    panies, 878, 972; — exemption laws should be uniform, 973;
    special laws prohibited, IX, 232, taxation, New York and
    Brooklyn bridge, 91.
    VETOES. Jurors, X, 808, 953; jury duty, Flatbush, firemen, VIII,
        728; jury, Kings county, 1037; jurors, New York, IX, 631;
        Soldiers and Sailors' Home from General Excise Law, 625;
        Supreme Grange Life Association, payment before com-
        mencing business, 802; real property, report on, X, 439;
        poll tax, Westchester county, 952.
    TAXATION. Railroad receiving local aid, VI, 164; Industrial
        Exhibition Company, 331, 482; New York Hospital, 703;
        Rockland County House of Good Shepherd, VII, 266; In-
        ternational Fire Association, 413; library company, 345;

EXEMPTION, VETOES —(*Continued*).

Ebenezer Baptist church, 931; West Side German Dispensary, New York, VIII, 294; Young Women's Association, Troy, 332; German American School Society, 460; Masonic Hall Association, Buffalo, 464; Methodist Episcopal Hospital, Brooklyn, 464; Bedford Reformed Dutch church, 465; S. R. Smith Infirmary, 538; agricultural and horticultural societies, 619; Gallaudet Home, 623; Catholic Union, Albany, 623; Sanitarium for Hebrew Children, 1036; property purchased with pension money, repeal, IX, 113; Sanitarium for Hebrew Children, New York, 152; Ladies' Deborah Nursery and Child's Protectory, 232; Rochester Homeopathic Hospital, 235; St. Vincent's Retreat for the Insane, 253; Larchmont Manor Park Society, 431; Oneida, refunding bonds, 432; Pythian Association, Amsterdam, 449; Syracuse bonds, 450; Grand Army of the Republic posts, 470; property of clergymen, 722; Masonic Association, Utica, 791; University Settlement Society, New York, and Educational Alliance, 794; Beth Israel Hospital Association, 806, 810; Spalding Literary Union, New York, 810; House of Good Shepherd, 868; Missionary Society of the Most Holy Redeemer, release from existing assessments, 868; Young Men's Hebrew Association, 869; X, 179; Missionary Society of the Most Holy Redeemer, New York, 176; St. Joseph's Asylum, New York, 176; New York University, 179; St. John's Armenian Apostolic church, 326; corporations, acquiring property without State, 521; assessments for local improvements, 595; colleges and universities, amending act, 947.

EXPATRIATION. Voluntary, prohibited without Leisler's consent, I, 16; effect of joining enemy, II, 203; act of Congress, 1907, VI, 365.

EXPERT EXAMINER OF MACHINERY. Compensation, office abolished, veto, X, 787.

EXPORTS. Corn and flour, I, 116; of military stores and provisions restricted, 564; of flour and wheat in exchange for salt, II, 79; embargo on, 126; to West Indies, restricted to British vessels, 197; increase of, 596; relation to imports, 1091; from State, not to be taxed, IV, 667; amount from New York, V, 410.

EXPOSITION. See COLUMBIAN EXPOSITION; INTERNATIONAL EXPOSITIONS; WORLD'S FAIR. Tennessee Centennial, 1897, IX, 852.

EX POST FACTO LAW. Taxation, II, 65; suspending finance acts, 129; rights of citizens as result of war, 215; act relating to sequestrations

Ex Post Facto Law — *(Continued).*
    and forfeitures, 234; widows of attainted persons, 582; capital punishment, V, 264.

Expressmen's Savings Bank, New York. Charter, veto, VI, 326.

Extortion. Repeal of act relative to, I, 144; prevention of, II, 77; by railroads, prevention of, veto, VIII, 1128.

Extra Compensation. To executive and judicial officers, II, 449, 460; of judges, 509; prohibited, VI, 403, 540; VII, 49, 158, 223, 259, 372; meaning of, 257, 550; Swift case, quarantine buildings, claim rejected, VII, 373; sums awarded to captain of the port and harbor masters not extra compensation, 1048; to canal contractors, prohibited, VII, 626; IX, 431.

Vetoes. Legislative employees, VII, 372; Sullivan case, new capitol contractor, 499, 791; Erie county, court officers, 539; Sullivan county, town officers, 540; Seneca county, judge and surrogate, salary, 550; Binghamton, police force, 753; keepers of city prison, New York, 773; Troy, increasing salaries of officers, 777; captain of the port and harbor masters, 1055; supervisors, 1115; sheriff, Nassau county, X, 243.

Extradition. Under treaty with Great Britain, II, 1104; act relating to, 1105; under Federal Constitution, III, 350, 596, 777, 778, 852, 869, 915, 917, 922, 1030; IV, 8; Canada's construction of right of, III, 599; Williams case, 583, 594; Philbrook and Kelleran case, 748, 822; application of rule, 777; executive discretion not subject to legislative control, 778, 1030; Johnson, Smith and Gansey case, 852, 869, 920, 932, 936; IV, 47; Curry case, forgery, III, 910, 915; what crimes subject to, 920; case of stealing a slave, 937, 938; Greenman case, 937; Rhode Island case, 1037; international, 1038; conference of Governors relative to, VIII, 689; case of William R. Foster, X, 59, 473; claim of New York Produce Exchange for services, Foster case, veto, 473.

Extraordinary Session (Colony). Tenth Assembly, I, 119.

Extraordinary Session (State). Meaning of term, II, 251, 278, 280; III, 51; recommended by Congress on Tariff Act, II, 277; of Congress, 398; Senate alleges Governor's proclamation indiscreetly issued, 1824, III, 51; requested by Legislature following resignation of twelve senators, IV, 578; Governor King declines to call (panic of 1857), V, 44; constitutional provision, VII, 728; VIII, 132, 135; IX, 154; X, 820, 821; what subjects may be considered at, VIII, 135; X, 821; enumeration bill, cannot include subjects not recommended by Governor, VIII, 135; journal of proceedings, 1905, X, 830; 1778, October, II, 50; 1779, August, 78; 1780, January, 87; 1780, May, 96; 1780, September, 105; 1781, January, 114; 1781, October, 146; 1782, February, 163; 1788, December, 289; 1789,

EXTRAORDINARY SESSION (State) — (*Continued*).

July, 301; 1798, August, 420; 1814, September, 800; 1824, August, III, 38; 1827, June (Senate), 195; 1832, June, 392; 1851, June, IV, 578; 1853, April, 694; 734; 1876, May, Senate, trial of charges against Superintendent Ellis, VII, 58, 122; 1885, May, VIII, 43, 132; 1838, July, 643; 1892, April, 1057; IX, 84, 154; 1898, July, 876, 1899, May, X, 64; 1905, June, 828; 1907, July, 852.

F.

FACTOR. Relations to principal, III, 89.

FACTORY INSPECTOR. Office created, VIII, 164; duties as to apprentices, 323; women deputies, appointment of, 837; cost of, 1891, IX, 11; act of 1892, scope of, 163; additional inspectors and deputies, 160; additional deputies, 1899, X, 7; service should be efficient, 10; proposed appointment of unsalaried, 96; appropriation, 1900, 188; office abolished, 1901, 189; additional legislation needed, 857.

VETOES. Female deputies, appropriation, VIII, 885; reports of accidents, 1039; counsel, appointment by Attorney-General, IX, 403; deputy, labor on public works, 864.

FAENGER, FRITZ. Escheat, veto, VI, 692.

FAIRBANKS, JASON. Keeper of arsenal, Watertown, report on seizure of arms, III, 683.

FAIRCHILD, CHARLES S. Attorney-General, opinion, vacancies in office, failure to take oath, VII, 44; special counsel, Sage case, appropriation, 582, 905; communication to Governor, relative to appointment of William Church Osborn as State commissioner in lunacy, X, 43.

FAIRCHILD, EGBERT H. Relief, veto, VI, 595.

FAIRCHILD, NANCY. Relief, veto, II, 716.

FAIRFIELD. VETOES. Normal school at, VIII, 888; separate road district, amending act, IX, 250.

FAIRFIELD COLLEGE OF PHYSICIANS AND SURGEONS. Prosperous condition of, II, 904; III, 118, 408; course of instruction in, II, 904; work of, III, 297, 338.

FAIRS. Recommended, III, 386.

FALCONER, WILLIAM. See FAULKENER.

FALKLAND ISLAND. Fort Egmont, Spanish seizure of, I, 737.

FALSE PRETENSES. Evidence, veto, IX, 259.

FANCHER, ALBERT T. Senate, member of joint legislative committee on services in memory of former Governor Higgins, X, 963.

FANCHER, E. L. Approves Harvey claim against New York city, VIII, 1162.

FANNING, WILLIAM. Bond for return of arms, II, 774.

FANWOOD. New York Institution for the Instruction of the Deaf and Dumb located at, IV, 793.

FAREWELL, GEORGE. Appointed to draft bills for Assembly, I, 20.

FAR INDIANS. Negotiations with, I, 201; trade with, 206, 214, 218, 223, 225, 315; delegation from, to trade at Albany, 206; trade increasing, 212; trade laws not well executed, 217; encouragement of, 243; effect of abandonment of Oswego, 326; negotiating with English, 426; smith for, at Oswego, 460; securing fidelity of, 516; fur trade, French interference with, 535; retaining friendship of, 592.

FARMERS' BANK OF ORLEANS. Securities in trust for redemption of notes, IV. 36.

FARMERS OF EXCISE. Appointment and bond of, I, 188; act relating to, 194, 240; office discontinued, 529.

FARMERS' INSTITUTES. Cost of, 1891, IX, 11; appropriation, X, 121, 217.

FARMERS AND MECHANICS' SAVINGS BANK, NEW YORK. Charter, veto, VI, 342.

FARMERS AND MECHANICS' SAVINGS BANK, SCHENECTADY. Charter, veto, VI, 214.

FARRELL, THOMAS J. Assembly, member of joint legislative committee on services in memory of former Governor Higgins, X, 963.

FAR ROCKAWAY. VETOES. Claim of Gamewell Fire Alarm Telegraph Company, X, 324; claim of Eureka Fire Hose Company, 324.

FASSETT, J. SLOAT. Senate, introduces amendment abolishing common school fund, VIII, 148.

FAST DAY. Recommended on account of blast on corn, I, 24; Congress appoints, II, 170; Legislature recommends, 715.

"FATHER OF HIS PEOPLE." Title given to George III, I, 702.

FATHER MATHEW TOTAL ABSTINENCE BENEFIT SOCIETY, No. 6, NEW YORK. Charter, veto, V, 654.

FAULKENER, WILLIAM. Nominated as sheriff of Orange county, proceedings in Council of Appointment, II, 475, 493.

FAUNA. Number and description of, III, 761, 993.

FAY, JOHN. Bond for return of arms, II, 772.

FAY, THEODORE S. United States Minister at Berne, Switzerland, communication from, foreign acknowledgments, V, 111.

FAYAL. Naval engagement at, II, 859.

FAYETTEVILLE. Purchasing fire apparatus, veto, VII, 848.

FEATHERSTONE, THOMAS. Board of Claims, veto, VII, 1120.

FEELY, MATTHEW M. Assistant expert accountant, New York, claim, veto, X, 690.

FEES. Communication relative to, I, 34; Governor and Council may establish, 84; repeal of act establishing, 144; to be established by Council, 144; taking unlawful, II, 22; in Court of Chancery,

FEES — (*Continued*).

542, 702; of judges for chamber business, 622; of New York pilots, 888; of New York pilots, British vessels, 918; of court officers, III, 720, 774, 871; of attorneys and solicitors, 774, 871; of judicial officers prohibited, IV, 684, 686, 777; of district attorneys in criminal cases, V, 698; of local officers under Transfer Tax Law, X, 109.

VETOES. Justices, fixing their own, II, 86; of court officers, 275; sheriffs, V, 875; Albany county clerk, VII, 805; referees in highway proceedings, VIII, 470; witnesses, amending Code, IX, 446; for transcripts of testimony in certain cases, 722; jurors, amending Code, 792; X, 62; commissions of receivers and trustees, 589.

FELLER, GEORGE. Escheat, veto, VIII, 882.

FELLOWS, JOHN R. District attorney, New York, payment of unearned salary to widow, veto, IX, 805.

FELLOWS, LIZZIE M. Widow of John R. Fellows, late district attorney of New York, payment of unearned salary to, veto, IX, 805.

FELONY. Act relating to privateers and pirates, I, 29; counterfeiting bills of credit, II, 66; punishment of, 363, 451; right of a State to define and bind other States, III, 929.

VETOES. Second offense, trial, VI, 849; committed on Indian reservations, expense of trials and proceedings, X, 164.

FEMALE ACADEMY. At Waterford, incorporated, II, 972; usefulness of, 1018.

FEMALE ACADEMY OF THE SACRED HEART, NEW YORK. Charter, veto, IV, 531.

FENCER, THOMAS. Member of Prison Labor Commission, VI, 234.

FENCES. See also DIVISION DITCHES. Act relating to, I, 11; division, amending Town Law, veto, X, 440; fence viewers in villages, veto, 812.

FENTON, REUBEN E. Governor, portrait, V, 582.

1865. Annual message, V, 582; public charities, 582; repeal of law authorizing sending of insane female convicts to Utica asylum, 583; condition of insane poor, 583; asylum for incurable insane, 583; care of soldiers and families, 584; military State agency and soldiers' home, 585; banking and currency, 585; number of national banks, 586; New York banking system becomes basis of national banks, 586; benefits of national banking system, 587; State banks may become national banks, 587; finances, 588; general fund, 588; State debt, 589; State tax, 589; canals and canal funds, 589; canal debt, 590; gross earnings of canals, four years, 591; claims against State, 591; condemns loan for

Fenton, Reuben E., 1865 — (*Continued*).

interest, 592; increase of commerce resulting from war, 593; effect of railroad competition on canal revenues, 593; tonnage on railroads and canals, 594; increase of foreign trade, 594; agriculture, 595; aid to Agricultural College, 596; codification of laws, 596; commission of appeals, 597; metropolitan police, 598; Central park, 598; immigration, 598; new hospital buildings at quarantine, 599; State prisons, 599; confinement of female convicts from western part of State, 599; conditions at Clinton prison, 600; duties of Prison Association, 601; census, 601; increase in number of voters, 602; education, 602; school statistics, 603; more teachers needed, 604; condition of higher institutions of learning, 605; elective franchise, 605; registration of voters, 605; vote of absent soldiers, 606; number of men sent into the field, 607; quotas of 1864, 607; appointment of military officers, 608; bureau of military statistics, 608; bounties and recruiting, 609; recruits for two year regiments, 610; National Guard, 611; importance of militia organization, 612; local legislation and economy, 613; general considerations, 614; extinction of slavery, 614; republican governments, 616; correspondence between Secretary Seward and Venezuelan minister, 617; information concerning quotas, 618, 621, 624, 634; constitutional amendment, slavery abolished, 623; conference with Washington authorities concerning quotas, 628; telegram to General Fry, quotas, 631; communication from Department of State, statues for hall of House of Representatives, 634; national cemetery, Gettysburg and Antietam, 636; quarantine matters, 638; warehouse for sanitary and commercial reasons in lower and upper bay, 639; jurisdiction of State over waters of lower New York bay, 640; Commission on Quarantine Regulations, 640; boarding stations deficient, 640; corporation for erecting warehouse and docks at quarantine, 641; purchase of Exchange building by United States, 641; claims of 32d Regiment, 642; repair of arsenals, 642; repair of Dunkirk arsenal, 643; announces death of President Lincoln, 648, 677; assault on Secretary Seward, 649; remonstrance against bill for care and improvement of Albany streets, 655; proclamation, announcing fall of Richmond, 676; proclamation, announcing President Lincoln's death, 677.

FENTON, REUBEN E., 1865 — (*Continued*).

    VETOES. German Association Erheiterung, charter, V, 643; German American Colonization Society, charter, 643; Gladiator Benevolent Association, New York, charter, 644; National Glee Club, New York, charter, 645; Atlantic Base Ball Club, charter, 645; Dry Dock, East Broadway and Battery Railroad Company, extension of road, and use by another company, 646; care and improvement of streets, Albany, 650; Susquehanna river dam, 652, veto withdrawn, 659; street railroad fares, Erie, Albany and Rensselaer counties, 653; Father Mathew Total Abstinence Benefit Society No. 6, New York, charter, 654; Young Men's Father Mathew Total Abstinence Benefit Society No. 1, charter, 654; plankroad and turnpike road companies, additional tolls, 656; New York Central Railroad Company, authorizing increase of passenger fare, 659; final closing of incorporated banks, 665; Second Avenue Railroad Company and Third Avenue Railroad Company, 667; Metropolitan Railroad Company, tunnel under Broadway, 669; Pneumatic Railway and Express Company, 670; increasing price of gas, Manhattan Gas Company, 670; Knickerbocker Gas Company, charter, 673; legalizing military bounties, 673.

1866. Annual message, V, 680; termination of war, 680; New York soldiers, 681; military agencies, 681; claim agencies, 683; soldiers' claims, 683; pensions, 683; soldiers' homes, 684; soldiers' depot, 684; military departments, 686; National Guard, 686; general encampment of National Guard, 687; defense of northern frontier, 688; Bounty Law, 688; amount expended for bounties, 689; staff reports, 689; Bureau of Military Record, 689; building for military records and trophies, 689; finances and taxation, 690; general fund, 690; defective methods of assessing personal property, 691; banking and currency, 692; benefits of national banks, 693; agriculture and manufactures, 693; improvement of agricultural implements, 693; Cornell University, 693; education, 694; more normal schools needed, 695; member of Commission on Normal Schools, 695; free tuition to children of deceased soldiers, 696; prisons and crime, 696; State prisons should be free from partisan influence, 697, 757; suppression of crime, 698; asylums and

FENTON, REUBEN E., 1866 — (*Continued*).

    other public institutions, 698; quarantine and public health, 699; Eastern Asia epidemic, 699; Asiatic cholera in New York, 700; inadequate quarantine accommodations, 700; public health in New York city and Brooklyn, 701; metropolitan sanitary district and metropolitan board of health, 702; claims against United States, 702; adjustment of Federal direct tax, 703; canals and internal improvements, 704; probable early payment of canal debt, 706; Hudson river improvement, 707; resolution of Detroit Convention on enlargement of canal locks, 707; no adequate outlet through Canada for western products, 709; railroad competition with canals, 709; special legislation, 711; objections to legislation for relief of canal contractors, 711; slavery destroyed, 713; reconstruction of southern States, 714; general beneficial results of Civil War, 715; charges against New York city officers, 715; proceedings for removal of officers, commissioners, 716; report of commissioners of quarantine and health officer, 717; acquisition of property for quarantine purposes, 718; report of commissioners on quarantine warehouses, 719; Vermont statute, fishing in Lake Champlain, 719; memorial, exploration of ancient mounds, 720; resolutions, canal board, Federal fees on canal boats, 721; proceedings in erection of new capitol, 721; charges against Judge George W. Smith, 723; Antietam national cemetery, 725; additional land for Brooklyn navy yard, 728.

    VETOES. Relative to contracts, New York city, V, 724; Amsterdam and Florida, towns, relief, 725; American Exploring and Mining Company, charter, 726; New York city, contracts for filling certain lots, 728; navigation of Oneida Lake canal, 730; revising charter of Buffalo, 734; aiding Whitehall and Plattsburgh Railroad and Albany and Susquehanna Railroad, 737.

1867.   Annual message, V, 741; general review, 741; fourteenth amendment, 742, 790; Constitutional Convention, 744; comment on Constitution of 1846, 745; defects in judiciary system, 746; organization and powers of Court of Appeals, 746; resignation of judges of Court of Appeals, 747; method of selecting delegates to convention, 748; finances, 749; general fund, 750; State tax, 751; assessment of personal property, 751; economy necessary, 751; amount of

FENTON, REUBEN E., 1867 —(*Continued*).

State debt, 751; reduction of imposts, 752; amount of State debt caused by Civil War, 752; estimated amount of national debt, 753; estimated population of United States in 1900, 753; claims against United States, Civil War, 754; Commission on War Claims against United States, 756; prisons and crime, 756; convict labor, 757; report of Prison Association, 757; procedure in pardon cases, 758; Bureau of Pardons, 758; responsibility of district attorney in criminal cases, 759; new capitol, 759; public charities, 760; supervision of charitable institutions, 760; State Board of Charities, 760; investigation of management of inebriate asylum, 761; Batavia Institution for the Blind, 762; Willard Asylum for the Insane, 762; Hudson River Asylum for the Insane, 763; national cemetery at Antietam, 764; New York city quarantine and public health, 764; cholera in New York, 765; West Bank, quarantine establishment, 767; metropolitan sanitary district and board of health, 767; military departments, 768; improvement in National Guard, 769; use of rifles, 769; reserve militia, 770; bureau of military statistics, 771; hall of military record, 772; room in new capitol for military relics, 772, 835; military agencies, 772; congressional equalization bounty bill, 774; temporary home for disabled soldiers, 774; population, manufactures and agriculture, 775; census, 1865, 775; number and capital of manufactories, 777; general improvement in agriculture, 777; education, 778; common school statistics, 778; abolition of rate bill, 780; advantages derived from normal schools, 780; additional normal schools, 780; colleges and academies, 781; State Cabinet of Geology and Natural History, 781; canals and internal improvements, 782; canal fund, 782; canal debt, 783; tonnage capacity of canals, 785; canals needed for transportation of western products, 785; steam power on canals, 786; early payment of canal debt, 787; enlarging locks on Erie and Oswego canals, 787; beneficial results of canals, 788; Hudson river improvement, 789; various annual reports, 791; report of commission, sale of quarantine, 791; anti-rent troubles, Albany and Rensselaer counties, 792; announces death of ex-Governor Washington Hunt, 793; cession of certain property adjacent to Brooklyn navy yard, 794; monument of Abraham Lincoln, 794; communication from pilot com-

FENTON, REUBEN E., 1867 —(*Continued*).

    missioner, encroachments on New York harbor, 796; comment on railroad tolls, 803.

    MEMORANDUM OF APPROVAL. Aid to Oswego and Midland, and Southern Central Railroad, V, 813.

    VETOES. New York, railroads in Christopher street, V, 796; New York Central Railroad Company, increasing fare, 802; New York, railroads in Broadway and other streets, 809; railroads, aiding construction, 814.

1868. Annual message, V, 818; finances, 818; State debt, 819; State's wealth and resources, 819; New York's contribution to Federal revenue, 820; lessons derived from Civil War, 822; national debt not burdensome, 822; national banks and State banks, 823; labor should be relieved from oppressive burdens, 824; United States taxes should be revised and reduced, 824; low price of gold, 824; taxation of personal property, 825; returns by owners of personal property as basis of assessment, 826; proposed tax commission, 826; canals and canal fund, 827; canal debt, 828; improvement of Champlain canal, 829; Genesee Valley canal improvement, 829; Chenango canal extension, 830; claims against general government, 831; military departments, 832; National Guard, 832; militia necessary to free government, 832; encampments of militia, 833; Soldiers' Agency and Home, 834; bureau of military statistics, collections, 834; military agencies, 835; Soldiers' Home, 836; public charities, 837; care of insane, 837; State Institution for the Blind, Batavia, 838; Binghamton Inebriate Asylum, property transferred to State, 839; State Board of Charities, 839; report of commissioner, Antietam cemetery, 840; State prisons, 841; prison labor, 842; quarantine, public health, harbor of New York, 842; alien emigrants, 842; immigration, 843; immigrant fund, 843; Metropolitan sanitary district, 844; number of vessels under quarantine, 844; West Bank quarantine hospital, 845; warehouses for quarantine purposes, 845, 846; quarantine establishment at Coney Island, 845; proceedings against New Jersey Central Railroad Company, piers and docks in New York bay, 846; special legislation, 848; bills signed after adjournment, 849; education, 850; common school statistics, 851; normal schools, 852; good effect of abolition of rate bills, 852; inefficient school accommodations, 854; Cornell University,

FENTON, REUBEN E., 1868 —(*Continued*).

854; State Cabinet of Natural History, 854; report of Regents, 855; State and national interests, 855; beneficent effects of emancipation, 855; negroes receive right of suffrage, 856; civil government destroyed in States composing Southern Confederacy, 856; purpose of thirteenth and fourteenth amendments, 858; reconstruction of seceding States, 858; new Constitutions in seceding States, 860; cession of David's island to United States, 861; land for navy yard, 862; report of Commissioner to Paris Exposition, 862; registration of births, marriages and deaths, 863; report of commissioner to ascertain damages on reservations by trespassers, 863; New York, annual tax levy, 868; report of special commissioner on Antietam national cemetery, 869; list of soldiers buried in Antietam cemetery, 870; report of Auditing Board, claims against State for expense in raising volunteers, 870; expected financial panic, 876; memorandum filed with supply bill, 881; approves New York Avenue C railroad bill, VI, 63; official service, I, pref., xiii.

VETOES. Aiding construction of Whitehall and Plattsburgh Railroad, V, 864; New York, railroad in 125th street, 871; increasing fees of sheriffs, 875; New York, widening West street, 878.

FERRIS, ROBERT M. Deceased, bounties to heirs, veto, VI, 324.

FERRIS, TYRUS H. St. Lawrence county clerk, expenses, notaries public, appropriation, veto, VII, 83.

FERRY. On St. Regis river, II, 520; at Black Rock, 526, 605, 1029; at Queenstown, 526; on Harlem river, New York's control of, 783; on Niagara river, Six Nations entitled to free use of, 1029; on Cattaraugus reservation, privileges, 1030; New York, amending charter, X, 280.

VETOES. On Hudson river, Mount Pleasant and Clarkstown, II, 476; Youngstown, motive power on, VI, 593; New York and Brooklyn, 697; People's Water Transit Company, East river, 703; Troy and West Troy, 705; Hudson river, at Phillipstown, 813; Seneca lake, Lodi Landing, 1033; Genesee river, Rochester, VII, 417; Chadeayne, Hudson river, Cornwall Landing, 664; Sammis, Babylon to Fire Island Beach, 936; Barber's Point across Lake Champlain, VIII, 410; Crown Point across Lake Champlain, 463; Great South bay, fees, 639; between Tarrytown and Nyack, continuance, 880; Conesus lake, Long Point to

FERRY, VETOES — (*Continued*).

McPherson Point, 1098; Lake Champlain at Ticonderoga, 1099; Thirty-fourth street, New York, relief, 1119; Fulton, Wall and Cortland Streets Ferry Railroad Company, relief, 1119; Seneca lake, extending Goodwin franchise, IX, 372; New York, amending charter, X, 325; across Lake Champlain, Essex county, 953.

FERRY AND EXCURSION BOATS. Life saving crews, veto, X, 807.

FERTILIZERS. Preventing fraud in manufacture and sale, veto, VII, 130; manufacture of, nuisance, report of State Board of Health, 547.

FETTRETCH, JOSEPH. New York school trustees, 19th ward, action against, legal services and expenses, veto, IX, 871.

FEUDAL SYSTEM. Abolition of, IV, 358.

FEUDAL TENURES. Abolished, IV, 409, 559.

FEVER HOSPITAL. Established, III, 12.

FIEDERONDEQUAT. French designs on, I, 241.

FIELD, BEN. Member of Connecticut Boundary Commission, V, 112.

FIELD, DAVID DUDLEY. Member of Procedure Commission, IV, 366; delegate to Washington Peace Convention, V, 310; quoted, cost of legislation, VIII, 346.

FIELDS, STILLMAN A. Preventing damage to lands of, veto, VI, 852.

FIESEL, JOSEPH, JR. Claim against Long Island City for services, board of education, veto, X, 950.

FIFTH AVENUE HOTEL, NEW YORK. French delegates to Yorktown Celebration entertained at, VII, 739; German delegates to Yorktown Celebration entertained at, 741.

FIFTH AVENUE PRESBYTERIAN CHURCH, NEW YORK. Sale of liquor within 200 feet of, Gotham Hotel, veto, X, 779.

FIFTH AVENUE SAVINGS BANK OF NEW YORK. Charter, veto, VI, 97, 211.

FIFTH JUDICIAL DISTRICT. Additional justices for, VII, 837; X, 850, 936; included in fourth judicial department, IX, 546.

VETOES. Law library, purchase of books, VIII, 856; law library, Owego, IX, 130; clerks to justices, 812; law library, Utica,— librarian, increasing compensation, X, 519;— books and rebinding, appropriation, 556.

FILKINS, MR. Interference in service of process, Van Rensselaer rent, III, 826.

FILLMORE, MILLARD. Comptroller, communication from, marine hospital, IV, 451; President, succeeding Zachary Taylor, 572; petition, enlargement and use of canals, V, 506; death of, legislative action thereon, VI, 662.

FINANCES. See also GENERAL FUND. Acts relating to, II, 9; Federal system adopted, 97; approved by New York, 97; acts relating to, suspension of, veto, 128; letter from Robert Morris, 152; funding public debt, 158; Federal, general note, 180; Congress authorized to settle New York's share of expenses, 184; payment of public debt, 199; national debt, arrears of interest, 218; restoring public credit, 254; Federal requisition on New York, 263; Federal revenue system, general note, 275; public accounts, settlement of, veto, 288; State, condition of, 304; permanent system of ways and means, 312; good condition of, 320; IV, 539; aid to navigation companies, II, 321, 335; office of Comptroller created, 383; replenishing treasury, 422; loan from Bank of New York, 436; condition of, 506, 526; estimated revenue, 1806, 576; military expenses, 654; statement of common school fund, 722; expenses, War of 1812, 750, 757; funds advanced by United States, 1812, 763; Federal direct tax, 788; resources and debts, 906; funding State debt, 907; economy necessary, 909, 1013; III, 321, 720; IV, 24; V, 73; general statement, II, 967; III, 10, 28, 321, 371, 473, 671, 707, 763, 855; IV, 87, 252, 386, 423, 595, 780, 830; V, 1, 64, 252, 360, 451, 529, 588, 690, 750, 818; VI, 5, 99, 524, 614, 720; VII, 2, 137, 273, 418, 511, 678, 815, 940; VIII, 4, 145, 303, 496, 663, 933, 1082; IX, 7, 157, 533, 647, 738, 820; X, 108, 180, 327, 484, 595, 718; general financial situation, II, 980; loan of public funds, 1004; loans for canal construction, 1097; III, 10, 26; State debt, II, 1098, see that title; aid to Delaware and Hudson Canal Company, III, 167; condition of, 1828, 201; public funds, 232; important element of public administration, 273; common schools, 296, 411, 500, 539, 618, 653; V, 12, 51, 81, 173, see also COMMON SCHOOLS; canals, III, 304, 333, 410, 952, see CANALS; expenditures usually exceed estimates, 322; borrowing money for current expenses, 323; character of public debt, 325; fiscal year established, 327, 369; special fund for internal improvements, 373; funds insufficient for expenses, 413; debt for current expenses an evil, 415; loan for Chenango canal, 419; State loan, 481, 491, 496, 505; treasury exhausted, 504, 543; borrowing money to pay interest, 544, 546; defective financial policy, 545; mortgaging the future, 547; under-estimating expense of canal construction, 791, 891; new financial policy needed, 796, 957; opposition to internal improvements, 801; results of internal improvements, 813; income sufficient for wants, 816; fortifying credit, 970; State debt, act to provide for payment of, and preserve public credit, 1008; policy of 1842, 1008, 1044; IV, 15, see that title; new method of stating accounts, 1045; due on suspended public works, IV, 13; proposed amendment confirming policy of 1842, 60; diversion of

FINANCES — (*Continued*).

funds, 96; State stock debt, 212; loans for deficiencies in sinking fund, 422; proposed loan for completion of canals, 549; depressed condition in 1841, 664; condition not satisfactory, 678; interest on canal certificates, 700; contracts not to exceed available appropriations, 744; State prison indebtedness, 786; public securities, standard of value, how fixed, 806; canal revenues, 820; schools, 838; administration of school moneys, 842; canal revenues inadequate for required constitutional purposes, V, 211; high credit of State, 359; appropriations should be accompanied by means of payment, VI, 524; excessive speculation, 962; unappropriated balance, how used, VII, 277; monthly estimates of expenses in State hospitals, IX, 190, 229, 436; monthly estimates of expenses in charitable institutions and reformatories, IX, 436; State Finance Law, 1897, monthly estimates, 436; economy needed, 542, 574; X, 22; Comptroller's estimate, 1895, IX, 683; Governor Morton's special message, 1896, urging economy in appropriations, 682; payment of fees into State treasury, X, 73; proposed auditing department, 346; general funds, payments from, constitutional amendment, 1905, 577; appropriations, comparative statement, 1903, 578.

FINES. Recovery of, in Albany county, I, 233. VETOES. Oneida county, misdemeanors, VI, 696; remission of, IX, 793.

FINGAR, PETER R. Board of Claims, veto, VIII, 1124.

FINN, ROBERT. Will of, act relative to, II, 1036.

FIRE. Public buildings, New York, I, 297, 302; in Boston, 646; in Montreal, 701; second, at Montreal, 725; in New York, Governor's house, 753; Dutchess county courthouse and jail, II, 224; partially destroys New York prison, 547; Champlain barracks, 770; State standard of weights and measures, III, 142; in New York, 534, 584, 696; The Caroline, 678; at Rouse's Point, 760; Genesee Wesleyan Seminary, 1033; Canadian Parliamentary Library, IV, 573; Congressional Library, 613; at State lunatic asylum, V, 54, 86; Staten Island, quarantine buildings, 79, 100; at Sing Sing prison, 272; in New York, draft riots, 547; Chicago, 1871, VI, 355, 547; Chicago Law Library, 364; The Andrew Fletcher, 533; provision for extinguishing, 548; number of, and insurance losses, 1878, VII, 426; destructive effects in Adirondack region, 721; prevention in Adirondack region, 985; caused by operation of railroads, protection from, VIII, 323, 481; compulsory investigation of, 689, 929, 1080; statement of losses in United States, 690; at Auburn and Clinton prisons, IX, 25; investigating causes of, 332; in forests, should be prevented, X, 101; fire patrol, forest preserve, 607; in forest preserve, preventing waste

FIRE — (*Continued*).

from, 706; San Francisco, New York's relief appropriation, 890.

VETOES. Syracuse armory, replacing property destroyed, VI, 875; New York, prevention and extinguishment of, 911; State fair buildings, Elmira, reconstruction, VII, 90; New York, prohibiting construction of wooden buildings, 444; Carthage union schoolhouse, appropriation for new building, VIII, 117; districts in unincorporated villages, 872; Utica commissioners, amending act, 888; fire escapes on school buildings, IX, 355; Brooklyn, fire limits, 734, 876; fire wardens, compensation, 768; in forests, services at, X, 161; New York, prevention of, 313; 71st Regiment armory destroyed by, reimbursement for private property lost, appropriation, 566; White Plains, water, fire protection tax, 592; Greenwood fire district, water supply, 704; protection from, excursion boats and barges, 805.

FIREARMS. See ARMS.

FIRE COMPANIES. In towns, VI, 119, 548; act providing for, 548; participation in Centennial celebration of Washington's inauguration, VIII, 695; exemption from taxation, 878, 972; tax on foreign insurance companies, IX, 249.

VETOES. Brewer Fire Company, Monsey, charter, VII, 268; Gouverneur Fire Company, charter, 327; Highland Fire Engine and Hose Company No. 3, Florida, charter, VIII, 462; Flatbush, amending charter, 728; Firemen's Benevolent Fund Association, Mount Vernon, charter, IX, 469; in certain cities, compensation of officers, 727; Long Island City, improvement, 786; Washington Hook and Ladder Company No. 1, Lawrence and Cedarhurst, changing name, conferring additional powers, X, 261; Eureka Fire Hose Company, claim against Far Rockaway, 324.

FIRE DEPARTMENT. VETOES. Albany, reorganizing, VI, 331; Andes, organizing, VII, 65; Brooklyn,— insurance fund, IX, 475; — legalizing appointment, 874; — pension fund, VIII, 131; — salaries, IX, 262; Buffalo,— relative to, VII, 413, 870; VIII, 889; — holidays, IX, 51; — storekeeper, X, 776; Elmira, building bonds, IX, 734; Glenville, school district, VI, 1035; Gloversville, term of service, VIII, 409; Long Island City, improvement, IX, 786; New Brighton, relative to, VIII, 532; Ossining, relative to, X, 443; Plattsburgh, relative to, VII, 64; Saratoga Springs, relative to, 413, 1102; Savannah, relative to, VIII, 410; Syracuse, relative to, VII, 1098; IX, 789, 790; New York, sites for buildings, 235; Edgewater, fire department, charter, VIII, 616; X, 473; Poughkeepsie, associated fire department, amending charter, VIII, 878, 972; Oswego, amending charter, 1040; Flatlands, fire department, charter, 1097; Rochester, pension fund,

FIRE DEPARTMENT — (*Continued*).

IX, 249; X, 713, 714; New York,— relative to, IX, 728; — uniforms, 732; — employees, appointment to uniform force, 732; X, 850; — life insurance fund, deposit, 321; — promotion for bravery, 580; — pensions, 582; employees, relative to, 583; — claims for labor, services and material, 663; — assignments and promotions, 634; — reinstatements, 713; — deputy chiefs, Brooklyn and Queens boroughs, 818; — Parker claim, relief of minor daughter, 818; — Sweeney, reappointment, 818.

FIRE DISTRICTS. Purchases for, veto, IX, 622.

FIRE ESCAPES. Required on certain buildings, IX, 163; on tenementhouses, X 746. VETOES. Erection of, VII, 267; on school buildings, IX, 355; on hotels, X, 701, 709.

FIRE AND INLAND NAVIGATION COMPANIES. Reports, veto, VII, 416.

FIRE INSURANCE COMPANIES. Statistics, V, 275; VII, 426, 690, 824, 950; general act, VI, 197; losses by Chicago fire, 1871, 355; joint stock, number of, VII, 950.

VETOES. Preventing false and deceptive statements, VII, 267, 322; policies, construction, 332; X, 441; amending general act, VII, 507; securities, investments, 891; amending Insurance Law, X, 583.

FIRE ISLAND. Ferry at, amending act, veto, VII, 936; part of, purchased for quarantine purposes, IX, 204.

FIREMEN. Buffalo, disabled, half-pay, VIII, 561.

VETOES. New York volunteers, preference, X, 580, 717; Exempt Firemen's Benevolent Fund Association, Bronx borough, headquarters, 581; volunteers, death from injuries received while on duty, payment to estate, IX, 815; volunteer, peddler's license, 866; Buffalo, vacations and leaves of absence, 869; volunteers, Westchester annexed district, services after annexation, compensation, 871; Brooklyn, Flatbush, payment for services, 876; New York, reinstatements, X, 53; volunteer, Queens and Richmond boroughs, 60; New York pension fund, Bowen case, 321; veteran volunteers, exemptions, Queens and Richmond boroughs, 323; New York volunteer associations in certain towns, appropriation, 472; New York, qualifications, 476, 580, 581; Utica pension fund, 476; New York, Murphy relief, 581; New York, Kenehan relief, 581; volunteer, Queens and Richmond, relative to, 715; New York, pensions, 717; Brooklyn, confirming appointment, 806; New York,— appointment to uniformed force, 806; — Davis, relief 817; — Lyons, reinstatement, 950; — Weise, reinstatement, 950; — McCullen, reinstatement, 951.

FIREMEN'S BENEVOLENT FUND ASSOCIATION, MOUNT VERNON. Charter, veto, IX, 469.

FIREMEN'S RELIEF FUND. Tax on foreign insurance companies, VI, 1028.

FIREPROOF WAREHOUSE COMPANY. Amending charter, veto, VI, 328.

FIRES. Prevention of incendiary, I, 298. See also FIRE.

FIRE WARDENS. VETOES. Indian Lake, services, claim bill, X, 946; Jefferson county, 954.

FIRE-WOOD. For garrisons, I, 131, 138, 608; permission to cut, granted to certain persons in Tryon county, II, 168.

FIRST BAPTIST CHURCH, GREENPOINT. Changing name to Noble Street Baptist church of Brooklyn, veto, IX, 348.

FIRST BAPTIST CHURCH, KENDALL. Sale and division of property, veto, VII, 881.

FIRST-CLASS CITIES. Railroads, right of way, use of, in certain cases, IX, 791; Tenement-House Commission, 1900, X, 96, 206; fireproof tenements, act of 1904, 632; free employment bureau, 880, 885; elections to be in odd-numbered years, 911.

    VETOES. Banks, bonds for security of certain depositors, IX, 791; private bankers, security for deposits, 867; railroads, terminal facilities, X, 466.

FIRST CONGREGATIONAL CHURCH AND SOCIETY OF CAMBRIA. Authorizing sale of property, veto, V, 150.

FIRST CONGREGATIONAL CHURCH, KENDALL. Sale and division of property, veto, VII, 881.

FIRST CONGREGATIONAL CHURCH, POUGHKEEPSIE. Changing name, veto, VI, 431.

FIRST CONGREGATIONAL SOCIETY, BYRON. Changing name, veto, VIII, 205.

FIRST GERMAN METHODIST EPISCOPAL CHURCH, NEW YORK. Land for cemetery purposes, veto, IX, 254.

FIRST JUDICIAL DEPARTMENT. How constituted, IX, 546; stenographers, increasing salaries, X, 152; Supreme Court, relief from large calendar, 371; trial judges, suggested increase of hours of work, 374.

    VETOES. Appellate Division, attendants, compensation, IX, 727; X, 716; law library, Appellate Division and trial courts, appropriation, IX, 770; referees, appointment, X, 318; Appellate Division, special deputy clerk, 717.

FIRST JUDICIAL DISTRICT. Increasing number of justices, IV, 615, 857; additional justices, VII, 837; X, 850, 936; constitutes first judicial department, IX, 546; commission on law's delay, X, 515, 516; defined, 1906, 850.

First Judicial District — (*Continued*).

  Vetoes. Supreme Court, attendants, compensation, IX, 727; court interpreter, classification of, 812; court attendants, X, 716; additional justices, 947.

First Methodist Episcopal Church, Carlton. Burial ground, preventing interments in, veto, VII, 120.

First Methodist Episcopal Church, New York. Relief, veto, X, 60.

First Methodist Episcopal Society, Watkins. Relative to, veto, VII, 121.

First National Bank, Ballston Spa. Refunding taxes erroneously paid, veto, X, 452.

First National Bank, Buffalo. Settlement of claims against sureties, veto, VII, 874.

First Presbyterian Church, Batchellerville. Legalizing acts of trustees, veto, VII, 1106.

First Presbyterian Church, Perry. Sale of real estate, veto, VI, 45.

First Regiment New York Mexican Volunteers. Relief, veto, VII, 882; former relief acts, 883.

First Universalist Society, Mount Vernon. Vetoes. Relative to, X, 59; relief from assessment, 254.

First Wesleyan Methodist Church, Chazy. Confirming reorganization, veto, VII, 357.

Fiscal Supervisor. Office created, duties, IX, 436; X, 336, 496; office expenses, services of examiner of accounts of institutions, veto, 554.

Fiscal Year. Established, III, 327, 369; for State institutions, VII, 297.

Fish. See also Game and Game Law. Inspector of, III, 98; protection of, Jamaica bay, VIII, 1025; propagation of, IX, 191; use as food, 335; stocking Lake Ontario with whitefish, 192, 335; nets, regulating size of meshes, 336.

  Vetoes. Shell, protection in certain waters, VII, 415; replenishing waters with, VIII, 75; killing, 130; method of taking, 131; preservation in Lake Erie, 457; protection of, Lake Ontario, 627; shad and game fish, Delaware river, protection of, 888; in Lake George, 888; black bass in Brant lake, 975; protection in Erie county, 979; giving free access to private streams and ponds stocked by State, IX, 444; seines and spawning beds south of Croton Point, 470; bass, not to be fished for in certain waters, 623; taking by drawing off water from ponds or reservoirs, 798; Lake Ontario and other waters, 798; sturgeon in Lake Ontario, 800; catching in certain waters, X, 61; transportation of, 590; spearing in Lake Ontario, 954.

Fish Carrier. Cayuga Indian, memorial from, lease of lands, II, 328.

FISH CREEK. Indian lands at, purchase of, II, 644; cleaning and deepening, veto, IX, 81.

FISH CREEK RESERVATION. Acquisition of, II, 999.

FISH, HAMILTON. Governor, first under third Constitution, portrait, IV, 421.

    1849. Annual message, IV, 421; general condition of State, 421; loans for deficiencies in sinking fund, 422; State debt, 422; canals, 424, canal boats, 425; basins, 426; education funds, 426; reports of Comptroller, commissioners of the canal fund, inspectors of State prisons, pardons, Adjutant-General and Commissary-General, 427; militia legislation, 427; common school system, 427; libraries, 428; Astor Library, 428; restoration of county superintendent of schools, 429; normal school, 429; State lunatic asylum, 429; visits institution for the deaf and dumb, 430; New York Institution for the Blind, 430; New York Hospital, 431; Bloomingdale asylum, 431; State fair, 431; wide range of legislation, 431; agricultural school, 432; school for instruction in mechanic arts, 432; gubernatorial succession, 433; vacancies in office, 433; local laws, transferring power to board of supervisors, 433; modification of Criminal Code, 434; procedure in pardon cases, 435; revision of tax laws, 435; claims against State, canal contracts, 437; appropriation for canal damages, 438; quarantine excitement in Richmond county, 438; New York, health officer, compensation, 439; emigration, 439; liability of bank stockholders, 441; Code of Procedure, 442; judicial system, 442; number of judges in New York, 443; tribunals of conciliation, 443; war with Mexico, termination of, 444; acquisition of territory by Mexican War, 445; slavery in Mexico, 445; abolition of slavery in New York, 446; Missouri compromise, 447; admission of New Mexico, slavery, 448; recent presidential election, 449; quota of arms from United States, 450; aid to hospitals at quarantine, 451, 452; location of gunhouses, 452; medals and engravings from Pope Gregory, XVI, 453; new library building needed, 453; presents boundary record to Rhode Island, 456; Seneca Indians, new form of government, 457; geological survey, 460; cession of land for Brooklyn navy yard, 465, 506, 512; interchange of publications with France, 465; South Carolina and Virginia resolutions, 466; Missouri resolutions, 466.

    1850. Annual message, IV, 467; Asiatic cholera epidemic, 468; public health, 469; medical education, 470; financial condition, 470; Albany basin, 474; canals, 474; Hudson river improvement, 475; school finances, 475; Free School Act,

Fish, Hamilton, 1850 —(*Continued*).

475; school statistics, 475; normal school, 476; Indians in normal school, 477; agricultural college and experimental farm, 477; State fair, 478; banks, 478; branch mint, New York, 479; renewal of former recommendations, 479; pardons, 480; houses of refuge, 480; State prisons, 482; lunatic asylums, 483; charitable institutions, 483; care of idiots, 484; alien passenger tax, 485; quarantine establishment, 485; emigration, 485; State library buildings, 486; more room needed for specimens of geological survey, 487; colonial laws, 488; Codification Commission, 488; criminal actions, challenges and exceptions, 489, 505; vagrancy, 490, 505; homestead exemption, 492; militia, 493; arsenals, 495; railroads, 495; slavery in newly-acquired territory, 497; Washington's headquarters, Newburgh, 502; protest by certain Seneca chiefs against new form of government, 503, 506; Vermont resolutions, 504, 507; Connecticut resolutions, 506; cholera, 506; Indian citizenship and taxation, 507; protest against repeal of confirming act, Seneca's new form of government, 507; Rhode Island and Virginia resolutions on slavery, 507; Georgia resolutions, 507; international literary exchanges, report, 508; exhibition of works of industry of all nations, 509; Rhode Island resolutions, 510; report from New York Marine Hospital, 512; Mississippi resolutions, 512; Maryland resolutions, 513; returning Coeymans road bill, 513; announces death of John C. Calhoun, 516; large number of bills at close of session, 523; Mississippi resolutions, pensions, 524; French publications, 524; Texas resolutions, 526; cited, veto of bill extending charter, 637; V, 147; quoted, object of constitutional provisions as to general corporation laws, 130, 134, 232; pardon reports, 137; official service, I, pref., xiii.

Vetoes. Speedy disposition of suits, IV, 510; extending charter of Schoharie Central Bridge Company, 513, 637; Buffalo, subscribing to stock of Buffalo Waterworks Company, 517; Society for the Reformation of Juvenile Delinquents, relative to, 518; Barryville and Shehola Delaware Bridge Company, charter, 521; Buffalo, floating debt, amending charter, 524; Oswego Dry Dock and Marine Railway Company, 525; New York Juvenile Asylum, charter, 526; Thistle Benevolent Association, New York, Female Academy of the Sacred Heart, New York, Firemen of the Village of Williamsburgh, charters, 531; Court of Appeals, relief, 532, 772.

FISH, HAMILTON, JR. Member of Yorktown Centennial Commission, VII, 734.

FISH, NICHOLAS. Minister to Switzerland, appointment of successor, VII, 555.

FISHER, D. W. Canal department, appropriation for services, veto, IX, 716.

FISHER, JOHN. Services in exchange of prisoners, I, 510.

FISHER, JOHN. Court of Claims, veto, X, 165.

FISHER, LEWIS F. Court of Claims, veto, X, 165.

FISHER'S ISLAND. Connecticut requests transfer from New York, VII, 536.

FISHERIES. New Utrecht, V, 123; commissioners, stocking certain waters, veto, VIII, 75.

FISH HATCHERY. Governor Flower criticises location of, IX, 191; two established, 1893, 192.

    VETOES. Jefferson county, VII, 632; VIII, 249; Caledonia, VII, 902; Cold Spring, 902; Palenville, 902; Caledonia, purchase of additional land, VIII, 249; shad hatching car, equipment, 1136; Sullivan county, IX, 38; southern tier, 43; Theresa, State co-operating with United States, 81; Oneida county, Watkins creek, 221; stocking private ponds and streams, giving free access to, 444; Schroon, 777; Catskill, Middletown, rearing ponds, X, 562; trout, Ellington, 787.

FISHKILL. Number of excise licenses, 1887, VIII, 360. VETOES. Road commissioner, creating office, VIII, 388; registration of voters, 719.

FISH OIL. Inspector of, III, 95.

FISHWAYS. VETOES. Oswego, Oneida and Seneca rivers, VII, 61; relative to, 805; Chittenango creek, amending act, VIII, 713; Chenango Forks, 888; Oswego and Seneca rivers, 888; Cattaraugus creek, 890; Ogdensburg dam, IX, 80; Rossie dam, 80; Delaware river, dam at Deposit, X, 787; Chenango river, Fort Dickinson, 787.

FISK, JONATHAN. United States district attorney, letter from, fees of New York pilots, II, 888.

FITCH, JOHN. Steamboat privilege, repeal, II, 415.

FITCH, THOMAS. Governor of Connecticut, report as to levies, I, 570; raises large force for Crown Point expedition, 575, 594; letter from, relative to New York appropriation for Connecticut volunteers, 577.

FITZGIBBONS, JAMES. Relief, veto, X, 177.

FITZGIBBONS, JOHN. Relief, veto, X, 53, 177.

FITZPATRICK, JEREMIAH. New York school trustee, 19th ward, action against, legal services and expenses, veto, IX, 871.

FITZPATRICK, JOHN. Relief, veto, new act passed, VI, 159.

FITZSIMONS, JAMES M. Appointed justice New York City Court, VIII, 935.

FIVE NATIONS. Referred to, I, 30; alliance with, 35; reported negotiations with French, 46, 129; covenant chain renewed, 65; necessity of protecting, 71; Bellomont's conference with, 82; importance of amicable relations with, 85, 86, 201; convey land to Crown, 94; expected attack from Waghana Indians, 114; presents to, 129, 196; treaty with Waghanas, 134, 136; possible results of engaging them in war with French, 157; reported negotiations with French, 161; proposed alliance with Tuscaroras, 170; return wampum belt in Flathead matter, 170; becoming uneasy, 173; presents from French, 176; French negotiations, 192; send commissioners to eastern Indians, 203; invited to treat with Boston commissioners, 206; peltry trade with, 212; letter from agent Schuyler, 219; means used to secure allegiance of, 225; encouragement of, 243; posting party of men with Senecas, 316; efforts to retain fidelity of, 391, 398, 529; former custom in peace negotiations, 487; Governor to confer with, 510; conquest and extirpation of Eries, 542; British dominion over, 542.

FIVE POINTS HOUSE OF INDUSTRY, NEW YORK. Powers of, veto, VII,' 334.

FIZZELL, WILLIAM. Administrator Maude Fizzell, Court of Claims, veto, X, 445.

FLAG. See also STATE FLAG. Colony to furnish, I, 295; none for forts, 310; French, alleged indignity to, II, 246; for St. Regis Indians, 520; militia deficient in colors, 601; symbol of national greatness, V, 560; again hoisted on Fort Sumter, 676; State, description of arms, VII, 727; on public buildings at half staff on General Sherman's death, VIII, 1087; on public buildings, half staff on former Governor Robinson's death, 1095; to be displayed on schoolhouses, IX, 564, 661.
    VETOES. On school buildings, VIII, 1038; foreign, preventing display on public buildings, IX, 527, act passed 1895; national or State, improper use of, 860; X, 62; battle flags, permitting use of, in Oswego county, Old Home Week, 919.

FLAG OF TRUCE. Expenses of, from Canada, I, 144; for exchange of English prisoners, 409, 487, 510; obtaining goods under, II, 57; by Samuel Hake, 58; act to prevent improper use of, 58.

FLAGG, AZARIAH C. Comptroller, report, payments, Oneida land, VI, 666; canal policy commended, 749.

FLANAGAN, JOHN. VETOES. Judgments for costs, VII, 230; interest on judgments, 230.

FLANDERS. American property owned in, II, 1033.

FLANDERS, HENRY J. Member of Commission on St. Regis River Improvement, VIII, 115.

FLANNAGEN, CHARLES ·A. Relief, veto, X, 178.

FLATBUSH. Act removing courts to, from Gravesend, I, 12; hospital for insane, IV, 78; fire company, aid to, VI, 183; annexed to Brooklyn, VIII, 1111.

    VETOES. Brooklyn, railroad, VI, 597; licensing public hacks, etc., VII, 1111; Parkville, streets and avenues, VIII, 615; fire company, 728; lighting streets, 1036; increasing number of policemen and salaries of officers, 1110; police department, — increasing salaries, IX, 107; — captain, increasing salary, 117; Remsen avenue improvement, 275; street and sewer commissioners, 29th ward, transferring powers and duties to Brooklyn commissioner of city works, 720; taxes, sale for, cancellation, Gilmour claim, 810; Prospect avenue opening, 874; firemen, payment for services, 876; Prospect ·avenue, assessments, X, 177; Prospect avenue, refunding assessments, 325; Volunteer Firemen Association, appropriation, 472.

FLATBUSH FIRE COMPANY. Aid to, veto, VI, 183.

FLATHEAD INDIANS. Five Nations return wampum belt, I, 170.

FLATLANDS. Annexed to Brooklyn, VIII, 1098.

    VETOES. Public hacks and amusements, licensing, VIII, 975; Remsen avenue improvement, IX, 275; amending Annexation Act, 634; Volunteer Firemen's Association, appropriation, X, 472.

FLATLANDS FIRE DEPARTMENT. Charter, veto, VIII, 1097.

FLAT ROCK BATTERY, NEW YORK. Banquette at, I, 323.

FLAX. Carding and spinning, II, 534; cultivation, 1092; III. 126, 506.

FLAXSEED. Inspector of, appointed, II, 1091.

FLEECK, FRANK. Court of Claims, veto, X, 165.

FLEET. French, defeated on coast of Algrave, I, 640; English and French, battle off coast of France, 642; Spanish, at Havana, destruction of, 669; French,· supplies for, II, 108, 111.

FLEMING, GEORGE. Lieutenant-colonel, commands troops at Oswego, 1812, II, 746.

FLEMING, HENRY AND MARY. Estate, escheat, veto, X, 958.

FLEMING, MARY 2D, THOMAS, MARGARET AND ELIZABETH. Escheat, veto, X, 958.

FLETCHER, BENJAMIN. Appointed Governor, I, 25; assumes office, 28; also Governor of Pennsylvania, 25, 37, 45; remarks on defense of northern frontier, 28; decay of trade, 28; loans on excessive interest, 28; status of Assembly, 28; transmits to Assembly proposed act relative to privateers and pirates, 29; conference committee on address to Crown, 29, 59; dissolves first Assembly, 31.

Fletcher, Benjamin — (*Continued*).

Opening Speech. Second Assembly, first session, I, 32; support of ministry, 32, 34, 38, 39, 42; Sabbath observance, 32, 34, 38, 59; public debts, 32, 34, 52, 64; Indian alliance, 32, 34, 44, 45, 46, 65; defense of frontier, 33, 34, 36, 38, 48, 52, 53, 54, 56, 57, 59, 62, 64, 73; support of government, 33, 40, 42, 44, 63; courts, 33, 49, 60; relief of Albany, 34, 37, 43, 44, 49, 68; recommends establishment of a post-office, 34; remarks on official fees, 34.

Opening Speech. Second Assembly, second session, I, 34; Canadian expedition, 35; fort at Albany, 35; New York weighhouse, 36, 38; royal aid to colony, 36, 40, 48, 49, 52, 61; changing name of Long Island to Nassau, 36, 38; burdensome taxes, 37, 44, 58; dissolves second Assembly, 39.

Opening Speech. Third Assembly, first session, I, 39; defense of New York, 41, 44; King's chapel, 41, 44, 51, 62, 64; transmits memorial relative to post-office, 42; transmits petition from Westchester freeholders on unequal taxation, 42; power as to clergy, 42; Assembly's assumption of unauthorized power, 43; dissolves third Assembly, 43.

Fourth Assembly, abstract of opening speech, I, 43; payment of fusileers, 43, 48, 49, 64, 66; Governor's military powers, 45; receives commission to command Connecticut militia, 45; calls meeting of Pennsylvania Assembly, 46; reported defection of Indians, 46.

Opening Speech. Fourth Assembly, second session, I, 47; barracks in New York, 48; transmits letter from Governor Phipps, 49; troops from England, 48, 49, 58, 59.

Opening Speech. Fourth Assembly, third session, I, 51; aid from other colonies, 53, 67; muster rolls, 53; vetoes bill for frontier defense, 54; denies Assembly's power to call dissenting minister, 55; reproves Assembly, 55; printing Assembly's votes, 55; dissolves fourth Assembly, 56.

Fifth Assembly, first session, abstract of opening speech, I, 56; vetoes bills relating to deserters and for a present to himself, 56.

Opening Speech. Fifth Assembly, second session, I, 57; appointment of agent to represent colony in England, 57, 59, 67, 72, 74; bill relating to attorneys, 59; vetoes appropriation for levy money, 59; conference committee on quota of troops, 60; disorders in colony, 60.

Opening Speech. Fifth Assembly, third session, I, 61; conference committee on public expenditures, 63.

FLETCHER, BENJAMIN — (*Continued*).

OPENING SPEECH. Fifth Assembly, fourth session, I, 64; French invasion of Indian country, 65, 66; visits Albany, 65, 68, 69, 70; militia desertions, 66, 70; conference committee on spending winter in Albany, 67, 68; French attempt on Kinderhook, 68; committee on address to King, 69.

OPENING SPEECH. Fifth Assembly, fifth session, I, 69; absence of Westchester members, 69; spends winter in Albany, 70; defection of towns of Rye and Bedford, 73; conference committee on appropriation for frontier defense, 73; statement of arrears of taxes, 73; retires from office of Governor of New York, 25, 74; official service, I, pref., ix.

FLINT, CHARLES R. Approves Harvey claim against New York city, VIII, 1162.

FLINT, ROYAL. Commissary-General of Purchases, letter from, scarcity of wheat and flour, II, 54, 82.

FLOATING BATTERY. Proposed construction of, I, 555.

FLOATING DOCK. Use of, veto, VII, 569.

FLOOD, JEREMIAH. Relief, veto, VI, 185.

FLORA. Number and description of species, III, 761, 993.

FLOUR. Exportation of, encouraged, I, 116, 530; inspection of, 246, 749; II, 436; market affected by importations, I, 256; good reputation of, should be preserved, 302; false taring of casks, 530; exportation of unmerchantable, prohibited, 617; exportation of, veto, II, 26; scarcity of, 54, 82; proposed suspension of embargo on, 68; scarcity in Massachusetts, 69; Legislature declines to permit exportation of, 74; exportation permitted in exchange for salt, 79; for army, 88, 114; embargo on, 114, 120; supply to army authorized, 161; impressment of, suit against Trimble for, 186; poor quality of, 970; reduction of tolls on, III, 505; transported on Erie canal, 893.

FLOWER, ROSWELL P. Governor and portrait, IX, 1.

1892. Annual message, IX, 1; Legislature in political accord with executive, 2; enumeration and apportionment, 2; inequalities in representation, 4; legislative power to enact apportionment bill continuing, 5; congressional reapportionment, 5; State finances, 7; State debt paid, 9; sources of revenue, 9; proper principles of indirect taxation, 10; taxation of bonded indebtedness of corporations, 10; committee to investigate corporation laws of neighboring States, 10; economy in public expense, 10; cost of various boards and commissions, 1891, 11; Constitutional Convention, 13; education and the State, 14; decline in attendance on common schools, 14; common schools, cause of country's prosperity, 16; university extension, 17; not

FLOWER, ROSWELL P., 1892 —(*Continued*).

   self-supporting, 20; executions by electricity, 21; publishing details of executions in newspapers, 22; separate building for executions, 23; World's Fair, 23; State prisons, 24; more prison room needed, 24; financial condition of prisons, 25; revision of statutes, 26; National Guard, 28; municipal government, 28; local self-government, 29; State care of insane, 31; canals, 32; electoral reform, 33; registration of electors, 34; personal registration throughout State, 34; contested elections, 34; announces death of Chief Judge Ruger, 36; various annual reports, 36, 37, 38; franchises in New York and Brooklyn, 39; pardon report, 49; compliments Legislature on appropriation bill, 69; Adirondack park should be self-sustaining, 146; proclamation convening Legislature in extraordinary session, 84.

   1892. Extraordinary session, IX, 154; message, 154; apportionment of Legislature, 154.

   MEMORANDUMS OF APPROVAL. Rochester, wards, increase of, IX, 85; Young Women's Christian Association, State executive Committee, charter, 86; Commercial Travelers' Home Association of America, charter, 87; Watervliet, police justice, amending act, 87; new capitol, appropriation, 89; East River Bridge Company, charter; rapid transit railways, New York, 90; taxation, restricting deduction of debts, 93; women authorized to vote for school commissioners, 94; submitting constitutional amendment increasing number of Supreme Court justices, 97; General Electric Company, charter, 99; New York, railroads in annexed district, 99; New York city, election boards, 102; excise laws, revision, 1892, 105; New York, additional surrogate, 122; tax rate, 1892, 122; statutory revision bills, 1892, 135; railroads, limiting hours of service on, 145; Adirondack park, 145.

   VETOES. Reformed Protestant Dutch church of Cattsbane, changing name, IX, 37; fish hatchery, Sullivan county, 38; county clerk, Seneca county, transcribing certain records, 39; fish hatchery, southern tier, 43; Code of Civil Procedure, evidence, confidential communications, 44; Code of Criminal Procedure, appeal from special sessions, stay of execution, 45; law library, sixth judicial district, Elmira, establishing, 45; Penal Code, gilded ware, deception in manufacture and sale, 47; Erie canal, Royalton, vertical wall, 48; Board of Claims, appropriation, undetermined awards, 49; Board of Claims, Burhans, 50; Cohoes, Schuyler street extension, 51;

FLOWER, ROSWELL P., 1892, VETOES —(*Continued*).

Buffalo, fire department, holidays, 51; New York, park
police, 52; Waterford, sidewalks, injuries from defects,
notice, 54; Erie canal, Oak Orchard creek and canal feeder,
improvement, 55; Society for the Relief of Orphan and
Destitute Children, Albany, changing name, enlarging property limit, 56; Union Literary Society, Ellisburgh, changing
name, enlarging income limit, 56; Catholic Mutual Benefit
Association, Supreme Council, amending charter, 57; Congregational Society, Worcester, removing remains from
cemetery, 57; State Treasurer, deposit of funds, 57; Erie
basin, dredging Black Rock harbor, 58; Erie canal, Rochester,
bridge, Monroe avenue, 59; taxes, York, confirming and
levying assessments, 59; Yonkers, bonds for election purposes, 61; villages, poll tax, action to recover, 62; Saranac
river, improvement, 62; Penn Yan, changing boundary, 63;
Cohoes, election inspectors and poll clerks, 64; Board of
Claims, Bassler hearing, 66; Board of Claims, Milliete, 66;
Board of Claims, Morgan, 66; New York, tenement-houses,
67; poor, non-residents, care of, 68; items in appropriation
bill, 68; State printing, office and superintendent, 70; Mount
Morris, consolidation of school districts, 73; State Asylum
for Insane Criminals, Matteawan, acquiring land for sewer,
74; New York, evening high school, 74; Norwich, recorder,
creating office, 75; items in supply bill, 75; appropriation
for Cortland normal school, 106; Conewango creek, improvement, 106; Flatbush, police department, increasing salaries,
107; Rensselaer county judge and surrogate, increasing
compensation, 107; Rensselaer county surrogate, increasing
compensation, 108; encouragement of agriculture, 109; commerce on canals, improvements for promoting, 110; taxation, exemption of property purchased with pension money,
repeal, 113; stenographers, Surrogates' Courts, transcribing
notes, 115; United States deposit fund loan commissioners, increasing fees, 115; common schools, study of
music, 116; medical science, 117; Bath, town meetings,
time and place of meeting, 117; Flatbush, police department
captain, increasing salary, 117; collateral inheritance, 118;
State hospitals, inmates, letters by or to, regulations concerning, 118; Board of Claims, Powell and others, 119;
Brooklyn, police and excise departments, engineer, qualifications, 119; Rochester, police vacations, 120; Cohoes,
bonds for taxes, 120; Brooklyn, wards, increasing number,

FLOWER, ROSWELL P., 1892, VETOES —(*Continued*).

121; Salmon and Mad rivers, public highways, repealing act, 121; Cayuga county clerk, salaried office, Oneida county officers, abolishing fee system, 124; villages, electric light companies, contracts with, 126; mechanics' lien, dredging and improving low lands, 127; mechanic's lien, claims against contractors, notice to owner, 128; Court of Special Sessions, jury, method of selecting, 129; law library, fifth judicial district, Oswego, 130; highways, Kings county, special, 130; villages, ordinary expenditures, 131; wills, probates, effect of, 131; taxes, assessments, review, railroad and telegraph companies, 132; New Utrecht, board of improvement, powers, 133; Jamaica normal school, 134; Elmira Reformatory, transportation facilities, 135; penal institutions, manufactures in, branding and marking, 138; Court of Special Sessions, method of trial, defendant's right to select, 139; Champlain canal, Whitehall, bridge, Rathbun crossing, 139; insolvent debtors, assignments, costs in actions for fraud, 139; Board of Claims, awards, interest on, 140; Owasco lake, protection of highway along outlet, 141; Long Island City, police patrolmen, salaries, 141; elevated railroads, Harvey claim, 141; Hudson House of Refuge for Women, new buildings, 143; street railroads, hours of labor, 144; omnibus veto, 147.

1893. Annual message, IX, 156; visits various State institutions, 156; State finances, 157; taxation, 158; joint committee on taxation, commission to examine tax laws of other States, 158; restricting deduction of debts, assessment of personal property, 158; Buffalo, strike, 159; labor interests, 163; Factory Inspection Act of 1892, 163; sweating system, 164; manufacturers, registry of employees, 166; more inspectors needed, 166; common school education, 166; Compulsory Education Law, 167; improvement of canals, 167; rapid transit on canals needed, 168; electricity as motive power on canals, 168; various canal improvements, 169; World's Fair, 170; agricultural interests, 170; various plans for improvement of agriculture, 171; proposes bureau of agriculture, 172; high rank of State in agriculture, 174; scientific work in agriculture, 175; registration in towns and villages, 180; prisons and pardons, 180; prisons, manufacture of articles for State hospitals, 181; employment of Clinton prison convicts in road building, 181; separate prison for women, Auburn, 181; visits prisons, hears ap-

FLOWER, ROSWELL P., 1893 —(*Continued*).

plications for pardon, 182; new homes for prisoners after discharge, 182; coal combination, 183; Adirondack park, 184; restrictive contracts with private owners, 185; special Forest Commission, 186; leases of lands for cottage purposes, 187; tax sales, reform needed, 187; uniformity of legislation, 188; care of insane, 188; separate tax bill for State care of insane, 189; monthly estimates of expense of State hospitals, 190; propagation of fish, 191; location of fish hatchery, 191; stocking lakes and rivers, 192; oyster culture, 193; value of oyster beds, Long Island sound, 193; Constitutional Convention, 194; postponement of election of delegates, 194; appointment of delegates to Constitutional Convention, constitutionality questioned, 195; minority representation in Constitutional Conventions, 195; use of money in elections, 196; statements of receipts and expenditures by political committees, 197; conviction of bribery, forfeiture of office of candidate, 198; good roads, 198; cost of labor system on highways, 199; market roads, 203; county roads, 203; quarantine, 204; cholera epidemic, 1892, 204; purchases part of Fire island for State, 204; improvements on Hoffman and Swinburne islands, 205; disapproves exclusive national quarantine, 206; public health should be a subject of State jurisdiction, 207; inefficient measures of protection against cholera by consuls at foreign ports, 208; careless engrossing and construction of legislative bills, 209; legislative counsel, 210; various annual reports, 210; cession of land to United States, Old Orchard shoal, 211; Minnesota resolutions, Pacific Railroad bonds, 211; adulterated dairy products in State institutions should be prohibited, 214; communication from American Federation of Labor, New York branch, approving recommendations concerning coal combinations, 216; pardon report, 218; forest preserve, cancellation of tax sales, pecial message, 218; land in forest preserve owned by State, 219.

MEMORANDUMS OF APPROVAL. New capitol, continuing work, IX, county, Brooklyn, supervisors, filling vacancies, 223; Rens-223; Kings county, Brooklyn, supervisors, filling vacancies, 223; Rensselaer county surrogate, increasing salary, 224; New York water supply, sanitary protection, 225; insane, State care, 226; Yonkers Railroad Company, completion of road, 270.

FLOWER, ROSWELL P., 1893, MEMORANDUMS — (*Continued*).

VETOES. Kings county, soldiers and sailors' memorial arch, legalizing acts, IX, 211; Oswego canal, Phœnix bridge, Bridge street, 216; New York, evening high school, 216; Onondaga Historical Association, Southside Sportmen's Club, Long Island, amending charters, 217; Rochester, streets, restricting right to lay out, repeal, 217; Executive Law, amending, 218; fish hatchery, Oneida county, Watkins creek, 221; State memorial hall, White Plains, 221; statue of Hendrick Hudson, 222; civil service, exempting physicians from examinations for municipal appointments, 230; Oneida county, board of supervisors, legalizing audits of accounts, 231; railroad aid, Berlin, railroad commissioner, abolishing office, 232; Agricultural Experiment Station, Long Island, establishing, 232; Ladies' Deborah Nursery and Child's Protectory, exempting from taxation, 232; Bayard Homeopathic College Hospital and Dispensary, charter, 233; Game Law, trespasses on private fish ponds, 233; Game Law, amendments, 233, 258; Game Law, board of supervisors, powers of, 234; public health, sanitary inspection of steamboats, railroad stations and cars, State Sanitary Commission, 234; Rochester Homeopathic Hospital, exempting property from taxation, 235; New York, fire department, sites for buildings, 235; New York, dock department, 235; New York, Twenty-second street sewer, reconsidering assessments, 236; New York, land for public use, acquisition of, 236;; Board of Claims, Brock and Wiener, National Guard uniforms, 237; Board of Claims, Ross and Sanford, 237; taxes, New York, McCaddin property, settlement of, 238; Corning, amending charter, 238; public health, vital statistics, registration of, 238; Cayuga and Seneca canals, berme bank, repairs, Geneva, 239; Erie canal, Rome, canal feeder wall, 239; Owasco lake, highway on west shore, protection of, 239; Herkimer monument, 240; epileptic colony, establishing, 240; Ulster county insane asylum, purchase by State, 243; Elmira Reformatory, improving transportation facilities, 244; rifle range, Bath-on-the-Hudson, additional land, 244; State dam, Black

FLOWER, ROSWELL P., 1893, VETOES —(*Continued*).

river, waste gates, 244; Erie canal, Syracuse, bridge, Crouse avenue or Beach street, 245; Walton armory, repairs and improvements, 245; Eastern New York Reformatory, commission to establish institution for inebriates, Boys' Industrial Home, 246; wages, judgments for, 246; railroads, electric light and power companies becoming railroad companies, 246; surface water, obstructing flow of, 247; Myers' automatic ballot machine, authorizing use of, in villages, ·247; Wolf Island Bridge Company, charter, 248; White Plains, amending charter, 248; Penn Yan, amending charter, 249; Rochester, paid fire department, pension fund, 249; highways, separate district in certain towns in Herkimer county, 250; Board of Claims, Roberts, 250; Mentz, consolidating school districts, 252; villages, crosswalks, assessment on property benefited, 252; penitentiaries, medical treatment of persons convicted of intoxication, 252; St. Vincent's Retreat for the Insane, exempting property from taxation, 253; Long Island City,—rent of buildings for educational purposes, 253; — sick poor, medical and surgical aid, 253; — Grand avenue and Main street improvement, 254; First German Methodist Episcopal Church, land for cemetery purposes, 254; Long lake, bridge over, 255; nautical school, establishing, 256; Erie canal, Buffalo, dredging Ohio basin, 256; New York Finance Company, charter, 256; Citizens' Loan Agency and Guarantee Company, amending charter, 257; Saranac Lake, village charter, 258; Bellis, police justice, legalizing acts, 258; County Law, amending, 259, 289; mechanics' lien, amending general act, 259; false pretenses, evidence, 259; Court of Special Sessions, jurisdiction, 260; actions, railway construction damages, limitation of time, 260; New York, parks, West End avenue, 262; Brooklyn,—fire department, salaries, 262; — water front, 262; — 8th ward, improvements, 263; — Clymer and Heyward streets, closing portions of, 263; Catskill armory, completion, 263; Minisceongo creek, declaring jurisdiction of, 264; New Utrecht, highway improvement in, 264; Seneca Falls, school for anatomy, dissections, 264; State Board of Undertakers, establishing, 265; Board of Claims, county insane asylums, 265; street railroads, hours of labor in certain cities, 266; acknowledg-

FLOWER, ROSWELL P., 1893, VETOES —(*Continued*).

    ments, proof of, and effect as evidence, 266; bottles, boxes,
syphons and kegs, used in connection with certain drinks,
267; Ontario county, excise moneys, disposal of, 267; Buffalo, Parkside avenue extension, 268; Board of Claims,—
Morgan, 268; — Putnam, 269; — McKinstry, 269; — Benway, 270; county clerk, Erie county, salaried office, 272;
political divisions, general act, 272; executors and administrators, amending Revised Statutes, 272; anthracite coal, regulating grade and sale of, 272; taxable transfers, surrogate's
transfer tax clerk's fees, 273; transfer tax, New York,
salaries, 273; salt springs, renewing leases, 274; highways,
bridges broken by heavy loads, when town not liable, 274;
Flatlands and Flatbush, Remsen avenue improvement, 275;
transfer tax, Kings county, appointment of special officer,
275; excise commissioners, compensation, 275; Board of
Claims, general awards, 1893, 276; Board of Claims, corporation taxes unlawfully collected, claims for, 278; Rockland, taxes, collection, 282; taxes, Clinton county, collection, 282; taxes, non-residents, sales for non-payment, 282;
Penal Code, general amendments, 282; executors and administrators, judicial settlement of accounts, 283; infants,
lunatics and habitual drunkards, real property, sale of, 283;
appeals, exceptions and case, 283; escheat, Frost, 284; State
lands under water, Tonawanda, conveyance to Munch, 284;
escheat, Winship, 285; Board of Claims, Holdridge, 285;
Champlain canal, Mechanicville, bridge, North street, 285;
New York, dock department, 286; stenographers, eighth
judicial district, additional, 286; towns, division ditches,
286; personal property, conditional sales, amending act,
287; cheese, promoting consumption of, 287; Board of
Claims, awards, interest on, 288; gunpowder, keeping, unauthorized use, 289; Norwich, revised charter, 289; Board
of Claims, Rochester, 290; items in supply bill, 290.

1894. Annual message, IX, 296; State out of debt, 296; large receipts from indirect taxation, 296; lower tax rate, 297;
forest preservation, 298; contracts with private owners,
restricting timber cutting, 298; municipal consolidation,
New York and Brooklyn, 300; canals, 301; tonnage on
canals, 301; general canal improvements, 302; suggestions
for promoting usefulness of canals, 302; motive power on

FLOWER, ROSWELL P., 1894 — (*Continued*).

canals, 305; use of Niagara Falls to create electric power, 307; road improvement, 308; changes in Election Law, 308; blanket ballot, 308; bi-partisan election boards, 309; personal registration, 309; publication of registry lists in cities prior to election, 310; use of money at elections, statements by political committees, 310; amendments to Civil Service Law, certification of appointments, 311; State care of the insane, 311; World's Fair, 317; international expositions, 317; California Mid-Winter International Exposition, 317; Antwerp International Exposition, 317; agricultural interests, 318; oleomargarine, alleged violations of law, 319; expert instruction in agriculture, 321; harvest holiday, 322; State topographic survey, 323; honors to Union soldiers, 323; labor interests, 325; industrial classification of inhabitants, 326; public health, 327; preventing spread of tuberculosis in cattle, 327; common school statistics, 328; State prisons, 328; indeterminate sentences at Elmira Reformatory, 330; reformatory management, 331; power of removal of superintendents of reformatories, 332; prevention of waste by fire, 332; amendments to Banking Law, 333; fish propagation, 334; registration of nets, 335; National Guard and Naval Militia, 336; municipal government, home rule, 337; report of Comptroller's agent for examination of charitable institutions, 339; various annual reports, 339, 343; communication from Thomas Asylum for Orphan and Destitute Indian Children, increase of appropriation, 339; monuments at Antietam, 340; pardon report, 343; communication from commissioner of capitol, unsanitary plumbing, 357; redemption of lands sold for taxes, 377; power of removal of superintendents of reformatories and other State institutions, 387; power of removal essential to good government, 387; investigation of Elmira Reformatory, charges against managers, 1893, 387, 388; transfers of inmates from Elmira Reformatory to State prisons, 389; special message, blanket ballot, 393; protest against riders in appropriation bills, 404.

MEMORANDUMS OF APPROVAL. Attorney-General, appearance before grand juries, IX, 409; Penn Yan, water supply, 411; New York, teachers' retirement fund, 411; New York, sheriff, salaried officer, 413; charitable institutions and reformatories,

FLOWER, ROSWELL P., 1894, MEMORANDUMS—(*Continued*).

monthly estimates in certain cases, 436; police patrolmen, pay in certain cities, 498; New York, elevated railroads, rates of fare, 500; New York, rapid transit, 504.

VETOES. Troy, bi-partisan election boards, IX, 343; Sherman, justice of the peace, Marion, legalizing acts, 346; county clerk, fees in relation to notaries public, 346; Brooklyn, aldermen, election by wards, 347; First Baptist church, Greenpoint, German Social Turn-Verein of Rochester, changing names, 348; Tonawanda Indian reservation, bridges over Tonawanda creek, 348; transfer tax, release of tax on Cullum legacy to United States, 349; villages, licensing temporary or transient business, 350; Hornell cemetery, Hornellsville, removal of remains, 352; civil service, preference, persons holding life saving medals, 353; Board of Claims, Putnam, 353; compensation of agent to examine yellows or black knot in peach trees, 354; fire-escapes, school buildings, 355; Buffalo, Main street road improvement, 356; Davenport Institution for Female Orphan Children, changing name, 356; Cornell University, college land scrip fund, loan to State, 357; Oswego, electoral college for appointment of officers, 360; union free schools, academic departments, use of academies, 364; taxpayer's action against public officer, 364; Brooklyn, fire, police and excise departments, supplies, 364; notary public, Cantwell, legalizing acts, 365; school commissioner districts, formation in certain counties, 365; banks, conferring trust company powers on certain moneyed corporations, 366; State Board of Health, rules and regulations, 367; commissioner of deeds, Prime, legalizing acts, 368; Curtis, justice of the peace, legalizing acts, 369; Suffolk county judge and surrogate, salaries, 369; Board of Claims, Linus Jones, Peck & Co., 369; escheat, Sullivan, 370; Port Jervis, public building, 371; Brighton, assessors, compensation, 371; Buffalo, redemption of outstanding bonds, 372; Seneca Lake ferry, extending Goodwin franchise, 372; board of supervisors, licenses to peddlers, 372; Troy Female Seminary, trustees, increasing method of appointment, 373; attorneys, Queens county justice's court, laymen not to practice in, 373; Amsterdam, legalizing assessments, 374; justices of the peace, fees, 375; fraudulent transfers, prevention of, 376; veterinary medicine and surgery, practi-

FLOWER, ROSWELL P., 1894, VETOES —(*Continued*).

tioners, legalizing acts, 376; Metropolis Finance Company, New York, charter, 379; nautical school, establishing, 380; College of the City of New York, acquiring new site, 381; escheat, Dickinson, 384; public health, depositing refuse matters in waters about New York, repeal, 384; appeals, exceptions and case, 390; town meetings, continuance and adjournment, repeal, 392; New York, parks, compensation of laborers and employees, 393; Dean, estate of, 393; Sons of Veterans, parading with fire arms, 398; taxes, Richmond county, collection, 399; towns, division fences, compelling erection of, 401; items in supply bill, 401; escheat, Elizabeth Smith, 403; appropriation bill, 403; New York, department heads, appointment and removal, 415; Albany, water supply, water commissioners, 420; State survey, appropriation, 423; savings banks deposits, publishing statements of, 425; Baron Steuben statue, 427; justices' courts, jurors' fees, 427; State prisons, clerk of prison, 428; escheat, Hyne and Kilgour, 428; Board of Claims,— Crouse and Fyler, 428;— Jarvis, 429;— Drury and Van Arnum, 430;— Moore, 430; Larchmont Manor Park Society, exemption from taxation, 431; Lyons, union school, clerk of trustees, 431; Oneida, refunding bonded indebtedness, 432; Oswego, electoral college for appointment of officers, 432; Ulster, amending village charter, duplicate bill, 432; Plattsburgh, normal school, reducing number of managers, 433; Plattsburgh, stone crusher for highways, 433; Brooklyn, park lands, duplicate bills, 434; Brooklyn, local improvements, duplicate bill, 434; Kings county, coroner's physician, eastern district, 434; New York, park commissioners, appointment, 434; Brooklyn, pier near navy yard, 438; charitable and benevolent institutions, trustees and directors to receive compensation in certain cases, 439; towns, balloting outside incorporated villages, 439; Kings county, charities and corrections, board of, reorganization, 440; New York and Brooklyn bridge, trustees, legislating out of office, 441; benevolent and charitable institutions, establishing cemeteries, 442; street railroads, abandoning part of road, 443; canals, lift and swing-bridges, compulsory operation by State, 444; fish, giving free access to private streams and ponds stocked by State, 444; New York, buildings,

FLOWER, ROSWELL P., 1894, VETOES —(*Continued*).

elevators in, 445; Game Law, fishing through ice, 446; Supreme Court, second judicial department, 446; witness fees, 446; transfer tax appraisers, increasing compensation, 447; general laws, correcting manifest errors, 447; poisons, liquid, preparation and sale, 447; laborers, Brooklyn, fixing rate of wages, 448; Brooklyn, pier North Seventh street, 448; Pythian Association, Amsterdam, exemption from taxa-tion, 449; Erie canal, Buffalo, towing-path wall, Austin street, 449; unpaid taxes, Mount Vernon, bonds for, 450; Syracuse, exempting bonds from taxation, 450; Children's Aid Society, Rochester, charter, 450; Watertown, legaliz-ing local assessments, duplicate bill, 451; Vandevoort relief, 451; Board of Claims,—McIntyre, 451;—Bray, Auburn prison keeper, injured by convict, 452;—National Guard uniforms, 452; canals, electrical conductors, repeal, 453; Yonkers, Watertown, Little Falls, amending charters, elec-tion inspectors, 458; New York, snow and ice, removal from streets, 459; New York, sheriff's deputies, appointment and compensation, 459; New York, real estate, 23d and 24th wards, recording documents, 460; New York, elevators in buildings, 461; towns, highway commissioner, compen-sation, 462; county clerk, office hours in certain counties, 462; railroads, local authorities, definition, 462; teachers, conditional compensation in towns after twenty-five years' service, 463; election officers, compensation, 463; prison labor, prohibiting manufacture of certain articles in penal institutions, 464; manufactures, branding prison-made goods from other States, 464; licenses, itinerant venders of goods, 465; escheat, Reilly, 467; Long Island City, rent of buildings for school purposes, legalizing certain claims, 468; New York, claim of John C. Ham, 468; Erie canal, Verona wall, 469; Firemen's Benevolent Fund Association, Mount Vernon, charter, 469; Grand Army of the Republic, posts, exempting property from taxation, 470; union free schools, Ontario, district No. 6, bonds for new schoolhouse site and building, 470; fish seines and spawning beds south of Croton Point, 470; Dansville, police justices, 471; co-opera-tive savings and loan associations, amending Banking Law, 472; railroads, receipts for freight, 472; surface water, obstructing flow of, 473; Board of Claims, Lockman and

FLOWER, ROSWELL P., 1894, VETOES —(*Continued*).

Devery, 473; attachments, liens on real property, 474; New York, streets, etc., cleaning, 474; tunnel under Newtown creek, 474; Brooklyn, fire department, 475; Brooklyn, justices' courts, 476; Brooklyn, street cleaning department, 476; manufacturing establishments, employment of children in brickyards, 477; elections, official ballot, pasters, 477; Constitutional Convention,— submission of amendments, 480;— contested elections, fees of judicial officers, 481; teachers, professional training, promotion of, 482; Senate investigating committee, New York police department expenses, 484; Albany, police department, reorganization, Troy, police department, Richmond county, police force, and New York, reorganization, 489; Brooklyn, police justices, police courts, appointments, 502; public health, penalties, collection, 504; jurors, commissioners in certain counties, general regulations concerning lists of jurors, qualifications, etc., 514; New York,— parks, protection of, 517; — amending charter, 520; — stables near churches, 520; — lien, discharge of, 520; — fire commissioners not to be candidates for other office, 521; Brooklyn, officers, tenure, 521; New Utrecht, local improvements, 522; coal, protection of purchasers in certain cities, 522; towns, division ditches, 522; villages, taxes, non-resident, report to county treasurer, 523; attorneys, compensation, 523; Board of Claims, jurisdiction, escheats, 524; highways, labor commutations, money system, 524; Western House of Refuge for Women, commitments, 525; Highway Law, joint bridges, apportionment of expenses, Oneida county joint bridges, apportionment of expenses, 525; Court of Special Sessions, New York, appeals, disorderly persons, neglect to support family, 526; flag, foreign, preventing display on public buildings, 527; stock corporations, foreign, licensing, 529; State lands, trespasses, procedure, 530; highways, Fulton Chain of Lakes, public highway, 531; public health, pharmacy, practice of, 532; items in supplemental supply bill, 533; omnibus veto, 534.

Death of, IX, 534; memorial services, 534; quoted, management of State hospitals, 409; Governor Odell's comment on administration of, 461; official service, I, pref., xiii.

FLOOD, CHARLES. Relief, veto, X, 176.

FLOOD, MICHAEL. Land devised by, relative to, veto, IX, 811.

FLORENCE. Town, establishing highways, veto, VI, 182.

FLORIDA. Secession ordinance, V, 396; presidential election of 1876, action by Electoral Commission, VII, 32; action by State Canvassing Board, 37; court to render opinion as to constitutionality of pending bills, VIII, 947; proclamation by Governor, International and Isthmian Exposition, X, 866.

FLORIDA. Town, relief of, veto, V, 725.

FLOYD, WILLIAM. Delegate to Continental Congress, I, 768.

FLOYD, WILLIAM. Trustee, Mechanics and Traders' Savings Institution, testimony, VII, 57.

FLUIDS. Illuminating, regulating standard, veto, VII, 659, 751; act passed, test required, 751.

FLYNN, CORNELIUS. Assistant clerk, District Court, New York, relief, VII, 452.

FLUSHING. Included in metropolitan police district, V, 183; number of excise licenses, 1887, VIII, 360; merged in Greater New York, IX, 300.

    VETOES. Creating board of health, VII, 113; correcting assessment maps, 413; armory, 17th Separate Company, erection, 482, 778; new armory, 953; street improvements, VIII, 724, new bill passed; free schools, increasing tax rate, IX, 718; tax on foreign fire insurance companies, payment of, 817; school district No. 7, conveyance of land by College Point, 819; surplus of certain bonds, authorizing use for other purposes, 819; bonds for arrears of taxes, 819; unpaid taxes, X, 62, 322.

FLYTSEN, FREDERICK. Member of first legislative Council, I, 9.

FOLEY, JOHN. New York, supervisor, salary, veto, VII, 643, 933.

FOLGER, CHARLES J. Chief judge Court of Appeals, law library, relative to, veto, VII, 902.

FOLKS, HOMER. Communication to Governor relative to appointment of William Church Osborn as State commissioner in lunacy, X, 42.

FOLLETT, DAVID L. Justice Supreme Court, law library, appropriation, veto, X, 784.

FOLLETT, NATHAN. Report on seizure of military stores at Batavia arsenal, III, 683.

FOLSOM, GEORGE. Memorial, New York Historical Society, colonial history, IV, 166.

FONDA. Number of excise licenses, 1887, VIII, 360.

FONDA, JELLIS. Guardian of Sir William Johnson's Indian children, II, 273.

FONDA, JOHNSTOWN AND GLOVERSVILLE RAILROAD COMPANY. Asks State aid, VI, 71.

FOOD. Acts relating to, VIII, 320; use of fish, IX, 335; poisonous coloring matter prohibited, X, 30; sample colors, report of State Board of Health, 148; use of fish, IX, 335.

VETOES. Adulteration, VII, 924, 1113; horse flesh, prohibiting sale, amending Penal Cole, IX, 793; sale and delivery of uncooked flesh food on Sunday, X, 280, 292; prohibited articles, seizure and sale, evidence, 776.

FOOT, LEMEN, CAPTAIN. Funds received by, II, 766.

FORAGE. Scarcity of, II, 54, 56; impressment of, 67; in Westchester county, 151, 165; collection by State agent, 169; act to provide for, 185.

FORAGE-MASTER-GENERAL. Deputy, letter from, public contracts, II, 208.

FORBES, JOHN, BRIGADIER-GENERAL. Drives French from Fort Duquesne, I, 630.

FORD, JAMES. Relief, veto, II, 688.

FORD, RODNEY A. Trustee Binghamton Insane Asylum, charges against, not removed, VII, 443.

FORDHAM. St. Joseph's Institution for the Improved Instruction of Deaf-Mutes, deficiency appropriation, veto, VII, 470.

FOREIGN CORPORATIONS. Taxation of, X, 367; license fee, basis of computation, 837.

VETOES. Exercising powers in this State, IV, 827; railroads, amending general act, 1097; stock, licensing, IX, 529; certificate of surety, 864.

FOREIGN INSURANCE COMPANIES. Tax on, appropriation of, VI, 1028; fire and marine companies, deposit of securities, VII, 427; tax on, for benefit of volunteer firemen, IX, 249; canceling authority, retaliatory act, 1896, 691.

VETOES. Preventing removal of causes, VII, 265; removal of actions to Federal court, 573; mutual, insuring tobacco, authorizing business in this State, 934; foreign fire companies, agent's authority, IX, 721, 802; foreign fire companies, tax on, Jamaica and Flushing, 817; New York, taxes, X, 177; life, taxation of, 590.

FOREST COMMISSION. Established, VII, 1110; VIII, 23; cost of, 1891, IX, 11; new commission, 1893, 187.

VETOES. Act to create, VII, 1110; reimbursing maintenance fund, IX, 76; surveys by State Engineer, appropriation, X, 560.

FOREST, FISH AND GAME COMMISSION. Employment of counsel, X, 187; appropriation for salaries and office expenses, 1900, 193; reorganized, 1901, 193, 461.

VETOES. Office expenses, IX, 768; stenographer and clerk, salary, XI — 33

Forest, Fish and Game Commission, Vetoes —(*Continued*).
    X, 421; reforesting burned and barren lands, publication and
    distribution of forest information, 562; office, mezzanine gallery
    and filing cases, 563; general expenses, forest preserve matters,
    appropriation, 786.
Forest, Fish and Game Commissioner.   Office created, X, 193, 461;
    Governor's approval ·of expenses of attorneys or counsel, 194.
Forestport.   State road to Woodhull, repairs, veto, VIII, 850, 1138.
Forest Preserve.   Established, 1885, VIII, 23, 476; ·purchase and sale
    of land in, VIII, 938, 999; should be self-sustaining, IX, 146,
    186, 299; proposed restrictive contracts with private owners,
    185; new Forest Commission, 186, 187; general act, 1893, 187;
    constitutional provision, 187, 300, 569; X, 753; amendment of
    1896 rejected, IX, 187, 669; Governor Flower's special message,
    1893, 213; land in, owned by State, 1893, 219; tax sales, can-
    cellation of, 219, 300, 377; contracts with owners restricting
    timber cutting, 298; acquiring lands for, 299; constitutional
    provision unanimously adopted by Convention. of 1894, 569;
    proposed amendment, 1896, leases and camp sites, not approved,
    569; revision of 1895, 569; devastations should be stopped, 751;
    board established, 752; appropriations for purchase of land by
    State, 752; monument to founders, X, 22; extension in certain
    counties, 22; scientific cultivation, 339, 755, 862; leases and camp
    sites, 339, 512; proposed amendments, 1902, 339; overflowing
    of lands prohibited, 458; Assembly investigating committee,
    1903, 512; proposed constitutional amendments, 1903, 512;
    adoption of plans to attract tourists, 513; purchase of land
    discontinued, 606; acreage of private preserves and other hold-
    ings, 607; assessment of State lands for local purposes, 607;
    Governor Higgins' special message, 1905, 753; scope of restric-
    tion as to removal of timber, 754; lumbering necessary to forest
    production, 755; removal of dead timber, 756.
    Vetoes.   Establishing, VII, 412; map of, in certain counties, IX,
       776; land acquired by tax sale, cancellation of tax, X, 263; ex-
       tending boundaries in Catskills, 291; surveys for Forest Com-
       mission, appropriation, 560; preventing waste of timber killed
       by forest fires, 706; investigation as to trespasses, appropria-
       tion for counsel fees and expenses, 796; commission to investi-
       gate titles, 814.
Forest Preserve Board..   Established, 1897, IX, 752; appropriation,
    1900, X, 193; abolished, 1901, 193, 461.
Forests.   Rapid destruction of, II, 1094; cultivation of, III, 203; IX,
    835; X, 339; furnish abundant fuel, III, 1036; preservation of,
    VI, 629; preservation, importance in maintaining water supply,

FORESTS — (*Continued*).

VII, 983; VIII, 22; IX, 668; prevention of fires, VII, 985; preservation and cultivation, communications relative to, 1000; commission to investigate condition of, VIII, 23; Forest Commission, see that title; forest preserve, see that title; Adirondack, possible revenue from, 937; preservation, beneficial results of recent legislation, 1894; IX, 298; large acquisitions by State, 1897, 834; pulp mills absorb large numbers of trees, 836; scientific cultivation in other States and countries, 836; purchase of land for experiments, 837; Cornell University Experiment tract, 837; X, 32; preservation, importance of, 100; fires should be prevented, 101; fire patrol, 607; preservation policy adopted by Federal government, 755; State should derive revenue from, 862.

VETOES. Parks, preserves and hunting grounds, VII, 412; replanting, promotion of, 932; St. Lawrence county, appointing commissioner, 933; Forest Commission, act to create, 1110; fires, service at, X, 161; assistant superintendent of forests, salary, 421, 424, 553, 563; classifying and describing, 640.

FORFEITURES. See ESTATES. Recovery of, in Albany county, I, 233.
VETOES. Relative to, II, 70;—indemnification of commissioners, 233.

FORGERY. Act to prevent, I, 11; II, 224; classification of, suggested, 550; of certain public records, 952; extradition for, 1104; III, 910; punishment of, 285.

FORGES. Traveling, construction of, II, 629.

FORMAN, JOSHUA. Communication to Governor Van Buren on bank safety fund, III, 261.

FORREST, DAVID P. State prison inspector, conference with Superintendent Pilsbury, V, 433.

FORT. See also specific names. At Albany, I, 33, 35, 93, 143, 147, 157, 179, 315, 460; at Schenectady, 33, 93, 143, 147, 157, 247, 249, 338; in Indian country, 86, 87, 89, 92, 156, 536; royal aid for, 95; weakness of, at New York, 179; at Albany, repair, 203; in New York, repair of, 120, 125, 137, 208, 210, 213, 216, 222, 227, 231, 238, 244, 249, 305, 315; new, at Albany, 238, 247, 249, 338, 390, 460; proposed at Wood creek, 272; proposed acquisition of land for, at Tierondequat, 277; new forts on frontier, 333; Saratoga, 364; Carrying Place, 364, 584; on Hudson river above Albany, 548, 533, 555, 563; new, recommended at several places, 567; at or near Crown Point, 569; on Lake George, 584; at Oneida Station, 625, 626; at Niagara, reduction of, 640.

FORT ANN. VETOES. Champlain canal, raising roadbed, VII, 114, 457, bridge, Dewey's, 577.

Fort Anne. Protection of powder magazine, I, 156.

Fort Brewster. Acquiring site of, veto, X, 435.

Fort Clinton. Supplies for garrison at, I, 462.

Fort Covington. Vetoes. Bridge, amending act, VI, 46; townhouse, 910; annual school meeting, VIII, 130.

Fort Dayton. Petition for appointment of Dr. Petri as surgeon at, II, 117.

Fort Defiance. Perpetuating memory of defenders, appropriation, veto, VIII, 886.

Fort Diamond. Sea fencibles in, II, 810.

Fort Donelson. Successes of Union army at, Maine resolution, V, 459.

Fort Dummer. Orondax Indians in vicinity of, I, 355.

Fort Duquesne. French abandon and destroy, I, 630.

Fort Edward. Garrison at, I, 585, 588; General Webb at, 614; service of New York troops at, 627.

    Vetoes. Canal bridge, VI, 448; VIII, 234; canal bridge, Main street, VII, 115; board of education, contract with Fort Edward Collegiate Institute, 205.

Fort Edward Collegiate Institute. Contract with Fort Edward board of education, veto, VII, 205.

Fort Edward Feeder. Completing bridge, VI, 855.

Fort Egmont. Spanish seizure of, I, 737.

Fort Erie. American successes at, II, 806.

Fort Frontenac. Capture and destruction of, I, 625; New York troops at, capture of, 627.

Fort Gates. Sea fencibles in, II, 810.

Fort George (Canada, War of 1812). Taken by Americans, II, 786.

Fort George (Lake George). Lands at, ceded to Regents, resumption of, II, 376.

Fort George. At New York, providing for completion of, I, 216, 218; repair of chapel and barracks, 222, 227, 231, 238; repairs at, 227, 231, 238, 241, 260, 265, 270, 277, 305, 309, 339, 736, 748; Legislature meets at, 258; public buildings in, destroyed by fire, 297, 302; stable and coachhouse at, 306, 339, 460; repair and improvement of, 322, 763; powder magazine, 322; completion of house and stables, 511; injured by storm, 528; repair of battery at, 748, 763; demolition of, II, 305.

Fort Green. Monument, prison-ship martyrs, veto, VII, 85.

Fort Hamilton. Strengthening works at, III, 309.

Fort Henry. Success of Union army at, V, 439.

Fort Herkimer. Petition for appointment of Dr. Petri as surgeon at, II, 117.

Fort Hudson. Improvement of, II, 864.

FORT HUNTER. Ruinous condition of, I, 256, 265, 277, 280; proposed removal of garrison to Carrying Place, 258, 260; cannon and military stores for, 316; improvement of Schoharie creek, veto, VIII, 886.

FORT JAMES. First Assembly meets in, I, 9.

FORT LEE. Southern boundary of Palisades park, IX, 736.

FORT MONTGOMERY. Taken by British, II, 16; soldiers at, relief of families, 21.

FORT MORTON. Improvement of, II, 864.

FORT NIAGARA. Surrender of, II, 786; dangerous situation of, 791; William Morgan confined at, III, 251; cession of land at, 850.

FORT ONTARIO. Providing for company at, I, 675; land in front of, cession to Oswego, IV, 591.

FORT PILLOW. Riot at, V, 858.

FORT PLAIN. Act relative to, III, 1023.

FORT PULASKI. Ceded by Georgia authorities, V, 315.

FORT RICHMOND. Erection of, II, 658; improvement of, 864; guard at, 865; repairs recommended, III, 35; sale to United States, IV, 72.

FORT SCHUYLER. Conduct of garrison at, II, 8, 11; supplies for garrison, 122; Indian treaty at, lands embraced in, 273.

FORT SMITH. Improvement of, II, 864.

FORT STANWIX. Indian treaty at, I, 727; canal to Wood creek, II, 312, 320; relieved by General Herkimer, III, 228; development of neighboring country, 805.

FORT STEVENS. Sea fencibles in, II, 810.

FORT WILLIAM. Repairs on, I, 338.

FORT SUMTER. Attacked by South Carolina forces, V, 306; Major Anderson in command, 399; surrendered to rebels, 399; national flag again hoisted, 676.

FORT TOMPKINS. Injured by storm, II, 1038; plan of construction, 1081; sale to United States, IV, 72.

FORT WILLIAM HENRY, LAKE GEORGE. Garrison at, I, 585, 588; distressed condition of garrison, 597; surrenders to French, 614; New York troops cut road to, from Fort Edward, 627.

FORT WILLIAM HENRY, NEW YORK. Sloughter Assembly meets at, I, 20; chapel in, proposed repair of, 41, 44, 63; repair of barracks in, 48.

FORTIFICATIONS (Colony). Governor urges repair of, I, 133, 144; act for repair of, 155, 179, 193, 522; at New York, 187, 247; on frontier, 196, 247; completion of, 256, 260, 265, 270, 277, 285; general act, 250, 296, 314, 345, 547; act for completing, in Albany, 318; plan of, at New York, 322; for frontier defense, 323; at Albany, 460; New York, engineer's report on, 467; at Crown Point, 548; plan of, for frontier posts, 572; repairs at New York, 741.

FORTIFICATIONS (State). Appropriation for, II, 113; at New York, 334, 349, 370, 413, 414, 418, 422, 440, 550, 568, 618, 637; on Governor's island, 360; on Bedlow's island, 360; on Oyster island, 360; expense of, payment, 438, 507; negotiations with national government, 469; report of engineer and commissioners, 667; on Staten Island, 676, 1037; III, 309; statement of expenditures, 750, 757; on Hendrick's reef, 777; on Signal hill, 778; for defense of New York, 797; Governor urges completion of, 830; on Staten Island, improvement of, 864; sale to United States, 865, 940, 1031; III, 178, 309, 972; IV, 72, 288.

FORTUNE, THE. Bellomont recommends relief of, against certain judgment, I, 84.

FORTY-SECOND STREET AND GRAND STREET FERRY RAILROAD COMPANY. Extending tracts, veto, VI, 335.

FOSDYCK, NICHOL, JR. Bond for return of arms, II, 774.

FOSTER, EDWARD W. Member of Tax Revision Commission, 1881, VII, 538.

FOSTER, HENRY. New York, relief, veto, X, 176.

FOSTER, HENRY A. Appointed United States Senator, IV, 154.

FOSTER, WILLIAM. Dock on Oneida lake, veto, VI, 156.

FOSTER, WILLIAM R. (F.) Extradition, veto, X, 59; claim of New York Produce Exchange, services, veto, 473.

FOUNDLING ASYLUM OF THE SISTERS OF CHARITY, NEW YORK. Changing name, veto, VIII, 376.

FOUNDRY. Proposed, for making cannon, II, 813, 814.

FOURTH JUDICIAL DEPARTMENT. How constituted, IX, 546.

FOURTH JUDICIAL DISTRICT. Additional justices for, VII, 837; included in third judicial department, IX, 546.

    VETOES. Law library, Canton, VII, 82; law library, 218; additional justice, X, 947.

FOURTH OF JULY. A public holiday, VI, 679.

FOWLER. VETOES. Highway over certain lands, VI, 188; breakwater in, 331; highway, repairs, appropriation, X, 428, 791.

FOWLER, CHARLES A. Senate, remarks on opening of new Senate chamber, VII, 540; member of insane asylum investigating committee, IX, 312.

FOWLER, CHARLES W. Court of Claims, veto, X, 165.

FOWLER, RICHARD C. Service of process on, Van Rensselaer rent, III, 825.

FOX, AUSTEN G. Appointment, X, 77; special counsel to examine report of Canal Investigating Commission, 1898, communication to Governor, 40; appropriation for expenses, 40.

FOX, CHARLES J. Nominated as trustee of Soldiers' Home, VIII, 236.

Fox, HENRY. Secretary of State, letter from, Earl of Loudoun appointed commander-in-chief, I, 597.

Fox, H. F. Canal department, appropriation for services, veto, IX, 716.

Fox, JABEZ. Suggested appointment as postmaster at Herkimer, II, 1070.

FOXALL, HENRY. Superintendent of Georgetown foundry, II, 608.

FOXTON, THEODORE S. State lunatic asylum commissioner, communication from, III, 930.

FRANCE. English subjects required to leave, I, 5; trade with, prohibited, 117; preparations for settlements on Mississippi river, 178, 192; protests against encroachments at Niagara, 227; effect of possible rupture with, 244; expected rupture with, 295, 304, 307; fleet of, battle with English in Mediterranean, 314; declares war against England, 316; King of, accused of violating treaties, 317; extensive preparations for war, 401; treaty of peace, Aix-La-Chapelle, 471, 481; sends more troops to Canada, 591; England declares war against, 602; defeat of fleet, 640, 642; intended invasion of Great Britain defeated, 642; insincerity in negotiations, 662; war with, purpose of, 667; Languedoc canal, 728; treaty with United States, II, 44, 67; privileges and immunities of subjects of, 91; supplies for fleet and army, 108, 111; aid to American cause, 148, 154, 159; only European power acknowledging American independence, 153; birth of dauphin, 182; alleged indignity to flag by British seamen in New York, 245; relations with United States, 420, 423, 442 (general note); depredations on American commerce, 445; Louisiana sold to United States, 535; IV, 813; John Armstrong, appointed minister to, II, 546; violates international law, 616; diminution of commercial enterprise, 617; revokes decrees relative to neutral commerce, 672, 690; improved political conditions in, III, 320; description of roads in, 374; obtaining colonial records from, 752; silk culture, 946; designs on English colonies, documents relating to, 1019; American colonial documents, examination of, IV, 185; New York geological survey transmitted to, 384; interchange of publications, 465; instruction of idiots, 555; authentication of instruments in Great Britain and France, V, 212; right to hold real estate, equality of American citizens, VI, 551; financial experience in, following German war, 976; joins in Yorktown Centennial Celebration, VII, 736; sends delegates and naval escort, 738; participation in Cotton States Exposition, IX, 581; forest cultivation, 836; canal development should keep pace with railroads, X, 135; illiteracy as compared with New York, 859.

FRANCHISE. Banks, sale of, III, 470, 632; municipality should derive benefit from, V, 189, 238, 517, 648, 799, 811, 873; VI, 63, 74, 206, 694, 703; VII, 793, 1068; IX, 41, 91, 101; X, 44, 304, 487, 658; extent of grant should be certain, V, 647; should not convey irrevocable vested right, 874; people own street railroad grants, VI, 64; use of steam on canals, 107; exclusive, constitutional provision, 662, 683, 691, 814, 949, 1034; VII, 845; VIII, 411, 463, 880; X, 399; corporations, Tax Act of 1880, VII, 454, 682, 816; New York, percentage of net income payable by West Side and Yonkers Patent Railway Company, 852; payments to local treasury, 1068; proposed sale to highest bidder, 1069; sale at auction, VIII, 200; given away in New York, 201; New York and Brooklyn, Governor Flower's special message, relative to, IX, 39; sale under Cantor Act, 41, 101; should yield return to government, X, 36, 43; taxation, general act, 1899, 46, 71, 83, 196, 490; taxation by State authorities, 64; Tax Act of 1899 constitutional, 71; taxation, amending act of 1899, 171; tax on trust companies, 200; tax on savings banks, 200; tax on foreign corporations, 367; Pennsylvania Railroad Company, terminal facilities in New York, 396; Hudson river dams, State or locality should derive remuneration from, 453; earning capacity as basis of taxation, 487; local control of, 624; special, taxation of, review, employment of counsel, 845.

VETOES. Exclusive, carding machines, II, 534; exclusive, street railroads in New York, V, 800; corporations, equalizing tax on, VIII, 640; New York, requiring certain corporations to afford special facilities to city officers and employees, IX, 719; corporations using pneumatic tubes, tax on, 794; taxation as real property, X, 63; tunnel railroads, New York, 471; corporations, amending act, 706.

FRANCIS, JACOB. Appointed trustee of St. Regis Indians, II, 938.

FRANCIS, SAMUEL. Claim of, support of prisoners, II, 259.

FRANCISCO, JOHN L. Bond for return of arms, II, 772.

FRANKING PRIVILEGE. Proposed extension of, III, 637; abolition recommended, IV, 45, 84.

FRANKFORT. VETOES. Better administration of justice, IX, 867; Court of Claims, claims of residents, X, 706; payment of certain indebtedness, town bonds, 815.

"FRANKLIN, THE." Brings cholera to New York, VI, 360.

FRANKLIN, BENJAMIN. Commissioner from Pennsylvania to Albany Convention, I, 578; prepares plan of union, 579; works of, text of plan, 579; member of Continental Congress, 583; presents to Lord Dart-

FRANKLIN, BENJAMIN —(Continued).
mouth petition of Continental Congress, 770; payment of bills drawn by Congress, II, 160.

FRANKLIN BRIDGE COMPANY. Charter, veto, IV, 694.

FRANKLIN COUNTY. Defense of, II, 713; militia from, 1812, 744, 807; troops stationed in, 745, 746; arsenal in, 758; arms and supplies for, 770; rewards for destruction of wolves, 1107; arsenal and equipments to be sold, IV, 495; increase of population, VI, 578; land in, State park, 629; highways, facilitating travel on, VII, 650; boundaries relocated, 720; timbered lands, acquisition by State, 722; average excisé license fees, 1889, VIII, 686; highways, cost of labor system, 1892, IX, 199; insane, care of, county and State systems compared, 228.

VETOES. Special road district, VI, 481; Fort Covington, townhouse, 910; Saranac river, removing obstructions, VII, 382; escheat, Schroeder, 1116; St. Regis Indian lands, removing intruders, VIII, 115; State land in, conveyance to Schroeder, 131; Harrietstown, town hall, 508; Saranac river improvement, IX, 62; changing boundaries, X, 320; exemption from act relating to rebate of taxes for wide tire wagons, 393.

FRANKLIN LOAN AND TRUST COMPANY, NEW YORK. Amending charter, veto, VIII, 630, 890.

FRANTZ, FERDINAND. Relief, veto, VI, 312.

FRASER, CHARLES E. Relief, veto, VI, 185.

FRAUD. VETOES. Definition of, VII, 350; sale or exchange of merchandise, 388; in mánufacture and sale of sugars, syrups, molasses and honey, 648; transfers, prevention of, amending act, IX, 376, new act passed; prevention of, licensing itinerant venders of goods, 465.

FRAWLEY, JAMES J. Senate, member of joint legislative committee on services in memory of former Governor Higgins, X, 963.

FRAZEE, JAMES. Board of Claims, veto, VIII, 887.

FREDERICA. Captain Horton at, letter from, I, 338.

FREDERICKSBURGH. Washington at, letter from, II, 54.

FREDONIA. Normal school at, V, 695, 780. VETOES. Darwin R. Barker Literary Association, charter, VII, 845; amending charter, VIII, 457.

FREDONIA NORMAL SCHOOL. Established, V, 695, 780, 852; Hattie L. Burhans injured at, claim for damages, IX, 50.

VETOES. Repairs and improvements, VII, 468; VIII, 863, 1138; rooms for school societies, X, 649.

FREEDOM. Of State, act relating to, veto, II, 215.

FREEDOM OF DEBATE. Legislature granted, I, 8.

FREEHOLDERS. To choose members of Assembly, I, 6.

FREEMAN, JOHN R. New York, water supply expert, using city water for generation of electricity, X, 805.

FREEMEN'S RIGHTS. Guaranteed by Leisler's Assembly, I, 16; freedom of action, II, 29; under Election Law, 36; equality of tax, 40, 60.

FREE SCHOOL DISTRICT No. 12, NEWTOWN. Charter, veto, VIII, 338.

FREE SPEECH. Secured by Constitution, III, 589, 645; IV, 581; V, 483, VIII, 578; anti-slavery agitation, III, 589; value of public discussion, IV, 581; discussion of questions relating to slavery, 829.

FREE TRADE ASSOCIATION, NEW YORK. Recommends repeal of inspection laws, IV, 45.

FRELINGHUYSEN, FREDERICK T. Member New Jersey commission to procure Constitutional Convention, V, 325.

FRELINGHUYSEN, THEODORE. New Jersey commissioner on New York boundary, VI, 779.

FRENCH. Of Canada, attempt on frontiers, I, 35; derive information from prisoners among Indians, 36; squadron threatens New York, 41; reported negotiations of, with Five Nations, 46; approach to Cadaracqui, 52; occupy and fortify Cadaraequi, 57, 58; attack Oneidas and Onondagas, 65; defeated by Indians near Kinderhook, 68; attack on Pemaquid, 69; detain Indian prisoners after treaty of peace, 82; support Pretender, as King of England, 97; expected attack of, on New York, 103; movement against Five Nations, 114; act to prevent slaves from running away to, 116; privateer near New York, 117, 119, 128, 131; trade with France prohibited, 117; expected attempt on colony, 119, 137; attack on New England, 142; engaging Five Nations against, 157; negotiations with Five Nations, 161; maintenance of prisoners, 166; presents to Indians, 176, 310; learning Indian language, 176; negotiations with Onondagas, 177; plans for American settlements, 178, 192; encroachments on frontier, 192; trading-house at Niagara, 193, 222, 227; prohibiting Indian trade, 193; continued aggressions against colony, 196; clandestine trade with, prohibited, 200; restricting trade with, 209, 212, 600; attempts to seduce Indians, 210, 222, 225; artifices to secure Indian trade, 217; King vetoes bills prohibiting sale of Indian goods to, 236, 237; occupation of Crown Point, 241; propose to occupy Fiederondequat, 241; aiding Indians, 248; Cœur obtains leave to build house at Tierondequat, 262, 265; encroachments on northern frontier, 271, 272; proposed acquisition of Tierondequat, 271, 272; defending Oswego against, 296; encroachments in Indian country, 301; preparing to invade King's dominions, 314, 318; Indians reluctant to engage in war with, 319; Crown Point a convenient place of operations, 324; designs on Oswego, 328; attempt on

FRENCH — (Continued).

Annapolis Royal, 331, 336; Massachusetts movement against, 331; armament at Martinique, 340; expected attack on British dominions in South America, 340; alleged negotiations of Six Nations with, 341; intrigues with Six Nations, 342, 355, 366, 381, 464; invade Nova Scotia, 346; murders by French Indians, 355; Indians declare war against English, 355; Six Nations agree to join in war against, 359; with Indians, reported near Stockbridge, 363; expected invasion of, 366; fleet reported off Nova Scotia, 383; extensive preparations for war, 401; exchange of English prisoners, 409; incursion on Burnett's Field, 410; with Indians, near Crown Point, movement against, 410; sachems in interest of, 425; projected movement against, 464; danger of Indian defection to, 466; privateers infesting American coast, 467; war with, conclusion of, 471, 481; exchange of prisoners, 476, 486, 489, 492, 507, 519; designs to alienate Indians, 486, 504, 508, 515; alleged encouragement of war among Indians, 504; commissioners on exchange of prisoners, entertainment of, 510; emissaries among Indians, 517; encroachments in western country, 534, 535, 538, 541, 549; interference with fur trade, 535; fort at French creek, 541; acknowledge Great Britain's dominion over Five Nations, 542; sending troops to the Ohio, 543; with Indian allies, defeat Washington on Ohio frontier, 546, 549; build fort on Monongahela river, 546, 549; campaign against, 547; fort on Beeve park, 549; plans for conquest of America, 550; Indians attack Hoseck and Sinkbaick, 553; access to New York, if Albany be taken, 563; obtain goods through Louisburg trade, 564; Indians attack Brimmer family at Hoseck, 571; Braddock's defeat, 572; under Baron de Dieskau, defeat of, 583; capture Oswego, 602; invade Minorca, 602; neutrals, settlement in New York, subsistence of, 607; attack Fort William Henry, 614; navy defeated, 624; intended irruption into Mohawk valley, 625; defeat at Cadaracqui, 625; desire to possess New York, 629; abandon and destroy Fort Duquesne, 630; army defeated near Minden, 640; fleet defeated on coast of Algrave, 640; driven from Crown Point and Ticonderoga, 640; defeat of army for relief of Niagara, 640; Quebec taken, 640; fleet defeated on coast of France, 642; conquest of Canada, 648; insincerity in negotiations, 602; again lose St. John's, Newfoundland, 669; invasion on northern frontier, II, 7; fleet and army (Revolutionary War) supplies for, 108, 111; designs on English colonies, documents relating to, III, 1019; spoliation claims, IV, 83, 85, 865.

FRENCH, EDWARD H. Canal contractor, appropriation for interest, veto, VI, 1008.

FRENCH CREEK. Fort at, I, 541; militia at, III, 694.

FRENCH HOUSE OF DEPUTIES. Small number of laws enacted, V, 849.

FRENCH MILLS. Militia captured at, II, 770; purchase of St. Regis lands at, 866.

FRENCH NEUTRALS. Settled in province, subsistence of, I, 607.

FRENCH PRISONERS. Maintenance of, I, 166, 327, 375, 388, 445; to be sent out of colony, 329, 330, 624; sent to St. Domingo, 334; Colonel Johnson's certificate as to, 441; exchange of, 467, 470, 474, 476, 486, 489, 492, 507, 510, 519; claims for subsistence of, 478, 508, 608; medical service for, 511; subsistence of, 603, 616.

FRENCH SPOLIATION CLAIMS. Resolutions relating to payment of, IV, 83, 85, 865.

FREWSBURG CEMETERY ASSOCIATION. Charter, veto, VI, 186.

FREY, HENDRICK. Guardian of Sir William Johnson's Indian children, II, 273.

FRIENDS. See QUAKERS.

FRINK, ADAM. Bond for return of arms, II, 774.

FRINK, JAMES. Commissioner, Allegany reservation, Red House bridge, veto, VII, 587.

FROELICH, ELIZABETH. Widow of Jacob Froelich, escheat, veto, X, 312.

FROELICH, JACOB. Estate, escheat, veto, X, 312.

"FROLIC, THE." Captured by Paul Jones, II, 780.

FRONTIER GASLIGHT COMPANY, WATERTOWN. Charter, veto, VI, 215.

FRONTIERS. Governor Fletcher urges defense of, I, 28, 33; attempt on, by French and Indians, 35; aid from Crown, 41; veto of act for defense of, 54; engineer to examine fortifications, 77; defense of, 19, 23, 25, 37, 44, 48, 52, 56, 57, 62, 71, 73, 99, 103, 105, 108, 112, 114, 118, 124, 125, 130, 137, 138, 149, 154, 155, 160, 166, 193, 196, 202, 239, 247, 276, 290, 315, 362, 421, 455, 537, 563, 680; Engineer Redknap visits Albany, 130; situation at Wood's creek, 139; situation on, 142; more advanced settlements needed, 181; French encroachments on, 192; Albany county, ordnance for forts in, 295; cannon and military stores for, 316; repair and improvement of fortifications, 323; colonies should join in defense of, 324; additional forts on, 333; dangerous situation of settlers on, 342; danger of attack from French Indians, 358; fort at Saratoga, 364; new blockhouses, 368; outscouts for, 462; continuing protection of, 470; conditions on, 474; Ohio, French encroachments on, 534; western, defense of, 607, 616, 626; II, 26, 70, 92, 106; settlements on, consideration of plans for, 631; volunteers for service on, 670; western, Indian ravages on, II, 50; northern, conditions on, 101; act for defense of, 106, 148; defense of settlements on, 115, 174, 180; precarious conditions on, 123; improved conditions on, 147; troops for, 188; condition of posts on western, 201; defense of northwestern, 245; British occupy western

FRONTIERS — (*Continued*).

posts, 253, 334; western, proposed route of march of forces for, 273; proposed fortifications on northern and western, 334; defense of northern and western, 618, 636, 713; exposed condition of northern, 743; western, devastations by British, 787; western, defense of, III, 691; northeastern, disturbances on, 759; colonial documents relative to expeditions on, 1019; commission on defense of, V, 545; northern, expected attack by southern refugees, 550; northern, band of desperadoes on, 612; northern, importance of adequate defense, 638.

FROST, HENRY A. Board of Claims, IX, 721.

FRY, ALFRED B. Member Canal Advisory Board, X, 629.

FRY, JAMES B., COLONEL. Informed of overcrowded condition at Elmira, V, 562; communication to Governor Fenton relative to New York quotas, 621; telegram, quotas, 628, 631.

FUEL. Impressment of, II, 109; scarcity of wood for, 1094; coal used in manufacture of salt, V, 176.

FUGITIVES FROM JUSTICE. Extradition of, II, 1105; III, 350, 584, 596, 777, 778, 852, 869, 915, 917, 922, 1030; IV, 8; extradition, Williams case, III, 584, 594; meaning of term, 594, 604; Georgia protests against Maine's refusal to surrender Philbrook and Kellcran, Atticus case, 748; act regulating procedure, 748; Virginia case (Johnson, Smith and Gansey), 777, 852, 869, 920, 932, 936; IV, 47; Curry case, forgery, III, 910, 915; Greenman case, 937; expense of proceedings, V, 291; proceedings against, veto, IX, 793.

FUGITIVE SLAVES. Surrender of, III, 572, 574, 917, 922, 937; IV, 7, 569, 810, 823; V, 302; trial by jury in cases of, III, 779, 911, 925, 936, 981, 1028, 1037; IV, 7; V, 301; Federal act relating to, IV, 7; trial by jury, unconstitutional, 7; V, 301; Virginia resolutions, IV, 466; Lemmon case, 810; New York condemns law, 828; Vermont demands repeal of law, 865; proposed liability of States for refusing to surrender, V, 316; proposed liability of United States for failure to recover, 355.

FULLER, RUDOLPH C. Senate, member of Prince Henry reception committee, X, 479.

FULTON. VETOES. Amending city charter, X, 583; sidewalks and paving, 715.

FULTON CHAIN OF LAKES. Making public highway, veto, IX, 531.

FULTON COUNTY. Agricultural society in, III, 945; refunding illegal taxes, VI, 278; average excise license fees, 1889, VIII, 686; highways, cost of labor system, 1892, IX, 200; insane, care of, county and State systems compared, IX, 228.

VETOES. Special highway, VI, 598; Northville, amending General Village Law, VII, 214; bridge over Sacandaga river, Northville,

FULTON COUNTY, VETOES—(*Continued*).
474; board of supervisors, equalizing representation, 769, 860, new bill passed; superintendent of the poor, election, 930; excepting from County Treasurer's Act, 1010; relief of poor, VIII, 130; tax sale, Walker case, X, 589.

FULTON, ALFRED. Commissioner to build road on St. Regis reservation, veto, VII, 91, 475.

FULTON, ROBERT. Aid to heirs, III, 134, 150; application of steam to navigation, 150; exclusive privileges granted to, 151; proposed statue of, VI, 435; application of steam to navigation, Centennial Celebration, X, 874.

FULTON INSURANCE COMPANY. Bill incorporating, recalled for amendment, IV, 751.

FULTON MARKET FISHMONGERS ASSOCIATION. Relative to, veto, X, 177.

FULTON SAVINGS BANK, NEW YORK. Charter, veto, VI, 322.

FULTONVILLE. VETOES. Rebuilding canal bridge, VI, 1007; enlarging canal bridge, VII, 508; iron draw-bridge, VIII, 453.

FULTON, WALL AND CORTLAND STREETS FERRY RAILROAD COMPANY. Relief, veto, VIII, 1119.

FUR. Trade in, affected by colonial restrictive bills, I, 237; how to increase trade at Oswego, 239; danger of French interference, 241, 535; trade at Oswego, possible interception by French, 262, 296; act to regulate trade in, 265; danger to trade by French acquisition of Tierondequat, 272; trade, protection of, at Tierondequat, 277; traders retreat from Oswego, 326.

FURNACES. Colonel Livingston offers use of, II, 20.

FUSILEERS. At Albany, discharge of, I, 36; weekly payment of, 43; provided for, 57, 99, 105; difference between Governor and Assembly as to officers of, 109; for frontier defense, 118; at Albany, provision for, 409.

FYLER, SILAS B. Board of Claims, veto, IX, 428.

G.

GAFFIGAN, WILLIAM. Troy school janitor, claim, veto, X, 634.

GAGE, FRANKLIN. Relief, veto, VI, 344.

GAGE, THOMAS, LIEUTENANT-COLONEL. At Schenectady, I, 591; return of troops for New York, 708; papers from, Indian trade, 733; claim for quartering troops, 744, 751.

GAINES, EDMUND PENDLETON, GENERAL. Success in Niagara campaign, II, 802; thanked by Legislature and presented with sword, 832; letter from Governor Tompkins, 836; reply, 837.

GALEN. Legalizing contract with Reynolds, VIII, 1148.

GALLAGHER, WILLIAM J. Dam across Hudson river, North Creek, veto, X, 705.

GALLAUDET HOME. Exempting property from taxation, veto, VIII, 623, 733.

GALLIEN, ELIZA M. (MRS.) Widow of Henry Gallien, former Deputy Comptroller, salary, appropriation, veto, VII, 1081; VIII, 109.

GALLIEN, HENRY. Notary public, Sullivan affidavit, VII, 499, 790; former Deputy Comptroller, salary, appropriation for widow, veto, 1081.

GALLIGAN, LOUIS M. New York, action against school trustees, 19th ward, IX, 871.

GALSTER, JACOB. Canal department, appropriation for services, veto, IX, 716.

GALVIN, PETER J. Injuries received while at work on capitol, Court of Claims, veto, X, 267.

GALWAY, JAMES. Relief, veto, VI, 573.

GAMBLING. See also POOL-SELLING. Encouraged by lotteries, III, 187; stockjobbing, 565; in stocks, IV, 807; bucket shops, business prohibited, VII, 1090; racing, Pool-Selling Act regulating, VIII, 434; bucket shops, act of 1889, 815; prohibited, IX, 548, 602; X, 892; act of 1895, IX, 601.

VETOES. Bucket shops, taxation of, VIII, 445; race track, amending act, X, 891.

GAME AND FISH PROTECTORS. Cost of, 1891, IX, 11. VETOES. Amending act, IX, 151; compensation, 768; X, 810; game protectors, amending Game Law, 319; Jamaica bay, etc., 815, 949.

GAME LAW. Power of supervisors to enact, should be abrogated, VII, 301; general act, 1879, 302; fishing in Lake Ontario, act relative to, VIII, 432; game and fish protectors, act reorganizing, 607; revision commission created, 1890, 975; revision of 1895, IX, 569; deer, more strict regulations for protection of, 669; improvement in administration needed, X, 100; birds should not be killed to obtain ornaments, 102; uniform open season, 102; revision of 1900, 102; bond by person in possession of game, 346; proposed regulations by boards of supervisors, 504; spring shooting, Wild Fowl Act, 1903, 536.

VETOES. Amending act, VI, 505, 906; VII, 264, 507, 508, 611, 938; IX, 233, 258, 798, 863; X, 448, 810; close season, VI, 274; Sunday observance, 505; Wyoming county, fishing in Tonawanda creek, 906; fishing in Clinton county, 906; fishing in St. Lawrence river, 911; trout, Owasco lake, taking prohibited, VII, 69; Ulster county, protection in certain waters, 131; Ulster

GAME LAW, VETOES —(Continued).

county, protection of fish in Esopus creek, 234; special game
constables, 263; preservation of certain animals, 264; preservation of fish, Monroe county, 264; private parks, protection of,
264; Hudson river, protecting spawning fish, 264; Kings county,
preservation of fish, 264; Loon lake, taking certain fish prohibited, 264; protection of shellfish in certain waters, 415;
Jefferson and Oswego counties, releasing certain waters from
operation of, 442, new bill passed; Steuben county, fishing in
Loon lake, 446; replenishing lakes and rivers, 458; taking fish
from Wallkill river, 506; Monroe county, protection of fish, 507;
fish hatchery, Jefferson county, 632; Salmon river, preservation
of fish in, 807; preservation of game, 1095; killing wild fowl
and fish, VIII, 130; method of taking fish, 131; Lake Erie,
preservation of fish, 457; game and fish constables, auditing
accounts, 469; Hudson river, pound and purse nets, 627; Oneida
county, 716; Delaware river, shad and game fish, protection of,
888; Lake George, fish in, 888; Brant lake, black bass in, 975;
snares and nets, use of, 976; Erie county, protection of ducks
and fish, 979; fish, private ponds, trespasses on, IX, 233; board
of supervisors, powers of, 234; fishing through ice, 446; amending act of 1895, 717; fishing with certain devices prohibited,
717; wild fowl, 721; fishing through ice in certain lakes, 721; eel-
weirs in Chemung river, 721; fur-bearing animals, protection,
722; deer, hounding in certain towns in Washington county, 723;
fish and game protectors, foresters, compensation, 768; fire
wardens, compensation, 768; taking fish through ice in certain
waters, 798; grouse and other birds, 798; publication and distribution, 798; Jamaica bay, nets in, 798; squirrels, hares and
rabbits, amending, 798; amendments, 798, 863; fishing in Fall
creek, Ithaca, 798; sturgeon, method of taking, Thousand Islands,
798, 863; disseminating knowledge of birds and wild animals,
798; protector's right of search, 798; hounds running at large
where deer inhabit, 798; fire wardens and assistants, Sullivan
county, 799; elk, protection of, 799; recoveries in actions by
people, disposal of, 799; venison, possession of, 799; Crystal
lake, black bass, close season, 799; use of nets, 799; salmon, close
season, 799; sale of bird skins, 799; protectors and foresters,
amending act, 862; taking bass in St. Lawrence county, X, 61;
Lake Erie, fishing in, 61; Honeoye lake, fishing with set lines,
64; fishing in Ouleout creek, 161; forest fires, services at, 161;
fishing in certain waters in Seneca county, 168; fishing in

GAME LAW, VETOES—(*Continued*).

Canandaigua and Honeoye lakes, 173; fishing in Chautauqua lake, 174; fishing in Skaneateles lake, 174; black bass, close season, 308, 313; Antwerp or homing pigeons, interference with, 309; fishing through ice in Washington county, 309, 313; game, places of refuge for, 309; grouse, close season, 311; fishing with set lines, 312; Adirondack park, amending description, 317; fishing in Orange county, 319, 320; woodcock, close season, 382; bass, striped, in Hudson river, 392; fish culturist, salary, 421, 553; assistant superintendent of forests, salary, 421; woodcock and grouse, close season, 439; spearing suckers and eels, Long Point, 440; woodcock on Long Island, close season, 440; supervisors, powers in certain counties, 441; grouse, relative to, 442; nets in Hudson and Delaware rivers, 443; trout season, Keuka lake, 443; squirrels, close season, 444; Rockland county, taking game in, 444; lake trout, taking or possession of, 445; nets and set lines, 445; shellfish, taking by non-residents, 448; fishing, destruction of illegal devices, 448; Cattaraugus county, hunting with ferret, 587; Sullivan county, hunting and fishing on Sunday prohibited, 589; fish, transportation of, 590; grey squirrels, 700; wild fowl, taking in Black River bay, 700; sale of trout, 708; game protectors, compensation, 810; pollution of streams, 810; general amendments, 810; stocking Adirondack region with game, 814; fire wardens, Jefferson county, 954; Orange county, close season, 954; Kayutah lake, 954; hares and rabbits, close season, 954; fishing through ice, 954; fishing through ice, Lake Neahtahwanta, 954.

GAMEWELL FIRE ALARM TELEGRAPH COMPANY. Claim against village of Far Rockaway, veto, X, 324.

GAMING. Suppression of, recommended by Congress, II, 56.

GANGHAM, CHARLES H. New York, Municipal Court attendant, claim, veto, X, 168.

GANONOQUE RIVER. Terminus of Oswegatchie reservation, II, 553.

GANSEVOORT, LEONARD. Commissioner to Commercial Convention, II, 260.

GANSEVOORT, PETER, DR. Claim, subsistence of French prisoners, I, 608.

GANSEVOORT, PETER, MAJOR-GENERAL. Claim of, payment, II, 356.

GANSEVOORT, PETER, JR. Chosen Regent, II, 629; death of, 753.

GANSEY, ISAAC. Extradition of, III, 852, 869, 920, 932, 937, 982; IV, 47; legislative action, III, 1030.

GARD, WILLIAM. Court of Claims, Auburn prison, veto, X, 702.

GARDES LAFAYETTE. Escort of French delegates, Yorktown Celebration, VII, 740.

GARDINER, ADDISON. Circuit judge, letter from, Morgan case, III, 355; appointed delegate to Washington Peace Convention, V, 310; declines appointment, 311.

GARDNER, CHARLES K., COLONEL. Prepares book on military tactics, II, 996.

"GARDNER'S COMPEND." On military tactics, purchase of, II, 995, 996.

GARFIELD, JAMES A. President, action on New York appointments, VII, 556, 559; quoted, regulation of civil service, 561; assassination of, 677; death of, 678.

GARFIELD MEMORIAL HOME. Changing name to Brooklyn Home for Consumptives, veto, VII, 931.

"GARLAND, THE." Brings stamped paper to New York, I, 711.

GARRISON. At Albany, I, 19, 26, 52, 131, 239; Schenectady, 26, 52, 108, 131, 366; Half Moon, 26, 108; Connestaguicena, 26; fort in Indian country, 89, 160; Nistigaone, 108; Kinderhook, 108; New York, 131; French at Cape Breton, 179; at Oswego, 228, 243, 265, 290, 296, 304, 308, 315, 318, 410, 416, 421, 477, 503, 518, 546; at Fort Hunter, proposed removal of, to Carrying Place, 258; supplies, by whom furnished, 282; powder magazines, 314; Fort Clinton, 462; repairs of, 511; gunpowder for, 540; at Carrying Place and Lake George, 584; at Fort William Henry, Lake George, 585, 588; at Fort Edward, 585; at Saratoga, II, 151; posts on western frontier, action of Congress, 201; British at Point A'fere, conduct of, 318.

GARRISON AND WEST POINT FERRY COMPANY. Exclusive franchise, veto, VI, 813.

GARTER, GERTRUDE. Petition for relief, II, 117.

GARVEY, JOSEPH H. Claim against New York city as superintendent of Bellevue Hospital Dispensary, veto, X, 169, 311.

GAS. Inspector, office abolished, VI, 284; New York, limiting price of, VIII, 241; State commission established, transfer of powers, 244, 312; X, 764; Brooklyn, regulating price, act relative to, VIII, 431; illuminating, regulating price in certain cities, 1021; New York, inspection and tests, X, 763; New York, illuminating, price to city, 764; price in Great Britain and United States, 854; New York, eighty-cent bill, 900.

VETOES. Manhattan Gas Company, authorizing increase of price, V, 670; supplying New York, VI, 180; Frontier Gaslight Company, Watertown, 215; Senate investigating committee, printing testimony, VIII, 118; gas regions in State, proposed survey, IX, 774; Auburn, regulating price, X, 907; Seneca Falls and Waterloo, regulating price, 907.

GAS COMPANIES. New York, organization, general act, VIII, 240; proposition to place under supervision of Railroad Commission, X, 220.

VETOES. Preventing extortion by, VI, 589; Tonawanda Gas Company, charter, VII, 807; New York, Senate investigation, printing testimony, VIII, 251; East River Gas Company, Long Island City, relative to, X, 582; Consolidated Gas Company, litigation with, legal services, appropriation, 785.

GAS AND ELECTRICITY COMMISSION. Created, VIII, 244, 312; powers transferred to Public Service Commissions, 244, 312; X, 855.

GASLIGHT COMPANIES. VETOES. Amending act, VII, 808; use of electricity, 864; Kings county, relative to, 1119; Brooklyn, use of electricity, VIII, 132; New York, relative to, 240; Brooklyn Equity Gaslight Company, relative to, 469; Queen City Company, Buffalo, supplying city with gas, repeal, IX, 723.

GAS METERS. Inspectors, office abolished, VI, 284; X, 855.

VETOES. Inspection, amending acts, VI, 282; inspectors of, amending act, IX, 722; New York, inspection of, X, 60.

GATES. Commissioner of common schools to be trustee of Rochester Colored School, III, 378.

GATES, HORATIO, MAJOR-GENERAL. Army of, to be strengthened, II, 8.

GAUTINONTY. Oswegatchie Indian, presents claim, II, 583.

GAVIN, MICHAEL. VETOES. Relief, X, 53, 60; claim, extra work, 323.

GAVITT AND DUTHIE. Contract for printing and engraving plates geological survey, IV, 464.

GAYLE, JOHN. Governor of Alabama, demands surrender of Robert G. Williams, III, 594.

GAZETTE. Official organ of colony, publications of, I, 446.

GAZLEY, JAMES. Aid to, veto, II, 713.

GEARY, JOHN W. Governor of Pennsylvania, communication from, Centennial Celebration, 1876, VI, 303; member of Centennial Celebration committee, 303.

GEDDES. Prosperity from manufacture of salt, III, 708; laying out salt lots, 709; salt spring in, 856; property of State Agricultural Society at, transferred to State, X, 120.

VETOES. Canal bridge, Magnolia street, VII, 361, 576; village, relative to, 806.

GEDDES, GEORGE. Builds canal raceway at Syracuse, VI, 869; member of Tax Revision Commission, 1881, VII, 538; commissioner of State survey, death of, VIII, 255.

GEDDES, JAMES. Surveys canal route between Seneca lake and Tioga river, III, 98.

Geib, Laura C. Escheat, veto, X, 451.

"General Armstrong, The." Frigate, engagements with British vessels at Fayal, II, 859.

General Assembly of Presbyterian Church. Joins in movement for fast day, II, 715.

General City Law. Enacted 1900, IX, 547.

General Corporation Law. Enacted, 1890, IX, 28, 135.

General Electric Company. Charter, IX, 99; refunding franchise tax, veto, 713.

General Fund. Statistics, IV, 830; V, 3, 368, 529, 588, 690, 750; VI, 5, 526, 614, 720, 792, 914; VII, 2, 138, 275, 420, 512, 680; payments from, amendment of 1905, X, 577, 601, 731, 848, 923; how composed, II, 1098; III, 232, 299, 371; IV, 780; V, 71, 529; possible increase from distribution of Federal revenues, III, 307; diminution of capital, 321, 412, 503; transfer of funds, 371; salt and auction duties restored to, 414, 505, 544, 552; IV, 53; transfer of securities to literature and common school funds, III, 499; borrowing from canal fund, 544; debt against, 619, 707, 736, 867; IV, 92, 260, 386, 422, 470, 540, 595, 743, 782, 830; V, 3, 64, 151, 252, 360, 451, 529, 588, 691, 750; VI, 6, 7; to bear expense of Chenango canal, III, 621; due United States deposit fund, IV, 270; sinking fund, 371, 661, 679; V, 3, 368; VI, 10; interest on debt, payment of, V, 491; debt, payment in coin, premium, VI, 167; repayments from canal revenues, 792; debt, payment of, VII, 141; debt paid, 273, 275, 420.

General Laws. Creating corporations, IV, 379, 513, 522, 526, 531, 574, 593, 633, 636, 638, 639, 823; V, 129, 133, 147, 191, 231, 645, 655, 658, 711, 848; VI, 168, 246, 353, 640; VII, 202, 233, 241, 336, 357, 371, 546, 565, 745, 845; VIII, 52, 197, 297; bridge companies, IV, 514, 636; VI, 221; academies, IV, 575, 648; purpose of constitutional provision, 634; V, 129, 657; VI, 353; benevolent, charitable, scientific and missionary, IV, 635, 638; V, 131, 233; VI, 55, 168, 187, 578, 673; VII, 240, 241; VIII, 379; colleges, IV, 648; agricultural societies, 648; horticultural societies, 648; navigation companies, V, 133; county penitentiaries, contracts with, 337; public bridges, 347; societies for social and esthetic purposes, 643, 644, 645; VI, 195, 661; temperance and benefit societies, V, 655; VI, 187, 192, 309; gas companies, V, 673; VI, 180, 215; fire, hook and ladder and hose companies, 55, 825; should be amended to avoid special laws, 117; town insurance companies, 153; literary societies, 196; musical societies, 289; number of special laws should be reduced, 399; boards of supervisors, powers of, 402; library companies, 691; VII, 336, 845; constitutional require-

GENERAL LAWS — (*Continued*).

ments, VI, 726; VIII, 343; camp meetings, VII, 867; railroads, constitutional provision, 1063, 1064; general building law recommended for cities, VIII, 36; gas companies in New York, 240; trade unions, general law recommended, 35, 163, 303; mutual benefit associations, 336; Governor Hill urges more general legislation, 342; commission recommended, 347; Young Men's Christian Associations, general act, 379; unpaid taxes, sales for, general law needed, 751; fraternal and benefit societies, 876; escheats, general act, 1890, 1014; corporations, towns, highways, 1890 (Statutory Revision Commission bills), 1027; IX, 26; decisions involving general laws, VIII, 1029; navigation act, 1897, 1121; Statutory Revision bills, 1892, IX, 28; what is a general law, 510; General City Law, 1900, 547; special should be limited, 676; X, 626; second and third-class cities, commissions on, IX, 677; Statutory Revision bills, 1896, 680; comparative statement, 1894–1900, X, 504.

VETOES. Ichthyological societies, general act, VIII, 878, 1039; correcting manifest errors, IX, 447; corporations to make loans on personal property, 534.

GENERAL MUNICIPAL LAW. Enacted, 1892, IX, 28.

GENERAL SYNOD OF THE REFORMED DUTCH CHURCH IN THE UNITED STATES. Communication from, relative to day of humiliation, fasting and prayer, II, 715.

GENERAL TERMS, SUPREME COURT. See COURT, GENERAL TERMS.

GENESEE ANNUAL CONFERENCE. Amending charter, veto, VI, 92.

GENESEE CAMP GROUND ASSOCIATION. Supplemental act, trustees, veto, VII, 1019.

GENESEE COLLEGE, LIMA. Aid recommended, IV, 603; gift from Ezra Cornell, V, 596.

GENESEE. Deposit of arms in, II, 682; militia from, 1812, 743, 744; arsenal in, 758; British devastation in, 787; abduction of William Morgan, III, 185, 365; agricultural society in, 945; silk culture in, 945; includes part of Tonawanda reservation, V, 199; exempted from Town Auditor's Act, VIII, 49; average excise license fees, 1889, 686; Erie county boundary, act relative to, 1102; highways, cost of labor system, 1892, IX, 200; insane, care of, county and State systems compared, 228.

VETOES. Support of insane, VI, 1035; recording and indexing notices of pendency, VIII, 70; boundary, Erie and Niagara counties, 1102; authorizing annual appropriation to corporations for prevention of cruelty, X, 812.

GENESEE RIVER. Improvement of, II, 965; Bayard's reservation, purchase of, 1030; lighthouse at mouth of, 1054, 1056, 1113; canal
connection with Susquehanna and Allegany rivers, III, 70;
Erie canal, aqueduct over, changing location, 552, 670; fortifications at mouth of, IV, 294; canal bridge at Mount Morris,
VI, 862.

    VETOES. Ferry at Rochester, VII, 417; State dam, Mount Morris,
908; removing obstructions, Allegany county, VIII, 847; State
dam, IX, 609.

GENESEE RIVER FEEDER. Stop gate, Rochester, veto, VII, 233, 362.

GENESEE RIVER RESERVATION. Number of Indians on, 1819, II, 976.

GENESEE VALLEY CANAL. Suggested, III, 104, 509; construction authorized, 510, 789; IV, 369; loan for, III, 620, 711, 816, 865;
banks authorized to subscribe to loans for, 633; work of construction, 669, 887, 953; debt, 736; IV, 252; estimated cost
of, III, 790, 865, 963; suggested discontinuance of construction,
798; northern part open to navigation, 865; construction suspended, 959, 1009, 1043, 1049; IV, 13, 102; work should be
resumed, 18, 59; expense charged on canal fund, 206; construction resumed, 369, 390, 424, 586; suspension of work a mistake (Young), 339; appropriation, 391, 425, 474, 678, 735, 743;
progress of work, 474, 599; expense of completing, 544, 670;
importance of early completion, 696; extension provided for,
835; tolls, V, 66, 154, 257, 361; relation to canal system, 789;
not self-supporting, 830; bridge over Genesee river at Mount
Morris, VI, 862; financial statement, 930; VII, 5; commission
to examine, VI, 933; sale recommended, VII, 8; drainage, 517.

    VETOES. Appropriation for work of, IV, 194; bridge at Portville,
VI, 709; fall of bridge, death resulting from, damages, VII,
88; extending time for sale, 216; new act passed, 217; release
to adjoining owners, VIII, 463.

GENESEE WESLEYAN SEMINARY. Destroyed by fire, III, 1033.

GENESEO. Normal school at, V, 695; public building, veto, X, 960.

GENESEO NORMAL SCHOOL. Established, V, 695, 852; building for school
of practice, veto, VIII, 116; new buildings, relative to, IX, 593.

GENET, EDMUND C. Survey of ship canal along Hudson river, III,
465.

GENEVA. Agricultural Experimental Station, VII, 697; VIII, 33; centennial celebration of Sullivan's campaign, VII, 1084; number
of excise licenses, 1887, VIII, 360; overseers of the poor, compensation, 696.

    VETOES. Appointment of police justice, VI, 216; railroads, VII,
1105; new armory at, VIII, 887; Indian mound, purchase of,

GENEVA, VETOES —(*Continued*).

887; Cayuga and Seneca canal, repairs, IX, 239; depositories of city funds, X, 583; assessment on State property, Seneca lake, and Seneca and Cayuga canal, 648; finances, sinking and highway funds, 716; street improvements, sewer extension, 806.

GENEVA COLLEGE. Proposed aid to, III, 117; struggling under difficulties, 297; lack of endowments, 540; appointing delegate to State Medical Society, veto, 593; aid from United States deposit fund, 613, 711; condition of, 739, 767, 857; appropriation for medical department, 857.

GENEVA HARBOR. State piers, repairs, veto, VI, 857.

GEOLOGICAL SURVEY. Provided for, III, 567, 568, 634; Eaton claim, 591; appointments, 638; convention of geologists, 642, 681; expense of, 644, 682, 935, 991, 994, 996; IV, 460; progress of, III, 677; report of, 680, 753, 820, 909, 935; flora, number and description of species, 761, 993; fauna, number and description of, 761, 993; continuance of, 769, 935; State museum, see that title; completion of, 859; distribution of report, 860, 1036; IV, 81, 289, 384; special message by Governor Seward, III, 990; publication of, 993; IV, 81; map and illustrations, III, 994; appropriation overdrawn, 995; coal not found, 1036; general results, 1036; contract for printing and binding, IV, 162; publications sent to Pope, 453; special message from Governor Fish, 460; continuing and completing work, 464; more room needed for specimens, 487; copies for Canadian Parliamentary Library, 573.

VETOES. Map, Catskill region, VII, 469, 495; map, printing and distributing, VIII, 252; United States co-operating with, appropriation, X, 785; United States hydrographic work, water supply, 785.

GEORGE I. Accession of, I, 174; commission to Governor Hunter, 141; address to, 174; vetoes Colonial Tariff Act, 198; address to, on deliverance from conspiracy, 205; instruction relative to private laws, 210; relations with colony, 213, 216; death of, 225.

GEORGE II. Accession of, I, 225; address to, 228; vetoes,—partition and township division bill, 231;—bill to prevent prosecutions by information, 236; — bills prohibiting sale of Indian goods to French, 236; — act fixing Assembly term at three years, 269, 273, 279; address of condolence on death of Queen Caroline, 269; birth of Prince, 275; approves Partition Act, 285; declares war against Spain, 286; instruction as to expedition against West Indies, 288; approves Oyster Bay Partition Act, 292; address to, requesting

GEORGE II — (*Continued*).

aid in restoring public buildings destroyed by fire, 304; orders expedition against Canada, 373; care of American colonies, 374, 395; secures friendship of Six Nations, 391; colony must contribute to expense of war, 410, 412, 415; requested to send naval force to St. Lawrence river, 420; grants of money from, how used, 424; approves projected movement against French, 464; sends presents to Indians, 466; intrusions on land of, 523; urges colonies to join in opposing invasion, 531; criticises conduct of Assembly, 532; sends troops to aid Virginia against French, 535; Albany plan of union presented to, 581; directs preparation of plan of union, 581; furnishes troops, artillery and stores for Crown Point campaign, 598; offers land for military service, 598; grants financial aid to colonies, 598, 604; declares war against France, 602; consents to annual appropriations, 605; approves conduct of New York Assembly, 607; sends troops to America, 609; permits Governor Hardy to resign, appoints him rear admiral, 613; furnishes stores and supplies for Canadian expedition, 620, 634, 643; death of, 649.

GEORGE III. Accession of, 649, 650; furnishes stores and supplies for Canadian expedition, 654, 663; congratulatory address on his marriage, 662; war against Spain, 666; birth of Prince of Wales, 669; petition from New York Assembly, 687, 703, 729, 768; called the Father of his People, 702; protest against parliamentary encroachment on rights of colony, 703; vetoes New York act for support of King's troops, 710, 716, 722; Parliament declares authority in New York colonies, 712; revokes instruction prohibiting bills of credit, 714, 715; vetoes bill erecting Cumberland county, 722; grants charter to New York Hospital, 743; receives petition from Continental Congress, 770.

GEORGE, "STIFF-ARMED." Convicted of murder, pardoned, II, 531.

GEORGETOWN, D. C. Requests retrocession to Maryland, III, 907; manufacture of ordnance at, II, 608, 629.

GEORGIA. Agent for, how appointed, I, 732; approves Kentucky resolution relative to jurisdiction of Federal court, doubts efficacy of North Carolina resolution relative to importation of slaves, disapproves Massachusetts resolution relative to basis of representation, II, 586; constitutional amendment, reducing terms of Senators, 827, 830; disapproves North Carolina proposition relative to election of Representatives and presidential electors, approves Kentucky proposition relative to salary of Representatives, 953; Constitution, procedure to amend, 1057; disapproves Pennsylvania proposition as to banks, III, 14; constitutional amendment, prohibiting importation of colored persons into a State without its consent, 34; disapproves

GEORGIA — (*Continued*).

Ohio proposition as to abolition of slavery, 94; constitutional amendment, House of Representatives no power to determine election of President, 182, 314; Governor of, communication from, treaty with Creek Indians, 183; protests against congressional encouragement of manufactures and internal improvements, and increase of tariff duties, and gives notice of resistance to such policies, 221; approves South Carolina resolution relative to rights of States, 261; disapproves Louisiana proposition to extend presidential term, 314; approves Missouri proposition for direct election of President, 314; opposes appropriation of Federal revenues to States, recommends constitutional convention to consider various constitutional amendments, 431, 433; opposes disposition of proceeds of public lands and of Federal revenues derived from tariff, 482; resolutions relative to anti-slavery agitation, 588; protests against Maine's refusal to surrender Philbrook and Kelleran, Atticus case, 748, 822, 908; publication of colonial records, 751; demands surrender of Alanson Greenman, charged with stealing a slave, 937; resolutions relating to national affairs, 977; opposes repudiation of public debts, IV, 46, 86; declares that negroes are not citizens, 46; on slavery, 507; action on independence monument, V, 122; seizure of national forts and property, 306; resolutions approving seizure of Fort Pulaski, 314; secession ordinance, 318, 396; assessment of personal property, 825; alleged subjection to military power, Governor Hoffman's protest against, VI, 131; resolutions protesting against Federal interference in Louisiana, 785; cedes to United States jurisdiction over Chickamauga battle field, VIII, 1076; communication from Governor, Cotton States Exposition, IX, 581; retail liquor licenses, 1892, 666.

GERICHTEN, CHARLES. New York, police commissioners to reconsider application, veto, X, 62.

GERMAN AMERICAN COLONIZATION SOCIETY. Charter, veto, V, 643.

GERMAN AMERICAN SCHOOL SOCIETY. Exempting property from taxation, veto, VIII, 460.

GERMAN ASSOCIATION ERHEITERUNG, STATEN ISLAND. Charter, veto, V, 643.

GERMAN BANK, BUFFALO. Investigation, appropriation for legal services, veto, X, 784; relation to investigation of bank department, 872.

GERMAN FLATS. Troops concentrate at, I, 603; relief of distressed families at, II, 112, 117; creating board of alms, veto, VII, 215.

GERMAN HOSPITAL DISPENSARY, NEW YORK. Relief, veto, X, 449.

GERMANIA (THE), BROOKLYN. Charter, veto, VIII, 704.

GERMAN LOOKING GLASS PLATE COMPANY. Refunding franchise tax, veto, IX, 713.

GERMAN MISSIONARY CHURCH, BUFFALO. Charter, veto, IV, 633.

GERMAN SAVINGS BANK, MORRISANIA. Financial condition of, VII, 66.

GERMAN SOCIAL TURN-VEREIN OF ROCHESTER. Changing name, veto, IX, 348.

GERMAN SOCIETY OF NEW YORK. President, *ex officio* commissioner of emigration, VI, 117; VII, 832, 966.

GERMANS. See also PALATINES. Immigration of, I, 143, 146.

GERMAN SOCIETY FOR PROMOTING EMIGRATION. Charter, veto, II, 243.

GERMANTOWN. Part of Columbia county, IV, 329.

GERMANY. Instruction of idiots, IV, 555; large number of emigrants from, VI, 999; participation in Cotton States Exposition, IX, 581; forest cultivation, 836; canal development should keep pace with railroads, X, 135; Prince Henry's reception by New York Legislature, 478; supervision of insurance companies, 840; illiteracy as compared with New York, 859.

GERRY, ELBRIDGE T. Member of Commission on Method of Inflicting Death Penalty, VIII, 484.

GETTYSBURG. Cemetery for New York soldiers at, V, 636, 638, 686; report of commissioners, VI, 61; battlefield, marking positions of New York troops and defensive works, VII, 1083; battlefield monuments, appropriations, veto, VIII, 253; commission consolidated with Chattanooga Commission, 1077; battle of, repulse of Longstreet, Walker's painting, purchase of, veto, IX, 291; dedication of New York monuments, 323; marking positions of New York troops in battle, 324.

GETTYSBURG BATTLEFIELD MEMORIAL ASSOCIATION. Marking position of New York troops and defensive works, appropriation, veto, VII, 1083.

GETTYSBURG AND CHATTANOOGA BATTLEFIELD COMMISSION. Publishing and distributing report, veto, X, 302.

GHENT. Treaty of peace between United States and Great Britain, War of 1812, II, 824; unsettled question relative to Grand island, 995; adjustment of unsettled boundary questions, III, 389.

GHERARDI, BANCROFT. Rear-admiral, objects to Brooklyn pier bill, IX, 438.

GIBBONSVILLE. Water from Erie canal for Watervliet arsenal, III, 356.

GIBBS, JACOB. Bond for return of arms, II, 772.

GIBIER, PAUL. Estate, Court of Claims, veto, X, 591.

GIBSON, HENRY C. Escheat, veto, X, 952.

GILBERT, FRANK B. State Law Librarian, acknowledgments to, I, pref., xv.

GILBERT, G. Bond for return of arms, II, 772.

GILBERT, JAMES H. Notary, legalizing acts, veto, VI, 690.

GILBERT, SAMUEL. Bond for return of arms, II, 772.

GILBERT ON TENANTS. Cited, IV, 358.

GILCHRIST, WILLIAM. Relief, veto, II, 249.

GILDED WARE. Manufacture and sale, preventing deception, veto, IX, 47.

GILGAN, THOMAS. Board of Claims, veto, IX, 797.

GILLINS, MARGARET. Life interest in McNamara estate, sale, veto, VIII, 1090.

GILLIS, WILLIAM. Commission, highway, St. Regis reservation, veto, VII, 909.

GILMER, THOMAS W. Governor of Virginia, resignation of, III, 915.

GILMOUR, LUCIE W. Application for cancellation of taxes, Flatbush, Comptroller to hear, veto, IX, 810.

GILSON, THOMAS D. Heirs, claims, State prisons, veto, VI, 703.

GINGER BEER. Composition of, VIII, 354.

GINLEY, PATRICK. Relief, veto, X, 53, 63.

GISEL, JOHN. Claims against Buffalo, audit, veto, VIII, 1038.

GLADIATOR BENEVOLENT ASSOCIATION, NEW YORK. Charter, veto, V, 644.

GLADSTONE, WILLIAM E. England, Prime Minister, adoption of ballot at elections, VIII, 585.

GLANDERS. Animals affected with, destruction of, veto, VIII, 1166; supervision of, transferred to Department of Agriculture, X, 192, 217.

GLEBE. Land purchased from Mohawks, I, 553.

GLEN. Town, leasehold estates in, IV, 331.

GLEN, HENRY. President, commissioners of Indian affairs, papers from, II, 221.

GLEN CREEK. VETOES. Improvement of, VIII, 1123; reconstructing banks and channel, X, 314, 435.

GLENDENNING, GEORGE E. Sealer of weights and measures, New York, salary, veto, X, 308.

GLENEIDA SAVINGS BANK. Charter, veto, VI, 310.

GLENS FALLS. City charter, 1908, IX, 679; bridge over feeder, veto, VI, 504; new armory, veto, VIII, 887.

GLENS FALLS FEEDER. Completion of, III, 120; payments for, 763; provision for arrearages, IV, 18; repairing lock, VI, 855.
VETOES. Bridge over, VI, 504, 1007; VII, 361; bridge over, removal, IX, 755; repairs, X, 427, 434.

GLENHAM. Dutchess county, decline of, X, 693.

GLENVILLE. VETOES. Highway assessments, VI, 701; school district, fire department, 1035; purchasing bridge, amending act, VII, 1102.

Glidden, Henry A. Senate Clerk, resolution requesting extraordinary session, VII, 122; index to legislative documents, veto, 225, 461.

Globes. Standard geographic time, purchase for executive chamber, legislative libraries and State library, veto, VIII, 108.

Gloucester County. Included part of New Hampshire grants, II, 103.

Gloversville. Vetoes. Village, gas supply, VI, 329; savings bank, 333; fire department, term of service, VIII, 409.

Gloversville, Mayfield and Northville Railroad Company. Asks State aid, VI, 71.

Gloversville Savings Bank. Charter, veto, VI, 333.

Godkin, Edwin L. Member of Tilden Municipal Reform Commission, 1875, IX, 417.

Gold. See also Coin, Currency, Money, Silver. Exportation of coin prohibited, I, 133; act relative to rates of foreign coin, 134; continental bills of credit, interest to be paid in gold or silver, II, 97; coin, counterfeiting prohibited, 224; duties payable in, 277; encouraging circulation of, III, 517; from California, IV, 729; low price of, V, 824; income from imports, VI, 135; effect of treasury sales of, 140; reduction of premium, 249; production and coinage, 645; payment to foreign creditors, 958; taxes to be paid in, VII, 170, 310; stamping articles made of, veto, X, 705.

Gold, Mr. Communication from, Oneida Indians, II, 472.

Golden Hill Creek. Niagara county, deepening for canal drainage, veto, X, 645.

Goldsborough, Charles W. Washington committee, lottery memorial, II, 1126.

Gold and Stock Telegraph Company. Judgment against, for franchise tax, IX, 279.

Gooch, Sir William. Recruits for regiment, I, 306; Governor of Virginia appointed to command expedition against Canada, 373; letter from, declines to join in expense of furnishing provisions to Indians, 378; declines to command Canadian expedition, 382.

Goodelle, William P. Counsel for State Bar Association at trial of Justice Hooker, X, 829.

Gooderson Fire Engine Company No. 2, Winfield. Changing name, veto, VII, 743.

Goodrich, William W. Counsel for Justice Hooker, X, 829.

Goodwin, Alexander T. Senate, member of committee on arrangements, opening of new capitol, VII, 270; mayor of Utica, objects to engine house bill, VIII, 1003.

Goodwin, Erminda. Ferry, Seneca lake, extending franchise, veto, IX, 372.

Goodyear. See Chapman Church case, IV, 149.

GORDON, GEORGE L. Court of Claims, veto, X, 165.

GOSHEN. Petition from, protection against Indians, I, 589; murder by Indians near, 593; town, opening highway, VI, 213.

    VETOES. Holding biennial town elections on general election day, IX, 816; — water supply, X, 232.

GOSHORN, A. T. Director-General Centennial Celebration, communication from, VI, 785; communication from, awards, VII, 55.

GOSPEL AND SCHOOL LOTS. Act providing for, II, 291; act relating to, 1050; fund, Stockbridge Indians, IV, 831; V, 159; general references, 603; VI, 22.

GOTHAM HOTEL, NEW YORK. Authority to sell liquor within 200 feet of a church, veto, X, 779.

GOTTENBURGH. Proposed conference at, between Great Britain and United States, II, 785.

GOUVERNEUR. VETOES. Declaring John street a public highway, VI, 76; fire company, charter, VII, 327.

GOUVERNEUR, ABRAHAM. Chosen Speaker, Seventh Assembly, I, 84.

GOUVERNEUR FIRE COMPANY. Charter, veto, VII, 327.

GOVERNMENT. Early forms of, I, 1; Council assumes executive authority, 23; threat to assert Queen's prerogative in colony, 166; alleged libel on, 499; duty of individual, 528; State established, 779, 780; II, 1, 5, 9; no department should encroach on another, 10, 12, 21, 246, 250, 278, 449, 465, 472; IV, 534, 779; VI, 455; IX, 537; X, 831; sources of authority, II, 27; limitation as to power of punishment, 61; probable effect of creation of Council of Safety, 114; defects under Articles of Confederation, proposed convention to revise, 194; State can do no wrong, 234; representative, all people should share in, 237; needs confidence and good-will of people, 290, 293; duty to protect citizens, 452; republican, blessings of, 541; State, should manufacture arms for militia, 572; danger of encouraging accumulation of wealth, 701; importance of popular education, 719; right to punish with death, 730; should promote internal communications, 966; aiding people by loan of public funds, 1004; parties, proper function of, 1019; III, 274; danger of permitting foreign control of property, II, 1032; people sit in judgment on form of, 1088; proper functions of, III, 272; benefits of public scrutiny, 282; forms of, instruction of children at Polytechnic, 299; dangers of unguarded taxation, 333; powers vested in classes, 744; management of railroads, 961; must be just to creditors, 968; dangers of excessive party strife, IV, 2; stability under Constitution, 51; combinations to obstruct, dangers of, 829; necessity of well-organized militia, V, 832; municipal corporations, problems relative to, VI, 735; local, progress of, 832; municipal, New York a conspicuous example, 836; "abuses of power follow power," 838.

GOVERNMENT HOUSE. Care of, II, 368; furniture, removal to Albany, 516.

GOVERNOR (COLONY). See also INSTRUCTIONS TO GOVERNOR, and names of Governors. Powers of, I, 1, 13; Twelve Men associated with, 1; Eight Men associated with, 2; Nine Men associated with, 2; power of, in relation to bills, 7, 18; Thomas Dongan, Governor, 9; power to adjourn or dissolve Assembly, 7, 18; opening speech to Legislature, 10; act to provide present for, 11, 56; Jacob Leisler assumes executive authority, 14; Edmund Andros, Governor, 14; Henry Sloughter, Governor, 17; communication from, to be in writing, 20; power of, devolves on Council, 23; Richard Ingoldesby, commander-in-chief, 23; Benjamin Fletcher, Governor, 28; power as to clergy, 42; admonishes Assembly relative to public business, 54, 55; Earl of Bellomont, Governor, 74; power of, with Council to establish fees, 84; succession in office, 90; John Nanfan, Lieutenant-Governor, 93; Lord Cornbury, Governor, 98; presents to, prohibited, 106, 116, 143, 145, 148, 530, 738; controversy with Assembly concerning legislative power, 110; power to act while out of colony, 126, 127, 149, 195; Assembly denies power, 150; Lord Lovelace, Governor, 132; Richard Ingoldesby, Lieutenant-Governor, 134; Robert Hunter, Governor, 141; status of, in congress of Governors, 158; William Burnet, Governor, 190; change of, does not dissolve Assembly, 196, 311; John Montgomerie, Governor, 229; Rip Van Dam, President of the Council, 238; William Cosby, Governor, 242; relation to Legislature, general note, 253; charges against Governor Cosby, 253; third part of Legislature, veto power, 254; to act in King's name, 254; George Clarke, President of the Council, 254; George Clarke, Lieutenant-Governor, 258; George Clinton, Governor, 305, 310; appointment of new, effect on status of Assembly, 311; declines to express opinion as to probable action on bill, 371; Assembly asserts independence in legislative action, 422; refuses to receive Assembly remonstrance, 423, 432; exercises powers independent of Legislature, 430, 438; entitled to inspect Assembly proceedings, 431; rule as to reception of Assembly communications, 432, 475, 484; difference with Assembly as to military authority, 454; alleged interference with civil tribunals, 468; salary payable annually, 473; Assembly's right of access to, 478, 494; no power to veto separate provisions in appropriation bills, 489; Sir Danvers Osborn, Governor, 526; James De Lancey, Lieutenant-Governor, 526, 613; compensation of, 530; Sir Charles Hardy, Governor, 576; Cadwallader Colden, President of Council, 647; Cadwallader Colden, Lieutenant-Governor, 656, 659, 673, 734, 759; Robert Monckton, Governor, 659, 669; Sir Henry Moore, Governor, 700; Earl of Dunmore, Governor,

GOVERNOR (COLONY)—(Continued).

736; declines salary voted by Assembly, 738, 745; William Tryon, Governor, 739; James Robertson, Governor, 779; reports, instructions and commissions, III, 1018; list of, I, pref., ix.

GOVERNOR (STATE). Continued from colonial period, II, 1; sources of authority, 2; general duties, 2; communications to Legislature, 2; III, 1003; President of Council of Appointment, II, 3; powers in, 3, 473; President of Council of Revision, 4; first election of, 6; George Clinton, 6; when to be chosen, 10; official term, beginning of, 10; powers in Council of Safety, 16; improper duties imposed on, 30; cannot be controlled by Council of Safety, 114; prorogation of Legislature, 7, 144; authorized to leave State on military service, 271; John Jay, 358; Council of Appointment, right of nomination, 361, 473, 479, 494; commander-in-chief of militia, 403; relations with Council of Appointment, general note, 489; status as member of Council of Revision, 495; Morgan Lewis, 545; Daniel D. Tompkins, 616; veto power cannot be evaded by adopting a concurrent resolution instead of passing a bill, 740; authorized to negotiate treaties for purchase of Indian lands, 754; authorized to appoint military secretary, 818; authorized to cede land to United States, 825; when to provide for employment of convict labor, 875; Governor Tompkins resigns to become Vice-President, 883; Lieutenant-Governor John Tayler becomes acting Governor, 887; election to fill vacancy, 887; De Witt Clinton, 897; III, 53; power to make brevet appointments in militia, II, 992; authorized to procure removal of General Montgomery's remains, 1000; salary, 1013; answer to speech discontinued, 1014; criticism by Senate, 1059; answers to legislative request for information, 1061; powers in extradition cases, 1105; election and official term under second Constitution, III, 1; vested with pardoning power, 1; V, 93; vested with veto power, III, 2; exclusive right of nomination to office, 2; Joseph C. Yates, 2; appointment of justices of the peace, 17; appointment of auctioneers, 18; duties under Militia Law, 19; power of removal, 133; V, 716; appointments to fill vacancies, III, 176; Nathaniel Pitcher, acting Governor, 221; to see that laws are faithfully executed, 222, 833, 1002, 1031; IV, 149, 729, 778; V, 105, 466, 753; X, 831; Martin Van Buren, Governor, III, 230; Enos T. Throop, Lieutenant-Governor, becomes acting Governor, 269; elected Governor, 318; William L. Marcy, 299; William H. Seward, 706; appointment of commissioners to take acknowledgments, 770; discretion in extradition cases not subject to legislative control, 778, 1030; relation to legislation, 973, 975, 1009; duty to preserve power of his department, 976, 1007; appointing power, 1002; IV, 109; removal of

GOVERNOR (STATE)—(*Continued*).

officers, III, 1021; William C. Bouck, IV, 1; Silas Wright, 87; abolishing property qualifications, 137; when may call militia to aid sheriff, 146, 707, 728; loan of arms for local purposes, 150, 155; first election under Constitution of 1846, 363; John Young, 363; propriety of recommendations to amend Constitution, 373; Hamilton Fish, 421; gubernatorial succession, IV, 433; procedure in pardon cases, 405, 435; effect of hasty consideration of bills near close of session, 523; action on bills after adjournment of Legislature, 524; V, 849; Washington Hunt, IV, 538; Horatio Seymour, 640; V, 445; power of removal, veto, IV, 772; Myron H. Clark, 780; John A. King, V, 1; Edwin D. Morgan, 64; office becomes an office of record, 116; expenses in pardon cases, 172; power of removal should be extended, 190, 294, 387; member of commission to organize militia, 281, 400; certifying accounts, 292; communications to Legislature, 458, 582, 789; VI, 4, 644; VIII, 2; power to remove mayor of New York, V, 519; member of commission to care for recruits and returning volunteers, 563; Reuben E. Fenton, 582; appointment of military officers, 608; member of Commission on Normal Schools, 695; proposed bureau of pardons, 758; John T. Hoffman, VI, 1; cannot remove health officer, 361; should be responsible for all branches of State's affairs, 396; should appoint State officers, 396; term extended to three years, 398; errors in engrossing bills, 419; judicial aid in considering bills, 430; member of Commission on Statues, 435; extraordinary term of court, 492; John A. Dix, 522; Samuel J. Tilden, 719; accountability for appropriations, 925; Lucius Robinson, VII, 1; passage of bills, emergency certificates, 43; responsibility for canal administration, 50; executive residence, 178; Alonzo B. Cornell, 418; first simultaneous election with Legislature, 1879, 438; custodian of privy seal, 439; Governor's Guard, charter, veto, 506; member of Commission on State's Property Rights, War of 1812, 601; consideration of bills, ten-day period, 669; Grover Cleveland, 315; *ex-officio* trustee of public buildings, 837; Governor Cleveland declines to furnish facts in response to Senate resolution, 998; David B. Hill, VIII, 1; counsel, office created, 27; member of New Capitol Advisory Board, 31; when may not review discretion of Legislature, 85, 89; *ex-officio* Regent of University, 169; member of Board of Capitol Construction, veto, 213; salary fixed by Constitution, 227; proposition to deprive him of power to appoint quarantine commissioners, veto, 555; proper rule in disposing of constitutional questions, 605; to execute deeds under Cessions Act, 1113; Roswell P. Flower, IX, 1; removal of officers, expense of investigation, appropriation, veto, 75; Levi P.

GOVERNOR (STATE)—(*Continued*).

Morton, 536; taking initiative in legislation, 537; executive consideration of bills, 537; should not interfere in legislation, 537; designation of justices to Appellate Division, 546; jurisdiction to act on bills, 618; commander-in-chief of military and naval force, 640; term reduced to two years, Constitution, 1894, 645; investigation of State officers, appropriations, veto, 712; Frank S. Black, 738; staff, Governor Black's comment on, 743; Theodore Roosevelt, X, 1; Benjamin B. Odell, Jr., 180; approval of services and expenses of attorneys or counsel in forest department, 194; limitation of power as to New York city administration, 209, 230; judicial designations, 374; expense of confidential investigations, 422; office, notarial clerks, veto, 442; Frank W. Higgins, 718; list of, I, pref., xii.

GOVERNOR'S GUARD. Charter, veto, VII, 506.

GOVERNOR'S HOUSE. New York, destroyed by fire, I, 297, 302; King requested to aid in rebuilding, 304; rebuilding of, recommended, 306, 312; act passed for erecting Governor's house, 313, 314; description of new house, 314; additional appropriation for, recommended, 339, 349, 460; rent for, 460; completion of, 511; repairs on, 673, 717, 739, 748; destroyed by fire, 753, 756, 758; rebuilding of, considered, 758.

GOVERNOR'S ISLAND. See also NUTTEN ISLAND. Sale of, veto, II, 287; fortifications on, 360; lazaretto on, 381; yellow fever patients, VI, 237.

GOWANDA STATE HOSPITAL. Board of managers, alleged improper contracts with treasurer and architect, X, 412.

GOWANUS. North Protestant Dutch church, changing name, veto, V, 127.

GRACE, WILLIAM R. Mayor of New York, appointment of excise commissioners, VIII, 275.

GRADE CROSSINGS. Statistics, VII, 972; general act, 1897, IX, 744; appropriation for, 822; X, 28, 119, 227, 620; number of accidents, 1898, 29; State aid, Schenectady, 619; policy should be carefully defined, 620.

 VETOES. Amending act, VIII, 1037; New York, abolition of, X, 176; Mount Vernon, Harlem Railroad, cost of changing, 454; Buffalo, damages, 474; appropriation, 568; Mount Vernon, over New York and Harlem Railroad, 590; amending Railroad Law, 591; Railroad Commission, reappropriation, 647, 653; Brooklyn borough, 714.

GRADY, FRANKLIN. Escheat, veto, X, 705.

GRADY, THOMAS F. Senate, member of joint committee on taxation, 1899, X, 801.

GRADY, WILLIAM. Sealer of weights and measures, New York, salary, veto, X, 308.

GRAEFF, JAMES M. Assembly, member of Prince Henry reception committee, X, 479; escorts Admiral von Eisendecher at reception, 480.

GRAHAM, DANIEL. Impressments for army service, II, 99.

GRAHAM, DAVID. Member of Procedure Commission, IV, 366; VII, 183.

GRAHAM, JAMES. Speaker of first General Assembly, I, 20; appointed as draftsman of Assembly bills, 20; member of conference committee, 78; appointed member of Council, 84.

GRAHAM, JAMES G. Secretary to Governor, accompanies Prince Henry to Assembly chamber at his reception, X, 480.

GRAHAM'S PRACTICE. Cited, powers of Supreme Court commissioners, X, 670; reference of causes for trial, 682.

GRAIN. Exportation of, veto, II, 26; production of, IV, 42; supply, New York's dependence on other States, VI, 240.

GRAMMAR SCHOOL. Governor Lewis suggests plan of, II, 558; connected with University of City of New York, III, 766; statistics, 857.

GRAND ARMY OF THE REPUBLIC. Unauthorized wearing of badges prohibited, VII, 1108; members attending Centennial Celebration of Washington's inauguration, provision for, VIII, 695; opposes repeal of law exempting from taxation property purchased with pension money, IX, 114.

    VETOES. Sunday processions, music, VII, 335; national camp, 1879, Assembly committee, expenses, 463; prohibiting wearing of badges, 1108; Seth N. Hedges Post No. 216, Dansville, charter, VIII, 462; preservation of records, 528, new bill passed; Sherman Post, Rose, use of room in town hall, 528; unincorporated posts taking and holding property, 878; posts, exempting property from taxation, IX, 470; badges or buttons, relative to, X, 62; towns, renting rooms for, 535; lease of buildings from municipal corporations, 585; relief of soldiers, 809.

GRAND ARMY OF THE REPUBLIC SOLDIERS' HOME. Incorporated, V, 490.

GRAND ISLAND. Intrusions on, II, 995, 1026, 1106; sale of, use of proceeds, 1010; III, 26; part of unproductive canal fund, II, 1099; ship timber from, finds market in New York, III, 815; bridge over Niagara river, veto, X, 63, 703, 774.

GRAND JURY. New York, petition against vendues and peddlers, I, 170; Ontario county, memorial, George case, II, 531; New York, communication from, relative to poor debtors, 923; New York, indictment of lottery, III, 404; indictment for infamous crime, V, 471; New York, report on usury laws, VI, 564; Attorney-General may appear before, IX, 409.

GRAND JURY — *(Continued).*

VETOES. Proposed power to investigate offenses in other counties, II, 130; stenographer's compensation, VIII, 468; preparation of list, IX, 148; stenographers for, 725, 811; Madison county, clerk, X, 61; stenographer for Westchester county, 387; who may be present at sessions of, 392; New York, selection of, 634.

"GRAND LEGISLATURE OF THE NATION." Title given to Parliament, I, 710, 772.

GRAND MARAIS HARBOR, LAKE SUPERIOR. Proposed harbor of refuge at, VII, 60.

GRAND RIVER. Indians from, visit of, II, 346.

GRAND STREET SAVINGS BANK, BROOKLYN. Charter, veto, VI, 342.

GRANGER, FRANCIS. Resigns as Representative in Congress, III, 909; delegate to Washington Peace Convention, V, 311.

GRANGER, GIDEON, Communication from, purchase of Holland Land Company's property, II, 1031.

GRANGER, HEZEKIAH L. Postmaster in Manlius, removal of, II, 1068.

GRANITE. Discovered in Highlands, IV, 29.

GRANITE LAKE COMPANY. Charter, veto, VI, 270.

GRANT, ELEAZER. Communication from, Massachusetts boundary, II, 260.

GRANT, ULYSSES S. Commander of Union army, receives surrender of General Lee, V, 676; Secretary of War *ad interim,* communication from, cession of David's island, 861; President, cited, policy of resumption, VI, 141; re-elected President, 1872, 522; proposed nomination for third term, VII, 563; death of, Mount McGregor Memorial Association, incorporated, VIII, 625; as life Senator, possible length of service, 694; monument, New York, act of 1897, IX, 755.

GRASS RIVER. St. Regis lands on, II, 454; purchase of, 472, 520; improving navigation of branches, VIII, 560.

VETOES. Improvement, VI, 575; bridge, Russell, VII, 474; improving navigation of branches, VIII, 846; State dam, repairs, X, 789.

GRATTAN, PATRICK. Relief, veto, VI, 213.

GRATUITY. See also PUBLIC FUNDS. To public printer, I, 500; bounty land, Trotter case, II, 343; to executive and judicial officers, Governor Jay's comment on, 449; prohibited, constitutional provision, VII, 47; reimbursing officer for loss of public funds, X, 275.

VETOES. New York, payment of court clerks illegally appointed, VII, 47; to convicts on discharge, 264; Catherine Hogan, death of husband, appropriation, 464, 910; Brandow, Sing Sing keeper, injuries from assault by convict, 464; Ann Higgins,

Gratuity, Vetoes —(*Continued*).

     death of son, appropriation, 464; Lawrence, corporal, 22d
Regiment, National Guard, permanent injuries, damages, 465,
910; Johnson, laborer, injuries, appropriation, 465; Strong,
keeper Auburn prison, injuries, 465; Hagar, death of son,
466; Kennedy, damages, death of husband, 466; Canandaigua,
reimbursing public officer for loss of property, 569; election
contest, salary and expenses of successful contestant, 617; election contest, Kessel case, Kings county, reimbursing expenses,
651; New York, Stemmler case, salary, 661; Sangerfield, refunding surety for payment on supervisor's bond, 753; towns,
aiding railroads, 848; Onondaga county, donation of clerk's
office and lot, 867; McAvoy claim, new capitol, 910; Meissner
claim, National Guard, damages, 910; O'Keef, damages, new
capitol, 910; Humo, damages, Hudson River Hospital, 910;
Taylor and Young, damages, new capitol, 911; Mary T. Creney,
widow of James Creney, 917; Catherine D. Pierson, widow
of William W. Pierson, 917, 1082; VIII, 109; Delia Weatherwax, widow of James H. Weatherwax, VII, 917; Onondaga
Historical Association, donation of land to, 932; judgment
against Binghamton superintendent of streets, proposed payment by city, 1018; Orleans county poorhouse, claims for construction, 1047; appropriation to widow of Henry Gallien,
Deputy Comptroller, 1082; VIII, 109; Denmark, conveyance
of land to private corporation, VII, 1106; Amsterdam waterworks, claims for labor, 1107; appropriation to widow of Justice Westbrook, former justice of Supreme Court, VIII, 250;
Schuylerville battlefield monument, appropriation, 253; Gettysburg battlefield monument, appropriation, 253; Rose, town hall,
room for G. A. R., 529; sheriff, Nassau county, reimbursement
for services and expenses after expiration of term, X, 243; city
employees serving in Spanish War, continuing compensation,
264; sheriff, New York county, reimbursement for services and
expenses after expiration of term, 321; Fredonia normal school,
furnishing rooms for school societies, 649; New Hartford, aid
to Bridgewater turnpike, 811; counsel in criminal cases, allowance for past services, 942.

Graves, George B.   Assistant in Governor's office, acknowledgments to,
     I, pref., xv.

Graves, John.   Bond for return of arms, II, 774.

Gravesend.   Act to remove courts of, to Flatbush, I, 12; blockhouses,
     sea fencibles in, II, 810; annexed to Brooklyn, VIII, 1112;
     Bensonhurst park, amending act, 1157.

GRAVESEND — (*Continued*).

VETOES. Common lands, VII, 665, 804; IX, 729; common lands, Senate investigation, counsel fees, VII, 905; sewer property, sale of, VIII, 1036; peace, preservation of, 1037; police department, authorizing increase of expenditures for, 1111; taxes, arrearages, settlement, IX, 782; local improvement bonds, relative to, 872; Surf avenue, relative to, 872; Volunteer Firemen's Association, appropriation, X, 472; Surf avenue improvement, amending act, 476; common lands fund, 714.

GRAY, BRIDGET. Relief, veto, VII, 507.

GRAY, WILLIAM. Trustee, St. Regis Indians, II, 938; taken prisoner, War of 1812, death of, 938.

GRAY, WILLIAM L. Indian interpreter, II, 939.

GREAT BARN ISLAND. General Van Orden's brigade on, II, 810.

GREAT BRITAIN. Bankrupts, estates in colony, relief of creditors, I, 143; colonial agent to, 175, 222; rebellion in, suppressed, 180; pitch and tar imported from colony, communication relative to, 188; prosperity of, 193; war with Spain, 187, 286; South American dominions, expected French attack on, 340; expense of defending liberties of Europe, 412; treaty of peace, Aix-La-Chapelle, 471, 481; domination over Five Nations, 542; war with France, 602; intended French invasion of, defeated, 642; declares war against Spain, 666; Sugar Act, mischiefs of, 684; possibilities of American colonies, 690; alleged discriminations against colonies, 690; dominion and trade extended by colonies, 698; union of colonies with, importance of, 729; disputes with colonies, 766; treaty of peace with United States, 780; II, 191, 192, 195; peace overtures, II, 45; subjects of, harsh legislation against, 71; loses several West India islands, 89; attempt to monopolize West India trade, 197; statutes continued, revision recommended, 219, 255; proposed treaty of commerce with United States, 236; commercial prosperity of, 597; impressment of American seamen, 616, 656; violates international law, 616; exchequer standard yard measure adopted in New York, 641; Orders in Council, Berlin and Milan decrees, 672, 690; tenders reparation in Chesapeake case, 690; United States declares war against, 735; Emperor of Russia offers mediation with United States, 785, 801; treaty of peace with United States, War of 1812, 824; commercial convention, complaint relative to New York pilot fees, 888; vessels of, pilot fees at New York, 918; certain officers not eligible to House of Commons, 1063; commercial treaty with United States, 1104; act regulating commercial intercourse between Canada and United States, III, 23; care of insane criminals, 84; infant schools, 114, 213; minis-

GREAT BRITIAN — (*Continued*).

ter from, complaint relative to New York public administrator, 216; beginning of public debt, 324; oppressive taxation, 325; reluctance in offering opportunties to examine colonial documents, 935, 1008; IV, 169; McLeod case, III, 941; naval armament on border lakes, 945; minister, Georgia opposes appointment of, 977; relations with colonies, documents concerning, 1019; grants consent to examine colonial documents, 1020; treaty with United States, Canadian boundary, 1038; Oregon, claims to territory, IV, 285; authentication of instruments executed in, V, 212; report of Commission on Harbor Defenses, 569; slow growth of wealth, VI, 958; question with Venezuela, relative to boundary, IX, 646; price of gas, X, 854.

GREAT CHAZY RIVER. Improvement of, VI, 94; dam at Chazy Lake, veto, X, 739.

GREAT DOCK, NEW YORK. Battery proposed, at, I, 325.

GREATER NEW YORK. Established, VIII, 300; IX, 708; act of 1894, submitting question of consolidation to people, approved, 300, 552, 708; description of territory, 300, 705; Charter Commission created, 1896, 553, 674, 705; charter, 1897, 753; judicial construction of charter, 753; consolidated municipalities, legalizing transfer and assignment of clerks and employees, veto, 874; new Charter Commission, 1900, X, 122, 144, 206; Governor's memorandum on appointment of, 122; Commission's report, 1901, 122, 206, 229; charter amendments, 1901, 267; valuation and assessment of property, 1903, 620; pays more than its share of personal property tax, 620.

GREAT GULL ISLAND. Cession for lighthouse, II, 530.

GREAT MEADOW. French Indians attack, I, 360.

GREAT SHANDAKEN. Road from, to Walton, II, 312.

GREAT SODUS BAY. Harbor at, II, 986; proposed connection with Erie canal, III, 166; bridge over, veto, VI, 212.

GREAT SOUTH BAY. VETOES. Ferry, amending act, VII, 936; ferriage, VIII, 639; dredging channel to Shinnecock bay, X, 786.

GREAT VALLEY. VETOES. Highway encroachments, VI, 160; State road, Allegany reservation improvement, VIII, 847.

GREAT WESTERN TURNPIKE COMPANY. Albany county, tolls, veto, VI, 209.

GREECE. Efforts for freedom of, American interest in, III, 19.

GREEN, ANDREW H. Comptroller, New York city, report on funded debt, VI, 405; letter to Governor Hoffman, 413; letter from, Loutrel relief bill, 574; reduces payments to newspapers, 607.

GREEN, CHARLES H. Relief, veto, VI, 185.

GREEN, GEORGE E. Member of Canal Investigating Commission, 1899, X, 75.

GREEN, H. NOYES. Notary public, legalizing acts, veto, IX, 720.

GREEN, WARDELL. Nominated sheriff of Schoharie county, proceedings of Council of Appointment, II, 475.

GREEN BAY. Lands at, purchased for Indians, II, 1107; removal of Indians to, III, 96; Oneidas remove to, 310, 349.

GREENBURGH. VETOES. Highway improvement, VI, 328; including part of White Plains, repeal, VII, 931; election of highway commissioners, VIII, 54; assessment, when to be made, compensation of assessors, IX, 817.

GREENBUSH. Troops at, I, 407; on east side of Hudson river, 407; village, amending charter, VII, 806; poor, relief of, VIII, 699.

GREENE, DAVID M. Nominated as commissioner of State survey, VIII, 255.

GREENE, FRANCIS V. Member of Canal Investigating Commission, 1899, X, 75.

GREENE, MARY. Escheat, veto, VIII, 882.

GREENE, WILLIAM. Governor of Rhode Island, letter from, scarcity of bread, II, 68.

GREENE COUNTY. Williams murder case, II, 621; agricultural society in, III, 945; tenants represented before Assembly committee on anti-rent troubles, IV, 238; Livingston leases, 332; Hunter and Overing's leases, 333; forest lands included in forest preserve, VIII, 23; average excise license fees, 1889, 686; highways, cost of labor system, 1892, IX, 200; insane, care of, county and State systems compared, 228; extending forest preserve in, X, 22.

VETOES. Subjecting to Railroad Act, VI, 214; Hunter and Jewett, bonding, 328; police justice, repealing act, 1035; mutual insurance companies, Catskill and Athens, 595; VII, 132; exempting from Town Auditor's Act, 554; VIII, 49; judge, repealing Salary Law, VII, 807; Palenville, fish hatchery, 902; mutual insurance companies in certain towns, 1097; Cairo, bridge over Catskill creek, VIII, 383; map of forest preserve in, IX, 776; extending forest preserve, X, 291; institutions, purchase of supplies, 700.

GREENFIELD, GEORGE, HENRY AND ELIZABETH. New York, taxes, assessments and water rates, cancellation, veto, X, 325.

GREEN ISLAND. Number of excise licenses, 1887, VIII, 360.

VETOES. Canal bridge, Arch street, VII, 115; annexing territory from Watervliet, X, 179; restoring territory from Watervliet, 179.

GREENMAN, ALANSON. Extradition of, III, 937.

GREENPOINT. VETOES. Ferriage to New York, VI, 697; First Baptist church, changing name, IX, 348.

GREENPOINT FERRY COMPANY. Boats on East river, veto, VI, 336.

GREENPORT. Village, relative to, veto, VII, 805.

GREENWICH. Assembly meets at, I, 367; smallpox at, 367; General Curtenius' brigade at, II, 810; aiding Union Village and Johnsonville Railroad Company, veto, VI, 164; bridge to Northumberland, veto, X, 699.

GREENWICH ELEVATED RAILROAD COMPANY. Successor to West Side and Yonkers Patent Railway Company, VI, 715.

GREENWOOD. Fire district, waterworks bonds, veto, X, 704.

GREENWOOD CEMETERY. Charges against management, report of investigating commission, VIII, 70.

GREGG, JOHN. Stockbridge land conveyed to, II, 1119.

GREGORY XVI. Pope, geological survey presented to, IV, 453.

GREGORY, IRA W. Trustee, Mechanics and Traders' Savings Institution, testimony, VII, 57.

GREIG. Town, aid to Utica and Black River Railroad Company, amending act, veto, VI, 92.

GREIG, JOHN. Appointed Regent, III, 94.

GRELL, WILLIAM F. Sheriff, New York, allowance for expenses after expiration of term, veto, X, 594.

GRENADIERS. Sent to colony, I, 36; organization of, II, 339.

GREVILLE, CHARLES CAVENDISH FULKE. Clerk, Privy Council, examination of colonial documents, IV, 182.

GREY, WILLIAM. Capture and adoption of, II, 391; claim of, payment, 392.

GRIDLEY, PHILO. Justice Supreme Court, communication from, vagrants, trial jurors, IV, 505.

GRIFFIN, JAMES. New York, relief, veto, X, 177.

GRIFFIN, MARGUERITE E. Editor's reader and stenographer, acknowledgments to, I, pref. xv.

GRIFFIN CREEK FEEDER. Relative to, veto, VII, 805.

GRINNELL, CLARK S. Assembly, member of select committee on anti-rent troubles, IV, 323.

GRIST MILLS. Act for erection of, II, 485.

GRISWOLD, JOHN A. Member of Arcade Railway Company, VI, 198.

GRISWOLD, NATHANIEL. Communication from, IV, 381.

GROCERS. License to sell liquor, IV, 753.

GROCERS' TRUST COMPANY, NEW YORK. Charter, veto, VIII, 292.

GROTE, GEORGE. England, favors use of ballot at elections, VIII, 585.

GROTON CEMETERY ASSOCIATION. Changing name, veto, VIII, 974; legalizing bill passed, 974.

GROW, SIDNEY G. Commissioner to build road on St. Regis reservation, veto, VII, 91, 475.

GUADALUPE. Conquest of, I, 640.

GUAM. Acknowledgment of instruments executed in, veto, X, 63.

GUARANTORS AND SURETIES. Amending Insurance Law, extending powers to foreign corporations, IX, 596.

GUARANTY COMPANIES. Statistics, VII, 428, 521, 690, 823, 949; VIII, 6; general act, 463.

GUARDHOUSE. At Schenectady, burned, I, 125.

GUARDIANS. Act authorizing persons over fourteen to choose, I, 11; status of persons pardoned after life sentence, II, 1108; natural right of father, III, 845; relief of sureties, VII, 508.

> VETOES. Appointment of, II, 488; amending act, VI, 505; appointment in certain cases, VIII, 631; in socage, real property sold to, X, 62.

GUARD-SHIP. To secure trade and navigation, I, 276.

GUATEMALA. Participation in Cotton States Exposition, IX, 581.

GUBERNATORIAL SUCCESSION. In colony, I, 90, 94; under first Constitution, II, 674, 887; under second Constitution, III, 221, 269; Speaker added, IV, 433.

GUDEN, CHARLES. Sheriff of Kings county, proceedings against, X, 559.

"GUERRIERE, THE." Destroyed by Captain Hull, II, 780.

GUIDE POSTS. Provided for, II, 385.

GUILDERLAND. Van Rensselaer leases, description of, IV, 329.

> VETOES. Reformed church, sale of property, VI, 209; special highway, 670; justice of the peace, appointment in first district, IX, 816.

GUILDERLAND CENTER TURNPIKE COMPANY. Charter, veto, VI, 339.

GUIMAN, JOHN. New York, relief, veto, X, 176.

GUION, J. MARSHALL. Justice of the peace, Seneca Falls, legalizing act, veto, VII, 44, new act passed.

GUIZOT, M. Letter from, French Canadian archives, IV, 188.

GUNBOATS. For defense of New York harbor, II, 569.

GUNHOUSES. Proposed erection of, II, 630; location of, IV, 452.

GUNNER. At Albany, claim for arrears, I, 202.

GUNPOWDER. Supplies for magazines, I, 314, 322; for Oswego and other frontier garrisons, 315; powder duty recommended, 357; for garrisons, 540; seizure of, by New York collector, 532, 543, 552; purchase of, authorized, 751, 758; seizure of, Curson case, II, 82; Congress requested to loan to State, 181; encouraging manufacture of, 254; keeping, unauthorized use, veto, IX, 289.

GUNSMITHS. See SMITHS.

GUTHRIE, JAMES. Delegate from Kentucky to Washington Peace Convention, V, 329.

GYPSUM. Discovery of, II, 1009; transportation facilitated by canals,

GYPSUM — (*Continued*).

  III, 815; market for, 953; accumulations of, 1036; bounties on, IV,
  69.

GYPSUM CEMETERY ASSOCIATION. Revival, veto, VII, 412.

H.

HABEAS CORPUS. Restraint of, II, 14; disorderly persons, 223; exten-
  tension of right, 943; power to take bail on, III, 941; abuses in
  use of writ, 1034; slaves, Lemmon case, IV, 809; suspension of
  writ by Federal government, Kentucky protest, V, 500; writ suspended, Civil War, 551; Edymoiñ case, expenses, veto, VI, 678;
  presidential elector, violation of Election Law, United States Circuit Court no power to grant, VII, 33; South Carolina election
  cases, 1876, 38; amending Revised Statutes, veto, 197, 343; constitutional provision, 504.

HABITUAL DRUNKARDS. VETOES. Ontario county, publication of, VII,
  266; sale of property, VIII, 1041; IX, 283.

HACKETT, JOHN C. Assembly, member of joint legislative committee
  on services in memory of former Governor Higgins, X, 963.

HACKNEY COACHES. Licensing in New York, veto, II, 315.

HACKS. VETOES. License, Flatbush, VII, 1111; stands, Saratoga
  Springs, 1112.

HADCOCK, JOHN. Stockbridge land conveyed to, II, 1119; testimony
  on Oneida claim, VI, 666.

HADLEY. Union free school district No. 1, legalizing proceedings relative to new site and school building, veto, X, 811.

HAERLEM BRIDGE COMPANY. Amending charter, veto, II, 782.

HAERLEM HEIGHTS. General Hermance's brigade on, II, 810.

HAGAR, CHARLES. Death of, appropriation to father, veto, VII, 466.

HAGAR, LAWRENCE. Damages, death of son, appropriation, veto, VII,
  466.

HAGGERTY, HENRY F. Brooklyn, police justice, expiration of term, 1895,
  IX, 503.

HAGUE, THE. Early ecclesiastical documents, translation of, veto, X,
  298, 563.

HAHN, FREDERICK. Court of Claims, veto, X, 165.

HAIGHT, ALBERT. Court of Appeals, opinion, Oneida county courthouse bill, X, 768.

HAIGHT, SAMUEL. Sheriff of Westchester county, memorial from, Ryer
  case, II, 345.

HAIGHT, SAMUEL, BRIGADIER-GENERAL. Commands brigade, stationed
  at Brooklyn, II, 800.

HAIT, THADDEUS. Member of Tax Revision Commission, 1881, VII, 538.

HAKE, SAMUEL. Obtains flag of truce, II, 58; arrest of, 58.

HALE, MATTHEW. Attorney, Buck case, VI, 681; member of Commission on Method of Inflicting Death Penalty, VIII, 484.

HALE, WILLIAM. Justice of the peace, Johnstown, legalizing acts, veto, IX, 725.

HALF MOON. Garrison at, I, 26, 108; troops, 397; boundary question, Schenectady church lands, II, 117; patent, rights under, 354; school district No. 10, regulating elections in, veto, IX, 817.

HALF-MOON, THE. Yacht, Hudson's voyage of discovery, IV, 173.

HALL, AMOS, MAJOR-GENERAL. Detachment of militia, 1812, II, 743; service on Niagara frontier, 746, 791; General McClure to transmit statement to, 791; commands all troops west of Onondaga, 792; calls out militia, 796, 822; called on for militia, 806.

HALL, AMOS C. Court of Claims, veto, X, 441.

HALL, CHARLES H. Heirs, relief, veto, VI, 589.

HALL, DOMINICK AUGUSTINE. Judge, District Court, Louisiana, imposes fine against General Jackson, IV, 46.

HALL, EDWARD, DR. Superintendent of Asylum for Insane Convicts, conference with Superintendent Pilsbury, V, 438.

HALL, JAMES. Geological survey, appointed geologist, fourth district, III, 681, 754, 991; IV, 461; report of, III, 683, 754; IV, 81; V, 781; supervision of State Museum, VI, 619.

HALL, JAMES. VETOES. Board of Claims, IX, 797; Court of Claims, 858.

HALL, JAMES D. Claim against New York, audit, veto, VIII, 467.

HALL'S LECTURES ON SCHOOL KEEPING. To be furnished to school districts, III, 378.

HALLIDAY, SAMUEL D. Trustee, Binghamton Insane Asylum, charges against, not removed, VII, 443.

HALLIGON, JULIEN LOUIS VICTOR, REAR-ADMIRAL. Commander of French naval escort, Yorktown Centennial Celebration, VII, 738.

HALSEY, JEREMIAH. Communication from, Connecticut claim, II, 371.

HAM, JOHN C. Claim against New York city, veto, VIII, 131; IX, 468.

HAMBOROUGH ARMS. Report relative to, II, 561.

HAMBURG. Town, fixing bail of overseer of highways, veto, VI, 91.

HAMBURG CEMETERY ASSOCIATION. Changing name to Prospect Lawn Cemetery Association, legalizing conveyances, veto, X, 256.

HAMILL, JAMES. Injuries received in Clinton prison, Court of Claims, veto, X, 259.

HAMILTON, ALEXANDER. Appointed receiver of Continental taxes, II, 185; letter from, 190; commissioner to Commercial Convention, 260; delegate to Federal Constitutional Convention, 271; counsel to examine dower cases, 374; statue in United States capitol, VI, 555;

HAMILTON, ALEXANDER — (*Continued*).

    draft of Federal Constitution, Congress determining questions relating to election of members, VIII, 985. VETOES. Memorial building, New York, X, 324; — statue at Albany, 586.

HAMILTON, ANDREW. Appointed Postmaster-General of Colonies, I, 34; memorial from, relative to post-office, 42.

HAMILTON, ELIZABETH (MRS.) Communication from, New York Orphan Asylum, III, 265.

HAMILTON, JAMES. Commissary, claims of, II, 185.

HAMILTON, JAMES. Lieutenant-Governor, Pennsylvania, letter from relative to Indian affairs, I, 508, 511; letter from, 538.

HAMILTON, MICHAEL. Murder of, Clinton prison, VII, 782.

HAMILTON, ROBERT RAY. Member of Yorktown Centennial Commission, VII, 734.

HAMILTON, THOMAS. Contract, materials for Sing Sing prison, assignment, appropriation, veto, VII, 485.

HAMILTON COLLEGE. Aid to, II, 973; condition of, III, 296, 739, 767, 857; lack of endowment, 540; aid from United States deposit fund, 613, 711.

HAMILTON COUNTY. Agricultural society in, III, 945; united with Fulton in election of member of Assembly, V, 226; land in, State park, VI, 629; boundaries relocated, VII, 720; timbered lands, acquisition by State, 722; average excise license fees, 1889, VIII, 686; highways, cost of labor system, 1892, IX, 200; insane, care of, county and State systems compared, 228.

    VETOES. Publication of legal notices, V, 508; highways, VI, 82; opening road, 93; non-resident highway taxes, 338; separate road district, taxes, 442; special highway, 502; VII, 215, 932; Totten and Crossfield's purchase, exemption from highway taxes, 701; highway, Johnsburgh to Long Lake, 133, 320; unpaid taxes, Morehouse, relief, X, 274; cleaning Brown's Tract inlet and other streams, 320; repayment to, by Comptroller, 558; tax sale, Ostrander, 446, 588; taxes, redemption, Robinson, 953.

HAMILTON GRANGE. New York, acquiring and maintaining, veto, X, 324.

HAMILTON SAVINGS BANK. Amending charter, veto, VI, 187.

HAMILTON SCHOOL. Appropriation for, veto, II, 1111.

HAMILTON (TOWN). Canal bridge, veto, VIII, 453.

HAMLIN, HANNIBAL. Elected Vice-President, 1860, V, 326.

HAMLIN, JACOB J. Relief, veto, VIII, 292.

HAMMOND. Relief from railroad burdens, veto, VII, 847, new bill passed.

HAMMOND, JABEZ D. Agent to settle claims against United States, report of, III, 106; State road commissioner, 124; appropriation for compensation as claim agent, 145.

HAMMOND, ROBERT. Clerk of first Assembly, second session, I, 11; id., second Assembly, 12.

HAMMOND, WILLIAM. Bond for return of arms, II, 772.

HANCOCK. Compromising railroad indebtedness, VIII, 128. VETOES. Town meetings, voting in three different places, IX, 817; Delaware river, dykes, X, 788.

HANCOCK, JOHN. Governor of Massachusetts, letter from, Convention on Taxation, II, 190.

HANCOCK, THEODORE E. Attorney-General, opinion, extent of forest preserve restriction as to timber, X, 754.

HANCOCK, WINFIELD S. Major-General, accompanies French delegates to West Point, VII, 740.

HAND, AUGUSTUS C. Keeper of Elizabethtown arsenal, letter from, III, 684.

HANKS, BRIGHAM. Police justice, Wellsville, legalizing acts, veto, VIII, 132.

HANOVER. Reigning house of, I, 689; Empress of, partition of Poland, II, 138.

HANSEN, HENDRICK. Appropriation for subsistence furnished, I, 128; expenses in Indian service, payment of, 172.

HANUS, GUSTAVUS C. Board of Claims, veto, VIII, 1039.

HARBORS. Improvement of, IV, 391; bill for improvement of, veto, 292; legislative resolutions, 393; improvement, neglect of Congress, 571; Federal expenditures on, X, 730.

HARBORMASTERS. New York, fees of, V, 187; employment of assistants condemned, 285, 380; revision of law, 381; VII, 1049; complaints against, VI, 360, 548; compensation a tax on commerce, VII, 163; fees, New York act unconstitutional, 435, 531, 713, 834, 969, 1049; duties and compensation, 834; new act passed, 835, 969, 1049; abolition of office recommended, 997; duties assumed by dock department, 1051; claim submitted to Board of Claims, 1048.
    VETOES. Albany, amending act, VII, 121; New York, compensation, 1048; Port Chester, creating office, X, 590.

HARDENBERGH, JOHANNES, JR., COLONEL. Service in Ulster and Orange counties, I, 626.

HARDENBROOK, MR. Standard yard measure, II, 640.

HARDENBROOK, ABEL. Keeper of powder-house, appointment of counsel for, I, 532.

HARDENBROOK, THEOPHILUS. Claim for services at Fort George, I, 750, 756.

HARDENBURG PATENT. Leasehold estates in, IV, 333.

HARDENBURGH, NICHOLAS. Relief of, veto, II, 663.

HARDY, SIR CHARLES. Appointed Governor, assumes office, I, 576; payment of Connecticut volunteers, 577.

OPENING SPEECH. Twenty-seventh Assembly, seventh session, I, 583; General Johnson defeats French, 583; goes to Albany, 583; fortifying northern frontier, 584; urges new Revenue Law, 584; recommends permanent funds for fixed charges, 584; new Militia Law, 584; Assembly's revenue suggestions, 586; Indians at Minisink, 587; draft for northern garrisons, 588; troops for Crown Point expedition, 588, 591, 592, 595; New Jersey and Massachusetts boundaries, 588, 589; quartering soldiers, 589, 604; expedition against Ticonderoga, 589, 591; Indians on frontiers, 589; blockhouses in Ulster and Orange counties, 590; council of war, Crown Point expedition, 591; Governor Burnet's claim against colony, 592; recommends erection of pesthouse, 592; Indian raid in Ulster county, 593, 594; Massachusetts offers bounties for scalps, 595; letters from Governor Morris, 596; restricting exportation of provisions and military stores, 596, 600; rates on impressments, 596; distressed condition of garrison at Fort William Henry, 597; Earl of Loudoun appointed commander-in-chief, 597; King offers military bounties, 598; financial aid from Crown, 598, 604; reimbursing masters for enlisted servants, 599; fraudulent grants of Indian lands, 601, 606, 611, 687; additional barracks, 602.

OPENING SPEECH. Twenty-seventh Assembly, eighth session, I, 602; French attack Oswego, 602; war with France, 602; subsistence of French prisoners, 603; King consents to annual appropriation, 605; urges increase of revenues, 606; indirect taxes suggested, 606; various recommendations, 607; quarters for King's troops, 608.

OPENING SPEECH. Twenty-seventh Assembly, ninth session, I, 609; more troops from England, 609; Earl of Loudoun urges colonial enlistments, 609, 612; Massachusetts and New Jersey boundaries, 610, 612; township settlements, 613; resignation of, 613; official service, I, pref. x; appointed rear-admiral, 613.

HARDY, HENRY F. Escaped convict, claim for capture of, veto, X, 62.

HARDY, THOMAS E. Auburn prison convict, crime committed by, trial, reimbursing Cayuga county, veto, VI, 876; VII, 87, 227, 471, 781.

HARLAEM LIBRARY. Appropriation for, veto, II, 1111.

HARLAEM SAVINGS BANK. Incorporated, V, 512.

HARLEIAN COLLECTION. British Museum, IV, 183.

HARLEM. Representation in first Assembly, I, 9. VETOES. Common lands, relative to, II, 1110; schools in, appropriation for, 1111; religious societies, appropriation for, 1111; Reformed Low Dutch church, appropriation for, 1111; Episcopal church, appropriation for, 1111; Second Baptist church, relief from assessment for street improvements, VI, 710.

HARLEM HOSPITAL, NEW YORK. Charter, veto, VI, 323.

HARLEM RAILROAD COMPANY. Franchise in New York streets, V, 518.

HARLEM RIVER. VETOES. New bridge over, II, 782; granting to United States right to acquire jurisdiction over, VII, 406; improvement, payment of expense by State, 407; bridges, increasing elevation, VIII, 1035; bridge commissioners, closing affairs of, IX, 154; bridge, 145th street, 807.

HARLEM YACHT CLUB. Charter, veto, VI, 90.

HARMONY. Town, compensation of supervisor, special services, veto, VI, 588.

HARPER, JOHN. Alleged fraud on purchase of Oneida Indian land, II, 223.

HARPER'S. Publishers of school district library, III, 878.

HARPERSVILLE CEMETERY ASSOCIATION. Granting certain powers, veto, VII, 98.

HARPUR, RODERT. Clerk of Council of Appointment, II, 315.

HARRIETSTOWN. Town hall, veto, VIII, 508.

HARRIS, ELISHA. Governor of Rhode Island, application for boundary record, IV, 457.

HARRIS, HAMILTON. Member of New Capitol Commission, VI, 229; Senate, member of committee of arrangements, opening of new capitol, VII, 270.

HARRIS, IRA. Assembly, member of select committee on anti-rent troubles, IV, 328.

HARRIS, JOHN. Convicted of murder, pardoned, II, 923.

HARRIS, ORRIN. Relief, veto, VI, 698.

HARRIS, SAMUEL C. Assembly doorkeeper, compensation, veto, VII, 1078.

HARRISON, FRANCIS. Bond as farmer of excise, I, 188.

HARRISON, WILLIAM HENRY. Elected President, III, 904; death of, 905, 914, 934; legislative proceedings on death of, 914; widow, relief of, Georgia opposes bill for, 977.

HART, EDWARD, CAPTAIN. Account for war expenses, I, 394.

HART, JAMES I. Senate, assistant sergeant-at-arms and postmaster, expenses, attending Abbott funeral, veto, VII, 586.

HART, LEWI. Bond for return of arms, II, 775.

HART, PHEBE B. Estate of, veto, II, 713.

HART, WILLIAM H. New York, relief, veto, X, 581.

HARTFORD, CONNECTICUT. Meeting of Massachusetts Boundary Commissioners at, I, 755; conference of Governors Tryon and Hutchinson, 756; proposed improvement of road to New York, 757; proposed convention at, for regulating prices, II, 83; convention at, on national affairs, 108; convention at, on taxation, 190; hospital for insane, successful treatment at, III, 379.

HARTFORD, CORTLAND COUNTY, NEW YORK. Southern Central Railroad, school taxes, distribution, veto, VI, 1035.

HARTFORD, WASHINGTON COUNTY, NEW YORK. Postmaster at, removal of, II, 1069.

HARTLAND. Canal drainage, deepening Golden Hill creek, etc., veto, X, 645.

HARTS FALLS. Village, changing name, veto, VI, 341.

HART'S ISLAND. Annexation to New York, veto, VIII, 1035.

HARTSTENE, HENRY J. Search for Dr. Kane, V, 59; medal for, 59.

HARVARD UNIVERSITY. Law school graduates, relative to, veto, VII, 416.

HARVEY, CHARLES T. Rapid transit experiments, act relative to, VIII, 125; unconstitutional, 127; claim, veto, 886, 1160; IX, 141.

HARVEY, HERBERT S. New York, assistant clerk, city magistrate's court, claim for services, veto, X, 172.

HARVEY, MARTHA. Escheat, veto, VII, 550.

HASBROUCK, GILBERT D. B. Board of Claims, veto, VIII, 1128.

HASBROUCK, LOUIS, JR. Court of Claims, veto, X, 449.

HASKIN, JOHN B. Appropriation for Flanagan judgment, VII, 230.

HASSALL ON FOOD AND ADULTERATIONS. Quoted, composition of lemonade, ginger beer and cider, VIII, 354.

HASTINGS, GEORGE S. Secretary to Governor Fenton, proclamation on death of Lincoln, V, 677.

HASTINGS, HUGH. State Historian, publication of Clinton papers, VII, 814.

HASTINGS-ON-THE-HUDSON. Changing boundaries, veto, X, 233.

HASTINGS, OSWEGO COUNTY. Fort Brewster, acquiring site of, veto, X, 435.

HASWELL, CHARLES H. Requests approval of Harvey rapid transit bill, VIII, 125.

HATFIELD, ROBERT G. Architect, examines Hudson River Asylum and Elmira Reformatory, report, VI, 567.

HATHAWAY, SAMUEL A. Administrator Bessie G. Hathaway, Court of Claims, veto, X, 445.

HATHORN, JOHN. Seat in Senate declared vacant, II, 310.

HATZEL, JACOB A. New York alderman, election contest, relief, veto, VII, 616.

HAVANA, CUBA. Taken by English, I, 669; vessels from, detained for observation, yellow fever, VI, 533, 626.

HAVANA, NEW YORK. People's College located at, V, 178; village, bridge over Fall creek, veto, VI, 327.

HAVEMEYER, WILLIAM F. Mayor of New York, administration commended by Governor Dix, VI, 544.

HAVEN, WILLIAM. Board of Claims, veto, VIII, 1166.

HAVERSTRAW. Persons driven from, II, 82; highways, amending charter, veto, VIII, 1040.

HAVERSTRAW SAVINGS BANK. Charter, veto, VI, 186.

HAWAII ISLANDS. Acknowledgment of instruments executed in, veto, X, 63; proposed illustration of social conditions at Pan-American Exposition, 125.

HAWK, SIR EDWARD. Commands English fleet in naval battle off coast of France, I, 642.

HAWKING, GEORGE. Legislative employee, compensation, veto, VII, 372.

HAWLEY, EBENEZER R. Sheriff, Onondaga, execution sale of land in military tract, II, 689.

HAWLEY, JESSE. Resigns as Niagara courthouse commissioner, II, 1117.

HAY, JOHN. Secretary of State, United States, correspondence relative to Canadian branch of Cayuga Indians, X, 128.

HAY, UDNY, COLONEL. Deputy Quartermaster-General, letter from, scarcity of forage, II, 56; letters from, army supplies, 66, 90; letters from, various matters, 108; appointed Deputy Commissary-General of Purchases for New York in the Continental army, 109; account of, 124; papers from, 133; State agent, difficulties of administering office, 134; forage in Westchester county, 165; letter from, public contracts, 208.

HAY, WILLIAM. Canal department, appropriation for services, veto, IX, 716.

HAYES, EDWARD. New York, Municipal Court attendant, claim, veto, X, 168.

HAYES, RUTHERFORD B. President, receives majority of electoral votes, 1876, VII, 33; New York appointments, 559; quoted, protest against riders in appropriation bills, IX, 406.

HAYNES, JAMES A. Claim against Stockport, legalizing settlement, veto, X, 814.

HAYS, WILLIAM, BRIGADIER-GENERAL. Enlistment of volunteers, V, 538; superintendent of volunteer recruiting service, 561.

HEAD OF ELK. Troops receive pay at, II, 149.

HEAD, HENRY. Dock department engineer, New York, rehearing
    charges, veto, X, 951.
HEADLEY, JOEL T. Secretary of State, report, publication of colonial
    history, VIII, 425.
HEADS. Bounty for, I, 71.
HEALTH INSURANCE COMPANIES. VETOES. Amending act, VIII, 1040;
    amending general law, IX, 802.
HEALTH OFFICER. Compensation, II, 344, 382; letter from, 520, 586;
    reducing compensation, IV, 439, 480; VII, 833, 968; act rela-
    tive to, V, 450; report, 563, 717; VI, 776; VII, 538; VIII, 338;
    IX, 38, 222, 363, 581, 683, 756, 852; X, 46, 149; member of
    metropolitan board of Health, V, 702; communication from,
    expected visitation of cholera, 863; member of New York
    health department, VI, 129; complaints against, 360; exten-
    sion of powers, removal, 534; Senate investigation of fees,
    VII, 967; political contributions, 968; regulation of quaran-
    tine fees, congressional action requested, 968; salary fixed, fees
    regulated, 968; ex-officio member of State Board of Health,
    VIII, 175; nominations not acted on, 426; act fixing salary,
    557.
    VETOES. Various appropriations, VII, 1085; residence, painting
    and repairs, VIII, 425; landing at Clifton Station, X, 567;
    repairs to steamers, 792; plumbing, office, laboratory and house,
    792; mason work, 792; heating apparatus, 792; gas apparatus,
    792.
HEANEY, JOHN F. New York, Municipal Court attendant, claim, veto,
    X, 168.
HEAP, D. P. Engineer third lighthouse district, communication from,
    cession of land to United States at Old Orchard shoal, IX, 211.
HEATH, SAMUEL. Deputy weighmaster, matter of, I, 195.
HEATH, WILLIAM, MAJOR-GENERAL. Letter from, II, 20; supplies ob-
    tained by enemy in Westchester county, 90; need of army supplies,
    90; scarcity of bread for troops, 161.
HEATHCOTE, CALEB. Account of revenue and taxes, I, 63.
HEBREW FREE LOAN ASSOCIATION. Charter, veto, X, 813.
HECTOR. VETOES. Part of, bonding for railroad, VI, 187; town meet-
    ing, fixing time of, VII, 842.
HEFFLEY COLLEGIATE INSTITUTE. Charter, veto, X, 709.
HEGEMAN, FREDERICK. New York, relief, veto, X, 177.
HEIMATH, ISABELLA. Relief, veto, X, 59.
HELL GATE. Pilotage,— Maine protests against, VI, 561; — Connecticut
    protests against, VII, 47, 411.
    VETOES. Pilots, reducing fees, VII, 568; pilots, relative to, IX, 728;
    X, 316.

HELL GATE NAVIGATION COMPANY. Incorporation, remonstrance by New York Chamber of Commerce, IV, 824.

HEMP. Soil of colony adapted to, I, 255; English bounty on, 256; cultivation of, recommended, 260; failure of, 682; lottery to promote cultivation of, 682; carding and spinning, II, 534; cultivation of, 1092; III, 126, 206, 253, 298.

HEMPSTEAD. Number of excise licenses, 1887, VIII, 360; school district No. 1, increasing tax for school purposes, 1156; part of, merged in Greater New York, IX, 301.

VETOES. Town, special meeting, sale of Hempstead Plains, VI, 97; Jamaica bay, Hummel dock, 705; unpaid taxes, VII, 415; X, 62, 322; free schools, amending act, VIII, 701; exempting from taxation, property of Sanitarium for Hebrew Children, IX, 152; personal property of, relative to, 817.

HEMPSTEAD BAY. Canal to Jamaica bay, survey, veto, X, 649.

HEMPSTEAD CONVENTION. Meeting, promulgates Duke's laws, I, 2.

HEMPSTEAD PLAINS. Sale of, veto, VI, 97.

HENDERSON. Arms and supplies for, II, 774.

HENDRICKS, GEORGE. Relief, veto, VI, 185.

HENDRICKS, HARRIET M. Board of Claims, veto, VIII, 888.

HENDRICK'S REEF. Fortifications on, II, 777.

HENDRICKS, THOMAS A. Electoral vote for Vice-President, 1876, VII, 33.

HENDY, JAMES. Estate, Court of Claims, veto, X, 944.

HENRY IV. France, benevolent wish for comfort of people, III, 197.

HENRY VI. Reign of, beginning of public debt, III, 324.

HENRY, CHARLES J. Assembly, introduces Brooklyn aldermanic bill, 1883, quoted, VIII, 744.

HENRY, JOHN. Relief, veto, II, 309.

HENRY, NELSON H. Adjutant-General, accompanies Prince Henry to Assembly chamber at his reception, X, 480.

HENRY, PRINCE (Prussia). Visit of, X, 375; reception by Legislature, 478; replies to address by Lieutenant-Governor Woodruff, 479.

HENSHAW, JOHN. Director Western Railroad Company, communication from, III, 750.

HERDER, HENRY, CAPTAIN. Petition from, appointment of surgeon, II, 117.

"HERDER, THE." German steamer, brings delegates to Yorktown Celebration, VII, 741.

HERKIMER, NICHOLAS. Gallantry of, II, 8, 11; orders to, relative to troops, 13; relief of families of men killed in battle under, 25; monument to, III, 179, 214, 226, 989; sketch of services, 228; monument, veto, IX, 240; Monument Act, 1895, 240; report of Monument Commission, 685.

HERKIMER COUNTY. Sheriff, letters from, removal of intruders from Indian lands, II, 320; militia from, 1812, 743; convicts to be sent to Sing Sing prison, III, 316; Clark Patent, IV, 332; refunding illegal taxes, VI, 278; increase in population, 578; land in, State park, 629; boundaries relocated, VII, 720; timbered lands, acquisition by State, 722; average excise license fees, 1889, VIII, 686; highways, cost of labor system, 1892, IX, 200; insane, care of, county and State systems compared, 228.

VETOES. Repairing courthouse and jail, II, 388; highways, VI, 193; manufacturing corporations, facilitating dissolution, VII, 59; taxes, rejected, reassessment, 664; establishing Lewis county boundary, appropriation, 783; Oswegatchie river improvement, VIII, 848; State road repairs, 850; separate road districts in certain towns, amending act, IX, 250; Lewis county boundary, survey, 856; county clerk, special deputies, X, 811.

HERKIMER (Village). Postmaster at, suggested removal of, II, 1070.

VETOES. Police justice and police constables, VIII, 330; Erie canal, completing vertical wall, 1112.

HERMAN. Highways, repair, appropriation, veto, X, 428.

HERMANCE, BRIGADIER-GENERAL. Commands brigade at Haerlem Heights, II, 810.

HERRIMAN, A. R. President board of education, Ogdensburg, communication favoring school bill, X, 912.

HERTEL, JOHN S. Board of Claims, veto, VIII, 1166.

HESS & COMPANY, S. F. Court of Claims, veto, X, 315, 588.

HETH, H. Communication from, Federal Antietam board, IX, 343.

HEUVELTON. Highway from, to Depeyster town line, repairs, appropriation, veto, X, 428.

HEWITT, ABRAM S. Mayor of New York, objections to police and fire commission bill, VIII, 637; House of Representatives, army bill, 1879, prohibiting use of troops at polls, IX, 405.

HEWITT, JOHN. Murder of, II, 531.

HIBBARD, ENOS S. Commissioner, repairing highway, Cattaraugus reservation, veto, VII, 476.

HIDES. Inspector of, III, 748.

HIGBY, CAPTAIN. Defense of frontier, I, 124, 128, 144.

HIGGINS, ANN. Damages, death of son, appropriation, veto, VII, 464.

HIGGINS, FRANK W. Senate, member of joint committee on taxation, 1899, X, 801; Governor, appoints counsel, VIII, 27; portrait, X, 718.

1905. Annual message, X, 718; State debt, 718; receipts and expenditures, 719; corporations, capital employed in State,

HIGGINS, FRANK W., 1905 — (Continued).

720; tax on premiums of life insurance companies construed, 720; appropriations and taxation, 720; tax legislation, 721; repeal of tax on surplus and undivided profits of savings banks, 721; taxation of insurance premiums, 722; census, 722; insane and charities, 723; boards of managers for State hospitals, 724; enlargement of State hospital accommodations, 724; who entitled to State support in State hospitals, 725; additional accommodations for feeble-minded, 725; progress in reformatory system, 726; more public competitive bidding in purchases for State institutions, 727; all appropriations for charitable and reformatory institutions should be in one bill, 727; transfer of inmates from one charitable or reformatory institution to another, 727; instruction and employment of adult blind, 728; election reforms, 728; identification of naturalized citizens, 729; right of women to vote at special tax elections in cities of the third-class, 730; canals, 730; expenditures by United States for rivers and harbors, 730; abandonment of part of Black River canal, 731; good roads, 732; banks, 732; restricting loan to individuals, 734; insurance, 735; excise, 736; local option in cities, 736; education, 736; child labor, 738; agriculture, 739; prisons, 740; transfer of imbeciles and idiots from penal institutions, 740; State Architect, additional inspectors, 740; public buildings, 741; State library building, 741; plumbing, heating, lighting and drainage of capitol, 741; civil service, 741; merit system should be extended to large counties, 742; civil service should be extended to New York House of Refuge, 742; public health, 743; source of water supply should be inspected by Public Health Department, 743; Water Storage Commission, 1904, 743; State Water Supply Commission, 744; fish, game and forests, 744; United States deposit fund, 744; change in method of investment of fund, 745; Tenement-House Law, 746; preservation of places of scenic and historic interest, 746; Louisiana Purchase Exposition at St. Louis, 747; large number of awards to State at exposition, 747; executive office hours, 747; additional water supply for New York city, 748; special message on forest preserve, 753; policy of Federal government as to forests, 755; recommendations as to forest preserve, 757; special message, repeal of tax on surplus of savings

HIGGINS, FRANK W., 1905 — (*Continued*).

      banks, 766; review of current legislation, 782; certificates
of necessity of immediate passage of bills, 759, 763, 764,
765, 766, 767.   ·

   MEMORANDUMS OF APPROVAL. Utica courthouse, X, 768; stock
transfers, taxation of, 769; railroads, inspection of locomotive boilers, 772; liquor tax, inspection of hotels, revocation
of certificates, local option, 780; appropriation bill, 781;
State hospital in northern part of State, reappropriation,
794; railroads, incorporation and powers, 799; mortgage
tax, 800; New York water supply, using for generation of
electricity, 804.

   VETOES. Palmyra union school, additional building, X, 752;
divorce, when action may be maintained, 758; labor, protection of persons employed on buildings in cities, 760; Condemnation Law, 761; New York Memorial Day Celebration,
Richmond borough, 762; transfer tax, appraisers and surrogates' assistants, 770; Barker, relief, 770; Kings county,
register and sheriff, additional subordinates, salaries, 770;
sheriff, New York, salary, 773; civil service, claims of
persons employed in violation of law, 773; Niagara river,
bridge at Grand Island, 774; canals, private claim bills,
waiving statutes, 775; Buffalo, fire department, storekeeper,
776; Agricultural Law, condensed milk, 776; Buffalo, Union
Railroad Passenger Station Commission, 777; escheat, various bills, names not given, 778; Liquor Tax Law, sale
within prohibited distance of a church, Gotham Hotel, 779;
items in supply bill, 784; item in appropriation bill, 783;
items in supplemental supply bill, 795; omnibus veto, 805.

   PROCLAMATION. Extraordinary session, Hooker case, X, 819;
charges against Warren B. Hooker, justice of the Supreme
Court, 819; appropriation for expenses of extraordinary
session, 820; certificates of necessity of immediate passage
of bills, 821; insurance investigation, 822; Hooker case,
note, 825.

1906.   Annual message, X, 831; State debt, 832; receipts and expenditures, 833; barge canal bonds, 833; highway improvement bonds, 833; taxation, 834; cost of New York city
government, comparative statement, 834; mortgage tax,
835; repeal of law taxing savings banks' surplus, 836;
license tax on foreign corporations doing business in State,
836; Tax Commission, 837; insurance, 837; life insurance

HIGGINS, FRANK W., 1906 — (Continued).

statistics, 838; more thorough regulation by Department of Insurance, 840; recommendations concerning Insurance Law, 841; canals, 842; barge canal work, 844; Attorney-General, 845; receivers and counsel fees, defunct corporations, 845; franchise tax, review, employment of counsel, 845; election reform, 846; political contributions by corporations should be prohibited, 847; direct nominations for political office, 847; Ballot Law should be simplified, 847; constitutional amendments, 848; State debt, extending period, 848; judiciary, 849; labor, 850; improvement of highways, 850; shade trees along highways, 851; debt limitations of New York city, 851; alteration of Senate districts and apportionment of Assemblymen, 851; protection of Niagara Falls, 852; local option, 853; regulation of public utilities, 854; submission of maps of sources of water supply by persons and private corporations, 855; charities and insane, 856; additional accommodations needed at Craig Colony, 857; labor, 857; State free employment bureau discontinued, 858; education, 858; illiteracy in State, 859; public health, 860; agriculture, 861; State fair, 861; Forest, Fish and Game Commission, 862; scientific cultivation of forests, 862; State should derive revenue from forests, 862; prisons and penal legislation, 863; Commission on Prison Buildings, 863; Commission on Probation System, 863; punishment of boys sixteen years of age, 863; Massachusetts and New York boundary line, 864; special legislation, 864; work and early adjournment, 865; number of thirty-day bills, 1905, 865; annual reports, 866; report of delegation at National Immigration Conference, 866; communication from Governor of Florida, proposed International and Isthmian Exposition, 866; tabulation of census statistics, 868; transmits papers to Senate relative to charges preferred against Bank Superintendent Kilburn, 872; certificates of necessity of immediate passage of bills, 876, 878, 880, 885, 890, 891, 892, 893, 894, 895, 896, 897; Hudson-Fulton Celebration, 874; requests return of Kilburn papers from Senate, 878; transmits Kilburn papers to Assembly, 879; San Francisco earthquake and fire, appropriation for relief of sufferers, 890; changing time of election of directors in domestic mutual life insurance corporations for 1906, 894; summary of important legislation, 931.

HIGGINS, FRANK W., 1906 — (*Continued*).

 MEMORANDUMS OF APPROVAL. New York, railroads, terminating use in certain streets, 897; mutual life insurance companies, election of directors, 899; New York, gas, fixing price, 900; Liquor Tax Law, inspection of hotels, 902; Legislature, persons appearing before committees, notice of employment, 904; perjury, presumption outside contradictory statements, 905; Insurance Law, amendments, 906; highways, amending act of 1898, improvement bonds, 909; Ogdensburg, amending charter, school officers, elections, 910; labor, hours and wages, 914; mortgages, recording tax, 920; canal debt interest, highway improvement debt interest, highway improvement fund appropriation, canal debt sinking fund appropriation, 922; railroads, injuries to employees, 924; Oswego canal, Syracuse, bridge, North Salina street, 929; appropriation bill, 1906, 930; Supreme Court, additional justices in certain districts, 936; Palisades, extending park, acquisition of Watkin's Glen, Johnson Mansion and blockhouse, 940; free school fund, apportionment, 941.

 VETOES. Tompkins, bridge over Delaware river, X, 873; Buffalo, police pension, Dowd case, 875; taxation, personal property of non-residents, 876; costs in action, 880, 916; street railroads, fares in Brooklyn and Queens boroughs, 882; taxation, mortgages, 885; racing associations, annual tax on gross receipts, 891; Auburn, Seneca Falls and Waterloo, regulating price of gas, 907; Schenectady, diverting fourth of July appropriation to San Francisco relief, 908; Elmira Reformatory, sentences, 917; Niagara river, limiting use of water, 918; flags, battleflags, permitting use of, in Oswego County Old Home Week, 919; civil service, retiring veterans, 924; railroads, freight transportation, 926; appeals, criminal cases, from order denying motion for new trial, 927; personal property, transfers of goods in bulk, 929; Erie canal, bridge, Rochester, Lyell avenue, 929; items in supply bill, 933; counsel in criminal cases, allowance, 942; dentists, examination and practice, 942; omnibus veto, 943.

 Appoints editor of Governor's Messages, I, pref. iii; official service, I, pref. xiii; death of, note on, X, 961; legislative memorial services, 963.

HIGGINS, WILLIAM. Death of, appropriation to mother, veto, VII, 464.

HIGHLAND, SULLIVAN COUNTY. VETOES. Town, appropriation of certain moneys, VI, 592; dyke, Delaware river, X, 935.

HIGHLAND FIRE ENGINE AND HOSE COMPANY No. 3, FLORIDA. Charter, veto, VIII, 462.

HIGHLAND INDIANS. Presents to, I, 341.

HIGHLAND AND MODENA TURNPIKE ROAD COMPANY. Tolls chargeable by, veto, VIII, 1112.

HIGHLANDS. British movements in, II, 7; condition of posts in, 8; British take forts in, 15, 16, 18; discovery of granite, IV, 29.

HIGHLAND TRANS-HUDSON RAILROAD COMPANY. Bridge across Hudson river, veto, VII, 937.

HIGH SCHOOLS. Proposed establishment of, IV, 840; should not be supported by taxation, VII, 156; free tuition in, X, 514, 539, 859; comparative statement, 1905, 737; increase in attendance, 1905, 858.

    VETOES. Brooklyn, establishing, VII, 134; evening, New York, VIII, 637, 638; IX, 74, 216; Richmond borough, changing site, erecting buildings, X, 447; university grants to, 551; Auburn, enlarging building, 717.

HIGHWAY LAW. General, 1890, VIII, 1027.

HIGHWAYS. See also ROAD. General act relating to, I, 103; supplemental act, 129; petitions for new, 758; for interior communication, 762; revision of laws, II, 219; right of soil in, 331, 385; general act, 385; act amended, 410; public, certain streams in Chenango and Steuben, 521; carriages passing each other, 554; laws relating to, should be uniform, 591; road between Albany and St. Lawrence river, report of commission, 756, 795; crossing canals, 1010; money tax superior to labor system, III, 376; appropriations by town meetings, 377; benefits not equal to burdens, 469; railroad crossings, 511; improvement of, 739; labor, militia exempt from, IV, 557; annual expenditure for, in towns, VI, 47; borrowing money for, 55; damages, vested right, 158; on Indian reservations, State's right to build, VII, 222; commissioners, when residents of village may not vote for, VIII, 55; effect of declaring stream a public highway, 381, 407, 454; improvement of, 923, 1068; IX, 308; State roads, see that title; General Law, 1890, VIII, 1027; improvement, general note, 1041; State aid to towns, 1042; constitutional amendment, State debt, 1043; act of 1906, 1043; bad condition of, 1069; near Clinton prison, employment of prisoners on, IX, 181, 329; labor system, cost of, by counties, 1892, 199; macadam roads, estimated cost, 201; county roads, VIII, 1041; IX, 203, 559; prison labor on, 181, 329; employment of State and

HIGHWAYS —(*Continued*).

county convicts on, 668, 740; New York and Albany post road, act of 1896, 668; improvement needed, 1897, 745; money system, 844; State Engineer's supervision, X, 340; stone crushers, regulations as to purchase, 380; good roads, comparative statement, of appropriations, 1893–4; 1901–2, 464; improvement, constitutional amendment 1905, 513; Improvement Act of 1898 not applicable to villages, 523; total mileage in State, 1904, 618; improvement, appropriation, 1904, 619; removal of snow, act of 1904, 632; State debt for, constitutional amendment, 732, 833, 850, 900; improvement bonds, 1906, 834, 851, 909; shade trees recommended, 851; reports to State Engineer, 893; amending act of 1898, 909; provision for interest and sinking fund, 1906, 922.

VETOES. In certain counties, relative to, II, 348; in Westchester county, 592; proceedings against residents of Connecticut, 592, 593; Canandaigua, IV, 771; Hamilton county, VI, 82; opening road, Warren and Hamilton counties, 93; Westchester and West Farms, amending act, 158; Great Valley, encroachments, 160; Florence, highway commissioner to establish, 182; Fowler, special, 188; separate road district, Worcester, 196; Goshen, opening, 213; town auditors, raising money, 329; non-resident taxes, Essex and Hamilton, 338; acquiring right of way, special method, 340; taxes, Hamilton and Warren counties, 442; Franklin county, special road district, 481; Hamilton county, special, 502; VII, 215, 932; Morrisania, 167th street improvement, VI, 566; Westchester county, public roads in certain towns, 589; Morrisania, changing grade of certain streets, 590; special, less than three rods wide, Guilderland and New Scotland, 670; amending Revised Statutes, 695; assessments, Glenville, 701; Totten and Crossfield's purchase, exemption of certain townships from taxes, 701; Livonia, road two rods wide, 707; new lots, Bushwick avenue, special act, VII, 63; system of repairs, amending act, 69; St. Regis reservation, 91, 909; Onondaga reservation, 92, 223, 384; IX, 80; Eastchester, VII, 130; Camden and Amsville, assessment for highway labor, 130; Northfield, macadamizing certain roads, 132; Hamilton county, Johnsburgh to Long Lake, 133, 320; discontinuance, 201; Mentz, overseers of highways, appointment, special act, 208; Cattaraugus reservation, 221; Thurman, non-resident taxes, 268; labor, 325; Black creek, public, 358; laying out and altering, 367, 372; Saranac river, removing obstructions, floating logs, 382; Middleburgh, separate road district, 414, 440; plankroad in-

HIGHWAYS, VETOES— (*Continued*).

spectors, exempting Ulster county, 414; streets in territory adjoining city, 416; Middletown (Richmond county), separate road district, 497, 507; Piermont, macadamizing, 509; deposit of ashes and rubbish in, 646; Franklin county, facilitating travel on, 650; defective, liability of town for damages, 767; Washington county, near Fort Miller bridge, 805; facilitating improvement, 807; damages resulting from defects, notice before accident, 843; opening in one town on application of freeholders of another town, 835; Washington county, special, 886; public, Bonaparte creek, Lewis county, 934; New York, permanent exterior street, 1087; weeds and brush, 1095; orchards and vineyards, excepting Pultney, 1098; Wilmington and North Elba, repair, 1099; Northfield, separate road district, 1099; obstruction by snow, 1108; Greenburgh, election of highway commissioners, VIII, 54; Onondaga reservation, repairs, 116, 845; X, 426; Westchester, bonds for, 292; Salmon river, protection of banks, 380; New Baltimore, consolidation and repairs, 387; Fishkill, road commissioner, creating office, 388; Washington and Saratoga counties, damaged by Champlain canal, repairs, 453; Deer river, bill declaring public highway, 454; X, 444; commissioners to assess damages, compensation, VIII, 459; number of highway commissioners in towns, 461; Eastchester, number of commissioners, 461, 616; Newtown, road improvement, 469; referee's fees, 470; New Utrecht, Franklin avenue, special act, 615; Flatbush, Parkville streets and avenues, 615; Westerlo, Chesterville separate road district, 616; Onondaga county, amending local act, 617; Sacandaga river, public highway, 621; boulevard, Buffalo to Niagara Falls, 639, 879; over tidal streams, 640; Cattaraugus reservation, repairs, 845; St. Regis reservation, repairs, 850; X, 427; Lewis county, No. 4, to Stillwater reservoir, repairs, 851; road implements, purchase of, 873; Portland, special act, 879; between towns divided by navigable tidal streams, construction of, 888; Springfield Center, separate road district, 1039; Haverstraw, amending charter, 1040; Virgil, opening, extending time, 1086; tax, amending Revised Statutes, 1106; New Utrecht, board of improvement, 1134; Queens county, highway labor, 1154; traction engine on, damages, 1156; Kings county, special, IX, 130; New Utrecht, special act, 134; use of, amending act, 150; separate district, certain towns in Herkimer county, 250; New Utrecht, improvement, 264; bridges broken by heavy loads, when town

Highways, Vetoes — (Continued).

not liable, 274; Plattsburgh stone crusher, 433; commissioner, towns, compensation, 462; labor commutations, 524; money system, 524; joint bridges, apportionment of expense, 525; Oneida county, joint bridges, apportionment of expense, 525; Fulton chain of lakes, public highway, 531; amending general law, 624, 628; X, 317, 445, 446; altering, discontinuing or laying out, amending, IX, 625; roads and streets, Kings county, altering commissioner's map, 628; sidepaths, Niagara county, 629; Westchester county, special, 722; sidepaths, Oneida county, 726; — Chemung county, 729; — Monroe county, 731; Olive, protection of, 768; near Sing Sing prison, convict labor on, 775; Queens county system, making Thompson avenue, Long Island City, a part of, IX, 786; Schenectady, street on canal land, 788, 789; Buffalo, Main street, road improvement, 795; alteration and discontinuance, compensation of commissioners, 801; water, free flow in rivers and streams, 801; bridges, inspection by State Engineer and Surveyor, 801; overseers, annual report, 801; railroads, highway labor, assessments, 801; convict labor on, 814; Clinton county, exempting from certain provisions relative to commissioners for laying out, 861; labor, commutation for, 864; laying out, damages, compensation of commissioners, 864; county roads, amending general law, 864; laying out, commissioner's notice of meeting, 864; Hastings-on-the-Hudson, exempting from village limits property required for State highways, X, 233; Dewitt, special system, 234; Albany county, Delaware turnpike improvement, Leith claim, 236; plowing, digging and cropping, 276; in two or more towns in same county, 316; through Cypress Hill cemetery, New York, 325; improvement, acquisition of materials, 384, new bill passed; rebate of taxes for wide tire wagons, exempting Franklin and Oswego counties, 393; county, supervision, amending law, 404; Piercefield, repairs, appropriation, 428; Herman, repairs, appropriation, 428; Fowler, repairs, appropriation, 428; from Heuvelton to Depeyster town line, repairs, appropriation, 428; Allegany reservation, repairs, 429; Tonawanda reservation, repairs, 429; Rome, outside of tax district, 438, 446; connecting, construction of, 439; St. Lawrence county, improvement, 439; automobiles, regulating use of, 441; South Sandy creek, public highway, 444; noxious weeds, 450; streams as public, condemnation proceedings, 457; Improvement Act, 1898, Rome included in, 522; Black river,

HIGHWAYS, VETOES — *(Continued)*.

Castorland dyke road, Croghan, repairing and improving, 570; Improvement Act of 1898, appropriation, 572; State aid to towns, 585; Queens and Nassau counties, street railroads on, 587; Colonie, collection and disbursement of money, 589; commissioners in certain towns, 590; appointment of overseers, 594; snow, removal of, 594, 707; sidepaths, amending general act, 594; over Madison reservoir, repairs, 645; Montezuma turnpike repairs, 646; Owasco lake, highway on west shore, protection of, 646; Ulster and Delaware road, No. 16, Shandaken, 696; Yates county improvement, 703; White Plains, road improvement, Bronx borough, 712; Irondequoit, Hudson avenue improvement, reimbursement, 785; Irving, widening and raising embankment, 789; Fowler, along Oswegatchie river, 791; Croghan breakwater, Black river, 791; instruction in methods, good roads school, 793; State aid, appropriation, 796; laying out, notice of meeting, 809; limitation on laying out, 809; private roads, amending Highway Law, 809; laying out, decision of commissioners denying application, 809; improvement, repairs and maintenance, 946; qualified abandonment, 948; State aid in towns under money system, 952; Westchester county, exemption from poll tax, 952; poll tax in Suffolk and Westchester counties, 955; poll tax in towns under money system, 956.

HIGLEY, BRODIE G. Dam across Hudson river, North creek, veto, X, 705.

HILL, AARON. Son of Captain David, Mohawk delegate, II, 378, 379.

HILL, AARON HENRY. Son of Brandt, Mohawk delegate, II, 378, 379.

HILL, DAVID B. Lieutenant-Governor, becomes Governor on resignation of Governor Cleveland, VII, 1126; I, pref. xii; portrait, VIII, 1.

1885. Annual message, VIII, 1; Governor and Legislature not in political accord, 2; numerous State departments, 3, 140; condition of State, 4; finances, 4; summary of important legislation, 1884, 4; commends Governor Cleveland's administration, 5; banks, 6; general law for trust companies, 6; restricting individual bankers, 6; supervision, 7; insurance, 7; State prisons, 8; convict labor, sketch of movement to abolish, 8; results of abolition of contract system, 10; canals, 12; Erie canal improvement, 13; National Guard, 14; camp of instruction, 14; service uniforms, 14; Board of Claims, 14; spring elections, New

HILL, DAVID B., 1885 — (*Continued*).

York, 15; civil service, 18; practical tests suggested, 19; naturalized citizens, 20; registration of naturalized citizens, production of papers, 20; forest preservation, 22; commission to investigate condition of forests, 23; freedom of worship in penal and reformatory institutions, 23; legislative counsel, 25; constitutional amendment, limitation of municipal indebtedness, 27; new capitol, 29; Advisory Board created, 31; New Orleans Exposition, 31; agricultural interests, 32; experiment station, 33; dairy interests, 33; labor interests, 35; general building laws for cities, 36; assignments, preference, 36; mode of inflicting death penalty, 37; repeal of statutes superseding Penal and Criminal Codes, 37; revision and promulgation of Penal Code, 38; list of revisions of statutes, 38; statutory revision, 38; corporations, restricting power of dissolution, 39; railroad supervision, transportation problem, 39; State census, 40; omission of statistical information, 41, 59; change of time for completion of State census, 42, 59; enumerators, method of appointment, 42; civil service laws should apply to census enumerators, 42, 60; pardon report, 43; audit of town accounts, historical sketch, 48; appropriation for Civil Service Commission, expenses and enumerators, 57; report of commission to investigate charges against Greenwood Cemetery Corporation, 70; delay in inflicting death penalty after conviction, 80; urges passage of enumeration bill, 83.

MEMORANDUMS OF APPROVAL. Troy, police, VIII, 84; Amsterdam charter, 88; capitol appropriation bill, 93; Ogdensburg, sewers, 96; taxation, collateral inheritance, 102; rapid transit, Harvey experiments, 125; International Prison Congress, delegate to, 127; Hancock, compromising railroad indebtedness, 128; Sunday Mercury, relief, 128; Brooklyn Elevated Railroad bill, 129.

VETOES. Additional notaries public, Monroe and Onondaga counties, VIII, 43; New York, water supply, amending Aqueduct Act, 45; common schools, Palmyra, permitting supervisor to hold office, 47; Hornellsville, town auditors, 48; Lowell Cemetery Association, reducing number of trustees, 52; conveyance of State lands under water at Yonkers, 53; Greenburgh, highway commissioners, 54; Board of Claims, appeal to Court of Appeals, 56; Middle-

Hill, David B., 1885, Vetoes — (*Continued*).

town, village hall, 61; Elmira Female College, changing name, 62; Rensselaer county coroners, compensation and proceedings, 62; Elmira, revising charter, new ward, 64; census bill, 66; county clerks, recording and indexing notices of pendency in certain counties, 70; items in appropriation bill, 71; Newburgh, increasing tax for contingent expenses, 76; Chautauqua county, legalizing acts of board of supervisors, fishing in Lake Erie, 79; Pomfret union free school district, 82; New York, Surrogate's Court, stenographer, salary, 82; Oswego, water supply, 98; New York, sinking fund, improving condition, 99; New York College of Medicine and Surgery, charter, 100; New York, Arcade Railway Company, extending powers, 102; items in supply bill, 106; Long Island City, unpaid taxes, assessments and water rents, 120; New York and Brooklyn bridge, completion, 123; Kings county, clerk and register, 124; omnibus veto, 129.

Proclamation convening Legislature in extraordinary session, VIII, 132; message at extraordinary session, enumeration of inhabitants, 133; veto, census, general act, 134.

1886. Annual message, VIII, 143; enacting clause, 143; source of legislative power, 143; general laws needed, 144; finances, 145; no public debt, 145; increasing taxation, 145; new sources of taxation needed, 146; tax rate, comparative statement, 146; abolition of common school fund, 147; civil service, 148; number of positions in classified civil service, 148; principles of civil service system, 150; preference of veterans, 151; revision of tax laws, 152; disproportionate taxation of personal property and real estate, 152; deduction of debts, 153; enumeration and apportionment, 155; municipal reform, New York, 158; separating city elections from State and national, 158; non-partisan board of elections, New York, 159; proposed Charter Revision Commission, 160; home rule for cities, 160; sinking fund and public improvements, New York, 161; industrial interests, 162; child labor, 163; arbitration of differences between capital and labor, 164; State prisons, 165; employment of convicts on State account, 165; abolition of unnecessary offices and concentration of official responsibility, 168; abolition of Board of Regents, 168, 171; abo-

Hill, David B., 1886 — (*Continued*).

lition of State Board of Charities, 171; abolition of State Surveyor should have charge of all surveys, 176; Consti- Board of Health, 173; surveys, 175; State Engineer and tutional Convention, 177; religious liberty, 178; limitation of power of corporations to issue stock and bonds, 179; speedy enforcement of criminal law, 180; registration in Brooklyn, 181; sea-coast defenses, 182; special message, New York, sinking fund, improvements, 183; total debt and valuation, New York, 1885, 185; origin of New York sinking fund, 189; various annual reports, 195, 197; an- nounces death of Horatio Seymour, 195; legislative power to annul or dissolve corporation, 204; confirmation of ap- pointments, 235; State Gas Commission, 244; nomination of commissioners of State survey, 255.

Memorandums of Approval. Street railroads, operation in cities and villages, VIII, 200; New York, gas companies, organization, 240; New York, gas companies, limiting price of gas, 241; Milo, new assessment authorized, 257; Syracuse, water department, 258; Monroe county clerk's salary, 260; New York, additional evening high school, 261; New York, Arcade Railway Company, 261; New York, water supply, 270; Suffolk county, annexation of Lloyd's Neck, 289; free libraries, encouraging growth of, 290.

Vetoes. Retail Grocers' Union, New York, charter, VIII, 197; Brooklyn Retail Grocers' Association, charter, 198; ap- peals from superintendents of the poor, 199; First Con- gregational Society, Byron, changing name, 205; Erie canal, bridge, Utica, Genesee street, 206; Comptroller, an- nual report, 208; New York, police captains, increasing salaries, 211; new capitol, Board of Commissioners of Con- struction, 213; Colton, lockup, 229; Code of Civil Proce- dure, Court of Appeals, jurisdiction, 229; Ulster County Loan and Trust Company, Kingston, charter, 230; Cham- plain canal, exchange bridge, Fort Edward, 234; extend- ing time for completion of railroads, 237; payment of teachers' wages, 240; New York, gas companies, 240; items in supply bill, 245; printing message in German, 251; item in appropriation bill, 255; Ithaca, police department, 256; New York, excise commissioners, 273; New York, mayor, aldermen, comptroller and president of the board of aldermen, election, terms of office and powers, 278; omnibus veto, 291.

HILL, DAVID B.—(*Continued*).

1887. Annual message, VIII, 294; permanent system for employment of prison labor, 295; spring municipal elections, New York, 296; registration of naturalized voters, 296; general law for trust companies, 296; assignment for creditors, 297; counsel for Legislature, 298; revision of tax laws, 298; enumeration of inhabitants, 298; commission to revise New York charter, 299; abolition of Regents of University, 301; abolition of State Board of Charities, 301; abolition of State Board of Health, 301; religious toleration in penal institutions, 302; speedy enforcement of criminal law in cases of murder, first degree, 302; limiting power of corporations to issue stock and bonds, 303; general law for trades unions, 303; finances, 303; taxation, 304; Corporation Tax Law, 304; collateral inheritance tax, 304; organization tax on corporations, 305; tax on notaries public, 305; tax on stock transfers, 305; taxation of bonds or other evidence of debt of corporations, 305; taxation of personal property, 307; Constitutional Convention, 308; all political parties should be represented in convention, 310; congressional district representation in convention, 310; minority representation in convention, 310; State Gas Commission, 311, 431; interests of labor, 312; regulating hours of labor, 314; increased compensation of laborers, 315; Saturday half-holidays, 316; Labor Day, 316; regulation of tenement-houses, 317; recovery of damages in case of death, 318; meetings of labor to promote interests should be permitted, 318; collection of wages, 318; special Labor Commission, grievances of labor, 319; adulteration of food, 319; arbitration of labor disputes, 320; manual training in schools, 322; decline in apprentice system, 322; protection from railroad fires, 323; abolition of office of State agent for discharged convicts, 324; various annual reports, 325; relief from special legislation, 342; commission to prepare general laws, 347; urges action on nomination of railroad commissioners, 373; pardon report, 399; urges confirmation of nomination of quarantine commissioners, 426.

MEMORANDUMS OF APPROVAL. Oswego, city chamberlain, reducing number of aldermen, VIII, 427; United States deposit fund, Steuben county, local custody of fund, 429; Oswego county jail, changing site, 429; New York, public health,

HILL, DAVID B., 1887, MEMORANDUMS — (Continued).

430; New York, park commissioners, extending jurisdiction, 430; Brooklyn, gas, regulating price, 431; Game Law, fishing in Lake Ontario, 432; New York, comptroller, fire insurance, 433; pool selling, 434; excise, five gallon sales, 440; Poughkeepsie bridge, 443; Albany, public market, 447; New York, electrical subways, 450.

VETOES. St. Luke's Home, Utica, changing name, VIII, 326; Oneonta, prohibiting new cemeteries, 327; Pittsburg, Lackawanna and Northeastern Railroad Company, changing name, 327; justices of the peace, legalizing acts, taking oath and filing bond, 328; Herkimer, police justice and police constables, 330; Saratoga Springs, sewers in Church street, 331; Young Women's Association, Troy, exempting property from taxation, 332; union free school district, Orangetown, date of annual meeting, 334; Teachers' Mutual Benefit Association, New York, charter, 336; Sherburne, raising money for new bridge, 336; American Female Guardian Society, changing name, 337; Yorkshire, additional justice of the peace, 338; free school district No. 12, Newtown, charter, 338; inspectors of election and poll clerks, Queens county, fixing compensation, 340; Willard Insane Asylum, prohibiting sale of liquor within half a mile of, 340; Oswego County Agricultural Society, mortgage for indebtedness, 341; Canandaigua, sewers and drains, 348; New York, park department, altering map, 23d ward, 350; — 24th ward, 350; prohibiting sale of liquor on State property, 351; Commissioners of Excise McCollum and McCleary, legalizing acts of, 354; excise, amending general act as to New York and Brooklyn, 355; railroad aid, relief of certain towns, 371; New York Investment Company, charter, 376; peach trees, preventing spread of yellows, 376; Oswego canal, improving State ditch, 377; agricultural and horticultural societies, protection of property, appointment of policemen, 378; Young Women's Christian Association, Ogdensburg, charter, 379; Salmon river, protection of banks, 379; Cortland Opera House Company, mortgage for indebtedness, 381; West Troy, contract with West Troy Waterworks Company, water for sewers, 382; Cairo, bridge over Catskill creek, 383; Elmira, political primaries and conventions, 386; Ot-

HILL, DAVID B., 1887, VETOES — (*Continued*).

sego County Agricultural Society, mortgage of property, 388; Fishkill, road commissioner, creating office, 388; New York, Nineteenth street, repaving, 389; Rome, fire commissioners, extending jurisdiction over police department, 390; Mohawk, village cemetery, revising act, 391; unpaid taxes, Binghamton, sales for, 392; Constitutional Convention, providing for, 393; Troy, sewers, expense, how assessed, 399; United States deposit fund, loan commissioners, Ontario county, transferring funds, 401; Steuben county, increasing school commissioner districts, 402; New York, dock department, 403; Veteran Association, Seventy-first Regiment, National Guard, charter, 404; district attorneys, compensation, retaining taxable costs, 404; Beattie escheat, 405; Code of Civil Procedure, appeal to County Court, 406; villages, taxation for water, qualifications of voters on proposition, 406; normal school, secretary to board, right to salary, 407; Delaware river improvement, 407; Rome, defining boundary, 408; Board of Claims, Dudley claim, 408; Gloversville, fire department, term of service, 409; Savannah, engine house and fire department, 410; ferry, Barber's Point, across Lake Champlain, 410; unpaid taxes, Madison county, sale for, 411; collateral inheritance tax, New York, fees of county treasurer and comptroller, 412; canals, State ditch, Mentz, 413; Cayuga and Seneca canals, sewer under, Waterloo, 413; Provident Industrial Insurance Company, charter, 414; registration of voters, requiring personal appearance of voter, 415; items in supply bill, 418; excise, tax on sales, 436; item in appropriation bill, 439; bucket shops, taxation of, 445; teachers' licenses, 448; New York Central park, zoological collection, 449; omnibus veto, 452; committee report on veto of Constitutional Convention bill, 470.

1888. Annual message, VIII, 475; review of legislation, 476; regulating employment of prison labor, 477; spring municipal elections in New York city, 478; counsel to Legislature, 478; revision of tax laws, 478; Commission to revise New York Charter, 479; abolition of Board of Regents, 479; abolition of State Board of Charities, 479; abolition of State Board of Health, 479; religious toleration in penal institutions, 479; power of corporations to issue stock and

HILL, DAVID B., 1888 — (*Continued*).

   bonds, 480; taxation of indebtedness of corporations, 480;
   State Gas Commission, 481; increasing amount recoverable
   from injuries resulting in death, 481; railroad companies
   liable for fires caused by locomotives, 481; abolition of
   office of State agent for discharged convicts, 481; special
   Labor Commission, 482; manual training in schools, 483;
   veterans' rights, elective franchise, Soldiers' Home, 483, 497;
   capital punishment, 483; Constitutional Convention, 484;
   commitment of insane, 484; revision of insanity laws, 485;
   reform in Criminal Law, 486; constitutional amendment,
   second division, Court of Appeals, 486; abolition of confirming power, 487; enumeration and apportionment, 491;
   inequalities in representation under apportionment of 1879,
   494; finances, 496; right of inmates of Soldiers' Home to
   vote in Bath, 497; communications from Eidlitz, Richardson
   & Company, defects in Assembly chamber, 501; revision and
   amendment of excise laws, 509; Commission to Revise Excise
   Laws, 515; urges confirmation of quarantine commissioners,
   519; report of committee of Academy of Medicine, condition of quarantine establishment, 527; pardon report, 534.

MEMORANDUMS OF APPROVAL. Quarantine, amending act,
   VIII, 557; Brooklyn, Lee and Nostrand avenues, 559; items
   in supply bill, 559; Buffalo, fireman, disabled, half pay,
   561; canal improvements, 561; Lockport, sewer, 562; Middletown, city charter, 564; increasing salary of Deputy
   Superintendent of Public Instruction, 565; grain elevators,
   regulating charges, 603; game and fish protectors, 607; New
   York city normal college, 607; Assembly chamber, repairs
   to ceiling, 608; new capitol, continuing work, 610; Albany,
   Hawk street bridge, 612.

VETOES. Auburn, railroad aid bonds, VIII, 504; normal school,
   free privileges of, 506; trust companies, organization in
   villages, 507; Harrietstown, town hall, 508; Parishville,
   town house, 516; commissioner of deeds, Reevs, Yonkers,
   legalizing acts, 518; Westfield, establishing water department, 518; Erie canal, Ilion, vertical wall, 521; Brooklyn,
   police pension fund, 523; New York, police sergeants and
   detective sergeants, salaries, 524; Brooklyn, soldiers' monument, 527; Grand Army of the Republic, preservation of
   records, 528; Grand Army of the Republic, Sherman Post,
   Rose, use of room in town hall, 528; Northern New York

HILL, DAVID B., 1888, VETOES — (*Continued*).

Institution for Deaf-Mutes, general improvements, 531; New Brighton, fire department, 532; divorce, advertising business of procuring, prohibited, 534; Vienna, police regulations, 534; holidays, amending Saturday half-holiday provision, 535; superintendent of the poor, Clinton county, keeper of poorhouse, 537; S. R. Smith Infirmary, exempting property from taxation, 538; Susquehanna Turnpike Company, abandoning part of road, 539; law library, Delhi, purchase of Justice Murray's library for, 539; excise, regulating sale of intoxicating liquors, 540; items in supply bill, 546; item in appropriation bill, 553; quarantine commissioners, method of appointment, 555; Corning, city charter, 562; independence of voters, secrecy of ballot, 566; Edison Electric Illuminating Company, Brooklyn, right to use streets, 591; Kings county, farm at St. Johnland, changing supervision of, 594; bribery at elections, 598; omnibus veto, 613; Senate report on Excise Law, 640.

Proclamation, extraordinary session, VIII, 643; message, 643; proper employment of convicts, 643, 651; communication from Superintendent of State Prisons, 644; changes in plans for completion of State library apartments, 650; revision of conspiracy laws, 650; enumeration of inhabitants, Constitutional Convention, 652; new Croton Aqueduct Commission, 652.

MEMORANDUMS OF APPROVAL. New York aqueduct, new commission, VIII, 656; convict labor, 658.

1889. Annual message, VIII, 662; finances, 663; tax rate, 663; reform in election methods, 664; presidential election, 1888, use of money, 664; bribery laws not enforced, 666; electioneering near polls should be prohibited, 666; coercion of workmen at elections, 667; ballots furnished at public expense, 667; Australian system of voting, 668; candidate's contribution for expenses, 668; ballot clerks, 669; marking ballots, 670; smaller election districts, 670; electioneering by pay envelopes, 671; candidate's statement of expenses, 672; privileges of employees, 673; compulsory voting, 674; enumeration demanded, 676; prison labor question, 678; abolition of Board of Regents, State Board of Charities, State Board of Health, 680; limiting power of corporations to issue stock and bonds, 680; State Gas Commission, 680;

HILL, DAVID B., 1889 — (*Continued*).

     Special Labor Commission, 680; Constitutional Convention,
680; abolition of Senate's confirming power, 680; revision
of tax laws, 680; weekly payment of wages, 680; excise
legislation, 681; license fees in force, 1889, 685; marriage
and divorce, 688; extradition, conference of Governors
relative to, 689; compulsory investigation of fires, 689;
presidential term and provision for ex-Presidents, 691;
commends administration of President Cleveland, 692;
President Washington's inauguration celebration, 694; General Registration Law recommended, 720; rapid transit, New
York, 759; historical sketch of ballot, 778; pardon report,
789.

MEMORANDUMS OF APPROVAL. The Isabella Heimath, charter,
VIII, 789; Albany, paving certain streets, 790; teachers'
classes, transfer from Regents to Department of Public Instruction, 791; legislative printing, legalizing Bloomingdale
asylum investigation, 793; New York, police justices, increasing number, 794; Convict Labor Act, 1889, 814;
bucket shops, 815; dog tax, 823; New York Historical
Society, changing site, 824; New York Hospital, changing
site, continuing exemption from taxation, 824; Auburn,
increasing salaries, 825; naval militia, 829; New York, dock
commissioners, 832; East river bulkhead lines, 834; Northern New York Institution for Deaf-Mutes, appropriation,
835.

VETOES. Overseers of the poor, Ontario county, compensation
in certain towns, VIII, 697; Newburgh, alteration of map,
697; Batavia, place of holding elections and town meetings, 698; poor, Greenbush, relief, 699; stenographers,
Supreme Court, third judicial district, salaries, 699; Hempstead, free school, amending act, 701; Lyons, school district No. 6, additional accommodations, 702; St. Lawrence
University and Theological Seminary, amending charter,
703; Germania, Brooklyn, charter, 704; county clerks, Cattaraugus and Columbia counties, recording notices of pendency of actions, 705; Jefferson county taxes, collection of,
706; New York Post-Graduate School and Hospital, amending charter, 707; Polytechnic Institute, Brooklyn, charter,
708; Century Association, amending charter, 709; Erie
canal, Utica, sewer or culvert under, 710; Code of Civil
Procedure, New York marine court, jurisdiction, 711;
Milford Center Cemetery Association, extending powers,

HILL, David B., 1889, Vetoes — (*Continued*).

712; fishways, Chittenango creek, 713; school commissioner districts, Cattaraugus county, increasing number, 713; New York, park department, extending jurisdiction, 714; Game Law, Oneida county, protection of, 716; Weedsport, union school, amending act, 717; General Terms, appeals from, 718; registration of voters, Fishkill, 719; town meeting, Pelham, restricting powers, 722; Racka escheat, 722; Brunn escheat, 723; Flushing, street improvements, 724; McKenna escheat, 725; Board of Claims, Kowalski, 727; Flatbush, fire company, 728; Vassar College, right to hold additional property, 728; Poughkeepsie, street railroads, changing motive power, 729; animals, infectious and contagious diseases, 730; Thebaud escheat, 731; Young Men's Association, Buffalo, amending charter, 732; Straack escheat, 734; Niagara county, board of equalization of taxes, 737; Sons of Liberty, Grand Lodge, charter, 737; New York, 111th street, closing portion of, 738; Brooklyn, board of aldermen, method of electing, 739; taxes, delinquent, statements by county treasurers, 749; Poughkeepsie, employees' term of service, 751; taxation, Erie county, equalizing real estate, 752; Binghamton, enlarging boundaries, 753; Wayne county, taxes, collection of, 754; counties, claims against State, adjustment, 755; Washington escheat, 755; New York, bi-partisan police commissioners, 756; New York, bi-partisan park commissioners, 758; ballot bill, 1889, 762; excise, tax on beverages, 797; excise, revision bill, 1889, 801; compulsory education, 817; reformatory for women, 819; employment of women and children in manufacturing establishments, 837; items in supply bill, 839; item in appropriation bill providing incidental expenses of lunacy commissioner, 867; items of appropriation for State ditch, Cayuga creek, 867; item in canal awards, appropriation bill, 868; new capitol, work on, new commission, 869; State agent for discharged convicts, bill to abolish office, 870; omnibus veto, 871.

1890. Annual message, VIII, 891; enumeration and apportionment, 892; electoral reform, 895; Australian system of voting, 897; booths for voters, 900; General Registration Act, 904; official and unofficial ballots, 906; ballot defined, 913; privileges of employees on election days, 918; use of pay envelopes, 918; candidate's statement of expenses, 918;

HILL, DAVIL B., 1890 — (*Continued*).

    small election districts, 919; prohibition amendment, 920;
constitutional amendments, principles which should govern
legislative consideration of, 921; improvement of country
roads, 923; State roads in each county, 925; new methods
of taxation, 926; collateral inheritance tax, 928; Constitutional Convention, 929; General Excise Law, 929; revision
of Tax Law, 929; compulsory investigation of fires, 929;
uniform marriage and divorce laws, 929; weekly payment
of wages, 930; State Gas Commission, 930; compulsory
voting, 930; rapid transit, New York city, 930; abolition of
State Board of Charities and State Board of Health, 931;
limiting power of corporations to issue stocks and bonds,
931; World's Fair in 1892, 931; finances, 933; Justice
Pitshke's case, 935; Adirondack forest, 936; State park in
Adirondacks, 937; World's Fair bill, 938; ballot reform,
946; suggests application to Court of Appeals for opinion
as to constitutionality of ballot bill, 1890, 948, 1009, 1044;
essential features of an electoral reform measure, 962;
corrupt practices at elections, 970; Game Law Revision
Commission, 1890, 975; pardon report, 980; change in
method of determining contested elections, 982; contested
elections, House of Commons, 983.

MEMORANDUMS OF APPROVAL. World's Fair bill, VIII, 996;
Queens county treasurer, appointment of deputy, 998; forest
preserve, purchase of lands, 999; Board of Claims, awards,
1000; Corrupt Practices Act, 1890, 1001; Utica, additional
enginehouse, 1003; State laborers, regulating pay of, 1003;
Ballot Reform Act, 1005; escheats, general act, 1014; Syracuse Water Act, 1015; new capitol, appropriation, 1017;
Brooklyn, street improvements, 1021; regulating price of
illuminating gas in certain cities, 1021; New York, sheriff's
office, 1023; Jamaica bay, protection of fish in, 1025; Chautauqua county clerk, salaried office, 1025; Baldwinsville,
legalizing water bonds, 1026; tax rate, 1026; general laws,
corporations, towns and highways, 1027; Constitutional
Commission, 1890, 1034.

VETOES. Malone Waterworks Company, sale of water, VIII,
941; villages, amending general act, New Rochelle, 942;
Port Chester, legalizing sewer bonds, 942; Howe, justice of
the peace, legalizing acts, 943; Amsterdam, official newspapers, 943; Onondaga county penitentiary property, sale

HILL, DAVID B., 1890, VETOES — (*Continued*).

of, 945; ballot bill, 949; taxes, Chautauqua and Cattaraugus counties, collection, 967; Brooklyn, dispensaries, increasing number, 969; Poughkeepsie Associated Fire Department, exemption from taxation, 972; boards of excise, amending act of 1874, 973; Groton Cemetery Association, changing name, 974; Young Men's Christian Associations, amending general act, 974; Flatlands, licensing public hacks and amusements, 975; Game Law, black bass in Brant lake, 975; Game Law, use of snares and nets, 976; Board of Claims, Myers, 976; Oyster Bay school district No. 5, new schoolhouse, 977; Hudson, public schools, legalizing official acts, 978; Game Law, Erie county, protection of ducks and fish, 979; Bruno escheat, 980; Union Literary Society, Ellisburgh, changing name, 980; Citizens' Loan Agency and Guarantee Company, changing name, 981; appeals by people in criminal cases, 981; item in appropriation bill, expenses of investigating committees, 989; Lansingburgh, new wards, sidewalks, repairs, 991; New York and Brooklyn bridge, policemen, compensation, 992; Ogdensburg, board of public works, 993; New York, soldiers and sailors' memorial arch or monument, 1029; Buffalo, revised charter, 1030; constitutional amendment, Supreme Court, additional justices, submission, 1890, 1033; police matrons, 1034; omnibus veto, 1035.

1891. Annual message, VIII, 1054; chosen United States Senator, 1054; enumeration of inhabitants, 1055; defects in Federal census, 1890, 1056; just and reasonable excise law, 1058; excise fees for local benefit, 1059; prohibition amendment, 1060; power to call special election by concurrent resolution, *quære*, 1061; judiciary amendment, 1062; reform in methods of taxation, 1062; taxation, deducting debts, 1065; personal property escapes taxation, 1066; probate and succession tax, 1067; marriage and divorce, 1067; Commission on Uniform Laws, 1068; improvement of country roads, 1068; bad condition of highways, 1069; rapid transit, New York, 1070; labor interests, 1071; labor arbitrations, compulsory, suggested, 1072; private detectives, strikes, 1073; use of *posse comitatus* in labor strikes, 1074; contested elections, 1074; Chickamauga and Chattanooga National Military park, 1076; World's Fair, 1077; constitutional convention, 1078;

HILL, DAVID B., 1891, (*Continued*).

compulsory voting, 1078; State Gas Commission, 1078; weekly payment of employees on railroads, 1078; statements of expenses by political committees and candidates, 1079, 1092; bribery by successful candidate, exclusion from office, 1079, 1092; compulsory investigation of fires, 1080; abolition of confirming power of Senate, 1080; Special Labor Commission, 1080; abolition of State Board of Charities and State Board of Health, 1081; manual training in public schools, 1081; State park in Adirondacks, 1081; finances, 1082; dangerous Federal legislation, force bill, 1083; acknowledgment to State officers, 1085; various annual reports, 1085; announces death of General Sherman, 1087; Texas resolutions, tenure of office, 1091; special message, contested elections, corrupt practices, 1091; announces death of former Governor Robinson, 1094; pardon report, 1107; direct taxes, United States, amount refunded to New York, 1107; proposed disposal of, 1108.

MEMORANDUMS OF APPROVAL. New York rapid transit, VIII, 1142; United Life and Accident Insurance Association, changing name, 1144; Utica, river improvement, 1145; police matrons, 1147; Wayne county, legalizing contracts, county agricultural society and town of Galen, 1148; United States deposit fund, reducing rate of interest, 1149; new capitol, appropriation, 1149; collateral inheritance, graduated tax, 1150; medical examiners, 1152; Little Falls highway commissioners, legalizing acts, 1156; Hempstead free school, amending act, 1156; Bensonhurst park, amending act, 1157; Rochester Athenæum, changing name and number of directors, 1162; Madison Forks Obituary Society, changing name, 1163; New York board of electrical control, extending duration of, 1163; tax rate, 1164.

VETOES. Virgil, opening highway, extending time, 1086; Johnstown, voting by ballot on bridge appropriation, 1087; Cattaraugus county, South Valley, division of, legalizing action of board of supervisors, 1089; McNamara estate, sale, 1090; religious corporations, African Methodist Episcopal churches, special provisions, 1095; United Presbyterian church, North Hamden, changing name, 1096; Oneida county, surrogate, new seal, 1096; Flatlands, fire department, charter, 1097; ferry, Conesus lake, Long Point to McPherson Point, 1098; ferry, Lake Champlain at Ticonderoga, 1099; Chappell and

HILL, DAVID B., 1891, VETOES — (*Continued*).

Curell, 1100; New York Building and Improvement Company, increasing or diminishing capital stock, 1101; New York Conference of the African Methodist Episcopal Church, charter, 1101; Genesee, Erie and Niagara counties, boundaries between, 1102; Brooklyn, commissioner's map, 1102; Cayuga county clerk, salaried office, 1103; Perry, railroad aid, using fund for general town purposes, 1105; highway tax, amending Revised Statutes, 1106; Buffalo, water commissioners, increasing salary, 1106; Flatbush, increasing policemen, salaries of officers, 1110; Gravesend, police department, authorizing increase of expenditures for, 1111; Highland and Modena Turnpike Road Company, tolls chargeable by, 1112; Erie canal, completing vertical wall, Herkimer, 1112; United States, cession of land in Queens county, 1113; villages, general act of 1870, Tonawanda, special powers, 1115; West Troy Electric Light Commission, 1117; West Side Street Railway Company, relief from certain obligations, 1117; Scriba, Old Burt cemetery, removal of remains, 1118; Thirty-fourth Street Ferry and Eleventh Avenue Railroad Company, relief, 1119; Fulton, Wall and Cortland Street Ferry Railroad Company, relief, 1119; societies and clubs, maximum amount of property, 1119; St. Regis Indians, regulating occupation of land, 1120; Board of Claims, Myers, 1120; poor, Jefferson county, amending act, 1121; navigation, inspection of vessels on certain lakes, 1121; Clifton Springs, legalizing village election, 1122; Glen creek, improvement, 1123; street railroads, percentages payable by, 1124; Board of Claims, Fingar, 1124; Board of Claims, Milliete, 1125; Oneida county, taxes, redemption, 1126; Union Mission Chapel Association, Brooklyn, trusts, legacies and donations, 1127; Board of Claims, Hasbrouck, 1128; railroads, prevention of extortion, 1128; New York, police pension fund, 1129; Board of Claims, David T. Smith, 1129; Rome, Watertown and Ogdensburg Railroad Company, purchasing bridge company stock, 1130; Vienna, police regulations, 1131; notaries public, notarial clerks in certain counties, compensation, 1131; culvert under Erie canal, Utica, 1132; Niagara Street Railroad Company, Niagara Falls, changing route, 1132; Olean, amending village charter, 1133; New Utrecht, highways and bridges,

HILL, David B., 1891, Vetoes — (*Continued*).

1134; New York and Brooklyn Tunnel Company, charter, 1135; items in supply bill, 1135; Erie county coroners, fees and post mortem examinations, 1153; Queens county, highway labor, 1154; board of supervisors, amending general act, 1154; North Tonawanda, highway improvement, 1155; traction engines on highways, damages, 1156; Oswego, method of letting contracts, 1158; Westchester county, care of indigent children, 1159; New York, soldiers and sailors' memorial arch, 1160; elevated railroads percentage tax receipts, 1160; deaf-mutes, care and education of, 1166; Board of Claims, Humphrey and others, 1166; jurors in justices' courts, 1166; animals affected with glanders, destruction of, · 1166; Board of Claims, Weed-Parsons & Company, 1166; evidence, 1167.

United States Senate, introduces bill regulating transportation of imitation dairy products, IX, 321; quoted, management of charitable institutions, X, 409; official service as Governor, I, pref. xiii.

HILL, John W. Geological survey draughtsman, III, 753.

HILL, Millen T. Commissioner repairing highway, Cattaraugus reservation, veto, VII, 221, 475.

HILL, Nicholas, Jr. Appointed member of Procedure Commission, resigns, IV, 366; member of Procedure Commission, VII, 183.

HILL, Rufus. Convicted of murder, pardoned, II, 635, 636, 639.

HILL Land Horticultural Society of Southern Central New York. Charter, veto, VIII, 876.

HILLSIDE Cemetery Association, Madison County. Control of certain lands, veto, VII, 807.

HILLSIDE Cemetery Association, Middletown. Raising money for improvements, veto, IX, 794.

HINCKLEY, Gardner. Bond for return of arms, II, 774.

HINGSTON, Edward J. Claim against Buffalo, settlement, veto, IX, 869.

HISTORICAL Societies. Exemption from taxation, VIII, 824; Westchester county, books and records to be delivered to, veto, IX, 862.

HISTORIC Places. Should be preserved, X, 746.

HITCHMAN, William. Speaker of Assembly, member of Centennial Celebration Committee, VI, 302.

HOBART, John Sloss. Supreme Court, member of Council of Revision, II, 21; commissioner to Hartford Convention, 107; resigns as Senator in Congress, 424.

HODGES, JACK. Convicted of murder, pardoned, II, 997.

HODGSON, GEORGE. New York, Municipal Court attendant, claim, veto, X, 168.

HOENIG, LAURA BALL. Escheat to heirs, veto, VII, 549.

HOFF, JOHN H. Devise to widow, relative to, veto, X, 584.

HOFF, SARAH ELIZABETH. Devise from husband, John H. Hoff, relative to, veto, X, 584.

HOFFMAN, ALLAN H. Sheriff, Dutchess county, legalizing audit of accounts, veto, X, 956.

HOFFMAN, HERMAN. Letter from, relief, II, 167; bond for return of arms, 771.

HOFFMAN, JOHN T. Governor and portrait, VI, 1.

1869. Annual message, VI, 1; Legislature not in political sympathy with Governor, 1; relation of New York city to remainder of State, 2; broad policies of government needed, 3; opposes suggested division of State, 3; agricultural interests, 4; finances and indebtedness, 5; general fund, 5; taxes, 6; State debt, 6; canals, 8; canal fund, 8; canal revenues and expenditures, 9; canal debt, 11; canal debt paid, 14; importance of Erie canal, 14; neglect of repairs and improvements on Erie canal, 15; contract system of repairs on canals, 16; protests against Federal control of canals, 16; salt springs, 16; State prisons, 17; politics in prison management, 18; prison labor should be on State account, 18; commutations for good behavior, 18; payments to convicts on discharge, 18; houses of refuge, 19; detention of witnesses, 19; insurance, 19; banks, 19; militia, 21; education, 22; opening of Cornell University, 22; increase of annuity from United State deposit fund to academies, 22; State Library and cabinet of natural history, 22; common school statistics, 22; normal schools, 23; charities and asylums, 24; visitations by State Board of Charities, 24; management of inebriate asylum, 24; new capitol, 24; quarantine and public health, 25; quarantine establishment at West Bank, 26; boarding station at West Bank, 27; cattle disease, 27; immigration, 28; labor exchange, Castle Garden, 28; Civil and Criminal Codes, etc., 29; murder, second degree, 29; metropolitan districts and commissions, 29; repeal of laws creating district commissions, 30; municipal government, 31; too many commissions in New York city, 32; Legislature should not interfere in New York local affairs, 32; executive responsibility in cities, 34; minority representation in municipal

HOFFMAN, JOHN T., 1869 — (*Continued*).

government, 34; New York city, wharves and piers, 34; Excise Law in metropolitan district, 35; purity of elections, 36; use of money at elections, 36; election laws should apply equally to all citizens, 37; Federal centralization, 37; Federal control of elections, 37; naturalization and citizenship, 39; alien soldiers, 40; national affairs, 41; slow progress of reconstruction of seceding States, 41; various reports, 43, 44; modification of New York's appropriation to Lincoln monument, 44; importance of Albany basin, 44; pay of patrolmen, metropolitan police department, 44; Fifteenth Amendment, 50; proposed exposition of articles of daily use, Utrecht, 50; towns borrowing money for roads and bridges, 54; overcrowded condition of State prisons, 57; new prison needed, 57; commission to select site for State penitentiary, 58; town meetings, 59; power to alter or erect towns, 60; appropriation for soldiers' home, Albany, 61; national asylum for disabled volunteer soldiers, 61; people own street railroad grants, 64; value of railroad grants in cities, 66.

VETOES. First Presbyterian church of Perry, sale of real estate, VI, 45; Fort Covington, bridge, 46; Ellicott, improvement of roads and bridges, 47; Lowville, vacancies in office of justice of the peace, 48; metropolitan police board, temporary president, 50; Addison, borrowing money for bridges, 52; Excelsior Temple of Honor No. 23, Albany, charter, 55; Rescue Hook and Ladder Company No. 1, Bath, charter, 55; Ours Hose Company, No. 4, Elmira, charter, 56; Sodus, election districts, 58; New York, railroad in 125th street, 62; Whitehall and Plattsburg Railroad, aiding completion, 68; New York, Avenue C Railroad extension, 74; justices of the peace, vacancies in office, 74; Gouverneur, declaring John street a public highway, 76; Chateaugay, village charter, 76; Adams, aiding Hungerford Collegiate Institute, 77; Cuyler, bridge over Tioughnioga river, 78; Owego, amending village charter, 79; Jordan Academy and free school district No. 4, Elbridge, 81; Hamilton county, highways in, 82; Oswego Pier and Dock Company, charter, 84; Johnstown, consolidating school districts and establishing graded school, 86; Oswegatchie, assessment-roll, 88; convicts, commutation for good behavior, increasing rate, 89; Bethlehem Mutual Insurance Association, charter, 90;

HOFFMAN, JOHN T., 1869, VETOES — (*Continued*).

Jamaica, amending village charter, 90; Harlem Yacht Club, charter, 90; Schoharie Valley Railroad extension, 90; New York and Long Island Bridge Company, amending charter, 91; Staten Island Bridge Company, charter, 91; Hamburgh, fixing bail of overseer of highways, 91; Olean, acquiring land for Buffalo and Washington Railroad Company, 91; Rockland county, dogs running at large, 92; Genesee Annual Conference, amending charter, 92; mortgages, foreclosure by advertisement, surplus moneys, 92; Brooklyn, improving North Second street, 92; Utica and Black River Railroad Company, aid by certain towns, 92; New York, widening West street, 93; Warren county, opening road, 93; New York, city market in 21st ward, 93; Oswegatchie river, repairing State works, 94; excise, amending general act of 1857, 94; Homer, aiding Cortland Academy, 95; Columbia county, equalizing assessments, 95; public schools, preventing nuisances near, 95; Clyde Waterworks Company, charter, 95; aid to railroads, Allegany and other counties, 95; Smith and Parmelee Gold Company, issuing preferred stock, 96; Oswego river, restoring channel, 96; Carrol, bridge, 96; metropolitan police, inspecting steam boilers, 96; excise, prohibiting sales of liquor on Allegany and Cattaraugus reservations, 97; Mill Brook Log Company, improving Mill brook, 97; Fifth Avenue Savings Bank, New York, charter, 97; Hempstead, special town meeting, 97; Ellisburgh, bridges, 98; New York River Road Company, constructing roads, 98.

1870. Annual message, VI, 99; State debt, 99; interest on State debt should be paid in coin, 100; bounty fund debt, 100; receipts and payments of the State treasury, 101; taxes, 101; canal fund, 102; duty of State in relation to canals, 103; canals keep down transportation rates, 104; delegates to Iowa Canal Convention, 104; canals should be made free as soon as practicable, 105; abolition of canal contract system for repairs, 105; extending powers of Canal Board 106; reduction of canal tolls, 106; canal improvements, 107; education, 108; common school statistics, 108; State prisons, 109; opposes contract system of prison labor, 109; punishment in State prisons, 109; prison management, 109; new State penitentiary, 110; pardons and commutations, 110;

HOFFMAN, JOHN T., 1870 — (*Continued*).

salt springs, 110; insurance, 111; banks, 111; savings banks, 112; supervision of savings banks, 112; military affairs, 112; National Guard, 112; transfer of arsenals to counties, 113; Military Code, 113; military agencies, 113; redemption of militia certificates, War of 1812, 113; parade ground, first division, National Guard, 114; charities and asylums, 114; care of insane poor, 114; Buffalo Asylum for Insane, 115; special pathologist for Utica Insane Asylum, 115; new capitol, 116; quarantine, 116; immigration, 117; general and special laws, 117; Revision Commission, 118; legislative powers of boards of supervisors, 118; highways in Westchester county, parts of Long Island, 118; payment of canal damages, 119; general law for savings banks, 119; amendment of general law incorporating fire companies, 119; increasing amount of property held by literary, musical and other societies, 119; changing names of corporations, 119; General Village Law, 120; uniformity in town governments, 120; vacancy in office of justice of sessions, 121; conspiracy laws, 121; injunctions and receivers, 122; apprentice laws, 123; revision of statutes, 123; new judiciary, 124; registration and election laws, 125; use of money at elections, 125; smaller polling districts, and free exercise of challenge privilege, 125; criminal law, murder, lack of premeditation, 126; new trials, 126; trial of accessory to the felony, 126; excise laws, 126; repeal of Metropolitan Excise Law, 126; excise laws should be uniform, 127; abolition of county boards of excise, 127; commission and city governments, 128; executive responsibility in cities, 129; city charters need revision, 129; early consideration of appropriation bills, 129; Federal affairs, 130; Georgia under military authority, 131; tariff, 131; monopoly resulting from high tariff, 132; general finances, 133; redemption of legal tender notes, 134, 136; panic in New York, 1869, 134; money should have stable value, 134; specie payments, 135; legal tender notes, 135; income of gold from imports, 135; England specie payments, 135; coin should be restored to its proper place, 137; causes of depreciation, 138; payment of bonds, 139; effect of treasury sales of gold, 140; policy of resumption of legal tenders, 141; various reports, 142, 143; pardon report, 143; general law for incorporation of villages, 145; payment of interest on State debt, 166; recall of O'Brien bill, 167.

HOFFMAN, JOHN T., 1870 — (*Continued*).

VETOES. Washington county, assistant district attorney, VI, 143;
Phœnix, protection of bridge at, 147; Binghamton, preservation of bridges, 149; county treasurers' fees, excepting
Oneida and Schoharie counties, 151; town insurance companies, amending act, 153; bridge over Champlain canal
at Whitehall, 154; Oneida lake, construction of dock, 156;
Bashford escheat, 157; Chamberlain escheat, 158; Westchester and West Farms, avenues in, amending act, 158;
Fitzpatrick, relief bill, 159; highway encroachments in Great
Valley, 160; Whites' Corners and Buffalo Plankroad Company, extending charter, 161; East Hamburgh Turnpike
Road Company, extending charter, 162; soldiers' monument, St. Lawrence county, 162; rural cemeteries, acquir-
ing property by eminent domain, 162; Webster Plank Road
Company, extending charter, 163; Greenwich, aiding rail-
road, 164; Albany county, supervisors, 165; United States
Mutual Benefit Company, New York, charter, 167;
Hopkinton Manufacturing Company, relief, 169; Erie
county, coroners, 170; Peabody Mutual Benefit Company,
New York, charter, 171; National Mutual Benefit Association, Buffalo, charter, 172; facilitating construction of
Adirondack, New York and Oswego Midland, Whitehall and
Plattsburgh, Buffalo and Washington, Cattaraugus, Carthage, Watertown and Sacketts Harbor railroads, and Pine
Hills tunnel, 172; manufacturing corporations, payment of
capital stock, 179; Protection Hose Company No. 3, Binghamton, charter, 179; New York, gas supply, 180; Hornellsville, establishing manufacture of machinery, 180; Saratoga Agricultural Society, improvement of grounds, 181;
Saratoga county, removal of insane from State asylum
to poorhouses, 182; Saratoga Springs, union schools, consolidation of districts, 182; Florence, establishing highways,
182; Flatbush Fire Company, aid to, 183; Snook, relief,
183; White Plains, consolidation of school districts, 183;
New Hartford, village charter, 183; Evans Mills Cemetery
Association, raising money for fences, 184; Shenandoah,
relief, 184; omnibus veto of relief bills, 185; Frewsburg
Cemetery Association, charter, 186; Brooklyn, alteration of
map, Pratt street, 186; Barnes' Corners Burial Association,
charter, 186; Haverstraw Savings Bank, charter, 186;
Hamilton Savings Bank, amending charter, 187; Cascade

XI — 38

HOFFMAN, JOHN T., 1870, VETOES — *(Continued)*.

Fire Company No. 1, Little Falls, charter, 187; American Mutual Benevolent Association, New York, charter, 187; Canton Lodge No. 558, Independent Order of Good Templars, charter, 187; Hector, railroad aid, 187; Canastota, amending village charter, 187; Essex county, assessment of certain taxes, 188; Niagara, school trustees, 188; Fowler, highway over certain lands, 188; barrels, size of, for fruits and vegetables, 188; American Popular Life Insurance Company, amending charter, 189; Knox Railway Clamp Company, changing name, 189; Cicero and Clay, drainage, 189; De Ruyter, extending boundaries, 189; railroad aid, amending act, 190; Clifton, aiding railroad, 190; drainage, amending Revised Statutes, 190; New York Advertising Company, charter, 191; Commercial Credit Guaranty Company, New York, charter, 191; Lyons cemetery, taxing lots, 191; Richmond county, laying out Central park, 191; Cohoes, legalizing construction of sewers, 192; Association of the Bar of the City of New York, charter, 192; Brooklyn, improving Fourth street, 192; Brooklyn, improving Banker street, 193; Charlotte, police office and lockup, 193; Newtown, election districts, 193; Lewis county, highways, 193; medicine, practice of, elevating standard, 194; Warren county, State loan to, 194; Paris, election of railroad commissioners, 194; Unadilla, sidewalks, 195; Palatine, bridge, amending village charter, 195; Ione Yacht Club, charter, 195; Buffalo, plank road, improvement, 195; Newtown, construction of highways, 195; Eagle Hose Company No. 2, Buffalo, charter, 196; Worcester, separate road district, 196; Richmond county, construction of certain avenues, 196; Mental and Moral Improvement Society, Irvington, charter, 196; Saratoga County Mutual Fire Insurance Company, amending charter, 197; Cohoes, amending city charter, 197; New York Arcade Railway, charter, 197; New York Annuity Company, charter, 208; Deer Park, additional justices of the peace, 208; rural cemetery, Oneida county, acquiring property by eminent domain, 208; Reformed church of Helderberg, sale of property, 209; stenographers in second district, 209; Albany county, plank roads, tolls, 209; New York, market, 13th ward, 209; minors, protection of, 210; Malone, compensation of assessors, 210;

HOFFMAN JOHN T., 1870, VETOES — (*Continued*).

Albany, land under water, 210; VIII, 54; Security Bank, Brooklyn, charter, VI, 210; Newark, public hall, 210; railroad between Long Wharf and Matteawan, 211; Oneida river road, charter, 211; Fifth Avenue Savings Bank, New York, charter, 211; bridges, Oswego county, 212; bridge over Great Sodus bay, 212; Goshen, opening highway, 213; Eighth Ward Savings Bank, New York, charter, 213; Grattan and others, relief, 213; mechanics' liens, New York, 213; Farmers and Mechanics' Savings Bank, Schenectady county, charter, 214; railroads, municipal aid, 214; Frontier Gaslight Company, Watertown, charter, 215; Humphrey, relief, 215; Oswego city, fixing value of certain lots, 215; Corn Exchange Warehouse Company, charter, 215; Pawling and Beekman Turnpike Company, surrender of part of road, 215; Otisville and Wurtsboro Turnpike Company, rates of toll, 216; Geneva, charter, Copenhagen, charter, Clyde, charter, 216; Buffalo and Williamsville McAdam Road Company, amending charter, 218; Calrow, relief, 219; Mutual Loan and Depositors' Institution, New York, charter, 219; New York, improvement of streets, avenues and public places, 220; Nassau Savings Bank, Brooklyn, charter, 220; New York, map, alteration of, 220; Chemung and Tioga Bridge Company, charter, 221; Buffalo, legalizing street improvements, 221; Stock Exchange, New York, charter, 221; foreign insurance companies, 221.

1871. Annual message, VI, 225; summary of recent legislation, 225; burdensome taxation, 226; too many special laws, 227; taxes, 228; new capitol, 228; executive residence in new capitol, 229; State debt, 229; bounty debt, 229; salt springs, 230; banks, 231; savings banks, 231; examination of savings banks, 232; insurance, 232; State prisons, 233; punishments in State prisons, 233; Elmira Reformatory, 233; Prison Labor Commission, 234; visits State prisons, 234; applications for pardon, 234; charities and asylums, 234; care of insane poor, 235; poor children, 235; education, 235; State militia, 236; arms for National Guard, 236; quarantine, 236; yellow fever, 237; smallpox, 237; ship fever, 237; immigration, 238; Commission on Statutory Revision, 238; Commission on Tax Revision, 238; canals, 239; reduction of tolls, 239; canal tolls should be limited to

HOFFMAN, JOHN T., 1871 — (*Continued*).

    maintenance and debt, 241; canals not constructed primarily
for revenue, 241; steam power on canals, 242; death of
Senator Blood, vacancy in Senate, 242; modification of
laws relating to murder, 242; detention of witnesses, 243;
new trials, 244; amendment to Village Law, election of
police justices, 244; rapid transit, New York, 244; elevated
railroads, 245; commissioners of rinderpest, 245; Federal
affairs, 246; tariff, 247; decline of shipbuilding, 247; Federal finances, 249; premium on gold, 249; treasury notes,
249; resumption of specie payments, 250; amount of coin
received in United States treasury, 251; legal tender notes,
251; contraction of legal tender notes, 253; repealing Federal income tax, 254; Federal interference in elections, 255;
Convention of Judges, 260; admission of attorneys, 260;
payment of money into court, 261; General Terms of Supreme Court, 261; Supreme Court reporter, 261; appropriation for Antietam cemetery, 261; report of Emigration Convention, Indianapolis, 263; use of money at elections, 263; bribery amendment, 1853, 264; pardon report,
268; report of Tax Commission, 269; memorial from New
York Chamber of Commerce, reducing canal tolls, 276;
communication from Governor of Pennsylvania, Centennial Celebration, 1876, 302; member of Centennial Celebration Committee, 302.

    VETOES. Castleton school district No. 4, borrowing money, VI,
262; Monroe county, assistant and special deputy county
clerks, 266; Methodist Episcopal church, Tompkinsville,
changing name, 270; Granite Lake Company, charter, 270;
Orleans county, lockup at Medina, 273; Game Law, close
season, 274; Deer Park, additional justice of the peace,
276; Cascade Association, Little Falls, charter, 277; taxation, relief, in certain counties, extending act, 278; New
York, district courts, additional clerk, 281; gas meters, inspection, 282; Little Valley Waterworks Company, charter,
284; closing sheriffs and county clerks' offices on holidays,
287; Oswegatchie, assessment-roll, 288; New York Musical
Instrument Saving and Loan Society, charter, 289; pneumatic tubes, amending act, 289; Auburn, enlarging boundaries, 304; Knickerbocker Loan and Trust Company, New
York, charter, 305; De Graff and others, relief, 306; Central
Savings Bank, New York, amending charter, 308; Hopkin-

HOFFMAN, JOHN T., 1871, VETOES — (*Continued*).

ton, tax for town hall, 309; Idlewild Temperance Association, Cornwall, charter, 309; Queens county, new indices,
310; Gleneida Savings Bank, charter, 310; Wellsville, tax
for bridge, 311; Frantz, relief, 312; New York Real Estate
Banking Company, charter, 315; road from Carthage to
Lake Champlain, 315; stenographers, Surrogates' Courts,
second and third districts, 317; Lowville, commissioners of
highways, borrowing money, 318; Mutual Fire Insurance
Company, amending charter, 319; South Hill Waterworks
Company, Ithaca, charter, 320; Fulton Savings Bank, New
York, charter, 322; New York city, manure, deposits of,
323; Richmond county, recording notices of pendency of
actions, discharges of mortgages, 323, 331; Staten Island
Northside Railroad Company, charter, 323; Harlem Hospital, New York, charter, 323; Southern Tier Savings
Bank, Elmira, amending charter, 324; New York, protection
of health, 324; New York, insane and idiots, 324; Ferris,
bounty to heirs, 324; canal bridge at Syracuse, 324; medicine, prescriptions and remedies, 325; New York, prevention
of contagious diseases, 325; Madrid, union free school district No. 1, borrowing money, 325; Immaculate Conception Total Abstinence Beneficial Society, Yonkers, charter,
325; Clarkson cemetery, charter, 325; United States Commission and Storage Company, charter, 325; Philipstown,
opening highway, 326; Expressmens' Savings Bank, New
York, charter, 326; Verona, additional justice of the peace,
326; New York, improving certain streets, 326; Peoples'
Mutual Benefit Association, charter, 326; Workingmens'
Friendly Society of America, charter, 326; railroads, amending general act, 326; Onondaga County Court, stenographer,
326; Mohawk, village, amending charter, 327; American
and Foreign Bible Society, consolidating with American
Baptist Publication Society, 327; Indian river, public highway, extending act, 327; Havana, bridge over Fall creek,
327; Oneida county, compensation of supervisors, 327; Port
Morris Warehouse and Elevator Company, charter, 328;
Hunter and Jewett, bonding, 328; National Book Exchange,
New York, charter, 328; Scarsdale and Greenburgh, highway
improvement, 328; Fireproof Warehouse Company, amending charter, 328; Metropolitan Nautical Institute, New York,

HOFFMAN, JOHN T., 1871, VETOES — (*Continued*).

charter, 328; towns, reducing expenses, 329; Protectives
No. 1, Rochester, amending charter, 329; town auditors,
raising money for roads and bridges, 329; Baywood Land
Improvement Company, charter, 329; Gloversville, village
gas supply, 329; Mount Pleasant, opening highway, 330;
Owego, village, railroad in certain streets, 330; Journeymen
Pork Butchers' Union Benevolent Society, New York, charter,
330; New York, vagrants, amending act, 330; Newtown,
opening highway, 330; Port Richmond, improving road to
New Springville, 330; New York, oyer and terminer, stenographer's notes, 330; Chautauqua county, taxes, 331;
Albany, reorganizing fire department, 331; Industrial Exhibition Company, amending charter, 331; Oswegatchie
river breakwater, 331; Wayne county, highways and bridges, 332; Jay, separate road district, 332; Progress Health
Insurance Company, charter, 332; Cherry Creek cemetery,
taking charge of public burying ground, 332; State tax,
equalizing among counties, 332; Rensselaer county, treasurer, 333; Lake George Baptist Association, charter, 333;
Jamestown Savings Bank, charter, 333; Homeopathic Insane Asylum, Middletown, fund in aid of, 333; Brooklyn,
disorderly persons, 333; Mechanicville Bridge Company,
charter, 333; South Hampton, discontinuing road, 333;
Gloversville Savings Bank, charter, 333; Robinson, relief,
334; Schaub, relief, 334; Dunkirk, purchasing steam fire
engine, 334; State prisons, repealing part of act, 334; patent rights, frauds in sale, 334; Brooklyn, map, alteration,
335; Forty-second Street and Grand Street Ferry Railroad
Company, extending tracks, 335; Associated Hotel Company, amending charter, 335; Mount Pleasant, improving
Railroad avenue, 335; manufacturing corporations, amending act, 335; Greenpoint Ferry Company, boats on East
river, 336; Seneca Indians, leases, ratification, 336; Westchester and Richmond counties, highway labor, 336; Williamsville Academy, sale of property, 336; City Loan and
Trust Company, New York, amending charter, 336; Republic Life Insurance and Trust Company, New York,
charter, 336; Benton, school district No. 11, tax for new
schoolhouse, 337; Deer Park, union free school district No.
1, examination of teachers, 337; New York Coal Exchange,

HOFFMAN, JOHN T., 1871, VETOES — (*Continued*).

charter, 337; New York State Loan and Trust Company, amending charter, 337; medicine, regulating practice of, 337; Rockland Lake, highway improvement, 338; Essex and Hamilton counties, non-resident highway taxes, 338; St. John's College, Brooklyn, charter, 339; Jefferson Medical University, charter, 339; Rensselaer county, support of poor, 339; Cayuga and Seneca canal, sewer, Waterloo, 339; Co-operative Savings and Loan Association, charter, 839; Guilderland Center Turnpike Company, charter, 339; Surrogate's Court, costs, 340; National Improvement Company, New York, charter, 340; New York Financial Association, charter, 340; Rossville, road extension, 340; Insurers' Indemnity Company, New York, amending charter, 340; Commercial Travelers' Association, New York, charter, 340; Veteran Association, Corcoran Irish Legion, charter, 341; Kings county, Supreme and County Court, messengers, doorkeepers and attendants, 341; villages, amending general act, 341; Memphis, village charter, 341; Harts Falls, village, changing name, 341; Monhagen Hose Company No. 1, Middletown, charter, 341; Teutonia Singing Society, Winfield, charter, 341; several bank and trust companies, charters, 341, 342, 343; New York Tunnel Company, relief, 343; Code of Procedure, amendments, 343; International Improvement and Loan Company, charter, 343; Wright and Hubbard, relief, 343; New York Stock Exchange, charter, 343; superintendent of canal repairs, abolition of office, 344; Sackett and Gage, relief, 344; unfinished railroads, aiding, 345; Erie canal, locks, western division, 347; Erie canal, constructing walls, 347; Assembly, filling vacancies, 347; Racket river, improving navigation, 348; Black River and St. Lawrence Railroad Company, town aid to, 348.

1872. Annual message, VI, 348; State debt, 348; bounty debt, 350; taxes, 349; new capitol, 350; salt springs, 350; banks, 350; savings banks, 351; limiting individual deposits in savings banks, 353; Insurance Department, 354; losses by New York insurance companies, Chicago fire, 355; State prisons, 355; change of prison management, 355; pardons, 355; charities and asylums, 355; condition of pauper children, 356; education, 356; State militia, 357; claims against

HOFFMAN, JOHN T., 1872 — (*Continued*).

United States, 357; quarantine, 358; completion of buildings at West Bank, 360; complaints against health officer and harbor masters, 360; immigration, 362; revision of statutes, 362; canals, 362; low canal tolls, 363; communication from President of United States, proposed reciprocity with Canada in use of canals, 363; books for Chicago Law Library, 364; status of children of American women marrying foreigners, 365; right of aliens to take and hold property, 365; abuses in referee system, 365; vacancies in Senate and Assembly, 365; detention of witnesses, 366; new trials in criminal cases, 366; revision of laws relating to insane, 366; greater precautions needed against improper incarceration of insane persons, 367; supervision of private lunatic asylums, 367; amendment of laws relating to murder, 368; early passage of appropriation bills, 368; repeal of Town Bonding Act, 369; Eight Hour Law, 369; tax revision, 370; New York not sufficiently liberal in tax exemptions, 371; exemption of personal property, 372; street processions, 374; popular election of United States Senators, 377; reform in New York city government, 378; New York, charter of 1879, 379; city charters should be permanent, 383; plan of charter for New York, 384; purity of elections, 387; registration laws do not prevent election frauds, 389; purity of legislation, 391; constitutional reform, 391; defects of Constitution, 392; Constitutional Commission, 393; executive power defective, 395; Governor should be responsible for all branches of State's affairs, 396; State officers should be appointed by Governor, 396; Attorney-General should have supervision of district attorneys, 396; Superintendent of State Prisons, 397; proposed appointment of State Treasurer and Superintendent of Public Instruction by Legislature, 398; extension of term of Governor, 398; number of special laws should be reduced, 399; large number of bills vetoed or recalled, 399; three readings of bills, 400; compensation of members of Legislature, 400; power to prorogue Legislature, 401; object and composition of Senate, 401; increasing size of Senate districts, 401; abolition of single Assembly districts, 401; limiting municipal indebtedness, 402; uniform laws for counties, towns and villages, 402; extra compensation, 402; veto of separate items in appropriation

HOFFMAN, JOHN T., 1872 — (*Continued*).

bills, 403; decentralization, 403; financial condition of New York city, 404; correspondence with Tax Commission, 404; relation of taxation to population and property, 412; letter from Andrew H. Green, comptroller of New York city, 413; cession to United States, lighthouse-keeper's dwelling, Clinton county, 414; various reports, 415; memorial, Stockbridge Indians, 415; memorandum approving New York tax bill, 415; errors in engrossing bills, 418; pardon report, 426, 554; proposed Tax Code, 428; statues for Hall of Representatives, 434; charges against Judge Prindle, 440; death of Inventor Morse, 444; revision of exterior line of New York harbor, Brooklyn side, 452; cumulative voting, 453; minority representation, 460; religious instruction in charitable institutions, 468; proposed board of safety, New York, 471; local authority, 496; charges against Judge McCunn, 497; charges against Judge Curtis, 498; correspondence with Court of Appeals concerning validity of taxpayers' bill, 430; VIII, 950, 1050.

VETOES. Clute, superintendent of the poor, Schenectady, legalizing election, VI, 424; Utica, recorder's court, increasing salary, 427; protection of taxpayers, 429; First Congregational church, Poughkeepsie, changing name, 433; Utica, Chenango and Cortland Railroad, extension, 433; town auditors, Lenox, 435; Methodist Episcopal church, Northville, sale of property, 437; Townsend, relief, 438; Port Chester Savings Bank, amending charter, 441; highway taxes, Hamilton and Warren counties, 442; Albany, police, 445; Champlain canal, bridge at Fort Edward, 448; Albany, cession for United States public buildings, 449; Newtown, local government, 449; Lenox Farmers and Mechanics' Association, charter, 451; New York, charter, 453; VII, 1061; VIII, 16; New York, city elections, VI, 479; Seymour, justice of the peace, legalizing acts, 479; leaf tobacco, regulating sale in New York, 480; Franklin county, special road district, 481; Industrial Exhibition Company, amending charter, 482; Baldwin escheat, 483; Clarence, teachers' employment fund, 484; pneumatic tubes, supplemental act, 485; Westchester county, Marmaroneck avenue, repayment of money, 488; Brooklyn, board of excise, 489; oyer and terminer, trial of special causes, 490; congressional apportionment, 493; New York, charter,

HOFFMAN, JOHN T., 1872, VETOES — (*Continued*).

election, 495; New York, local government, 499; Washington Park Association, Dairyman's Manufacturing Association, Perth, Quincy Rural Cemetery Association, Ripley, New Baltimore Chestnut Lawn Cemetery Association, charters, 501; Quincy Rural Cemetery Association, acquiring additional land, 501; social clubs, amending act, 501; manufacturing corporations, mercantile companies, 501; Buffalo and New York Oil Tankage and Transportation Company, charter, 502; dower, procedure, 502; villages, amending general act, Akron, 502; patent rights, frauds in sale, 502; Hamilton county, special highway, 502; life saving stations, buildings for, 502; Rome, amending charter, 503; Howard relief, 503; Lockport, Home for the Friendless, care of poor children, 503; Richmond county, survey, water supply; three bank charters, 503; canal farm bridge, Saratoga, 504; canal bridge, Glens Falls feeder, 504; Albany county, superintendent of the poor, 504; Nyack Waterworks Company, charter, 504; Binghamton, schools, 504; wills and decedents' estates, 505; excise, amending act of 1870, 505; Game Law amendments, 505; Game Law, Sunday observances, 505; Westchester county, Fordham and Pelham avenues, 505; excise, local option, 506; life insurance companies, reserves and transfers, 506; Huntington school district No. 4, sale of schoolhouse, 506; Kings county, Court of General Sessions, deputy clerk, 506; New York Tunnel Company, relief, 507; State prisons, accounts of purchases and sales, 507; State prisons, reducing force, 507; Newburgh, amending Free School Act, 507; slung shot, preventing use of, 507; New York, duplicate docket books, 507; Troy, board of school commissioners, 508; canals, settling claims, Chenango canal, 508; county treasurers' fees, 508; New York, Consolidation Act, 508; Buffalo, Corry and Pittsburgh Railroad Company, extending road and changing name, 508; Erie county, support of poor, 509; town insurance company, amending act, 509; notices and citations, publication of, 509; Watertown, amending charter, 509; drainage, amending act of 1869, 509; Kings county, courthouse property, 510; canal boats, liens on, 510; United States deposit fund, Jefferson county, 511; emigration commissioners, creating board, 511; Richmond county,

HOFFMAN, JOHN T., 1872, VETOES — (*Continued*).

police force, 511; Brooklyn, inferior courts, 512; Kings county, penitentiary, sentences, 512; Kings county, Supreme Court, messengers and attendants, 512; Westchester county, highways in Yonkers and Eastchester, 512; practice of medicine, licenses, 512; Brooklyn, board of health, extending jurisdiction, 517; Brooklyn, amending charter, appointments, 517; Brooklyn, Van Brunt Street and Erie Basin Railroad Company, relief, amending act, 518; New York, settlement of certain claims, 518; orphan asylums, instruction in, 518; Kings county, board of health, establishment of, 518; New York, local improvement expenses, 519.

Quoted, New York, mayor's power of appointment, VII, 1062; approves Poughkeepsie bridge extension bill, VIII, 444; quoted, uniform registration laws needed, 720; official service as Governor, I, pref. xiii.

HOFFMAN, JOSIAH OGDEN. Attorney-General, communication from Connecticut commissioners, II, 407.

HOFFMAN, OGDEN. Attorney-General, to represent State in Lemmon case, IV, 811, 860; V, 61.

HOFFMAN ISLAND. Quarantine station, VI, 533; improvements, appropriation, 1892, IX, 205; repairs and improvements, 1893, IX, 292; building for cabin passengers, X, 119.

VETOES. Quarantine repairs and improvements, VII, 588; continuing sea wall, repairs, VIII, 426; artesian wells, IX, 292; painting buildings, 292; enlargement, 292; quarantine repairs, X, 792.

HOGAN, CATHERINE. Widow of Patrick Hogan, damages, death of husband, veto, VII, 464, 910.

HOGAN, PATRICK. Death of, appropriation for widow, veto, VII, 464, 910.

HOGEBOOM, PETER. Dock on Oneida lake, veto, VI, 156.

HOHENHOLZ, AUGUSTE LOUISE. Escheat, veto, VII, 548.

HOLDERNESSE, EARL OF. Secretary of State, letter from, expected invasion of colony, I, 531, 539.

HOLDRIDGE, HARRISON. Board of Claims, veto, VIII, 1041; IX, 285.

HOLIDAYS. Easter, Assembly adjourns over, I, 219; election day, V, 196; list of, VI, 679; Saturday half-holidays suggested, VIII, 316; established, 476; Labor Day established, 316, 476; October 12, 1892, special, IX, 24; harvest day recommended, 322;

HOLIDAYS—(*Continued*).

days set apart for reception of Admiral Dewey, 1899, X, 72; application extended to contracts, 369.

VETOES. Closing certain offices on, VI, 287; VII, 201; payment of bank paper, VI, 679; amending act, VIII, 291; amending Saturday half-holiday provision, 535; Buffalo, fire department, increasing number, IX, 51; Jamestown, union school, authorizing designation of special, X, 173; amending act, adding Columbus Day, 584, new bill passed, 1909.

HOLLAND. States-General, supervision of colony, I, 1; government of colonies, 492; loans expected from, II, 154, 159; emigration from, practical termination of, 955; American property owned in, 1033; description of roads in, III, 374; obtaining historical records from, 751; IV, 169.

HOLLAND, HENRY. Claim for arrears, I, 202.

HOLLAND, SAMUEL. Survey of Pennsylvania boundary, I, 761.

HOLLAND LAND COMPANY. Conveyance of land to State, II, 994; purchasing property of, 1031; quantity of unsold land, 1034; office closed, papers deposited with Secretary of State, III, 755, 756.

HOLLENBECK, JOHN R. Free road, veto, II, 591.

HOLLENBEN, VON. German Ambassador, accompanies Prince Henry to Assembly chamber at his reception, X, 480.

HOLLIDAY, JOSIAH, JR. Bond for return of arms, II, 774.

HOLLINGWORTH, GEORGE T. National Guard, service medal, veto, X, 173.

HOLLISTER, MR. Suggested appointment as postmaster at Little Falls, II, 1070.

HOLLS, FREDERICK W. Constitutional Convention, 1894, compulsory voting, VIII, 676; member of Education Unification Commission, 1899, X, 114.

HOLMES, BENJAMIN. Convicted of murder, pardon denied, II, 454.

HOLMES, JOSEPH W. Commissioner, bridge, Tonawanda reservation, veto, VII, 477.

HOLT, JOHN. Deceased, estate of, suit against State, II, 330, 351.

HOLT, MR. Postmaster at Herkimer, removal of, II, 1070, 1071.

HOLTROP, J. W. Librarian, Royal Library at the Hague, IV, 174.

HOMEOPATHIC ASYLUM FOR THE INSANE. Established at Middletown, VI, 115; estimates and expenditures, 650; statement of appropriations, 872, 939; change of management, 874; expense of construction, VII, 283; number of inmates, 958; excessive cost *per capita*, X, 410; number of visits of local managers, 415.

VETOES. Fund in aid of, VI, 333; improvements, appropriation, VII, 583, 786; claim of Henry R. Low, 665; various appropriations, 913, 1081; house for gardener, VIII, 853.

HOMŒOPATHIC MEDICAL COLLEGE, BUFFALO. Charter, veto, VII, 266.

HOMER. Aiding Cortland Academy, veto, VI, 94.

HOME RULE. Indian trade, I, 723, 735, 738; demanded by Assembly, 765; trial by jury, 769, 772; general rights of, declared, 776; local officers, II, 41; IV, 684; in New York, discussed by Governor Robinson, VII, 101; erection of county buildings, III, 193; New York city, people to manage their own affairs, VI, 382; essential conditions of, 835; people should remedy evils of local government, VII, 31; highways, 368; care of streets, 370; right and duty of people, 840; New York, mayor, appointments without confirmation, 1056; Newburgh, increasing tax for contingent expenses, VIII, 77; Troy, police bill, 84; Amsterdam, people vote for city charter, 89; for cities, recommended by Governor Hill, 160; New York, additional evening high school, 261; regulating cemeteries, 327; municipal corporations, 332, 345; sales of liquor, 441, 683; in local public improvements, should be encouraged by legislation, 516; New York, Croton aqueduct, 653, 656; in villages, 724; private corporations, 732; limitations as to cities, 827; principles properly applicable to, 993; World's Fair, New York, selection of commissioners by Legislature, 997, 1071; rapid transit in New York, 1071, 1142; necessary in municipal reform, IX, 29; salaries of local officers, 88; establishment of Greater New York, 300; special city laws, constitutional provision, 1894, 339; principle violated by New York city college bill acquiring new site and buildings, 381; town collectors in Richmond county, 400; police boards in various cities, 490; bi-partisan boards, 591; Assembly resolution in favor of, 592; power of cities to reject proposed legislation, 619; sketch of subject in Constitutional Convention, 1894, 620; New York, compensation of teachers, 855; meaning of, 880; metropolitan police, X, 210; proper scope of, 354; principle violated by requiring municipality to refund taxes, 453; tuberculosis hospitals, 575; secured by Constitution, 1894, 624; employees in county offices, 771.

VETOES. Middletown, separate road district, VII, 497; opening highways, 885; Broadway Underground Railroad, construction without consent of city authorities, 1040; New York, police captains, increasing salaries, VIII, 212; use of streets by electric light company, 591; Brooklyn, additional dispensaries, 970; selection of board of public works, Ogdensburg, 993.

HOMESTEAD. Exemption from execution, IV, 493, 558.

HONDURAS. Participation in Cotton States Exposition, IX, 581.

HONEOYE FALLS. McKenna escheat bill, veto, VIII, 725.

Honeoye Lake. Vetoes. Fishing with set lines, X, 64; fishing in, amending Game Law, 173.

Honey. Fraud in manufacture and sale, veto, VII, 648.

Honeywood, St. John. County clerk, authorized to act as attorney, veto, II, 395.

Honyoust, Widow. See Shenandoah claim, VI, 184.

Hook Mountain. Proposed inclusion in Palisades park, veto, X, 451.

Hook and Ladder Companies. Act providing for, VI, 548.

Hooker, Warren B. Justice of Supreme Court, trial, X, 819, 826; communication to Speaker Nixon requesting investigation, X, 826; nature of complaint against, 827; proceedings of Legislature, 828; challenges right of members of Assembly Judiciary Committee to sit in case, 830; result of vote in Assembly, 830.

Hoosick. Vetoes. Baptist church, removing dead from burying ground, VII, 76; board of education, additional powers, 934.

Hope Cemetery. Perry reinterments, veto, VII, 870.

Hope Savings Bank, Albany. Dissolution, veto, VIII, 469.

Hopewell (Ulster County). Petition for grant of land at, for congregation, II, 82.

"Hopkins, The N. K." Steamboat, repairs, veto, VII, 791, 929.

Hopkins, Nelson K. Comptroller, action on Buck case, VI, 683; commissioner on quarantine jurisdiction, report, 778; interest on bounty debt, 1013.

Hopkins, Samuel M. Member of Prison Investigating Commission, III, 22.

Hopkins, Stephen. Member of Albany Convention and of Continental Congress, I, 583.

Hopkins, Timothy S. Brigadier-General, commandant of Niagara brigade, II, 791; calls out militia, 796.

Hopkinton. Cavalry company petition for use of arms, III, 180; town tax for town hall, veto, VI, 309.

Hopkinton Manufacturing Company. Relief, veto, VI, 169.

Hop Boxes. Regulating size, veto, VIII, 1040.

Hops. Premium for cultivation of, veto, VII, 1078.

Hornblower, William B. Opinion, voter's freedom of selection of candidate cannot be restricted by form of ballot, IX, 395, 479.

Hornellsville. Riots of 1877, VII, 152; town auditors, VIII, 48; number of excise licenses, 1887, 360; excise license fees, 1889, 685.

    Vetoes. Establishing manufacture of machinery, VI, 180; St. Ann's Total Abstinence and Benevolent Society, charter, 672; extending time for collection of taxes, VII, 878; amending village charter, 935; courthouse for Steuben county, VIII,

HORNELLSVILLE, VETOES — (*Continued*).

880; sewerage system, 880; Hornell cemetery, removal of remains, IX, 352, new bill passed; excise money, payment to St. James Mercy Hospital, 723; elections and officers, X, 819.

HORNTHAL, LEWIS M. New York, school trustee, 19th ward, action against, legal services and expenses, veto, IX, 871.

HORSEHEADS. VETOES. Dam at, Chemung canal, VII, 268; amending charter, regulating sales of gas, VIII, 622; Newtown creek improvement, Court of Claims, X, 588, 708.

HORSES. Impressment of, I, 374, 631, 671; II, 99, 109; associations to improve breed of, authorized, IX, 548, 601; horse flesh, prohibiting sale as food, veto, 793.

HORSERACING. Suppression of, recommended by Congress, II, 56; act to prevent, veto, 85; regulation of, IX, 548, 601; State Commission established, 1895, 601; racing associations, see that title.

HORSESHOEING. Regulating practice in certain cities, veto, IX, 622.

HORSE STEALING. Societies for prevention of, amending act, veto, VIII, 1039.

HORSE THIEF. Proclamation for arrest of, I, 238.

HORSMANDEN, DANIEL. Commissioner on colonial union, I, 370.

HORTICULTURAL SOCIETIES. Incorporated, III, 64; general act, IV, 648; general act amended, mortgages authorized, VIII, 388. VETOES. Protection of property, appointment of policemen, VIII, 378; exempting from taxation, 619.

HORTICULTURE. Improvement of, III, 64; instruction, investigations and experiments, appropriation, veto, X, 552.

HORTON, DANIEL E. Board of Claims, veto, VIII, 1166.

HORTON, DAVID. Judgment against United States deposit fund, sale of, veto, VII, 877.

HORTON, H. P. Justice of the peace, legalizing acts, veto, VII, 413.

HORTON, WILLIAM, CAPTAIN. Letter from, I, 338.

HOSACK, DAVID. Professor in Columbia College, establishes botanic garden, II, 579.

HOSECK. French Indians attack, I, 553; attack on Brimmer family, 571.

HOSE COMPANIES. Act providing for, VI, 548; Excelsior Hose Company, Warwick, charter, veto, VII, 507.

HOSKINS, GEORGE G. Lieutenant-Governor, remarks on opening of new Senate chamber, VII, 540.

HOSPITAL. Proposed, in New York, I, 733, 743; charter granted, 743; who entitled to relief, 743; excise moneys appropriated for, 743; nurses in, letter relative to, II, 95; officers, pay of, 134;

HOSPITAL—(*Continued*).

for fever patients in New York, III, 12; erection at quarantine, 164; naval, at Brooklyn, 181; floating, established at New York, V, 184, 278, 378; for soldiers, 488; new buildings at, quarantine, 599; Ira Harris, Albany, 684; floating, used for cholera patients, 700; for immigrants on Ward's island, 844; The Isabella Heimath, incorporation of, VIII, 789; New York Hospital, changing site, continuing exemption from taxation, 824; property exempt from taxation, general act, 824. VETOES. Marine, New York, II, 565; New York, additional, 1086; Methodist Episcopal Hospital, Brooklyn, amending charter, VIII, 464; New York Post-Graduate School and Hospital, amending charter, 707; Nassau Association, support of patients from North Hempstead, IX, 818; New York, tuberculosis hospital, X, 178; Buffalo, quarantine hospital, purchasing land for, 475; New York, public, 806; New York, stables near, 807.

HOTCHKISS, FRANK. Canal Department, appropriation for services, IX, 716.

HOTCHKISS, LEMAN. Contested election, Wayne county, expenses, veto, VII, 917.

HOTELS. To furnish State excise commissioner with lists of guests, X, 202; inspection of, X, 765, 780, 902. VETOES. Fire escapes on, VII, 267; X, 701, 709; soliciting patronage for, VII, 415; liens on, X, 593; Gotham, New York, authority to sell liquor within 200 feet of church, 779.

HOTTENROTH, CHRISTIAN C. Claim against New York, veto, VIII, 883.

HOUGH, FRANKLIN B. Member of Adirondack Park Commission, 1872, VII, 722.

HOUGH, GORDON. Board of Claims, veto, IX, 119.

HOUGH, KATE P. Board of Claims, veto, IX, 119.

HOUGH'S CLASSIFIED ABSTRACT OF LAWS OF NEW YORK. Purchase of, veto, VII, 469.

HOUNSFIELD. Town, aid to Utica and Black River Railroad Company, veto, VI, 92.

HOUSE OF COMMONS. Committee for grievances, I, 60; Assembly claims rights of, as to money bills, 162; Assembly memorial to, relative to importation of salt, 233; Assembly's power compared with, 430; what rights of, possessed by Assembly, 479; petition from Assembly, 687, 698, 703, 768, 776; protest against parliamentary encroachment on rights of colony, 703; extent of parliamentary authority in colony, 712; certain officers not eligible to, II, 1063; expulsion of members from, improper influence, VII, 564; members, question relating to election of, historical sketch, VIII, 983, 1075; con-

HOUSE OF COMMONS —(*Continued*).
tested elections, transfer of jurisdiction to courts, 1863, 984; Grenville Act, 1770, 984.

HOUSES OF DETENTION. Suggested, III, 1034; at Soldiers and Sailors' Home, Bath, veto, X, 546.

HOUSE OF DETENTION FOR WITNESSES. In metropolitan police district, V, 181.

HOUSE OF GOOD SHEPHERD. VETOES. Exemption from taxation and water rates, IX, 863; cancellation of assessments, X, 179.

HOUSE OF GOOD SHEPHERD, ROCKLAND COUNTY. Exempting property from taxation, veto, VII, 266.

HOUSE OF LORDS. Petition from New York Assembly, I, 687, 696, 703, 768, 775; protest against parliamentary encroachment on rights of colony, 703; proceedings relative to colonial opposition to Stamp Act, 712.

HOUSE OF REFUGE. Established in New York, III, 82, 130; good work of, 163; petition for Western, 743; Western, at Rochester, IV, 408; employment of children by contract, veto, VII, 764; employment of children by contract prohibited, 957; freedom of worship in, VIII, 23, 178, 479; temperance instruction in, IX, 616; amending Penal Code, veto, 718; commitment of women to, X, 117.

HOUSE OF REPRESENTATIVES. Resolution relating to first meeting of, II, 297; member of, cannot hold seat in Legislature, 310; apportionment of, 324, 546, 705; III, 387, 392, 939, 1033; IV, 590; VI, 493; VII, 725, 837; VIII, 135, approval of treaty, II, 366; committee report, militia system, 531; basis of representation, proposed amendment, 827; proposed amendment, not to determine election of President, III, 182, 199, 314, 315, 589; hall of, statues for, communications relative to, V, 635; VI, 434, 555; old hall set apart for statuary hall, 636; apportionment of members, Fourteenth Amendment, 790; when basis of representation to be reduced, 790; participation in counting presidential vote, VII, 41.

HOUSEHOLD FURNITURE. Sale on installment plan, veto, VII, 758.

HOWARD, GEORGE. Relief, veto, VI, 503.

HOWARD, JOHN. Anticipates self-support of prisons, III, 207.

HOWARD, JOHN P. Estate of, restitution of collateral inheritance tax, veto, VIII, 1139.

HOWE, JOHN W. Justice of the peace, York, legalizing acts, veto, VIII, 943.

HOWE, WILLIAM, SIR. British general, movements in Highlands, II, 7, 8; invasion of colonies, III, 227.

XI — 39

Howell, Mr. Postmaster at Bath, suggested removal of, II, 1070.

Howell's Early History of Southampton, Long Island. Quoted, rule as to compulsory voting, VIII, 675.

Howland College for the Education of Young Men. Charter, veto, VI, 671.

Hoyland, William P. Court of Claims, veto, X, 165.

Hoyt, William B. Counsel for Justice Hooker, X, 829.

Hubbard, W. C. Board of Claims, veto, VIII, 1166.

Hubbard, William O. Relief, veto, VI, 185, 343.

Hubble, Richard. Report on Montauk Indians, II, 931.

Huddy, Lieutenant. Protest against selling liquor to Indians, I, 170.

Hudson. Sanitary regulations, II, 537, 542; hospital for insane, III, 379; IV, 77; Lancaster school, two-thirds bill, III, 533; application to Governor for aid, anti-rent trouble, IV, 147; House of Refuge for Women, VII, 529; number of excise licenses, 1897, VIII, 359; excise license fees, 1889, 685; armory proposed at, IX, 573.

　　Vetoes. Charter of, II, 246; night watch, 395; extending time for collection of taxes, VII, 199; amending charter, 935; VIII, 889; public schools, legalizing official acts, 978; armory, IX, 626; water system, commissioner of public works, X, 583; removal of poles and wires from certain streets, 805.

Hudson, Hendrick. Discovery of Manhattan, III, 1017; in service of East India Company, IV, 173; proposed statue of, veto, IX, 222; discovery of Hudson river, tercentennial celebration, X, 874.

Hudson, Margaret. Pension claim, New York fire department, veto, IX, 728; X, 59.

Hudson Bank. Stock as part of common school fund, II, 722; failure, loss of bank stock, III, 299.

Hudson and Berkshire Railroad Company. State aid to, IV, 10.

Hudson-Fulton Celebration Commission. Incorporated, X, 875.

Hudson House of Refuge for Women. Established, VII, 529; purchase of land for, 703; accommodations available at, VIII, 821; classed as a reformatory, X, 334; made a State training school for girls, 726.

　　Vetoes. Nursery cottage, VIII, 1137; new buildings, IX, 143; reconstruction of administration building and prison, X, 545; electric-light plant, 647; coal pockets and driveway, repairs and equipment, 654.

Hudson River. Sloops on, to carry stones to Albany for fort, I, 35; settlement of Palatines on, 146; expected Indian raid, 161; proposed batteries on, at New York, 295; Albany on west

HUDSON RIVER —(*Continued*).

side, 407; Greenbush on east side, 407; width at Albany, 407; new fort above Albany, 547, 548, 553, 555, 563; situation on, following defeat at Ticonderoga, 625; survey of, relative to Massachusetts boundary, 757; obstructions in, II, 8, 19, 34; loss of forts on, 18; defense of, 31, 34; Vermont's claims extended to, 145, 177; canal from, to Wood creek, 312, 320; canal to Lake Ontario, 321; improvement of, between Albany and Meadow creek, 365; improvement of, 527, 540, 562, 900, 954, 1011, 1031, 1045, 1046; III, 26, 48, 124, 462, 511, 733; V, 453, 534, 707, 789; canal connection with Lakes Erie and Ontario, II, 675; good roads recommended connecting with western and northern lakes, 853, Commission on Canal Communication with Western and Northern Lakes, 854; regulating fishing in, 1011; canal along east bank of, III, 26; canal connection with Delaware river, 70, 165; sloops on upper part of, 72; State road to Cayuga lake, 80; proposed State road to Lake Erie through southern tier of counties, 81; steamboats on, rule for passing, 135; New Jersey boundary, 156; New Jersey's claim of jurisdiction, 356; Federal government authorized to take property for purpose of improvement, 511; above tide water, proposed improvement of, 748; improving upper part of, IV, 475; improvement, neglect of Congress, 571; removing obstructions in, V, 40, 56; Improvement Commission, 453; obstruction by deposits, VI, 557; Poughkeepsie bridge, extending time for completion, VIII, 444; source in Adirondack region, IX, 147; Palisades, preservation of, IX, 670, see PALISADES; ice in, rights of riparian owner, X, 689; discovery, tercentennial celebration, 874.

VETOES. Ferry between Mount Pleasant and Clarkstown, II, 476; MacGuire dock, Phillipstown, VI, 705; ferry, Troy and West Troy, 705; ferry at Phillipstown, 813; improving navigation, 908; protection of spawning fish, VII, 264; repairing dock, Lansingburgh, 366; Chadeayne, ferry, Cornwall Landing, 664; bridges over, 808; bridge, Highland Trans-Hudson Railroad Company, 937; land under, Yonkers, conveyance of, VIII, 53; pound and purse nets, prohibiting use of, 627; dyke at Albany, IX, 606; bridge over, authorizing Albany Railroad Company to construct, X, 52; nets in, amending Game Law, 443; dam in Warren county, Johnsburgh Electric Light, Heat and Power Company, 445, 452; dam in Warren county, Warren County Electric Light, Heat and Power Company, 446, 453; dam, Warren county, North creek, 705.

HUDSON RIVER ASYLUM FOR THE INSANE. Located at Poughkeepsie,
    V, 763; site donated by Dutchess county citizens, 763; report
    of commissioners, 791; erection of buildings, 838; appropria-
    tion, 838; architect's report on examination of, VI, 567; esti-
    mates and expenditures, 650; statement of appropriations, 872,
    939; appropriations for, VII, 123; expense of construction,
    283; number of inmates, 958.
    VETOES. Improvements, appropriation, VII, 89; deficiency appro-
        priation, 487; various repairs and improvements, 487, 785;
        limiting use of maintenance fund, 785, Humo, claim, damages,
        910; various buildings, VIII, 853.
HUDSON RIVER STATE HOSPITAL. Excessive *per capita* cost of, X, 410;
    number of visits by local managers, 415; decrease in number
    of recoveries, 1902, 498.
    VETOES. Purchase of land, VIII, 1138; electric light, IX, 78; fire
        protection, 78; house for night nurses, 294; State care cottages,
        295; Marningham claim, injuries received at, X, 704; extending
        water main, 934.
HUDSON RIVER TELEPHONE COMPANY. Renewal of Senate telephone,
    appropriation, veto, VIII, 245.
HUDSON VALLEY ELECTRIC RAILROAD. Strike on, X, 510.
HUEY, JAMES. Petition from, requesting grant of land for congregation,
    II, 82.
HUGHES, BISHOP. Letter from, transmitting medals, etc., from Pope,
    IV, 453, 454.
HUGHES, CHARLES E. Counsel to Insurance Investigating Committee,
    1905, X, 825; Governor, recommends abolition of railroad and
    other commissions and the creation of public service commissioners,
    act passed, 1907, IX, 761; special message announcing death of
    former Governor Higgins, X, 961; presides at Higgins memorial
    services, 963.
HUGHES, FRANCIS J. New York patrolman, reinstatement, veto, X, 950.
HUGHES, HUGH. Deputy Quartermaster-General, letter from, Hudson
    river obstructions, II, 19; loan to, 19; public contracts, 208.
HUGHES, JOHN. Murder of, III, 32.
HULL, ISAAC, CAPTAIN. Gallant conduct of, commended by Legislature,
    II, 780.
HUMMEL, LOUIS. Dock on Jamaica bay, Hempstead, VI, 705.
HUMO, BENNETT A. Damages, Hudson River Hospital, veto, VII, 910.
HUMPHREY, DAVID. Secretary to Society for the Propagation of the
    Gospel in Foreign Parts, communication from, relative to library,
    I, 234.
HUMPHREY, JOHN M. Relief, veto, VI, 215.
HUMPHREY, RICHARD. Board of Claims, veto, VIII, 1166.

HUN, THOMAS, DR. Albany physician, letter from, Medical Law, VI, 513.

HUNGERFORD, MR. Service of process on, anti-rent troubles, III, 824.

HUNGERFORD COLLEGIATE INSTITUTE. Aid by village of Adams, veto, VI, 77, 94.

HUNSDON, JOHN. Memorial, St. Regis land, II, 941.

HUNT, SUMNER L. Member of commission, Onondaga reservation highways, VIII, 116.

HUNT, WASHINGTON. Governor and portrait, IV, 538.

    1851. Annual message, IV, 538; popular rights under new Constitution, 538; general prosperity, 539; finances, 539; reduction of canal tolls, 541; railroad competition, 541; scarcity of water for canals, 542; Erie canal enlargement, 542, 543; importance of canals, 542, 582; expense of completing unfinished canals, 544; issue of canal certificates, 545; pledging canal revenues, 546; constitutional amendment, canal debt, 547; common school fund, 549; Free School Act, 549, 551; literature and United States deposit funds, 551; colleges, 552; education of common school teachers, 552; institution for the advancement of agricultural science and mechanic arts, 552; agricultural college and experimental farm, 553; charitable institutions, 554; asylum for idiots, 555; State prisons, 556; houses of refuge, 556; militia, 557; emigrant passengers, 557; homestead exemption, 558; proposed survey of State lands, 558, 615; proposed purchase of manorial titles, 560; revision of statutes, 560, 615; codification, 561; enlarging jurisdiction of County Court, 562; punishment of embezzlement, 562, 615; new building for State Library, 563; bribery at elections, 563; banks, 563; Bank Department, 564; assessment of property, 564; pardon report, 564; oyster fishery controversy, 564; national affairs, 565; ordinance of 1787, status of slavery, 567; fugitive slaves, 569; ill effects of tariff of 1846, 570; Hudson river, harbor improvement, 571; announces death of President Taylor, 572; World's Fair, London, 572; gift to Canadian Parliamentary Library, 573; cession of land, Brooklyn navy yard, 573; remonstrance against interruption of navigation between Missisquoi bay and Richelieu river, 574; census of 1850, apportionment of representatives, 577, 590, 592; twelve members of Senate resign, 577; proclamation calling extraordinary session, 578; orders special elections to fill vacancies in Senate, 580; canal policy, 582; enlargement of

HUNT, WASHINGTON, 1851 — (Continued).

    Oswego canal, 588; completion of New York and Erie Railroad, 589; cession of land under water to Oswego, 591.

    VETOES. Monticello Academy, charter, IV, 574; Plattsburgh, amending village charter, 592; Madison Association, charter, 592.

1852. Annual message, IV, 594; sketch of early State government, 594; present conditions, 595; finances, 595; large increase in assessments of real estate, 597; reduction of tax rate, 598; taxation of personal property, 598; canal revenues, 598; canal revenue certificates, 598; canal policy, 600; reduction of canal tolls, 601; Canal Loan Act of 1851, unconstitutional, 602; common school statistics, 602; common school code, 603; colleges, 603; agricultural college, 603; charitable institutions, 604; number of insane, 1850, 605; houses of refuge, 605; State prisons, 606; convict labor, 608; number of convicts, 609; number of pardons, 609; punishment of petit larceny, 609; increase in number of crimes, 609; proposed review of convictions in capital cases, 610; Albany penitentiary, 611; emigrants, 611; militia, 612; banks, 612; railroads, 612; State Library building, 613; destruction of Congressional Library, 613; corrupt practices at elections, 613; manorial titles, 614; delays in administration of justice, New York city, 614; proof of wills, 615; renewal of former suggestions, 615; national affairs, 615; sectional differences, 617; ultimate destiny of African race, 619; slavery, 619; number of negroes, 620; American Colonization Society, 621; proposed monument to commemorate independence, 624; pardon report, 624; Pennsylvania resolutions, 625; report of agent, World's Fair, 1851, 625; completion of unfinished canals, act unconstitutional, 627; validity of canal revenue certificates, act of 1851, 631; counsel for State in canal cases, 633; report on pardons, V, 116; quoted, object of constitutional provision as to general corporation laws, 129, 133, 148, 231; quoted, special charters, variations from general law, 136; death of, 793; official service, I, pref. xiii.

    VETOES. County judges exchanging terms, IV, 625; German Missionary Church, Buffalo, Presbyterian Society, Stephentown, American Geographical and Statistical Society, charters, 633; extending charter of Unadilla Bridge Company, 636.

HUNTER. Town, landing, veto, VI, 328.

HUNTER, MR. Leasehold estate, IV, 333.

HUNTER, ANDREW. Washington committee, lottery memorial, II, 1126.

HUNTER, JOHN W. Mayor of Brooklyn, appointing power, VI, 1025.

HUNTER, ROBERT. Governor, I, 141; letter from Lords of Trade relative to Governor's power to act outside of colony, 127; appointment and accession of, 141; also Governor of New Jersey; previously Governor of Virginia, 141.

    OPENING SPEECH. Thirteenth Assembly, first session, I, 141; support of government, 141; public credit, 142; revenue, 142; unhappy situation on frontier, 142; frontier defense, 143; militia, 143; payment of public creditors, 143; burning of woods, 143; naval stores, 143; relief of creditors of bankrupts, 143; protests against presents, 143, 145; royal repeal of certain acts, 144; expenses of flag of truce, 144; Captain Higby's claim, 144; revival of post-office, 144; Schenectady fortifications, 144; smith for Indian country, 145; claim of Governor Lovelace, 145; Palatine immigration, 146; frontier forts, 147; expedition to Canada, 147; prorogues Assembly, 147.

    OPENING SPEECH. Thirteenth Assembly, second session, I, 148; official salaries, 148; Queen's instruction relative to presents, 148; criticises Assembly's disposition of revenue, 148; power to act out of colony, 149; Assembly denies power, 150; dissolves thirteenth Assembly, 150.

    OPENING SPEECH. Fourteenth Assembly, first session, I, 150; expedition to Canada, 151; New York's quota for expedition, 151; naval preparations, 153; exempting transports from tonnage duty, 153; address to Queen, 153; preparing for expedition, 153; Assembly prorogued, 153.

    OPENING SPEECH. Fourteenth Assembly, second session, I, 154; failure of expedition, 154; condition of colony, 154; new Militia Law, 155; proposed visit to Albany, 155, 156; protecting Fort Anne powder magazine, 156; transactions at Albany, 156; Connecticut's claim for extra Indian enlistments, 156; Palatines in military service, 156; compensation of British officers, 157; address to Queen, 157; sale of liquor to Indians, 157; money bills, 157; relations with Indians, 157; Assembly's views as to congress of Governors, 158.

    OPENING SPEECH. Fourteenth Assembly, third session, I, 159; claims of public creditors, 159; money bills, 159, 162; conditions on frontier, 160; use of military stores remaining from Canadian expedition, 161; repair of magazines, 161; slaves and servants, 161; new Militia Law recommended, 161; thanks Assembly for address, 161; communication from Albany justices,

HUNTER, ROBERT — (*Continued*).

161; reported negotiations between French and Indians, 161; proposed Indian raid, 161.

OPENING SPEECH. Fourteenth Assembly, fourth session, I, 163; financial affairs, 163; no money to be drawn from treasury except by warrant, 164; new financial methods proposed, 164; frontier defense, 166; maintenance of French prisoners, 166; conspiracies of slaves, 166; threatening letter from Lords of Trade, 166; claims for expenses in Indian service, 167; dissolves fourteenth Assembly, 167.

OPENING SPEECH. Fifteenth Assembly, first session, I, 167; new Revenue Act, 168; declares limitation of Assembly's authority over public funds, 168; compensation of officers, 168; advises frequent meetings between Assembly and Council, 169; relief of Lady Lovelace, 170; vendues and peddlers, 170; sale of liquor to Mohawks, 170; proposed alliance between Tuscaroras and Five Nations, 170; proposed commission to Onondagas, 170.

OPENING SPEECH. Fifteenth Assembly, second session, I, 171; appropriation of excise money, 171; duty on tonnage and slaves, veto, 171; Hansen claim, Indian service, 172; salary bill, veto, 172.

OPENING SPEECH. Fifteenth Assembly, third session, I, 172; urges payment of public debt, 172; support of government, 173; Five Nations becoming uneasy, 173; fifteenth Assembly dissolved by Queen Anne's death, 174.

OPENING SPEECH. Sixteenth Assembly, first session, I, 174; address to King, 174; Governor's commissions renewed, 175; defends his administration, 175; colonial agent to Great Britain, 175; act for support of government, 176; French negotiations with Indians, 176, 177; Connecticut boundary, 176; South Carolina refugees, 177; sixteenth Assembly dissolved, 177.

OPENING SPEECH. Seventeenth Assembly, first session, I, 178; commends loyalty of colony, 178; treaties of peace unsatisfactory, 178; French plans in America, 178; urges payment of public creditors, 179; address to King, 180; expenses in procuring royal assent to public debts bill, 180.

SEVENTEENTH ASSEMBLY, second session, I, 180; Mulford libel case, 180, 183.

SEVENTEENTH ASSEMBLY, third session, I, 181; new bills of credit, 181; frontier settlements, 181; letter from Ambrose Philips, colonial agent, 181; memorial for schoolhouse, 181.

HUNTER, ROBERT—(*Continued*).

SEVENTEENTH ASSEMBLY, fourth session, I, 182; memorial against colony, 182; Assembly's action thereon, 182; New Jersey boundary, 183; Indian complaints, 183.

SEVENTEENTH ASSEMBLY, fifth session, I, 183; trade and navigation, 184.

OPENING SPEECH. Seventeenth Assembly, sixth session, I, 184; Lords of Trade object to revenue and tonnage acts, 184, 185; explanatory act passed, 185; thanks Assembly for address, 186; Spanish seizure of mayor's sloop, 186.

SEVENTEENTH ASSEMBLY, seventh session, written message instead of opening speech, I, 186; war against Spain, 187; defense of New York, 187; act for support of government, 188; bills of credit, 188; communication from Lords of Trade relative to pitch and tar exported, 188; bond for farmers of excise, 188; recommends second judge, 188; custom house repairs, 188; gives notice of intention to go to England, 189; Assembly's address, 189; sails for England, 190; warrant to, for Indian presents and expenses, 194; support of government under, acts in force five years, 470; official service, I, pref., ix.

HUNTERDON COUNTY (NEW YORK). Questions relating to New York boundary, I, 227.

HUNTER'S POINT. Removal of nuisances, VII, 710.

HUNTING GROUND. Establishing, veto, VII, 412.

HUNTINGTON, SAMUEL. President of Congress, letter from Governor Chittenden of Vermont, II, 142.

HUNTINGTON. Deposit of military stores in, II, 769; school district No. 4, sale of schoolhouse, veto, VI, 506.

HUNTINGTON BAY. Cession near, Eaton's Neck lighthouse, II, 415; protection of shellfish in, veto, VII, 415.

HUNTINGTON HARBOR. Protection of shellfish in, veto, VII, 415.

HURD, JABEZ N. M. Brigadier-General, detachment of militia, 1812, II, 743.

HURD, WILLIAM B., JR. Counsel for Brooklyn City Bar Association, at trial of Justice Hooker, X, 829.

HURFORD, HARRY D. Escheat, veto, VIII, 882.

HURLEY. Council of Safety meets at, II, 17; town meetings by election districts, veto, VI, 674, 690.

HURLEY, BARON OF. See JOHN LOVELACE.

HUSBAND AND WIFE. When incompetent as witnesses, II, 704; equality of relations between, 704; dissolution of marriage by Legislature, 920, 947; joining Shakers, effect of, 948; imprisonment for life, pardon, effect of, 1108; duties of wife, III, 847;

HUSBAND AND WIFE —(*Continued*).

     rights as to property, V, 291; contracts with each other, VII, 332.

    VETOES. Legacies to wife, relative to, III, 262; right of inheritance from each other, VII, 351; partition of land held by, 416; wife's testimony to disprove adultery, 1093; liabilities and remedies, IX, 148.

HURST, F. Z. W. Collection of zoological specimens, proposed sale to State, veto, VIII, 108.

HUSTED, JAMES W. Assembly, member of committee on arrangements, opening of new capitol, VII, 270; member of committee, first occupation of new Senate chamber, 540; remarks at ceremonies, 540; Speaker, trustee of public buildings, VIII, 502.

HUTCHINSON, JOHN D. Board of Claims, veto, VIII, 888, 1037.

HUTCHINSON, THOMAS. Governor of Massachusetts, communication relative to boundary, I, 747, 749; conference with Governor Tryon, 757.

HYDE, EDWARD. See CORNBURY, LORD.

HYDE, HIRAM. Canal Department, appropriation for services, veto, IX, 716.

HYDE, LORD. Papers, selections from, IV, 190.

HYNE, GEORGE. Escheat, veto, IX, 428.

I.

ICE. In Hudson river, rights' of riparian owners, X, 689; VETOES. Cutting in Cazenovia lake, failure to guard openings, misdemeanor, VIII, 461; preventing deception in sale of, 633; New York, removal from streets, IX, 459; New York, removal from sidewalks, X, 60.

ICHTHYOLOGICAL SOCIETIES. Charter, veto, VIII, 878, 1039.

IDIOTS. See also STATE ASYLUM FOR IDIOTS. Number of, IV, 484, 643; V, 10; asylum for, IV, 485, 555; instruction in other counties, 555; asylum established at Albany, 555; new site near Syracuse, 555; name of asylum changed to Syracuse State Institution for Feeble-Minded Children, 556; ascertaining number and residence, 605; fiscal year established, VII, 297.

    VETOES. New York, act relative to, VI, 324; care of estates, VII, 415; sale of property, VIII, 1041.

IDLEWILD TEMPERANCE ASSOCIATION, CORNWALL. Charter, veto, VI, 309.

ILION. VETOES. Vertical wall, Erie canal, VIII, 521; amending village charter, IX, 148.

ILLINOIS. Constitution, procedure to amend, II, 1058; approves Pennsylvania proposition as to national banks, Vermont's proposition for election of Representatives and presidential electors by districts, disapproves Kentucky's proposition as to compensation of Representatives, 1082, 1083; canal project, III, 123; approves Ohio proposition relative to abolition of slavery, 136; exchanges maps with New York, 225; recommends reorganization of militia, 431; wheat and flour from, transported on Erie canal, 894; embarrassments in prosecuting works of internal improvement, 901; stock of, security in New York banks, IV, 36; sends delegates to Washington Peace Convention, V, 342; gallant conduct of troops at Fort Donelson, 439; State stock held by New York banks, 449, 527, 586, 692; resolutions relative to New York canals, 507; communication from Governor, monument to Abraham Lincoln, 794; appropriation for Lincoln monument, 794; cumulative voting, VI, 544; VIII, 286; assessed valuation of personal property, 1880, 307; uniform liquor tax, 437; excise taxes used for local purposes, 438; retail liquor licenses, 1892, IX, 666.

"ILLINOIS, THE." Used in cholera epidemic, V, 718, 765; hospital-ship, repairs, veto, VII, 791, 929; VIII, 425.

ILLINOIS CANAL. Description of, III, 902, 903.

ILLINOIS RIVER. Canal connection with Lake Michigan, II, 1011, 1096.

ILLUSTRATIONS. See PORTRAITS AND ILLUSTRATIONS.

IMMACULATE CONCEPTION TOTAL ABSTINENCE BENEFICIAL SOCIETY, YONKERS. Charter, veto, VI, 325.

IMMIGRATION. Consequence of excessive, II, 243; increase of, III, 177; adds labor as a source of wealth, 728; should be encouraged, 729; obstructed by English government prior to Revolution, 803; increase of, 1039; revision of laws, IV, 439; influence on national development, V, 843; importance in national development, VI, 1000; national conference, report, X, 866.

IMMIGRANT REFUGE HOSPITAL. Number treated at, IV, 644.

IMMIGRANTS. See also EMIGRANTS, PALATINES. From North Britain, proposed settlement at Wood creek, I, 272, 278; to be encouraged, II, 232; instruction of, III, 729; care of, IV, 439; from all nations of Europe, 711; protection of, 793; V, 24; number of, 644, 719, 793, 849; V, 22, 84, 188, 278, 377, 450, 535, 599, 842; VI, 28, 117, 238, 362, 534, 627; VII, 15, 309, 432, 530, 711, 831, 965; care of insane, V, 278; investigation of condition of vessels, 844; indemnity bond, act unconstitutional, VI, 997, 1001; VII, 14, 432; improved quality of, 529; fund created by Congress, 802, 832; State inspection of, X, 609, 610.

IMMORALITY. Suppression of, II, 416.

IMPEACHMENT. Court for trial of, how composed, II, 325; suggested in Council of Appointment controversy, 502, 504; John C. Mather, canal commissioner, IV, 695.

IMPORTS. From other colonies, taxation of, proposed, I, 115; naval stores from other colonies, 117; Congress authorized to levy on foreign merchandise, II, 120, 121; from West Indies, restricted to British vessels, 197; act imposing duties on, 199, 220; explanatory act, veto, 236; resolutions of Congress on, 276; relation to exports, 1091; speculation based on, III, 486; unrestricted, Governor Seward's objections to, 878; large amount collected at New York, V, 186; received by New York, 410; gold, income from, VI, 135.

IMPOST. Act relating to, II, 220; explanatory act, veto, 236; suggested reduction of, V, 752.

IMPRESSMENTS (Colony). For Canadian expedition, I, 374; of provisions for Carrying Place, 498, 499; act providing for, 565, 631; rates for carriages, 596; for Spanish war, 667; recommended, 671, 673.

IMPRESSMENTS (State). Of forage and carriages, II, 67; for service on northern frontier, 99; of provisions, 134; of flour, suit against Trimble for, 186.

IMPRISONMENT FOR DEBT. Limiting duration of, II, 427; relief on surrender of property, 914; relief from, III, 343; abolished, 345, 384, 445; petitions and remonstrances relative to, 446; non-resident debtors, 770, 876; on process of Federal courts, 876; facilitating discharge in cases of, veto, VII, 265; law abolishing, not effective, 534, 708.

IMPRISONMENT FOR LIFE. Civil deaths, results from, II, 399, 427; III, 863; restrictions on, effect of, II, 1108; imposed as condition of pardon, III, 83; certain offenses subject to, 285; on second conviction, 286; should be rarely inflicted, 340; proposed substitute for capital punishment, 863, 940; murder, second degree, VI, 243; commutation for good behavior, veto, 899.

INCOME TAX. On traders and manufacturers, II, 39; "faculty or means," 59, 60; Federal act of 1861, V, 391; United States, Legislature recommends repeal, VI, 254.

INDEMNITY COMPANIES. General statistics, VI, 953; VII, 521, 949; VIII, 6.

INDEPENDENCE. See also DECLARATION OF INDEPENDENCE. Suggested in colony, I, 79; Assembly denies intended movement for, 294; of Assembly in legislative action, 422; Assembly's observations on taxation, 683; not involved in protest against taxation without representation, 697; inclination toward, denied, 729, 771, 772, 776; not acknowledged by European powers, except France, II, 153; fully

INDEPENDENCE — (*Continued*).

established, 195; of State, act relating to, veto, 215; of municipal corporations, 247; duty to defend, 423; proposed monument to commemorate, IV, 624, 681; V, 121; Centennial Celebration, 1876, VI, 302.

INDEPENDENCE RIVER. VETOES. Canal dam on, VII, 457; relative to, 507.

INDETERMINATE SENTENCES. In Elmira Reformatory, VII, 955; judge should fix definite term, Elmira Reformatory, IX, 832; Governor Odell's suggestions, 1901, X, 205; required in certain cases, 205; purpose of, 918.

INDIA. Trade with, encouragement of, II, 254.

INDIANA. Approves Pennsylvania proposition as to national banks, II, 1030; Constitution, procedure to amend, 1058; disapproves Georgia's proposition relative to importation of colored persons, III, 104; approves Ohio proposition relative to abolition of slavery, 105; disapproves Tennessee proposition relative to election of President and Vice-President by popular vote, and making a member of Congress ineligible to civil appointments by the President, 144; recommends Revolutionary pensions, reorganization of militia, 391; resolutions on South Carolina nullification proceedings, 434; stocks of, securities in New York banks, 725; IV, 36; protest against anti-slavery agitation, III, 756; resolutions relative to northeastern boundary controversy, 852; wheat and flour from, transported on Erie canal, 894; rapid increase of population, 899; embarrassments in prosecuting works of internal improvement, 901; approves Vermont's proposition limiting eligibility of President, 908; uniform day for choosing presidential electors, 908; favors distribution of proceeds of public lands, 909; negroes excluded, IV, 621; joins in Washington Peace Convention, V, 331; recommends Constitutional Convention, 350; memorial relative to use of New York canals and railroads, 493; appropriation for Antietam cemetery, 840; assessed valuation of personal property, 1880, VIII, 307; Supreme Court, opinion, ballot must be secure, 586; Employers' Liability Law, X, 190.

INDIAN AGENTS. Proposed, for Senecas and Onondagas, I, 212, 217; of colonies at Albany, 572; compensation, II, 364, 368; for Onondaga Indians, 888; III, 105; Onondagas, suggested change of, 995; Jasper Parish, communication from, III, 35; removal of Oneidas, 310, 349.

INDIAN ATTORNEY. Office created, II, 433; for Onondaga Indians, 587, 588; Oneidas, payment of salary, III, 909; for Senecas, IV, 291.

INDIAN CONTRACTS. Relative to Oneida lands, II, 224; enforcement of constitutional provision, 302; with individual invalid, 695; regulation of, 1076; congressional ratification when needed, VII, 73; actions against Indians, veto, X, 590.

INDIAN COUNTRY. Smith for, I, 145; two new forts, 156, 160; more advanced settlements, 181; French encroachments, 192, 301; payment of persons serving in, 270; scarcity of provisions, 300; ordnance for forts, 305; importance of posting party of men in, 316; new forts, 346, 416, 421, 536; victualling troops, 460.

INDIAN LANDS AND RESERVATIONS. Act relative to purchase of, I, 11; certain grants claimed to be fraudulent, 601, 606, 611, 685, 751; Assembly memorandum relative to, 686; boundary agreement, 724, 727; deed, Fort Stanwix treaty, 727; survey of line, 744; alleged fraud on purchase from Oneidas, II, 223; survey of, 267; what deemed embraced in Fort Schuyler treaty, 273; title as affected by Pennsylvania boundary, 273; division into townships, 291; contracts for, act regulating, 302; act relative to certain claims, 307; intrusions, 319, 553, 586, 694, 695, 888, 895, 939, 1076; III, 183; V, 202; memorial from Cayugas relative to leases, II, 328; trustees, powers of, 339; at Brothertown, act relating to, 364; treaty with Seven Nations, 381; purchase from Cayugas, 435; survey of St. Regis reservation, 435; map of St. Regis reservation, 454; on Grass river, purchase of, 472; on Cayuga lake, purchase of, 605, 607; purchase from Oneidas, 412, 441, 607, 644, 651, 670, 678, 753; III, 47, 143, 310; purchase from Senecas, II, 677, 857; when contract for purchase of, invalid, 695; Governor authorized to negotiate treaties for purchase of, 754; purchase of St. Regis lands, 866, 941; III, 36, 47; purchase from Onondagas, II, 887, 888, 1118; III, 13; exchange of land with Second Christian Party of Oneidas, II, 894; quantity in reservations, 915, 976; on White river, Indiana, treaties relative to, 987; purchased from Stockbridge Indians, 989, 1119; III, 13; Fish Creek reservation, II, 999; criminal jurisdiction over, 1119; purchase from New Stockbridge, 1120; purchase of St. Regis, Mile Square tract, III, 36; purchase of residue of Stockbridge land, 96; New Jersey, tax on, invalid, 1024; contracts, constitutional provision, IV, 295; Stockbridge claims, 857; VI, 415; sale for taxes, release of, V, 36, 202; taxation of, 200; trespasses on certain reservations, commissioner to ascertain damages, 863; Oneidas claim certain land as not ceded to State, VI, 664; villages, survey under act of Congress, 704; taxation prohibited, 704; leases, 704; highways, State's right to build,

INDIAN LANDS AND RESERVATIONS—(*Continued*).

VII, 222; reservations, State's relation to, 383; allotments in severalty, 709.

VETOES. Allegany and Cattaraugus reservations, prohibiting sale of liquor on, VI, 97; Shenandoah claim, 184; Allegany reservation, highways and bridges, 690; incorporation of village, Salamanca, 704; Allegany reservation pipe line lease, VII, 73; felonies committed on, expense of trials and proceedings, X, 164.

INDIAN LAKE. Services of fire wardens, Court of Claims, veto, X, 946.

INDIAN LAW. Provisions relating to leases and municipal corporations, VI, 704; enacted, 1892, IX, 28.

INDIANAPOLIS. Emigration Convention, report of delegates, VI, 263.

INDIAN RIVER. VETOES. Public highway, extending act, VI, 327; reclaiming overflowed lands on, VII, 934, 1115; improvement, IX, 80.

INDIANS (COLONY). See also INDIAN LANDS. Twelve men chosen to advise concerning relations with, I, 2; negotiations with, 25, 26; Five Nations, relations with, 30; arms and presents for, recommended, 32; with French, attempt on frontiers, 35; alliance with Five Nations, 35; presents to, 25, 44, 45, 46, 65, 82, 95, 128, 130, 132, 161, 173, 194, 196, 200, 257, 304, 310, 312, 319, 341, 346, 354, 376, 391, 406, 416, 417, 419, 421, 424, 434, 466, 505, 510, 513, 517, 526, 531, 537, 540, 568; II, 273, 342, 352, 377; information from prisoners among, I, 36; Five Nations negotiate with French, 46; make peace with Canada, 47; Governor Fletcher recommends aid to, 52; Oneidas and Onondagas attacked from Canada, 65; covenant chain with Five Nations renewed, 65; defeat French near Kinderhook, 68; Bellomont's conference with Five Nations, 82; detained by French after treaty of peace, 82; appointment of conference committee on affairs of, 83; commissioners appointed to visit, 84; ask for Protestant ministers, 86; act providing for fort in Indian country, 86, 87, 89, 92; conveyance of land by Five Nations, 94; expected attack from Waghanas, 114; slaves, fugitives from service, 116; Peter Schuyler's visit to Onondagas, 124; treaty between Five Nations and Waghanas, 134, 136; attack on New England, 142; smith for Oneidas, 145; in Canadian expedition, 152; forts and missionaries for, 156; sales of liquor to, prohibited, 157, 161; possible results of engaging them in war with French, 157; reported negotiations with French, 161; expected raid along Hudson river, 161; expense of commissioners to Onondagas, 167; proposed prohibition of sale of liquor to Mohawks, 170; proposed alliance between Tuscaroras and Five Nations, 170; Five Nations return wampum belt received in Flathead matter, 170; Hansen claim, visit

INDIANS (COLONY)—(*Continued*).

to Onondagas, 172; Five Nations becoming uneasy, 173; presents from French, 176; interpreters, 176, 459; French negotiations with Onondagas, 177; war in South Carolina, 177; to be warned against effect of false memorial, 182; Complain as to price of goods, 183; Canadian trade, 183; French attempts to seduce, 192, 210, 222, 225; prohibiting trade with French, 193; foreign, arrive at Albany, 197; encouraging trade with, 198; conference with, at Albany, 200, 376; Far, negotiations with, 201; interpreters and smiths recommended for, 201; houses to be built at Albany, 202; Eastern, Massachusetts declares war against, 203, 219; trade with Far, 206, 214, 225, 315; Five Nations to treat with Boston commissioners, 206; Far, trading at Albany, 206; promoting trade with, 208; instruction of youth in Mohawks' language, 211; peltry trade with Five Nations, 212; persons to reside among Six Nations, 215; agents for Senecas and Onondagas, 212, 217; trade on Onondaga river, 217, 223; conference between Governor and Six Nations, 222, 224, 232; regulating trade with, at Albany and westward, 223; claim for board of Michael, 224; means used to secure allegiance of Five Nations, 225; treaty with Six Nations, 233; King vetoes bills prohibiting sale of goods to French, 236, 237; importance of maintaining Oswego, 236, 239, 299, 315; regulating trade with, 243; Oswego commissary not to trade with, 245; Six Nations need smiths, 248; renewal of covenant chain with Six Nations, 251; smith and presents for Senecas, 257; Governor to meet Six Nations, 262, 265; Senecas authorize building of house at Tierondequat by Frenchman, 262, 265; interpreter and smith for Senecas, 265, 323, 548; payment of persons serving among, 270; sachems visit Quebec to negotiate with French, 271, 272; danger of French acquisition of Tierondequat, 272; acquisition of land at Tierondequat, 277, 548; proposed conference with Six Nations, 278, 286, 296, 392, 466, 512, 537; growth of Christian faith among, 291; services of Six Nations at Oswego, 290, 296, 319; employment of, as spies, 296; scarcity of provisions among, 300; smith for three tribes, 306; danger of defection of, if Oswego lost, 308; French make presents to, 310; friendship of, important to British interests, 312, 320, 458, 462; employment of, as scouts, 318, 325, 439; reluctant to engage in war with French, 319; confer with representatives of other colonies, 319; armorer for Senecas, 323; expected benefits of new forts, 333; presents to Wapingo and Highland tribes, 341; preserving friendship of, 346; neutrality treaty with Six Nations broken by Canada Indians, 352, 356, 358; from Canada, attack New England settlements, 353, 356, 360; uneasiness among Six

INDIANS (COLONY)—(Continued).

Nations, 353, 355; Chonodado and Attowas invited to join conference with Six Nations, 354; from Six Nations visit Canada, 353, 355; Orondax and Caghnawaga Indians, relative to, 355; murders by French Indians, 355; Six Nations invited by Governor of Canada to join in war against English, 355, 356; complain of lack of hospitality at Oswego, 357; result of conference with Six Nations, 359; new treaty with Six Nations, 359; Six Nations agree to join in war against French, 359, 362; refuse to engage in war, 368; subsistence of, in Canadian expedition, 376; Six Nations agree to join in Canadian war, 382; rewards for scalps, 389, 400; efforts to retain fidelity of, 391, 395, 411, 511; Western, negotiations with, proposed, 391; loyal to England, 405, 414; enlistments in Crown Point expedition, 419; Six Nations sent against Canada, 425; Colonel Johnson's influence over, 425; receive belts from Governor of Canada, 425; families to be protected while warriors are in service, 421, 426; smith for each nation, 439; smith at Oswego, 460; Colonel Johnson's negotiations with, for Crown Point expedition, 466; restricting trade with, 466, 549; exchange of prisoners, 467, 492, 507, 519; Canadian Governor's designs to alienate, 486; Mohawks deliver prisoners to Johnson, 486; refuse to send deputies to Canada, 487, 495; French attempts to prejudice against English, 504, 515; French encouragement of war among tribes, 504; uneasiness among, owing to French influence, 508; Ohio river, securing fidelity of, 508; conference with Five Nations, 510; Mohawks complain against duties on goods, 514; Colonel Johnson appointed to confer with, 526; expected invasion by, 531; fur trade, French interference with, 535; alarmed at French encroachments, 536; Erie, former possessions of, 542; Five Nations under British dominion, 542; with French defeat Washington on Ohio frontier, 546; smith for Onondagas, 548; pernicious effects of use of rum, 549, 569; French, invade colony, 553; church for Mohawks at Canajoharie, 554; Mohawks friendly to English, 554; procuring assistance from, 567; continue attached to British interests, 570; French, attack Brimmer family at Hoseck, 571; colonial agents at Albany, 572; effect of Braddock's defeat, 573; incursions in northern part of Pennsylvania, 587; at Minisink, 587; on southern frontier, 589; from settlements, go into towns, 589; destroy Swartwout house and family, 593; expedition against, 593, 594; ask annulment of certain land grants, 601, 606, 611, 685, 751; River, come into settlements, 607; incursions in Orange and Ulster counties, 616, 626; effect of destruction of Fort Duquesne, 630; English restrain from acts of cruelty. 648; uneasiness in Orange and Ulster counties, 657,

INDIANS (COLONY)—(*Continued*).

658; attacks on western frontier, 674; submission of western
Indians, 680; peace with, 681, 682; conference with Mohawks relative
to land grants, 686; trade with, colony to regulate, 723, 735, 738;
boundary line, agreement for, 724, 727; Fort Stanwix treaty, 727;
trade with, injuriously affected by Quebec tariff regulations, 773.

INDIANS (STATE). Uneasiness on western frontier, II, 26; ravages
on western frontier, 50; expected irruption of, on western
frontier, 92, 98; company to be raised for defense of frontier,
117; not taxed, not included in basis of apportionment of
public expense, 184; commissioners, settling accounts of, 220,
221; depredations of, protection against, 245; clothing and
supplies for, 262; survey of lands, 267; Fort Schuyler treaty,
land deemed embraced in, 273; treaty with Oneidas and Onondagas, 291; treaty with Cayugas, 296; annuities, 311, 381;
raids in other States, 324; murder of chief, 324; chiefs of
Seven Villages, Canada, claim of, 328, 343; Chemung Point
treaty, 328; conference with certain tribes, 338, 340, 341, 342,
343, 344, 356; trustees for, appointed, 339; at Buffalo creek,
visit from, 344, 346; lands at Brothertown, 364; Northwest,
treaty with, 367; treaty with Seven Nations of Canada, 368;
friendly relations with, 381; entertainment of, 408, 410; expect
hospitality, 410; ignorance in legal proceedings, entitled to protection, 432, 433; conviction and pardon of "Stiff-Armed
George," 531; agent for Onondagas, office created, 684; amel-
iorating condition of, 694; contracts with, 695; subjugation of
Western, War of 1812, 786; defeat of Creeks, 786; church for
Oneidas, 894, 930, 951; deteriorating in character and diminishing in numbers, 915; migration of, 916; documents relating
to, Governor Clinton urges preservation of, 931; commissioners
appointed to investigate condition of Montauks, 931; address
from Seneca chiefs, 941; Governor Clinton on migration of,
975; number of, 1819, 976; reservations, quantity of land in,
976; proposed change of administration, relative to, 976;
board of commissioners proposed, 977; removal to western
country, 1107; removal to Green Bay, III, 96, 135; liquor not
to be sold to, 143; advantages of removal to Green Bay, 310;
migration to western reservations, 635; colonial documents relating to, 1018; number, census of 1854, IV, 249; Massachusetts
claim to land, 290, 295; sachems' power to make treaties, 295;
instruction of youth in Albany normal school, 477; Senecas,
new form of government, early method of choosing chiefs, 503,
504; female suffrage among, 504; Tuscaroras protest against

INDIANS (STATE)—(Continued).

citizenship and taxation, 507; number increasing, 776; contest right to incorporate village on reservation, VI, 704; legislation needed, VII, 436; decline of mental and moral condition, 709; allotments of land in severalty, 709; instruction of youth in normal schools, 709; compulsory education of children, 710; Cayugas, Canadian branch, claim against State, X, 31.

VETOES. Prohibiting sale of liquor on Allegany and Cattaraugus reservations, VI, 97; manual labor school, Tonawanda reservation, VII, 132; Thomas Asylum for Indian Children, repairs and improvements, 489; X, 295; Six Nations, Sullivan's expedition against, publication of records, VII, 934, 1084; Assembly investigation, 1888, attorney and stenographer, appropriation, VIII, 842; mound at Geneva, purchase of, 887; welfare, providing for, 1037; St. Regis, regulating occupation of land, 1120; poor, support of, IX, 802; undertaking given by, prosecution of, X, 169; actions against, on contract, 590; schools, inspectors of, compensation, 637.

INDICTMENT. Grand jury, extending authority to other counties, veto, II, 130; for infamous crime, V, 471.

INDIGO. Encouraging manufacture of, I, 507.

INDIRECT TAXATION. Poll tax on slaves suggested, I, 574, 606, 618; excise on tea, 574, 606, 617; stamp duty, 574, 606, 617; tonnage on foreign vessels, 618; income tax on traders and manufacturers, II, 39; arbitrary assessment on certain kinds of business, 59; sale of lands, 199; duties, 199; excise, 199; marine passes, 199; auction duties, 199; carriage license, 315; fees on commissions and grants, 509; duty on salt, 902, 1010; III, 330; canal tolls, 908, 965, 1050, 1098; tavern license, proposed for agricultural purposes, 958; sources of public funds, III, 232; insufficient for current expenses and interest, 326, 413; V, 140; advantages over direct tax, 332; inequality of, 439; by United States, distribution of proceeds, 708; rate bills, common schools, IV, 66; see RATE BILLS; passengers on foreign vessels, 75; proposed tax on suits in Supreme Court, 363; on incomes, by Federal Direct Tax Act of 1861, V, 391; plan of Tax Commission of 1870, VI, 372, 411; corporations, VII, 514; VIII, 145; plan of Tax Revision Commission, 1881, VII, 570; savings banks surplus, 571; sale of liquor, 571; transfer of property, 571; trust companies, surplus, 571; mortgages, 571; X, 347, 800; transfers of stock, VII, 571; VIII, 305; X, 769; franchise tax receipts, VII, 682; new sources needed, VIII, 146, 539; corporations, organization tax, 305; notaries public, tax on, 305; license fees, 357; proper principles underlying policy, IX, 10;

INDIRECT TAXATION.—(*Continued*).
  large receipts from, 296; X, 482; receipts and estimates, IX, 539, 821; X, 26, 328, 460, 485, 595; traffic in intoxicating liquors, IX, 666; recommended by joint legislative committee, 1900, X, 81; Erie county's contribution, 1902, 483; notary certificates, 490; recording tax, 490; new revenues needed for barge canal, 602; only source of State revenue, 923.

INDUSTRIAL EXHIBITION COMPANY. Amending charter, veto, VI, 331, 482.

INDUSTRIAL SCHOOLS. Usefulness of, III, 381; Aurora Manual Labor Seminary, 407; department in New York Institution for the Instruction of the Deaf and Dumb, IV, 282, 793; department in New York Institution for the Blind, 430; manual training in common schools recommended, VIII, 322, 483, 1081; training in public and normal schools, 483.
  VETOES. Manual labor, Tonawanda reservation, VII, 132, 477; State school, act to establish, 631; school of technology, Western House of Refuge, 1082; Boys' Industrial Home, establishing, IX, 246.

INEBRIATES. Asylum for, at Binghamton, V, 86, 180; asylum in New York, 521. VETOES. Institution for, establishing, IX, 246; — Inebriates' Home, New York, charter, X, 323; — amending charter, 586.

INEBRIATES' HOME, NEW YORK. Charter, veto, X, 323; amending charter, 586.

INFANTRY. Light, organization of, II, 339; enrolled for Mexican War, IV, 415.

INFANTS. See MINORS.

INFANT SCHOOLS. In Great Britain, III, 114, 213; in New York, 290; general establishment of, 381.

INFECTIOUS DISEASES. Governor Clinton urges prevention of, I, 315, 316; act to prevent spread of, 592; preventing spread of, II, 336, 344, 364, 372, 382, 440, 451, 536; III, 12; V, 845; act relative to, II, 529; New York Health Act, 1018; Asiatic cholera, III, 394; New Jersey, complaint relative to, V, 35; prevention among cattle, sheep and swine, VI, 28; dangers from foreign commerce, 237; detaining vessels for observation, 533, 626; yellow fever, historical sketch, 782; animals, amending general act, veto, VIII, 730; investigation concerning, 1904, X, 624; investigations by State Department of Health, appropriation, veto, 787.

INFORMATION. Prosecutions by, bill to prevent, veto, I, 236.

INFORMERS. Testimony in certain cases, veto, VII, 624.

INGHAM, CHARLES. Paints portrait of Lafayette, III, 112.

INGLIS, WILLIAM. Judge, Court of Common Pleas, proceedings for removal of, III, 906.

INGOLD, JOHN. Nominated sheriff of Schoharie county, proceedings by Council of Appointment, II, 475.

INGOLDESBY, RICHARD. Commander-in-chief, becomes acting Governor, I, 23, pref. viii; message to Assembly, 23; remarks on defense of frontier, 23, 25, 26; expedition to Canada, 24; proclamation for fast day, 24; recommends present to Indians, 25.

    OPENING SPEECH. First Assembly, fourth session, I, 25; affairs at Albany, 26, 27; payment of public debt, 26, 28; execution of laws, 27.

    Appointed Lieutenant-Governor, I, 135; claims right to act in Governor Cornbury's absence in New Jersey, 127; assumes executive office on death of Governor Lovelace, 134; appointment revoked, 135; proposed expedition to Canada, 135, 136; proposed post between Albany and Boston, 136.

    TWELFTH ASSEMBLY, second session, I, 136; presents Cockerill's accounts for Indian service, 136; proposed conference with Governors, 137; camp at Wood's creek, 137; forts at Albany and New York, 137; troops for frontier defense, 138; requests funds for expenses to Rhode Island, Assembly refuses, 139, 140; Canadian expedition abandoned, 140; Justice Milward's salary, 140; address to Queens, 140; official service, I, pref. ix.

INJUNCTIONS. Extravagant grants of, V, 56; limiting issue of, 57; regulating grant of, VI, 122; against sale of liquor without certificate, IX, 701; amending Code, relative to, veto, 791.

INN. Quartering soldiers in, I, 604.

INNHOLDERS. Fixing prices to be charged by, II, 25, 46.

INSANE. Provision for care of, II, 650; III, 292; convict, conditional pardon of, II, 874; III, 32; New York Hospital, transfer of insane convicts to, II, 945; New York, asylum for, 974; III, 83; enumeration of, 84, 293; indigent, hospital recommended for, 293, 345, 378, 451, 543; State Lunatic Asylum established, 379, 452, 516, 543, 617, 676, 713; number of, 900; IV, 77, 605, 642; V, 10; VI, 623; VII, 527, 800, 958; IX, 567; hospitals for, IV, 77; aid to private hospitals, 127; another asylum recommended, 642, 718, 791, 848; V, 86; county asylums, 55; immigrants, care of, 278; Commission in Lunacy, office created, 448; in poorhouses, investigation, 583; Willard Asylum established, 584, see that title; Hudson River Asylum, 763, see that title; poor, care of, VI, 114; Buffalo Asylum, 115, see that title; Homeopathic Asylum at Middletown, 115, see that title; revision of laws, 366, 628; greater precautions needed

INSANE —(*Continued*).

    against improper incarceration of, 367; supervision of private asylums, 367; expensive accommodations for, 873; accommodations for, VII, 283; number, report of State Board of Charities, 283, 430; extravagant expenditures for care of, 527; New York, transfer to State institutions, 527; number increasing, 705; asylum for emigrants, number of inmates, 958; revision of laws needed, VIII, 484; State Asylum districts, report of board, 1085; State care of, cost of, 1891, IX, 11; State care of, established, 31, 188, 226; X, 23; State hospitals, see that title; separate tax for State care of, IX, 189, 226, 568, 653; State Commission in Lunacy, constitutional provision, 191; number in institutions, 1892, 191; care of, county and State systems compared, 228; new method of apportioning appropriations recommended, 566; State care, New York first to adopt policy, 650, 747; large number cured, 1897, 830; State care, Governor Odell's review, X, 461; increase in number of, 463; comparative statement of appropriations, 1893-4; 1901-2, 464; proposed new hospital in northeastern part of State, 500; chronic and acute should be separated, 609; board of alienists for examination of immigrants, 610; acute, hospitals for, 724; hospital for chronic, 724; who entitled to State support, 725; annual expenditures for, 856.

VETOES. Removal from State asylums to poorhouse, Saratoga county, VI, 182; New York, act relative to, 324; married women, releasing dower in certain cases, 597; Genesee county, support of, 1035; Willard Asylum, new buildings, VII, 88; Buffalo asylum, improvements, 88; Utica asylum, land for, 89; Hudson River Asylum, improvements, 89; care and custody, 413, 506; Buffalo asylum, garden improvements, 486; care and custody, county charges, VIII, 132; Kings county farm, amending act, 292; custody and discharge of, regulation, 891; lunacy examiners, New York, board of, X, 60; criminals, commutations for good behavior, 309; criminals confined in asylums, 317.

INSANE ASYLUMS. Utica, see STATE LUNATIC ASYLUM, UTICA STATE HOSPITAL; Ovid, see WILLARD ASYLUM; Middletown, see HOMEOPATHIC ASYLUM; Poughkeepsie, see HUDSON RIVER ASYLUM FOR THE INSANE, HUDSON RIVER STATE HOSPITAL; Buffalo, see BUFFALO ASYLUM FOR THE INSANE, BUFFALO STATE HOSPITAL. Report of investigating commission, VI, 554; extravagance in construction, VII, 12; X, 330; Binghamton asylum established, VII, 286, see that title; fiscal year

INSANE ASYLUMS —(*Continued*).

established, 297; receiving patients from New York, 527; comparative statement of expense of maintenance, 962; private licensed, inmates, 1891, IX, 32; general, inmates, 1891, 32; New York and Kings counties transferred to State, 541, 651; asylum districts, board on, report, 1895, 575; near New York, need improvement, 830; duplication of administration, X, 330; increase in number of inmates, 1894–1902, 463.

VETOES. Inmates, letters by or to, regulations concerning, IX, 118; Ulster county, purchase by State, 243; county, claims against State, hearing, 265; value of, claims by counties against State, Court of Claims, 858.

INSANE CRIMINALS. Transfer from State prisons, II, 945; Auburn asylum for, V, 78, see AUBURN PRISON; asylum at Clinton prison, IX, 653; X, 588; confined in asylums, veto, 317; excessive cost of maintenance, 342; should be under supervision of State Commission in Lunacy, 342.

INSANITY LAW. Enacted, 1896, IX, 191; general amendments, veto, X, 538.

INSOLVENT DEBTORS. Imprisonment of, II, 427; absconding, revision of laws relating to, 554; relief from imprisonment on surrender of property, 914; communication from New York grand jury, relative to, 923; difference between Insolvent Law and Bankruptcy Law, IV, 5; act of Congress, 5; assignments, limiting preference, VIII, 36, 297, 476.

VETOES. Bill relating to, II, 190; V, 292; assignments, amending act, VIII, 130; X, 815; assignments, cost in actions for fraud, IX, 139; to mature debts, 866.

INSPECTION (Commodities). Of flour, I, 246, 749; II, 436, 471; beef, I, 617, 749; II, 436, 439, 457, 513; III, 99; pork, I, 617, 749; II, 436, 439, 457, 513; III, 99; meal, II, 436, 471; potash, 457, 471, 1093; lumber, 457; pearl ash, 471, 1093; staves and heading, 477, 518; proposition to restrict, III, 722; of merchandise, discontinued, 722; VI, 282; VII, 659, 751; of New York vessels, proposed by Virginia, III, 910; all laws repealed except as to salt, IV, 32.

INSPECTORS (Commodities). See also INSPECTION. Of flour recommended, I, 246; act relating to, II, 385, 436, 457; required to make annual reports, III, 182; of merchandise, office discontinued, 722; office abolished except as to salt, IV, 32; office abolished, constitutional provision, VII, 659, 751; IX, 522.

INSPECTORS OF BEEF AND PORK. Madison county, III, 315, 749; Albany county, 315; New York county, 315; Tompkins county, 315.

INSPECTORS OF COMMON SCHOOLS. Provided for, II, 967; office abolished, IV, 23.

INSPECTOR OF CUSTOMS, STATEN ISLAND. Alleged improper conduct at elections, II, 1066.

INSPECTOR OF DISTILLED SPIRITS. Report, III, 749.

INSPECTOR OF ELÉCTIONS. Bi-partisan boards, act and Constitution of 1894, IX, 309.

    VETOES. In cities and towns, amending Revised Statutes, VII, 130; — minority representation, 203; — Queens county, compensation, VIII, 340; — New York, amending charter, IX, 151; — compensation in certain counties, 722.

INSPECTOR OF FISH. Report, III, 98, 104.

INSPECTOR OF FISH OIL. Report, III, 95, 748.

INSPECTOR OF FLAXSEED. Appointed, II, 1091.

INSPECTOR OF FLOUR AND MEAL, NEW YORK. Report, II, 796, 828, 857, 887, 944, 991, 1078, 1120; III, 14, 35, 105, 144, 186.

INSPECTOR OF GREEN HIDES AND CALF SKINS. Report, III, 748.

INSPECTOR OF LIVER OIL. Report, IV, 84.

INSPECTORS OF LUMBER. Albany, III, 315; Kings, 315; New York, 749.

INSPECTOR OF PUBLIC WORKS. Proposed by Governor Tilden, VI, 806.

INSPECTOR OF RIFLE PRACTICE. Office created, VI, 621.

INSPECTOR OF SALT. Office created, III, 82; duties of, 149.

INSPECTORS OF SOLE LEATHER. St. Lawrence county, III, 315; New York, 749.

INSPECTOR OF STATE PRISONS. Office created, II, 364; letter from, escapes, 473; employment of convict labor, 875; powers of, 985; removal of New York prison, 1016; inadequate administration by, 1051; to receive convicts pardoned on condition of life imprisonment, III, 33; report on convict labor, IV, 48; constitutional provision, 777; V, 77, 268, 437, 758; VI, 355; method of selection, V, 437; abolition of office, 78, 373.

INSPECTOR OF STEAM BOILERS. Report, VI, 43.

INSPECTOR OF TOBACCO. Provided for, III, 207.

INSPECTORS OF TURNPIKES. Act relating to, II, 593.

INSPECTOR OF WEIGHTS AND MEASURES. New York, appointment of, VIII, 131.

INSPECTOR-GENERAL (Militia). Letter from, condition of New York troops, II, 88; appointed, IV, 612; annual report, 624, 681; V, 63, 242, 413, 486, 578, 719, 863; special report on arms for militia, 570; communication from, lists of volunteers, 577; communication from, claim of 32d Regiment, 642; member of Military Code Revision Commission, VII, 428.

INSPECTOR-GENERAL OF BEEF AND PORK. Report, II, 513, 518, 529, 1113; III, 314.

INSPECTOR-GENERAL OF PROVISIONS. Report, II, 457, 476.

INSPECTOR-GENERAL OF STAVES AND HEADING. Report, II, 518, 529, 560, 606, 628, 644, 665, 677, 707, 750, 795, 828, 857, 882, 938, 989, 1027, 1078, 1113; III, 98, 183, 314, 354, 749, 853; IV, 84.

INSTITUTION FOR THE BLIND AT BATAVIA. Established, V, 762. See BATAVIA INSTITUTION FOR THE BLIND.

INSTRUCTIONS TO GOVERNOR (Colony). To Governor Dongan, extracts from, I, 6; to Governor Hunter, relative to use of public funds, 164; trade and navigation, 184; to Governor Burnet, relative to quotas of troops, 203; relative to private laws, 210; possible violation of seventeenth item by Governor Cosby, 250; to Lieutenant-Governor Clarke, different subjects not to be united in same bill, 272; to Lieutenant-Governor Clarke, expedition against West Indies, 288; relative to union for colonial defense, 336, 337; to Governor Clinton recommending powder duty, 357; to Governor Clinton, method of using appropriations, 484, 505; statutes, how long to be in force, 484; to Governor Clinton, enacting clause, different subjects not to be united in bill, 493, 506; Governor Clinton, revision of statutes, 521; to Governor Osborn, relative to forms and methods of legislation, 528, 532; to Governor Monckton, judicial commissions not to be limited, 670; prohibiting bills of credit, revoked, 714, 715; to Governor Tryon, powder duty, 744.

INSURANCE. Of lottery tickets, II, 613; III, 187; rights of non-resident insurers, II, 613; III, 173; relief of companies made insolvent by New York fire, 535, 585; examination of companies, 564; department established, V, 75; mutual insurance companies, see that title; legislative administration not expedient, VII, 304; county and town companies, 387, 692; fires and losses, 1878, 426; casualty companies, 824; revision of 1892, IX, 565; department self-supporting, X, 119; revision of laws needed, 824; government supervision in Germany, 840; legislation of 1906, 842, 906.

VETOES. Town companies, amending act, VI, 153; foreign companies, equality with domestic companies, 221; plate glass companies, deposit of securities, VII, 55; policy, fixing amount to be paid on, 506; steam boilers, 507; life, exempting benevolent corporations from laws relating to, 543; tontine, Assembly investigating committee, legal services, VIII, 247; policy not to be forfeited without notice, IX, 864; limitation of risks, X, 312; minors, 320; fire policies, construction of, 441.

INSURANCE COMPANIES. Changing name, act of 1893, VIII, 1144; number, 1897, IX, 821; public interest in, 821; limiting right to use certain names, X, 104; proposed tax on surplus, 199; tax

Insurance Companies —(*Continued*).

　　on premiums, 200; number, 1900, 218; Church Insurance Association, amending charter, 278; receivers, limiting expense of administration, 352; amount invested in mortgages, 1903, 531; filing certificates in Insurance Department, 621; increase of business, 735.

　Vetoes. Insolvent, settlement of affairs, VII, 797; Provident Industrial, charter, VIII, 414; life, health and casualty companies, amending act, 1040; Supreme Grange Life Association, exemption from payment before commencing business, IX, 802; life, health and casualty companies, incorporation, 802; credit guarantee, relative to, 802; New York Mutual Title Insurance Company, charter, 861; Niagara Fire Insurance Company of Erie County, changing name, X, 242; fraternal beneficiary societies, incorporation, 812.

Insurance Department. Established, V, 75; statistics, 275; VI, 111, 232, 354, 530, 624, 954; VII, 426, 522, 690, 824, 950; VIII, 7; companies pay expense of, V, 276; report, 376; VI, 19; charges against Superintendent Smyth, VII, 180; Governor Robinson's comment on administration of, 304; abolition recommended, 304; occupies rooms in new capitol, 694; amount of securities on deposit, 950; office force reduced, 951; supervision of fraternal and benefit societies, VIII, 876.

　Vetoes. Amending act, VII, 126, 134; National Life Insurance Company, distribution of funds, 267; printing reports, 490.

Insurance Law. Enacted, 1892, IX, 28, 135; guarantors and sureties, extending powers to foreign corporations, 596; general amendments, 1906, X, 906.

　Vetoes. Superintendent's examinations, VII, 266; investments by insurance companies, 266; amending, 1895, IX, 625; general provisions, limiting application of, 802.

Insurers' Indemnity Company, New York. Amending charter, veto, VI, 340.

Insurrection. What constitutes, III, 690; suppression of, debt for, IV, 104; in Delaware county, anti-rent troubles, 235, 238, 297, 326; New York city draft riots, V, 547.

Intemperance. A source of crime, IV, 610; a topic of public discussion, 745; excise laws inadequate, 745; bill to suppress, veto, 752; unhappy consequences of, 800; Prohibitory Act of 1855, 858; act unconstitutional, V, 19; act to suppress, 1857, 20; a cause of crime, VII, 707, 714; among Indians, 709; evils of, cannot be hidden, VIII, 364.

INTEREST. Governor Fletcher protests against 10 per cent. rate of, I, 28; loans for, condemned, II, 158; III, 508, 544; IV, 821; V, 592; VII, 334, 391; violation of laws relating to, II, 400; reducing rate of, 1047; III, 88; IV, 81; X, 359; rate reduced, III, 88; VII, 404; compound on State debt, III, 323; laws cannot control, 472; on State debt should not exceed surplus revenues, 797, 892, 970; increase on State loans, 967; on State loan, IV, 422; on State debt, payment of, V, 490, 578; usury laws should be repealed, VI, 551; on taxes due, State entitled to, 631; on insurance reserves, VII, 522; high rates in commercial transactions, 718; on United States deposit fund, act reducing, VIII, 1149; on breach of contract by State, when not recoverable, IX, 277.

VETOES. On certain canal drafts, V, 143; on unpaid taxes, remission of, VII, 200; on awards by Board of Claims, VIII, 885, 1000; IX, 140, 288; Brooklyn, assessments, X, 176; on unpaid assessments, New York, 476.

INTERNATIONAL EMPLOYMENT GUARANTY AND DEPOSIT COMPANY. Charter, veto, VI, 341.

INTERNATIONAL EXPOSITION. London, 1851, IV, 509, 572; agent's report, IV, 625; in New York, 656, 708; educational, London, 752; Paris, report of commissioners, 865; Centennial Celebration, Philadelphia, 1876, VI, 302; proposed, in New York, VII, 718; at New Orleans, VIII, 31; at California, New York asked to participate, IX, 317; at Antwerp, 1894, 317; Cotton States, 1895, Atlanta, Georgia, 581, 672; Mexican Exposition, 1896, 671; Trans-Mississippi, report of commission, X, 34; Pan-American Exposition, 1901, 124; Louisiana Purchase, St. Louis, 350; Lewis and Clark, expenses of commission, appropriation, veto, X, 799; Jamestown Ter-Centennial Exposition, New York's participation in, appropriation, veto, 815; International Isthmian Exposition, 866.

INTERNATIONAL FAIR ASSOCIATION. Exemption from taxation, veto, VII, 413.

INTERNATIONAL FRATERNAL ALLIANCE, GRAND ASSEMBLY. Charter, veto, IX, 150.

INTERNATIONAL IMPROVEMENT AND LOAN COMPANY. Charter, veto, VI, 343.

INTERNATIONAL AND ISTHMIAN EXPOSITION. Proposed by Governor of Florida, X, 866.

INTERNATIONAL LAW. British and French violations of, II, 616, 656; extradition in absence of treaty, 1104; extradition, limitation of right, III, 777; McLeod case, 942; transportation of slaves from

INTERNATIONAL LAW —(*Continued*).

one State to another, IV, 810; authentication of written instruments, V, 213.

INTERNATIONAL LOAN, TRUST AND GUARANTEE COMPANY. Charter, veto, VIII, 463.

INTERNATIONAL PENITENTIARY CONGRESS, LONDON. Report of New York commissioner, VI, 554.

INTERNATIONAL PRISON CONGRESS. Delegate to, VIII, 127.

INTERNATIONAL TRUST AND BANKING COMPANY. Charter, veto, VI, 342.

INTERPRETATION OF LAWS. Assembly no jurisdiction of, limited to courts, I, 55.

INTERPRETER. Kings county, compensation, X, 158. VETOES. New York, thirteenth civil district court, legalizing appointments, IX, 809; — court, first and second judicial districts, classification of, 812; — New York courts, 875; — New York Municipal Court, compensation, X, 168, 474, 714.

INTERPRETER (INDIANS). Report of Lawrence Claesen, I, 176; recommended for Indian service, 201; mission to Five Nations, 206; instruction of Indian youth, 211; for Senecas, 265; for Oswego, 318; Wieser, journal of, 355; Aaron Stevens appointed, 459; de Joncourt, compensation of, 478; at Niagara and Detroit, 733; Jasper Parish, II, 605, 607, 857, 1076; William L. Gray, 939; Harry Work, 943; Horatio Jones, III, 189.

INTERREGNUM. After Governor Bellomont's death, I, 90.

INTESTATES' ESTATES. Relative to, veto, II, 257, 267.

INTOXICATING LIQUOR. See LIQUOR.

INTRUSIONS. On land in colony, I, 523; on Indian lands, II, 319, 553, 694, 695, 1076; on State lands, 302, 370, 527; on Onondaga lands, 586, 888; Oneida land, 895; on New Stockbridge land, 939, 1076; on Brothertown land, 939; III, 183; on Grand Island, act relative to, II, 995; status of Indian missionaries, III, 36.

INVASION. Expense of repelling, debt for, IV, 104.

INVESTIGATION. As to surrender of Ticonderoga and Mount Independence, II, 15; Astor claim, 867; Clark land title, 883; power of Legislature, V, 38.

IONA ISLAND. Cession to United States, X, 143.

IONE YACHT CLUB. Charter, veto, VI, 195.

IOWA. New York sends delegates to Canal Convention, VI, 104.

IRA HARRIS HOSPITAL, ALBANY. Use of, for soldiers, V, 684.

IRELAND. Lord Lieutenants, power to act while out of country, I, 150; Spanish attempt against, 187; Parliament continued under successive Governors, 196; exportation of linen, importation of lumber, 693;

IRELAND —(*Continued*).

unhappy conditions in, IV, 398; commissioners of deeds in, V, 214; slow growth of wealth, VI, 958; large number of emigrants from, 999.

IRISH EMIGRANT SOCIETY. President *ex officio* commissioner of emigration, VI, 117; VII, 832, 966.

IRON. Production of, recommended, I, 260; act of Parliament relating to, 507; scarcity of, II, 19, 20; encouraging manufacture of, 254, 255; abundance of, 899, 1092; III, 1036; on Lake Champlain, 72; found in connection with coal, 204; in northern counties, making markets for, 372; transportation facilitated by canals, 815; market for, 953; manufacture at Clinton prison, IV, 74, 124, 277; V, 165, 426, 601; manufacture neglected at Clinton prison, IV, 607.

IRONDEQUOIT. See also TIERONDEQUAT. Hudson avenue improvement, reimbursement, veto, X, 785.

IRVINE, WILLIAM. Adjutant-General, communication from, quotas under President's call for troops, V, 619.

IRVING. Highways, widening and raising embankment, veto, X, 789.

IRVING, JAMES. Assembly, resignation of, VI, 347; alleged assault on Smith M. Weed, VII, 81.

IRVING, JOHN T. Judge of common pleas, communication from, costs in action for slander and assault and battery, III, 219.

IRVING, WASHINGTON. "Life of Columbus," to be used in schools, III, 406.

IRVINGTON. Mental and Moral Improvement Society, charter, veto, VI, 196.

ISABELLA HEIMATH, THE. Incorporation, VIII, 789.

ISLAND CITY TRUST COMPANY. Charter, veto, VI, 342.

ISLAND POINT. Ceded to United States, II, 919.

ISLE-LA-MOTTE. Proposed fortifications on, III, 318.

ITALY. Exportation of silk, III, 878; silk culture in, 946; participation in Cotton States Exposition, IX, 581.

ITALY (New York). Division, annexing part to Naples, veto, V, 126.

ITHACA. Cornell University located at, V, 596; number of excise licenses, 1887, VIII, 360; excise license fees, 1889, 685.

   VETOES. South Hill Waterworks Company, charter, VI, 320; Ithaca Company, charter, 700; school system, 1105; police department, VIII, 256; amending charter, IX, 719; Fall creek, fishing in, amending Game Law, 798; dredging Cayuga Lake inlet, repairing State pier, X, 570, 644.

ITHACA COMPANY. Charter, veto, VI, 700.

ITHACA AND OWEGO RAILROAD. State aid to, III, 887; IV, 10; default in payment of interest on State loan, III, 952; affords access to markets, 953; sold at auction, IV, 10.

ITHACA SAVINGS BANK. Exclusive privilege, veto, VII, 1105.

ITHACA AND TONAWANDA RAILROAD COMPANY. Asks State aid, VI, 70.

IZARD, GEORGE, GENERAL. Calls for militia, II, 807, 823.

J.

JACK, MARGARET J. Janitress, Senate Committee on Cities investigation, compensation, appropriation, veto, VIII, 1140.

JACKETT, JOHN. President of Seneca Nation of Indians, protest against Allegany reservation pipe line bill, VII, 74.

JACKSON, ANDREW. Major-general, commands American Army at battle of New Orleans, thanked by Legislature, II, 858; letter from Governor Tompkins, 859; reply, 860; defeated for President by John Quincy Adams, III, 199.

President, election of, III, 606; appoints Governor Van Buren Secretary of State, 269; veto of Lexington and Maysville road bill, 319, 391; Governor Marcy's tribute to, 607; quoted, distribution of Federal revenues, 898, 986; fine against, refunded, IV, 44, 45, 46, 82, 84, 85; views approved by President Pierce, 748; quoted, denying right of secession, V, 322; quoted, spirit of nullification not crushed, 394; death of, IV, 45; as life Senator, possible length of service, VIII, 694.

JACKSON, BENJAMIN. Nominated sheriff of Orange county, proceedings of Council of Appointment, II, 474, 493.

JACKSON, NOBLE. Relief, veto, VI, 185.

JACKSON, WILLIAM. Secretary National Constitutional Convention, II, 297.

JACOBS, CHARLES. Relief, veto, X, 177.

JAIL. In New York, I, 83; Albany, 89, 234; United States prisoners to be confined in, II, 304; Herkimer county, repair of, 388; Albany county, condition of, 392; escape from, reward for recapture, 393; in New York, condition of, 394; Queens county, completion of, 417; Rensselaer county, repair, 417; Delaware county, building, 417; Schoharie county, building, 417; Columbia county, repair, 419; in New York, prisoners escape from, 426; reform needed, III, 286, 342, 380, 449, 515, 542, 765, 941; IV, 723, 845; VII, 706; transfer of insane to State asylum, V, 374; inspection by Prison Association, 526, 601; investigating commission created, VII, 287, 432, 528; bad condition of, 431, 528, 706; freedom of worship in, VIII, 23, 302, 479; Oswego county, changing site, 429.

JAIL—(*Continued*).

VETOES. Onondaga county, relative to, III, 190; Westchester county, addition to, VII, 130; limits, Orange county, 234; Ulster county, extending limits, 265; Erie county, construction and custody of, 316; board of supervisors, changing location, 412; vagrants, sentenced to hard labor, VIII, 132; limits, Onondaga county, 632; New York, relative to, X, 179, 582.

JAMAICA (New York). Legislature meets at, I, 98, 521; adjournment to New York, 101; smallpox at, 367; included in metropolitan police district, V, 183; normal school at, 695; IX, 134; number of excise licenses, 1887, VIII, 360; merged in Greater New York, IX, 300.

VETOES. Village, amending charter, VI, 90; creating board of health, VII, 113; normal school at, VIII, 888; IX, 134, 627; tax on foreign fire insurance companies, payment of, 817; unpaid taxes, X, 62, 322.

JAMAICA BAY. Protection of fish in, act relative to, VIII, 1025.
VETOES. Hummel dock, VI, 705; use of nets in, IX, 798; canal to Hempstead bay, survey, X, 649; game and fish protectors for, 815, 949.

JAMAICA AND BROOKLYN PLANKROAD. Adjusting assessments, veto, X, 178.

JAMAICA ELECTRIC LIGHT COMPANY. Assignee's claim against New York, veto, X, 316.

JAMAICA ISLAND. Recruits sent to, I, 308.

JAMAICA NORMAL SCHOOL. Established, 1893, V, 695; IX, 134; establishing, veto, VIII, 888; IX, 134, 627; Waters case, veto, X, 561.

JAMES I. Statute of, conviction under, murder, II, 68; House of Commons address on privileges, VIII, 984.

JAMES II. Duke of York becomes, I, 12, 14; letter to Governor Dongan relative to change of government, 12; issues new commission to Governor Dongan, 13; abdicates, 14; supervision of colonial affairs, IV, 178, 180; expulsion from throne, VI, 773.

JAMES, AMAZIAH B. Delegate to Washington Peace Convention, V, 310.

JAMES, D. WILLIS. Member of Forest Investigating Commission, 1884, VIII, 23.

JAMES, THOMAS, MAJOR. Property destroyed by New York mob, I, 711; sails for England, 712; claim paid by colony, 713.

JAMES, THOMAS L. Postmaster-General, consulted on New York appointments, VII, 556; protests against appointment of William H. Robertson, collector of New York, 557.

JAMESON, T. T. Clerk, Seneca Nation, protest against Allegany reservation pipe line bill, VII, 74.

JAMESTOWN. Number of excise licenses, 1887, VIII, 359; excise license
        fees, 1889, 685.
    VETOES. Savings bank charter, VI, 333; amending charter, VIII,
        469; water supply, IX, 785; public schools, maintenance and
        government, 858; water supply, acquiring property, 858;
        schools, designating special holidays, X, 173; police pensions,
        322; police, care of indigent sick, 472; acting police justice,
        salary overseer of the poor, 717.
JAMESTOWN BAR ASSOCIATION. Complaint against Justice Hooker, X,
    826; represented by counsel at trial of Justice Hooker, 829.
JAMESTOWN SAVINGS BANK. Charter, veto, VI, 333.
JAMESTOWN TER-CENTENNIAL EXPOSITION. New York's participation in,
    appropriation, veto, X, 815.
JANSEN, CORNELIUS S. Estate, partition of, II, 663.
JANSEN, THOMAS C. Relief, veto, II, 663.
JAPAN. First embassy to United States, V, 297.
JARVIS, MILTON B. Board of Claims, veto, IX, 429.
JAUNCEY, JAMES. Appointed master of rolls, I, 763.
JAVA, THE. Destroyed by Commodore Bainbridge, II, 780.
JAY (TOWN). Separate road district, veto, VI, 332.
JAY, JAMES. Senate, resolution, use of flags of truce, II, 57.
JAY, JOHN. Delegate to Continental Congress, I, 768; chief justice,
    member of Council of Revision, II, 21; opinion, veto of ex-
    portation bill, 26; appointed minister to Spain, 83; order on
    Connecticut for cannon and ball, 101; commissioner on Massa-
    chusetts boundary, 217; becomes Secretary of State, 237; re-
    signs as Regent of University, 301; Governor, 358; IX, 688;
    portrait, II, 358.
    1796, JANUARY. Opening speech, II, 358; happy conditions of
        public affairs, 358; continuance of national prosperity, 359;
        fortifying New York, 359; scarcity of arms and ammunition,
        360; magazines of warlike stores, 360; militia, 360; Council of
        Appointment, 360; keeper of great seal, 361; judicial salaries,
        362; assistant Attorney-Generals, 363; Criminal Code, 363;
        Indian affairs, 363; epidemics in New York and Albany, 364,
        366, 372; St. Domingo refugees, 364; poor, 365; emigrants,
        365; internal communications, 365; Virginia resolutions, con-
        stitutional amendments, 366; treaty with northwest Indians,
        367; military stores, 367; government house, 368; treaty with
        Seven Nations of Canada, 368, 380, 381, 386, 390; report of
        Adjutant-General, 369; communication from Council of Re-
        vision, 369; Connecticut land claims, 370; exchange of laws
        with Virginia, 371; claim of Mohawk Indians, 372, 378; New

JAY, JOHN, 1796 — *(Continued)*.

York tax bill, 1796, veto, 373; petition from Stockbridge Indians, 373; attainder, effect on dower, 374; Columbia College, 375; John McDonald resigns as Regent, 375; notice of appointment to office, 375; claim of Seven Nations, 376; lands ceded to Regents, resumption of, 376, 377; address from Oneida, Tuscarora and Stockbridge Indians, 379.

1796, NOVEMBER. Opening speech, II, 379; election of President, 380; Washington's retirement, 380; Mohawk Indian claim, 381; Indian annuities, 381; lazaretto, 381; infectious diseases, 382; fortification of New York, 382; office of Comptroller established, 383; finances, 383; revision of tax system, 383; St. Domingo refugees, 383; indemnity against expense of maintaining emigrants, 384; resignation of Senator Rufus King, 384; salt, 384; State map, 385; highways, 385; militia, 385, 388; inspection laws, 385; Connecticut claim, 385; papers on fortifying New York harbor, 387; prisons at New York and Albany, 387; Mallory Relief Act, 388; anatomical museum, Columbia College, 389; Massachusetts boundary, 391; Grey claim, 391; Albany jail, 392; additional expense of New York prison, 393; Cayuga Indians, 393; New York jail, 394; agreement with Mohawk and Stockbridge Indians, 394.

VETOES. Herkimer county courthouse and jail, II, 388; Hudson night watch, 395; Honeywood matter, 395; Albany, lamps and night watch, 396.

1798, JANUARY. Opening speech, II, 397; extraordinary session of Congress, 398; detachments of militia under act of Congress, 398; civil death, 399; assistant Attorney-General, 399; quitrents, 399; militia, 399; taxation, 400; violation of Usury Law, 400; Sabbath observance, 400; arsenals, 400; great seal, 404; Connecticut's land claim, 404, 406; Onondaga land claims, 404; New York prison, 405; St. Domingo refugees, 405, 413; visit of Onondaga chiefs, 408; distributing acts of Congress, 409; highways, 410; visit of Tuscarora chiefs, 410; survey of Niagara lands, 411; disorders in town of Livingston, 411; purchase of Oneida Indian lands, 412; fortifications at New York, 413, 418; lighthouse at Eaton's Neck, 414; change of venue, 415; loan of cannon to United States, 416; proclamation convening Legislature at Albany, 420.

JAY, JOHN, 1798 — (Continued).

VETOES. Troy and Lansingburgh, municipal powers, II, 402; militia bill, 403; Breadbake relief, 406; paper, use of, in legal proceedings, 409; Fitch steamboat privilege, repeal, 415; immorality, suppression of, 416; Queens county court-house and jail, Rensselaer county courthouse and jail, Delaware county courthouse and jail, Schoharie county courthouse and jail, Columbia county courthouse and jail, 419.

1798, AUGUST. Opening speech, II, 420; national affairs, 420; New York fortifications, 422, 440; militia, 422; finances, 422; Tax Law, 423; Massachusetts resolution, foreign influence in national councils, 424; resignation of Senator Hobart, 424; arsenals, 424, 425; Connecticut resolutions, amendments to United States Constitution, eligibility of President, Vice-President, Senators and Representatives in Congress, 425; punishment for escape, 426; civil death, 427; petit larceny, 427; imprisoned debtors, 427; money paid into court, 427; resolutions from Virginia and Kentucky, 428; communication from Attorney-General, suits in which people of State are in-terested, 431; survey of patented lands, 432; Indian attorney, 432, 433; New Hampshire resolutions, 433; memorial from New York, public health, 433; report of commissary of military stores, 433; Maryland resolutions, 434; purchase of Cayuga Indian lands, 435; survey of St. Regis land, 435; inspection laws, 435; loan from bank of New York, 436; Watervliet arsenal, 436, 437; claim of United States against State, 437; Delaware resolutions, 438; Virginia resolutions, 438; chamber of commerce memorial, 439; account of expenses, preventing spread of infectious diseases, 440; treaty with Oneida, limita-tion of actions, veto, 441; Senate's address, relations with France, 442; reply, 444; Assembly's address, relations with France, 444; reply, 445; Legislature's address to President Adams, 445.

1800, JANUARY. Opening speech, II, 448; death of Washington, 448, 461; Connecticut controversy, 448; separation of powers of government, 449, 465, 472; III, 254; compensation of officers, II, 449; private laws, 449; corporations, 450; trial of small causse, 450; perjury, 450; infectious diseases, 451; resistance to judicial authority in Columbia county, 451, 456; preparations for national defense, 452; education, 453; colleges, 453; Holmes

JAY, JOHN, 1800 — (*Continued*).

and Pastano murder cases, 454; map of St. Regis lands, 454; salt lands, 456; inspection laws, 457; Onondaga controversy, 457; Watervliet arsenal, 458, 477; oath and bond of State Treasurer, 459; power of magistrates as to seamen in foreign service, veto, 459; resignation of Senator Watson, 460; Salaries Act, veto, 460.

1800, NOVEMBER. Opening speech, II, 463; presidential election 463; local expenditures, 464; taxation, 465; wills, 465; religious corporations, 467; assessment of members of religious corporations, 467; number of members of Senate and Assembly, 468; proposed convention for reorganizing Legislature, 468; resignation of Senator Lawrence, 469; defense of New York, 469; reply to Senate's address, 470; inspection of flour, 470; Maryland resolution, 471; inspection of pot and pearl ashes, 471; communication relative to Oneida Indians, 472; St. Regis Indians, 472; powers of Council of Appointment, 472; inspection of staves and heading, 477; Indian affairs, 477; punishment for escapes, 478; letter to chancellor and judges, Council of Appointment, 479; reply, 481, 483; relations between Governor and Council of Appointment, general note, 489.

VETOES. Ferry on Hudson river, II, 476; Marshall and Brown grist mills, 485; deeds and conveyances, proof of, 486; mortgages, 486; masters in chancery, appointment of guardians, 488.

Succeeded by Governor Clinton, II, 506; quoted by Governor Van Buren, III, 254; bust in United States capitol, VI, 555; Governor, correspondence with judges as to construction of article 23, VIII, 1053; office service as Governor, I, pref. xii.

JAY, JOHN. Commissioner from New York in Antietam Cemetery Board, report, V, 840, 869.

JAY, PETER A. Commissioner on New Jersey boundary, VI, 779.

JAY, WILLIAM. Member of Yorktown Centennial Commission, VII, 734; member of Capital Centenary Commission, IX, 689.

JEFFERSON, THOMAS. President, II, 604; address to, by New York Legislature, 624; reply, declining a third term, 626; services in establishing university, 1100; report on weights and measures, III, 101; death of, 178; favors appropriations for education and internal improvement, 805, 898, 985; quoted, naturalization, 883; quoted, duty of citizen to respond to sheriff's call, IV, 145; views

JEFFERSON, THOMAS —(*Continued*).

approved by President Pierce, 748; as life Senator, possible length of service, VIII, 693.

JEFFERSON COUNTY. Arms and ammunition for, II, 636; militia from, 1812, 743; defense of, 744; agricultural society in, III, 945; silk culture in, 945; arsenal and equipments to be sold, IV, 495; average excise license fees, 1889, VIII, 686; unpaid taxes, sales under special act, 749; highways, cost of labor system, 1892, IX, 200; insane, care of, county and State systems compared, 228.

VETOES. Rural cemetery associations, acquiring land, VI, 162; United States deposit fund, 511; Carthage, amending village charter, VII, 78; Black creek, public highway, 358; Orleans, railroad bonds, 412; Game Law, releasing certain waters from operation of, 442; fish hatchery, 632; VIII, 249; Clayton, amending Village Law, VII, 664; taxes, enforcement, 805; assessments for railroad purposes, 807; relieving certain towns from railroad burdens, 847; new bill passed, reclaiming over-flowed lands, 934, 1115; Carthage, new union school building, appropriation, VIII, 117; taxes, collection, 706, 750, 1039; poor, amending act, 1121; legalizing creation of school commissioner districts, IX, 365; special county judge and surrogate, term of office, X, 701; fire wardens, 954.

JEFFERSON MEDICAL UNIVERSITY. Charter, veto, VI, 339.

JENKINS, ELISHA. Secretary of State, letter from, standard of measures, II, 640.

JENKINS, HARRIET. Canal award, veto, VII, 456.

JENNEY, ROBERT. Memorial for schoolhouse and master's dwelling, I, 181.

JENNINGS, RICHARD. Murder of, II, 997.

JERSEY BANK. Dissolution of, II, 705; incorporation, 709.

JESUITS. Charged with influencing Indians against English, I, 30; seducing Indians to French interest, 86.

JEWELL, ELIPHALET. Buys Oneida land, VI, 666.

JEWELL, GUSTAVUS. Act authorizing erection of dam, III, 37.

JEWETT. Town, bonding, veto, VI, 328.

JEWISH PROTECTORY AND AID SOCIETY. Authorizing appropriation for, veto, X, 475.

JEWISH THEOLOGICAL SEMINARY ASSOCIATION, NEW YORK. VETOES. Relief, IX, 628; relative to, X, 60.

JILLSON, HENRY C. Canal department, appropriation for services, veto, IX, 716.

JOACHIMSEN, P. J. Attorney for Edye and Volckens, judgment against people, payment, veto, VII, 926.

JOHNSBURGH. Highway to Long Lake, veto, VII, 133, 320.

JOHNSBURGH ELECTRIC LIGHT, HEAT AND POWER COMPANY. Dam across Hudson river, veto, X, 445, 453.

JOHNSON, ALEXANDER S. Court of Appeals, quoted, power of Legislature to determine municipal taxation, VII, 453.

JOHNSON, BENJAMIN P. State agent at World's Fair, report, IV, 625.

JOHNSON, BRADISH. Estate, amending act relative to, X, 283.

JOHNSON, EDWARD M. Preparing appendix to Clerk's Manual, appropriation, veto, VII, 459.

JOHNSON, GUY. Member of Assembly, papers in Mohawk matter, I, 751.

JOHNSON, JAMES F. Laborer, injuries, appropriation, veto, VII, 465.

JOHNSON, JAMES G. Board of Claims, veto, VIII, 1040.

JOHNSON, JEREMIAH. Brigadier-general, commands brigade stationed at Brooklyn, II, 809.

JOHNSON, JOHN. Legislative employee, compensation, veto, VII, 372.

JOHNSON, JOSEPH. Captain, Orange County Rangers, II, 43.

JOHNSON, MILES. Farm bridge over Champlain canal, veto, VI, 154, 584.

JOHNSON, PETER. Extradition of, III, 852, 869, 920, 932, 937, 982; IV, 47; legislative action on, III, 1030.

JOHNSON, R. A. Sale of land to State for site of State hospital, X, 794.

JOHNSON, RUSSELL S. Assembly, 1891, election contest, appropriation, veto, VIII, 1142.

JOHNSON, SIR WILLIAM. Contracts for supplies at Oswego, I, 389, 410, 473; movement against French near Saratoga, 410, 411; visits New York with sachems, 418; examined as to condition of Six Nations, 421; influence with Indians, 425; certificate as to French prisoners, scalps, 440; provisions for Oswego garrison, 459; smith at Oswego, 460; advances money to smiths for Indians, 460; negotiations with Indians, 466; appointed to command new levies, 468; unpaid claim against colony, 473, 490; accounts against colony, 478; receives prisoners from Mohawks, 487; appropriation for, 504, 522; supplies for French prisoners, 508; letter from, relative to Indian affairs, 508; letter and papers from, 511, 529, 531; value of services among Indians, 515, 519; claims for services, 518, 553; payment of claim, 522; appointed commissioner to confer with Indians, 526; service on Crown Point expedition, 567, 571; sale of rum to Indians, 569; expenses, apportionment among colonies, 571; papers from, 572, 727; council of war, 575; defeats French under de Dieskau,

JOHNSON, SIR WILLIAM — (*Continued*).

583; rendezvous at German Flats, 603; letter from, Indian war, 678; peace negotiations with Indians at Niagara, 681, 682; suggested that he intercede in Mohawk claims, 687; boundary line agreement with Indians, 724, 727; settlement of Mohawk claims, 751; Indian children, guardians of, letters from, II, 273; letters, Mr. Brodhead makes copies of, IV, 184; acquisition of mansion and blockhouse, X, 941.

JOHNSTON, DAVID J. Nominated commissioner of State survey, VIII, 255.

JOHNSTON, SIR JOHN. Establishes Indian boundaries on Cat island, II, 553.

JOHNSTOWN. Voting by ballot on bridge appropriation, VIII, 1087; Johnson mansion and blockhouse, acquisition, act for, X, 941.

VETOES. Consolidating school districts and establishing graded school, VI, 86; highway to Caroga, 598; officers, method of voting for, VIII, 1041; Dickson escheat, IX, 384; Hale and Reid, legalizing acts, 725; amending charter, 785, 870; streets, opening, X, 327.

JOHNSTOWN ACADEMY. Proposed lease or transfer to village, VI, 86.

JOHNSTOWN LOAN AND TRUST COMPANY. Charter, veto, VI, 342.

JOINT TENANTS. Relative to, veto, II, 239, 779.

JONES, ALBERT. Administrator Inez Jones, Court of Claims, veto, X, 445.

JONES, ANDREW. Estate, relief, veto, II, 685.

JONES, ANNIE. Escheat, veto, X, 958.

JONES, EDWARD F. Lieutenant-Governor, trustee of public buildings, VIII, 501; member of New Capitol Commission, 1888, 650.

JONES, HORATIO. Purchase of Cayuga land, II, 478; Indian interpreter, compensation, III, 189.

JONES, JAMES. Cancellation of tax sale, veto, X, 960.

JONES, JOHN E. Canal Department, appropriation for services, veto, IX, 716.

JONES, PAUL. Captain, gallant conduct commended by Legislature, II, 780.

JONES, R. Remonstrance against interruption of navigation between Missisquoi bay and Richelieu river, IV, 574.

JONES, SAMUEL. Commissioner to revise statutes, II, 255.

JONES AND VARICK. Revision of statutes, noted, VIII, 38.

JONES, WALTER R. President, Board of Underwriters, letter from, encroachments on New York harbor, IV, 704.

JORDAN ACADEMY AND FREE SCHOOL DISTRICT NO. 4. Merged in free school district No. 4, Elbridge, VI, 81.

JOURNAL. Legislature to keep, III, 975; Assembly, first meeting, 1780, presented to State, V, 132; irregularities in, VI, 98; Senate and Assembly, relative to, veto, VII, 264; votes to be entered on, 672.

JOURNEYMEN'S PORK BUTCHERS UNION BENEVOLENT SOCIETY, NEW YORK. Charter, veto, VI, 330.

JOY, ABIATHER. Bond for return of arms, II, 774.

JOYCE, MARGARET. Heirs, escheat, veto, VII, 805.

JOY'S BANK. Holder of State securities, V, 257, 364.

JUDEVINE, WILLIAM. Commissioner of excise, Canandaigua, reimbursement for loss of property, veto, VII, 569.

JUERGENS, ERNEST H. New York law department, claim, office boy, veto, X, 816, 957.

JUDGE-ADVOCATE. Settling claims of, II, 150; communication from, procedure in courts-martial, 996.

JUDGE-ADVOCATE GENERAL. Communications from, procedure in courts-martial, II, 996; report on militia system, V, 393, 412; annual report, 412, 486; communication from, pay of volunteers discharged on inspection, 421.

JUDGES. Act relating to compensation of, I, 11; exclusive power to interpret laws, 55; second judge recommended, 188; additional judge of Supreme Court, 641; tenure of office, 670, 774; II, 461, 740; increasing salaries of, I, 750; of Supreme Court, members of Council of Revision, II, 4; of probates, powers of, 257; not to hold other office, 325, 647; III, 6; IX, 47; X, 679; Aaron Burr declines appointment as puisne judge, II, 327; salaries of, 362; age limit, 362, 622; pensions, 363; extra compensation, 449, 460, 509; Governor Jay's letter to, Council of Appointment, 479; reply, 483; compensation, 622; III, 5, 256, 444, 498; IV, 368; fees for chamber business, II, 622; circuit, III, 5; of Supreme Court, resign to become clerks, 720; removal of, principles applicable to, 929; long continuance in office, effects in criminal administration, 1011; appointment under Constitution, 1012; removal of, procedure, IV, 55, 109, 137; first election under Constitution of 1846, 363; difficulty of resuming general practice, 368; should not be vested with administrative functions, V, 26; X, 679; election, how determined, V, 58; removal, constitutional provision, 723; VI, 440, 498, 833; VII, 533, 534; VIII, 935; X, 928; Court of Appeals, resignation of, V, 747; opinions on pending bills, VI, 431; power of appointment, when not local authority, 496; New York, marine court, filling vacancy, 936; disabled, removal of, VII, 533; continuing portion of salary after removal for disability, 533; Court of Claims, official term, 821; when not

JUDGES — (*Continued*).

    entitled to fees, IX, 481; candidates not to make political contributions, X, 123, 516; assignment to other districts, 336; Legislature to determine what constitutes cause of removal, 829.

    VETOES. Supreme Court II, 740; exclusion from oyer and terminer, VI, 491; third judicial district, increasing salaries, VII, 257; second judicial district, additional compensation, 780; Justice Westbrook, investigation, counsel fees, 924; Justice Balcom, salary, payment, 931; orders at chambers, amending Code, VIII, 629; compensation in certain counties having commissioners of jurors, X, 710.

JUDGES (United States). Ineligibility to other office, II, 366; eligibility, 439; proposed amendment, relative to removal of, 627, 630.

JUDGMENT. Act relating to proceedings on, I, 11; Legislature cannot vacate, II, 250; where to be docketed, III, 873; Legislature cannot annul, IV, 535, 772; treason, Dorr case, annulled by Rhode Island Legislature, 817; against New York, act requiring payment of, V, 237; in divorce cases, regulating entry of, X, 366.

    VETOES. Against Potsdam and Watertown Railroad, discharge of, IV, 693; canal claims, opening, VI, 673; making effectual against unknown owners, VII, 266, 508; Binghamton, payment of, submitting question to people, 1017; in attachment cases, 1093; justice's court, execution, 1094; real property, levy after ten years, VIII, 468; United States courts, docketing in county clerk's office, 1039; for wages of employees, enforcement, IX, 246; entry of, 624; New York, claims arising from contests of, X, 307; notice of application, 444; foreign divorce, enforcement in this State, 594; application for, 707; docket of, 814.

JUDGMENT CREDITORS. Actions by, veto, IX, 792.

JUDICIAL AID IN LEGISLATION. Note on, VIII, 1044.

JUDICIAL DEPARTMENTS. Under Constitution of 1894, IX, 545; established, act of 1895, 546.

JUDICIAL DISTRICTS. Established, III, 5, 6; proposed reorganization of, 648; under Constitution of 1846, IV, 365, 857; additional, recommended, 857; ninth, created, 857; first district, additional justices, 615, 857; law libraries, veto, VII, 82, 220; legislation relative to, 1906, X, 850.

JUDICIAL PENSIONS. Suggested, II, 362; plan adopted, 363; abrogated, 363.

JUDICIAL POWER. See various courts. Exercised by Dutch West India Company, I, 1; by Nine Men, 2; first Judiciary Act, 10, 11; Supreme Court, 19; exclusive jurisdiction to interpret laws, 55; Legislature cannot exercise, II, 249, 250, 581, 583, 665; IV, 772; VI, 907, 1031, 1034; resisted in Columbia county, II, 451; limitations of, 482; United States, proposed limitation of, 560; conflict of jurisdiction between State and Federal, 665; Federal Supreme Court, extent of authority, III, 79, 312; Federal Senate, proposed tribunal to settle controversies between State and National governments, 79; of United States, 364, 1026.

JUDICIARY. Revision of system under second Constitution, III, 5, 719; defects of system, 210, 443, 498, 536, 609, 647, 718, 772, 871, 1034; IV, 30, 53; V, 291; State Superior Court proposed, III, 498; commission appointed to investigate system, 611, 648; report of commission, 648; new article proposed, 936; judicial and administrative functions should not be mingled, 1011; frequent revision needed, IV, 53; act of 1847, 365; proceedings in law and equity, alteration of, 367; tribunals of conciliation, 443; powers considered by Governor Fish, 534; confusion of statutes relative to, 560; under Constitution of 1846; V, 746; opinions on pending bills, VI, 431; relative to, veto, VII, 414; extending powers, limitations of Legislature, 615; Court of Claims established, 821; amending act of 1847, veto, VIII, 470, 621; Constitutional Commission, 1890, 1034; aid in legislation, note, 1044; should have power to compel performance of administrative duty, IX, 588; cost of, 1900, X, 182; growing expense of, 194; power to review findings of military courts of inquiry, 350; should have power to interfere in disputes between capital and labor where necessaries are involved, 509.

JUDICIARY ACT. Passed, I, 10, 11, 19. 20, 33.

JUDICIARY ARTICLE, 1869. Adopted, V, 749; VI, 124; enlarging jurisdiction of County Court, IV, 562; powers of county judge, 627; VII, 614; Court of Appeals, VI, 124; Commission of Appeals, 124; New York, common pleas, 124; Supreme Court, 124; County Court, 124; county clerk to be clerk of Supreme Court, 266; removal of judges, 440, 498; VII, 533; justices of the peace, VI, 480; VII, 44; police justice, Brooklyn, VI, 512, 517; Supreme Court, equity powers, VII, 80; jurisdiction of Supreme Court, 238, 798; compensation of judges, 259; clerks of Supreme Court, 356; surrogate, when separate may be chosen, 615; new section 28, 1882, Supreme Court, additional justices and General Term, 728, 837; county judge, compensation, IX, 107; surrogate, salary, how fixed, 124; judicial officers not to receive fees, 481; judges not to hold other office or

Judiciary Article, 1869 — (*Continued*).
    public trust, 515; second division, Court of Appeals, amendment, 1888, X, 373.

Junction Canal. Purchase by State, III, 816.

Jurisprudence. Of New York, source of, II, 350; colonial documents relating to, III, 1018.

Jurors. Qualifications, I, 101; new law proposed, 278; fined without hearing, II, 171; challenges in criminal cases, IV, 489; qualifications in criminal cases, 855; New York, special commissioner, 1896, expenses of administration, X, 195; commissioners, general act, 1901, 195.
    Vetoes. New York, commissioner of, VII, 129, 251, 803; Kings county, certificate of attendance, 938; justices' courts, amending Code, VIII, 1166; justices' courts, fees, IX, 427; commissioners in certain counties, general regulations concerning list of jurors, qualifications, etc., 514; New York, exemptions, 631; compensation, 726; in certain counties, 791; fees, 792; X, 62, 947; Richmond county, commissioner, creating office, IX, 796; commissioners in certain counties, 811, 866; commissioner, Albany, X, 44; commissioner and special commissioner, Kings county, abolishing office, 178; fees of, Syracuse, Municipal Court, 441; commissioners, salaries, 450; commissioner, notice server, amending act, 532; commissioners, amending act of 1895; qualifications and exemptions of jurors in certain counties, 587; powers of commissioner, exemptions, 701; commissioners, compensation of jurors, 710; exemptions, 808, 953; peremptory challenges in criminal cases, 956.

Jury. See also Trial by Jury. Struck, in proceedings to acquire land for United States, II, 753, 777, 878; exemption of persons engaged in certain manufacturing establishments, 876; militia exempt from, IV, 557; raising standard of qualifications, VI, 546; right of trial by, United States Constitution, VII, 613.
    Vetoes. Sheriffs, New York, VII, 595; exempting firemen, Flatbush, VIII, 728; exemptions, Kings county, 1037; courts of special sessions, method of selecting, IX, 129; notices, service of 792; New York, jury servers, fixing salary, 807; coroner's, bill to abolish, 860; membership corporations, drawing juries on exhibition grounds, X, 450.

Justices. Act relative to fees of, I, 10; act requiring them to attend court, 11; given power to try title to land, 60; reduction of number recommended, 78; of Albany, ask for law against sale of liquor to Indians, 161; of Albany, relative to jail, 234; of Supreme Court, inquiry as to destruction of property, II, 162.

JUSTICES' COURTS. See COURT, JUSTICES.

JUSTICES OF THE PEACE. To be members of militia reserves, I, 549; cannot exercise power of taxation, II, 95; prevention of abuses by, 1015; how chosen, III, 17, 57, 135, 158, 161, 1012; VI, 75; to be elected by people, III, 57, 135, 158, 161; IV, 52, 684; VI, 208; VII, 44; resignation of, III, 106; duties of commissioner of deeds transferred to, 770; Delaware county, join anti-rent associations, IV, 301; removal, constitutional provision, VI, 49, 74; Legislature cannot appoint, 76; acting as justices of sessions, 121; limiting jurisdiction, 327; number should be increased for special necessity, VII, 78; *de facto*, when acts of, cannot be questioned, VIII, 328, 943; Constitution of 1846, X, 673.

VETOES. Fixing their own charges, II, 86; warrants of, arrest on, 210; Lowville, filling vacancies in office, VI, 48; vacancies in office, 74; additional, Deer Park, 208, 276; additional, Verona, 326; Brooklyn,— election, VII, 415; — reducing number, 804; execution on judgment, 1094; Brooklyn, increasing number, 1119; Yorkshire, additional justice, VIII, 338; fees, IX, 375; bill relative to, 534; Owasco, power to appoint special officers, 623; criminal docket, 722; Cortland, salaries for, 722; jurisdiction in certain towns, 792; Guilderland, appointment in first district, 816; jurisdiction, X, 704, 808; defining term, 704; meaning of term, 808.

LEGALIZING ACTS. Relative to, VI, 479; VIII, 639; X, 163; failure to take oath, VII, 44; Noyes, 412; Horton, 413; Weller, 413; Williams, 507; taking oath and filing bond, VIII, 328, 518; Howe, 943; Sherman, IX, 346; Curtis, 369; Bagg, filing oath and bond, 725; Hale and Reid, Johnstown, 725; Steele, X, 62; Orange, Rockland and Sullivan, 62; Richardson, 63; McCormick, Potsdam, 813; Tibbitt, Fabius, 948.

JUSTICES OF SESSIONS. Vacancies in office, how filled, VI, 121; Kings county, compensation, veto, VII, 1090.

JUSTIN, A. A. Board of Claims, veto, VIII, 1166.

K.

KAISER, KATHARINA. Escheat, veto, X, 588.

KANE, CORNELIUS J. Attendant, Senate Committee on Cities Investigation, compensation, veto, VIII, 1140.

KANE, DR. ELISHA K. Arctic explorer, medal for, V, 59; death of, legislative action thereon, 59.

KANSAS. Territory organized, IV, 827, 860; struggle over slavery, 861; Vermont resolutions, 865; slavery troubles in, V, 32; sufferers, appropriation for, 34; President Buchanan's comment on status of slavery, 60; Lecompton Constitution, New York opposes, 61; Indian lands in, relinquishment of interest, 200; various papers relating to, 345; act for relief of, 345, 387; report of commissioners on relief fund, 350, 388; women may vote for school officers, IX, 96.

KAYADEROSSERAS. Mohawks deny sale of, I, 553, 685; Indian land grants claimed to be fraudulent, 601, 611, 685, 687, 751; patent rights under, II, 354.

KAYUTAH LAKE. Amending Game Law, veto, X, 954.

KEARSARGE, THE. Conveys French delegates to West Point, VII, 740; conveys German delegates from naval station to New York, 741.

KEEFE, THOMAS. Canal Department, appropriation for services, veto, IX, 716.

KEELER, ISAAC. Report on Montauk Indians, II, 931.

KEENAN, PETER, MAJOR. Monument to, veto, X, 163.

KEENE. Arms and supplies for, II, 772.

KEENEY, ABNER C. Brooklyn, contract, construction of storage reservoir, payment, veto, VII, 617.

KEEPER OF GREAT SEAL. Governor acting as, II, 361.

KEGS. Used in connection with certain drinks, amending act, veto, IX, 267.

KEHR, PETER. Relief, veto, VII, 601.

KEITH, SIR WILLIAM. Governor of Pennsylvania, letter from, relative to importation of salt, I, 219.

KELLERAN, EDWARD. Extradition of, III, 748.

KELLEY, DANIEL. Bond for return of arms, II, 775.

KELLNER, JOHN A. Relief, veto, VII, 601.

KELLOGG, GILES, CAPTAIN. Funds received by, II, 766; arms received by, 773.

KELLOGG, O. C. Committee on procuring readjustment of quotas, V, 537, 572.

KELLY, GEORGE V. Coroner's clerk, New York, claim for services, veto, X, 956.

KELLY, JOHN. Commissioner to build road on Onondaga reservation, veto, VII, 92, 223.

KELLY, RICHARD. New York school trustee, 19th ward, action against, legal services and expenses, veto, IX, 871.

KELSEY, OTTO. Assembly, member of Prince Henry reception committee, X, 479; escorts Ambassador von Hollenben at reception, 480.

KEMBLE, GOUVERNEUR. House of Representatives, communication from, fortifications on Lake Champlain and at Black Rock, III, 850.

KEMP, FRANCOIS ADRIAAN vander. Translates Dutch records, III, 162.

KENDALL. First Congregational and First Baptist churches, sale and division of property, veto, VII, 881.

KENEHAN, JAMES F. New York firemen, relief, veto, X, 581.

KENHAWA SPRINGS. Salt at, III, 477.

KENMORE. Frontage tax for water purposes, veto, X, 812.

KENNEDY, ALEXANDER. Auction agent, award, veto, VIII, 247.

KENNEDY, ARCHIBALD. Memorial, supplies for troops, I, 202; claim, money advanced for use of colony, 517; collector of customs, seizure by, 532.

KENNEDY, BARBARA. Damages, death of husband, appropriation, veto, VII, 466.

KENNEDY, JOHN, JR. Captain of Eighth Regiment, National Guard, Syracuse, death of, appropriation for widow, veto, VII, 466.

KENNEDY, ROBERT D. Canal Department, appropriation for services, veto, IX, 716.

KENNEDY, ROBERT J. New York, relief, veto, X, 177.

KENSINGTON. Quoted, composition of cider, VIII, 354.

KENT, JAMES. Counsel to examine dower cases, II, 374; judge, correspondence with Governor Jay, Council of Appointment, 483; chancellor, prepares veto of constitutional convention bill, 1059; appointed statutory revision commissioner, III, 18; signs cession to United States, 140; cited, franchise considered real property, X, 68.

KENT, PHINEAS. Relief, veto, VII, 805.

KENT'S COMMENTARIES. Cited, IV, 359; condition not to alien void, 359.

KENT AND RADCLIFF. Revision of statutes, noted, VIII, 38.

KENTUCKY. Resolutions, relation of States to United States, II, 428, 431; laws of, received, 530; proposed amendments, jurisdiction of Federal courts, 560, 586; protests against change in plan of apportioning Representatives, 560; pledges fidelity to Union and support of administration, 606; protests against unlawful taxation of commerce of Mississippi river, 606; constitutional amendment, prohibiting increase of salary of Representatives during term, 919; Constitution, procedure to amend, 1058; approves Maryland proposition for disposition of public land, 1114; canal project, III, 123; disapproves Georgia's proposition relative to importation of negroes or colored persons, 143; resolutions, protest against anti-slavery movement, 589; resolutions, Federal financial affairs, 690; communication from Governor relative to cultivation of silk and beet sugar, 821;

KENTUCKY — (*Continued*).

    resolutions on public lands, 851; constitutional amendment, limiting eligibility of President to one term, 909; preserving faith pledged to public creditors, 978; resolutions, ascertaining survivors of Revolutionary Army, 979; constitutional amendments, 1020; stocks of, securities in New York banks, IV, 36; apportionment of direct taxes, 86; Governor and Legislature invited to visit Albany, V, 203; proposes Federal Constitutional Convention, 328; approves Crittenden resolutions, 328; delegates to Washington Peace Convention, 329; adheres to Union, 476; resolutions on national affairs, 499; protests against Emancipation Proclamation, 500; recommends Constitutional Convention, 501; election booths, VIII, 902.

KEPPEL, AUGUSTUS (first Viscount Keppel), COMMODORE. Commands British North American fleet, I, 568.

KERNAN, WILLIAM. Member of Education Unification Commission, 1899, X, 114.

KERR, CHARLES. Petition for appointment of, as surgeon at Oswego, I, 258.

KESLER, ABRAHAM. Convicted of murder, II, 921; application for pardon refused, execution directed by Legislature, 922.

KESSEL, MOSES. Commissioner of charities, Kings county, contest, reimbursing for expenses, veto, VII, 651.

KETCHUM, JOSEPH. Petition from, exportation of provisions, II, 127.

KETTLES. For King's troops, Assembly declines to furnish, I, 282.

KEUKA LAKE. VETOES. Lighthouse and breakwater, IX, 713; trout season, X, 443.

KEYSER, JOHN H. Farm bridge over Erie canal, veto, VI, 854.

KIDD, WILLIAM, CAPTAIN. Governor Sloughter recommends reward for services to colony, appropriation for, I, 21.

KIDDER, ———. See Chapman Church case, V, 149.

KIDNAPPING. An extraditable offense, III, 938; punishment of, veto, X, 699.

KIERNAN, JOHN J. Senate, offers amendments to Brooklyn aldermanic bill, VIII, 744.

KILBURN, FREDERICK D. Superintendent of Banks, charges against, X, 872.

KILGOUR, DAVID and JOHN. Escheat, veto, IX, 428.

KILLMEYER, ALBERT. School supplies, Westfield, Richmond county, claim, veto, X, 320.

KILL VON KULL. Quarantine jurisdiction over, VI, 780.

KIMBALL, WILLIAM H. Treasurer Manhattan State Hospital, reimbursement for premiums on bonds, veto, X, 642.

KINDERHOOK. French designs on, I, 68; garrison at, 108; petition for relief, 394, 463; rangers at, 439; company sent to, 463; plan of fortifications, 572.

KINEALLY, MARY. Escheat, Court of Claims, veto, X, 310.

KINEALLY, WILLIAM A. Estate, Court of Claims, veto, X, 310.

KING, ANDREW. Regent, death of, II, 857.

KING, HENRY. Clinton prison convict, crime committed by, trial, reimbursing Clinton county, veto, VII, 782, 887.

KING, JOHN A. Becomes owner of part of Blenheim patent, IV, 331; Governor and portrait, V, 1.

1857. Annual message, V, 1; state of treasury, 1; canals and canal debt, 3; canals not to be sold, 7; extending term of credit, 7; banks, 8; failure of appropriation and supply bills, 1856, 8; census statistics, 9; militia, 11; common school statistics, 12; more adequate compensation of teachers, 13; influence of school commissioners, 14; State normal school, 15; agricultural college, 16; Dudley Observatory, 17; State prisons, 17; houses of refuge, 18; State charitable institutions, 18; excise laws, 19; Prohibitory Act of 1855 unconstitutional, 19; salt manufacture, 20; New York harbor encroachments, 21; care of emigrants, 22; marine hospital, 22; amount of emigrant passenger fund, 22; aid to commissioners of emigration, 23; opening northern wilderness, 24; New York city affairs, 25; abuses in elective franchise, 25; reorganization of New York city police system, 26; removal of quarantine establishment, 28; New York opposed to extension of slavery, 28; attitude of free States toward slavery, 29; Missouri Compromise, 31; slavery troubles in Kansas, 32; New Jersey complains of New York's violation of quarantine agreement, 35; sale of Indian lands for taxes, 36; obstructions in Hudson river, 40.

VETOES. Appropriation bill, deficiency, V, 36; compensation of legislative committees, 41 (two bills).

1858. Annual message, V, 42; financial panic of 1857, 42; suspension of specie payments, 43; declines to call extraordinary session, 44; specie payments resumed, 44; condition of Bank of England, 45; reserve deposits of coin in banks, 46; restoration of railroad tolls, 47; increasing railroad transportation charges, 47; no State aid to private enterprise, 48; salt springs, 48; canals, 48; canal revenues, 49; tax for canal debt, 50; condition of public schools, 51; militia commutations, 51; number of militia, 53; Registry Law, 53; metropolitan police district, 53;

KING, JOHN A., 1858 — (*Continued*).

 port wardens, 53; removal of quarantine, 54; constitutional amendments sent to Governor by mistake, 54; fire at State Lunatic Asylum, 54; condition of insane paupers, 55; clearing out obstructions in Hudson river, 56; pier and bulkhead lines, New York harbor, 56; practice of granting injunctions, 56; mode of declaring election of judges, 58; discrimination in degrees of criminality, 59; medal for Dr. Kane, 59; medal for Lieutenant Hartstene, 59; condition in Kansas, 59, 345; Lemmon slave case, 61; revision of school laws, New York city, 62; United States loan commissioners, 63; New York and Harlem Railroad Company, amending charter, veto, 63; declares Richmond county in state of insurrection, 79, 88; reimbursed for expenses incurred in quarantine disturbance, 89; letter to Governor Morgan, quarantine affairs, 99; correspondence with emigration commissioners, 99; proclamation by, Staten Island quarantine, 99; correspondence with Attorney-General, quarantine affairs, 99; correspondence with Comptroller, quarantine affairs, 100, 105; instructions to Captain Benham, 100; delegate to Washington Peace Convention, 310; president Yorktown Centennial Commission, VII, 734, 743; president New York Historical Society, communication from, centennial anniversary of New York's ratification of Federal Constitution, VIII, 506; official service, I, pref. xiii.

KING, PATRICK. Commissioner, special highway, Onondaga highway, veto, VII, 474.

KING, REUBEN, CAPTAIN. Funds received by, II, 766.

KING, RUFUS (Albany). Adjutant-General, correspondence relative to disturbance in northeastern part of State, III, 760, 762.

KING, RUFUS (New York). Chosen Senator in Congress, II, 301; appointed Minister to Great Britain, 384; re-elected Senator, 1021; succeeded by Nathan Sanford, III, 85, 132.

KINGSBRIDGE. Annexed to New York, VI, 712. VETOES. Annexation Act, amendment, 911; exempt firemen, VIII, 1036.

KINGSBURY, E. Pennsylvania, committee on canal connecting North Branch canal with Chemung canal, III, 759.

KING'S COLLEGE. Act to establish, I, 523; changed to Columbia, II, 200; VIII, 168; trustees, power to fill vacancies, II, 610; foundation of State university, VIII, 168.

KINGS COUNTY. Burning of woods in, prohibited, I, 143; sheriff of, account for subsistence of French prisoners, 388; Simon Boerum, Assembly, favors colonial union, 767; cessions of land in, how made, II, 825; convict labor in, 875; general elections in, III, 771; agricultural society in, 945; hospital for insane at Flatbush, IV, 78; included in metropolitan police district, V, 27; VI, 30; board of supervisors, report of charitable and penal institutions, VII, 537; exempted from Dog Tax Law, VIII, 823; Bensonhurst park, amending act to establish, 1157; increase in population, IX, 3; State care of insane, 31, 189; insane asylums, inmates, 1891, 32; highways, cost of labor system, 1892, 200; Brooklyn, supervisors, filling vacancies, act relative to, 223; insane, care of, county and State systems compared, 228; territory included in Greater New York, 300; insane asylums transferred to State, 541, 575; consolidated with Brooklyn, 1896, 585, 588; board of supervisors abolished, 585; supervisors-at-large, powers of, 585; coroners, term of office, 704; included in metropolitan elections district, 885; sheriff, county clerk, and register, salaried offices, X, 25, 208, 290; transfer tax assistant, 108; interpreter's compensation, 158; sheriff, clerk and register, extravagant compensation, 207; district attorney's chief clerk, 279; commissioner of jurors, 395.

.VETOES. Register, closing office on holiday, VI, 287; Supreme and County Courts, messengers, doorkeepers and attendants, 341; court of general sessions, deputy clerk, 506; courthouse property, 510; penitentiaries, sentences, 512; Supreme Court, messengers and attendants, 512; Brooklyn board of health, extending jurisdiction, 517; board of health, establishment of, 518; Tyrian Hall Association, New Lots, charter, 590; maintenance of civil prisoners, 596; board of charities, 1018; VIII, 596; notaries public, relative to, VI, 1036; New Lots, Bushwick avenue, VII, 63; clerk, expenses, notaries public, 83; notaries public, powers of, 131; preservation of fish, 264; county treasurers, amending act, 266; clerks of board of supervisors, courthouse engineers, 440; site for armory, 541; reimbursing Commissioner Cunningham for expenses in action, 544; VII, 294; commissioner of charities ousting incumbent, Kessel case, VII, 651; closing certain offices on Saturday, 757; stenographers, second judicial district, appointment and removal, 769; armory, reappropriation, 795; court officers, appointment and dismissal, 804; New Lots, police commissioners, 804; Gravesend, common lands, 665, 804; contested election, Assembly, Lindsay, expenses,

KINGS COUNTY, VETOES — (*Continued*).

918; contested election, Assembly, Sheridan, expenses, 918; sale of drugs, medicines and poisons, 936; New Lots, sidewalks and streets, improvement, 936; jurors, certificate of attendance, 938; justices of sessions, compensation, 1090; gaslight companies, 1119; clerk, VIII, 124; register, 124; poor and insane, farm, amending act, 292; religious societies, relief of, 468; farm at St. Johnland, changing supervision of, 594; pension, Abraham Dalley, 638; coroner's clerk, 638; coroner's stenographer, 890; farm commissioners, 1037; special highway, IX, 130; Coney Island, improvement of concourse land, 152; soldiers and sailors' memorial arch, legalizing acts relative to, 211; Flatlands and Flatbush, Remsen avenue improvement, 275; appointment of special officer, transfer tax, 275; coroner's physician, eastern district, 434; charities and corrections, board of, reorganization, 440; tunnel under Newtown creek, 474; Charities Commission, reorganization, 583; roads and streets, commissioner's map, alteration, 628; public administrator, amending Code, 792; armory, Forty-seventh Regiment, Richmond, 777; County Court and court of sessions, clerks and records, 795; Supreme Court, amending order, transferring employees from Brooklyn City Court to, 795; Hall of Records, keeper, 861; public buildings inspector, duties, 861; Sherman street, closing part of, 872; new inferior court, 873; County Court, clerks, relief, X, 59; removal of penitentiary, 177; commissioner and special commissioner of jurors, abolishing office, 178; county clerk, register and sheriff, salaried offices, 179 (three bills); register, salaries of clerks, 449; Charles Guden, sheriff, proceedings against, appropriation for counsel for successor, 559; county clerk, employees, 584; county clerk, office fees, 588; register, employees, 592; register, salary, 594; county clerk, salary, 594; register and clerk's office, transcribing records, compensation, 710; sheriff, assistant deputies, 710, 711; county clerk, management of office, 711; register, management of office, 711; county clerk, office, index clerks and custodians, compensation, 711; register and sheriff, additional subordinates, appointment and salary, 770; map, closing part of East Ninety-second street, repealing act, 815; county detectives, fixing salaries, 955; McNeile, coroner's clerk, compensation, 957.

KINGS COUNTY PENITENTIARY. Sentences, veto, VI, 512.

KING'S DISTRICT. Memorial from inhabitants of, II, 55.

KING'S FERRY. Vessel at, with contraband goods, II, 58; persons driven from, 82.

KINGSLAND. Petition from, defense of frontier, II, 117.

KINGSLAND, JACOB D. Prison claims, commission to examine, V, 167, 272; labor contracts, Clinton prison, 425, 427.

KINGSLEY, WILLIAM C. Member of New Capitol Commission, VI, 229; Brooklyn contract, construction of storage reservoir, payment, veto, VII, 617.

KING'S PARK STATE HOSPITAL. Building for industries, veto, X, 935.

KINGSTON. Blockhouses for protection of, I, 627; canvass of first election, II, 6; first meeting of Legislature at, 7; IX, 688; Legislature adjourns from, II, 15, 16; destroyed by British, 17; Legislature meets at, 75, 96, 186; armory at, V, 175; number of excise licenses, 1887, VIII, 359; excise license fees, 1889, 685; law library, IX, 46; consolidation of school districts, act of 1902, X, 437.

VETOES. Memorial, organization of State government, appropriation, VII, 85; officers, relative to, 416; election case, printing testimony, 491; Cornell Hose Company No. 2, charter, 600; Ulster County Loan and Trust Company, charter, VIII, 230; law library, appropriation, IX, 776; City Court, jurisdiction and powers, 785.

KIP, ISAAC L. Clerk, General Synod of Reformed Church, communication from, fast day, II, 716.

KIPPEN, CAPTAIN. President and Council meet at house of, I, 239.

KIRBY, FRANCES. Murder of, III, 32.

KIRBY, WILLIAM. Convicted of murder, sentence changed to life imprisonment, III, 32.

KIRKER, THOMAS. Speaker, Ohio House of Representatives, communication from, Erie canal, II, 891.

KIRKHAM, HENRY P. Repairs to hospital ships, veto, VII, 792, 929; claim submitted to Board of Claims, 792.

KIRKVILLE. Canal leakage ditch at, veto, VIII, 850.

KIRKWOOD, SAMUEL J. United States Senator, approves appointment of Edwin A. Merritt as collector of New York, VII, 560.

KISSELBURGH, WILLIAM E. Counsel for Justice Hooker, X, 829.

KLEINDINST, GEORGE. Escheat, veto, IX, 815.

KLOCK, JACOB, COLONEL. Letter from, militia losses, II, 93; conditions in Tryon county, 116, 117; claim of, militia services, 262.

KNAPP, SOLOMON. Bond for return of arms, II, 772.

KNEASKERN, MARY. Board of Claims, veto, IX, 119.

KNICKERBOCKER GAS COMPANY. Charter, veto, V, 673.

KNICKERBOCKER LOAN AND TRUST COMPANY, NEW YORK. Charter, veto, VI, 305.

KNIGHT, WILLIAM E. Trustee Binghamton Insane Asylum, charges against, not removed, VII, 443.

KNIGHTS OF HONOR, GRAND LODGE. Charter, veto, VII, 509.

KNIGHTS OF MACCABEES OF THE WORLD. Charter, veto, VII, 506.

KNOWLES, SIR CHARLES. Governor of Cape Breton, dispatches from Duke of Newcastle, I, 410; retaining forces at Albany, 418.

KNOX. Proceedings for collection of Van Rensselaer rent, III, 823; Van Rensselaer leases, description of, IV, 329.

KNOX, JAMES. Escheat, veto, IV, 693.

KNOX, JOHN J. Approves Harvey claim against New York city, VIII, 1162.

KNOX, WILLIAM. Escheat, veto, IV, 693.

KNOX RAILWAY CLAMP COMPANY. Changing name, veto, VI, 189.

KOCH, ELIZABETH. Escheat, veto, X, 588.

KONKAPOT, JACOB. Claim for relief, II, 1120.

KORTRIGHT. Town, leasehold estates in, IV, 332.

KORTRIGHT PATENT. Land in Delaware county, IV, 332.

KOSCIUSKO, THADDEUS (TADEUSZ). General, treatise on horse artillery, II, 639.

KOWALSKI, WILLIAM. Board of Claims, veto, VIII, 626, 727.

KRAFT, HENRY. Canal Department, appropriation for services, veto, IX, 716.

KREISCHER, B., & SONS. Westfield, Richmond county, school supplies, claim, veto, X, 320.

KRENKEL, MARTHA. Administratrix, claim against New York city, veto, VIII, 132, 291, 1036.

KRENKEL, KASMIRE. Estate, claim against New York city, veto, VIII, 132, 291.

L.

LA BAU, NICHOLAS B. Member of Arcade Railway Company, VI, 198.

LABELS. False, veto, VIII, 632.

LABOR. Fixing prices of, II, 25, 46; advance in price of, 349; of immigrants a source of wealth, III, 728; free, following abolition of slavery, V, 713; should be relieved from oppressive burdens, 824; exchange at Castle Garden, VI, 28; efforts to increase wages, when not conspiracy, 122; Eight Hour Law, 369; children, compulsory education, 617; unemployed, VII, 148; railroad riots, 1877, 151; unhappy results of inflation of currency, 311; agriculture underlies all other industries, 312; revival of business, 313; Bureau of Labor Statistics established, 409, 977; employment bureau at Castle Garden, 432; interests considered

LABOR — (*Continued*).

by Governor Hill, VIII, 35; arbitration of disputes between employers and employees, 36; protection of life and limb, 36; payment of wages, 36; industrial interests, 162; child labor, 163, 477; arbitration of differences between capital and labor, 164; boards of arbitration created, 165; trades-unions, general law recommended, 35, 163, 303; regulating hours of, 314, 316; increasing compensation, 315; Saturday half-holiday, 316; Labor Day a holiday, 316; meetings to promote interests of, should be promoted, 318; wages, preference in collection of, 318; investigating commission suggested, 319, 482, 680, 1080; apprentices, 322; day's work, reduction in hours of, 530; coercion of workmen at elections, 667; electioneering by pay envelopes prohibited, 671, 918, 1001; weekly payment of wages, 680, 930; employees, time allowed at elections, 918, 1013; State laborers, regulating pay, 1003; strikes, private detectives, 1073; strikes, use of *posse comitatus*, 1074; monthly payment of wages by railroad companies, 1079; hours of service on railroads, act regulating, IX, 145; strike of railroad switchmen, Buffalo, 1892, 159; Factory Act of 1892, scope of, 163; sweating system, 164, 325; Lehigh Valley Railroad, strike, 1893, 326; industrial classification, census of 1892, 326; general conditions, 1896, 741; university extension, investigations by means of, 742; questions relating to, proposed application of university settlement, 833; foreign, free importation should be discouraged, 833; general act, 1899, X, 7, 48; sweat shops condemned, 8; Eight Hour Law, enforcement, 9; protection of employees, 91; strikes, 1899, 94; employment bureaus should be licensed, 95; employer's liability, 97, 189, 365; railroads, actions by employees for personal injuries, 97; public works, protection of employees, constitutional amendment, 97, 190, 850, 916; State department established, 1901, 189, 365, 461; suggested codification of judicial decisions, 364; proposed boards of arbitration, 365; disputes with capital, courts should have power to interfere as to necessaries, 509; strike, Hudson Valley Electric Railroad, 510; child labor, act of 1903, 515; 1905, 738, 739; employer and employee both entitled to protection, 616; free employment bureaus abolished, 858, 880; minors, limiting hours of, 860; statistical information included in census of 1905, 869; Free Employment Bureau Act of 1905, 869; Free Employment Bureau Act of 1906 limited to first-class cities, 880, 885; hours and prevailing rate of wages, act of 1906, 914; railroads, liability for injuries to employees, 924.

Labor — (*Continued*).

   Vetoes. Statistics, collection of, VII, 409; New York and Brooklyn, protection of female employees, 509; of children, restriction of, compulsory education, VIII, 817; State laborers, wages, regulating pay of, 1041; hours on street railroads, IX, 144; judgments for wages, enforcement, 246; street railroads, hours in certain cities, 266; employment of children in brickyards, 477; stone cutters, etc., filing liens, 623; mechanical employments on Sunday, 623; hours on street surface and elevated railroads, 626; free public employment bureaus, 630; hours in State service, 724; Brooklyn, public works, wages of employees, 733; servile, 793; on public works, deputy factory inspector, 864; Buffalo, labor organizations, no discrimination against, 869; wages, prevailing rate, how determined, 864; employees, safety appliances, X, 52; employer's liability, 305; New York employment agencies, 308; preferences on public works, 424; mediation and arbitration, amending act, 439; Buffalo free employment bureau, appropriation, 554, 564; protection of persons employed on buildings in cities, 760, new bill passed.

Labor Day. Established as a holiday, VIII, 316.

Laborers. Act relating to, I, 11; Governor Sloughter's recommendation concerning wages, 22; impressment of, 374; fixing wages of, II, 25, 46; employed on enlargement of Erie canal, III, 958; resident, preferred on new capitol work, VI, 299; right to strike, IX, 162; appliances for protection of, X, 6, 8; liability of employers, 96, 189, 365.

   Vetoes. State, regulating payment of, VIII, 1041; Brooklyn, fixing rate of wages, IX, 448; wages, preferences in Lockport, 719; actions for wages and materials, 726; working men and women, lectures for, amending act, 807; safety appliances, X, 52; employed on buildings in cities, protection of, 62; employer's liability, 305.

Labor Law. Enacted, 1897, IX, 743; hours of labor, VIII, 316, 317; judicial decisions, 317.

Labor Union. Expulsion of member for service in National Guard, X, 510; protection of members who are also members of National Guard, 510; bribery of representative a misdemeanor, 616.

Lacona. Legalizing sale of bonds, X, 285.

Ladies Deborah Nursery and Child Protectory, New York. Vetoes. Relative to, VII, 267; exempting property from taxation, IX, 232.

Ladies Soldiers' Relief Association. Aid to soldiers, V. 685.

LAFAYETTE, GILBERT DE M. Visits United States, honors to, III, 46; reception of, 85, 110, 133; letter from, 104, 111; portrait, 110, 112, 143; expense of reception, 146; courtesies to family, Yorktown Centennial, VII, 733, 736, 737; portrait and letters, New York Historical Society, 742; letters to Governor George Clinton, noted, 812. See GARDES LAFAYETTE.

LA GRANGE. Defective highway, claim against town for damages, VII, 767.

LAKE AWASTING. Protection of trout in, veto, VII, 131.

LAKE CADARACQUI. Trading-house on, I, 201; French on southern shore of, 241. See ONTARIO.

LAKE CHAMPLAIN. See also CORLAR'S LAKE. Unpatented lands on, petition for grant of, II, 117; territory west of, erection of Clinton county, 271; claim of de Lolbiniere to lands on, 295; loss of vessel on, 770; naval battle on, MacDonough's victory, 803, 808; good roads recommended, connecting with Hudson river, 853; Commission on Canal Communication with Hudson River and Western Lakes, 854; canal connection with St. Lawrence river, 1011; III, 68, 69; fortifications at outlet, cession for, 850; railroad to St. Lawrence river, 866, 964, 983; fishing in, Vermont statute, V, 719; ship canal connecting with St. Lawrence river, VI, 539; railroad to Dannemora, VII, 281.

VETOES. Road to Carthage, VI, 315; ferry from Barber's Point, VIII, 410; ferry from Crown Point, 463; ferry at Ticonderoga, 1099; ferry across, Essex county, X, 953.

LAKE ERIE. French forts on, I, 534, 549; Indian war on, 676; military post at Black Rock, II, 512, 513; canal connection with Hudson river, 675; Perry's victory on, 799; good roads recommended, connecting with Lake Ontario and Hudson river, 853; Commission on Canal Communication with Hudson River, 854; canal communication with Ohio river, 1011, 1046, 1096; III, 75; proposed State road to Hudson river, through southern tier of counties, 81; canal connection with Allegany river via Chautauqua lake, 96; number of vessels on, 460; commerce on, IV, 61. VETOES. Preservation of fish, VIII, 457; — fishing in, X, 61.

LAKE GEORGE. Fort on, I, 584; Indian treaty at, II, 368. VETOES. Islands, preservation of trees and shrubbery, VII, 655; — fishing in, amending Game Law, VIII, 888; battle of, acquiring land to commemorate, reappropriation, X, 423.

LAKE GEORGE BAPTIST ASSOCIATION. Charter, veto, VI, 333.

LAKE MICHIGAN. Canal connection with Illinois river, II, 1011, 1096.

LAKE NEAHTAHWANTA. Fishing through ice, veto, X, 954.

LAKE ONTARIO. Destruction of French vessels on, I, 625, 627; canal to Hudson river, II, 321, 675; good roads recommended, connecting with Lake Erie and Hudson river, 853; canal connection with Erie canal, 965, 1011; III, 68, 69, 166; colonial documents relative to, 1019; fishing in, act relative to, VIII, 432; stocking with whitefish, IX, 192, 335.

VETOES. Stocking with fish, VIII, 75; protection of fish, 627; fishing in, amending Game Law, IX, 798; fishing for sturgeon in, 800; spearing fish in, X, 954.

LAKE ONTARIO SHORE RAILROAD COMPANY. Asks State aid, V, 866.

LAKE PLEASANT. Arms and supplies for, II, 772.

LAKE SACRAMENT. Scouts sent to, I, 396; French and Indians near, movement against, 411.

LAKE ST. FRANCOIS. Terminus of survey of Quebec boundary, I, 755.

LAKE SHORE RAILROAD COMPANY. Asks State aid, VI, 71.

LAKE SUPERIOR. Stannard's Rock, proposed lighthouse on, VII, 46; Grand Marais harbor, proposed harbor of refuge at, 60.

LALOR'S CYCLOPEDIA OF POLITICAL SCIENCE. Quoted, definition of ballot, VIII, 584.

LAMB, ANTHONY, COLONEL. Deputy quartermaster, communication from, Greenbush magazine, II, 713; sent to Niagara frontier, 792; Commissary-General, communication from, improvement of streets about New York arsenal, repairs to Albany arsenal, 895; settlement of claims against United States, 924, 927.

LAMBETH. Archiepiscopal Library, colonial documents in, IV, 183.

LAMONT, DANIEL S. Secretary of War, communication from, dedication of Chickamauga and Chattanooga National Military park, IX, 577.

LAMONT, MRS. Providing for certain payment to, veto, VII, 805.

LANCASTER. Amending charter, veto, VII, 416.

LANCASTER, JOSEPH. Books relating to education, II, 725.

LANCASTRIAN SCHOOLS. Efficiency of, II, 725, 903, 1100; instruction of teachers for, 972; number of, 1820, 1048; incorporation provided for, 1050.

LAND. See REAL ESTATE, LAND GRANTS, STATE LANDS. VETOES. Defining, amending Revised Statutes, VII, 506; in Richmond county, judicial sales, 933.

LAND BOARD. Governor Clinton requests exemption from service on, II, 521.

LAND GRANTS. Revocation of, I, 146; to Palatines, 146; for military service, 598; of certain Indian lands, claimed to be fraudulent, 601, 606, 611, 685, 751; Assembly memorandum relative to Indian lands, 686; by New Hampshire, 756, 758, 765; confirmed, II, 164; Remsen

LAND GRANTS — (*Continued*).

claim, Montgomery county, 261; to Nova Scotia refugees, 308; to western settlers, seizure of land by British, 334; occasioned by establishment of Massachusetts boundary, 351; on condition of settlement, inquiry concerning, 432; gift to Commodore MacDonough, 832, 833; colonial documents relating to, III, 1018; English, bill relative to, veto, X, 450.

LANDLORD AND TENANT. Anti-rent troubles, III, 774, see that title; Rensselaerwyck manor, leases described, 775; disputes between, IV, 141, 233; Van Rensselaer leases, change of tenures, 240; distress for rent abolished, 241, 242, 338; taxation of reserved rents, 242, 338, 357; commutation of leasehold titles, 245; duty of, anti-rent troubles, 307; Van Rensselaer leases, claim of tenants, 338; landlord's title, denial by tenants, 338, 352, 410; ejectment to test validity of Van Rensselaer titles, 412; summary proceedings, veto, VII, 1094.

LAND OFFICE. See COMMISSIONERS OF THE LAND OFFICE.

LANE, J. H. Chairman Executive Committee, Kansas Territory, communication from, expected invasion from Missouri, IV, 864.

LANG, KONRAD, 2D. Escheat, veto, X, 588.

LANGDON, RICHARD. Captain, service in French War, I, 396.

LANGUEDOC. Canal mentioned, I, 728.

LANSDOWNE COLLECTION. British Museum, IV, 183.

LANSING, MR. Treatment of, anti-rent troubles, III, 826.

LANSING, ABRAHAM. Commissioner to examine Oneida Indian claims, report, VI, 663.

LANSING, CHRISTOPHER Y. Private secretary, attests proclamation calling extraordinary session, III, 40.

LANSING, JACOB J., CAPTAIN. Muster master, claim of, II, 151.

LANSING, JOHN. Commissioner to Hartford Convention on Taxation, II, 190.

LANSING, JOHN, JR. Delegate to Federal Constitutional Convention, II, 271; chief justice, correspondence with Governor Jay on Council of Appointment, 480, 483; chancellor, communication from, transcribing court records, 609, 754; court fees, 702; signs cession to United States, III, 140; purchases Blenheim patent, IV, 331.

LANSINGBURGH. Amending charter, police justices, Governor's objections, return of bill for amendment, V, 137.

VETOES. Powers of, II, 402; eligibility to office, VII, 323; repairing Hudson river dock, 366; new ward, sidewalk, repairs, VIII, 991.

LANSINGKILL CREEK. Damages, hearing claims for, veto, VII, 417.

LAPHAM, ELBRIDGE G. Elected United States Senator in place of Roscoe Conkling, resigned, VII, 555.

LARCENY. Petit, punishment of, II, 222, 427, 612; III, 173; from church, death penalty, II, 363; discrimination in punishment of, 598; petit, whipping for, 633; petit, second conviction, large number of, III, 287; when subject to extradition, 938, 1030; IV, 8; petit, increasing money limit, 435, 480, 609; abolishing distinction between grand and petit, 855; by false pretenses, veto, IX, 860.

LARCHMONT MANOR PARK SOCIETY. Exemption from taxation, veto, IX, 431.

LARD. Imitations, regulating manufacture and sale, VII, 700.

LARKIN, JOHN. Notary public, New York, legalizing acts, veto, IX, 812.

LATERAL CANALS. Canal at Salina, II, 1007; statement relative to, III, 304; new canals authorized, 308, 419; connection with Erie canal, 329; not self-supporting, 466, 506, 549, 621, 668, 710, 799; VI, 535, 747; VII, 5, 145; loan for, III, 620; banks authorized to subscribe to loans for, 633; constructed without expectation of immediate revenue, 798; indirect benefits of, 799; connection with Pennsylvania railroads, 901; sale permitted, VI, 540, 749, 796; use as feeders, 749; commission to consider question of disposal, 750; report, 933, VII, 8; new commission created, VI, 933; Genesee Valley, extending time for sale, VII, 217; cause malaria, 517; Chemung and Genesee Valley, drainage, 517; Black River canal not to be sold, 685.

VETOES. Abandoned, drainage of, VII, 412; Chenango, abandoned, De Groat escheat, 643; Genesee Valley, release to adjoining owners, VIII, 463.

LATHROP, AUSTIN. Superintendent of State Prisons, communication from, convict labor, VIII, 644.

LAUGHLIN, JOHN. Senate, 1891, resolution for canal investigation, VIII, 1117.

LAURENS, JOHN. Colonel, order for stores, II, 156; French loan, 160.

LAUTERBACH, EDWARD. Constitutional Convention, 1894, duty of citizen to vote, VIII, 676.

LAW, JONATHAN. Governor of Connecticut, letter from, relative to Indian depredations, I, 355; letter from, declines to join in expense of furnishing provisions to Indians, 378; letter from, relative to agreement for union, 461; communication from, relative to Connecticut troops, 463.

LAW'S DELAY. Commission on, report, X, 516, 620, 621, 628.

LAW OF THE LAND. Includes national treaties, II, 274; meaning of, 466; III, 262; under Federal Constitution, 364.

LAW LIBRARIES. Delhi, appropriation, VII, 219; Elmira, established, 1895, IX, 45; number of, 45.

LAW LIBRARIES — (*Continued*).

VETOES. Judicial districts, appropriation, VII, 81, 220; Canton, appropriation, 82; fourth judicial district, 218; eight judicial district, 220; sixth judicial district, Binghamton, 220; IX, 83; seventh judicial district, Rochester, VII, 220; Court of Appeals judges, 902; VIII, 856; Delhi, purchase of Justice Murray's library for, 539; fifth judicial district, purchase of books, 856; Court of Appeals, Rochester, purchase of books, 856; Syracuse, purchase of books, 856; Supreme Court, Newburg, appropriation, 856; IX, 769; sixth judicial district, Elmira, establishing, 45, 130; library established, 1895, 45; fifth judicial district, Oswego, 130; Elmira, appropriation, 769; first department, Appellate Division, and trial courts, 770; Kingston, purchase of set of Federal Cases, 776; New York court of general sessions, custodian, X, 390; New York court of general sessions, 475; Utica, librarian, increasing compensation, 519; Albany, Court of Appeals, 549; Court of Appeals, Syracuse, 550; Kingston, rebinding books, 556; Elmira, books and rebinding, 556; Utica, books and rebinding, 556; Delhi, books and rebinding, 556; sixth judicial district, Follett, 784; Court of Appeals, Rochester, librarian, 952.

LAWS. See STATUTES.

LAW SCHOOLS. Number of, VI, 618. VETOES. Harvard University and Yale College graduates, relative to, VII, 416; — Buffalo, relative to, VIII, 1038.

LAWLOR, THOMAS. VETOES. State Board of Audit, VII, 938; State Board of Claims, 1121.

LAWYER, GEORGE A. Counsel for State Bar Association at trial of Justice Hooker, X, 829.

LAWRENCE (Kansas). Center of conflict over slavery, IV, 862.

LAWRENCE, JOHN. Judge-Advocate, claim, settlement of, II, 150; seat in Senate declared vacant, 310; chosen United States Senator, 384; resignation of, 469.

LAWRENCE, HENRY. Assault on, IV, 705, 727.

LAWRENCE, PETER. Legislative employee, compensation, veto, VII, 372.

LAWRENCE, RICHARD. Agent to dispense aid to St. Domingo refugees, II, 405, 413.

LAWRENCE, THOMAS J. Corporal, 22d Regiment, National Guard, permanent injuries, damages, appropriation, veto, VII, 465, 910.

LAWRENCE, WILLIAM F. Conveyance of land under water, Yonkers, veto, VIII, 53.

LAWRENCE'S TAVERN. Transaction at, anti-rent troubles, III, 826.

LAWTON, ELIJAH H. Commissioner, repairing highway, Cattarangus reservation, veto, VII, 476.

LAY, R. G. Canal Department, appropriation for services, veto, IX, 716.

LAYCOCK LUMBER COMPANY. Board of Claims, veto, VIII, 1166.

LAZARETTO. On Bedlow's and Governor's island, II, 381.

LEAD. French furnish Indians, I, 248; deposits in New York, III, 1036; canal tolls on, IV, 18; bounties on, 69.

LEASES. Rensselaerwyck manor, leases described, III, 775; disputes between landlord and tenant, IV, 141, 233; Van Rensselaer, change of tenures, 240, 307; distress for rent abolished, 241, 242, 653; taxation of reserved rent, 242, 653; agricultural, limiting term of, 244, 356, 409, 653; commutation of leasehold titles, 245; in Rensselaerwyck manor, description of, 329; Van Rensselaer, when conveys a fee, 354; manorial, quantity of lands in 1848, 408; disadvantages of leasehold estates, 559; Indian lands, act of Congress, VI, 704; of land for oyster beds, IX, 194.

VETOES. "Campbell Leases," tenants, protecting rights under, VI, 584; Allegany reservation, pipe line, VII, 73; termination on taking land for public use, new contract, 1015.

LEARY, ARTHUR. Nominated as quarantine commissioner, VIII, 520.

LEATHER. See INSPECTORS OF SOLE LEATHER. Inspector of, III, 315.

LECHMERE, CHARLES. Deputy keeper, State paper office, aid to Mr. Brodhead, IV, 182.

LECOMPTON CONSTITUTION. Kansas, New York opposes, V, 61.

LECOUTEULX ST. MARY'S INSTITUTION FOR THE IMPROVED INSTRUCTION OF DEAF-MUTES, BUFFALO. VETOES. Deficiency appropriation, VII, 470; new buildings, VIII, 888.

LEDYARD, ISAAC. Health officer, letter from, II, 520.

LEE, ARTHUR. Presents to Lord Dartmouth petition of Continental Congress, I, 770.

LEE, EDMUND C. Stenographer, Assembly committees, 1889, appropriation, veto, VIII, 839.

LEE, FRANCIS LIGHTFOOT. Member of Congress, letter from, II, 18.

LEE, ROBERT. Prisoner, Fort Niagara, affidavit, II, 793.

LEE, ROBERT E. General, invasion of Pennsylvania, V, 544; surrenders to Grant at Appomatox, 676.

LEE, SIR WILLIAM. Lord chief justice, opinion in Paterson case, factors, III, 88.

LEECH, DAVID C. Cancellation of tax sale, veto, X, 317.

LEET, THOMAS R. Board of Claims, veto, VIII, 1039.

LE GAL, EUGENE. Colonel, 55th Regiment, supplies from Union Defense Committee, VII, 501.

LEGAL TENDER. Lords of Trade think bills of credit should not be, I, 558; Assembly expresses opposite view, 559; restricted use of paper currency, 773.

LEGALIZING ACTS. Indian reservations, villages, school districts, proceedings by municipal officers, VI, 704; New York Elevated Railroad Company, acquisition of property, 716; defects should be specified in bill, VIII, 943, 978, 1089, 1123, 1156; IX, 59, 258; Baldwinsville water bonds, VIII, 1026; should contain saving clause, 355; should not affect pending litigation, IX, 61, 231; sale of bonds, Lacona, X, 285; could be avoided by greater care of local authorities, 518; Syracuse local assessments, 634; services of captain of the port and harbor masters, VII, 1048; legislative printing, Bloomingdale Asylum investigation, VIII, 793; Assembly select committee, 1887, employment of counsel, 976; contracts, Wayne County Agricultural Society and town of Galen, 1148; highway commissioners, Little Falls, 1156; Madison Forks Obituary Society, acquisitions of land, 1163; New York, 31st Assembly district, ratifying nominations, X, 130; town meetings, legalizing action of boards of supervisors in changing time, 236; Warwick union free school district, legalizing bonds, 283; East Aurora bonds, 284; Utica, legalizing Central Advance school bonds and Mary street school bonds, 285; Brockport, special election for establishment of sewer system, 518; Cobleskill, election for public improvements, 892.

VETOES. Bounties, V, 673; special municipal contract, 730; Hopkinton Manufacturing Company, VI, 169; Cohoes, construction of sewer, 192; Buffalo street improvements, 221; Schenectady superintendent of the poor, election, 424; Seymour, justice of the peace, 479; New York police court, assistant clerk, 564; Shawangunk, resolution fixing place of town meeting, 581; Morristown, railroad aid bonding proceedings, 583; Gilbert, notary public, 690; New Hartford, town meeting, 701; dower, releasing inchoate rights of, 820; Elmira common council, 845; Ontario, town meeting, 1031; Alden, town meeting, 1034; Cohoes, State and county taxes, 1035; Guion, justice of the peace, VII, 44; Allegany reservation pipe line lease, 73; Cohoes taxes, 133; Bath excise commissioners, 178; Saratoga Springs, cemeteries, purchase of land for, 391; Noyes, justice of the peace, 412; Horton, justice of the peace, 413; Weller, justice of the peace, 413; Livingston county election, 415; Cornell,

LEGALIZING ACTS, VETOES — (*Continued*).

notary public, 507; Whitney, notary public, 507; Williams, justice of the peace, 507; New York common council, 509; Erie county board of supervisors, compensation of court officers, 538; Canandaigua, local tax, reimbursement for loss of property, 569; New York, Kehr relief, 601; Brooklyn, Sackett street improvement, 605; Brooklyn, storage reservoir, extra compensation, 617; Sangerfield, refunding surety for payment on supervisor's bond, 754; charters of certain medical and charitable corporations, 937; Ulster county, legalizing bond resolution of board of supervisors, 994; St. Paul's Methodist Episcopal church, Onondaga Valley, title to land, 1100; First Presbyterian church, Batchellerville, acts of trustees, 1106; Chautauqua county, board of supervisors, fishing in Lake Erie, VIII, 79; Wellsville, police justice, 132; Wells, notary public, 291; justices of the peace, 328, 639, 943; X, 163; notaries public, VIII, 334; X, 813; commissioners of excise, Salem, VIII, 354; Stier, notary public, 387; Reevs, commissioner of deeds, 518; Oswegatchie, town meeting, 885; boards of supervisors, confirming audits of accounts, 886; Phelps, town meeting, 887; Port Chester, sewer bonds, 942; Howe, justice of the peace, 943; Groton Cemetery Association, use of another name, 974; Hudson board of education, 978; Buffalo, Guilford street excavation, 1038; foreclosure by advertisement, 1039; Cattaraugus county, division of South Valley, 1089; Clifton Springs, election of officers, 1122; York, assessments for taxes, IX, 59; Swikehard, commissioner of deeds, 150; Kings county and Brooklyn, soldiers and sailors' memorial arch, 211; Oneida county board of supervisors, audits of accounts, 231; Penn Yan, Bellis, police justice, 258; Sherman, justice of the peace, Marion, 346; Cantwell, notary public, 365; Jefferson county board of supervisors, creation of school commissioner districts, 365; Prime, commissioner of deeds, Yonkers, 368; Curtis, justice of the peace, 369; Amsterdam, assessments for local improvements, 374; veterinary practitioners, 376; Watertown, local assessments, duplicate bill, 451; Long Island City, legalizing certain claims, 468; Newburgh, Water street paving bonds, 719; notary public, Green, 720; Bagg, justice of the peace, West Turin, filing oath and bond, 725; Hale and Reid, justices of the peace, Johnstown, 725; Broome county board of supervisors, 795; McMaster, legalizing claim against State, 797; New York, East River park, legalizing laying out, 808; New York, 13th civil district court, appointment of at-

LEGALIZING ACTS, VETOES — (*Continued*).

tendants and employees, 809; Larkin, notary public, New York, 812; legislative resolutions, providing for certain, printing, 814; Oyster Bay, town election, 1897, 818; West Turin election districts, 818; New York district court justices, 872; Brooklyn fire department, appointments, 874; New York, clerks, employees, legalizing transfer and assignment from consolidated municipalities, 874; Steele, justice of the peace, X, 62; justices of the peace, Orange, Rockland and Sullivan counties, 62; Richardson, justice of the peace, Chesterfield, 63; appointments, fire commissioners, Brooklyn and Long Island City, 178; conveyances, Hamburg Cemetery Association, 256; New York permits for projections on certain streets, 323; Bronx borough, opening Pelham avenue, 326; New Rochelle public improvement bonds, 636; Newark Valley, water bonds, 702; Syracuse assessment, 705; Camden, legalizing proceedings for electric light system, 708; various items of public printing, 797; taxes, Utica, 806, 819; union free school district No. 1, Luzerne and Hadley, relative to new site and school building, 811; aid to Bridgewater turnpike, New Hartford, 811; Boughton, coroner, Wyoming county, 813; McCormick, James C., notary public, 813; William McCormick, justice of the peace, Potsdam, 813; Stockport, Haynes claim, 814; Tibbit, justice of the peace, Fabius, 948; O'Toole, commissioner of deeds, 948; Hoffman, sheriff, legalizing accounts, 956; Simon, commissioner of deeds, 958; Sandy Hill, trustees, borrowing money, 960.

LEGGETT, JAMES. Service of process on, Van Rensselaer rent, III, 825.

LEHIGH VALLEY RAILROAD COMPANY. Strike of employees, 1893, IX, 326, 594.

LEITH, SARAH E. Court of Claims, highway damages, veto, X, 326.

LEGISLATIVE COUNCIL. How constituted, I, 6, 9, 13; relation of, to colonial Legislature, 9; re-established under Governor Sloughter, 18.

LEGISLATIVE COUNSEL. See COUNSEL TO LEGISLATURE.

LEGISLATIVE LAW. Enacted, 1892, IX, 28.

LEGISLATIVE POWER. See also DELEGATION OF LEGISLATIVE POWER. Exercised by Dutch West India Company, I, 1; by Governor and Council, 1, 13; people demand share in, 1; exercised by Eight Men, 2; petition to Court of Assizes for representative government, 2; Assembly granted, power of, 6; revenue bills, 8; temporary laws, 8; Assembly's share in legislation, 43; controversy between Governor and Assembly concerning, 110; not subject to royal prerogative, 730; how to be exercised, II, 26; where vested, 42; control of private

LEGISLATIVE POWER — (*Continued*).

property, 581, 583; dissolution of marriage, 947; modification of will, 1036; dissolution of corporations, 1082; interference with private rights, III, 263; creating corporations, 521; defining "resident" under elective franchise, 772; does not usually include appointments to office, 1002; removal of officers, 1021; nature of, IV, 231; proceedings in law and equity, alteration of, 367; submitting act to people for approval, 475; creating corporations by special act, 513; police justice, 685; general scope of, 709; prohibition of liquor traffic, 801; cannot abridge qualifications of voters, 825; investigations, V, 38; when cannot appoint to office, VI, 76; Legislature cannot appoint successors, 186; bank failure, deposit of public funds, cannot direct reimbursement of officer, 334; when cannot legalize election, Clute case, 425; cannot appoint justices of the peace, 480; cannot determine election of town officers, 1031, 1034; cannot appoint governors of Rensselaer House of Industry, 1033; cannot appoint New York city commissions, VII, 107; cannot appoint public administrator in New York, 108; cannot appoint members of Brooklyn commissions, 126; continuing in office excise commissioners after failure to give bond, 179; cannot appoint overseers of highways, 208; cannot appoint town auditors, 216; cannot appoint commissioners of city and county hall, Buffalo, 317; cannot direct local tax to reimburse officer for loss of property, 569; cannot interfere with patents, 571, 591; cannot deprive Federal courts of jurisdiction, 574; cannot extend powers of surrogate, 615; cannot interfere with jurisdiction of Supreme Court as to insolvent corporations, 798; vested in people, VIII, 143; apportionment and enumeration, power is a continuing one, 156, 299, 484; when may annul or dissolve a corporation, 204; restriction as to limiting qualifications of voters, 566; cannot authorize cemetery association to take charge of adjoining burial grounds without consent, 712; limitation as to legalizing acts, 943; election of officers, property qualifications cannot be imposed on voters, 1117; may regulate sale of oleomargarine, IX, 320; cannot revive claim or waive limitation, 370; prescribing courses of study in schools, 616; may increase, diminish or modify Attorney-General's powers, X, 187; forest preserve, land acquired by State under tax sale, power to authorize cancellation of tax, veto, 263; when cannot direct a refund of local tax, 453; may provide for buildings and accommodations for courts, 768.

LEGISLATIVE RECORD. Printing and distributing, veto, VIII, 891.

LEGISLATURE (Colony). Established, I, 1; Duke of York rejects propositions for Assembly, 3; petition for Assembly, 4; letter from Werden to Brockholls, relative to Assembly, 4; Assembly promised,

LEGISLATURE (Colony) — (*Continued*).

5; Assembly granted, 5; powers of Assembly, 6; Governor's power in relation to bills, 7; freedom of debate in, 8; first Assembly called, 9; first legislative council, 9; Governor's opening speech, 10; second Assembly, 12; Leisler's Assembly, 15, 16; prorogation, 7, 18; powers of, how distributed, 43; Governor's relation to, general note, 253; each part has equal authority, 661; character and powers of, 730; II, 2; proceedings, documents relating to, III, 1018.

LEGISLATURE (State). Governor's communications to, II, 2; first election of, 6; first, meets at Kingston, 7; IX, 688; act regulating election of, II, 10; sudden adjournment of, 15; meets at Poughkeepsie, 17, 43, 50, 105, 132, 146, 163, 182, 281, 348; IX, 688; ratifies Articles of Confederation, II, 18; powers of, how affected by veto, 21; no power to establish conventions or councils of safety, 27; provision relating to meeting of, 39; cannot designate supervisors to act as assessors, 41; only source of legislative power, 42; action on Vermont controversy, 47, 51; cannot delegate power to determine amount of taxes, 61, 95; first pardon granted by, 68; resolutions on export of provisions, 72; declines to permit exportation of flour or wheat, 74; meets at Kingston, 75, 96, 186; pardons Thomas Cummings, convicted of treason, 82; meets at Albany, 87, 114, 289, 301, 322, 386; cannot delegate power to Council of Safety, 113; recommends thanksgiving day as suggested by Congress, 152; recommends fast day as suggested by Congress, 170; denies power of Congress to erect Vermont, 179; action on communication from Superintendent Morris, 180; requests loan of gunpowder from Congress, 181; proposes convention to revise Federal system of government, 194, 270; meets at New York, I, 780; II, 195, 217, 251, 263, 304, 311, 319, 323, 351, 358, 379; IX, 688; condemns British methods of conducting war, II, 206; cannot exercise judicial powers, 249, 250, 581, 583, 665; IV, 772; cannot vacate judgment, II, 250; annual meeting of, 252, 448, 960; V, 251; consents that Governor leave State on military service, II, 271; cannot construe or limit national treaty, 274; presidential electors, houses unable to agree on method of choosing, 299; Senators and Representatives in Congress cannot hold seat in, 310; apportionment under first census, 312; chooses Presidential electors, 323; declines to concur in Virginia resolutions proposing amendments, 367; to meet in Albany except in special cases, 397; duty to maintain militia, 399; declares its relations to Federal government, 428, 429; address to President, relations with France, 445; action on death of Washington, 462; power

Legislature (State) — (Continued).

to grant exclusive privileges, 466; convention to reorganize, 468, 511; constitutional amendment, presidential electors and elections, 513; report of joint committee on education, 560; urges congressional aid for defense of New York, 569; cannot prefer creditors, 583; address to President Jefferson, 624; President Jefferson's reply, 626; apportionment of, 651, 1047; III, 133, 567; IV, 250; prorogued by Governor Tompkins, II, 708; III, 1005; appoints day of humiliation, fasting and prayer, II, 715; cannot evade veto power by adopting concurrent resolution instead of passing a bill, 740; commends gallant conduct of naval officers, 780; proposed session in New York, 805; protests against terms of peace proposed by Great Britain, 826; adopts resolutions of thanks and presents swords to several army and navy officers, 832; resolutions thanking American officers for gallant services, 859, 860; short sessions recommended, 1014; answer to Governor's speech discontinued, 1014; resolution protesting against extension of slavery, 1023, 1041; IV, 814; cannot interfere with vested rights of property, II, 1036; apportionment of 1821 based on United States census, 1047; power to call constitutional convention, 1056; Governor's reply to request for information, 1061; who not eligible to, 1062, 1063; disapproves Maryland's plan as to proceeds of public land, 1080; power to dissolve corporation, 1082; election and official term under second Constitution, III, 1; power to pass bill over veto, 2; disapproves Pennsylvania proposition as to national banks, 13; resolutions recommending a protective tariff, 24; resolutions protesting against canal boat licenses or tonnage duties claimed by United States, 49; not bound by precedents, 194; proceedings on death of Governor Clinton, 220; interference with private rights, 263; committee on visitation of State prisons, 290; miniature, for children at Chittenango Polytechnic, 299; disappearance of lobby, 313; recommends revolutionary pensions, 388; urges reform in national militia system, 406; denies power of a State to nullify acts of Congress, 429; duty to suppress lotteries, 526, 567; resolutions on abolition of slavery, 582; action on death of former Governor Yates, 645; pledges support to national government on New Brunswick boundary question, 758; cannot control Governor's discretion in extradition cases, 778; resolutions on public lands, 819, 903; proceedings on death of President Harrison, 914; declares that stealing a slave in Virginia is an extraditable crime, 937; IV, 8; responsibility for enactment of laws, III, 973; to keep

LEGISLATURE (State) — (*Continued*).

journal, 975; when members not eligible to civil appointment, 1001; appointing power not usually vested in, 1002; removal of officers, 1021; abrogation of contract, 1022; when may not rescind action of predecessor, 1024; disagrees with Governor of Virginia, extradition case, 1030; printing proceedings of, IV, 32; limiting power over appropriations, 54; removal of judicial officers, procedure on, 55, 109; favors a reduction of letter postage, the abolition or better regulation of the franking privilege, and a more rigid economy in the Post-Office Department, 84; majority responsible for legislation, 105; apportionment, 1846, 250; urges Congress to revise militia laws, 283; action on death of former Governor Wright, 384; resolutions, appropriations for rivers and harbors, 393; resolution to investigate manorial titles, 413; invites General Taylor to visit New York, 420; journals and documents, international exchanges, 466; recommends branch mint in New York, 479; action on death of John C. Calhoun, 516; cannot annul judgment, 535; resolutions requesting extraordinary session, 578; attends opening of New York Crystal Palace, 709; recall of bills from Governor, 751; members of, compensation, V, 37, 41, 42; VI, 400, 550, 726; committees, compensation and expenses of, V, 36, 41; resolutions, militia, arms and organization, 53; resolutions recommending lake harbor improvement, 71; lobbying, 95, 194; resolutions for appointment of Connecticut boundary commissioners, IV, 863; V, 112; resolutions inviting Governors of Kentucky, Tennessee and Ohio to visit Albany, 203; duration of session, 251; reducing number of employees, 293; approves President's message on secession movement, 306; tenders hospitalities to President-elect Lincoln, 333; thanks Union Army, 439; resolutions on adjustment of quotas, 457; resolutions on war claims, 1812, 458; resolutions recommending constitutional amendment prohibiting slavery, 616; ratifies Thirteenth Amendment, 616, 623; resolutions on assault of Secretary Seward, 649; resolutions on death of President Lincoln, 677; ratifies Fourteenth Amendment, 744; resolutions on death of ex-Governor Hunt, 793; should not interfere in New York local affairs, VI, 32; ratifies Fifteenth Amendment, resolution rescinded, 50; resolution authorizing reduction of canal tolls, 107; cannot bind successors, 186; recommends repeal of Federal income tax, 254; Centennial Celebration Committee, provision for, 302; proposed amendment, prison management, 355; purity of legislation, 391; removing limitation on length

Legislature (State) — (*Continued*).

    of session, 400; action on death of Samuel F. B. Morse, 444; action on death of Chief Justice Chase, 566; duty to maintain common schools, 617, 945; action on death of ex-President Fillmore, 663; resolutions against inflation of currency, 670; resolutions on Louisiana disturbance, 774; resolutions for Commission on New York Harbor Encroachments, 776; joint committee to investigate canals, 809; interference with local government, 838; resolutions on specie payments, 975; VII, 150; resolution urging Federal legislation concerning emigration, VI, 1001; action on bills after veto, 1003; resolution reducing canal tolls, VII, 7; vacancies in office, power to declare, 45; resolution fixing date of occupancy of new capitol, 175; first occupation of new capitol, 269, 271; formal observances on removal to new capitol, 270; resolution as to park at Niagara Falls, 300; resolutions congratulating people on resumption of specie payments, 312; members of, ineligible to certain other offices, 322; X, 46; resolutions on death of former Governor Dix, VII, 329; joint committee on taxation, 1880, 422; railroad investigating committee, report, 434; first simultaneous election with Governor, 1879, 438; action on death of Chief Judge Church, 449; resolutions requesting congressional action on pleuro-pneumonia, 537; meaning of term as applied to adjournment, 669; contested elections, legislation needed, 723; biennial sessions, 728; IX, 753, 847; responsibility should not be transferred to future Legislatures, VII, 795; determining elections and qualifications of members, 918; VIII, 983; investigations as to election of members, VII, 919; results of unnecessary recesses, 939; requests Congress to establish quarantine fees at New York, 968; resolution prohibiting political tests in employment on new capitol, 982; pleuro-pneumonia, Federal legislation requested, 990; legislative counsel, VIII, 25, 125, 298, 351, 456, 459, 462, 478, 620; IX, 210; when discretion in passing bills may not be reviewed by Governor, VIII, 85, 89; denying opponents of bill an opportunity to be heard, 102; extraordinary session, 1885, 132, 133; constitutional duty may be performed by successor, 142, 156, 299, 484, 1062; IX, 4; memorial services on death of former Governor Seymour, VIII, 196; power to annul or dissolve a corporation, 204; may interpret its own enactments, 264; should not assume to settle questions of title to office, 274, 355; expense of enacting laws, 346; inequalities of representation under apportionment of 1879, 494; appoints joint committee to attend Centennial Celebration

LEGISLATURE (State) — (*Continued*).

of New York's ratification of Federal Constitution, 506; extraordinary session, 1888, 643; contested elections, transferring powers to courts, proposed amendment rejected, 982; investigating committees, traveling and incidental expenses, 1890, 989; asserts constitutionality of ballot bill, 1890, 1049; resolutions accepting amount refunded under United States direct tax, 1107; deadlock over canal investigation, 1891, 1117; IX, 26; of 1892, in political accord with executive, 2; judicial power, should not affect pending litigation, 61; membership increased, 1894, 155; resolution requesting Federal statute making imitation dairy products transported to another State subject to its police regulations, 321; should not interfere with pending litigation, 429; memorial services on death of former Governor Flower, 535; joint committee, 1895, to investigate State departments, bureaus and institutions, 544; prison labor amendment, 1895, 550; joint committee to attend dedication of Chickamauga and Chattanooga National Military park, 576; joint committee to attend Cotton States Exposition, 582; vote of majority necessary to pass bill, 618; of 1896, first composed of 200 members, 644; procedure, commission on, 1895, 676; first meeting at Albany, 1797, 688; extraordinary session, July, 1898, 876; appropriation for expenses, 884; joint committee on taxation, 1899, X, 3, 37; extraordinary session, May, 1899, 64; joint committee on revision bills, 1900, 107; custom as to reading emergency certificates, 145; cost of, 1900, 182; employees, act of 1901, 183; comparative statement of appropriations, 1893-4, 1901-2, 464; joint committee on reception of Prince Henry, 479; joint educational investigating committee, 1903, 537, 604; joint committee to investigate life insurance companies, 825; trial of Justice Hooker, 827; removal of judges, should determine what constitutes cause, 829; Apportionment Act of 1906 unconstitutional, 852; new act passed, 1907, 852; persons appearing before committees, notice of employment, 904; 1906, commended by Governor Higgins, 931.

VETOES. Appointment of bank commissioners by, III, 1000; employees and investigating committees, VII, 133; VIII, 107; index to documents, VII, 225; employees, compensation, 372; proceedings on removal from old to new capitol, printing, 492; bill file boards for State officers, 493; file boards for Assembly clerk, 494; expenses of committees, appropriation, 586; investigating committee, services of counsel, 647; expenses of committees, reception of Massachusetts delegates, 779; expenses of

LEGISLATURE (State), VETOES — (*Continued*).
committees, compensation of witnesses, 779; employees, 806; VIII, 639; contingent expenses, VII, 903; compensation of certain officers after adjournment, 1078; VIII, 106; investigating committees, composing and printing testimony, VII, 1079; legislative printing, defining, 1120; printing Clerk's Manual, VIII, 118; enumeration bill, 134; printing, continuing appropriation of 1885, 252; legislative printing, 1886, appropriation, 255; investigating committees, expenses, 419; investigating committees, expenses, reappropriation, 420; committees, deficiency appropriation, counsel, stenographers, printing testimony and contingent expenses, 549, 550, 551; proposed appointment of quarantine commissioners by, 555; furniture for clerk's rooms, appropriation, 841; clerks, advances, purchase of file boards, 857; printing and distributing, 1889, 891; contingent expenses, additional appropriation, 1037; printing, 1037; officers and employees, compensation, IX, 802; legalizing resolutions relative to printing, 814; clerk's books, stationery, etc., X, 793; parliamentary rules and precedents, revision, 795; contingent expenses, appropriation, 933.

LE HEUP, PETER. Letter from, I, 214; suggested as colonial agent, 215; agent at London, communication from, 219; reappointed agent, 233; letter from, relative to Triennial Assembly Act, 271.

LEISLER, JACOB. Assumes executive authority in colony, I, 14, 18; issues writs for Assembly, pref. vi, 14, 15, 18; Assembly meets, records lost, 15; second meeting, 16; convicted of treason, 21; suggested reprieve of, Assembly declines to act, 21; execution, 22; official service, I, pref. ix.

LEISLER'S ASSEMBLY. See LEISLER, JACOB.

LELAND, C. R. Attorney for Seneca Indians, IV, 291; communication from, relative to Indian elections, 291.

LEMMON, JONATHAN. Brings slaves to New York, IV, 809, 860; action concerning slaves, decision, V, 61.

LEMON, ROBERT. Chief clerk, State paper office, aid to Mr. Brodhead, IV, 182.

LEMONADE. Composition of, VIII, 354.

LENG, MARY. Claim against Buffalo, veto, X, 806.

LENOX (New York). VETOES. Town auditors, creating board, VI, 435; extending union school district boundaries, VIII, 130; reimbursement for bridge over Douglass State ditch, IX, 817.

LENOX FARMERS AND MECHANICS' ASSOCIATION. Charter, veto, VI, 451.

LENOX LIBRARY. Report, VI, 261, 415.

LENT, MR. Sale of land to Federal government, II, 628.

LENWAY, WILLIAM A. Canal Department, appropriation for services, veto, IX, 716.

LEONARD, DANIEL I. Employed to serve process, anti-rent troubles, III, 824; assault on, 825; affidavit by, 829.

LEONARD, JAMES H. Bond for return of arms, II, 775.

LEONARD, STEPHEN B. Postmaster at Owego, removal of, II, 1072.

LE ROY. VETOES. Aid to Utica and Black River Railroad Company, amending act, VI, 92; trustees, additional powers, VII, 337; Oatka Hose Company, charter, 806, 877.

LEVY MONEY. Veto of bill for, I, 59.

LEVY, BENJAMIN C. Court of Claims, veto, X, 309.

LEWIS, COLONEL. Speech of, St. Regis Indians, II, 343, 345.

LEWIS, BENJAMIN. Seneca Indian, pipe line lease, veto, VII, 73.

LEWIS, FRANCIS. Letter from, clothing for New York troops, II, 91.

LEWIS, MORGAN. Account of, II, 124; Deputy Quartermaster-General, letter from, public contracts, 208; Governor and portrait, 545.

1804, November. Opening speech, II, 545; presidential election, 545; Twelfth Amendment ratified, 546; Massachusetts plan of congressional apportionment, 546; Senator Armstrong appointed Minister to France, 547; New York prison damaged by fire, 547; capital punishment, 547; revision of Criminal Code, 548; fortifying New York, 550; education, 550; New York Free School Society, 551; common school fund, 551, 555, 560; North Carolina resolution, importation of slaves, 552; intrusions on Cayuga Indian land, 553; carriages in highways, 554; absconding debtors, 554; publication of statutes in newspapers, 555; trustee of Columbia College, 559; Kentucky amendment, jurisdiction of Federal courts, 560; aid to New York Hospital, 561; Hudson river improvement, 562; militia appointments, 563; reviving Comptroller's office, 565.

VETOES. Libels, II, 551; St. Ann's church, Brooklyn, sale of property, 561; Shaler relief, 563; New York Marine Hospital, charter, 565.

1806, January. Opening speech, II, 567; threatening aspect of national affairs, 568; providing for defense of New York city, 568; public health, 570; militia, 571; scarcity of drummers, 572; finances, 573; debts due State, 574; turnpike companies, 574; auctioneers, 574; Arnold murder case, 575; revision of Criminal Code, 577; Williams murder case, 578; botanic garden, 579; beacon on Staten Island, 586;

LEWIS, MORGAN, 1806 — (*Continued*).

     Georgia resolutions, 586; trespasses on Onondagas' lands, 586; Indian attorney, 587; national affairs, 587; Francisco Son murder case, 588; Tennessee resolution, 589.

   VETOES. Smith, conveyance by, II, 580; dower, 581; Reynolds relief, 582; death penalty, 583; Newburgh Aqueduct Association, charter, 584; relative to crimes, 589; Hollenbeck free road, 591; Westchester county, highways, 592; turnpike road inspectors, 593; actions, small causes, amendatory, 594.

   1807, January. Opening speech, II, 595; commercial growth of State, 596; agriculture, 597; common school fund, 598; revision of Criminal Code, 598; needed reform in justices' courts, 599; militia, 600; New Jersey boundary, 601; reply to criticisms, 604; purchase of Cayuga Indian land, 605, 607; Maryland and New Jersey resolutions, 606; Kentucky resolutions, 606; communication from Vermont relative to Canadian boundary, 606; purchase of Oneida land, 607; purchase of ordnance and ammunition, 608; communication from Chancellor Lansing, transcribing records of court, 609; changing punishment of petit larceny, 612; succeeded by Governor Tompkins, 616; leasehold estates, IV, 333; official service, I, pref. xii.

   VETOES. Punishment of crimes, II, 602; forfeited and unappropriated lands, 603; Columbia College, 610; lottery insurance, 613.

LEWIS, REUBEN. Assembly, member of select committee on anti-rent troubles, IV, 328.

LEWIS AND CLARK CENTENNIAL EXPOSITION. Expenses of Commission, appropriation, veto, X, 799; report, 897.

LEWISBOROUGH. Public roads in, veto, VI, 589.

LEWIS COUNTY. Militia from, 1812, II, 743; defense of, 744; silk culture in, III, 945; land in, State park, VI, 629; boundaries relocated, VII, 720; timbered lands, acquisition by State, 722; average excise license fees, 1889, VIII, 687; unpaid taxes, sales under special act, 749; highways, cost of labor system, 1892, IX, 200; insane, care of, county and State systems compared, 228.

   VETOES. Highways, VI, 193; Deer river, water supply, VII, 505; rejected taxes, reassessmennt, 664; establishing Herkimer county boundary, appropriation, 783; Bonaparte creek, public highway, 934; bridge over Black river, VIII, 292; one superintendent of

LEWIS COUNTY, VETOES — (*Continued*).
the poor, 461; Oswegatchie river improvement, 848; highway, No. 4 to Stillwater reservoir, repair, 851; sales for nonpayment of taxes, IX, 804; Herkimer county boundary, survey, 856; Castorland dyke, Croghan road, repairing and improving, X, 570.

LEWIS ON EMINENT DOMAIN. Quoted, compensation required, X, 761.

LEWISTON. Militia in service at, II, 736; burned by British, 791; Alexander McLeod arrested at, III, 933.

LEWISTON SCHOOL FUND. Amount of, II, 1099.

LEXINGTON. Battle of, I, 765.

LEXINGTON AVENUE BAPTIST CHURCH, NEW YORK. Canceling assessment on opening portion of Lexington avenue, veto, IX, 809.

LEXINGTON AND MAYSVILLE TURNPIKE ROAD. President's veto of, III, 391, 464.

LEXOW, CLARENCE. Senate, 1894, New York Park Commission bill, IX, 435.

LEYDEN. Arms and supplies for, II, 775.

L'HOMMEDIEU, EZRA. Commissioner to Hartford Convention on Taxation, II, 190; commissioner on purchase of Oneida lands, 519; Senate, negotiates purchase of Cayuga land, 605; negotiates purchase of Oneida land, 607; receives grant of Oneida land, VI, 666; Regent, death of, II, 707.

LIBEL. Milford case, I, 180, 183; alleged publication of, against government, 499; act relating to, veto, II, 551.

LIBERIA, AFRICA. Negro colonization in, IV, 621; republican government in, 622.

LIBERTY. Spirit of, indestructible, II, 11.

LIBERTY NORMAL INSTITUTE. Amending charter, veto, VII, 935; VIII, 130.

LIBRARY. Proposal to establish in New York, I, 234; room to be provided by city authorities, 235; in academies, III, 654; Royal, at The Hague, examination of, IV, 174; State paper office, London, 177; British Museum, 182; Archiepiscopal, Lambeth, 183; Royal, Paris, colonial documents in, 188; Astor, 428; Canadian Parliamentary, destruction of, books for, 573; Congressional, destruction of, 613; in State prisons, V, 270; at New York Soldiers' Depot, 635; Chicago Law, destroyed, New York's donation, VI, 364; free, encouraging growth of, VIII, 290; trusts for, act of 1892, IX, 21; value in educational system, 829; traveling, sketch of, 829.

VETOES. Corning, acquiring property, fixing annual election, VI, 691; Sing Sing prison, appropriation, VII, 483; Auburn prison,

Library, Vetoes — (*Continued*).

    appropriation, 484; Clinton prison, appropriation, 484, 920; Senate and Assembly, removal to new capitol, 581; medical, Homeopathic Insane Asylum, 786; sixth judicial district, use of books, 807; Darwin R. Barker Library Association, charter, 845; Senate, arrangement and classification, 906; medical, Middletown Hospital, 913; foreign, presentation of "New York Public Service" to, 920; Orange County Reference Law Library, appropriation for, 1025; Senate, stairs and bookcases, VIII, 422; Senate, removing and rearranging books, 422; Young Men's Association, Buffalo, membership, exemption from collateral inheritance tax, 732; Senate, furnishing various books for, 859; State Medical, books and binding, IX, 69; Senate and Assembly, promoting usefulness of, 153; Senate, books and binding, 773; Brooklyn Free Library, transfer of certain land to, 867; Brooklyn Public Library, transfer of certain land to, 873; Labor Department, cataloging, X, 564; Plattsburgh Free Public Library, charter, 713, 717.

Library (School). Suggested by Governor Clinton, III, 160; established, 499, 538, 767; United States deposit fund, 613, 652; policy not generally adopted, 651; act relating to, 743; treatise on agriculture proposed for, 745; number of volumes, 858, 946; IV, 22, 113, 264, 378, 396, 428, 476, 646, 795, 839; V, 523, 604, 779, 851; VI, 23, 528, 618, 946; VII, 19, 155, 297, 424, 519, 687, 821, 946; usefulness of, III, 858; books for prisoners, 861; books on political economy and agriculture, 878; number of, 946; decline of, VII, 686, 947; should include Penal Code, VIII, 38; reorganized, 1892, IX, 16.

Licenses. See also Excise. For exports, II, 30, 126; for certain manufactures, 382; Federal tax on, 789; tavern, proposed for agricultural purposes, 958; Federal imposition on canal tolls, protest against, III, 50, 78; for auction sales, 247; to pilots, 637; IV, 157; taverns, 753; grocers, 753; excise, revision needed, V, 386, 450; imposed for revenue, equivalent to taxation, VIII, 357; excise fees in force, 1889, 685; required for sale of foreign prison-made goods, IX, 329; buildings for manufacturing purposes, X, 8; by employment bureaus, 95; to foreign corporations, basis of computation, 837.

Vetoes. Of carriages in New York, II, 315; places of amusement, V, 220; excise, method of revoking, VI, 94; public hacks, etc., Flatbush, VII, 1111; for marriage, VIII, 470; Flatlands, public hacks and amusements, 975; villages, temporary and transient business, IX, 350; peddlers, board of supervisors, 372; itinerant

LICENSES, VETOES — (*Continued*).

> vendors of goods, 465; stock corporations, 529; peddlers', to veterans, 811; peddlers', to volunteer firemen, 866; manufacturing certain articles in tenement-houses, X, 37; peddlers, 163; fees, sale of concentrated commercial feeding stuffs, 447; trading stamps, Lockport, 636; New York auctioneers, 957.

LIEBER, FRANCIS, DR. Quoted, supervision of elections, V, 514.

LIEFER, EDWARD and MAX. Claim against Niagara Falls board of education, veto, X, 716.

LIENS. VETOES. Conditional contracts, goods and chattels, amending act, IX, 865; personal property, sales to satisfy, 865; filing notice of, 865, X, 310; livery-stable-keepers, IX, 866; hotels, boarding and lodging-house-keepers, X, 593.

LIEUTENANT-GOVERNOR (Colony). Francis Nicholson appointed, I, 14; Leisler assumes title and powers of, 15; John Nanfan, 90; powers of, 91; presents to, prohibited, 106; Richard Ingoldesby, 127; George Clarke, 255; James De Lancey, 526; Cadwallader Colden, 656.

LIEUTENANT-GOVERNOR (State). When president of Council of Appointment, II, 3; George Clinton chosen, declines, 6; when to be chosen, 10; official term, beginning of, 10; act for election of, 674, 887; authority as to distribution of military stores, 768; member of commission to make cessions to United States, 825; John Tayler becomes acting Governor, 887; member of Canal Board, 901; election and official term under second Constitution, III, 1; Erastus Root, 1; Nathaniel Pitcher becomes acting Governor, 221; Enos T. Throop becomes acting Governor, 269; vacancy in office, succession, IV, 433; joins in instructions to Captain Benham, quarantine affairs, V, 100; member of Commission to Organize Militia, 281, 400; member of Commission on Normal Schools, 695; member of Centennial Celebration Committee, VI, 302; term extended to three years, 398; *ex officio* trustee of public buildings, VII, 837; when to assume duties of Governor, VIII, 1; *ex officio* Regent of University, 169; member of Board of Capitol Construction, veto, 213; salary fixed by Constitution, 227; New Capitol Commission, 1888, 610; New Capitol Commission, 1895, IX, 545; first, Pierre Van Cortlandt, 688; Stephen Van Rensselaer, 1797, 689; *ex officio* member of State Fair Commission, X, 120; Timothy L. Woodruff, address on reception of Prince Henry, 479; M. Linn Bruce, presides at trial of Justice Hooker, 829.

LIFE INSURANCE COMPANIES. Statistics, V, 275; VI, 955; VII, 522, 691, 824, 950; X, 838; general act, VI, 168; mutual benefit companies, 326; origin and growth of, VII, 165; extravagant admin-

Life Insurance Companies — (*Continued*).

    istration condemned, 167; failure of adequate supervision, 167; lapsed policies, protection of holders, 305; interest on reserves, 522; premium tax on, law construed, X, 720; premiums, taxation, new rule, 722; legislative committee of investigation, 1905, 825; report and action thereon, 1906, 825; conditions in 1906, 838; mutual, special election of directors, 1906, 894; mutual, election of directors, general act of 1906, 899.

    Vetoes. Peabody Mutual Benefit Company, New York, VI, 171; National Mutual Benefit Association, Buffalo, 172; American Popular Life Insurance Company, 189; reserves and transfers, 506; forfeitures of policies, 602; co-operative, exempting from insurance laws, VII, 543, 692; suicide as defense, 1093; amending act, VIII, 1040; incorporation, amending general law, IX, 802.

Life Saving Benevolent Association, Buffalo. Charter, veto, VII, 414.

Life Saving Stations. Long Island, buildings for, veto, VI, 502.

Lighting Companies. Contracts with villages, veto, IX, 814.

Lighting Districts. Vetoes. In towns, amending act relative to, IX, 814; Westchester county, lighting highways and public places in towns, X, 948.

Lighthouses. At Sandy Hook, I, 655; ceded to United States, II, 304; at Eaton's Neck, 414, 415; Great Gull and Little Gull islands, 530; at Watch Point, 636, 641; at mouth of Genesee river, 1054, 1055, 1113; at mouth of Oswego river, 1055; Lake Champlain, Clinton county, keeper's dwelling, VI, 414; on Stannard's Rock, proposition for, VII, 46; Cold Harbor, cession for, 393. Vetoes. On Keuka lake, IX, 713; — Cayuga lake, lamp for, X, 791.

Lima. Amending village charter, veto, VIII, 621.

Lime. Oyster shells not to be burned for, in New York, I, 103; accumulations of, III, 1036.

Limestone. Discovery of, II, 1010; used for State Lunatic Asylum, III, 713.

Limitation of Actions. Claims against State, two years, VIII, 977; against State for negligence, X, 255, 259.

    Vetoes. Person dying within State, VII, 665; claims against New York city, 1089; railway construction and operation, damages, IX, 260; extending time to sue, Chiesa case, New York, X, 473; cause of action arising in another State, 703.

Lincoln, Abraham. Elected President, 1860, V, 326; letter from, accepting hospitalities tendered by Governor and Legislature, 334; speech at reception, 334; Wisconsin pledges support of administration, 348;

LINCOLN, ABRAHAM — (*Continued*).
  calls for militia, 356, 400; receives New York electoral vote, 1860, 395; calls special session of Congress, 399; asks additional troops from New York, 403; calls for 300,000 men, 453; proclamation of emancipation, 473; message to Congress, New York canals, 506; receives thanks of New York Chamber of Commerce, 507; last call for troops, 300,000, quotas, 618, 621; death of, 648, 677; day of mourning, 677; legislative resolutions, 677; funeral observances in Albany, 679; proposed monument to, 794; VI, 44; frame for portrait of, appropriation, veto, VII, 86; portrait in new capitol, 743; proposition to exchange portraits, 769; portrait, V, 676.

LINCOLN, BENJAMIN, GENERAL. Of Massachusetts, letter from, Shays' rebellion, II, 271.

LINCOLN, CHARLES Z. Appointed editor of Governors' Messages, I, pref. iii.

LINCOLN, ROBERT T. Secretary of War, communication from, cession Cypress Hills National cemetery, VII, 998.

LINDSAY, DAVID. Contested election, Assembly, Kings county, expenses, veto, VII, 918.

LINEHAN, MICHAEL. New York policeman, relief, veto, X, 581.

LINEN. Importation of, from Ireland, I, 693; manufacture exempt from taxation, II, 876.

LINKIE, CARRIE and CHARLES E. Court of Claims, veto, X, 165.

LINN, WILLIAM, REV. DR. Regent, death of, II, 629.

LINSON, JOHN J. Senate, fixing salary of health officer, VIII, 558; introduces general registration bill, 720.

LINTNER, W. H. Canal Department, appropriation for services, veto, IX, 716.

LINUS, DAVID. Convicted of murder, pardoned, II, 923.

LIQUOR. See also EXCISE. Sale to Indians prohibited, I, 157, 161; proposed prohibition against sale to Mohawks, 170; not to be sold to Indians, 466, 549, 569; III, 143; immoderate use by King's troops, I, 617; excessive consumption of, 641; sale on Sunday prohibited, II, 400; restricting licenses, 427; sale, prohibited to paupers, III, 516; inspector of distilled spirits, 749; license system inadequate, IV, 745; evidence of sale, 758; destruction of, 759; damages for sale, 765; power to prohibit sale, 801; act to regulate sale, V, 20; intoxication, punishment of, 285; tax on sale, VII, 571; alcoholic beverages, statement by board of health, VIII, 353; is property protected by Constitution, 361, 367; five gallon sales, act relative to, 440; excessive number of saloons in State, IX, 665; sale without certificate, injunction against, 701; sale on Sunday should not be permitted, X, 356; sales by pharmacists, act of 1903, 542.

Liquor — (*Continued*).

    Vetoes. Sale prohibited, IV, 753; prohibiting sale on State property, VIII, 291, 351; prohibiting sale within half a mile of Willard Insane Asylum, 340; regulating sale, 540; tax on beverages, 1889, 688, 797; intoxication, persons convicted of, medical treatment in penitentiaries, IX, 252; bottles, etc., used in connection with certain drinks, protection of owners, 267; adulteration of beer, X, 55; persons habitually intoxicated, New York, 806.

Liquor Tax Law. Tax on sales, VII, 571; VIII, 929; IX, 696; distribution of excise moneys, VIII, 1059; IX, 666, 701; injunction against sale without certificate, 701; receipts, 738, 821, 823; X, 26, 108, 115, 181, 200, 460, 736; operation of, 1897, IX, 748; good effects of, 823; large revenue from, X, 30; decrease in number of saloons, 201, 460; actions under, State commissioner to be party, 201; hotels, alleged colonization of voters in, 202; hotels and boarding-houses to furnish lists of guests, 202; amendments, 1901, 290; New York's contribution to, 1902, 483; additional means of enforcement needed, 513; general amendments, 1903, 540; sales by pharmacists, act of 1903, 542; local option, proposed extension to cities, 736; local option amendment, 1905, 764, 780; inspection of hotels, revocation of certificates, act of 1905, 780; inspection of hotels, 902.

    Vetoes. Buildings for hotel purposes, consents, IX, 802; amending, 865; X, 948; sale of liquor on election days, 162; certificate, cancellation, hearing by Court of Claims, 170; refund on certificates, 553; rebates, payment of, 590, 638; sale within prohibited distance of a church, Gotham Hotel, 779; sale within 200 feet of church or school, 959.

Lisk, Charles R. Canal Department, appropriation for services, veto, IX, 716.

Literature Fund. Distribution of, II, 967; III, 412; receipts from quitrents, II, 968; lottery for, 990, 1027; amount of, 1099; income, III, 232, 480, 501, 544, 618, 673, 711, 764, 857, 946; IV, 21, 64, 88, 117, 269, 377, 397, 426, 475, 551, 602, 645, 782, 831; V, 2, 74; New York Institution for Instruction of Deaf and Dumb to share in, III, 292; transfer to general fund, exchange of securities, 371, 499; used for instruction of teachers, 454, 499; United States deposit fund, 613, 652; due from general fund, 707; distribution to academies, rules for, IV, 117; appropriation for Albany normal school, 267; not to be diverted, 782; IX, 69; increasing, veto, VIII, 291.

Littauer, Lucius N. Offer of land for tuberculosis hospital declined, X, 351.

LITTHAUER, GOTTHARDT A. Assembly, member of Prince Henry reception committee, X, 479; escorts Admiral von Baudissin at reception, 480.

"LITTLE BELT, THE." Attacks frigate President, II, 690.

LITTLE EQUINUNK BRIDGE COMPANY. Charter, veto, VIII, 874.

LITTLE FALLS. See also ROCKTON. Postmaster at, removal of, II, 1070, 1071, 1072; highway commissioners, legalizing acts of, VIII, 1156.

    VETOES. Cascade Fire Company No. 1, charter, VI, 186; Cascade Association, charter, 277; amending charter, VII, 416; VIII, 1040; separate road district, IX, 250; election inspectors, 458; amending city charter, 785; X, 714; public buildings, IX, 785; annual tax levy, X, 686.

LITTE FALLS, VAN HORNESVILLE AND OTSEGO LAKE NARROW GAUGE RAILROAD COMPANY. Extending time to begin construction, veto, X, 258, 959.

LITTLE GULL ISLAND. Cession for lighthouse, II, 530.

LITTLE SODUS BAY. Harbor at, II, 936.

LITTLE VALLEY WATERWORKS COMPANY. Charter, veto, VI, 284, 321.

LIVER OIL. Report of inspector, IV, 84.

LIVERPOOL, ENGLAND. Railroad to Manchester, III, 327; proceedings against public officers for misconduct, VI, 731; stopping waste of water, VII, 636.

LIVERPOOL, NEW YORK. Prosperity resulting from manufacture of salt, III, 708; salt spring in, 856.

LIVERPOOL AND MANCHESTER RAILROAD. Freight and passenger rates on, III, 375; average speed on, 397.

LIVERY STABLES. Quartering soldiers in, I, 604.

LIVERY-STABLE-KEEPERS. VETOES. Liens, amending act, VIII, 457; liens, extension of, IX, 866.

LIVINGSTON, BROCKHOLST. Supreme Court, letter from, George case, II, 531.

LIVINGSTON, EDWARD P. Lease in Greene county, IV, 332.

LIVINGSTON, GILBERT. Bond as farmer of excise, I, 188.

LIVINGSTON, HENRY, CAPTAIN. Account for supplies, I, 462.

LIVINGSTON, HENRY BEEKMAN, COLONEL. Regiment in national service, II, 18; offers use of iron furnaces, 20.

LIVINGSTON, HENRY W. Lease from, description of, IV, 330.

LIVINGSTON, JOHN. Owner of Scott patent, IV, 331.

LIVINGSTON, LEWIS. Commissioner to receive Montgomery's remains on removal from Quebec, II, 1000.

LIVINGSTON, MARY. Lease from, description of, IV, 330.

LIVINGSTON, PETER R. Senate, action on removal of Jacob Van Ness, Dutchess county clerk, II, 1069.

LIVINGSTON, PHILIP (Albany). Secretary of Indian Affairs, petition for payment of salary, I, 200; statement from, relative to Indian trade, 214; appointed commissioner on colonial union, I, 370.

LIVINGSTON, PHILIP (Livingston manor). Assembly, favors colonial union, I, 767; resolutions, relating to state of colony, 768; resolution thanking merchants for declining to receive British importations, 768.

LIVINGSTON, PHILIP (New York). Assembly, favors colonial union, I, 767; delegate to Continental Congress, 768.

LIVINGSTON, ROBERT. Claim of, action on, recommended, I, 84; absence from Council meeting noted, 91; sells land for Palatine settlements, 147; chosen Speaker of Assembly, 183.

LIVINGSTON, ROBERT, JR. Lease from, description of, IV, 330.

LIVINGSTON, ROBERT C. Commissioner to Commercial Convention, II, 260.

LIVINGSTON, ROBERT E. Member of Yorktown Centennial Commission, VII, 734.

LIVINGSTON, ROBERT R. Member of committee on frontier settlements, I, 631; chancellor, member of Council of Revision, II, 21; elected delegate to Congress, 83; letter from, 112; letter from, destruction of property, 162; commissioner on Massachusetts boundary, 217; commissioner to Commercial Convention, 260; steamboat privileges granted to, 415; chancellor, correspondence with Governor Jay, Council of Appointment, 481; commissioner Louisiana Purchase, 535; engages in agriculture, 958; heirs of, leases in Ulster and Sullivan counties, IV, 332; leasehold estates, 333; statue in United States capitol, VI, 435, 555; statue of, appropriation, veto, VII, 382, 469; letter from George Clinton, 811.

LIVINGSTON, ROBERT SWIFT. Lease from, description of, IV, 330.

LIVINGSTON, WALTER. First Speaker of Assembly, 1777, IX, 688; commissioner on Massachusetts boundary, II, 217.

LIVINGSTON, WILLIAM. Appointed counsel for keeper of powder-house, I, 532; member of committee on frontier settlements, 631.

LIVINGSTON COUNTY. School for instruction of teachers, III, 160, 213; agricultural society in, 945; exempted from Town Auditor's Act, VIII, 49; average excise license fees, 1889, 687; unpaid taxes, sales under special act, 749; highways, cost of labor system, 1892, IX, 200; insane, care of, county and State systems compared, 228; Craig Colony for Epileptics, Sonyea, 240.

VETOES. Bridge over Genesee river, relief of De Graff and others, VI, 306; Livonia road, two rods wide, 707; legalizing election, VII, 415; Livonia, auditing Reed claim, VIII, 889; York, John W. Howe, justice of peace, legalizing acts, 943; York taxes,

LIVINGSTON COUNTY, VETOES — (*Continued*).

confirming and levying, IX, 59; compensation of under sheriff, jailer and attendants, X, 811.

LIVINGSTON MANOR. Riot in, I, 610; ancient charter of, 612; Philip Livingston, Assembly, favors colonial union, 767; description of, IV, 329.

LIVINGSTON (Town). Disorders in, II, 411.

LIVONIA. VETOES. Road two rods wide, VI, 707; auditing claim of Reed and others, VIII, 889.

LLOYD'S HARBOR. Protection of shellfish in, veto, VII, 415.

LLOYD'S NECK. Annexed to Suffolk county, VIII, 289.

LOAN. By General Amherst for war purposes, I, 637, 695; partial payment of, 639; payment of, 646; to Hughes, II, 19; expected from Holland, 154; obtained from Spain, 154; from France, 155; for interest, condemned, 158; statement relating to French, 159; of gunpowder, requested from Congress, 181; of public funds, 320; from Bank of New York, 436; of common school fund, 660, 722; State certificate, cashier appointed to issue, 907; of State funds, 1004; for canal construction, 1097; III, 10, 26, 620, 711, 816, 865; IV, 61; for public expenditures, III, 323; for Chenango canal, 419, 507, 554; to banks and citizens, 481, 491, 496; for general purposes, 505, 619; by New York city to banks, 535; policy of transferring payment to future generations, 547; to New York and Erie Railroad Company, 551; United States deposit fund, 613; IV, 120; for lateral canals, banks authorized to subscribe to, III, 633; for Erie canal enlargement, 671, 816, 865; to railroads, 887; IV, 10, 62, 92, 831; State, rate of interest increased, III, 967; to pay arrearages to canal contractors, IV, 18, 63; United States deposit fund, collection postponed, 47; for State debt, when people must approve, 104; for canal damages, 260; for deficiencies in sinking fund, 422, 473, 782; for casual deficits, 473, 589, 660; V, 152, 360, 890, 923; VII, 399; proposed for completion of canals, unconstitutional, IV, 549; for interest on canal certificates and Oswego loan, 700; payable from canal revenues, 781; for canal enlargement, 783, 834; from United States deposit fund, to State Agricultural College, 853; V, 16; to emigration commissioners, 24; for canals, act approved by people, 70, 152, 159, 256; by United States, based on deposit fund, 330; for military bounties, 530; for Civil War bounties, 610; new, on redemption of State stock, VI, 615.

LOAN — (*Continued*).

     VETOES. By colony due State, payment of, II, 240; to Warren county, VI, 194; on personal credit, IX, 534; on salary, X, 700; Personal Property Loan Company, charter, 594, 708.

LOAN COMMISSIONERS. Office created, II, 320; United States deposit fund, III, 613; in New York city, V, 63.

     VETOES. Delaware county, Horton, judgment, sale of, VII, 877; — Ontario county, transferring funds to, VIII, 401; — increasing fees, IX, 115.

LOAN COMPANIES. General statistics, VI, 953; VII, 521, 690, 823, 949; VIII, 6; annual expense limited, X, 222.

     VETOES. Insolvent, settlement of affairs, VII, 797; Ulster County Company, charter, VIII, 230; investments by, 891; co-operative associations, charter, IX, 148; personal property, amending act, X, 317.

LOANERS' BANK. Financial condition of, VII, 66.

LOBBY. Disappearance of, noted by Governor Throop, III, 313.

LOBBYING. Condemned by Governor Morgan, V, 95, 194; for railroad appropriations, VI, 72.

LOBDELL, MR. Land for Utica asylum, veto, VII, 89.

LOBDELL, JAMES. Bond for return of arms, II, 772.

LOCAL ASSESSMENTS. Needed reform in, 437; relief from, veto, VI, 573.

LOCAL AUTHORITY. Buffalo, presiding judge of Superior Court, VI, 496; village trustees cannot appoint town officer, VII, 1098; president of Troy common council, VIII, 86; meaning of term, 87; minority of common council not, 85; president *pro tem.*, board of supervisors, 85; supervisor-at-large, IX, 584.

     VETOES. Power of appointment, New York Superior Court judges, VI, 496; Railroad Law, definition, IX, 462.

LOCAL LAW. See next two titles, also PRIVATE LAWS. Reducing number of, transferring power to board of supervisors, IV, 433; reducing number of, VI, 52, 117, 550; vetoes sustained by Legislature, 117; meaning of, third judicial district, VII, 260; must have title, VIII, 617, 618; notice of introduction, IX, 676; comparative statement, 1894–1900, X, 504.

LOCAL (AND PRIVATE) LAWS. CONSTITUTION, ARTICLE 3, SECTION 16. Object of provision, IV, 775; V, 387, 798; VI, 271.

     VETOES. Binghamton Masonic Board of Trustees, charter, VIII, 460; Black Rock drainage, 614; Buffalo,— funding floating debt, IV, 524; — subscribing to stock of Buffalo Waterworks Company, 517; Chenango canal, settling claims, VI, 508; Clifton Springs, legalizing election of officers, VIII, 1122; Clyde, bor-

LOCAL (and Private) LAWS, VETOES — (*Continued*).

rowing money, VI, 706; Croton Water Act, IV, 773; Delaware river improvement, VIII, 407; Dudley claim, 408; Elmira, primary elections, 386; Five Points House of Industry, New York, powers of, VII, 334; gas light companies, Kings county, 1120; Granite Lake Company, VI, 270; highway, Wilmington to North Elba, VII, 1099; Huntington, sale of schoolhouse, VI, 506; Ithaca, School Act, VII, 1105; Kings county and Brooklyn, soldiers and sailors' memorial arch, IX, 211; Mutual Insurance Company, amending act, VII, 1098; National Book Exchange, New York, VI, 328; New York,—altering map, VII, 1088; — Croton water supply, VI, 596; — district court, janitors, VII, 326; — engineers, VI, 715; — general sessions, compensation of stenographers, VII, 768; — grading street, 658; — local government, 1876, VI, 1030; — Spuyten Duyvil road, VII, 631; New York and Kings counties, closing certain offices on Saturday, 758; New York Central Railroad, terminating use of Eleventh avenue, X, 898; New York Orthopœdic Dispensary, amending charter, VI, 693; Norwich, recorder, IX, 75; Oswegatchie river breakwater, VI, 331; Owego, charter, 80; Port Morris Warehouse and Elevator Company, 328; railroad aid, 190; Rome, fire commissioners, jurisdiction of, VIII, 390; Schoharie Valley Railroad extension, VI, 90; Society for the Reformation of Juvenile Delinquents, relief fund, V, 219; Sodus, election districts, VI, 60; Staten Island Bridge Company, charter, 91; State Woman's Hospital, amending charter, VIII, 458; street railroads in New York, V, 797; Syracuse Water Company, supplying adjacent villages, VII, 1100; Totten and Crossfield's Purchase, exemption from highway taxes, VI, 702; town insurance companies, amending act, 509; Troy and West Troy ferry, 705; Ulster county treasurer's fees, 508; Watervliet police justices, 1032; Workingmen's Friendly Society of America, 326; Yonkers bonded debt, 714; Yonkers Railroad Company, completion of road, IX, 271.

LOCAL LAW, CONSTITUTION, ARTICLE 3, SECTION 18. Limiting subjects, general references, VI, 402, 550; VII, 158, 729, 763.

VETOES. BRIDGES. Cattaraugus Indian reservation, VII, 383, 909; Chemung river, 578; Rochester, 589; Tompkins, Delaware river, X, 874.

DRAINAGE. Black lake, VIII, 614; Cato, 614; Cayuga lake, VII, 406; Long Island City, 369.

ELECTIONS. Brooklyn, counting ballots, VII, 370; places and conduct of, Albany, 263.

LOCAL LAW, ETC., VETOES — (*Continued*).

EXCLUSIVE PRIVILEGE. Not to be granted, VI, 662; ferry, Seneca lake, 1034; street processions, music, G. A. R., VII, 336; teachers, State certificates, VI, 949.

FEES, PERCENTAGE AND ALLOWANCES. Not to be increased, Albany county clerk, VII, 604; Albany sheriff, 1121; Binghamton police, 753; canal auditor, IV, 877; captain of the port and harbor masters, VII, 1055; cities, public burdens, 252; judges, third judicial district, 259; New York commissioner of jurors, 251; New York county treasurer and comptroller, VIII, 412; Rensselaer sheriff, VII, 1115; Richmond county clerk, 497; Seneca county judge and surrogate, 549; Sullivan county town officers, 540; supervisors, 1115; Syracuse fire department, 1098; Troy local officers, 777.

GENERAL LAWS. Brooklyn schools, VII, 628; cemeteries, application to local association, VIII, 52; changing names of corporations, VII, 748; Game Law, powers of boards of supervisors, 69; medical colleges, VIII, 101; office hours, Albany county clerk, VII, 757.

HIGHWAYS. Black creek, VII, 358; Buffalo and Niagara Falls boulevard, VIII, 879; Cattaraugus Indian reservation, VII, 222; Dewitt, special act, X, 235; Eastchester commissioners, VIII, 616; Flatbush, Parkville streets and avenues, 615; Hamilton county,— Johnsburgh to Long Lake, VII, 320; — special, 215; Mentz, application of railroad tax, 208; Middleburgh, special road district, 440; New Baltimore, special, VIII, 387; New Lots, Bushwick avenue, VII, 63; New Utrecht,— board of improvement, IX, 134;— Franklin avenue, VIII, 615; New York, Spuyten Duyvil road, VII, 630; Onondaga reservation, 92, 384; Cortland special act, VIII, 879; St. Regis reservation, VII, 91; Virgil, special, 1086; Washington county, special, 887; Westerlo, Chesterville, separate road district, VIII, 616.

JURORS. Commissioners, general regulations, IX, 516.

RAILROADS. General, X, 542; Brooklyn, Atlantic avenue, VII, 395; court order extending time for completion of road, IX, 271; laying down tracks, VII, 593; New York rapid transit, IX, 509; special acts prohibited, VII, 1063; White Plains to Connecticut line, VIII, 615.

STREET RAILROADS. Consent of adjoining owners, VII, 1037,

LOCAL LAW, ETC., VETOES — (*Continued*).

1064; consent of local authorities, 1040, 1064; extensions, 592; general act, special provisions for New York, 895.

SUPERVISORS. Fulton county, equalizing representation, VII, 769, 860; Hector, election, 843.

VILLAGES. Special acts, VIII, 330; Canajoharie, reorganization, VI, 825; Dresden, amending general act, VII, 645; Hastings-on-the-Hudson, changing boundaries, X, 233; Lyons, new charter, VII, 879; Newark, revising charter, 1123; North Tonawanda, special act, VIII, 1155; Northville, VII, 214; Saranac Lake, special charter, IX, 258; Sylvan Beach, special act, VIII, 1131, see note.

LOCAL OFFICERS. How chosen, IV, 684; VI, 30, 75, 128, 425, 496, 504, 507, 512, 517, 734; VII, 179, 218; IX; 29; X, 750; justices of the peace, vacancies in office, how filled, VI, 75; village elections, property qualifications, 77; local authority, New York Superior Court judges, 496; city officer cannot be given jurisdiction over county, 504; Legislature cannot appoint school trustee, 507; Brooklyn police justice, 512, 517; Brooklyn board of health cannot be given jurisdiction in towns, 517; method of choice, change from first to second Constitution, 832; judicial, cities and villages, how chosen, 987; Legislature cannot appoint district court clerks, 1029; New York commissioners, water supply, VII, 901; Albany police board, method of appointment unconstitutional, VIII, 84; Troy police commissioners, 86; new offices, how filled, IX, 96; Penn Yan water commissioners, 411; New York rapid transit commissioners, 511; supervisors of counties, 584; West Troy police commissioners, 591; Syracuse board to audit certain claims against city, X, 288; Ogdensburg school officers, 913.

VETOES. Police justice, Geneva, VI, 216; Kings county board of charities, 1019; New York district court clerks, 1029; Ontario, confirming election of officers, 1031; Union College, appointment of policemen, 1032; Rensselaer county, House of Industry, board of governors for, 1033; New York, department of docks, VII, 106; New York, various commissions, 107; New York public administrator, 108; Brooklyn, members of commissions, 126; Bath excise commissioners, failure to give bond, 179; Mentz, overseers of highways, 208; German Flats, board of town auditors, 216; Scio, constables, appointment by county judge, 218; commissioners of city and county hall, Buffalo, 317; recorder, Cohoes, chamber powers of Supreme Court justice

Local Officers, Vetoes — (*Continued*).

  vested in, 327; Supreme Court clerk, Erie county, 357; agent of Society for Prevention of Cruelty to Animals, powers of constable, 746; Brooklyn, board to adjust unpaid taxes, 771; Saratoga Springs, health office, 1098; Westfield water commissioners, VIII, 519; Kings county farm, commissioners, 594; Long Island City, Greenpoint avenue improvement, commissioners, 635; Utica park commissioners, Hornellsville sewer commissioners, 880; Ogdensburg board of public works, 995; Port Jervis commissioner to erect public building, IX, 371; Richmond county, deputy county treasurers as town officers, 399.

Local Option. Excise, general act, veto, VI, 506, 568; five-gallon sales, act of 1887, VIII, ·440; generally approved, 683; continued by Liquor Tax Law of 1896, IX, 701; properly applicable to cities, 701; defined, X, 354; application to cities, 355; proposed extension to cities, 736, 854; amending Liquor Tax Law, 1905, 764, 780.

Local Purpose. Question as to meaning of, IV, 56.

Locke, Henry. Commissioner, repairing highway, Cattaraugus reservation, veto, VII, 475.

Lockman, William. Board of Claims, veto, IX, 473.

Lockport. Number of excise licenses, 1887, VIII, 359; sewer, act for construction, 562; excise license fees, 1889, 685; water supply, X, 418.

  Vetoes. Lift bridge, Exchange street, VI, 1005; VII, 115; iron bridge, Prospect street, VI, 1007; hose carriage, purchase of, VII, 267; bridge, Mill street, 363; Episcopal cemetery, removing bodies from, VIII, 887; lifting locks at, IX, 606; wages and preferences of laborers, 719; electric light system, 730, 786; poor fund, maintenance of provident woodyard, 785; salary and lift bridge funds, X, 583; trading stamps, license for, 636; lighting contracts, 636.

Lockport Bank. Debt to safety fund, III, 711.

Lockport Home for the Friendless. Care of poor children, veto, VI, 503.

Lock-Up. Vetoes. Colton, providing for, VIII, 229; Parishville, authorizing, 1039; at Soldiers and Sailors' Home, Bath, X, 546.

Locomotive Engineers' Mutual Benefit Association. Relief, veto, VII, 414.

Lodging-Houses. Metropolitan elections district, register of guests, X, 213; liens of, veto, 593.

LOG ROLLING. Legislation, Governor protests against, III, 91; suggested, railroad aid bills, VI, 174; New York charter, 1876, 1030.

LOGS. Floating on rivers, veto, VII, 506; VIII, 1041; IX, 815.

LONDON. Merchants remonstrate against Colonial Tariff Act, I, 198; mayor of, acknowledgments by, II, 488; proposed conference at, between Great Britain and United States, 785; prison in, noted, 1051; horticultural society, basis of New York society, III, 64; International Exposition, 1851, IV, 509, 572; International Educational Exhibition, 752.

LONDON GAZETTE. Announces declaration of war by France against England, I, 316.

LONDON SOCIETY FOR THE EXTENSION OF UNIVERSITY TEACHING. England, extension movement, IX, 17.

LONG, JOHN D. Secretary of the Navy, requests cession of Iona island, X, 143.

LONG ISLAND. Delegates of, to Hempstead Convention, I, 2; ridings on, representation in first Assembly, 9; name changed to Nassau, 36, 38; ministers on, 115; eastern part of, placed in New York collector's district, 213; defense of, 295; proclamation to prevent plundering inhabitants of, II, 80; prisoners of war, relief of, 116; Eaton's Neck lighthouse, 415; lighthouse, Great Gull and Little Gull islands, 530; jurisdiction over adjacent waters in New York harbor, 540; troops stationed on, 1812, 746; situation of Montauk Indians, 931; peat, discovery of, 1094; proposed canals on, III, 70, 71, 122, 165; Willet's Point, cession of land at, VI, 774; Cold Harbor, lighthouse, cession for, VII, 393; Cypress Hills cemetery, cession of land for, 998.

VETOES. Life-saving stations, buildings for, VI, 502; agricultural experiment station, establishing, IX, 232; woodcock, close season, X, 440.

LONG ISLAND CITY. Incorporated, VI, 193; number of excise licenses, 1887, VIII, 359; excise license fees, 1889, 685; probable benefits to be derived from East river bulkhead bill, 835; smallpox in, 1893, IX, 253; mayor of, member of New York Charter Commission, 553; accepts Greater New York bill, 1896, 709; merged in Greater New York, 300.

VETOES. Unpaid taxes, VII, 265; X, 62; relative to certain streets in, VII, 266; Steinway avenue improvement, 353; Flushing avenue improvement, 368; Astoria, certain streets and avenues, improvements, 369; intersection of certain avenues, 417, Jackson avenue improvement, 603, 862; closing Ninth street, 609; salary for aldermen, 641; unpaid taxes, assessments and water rents,

LONG ISLAND CITY, VETOES — (*Continued*).

    VIII, 120; IX, 726; reducing expenses, repealing part of act, VIII, 130; Greenpoint avenue improvement, 635; overseer of the poor, 886; parks and parade ground, 888; charter amendments, 1038; IX, 629, 786; police patrolmen, salaries, 141; rent of buildings for educational purposes, 253, 468; Grand avenue and Main street improvements, 254, 786; legalizing certain claims, 468; street improvement, 633, 731; Ward's Island Bridge Company, charter, 725; unpaid taxes and water rates, 726; additional water supply, 726; moneys received by treasurer, 730; Second avenue, reducing width, 734; Newtown creek, abatement of nuisance, 773; Thompson avenue, making part of county road system, 786; schools, additional accommodations, 786; expense of government, amending act, 786; fire department, 786; improvement commission, amending act, 786; Bach claim, audit of, 786; claims against, X, 60; fire commissioners, legalizing appointments, 178; Pender's claim, work and material for board of education, 322; claim of Woodside Water Company, 326; East River Gas Company, relative to, 582; Fiesel claim for services, board of education, 950.

LONG ISLAND CITY SAVINGS BANKS. Charter, veto, VI, 342.

LONG ISLAND HISTORICAL SOCIETY. Relative to, veto, IX, 794.

LONG ISLAND RAILROAD. Construction of, III, 786; progress of construction, 953; State aid to, IV, 10, 831; VI, 720; relation to rapid transit in New York, X, 401; on Atlantic avenue, Brooklyn, relative to, veto, 582; grade crossings in Brooklyn, 714.

LONG ISLAND SOUND. Line in, between New York and Connecticut, VIII, 172; value of oyster beds, IX, 193.

LONG ISLAND CITY HOSPITAL. Established 1895, IX, 541, 575; purchase of Dady property, veto, 773; extravagance in purchase of coal, X, 411; alleged improper letting of contract, 412; number of visits of managers, 415.

LONG LAKE. VETOES. Highway to Johnsburgh, VII, 133, 320; town hall, VIII, 1041.

LONG LAKE. Bridge over, veto, IX, 255.

LONG POND. See also LAKE AWASTING. Spearing suckers and eels in, veto, X, 440.

LONG WHARF. Railroad to Matteawan, veto, VI, 211.

LOOKOUT MOUNTAIN. Roads on, ceded by Tennessee to United States, VIII, 1076; battle of, monuments to New York troops, 1077; IX, 324, 577.

LOOMIS, ARPHAXED. Member of Procedure Commission, IV, 366; VII, 183.

LOON LAKE. VETOES. Taking certain fish prohibited, VII, 264; protection of fish, Steuben county, 446.

LORD, MINNIE A. Cancellation of tax sale, veto, X, 317.

LORDS OF ADMIRALTY. Notice to, of need of fleet, I, 321; directions to colonial governors to aid in Cape Breton expedition, 351.

LORDS JUSTICES. Memorial to, I, 72, 73; letter from, relative to military preparations, 314; recommend revision of colonial statutes, 521; New Jersey boundary, 588.

LORDS LIEUTENANTS. Power to act out of territory, I, 150.

LORDS OF TRADE. See COMMISSIONERS OF TRADE AND PLANTATIONS.

LORDVILLE AND EQUINUNK BRIDGE COMPANY. Amending charter, veto, VIII, 1041.

LORING, GEORGE B. United States commissioner of agriculture, communication from, preservation of forests, VII, 1000.

LORRAINE. Borrowing money for vault, veto, VIII, 639.

LOS ANGELES. Bonds of, savings banks authorized to invest in, X, 454.

LOTT, ABRAHAM. Treasurer, appointment approved, I, 722.

LOTT, JOHN A. Judge, Brooklyn, chairman citizens' committee, Kings county board of charities bill, VI, 1020.

LOTTERY. Authorized to raise money for fortifying New York, I, 345, 363; for Kings College, 523; foreign, sale of tickets prohibited, 641; for Sandy Hook lighthouse, 655; for cultivation of hemp, 682; recommended for erection of prisons, II, 336; for State roads, 385; proceeds of, invested for educational purposes, 528, 908; III, 187; for Union College, II, 551; for purchase of botanic garden, 579; insurance of, act relating to, 613, 908, 950; III, 187; for Union College, payment of prizes, II, 678; proceeds of certain, devoted to canal fund, 902; acts relating to, 908; promotion of medical science, 908; regulation of, 908, 950, 968; for literature fund, 990, 1027; pernicious effects of, 1052; report of managers, 1054; Washington, 1103, 1123; constitutional prohibition against, 1127; III, 526, 567; IV, 807; VII, 532, 625, 715; IX, 603; tickets, relative to, veto, III, 186; regulating sale of tickets, 186; indicted as a nuisance, 404; abolished, 404; duty of Legislature to suppress, 567; VII, 532; persistent violation of law, 625, 715; amending Penal Code, veto, IX, 534.

LOUISBURG. Expedition against, I, 347, 350, 351; capture of, 352; New York requested to aid in defending, 358; troops needed for, Assembly declines assistance, 370, 371; trade with French, profit by, 564; reduction of, 624, 635.

LOUISIANA. Purchase of, II, 535; IV, 813; Missouri Compromise prohibiting extension of slavery, II, 1023; Constitution, procedure to amend, 1058; approves Georgia's proposition relative to importation of colored persons, III, 145; disapproves Ohio proposition relative to abolition of slavery, 145; constitutional amendment, extending term of President to six years and making him ineligible to re-election, 281; approves tariff of 1828, 354; fine imposed on General Jackson, IV, 44, 45; seizure of national forts and property, V, 306; secession ordinance, 341, 396; asserts right of free navigation of Mississippi river, 341; political disturbances, VI, 769; action of New York Legislature, 774; protests against Federal interference in, 776, 785, 787; presidential election of 1876, action by Electoral Commission, VII, 33; Federal interference in election, 1876, 34.

LOUISIANA PURCHASE EXPOSITION, ST. LOUIS. Commission, X, 350; appropriation, 350; New York's large number of awards at, 747; report, publication, veto, 796.

LOUTREL, GEORGE L. VETOES. Relief, VI, 573; claim against New York, VIII, 883.

LOVE, HENRY M. Court of Claims, veto, X, 709.

LOVE, JOHN. Member of Commission on Readjustment of Quotas, V, 537, 572.

LOVELACE, JOHN. Appointed Governor, I, 132; assumes office, 132; dissolves Eleventh Assembly, 132; calls new Assembly, 132.
    OPENING SPEECH. Twelfth Assembly, first session, I, 132; aid from Crown, 132; financial condition, 132; support of government, 132; fortifications, 133; quartering soldiers, 133; coast defense, 133; exportation of gold and silver coin, 133; proposed Indian treaty, 134; act of Parliament relative to rates of foreign coin, 134; death of, 134; widow's claim against colony, 145; missing letters from, IV, 184; official service, I, pref. ix.

LOVELACE, LADY. Claim against colony, I, 145; act for relief of, 170.

LOVELAND, JOSEPH D. Relief, veto, VI, 185.

LOW, HENRY R. Claim against State, Middletown Homœopathic Asylum, veto, VII, 665; Senator, member of New Capitol Commission, 1888, VIII, 650.

LOW, ISAAC. Delegate to Continental Congress, I, 768.

LOW, SETH. Mayor of New York, communication to Governor Odell relative to tunnel railroads, X, 396.

LOWELL CEMETERY ASSOCIATION. Reducing number of trustees, veto, VIII, 52.

LOWER, ANNA. Petition for relief, II, 117.

LOWVILLE. Arms and supplies for, II, 775. VETOES. Vacancies in office of justice of the peace, VI, 48; — commissioners of highways, borrowing money, 318.

LUDDEN, WILLIAM J. Counsel for Senate Committee on Investigation of Election Frauds, 1894, veto, IX, 533; appropriation, 1895, 533.

LUDLOW, GEORGE D. Reimbursed for fire losses, I, 758.

LUMBER. Exportation of, to Ireland prohibited, I, 693; inspection of, II, 457; from interior of State finds market in New York, III, 815; floating on streams, veto, VII, 415; VIII, 1041; IX, 815.

LUNATIC ASYLUMS. See INSANE ASYLUMS.

LUNATICS. See also INSANE. Provision for care of, II, 650; estimated number of, III, 452; State asylum established, 452, see STATE LUNATIC ASYLUM and INSANE; number of, 900; IV, 77; sale of property, veto, VIII, 1041; IX, 283.

LUTHERAN CEMETERY, MIDDLE VILLAGE. Amending charter, veto, VI, 595.

LUTHERAN CEMETERY, NEWTOWN. Relief of, veto, VII, 268.

LUTHERAN LEAGUE, ROCHESTER. Changing name to Lutheran. Mission Union, etc., veto, IX, 793, 794.

LUXURIES. Foreign, profuse use of, II, 283.

LUZERNE. Union free school district No. 1, legalizing proceedings relative to, veto, X, 811.

LUZERNE, CHEVALIER DE LA. Deposits with, French loan, II, 160.

LYDIAS, MR. Offers blockhouse for use of colony, I, 357.

LYMAN, JOSEPH S. Affidavit, removal of Little Falls postmaster, II, 1072.

LYMAN, PHINEAS. Major-General, commands Connecticut troops, I, 575.

LYNCH, EDWARD. New York, relief, veto, X, 177.

LYNCH, JANE E. Adm. Morris Lynch, Board of Claims, veto, IX, 979.

LYNCH, MORRIS. Estate of, Board of Claims, veto, IX, 797.

LYONS. Number of excise licenses, 1887, VIII, 360.
VETOES. Revising charter, VII, 878; school district No. 6, additional accommodations, VIII, 702; union school, clerk of trustees, IX, 431; canal bridge, Water street, X, 314.

LYONS, GEORGE A. Colonel, Eighth Regiment, supplies from Union Defense Committee, VII, 500.

LYONS, JOHN J. New York fireman, reinstatement, veto, X, 950.

LYONS CEMETERY. Taxing lots, veto, VI, 191.

LYONSDALE. Reimbursement for bridge over Moose river, veto, VIII, 552.

LYME. Additional justices for, II, 1121.

LYSANDER. VETOES. Union school district, VII, 1106; bridge over Seneca river, X, 697.

M.

MACAULAY, THOMAS BABINGTON. Favors use of ballot at elections, VIII, 585; quoted, comparison between Middlesex and Utopia, 788.

MACDONALD, JAMES. New York, relief, veto, X, 581.

MACDONOUGH, THOMAS. Commodore, defeats British on Lake Champlain, II, 803; thanked by Legislature and presented with sword and land, 832; letter from Governor Tompkins, 832; reply, 833; proposed monument to, III, 134.

MACEDON. Rebuilding canal wall, veto, VI, 860.

" MACEDONIAN, THE." Captured by Commodore Decatur, II, 780.

MACEVERS, JOHN. Appointed counsel for keeper of powder-house, I, 532.

MAC FARLANE, WALLACE. Special counsel to examine report of Canal Investigating Commission, 1898, appointment, X, 77; communication to Governor, 40; appropriation for expenses, 40; counsel for New York City Bar Association at trial of Justice Hooker, 829.

MACGUIRE, DAVID. Dock, Philipstown, Hudson river, VI, 705.

MACHACKAMACK. Line of blockhouses from, I, 590.

MACHPELAH CEMETERY ASSOCIATION, LE ROY. Amending charter, veto, VI, 585.

MACK, JOHN. Charges against Bank Superintendent Ellis, VII, 66.

MACK, RALPH. Bond for return of arms, II, 772.

MACKAY, DONALD. Executor, Howard estate, restitution of collateral inheritance tax, veto, VIII, 1139.

MACKENZIE, MERVYN. Admission to practice as attorney, veto, X, 262.

MACNEVEN, DR. Communication from, Kesler case, II, 921.

MACOMB, ALEXANDER. Brigadier-general, commands American troops at battle of Plattsburgh, II, 803; military property occupied at Plattsburgh, purchase by United States, 825; thanked by Legislature and presented with sword, 832; letter from Governor Tompkins; reply, 841.

MACOMB, ROBERT. Member of Commission on Common School System, II, 707.

MACOMB'S PURCHASE. Of Indian lands, II, 456.

MADISON, JAMES. President, appoints thanksgiving day after War of 1812, II, 824; letter from, on New York resolutions, 826; as life Senator, possible length of service, VIII, 694.

MADISON ASSOCIATION. Charter, IV, 592.

MADISON COUNTY. Militia from, 1812, II, 743; purchase of Stockbridge land, 989; gypsum, market for, III, 815; charges against county judge, 928; agricultural society in, 945; refunding illegal taxes, VI, 278; disbandment of separate military company, VII, 826; one town excepted from repeal of Town Auditor's Act, VIII, 50; average excise license fees, 1889, 687; county clerk, salaried office, 1103; highways, cost of labor system, 1892, IX, 200; insane, care of, county and State systems compared, 228.

VETOES. Town auditors, VI, 435; excepting from provisions of County Treasurer's Act, VII, 265; Hillside Cemetery Association, control of certain lands, 807; unpaid taxes, sale for, VIII, 411; clerk, grand jury, X, 61.

MADISON FORKS OBITUARY SOCIETY. Changing name, acquiring land, VIII, 1163.

MADISON RESERVOIR. Repair of highway and bridge over, veto, X, 645.

MADISON (Town). Canal bridge, veto, VIII, 453.

MADRID. Union free school district No. 1, borrowing money, veto, VI, 325.

MAD RIVER. Public highway, repealing act, veto, IX, 121.

MAGAZINES. Repair of, recommended, I, 161; supplying with gunpowder, 314; at Fort George, 322; province powder to be stored in, 352; at northern Carrying Place, 392; condition of, II, 54, 98; proposed deposit of provisions in, 109; powder exhausted, 149; supplies for, 220; of warlike stores, to be maintained, 360, 510, 524, 600, 911; at Greenbush, 714; in New York, 751.

"MAGICIENNE, THE." French frigate, escort to French delegation to Yorktown Centennial Celebration, VII, 738.

MAGISTRATES. Powers of, seamen in foreign service, veto, II, 459; number of local, IV, 764; should not be vested with administrative functions, V, 26.

MAGNA CHARTA. Rights of citizens, arrest without warrant, II, 820; justice not to be diverted, V, 291.

MAGOFFIN, BERIAH. Governor of Kentucky, invited to visit Albany, V, 203.

MAGONE, DANIEL, JR. Member of Canal Investigating Commission, 1875, VI, 928.

MAHON, CATHERINE F. New York, pension, veto, X, 807.

MAHONEY, WILLIAM. New York, fire department, pension claim, veto, IX, 732.

MAIL. Railroad transportation of, veto, III, 592; franking privilege, proposed extension of, 637; transmission of opinions, 645.

MAINE. Disapproves Georgia's proposition as to importation of colored persons, III, 35; disapproves Tennessee proposition relative to election of President and Vice-President by popular vote and making members of Congress ineligible to civil appointments by President, 144; resolutions on distribution of Federal revenues, 186; protests against Federal duties, taxes, imposts and excises, urges tariff reform and distribution of surplus revenues, 387; northeastern boundary question, 390, 756; protests against South Carolina nullification proceedings and protective tariff policy, approves President's course, 438; protests against anti-slavery agitation, 590; election of President and Vice-President, 591; stocks of, securities in New York banks, 725; IV, 36; refuses to surrender Philbrook and Kelleran, Atticus case, III, 748; resolutions on public land, 821, 1020; resolutions on northeastern boundary controversy, 851; constitutional amendment, limiting eligibility of President to one term, 972; recommends refunding fine imposed on General Jackson, IV, 46, 84; recommends abolition of West Point Military Academy, 46; protection of colored citizens, 48; proposes international decimal system of weights, measures and currencies, V, 323; urges increase of tariff on wool and other agricultural products, 423; resolutions, success of Union Army, 439; appropriation for Antietam cemetery, 840; National Soldiers' Home, VI, 61; tax exemptions, 371; protest against Hell Gate pilotage, 561; court to render opinion as to constitutionality of pending bills, VIII, 947.

MAIN AND HAMBURG STREET CANAL. Appropriation for, IV, 391, 475; repairing dock, veto, VI, 1007.

MAHER, JAMES. Captain, funds received by, II, 766.

MAITLAND, S. R., REV. Librarian, Archiepiscopal Library, Lambeth, IV, 183.

"MAJOR ANDERSON, THE." Canal boat, claim for loss of, veto, VI, 312.

MALCOLM, ANNA M. Board of Claims, veto, VIII, 1166.

MALCOLM, WILLIAM. Colonel, claim, pay for troops, II, 117.

MALLET, JOSEPH. Bond for return of arms, II, 772.

MALLON, EDWARD. Charges against Bank Superintendent Ellis, VII, 67.

MALLORY, NATHANIEL. Relief of, II, 388.

MALONE. Deposit of military stores at, II, 771. VETOES. Compensation of assessors, VI, 210; — new armory at, VIII, 886.

MALONE WATERWORKS COMPANY. Amending charter, sale of water, VIII, 941, new bill passed.

MALTBY, ISAAC. Proposition to furnish system of military tactics, II, 953.

MAMAKATING. VETOES. Railroad commissioners, bonds to retire outstanding bonds, X, 235; State dam, cleaning, 791.

MAMARONECK AND NEW ROCHELLE STEAM NAVIGATION COMPANY. Charter, veto, V, 133.

MANCHESTER. Railroad to Liverpool, III, 327.

MANHATTAN BANK. Deposit of canal funds, IV, 254; advances, repayment of, V, 160; deposit of remainder of bounty debt, VII, 141.

MANHATTAN BAY. Discovery by Hendrick Hudson, III, 1017.

MANHATTAN BOROUGH. Tunnel connection with Queens borough, X, 396; Municipal Court, maintenance claims, veto, 817.

MANHATTAN EAST SIDE MISSION. Relief, veto, X, 59.

MANHATTAN GAS COMPANY. Increasing price of gas, veto, V, 671.

MANHATTAN INDEMNITY AND LOAN COMPANY, NEW YORK. Charter, veto, VI, 342.

MANHATTAN LOAN AND TRUST COMPANY, NEW YORK. VETOES. Charter, VI, 503; supplemental act, 911; amending charter, VIII, 293.

MANHATTAN RAILWAY COMPANY. Operating elevated railroads, New York, VII, 851; dividend, 1894, IX, 501.

MANHATTAN STATE HOSPITAL. Established, 1896, IX, 541, 651; alleged extravagance in management, X, 412.

VETOES. Establishing, 1895, IX, 617, 650; claim of Commercial Construction Company, X, 589; Kimball, treasurer, reimbursement for premium on bonds, 642.

MANHATTANVILLE. VETOES. Schools in, appropriation for, II, 1111; New York, opening road, VI, 692.

MANHEIM. Separate road district, amending act, veto, IX, 250.

MANLIUS. Postmaster at, removal of, II, 1068. VETOES. Canal ditch, VIII, 849; — soldiers' monument, changing location of, IX, 817.

MANN, MORRIS. Troy school janitor, claim, veto, X, 634.

MANNIX, PATRICK. Sealer of weights and measures, New York, salary, veto, X, 308.

MANORIAL TITLES. Leases, quantity of land in, 1848, IV, 408; investigation of, titles sustained, 413, 614, 654; disposition of certain actions, veto, 511; proposed purchase by State, resale to tenants, 560; considered by Governor Seymour, 653; progress of adjustment, 727.

MANSION HOUSE. See GOVERNOR'S HOUSE.

MANSLAUGHTER. Punishment of, III, 173.

MANVILLE, GEORGE E. Court of Claims, veto, X, 945.

MANVILLE, M. M. Canal Department, appropriation for service, veto, IX, 716.

MANZANILLA. Vessels from, detained for observation, yellow fever, VI, 533.

MANUFACTURERS. Income tax on, veto, II, 39.

Manufactures. Encouragement of, I, 255, 260, 266, 506, 749; II, 254, 312, 854; III, 297; British, premium on exportation of, I, 198; inquiry from Lords of Trade as to, 250; iron, production of, recommended, 260; iron and indigo, 507; naval stores, 555; British, increasing consumption of, in colonies, 690; fixing prices of goods and commodities, II, 25; encouraged by bounties, 40; sulphur and copperas, 92; home, encouragement of, 283; maple sugar, 313; arms and ammunition, 360; salt, act relating to, 384; American, should be preferred, 525, 572, 658; extension of, 658; improvement and extension of, 673; encouraging domestic, 702; III, 23; domestic, act to encourage, II, 876; Governor Clinton on promotion of, 899; domestic, appropriation for promotion of, 970, 1006, 1089; militia uniforms, 979; depressed condition of, 1003; statistics of, 1048; coal needed, 1094; beneficial results of encouragement, III, 65, 204; instruction of mechanics, 127; Georgia protests against congressional encouragement of, 221; improved condition, 352; importance, 420; large investment in, 458; statistics to be included in census, 526; in State prisons, 931; woolen, statistics of, IV, 42; cotton, statistics of, 42; census statistics, 248; in Massachusetts, 400; languish for lack of tariff protection, 812; act regulating employment of women and children, VIII, 163; factory inspector, office created, 164; prison-made goods manufactured in and imported from other States, branding required; act unconstitutional, IX, 329; X, 9; license to sell foreign prison-made goods, IX, 329; license of buildings for, X, 8.

Vetoes. Sugars, syrups, molasses and honey, fraud in sales, VII, 648; illuminating oils and fluids, inspection of, 659; gilded ware, preventing deception in manufacture and sale, IX, 47; household, encouragement of, 109; in penal institutions, branding and marking, 138, 813; bottles, etc., used in connection with certain drinks, protection of owners, 267; in penal institutions, restriction of, 464; branding prison-made goods from other States, 465; convict-made goods, sales and license fees, 813; State prisons, restricting manufacture of school furniture, X, 165; articles made of gold, stamping, 705; transfers of goods in bulk, 929.

Manufacturing Corporations. Act relating to, II, 855; act revived, 899, 1041; act of 1848, IV, 404, 639; extending act, waterworks companies, VI, 580; mortgages, 582.

MANUFACTURING CORPORATIONS —(*Continued*).

    VETOES. Special charter, IV, 526; Hopkinton Company, relief, VI, 169; payment of capital stock, 179; mercantile and commercial business, 335, 501; Ithaca Company, powers too indefinite and comprehensive, 700; amending act, 708; VII, 414, 806; VIII, 130, 132; extending act, VI, 910; Herkimer county, facilitating dissolution, VII, 59; floating dock, 569; extending power, patent rights, 621; uniform standard of time, 1027; consolidation, VIII, 1038; relief, IX, 794.

MANUFACTURING ESTABLISHMENTS. Inspection, act of 1892, IX, 163; women and children, employment regulated, 163; women and children, employment in, veto, VIII, 837; IX, 477.

MANURES. Storage of, nuisance, report of State Board of Health, VII, 548; New York, facilitating removal of, veto, 553, 935.

MAN OF WAR. Sent from England for defense of colony, I, 36.

MAP. Military tract, II, 286; State and local, act providing for, 385; chart of New York harbor, 440; of St. Regis land, 454; of Massachusetts received by Governor, 514; submitted by Regents, 518; State, distribution, 531, 543; proposed new, of State, III, 96; State, purchase and distribution, 162, 391; exchanges with Virginia, Missouri, Illinois and Arkansas, 225; geological survey, 994; in State Library, IV, 486; of New York harbor, V, 186, 198; Adirondack survey, deposit recommended, VII, 937; relative to water supply, submission to State Commission, X, 744; water supply, approval by State Commission, 855.

    VETOES. Geological survey, Catskill region, appropriation, VII, 469; for Railroad Commission, 921; topographical, State survey, VIII, 73; geological, publication, 113; geological, printing and distributing, 252; State surveys, filing, 423; State and Adirondack surveys, publication of, 551; of forest preserve in certain counties, IX, 776; blue line, Erie, Champlain and Oswego canals, appropriation, X, 297, 423; New York, providing for, 713; Kings county, closing part of East Ninety-second street, repealing act, 815.

MAPES, JONAS. Lieutenant-colonel, commands troops, 1812, II, 747.

MAPLE SUGAR. Manufacture, II, 313.

MAPPA, ADAM G. Bond for return of arms, II, 774.

MARACAIBO. Vessels from, detained for observation, yellow fever, VI, 533.

MARBLE. For State Hall, from Mount Pleasant Prison, III, 764; accumulations of, 1036.

MARBLETOWN. Petition, defense of frontier, II, 70.

    VETOES. Bridge over Rondout creek, VI, 585; — free bridge, Ulster county to contribute to expense of, IX, 817.

MARCY, WILLIAM L. Supreme Court, designated to hold extraordinary term, Niagara county, III, 354; Governor and portrait, 399.

    1833. Annual message, III, 399; epidemic, 399; public health, 400; penitentiary establishments, 400; pardons, 402; separate prison for female convicts, 403; importation of convicts, 403; lotteries, 404; militia, 404; common schools, 406; medical institutions, 408; colleges, 408; instruction of deaf and dumb, 408; county poorhouse system, 409; canal finances, 410; common school fund, 411; literature fund, 412; general fund, 412; recommends resumption of direct tax, 413; auction and salt duties, 413; canals, 414; national debt, 415; internal improvements, 416; Chenango canal, 419; manufactures and commerce, 420; protection, 420; agriculture, 421; suit by New Jersey against New York, 422; political parties, 425; national affairs, 426; South Carolina nullification proceedings, 427; resigns as Senator in Congress, 429; Illinois resolutions, 431; resolutions from Pennsylvania, Georgia and South Carolina, 431; Indiana, New Hampshire, North Carolina and Massachusetts resolutions, 434; Delaware resolutions, 435, 437; Virginia resolutions, 436; New Jersey and Ohio resolutions, 437; Massachusetts resolutions, 437, 438; Mississippi, Alabama and Maine resolutions, 438; cullers of staves and heading, Rensselaer, veto, 438.

    1834. Annual message, III, 441; South Carolina nullification proceedings, 441; settlement of New Jersey boundary controversy, 441; prosperity of State, 442; judicial system inadequate, 443; recommends additional vice-chancellors, 443; compensation of judges, 444; imprisonment for debt, 445; penitentiary establishments, 446; prison for women, 448; county jails, 449; New York House of Refuge, 449; instruction of deaf and dumb, 450; insane poor, 451; instruction of blind, 452; county poorhouses, 453; education, 454; primary schools, 455; common schools, 456; academies, 456; colleges, 457; agriculture, 457; manufactures, 458; canals, 459; canal tolls, 461; Hudson river improvement, 462; sketch of canals, 465; highways, 469; banks, 469; sale of bank franchise, 470; reduction of interest on bank loans, 472; reducing bank circulation, 475; limiting circulation of small bills, 476; salt manufacture, 477; militia, 478; finances, 478; State loan to banks and citizens, 481, 491, 496; resolutions from other States, 481; receives laws and decisions from Maryland, 482;

MARCY, WILLIAM L., 1834 — (*Continued*).

Georgia and Massachusetts resolutions, 482; panic of 1834, 483, 494; State bank, 490; New York banks should be strengthened, 492.

1835. Annual message, III, 493; national affairs, 493; conduct of Bank of United States, 494; panic subsides, 496; reform in judicial system, 498; education, 498; finances, 501; urges resumption of direct tax, 503; auction and salt duties, 505; canals, 505; enlargement of Erie canal, 506; Chenango canal, 506; deficiency of revenues for internal improvements, 507; additional internal improvements, 509; Hudson river improvement, 511; highways, 511; penitentiaries, 511; convict labor, 512; prisons, 514; prison for female convicts, 515; county jails, 515; county poorhouses, 516; instruction of blind, 516; asylum for insane poor, 516; character of circulating medium, 516; limiting circulation of small bills, 519; reducing circulation of banks, 519; bank discounts, 520; bank corporations, 521; militia, 522; courts-martial, 523; riot in New York, 524; elective franchise, 525; lotteries, 526; census, 526; death of Surveyor-General De Witt, 526; Maryland resolutions, 527; railroad from Williamsport to Elmira, 527; New York fire, 534, 584.

VETOES. Weighing merchandise in New York, III, 528; Rochester market, 531.

1836. Annual message, III, 534; general condition of State, 535; judiciary system, 536; education, 536; instruction of teachers, 538; school district libraries, 538; academies and seminaries, 539; colleges, 540; penitentiaries, 540; silk manufacture, 541; county jails, 542; care of deaf and dumb, 542; care of insane, 543; finances, 543; internal improvements, 545; defective financial policy, 546; New York and Erie Railroad Company, 550; canals, 551; corporations interfere with individual enterprise, 554; banks, 555; speculation, 555; new bank charter, 561; discontinuance of Bank of United States, 562; assessed value of property in New York city, 563; examination of insurance companies, 564; limiting circulation of small bills, 564; stockjobbing, 565; unclaimed dividends and deposits, 566; lotteries, 567; apportionment of Legislature, 567; geological survey, 567; agriculture, 568; militia, 568; cession of land to United States for protection of New York harbor, 570; appoint-

MARCY, WILLIAM L., 1836 — (*Continued*).

    ment of canal commissioners, 570; Federal relations, 570; abolition of slavery, 571; South Carolina resolutions, 582; Williams extradition case, 583, 594; North Carolina, Georgia and Alabama resolutions, 588; Virginia resolutions, 589; Ohio resolutions, 589, 591; Michigan and Kentucky resolutions, 589; Pennsylvania and Mississippi resolutions, 590; Maine resolutions, 590, 591; Eaton claim, geological survey, 591; reply to Governor Gayle, Williams extradition case, 595.

    VETOES. Railroads to carry mail, III, 592; Geneva College, appointing delegate to State Medical Society, 593.

1837. Annual message, III, 605; schemes for abolishing domestic slavery, 605; commends President Jackson, 606; judiciary system, 608; Court of Appeals, 610; education, 612; United States deposit fund, 612, 622; proposed change of supervision of academies, 614; common schools, 616; colleges and academies, 616; State Lunatic Asylum, 617; State prisons, 617; finances, 618; internal improvements, 620; views on distribution of Federal revenues, 624; restraints on deposits and discounts, 628, 630; Usury Law, 630; increase of bank capital, 632; sale of bank franchise, 632; circulation of small bills, 633; geological survey, 634, 638, 680; militia, 635; migration of Indians to western reservations, 635; pilot laws, 636; Maryland resolutions, 637; Vermont resolutions, 645; death of former Governor Joseph C. Yates, 645; memorandum, Suspension Act, 645.

1838. Annual message, III, 647; judiciary department, 647; education, 649; United States deposit fund, 650; school district libraries, 651; common school teachers, 652; normal schools, 652; education statistics, 653; banking institutions, 654; Free Banking Law, 656; Restraining Law, 656; panic of 1837, 656; excessive importations, 657; suspension of specie payments by banks, 659; results of panic of 1837, 663; specie reserves, 666, 667; canals, 668; loan for completion of Erie canal enlargement, 671; finances, 671; loans of United States deposit fund, 673; penitentiaries, 674; State Lunatic Asylum, 676; geological survey, 677, 681; militia, 677; unlawful seizure of military property, 677; invasion of State from Canada, 678; Alabama resolutions, 683; unlawful seizure of military stores, 683; Kentucky resolutions, 690; Ohio resolutions, 691; militia on western frontier, 691; resumption of specie payments, 694; Arkansas resolution, 705; advances to geological survey, 995; official service, I, pref. xii.

MARINE COURT. See COURT, MARINE.

MARINE HOSPITAL. See also NEW YORK MARINE HOSPITAL. United States, Erie county, ceding land for, X, 394.

MARINE HOSPITAL, STATEN ISLAND. Persons treated at, IV, 644.

MARINE INSURANCE COMPANIES. Statistics, V, 275; VII, 691, 824, 950; regulating charges, veto, 804.

MARINERS' FAMILY ASYLUM, STATEN ISLAND. Various appropriations, veto, VII, 490.

MARINERS' FUND. How composed, IV, 75, 272; capital of, 272; loan to Seamen's Friend Society, 272; Alien Passenger Tax Act, unconstitutional, 272, 273.

MARION. Sherman, justice of the peace, legalizing acts, veto, IX, 346.

MARION RIVER. Cleaning and clearing shore, veto, X, 320.

MARITIME ASSOCIATION, NEW YORK. Charter, veto, VI, 585.

MARK, GEORGE. Relief, veto, VI, 591.

MARKELL, W. L. Relief, veto, X, 53.

MARKET. Rochester, act relating to, III, 531; Albany, public, act relative to, VIII, 447; market roads recommended, IX, 203.

VETOES. NEW YORK. Twenty-first ward, VI, 93; — 13th ward, 209; — general, VII, 450; — rebuilding Fulton, 507; — public, VIII, 292; Wallabout, Brooklyn, injurious effects of Brooklyn pier, IX, 438; Brooklyn, — Wallabout improvement, 781; — Wallabout market lands, 783.

MARL. Accumulations of, III, 1036.

MARNINGHAM, HENRY. Court of Claims, Hudson River State Hospital, veto, X, 704.

"MARQUIS DE LA FAYETTE, THE." Lost with public stores, II, 156, 160.

MARRIAGE. Act to prescribe procedure, I, 11; joining Shakers, ground for divorce, II, 920, 946; dissolved by Legislature, 947; registration of, V, 863; licenses for, VIII, 470; conflict of laws in different States, 688; uniform laws recommended, 929.

MARRIED WOMEN. Husband's interest in legacy to wife, III, 262; duties, 847; rights of, V, 291.

VETOES. Estates of, II, 703; releasing dower in certain cases, VI, 597, 820; insuring husband's life, amending act, VII, 80; contracts, 331.

MARSEILLES. New York, commissioners of deeds in, V, 213.

MARSHAL. Compensation in military courts, II, 989. VETOES. New York, relative to, VII, 509; — New York, amending charter, X, 175.

MARSHALL, CHARLES H. Communication to Governor relative to appointment of William Church Osborn as State commissioner in lunacy, X, 43.

MARSHALL, JOHN. Chief justice, opinion, jurisdiction of Federal courts, III, 1026; opinion, impairing obligation of contracts, 1027; quoted, power of taxation is power of destruction, X, 67.

MARSHALL, JOHN. Act authorizing erection of grist mill, II, 485.

MARSHALL, JOHN E. Communication from, Federal interference in elections, II, 1067.

MARTHA'S VINEYARD. Representation in first Assembly, I, 9.

MARTIAL LAW. In New York, I, 765, 779; in New Orleans, IV, 45; power of President to declare, V, 465; Governor Seymour's comments on, 468, 551; Kentucky protests against, 500; exercise of, resulting death, when murder, VI, 772.

MARTIN, CELORA E. Supreme Court Law Library, Binghamton, veto, VII, 220.

MARTIN, HENRY P. Colonel, Seventy-first Regiment, supplies from Union Defense Committee, VII, 501.

MARTIN, PHILIP. Captain, payment of losses incurred in New York riot, I, 713.

MARTIN, WALTER. Brigadier-general, arms and supplies delivered to, II, 775.

MARTINDALE, JOHN H. Agent, Tonawanda Indians, V, 202.

MARTINIQUE. French armament arrives at, I, 340.

MARTINSBURGH. Arms and supplies for, II, 775.

MARTINUS, GEORGE A. Senate messenger, appropriation, veto, VII, 459.

MARVIN, ANTHONY. Estate of, veto, II, 716.

MARVIN, HARRIET N. Escheat, veto, VII, 1107.

MARY, QUEEN OF ENGLAND. See WILLIAM AND MARY.

MARYLAND. Safety of, dependent on security of Albany, I, 30; troops from, in expedition against Canada, 373; Lords of Trade recommend colonial union, 578; represented in Albany Convention, 578; letter from Governor, II, 262; amendment, qualifications of Vice-President, Senators and Representatives, 434; amendment, election of presidential electors and Representatives by districts, 471; amendment, importation of slaves, 605; disapproves Virginia resolutions on removal of Senator, 649; opposes Massachusetts embargo amendment, 665; disapproves Pennsylvania proposition to reduce senatorial term, 829; report of Legislature, proceeds of public land, 1079; cession of territory for District of Columbia, III, 138; protests against South Carolina nullification proceedings, transmits copies of decisions and laws, 482; resolution favoring reorganization of militia, 527; proposition to extend franking privilege, 637; proposed retrocession of Georgetown to, 907; pledges support to national government in northeastern boundary matter, 909; right to

MARYLAND — (*Continued*).

define felony, 929; protests against Massachusetts apportionment proposition, IV, 86; protests against abolition of slavery in District of Columbia, 513; action on independence monument, V, 122; military to be subordinate to civil power, 470; adheres to Union, 476; appropriations for Antietam National cemetery, 764; cemetery originally a State enterprise, 840; tax exemptions, VI, 371; transfer of Antietam National cemetery to United States, VII, 172.

MASONIC ASSOCIATION, UTICA. Exempting from taxation, veto, IX, 791.

MASONIC HALL ASSOCIATION, BUFFALO. Charter, veto, VIII, 464, 624, 733.

MASONVILLE TURNPIKE ROAD COMPANY. Incorporated, III, 758.

MASSACHUSETTS (Colony). Establishes post from Boston to Westfield, I, 136; Governor Shute demands assistance in Indian War, 203; Assembly declines aid, 204; commissioners to treat with Five Nations, 206; petition to King for aid from New York in Indian War, 219; boundary disputes at Westenhook, 226; resolutions of Assembly, relative to New York boundary, 228; letter from Governor Belcher relative to boundary, 241, 283; commissioners confer with Indians at Albany, 319; negotiations for colonial union, 320; movement against French, 331; New York furnishes cannon and money, 332; sends aid to Annapolis Royal, 336; proximity to French settlements, 336; expedition against Cape Breton, 332, 346; letter from Lieutenant-Governor Phips, Louisburg campaign, 358; joins in Indian conference, 359; Indians attack Great Meadow, 360; letter from Lieutenant-Governor Phips, colonies should unite in war, 365, 366; appoints commissioners for colonial union, 370; asked to join in expense of engaging Indians in Canadian expedition, 376; estimated expense of attack on Crown Point, 393; joining other colonies in war measures, 404, 413, 584; presents to Indians, 417; agreement for colonial union, 419; share of expenses, Crown Point expedition, 419; approves joint agreement for colonial defense, 457, 461; legislative resolutions on agreement for union, 461; New York disapproves alterations in agreement, 462; treaty with Indians, 466; appropriations for Crown Point expedition, 571; troops for, 575, 594; Lords of Trade recommend colonial union, 578; represented in Albany Convention, 578; commissioners authorized to propose general union, 578; historical records, Albany plan of union, 579; bounties for Indian scalps, 595; distressed condition of forces at Fort William Henry, 597; financial aid from Crown, 599, 604; New Hampshire boundary, how settled, 610; alleged unwarrantable territorial claims of, 612, 721; troops for Canadian expedition, 620, 634, 644, 654; resolutions proposing western boundary, twenty-mile line, 722, 723.

Massachusetts (State). Militia at battle of Bennington, II, 8; conference on paper currency, 11; action relative to finances, 18; called on for militia, 31; land grants in Vermont, 48; scarcity of wheat and flour, 69; delegation from, visits Governor Clinton to present distressed condition of State, 72; communication from, relative to regulation of prices, 83; Assembly requests repeal of inland embargo laws, 91; boundary controversy with New Hampshire, 102; made no claim to Vermont, 140; letter from Governor Hancock relative to convention on taxation, 190; territorial claims of, 208, 217, 260; appoints boundary commissioners, 211; resolutions, boundary question, 261; letter from Governor, 261, 272; Shays' rebellion, 269; resolutions in Congress for general convention, 270; resolutions, suability of State, 334; resolution, amendment, foreign influence in national councils, 424; Constitution, appointment of officers, 499; interchange of maps and laws, 514, 530; land in Chenango and Steuben counties ceded to, 522; proposes constitutional amendment, apportionment of representatives, 546, 560, 586; amendment, importation of slaves from West Indies, 563; disapproves Virginia resolution on removal of Senators, 650; limiting duration of embargo, 665; constitutional amendments, basis of representation and direct taxes, admission of new States, limiting duration of embargo, interdiction of commerce, limiting power to declare war, only native citizens entitled to hold office, ineligibility of President to re-election, 827, 828, 864; amendment, election of Representatives and presidential electors by districts, 864; land claims in western New York, 916; distribution of statutes, 1026; Constitution, procedure to amend, 1057; resolutions relative to Ohio controversy over Bank of United States, 1118; resolutions relative to distribution of public lands, 1119; disapproves Pennsylvania proposition as to national banks, III, 13; superior inspection laws, 99; progress of education, 212; recommends reorganization of national militia, 364; affirms national character of Constitution, 364; resolutions on northeastern boundary question, 389; approves protective policy and opposes pending tariff bill, 434; protests against South Carolina nullification proceedings and approves President's course, 437; disapproves proposition for Constitutional Convention, 438; approves act of Congress distributing proceeds of public land, 438; recommends abolition of lotteries, 482; publication of colonial records, 751; resolutions on public lands, protective tariff, presidential term, presidential electors and northeastern boundary, 929; resolutions, imprisonment of its citizens in other States; choosing presidential electors, 1020; obtaining granite from, IV, 29; apportionment of Representatives, 84; urging pay-

MASSACHUSETTS (State)—(*Continued*).

ment of French spoliation claims, 85; opposes annexation of Texas, 85; claim to Indian lands in New York, 290, 295; manufactures in, 400; instruction of idiots, 555; Excise Law, 757; cedes Boston Corners to New York, 817; location of normal schools, 843; action on independence monument, V, 122; tenders aid to Federal government, 320; military to be subordinate to civil power, 470; letter from Governor, New York canals, 507; appropriation for Antietam cemetery, 840; usury laws repealed, VI, 552; VII, 719; assessed valuation of personal property, 1880, VIII, 307; statute relative to fires caused by operation of railroads, 324; Ballot Act of 1888, 670; protection of employees, act of 1888, 672, 918; weekly payment of wages, 681; general registration of voters, 906; experience under new Ballot Law, 908; voters must be able to read and write English language, 912, 959; court to render opinion as to constitutionality of pending bills, 947; Supreme Court declines to render an opinion on a legislative bill, 1048; factory inspectors, ratio to number of establishments, IX, 166; Corrupt Practices Act noted, 197; retail liquor licenses, 1892, 666; license of buildings for manufacturing purposes, X, 8; Employers' Liability Act, 190; information as to vital statistics, 870.

MASSACHUSETTS BAY. See MASSACHUSETTS.

MASSACHUSETTS BOUNDARY. Question relating to, at Westenhook, I, 226; resolutions of Massachusetts Assembly relative to, 228; letter from Governor Belcher relative to, 241, 283; papers relating to, 282; commissioners for, 541; proposed establishment of temporary line, 544; report of commissioners, 552; Governor Hardy recommends settlement of, 589, 610; Council's observations on, 611; act to facilitate settlement of, 685; difficulty of establishment, 714; commissaries appointed for settlement of, 718, 720, 747, 749, 752; New York's claim, 720; Massachusetts resolutions proposing western boundary, twenty-mile line, 722, 723; agreement by commissioners, 754; description of agreed boundary, 754, 755; proceedings relating to, II, 208; Massachusetts appoints commissioners, 211; Congress provides for hearing, 217, 260; New York appoints commissioners, 217, 260; Massachusetts resolutions, 261; line established, 265, 282; act to ascertain line, 306; exchange of land, 351, 391; colonial documents relative to, III, 1018; resurvey, 1889, X, 864.

MASSENA. St. Regis land in, purchase of, III, 36.

MASTER IN CHANCERY. Appointment of guardian, veto, II, 488; fees of, 702; county judge ineligible, 1053; general act for appointment of, III, 498; office abolished, IV, 414.

MASTER OF ROLLS. James Jauncey appointed, I, 763.

MASTERS. Act relating to, I, 11; reimbursement for enlistment of apprentices, 599.

MASTS. For King's ships, I, 93.

MATANZA. Vessels from, detained for observation, yellow fever, VI, 626.

MATHER, FREDERICK G. Preparation of papers, War of 1812, appropriation, veto, X, 784.

MATHER, JOHN C. Canal commissioner, impeachment, trial and acquittal, IV, 695.

MATHER, WILLIAM W. Geological survey, geologist, first district, III, 640, 754, 991; report, 644, 682, 754; IV, 81.

MATHER POWER BRIDGE COMPANY. Authorized to construct experimental power bridge, Niagara river, X, 54.

MATHEWS, THOMAS. Admiral, commands English fleet in Mediterranean, I, 314.

MATHEWS, WILBUR K. Court of Claims, veto, X, 312.

MATTHEWS, THOMAS F. Counsel fees and expenses, Assembly contested election, Palmer case, Kings county, veto, X, 795.

MATTEAWAN. State asylum for insane criminals at, VIII, 822. VETOES. Railroad to Long Wharf, VI, 211; — lighting streets, 704.

MATTEAWAN STATE HOSPITAL. VETOES. Additions, repairs and improvements, IX, 295, 296; propagating and greenhouse, X, 299; reception and maintenance of patients, 591; appropriations for, 655.

MATROSSES (Artillery). To be provided, I, 323.

MAUMIE INDIANS. Treaty, land on White river, Indiana, II, 988.

MAXWELL, SAMUEL. Bond for return of arms, II, 772.

MAYFIELD. Arms and supplies for, II, 772.

MAYHEM. Punishment of, III, 285.

MAYOR. Of New York and Albany to be commissioners of excise, I, 529; New York, — action concerning hospital, 743; — election by people, III, 212; IV, 53; election by people, 53; New York, Governor's power of removal, V, 519; concentration of executive responsibility in, VI, 34, 453, 477, 544; New York, charter of 1870, inadequate power of appointment, 381; Havemeyer, New York, administration commended, 544; of New York, appointments without confirmation, act relative to, VII, 1056; New York, powers of, IX, 416.

MAYSVILLE ROAD BILL. President's veto, III, 319, 464.

McADOO, WILLIAM. Assistant Secretary of Navy, objects to Brooklyn pier bill, IX, 438.

McALLISTER, JEANETTE. Board of Claims, veto, IX, 119.

McALPINE, C. L. Canals, engineer, certificate, appropriation, veto, VII, 231.

McALPINE, WILLIAM J. State Engineer and Surveyor, estimate, Erie canal enlargement, IV, 689.

McAVOY, THOMAS. Damages, injuries, new capitol, veto, VII, 910.

McCABE, DANIEL. Claim against New York, veto, VIII, 884.

McCABE, PATRICK. Assistant clerk, New York district court, relief, VII, 452.

McCANN, EDWARD P. New York, relief, veto, X, 176, 179.

McCARTHY, DENNIS. Senate, remarks on opening new Senate chamber, VII, 540.

McCARTHY, JOHN A. Contract for legislative printing, X, 270.

McCARTHY, PATRICK M. New York, relief, veto, X, 176.

McCAUGHEL, GEORGE. Escheat bill, veto, IV, 693.

McCLEARY, DANIEL. Excise commissioner, Salem, legalizing acts, veto, VIII, 354.

McCLELLAN, GEORGE B. Nominated as Superintendent of Public Works, VII, 51.

McCLELLAND, JOHN W. Canal Department, appropriation for services, veto, IX, 716.

McCLURE, FRANCIS. Lieutenant-colonel, commands volunteers, II, 765; commands troops on Niagara frontier, 791.

McCOLLUM, WILLIAM J. Excise commissioner, Salem, legalizing acts, veto, VIII, 354.

McCONNELL, WILLIAM. Bond for return of arms, II, 772.

McCORMICK, JAMES C. Notary public, Watertown, legalizing acts, veto, X, 813.

McCORMICK, WILLIAM. Justice of the peace, Potsdam, legalizing acts, veto, X, 813.

McCRARY ON "ELECTIONS." Quoted, secret ballot, VIII, 585.

McCREERY, JAMES. Approves Harvey claim against New York city, VIII, 1162.

McCULLEN, JAMES. New York fireman, reinstatement, veto, X, 951.

McCULLOCH, HUGH. Secretary of the Treasury, contraction of legal tender notes, VI, 253.

McCULLOUGH, JOHN. Appointed State Superintendent of Elections, metropolitan district, IX, 886.

McCUNN, JOHN H. Judge, New York Superior Court, charges against, removed, VI, 498.

McDONALD, CHARLES J. Governor of Georgia, communication from, Greenman extradition case, III, 937.

McDONALD, JOHN. Resigns as Regent, II, 375.

McDONALD, WILLIAM J. Substitute for Senate journal clerk, compensation, veto, VII, 907.

McDOUGALL, ALEXANDER. Major-general, supplies for forces under, II, 66; letter from, security of West Point, 165; depreciation in pay, 169.

McDOUGH, JOHN. Court of Claims, injuries received at Sing Sing prison, veto, X, 699.

McDOWELL, WILLIAM H. New York, relief, veto, X, 581.

McDUFFIE, ANGUS. Former sheriff, service of process, Van Rensselaer rent, III, 827.

McELROY, WILLIAM H. Poem at Capital Centennial Celebration, 1897, IX, 690.

McGEE, ANDREW. Escheat, veto, VII, 805.

McGOWAN, ELIZABETH. Claim, New York, refund taxes, veto, X, 806.

McGOWAN, JOHN F. Board of Claims, veto, VIII, 639, 886.

McGRAIN, JOSEPH. Canal Department, appropriation for services, veto, IX, 716.

McGRATH, FRANK. New York Municipal Court attendant, claim, veto, X, 168.

McGRATH, MICHAEL. Relief, veto, X, 53, 177.

McGRAW, JOHN J. Albany, relief, veto, X, 179.

McGUIRE, JOSEPH. Contestant, Stemmler case, VII, 661.

McGUIRE, THOMAS. Relief, veto, VI, 185.

McHALE, MARTIN. Legal services, Consolidated Gas Company case, appropriation, veto, X, 785.

McINTOSH, I. C. Land for Utica asylum, veto, VII, 89.

McINTOSH, WILLIAM C. Board of Claims, veto, VIII, 1166.

McINTYRE, ARCHIBALD. Comptroller, bond for return of arms, II, 772; communication from, relative to capitol, 936; report on removal of Montgomery's remains, 1001.

McINTYRE, ARCHIBALD. Board of Claims, veto, VIII, 887; IX, 152; Court of Claims, 451.

McKELWAY, ST. CLAIR. Regent, resignation, X, 518; withdrawal of resignation, re-election, 518.

McKENNA, BRIDGET. Escheat, veto, VIII, 725.

McKEON, JOHN. District attorney, communication from, vagrants, trial jurors, IV, 505.

McKEOWN, JOHN. Assembly, member of insurance investigating committee, 1905, X, 825.

McKESSON, JOHN. To deposit revolutionary records in office of Secretary of State, II, 543; correspondence with Governor George Clinton noted, VII, 812.

McKIM, JOHN A. Communication to Governor relative to appointment of William Church Osborn as State commissioner in lunacy, X, 43.

McKINLAY, JAMES. Bond for return of arms, II, 772.

McKINLAY, JOHN. Bond for return of arms, II, 772.

McKINLEY, WILLIAM. Assassination of, X, 340; monument, Buffalo, 394; memorial, printing and distributing, veto, 430.

McKINSTRY, CHARLES. Board of Claims, veto, IX, 149, 269.

McLACHLAN, ARCHIBALD C. Principal Jamaica normal school, Waters case, X, 561.

McLAREN, DANIEL. Bond for return of arms, II, 772.

McLAREN, DUNCAN. Bond for return of arms, II, 772.

McLEAN, DONALD, MRS. Member of Cotton States Exposition Commission, 1895, IX, 582.

McLEAN, JOHN. General, claim of, War of 1812, II, 946.

McLEER, JAMES. General, nominated as quarantine commissioner, VIII, 520.

McLEOD, ALEXANDER. Case of, III, 932, 941; tried and acquitted, 942, 943.

McLAUGHLIN, JOHN. Escheat, veto, VII, 748.

McMAHON, MARTIN T. Assembly, 1891, memorial and resolutions on General Sherman's death, VIII, 1088.

McMASTER, J. SMITH. Legalizing claim against State, Board of Claims, veto, IX, 797; Court of Claims, veto, X, 64.

McMILLAN, DANIEL H. Member of Educational Unification Commission, 1899, X, 114.

McMILLEN, DUNCAN C. Stenographer, Assembly, appropriation, veto, VII, 81.

McNAMARA, ROGER. Estate, sale, veto, VIII, 1090.

McNEILE, HECTOR. Coroner's clerk, Kings county, compensation, veto, X, 957.

McVEANY, JAMES E. Relief, veto, VII, 507.

MEAD, CHARLES W. Assembly, member of joint legislative committee on services in memory of former Governor Higgins, X, 963.

MEAD, THOMPSON. Lieutenant-colonel, commands 17th Regiment, II, 765; funds received by, 765.

MEADE, RICHARD W., JR. Captain, commander of the "Vandalia," visit of French delegates to West Point, VII, 740.

MEADOW CREEK. Northern terminus of proposed Hudson river improvement, II, 365.

MEADS, JOHN. Expense, coffin for General Montgomery, II, 1001.

MEAGHER, JOHN J. Relief, veto, X, 177.

MEAL. Exportation of, veto, II, 26; scarcity of, 54; embargo on, 114, 120; inspection of, 436, 471.

MEASURES. See WEIGHTS AND MEASURES.

MECHANICS. See also MECHANIC'S LIEN. Fixing wages, II, 25, 46; instruction of, III, 127; IV, 432, 603, 649; complaint against convict labor, III, 512, 930, 940; IV, 28, 72, 123, 608; proposed establishment of museum in old State Hall, 47; industrial exhibition, 509, 572; interest in work of Clinton prison, 651; residents preferred on new capitol work, VI, 229.

VETOES. Incorporating, II, 228; protection of, IX, 624, 724; hours of labor in State service, 724.

MECHANICS' BANK, NEW YORK. Bond, common school fund, II, 722.

MECHANIC AND SCIENTIFIC INSTITUTION, NEW YORK. Purposes of, III, 66.

MECHANICS AND FARMERS' BANK, ALBANY. Return from national to State system, VI, 20.

MECHANIC'S LIEN. Act of 1885, VIII, 36, 477.

VETOES. New York, VI, 213; effect on fire insurance policy, VII, 332; extending act, 417; amending act, cities, 665, 666; revision, 1125; amending act, VIII, 1040; IX, 259; dredging and improving low lands, 127; claims against contractors, notice to owner, 128; stone cutters, etc., 623; New York, repealing part of Consolidation Act, 872.

MECHANICS' SAVINGS BANK, TROY. Charter, veto, VI, 342.

MECHANICS AND TRADERS' SAVINGS INSTITUTION. Investigation of, VII, 56.

MECHANICS AND TRADESMEN. Charter, veto, II, 228; school for, III, 455.

MECHANICVILLE. VETOES. Bridge company, VI, 333; purchasing fire apparatus, VII, 849; lift bridge, Champlain canal, VIII, 130; fire commissioners, creating board, 621; bridge, North street, IX, 235; canal bridge, Burke avenue and Francis street, X, 434, 547.

MECHANICVILLE BRIDGE COMPANY. Charter, veto, VI, 333.

MEDALS. For Dr. Kane and Lieutenant Hartstene, Arctic explorers, V, 59.

MEDICAL COLLEGES. At New York, II, 317, 904; III, 117; at Fairfield, II, 904; III, 118; lottery for, II, 908; number of students, 1049; prosperous condition of, 1100; III, 62, 297, 338, 408; department in Geneva College, 857; number, VI, 618; VII, 947.

VETOES. Homeopathic Medical College, Buffalo, charter, VII, 266; legalizing certain charters, 937; New York College of Medicine and Surgery, charter, VIII, 100; New York Post-Graduate Medical School and Hospital, amending charter, 707; Seneca

MEDICAL COLLEGES, VETOES — (*Continued*).

Falls School of Anatomy, dissections, IX, 264; corpses to be delivered to, in certain cases, 627; medical department, University of Buffalo, cancer investigation, 772.

MEDICAL EXAMINERS. Providing for exemption of certain candidates, VIII, 1152.

MEDICAL SOCIETIES. General act for incorporation, II, 574; act amended, 974. VETOES. County, amount of property, VII, 412; — Rochester Electro-Medical Institute, charter, 416, 506.

MEDICINE. Act to regulate practice, I, 11; practice should be free, VI, 513; sketch of early legislation, 515; adulteration of, VII, 649; veterinary medicine and surgery, see that title.

VETOES. Practice of, elevating standard, VI, 194; prescriptions and remedies, 325; regulating practice, 337; licenses, 512; amending general act, VII, 353, new bill passed; amending general act, 415, 806; IX, 117; medical services, Auburn prison, audit, VII, 666; drugs, adulteration, 924; sale of, Kings county, 936; students, preliminary education, VIII, 131; dispensaries, Brooklyn, additional number, 969; State Board of Examiners, deficiency appropriation, IX, 76; intoxication, person convicted of, medical treatment in penitentiaries, 252; practicing without authority, penalty, 504; Metropolitan Post-Graduate School of Medicine, charter, 623; admission to examinations, 803; license to practice, 803; pharmacists and druggists, New York, regulating prescriptions, etc., 871; practice authorized by certain persons, X, 63; admission of Abbott to medical examination, 313; offenses connected with sale of, 592.

MEDINA. Canal improvements at, VI, 858. VETOES. Lock-up, VI, 273; bridge, Prospect street, VII, 577; armory, IX, 777; police department, X, 440.

MEDITERRANEAN SEA. Naval battle, I, 314.

MEEHAN, BERNARD. Relief, veto, X, 53.

MEEHAN, J. M., AND THOMAS. Relief, amending act, veto, IX, 152; X, 582.

MEEKS, JAMES. Affidavit by, anti-rent trouble, III, 829.

MEIGS, HENRY. Action in removal of postmaster, II, 1069; letter from Martin Van Buren, 1070.

MEIGS, R. J., JR. Letter to Stephen B. Leonard, II, 1072.

MEISNER, CARL. Battery G, Seventh Division, National Guard, damages, permanent injury, appropriation, veto, VII, 466, 910.

Mellon, Thomas G. Relief, veto, X, 53.

Membership Corporations Law. Cemeteries, taxing lots, VI, 184.

Vetoes. Amending general law, IX, 802; directors, quorum, annual reports, X, 432; drawing juries on exhibition grounds, 450; election of managers and trustees, 946.

Memorandum. Of Assembly, relative to Indian land grants, I, 686; of approval by Governor Seward, Senate refuses to receive, III, 974. See also Table of Memorandums on Approval of Bills.

Memorial. To Lords Justices, I, 72, 73; for schoolhouse, 181; against colony, 182; to King on Indian trade, 237; against aid to sugar colonies, 240; from Albany authorities relative to defense of city, 244; from Capt. John Morke, relative to floating battery and naval stores, 555; from General Winslow and others, pay of, 613; from John Beebe and others, II, 54; from army officers relative to supplies, 88; New York prisoners of war, 101; New York merchants, claims of, 241; Abijah Merril, distribution of public land, 256; from Cayuga Indians, lease of lands, 328; Samuel Haight, Ryer case, 345; Dr. Wright Post, anatomical museum for Columbia College, 389; from New York, public health, 433; New York Chamber of Commerce, inspection of provisions, 439; Ontario grand jury, George case, 531; from New York Society for Promoting Manumission of Slaves, abolition of slavery, 693; from John Hunsdon, St. Regis lands, 941; on revolutionary pensions, 1027; on Washington lottery, 1103, 1123; for canal between Lake Erie and Allegany river, III, 96; from American Colonization Society, 144; Seneca Indians, diversion of Tonawanda creek, 182; New York Law Institute, relief to Court of Chancery, 264; Amos Eaton, geological survey, 591; from Saratoga and Warren counties, Hudson river improvement, 748; New York Historical Society, publication of colonial documents, 751; IV, 166; by mechanics, against competition of convict labor, III, 930; by Ninth Regiment of Infantry, reorganization of militia, 983; New York Free Trade Association, repeal of inspection laws, IV, 45; New York pilots, 156; Seneca Indians, treaty rights, 295; Seneca Indians, new form of government, 507; Seneca Indians, protesting against repeal of Confirming Act, 507; New York Chamber of Commerce, encroachments on New York harbor, 704; New York Merchants' Exchange, encroachments on New York harbor, 751; Albany Board of Trade, obstructions in Hudson river, V, 40; from secretary of State Inebriate Asylum, 107; Kansas Legislature, 345; from Prison Association, 486; Indiana, use of New York canals and railroads, 493; New York Chamber of Commerce, use of canals, 506; to President, use of New York canals, 506; Canadian canals, 507;

MEMORIAL —(*Continued*).

Cheney, exploration of ancient mounds, 720; Albany and Rensselaer counties, anti-rent troubles, 792; New York Chamber of Commerce, reducing canal tolls, VI, 276; Stockbridge Indians, 415; New York Historical Society, centennial volume, 809; on uniform reports from railroad companies, VII, 28; Kingston, organization of State government, appropriation, veto, 85; Connecticut, Hell Gate pilotage, 441; American Forestry Congress, forest preservation, 1000; New York Historical Society, centennial anniversary of New York's ratification of United States Constitution, VIII, 505.

MEMORIAL DAY. VETOES. In towns, money for observance of, amending act, IX, 813; celebration in Richmond borough, X, 762.

MEMORIAL HALL. White Plains, bill to establish, veto, IX, 221.

MEMPHIS, NEW YORK. Village charter, veto, VI, 341.

MEMPHIS, TENNESSEE. Slaughter of Union soldiers at, V, 858.

MENOMINI INDIANS. Green Bay treaty, II, 1107.

MENTAL AND MORAL IMPROVEMENT SOCIETY, IRVINGTON. Charter, veto, VI, 196.

MENTZ. VETOES. Taxes, New York Central and Hudson River Railroad Company, application of, VII, 207; school district, 938; State ditch, bill relative to, VIII, 413; consolidating school districts, amending act of 1857, IX, 252.

MERCEIN, WILLIAM A. Prepares system of military tactics, II, 951, 953, 994, 996.

MERCHANDISE. Reduction of tolls on, III, 505; weighing in New York, veto, 528; inspection discontinued, 722; fraud in sale or exchange, VII, 388; sales in bulk, act relative to, X, 631.

MERCHANTS. London, remonstrate against Colonial Tariff Act, I, 198; colony opposes Canadian trade regulations, 212; oppose bills prohibiting sale of Indian goods to French, 237; of Albany, charged with opposing war, 399; of London, apply for relief from depreciated bills of credit, 560; of New York, Assembly rejects resolution of thanks to, 768; New York, claim of, II, 241.

MERCHANTS' BANK. Stock as part of common school fund, II, 722; defalcations in, 997, 998, 1029.

MERCHANTS' EXCHANGE SALESROOM. Charter, veto, VII, 417.

MERCHANTS' LOAN COMPANY. Charter, veto, VI, 587.

MERCHANTS' NATIONAL BANK, SYRACUSE. Drafts on Comptroller, veto, VI, 1001.

MERCHANTS' TRUST COMPANY. Relation to investigation of Bank Department, X, 872.

MERCHANTS' TRUST COMPANY, NEW YORK. Charter, veto, VIII, 292.

MERRIL, ABIJAH. Memorial, distribution of public lands, II, 256.

MERRIMAN, BENJAMIN. Bond for return of arms, II, 774.

MERRITT, EDWIN A. Quartermaster-General, member of Auditing Board of Enlistments, V, 870; report, VI, 44; member of New Capitol Commission, 229; collector of New York, appointment of successor, VII, 555.

MERRITT, FRANCIS E. Court of Claims, veto, X, 449.

MESEREAU, JOHN F. AND GRANT. Canal award, veto, VII, 774.

MESSAGE. From Governor and Council to be in writing, I, 20; first instance of, at opening of session, 186; substituted for opening speech, III, 1; annual, see ANNUAL MESSAGE; suppression by Senate, 976.

METCALF, SIMON. Claim for surveying Indian boundary, I, 744.

METEOROLOGICAL BUREAU. Cost of, 1891, IX, 11; established, 171. See STATE WEATHER BUREAU.

METHODIST EPISCOPAL CHURCH. Transfers and conveyances, veto, X, 704.

METHODIST EPISCOPAL CHURCH, NORTHVILLE. Sale of property, veto, VI, 437.

METHODIST EPISCOPAL CHURCH, TOMPKINSVILLE. Changing name, veto, VI, 270.

METHODIST EPISCOPAL CHURCH HOME, NEW YORK. VETOES. Relative to, VIII, 509; releasing from assessments, X, 175.

METHODIST EPISCOPAL HOSPITAL, BROOKLYN. Amending charter, veto, VIII, 464, 624, 733.

METROPOLIS FINANCE COMPANY, NEW YORK. Charter, veto, IX, 379.

METROPOLITAN BOARD OF EXCISE. Report, VI, 43, 143; repeal of law recommended, 126; metropolitan district abolished, 127.

METROPOLITAN BOARD OF HEALTH. Created, V, 702; good work of, 767; report of commissioners, 791; VI, 43, 142; documents for appendix to report, 44.

METROPOLITAN ELECTIONS DISTRICT. Created, 1898, IX, 885; John Mc-Cullough appointed superintendent, 886; lodging-houses, registry of guests, X, 213; salaries of deputy superintendents, veto, 429.

METROPOLITAN ELEVATED RAILWAY COMPANY. Leased to Manhattan Railway Company, VII, 851.

METROPOLITAN FIRE DEPARTMENT. Report of commissioners, V, 715, 791; VI, 43, 143.

METROPOLITAN MUSEUM OF ART. New York, Ward claim, settlement, veto, IX, 873.

METROPOLITAN NAUTICAL INSTITUTE, NEW YORK. Charter, veto, VI, 328.

METROPOLITAN POLICE DISTRICT. Created, V, 27, 53; organization of police force, 89; report of commissioners, 110, 193, 305, 413, 563, 598, 617, 699, 715, 791, 861; VI, 43, 142; efficiency of police, V, 181, 282; house of detention for witnesses, 181; finances, 181; territory enlarged, 183; number of commissioners reduced, 183, 282; area of, 282; increasing functions of police, 379; defective health laws, 701; commissioners to be members of metropolitan board of health, 702; act sustained, VI, 30; excise in, 35; communication from commissioners, pay of patrolmen, 44; inspecting steam boilers, veto, 96.

METROPOLITAN POST-GRADUATE SCHOOL OF MEDICINE. Charter, veto, IX, 623.

METROPOLITAN RAILROAD COMPANY. Tunnel under Broadway, veto, V, 669.

METROPOLITAN SANITARY DISTRICT. Established, V, 702; improved conditions in, 844; report of board of health, VI, 43; act repealed as to Brooklyn, 129. VETOES. Repeal as to Queens county, VII, 113; — amending act, Newtown, 267.

METROPOLITAN TRANSIT COMPANY. VETOES. Indirect amendment of charter, VI, 715; relative to, VII, 415; supplemental act, 592; discontinuing part of line, changing Harlem River bridge, VIII, 132.

MEXICO. Republic of, relations with, IV, 284; war with, slavery proviso in act relating to, 382; militia called out, 415; abolishes slavery, 445, 501; National Exposition of Industries and Fine Arts, 1896, IX, 671.

MEXICO (Oswego County). Arms and supplies for, II, 774; rebuilding town hall, veto, VII, 71; VIII, 516.

MEYER, LOUIS. Canal Department, appropriation for services, veto, IX, 716.

MEYER, WILLIAM. Escheat, veto, VII, 749.

MIAMI CANAL. Description of, III, 902; IV, 61.

MIAMI INDIANS. Convey to Stockbridge Indians land on White river, Indiana, II, 987.

MICHAEL. An Indian, claim for board of, I, 224.

MICHIGAN. Resolutions relative to anti-slavery movement, III, 589; stock of, securities in New York banks, 725; IV, 36; wheat and flour from, transported on Erie canal, III, 893; rapid increase of population, 899; difficulties in constructing roads connecting with Lake Erie, 901; requests congressional aid in construction of ship canal around St. Marie falls, 907; recommends additional river and harbor improvements, IV, 46; recommends ship canal around Niagara falls, 817; resolutions, improvement of St. Clair flats, V, 115; tenders aid to national government, 340; appropriation for Antietam cemetery, 840; communication from Governor, lighthouse on Stannard's rock,

MICHIGAN — (*Continued*).

VII, 46; communication from Governor, proposed harbor of refuge at Grand Marais harbor, Lake Superior, 60; uniform liquor tax, VIII, 437; excise taxes used for local purposes, 438; women may vote for school officers, IX, 96; retail liquor licenses, 1892, 666; information as to vital statistics, X, 870.

MIDDLEBURGH. Scott patent includes part of, IV, 331; separate road district, amending act, veto, VII, 414, 440.

MIDDLE DISTRICT BANK. Failure of, loss of common school funds, III, 295.

MIDDLEPORT. Repairing drain running into culvert under Erie canal, veto, X, 798.

MIDDLETOWN (Connecticut). Committees to meet at, Crown Point expedition, I, 420.

MIDDLETOWN (New York, Orange county). Homeopathic Asylum for Insane established at, VI, 115; armory, act of 1888, VIII, 455; city incorporated, 1888, 564.

    VETOES. Monhagen Hose Company No. 1, charter, VI, 341; payment of village bonds, VII, 131; village hall, 1042; VIII, 61, 516; armory, 455; city charter, 470, 564; extending boundaries, IX, 787; Hillside Cemetery Association, raising money for improvements, 794.

MIDDLETOWN (Richmond county). Separate road district, veto, VII, 497, 507.

MIDDLETOWN STATE HOMEOPATHIC HOSPITAL. See also HOMEOPATHIC ASYLUM FOR THE INSANE. VETOES. Cement walk, completing, X, 934; — fence on Monhagen avenue, 934.

MIDDLETOWN AND WURTSBORO TURNPIKE COMPANY. Extending charter, veto, VII, 265.

MIDDLE VILLAGE. Lutheran cemetery, amending charter, veto, VI, 595.

MIDWIFERY. VETOES. Practice of — Montgomery county, IX, 862; — New York, X, 172.

MILAN. Decrees of, noted, II, 672, 690.

MILBORNE, JACOB. Convicted of treason, I, 21; execution of, 22.

MILE POSTS. Providing for, II, 385.

MILES, BENJAMIN. Nominated sheriff of Schoharie county, proceedings of Council of Appointment, II, 475.

MILFORD CENTER CEMETERY ASSOCIATION. Extending powers, veto, VIII, 712.

MILITIA (Colony). Detachment of, burdensome, I, 51; deserters from, 48, 66; act for raising additional, 66; proposed revision of law,

MILITIA (Colony)— (*Continued*).

121; acts relating to, 11, 20, 99, 102, 128, 143, 155, 193, 309, 365, 529, 549, 585, 617, 741; exempts to serve as watchers, 297; equalizing service in, 306; detachments of, for service in Albany county, 325, 361, 366, 372; for Oswego, 329, 334; commissions-at-large declared invalid, 365; detachments from Albany for Canadian expedition, 374; rangers for Albany county, 377; independent companies on frontier, 440; pay of, 443; exempts to be organized as reserves, 549; detached for Indian service, 587; detached for northern garrisons, 588; difficulties of service, 596, 597; volunteers for King's regiments, 598; to be detached if necessary to fill quota, 610, 621, 636; ordered into service on northern frontier, 614; desertions at Fort Edward, 614; able-bodied men leave home to avoid service, 622; continuing troops in service, 638, 651; additional, for Canadian service, 651, 653.

MILITIA (State). See also NATIONAL GUARD. Various movements of, II, 8; new acts passed, 9, 89, 220, 255, 324, 339; III, 7; detachments for frontier service, II, 13; payment of, 13; exemption of deserters, 44; appropriation for, 53; payrolls, 57; returns of, 81; losses in service, compensation for, 92; claims of, 96, 262; delinquents, remedy against, 115; need powder, 149; responsibility for pay when called out of State, 167; prisoners of war, compensation recommended, 168; not suitable for permanent defense, 174; arrears, settlement of, 197; condition of, 266, 1016; Governor authorized to call, to resist Massachusetts insurgents, 271; equipment at public expense, 337; law amended, 360, 422; returns, 369, 529; revision of system, 388, 510; detachments under act of Congress, 398; duty of Legislature, 399, 600, 853, 911; supplemental act, 525; national system, 531; appointment of officers, 564; encampments, 565; State should furnish arms for, 571; III, 405; scarcity of drummers, II, 572; should be made more efficient, 600; deficient in colors and music, 601; organization under act of Congress, 619; statement relating to, 692; military schools, 692; called into service, War of 1812, 736, 796; pensions, 738, 748, 760, 794; exemptions from military duty, 739; New York's quota, 742; become United States troops, 744; State, duty under Federal Constitution, 748; in Federal service, same pay and supplies as regular army, 767; pay when called to repel invasion, 795; unequal operation of system, 803; organization and classification of, 804, 811; defense of New York, 807; number and location of, 1814, 809; compensation when called into service by State authority, 816; distribution of, 822; under Federal Constitution, 853; III, 345, 405; IV, 493, 726; V, 393,

Militia (State)—(*Continued*).

541; accounts with United States, II, 868; exemption of persons engaged in certain manufacturing establishments, 876; laws revised, 910, 1103; estimate of enrolled, 910; claims, War of 1812, 946; to conform to Federal Army tactics, 951; rearrangement of, 978; suggested exemption from personal tax on furnishing uniforms of domestic manufacture, 979; brevet appointments, 992; uniforms, 1050; not to borrow arms from arsenals, 1120; members of, expected to arm themselves, 1121; duties of Governor, III, 19; election of officers, 20; exemptions because of conscientious scruples, 85, 880; IV, 39; chaplains for, III, 103; Adjutant-General to issue commissions, 189; report on, 345, 385; number of, 385, 406, 478, 569, 635, 677, 713, 769, 868; IV, 39, 72, 655, 726; V, 11, 52, 88, 174, 281, 833; VI, 21, 112, 236, 357, 531; reorganization recommended, II, 853; III, 364, 388, 391, 431, 437, 478, 481, 482, 527, 677, 879, 983; IV, 283; V, 53; benefits of military training, III, 405; State should bear expense of, 405; aiding civil authorities, 523; courts-martial, 523; trial of delinquents, 523; service during New York fire, 568; called out for defense of frontier, 691, 694; services on northeastern frontier, 761; evasion of military service, 769; called out in anti-rent troubles, 775, 823, 830, 834, 840; IV, 147; parades, III, 879; IV, 288; report of infantry, Fifty-ninth Brigade, III, 1008; colonial documents relating to military affairs, 1018; required meetings of, IV, 38, 70; system inadequate, 70; uniform companies, 38, 70, 283, 288, 494, 557, 655; when may be called to aid sheriff, 146, 707; service in Delaware county, anti-rent troubles, 236, 238; number of persons liable to military duty, 248, 494; reserves, 283; V, 281, 770; reorganization acts, IV, 379, 427, 494; called out in Mexican War, 415; brigade inspectors, 427; enrollment, 557; inspector-general, 612; * commission to revise Code, 656, 726; constitutional provision, 726; V, 392, 456; commutations, 51; instructors for artillery and cavalry, 53; called into service on Staten Island, 88, 103; War of 1812, commission on services in, 175; 30,000 to be organized, 281, 400, 413; called into national service, 356, 400; New York's quota, 282, 400; report on new system, 393; National Guard, 394, see that title; places of rendezvous, Civil War, 400; number of men of military age, 1860, 455; ordered to Harrisburg, Pennsylvania, 544; biennial enrollment, 611; general references, 611, 768; VI, 21, 357, 531, 619; importance of organization, V, 612; necessary to free government, 832; enrollment once in five years, VI, 22;

MILITIA (State)—(*Continued*).

certificates, War of 1812, redemption of, 113; parade ground for New York city division, 114; commission to revise laws, VII, 428; supplies from Union Defense Committee, 500; changing method of selecting officers, constitutional provision, 797; appointments, confirmation by Senate, VIII, 487; naval, established, 829; right to occupy Palisades National park, IX, 735; active and reserve, constitutional provision, X, 15; definition, act of Congress, 1903, 15; subject to regular army organization, armament and discipline, 15; subject to call of President, 15; United States furnishes arms, equipments, and accoutrements for, 16; officers, instruction in national military schools and colleges, 16; Federal pension laws applicable to, 16; every citizen liable to duty, 510; member of, expulsion from labor union, 510.

VETOES. Amendatory act, II, 131, 403; certificates of service, 1812, VI, 902; revision of laws, VII, 411; Washington Rifles, charter, 412; counsel fees, Court of Claims, X, 945.

MILITARY ACADEMY. Cession of land for, on Staten Island, II, 676, 677; established at West Point, 677; III, 141; proposed instruction of State cadets at, II, 814, 865; flourishing condition, III, 53; proposed abolition of, IV, 45, 46, 83; additional land for, VI, 558, 788.

MILITARY AGENCIES. Provision for, V, 684; report of superintendent, 724; work of, 773, 835; VI, 113; appropriation for, V, 775.

MILITARY CODE. Need of revision, II, 1103; enacted, III, 7; new commission to revise, IV, 656, 726; amended, V, 772; enacted, 1870, VI, 113, 236; amended, excluding "white," 358; Revision Commission created, VII, 428, 523; new Code enacted, 523, 793, 827; enacted, 1883; amendments, 1884, 953; revised, 1898, IX, 827; definition of militia and National Guard, X, 15.

VETOES. Proposed revision of, VII, 411; amendments, 416; revision, 796; general amendments, VIII, 891; Sons of Veterans, parades with fire arms, IX, 398; armories, control of, amending, X, 707; pay and allowance, amending, 961.

MILITARY COMMISSION. Appointed by Governor Fenton, V, 770.

MILITARY COURTS. See COURT-MARTIAL.

MILITARY EXPENSES. Statement of, II, 806.

MILITARY GUARD. For New York, I, 99.

MILITARY POST. At Black Rock authorized, II, 512, 513.

MILITARY SCHOOLS. Established in several counties, II, 692; should be kept up in time of war, 812.

MILITARY SECRETARY. Office created, II, 818.

MILITARY STORES. To be provided, I, 118; furnished by Crown, 152; not used in Canadian expedition, application of, 161; for royal troops in colony, 202; from England for use in Spanish War, 292; King furnishes for colonial defense, 295, 312; for frontier defense, 316; at Saratoga, withdrawal of, 411; exportation of, restricted, 564, 596, 600; King furnishes for Crown Point campaign, 598; loss of, II, 156; permanent supply of, recommended, 200, 201; commissary, report of, 332; exhausting, 340; magazine for, to be maintained, 360, 510, 524; Governor's order relating to, 367; arsenals for, 400; collection and deposit of, 453; preservation of, 510; statement relating to, 755, 758, 768; purchase of additional, recommended, 797; report on, 814, 821; additional, to be purchased, 831; account with United States, 868; perishable, should be sold, 870; received on settlement with United States, 925, 987; offer to furnish for State, 1116; State offers to receive from United States in settlement of claims, III, 309; statement of, 385; unlawful seizure of, 683; deficiency in, V, 306, 392; contracts for, 406.

MILITARY TACTICS. Book on, proposed purchase of, II, 951, 953, 998; need of instruction in, 979; purchase of works on, 995, 1050; recommended in colleges and academies, V, 375.

MILITARY TRACT. Map of, II, 286; relief of occupants of escheated lands in, 991.

 VETOES. Survey of, II, 604; sheriff's sale of land in, 688; bill relating to land in, 779.

MILITARY WATCHES. In New York, act providing for, I, 298, 302.

MILK. Standard and products regulated, VIII, 34; impure, act amended, 320; large increase in product of, 1892, IX, 174; watering, penalties for, X, 120, 149; adulterated, sale of, 120.

 VETOES. Adulteration, VI, 710, 904; VII, 416; skimmed, regulating sale of, in certain cities, VIII, 1037; seizure and destruction, amending act, 1037; cans, unlawful detention, X, 447; condensed, amending general law, 776; pasteurized or clarified, encouraging formation of companies to supply, 813.

MILL BROOK. Improvement of, veto, VI, 97.

MILL BROOK LOG COMPANY. Improving Mill brook, veto, VI, 97.

MILL CREEK. Grist mills on, act for erection of, II, 485.

MILLEDGE, JOHN. Governor of Georgia, letter from, transmitting resolutions, II, 586.

MILLER, ABRAM H. Member of Elmira Reformatory Commission, VI, 233.

MILLER, EDWARD. Jail commissioner, letter from, II, 520.

MILLER, FRANK. Watchman, Richmond county park commissioners, compensation, veto, X, 959.

MILLER, FREDERICK. Major, service in collecting and returning arms, II, 776.

MILLER, HENDRICK. Bond for return of arms, II, 774.

MILLER, JAMES. Brigadier-general, detachment of militia, 1812, II, 743; thanked by Legislature and presented with sword, 832; letter from Governor Tompkins, 840; reply, 841.

MILLER, WARNER. Elected United States Senator in place of Thomas C. Platt resigned, VII, 555; Republican candidate for Governor, 1888, opposes excise commission bill, 1889, VIII, 805; approves Harvey claim against New York, 1162.

MILLERTON. VETOES. Frost escheat, IX, 284; normal school, 622, 712.

MILLGROVE POND. Southern terminus of Genesee Valley canal, IV, 835.

MILLIETE, JOSEPH. Board of Claims, military services, veto, VIII, 1125; IX, 66.

MILLINGTON, DR. Bequeaths library to Society for the Propagation of the Gospel in Foreign Parts, I, 234.

MILLINGTON, ASA. Buys Oneida land, VI, 666.

MILLS, JOHN. Letter from, relative to Indian affairs, I, 518.

MILLS, MYRON H. Member of Commission on Tall-Chief Monument, VIII, 110.

MILO. Failure to make assessment, new authorized, VIII, 257.

MILTON. School bonds, payment of, veto, VII, 391, new bill passed.

MILWARD, ROBERT. Justice of the Supreme Court, petition relative to salary, I, 140.

MINCHER, ISAAC. Canal Department, appropriation for services, veto, IX, 716.

MINDEN. French Army defeated near, I, 640; canal bridge, veto, X, 314.

MINES. Proposition to employ convict labor in, III, 1034; IV, 29, 73, 124.

MINING COMPANIES. Act for incorporation of, IV, 404; eminent domain, bill withdrawn, VI, 606. VETOES. Special act, IV, 824; V, 726; — reports, VII, 589.

MINISCEONGO CREEK., Penny bridge, declaring jurisdiction of, veto, IX, 264.

MINISINK. Indians at, I, 587; British irruption at, II, 76.

MINISTERS. Provision for, recommended by Governor Sloughter, I, 19; act for support of, 32, 35, 38, 39, 42, 115; for Indians, 86, 88; on Long Island, 115; glebe for, in Mohawk country, 553; ineligible to office, III, 103.

VETOES. Exempting property from taxation, IX, 722; — at Willard State Hospital, appropriation, X, 565, 783.

MINK, DAVID F. Board of Claims, veto, VII, 805.

MINNESOTA. Tenders aid to Federal government, V, 326; protests against interference with free navigation of Mississippi river, 327; communication to Governor from provost-marshal relative to quotas, 619; appropriation for Antietam cemetery, 840; excise taxes used for local purposes, VIII, 438; resolutions, Pacific railroad bonds, IX, 211.

MINORCA ISLAND. French invasion of, I, 602.

MINORITY REPRESENTATION. In municipal government, VI, 34; Governor Hoffman's discussion of, 385; proposed in New York charter, 459, 473; approved by Governor Dix, 545; New York, board of aldermen, 545; VIII, 281; proposed constitutional amendment as to cities, VII, 136; Syracuse, police and fire commissioners, 318; abolished in New York, VIII, 281; in Constitutional Conventions, 310; IX, 195; not fully provided for in convention bill of 1887, VIII, 393; bi-partisan boards, IX, 591.

VETOES. Inspectors of elections, method of choosing, VII, 203; Troy, police board, 1894, IX, 493.

MINORS. See also CHILDREN. Estates, legislation disposing of, II, 485; disposition of estates should be committed to Court of Chancery, 563, 664, 685, 688, 708; bank deposits by, 1016; schools for infants in Great Britain, III, 114, 213; prohibiting sale of liquor to, IV, 753; changing names, V, 191; limiting hours of labor, X, 860.

VETOES. Guardians, appointment of, II, 488; voting for members of Assembly, 685; protection of, III, 845; protection of, amending act of 1869, VI, 210; adoption, amending act, 816; adoption of, regulation, VII, 350; sale of property, VIII, 1041; IX, 283; insurance, X, 320; mortgaging property, 808.

MINSTREL FUND ASSOCIATION. Charter, veto, V, 231.

MINT. Branch in New York, IV, 479.

MISCELLANEOUS REPORTER. Office expenses, clerks, obtaining copies of opinions, appropriation, veto, X, 555.

MISDEMEANOR. Trespass on Indian land, II, 695; posting notices, veto, VII, 640; sale of imitation butter as genuine, 700; Cazenovia lake, cutting ice, failure to guard openings, veto, VIII, 461; bribery of labor representative, X, 616.

MISER, JOSEPH, JR. Canal award, payment, veto, VII, 666.

MISHKAN ISRAEL ANSHE SUWALKER CONGREGATION, NEW YORK. Relative to, veto, IX, 868.

MISNER, W. L. Canal Department, appropriation for services, veto, IX, 716.

MISSIONARIES. Among Indians, accommodations for, I, 156; alleged violation of Intrusions Act, III, 36.

MISSIONARY RIDGE. Roads on, ceded by Tennessee to United States, VIII, 1076; battle, monument to New York troops, 1077; IX, 324, 577.

MISSIONARY SOCIETY OF THE MOST HOLY REDEEMER. VETOES. Release from certain assessments, IX, 868; X, 175; exemption from taxation, 176.

MISSISQUOI BAY. Water connection with Richelieu, alleged interruption of, IV, 574.

MISSISSIPPI. Constitution, procedure to amend, II, 1058; approves Georgia proposition relative to importation of colored persons, disapproves Ohio proposition relative to abolition of slavery, III, 105; New Jersey proposition relative to colonization of colored persons, 144; disapproves Missouri proposition of January 23, 1829, 354; protests against South Carolina nullification proceedings and approves President's course, 438; opposes proposition for Constitutional Convention, 438; resolutions protesting against anti-slavery movement, 590; IV, 512; resolutions on extradition case, III, 910, 913; resolutions protesting against protective tariff, 913; favors annexation of Texas, 1051; IV, 85; protesting against acquisition of Texas by foreign power, 85; resolutions, pensions, War of 1812 and with Mexico, 524; secession ordinance, V, 396; assessment of personal property, 825.

MISSISSIPPI RIVER. French plans for settlements on, I, 178, 192; Spanish attempt to deprive Americans of free use of, II, 522; commerce on, Kentucky protests against unlawful taxation of, 606; canal connection with great lakes, 905; free navigation, Minnesota protests against interference with, V, 327; Louisiana asserts right to free navigation of, 341; commercial importance of free navigation, 479; blockade of, 494; water communication to New York, VI, 104; vessels from, detained at quarantine, 783; competition with New York canals, VII, 685.

MISSOURI. Admission of, slavery compromise, II, 1023; IV, 447, see MISSOURI COMPROMISE; approves Georgia proposition relative to importation or ingress of colored persons, disapproves Ohio proposition relative to abolition of slavery, III, 106; exchanges maps with New York, 225; resolutions relative to public lands, 758; protest against anti-slavery agitation, 821; resolutions, Federal Army, equalizing relations between officers and men, pensions, IV, 381; resolutions on extension of slavery, 466; people interfere in organizing Kansas government, 861; V, 33; adheres to Union, 476; resolutions protesting against Federal interference in Louisiana, VI, 785.

MISSOURI COMPROMISE. Adoption of, II, 1023; IV, 447, 860; V, 31; comments by Governor Fish, IV, 499; repealed, 813, 861; V, 31, 301; unconstitutional, IV, 813; V, 31; repeal approved by Arkansas, IV, 824; reasons for New York's acquiescence, V, 300.

MITCHEL, PATRICK J. Relief, veto, X, 178.

MITCHELL, SAMUEL L. Chosen Senator in Congress, II, 547.

MITTNACHT, JACOB A. Tax sale, application for cancellation, veto, IX, 815.

MOB. Riotous proceedings of, in New York, I, 711; attack on New York arsenal, III, 524; destruction of quarantine buildings, V, 79, 102, 279, VI, 783; county liable for property destroyed, V, 104; alleged interference in speakership contest, 485; draft riot in New York, 545.

MOHAWK. Armory proposed at, IX, 573. VETOES. Amending charter, VI, 327; armory, VIII, 294; cemetery, revising act, 391.

MOHAWK BANK. Sale of stock, III, 321.

MOHAWK BASIN. Green Island, iron bridge, Arch street, veto, VII, 115.

MOHAWK AND ILION HORSE RAILROAD COMPANY. Using bank of canal, veto, VI, 581.

MOHAWK INDIANS. Proposed prohibition of sale of liquor to, I, 170, 549; instruction of Indian youth in Mohawk language, 211; Fort Hunter, purpose of erection of, 256; condition of fort, 277, 280; chapel for, 290; ordnance for Mohawk country, 305, 316; visit Canada, 355; complaint regarding lands, 355; detained from hunting awaiting service in Canadian expedition, 391, 398; troops at castles, 397; rangers among, 439; country, victualling troops in, 460; deliver prisoners to Colonel Johnson, 486; refuse to send deputies to Canada, 487; complain of duty on goods, 513; speech of sachems, 524; proposed inquiry concerning conduct of, 524; deny sale of certain land, 553, 685, 751; friendly to English, 554; river Indians removed to castles, 607; conference with, relative to land grants, 686; high character of tribe, 687; visit of delegates, II, 372, 377, 378; claim of, 378, 381; agreement with, 394.

MOHAWK RIVER. Settlements on, open to enemy, I, 677; obstruction to navigation, 728; forces for western frontier, route of march along, II, 273; Canajoharie tool-bridge, 638; floods in, no claim against State for damages, V, 725; improvement at Utica, act for, VIII, 1145.

VETOES. Damages, hearing claims for, VII, 417; canal feeder wall, Rome, IX, 239.

MOHAWK VALLEY. Proposed location of Palatines in, I, 146; proposed new fort in, 256, 260; military operations in, 625; Washington visits, III, 804.

MOHAWK VALLEY RAILROAD COMPANY. Consolidation with other companies authorized, V, 803.

MOHEGAN INDIANS. Early location of, VI, 415.

MOLASSES. Distillation of, in New York prohibited, I, 103; fraud in manufacture and sale, veto, VII, 648.

MONAGHAN, JAMES A. VETOES. Relief, VIII, 636; claim, New York, 883.

MONAHAN, MARTIN F. Court of Claims, veto, X, 165.

MONCKTON, ROBERT. Appointed Governor, I, 658, 659; granted leave of absence, 659; resumes executive office, 669.

    OPENING SPEECH. Twenty-ninth Assembly, fifth session, I, 669; birth of Prince of Wales, 669; English take Havana, 669; English regain Newfoundland and St. John's, 669; volunteers for frontier service, 669; support of government, 670; judicial tenure, 670; relief of returning troops, 671; quartering soldiers, 671, 673; impressments, 671, 673; county boundaries, 672; Attorney-General's salary, 672; New Jersey boundary, 672; repairs on Governor's house, 673; returns to England, 673; official service, I, pref. x.

MONELL, ROBERT. Affidavit, removal of Little Falls postmaster, II, 1072.

MONEY. See also GOLD, SILVER and CURRENCY. Clipping and defacing foreign coin, I, 116; act relative to corruption of coin, 131, 134; exportation of gold and silver coin prohibited, 133; act relative to rates of foreign coin, 134; bills of credit, value of, 270; copper, act relating to importation of, 507; continental, ratio with specie, II, 94; exchanging old continental, for new, 147; continental, depreciation of, 241; excessive amount of bank capital, 696; counterfeiting, punishment of, III, 174; free trade in, 629, 631; coining, power of Federal government, 630; bills and notes, registry of, IV, 380; should have stable value, VI, 134; of the Constitution, 134, 142; two kinds of unequal value will not circulate together, 137; causes of depreciation, 138; payment into court, resolution of judges, 261.

MONEY BILLS. Assembly's power of, I, 118, 123, 493, 544, 545; Governor Cornbury declines approval of, 121; Council claims right to amend, 157, 159, 166; general note, 162.

MONHAGEN HOSE COMPANY No. 1, MIDDLETOWN. Charter, veto, VI, 341.

MONITORIAL HIGH SCHOOL. Proposed for each county, III, 212.

MONONGAHELA RIVER. French fort on, I, 546, 549; Braddock's defeat, 573.

MONOPOLY. Prevention of, II, 77; of cattle, act to prevent, 88; in West India trade, British attempt to secure, 197; auction sales, III, 246; protection against, 375; banking privileges, 470, 655, 1003; results from high tariff, VI, 132; prohibited, Stock Corporation Law, IX, 136; prohibited, act of 1893, 183; State's right to prevent, X, 93.

MONROE, JAMES. Commissioner, Louisiana Purchase, II, 535; Secretary of State, communication from, amendment, titles of nobility, 761; President, DeWitt Clinton's protest against Federal interference in State elections, 1064; notice of special session of Senate, III, 104; as life Senator, possible length of service, VIII, 694; Monroe Doctrine, IX, 645.

MONROE COUNTY. Morgan matter, proceedings in, III, 365; petition from, Western House of Refuge, 748; agricultural society in, 945; silk culture in, 945; supervisors request additional facilities for care of insane poor, V, 55; exempted from County Auditor's Act, VIII, 49; clerk's salary, 260; average excise license fees, 1889, 687; unpaid taxes, sales under special act, 749; increase in population, IX, 3; highways, cost of labor system, 1892, 200; insane, care of, county and State systems compared, 228; transfer tax assistant, X, 108.

VETOES. Aiding railroads, VI, 95; assistant and special deputy county clerks, 266; treasurer, collection of certain taxes, 1035; county treasurer, amending act, VII, 71; sale of property for unpaid taxes, 208; preservation of fish, 264; State school moneys, 412; county judge and surrogate, increasing salary, 414; protection of fish, 507; compensation of supervisors, exemption from general act, 883; supervisors, fixing compensation, 1115; VIII, 129; notaries public, additional number, 43; Honeoye Falls, McKenna escheat bill, 725; taxes, collection, IX, 148; sidepaths, establishing, 731; enrollment of political parties, X, 257.

MONROE COUNTY INSANE ASYLUM. State districts, report of investigating board, VIII, 1085.

MONROE COUNTY PENITENTIARY. To receive female convicts from seventh district, V, 599.

MONROE DOCTRINE. Suggested application in Venezuelan matter, IX, 646.

MONSEY. Brewer Fire Company, charter, veto, VII, 268.

MONTANA. Alleged improper seating of Senators in Congress, VIII, 987.

MONTAUK INDIANS. Report of condition of, II, 931.

MONTAUK POINT. Situation of Indians at, II, 931.

MONTEFIORE HOME FOR INVALIDS, NEW YORK. VETOES. Act relative to, VIII, 131; amending Consolidation Act relative to, 638.

MONTESQUIEU, CHARLES LOUIS DE SECONDAT. Quoted, education, II, 719.

MONTEZUMA. Salt Springs at, III, 856, 952; canal repairs at, VI, 858; amending charter, veto, VII, 934, 1104.

MONTEZUMA TURNPIKE. Repairs, veto, X, 646, 814.

MONTGOMERIE, JOHN. Appointed Governor, I, 229; dissolves Assembly recently called by Governor Burnet, 229.

OPENING SPEECH. Twentieth Assembly, first session, I, 230; need of ample revenue, 230; Governor Burnet's accounts for expenses at Oswego, 231; royal veto of partition and township division bill, 231.

OPENING SPEECH. Twentieth Assembly, second session, I, 232; conference with Six Nations, 232; Oswego trading-house, 232; agent at London, 223; treaty with Six Nations, 233; recovery of fines and forfeitures in Albany county, 233; importation of salt, 233; Connecticut boundary, 234; Albany jail, 234; Millington Library, 234; King's veto of bill to prevent prosecutions by information, 236.

OPENING SPEECH. Twentieth Assembly, third session, I, 236; King vetoes bill prohibiting sale of Indian goods to French, 236, 237; importance of maintaining Oswego, 236; Assembly memorial to King on Indian trade, 237; new fort at Albany, 238; repairs at Fort George, 238; arrest of horse thief, 238; letter from Governor Belcher to, relative to Massachusetts boundary, 241; death of, 238, 239; support of government under, acts in force five years, 470; official service, I, pref. ix.

MONTGOMERY COUNTY. Remsen claim, location of, II, 261; appointment of officers in, 302; militia called out, 807; militia called into service, anti-rent troubles, III, 834; troops discharged, 837; agricultural society, 945; communication from inhabitants relative to Erie canal, IV, 48; tenants represented before Assembly committee on anti-rent trouble, 328; leasehold estates in, 331; average excise license fees, 1889, VIII, 687; unpaid taxes, sales under special act, 749; highways, cost of labor system, 1892, IX, 200; insane, care of, county and State systems compared, 228.

VETOES. Highways in, relative to, II, 348; borrowing money, VII, 841; practice of midwifery, IX, 862; town meetings, X, 449.

MONTGOMERY, MRS. Leasehold estates, IV, 333.

MONTGOMERY, RICHARD. General, remains removed from Quebec to New York, II, 986; III, 746; act and report relative to, II, 999; expense of removal, 1000.

MONTHOLON, CHARLES DE. French Consul-General, communication from, authentication of instruments, V, 214.

MONTICELLO ACADEMY. Charter, veto, IV, 574.

MONTREAL. Six Nations invited to meet Governor of Canada at, I, 570; expedition against, 643; fire, 701; second fire, 725; exportation of grain, IX, 557.

MONTY, J. P. Canal Department, appropriation for services, veto, IX, 716.

MONUMENT. For Washington, II, 462; proposed, for General Herkimer, III, 179, 214, 226, 989; proposed, for General Woodhull, 214, 226; proposed, to DeWitt Clinton, 746, 905; proposed, to commemorate national independence, IV, 624, 681; V, 121; indifference to commemoration by, IV, 712; to Abraham Lincoln, V, 794; national, in Antietam cemetery, 841; at Yorktown, Federal appropriation for, VII, 735; expense of, is a city purpose, 846; to New York troops in battles of Chickamauga and Chattanooga, VIII, 1076; IX, 324; Brooklyn, memorial arch, act for, VIII, 1160; Herkimer, 1895, IX, 240; to New York troops at Gettysburg, 324; New York regiments on Antietam battlefield, 340; to General Grant, New York, act of 1897, 755; McKinley, Buffalo, act for, X, 394.

VETOES. Soldiers, St. Lawrence county, VI, 162; battle of Saratoga, appropriation, VII, 84; Fort Green, Brooklyn, prison ship martyrs, appropriation, 85; Sanford and Deposit, 806; soldiers and sailors, Chautauqua, 845; Gettysburg, marking positions of New York troops and defensive works, 1083; to William Tall-Chief, Seneca Indian, VIII, 110; Schuylerville battlefield monument, 253; Gettysburg battlefield monument, appropriation, 253; soldiers, Brooklyn, amending act, 527; soldiers and sailors, New York, 1029, 1160; soldiers' memorial arch, Brooklyn, legalizing act, IX, 211; Nicholas Herkimer, 240; soldiers' monument, Manlius, changing location of, 817; to prison ship martyrs, 874; soldiers, authorizing incorporation of associations for erection of, X, 63; to Maj. Peter Keenan, 163; Gen. James Clinton, 697; commemorating battle of White Plains, 698; Sweden, soldiers and sailors, 703; State boundary, restoring and placing, State Engineer's expenses, 786; soldiers' monuments, corporations relative to, 810.

MOODY, HORACE. Governor's secretary, attests Delaware county proclamation, IV, 327.

MOOERS, BENJAMIN. General, commands troops on Champlain frontier, 1812, II, 744, 764, 770; calls out militia, 796; commands militia at battle of Plattsburgh, 803; letter from, situation on Champlain frontier, 807; called on for militia, 807, 823; thanked by Legislature, and presented with sword, 832; letter from Governor Tompkins, 842; reply, 843; report of killed and wounded, 869.

MOOERS. Arms and supplies for, II, 770.

MOORE, BENJAMIN, REV. Resigns as Regent, II, 517.

MOORE, EDWARD M. State Board of Audit, veto, VII, 849.

MOORE, GREEN. Sheriff, Delaware county, letter from Governor Wright, IV, 309.

MOORE, SIR HENRY. Appointed Governor, I, 700.

OPENING SPEECH. Twenty-ninth Assembly, ninth session, I, 700; support of government, 701, 715; extension of commerce, 701; Montreal fire, 701; quartering soldiers, 702, 716; opposition to Stamp Act, 706.

OPENING SPEECH. Twenty-ninth Assembly, tenth session, I, 706; Stamp Act repealed, 706; riot in New York, 707; return of troops for New York, 708; requisition for support of King's troops, 708, 709, 710, 716, 732; joint address to Crown, repeal of Stamp Act, 710; unspiking cannon, 710.

OPENING SPEECH. Twenty-ninth Assembly, eleventh session, I, 714; revocation of instruction prohibiting issue of bills of credit, 714, 715; Massachusetts and New Jersey boundary, 714; Quebec boundary, 715; county boundaries, 715, 722; reimbursing New York for quartering troops, 717; repairs to Governor's house, 717; riot in Albany and Dutchess counties, 717.

OPENING SPEECH. Twenty-ninth Assembly, twelfth session, I, 717; Massachusetts boundary, 718; supplies for King's troops, 719, 721; Colonel Bradstreet's claim, 719.

OPENING SPEECH. Twenty-ninth Assembly, thirteenth session, I, 720; Massachusetts boundary, 720, 722; King's vetoes, 722; approves appointment of Abraham Lott as treasurer, 722; dissolves Assembly, 723.

OPENING SPEECH. Thirtieth Assembly, first session, I, 723; Indian trade, 723, 733; Indian boundary line, agreement for, 724, 727; Montreal fire, 725; riot in New York, 725; canal at Canajoharie Falls, 728; Lieutenant-Governor Colden's claim for salary and riot damages, 728; additional allowance to Attorney-General, 729; comment on Assembly resolutions, 729; dissolves Assembly, 731.

OPENING SPEECH. Thirty-first Assembly, first session, I, 731; method of appointing agent, 732; scarcity of paper currency, 733; hospital recommended, 733, 742; death of, 734; official service, I, pref. x.

MOORE, JOHN. Board of Claims, veto, IX, 430; X, 308.

MOOSE RIVER. VETOES. Dams for reservoir, VII, 118; dam, Old Brown Tract forge, 364; bridge over, Lyonsdale, reimbursing town, VIII, 552.

MORAVIA. Town auditors, veto, VII, 413.

MOREHEAD, C. S. Delegate from Kentucky to Washington Peace Convention, V, 329.

MOREHOUSE. Unpaid taxes, relief, veto, X, 274.

MORELL, GEORGE. State road commissioner, III, 124.

MOREY, MICHAEL. Canal Department, appropriation for services, veto, IX, 716.

MORGAN, CARTER H. Board of Claims, veto, IX, 66, 268.

MORGAN, EDWIN D. Governor and portrait, V, 64.

    1859. Annual message, V, 64; financial condition of State, 64; State debt created, 68; enlargement of canals, 69; steam navigation on canals, 69; loan for canals, 70; Buffalo basin, 71; condition of general fund, 71; summary of State tax, 73; economy in appropriations, 73; school funds, 74; banks, 74; insurance companies, 75; railroads, 75; State prisons, 77; revision of prison statutes, 78; asylum for insane convicts, 78; change of administration of State prisons, 78; destruction of quarantine buildings, 78, 99; removal of quarantine establishment, 79; too many health officials at New York, 81; public school statistics, 81; salt springs, 83; no coal deposits in State, 83; agriculture, 84; emigration, 84; Society for the Reformation of Juvenile Delinquents, New York, 85; Western House of Refuge, 85; State Lunatic Asylum, 86; additional insane asylum, 86; inebriate asylum, 86; deaf and dumb institution, 87; institution for the blind, 87; asylum for idiots, 88; militia, 88; new arsenals, 88; militia in service on Staten Island, 88; metropolitan police force, 89; right of aliens to take and hold property, 90; equalization of taxation, 91; Connecticut boundary, 91, 111; extension of time for collection of taxes disapproved, 91; reducing expense of printing, 92; registration of voters, 92; procedure in pardon cases, 93; sale of intoxicating liquors, 93; early consideration of appropriation bills, 94; duties of pilot commissioners and port wardens, 95; lobbying, 95; New York's attitude toward slavery, 96; letter from Governor King, quarantine affairs, 99, 100; memorial from New York State Inebriate Asylum, 107; commission on common schools, New York, report, 108; report on physical survey, New York harbor, 109; report of commissioners for removal of quarantine, 109; amendments to Metropolitan Police District Act, 110; foreign acknowledgments, 111; Michigan resolutions, improvement of St. Clair flats, 115; pardon reports, 115, 137; officers to be held to strict ac-

MORGAN, EDWIN D., 1859 — (Cont:nued).

count, 117; condition of State Agricultural College, 118; monument to commemorate Declaration of Independence, 121; opposed to monument, 123; New York Historical Society presents copy of Assembly journal, first meeting, 1780, 132.

MEMORANDUM OF APPROVAL of bill extending time for collection of taxes, V, 119.

RETURNING FOR AMENDMENT. Canal improvement bill, V, 128; canal debt bill, 128; militia claims, 1812, 131; amending charter, Sun Mutual Insurance Company, 136; Corpus Christi Ship Channel Company, charter, 137; Lansingburgh, amending charter, 137.

VETOES. Extending time for collection of taxes, V, 116; Sennett and Auburn Plank Road Company, assessing stockholders and making gravel road, 119; New Utrecht fisheries, 123; changing name of Protestant Reformed Dutch church, Duanesburgh, 125; dividing town of Italy, 126; North Protestant Dutch church, Gowanus, changing name, 127; Philomathian Society, Sherburne, charter, 129; Mamaroneck and New Rochelle Steam Navigation Company, charter, 133; facilitating construction of Albany and Susquehanna Railroad, 138; payment of drafts and certificates of canal commissioners, 143; Port Byron and Conquest Turnpike Road and Bridge Company, amending charter, 146; bill returned to Governor on request, and approved, 148; duties of assistant clerks, New York police courts, 149; relief of representatives of Chapman Church, deceased, 149; First Congregational church of Cambria, sale of property, 150.

1860. Annual message, V, 151; finances, 151; penalty for creation of State debt, 153; receipts from tolls, 153; reduction of canal tolls, 156; railroad competition, 157; increasing canal tolls, 157; speedy completion of canal enlargement, 158; canals not to be sold, 158; amount needed to complete canals, 159; railroad tolls, 161; recommends reimposition of railroad tolls, 163; State prisons, 163; prison for women, 165; location of Clinton prison an error, 165; enlargement of Clinton prison, 166; sale of part of farm at Sing Sing prison, 166; Asylum for Insane Convicts, Auburn, 166; settlement of Kingsland account against Clinton prison, 167;

MORGAN, EDWIN D., 1860 — (*Continued*).

Chittenden claim, 168; expense of transporting convicts, 168; attendance of Attorney-General at criminal trials, 169; procedure in pardon cases, 169; visits State prisons, 169; number of pardons, 170; minutes of testimony in criminal cases, 171; amendment of criminal laws, 171; appropriation for use in the exercise of pardoning power, 172; banks, 172; amount of trust securities, 172; school system, 173; militia system, 174; arsenals and armories, 174; adjustment of claims of militia, War of 1812, 175; State Board of Equalization, 175; assessment-roll, assessor's oath, 175; amount of salt manufactured, 176; State Lunatic Asylum, 176; asylum for idiots, 177; agricultural interests, 177; State Agricultural College, Ovid, 177; People's College, 178; houses of refuge, 178, 179; New York Institution for the Instruction of the Deaf and Dumb, 180; New York Institution for the Blind, 180; inebriate asylum, 180; New York police system, 181; house of detention for witnesses, 181; New York Central park, 183; removal of patients from marine hospital, 184; floating hospital, 184; quarantine hospital, 184; appropriation for New York pilots, 185; regulation of slips and wharves, New York, 185; map of New York harbor, 186; defense of New York, 186; warden's office, number of vessels surveyed, 187; fees of harbor masters, 187; captain of the port of New York, 188; number of alien passengers, 188; commissioners of emigration, expenditures, 188; railroads in New York city, 189, 238; public health, 189; Connecticut boundary commissioners, 189; truant officer, 190; breaches of trust, 190; power of removal, 190; right of aliens to hold real estate, 191; special legislation, 191; changing names of infants, 191; failure of railroad companies to pay interest, 191; additional railroad legislation needed, 192; rapid increase of pauperism, 192; excise licenses, 193; constitutional amendments, Court of Appeals, property qualifications, 193; Albany and Susquehanna Railroad bill, 194, 243; condemns lobbying, 194; constitutional amendment, registration of voters, 195; compulsory voting, 196; VIII, 676; election day a holiday, 196; extension of slavery, 196; invasion of Virginia, 197; various reports, 198, 199, 204; communication from Tonawanda band of Seneca Indians, 199; Governors and Legis-

MORGAN, EDWIN D., 1860 — (*Continued*).

latures of Ohio, Kentucky and Tennessee invited to visit Albany, 203; report of commissioners on Brooklyn park, 204; special message on canal revenues, 204; authentication of instruments executed in Great Britain and France, 212; commissioners of pilots ask to be relieved from certain duties, 223.

VETOES. Extending time for collection of taxes, V, 215; Society for the Reformation of Juvenile Delinquents, relief fund, 219; New York tax bill, 221; erection of Canisteo county, 223; Minstrel Fund Association, charter, 231; Delaware and Susquehanna Plank Road Company, assessments, 233; sale of State lands, 235; five railroads, New York, 238; Albany and Susquehanna Railroad, facilitating construction, 242; New York, legalizing act, 246; erecting Conhocton county, 249.

1861. Annual message, V, 249; short session, 251; too many statutes, 251; local and special legislation, 252; finances, 252; canal contracts under act of 1857, 254; Erie canal enlargement, 255; condition of canal fund, 256; receipts and payments on account of canals, 257; higher canal tolls, reimposition of railroad tolls, 259; general fund debt, 261; taxation, 262; appropriation and supply bills, 263; extension of time for collection of taxes, 263; capital punishment, 264; pardoning power, 266; more discrimination in punishments, 266; visits State prisons, 267; number of pardons, 267; severe punishments in State prisons, 268; recommends State prison investigating commission, 268; earnings and expenditures of prisons, 269, 270; recommends new prison, 271; number of convicts, 271; Asylum for Insane Convicts, Auburn, 272; Kingsland claim, 272; educational system, 273; academies and colleges, 274; banking capital, 274; Insurance Department, 275; report of State Engineer and Surveyor, 276; report on canal damages, 276; Onondaga salt springs, 276; visits salt springs, 277; emigration, 277; care of insane immigrants, 278; quarantine station, 278; floating hospital, 279; revision of laws relating to quarantine and emigration, 279; abolition of office of physician of New York Marine Hospital, 279; commission to ascertain damages resulting from destruction of quarantine buildings, 279; State Board of

MORGAN, EDWIN D., 1861 — (*Continued*).

Equalization, 280; militia, 281; member of Commission to Organize Militia, 281, 400; condition of arsenals and armories, 282; metropolitan police, 282; commissioners of pilots, 283; New York department of public charities and corrections, 284; punishment of intoxication, 285; revision of laws relating to harbor masters of the port, 285; commissioners of Central park, 286; Connecticut boundary, 286; supervision of State charities, 287; New York Institution for the Deaf and Dumb, 287; New York Institution for the Blind, 288; asylum for idiots, 288; inebriate asylum, 288; houses of refuge, 289; agricultural interests, 289; defects of judicial system, 291; Married Women's Act, 291; cost of transportation of convicts, 291; expense of proceedings in cases of fugitives from justice, 291; insolvent bill, 292; certifying accounts, 292; counsel for defendants in criminal cases, 292; importance of Registry Law, 293; expenses of Legislature too large, 293; renewal of former recommendations, 293; New York charter, 294; continental railway, 295; Federal census, 1860, 296; embassy from Japan, 297; visit of Prince of Wales, 297; secession movement, 298; movement to establish Southern Confederacy, 299; right of secession denied, 300; Missouri Compromise, 300; ordinance of 1787, 300; trial by jury, fugitive slaves, 301; effect of presidential election of 1860, 302; various reports, 305, 307; resolutions on secession movement, 306; Ohio resolutions, 307; Virginia resolutions, Washington Peace Convention, 309, 311; report of Cooper Union, 313; Tennessee, Virginia and Georgia resolutions, 313, 314; Tennessee resolutions, constitutional amendment, 315; Alabama resolutions, postal regulations, 318; Georgia secession ordinance, 318; Wisconsin resolutions, 319, 348; Massachusetts resolutions, 320; Pennsylvania resolutions, 321; Maine resolutions, uniform decimal system of weights, measures and currencies, 323; New Jersey resolutions, 324; Minnesota resolutions, 326; Kentucky resolutions, 327; North Carolina resolutions, 330; letter from Secretary of Treasury, national loan, 330; Indiana resolutions, 331, 349; returning for amendment bill to extend charter of New York Mills Fire Company, 332; resignation of Thurlow Weed as delegate to Washington Peace Convention, 333; letter from

Morgan, Edwin D., 1861 — (*Continued*).

President Lincoln accepting hospitalities of Legislature, 334; Michigan resolutions, 340; Louisiana secession ordinance, 341; Louisiana resolutions relative to navigation of Mississippi river, 341; Illinois resolutions, 342; Texas resolutions, 343; various papers relating to Kansas, 345; amendment to Federal Constitution securing perpetuity of slavery, 349; Arkansas resolutions, 352; militia called into national service, 350.

Vetoes. Onondaga county penitentiary, amending act, V, 336; Poughkeepsie, purchasing steam fire engine, 338; extending time for collection of taxes, Oneida county, 343; Allegany, bridge over Allegany river, 345; facilitating construction of Albany and Susquehanna Railroad, 350.

1862. Annual message, V, 357; Civil War, 358; number of men in national service, 359; banks aid national government, 359; financial situation, 360; canal tolls, 361; canal expenses, 362; completion of Erie canal enlargement, 365; publication of canal contracts, 365; railroad competition, 365; canal tolls increased, 366; appoints Samuel B. Ruggles commissioner to present to Federal government plan for use of New York canal for military purposes, 367; general fund debt, 368; State tax, 368; defects in assessment laws, 369; taxable valuation of real estate, 370; capital punishment, 370; classification of murder, punishment of arson, 370; pardoning power, 371; commission to examine system of prison management, appoints Amos Pilsbury to conduct investigation, 372, 423; defective discipline in State prisons, 372; recommends superintendent of prisons, 373; prison finances, 373; commutation of sentences for good behavior, IV, 723; V, 373; number of convicts, 374; transfer of insane from county jails to State asylum, 374; education, 375; military training in colleges, academies and common schools, 375; common schools, 375; People's College, 375; Banking Department, 376; Insurance Department, 376; salt works, 377; report of Superintendent of Weights and Measures, 377; number of emigrants, 377; floating hospital, 378; warehouse for infected cargoes, 378; revision of quarantine laws, 378; metropolitan police, 379; report of board of commissioners of pilots, 380; duties of harbor masters, 380; captain of the port, 381; Central park, 381; Children's Aid Society, 382; supervision of charitable institutions, 382; inebriate asylum, 383; houses of refuge, 383; aid

MORGAN, EDWIN D., 1862 — (*Continued*).

to sick and disabled soldiers, 383; comment on vetoed vagrancy
bill of 1861, 383; agricultural interests, 384; extending powers
of boards of supervisors, 385; cost of transportation of State
prison convicts, 386; excise licenses, 386; renewal of former
recommendations, 386; city and village charters, 387; private
and local bills, 387; relief for people of Kansas, 387; completion of Pacific telegraph line, 388; congressional apportionment, 383; direct tax levied by United States, 388; mode of
liquidating tax, 389; income tax, 391; militia, 391; Enfield rifles,
392; report on new militia system, 393; ratification of acts relating to military affairs, 394; presidential election of 1860, 394;
secession ordinances, 396; Washington Peace Convention, 397;
proposed amendment, perpetuation of slavery, 398; surrender of
Fort Sumter, 399; President calls for militia, 400; proclamation
for enlistment of militia, 400; militia sent to Washington, 400;
clothing and arms for troops, 401; arms purchased in Europe,
402; number of New York men in national service, 402, 404;
President asks for additional force of 25,000 volunteers, 403;
proclamation for volunteers, 403; commendation of New York
troops, 405; appointed major-general, 406; contracts for military supplies, 406; allotments of volunteers' pay for families,
407; harbor and lake coast defenses, 409; defense of New York,
409; tonnage and value of vessels, 410; foreign relations, 411;
report of Judge-Advocate-General, 412; report of Surgeon-
General, 412; report on purchase of arms, 413; purchase of
powder, 414; foreign purchase of arms discontinued, 416; report of engineer-in-chief, 416; pay of volunteers discharged on
inspection, 417, 421; purchase of ordnance, 418; classification
of quarantine diseases, 418; recommends repeal of law creating
board of commissioners of quarantine, 419; pensions for soldiers'
families, 420; Maine resolutions, 423, 439; instructions and report of Superintendent Pilsbury, State prison investigation, 424,
425, 430; Pilsbury report on Clinton prison, 425; Pilsbury report on Sing Sing prison, 431; Pilsbury report on Auburn
prison, 435; report of commissioners on defense of Narrows,
444; proclamation offering war bounties, 454; action ratified
by statute, 454; member of Commission on Harbor and Frontier
Defense, 545; approves Ninth avenue railroad bill, VI, 64;
Albany and Susquehanna Railroad, facilitating construction and
extending time, V, 439; official service, I, pref. xiii.

MORGAN, JOHN HILL. Assembly, 1903, seat contested, X, 571.

MORGAN, WILLIAM. Abduction of, III, 184, 222, 278; alleged murder of, 185; counsel appointed to investigate matter, 225, 251, 264, 350, 351; report of counsel, 250, 251, 314, 365; confined at Fort Niagara, 251; difficulties attending investigation, 350; statement concerning fate of, 365.

MORHOUS, ANDREW W. Board of Claims, veto, IX, 797.

MORIARITY, JOHN J. Court of Claims, X, 945.

MORIARITY, MICHAEL. Taxes, cancellation, veto, X, 590.

MORICHES BAY. Dredging channel connecting with Shinnecock bay, veto, X, 645.

MORKE, JOHN. Plan for construction of floating battery, I, 555.

MORRILL, JUSTIN S. House of Representatives, communication relative to statues for hall of house, V, 635.

MORRIS, CHARLES E., JR. Court of Claims, veto, X, 165.

MORRIS, EUGENIA. Administratrix, Phineas J. Morris, Court of Claims, veto, X, 445.

MORRIS, GOUVERNEUR. Delegate in Congress, letter from, advance of funds, II, 55; letter from, clothing for New York troops, 91; appointed Senator in Congress, 460; visits Washington in behalf of New York canal project, 706.

MORRIS, LEWIS. Lieutenant-colonel, letter from, depreciation in pay, II, 151.

MORRIS, MARY. Attainder, claim to land, II, 940; investigation of claim, III, 132, 174; settlement of claim, 175.

MORRIS, RICHARD. Court clerk, compensation of, I, 750.

MORRIS, ROBERT. Superintendent of Finance, letter from, national finances, II, 152, 180.

MORRIS, ROBERT HUNTER. Deputy Governor of Pennsylvania, letters from, troops for Crown Point expedition, I, 596.

MORRIS, ROGER. Attainder, claim to land, II, 940; investigation of claim, III, 132; settlement of claim, 174.

MORRIS, WILLIAM H. Brigadier-general, commissary-general of ordnance, report, VI, 143.

MORRISANIA. Annexed to New York, VI, 712.

VETOES. One Hundred and Sixty-seventh street improvement, VI, 556; collection of taxes, 589; changing grade of certain streets, 590; Annexation Act, amending, 911; VII, 417; exempt firemen, VIII, 1036.

MORRIS CANAL. Coal, transportation on, III, 204.

MORRISTOWN. VETOES. Legalizing town bonding proceedings, VI, 583; relief from railroad burdens, VII, 847, new bill passed.

Morse, Nathan B. Justice Supreme Court, communication from, vagrants, trial jurors, IV, 505.

Morse, Samuel F. B. Death of, VI, 444; legislative action thereon, 444.

Mortars. Proposed construction of, II, 629.

Mortgage Companies. General statistics, VII, 521, 690, 823, 949; VIII, 6; investments by, veto, 891.

Mortgages. Act confirming certain, I, 11; act concerning, II, 486; loans, part of common school fund, 722; foreclosure in chancery, regulation of, III, 722, 773; foreclosure by advertisement, 773; taxing, when not double taxation, IV, 341; foreclosure against Washington headquarters, 502; on school property should not be permitted, VI, 262; United States deposit fund, interest reduced to 5 per cent., VIII, 1149; tax on, VII, 571; X, 81, 197, 200, 347, 489, 524, 763, 800, 836, 885; tax paid by borrower, 487; taxation of, Governor Odell's plan, 1903, 489; — special message, 1903, 524; investments by various corporations, 531; tax on, Governor Higgins comment, 1906, 835; recording tax, act of 1906, 885, 920; taxation, recommendation of joint legislative committee, 1900, 886.

Vetoes. To State, foreclosure, II, 603; foreclosure judgments, New York sheriff's exclusive right to sell, V, 877; foreclosure by advertisement, surplus moneys, VI, 92; manufacturing corporations, 582; on lands under water, New York, 611; foreclosure, amending act, 678; foreclosure by advertisement, 707; foreclosure sale, publication of notice, New York, VII, 267; compelling assignments of, VIII, 469; corporations, consents of stockholders, 888; foreclosure by advertisement, legalizing act, 1039; foreclosure, costs, IX, 153; chattel, where to be filed, X, 63; stock corporations, consent of stockholders, 590; Tax Law, expense of State tax commissioners, 798; property of infants, 808; tax on, 809, 885.

Mortier, Abraham. Deputy Paymaster-General, to draw for Amherst loan, I, 637.

Morton, George W. Relief, veto, VII, 508.

Morton, Jacob. Brigadier-general, commands artillery, 1812, II, 746.

Morton, John. United States captain of ordnance, communication from, settlement of military claims, II, 929.

Morton, Levi P. Governor and portrait, IX, 536.

1895. Annual message, IX, 536; change of political control, 536; executive power and duty, 537; Governor should not interfere with legislation, 537; taxation and finances, 538; en-

MORTON, LEVI P., 1895 — (*Continued*).

largement of field of direct taxation, 539; State's financial needs, 540; transfer of New York and Kings counties insane asylums to State, 541; uniform date of payment of taxes into State treasury, 542; need of public economy, 542; extravagant increase of commissions, 543; committee to investigate State departments, bureaus, commissions and institutions, 543; new capitol, 544; constitutional amendments, 545; judiciary article, 545; special city laws, hearing, 547; pool-selling and bookmaking, 547; repeal of Ives Pool Law, 548; civil service, 548; canal improvement, 549; system of free common schools, 549; occupation and employment of prisoners, 549; sale of Onondaga salt springs, 550; general drainage laws, 550; visitation and inspection of State institutions, 550; reform legislation for New York city, 551; power of removal bill, 551; Greater New York, 552; commission to prepare charter for Greater New York, 553; election laws, 553; blanket ballot, 554; statements of expenses by political committees, 555; bi-partisan election boards, 556; State canals, improvement, 556; competition between railroads and canals, 556; deepening canals, 557; agricultural drainage, 558; roads and highways, 558; convict labor, 559; revision of civil service laws, 560; Bank Department, 561; amendments to Banking Law, 562; loose method of borrowing money from banking institutions, 562; surplus fund, 562; loans on capital stock should be prohibited, 562; savings banks should not be associated in business with discount banks, 563; public instruction, 563; Insurance Department, 565; dependent insane, 566; new method of apportioning appropriations, 566; number of insane, 568; maintenance of State charities, 568; State forestry, 568; State troops, 569; new arms needed for National Guard, 570; pardon report, 570; dedication of Chickamauga and Chattanooga National Military park, 575; reorganization of inferior criminal courts, New York, 578; communication from Governor of Georgia, Atlanta Exposition, 581; certificates of necessity of immediate passage of bills, 588, see that title.

MEMORANDUMS OF APPROVAL. West Troy police, IX, 589; Geneseo normal school, new buildings, 593; Tioga county, railroad strike, expenses of National Guard, 594; guarantors and sureties, 596; Mount Vernon, schools, licensing teachers,

MORTON, LEVI P., 1895, MEMORANDUMS. ETC — (*Continued*).

598; Board of Claims, Peek & Company, 600; horse racing, State Racing Commission, 601; schools, temperance instruction, 612.

VETOES. Ogdensburg armory, IX, 571; Whitehall armory, 575; Kings county charities commission, reorganization, 583; bridges on county lines, 587; items in supply bill, 604; items in supplemental supply bill, 605; Erie canal lifting locks, 606; Buffalo armory, 607; Genesee river State dam, 609; Manhattan State Hospital, establishment, 617; omnibus veto, 622.

Arms for National Guard, general note, IX, 634; Board of Examiners created, 634; decision as to improved firearms, 635.

1896. Annual message, IX, 643; Legislature composed of 200 members, 644; Venezuelan question, 646; State finances, 646; large number of corporations paying taxes, 647; care of insane, 649; prison labor, 653; insane criminals and capital punishment, 656; Asylum for Insane Convicts at Dannemora, 657; prison for confinement and execution of persons condemned to death, 658; condition of State prisons, 658; canals, 659; Improvement Act of 1895, 660; electricity as motive power on canals, 660; public education, 661; Compulsory Education Law, 661; one hundredth anniversary of inauguration of free school system, 662; civil service, 663; Ballot Law, 664; revision of Election Law, 665; excise question, 665; excessive number of saloons in State, 665; retail liquor licenses in several States, 1892, 666; road improvement, 667; National Good Roads Conference, Atlanta, 1895, 667; employment of State and county convicts in public road-making, 668; State Forest and Game Preserve, 668; preservation of deer in Adirondack forests, 669; State land survey, 669; preservation of Palisades, 670; Mexican Exposition, 671; Atlanta Exposition, 672; completion of capitol, 673; Greater New York, 674; extravagance in public printing, 674; protests against unbalanced bids, 675; legislative procedure, 676; large number of special city laws, 1895, 677; commissions on general laws for second and third-class cities, 677; revision of statutes, 679; commission on procedure, 1895, 680; Statutory Revision Commission appointed Code commissioners, 680; publication of colonial laws, 681; report of commission to recommend changes in

MORTON, LEVI P., 1896 — (*Continued*).

    legislative procedure, 682; various annual reports, 682, 685; strict economy in appropriation of public moneys, special message, 682; reform in public school system, New York city, 686; pardon report, 688; one hundredth anniversary of permanent establishment of the city of Albany as the capital, 688; certificates of necessity, 1896, 690.

    MEMORANDUMS OF APPROVAL. Foreign insurance companies, canceling authority, IX, 691; Liquor Tax Law, 696; Smithtown, relief, 703; Kings county coroners, term of office, 704; Greater New York, 705; Albany and Bath-on-the-Hudson Bridge Company, charter, 715.

    VETOES. Ramapo normal school, IX, 711; items in supply bill, 712; items in supplemental supply bill, 713; civil service, cities, assistant attorney or corporation counsel, exemption from examination, 715; canals, subordinates and employees, appropriation, 1896, 716; omnibus veto, 717.

    The Palisades, general note, IX, 735; official service, I, pref. xiii.

MORTON, MRS. LEVI P. Member of Cotton States Exposition Commission, 1895, IX, 582.

MORTON, OLIVER P. Governor of Indiana, transmits memorial relative to use of New York canals and railroads, V, 499.

MOSCOW (Russia). Capital transferred to Petersburg, II, 1124.

MOSELEY, DANIEL (Mosely). Appointed counsel to investigate Morgan matter, III, 225; report, 250, 251; resigns appointment as counsel, 265; appointed circuit judge, 265.

MOSER, JOSEPH. Convicted of murder, pardoned, II, 790.

MOTT HAVEN CANAL. New York, bridge over, veto, IX, 633.

MOULTON, R. G. Professor, quoted, university extension movement in England, IX, 19.

MOULTON, WILLIAM. Petition for grant of lands, II, 117.

MOUNDS. Ancient, exploration of, memorial, V, 720; Indian mound at Geneva, purchase of, veto, VIII, 887.

MOUNTAIN VIEW CEMETERY ASSOCIATION. Broome county, relative to, veto, VII, 807.

MOUNT INDEPENDENCE. Investigation as to surrender of, II, 15.

MOUNT McGREGOR MEMORIAL ASSOCIATION. Charter, veto, VIII, 625; act incorporating, 625.

MOUNT MORRIS. Canal bridge at, VI, 862. VETOES. Monument to William Tall-Chief, Seneca Indian, VIII, 110; consolidation of school districts, IX, 73, 817.

MOUNT PLEASANT. Prison at, III, 208. VETOES. Ferry to Clarkstown, II, 476; opening highway, VI, 330; improving Railroad avenue, 335; town meetings by election districts, 674; exempting from Rural Cemetery Associations Law, X, 446.

MOUNT PLEASANT PRISON. See also SING SING PRISON. No provision for female convicts, III, 207; separate buildings for women, 208; additional cells, 317; cholera at, 401; number of prisoners, 401, 447, 514, 540, 716, 764, 861; IV, 78, 122, 274; self-supporting, III, 447, 515, 541, 618, 675, 861; IV, 78; female prison at, III, 515, 618, 675, 716, 861, 874; IV, 79, 274; manufacture of silk at, III, 541; raises mulberry trees, 542; transfer of female prisoners from Bellevue, 618, 675; marble for State hall, 764; IV, 28; change of management, III, 765; judgment against University of the City of New York, 767; stone for New York Institution for the Blind, 857; chaplain at, 977; additional water for, IV, 125, 276; malignant fever at, IV, 275; poor quality of water, 275; transfer of convicts to Clinton prison, 276; statistics, 407.

MOUNT SINAI HOSPITAL, NEW YORK. Relief, veto, IX, 861.

MOUNT VERNON. Schools, licensing teachers, relative to, IX, 598. VETOES. Village, relative to, VII, 806, 807; tax on annexed territory, VIII, 456; amending General Village Act, 891; bonds for unpaid taxes, IX, 450; amending charter, VII, 936; IX, 629, 734, 787; X, 318; fire engines and apparatus, IX, 629; water supply, 734; Sinking Fund Commission, 787; Comptroller, 787; police department, 787; First Universalist Society, relative to, X, 59; street paving bonds, 59; grade crossing, Harlem Railroad, Mount Vernon avenue and Oak street, cost of changing, 454; tax budget, 1902, 471; city officers, 583; official newspapers, 583; grade crossings over New York and Harlem Railroad, 590; Young Men's Christian Association, relief, 806.

MOYNAHAN, BARTHOLOMEW. Stenographer, New York, claim for services, Supreme Court, criminal term, veto, X, 950.

MUD CREEK. Straightening, veto, VII, 414.

MUELLER, ELIZABETH. Straack escheat bill, veto, VIII, 734.

MUIR, ALEXANDER M. Commissary-General, death of, III, 430, 979.

MULATTO. Fugitives from service, I, 116; emancipated, denied right of suffrage, II, 237; in New York made free, 882.

MULFORD, SAMUEL. Prosecution against, for libel, I, 180, 183.

MULHERON, PATRICK. Court of Claims, veto, X, 945.

MULLIN, JOSEPH. Justice of Supreme Court, retired, residue of salary, appropriation for widow, veto, VII, 916.

MULLIN, LYDIA, MRS. Widow of Judge Joseph Mullin, residue of salary, veto, VII, 805, 916.

MUNCH, NICHOLAS. Land under water, Tonawanda, release, veto, IX. 284.

MUNICIPAL AID TO PRIVATE ENTERPRISE. Extravagant grants, IV, 805; prohibited, 806; VII, 206, 652, 661, 1106; VIII, 529; IX, 142, 512; X, 243, 264, 275, 777, 908, 942.

MUNICIPAL CORPORATIONS. Power to make by-laws, II, 246; called independent republics, 217; power of taxation, 315, 317; legislative power over, 317; charter amendments, persons affected, entitled to be heard, 544; taxation of State property, 680, 895, 953, 999; relation to State, III, 211; villages, general act for incorporation of, IV, 379; prevention of nuisances, 469; restricting powers of, 701, 730; V, 849; VI, 825; VII, 569; encroachment on rights of, V, 63; interfering with powers of local authorities, 149; aiding private enterprise, IV, 806; VI, 180; VII, 652, 848, 867, 1047; VIII, 239; IX, 142, 512; X, 777; should derive benefit from franchise, V, 189, 233, 799, 811, 873; VI, 63, 74, 206, 694, 703; VII, 793; IX, 41, 91, 101; X, 44, 304, 487, 658; improvements should be charged on property benefited, V, 652; taxing power, 735; Governor Hoffman's views on local administration, VI, 31; water supply, interference by private corporation, 272; eminent domain, waterworks, 285; limiting indebtedness, 402; VII, 31, 637, 846, 1088; right to acquire land in other municipalities, VI, 606; officers, embezzlements by, punishment, 638; attachments against officers for misappropriation of property, 730; official accountability, 734; problems of government, 735; ordinary subjects of administration, 832; essential conditions of home rule, 835; large indebtedness, 917; limiting expenditures and indebtedness, constitutional provisions, 917; VII, 47, 617, 637, 754, 1018; VIII, 239; compulsory creation of debts, VII, 31; State property should not be assessed for local improvements, VI, 869; VII, 86, 228, 472, 585; X, 640; heavy debt and taxation, VII, 298, 437; Legislature cannot interfere with property rights, 595; claims against, barred by limitation, 644; limiting indebtedness, amendment of 1884, 727; VIII, 27, 161, 184, 239; have power to issue bonds or notes for debts, VIII, 62; franchise, sale at auction, 200; hours of labor, contracts regulated, 316; home rule in, 332, 345; no expenditure except for local purpose, 880, 996; general Municipal Law, 1892, IX, 28; liability for injuries caused by defective streets and sidewalks, 54; payments for charitable institutions, 551; limiting indebtedness, Constitution 1894, X, 343, 804; better regulation of salaries needed, 344; bonds, proposition to author-

MUNICIPAL CORPORATIONS — (*Continued*).

ize boards of supervisors to validate, 519; local self-government, 541; bonds, proposed investment of United States deposit fund in, 622; tabulation of accounts and expenses, 764.

VETOES. Improvement of land at expense of adjoining owners, V, 729; railroad aid, VI, 214; reimbursement of officers for expense in suit, VII, 544; highways and bridges, notice of defects before accident, 843; railroad aid bonds, 937; actions against, in certain cases, X, 451; leasing buildings to G. A. R. posts, 585; negligence, limiting time to commence action, 709; assessments for local improvements, recovery of, 710.

MUNICIPAL LOAN COMPANY. Organization tax, veto, VIII, 638.

MUNICIPAL OWNERSHIP. New York rapid transit, people to vote on, 1894, IX, 505, 512; Syracuse subways, veto, 789; Governor Roosevelt's comment on, 1899, X, 36; New York rapid transit system, 43; public utilities, 85, 219; water rights, New York should own, 212; New York lighting plant, 805.

MUNICIPAL REFORM. Governor Tilden's special message, VI, 825, 1024; commission created, 844, 1025; work of commission, 951; general note, VII, 134; Governor Cleveland's comment on, 839.

VETOES. Election contest, salary and expenses of successful contestant, VII, 616; Oswego scheme, 1894, IX, 360, 432.

MUNICIPAL TAXATION. Act relating to, I, 10.

MUNN, STEPHEN. Land conveyed by, sale of, veto, X, 312.

MUNN, WILLIAM H. Trustee, land conveyed to, sale of, veto, X, 312.

MUNSEE INDIANS. Green Bay treaty, II, 1107.

MUNSON, SAMUEL. New York, relief, veto, X, 178.

MURDER. Act of James I, conviction under, II, 68; subject to death penalty, 363, 731; V, 265; classification needed, II, 549, 577; III, 128, 341; elements of, considered, II, 576, 577; revision of acts relating to, 635; extradition for, 1104; when death by duel constitutes, III, 209; number of convictions, 284; IV, 610; punishment of, III, 285; pardon, proposed constitutional amendment, 863; while committing another felony, IV, 309; classification of, act unconstitutional, V, 172, 264; two degrees of, 265, 371; second degree, lack of premeditation, VI, 126, 242, 368; increasing in New York, 545; second degree, definition and punishment, 547; as result of martial law, 772; judgment of conviction, direct appeal from oyer and terminer to Court of Appeals, VIII, 82, 180, 302; attempts to commit, punishments increased, X, 342; appeals, delays in, 344.

MURDER —(*Continued*).

VETOES. Second degree, punishment, commutation for good behavior, VI, 899; trial, giving defense right to make closing address, VII, 754; Patrick case, appeal from order denying motion for new trial, amending Code, X, 927.

MURLIN, EDGAR L. Assistant in Governor's office, acknowledgments to, I, pref. xv.

MURPHY, JULIA A. Widow of Lawrence Murphy, pension, New York fire department, veto, X, 816.

MURPHY, MATTHEW T. Relief, veto, X, 177.

MURPHY, RICHARD. Assembly, member of joint committee on taxation, 1899, X, 801.

MURPHY, THOMAS F. New York fireman, relief, veto, X, 581.

MURRAY. VETOES. Draining lands of Isaac U. Cole, VII, 457; State ditch, removing obstructions, VIII, 539.

MURRAY, MR. Governor Osborn found dead in garden of, I, 527.

MURRAY, DAVID. Secretary, Board of Regents, report on Clinton papers, VII, 809.

MURRAY, EDWARD. Heirs of, relief bill, VI, 213.

MURRAY, JOHN. See DUNMORE, EARL OF.

MURRAY, JOHN, JR. Member of Commission on Common School System, II, 707.

MURRAY, JOSEPH. Commissioner on colonial union, I, 370.

MURRAY, WILLIAM. Justice of Supreme Court, proposed purchase of library for Delhi Law Library, veto, VIII, 539.

MURTHA, WILLIAM H. Nominated as commissioner of immigration, VII, 833; special message urging confirmation, 888.

MUSEUM. See also State MUSEUM. Of mechanic arts, proposition to establish, IV, 47.

MUSIC. Martial, militia deficient in, II, 601. VETOES. Sunday processions, G. A. R., VII, 335; in public schools, IX, 116, new act passed; National Conservatory of Music, contracts with pupils for instruction, X, 63.

MUSKINGUM RIVER. Coal deposits on, III, 204.

MUSTEE. Emancipated, denied right of suffrage, II, 237; in New York, made free, 882.

MUSTER-MASTER. Assembly appoints, I, 52; custody of muster-rolls, 53.

MUSTER-ROLLS. Submitted to Assembly for examination, I, 52; examination of, requested, 53.

MUTUAL AID SOCIETY OF THE EAST GERMAN CONFERENCE, METHODIST EPISCOPAL CHURCH. Charter, veto, VI, 588.

MUTUAL FIRE INSURANCE COMPANIES. Regulating commencement of business, VI, 319; statistics, VII, 825.

MUTUAL FIRE INSURANCE COMPANY. Amending charter, veto, VI, 319.

MUTUAL INSURANCE COMPANIES. Statistics, 1900, X, 219; special election of directors, 1906, 894; election of directors, general act, 1906, 899.

VETOES. Organization authorized in certain towns, VI, 595; Catskill and Athens, formation of, VII, 132; Orange county, 412; foreign, insuring tobacco, authorizing business in this State, 934; Albany and Greene counties, 1097.

MUTUAL LOAN AND DEPOSITORS' INSTITUTION, NEW YORK. Charter, veto, VI, 219.

MUTUAL TRUST COMPANY. Charter, veto, VI, 342.

MYERS, MAMIE. Formerly Hines, Court of Claims, veto, X, 447.

MYERS, MATTHEW J. Board of Claims, veto, VIII, 976, 1120.

MYERS, MICHAEL S. Member of Prison Labor Commission, VI, 234.

MYERS, STEPHEN. Legislative employee, compensation, veto, VII, 372.

MYERS' AUTOMATIC BALLOT CABINET. See also VOTING MACHINES. Use authorized at town meetings, IX, 34; authorizing use in villages, veto, 247.

MYRES. See MYERS.

N.

NAGLE, ELLA. Court of Claims, veto, X, 944.

VII, 267, 506, 931, 938, 1000, 1006; VIII, 62, 326, 327, 337, VII, 267, 506, 931, 938, 1000, 1006; VIII, 62, 326, 327, 337, 617, 876, 974, 980, 981, 1144, 1162, 1163; IX, 56, 348, 356; X, 235, 242, 253, 256, 261, 705, 813; insurance companies, changing, act of 1893, VIII, 1144; corporations, limiting right to use, X, 104; protection of corporation pending change, 622.

VETOES. Religious corporations, VII, 133, 807; VIII, 205, 617, 1096; IX, 37, 348; X, 377, 700; business, continuing use of, VII, 415; Eastchester creek, changing to Eastchester river, VIII, 469; corporations, prohibiting use of, by others, IX, 625.

NANFAN, JOHN. Lieutenant-Governor, I, 90, 93; absent at time of Governor Bellomont's death, 90; Council assumes government, 90; letter from Lords of Trade to, 92; becomes acting Governor, 93; dissolves Seventh Assembly, 93.

OPENING SPEECH. Eighth Assembly, first session, I, 94; procures large tract of land from Indians, 94; royal aid to colony, 95; compensation of chief justice and Attorney-General, 95; revenue, support of government, 95; urges harmony in Assembly, 95; examination of Stephen Van Cortlandt's account, 96; defense of province, 96; thanks Assembly for address, 96; wharf in New York, 96.

NANFAN, JOHN —(*Continued*).

OPENING SPEECH. Eighth Assembly, second session, I, 96; opposition in Assembly, 97; French usurpation of English crown, 97; succeeded by Governor Cornbury, 98; official service, I, pref. ix.

NANTUCKET. Representation in First Assembly, I, 9.

NAPANOCH. Eastern New York Reformatory at, under supervision of Prison Department, X, 204.

NAPHTHA. Vessels on certain lakes, inspection, veto, VIII, 1121.

NAPLES. Town, annexing part of Italy, veto, V, 126.

NARROWS, THE. Act for batteries at, I, 103, 120; defense of, 125; beacons at, 151, 607; watchhouse at, 607; fortification of, II, 383; lands adjacent to, acquisition for fortifications, 642; erection of Fort Richmond at, 658; troops stationed at, 744; fortifications at, 750; III, 309; V, 186; troops at, arms for, II, 769; redoubt on Signal Hill, 778; fortifications at, improvement of, 864; fortifications and ordnance at, sale to United States, 940, 1081; cession of land at, III, 47; lighthouse at, 180; commissioners on defense of, V, 444; proposed obstructions at, 569.

NASSAU COUNTY. VETOES. Street railroads in villages, X, 145, 316, 431; taxation, relative to, 177; sheriff, reimbursement for services and expenses after expiration of term, 242; towns, preservation of records, 243; supervisors' powers under Game Law, 441; assessments in certain towns, 444, 450; town officers, compensation, 533, new bill passed; street railroads, exempting certain highways, 587.

NASSAU HOSPITAL ASSOCIATION. Support of patients from North Hempstead, veto, IX, 818.

NASSAU ISLAND. Long Island changed to, I, 36, 38; proposed battery on, 324; northern limit of privateer service, 333; Assembly meets at Brooklyn, 367; quota not filled, 570.

NASSAU LOAN AND SECURITY COMPANY. Charter, veto, VI, 342.

NASSAU SAVINGS BANK, BROOKLYN. Charter, veto, VI, 220.

NASSAU TRUST COMPANY. Charter, veto, VIII, 291.

NATIONAL ADVOCATE, THE. Federal statutes published in, II, 1068.

NATIONAL ASYLUM FOR SOLDIERS. Transfer of inmates from Albany Soldiers' Home, V, 684; VI, 62; homes established by, 61.

NATIONAL BANKS. Proposed, II, 159; proposition prohibiting, except in District of Columbia, 1025; Massachusetts sustains power of Congress as to establishment of, 1118; Rhode Island favors, III, 909; Georgia opposes, 977; State banks authorized to become, V, 528, 587; development of, 528, 693; large amount of paper currency, 550; number in State, 586; essential features derived from New York banking system, 586; number and capital, 822; return to State system, VI, 112, 231, 623; proposed tax on stock, X, 81.

NATIONAL BOOK EXCHANGE, NEW YORK. Charter, veto, VI, 328.

NATIONAL CONSERVATORY OF MUSIC. Contracts with pupils for instruction, veto, X, 63.

NATIONAL COTTON PLANTERS ASSOCIATION. Joins in inauguration of New Orleans Exposition, VIII, 31.

NATIONAL DEBT. A national evil, III, 415; when justified, 416; extinguished, 493, 817, 967; renewed by Civil War, V, 481, 553; probable duration of, 752; estimated amount of, 753; validity confirmed, Fourteenth Amendment, 791; not burdensome, 822.

NATIONAL GLEE CLUB OF NEW YORK. Charter, veto, V, 645.

NATIONAL GUARD. See also MILITIA. Organization of, V, 394; number of men of military age, 1860, 455; exemptions, 456; statistics, 611, 686, 769, 833; VI, 112, 236, 357, 531, 619, 944; VII, 23, 154, 293, 428, 523, 826, 951; IX, 28, 743, 827; X, 218; claim of 32d Regiment, V, 642; encampment recommended, 687, 833; maximum fixed at 50,000, 688, 769; improvement in discipline and efficiency, 769; Military Commission appointed, 770; condition of, 832; reducing maximum number, 833; VI, 21, 22, 113; colored persons eligible to, 358; rifle ranges, 358; independent organizations not encouraged, 598; improved inspection, 621; ordered out, riots of 1877, VII, 152; conduct commended, 154; separate companies in cities and villages, 154, 293; uniforms and equipments, 155, 294; arms for Albany Burgess Corps, 248; overcoats given to inmates of Soldiers' Home, 289; Revision Commission created, 428; report, 429; disbandments, 523, 693, 952; State should furnish uniforms, 694; detachments attend Yorktown Centennial Celebration, 736; 7th Regiment escort to French delegation to Yorktown Centennial Celebration, 739; review of first division, Yorktown Celebration, 739; camps of instruction, 747, 826, 952; VIII, 14; disbandment of several separate companies, VII, 826; instruction in camp, 826, 952; uniforms furnished by State, 952; VIII, 14; appointments, confirmation by Senate, 437; attendance at Centennial Celebration of Washington's Inauguration, 695; naval militia, act to establish, 829; military expenses, 1889, 830; called out, Buffalo railroad strike, IX, 159; called into service at Fire Island, 1892, 204; parades with firearms, organizations authorized, 398; new arms needed, 570; X, 14; expenses in railroad strike, Tioga county, 1892, IX, 594; arms, general note, 634; X, 15; board of examiners, report and decision, IX, 635; Savage military magazine rifle recommended by board, 635; question of supplying with arms used in Federal Army, 639; supplied with Springfield rifles, 643; right to occupy Palisades National park, 735; chief executive officers should have

NATIONAL GUARD—(*Continued*).

more permanent tenure, 743; war with Spain, 1898, appropriation for expenses, 853, 877; enlistments in Spanish War, 1898, 878; X, 11; using for national purposes, 11; employees of State departments and in Buffalo and New York receive compensation while absent in service, 13, 264; major-general actual head of guard, act of 1898, 13; arms should be uniform with those of Federal Army, 14; definition, Military Code, 1898, 15; subject to regular army organization, armament and discipline, 15; United States furnishes arms, equipments and accoutrements for, 16, 97; officers, instruction in national military schools and colleges, 16; volunteers, appointments in Federal Army, 97; need of practical experience in the field, 98; State debt, 1900, 180; expenses, including armories and arsenals, 1900, 182; not a Federal military reserve, 217; service at Croton Dam strike, 1900, 218; courts of inquiry, judicial review of findings, 350; member of, expulsion from labor union, 510; protection of members who are also members of labor unions, 510.

VETOES. Tompkins Square parade ground, VI, 698; Thomas J. Lawrence, corporal, 22d Regiment, permanent injuries, damages, VII, 465, 910; John Kennedy, Jr., captain, 8th Regiment, death of, appropriation to widow, 466; Carl Meisner, Battery G, 7th Division, permanent injury, damages, 466, 910; Remington rifles, altering sights, 478; funds for separate companies, 478; 27th Regiment, purchase of equipments, 479; 65th Regiment, replacing uniforms, 479; 74th Regiment, replacing uniforms and equipments, 480; 9th Regiment, replacing uniforms and equipments, 480; 12th Separate Company, replacing uniforms and equpiments, 480; 54th Regiment, replacing uniforms and equipments, 481; 7th Separate Company of Infantry, commutation for rations, 496; 9th Regiment, supplies for, 500; Mutual Relief Association, charter, 506; Buffalo Light Battery, 763; Military Code, 796; James Creney, Assistant Commissary-General, death of, appropriation for widow, 917; military storehouse, Binghamton, additional, 928; uniformed veterans, 23d Regiment, charter, 1108; Veteran Association, 71st Regiment, charter, 1108; VIII, 404; Veteran Reserve, charter, VII, 1111; commission to examine small-arms, VIII, 455; damages for injuries while in service, Bassler claim, IX, 66; rifle range, Creedmoor, repairs, 76; uniforms, Brock and Wiener claims, 237, 452; rifle range, Bath-on-the-Hudson, additional land, 244; to be furnished with cheese while on duty at State camp, 287; 74th Regiment, Buffalo, armory for, 607; new act, 1896, 607; 47th Armory, repairs and

NATIONAL GUARD, VETOES — (Continued).

enlargement, 777; uniforms, hearing, Court of Claims, 858; Hollingworth service medal, X, 173; New York city employees serving in Spanish War, amending act, 264; State employees serving in Spanish War, appropriation, 314; 71st Regiment armory, fire at, reimbursement for private property lost, appropriation, 566; Shaffer claim, blindness incurred in service, claim for damages, 592; counsel fees, Court of Claims, 945; pay and allowance, amending Military Code, 961.

NATIONAL GUARD MUTUAL RELIEF ASSOCIATION. Charter, veto, VII, 506.

NATIONAL IMPROVEMENT COMPANY, NEW YORK. Charter, veto, VI, 340.

NATIONAL LIFE INSURANCE COMPANY. Distribution of funds, veto, VII, 267.

NATIONAL LINCOLN MONUMENT ASSOCIATION. Memorial relative to monument to Abraham Lincoln, V, 794; requests modification of conditions of New York appropriation, VI, 44; request denied, 44.

NATIONAL MUTUAL BENEFIT ASSOCIATION, BUFFALO. Charter, veto, VI, 172.

NATIONAL SECURITY AND TRUST COMPANY. Charter, veto, VI, 341.

NATIONAL STATUARY HALL. Old hall of House of Representatives set apart for, V, 636.

NATIONAL TENT OF THE NATIONAL ORDER OF INDEPENDENT RECHABITES OF NORTH AMERICA. Charter, veto, VII, 415.

NATIONAL TRUST COMPANY. Depositary of highway funds, Westchester county, VI, 488; investigation of Receiver Best, counsel fees, veto, VII, 906.

NATURAL HISTORY. See also GEOLOGICAL SURVEY. Completion of cabinet, V, 781, 854; publication of, 855; duplicate specimens donated to American Museum, VI, 22; additional facilities for instruction in, IX, 564.

VETOES. Purchasing objects of, VII, 410; fossils, donation to Westfield Academy, 417; purchase of Wolcott collection, 467; printing volume five, paleontology, 491; printing report of State Cabinet, 493; State Museum, printing and binding for, 494; free instruction, continuing, VIII, 1037; nature study and extension bulletins, appropriation, X, 797.

NATURALIZATION. First law relating to, I, 10; Palatines to be immediately naturalized, 146, 147; encouragement of, II, 199; reducing term of probation, III, 883; alleged improper, Madison county, 928; policy should be liberal, VI, 39; Federal act of 1906, 39; X, 226; right extended to alien soldiers, VI, 40; act to prevent fraudulent certificates, 40; registration of voters, VIII, 20, 296; fraudulent use of papers, X, 226; additional safeguards needed, 729.

NAUTICAL SCHOOL. Establishing, veto, IX, 256, 380, 627.

NAVAL MILITIA. Established, VIII, 829; included in Constitution 1894, 829; called into service at Fire island, 1892, IX, 204; better opportunities for training needed, 743; chartering vessel for, veto, 777; war with Spain, 1898, appropriation, 853; defined, Military Code, 1898, X, 15; rendered efficient service in Spanish War, 17; importance of department, 218.

NAVAL STORES. Importation of, from other colonies, I, 117; proposed production of, in colony, 143, 146, 555; Palatine production of, abandoned, 147; inquiry from Lords of Trade as to production of, 250.

NAVIGATION. Act to encourage, I, 11; act relating to, 184; proposition to encourage, 246; convenience of, in colony, 255; secured by guardship, 276; expected benefits from Spanish War, 287, 302; powder duty recommended, 357; vessel for lake service, 567; inland, improvement of, 723; companies incorporated, II, 321, 329; of New York waters, Connecticut claims equal privileges in, 1025; needed inspection of steamboats, III, 46; sloops on Hudson river, 72; Fulton's experiments in use of steam, 151; of canals, proposed definite annual period of, 202; mileage from Chicago to Buffalo, New York and Europe, VI, 738; inspection of vessels on certain lakes, veto, VIII, 1121; general act, 1897, 1121; of canals, damages resulting from, when State not liable, IX, 270.

NAVIGATION LAW, 1897. Summary of provisions, VIII, 1121.

NAVY. Relative to masts for, I, 93; Canadian expedition, 153; desertions from, 290; vessels for, recommended, 321; French defeated, 624, 625; American successes in War of 1812, II, 786; deserters, bill relating to, veto, 819; hospital for, Brooklyn, III, 181.

NAVY ISLAND. Military stores deposited at, III, 686.

NAVY YARD. Brooklyn, see that title; proposed on lake frontier, IV, 625.

NEAL, THOMAS. Authorized to establish postoffice in colonies, I, 34.

NEBRASKA. Territory organized, IV, 827, 860; women may vote for school officers, IX, 96.

NEGOTIABLE INSTRUMENTS LAW. Uniform act passed by large number of States, VIII, 930.

NEGROES. See also SLAVES and SLAVERY. Slaves, act to prevent them from running away, I, 116; importation of, should be discouraged, 248; restricting assemblies, 298; plot of, 400; poll tax on, suggested, 574, 606, 618; emancipated, denied right of suffrage, 237; right to vote, veto, 686; presumed to be slaves, veto, 687; organization of volunteers for military service, 811; made free in New York, 882; purpose of statutes relating to, 977; encouraging improvement of,

NEGROES — (*Continued*).

978; importation into State without its consent, III, 34; foreign colonization proposed, 34; children in Rochester to constitute separate school, 378; ratio to whites, 717; schools for colored children, 887; IV, 476, 795; are not citizens, Georgia resolutions, 46; citizens, unlawful imprisonment of, Maine, 48; ultimate destiny of African race, 619, 621; treated as an inferior race, 620; excluded from Indiana, 621; colonization in Liberia, 621; suggested colonization in West Indies, 623; voters, abolishing property qualifications, V, 54, 99, 193; to be excluded from rights of citizenship, Arkansas proposition, 355; asylum for colored children, New York, destroyed in draft riots, 547; rights of, Fourteenth Amendment, 743; number, 1865, 776; receive right of suffrage, 856; eligible to National Guard, VI, 358.

NEISOR, LAURA M. Thomas Orphan Asylum, surgical services for, appropriation, veto, X, 799.

NELSON, PETER. Assistant archivist, State Library, acknowledgments to, I, pref. xv.

NERESHEIMER, EMIL AUGUST. Executor Gibier estate, Court of Claims, veto, X, 591.

NESDALL, THOMAS. Commissioner, repairing road, Onondaga reservation, VII, 384.

NETHERLANDS. Treaty with United States, II, 188; King of, arbitrator in northeastern boundary controversy, III, 390; offers facilities for transcribing colonial documents, 935; IV, · 169; Governor Seward transmits Regents' report to, III, 1051; richness of archives, IV, 170; illiteracy as compared with New York, X, 859.

NETHERLAND SOCIETY FOR THE ENCOURAGEMENT OF MANUFACTURES AND MECHANICAL INDUSTRY. Proposed exposition at Utrecht, VI, 50.

NEUSCH, FRANCISCA. Escheat, veto, VII, 805.

NEVIS ISLAND. Devastation on, I, 120.

NEWARK. Custodial Asylum for Feeble-Minded Women at, IX, 79.
     VETOES. Public hall, VI, 210; rebuilding canal wall, 860; bridge, Erie canal, VII, 1099; VIII, 131, 887; revising charter, VII, 1122.

NEWARK BAY. Right of oyster fishing in, IV, 564.

NEWARK AND ROSENDALE LIME AND CEMENT MANUFACTURING COMPANY. Power to purchase and hold land, veto, IV, 827.

NEWARK VALLEY. Legalizing water bonds, veto, X, 702.

NEW BALTIMORE. Southern terminus of proposed Hudson river improvements, V, 453; highways, consolidation and repairs, veto, VIII, 337.

NEW BALTIMORE CHESTNUT LAWN CEMETERY ASSOCIATION. Charter, veto, VI, 501.

NEW BALTIMORE AND RENSSELAERVILLE TURNPIKE ROAD COMPANY. Authorizing sale of road, veto, VII, 132.

NEW BERLIN HEMP COMPANY. Incorporated, III, 298.

NEW BREMEN. Aid to Utica and Black River Railroad Company, amending act, veto, VI, 92.

NEW BRIGHTON. Number of excise licenses, 1887, VIII, 360.

VETOES. Amending village charter, VI, 592; regulating use of dock, 907; fire department, VIII, 532, new bill passed.

NEW BRUNSWICK. Maine boundary question, III, 756.

NEWBURGH. Washington's Headquarters at, IV, 502; number of excise licenses, 1887, VIII, 359; excise license fees, 1889, 685; law library, IX, 46.

VETOES. Washington's Headquarters, care of, VI, 581; amending Free School Act, 507; armory, deficiency appropriation, VII, 482; boundaries, 1099; increasing tax for contingent expenses, VIII, 76; alteration of map, 697; amending charter, 1040; IX, 719, 787; legalizing Water street paving bonds, 719; St. Luke's Home and Hospital, payments for poor in, 723; law library, appropriation, 769; sewer, amending act, 787; bridge over Chambers creek, 818; armory, repairs and improvements, reappropriation, 857; land purchased at tax sales, X, 633.

NEWBURGH AQUEDUCT ASSOCIATION. Charter, veto, II, 584.

NEWBURGH AND COCHECTON TURNPIKE ROAD. Relative to, veto, IX, 793.

NEW CAPITOL. See also CAPITOL. Project for, Albany furnishes site, V, 722, 759; additional land for, 722; proposed postponement of erection of, 760; appropriation for, 759; VI, 24, 116, 229, 350, 938; VII, 13, 175, 293, 430, 524, 695, 836, 982; VIII, 31; room for military relics, V, 772, 835; work on, 835; VI, 24, 116; cost exceeds estimate, 223, 650; using part for executive residence, 229; new commission created, 229, 937; resident mechanics and laborers preferred, 229; probable expense not sufficiently considered, 877, 937; financial statement, 936; VII, 981; Governor Robinson's protest against, 12, 92; "a great public calamity," 92; appropriation for, memorandum, 123; slow progress of work, 173; completion of Assembly chamber, 174; completion of Senate chamber, 175; declared to be the capitol after January 1, 1879, 175; first occupation of, by Legislature, 269; historical sketch of, 289; Governor Robinson urges discontinuance of appropriations for, 292; new plans,

NEW CAPITOL —(*Continued*).

    limitation of expense, 293; liability of commissioners, liquida-
tion, 399; expenses not provided for, creation of debt, 400;
appropriation, 1879, memorandum, 403; completion of executive and Senate chambers, 430; proposed loan for completion
of, 430; appropriation, 1880, memorandum, 453; defects in
ceiling of Assembly chamber, 524; Senate occupies new
chamber, 539; executive chamber occupied, 694; rooms for
various departments, 694; location of Court of Appeals not
satisfactory, 694; portrait of Abraham Lincoln, 744; condition
of work on, 835; commission to examine building, report, 836;
commissioner, office created, powers and duties, 836; State
Architect, office created, 837; trustees and Superintendent of
Public Buildings, 837; southeastern staircase, 980; number of
men employed on, 981; political tests in employment prohibited, 982; orderlies and watchmen, veterans preferred, VIII,
20; work discontinued because of failure to make appropriations, 30; grounds, grading and improvement of, 31, 96; advisory board, powers and duties, appropriation, 31, 93, 213;
boiler-house and coal sheds, appropriation, 31; Governor Hill
protests against political patronage in selecting employees,
217; supervision of construction, single commissioner, act of
1883, 222; communications from Eidlitz, Richardson & Company,
defects in Assembly chamber, 501; continuing work, act of
1888, 610, 869; new commission created, 610, 650, 1149; IX,
545; completion of rooms for State Library, VIII, 650, 869;
continuing work, new commission created, 1890, 1017; sketch
of legislation relative to commissions, 1018; work on, commission of 1891, 1149; appropriation, 1892, IX, 89; cost up
to 1892, 89; continuing work, appropriation, 1893, 223; communication from Commissioner Perry relative to sanitary conditions, 358; appropriation for plumbing, 1895, 358; continuing work on, 1896, 674; capitol commissioner, office created,
1897, 746; lighting system, 746; completion, 1898, 827; appropriation, 827; plumbing, heating and lighting, X, 741;
illustration, VII, 268.

VETOES. Unappropriated tax, VI, 1002; Superintendent Eaton —
appropriation for counsel fees, VII, 83; — for expenses of
experts, 84; — for stenographer's services, 84; appropriation,
92, new item passed; death of Patrick Hogan, appropriation
for widow, 464, 910; death of William Higgins, appropriation
to mother, 464; James F. Johnson, laborer, injuries, appropria-

NEW CAPITOL, VETOES —(*Continued*).

tion, 465; death of Charles Hagar, appropriation to father, 466; printing legislative proceedings on removal to, 492; award, Timothy J. Sullivan, contractor, 498, 788; Senate and Assembly library, removal to, 581; work on exterior walls, 652; Eidlitz, Richardson & Company, advances, 903; water supply, 903; McAvoy and O'Keef claims, damages, 910; Taylor and Young claims, damages, 911; board of commissioners of construction, bill creating, VIII, 213; changing lighting appliances, appropriation, 422; continuing work on, new commission, 869; proposed purchase of Walker's painting of the repulse of Longstreet at Gettysburg, IX, 291; Senate chamber, rearranging lighting system, X, 51; claim for damages from injuries received while at work on, Galvin case, 267; Agricultural Department, repairs and furniture, 299; ventilation, reappropriation, 425; additional office facilities, 642; additional accommodations, finishing room and corridor on fifth floor for Department of Education, 643; Department of Education, additional accommodations, 643; former Adirondack survey rooms, fitting and furnishing, 788.

NEW CASTLE. Benjamin Fletcher, Governor of, I, 37.

NEWCASTLE, DUKE OF. Secretary of State, communication from, relative to recruits for expedition against West Indies, I, 299; letter from, relative to defense of colonies, 340, 346, 349; letter from, relative to expedition against Canada, 373, 375; reimbursement by King of colonial expenses in Canadian expedition, 379; dispatches from, 410; account of expenses of Canadian expedition to be sent to, 441; cultivating friendship of Indians, 462.

NEWCOMB. Lands in, repealing act, veto, VI, 699.

NEW COURT. Member of committee seizing unlicensed exports, II, 28; assessors under Tax Law, 61; Legislature, under Forfeitures Act, 70; justice of the peace in bill to prevent horse racing and theatrical performances, 85; referees, 205; inspectors and superintendents of election, 216; supervisors and New York city authorities under Tax Law, 235; Legislature, 249, 250, 309; judge of probates, 257, 268.

NEWELL, GRAHAM. Member of commission to distribute appropriation for Niagara frontier sufferers, II, 787.

NEW ENGLAND. Andros appointed Governor, I, 14; letters from, transmitted to Assembly, 68; letter from Governor of, situation on frontier, 142; importation of salt, 219; frontiers attacked by Canada Indians, 353, 356, 360; English immigration to, II, 956.

Newfoundland. Regained from French, I, 669.

New Hampshire (Colony). Proximity to French settlements, I, 336; joins in Cape Breton expedition, 350; murders in, by French Indians, 355; colonial union, 366; invitation to join in Crown Point expedition, 420; Lords of Trade recommend colonial union, 578; represented in Albany Convention, 578; land in, offered for military service, 598; financial aid from Crown, 599, 604; Massachusetts boundary, how settled, 610; troops for Canadian expedition, 620, 634, 644, 654.

New Hampshire (State). Militia at Battle of Bennington, II, 8; conference on paper currency, 11; act to prevent return of certain persons, 69; boundary controversy with Massachusetts, 102; boundary controversy with New York, 103; Vermont boundary, 140; letter from President of, legislative resolutions, 185; constitutional amendment, qualifications of President and Vice-President, Senators and Representatives in Congress, 433; Constitution, procedure to amend, 1058; disapproves Pennsylvania proposition as to national banks, 1076; urges reorganization of militia, III, 388, 481; resolutions, sustaining administration, approving Bank of United States charter, 434; exchange of judicial decisions, 481: recommends abolition of franking privilege and reduction of letter postage, IV, 45; refunding fine against General Jackson, 85; action on independence monument, V, 122; military to be subordinate to civil power, 470; communication from Adjutant-General of United States, dismissing Lieutenant Edgerly, Fourth Regiment Volunteers, 515; court to render opinion as to constitutionality of pending bills, VIII, 947; forest cultivation, IX, 836; means adopted to attract tourists, X, 513.

New Hampshire Grants. See also Vermont Controversy. Controversy concerning, I, 756, 758, 765; disturbances in, 764; aiding inhabitants, 764; confirmation of, recommended, II, 47; commutations for quitrents, 49; New York's claim under, 102; papers relating to, 148; confirmed by New York Legislature, 164; declared to be part of New York, 175.

New Hartford. Vetoes. Village charter, VI, 183; town, reimbursing collector, 701; legalizing aid to Bridgewater turnpike, X, 811.

New Haven. Labor convention at, II, 24, 46; manufacture of arms at, 667, 680.

Newington. Rector of, bequest of library, I, 234.

New Jersey (Colony). Sends men for defense of Albany, I, 45; pay of, 48; Lord Cornbury appointed Governor of, 98; Governor Cornbury while at Burlington dissolves New York Assembly, 126;

NEW JERSEY (Colony)—(*Continued*).

Robert Hunter Governor of, 141; Assembly votes money for Governor Lovelace, 145; William Burnet appointed Governor, 190; Millington library, clergy to use, 234; troops from, in expedition against Canada, 373; Lords of Trade recommend colonial union, 578; not represented in Albany Convention, 578; Indian incursions in northern Pennsylvania, 587; blockhouses in, 590; proposed joint expedition against Indians, 593; troops for Crown Point expedition, 596; financial aid from Crown, 599, 604; troops for Canadian expedition, 620, 634, 644, 654; Sandy Hook lighthouse, 655; requested to aid in Indian war, 676; act relative to New York boundary, 747.

NEW JERSEY (State). Governor to issue proclamation to prevent plundering, II, 80; laws of, received, 530; disapproves constitutional amendment limiting jurisdiction of Federal courts, 605; dissolves Jersey Bank, 705; joins in defense of New York, 810; disapproves amendments proposed by Massachusetts and Connecticut (see page 827), 828; constitutional amendment, election of Representatives and presidential electors by districts, 919; letter from Governor, boundary question, III, 94, 107; disapproves Georgia proposition relative to importation of colored persons, 99; proposes gradual abolition and colonization of slaves, 99; commissioners to authenticate instruments in other States, 210; suit against New York on boundary question, 312, 356; protests against South Carolina nullification proceedings, pledges support of government, 437; resolutions relative to public lands, 752; resolutions declaring power of State to determine election of Representatives in Congress, 820; favors protective tariff, 988; tax on Indian land, invalid, 1024; opposes repudiation of State debts, IV, 48; pilots acting in New York, 100; sends pupils to New York charitable institutions, 430, 792, 793; question as to oyster fishing in New York and Newark bays, 564; action relative to independence monument, 683; V, 122; resolutions, encroachments on New York harbor, 823; resolutions, Cape May breakwater, 866; complaint against New York for alleged violation of quarantine agreement, V, 35; opposition to location of quarantine station, 54; opposed to location of quarantine buildings at Sandy Hook, 79, 101; approves Crittenden resolutions, and recommends constitutional convention, 324; jurisdiction over Raritan bay, 640; negotiations with, relative to quarantine regulations, 640; appropriations for Antietam cemetery, 840; location of warehouses in New York harbor, 846; question concerning right to construct docks in New York harbor,

NEW JERSEYY (State)—(*Continued*).

847; tax exemptions, VI, 371; status of aliens, 551; removing anti-commercial restrictions, 553; boundary, communication from Governor, 775; communication from Governor relative to quarantine, 777; complaint against New York quarantine laws, 778; jurisdiction over lower New York bay and Raritan bay, 780; resolutions, commercial relations between United States and other countries, VII, 321; factory inspectors, ratio to number of establishments, IX, 166; commission on preservation of Palisades, 670; Palisades Park Commission, 736; comparative statement of general and special laws, X, 504; information as to vital statistics, 870.

NEW JERSEY BOUNDARY. Commissioners to establish, recommended, I, 183, 684; questions relating to, 227; papers relating to, 525; proceedings relating to, 540; New York submits question to King, 544, 555, 672, 684, 748; expense of ascertaining, 588, 610; Council's observations on, 611; Lords of Trade recommend commission on, 684; difficulty of establishment, 714; commissioners appointed, II, 601; Governor directed to preserve jurisdiction of State, 621; report of commissioners, 629; resolution of New Jersey Legislature, 941; Governor urges settlement of, 1105; III, 11, 86, 107; letter from Governor of New Jersey, 94, 107; in Hudson river, 156, 180; new commission appointed, 157; failure of negotiations, 212; suit by New Jersey against New York, 312, 349, 356, 422; controversy settled, 424, 442; VI, 779; colonial documents relative to, III, 1018; communication from Governor, New Jersey boundary, VI, 775; report of Quarantine Commission, 778; Regents authorized to establish, VII, 720.

NEW JERSEY CENTRAL RAILROAD COMPANY. Proceeding against, to prevent construction of docks in New York bay, V, 846.

NEW LEBANON. Manufacture of powder at, II, 681; explosion at mill, inquiry concerning, 681, 682.

NEW LONDON. Council of war at, I, 151.

NEW LOTS. VETOES. Tyrian Hall Association of East New York, charter, VI, 590; Bushwick avenue, VII, 63; register, 413; police commissioners, 804; annexing to Brooklyn, 936, 1110; sidewalks and streets, improvements, 936; grading Atlantic avenue, X, 177.

NEWMAN, T. H. President of Senate, Tennessee, invited to visit Albany, V, 203.

NEW MEXICO. Territory, admission to Union, status of slavery, IV, 382, 497, 501; New York resolutions, 448; territorial government, status of slavery, 501; territorial organization of, 565.

NEW NETHERLANDS. English conquest of, II, 1115; III, 1018; retaken by Dutch, II, 1115; papers relating to, III, 1017.

NEW ORLEANS. Spanish aggressions at, II, 522; battle of, 858; communication relative to charity hospital, III, 748; under martial law, War of 1812, IV, 45; condition of banks, V, 46; slaughter of ·Union soldiers at, 858; vessels from, detained for observation, yellow fever, VI, 626; World's Industrial and Cotton Centennial Exposition, see that title.

NEW ORLEANS EXPOSITION. Purpose of, VII, 31; appropriation for, 32.

NEW PALTZ NORMAL SCHOOL. Established, V, 695; repairs and improvements, veto, VIII, 864.

NEWPORT. Proposed conference of Governors at, I, 137, 138; Assembly protests against conference, 139; Assembly refuses appropriation for Lieutenant-Governor's visit, 140; French fleet at, supplies for, II, 111.

NEW ROCHELLE. VETOES. Drainage, VII, 392, 414; Harvey escheat, 550; amending General Village Act, VIII, 942, new bill passed; first city charter, IX, 858; election of comptroller, etc., X, 312; sewer, Residence park, 313; amending charter, 318; teachers' pensions, tax for, 435; teachers' retirement, 478; bond for public improvements, legalizing previous issues, 636; schools, sites and buildings, 717.

NEWSAM, WILLIAM. Relief, veto, X, 177.

NEWSCHAFFER, RUDOLPH. New York, relief, veto, X, 177.

NEW SCOTLAND. Van Rensselaer leases, description of, IV, 329; special highway, veto, VI, 670.

NEWSPAPERS. Publication of statutes in, II, 555; IV, 31; improper discussion of criminal cases, II, 578; publication of Federal statutes in, 1068; influence in promoting education, III, 538; use of mails for, 645; for deaf and dumb, 715; number of, 1855, V, 11; alleged suppression of, Civil War, 466; New York, improper use of patronage, VI, 607; Brooklyn Eagle, quoted on aldermanic bill, VIII, 744; New York, favor rapid transit bill, 1889, 760; favor naval militia bill, 832; publishing Session Laws in, 944; publishing details of electrocutions, IX, 22; prohibition repealed, 23; not to be sold by children under specified age, X, 739.

VETOES. New York, publication of legal proceedings, VI, 591; German, Erie county, publishing legal notices in, VII, 390; official, Albany, increasing number, 1121; publication of statutes, amending act, VIII, 130; official, Amsterdam, manner of designating, 944, 1039; designation of, for publication of

NEWSPAPERS, VETOES — (*Continued*).

    statutes, IX, 813; New York, advertising corporate notices, designation, 875; X, 59, 177; Mount Vernon, official, 583; official, second-class cities, designation, 589.

NEW STOCKBRIDGE INDIANS. Report of superintendent, intrusions, II, 939; report, 991, 1027, 1060, 1115; III, 96, 182; communication from, II, 1031; communication relative to squatters, 1076; communication from, advance of annuities, 1116; purchase of land from, 1120.

NEWTON, JOHN. Lieutenant-colonel, United States engineer, member of board on Brooklyn pier and bulkhead lines, VI, 452; communication from, 560; major-general, pilot commissioners, communication on obstructions in New York harbor and Hudson river, 557; surveys East river bulkhead lines, VIII, 834.

NEWTON, THOMAS. House of Representatives, report on canal tonnage, 1824, III, 50.

NEWTOWN (Elmira). Battle, Sullivan's campaign, celebration, VII, 1084.

NEWTOWN (Long Island). Included in metropolitan police district, V, 183; large number of cemeteries, IX, 254; merged in Greater New York, 300.

    VETOES. Election districts, VI, 193; construction of highways, 195; opening highway, 330; local government, 449, 558; creating board of health, VII, 113; amending Metropolitan Sanitary District Act, 267; Lutheran cemetery, relief, 268; free school district No. 12, charter, VIII, 338; road improvement, 469; unpaid taxes, relative to, X, 322.

NEWTOWN CREEK (Chemung County). VETOES. Restoration and protection of former work, X, 301; claim of Horseheads and Elmira, 588.

NEWTOWN CREEK (Long Island). VETOES. Pier and bulkhead lines, VII, 111; tunnel under, IX, 474; widening, bulkhead lines, 725; nuisance, abatement, 778; free public draw-bridge, 778; nuisance, repeal, X, 176; bridge, damages to owners of land abutting on Vernon avenue, Queens borough, 957.

NEW TRIALS. In criminal cases, VI, 126, 244, 366; New York board of police, veto, 848; capital cases, when Court of Appeals may grant, VII, 1091.

NEW UTRECHT. Highways and bridges, board of improvement, VIII, 1134; annexed to Brooklyn, 1134; Bensonhurst park, amending act, 1157.

NEW UTRECHT —(*Continued*).

VETOES. Fisheries, V, 123; Franklin and Eighteenth avenues, improvement, VIII, 468, 615; board of improvement, powers, IX, 133; fire hydrants, water supply, 151; highway improvement, 264; local improvements, 522; Volunteer Firemen's Association, appropriation, X, 472.

NEW UTRECHT POINT. Fortifications at, cession of land for, III, 48, 138.

NEW WINDSOR. Governor Clinton at, II, 17; bridge over Chambers creek, amending act, veto, IX, 818.

NEW YEAR'S DAY. A public holiday, VI, 679.

NEW YORK (Colony). Beginning of colonization, I, 1; English conquest, 1; powers of States-General, 1; Legislature established, 1; Governor and Council, powers before creation of Assembly, 1; Twelve Men, 1; Eight Men, 2; Nine Men, 2; Duke of York receives patent of, 2; Dyer's case, 4; Thomas Dongan, Governor, 9; first meeting of Assembly, 9; Assembly discontinued, 13; Leisler assumes executive authority, 14; Andros appointed Governor, 14; Leisler Assembly, 15, 16; Henry Sloughter, Governor, 17; Assembly revived, 18; Richard Ingoldesby, commander-in-chief, 23; Benjamin Fletcher, Governor, 28; postoffice established, 34; weighhouse, Crown to receive revenue from, 36, 38; Earl of Bellomont, Governor, 74; unhappy condition of, 75, 80, 98; charged with being receptacle of pirates, 75; independence of, suggested, 79, 294; reconciliation of parties in, 77, 82, 85; John Nanfan, Lieutenant-Governor, 93; Lord Cornbury, Governor, 98; should furnish arms, 124; Lord Lovelace, Governor, 132; Richard Ingoldesby, Lieutenant-Governor, 134; Robert Hunter, Governor, 141; William Burnet, Governor, 190; Governor urges defense of, 205; relations with King, 213, 216; importation of salt, 219; proposed fixing of boundaries, 226; John Montgomerie, Governor, 229; Rip Van Dam, President of the Council, 238; William Cosby, Governor, 242; George Clarke, President of the Council, 254; George Clarke, Lieutenant-Governor, 258; more whites needed, 266; Assembly terms fixed at three years, King vetoes act, 267, 271, 278, 279; importance of acquiring Tierondequat, 272; English troops in, 276; proposed settlements north of Saratoga, 278; receives special royal favors, 292; defense of, urged, 295; George Clinton, Governor, 305, 310; act for defense of, 318; suggestion of union with other colonies, 320; aids Massachusetts in Cape Breton expedition, 332; expected invasion of, by French and Indians, 366; engineer appointed for, 371; troops from, in expedition against Canada, 373; propose share of expense in French

New York (Colony)—(*Continued*).

War, 406; agreement for colonial union, 419, 457, 461; share of expenses, Crown Point expedition, 419; intrusions on land in, 523; Sir Danvers Osborn, Governor, 526; James DeLancey, Lieutenant-Governor, 526, 613; heavy expenditures in Canadian expedition, 551; high character of New York bills of credit, 560; results if French should take Albany, 563; apportionment for Crown Point expedition, 571; Sir Charles Hardy, Governor, 576; represented in Albany Convention, 578; Indian incursions in northern Pennsylvania, 587; troops for Crown Point expedition, 588, 591; troops of, not to serve outside North America, 598; land in, offered for military service, 598; financial aid from Crown, 599, 604, 629; King consents to annual appropriations, 605; troops for Canadian expedition, 620, 633, 644, 653; reimbursement for military expenses, 627, 634; extent of military service, 628; aid granted to other colonies, 629; French desire to obtain possession of, 629; frontier settlements, 631; foreign lotteries, sale of tickets prohibited, 641; share of parliamentary appropriation, 645, 647; Cadwallader Colden, President of Council, 647; Cadwallader Colden, Lieutenant-Governor, 656, 659, 673, 734, 759; Robert Monckton, Governor, 659, 669; recruits for King's regiments, 664; troops for Indian war, 676; English Sugar Act, mischiefs of, 684; Assembly petitions to home government, 687, 729; ruinous condition of colony, 692; trial by jury, 693; paper currency necessary, 694; Sir Henry Moore, Governor, 700; protest against parliamentary encroachment on rights of, 703; stamped paper for, destroyed, 706; authority of Parliament in, 712; receives from Pennsylvania overpayment of French War grant, 713; Parliament prohibits legislation until grant of supplies for troops, 721, 730, 773; to regulate Indian trade, 723, 735, 738; consultations with other colonies, 730; Earl of Dunmore, Governor, 736; influence in promoting intercourse between England and other colonies, 737; William Tryon, Governor, 739; courts needed in remote parts of, 762; Assembly demands home rule, 765; committee of fifty-one, 765; Assembly refuses to send delegates to Continental Congress, 769; grievances of, presented to home government, 771; provincial congresses, 778; martial law in, 765, 779; James Robertson, Governor, 779; British evacuate New York, 780; State government established, 780; statutes continued, revision recommended, II, 219, 255; loans by, act relating to payment of, veto, 240; Dutch records, translation of, 1115; III, 162; historical records, publication of, 162, 751, 935, 1008, 1013, see also Colonial History; J. R. Brodhead appointed agent to procure, 1013; English

NEW YORK (Colony)—(*Continued*).

records, where deposited, 1015; documents relating to, 1018; documents relating to commerce, 1019; Mr. Brodhead describes supervision of, IV, 179; French documents relating to, 185; statutes, publication of, 488; government by people first proclaimed in, IX, 645; grants from English Crown, bill relative to, veto, X, 450.

NEW YORK (State). Government established, I, 779, 780; II, 1, 5; need of written Constitution, 1; invasion of northern frontier, 7; first Tax Law, 9; debts due to, collection of, 9; United States claims against, payment of, 9; organizing government, 9; each department should keep within its own field, 10, 12, 21, 246, 250, 279, 449, 465, 472; III, 254; VI, 455; conference on paper currency, II, 11; claims against United States, 52; Congress advances funds for, 55; Governor requested by Congress to furnish supplies to Rhode Island, 69; principal seat of Revolutionary War, 73; tax to aid national government, 77; quota of assessments in aid of national government, 85; supplies for New York troops in continental service, 88; inability to comply with request of Congress for troops, 93; approves Federal system of finance, 97; balance of trade against, 98; account with Connecticut for cannon, ball and tents, 100; territorial claims under New Hampshire grants, 102; boundary controversy with New Hampshire, 103; compensation of troops for depreciation of currency, 110; bounties of unappropriated lands, 115; Washington expresses gratitude for support of, 122; accounts with United States for supplies, 134; Vermont demands relinquishment of claim to disputed territory, 135; troops march to Virginia, 149; Vermont offenses pardoned, grants confirmed, 164; protests against uniform scale of depreciation, 167; territory and jurisdiction of, 175; financial embarrassments, 180; tax for national expenses, 186; proposed convention to revise Articles of Confederation, 194, 270; act relating to freedom and independence of, 215; territorial claims of Massachusetts, 208, 217; consequence of excessive immigration, 243; appoints commissioners to Commercial Convention, 260; Federal requisition on, 263; proposes general convention of States, 270; appoints delegates to National Constitutional Convention, 271; repeals acts repugnant to treaty of peace, 275; Congress objects to Tariff Act, 279; convention to consider Federal Constitution, 283, 289; Constitution ratified, 283, 299; VIII, 505; convention proposes amendments, II, 290; V, 470; had no part in Washington's first election as President,

NEW YORK (State)—(*Continued*).

    II, 300; first Senators in Congress, 301; ratifies amendments to Federal Constitution, 304; V, 471; consents to erection of Vermont, II, 307; chiefs of Seven Villages, Canada, claim land in, 328, 343; Oswald case, 330, 335, 351; ratifies Eleventh Amendment, 335; source of jurisprudence, 350; John Jay, Governor, 358; exchange of laws with Virginia, 371; Connecticut's claim to land in, 370, 371, 386, 404, 406, 441; map, act providing for, 385; acquires Bedlow's island, 386; capital established at Albany, 397; proportion of national funded debt, payment of, 438; pledges support to national government, 446; judicial authority resisted in Columbia county, 451; map and laws, interchange and distribution of, 531, 543; ratifies Twelfth Amendment, 537; Morgan Lewis, Governor, 545; should manufacture arms for militia, 572; commercial growth of, 596; Daniel D. Tompkins, Governor, 616; adopts English Exchequer standard yard measure, 641; rejects amendment relative to titles of nobility, 678, 750, 761; military preparations, 691; War of 1812, New York's quota, 742; duty of militia under Federal Constitution, 748; receives arms from United States, 762; funds advanced by United States, 763; share of Federal direct tax, 788, 906; militia at battle of Plattsburgh, 803; number of troops furnished by, War of 1812, 804; Governor Tompkins urges abolition of slavery, 881; Lieutenant-Governor John Tayler becomes acting Governor on resignation of Governor Tompkins, 887; DeWitt Clinton, Governor, 897; III, 52; resources sufficient to construct canals, II, 902; share of expense of capitol, 936; loan of public funds, 1004; party spirit in, 1019; who not eligible to Legislature, 1063; estimated share in distribution of national domain for school purposes, 1080, 1101; Joseph C. Yates, Governor, III, 1; commercial intercourse with Canada, complaints relative to, 23; favors protective tariff, 24; protests against Federal claim of right to require license and tonnage duties on State canals, 49; capable of supporting 14,000,000 of inhabitants, 61; map, purchase and distribution of, 162; Nathaniel Pitcher, acting Governor, 221; Martin Van Buren, Governor, 230; Enos T. Throop, Lieutenant-Governor, becomes acting Governor, 269; capable of sustaining 8,000,000 people, 303; New Jersey brings suit on boundary question, 312, 356, 422; Enos T. Throop, Governor, 318; William L. Marcy, Governor, 399; all lotteries closed, 404; pledges support of national government, 429; judicial

NEW YORK (State)—(*Continued*).

system inadequate, 443; geological survey, 568, 634, 638; people attached to Federal compact, 578; accepts United States deposit fund, 613, 624; invasion from Canada, 678; resumption of specie payments, 694; William H. Seward, Governor, 706; independent in financial affairs, 724; stocks of, securities in New York banks, 725; disturbance in northeastern part, 759; may legitimately engage in railroad construction, 800; income sufficient for wants, 816; protests against exclusion of Representatives by Congress, 820; recommends enactment of National Bankrupt Law, 845, 876; distribution of volume of statistics, 907; Virginia attempts to restrict commerce with, 910, 925, 936, 980; asserts jurisdiction in McLeod case, 942; railroad connection with eastern States, 953; restoration of public lands, 966; requests repeal of act of Congress distributing public lands, 974; vessels, South Carolina act for search of, 980; compilation of colonial history, 1013; cannot abrogate contract without other party's consent, 1022; northern boundary treaty with Great Britain, 1038; foreign imprisonment of citizens aiding Canada, 1039; projector of system of internal improvements, 1042; William C. Bouck, Governor, IV, 1; should reserve control of railroad companies, 12; State stock held by banks, 36, 70; favors reduction of letter postage, abolition or better regulation of franking privilege, and a more rigid economy in Postoffice Department, 84; Silas Wright, Governor, 87; amount received from proceeds of public lands, 117; Pilot Act of 1837, 159; right to bring action to recover real estate, 345; John Young, Governor, 363; Mexican War, slavery in acquired territory, 382; urges appropriations for improvement of rivers and harbors, 393; Hamilton Fish, Governor, 421; early attitude toward slavery, 446; resolutions against slavery in New Mexico and California, 448; presents boundary record to Rhode Island, 457, 597; recognizes Seneca Indian Constitution, 459; interchange of publications with France, 465; opposes extension of slavery, 500, 502, 814; V, 300; Washington Hunt, Governor, IV, 538; proposed purchase of manorial titles, 560; respects rights of slave-holding States, 567; gift to Canadian Parliamentary Library, 573; colored population diminishing, 620; Horatio Seymour, Governor, 640; V, 445; joins in movement for independence monument, IV, 684; amount of stock debt, 702; has an honorable history, 710; scene of Revolutionary conflict, 712; leadership in education,

NEW YORK (State)—(*Continued*).

713; reluctant adoption of Federal Constitution, 750; Myron H. Clark, Governor, 780; sovereignty over domestic institutions (slavery), 811; Boston Corners ceded by Massachusetts, 817; protests against extension of slavery, 827; V, 28, 96; condemns Fugitive Slave Law, IV, 827; urges payment of French spoliation claim, 865; John A. King, Governor, V, 1; protests against Dred Scott decision, 34; opposes Lecompton Constitution for Kansas, 61; Edwin D. Morgan, Governor, 64; protests against reopening slave trade, 98; tenders aid to Federal government against secession movement, 300, 397, 439; delegates to Washington Peace Convention, reports, 310, 398; pledges to national government amount equal to United States deposit fund, 330; quota of militia under President's first call, 282, 356, 400; number of men in national service, 359, 553; use of canals for national defense, 367, 502; share of Federal direct tax, 388; buys arms in Europe, 402; Civil War, statistics of troops, 402, 404, 445, 553, 607; made a military department, 406; harbor and lake-coast defenses, 409; exports and imports, 410; bounties for volunteers, 454; adjustment of Civil War quotas, 457, 536, 572, 575; issues in State election of 1862, 468; consequence of failure to pay interest in coin, 581; Reuben E. Fenton, Governor, 582; banking system becomes basis of national banks, 586; share of public lands donated to States, 596; Civil War bounties, act approved, 610; ratifies Thirteenth Amendment, 616, 623; statues for hall of House of Representatives, 636; jurisdiction of lower New York bay, 640; primacy of, 710; when not liable for damages from floods, 725; ratifies Fourteenth Amendment, 744; Constitutional Convention of 1867, 744; increase of State debt resulting from Civil War, 752; wealth and resources, 819; contribution to Federal revenue, 820; appropriation for Antietam cemetery, 764, 840; John T. Hoffman, Governor, VI, 1; needs broad policies of government, 3; must not be divided, 3; should not relinquish control of canals, 16; local division, right of self-government, 30; liable for expense of bribery prosecutions, 37; ratifies Fifteenth Amendment, 50; not bound to restore channel of Oswego river, 96; not an insurer of canal boats, 312; VII, 599; gift of books to Chicago Law Library, VI, 364; defects of Constitution (Hoffman), 392; executive power defective, 395; John A. Dix, Governor, 522; retention of anti-commercial restrictions, 553; Samuel J. Tilden, Governor, 719; duty in

NEW YORK (State)—(*Continued*).

relation to canals, 738; interest in Federal financial policy, 750; partnership with canal boatmen, 788; VII, 7; Lucius Robinson, Governor, VII, 1; property should not be assessed for local improvements, VI, 869; VII, 86, 228, see also ASSESSMENTS AND PUBLIC FUNDS; liable for expense of trials for offenses committed in State prisons, 87; consents to transfer of Antietam National cemetery from Maryland to United States, 173; executive residence, purchase of, 178; relation to Indian reservations, 383; Alonzo B. Cornell, Governor, 418; first simultaneous election of executive officers and Legislature, 1879, 438; arms of, note on, 725; reception of French delegates to Yorktown Celebration, 733, 737; Grover Cleveland, Governor, 815; leads in establishing civil service system, 976; VIII, 20, 149; David B. Hill, Governor, 1; Columbian Exposition, board of managers, 933; military organizations in battle of Lookout Mountain and Missionary Ridge, 1076; memorial on Chattanooga battlefield, 1077; direct taxes, United States, amount refunded, 1107; Roswell P. Flower, Governor, IX, 1; cost of various boards and commissions, 1891, 11; representation at New York naval review, 1893, 24; high rank in agriculture, 174; should not engage in railroad business, Elmira Reformatory transportation facilities, 244; imprisonment of defendant on alleged improper conviction, when not liable for damages, 250; out of debt, 1894, 296; leads States in agricultural products, 319; Levi P. Morton, Governor, 536; change of political control, 1895, 536; troops in battle of Chattanooga, 576; pioneer in State care of insane, 650; retail liquor licenses, 1892, 666, 698; success at Cotton States Exposition, 1895, 672; Frank S. Black, Governor, 738; military expenses, Spanish War, 1898, I, 288; Theodore Roosevelt, Governor, X, 1; Benjamin B. Odell, Jr., Governor, 180; Frank W. Higgins, Governor, 718; large number of awards at Louisiana Purchase Exposition, 747; illiteracy in, 859.

VETOES. Council of Safety, bill to create, II, 113; colonial loans due State, payment of, 240; memorial, organization of government, VII, 85; citizens, claims against other States, 250; Harlem river improvement, expense of, 407; officers, expenses incurred by, 586; public records, preservation, 666; public service, publication of, proposed purchase, 920; judgment against, Edye and Volcken, payment, 926; accounts with counties, adjustment of, VIII, 640; memorial hall at White Plains,

NEW YORK (State), VETOES — (*Continued*).

IX, 221; certain waters of, protection of life and property on, 720; monuments on boundaries, expenses of State Engineer, X, 559; monuments on boundaries, restoring and placing, expenses, 786.

NEW YORK CITY (Colony). First Assembly to meet in, I, 6; representation in First Assembly, 9; postoffice established in, 34; weighhouse, Crown to receive revenue from, 36, 38; support of ministers in, 39; proposed battery in, 41; reported design against, by French ships, 41; key of province, 44; calling dissenting minister, 55; act for erection of city hall, 83; jail in, recommended, 83; petition for wharf, 96; defense of, 99, 103, 120, 123, 187, 247, 295, 340, 345; grammar free school established, 100; expected French attack on, 103, 120; rum not to be distilled, nor oyster shells burned in, 103; condition of fort at, 137; burning of woods in, prohibited, 143; repeal of Tax Law, 144; bounties for volunteers, Canadian expedition, 151; petition from, relative to maintenance of French prisoners, 166; petition of grand jury against vendues and peddlers, 170; weakness of fort at, 179; mayor's sloop seized by Spanish, 186; repair of custom-house, 188; garrison at, 131; powder magazine recommended in, 199; repair of fort, 208, 210, 213, 216; collector's district, restoring part of Long Island to, 213; providing for completion and repair of Fort George, 216, 218, 222, 229, 231, 238, 241, 260, 265, 270, 277, 305, 315; proposed gift of library to, 234; action of mayor and common council relative to Millington Library, 235; battery at, 41, 247, 280, 283, 295, 345; exempt militia to serve as watchers, 297; military watches, 298, 302; station ship at, 320; proposed plan of fortifications, 322; blockhouses recommended in, 340; lottery to raise fortifications' funds, 345; smallpox in, 367, 522, 616; mayor, recorder and aldermen to be commissioners of excise, 529; French scheme to attack, 550; more fortifications needed, 562; militia ordered to Fort Edward, 614; Earl of Loudoun arrives with troops, 615; authorized to raise money for barracks, 617; barracks sufficient for quartering soldiers, 703; riot in, 707, 725; proposed reimbursement of, for quartering troops, 717; hospital proposed in, 733, 742; repair of fortifications, 741; population in 1771, 743; fire in, 753; proposed improvement of road to Hartford, 757; evacuated by British, 780.

NEW YORK CITY (State). Evacuated by British, I, 780; II, 195; British occupancy of, 50; refugees from, 81; prisoners of war in, relief, 116; number of troops in service, 180; Legislature

NEW YORK CITY (State)—(*Continued*).

meets at, 195, 217, 251, 263, 304, 311, 319, 323, 351, 358, 379; IX, 688; condition at close of war, II, 195; local authorities, power under Tax Law, 235; merchants, claims of, 241; proposed erection of house for President in, 305; defenseless condition, 333; State prison at, 336, 364, 387, see NEW YORK PRISON; expenses in preventing spread of infectious disease, 336; importance of fortifying, 359; epidemic in, 364, 366, 372, 382, 451, 570, 1017; III, 12; fortifications at, II, 334, 349, 370, 413, 414, 418, 422, 440, 469, 550, 618; Bedlow's Island granted to State, 382, 386; health commissioners, report of, 387; condition of jail in, 394; court of general sessions, duties of Assistant Attorney-General, 399; arsenal in, 401, 425, 636, 642, 680, 751, 769, 999; prisoners escape from jail, 426; memorial from, public health, 433; authorized to purchase property deemed dangerous to public health, 451; letter from mayor relating to escapes from prison, 478; appointment of charter officers, 499; sanitary regulations, 537; charter elections, 544; providing for defense of, 567, 568, 636, 658; health officer, letter from, 586; oyer and terminer, Francisco Son murder case, 588; exports, comparison with Philadelphia, 596; population, 1807, 596; justices' courts, needed reform in procedure, 599; powder magazine in, 601, 618, 620, 636, 643, 649, 680; State lands in, sale of, 642, 679; banking capital, 1812, 710; militia in service at, 736, 746, 747; militia from, 1812, 744; fortifications, statement of expenditures, 750; magazine in, 751; deposit of military stores at, 755, 798; control of ferries, 783; proposed session of Legislature in, 805; militia for defense of, 807; sea fencibles organized, 808; reimbursement of war expenses, 1812, 809; advances for military expenditures, 816; vessels at, act relating to, 819; Thomas Burke convicted of murder, pardoned, 856; convict labor in, 875; Free School Law, amending, 877; street improvements about arsenal, 895, 953, 1115; bad effects of poor laws, 914; grand jury, communication from, relative to poor debtors, 923; General Montgomery's remains removed to, 986, 999; procuring water for, 1017; III, 87, 88; Health Board created, II, 1018; justices of Marine Court, III, 7; fever hospital in, 12; children instructed in schools, 61; prosperity resulting from canals, 75: house of refuge, 82; orphan asylum, 83; sealer of weights and measures, communication from, 101; Public School Society, 115, 159, 455; aldermen *ex officio* county judges, 161; Superior

NEW YORK CITY (State)—(*Continued*).

    Court established, 210; governmental powers of, 211; election of mayor by people, 212; IV, 53; public administrator, complaint relative to, III, 216; foreign poor, aid from auction duties, 246; prison for petty convicts, 288; schools for infants, 290; communication from mayor, importation of convicts, 403; grand jury, indictment of lottery, 404; militia aid in preserving peace, 523; riot in, 524, 527; common schools, two-thirds bill, 532; destructive fire in, 534, 584, 696; legislation resulting from fire, 535, 584; fire loan to banks, 535, 585; assessed value of property, 563; service of militia during fire, 569; abolitionists establish magazine in, 571; registration of voters, 771, 851 (mem.), 881, 988 (mem.); meeting to promote enactment of National Bankrupt Law, 841; trustees of common schools, 948; reorganization of common school system, 951; railroad to interior of State, 964; election riot, 1034; Croton aqueduct, 1034; new arsenal, IV, 72; V, 88, 175; dispensaries, aid from passenger tax, IV, 75; Blackwell's Island Hospital for Insane, 77; canal basin in, 426; Astor Library, 428; Superior Court, increasing number of judges, 443; Health Act of 1850, 470; almshouse, efficient administration of, 606; World's Fair in, 656; Crystal palace, 657; Tax Act, 695; Chamber of Commerce memorial relative to encroachments on harbor, 704; commercial center of United States, 732; V, 186; immigrant passengers, protection of, IV, 793; schools, union of various institutions, 798; board of brokers, powers of, 806; elections, regulation of ballot boxes, 808; violations of Prohibitory Law, 859; bulkhead and pier lines, V, 22, 56; bribery at elections, 25; reform in police system, 26; condition of banks, panic of 1857, 44; commission on common schools, 62, 108; communication from mayor, loan commissioners, 63; efficiency of police, 181; Central park, see that title; defenses of, 186; captain of the port, 188, see that title; more railroads needed, 189, 238, 294; authorized to buy certain State lands, 235; proportion of policemen to population, 283; department of public charities and corrections, 284; Charter Commission proposed, 294; rendezvous of troops, Civil War, 400; tonnage and value of vessels, 410; park barracks used for soldiers' hospital, 488; Harlem Railroad franchise, 518; Governor's power to remove mayor, 519; inebriate asylum, 521; national banks in, 529; unprotected condition of, 543; declared in state of insurrection, draft riots, 547; Asylum for Colored Children destroyed, draft

NEW YORK CITY (State)—(*Continued*).

riots, 547; Civil War, adjustment of quota, 574; increase of foreign trade during Civil War, 594; custom house, acquisition of property for, 642; rapid transit, importance of, 669; public property, diversion to corporate purposes, 669; aid to Soldiers' Depot, 685; mayor member of Commission on New Quarantine Establishment, 701; VI, 25; health laws need revision, V, 701; charges against certain officers, 715; affairs of, considered by Governor Fenton, 764; railroad in Broadway and other streets, 809; large increase in bank business, 819; insufficient school accommodations, 854; annual tax levy, Governor Fenton's message on, 868; widening West street, 878; VI, 93; relation to other parts of State, VI, 2; too many commissions, 32; interference in local affairs by Legislature, 32; wharves and piers, 34; Avenue C Railroad bill, 63; Ninth Avenue Railroad extension, 64; parade ground for militia, 114; Court of Common Pleas, additional judges, 124; elections, act relating to, 125; health department created, 129; authorized to take stock in New York Railway Company, 245; street processions, 374; charter revision needed, 378; charter of 1870, 379; permanency of charter, 383; police department, 384; financial condition, correspondence with Tax Commission, 404; estimated value of public property, 409; increasing population and wealth, 411; financial legislation, 1872, 414, 415; memorandum of approval on tax bill, 415; Townsend relief, 438; minority representation, 460; schools in good condition, 470; proposed board of safety, 471; needs real republican government, 476; Committee of Seventy, 478; pneumatic tubes, 289, 485; clerk, duplicate docket books, 507; charters, judicial construction, 519; extravagant salaries, 543; board of aldermen, minority representation in, 545; increase of crime, 545; extinguishment of fires, 548; grand jury, report of usury laws, 564; Produce Exchange, proceedings on canals, 564; bridge over East river to Queens county, 582; board of health reorganized, 627; comptroller to borrow money for State taxes, 632; cheap trains for laboring people, 658; annexation of Morrisania, West Farms and King's Bridge, 712; fraudulent audit of claims, 728; conspicuous example of municipal government, 836; charter of 1830, 837; charter of 1870, 839; charter of 1873, 840; limiting indebtedness, constitutional provisions, 917; marine court, appointment of Judge Sinnott, 986; objectionable legislation relative to, VII, 30; time of holding charter elections, 109; riots of 1877, 152; new charter

NEW YORK CITY (State) — (*Continued*).

needed, 162; Consolidation Act, 162, 309; expenses should be reduced, 437, 532, 715; district courts, relief of clerks and assistants, 451; repealing certain acts, 509; insane, transfer to State institution, 527; too many officers, 532; water inspectors, proposed appointment by Putnam county officers, 594; public debt, 1881, 635; Consolidation Act, 1882, 716, 802; water supply, Commission of Inquiry recommended, 717; percentage of net income payable by West Side and Yonkers Patent Railway Company, 852; increased water supply, 900; new armory, 1883, 953; civil service system established, 976; register and surrogate's bills returned for amendment, 1028, 1072; dock department assumes duties of captain of the port and harbor masters, 1051; mayor, appointments without confirmation, 1056; register, act relative to, 1072; officers chosen at general elections, VIII, 15; registration of naturalized citizens, production of papers, 20; reform in administration needed, 158; non-partisan board of elections, 159; proposed Charter Revision Commissions, 160, 299, 479; home rule recommended, 160; sinking fund and public improvements, 161, 183; total debt and valuation, 1885, 185; origin of sinking fund, 189; franchises given away, 201; Broadway Surface Railroad Company, charter annulled, 205; gas companies, organization, 240; gas companies, limiting price of gas, 241; additional evening high school, 261; Arcade Railway Company, relative to, 261; increasing water supply, 1886, 270; spring elections, 15, 278, 296, 478; board of aldermen, minority representation, 281; encouragement of free libraries, 290; consolidation with adjoining municipalities, 299; police detailed for tenement-house supervision, 317; number of excise licenses, 1887, 359; public health, act relative to, 430; park commissioners, act relative to, 430; comptroller and fire insurance, act relative to, 433; electrical subways, act relative to, 450; quarantine establishment, report on condition of, 527; normal college, incorporation and maintenance, act for, 607; Croton aqueduct, new commission created, 655, 656; excise license fees, 1889, 685; centennial anniversary of Washington's Inauguration, 695; rapid transit, Governor Hill's special message, 1889, 759; Subway Act of 1891, 761, 1071, 1142; number of election districts, 1889, 769; police justices, increasing number, 794; dock commissioners, act relative to, 832; suggested selection as site of World's Fair, 931; City Court, suspension of Justice Pitshke, 935; rapid transit, 1070; board of electrical control, extending duration of act of 1891, 1163;

NEW YORK CITY (State)—(*Continued*).

law library, IX, 45; rapid transit, amending act of 1891, 90; railroads in annexed district, amending act, 99; election boards, act relative to, 102; alleged interference in elections by Federal officers, 103; bi-partisan election boards, act of 1894, 102; X, 213; additional surrogate, act relative to, IX, 122; water supply, sanitary protection, act relative to, 225; consolidation with Brooklyn, 300; merged in Greater New York, 300; publication of registry lists, 310; College of the City of New York, acquiring new site and buildings, 381; teachers' retirement fund, act for, 411; power of removal bill, 1895, 420, 552; patrolmen, increasing salary, act for, 498; elevated railroads, rates of fare, act relative to, 500; Rapid Transit Act of 1894, 504; insane asylums transferred to State, 541; mayor member of Greater New York Charter Commission, 553; inferior criminal courts, reorganization, 578; police justice, office abolished, 580; city magistrates, office created, 580; public schools, Governor Morton's special message of 1896, 686; system reorganized, act of 1896, 687; rejects Greater New York bill, 1896, 709; Grant monument, act of 1897, 756; Rapid Transit Commission abolished, 1907, 761; affairs are not local but national, 825; Commission on commerce, 826; civil service, application of general act, 1897, 838; act of 1899, 854; decrease in commerce, 1899, X, 3; employees serving in Spanish War to receive compensation while absent, 13; special commissioner of jurors, office abolished, 24; reducing municipal expenses, 24; Garbage Disposal Act, 1900, 57; unpaid taxes in Long Island City, Jamaica, Flushing and Hempstead, 62; charter amendments of 1901, 122; Thirty-first Assembly district, ratifying nominations, 130; rapid transit, amending act, 130; Commerce Commission, report, 1900, 130; would pay large proportion of expense of canal enlargement, 140; law department, 144; teachers' salaries, 1900, 144, 154; Special Jury Law, 1896, expense of administration, 194; large compensation received by sheriff, 207; dock board abolished, one commissioner substituted, 208; better police system needed, 208; Governor's power limited, 209, 230; police system reorganized, 1901, 211; removal of employees, power limited, 211; water supply, charter amendments, 1901, 212; lodging-houses, registry of, 213; large number of tenement-houses, 237; charter amendments, 1901, 267; departments of education, act of 1901, 280; board of city record, act of 1901, 280; docks and ferries, act of 1901, 280; teachers' licenses, act

NEW YORK CITY (State)—(*Continued*).

of 1901, 281; excessive official salaries, 344; changing existing
salaries, 344; commerce as affected by canals, 359; alleged
railroad discrimination against, 364; tunnel railroads, mayor's
communication to Governor Odell, 396; indirect taxes received
from, 1902, 483; reform needed in police department, 505;
police commissioner's decisions should not be subject to judicial
review, 506; beneficent results of legislation of 1903, 579;
valuation and assessment of property, 1903, 620; city pays
more than its share of personal property tax, 620; classification of criminals and misdemeanants, 633; extent of water
rights, 691; fire marshals, 715; additional water supply, 748,
759; electric power, sale to city and to private consumers, 763;
illuminating gas, inspection and tests, 763; illuminating gas,
price to city, 764; manufacture of electricity, 764, 804; cost
of government, comparative statement, 1906, 834; authorized to
aid in Hudson-Fulton Celebration, 875; steam railroads, terminating use of, in certain streets, 897; gas, eighty-cent bill, 900.

VETOES. Tax bill, II, 211; taxes, petit larceny and disorderly
persons, 222; Mechanics and Tradesmen, charter, 228; tax,
support of poor, 247; license of carriages, 315; general tax
bill, 316; streets and highways, relative to, 331; tax bill, 1796,
373; actions for small debts, 532; laying out Canal street, 646;
surveys in, 661; relief of inhabitants, 665; weighing merchandise, III, 528; criminal courts, relative to, 1009; Croton water
tax, IV, 773; illegal voting, bill to prevent, 825; police courts,
assistant clerks, V, 149; taxes, 221; railroads in several streets,
238, 517; legalizing proceedings of mayor and common council,
246; police justices, compensation, 384; confirming street railroad ordinances, 667; street railroad tunnel under Broadway,
669; Pneumatic Railway and Express Company, 670; Manhattan Gas Company, increasing price of gas, 670; Knickerbocker Gas Company, use of streets, 673; board of revision of
assessments, 724; contracts for filling certain lots, 728; railroad in Christopher street, 796, 811; railroad in 125th street,
871; VI, 62; Avenue C Railroad extension, 74; aiding New York
and Long Island Bridge Company, 91; market in 21st ward, 93;
altering Central park map, 93; gas supply, 180; incorporating
New York Advertising Company, 191; Bar Association, charter,
192; Arcade Railway, charter, 197; market 13th ward, 209;
improvement of streets, avenues and public places, 220;
alteration of map, 220, 590; Stock Exchange, charter, 221;

NEW YORK CITY (State), VETOES — (*Continued*).

district courts, additional clerk, 281; register, closing office on
holiday, 287; deposit of manure, 323; protection of health, 324;
insane and idiots, 324; prevention of contagious diseases, 325;
street improvements, 326; vagrants, amending act, 330; oyer and
terminer, stenographic notes, 830; Forty-second Street and
Grand Street Ferry Railroad Company, extending tracks, 335;
new charter, 1872, 453; VII, 1061; VIII, 16; regulating sale
of leaf tobacco, VI, 480; special election commissioners, 495;
Consolidating Act, 508; claims, settlement of, 513; local improvement, expenses, 519; third police judicial court, salary of
assistant clerk, 564; Galway relief, 573; Loutrel relief, letter
from Comptroller, 573; streets, closing and changing grade,
583; public administrator, amending Revised Statutes, 583; public administrator, regulating bureau of, 584; Rapid Transit Company, charter, 585; Maritime Association, charter, 585; New
York Bridge Company, amending charter, 586; buildings, amending act, 590; publication of judicial proceedings and legal
notices, 591; Washington market, lease of, 594; Croton water,
amending act, 596; election districts, amending act, 596; Tenth
avenue and Ninety-third street improvement, 597; police and
district court janitors, 598; Eighty-sixth street improvement, 599;
street railroad, Wall street ferry to North river, 601; newspaper
claims, 607; mortgages on lands under water, 611; Warehouse
and Railway Company, charter, improving commercial facilities,
684; Bloomingdale road, Manhattanville, 692; Eastern boulevard, amending map, 695; ferry to Brooklyn, 697; Tompkins
square improvement, 698; alteration of map, Lewis street, 705;
Northeastern Dispensary, lease for, 706; telegraph, public use
of, 706; Harlem, Second Baptist church, relief from assessment, 710; poisons, regulating sale of, 710; Church of the
Resurrection, relief from assessments, 711; bonds for Yonkers
debt, 712; engineers, powers and duties, 715; New York Elevated Railroad Company, extending road, 715; West Farms,
board of education, relief, 718; coroners' inquests, expenses,
844, new act passed; board of police, granting new trials, 848;
police justices, 897; armories and drillrooms, payment for,
910; port, pilotage, 911; Westchester Annexation Act, amendments, 911; armories, 911; fire, prevention and extinguishment
of, 911; convicts and paupers, employment of, 982; volunteer
fire department, benevolent fund, 1028; district courts, clerks,

NEW YORK CITY (State), VETOES — (*Continued*).

1029; VII, 47, 451; local government, 1876, VI, 1029; notaries
public, relative to, 1036; VII, 131; charter, supplemental act,
VII, 99; securing better administration, 125, 129, 252; public
instruction, 127, 128; station-house, 30th precinct, 128; district
courts, revision of laws, 129; Boston and Third avenues, paving, 129; City Court, establishment, abolishing marine court,
129; docks, wharves, piers and bulkheads, management, 129;
coroners, duties and compensation, 129; water supply, 23d and
24th wards, 129; street improvements, 23d and 24th wards,
129; street repairs south of Fourteenth street, 129; local government, expenses, 129; commissioner of jurors, 129, 251; commissioners of deeds, additional number, 206; debt, payment of,
209, new act passed; public burdens, 252; public buildings, exemption from taxation, 267; Colored Home, relative to, 267;
Ladies Deborah Nursery and Child Protectory, relative to, 267;
foreclosure sale, publication of notice, 267; removal of refuse
matter, 268; preservation of records, 268; district courts, janitors, 326, 804, 933; Five Point House of Industry, powers of,
334; register, duties and compensation, 412; Washington Rifles,
charter, 412; summary proceedings, 413, 417; removal of officers,
procedure, 413; port, regulations, amending act, 414; police
department, 414; hackney coaches and carriages, amending act,
415; dock department, 416; VIII, 403; IX, 235, 286; livery
stables, VII, 416; improvements, 417; West Farms and Morrisania, amending act, 417; wooden buildings, construction prohibited, 444; rebuilding markets, 450; Senate investigating committee, 1875, 462; 111th street, relative to, 506; 126th and 127th
streets, opening, 507; public exchange, relative to, 507; Bachelor
Club, charter, 507; Fulton Market, rebuilding, 507; port, relative
to, 507; protection of female employees, 509; Croton water,
arrears of rent and charges, 509; marshals, relative to, 509; common council, legalizing proceedings, 509; Hohenholz escheat, 548;
additional public bath, 551, 873, new bills passed; Cottman
claim, proof of, 552; manure, facilitating removal of, 553;
Central Park refreshment house, 578; registry of voters, publication, 579, new bill passed; water supply, 1881, 593, 635, 716;
sheriff's jury, 595; city prison, compensation of keepers, 597;
Kehr, relief, 601; retirement of teachers, 606; Hatzel election
contest, alderman, relief, 616; docks, 622; VIII, 293; park
commissioners, alteration of map, Spuyten Duyvil road, VII,

NEW YORK CITY (State), VETOES — (Continued).

629; Foley, supervisor, salary, 643; Riverside park improvement, 655; streets, changing grades, 657; justice seventh district court, Stemmler case, payment of salary, 661; VIII, 294, 884; northwest section, laying out and improving, VII, 664; improvements, Eighth avenue and 155th street, amending act, 664; Tenth avenue and 145th street, improvements, 665; opening streets, amending act, 665; widening East 100th street, 666; general sessions, stenographer's compensation, 768; city prison, keepers, increasing compensation, 772; corporations, taxation of, 777; street railroads, maintenance and operation, 793; street cleaning, 803; IX, 631, 724; commissioner of jurors, VII, 803; police and fire departments, salaries, 803; Excise Law, amending, 803; teachers' pensions, 804, 931; public baths, additional, 804; surrogate, official term, expenses of proceedings, 804; preservation of public records, 804; elevated railroads, fares, 850; public works department, Senate investigation, counsel fees, 905; plumbers, registration, 933; common schools, 933; new armory, 933; park keepers, 934; police, salaries, 935; use of Pier 37, 935; stable refuse, removal, 935; amending charter, 1873, 936; police pensions, 937; X, 580; Consolidation Act, amendments, VII, 938; IX, 150; prohibiting tunnel under Washington park, VII, 999; Broadway Underground Railway, extending rights, powers and duties, 1031; district courts, increasing jurisdiction, 1045; captain of the port and harbor-masters, compensation, 1048; public officers, official terms, 1074, 1118; park department, 1075, 1118; park keepers, removal, 1086; hospital, upper part of city, 1086; places of amusement, exempting certain hall from license fee, 1086; sinking fund, improving condition of, 1087; police, additional patrolmen, 1087; street, permanent exterior, 1087; map, alteration of Morris avenue, 1088; Bartholdi statue fund, authorizing contribution, 1088; fire department pensions, Nunn and Wilson, 1088; Bailey and Bleakley claims, 1089; Fifth avenue, repavement, 1090; Safety Elevator Insurance Company, charter, 1113; marine (city) court, increasing jurisdiction, 1116; public health, summons, service in actions for penalties, 1117; erection of buildings, 1117; Aqueduct Commission, additional member, 1118; VIII, 45; North River pier, VII, 1119; water supply, 1885, VIII, 45; sinking fund, improving condition of, 99; Arcade Railway Company, extending powers, 102; Cedar park, discontinu-

New York City (State), Vetoes — (*Continued*).

ing proceedings relative to, 129; inspector of buildings, deputy, 130; map, College avenue, 130; Montefiore Home for Invalids, and canal boat pier in East river, amending Consolidation Act, 131; Donnelly claim, 131; Ham claim, 131; IX, 468; weights and measures, inspectors, VIII, 131; O'Connor claim, 131; Krenkel claim, 132; court officers, salaries, 132; Metropolitan Transit Company, discontinuing part of line, changing Harlem River bridge, 132; Retail Grocers' Union, charter, 198; police captains, increasing salaries, 211, 525; gas companies, 240; excise commissioners, 273, 656; mayor, aldermen, comptroller and president of board of aldermen, election, terms of office and powers, 278; cumulative voting for aldermen, 283; public market, 292; park department, jurisdiction over certain streets and avenues, 293; assessments for local improvements, 293; High Bridge park, 294; West Side German Dispensary, exempting from taxation, licenses, 294; Teachers' Mutual Benefit Association, charter, 336; park department, altering map, 23d and 24th wards, 350; amending General Excise Law, 355; Nineteenth street, repaving, 389; collateral inheritance tax, fees of county treasurer and comptroller, 412; Central park, zoological collection, 449; dockmasters, defining duties, 456; German American School Society, exempting property from taxation, 460; wooden buildings, 467; Melrose avenue, alteration of, 467; 23d ward, altering certain streets, 467; excise moneys, disposition of, 467; taxes, sales for, notice to unknown owners, 467; stands in streets, permits for, 467; Hall claim, audit of, 467; Central Park parade ground, 467; district courts, 469; police sergeants and detective sergeants, salaries, 524; commissioners of excise, charges against, stenographer's fees, 551; aqueduct extension and improvement, 636; police and fire commissioners, 636; evening high school for males, 22d ward, 637; evening high school for males, 19th ward, 638; Criminal Court building, 638; 12th ward, discharge of taxes, 638; Ophthalmic Institute, 638; Vogel relief, 638; local improvements, assessments, 638; election notices, 638; Montefiore Home, amending charter, 638; park police, 638; marine court, jurisdiction, 711; park department, extending jurisdiction, 714; 111th street, closing portion of, 738; bipartisan police commissioners, 756; bi-partisan Park Commission, 758; Monaghan, Dolan, Loutrel, Clarke and Hottenroth claims, 883; Dismore & Company, Vogel, McCabe, O'Connor

NEW YORK CITY (State), VETOES — (*Continued*).

and Roberts claims, 884; tenement-houses, 886; electrical conductors, right to construct, compensation for, 887; pavements, repair of, 887; poor adult blind, appropriations, 889; old armory building, 889; dock commissioners, salaries, 889; Van Cortlandt park, preservation of vaults and burial plats, 889; Hudson street, premises on, receiving testimony concerning, 889; patrolmen, acting as precinct detectives, salaries, 889; police pension fund, 891, 1129; IX, 728; X, 474; soldiers and sailors' memorial arch or monument, 1029, 1160; cable railroad, 1035; Harlem River bridges, 1035; Croton aqueduct, settlement of claims, 1035; Aqueduct Act, amending, 1035; public works, assessments for improvements, 1035; Waterbury claims, counsel fees, retaxation, 1035; X, 807; Central Park North and East River Railroad Company, claim against, settlement, VIII, 1035; Central park, railways in transverse roads, 1035; Hart's island, annexation of, 1035; hydrants, 1035; Sanitarium for Hebrew Children, exemption, 1035; poor and adult blind, relief, 1036; election days, amending charter, 1036; Krenkel, relief, 1036; Spicer escheat, amending act, 1036; firemen, exempt, Westchester annexed district, 1036; taxes, 120th street, settlement, 1036; Harvey claim, 1160; park police, IX, 52, new bill passed; tenement-houses, changing definition, 67; evening high school, 74, 216; normal college, instruction by American Museum of Natural History, 84; common council, powers of, 149; commissioner of street improvements, 23d and 24th wards, 151; inspectors of elections and poll clerks, 151; election districts, advertising boundaries, 151; fire department, sites for buildings, 235; Second street sewer, reconsidering assessments, 236; land for public use, acquisition, 236; taxes, McCaddin property, settlement of, 238; parks, West End avenue, 262; public health, depositing refuse matters in waters about, repeal, 384; parks, compensation of laborers and employees, 393; department heads, appointment and removal, 415; park commissioners, appointment, 434; buildings, elevators in, 445, 461; snow and ice, removal from streets, 459; real estate, 23d and 24th wards, recording documents, 460; streets, etc., cleaning, 474; police department, Senate investigation, 1894, expenses of committee, 484; police department, reorganization, 490; parks, protection of, 517; stables near churches, 520; liens, discharge of, 520; fire commissioners not to be candidates for

NEW YORK CITY (State), VETOES — (*Continued*).

Shill claim, audit, 807; lectures for working men and women, 807; fire department pension-roll, claims of chiefs of battalions to be placed thereon, 808; Westchester annexed district, public building in, 808; relief of Beth Israel Bikur Cholim Congregation, 808; East River park, legalizing laying out, refunding assessments, 808; St. Joseph's Seminary, relative to real estate, 808; criminal courts building, authorizing acceptance of, completion, 808; buildings, 809, 873; X, 175; St. Luke's church, relief from certain assessments, IX, 809; Wynn, relief, 809; Lexington avenue opening, canceling assessments on certain property, 809; Davenport, judge thirteenth civil district court, legalizing appointment of attendants and employees, 809; diseased animals, destruction of, compensation, repealing acts applicable to, 810, 870; Mott avenue, widening portion of, 810; teachers' salary bill, 854; inferior criminal courts, 859; Municipal Court, 859, 860; justices of special sessions and city magistrates, qualifications, 859; teachers' salaries, 859; election officers, compensation, 859; Mount Sinai Hospital, relief, 861; Brooklyn Free Library, transfer of land to, 867; tenements and lodging-houses, improvement of, 868; American Museum of Natural History, appropriation, 1898, 868; taxes, Westchester annexed district, cancellation, 870; Bronx, changing grade of streets and avenues, damages, 870; normal college, 871; pharmacists and druggists, regulating prescriptions, 871; school trustees, 19th ward, actions against, legal services and expenses, 871; volunteer firemen, Westchester annexed district, services after annexation, compensation, 871; sewer, Westchester annexed district, 871; mechanic's lien, repealing part of Consolidation Act, 872; assessments, cancellation, 872; Deering claim, settlement, 872; district court justices, legalizing acts, compensation, 872; Surf avenue, Gravesend, relative to, 872; X, 476; public exhibitions, license fees, payment to Actors' Fund of America, IX, 872; Metropolitan Museum of Art, Ward claim, 873; transferring property to Brooklyn Public Library, 873; East river, piers, slips and wharves, regulating use of, 873; prison ship martyrs, monument to, 874; Brooklyn maps, Strom claim, settlement, 874; clerks and employees, legalizing transfer and assignment from consolidated municipalities, 874; electrical subways, repealing act of 1897, 875; courts, clerks and interpreters, 875; newspapers for advertising corporate notices, designation, 875;

NEW YORK CITY (State), VETOES — (*Continued*).

X, 59, 177; dock board, leasing land for boathouse service, IX, 875; legislative department, members not eligible to certain appointments, X, 46; firemen and policemen, reinstatements, nineteen bills, 53; Brooklyn, confirming certain appointments by fire commissioners, 59; stoop lines, 59; Hudson claim, 59; elections, separate department, 59, 145; park, Fourth ward, 60; Jewish Theological Seminary, relative to, 60; First Methodist Episcopal church, relief, 60; Hamilton park, 60; trees and vegetation, cultivation of, 60; Long Island City, claims, 60; public schools, Queens and Richmond, 60; volunteer firemen, Queens and Richmond, 60; Evangelical Lutheran Church of St. James, relief, 60; lunacy examiners, board of, 60; public place, 24th ward, 60; Eagle Avenue German Baptist church, relief, 60; police pension fund, 60; sidewalks, removal of snow and ice, 60; Municipal Court, clerks and assistants, 60; engineers, relative to, 60; public driveway, 60; Gavin, relief, 60, 323; St. Nicholas park, 60; gas meters, inspection, 60; rapid transit, 60; commissioners of deeds, powers, 61; Wilson, policeman, relief, 61; application of Gerichten and Brown, police commissioners to reconsider, 62; Rehwinke, fireman, charges against, hearing, 63; Ginley, relief, 63; street improvements, 63; summary proceedings, amending Consolidation Act, 159, 175; health department, anti-toxin accountant, compensation, 160; Municipal Court, claims of attendants, 168; Garvey claim, 169; supply of teachers, 172; regulating practice of midwifery, 172; finance department, city magistrate's court, claims for services, 172, 176; Missionary Society of the Most Holy Redeemer, release from certain assessments, 175; Wasserman relief, 175; Williamsburgh Volunteer Firemen Association, headquarters for, 175; wharf property, 175; Woodside Water Company, claim, 175, 326; O'Connor, relief, 175; Methodist Episcopal Church Home, releasing from assessments, 175; marshals, 175; Municipal Court justices, 176; City College, site and buildings, 176; Dourigan, relief, 176; East Side bridge, Blackwell's Island, 176; Guiman, relief, 176; Cohen, policeman, 176; police department, 176; fire department relief fund, 176; Ward's island water rights, 176; McCarthy, relief, 176; Clifford, Sachs and Foster, relief, 176; Court of General Sessions, 176; water front improvement, corporate stock for, 176; grade crossings, abolition of, 176; Jerome park reservoir, bridge over, 176, 326;

NEW YORK CITY (State), VETOES — (*Continued*).

qualifications of patrolmen, 176; Flood, relief, 176; Thompson, relief, 176; Missionary Society of the Most Holy Redeemer, exemptions, 176; St. Joseph's Asylum, exemption from taxation, 176, 179; Newtown creek nuisance, repeal, 176; McCann, relief, 176; park, Twelfth ward, 176; court attendants, 176; Charles Smith, relief, 176; Dillon, relief, 177; Lynch, relief, 177; Kings county penitentiary, removal, 177; Wilson, Hegaman, McGrath and Kennedy, relief, 177; removal of garbage and night soil, 177; foreign insurance companies, taxes, 177; Fitzgibbons, John and James, relief, 177; Griffin, Murphy and Newschaffer, relief, 177; Fulton Market Fishmongers' Association, relative to, 177; Clifford and Newsam, relief, 177; schools, 177; Municipal Court Revision Commission, 177; Municipal Court employees, payment for services, 177; Jacobs and Cassidy, relief, 177; streets near schools, hospitals, etc., asphalting, 177; construction of conveyances, contracts and instruments, relative to assessments, 177; Enright, Meagher, Bohan, Scholes, Bolles, Mitchel, Munson, Cratz, Quinn, Wheeler, Dunn, Flannagen, Strauss, Curley, Darcy and Striebel, relief, 178; fire commissioners, Brooklyn and Long Island City, legalizing appointments, 178; ambulances, 178; tuberculosis hospital, 178; Municipal Court justices, salaries, 178; Jamaica and Brooklyn plank road, adjusting assessments, 178; trees in streets, cultivation of, 178; Cooper Union, releasing from assessment, 178; city magistrates, method of selection, 178; separate department of elections, 178; Barrett, relief, 178, 581; abandonment proceedings, undertaking on appeal, 178; parks, 178; condemnation proceedings, pay of commissioners, 179; New York University, exemption from assessments and water rates, 179; House of Good Shepherd, cancellation of assessments, 179; DuBois, relief, 179; park commissioners, powers, 179; city prison, third district, city magistrate's court and county jail, 179; employees serving in Spanish War, compensation, amending act, 264; New York and New Jersey Bridge Company, elevated railroad, West street, 303; claims arising under contests of certain judgments, 307; reservoirs, etc., assessment and taxation of, 308; Municipal Court, enforcement of judgments, 308; sealers of weights and measures, salaries, 308; dockmaster, White claim, 308; Municipal Court, O'Sullivan, stenographer, compensation, 310; Turner claim, finance department, 310; Dowling claim,

NEW YORK CITY (State), VETOES — (*Continued*).

310; Garvey claim, Charities Department, 311; Coyle, subpœna clerk, special sessions, compensation, 313; fires, explosives and combustible materials, prevention of, 313; City Court, 313; Williamson, assignee of Jamaica Electric Light Company, claim against New York, 316; Hell Gate pilots, 316; janitors of public schools, 319; Westfield, Richmond county, claims for school supplies, 320; dockmasters, Powers claim, 321; fire department, life insurance fund, deposit, 321; recorder, city judge and general sessions judges, fixing compensation, 321; firemen's pension, Bowen case, 321; unpaid taxes in annexed territory, 322; public building, 12th ward, Manhattan borough, 323; street projections, 323; park department, jurisdiction over certain streets and places, 323; veteran volunteer firemen associations, exemptions, Queens and Richmond boroughs, 323; streets, Bronx borough, settling claims for damages, 323; Hamilton Grange, acquiring and maintaining, 324; 135th street, improvement, 324; Pallandino, relief, 324, 581; Riverside drive extension, damages, 325; docks and ferries, 325; police department, 325; street through Cypress Hills cemetery, 325; taxes, assessments and water rates, Greenfield property, cancellation, 325; Beth Israel Hospital Association, taxes and water rents, relief, 326; St. John's Armenian Apostolic church, exempting property from taxation, 326; Diamond claim, school department, 326, 636; Manhattan street opening, compensation of commissioners, 326; notification of assessments, 389; court of general sessions, custodian, 390; public administrator, execution of provisions of Power will, 391; German Hospital and Dispensary, relief, 449; public dancing within half mile of cathedral in process of erection, 456; New York and Harlem Railroad Company, motive power and terminal facilities, 466; tunnel railroads, franchise, 471; Volunteer Firemen's Benevolent Association, Richmond Hill, charter, 472; assessments by boards of assessors, 472; taxes, levy and collection, 472; dockmasters, reinstatement, 472, 477; firemen, volunteer associations in certain former towns, appropriation, 472; Hamilton park, 473; claim of New York Produce Exchange, Foster extradition case, 473; Alger, acting supervisor of truancy, compensation, 473; amending charter, new section, 473; Municipal Court, additional justices, 473; St. Joseph's Asylum, releasing assessments, 473; Chiesa, relief, extending

NEW YORK CITY (State), VETOES — (*Continued*).

time to sue for personal injuries, 473; Diegan claim, Municipal Court attendant, 473; fire boat captains, retirement, 474; sewer, Brooklyn and Queens, construction and maintenance, 474; election officers, compensation, 474; department of correction, 474; Municipal Court interpreter and attendants, compensation, 474; docks and ferries, 475; water rents, apportionment, 475; places of amusement, 475; Jewish Protectory and Aid Society, authorizing appropriations for, 475; banks, repayment of penalties to certain, 475; banks, assessment of shares, correction, 475; law library, court of general sessions, 475; superintendent of buildings, appeals from, 475; patrolmen and firemen, qualifications, 476, 580, 581; Russel claim, 476; interest on unpaid assessments, 476; teachers' pensions, 477; department of education, services in, compensation, 477; piers for recreation, 580, 581, 582; police and fire departments, promotion for bravery, 580; fire department, volunteers, preference, 580; borough presidents, salaries, 580; Municipal Court, relative to, 580; code of ordinances, 580; acquisition of land by board of estimate and apportionment, 580; armory supplies, 580; Murphy, Bradley, Linehan, Cohen, Taylor and Pinkley, policemen, relief, 581; Kenehan, fireman, relief, 581; Richard E. Taylor, relief, 581; William H. Hart, relief, 581; Collins, relief, 581, 691, 813; Turner and Macdonald, relief, 581; McDowell, relief, 581; annual instalment payments, 581; Municipal Court justices, salaries, 581; fire department chaplains, compensation, 581; board of taxes and assessment, compensation, 581; playgrounds, acquisition of, 582, 634; fire commissioner, powers, 582, 806; city magistrate, qualifications, 582; Palmer, Cole, Mechan, Ryan, Boody, relief, 582; Devlin, roundsman, reinstatement, 582, 951; 6th ward, opening street, 582; general sessions, salary of attendants, 582; public building commissioners, costs, 582; additional public parks, 582; rapid transit railway commissioners, costs, 582; additional magistrates, police clerk, 582; local boards of improvement, meetings, 582; Walsh, relief, 582; court buildings and jail, 582; fire department, pensions, 582; fire department employees, relative to, 583; assessments, exempting religious corporations, 583; Municipal Court officers and marshals, 588, 633; Court of Claims, Park avenue improvement, claims for damages, 589; fire department, claims for labor, services and materials, 633; commitments to

NEW YORK CITY (State), VETOES — (*Continued*).

Bedford Reformatory, 633; fire department, assignments and promotions, 634; selection of grand jury, 634; damages, payment of awards, 634; special revenue bonds, 635; street and park openings, fund for, 635; purchase of supplies for departments, 635; Municipal Court, additional marshals, 635; City Court, relative to, 635; Feely claim, assistant expert accountant, 690; Russell claim, 690, 817; Daly claim, section superintendent, dock department, 691, 957; O'Neil claim, assistant clerk, Municipal Court, 691; commitment of females, 709; street improvements, 23d and 24th wards, 712; municipal clubhouses for boys, 712; medical examiner, abolishing office of coroner, 712; Municipal Court, salaries, 712; Crane estate, release, 712; street improvement damages, 23d and 24th wards, 712, 807; maps, providing for, 713; streets, change of grade, damages, 23d and 24th wards, 713; police qualifications, 713; Municipal Court, relative to, 713, 714; St. Nicholas park proceedings, rehearing by Supreme Court, 713; fire department, reinstatements, 713; police department, reinstatements, 713; assessments for local improvements, collection, 713, 715, 716; Municipal Court interpreter, salary, 714; retirement fund, 714, 806; summary proceedings, service of precept, 714, 717, 805, 806; Silver Lake park, Richmond county, 715; street opening, 6th ward, 715; refunding East River park assessments, 715, 806; volunteer firemen, claims, Queens and Richmond, 715; board of estimate and apportionment, powers, 715; commissioners of elections, term, 716; court attendants, compensation, 716; volunteer fire department, preference, 717; Municipal Court justices, 717; firemen's pensions, 717; Memorial Day celebration, Richmond borough, 762; excursion boats and barges, fire protection, 805; stenographers, City Court, 805; Brown claim, 806; habitual drunkards, 806; Duggan, patrolman, 806; Brooklyn firemen, confirming appointments, 806; Municipal Court attendants, 806; Taylor claim, 806; Campbell, patrolman, 806; McGowan, refunding taxes, 806; appointment of patrolmen, 806; public hospital, 806; condemnation proceedings, commissioners, 807; police clerks, 807; McGee, policeman, 807; Pelham avenue, laying out, 807; Mahon pension, 807; height of buildings, 807; Grand boulevard and Concourse, refunding assessments, 807; stables near churches and hospitals, 807; water supply department, Wydler claim for reinstatement, 815; law department,

NEW YORK CITY (State), VETOES — (*Continued*).

Juergens claim, 816, 957; Municipal Court officers and marshals, 816; fire marshals, 816; additional stenographer, City Court, 816; boards of aldermen and estimate and apportionment, powers, 816; fire department, Murphy pension, 816; Savage, patrolman, rehearing charges, 817, 950; Municipal Court, Manhattan borough, maintenance claims, 817; finance department, Wernberg claim, 817; Pinkley, appointment as policeman, 817; Davie, relief, volunteer fireman, 817; Dillon, policeman, rehearing charges, 817; dockmasters' claims, 818; fire department deputy chiefs, Brooklyn and Queens boroughs, 818; fire department, Parker claim, relief of minor daughter, 818; board of estimate and apportionment, powers, 715, 818; fire department, Sweeney, reappointment, 818; Municipal Court judges, designation and rotation, 818; Municipal Court, justice's clerk, 819; Carrigan, patrolman, reinstatement, 949; Douglass, service in water department, 949; Hughes, patrolman, reinstatement, 950; Carpenter, clerk, Municipal Court, claim, 950; Lyons, fireman, reinstatement, 950; Weise, fireman, reinstatement, 950; Brown and Fleming Contracting Company, Queens borough, highway department, materials, 950; Moynahan, stenographer, claim for services, Supreme Court, Criminal Term, 950; McCullen, fireman, reinstatement, 951; Phillips, coroner's clerk, 951; Head, dock department, engineer, rehearing charges, 951; Uvalde Asphalt Paving Company, labor and materials, Brooklyn, 951; court of general sessions, record clerks, salaries, 953; evidence, weather records, 955; establishing free college, Brooklyn, 956; City Court, justices' clerks, 956; Kelly, coroner's clerk, Queens borough, 956; McNeile, coroner's clerk, Kings county, 957; auctioneers, licenses, 957; Newtown creek bridge, damages to owners of land abutting on Vernon avenue, 957; general sessions, clerks and stenographers, compensation, 958; borough presidents, powers, 959; Ellett and Miller, secretary and watchman, Richmond county, park commissioners, 959; inferior criminal courts, 959.

NEW YORK COUNTY. Surrogate not to be appointed in, II, 258; nomination of sheriff, proceedings in Council of Appointment, 474; cessions of land in, how made, 825; included in metropolitan police district, V, 27; VI, 30; exempted from Dog Tax Law, VIII, 823; sheriff's office, salary established, 1023, 1103; offices of county clerk and register not self-supporting, 1024; increase

NEW YORK COUNTY — (*Continued*).

    in population, IX, 3; State care of insane, 31, 189; insane asylums, inmates, 1891, 32; highways, cost of labor system, 1892, 200; insane, care of, county and State systems compared, 228; sheriff a salaried officer, act for, 413, 459; officers to be elected in odd-numbered years, 705; board of supervisors reestablished, 1897, 753; included in metropolitan elections district, 885; transfer tax assistant, X, 108; estimated contribution to cost of barge canal, 602.

VETOES. Sheriff, increasing fees, V, 877; register, closing office on holiday, VI, 287; clerk, duplicate docket books, 507; publication of judicial proceedings, legal notices, 591; maintenance of civil prisoners, 596; coroners, stenographers for, 910; convicts and paupers, employment of, 982; notaries public, relative to, 1036; VII, 131; county clerk, duties and compensation, 413; Surrogate's Court, proceedings, 417; sheriff's jury, 595; Foley, supervisor, salary, 643, 933; closing certain offices on Saturday, 757; surrogate, official term, expense of proceedings, 804; Bliss, contested election, Assembly, expenses, 918; stenographer, Surrogate's Court, increasing salary, VIII, 82; Howard estate, restitution of collateral inheritance tax, 1139; transfer tax, salaries, IX, 273; sheriffs and deputies, appointment and compensation, 459; Tamsen, sheriff, charges against, expenses, 777; sewers in Bronx district, 805; sheriff, allowance for expenses after expiration of term, X, 321, 594, 716; sheriff, amending act, 581, 706; Surrogate's Court, preservation of records, 586; sheriff, salary, 711, 773, 948; register, compensation of copyists, 712; Surrogate's Court, referees and law assistants, 712; register, additional deputy, 956; sheriff, amending title to act, also amending act, 960.

NEW YORK ADVERTISING COMPANY. Charter, veto, VI, 191.

NEW YORK AGRICULTURAL COLLEGE. Incorporated, IV, 648.

NEW YORK AND ALBANY POST ROAD. Act to preserve, 1896, IX, 668.

NEW YORK AMERICAN. Cited, charges against Justice Van Ness, II, 1031.

NEW YORK ANNUITY COMPANY. Charter, veto, VI, 208.

NEW YORK ARCADE RAILWAY. Bill to incorporate, and to provide for the construction of a sub-surface railway, veto, VI, 197, 245; extending powers, veto, VIII, 102; act relative to, 261.

NEW YORK BAR ASSOCIATION. See ASSOCIATION OF THE BAR OF THE CITY OF NEW YORK.

NEW YORK BASEBALL CLUB. Preserving grounds of, veto, VIII, 738.

NEW YORK BAY. Right of oyster fishing in, IV, 564; quarantine jurisdiction, historical sketch, VI, 779; depositing refuse matters in waters of, repeal, veto, IX, 384; communication from State commissioner of health, pollution of waters, X, 523.

NEW YORK BOARD OF HEALTH. Established, II, 1018.

NEW YORK BRIDGE COMPANY. Amending charter, veto, VI, 586.

NEW YORK AND BROOKLYN BRIDGE. Completion and opening, VII, 450; exemption from taxation, IX, 91.

  VETOES. Investigation, printing testimony, VII, 491; completion, control and management, VIII, 123; maintenance and government, 637; policemen, compensation, 992; trustees, legislating out of office, IX, 441; lighting during fogs, 733; running of cars, regulation, 733; elevator at, 806; reports of commissioners, amending act of 1895, X, 477.

NEW YORK AND BROOKLYN SOCIETY FOR SCHOOL AND UNIVERSITY EXTENSION. Extension movement, IX, 18.

NEW YORK, BROOKLYN AND MANHATTAN BEACH RAILWAY COMPANY. Grade crossings in Brooklyn, X, 714.

NEW YORK AND BROOKLYN TUNNEL COMPANY. Charter, veto, VIII, 888, 1135; authorized to construct tunnel, 1895, 1135.

NEW YORK BUILDING AND IMPROVEMENT COMPANY. VETOES. Amending charter, VIII, 1036; increasing or diminishing capital stock, 1101.

NEW YORK AND CANADA BRIDGE COMPANY. Amending charter, veto, VIII, 469.

NEW YORK CANADIAN PACIFIC RAILWAY. Extending time for completion, veto, X, 949.

NEW YORK CATHOLIC PROTECTORY. Juvenile delinquents, maintenance, veto, VII, 914.

NEW YORK CENTRAL AND HUDSON RIVER RAILROAD COMPANY. Strikes and riots, 1877, VII, 151; taxes in Mentz, application of, veto, 207; courtesies to French delegates to Yorktown Celebration, 740; strike of employees, 1890, VIII, 1071; New York city, terminating use of Eleventh avenue by, X, 897.

NEW YORK CENTRAL RAILROAD COMPANY. Tonnage on, V, 207, 594; rate of fare limited, 261; Indiana memorial protesting against sudden increase of freight rates, 496; increase of passenger fare, veto, 659, 802, 804; fare of two cents per mile, 662; prosperity of, 806.

NEW YORK CHAMBER OF COMMERCE. Memorial from, inspection of provisions, II, 439; inquiry as to quality of flour, 971; suggestion as to weights and measures, III, 102; memorial from, encroachments on harbor, IV, 704; remonstrance against incorporation of Hellgate Navigation Company, 824; papers relative to use of canals by

NEW YORK CHAMBER OF COMMERCE — (*Continued*).
Federal government, V, 506, 507; memorial, reducing canal tolls, VI, 276; entertains French and German delegates to Yorktown Celebration, VII, 741; rapid transit bill, 1894, IX, 504.

NEW YORK CITY LIFE, POLICY, GUARANTY LOAN AND TRUST COMPANY. Charter, veto, VI, 343.

NEW YORK CIVIL LIST. Furnishing copies of, veto, VII, 493.

NEW YORK CLUB. Charter, veto, VI, 661.

NEW YORK COAL EXCHANGE. Charter, veto, VI, 337.

NEW YORK COLLEGE OF MEDICINE AND SURGERY. Charter, veto, VIII, 100.

NEW YORK COLLEGE OF PHYSICIANS AND SURGEONS. Established, II, 317; commended, 904; III, 338, 408; course of instruction in, II, 904; work of, III, 338.

NEW YORK COLONIAL DOCUMENTS. Cited,— correspondence relative to money bills, I, 162, 163; —Albany plan of union, 579; — Governor Hardy's resignation, 613; —opposition to Stamp Act, 706, 711.

NEW YORK COMMISSION FOR THE BATTLEFIELDS OF GETTYSBURG AND CHATTANOOGA. Established, VIII, 1077.

NEW YORK CONFERENCE OF THE AFRICAN METHODIST EPISCOPAL CHURCH. Charter, veto, VIII, 1101.

NEW YORK CUSTOM-HOUSE. Immense patronage of, II, 1066.

NEW YORK DOCUMENTARY HISTORY. Cited, Albany plan of union, I, 579.

NEW YORK ELEVATED RAILROAD COMPANY. Extending road, veto, VI, 715; lease to Manhattan Railway, VII, 851; successor of West Side and Yonkers Patent Railway Company, 851; rights confirmed by statute and judicial decision, 854.

NEW YORK AND ERIE RAILROAD. Survey for road, III, 510; State aid to, 551, 620, 731, 789, 866, 887, 959, 999; IV, 10, 661; V, 8; progress of work, III, 731, 786, 866, 953, 960, 1043; length of, 866; estimated cost of, 959; facilities afforded by, 960; extension of time for construction, 963, 999; IV, 12; difficulties attending construction, III, 999, 1049; default of, sale postponed, 999; IV, 10; company reorganized, 11; completion of, 589; tonnage, V, 207, 594; strikes and riots, 1877, VII, 151; courtesies to French delegates to Yorktown Celebration, 740.

NEW YORK EXPORTING COMPANY. Charter, veto, IV, 639.

NEW YORK EYE INFIRMARY. Appropriation from United States deposit fund, IV, 90, 118.

NEW YORK FINANCE COMPANY. Charter, veto, IX, 256, 379.

NEW YORK FINANCIAL ASSOCIATION. Charter, veto, VI, 340.

NEW YORK FREE SCHOOL SOCIETY. Incorporated, II, 551;. approves Lancastrian schools, 725; use of Bible in schools, 727; report of, 1027; name changed, III, 115; schools to become public, 115.

NEW YORK FRUIT AND SPICE EXCHANGE. Charter, veto, VII, 804.

NEW YORK GAZETTE. Proclamation in, for arrest of horse thief, I, 238.

NEW YORK HARBOR. Protection of, I, 295; III, 570; vessels in, Governor to direct disposition of, II, 246; papers relating to fortification of, 387; chart of, 440; lands ceded to United States, 457; jurisdiction over, 540; jurisdiction of cession commissioners, 620; interior defense of, 659; fortifications, statement of expenditures, 750; improvement of, III, 28, 124; importance of fortifications, 309; encroachments, memorial from Chamber of Commerce, IV, 704; proposed commission on encroachments, 732; memorial, New York Merchants' Exchange, encroachments, 751; New Jersey resolutions on encroachments, 823; Commission on Encroachments, work of, 857; survey of, V, 21, 95, 109, 186; duties of pilot commissioners, 95; protection of, 185, 294; map of, 186, 198; captain of the port, 187, see that title; defense of, 409, 414; commission on defense of, 545, 564; obstructions to prevent entry of vessels, 567; board of engineers, 568; jurisdiction over lower bay, 640; encroachments, Blunt report, 796; location of quarantine warehouses, 846; proceeding to prevent encroachment by New Jersey Central Railroad Company, 846; Brooklyn pier and bulkhead lines, revision of, VI, 452, 560; deposits in, 557, 654; always open, 736; Commission on Encroachments, 776; VII, 112; bulkhead lines, Staten Island side, report of United States Commission, 71; pier and bulkhead lines, report of Federal commissioners, 353; naval review, 1893, IX, 24.

  VETOES. New Utrecht fisheries, V, 124; pier and bulkhead lines, Newtown creek, VII, 111; port, regulations, 414; relative to, 507; bulkhead lines, Staten Island, VIII, 1037.

NEW YORK AND HARLEM RAILROAD COMPANY. VETOES. Amending charter, V, 63; motive power on Park avenue, New York, terminal facilities, X, 466; Mount Vernon, grade crossings over, 590.

NEW YORK HEALTH DEPARTMENT. Established, VI, 129.

NEW YORK HERALD. Quoted, proposed charter of 1872, VI, 475.

NEW YORK HISTORICAL SOCIETY. Charter revived, III, 118, 162; appropriation for, 162; publishes continuation of Smith's History, 162; memorial, publication of colonial documents, 751; work com-

New York Historical Society — *(Continued)*.

mended, IV, 165; communication from, presenting copy of Assembly journal, first meeting, 1780, V, 132; museum in Central park, 381; memorial, requests permission to prepare centennial memorial volume, VI, 809; visit of French and German delegates to Yorktown Celebration, VII, 742; Lafayette portrait and letters, Steuben manuscripts, 742; memorial, centennial anniversary of New York's ratification of United States Constitution, VIII, 505; changing site, continuing exemption from taxation, 824.

New York Hospital. See also Society of the Hospital of the City of New York in America. Annual report, II, 440, 529, 542, 560, 605, 630, 650, 678, 707, 750, 795, 829, 890, 944, 993, 1030, 1080, 1120; III, 14, 35, 105, 144, 184, 221, 264, 315, 391, 752; VI, 156, 557; appropriation for, II, 561; care of lunatics, 650; department for insane, 974; aid from auction duties, III, 245; aid from passenger tax, IV, 75; State aid to, 127; number of patients, 431; beneficent work of, 554; exempting property from taxation, veto, VI, 703; changing site, continuing exemption from taxation, VIII, 824.

New York House of Refuge. See also Society for the Reformation of Juvenile Delinquents. Established, III, 82; high character of, 130, 163, 291, 449, 716, 765, 876; IV, 650, 847; V, 18; to receive young convicts from State prisons, III, 292; accommodations and instruction at, 342; bill affecting, returned without action, 1032; overcrowded, IV, 481; territorial jurisdiction, 482; enlargement of, 556, 557; number of inmates, 606, 720, 789; V, 179, 289; new building, IV, 650; to receive children sentenced by United States courts, 650; increased accommodations, 720; supervision of, 720; removed to Randall's island, 789, 846; only reform school for girls, 789; counties may send girls to, V, 179; various appropriations, veto, VII, 489, 584; IX, 770; illiteracy, earnings, VII, 765; proposed transfer of title to State, IX, 771; classed as a reformatory, X, 334; proposed removal from Randall's island, 611; commitments to, veto, 705.

New York Institution. Establishment of, II, 905.

New York Institution for the Blind. State pupils at, III, 453, 716, 766; IV, 29, 128, 430, 605, 792; appropriation for, III, 716, 859; IV, 129; under supervision of superintendent of common schools, III, 716; good work of, IV, 74, 281, 554; V, 447; number of inmates, IV, 128, 430, 605, 643, 718, 792; V, 87, 180, 288, 521; industrial education, IV, 430, 848; assessment for sewers and street improvements, 644; embarrassed by financial depression, 792; sale of part of buildings authorized, V, 88.

NEW YORK INSTITUTION FOR THE INSTRUCTION OF THE DEAF AND DUMB. Incorporated, II, 974; appropriation for, 975; III, 450; IV, 430; State pupils at, III, 83, 292, 409, 450, 543, 766; IV, 29, 128, 430, 605, 643; V, 180, 447; to share in literature fund, III, 292; charter renewed, 543, 859; IV, 128; V, 382; Central Asylum consolidated with, III, 543; prosperous condition of, 715; IV, 74, 554; V, 447; supervision by superintendent of common schools, III, 292, 874; number of inmates, IV, 127, 282, 430, 605, 643, 718, 792, 848; V, 87, 180, 287, 521; removal to new site (Fanwood), IV, 718, 793, 848; V, 87; all indigent pupils made eligible to institutions, IV, 718; industrial occupations, 793; located at Washington Heights, V, 287.

NEW YORK INVESTMENT COMPANY. Charter, veto, VIII, 376.

NEW YORK JEWELERS' ASSOCIATION. Charter, veto, VII, 415.

NEW YORK JUVENILE ASYLUM. Charter, veto, IV, 526.

NEW YORK LAW INSTITUTE. Memorial, relief to Court of Chancery, III, 264.

NEW YORK LIFE AND TRUST COMPANY. Depositary of passenger tax, IV, 76.

NEW YORK LOAN AND INDEMNITY COMPANY. Assumes banking powers, VI, 622.

NEW YORK AND LONDON TRUST COMPANY. Purchase of stocks, and issue of debentures, veto, X, 586.

NEW YORK AND LONG ISLAND BRIDGE COMPANY. Amending charter, veto, VI, 91; VIII, 1037.

NEW YORK LUNATIC HOSPITAL. Insane convicts, transfer to, II, 945; condition of, III, 83; commended, 292.

NEW YORK MARINE HOSPITAL. See also SAILORS' SNUG HARBOR. Charter, veto, II, 565; annual report, 987; income of, appropriation for Society for the Reformation of Juvenile Delinquents, III, 252; necessity for, IV, 75; aid from Mariners' fund, 272; passenger tax in aid of, unconstitutional, 273; aided from commutation money, 451; V, 22; report of physician, IV, 512; removal of patients from, V, 184; physician, abolition of office recommended, 279.

NEW YORK MEDICAL COLLEGE. Condition of, II, 317, 904; III, 117, 297; incorporated, IV, 470.

NEW YORK MERCHANTS' EXCHANGE. Memorial, harbor encroachments, IV, 751.

NEW YORK MILLS FIRE COMPANY. Charter extended, V, 332.

NEW YORK MUSICAL INSTRUMENT SAVING AND LOAN SOCIETY. Charter, veto, VI, 289.

NEW YORK MUTUAL TITLE INSURANCE COMPANY. Charter, veto, IX, 861.

NEW YORK AND NEW JERSEY BRIDGE COMPANY. Elevated railroad, West street, New York, veto, X, 303.

NEW YORK NORTHERN RAILROAD COMPANY. Asks State aid, V, 866; VI, 70.

NEW YORK ORTHOPOEDIC DISPENSARY. Changing name and amending charter, veto, VI, 693.

NEW YORK AND OSWEGO MIDLAND RAILROAD COMPANY. Asks State aid, VI, 71.

  VETOES. Facilitating construction, VI, 172; aiding completion of, 345; bonds, postponing taxes, VII, 415; railroad aid bonds, relief of certain towns, VIII, 371.

NEW YORK PIPE LINE. Charter, veto, VII, 133.

NEW YORK POST-GRADUATE MEDICAL SCHOOL AND HOSPITAL. Amending charter, veto, VIII, 707.

NEW YORK PRISON. Proposed, II, 336; to be erected, 364, 387; additional expense of, 393, 405; escapes from, 478; partially destroyed by fire, 547; protection of, 712; overcrowded, 874; employment of convicts in, 913, 1015; transfer of insane convicts, 945; number of convicts in, 982; insurrection in, 985; removal of, 993, 1016; transfer of prisoners to Auburn, 1108; III, 22; to be sold, 82; condition of, 129; nearly self-supporting, 207; female department in, 207; to be used exclusively for women, 208.

NEW YORK PRODUCE EXCHANGE. Proceedings on canals, VI, 564; approves canal improvement, VIII, 13; claim against New York, Foster extradition case, veto, X, 473.

"NEW YORK PUBLIC SERVICE." Proposed purchase of copies for foreign distribution, veto, VII, 920.

NEW YORK AND QUEENS COUNTY BRIDGE COMPANY. Amending charter, veto, VI, 582.

NEW YORK RAILWAY COMPANY. Incorporated, VI, 245.

NEW YORK RAPID TRANSIT COMPANY. Charter, veto, VI, 585, 694.

NEW YORK REALTY BOND AND EXCHANGE COMPANY. Charter, veto, IX, 794.

NEW YORK REAL ESTATE BANKING COMPANY. Charter, veto, VI, 315.

NEW YORK REAL ESTATE GUARANTY COMPANY. Changing name and defining powers, veto, VIII, 617.

NEW YORK RIVER ROAD COMPANY. Constructing roads, veto, VI, 98, 419.

NEW YORK SACRED MUSIC SOCIETY. Incorporated, III, 281.

NEW YORK AND SHAWANGUNK MINING COMPANY. Amending charter, veto, IV, 323.

NEW YORK SOCIETY FOR THE PRESERVATION OF SCENIC AND HISTORIC PLACES AND OBJECTS. Appoints committee on Palisades, X, 127; changing name and extending powers, veto, 241; name changed to American Scenic and Historic Preservation Society, 241.

NEW YORK SOCIETY FOR THE PREVENTION OF CRUELTY TO CHILDREN. Recommends legislation regulating child labor, VIII, 163.

NEW YORK SOCIETY FOR THE PREVENTION OF PAUPERISM. Institutes inquiry as to prison system, II, 1052.

NEW YORK SOCIETY FOR PROMOTING THE MANUMISSION OF SLAVES. Memorial from, abolition of slavery, II, 692.

NEW YORK SOCIETY FOR THE PROMOTION OF EDUCATION AMONG COLORED CHILDREN. Communication from, V, 108.

NEW YORK STATE ASSOCIATION OF COUNTY AGRICULTURAL SOCIETIES. Three members of State Fair Commission to be chosen from, X, 120.

NEW YORK STATE CLOTHING COMPANY. Clinton prison contract, failure produces idleness of prisoners, VIII, 10.

NEW YORK STATE GRANGE. Three members of State Fair Commission to be chosen from, X, 120.

NEW YORK STATE LOAN AND TRUST COMPANY. Amending charter, veto, VI, 337; financial condition, VII, 66.

NEW YORK STATE MECHANIC ASSOCIATION. Memorial, proposition to establish museum in old State hall, IV, 47.

NEW YORK STATE SOLDIERS' DEPOT. Established, V, 577; report, 577; use of, 684; expenditures at, 686.

NEW YORK STATE TRUST COMPANY. Charter, veto, VII, 935.

NEW YORK STATE VETERINARY COLLEGE. Report, IX, 851; X, 32, 142.

NEW YORK STOCK EXCHANGE. See also STOCK EXCHANGE. Charter, veto, VI, 343.

NEW YORK SUPERIOR COURT. Established, III, 210.

NEW YORK TOWAGE COMPANY. Charter, veto, VI, 598.

NEW YORK TRANSIT COMPANY. Charter, veto, VII, 1104.

NEW YORK TUNNEL COMPANY. Relief, veto, VI, 343, 507.

NEW YORK UNIVERSITY. Exemption from assessment and water rates, veto, X, 179.

NEW YORK WAREHOUSE AND RAILWAY COMPANY. Charter, veto, VI, 684.

NEW YORK WATERWORKS COMPANY. Incorporated, III, 87.

NIAGARA. French trading-house at, I, 193, 222; protests against French stonehouse at, 227; supplied from Fort Frontenac, 625; defeat of French army of relief, 640; reduction of fort at, 640; providing for company at, 675; troops for Indian War to be concentrated at, 676; peace negotiations with Indians at, 681; interpreter and

NIAGARA — (*Continued*).

   smiths at, 733; Indian lands near, not in jurisdiction of State, II, 273; militia in service at, 736, 743.

NIAGARA CITY. Village, amending general act, veto, VII, 75.

NIAGARA COUNTY. Defense of, II, 713; militia from, 1812, 743, 744; British devastation in, 787; sheriff, removal of intruders on Grand Island, 995, 1026; entitled to share in appropriation for agriculture, 1006; commissioners appointed to locate court-house and jail, 1117; extraordinary circuit and oyer and terminer to investigate Morgan matter, III, 314, 351, 352, 354; proceedings in Morgan case, 365; agricultural society in, 945; silk culture in, 945; Assembly districts in, IV, 383; includes part of Tonawanda reservation, V, 199; exempted from Town Auditors' Act, VIII, 49; average excise license fees, 1889, 687; highways, cost of labor system, 1892, IX, 200; insane, care of, county and State systems compared, 228.

   VETOES. Subjecting to Railroad Aid Act, VI, 214; Lockport Home of the Friendless, care of poor children, 503; bridge over Tonawanda creek, 696; board of supervisors, poor expenses, VII, 328; support of poor, 367; board of equalization of taxes, VIII, 737; surrogate, compensation, 1038; boundary, Genesee and Erie counties, 1102; sidepaths, establishing, IX, 629; reconsideration of claim of Roswell park against, X, 268.

NIAGARA COUNTY SAVINGS BANK. Closing business, VI, 20.

NIAGARA FIRE INSURANCE COMPANY OF ERIE COUNTY. Changing name to Prudential Fire Insurance Company of Buffalo, veto, X, 242.

NIAGARA FALLS. Proposed canal around, III, 509, 816, 959; V, 533; establishment of park at, VII, 300; State reservation at, 301; visit of French delegates, 740; use for creation of electrical power, IX, 307, 455; should be preserved, X, 688, 918; protection of, 852.

NIAGARA FALLS. VETOES. Amending General Village Act, VII, 98; boulevard to Buffalo, VIII, 639, 879; State armory at, 887; Pierce avenue extension, IX, 534; amending city charter, 633, 731, 788; terms of officers, X, 322; board of public works, powers and contracts, 478; Liefer claims against board of education, 716.

NIAGARA FALLS RESERVATION. Commission to establish, VII, 301; X, 852; payment of awards for, government of, VII, 301; selection of land, 989; appropriation for, 989; debt for purchase of, VIII, 145, 303, 496, 663, 934, 1082; IX, 7, 157, 752; cost of, 1891, 11; debt paid, 1893, 296.

NIAGARA FALLS RESERVATION — (*Continued*).

VETOES. Roads, appropriation, X, 568; Turzkowska, injuries received at, Court of Claims, hearing, 707; labor saving machinery, appropriation, 788.

NIAGARA FRONTIER. British invasion of, II, 791; supplies for army on, 791; American successes on, 802; volunteers for service on, 815.

NIAGARA FRONTIER POLICE. Report of commissioners, V, 791, 861; VI, 43, 143.

NIAGARA, LOCKPORT AND ONTARIO POWER COMPANY. Amending charter, veto, X, 686.

NIAGARA RIVER. Lands on, survey of, II, 411; disposing of lands on, 526; ferries on, 526, 1029; islands in, purchased from Seneca Indians, 677, 857, 866; Grand Island, intrusions on, 955; Canadians, seize and destroy American vessel on, III, 678; colonial documents relative to, 1019; experimental power bridge, act of 1900, X, 54.

VETOES. Ferry at Youngstown, VI, 593; Erie county, fishing in, 906; power experiments, Mather plan, IX, 629, 813; X, 54; Grand Island bridge, 63, 703, 774; limiting use of water, 918.

NIAGARA STREET RAILROAD, NIAGARA FALLS. Changing route, veto, VIII, 1132.

NIAGARA (Town). School trustees, district No. 7, veto, VI, 188.

NIAGARA UNIVERSITY, SUSPENSION BRIDGE. Incorporating, VII, 947.

NICARAGUA. Participation in Cotton States Exposition, IX, 581.

NICHOLS, JOHN A. Senate election, 1891, elected by minority vote in consequence of rejection of irregular ballots cast for opposing candidate, VIII, 670.

NICHOLSON, FRANCIS. Appointed Lieutenant-Governor, I, 14; official service, I, pref. ix.

NICHOLSON, FRANCIS. General, commander of land force in Canadian expedition, I, 151; letter from, relative to Canadian expedition, 155.

NICHOLSON, JOHN. Captain, nominated sheriff of Orange county, proceedings in Council of Appointment, II, 475, 494.

NICOLL, BENJAMIN. Appointed counsel for keeper of powder-house, I, 532.

NICOLL, DELANCEY. Opposes New York and Brooklyn bridge bill, VIII, 637.

NICOLL, WILLIAM. Speaker, unable to preside, I, 183.

NICOLL, WILLIAM. Commissioner on colonial union, I, 370; Assembly, favors colonial union, 767.

NICOLLS, MATHIAS. Speaker of First Assembly, I, 9, 11.

NICOLLS, RICHARD. Governor of New York colony, missing letters from, IV, 184.

NICOLLS, WILLIAM. Appointed agent of colony, I, 58; letters from, 73.

"NIEW AMSTEL." Colony of, IV, 172.

NIEWENHOUS, SIEBRAND H. Court of Claims, New York, Park avenue improvement, veto, X, 699.

NIGHT WATCH. At Hudson, act for, II, 395; at Albany, 396.

NIGHT GUARD. Recommended, I, 298, 302.

NILES, SALLY ANN. Petition from, purchase of Niles' Register, III, 978.

NILES, HEZEKIAH. Publisher of Register, III, 978.

NILES' REGISTER. Proposed sale to State, III, 978.

NINE MEN. Powers of, I, 2.

NINTH BAPTIST CHURCH, SYRACUSE. Changing name to Lowell Avenue Baptist church, veto, X, 377.

NINTH JUDICIAL DISTRICT. Created, IV, 857; X, 337, 850; how constituted, IX, 547; X, 850; additional justices for, 850, 936.

NINTH REGIMENT. Of infantry, memorial from, reorganization of militia, III, 983.

NISTIGAONE. Garrison at, I, 108.

NITRE. Purchase for manufacture of powder, II, 681.

NIXON, S. FREDERICK. Speaker of Assembly, address at reception of Prince Henry, X, 480; communication from Governor's secretary, executive office hours, 747; communication from Justice Hooker requesting investigation of complaints, 826.

NOBLE, MARTIN W. Bath excise commissioner, legalizing acts of, veto, VII, 178.

NOBILITY, TITLES OF. Amendment relative to, rejected, II, 678, 750, 761.

NOLLE PROSEQUI. Court of general sessions cannot grant, II, 1002; McLeod case, III, 942.

NORBURY, CAPTAIN. Proposed reimbursement for expenses, I, 131.

NORFOLK, VIRGINIA. Epidemic in, IV, 852.

NORMAL COLLEGE, NEW YORK. VETOES. Instruction by American Museum of Natural History, IX, 84; relative to, 871.

NORMAL SCHOOLS. Proposed for each county, III, 652; academies used for, 743; at Albany, established, IV, 67, see that title; additional suggested, V, 604, 695; commission on additional, 695, 780; list of, 695; number of pupils, 779, 851; VI, 108, 236, 356, 528, 617, 946; VII, 19, 156, 297, 424, 519, 687, 821; 946; statistics, VI, 23; extravagant construction of, VII, 12; are they worth what they cost?, 21; Governor Robinson's criticism, 296; instruction of Indian youth, 709; industrial training, general act, VIII, 483; New York Normal College, incorporation and maintenance, act relating to, 607; alleged extension

NORMAL SCHOOLS — (*Continued*).

beyond original purpose of training teachers, 1138; instruction of music in, IX, 116; professional training of teachers, act of 1895, 564; large appropriations requested, 1895, 574; Geneseo, new buildings, 593; temperance instruction required, 613; training schools, act of 1894, X, 349.

VETOES. Cortland, repairs and improvements, VII, 468; Fredonia, repairs and improvements, 468; Brockport, additions and repairs, 468; Albany, repairs, furniture and books, 469; report of Assembly special committee, printing, 492; Oswego training school, instruction of kindergarten teachers, 792; Geneseo, building for school of practice, VIII, 116; Liberty Normal Institute, amending charter, 130; secretary of board, right to salary, 407; amending act, free privileges of, 506; Whitesboro, 888; Fairfield, 888; Watkins, 888; Saratoga Springs, 888; Jamaica, 888; IX, 134, 627; White Plains, VIII, 888; instruction by American Museum of Natural History, New York, IX, 84; Plattsburgh, reducing number of managers, 433; training classes in cities, 482; at Millerton, 622, 712; Ramapo, 711; Brockport, sewer system, X, 315; inspectors, compensation, 637; Fredonia, rooms for school societies, 649.

NORMAL TRAINING SCHOOL, BROOKLYN. Instruction by American Museum of Natural History, New York, veto, IX, 84.

NORMANBY, MARQUIS. Applied to, for leave to transcribe colonial documents, IV, 168.

NORMANS. Introduce improvements in agriculture, II, 956.

NORTH, ABIJAH. Member of Assembly, communication from citizens of Champlain, III, 760.

NORTH, WILLIAM. Appointed United States Senator in place of Hobart, resigned, II, 424.

NORTH AMERICA. Colonial troops not to serve out of, I, 598; possibilities of British colonies in, 690.

NORTH AMERICAN REVIEW. Cited, Speaker Reed's article on contested elections, VIII, 1075.

NORTH BRANCH CANAL. Proposed connection with Chemung canal, III, 759.

NORTH BRITAIN. Emigrants from, proposed settlement at Wood creek, I, 272, 278.

NORTH CAROLINA (Colony). Not represented in Albany Convention, I, 578; agent of, how appointed, 732; William Tryon, Governor of, 739, 742.

NORTH CAROLINA (State). Letter from Governor, II, 269, 308; resolutions, Eleventh Amendment, 347; resolutions, choosing presidential electors by districts, presidential elections, 513; laws of, received, 530; proposed constitutional amendment, importation of slaves from West Indies, 552, 586; constitutional amendment, election of representatives and presidential electors by single districts, 750, 864; disapproves Georgia proposition to reduce senatorial term, also disapproves Massachusetts resolutions (see page 827), 864; approves Massachusetts proposition for election of representatives and presidential electors by districts, 882; approves New Jersey proposition for election of representatives and presidential electors by districts, 924; encouraging internal communications, 1011; approves Maryland resolution as to distribution of public land, III, 13; disapproves South Carolina nullification proceedings, 434; recommends reorganization of militia, 482; resolutions protesting against anti-slavery agitation, 588; resolutions, protests against certain United States Senate resolutions, condemns President's financial policy and distribution of proceeds of public lands, 752; returns New York resolutions tendering aid to Federal government, V, 330; secession ordinance, 396; military to be subordinate to civil power, 470.

NORTH CASTLE. Public roads in, veto, VI, 589.

NORTH COLLINS. Town meetings and election districts, veto, VIII, 886.

NORTH CREEK. Proposed canal along, from upper Hudson to Corinth, III, 733.

NORTHEASTERN BOUNDARY. Massachusetts resolutions, III, 389, 929; Governor Seward's message, 756; Maine resolutions, 851; Indiana resolutions, 852; Maryland resolutions, 909.

NORTHEASTERN DISPENSARY, NEW YORK. Lease for, veto, VI, 706.

NORTH ELBA. Highway to Wilmington, repair, veto, VII, 1099.

NORTHERN AIR LINE RAILROAD COMPANY. Asks State aid, VI, 70.

NORTHERN CANAL. See CHAMPLAIN CANAL.

NORTHERN INLAND LOCK NAVIGATION COMPANY. Incorporated, II, 321; State aid to, 321, 335.

NORTHERN NEW YORK INSTITUTION FOR DEAF-MUTES. Appropriations, VIII, 835; X, 289; classed as an educational institution, 334.
     VETOES. Appropriation for improvements, VIII, 531; — reappropriation, unexpended balance, IX, 771.

NORTHFIELD. VETOES. Macadamizing certain roads, VII, 132; separate road district, 1099; board of education, amending act, VIII, 1039.

NORTH GREENBUSH. Excepting from Town Insurance Companies Act, veto, VI, 153.

NORTHAMPTON. Arms and supplies for, II, 772.

NORTH HAMDEN. United Presbyterian church, changing name, veto, VIII, 1096.

NORTH HAVERSTRAW. St. George's Methodist Episcopal church, changing name, veto, VIII, 617.

NORTH HEMPSTEAD. Lighthouse at, II, 641. VETOES. Support of patients in Nassau Association Hospital, IX, 818; — school district No. 2, refunding bonds, X, 961.

NORTHPORT BAY. Protection of shellfish in, veto, VII, 415.

NORTH PROTESTANT DUTCH CHURCH, GOWANUS. Changing name, veto, V, 127.

NORTH RIVER. Battery at Rutger's wharf, I, 322; battery on, 712; tunnel under, Pennsylvania, X, 396.

    VETOES. Pneumatic tubes, amending act, VI, 289; pier, New York, VII, 1119; depositing refuse matters in waters of, repeal, IX, 384.

NORTHRUP, DANIEL. Convicted of murder, pardoned, II, 874.

NORTH SHORE FIRE DEPARTMENT. Aid from New Brighton, veto, VIII, 532.

NORTH SHORE STATEN ISLAND FERRY COMPANY. Claims title to New Brighton pier, VI, 907.

NORTH TARRYTOWN. Construction of sewers, veto, VIII, 462.

NORTH TONAWANDA. VETOES. State ditch, bridges, Oliver and Foundry streets, VII, 363; highway improvement, VIII, 1155.

NORTHUMBERLAND. Bridge from Greenwich, veto, X, 699.

NORTHVILLE. VETOES. Methodist Episcopal church, sale of property, VI, 437; amending General Village Act, VII, 214; police justice, 932.

NORTHWEST TERRITORY. Slavery prohibited in, IV, 499, 567; V, 300.

NORTON, DANIEL. Commissioner, bridge, Tonawanda reservation, veto, VII, 477.

NORTON, CHARLES B. Commissioner to Paris Exposition, report, V, 862.

NORTON, PHILO. Carding machine, veto, II, 534.

NORWAY. Illiteracy as compared with New York, X, 859.

NORWICH. VETOES. Canal swing-bridge, VI, 588; recorder, creating office, IX, 75; revised charter, 289.

NORWOOD. Burial ground, removal of bodies, veto, VI, 1035.

NOTARIAL CLERKS. Amending Executive Law, veto, X, 442.

NOTARY PUBLIC. Tax on, VIII, 305, 663, 934, 1082; IX, 9; de facto, when acts cannot be questioned, VIII, 335; form of certificates, uniform legislation of States suggested, 930; commissions, act of 1899, X, 33; proposed tax on certificates, 490.

    VETOES. In certain counties, relative to, VI, 1036; VII, 131; additional number, 54, 415, 443, 863; VIII, 130; legalizing acts,

NOTARY PUBLIC, VETOES — (*Continued*).

—general, VIII, 334, 518; X, 813; — Daniel P. Cornell, VII, 507; — Whitney, 507; — Wells, VIII, 291; — Stier, 387, 518; — Cantwell, IX, 365; — Green, 720; — Larkin, 812; — McCormick, X, 813; Erie county, increasing number, VII, 1095; Monroe and Onondaga counties, additional number, VIII, 43; certificate of protest, evidence, 293; county clerk's fees, 1038; IX, 346; notarial clerks in certain counties, compensation, VIII, 1131; preventing traffic in office, X, 948.

NOTICES. Recording notices of pendency, general act of 1864, VIII, 705.

VETOES. Publication of, VI, 509; legal, Erie county, publishing in German newspaper, VII, 390; posting in certain places, misdemeanor, 640; of pendency,— recording, in Oneida and Columbia counties, VIII, 63; — recording and indexing in certain counties, 70; — recording in Cattaraugus and Columbia counties, 705; — directing record of certain, 887; — cancellation of, IX, 624, 627; of certain State contracts, VIII, 130; of liens, filing, IX, 865; assessment and grievance day, Tax Law, X, 809.

NOVA SCOTIA. Proximity to French settlements, I, 336; invaded by French, 346; fleet reported on coast of, 383; troops to be retained for defense of, 441; land in, offered for military service, 598; refugees, land grants for, II, 308.

NOYES, FALKNER E. Justice of the peace, legalizing acts, veto, VII, 412.

NOYES, WILLIAM CURTIS. Delegate to Washington Peace Convention, V, 310.

NUISANCE. Distilling of rum and burning of oyster shells in New York prohibited, I, 103; indictment of lotteries, III, 404; quarantine hospital indicted as, IV, 438; in populous districts, 469; under Public Health Law, V, 863; New York and Brooklyn, report of State Board of Health, VII, 547; abandoned Chemung canal, 575; at Hunter's Point, removal of, 710; telegraph and electric light wires and poles in streets, 865.

VETOES. Near public schools, VI, 95; trials in certain cases, VII, 416; Buffalo, abatement, 507; New York, facilitating removal of stable manure, 553; Spencerport, 805; summary destruction of fishing nets, VIII, 627; in cities and villages, relative to, IX, 151; Newtown creek, abatement, amending act, 778; New York, disposal of garbage, X, 57; Newtown creek, repeal, 176; Chemung canal, cleaning Catherine creek, 789.

NULLIFICATION. South Carolina proceedings, III, 427, 429, 434, 435, 436, 437, 438, 482; spirit not crushed, V, 394.

NUNN, GEORGE. New York fire department, pension, veto, VII, 1088.

NURSES. In hospitals, letter relative to, II, 95.

NUSSBAUM, MYER. Member of Capital Centenary Commission, IX, 689.

NUTTEN ISLAND. See also GOVERNOR'S ISLAND. Defense of, I, 295, 324; sale of, veto, II, 287.

NYACK. VETOES. Waterworks company, charter, VI, 504; ferry to Tarrytown, VIII, 880.

NYACK WATERWORKS COMPANY. Charter, veto, VI, 504.

O.

OAK ORCHARD CREEK. VETOES. Improvement of, IX, 55; deepening and straightening, X, 313.

OATH. See also OFFICIAL OATH. Of electors, II, 38; of allegiance required of suitors, 171; act relative to, 1106; of loyalty by challenged voter on election of delegates to Constitutional Convention, unconstitutional, V, 749; canals, administration of, veto, VII, 1115.

OATKA HOSE COMPANY, LEROY. Charter, veto, VII, 806, 877.

OBLIGATION OF CONTRACTS. Insolvent debtors, II, 427; power of Congress, Insolvent Law, IV, 6; relations between debtor and creditor, 40; Van Rensselaer leases, 240, 347; payment of national debt, VI, 668; elevated railroads, reducing rates of fare, IX, 500.

  VETOES. Purchases of forfeited estates, II, 112; executed trust, 354; right of dower, 582; turnpike companies, 594; trustees of Columbia College, power to fill vacancies, 610; estates of married women, 704; dissolution of corporation, 1082; diverting proceeds of Harlaem common lands, 1112; lotteries, III, 188; repeal of Public Printing Law, 1023; increasing railroad fares, VI, 518; Brooklyn Library Building Fund Association, liability of stockholders, VII, 96; remitting interest on unpaid taxes, 200; mechanic's lien, effect on fire insurance policy, 332; collectors' sureties, extension, 356; State rescinding contract, 375; railroad company, use of steam, changing motive power, 397; New York water supply, Putnam county, 595; New York Elevated Railway, fares, 856; New York Sinking Fund Act, repeal, VIII, 100; Poughkeepsie employees, term of service, 752; canals, permit to experiment with electrical conductors, IX, 453.

O'BRIEN, DENIS. Attorney-General, opinion, excise bill of 1887, unconstitutional, VIII, 362, 365.

O'BRIEN, JAMES. Convicted of murder, pardoned, II, 923.

O'BRIEN, JAMES. Board of Claims, veto, VIII, 886.

O'BRIEN, SARAH. Widow of Michael O'Brien, act relative to, VI, 167.

O'CALLAGHAN, EDMUND B. Documentary history of New York, cited, Albany plan of Union, I, 579.

OCKERMAN, JOHN. Petition from, distresses of, II, 81.

O'CONNELL, DANIEL. Parliament, 1830, proposes use of ballot at elections, VIII, 584.

O'CONNER, EDWARD. Convicted of murder of Deputy Sheriff Steele, IV, 309; jury asks for commutation of sentence, 319; personal description of, 321.

O'CONNOR, EDMUND. Senate, 1894, extract from speech on New York Park Commission bill, IX, 435.

O'CONNOR, JOHN. Claim against New York, examination of, veto, VIII, 131.

O'CONNOR, JOHN M. Quartermaster, service at Sackett's Harbor, II, 774.

O'CONNOR, THOMAS. Claim against New York, veto, VIII, 884.

O'CONNOR, W. W. Relief, veto, X, 53.

O'CONOR, PATRICK. Relief, veto, X, 175.

ODELL, BENJAMIN B., JR. Governor, portrait, X, 180.

    1901. Annual message, X, 180; financial condition, 180; more economical administration, 181; list of necessary expenditures, 182; excessive cost of administering Transfer Tax Law, 182; reduction of expenses, 183; legislative employees, 183; department expenses should be reduced, 183; corporation laws should be more liberal, 184; liability of directors of corporations for failure to make reports, 185; reduction of organization tax, 186; abuses of attorney system, 186; abolition of various commissions, 187; Department of Labor, consolidation of Board of Arbitration, Bureau of Labor Statistics and Factory Inspectors, 188; sweat shops, inspection, licenses, 189; employer's liability, 189; recommends abolition of State Board of Charities, 190; abolition of Prisons Commission, 191; reorganization of State Board of Health, 192; transfer of supervision of tuberculosis and glanders in cattle to Agricultural Department, 192; consolidation of Forest Preserve Board and Forest, Fish and Game Commission, 192; abolition of office of Superintendent of Weights and Measures, 194; expenses of judiciary and State printing, 194, 195; expenses of New York Special Jury Law, 195; repeal of Special Jury Law recommended, 195; duties of State Tax Commission, 196; taxation, 197; rights of corporations received from State, 197; taxation of public utilities, 198; tax on capital of trust companies and banks, 199; tax on surplus of savings banks and insurance companies, 199; tax on mortgages, 200; Excise Department, 200; actions under Liquor Tax Law, 201; alleged coloniza-

ODELL, BENJAMIN B., JR., 1901,— (*Continued*).

tion of voters in Raines Law hotels, 202; list of guests in hotels and boarding-houses, 202; public works, 202; decline in canal tonnage, 203; repeal of law limiting amount of capital of canal transportation companies, 203; State prisons, 204; unsanitary condition of Auburn and Sing Sing prisons, 204; Bertillon system of measurement, 205; indeterminate sentences, 205; municipalities, 205; commissions on New York charter and tenement-houses, 206; excessive salaries of sheriff, county clerk and register of New York and Kings, 207; single-headed commissions, 208; substitution of single-headed commission for present dock board, New York, 208; police department, New York, 208; single-headed Police Commission for New York, 210; city employees, 211; repeal of Ramapo Water Act, 211; New York should own water rights, 212; separation of bureau of elections from police department, 212; bi-partisan election board, 213; registry of all lodging-houses and guests, 213; good roads, 213; canals, 214; Palisades, 215; agriculture, 216; State fair, 216; sugar beet industry, 216; National Guard and Naval Militia, 217; Croton Dam strike, 218; Insurance Department, 218; public utilities, 219; Railroad Commission should have supervision of gas and electric light companies, 220; Banking Department, 221; defects of system of savings and loan associations, 221; statutory revision, 222; divorce laws, 224; State Lunacy Commission, 224; management of State hospitals, 225; fraudulent use of naturalization papers, 226; education, 226; grade crossings, appropriation, 227; Pan-American Exposition, 227; rule as to vetoes, 228; pardon report, 229; report of Charter Revision Commission, 229; certificates of necessity of immediate passage of bills, 236, 240, 244, 256, 267, 275, 278, 279, 280, 281, 282; report of Tenement-House Commission, 237; report of State Engineer and Surveyor, canal improvement, 244; has canal paid for itself?, 247; canal problems, 249; barge canal not desirable, 250; recommends submission of canal question to people, 252; increase in expense of public printing, 269.

MEMORANDUMS OF APPROVAL. Johnson estate, amending act, X, 283; Warwick union free school district, legalizing bonds, 283; East Aurora, legalizing bonds, 284; Utica, legalizing Central Advanced school bonds and Mary street school bonds,

ODELL, BENJAMIN B., JR., 1901, MEMORANDUMS, ETC.— (Continued).
sale of Lacona bonds, 285; Court of Claims, Deltry, Draper, and Borgersrud, 286; regulating construction of tenement-houses, 286; Syracuse, audit of claims against, 288; Northern New York Institution for Deaf-Mutes, appropriation, 289; Liquor Tax Law, amendments, 290; Kings county, sheriff, county clerk and register, salaried office (three bills), 290.

VETOES. Goshen water supply, X, 232; Hastings-on-the-Hudson, changing boundaries, 233; Dewitt, special system of working highways, 234; Troy Young Men's Association, changing name, 235; Mamakating, railroad commissioners, bonds to retire outstanding bonds, 235; Court of Claims, Leith, 236; public accountants, exemption from examinations, 239; Court of Claims, O'Keefe, 240; Society for the Preservation of Scenic and Historic Places and Objects, trustees of, amending charter, 241; Niagara Fire Insurance Company, Erie county, changing name, 242; Nassau county, sheriff, reimbursement for services and expenses after expiration of term, 242; Nassau county, preservation of town records, 243; Schuyler escheat, 252; Orphan Asylum of the Society of Reformed Churches, Brooklyn, changing name, 253; Surrogate's Court, appearance in proceedings, 253; Surrogate's Court, additional allowance on settlement of accounts, 254; First Universalist Society, Mount Vernon, relief from assessment, 254; Court of Claims, Dinehart, 255; Hamburg Cemetery Association, changing name, legalizing conveyance, 256; Monroe county, enrollment of political parties, 257; Little Falls, Van Hornesville and Otsego Lake Narrow Gage Railroad Company, extending time to begin construction, 258; stenographer, Richmond county, Surrogate and County Court, compensation, 259; Court of Claims, Hamill, injuries received in Clinton prison, 259; eminent domain, incomplete proceedings, restoring land to owner, 260; Washington Hook and Ladder Company No. 1, Lawrence and Cedarhurst, changing name, additional powers, 261; Mac-Kenzie, admission to practice as attorney, 262; Schenectady assessments, 262; taxes, cancellation, Cozine case, 262; New York employees serving in Spanish War, compensation, amending act, 264; dentists, admission of students to examination, 265; Peters escheat, amending act, 266; Court of

ODELL, BENJAMIN B., JR., 1901, VETOES — (*Continued*).

Claims, Galvin, 267; Niagara county, claim of Roswell Park, authorizing reconsideration, 268; poor, Westchester county, outdoor relief, 272; taxes, cities, proceedings by receiver of, 272; Cass escheat, 273; taxes, Morehouse, relief, 274; Chatfield, loss of public funds, Elbridge, relief, 275; highways, plowing, digging and cropping, 276; Buffalo police pensions, 276; Seneca Falls, bonds for bridge and cemetery addition, 278; elections, consolidation of registration and enrollment books, 279; executor's accounting, 282; Adirondack park and forest preserve, acquisition of land, extension of boundaries, 291; sale and delivery of uncooked flesh food on Sunday, 291; items in supplemental supply bill, 293; item in appropriation for Eastern New York Reformatory, 293; New York Soldiers and Sailors' Home, cement walks, 293; Syracuse Institution for Feeble-Minded Children, laundry machinery and sidewalks improvement, 294; Orthopedic Hospital, pavilion for contagious diseases, 294; items of appropriation for quarantine station, 294; items of appropriation for Rome Custodial Asylum, 294; items of appropriation for Thomas Asylum for Indian Children, 295; items of appropriation for Elmira Reformatory, 295; items in supply bill, 295; New York and New Jersey Bridge Company, elevated railroad, West street, 303; employer's liability, 305; New York, claims arising under contests of certain judgments, 307; omnibus veto, 308.

1902. Annual message, X, 327; financial condition, 327; inspects insane asylums, 329; extravagance in construction of asylums, 330; duplication of administration, 330; needed reform of procedure on admission of inmates to hospitals, 331; abolition of boards of managers, creation of boards of visitation of State hospitals, 332; State charitable institutions, 332; unreasonable demands for repairs and improvements, 333; classification of charitable institutions, 334; abolition of boards of managers of charitable institutions, creation of office of superintendent, 335; assignment of judges to districts other than their own, 337; temporary assignment of county judge to service in Supreme Court, 337, 373; forest preserve, 338; scientific cultivation of forests, 339; leases and camp sites, 339; good roads, super-

ODELL, BENJAMIN B., JR., 1902,— (*Continued*).

vision by State Engineer, 340; death of President Mc-
Kinley, 340; punishment for attempts at murder should
be increased, 341; bad condition of State prisons, 342;
excessive cost of maintenance of insane criminals, 342;
local expenses, 343; review of local assessments by State
tax commissioners, 343; excessive official salaries, New
York, 344; delay in appeals in capital cases, 344; prompt.
argument of appeals in capital cases, 345; new dormitory,
Soldiers and Sailors' Home, 345; game seizures, 346; bond
by dealers and warehousemen of game, 346; auditing department, 346; taxation of mortgages, 347; State normal
schools, 348; free school fund, 349; modification of plan of
distribution of school funds, 349; St. Louis Exposition to
commemorate the Louisiana Purchase, 350; National Guard,
350; judicial review of findings of courts of inquiry, 350;
tuberculosis hospital, 351; regulating admission of inmates
to hospital, 352; receiverships, 352; home rule for cities,
354; local option, liquor traffic, 354; traveling expenses
of departments, 357; savings banks, 357; increase of percentage on which loans may be made by savings banks, 357;
reducing rate of interest, 359; canals, 359; protection of
foreign commerce, 360; improvement of canal locks, 361;
recommendations concerning canal enlargement, 362; use of
canal bridges by street railroads, 363; alleged railroad discrimination against New York city, 364; labor interests,
364; employer's liability, 364; special boards of arbitration,
365; divorce laws, 365; corporations, 366; taxing foreign
companies, 367; building and loan associations, 369; making performance of contracts subject to rule as to holidays, 369; elections, 370; one ballot should be used, 370;
various annual reports, 371, 375; pardon report, 371; relief from overcrowded condition of calendars of first and
second judicial departments, 371; railroads, settlement of
negligence cases, 372; judicial designations, 374; increase
of hours of work of trial justices, 374; certificates of
necessity of immediate passage of bill, 375, 378, 385, 394,
395, 403, 404; memorandum from mayor of New York
relative to tunnel railroad bill, 395; visit of Prince Henry
of Prussia, 375; reception of Prince Henry, note, 478;
direct tax discontinued, 1902, 459; comment on Governor
Flower's administration, 460.

ODELL, BENJAMIN B., JR., 1902,— (*Continued*).

MEMORANDUMS OF APPROVAL. Insanity Law, State hospitals, boards of managers abolished, X, 404; political enrollment in towns, 417; Lockport water supply, 418; civil service, veterans, preference, removals, 419; Kingston, consolidation of school districts, 437; savings banks, investments, 454; highways, streams as public, condemnation proceedings, 457; tax rate, 459.

,VETOES. Peters escheat, X, 376; Ninth Baptist Church, Syracuse, changing name, 377; Court of Claims, White and Coughlin, extra work, Soldiers and Sailors' Home, 377; Adirondack park, extending boundaries, 379; Catskill, purchasing stone crusher, 380; Erie county sheriff, additional subordinates, purchase of supplies, 380; county clerks, fees for searches in certain counties, 381; Game Law, woodcock, close season, 382; Tonawanda armory, relief of contractors on construction, 383; improvement of highways, acquisition of materials, 384; control of armories, 385; tax collectors, notices to non-residents, 386; evidence, record of ancient deeds, 386; stenographer, grand jury, Westchester county, 387; county clerk, Onondaga, index and abstract clerks, 388; arrest on civil process, deposit in lieu of bail, 388; New York, notification of assessments, 389; law library, New York court of general sessions, custodian, 390; Power will, execution of certain provisions, 391; Game Law, striped bass in Hudson river, 392; who may be present at sessions of grand jury, 392; highways, rebate of taxes for wide-tire wagons, exempting Franklin and Oswego counties, 393; Primary Election Law, general amendments, 420; items in appropriation bill, 421; items in supply bill, 422; items in supplemental supply bill, 430; street railroads, Queens and Nassau counties, 431; St. Lawrence State Hospital, bridge over Tibbett's brook ravine, 432; Regents, evening examinations, 432; membership corporations, directors, quorum, annual reports, 432; corporation taxes, State fees and taxes, 433; Yonkers electric light wires and appurtenances, supervision and inspection, 433; Glens Falls feeder, repairs, 434; Champlain canal, Mechanicville bridge, Burke avenue and Francis street, 434; Watervliet recorder, 434; Fort Brewster, acquiring site of, 435; Glen creek, repairing banks and chan-

Odell, Benjamin B., Jr., 1902, Vetoes — (*Continued*).

nel, 435; Erie canal, Tonawanda bridge, North Niagara street, 435; New Rochelle, tax for teachers' pensions, 435; taxes, Cohoes, collection of arrears, 436; Erie canal, Royalton, drainage of flooded lands, 437; Yonkers, commissioners of deeds, additional property, 437; dams across Hudson river, Warren county, 453; Mount Vernon, grade crossing, Harlem Railroad, Mount Vernon avenue and Oak street, cost of changing, 454; New York, public dancing within half mile of cathedral in process of erection, 456; items in reappropriation bill of certain unexpended balances, 465; railroads, motive power, terminal facilities, first-class cities, Harlem Railroad, 466; Rochester police department, reorganization, 469; taxes, First National Bank, Ballston Spa, 452; New York tunnel railroads, franchises, 471; Mount Vernon, taxes and assessments, 1902, 471; Jamestown, police, care of indigent sick, 472; omnibus veto, 438, 472.

1903. Annual message, X, 482; small State debt, 482; benefits of indirect taxation, 482; financial condition of State, 484; franchise tax not satisfactory, 486; mortgage tax unfair, 487; proposed plan of taxing mortgages, 489; method of assessing franchise tax on corporations, 489; tax on public utilities, 489; tax on notary certificates, recording tax, 490; canal enlargement, 491; decrease of tonnage on canals, 492; recommends thousand ton barge canal, 493; extending debt period, 495; reimposition of canal tolls, 495; changes in government in insane asylums and charitable institutions, 496; Fiscal Supervisor, 496; decrease in number of recoveries in insane asylums, 498; insane pavilion, new insane hospital, 500; tuberculosis departments in State hospitals, 500; labor in charitable institutions, 500; proposed abandonment of Bedford Reformatory, 501; use of Elmira Reformatory by United States government should be prohibited, 501; new site for State Industrial School at Rochester, 502; good results of change of administration in Charities Department, 503; excessive number of private laws, 503; legislative counsel, 505; responsibility of mayor of New York, 505; New York police department, reform needed, 505; decisions of police commissioner should not be subject to review by courts, 506; transfer of voters on certificates prior to primaries, 507; identification of voters,

ODELL, BENJAMIN B., JR., 1903 — (*Continued*).

508; more perfect ballot system, 508; relations between capital and labor, 509; labor disputes with capital, courts should have power to interfere as to necessaries, 509; expulsion of member of labor union for service in National Guard, 510; amendments to Tenement-House Law, 511; purchase of land·in Adirondacks, 511; commission to ascertain ultimate cost of forest preserve, 512; good roads, 512; department to bring to attention of the public the attractions within State, 513; enforcement of Excise Law, 513; prisons and reformatories, 514; primary and secondary education, 514; free tuition in high schools, 514; child labor, 515; law's delay, first and second judicial departments, 515; civil service, 517; vacancy in office of Regent, resignation of St. Clair McKelway, 518; boards of supervisors to validate municipal bonds, 519; communication from State commissioner of health, pollution of waters of New York bay, 523; certificates of necessity of immediate passage of bills, 524, 535, 536, 537, 539, 540; mortgage taxation, special message, 524; heavy payments by railroad corporations for taxes, 528; mortgage investments by various corporations, 531; commission to investigate educational interests of State, 536.

MEMORANDUMS OF APPROVAL. Brockport, legalizing special election for establishment of sewer system, X, 518; Rochester, streets and water pipes, 540; Liquor Tax Law, sales by pharmacists, 542; tuberculosis hospitals, 575; savings bank investments, Buffalo Creek Railroad, 576; tax rate, 1903, 577.

VETOES. Law library, Utica, increasing compensation of librarian, X, 519; civil service, qualifications of applicants for examinations, 520; corporations, acquisition of property without State, 521; highways, improvement act of 1898, Rome included in, 522; Yonkers City Court, supplementary proceedings, 522; villages, changing boundaries, 523; commissioner of jurors, notice server, amending act, 532; towns, compensation of officers, 533; undertaking on discharge of judgment, 534; towns, G. A. R., renting rooms for, 535; Insanity Law, general amendments, 538; items of appropriation, Custodial Asylum for Feeble-Minded Women, 544; items for State Fair, 544; appropriations,— Thomas Asylum for Indian Children;— New York

Odell, Benjamin B., Jr., 1903, Vetoes — (*Continued*).

House of Refuge, 545; Hudson House of Refuge, 545; New York Woman's Relief Corps Home, 545; — Soldiers and Sailors' Home, 546; — Craig Colony for Epileptics, 546; —Agricultural Experiment Station, 546; — Western House of Refuge for Women, 547; — Batavia School for the Blind, 547; — Elmira Reformatory, 548; — Rome Custodial Asylum, 548; — quarantine stations, 549; canal bridge at Mechanicville, 547; items in appropriation bill, 549; items in supply bill, 555; items in supplemental supply bill, 571; railroads, consents for construction, 574; omnibus veto, 580.

1904. Annual message, X, 595; State's financial condition, 595; canal improvements, 596; tenure of office of canal advisory board, 596; special appraisers, barge canal, 597; manner of payment of barge canal debt, 598; special tax on counties, 599; new revenues needed for barge canal, 602; public education, 603; joint committee on educational interests, report, 604; Cornell School of Forestry, 605; forest preserve, purchase of land discontinued, 606; acreage in private preserves and other holdings, 606; forest preserve assessments, 607; charitable institutions, 608; State inspection of immigrants, 609; care of chronic and acute insane, 609; emergency hospitals, 609; increase in capacity of Rome Custodial Asylum, 610; Home for Juvenile Delinquents, Randall's island, complaints as to management, 610; removal from Randall's island, 611; amendments to Primary Election Law, 612; State prisons, 614; Central Prison for Condemned Prisoners, 614; Labor Department, 615; State employees, 616; State printing, 617; good roads, 618; total mileage of good roads, 618; supervision of roads by State Engineer and Surveyor, 619; grade crossings, 619; personal tax, assessments, 620; investigation of law's delays, 620; corporation laws, 621; filing certificates in Insurance Department, 621; protecting name of corporation pending change, 622; investment of United States deposit fund in municipal and local bonds, 622; Department of Health, 623; typhoid fever epidemic, 623; investigation concerning infectious and contagious diseases, 623; preservation of vital statistics, 624; home rule, 624; special laws, 626; agriculture, 626; agricultural education, 627; reports of departments, 628; certificates of necessity of im-

ODELL, BENJAMIN B., JR., 1904 — (*Continued*).

mediate passage of bills, 628, 629, 630, 631, 632, 633; members of Canal Advisory Board, 629; comparative statement of appropriations, 684; did not appoint counsel, VIII, 27; official service, I, pref. xiii.

MEMORANDUMS OF APPROVAL. Boy's Training School, X, 683; tax rate, 683; ice in Hudson river, rights of riparian owner, 689; Dutchess county, water rights, 691.

VETOES. Omnibus city veto, X, 633; items in appropriation bill, 637; items in supply bill, 639; items in supplemental supply bill, 648; appropriations — Custodial Asylum, Newark, 653; — Hudson House of Refuge, 654; — Woman's Relief Corps Home, 654; — Batavia School for Blind, 654; — Western House of Refuge at Albion, 655; — various State prisons, 655; — Reformatory for Women, Bedford, 656; — Craig Colony for Epileptics, 656; — Rome Custodial Asylum, 656; East River Gas Company, extending powers, 657; Supreme Court commissioners, 662; opinion of Attorney-General, 663; city bills not returned in time, 685; Niagara, Lockport and Ontario Power Company, amending charter, 686; acts relating to New York civil service, 690; adult blind, permanent commission, 696; highways, Ulster and Delaware road, No. 16, Shandaken, 696; Seneca river bridge, Salina and Lysander, 697; Rochester, assessment, State hospital, 697; monument, Gen. James Clinton, 697; Eastern New York Reformatory, continuing construction, 697; monument commemorating battle of White Plains, 698; Allegany river bridge, Elko, 698; drainage, Amherst and Clarence, 698; Seneca county, draining Gorman swamp, 698; Erie canal bridge, Amsterdam, 698; Champlain canal bridge, Greenwich to Northumberland, 699; omnibus veto, 699.

OFFICERS (Colony). See also particular offices; CANDIDATES FOR OFFICE AND REMOVAL OF OFFICERS. Act to punish, for refusal to serve under Leisler's commissions, I, 16; communication relative to fees, 34; compensation of members of Assembly, 43; of fusileers, relative to, 109; British in Canadian expedition, compensation of, 157; compensation of colonial, 168; salaries, veto, 172; of government entitled to protection, 213; King's prerogative to fix number and compensation of, 221; members of Assembly, veto of act fixing term at three years, 267; revenue, King's right to appoint, 293, 299; revenue, Assembly insists on

Officers (Colony) — (*Continued*).

　right to appoint, 294; nominations by Assembly, 456; compensation of King's, in colonial service, 459; commanding officer for new troops, 461; appropriations for salaries, 470, 471; salaries payable annually, 473; of courts to be members of militia reserve, 549; quartermaster, 572; salaries of, inadequate, 606; judges, tenure of office, 670; compensation of Attorney-General, 672.

Officers (State). How appointed under first Constitution, II, 3, 247, 1054; III, 1001; appointed by first Constitutional Convention, II, 6; act regulating elections, 10; compensation of public, 12, 190; failure to take oath, 23; local, right of people to choose, 41; medical and hospital, pay of, 134; staying suits against, 208; appointment in Montgomery county, 302; Council of Appointment, right of nomination, 361; notice of appointment, 375, 376; militia, appointment of, 403; eligibility, United States, 438, 439; gratuities to, protest against, 449; method of appointing in Massachusetts, 499; vacancies, provision for filling, 511; IV, 433; VI, 986; vacancies, presidential electors, provision for filling, 545; candidates, proper limits of criticism, 551; in military service, compensation of, 818; eligibility, limiting to citizens, proposed amendment, 828; vacancies, Governor and Lieutenant-Governor, provision for filling, 887; reducing salaries of, 1013; irregular methods of appointment, III, 7; militia, election of, 20; true principle of selection, 55; appointments, act revived, 142; of different departments, duty should not be interchangeable, 713; of courts, fees, 720; canal, not to be interested in contracts, IV, 18; inspectors of commodities, office abolished, 32; method of choosing, 109; property qualifications abolished, 109, 137; public, embezzlement by, 562, 615; judicial, fees prohibited, 684, 686, 777; to be held to strict account, V, 117; judicial, cities and villages, how chosen, 138; military appointments, Governor Seymour's rule, 446; should not be exempt from military service, 457; local, see Local Officers; deputies, VI, 267; members of Legislature prohibited from holding certain offices, VII, 322; property qualifications, amendment, 1845, 324; compensation, when subject to legislative change, 379; too many in New York and Brooklyn, 532; appointments not presidential perquisites, 560; militia, changing method of selection, constitutional provision, 797; questions as to title, Legislature should not assume to settle, VIII, 274, 355; reimbursement for loss of property or funds, see Public

OFFICERS (State) — (*Continued*).

    FUNDS; when successful contestant not entitled to salary, 661; *de facto*, when acts cannot be questioned, 328, 335; forfeits office by failure to take oath, 490; Senate's confirming power, abolition recommended, 487, 680, 1080; Federal, tenure should be limited, Texas resolutions, 1091; election of, property qualifications cannot be imposed on voters, 1117; in New York and Kings county to be elected in odd-numbered years, IX, 705; Governor Black opposes indefinite tenure, 839; New York, excessive salaries, X, 344; State departments, excessive traveling expenses, 357; allowance for expenses after expiration of term, 594, 716.

    VETOES. Staying suits against, II, 170, 173; public, payment of salaries, 249; of courts, fees of, 275; Brooklyn aldermen, holding Federal offices, VII, 321; property qualifications, Lansingburgh, 323; Kingston, 416; chosen at certain elections, 506; Sullivan county, town, pay of certain, repeal, 507; reimbursement for expenses in suit, 544, 651; IX, 871; X, 243; false impersonation of, VII, 573; candidates, report of financial transactions, 609; Sangerfield, supervisor's bond, refunding surety for payment on, 753; Cunningham, Kings county commissioner of charities, reimbursement for legal expenses, VIII, 294; Clifton Springs, legalizing election of, 1122; Oneida county, abolishing fee system, IX, 124; Oswego, scheme of an electoral college for appointments and removals, 360, 432; Brooklyn, tenure, 521; Brooklyn, fees, 778; Supreme Court commissioners, proposed establishment of, X, 662; commission on classification of salaries, allowance for expenses, 792.

OFFICIAL OATH. Act relating to, II, 376; constitutional provisions, III, 209; V, 38, 445; VI, 1; VII, 44; VIII, 892; United States Constitution, V, 849; failure to take, forfeiture of office, VIII, 490.

    VETOES. Act to require, II, 21, new bill passed; failure to take, legalizing acts, VII, 44; amending General Village Law, VIII, 1041.

OGDEN LAND COMPANY. Claims pre-emptive right to Indian lands, IV, 296; V, 199.

OGDENSBURG. Militia in service at, II, 736; troops stationed at, 745, 746; deposit of arms at, after expiration of service, 773; British invasion of, 773; railroad to Lake Champlain, III, 964, 983; armory at, V, 175; arsenal sold, refund from proceeds, VI, 620; amending charter, sewers, VIII, 96; number of ex-

OGDENSBURG — (*Continued*).
>   cise licenses, 1887, 359; excise license fees, 1889, 689; armory
>   provided, 1895, IX, 571; school officers and elections, X, 910.
VETOES.   City, assessment-rolls, VI, 88; Young Men's Christian
>   Association, charter, VIII, 379; board of public works, 993;
>   armory, IX, 571; amending charter, X, 584; street openings,
>   806.
OGLESBY, RICHARD J.   Governor of Illinois, communication from, Lincoln
>   monument, V, 795; VI, 44.
OGLETHORPH, JAMES EDWARD.   General, regiment of, I, 338.
O'GRADY, JAMES M. E.   Member of Capital Centenary Commission, IX,
>   689.
O'HARA, JOHN H.   Member of Assembly, death of, unearned salary,
>   appropriation, veto, VIII, 114.
OHIO.   Favors national aid to New York canal enterprise, II, 706; dis-
>   approves North Carolina resolution relative to election of Repre-
>   sentatives and presidential electors, and Georgia's resolution reduc-
>   ing senatorial term, 870; offers aid in constructing Erie canal, 891;
>   approves Pennsylvania proposition as to the limitation of national
>   banks, 1029; resolutions, case of Bank of United States against
>   State Auditor, 1077; resolutions on Maryland proposition for dis-
>   tribution of public land, 1117; proposes gradual abolition of slavery
>   and foreign colonization of colored persons, III, 34; disapproves
>   Georgia proposition as to importation of colored persons, 36; canal
>   project, 75, 122, 171; bituminous coal from, 127, 203; constitutional
>   amendment, popular election of President and presidential electors,
>   184; action on South Carolina resolutions (see page 218), 222;
>   sustains tariff of 1828, 318; declines to express opinion as to consti-
>   tutionality of Federal appropriations for Colonization Society, 356;
>   protests against South Carolina nullification proceedings and against
>   Constitutional Convention, approves President's South Carolina
>   proclamation, 437; tax for internal improvements, 507; constitu-
>   tional amendment, prohibiting House of Representatives from choos-
>   ing a President, and the Senate from choosing a Vice-President, 589;
>   protest against anti-slavery agitation, 591; protests against annexa-
>   tion of Texas, 691; pledges support to national government on north-
>   eastern boundary question, 761; reduction of tolls on New York
>   salt, 871; wheat and flour from, transported on Erie canal, 893;
>   slow progress of internal improvements, 901; provides for Mexican
>   War expenses, IV, 418; Governor and Legislature invited to visit
>   Albany, V, 203; protests against secession movement and tenders
>   aid to Federal government, 307; resolutions relative to New York
>   canals, 507; assessment of personal property, 825; appropriation

OHIO — (*Continued*).

for Antietam cemetery, 840; National Soldiers' Home, VI, 61; resolutions protesting against Federal interference in Louisiana, 785; failure of co-operative insurance companies, VII, 544; labor disputes, Allen G. Thurman appointed arbitrator, VIII, 165; assessed valuation of personal property, 1880, 307; uniform liquor tax, 437; excise taxes used for local purposes, 438; factory inspectors, ratio to number of establishments, IX, 166; provision for agricultural instruction, 178; retail liquor licenses, 1892, 666; taxation of corporate franchises, X, 69.

OHIO CANAL. Description of, III, 902.

OHIO FRONTIER. French encroachments on, I, 534, 538, 541, 542; French forts on, 543, 547; French troops on, 543; defeat of Washington, 546; French movements on, 549; French abandon and destroy Fort Duquesne, 630.

OHIO RIVER. Indians on, securing fidelity of, I, 508; French forts on, 534, 538, 541; French on, 549; Indians northwest of, treaty with, II, 367; canal connection with Lake Erie, 1011, 1046, 1096; III, 75; canal around Great Falls, 123, 171; canal connection with Potomac river, 171; improvement of, V, 564.

OILS. VETOES. Illuminating, regulating standard, VII, 659, 751; act passed, test required, 751; illuminating, preventing manufacture of dangerous, 924; oil regions in State, proposed survey, IX, 774.

OIL SPRING RESERVATION. Mentioned, II, 976; ascertaining damages caused by trespassers, V, 863.

O'KEEFE, MICHAEL. VETOES. Damages, new capitol, appropriation, VII, 910; Court of Claims, X, 165, 240, 584, 944.

OLCOTT, FREDERIC P. Comptroller, recommends central board for supervision of insane asylum appropriations, IX, 312.

OLDEN, CHARLES S. Governor of New Jersey, member of commission to procure constitutional convention, V, 325.

OLD HOME WEEK. Oswego, using battle flags at, veto, X, 919.

OLD ORCHARD SHOALS. Proposed establishment of quarantine station, V, 80, 109; land at, ceded to United States, IX, 211.

OLD STYLE. Calendar, change of, IV, 192.

OLEAN. Genesee Valley canal, extension of, IV, 835; number of excise licenses, 1887, VIII, 360; armory, act of 1888, 455.

VETOES. Acquiring land for Buffalo and Washington Railroad Company, VI, 91; armory, VIII, 455; amending village charter, 1133; completion of armory, IX, 147; powers of mayor, X, 478; commitments to Erie county penitentiary, 806.

OLEOMARGARINE. Legislation on, VII, 571, 699; regulating manufacture and sale, veto, 590, 699; State supervision limited, 699; coloring

OLEOMARGARINE — (*Continued*).

prohibited, 699; regulating manufacture and sale, 700, 808; VIII, 34; IX, 319; purchase prohibited for certain institutions, 214; alleged violations of law, 319; described, 319; further regulations, 1897, 745.

OLIVE. VETOES. Highways, protection from overflow of Bush creek, IX, 768; Bushkill creek improvement, bonds for, 818.

OLIVE OIL. Inspector of, III, 748.

OLMSTEAD CASE. Pennsylvania resolutions, II, 666.

OMNIBUS COMPANIES. Incorporation of, veto, VII, 807.

OMNIBUS AND STAGE LINES. Superseded by railroads, right to compensation, V, 517.

OMNIBUS VETO. Origin and description of, VI, 909; 1875, VI, 910; 1876, 1035; 1877, VII, 128; 1878, 264; 1879, 412; 1880, 505; 1881, 664; 1882, 803; 1883, 930; 1884, 1086; 1885, VIII, 129; 1886, 291; 1887, 452; 1888, 613; 1889, 871; 1890, 1035; 1892, IX, 147; 1894, 534; 1895, 622; 1896, 717; 1897, 776; 1898, 857; 1899, X, 59; 1900, 175; 1901, 308; 1902, 438, 472; 1903, 580; 1904, 633, 685, 699; 1905, 805; 1906, 943.

ONDERDONK, ANDRUS. Service of process on, Van Rensselaer rent, III, 825.

ONEIDA CARRYING PLACE. Indian land grants claimed to be fraudulent, I, 601, 606.

ONEIDA. VETOES. Spring Supply Water Company, changing name, VII, 1000; refunding bonded indebtedness, IX, 432; amending charter, X, 583.

ONEIDA COUNTY. Peters murder case, II, 514; militia from, 1812, 743; Linus murder case, 922; purchase of Stockbridge land in, 989; appropriation for agricultural purposes, 1089; agricultural school in, III, 298; convicts to be sent to Sing Sing prison, 316; trial of Alexander McLeod, 942; sheriff, compensation in McLeod case, 943; agricultural society in, 945; Clark patent, IV, 332; increase in population, VI, 578; tax to reimburse collectors for losses, unconstitutional VII, 753; X, 275; county clerk, recording notices of pendency, VIII, 63, 70; average excise license fees, 1889, 687; unpaid taxes, sales under special act, 749; surrogate, new seal, 1096; highways, cost of labor system, 1892, IX, 200; insane, care of, county and State systems compared, 228; transfer tax assistant, X, 108; Supreme Court commissioner, office created, 669; courthouse, expense of construction, increasing amount, 768.

VETOES. Extending time for collection of taxes, V, 264, 343; excepting from act relative to county treasurer's fees, VI, 151;

ONEIDA COUNTY, VETOES — (*Continued*).

rural cemeteries, acquiring land, 208; compensation of supervisors, 327; Utica recorder, increasing salary, 427; fines, 696; New Hartford, reimbursing collector, 701; Vienna real estate assessments, 1033; clerk, expenses, notaries public, VII, 83; Camden and Annsville, highway labor, 130; canal claims, Lansingkill creek, Mohawk river, 417; Sangerfield, supervisor's bond, refunding surety for payment on, 753; railroad aid bonds, VIII, 639; reservoir, completion of, 640; shipment of birds killed in, 716; State road, repairs, 850; taxes, redemption, 1126; county officers, abolishing fee system, IX, 124; fish hatchery, Watkins creek, 221; board of supervisors, legalizing audits of accounts, 231; joint bridges, apportionment of expense, 525; sidepaths, providing for, 726; sales for non-payment of taxes, 804; taxes, collection, X, 447; special county judge and surrogate, term of office, 701.

ONEIDA CREEK. Indian lands on, purchase of, II, 645.

ONEIDA FEEDER. To Erie canal, culvert under, veto, X, 935.

ONEIDA INDIANS. Country invaded from Canada, I, 65; smith for, 145, 419; alleged fraudulent contracts relating to land, II, 223; communication from chiefs, relative to lands, 267; treaty with, 291, 302, 523; annuities to, 311; intrusions on land, 319; act relating to lands of, 329; conference with, 338, 341, 343, 347; support of, act to provide for, 356, 364; address from, 379, 517; purchase of land, 412, 441, 519; attorney for, 433, 1076; communication relative to, 472; State purchases land of, 607; Fish creek lands, purchase of, by State, 644; separate contracts with Christians and Pagans, 644, 645, 651; purchase of land from Christian party, 670, 678, 753; III, 143; destruction of corn, advance from annuities, II, 882; exchange of lands with second Christian party, 894; church for, 894, 930, 951, 976; property of, 1819, 976; request advance of annuities, 989; lands in Fish Creek reservation, sale of, 999; Peter Otsequette, relief of, 1080; Green Bay treaty, 1107; purchase of lands of, migration to Green Bay, III, 310, 349; payment of attorney's salary, 909; Shenandoah claim, veto, VI, 184; claims, commission to examine, report, 663.

ONEIDA LAKE. VETOES. Construction of dock, VI, 156; steam and naphtha vessels on, inspection, VIII, 1121.

ONEIDA LAKE CANAL. Purchased by State, III, 816; debt, IV, 252; tolls, V, 66, 154, 257, 361; securing navigation of, veto, 730; relation to general system, 733, 789; completion, VI, 858; appropriation for, 862; financial statement, 1875, 930; extraordinary

ONEIDA LAKE CANAL — (*Continued*).

repairs, sum needed to settle contracts, new work, 992; completing reconstruction, veto, VII, 325.

ONEIDA RESERVATION. Stockbridge Indians on, petition from, II, 373; number of Indians on, 1819, 976.

ONEIDA RIVER. Wing dam in, III, 37; improvement of, 792; improvement work suspended, IV, 13; improvement debt, 252; improvement, tolls, V, 154, 258, 362; relation to canal system, 789; improvement, financial statement, 1875, VI, 930.

VETOES. Bridge over, VI, 212; fishway at State dam, VII, 61; draw-bridge, 94, 232, 366, 473, 576.

ONEIDA RIVER ROAD. Schroeppel, veto, VI, 211.

ONEIDA STATION. Fort at, I, 625, 626; New York troops at, 627.

O'NEIL, CHARLES J. Assistant clerk, New York Municipal Court, claim, veto, X, 691.

O'NEIL, PETER. Canal Department, appropriation for services, veto, IX, 716.

ONEONTA. Normal school at, V, 695; prohibiting new cemeteries, VIII, 327; city charter, 1908, IX, 679; armory, assessment for local improvement, appropriation, veto, X, 788.

ONEONTA FIRE DEPARTMENT. Charter, veto, VII, 415.

ONEONTA NORMAL SCHOOL. Established, V, 695; repairs and improvements, VIII, 864; appropriation for repairs, 1895, IX, 593.

ONONDAGA. Deposit of arms at, II, 682; deposit of military stores at, 755; reimbursement for expenses of road on Onondaga reservation, veto, VII, 588.

ONONDAGA COUNTY. Land claims, act relating to, II, 404, 405; report of commissioners, 457; sheriff's sale of land in military tract, 689; militia from, 1812, 743; appropriation for agricultural purposes, 1089; agricultural society in, III, 945; arsenal and equipments to be sold, IV, 495; refunding illegal taxes, VI, 278; exempted from Town Auditor's Act, VIII, 49; jail limits, 632; average excise license fees, 1889, 687; highways, cost of labor system, 1892, IX, 200; insane, care of, county and State systems compared, 228; transfer tax assistant, X, 108.

VETOES. Courthouse and jail, relative to, III, 190; draining certain lands, VI, 189; subjecting to Railroad Aid Act, 214; stenographer, County Court, 326; penitentiary, maintenance of convicts, 587; county clerk's office, records and indexes, 821; Simon contested election case, 866; Skaneateles, engine-house, VII, 97; excepting from provisions of County Treasurer's Act, 265; clerk's office, recording certain papers, 806; salary of supervisors, 806; disposing of old clerk's office and lot, 867;

ONONDAGA COUNTY, VETOES — (*Continued*).

notaries public, additional number, VIII, 43; State ditch, improvement, 377; inspection of steamboats, 469; highways, amending act, 617; penitentiary property, sale of, 945; town meetings, fixing time, IX, 718; Harbor brook and Onondaga lake, X, 321; county clerk, index and abstract clerks, 388, new bill passed.

ONONDAGA COUNTY PENITENTIARY. Amending act relative to, veto, V, 336.

ONONDAGA CREEK. Use of water for hydraulic purposes, III, 36.

VETOES. Bridge over, VII, 476; draining and filling up, IX, 735; Syracuse, bridge, West Water street, 790.

ONONDAGA HISTORICAL ASSOCIATION. VETOES. Donation of clerk's office and lot to, VII, 867; donation of salt lands to, 932; amending charter, IX, 217.

ONONDAGA INDIANS. Country invaded from Canada, I, 65; fort for protection of, 88; Peter Schuyler's visit to, 124; expenses of commissioners, 167; proposed commission to, 171; Hansen's visit to, expenses of, 172; French negotiations with, 177; agents to reside among, 212, 217; smith for, 306, 389, 419, 548; treaty with, II, 291, 302; annuities to, 311; request alteration of boundaries, 329; reservation of salt springs, 329; act relating to lands of, 329; quitclaim from, 338; conference with, 338, 341, 343, 344, 346, 347; request addition to reservation, 343; letter from chiefs, 353; support of, act to provide for, 356, 364; visit of chiefs, 408; offer to sell land, 477, 513; claim of, 514; trespasses on lands of, 586, 888; appointment of attorney for, 587, 684, 888; agent for, 684, 888, 1076; III, 105; destruction of corn, advance from annuities, II, 882; land purchased from, 887, 888; number of, 1819, 976; request appointment of Thaddeus M. Wood as agent, 995; Green Bay treaty, 1107; treaty with, for purchase of land, 1118; III, 13; separate school district for, 887; communication from chiefs, IV, 382; annuities, veto, VII, 417.

ONONDAGA LAKE. To be lowered, II, 1095; steam and naphtha vessels on, inspection, veto, VIII, 1121; relative to, veto, X, 321.

ONONDAGA POTTERY COMPANY. Court of Claims, veto, IX, 797.

ONONDAGA RESERVATION. Number of Indians on, 1819, II, 976; legislation needed, VII, 436; compulsory education of children, 710; roads and bridges, improvement, appropriation, VIII, 560.

VETOES. Highway, VII, 92, 223, 384, 474; bridge over Onondaga creek, 476, 909; repairing road, 587; road, reimbursing Onon-

ONONDAGA RESERVATION, VETOES — (*Continued*).
daga for expenses, 588; new schoolhouse, 909; repair of highways and bridges, VIII, 116; IX, 80; highways, repairs, VIII, 845; X, 426.

ONONDAGA RIVER. Successful trade on, I, 217, 223.

ONONDAGA SALT COMPANY. Charter renewed, III, 952.

ONOVILLE. Bridge over Allegany river at, VIII, 560; bridge, Allegany reservation, veto, 845.

ONTARIO. VETOES. Town meetings, legalizing proceedings, VI, 1031; school district No. 6, bonds for new schoolhouse site and building, IX, 470.

ONTARIO COUNTY. Connecticut land claims in, II, 370; George murder case, 531; militia from, 1812, 743, 744; abduction of William Morgan, III, 185; district attorney appointed special counsel in Morgan matter, 351; increase in population, VI, 578; exempted from Town Auditor's Act, VIII, 49; average excise license fees, 1889, 687; county clerk, salaried office, 1103; highways, cost of labor system, 1892, IX, 200; insane, care of, county and State systems compared, 228.

VETOES. Altering Assembly districts, V, 126; habitual drunkards, publication of, VII, 266; Gypsum Cemetery Association, revival, 412; United States deposit fund loan commissioners, transferring funds to, VIII, 401; overseers of the poor, compensation in certain towns, 696; excise moneys, disposal of, IX, 267.

"ONTARIO MESSENGER," THE. Federal statutes published in, II, 1068.

OOTHOUT, C. ELIZABETH. Communication to Governor, relative to appointment of William Church Osborn as State commissioner in lunacy, X, 43.

OPENING SPEECH (Colony). In Parliament, I, 10; in Colonial Legislature, 10; by Governor Sloughter, 19; acting-Governor Ingoldesby, 26; Governor Fletcher, 32, 34, 39, 43, 47, 51, 56, 59, 61, 64, 69; Governor Bellomont, 75, 79, 85, 89; Lieutenant-Governor Nanfan, 94, 96; Governor Cornbury, 98, 101, 105, 107, 111, 114, 119, 122, 127; Governor Lovelace, 132; Governor Hunter, 141, 148, 150, 154, 159, 163, 167, 171, 172, 174, 178, 184, 187; sent by secretary instead of delivered in person, 186; Governor Burnet, 190, 195, 197, 204, 207, 211, 216, 220, 225; Governor Montgomerie, 230, 232; President Van Dam, 239; Governor Cosby, 242, 244, 245, 251; President Clarke, 255; Lieutenant-Governor Clarke, 259, 262, 269, 275, 280, 285, 286, 289, 292, 301, 305, 307, 309; Governor Clinton, 311, 314, 317, 331, 345, 372, 381, 390, 413, 457, 469, 481, 503, 512, 515, 520,

OPENING SPEECH (Colony) — (*Continued*).

521; Lieutenant-Governor DeLancey, 527, 534, 545, 546, 618, 624, 630, 640; Governor Hardy, 583, 602, 609; President Colden, 647, 650; Lieutenant-Governor Colden, 656, 659, 662, 673, 679, 681, 734, 759; Governor Monckton, 669; Governor Moore, 700, 706, 714, 717, 720, 723, 731; Governor Dunmore, 736; Governor Tryon, 740, 746, 753.

OPENING SPEECH (State). Practice of, followed under first Constitution, II, 2; Governor Clinton, 7, 50, 75, 105, 146, 182, 195, 217, 251, 263, 281, 289, 301, 311, 319, 323, 332, 506, 522, 535; Governor Jay, 358, 379, 397, 420, 448, 463; Governor Lewis, 545, 567, 595; Governor Tompkins, 616, 632, 655, 671, 689, 735, 784, 800, 850, 872; Governor DeWitt Clinton, 897, 961, 1003, 1038, 1087; discontinued, message substituted, III, 1.

OPHTHALMIC INSTITUTE, NEW YORK. Relative to, veto, VIII, 638.

ORANGE COUNTY. Questions relating to New Jersey boundary, 1, 227, 540; militia sent against Indians at Minisink, 587; blockhouses proposed for, 590, 616; Indian incursions in, 594, 616, 626, 675; rangers in, 588, 595; militia engaged in frontier defense, 597; militia ordered into service, 614; expense of Indian raids, 631; uneasiness among Indians, 657, 658; rangers, expenses of, II, 43; Augur case, 67; commissioners of sequestration, Rush case, 250; nomination of sheriff, proceedings in Council of Appointment, 474, 493; drainage, redemption by infants, 685; Hodges and others, murder case, 997; discontinuance of wheat raising in, III, 815; agricultural society in, 945; silk culture in, 945; Drainage Act, V, 512; average excise license fees, 1889, VIII, 687; highways, cost of labor system, 1892, IX, 200; insane, care of, county and State systems compared, 228; included in ninth judicial district, 547; X, 850.

VETOES. Contingent expenses in, II, 95; highways in, 348; Deerpark, additional justice, VI, 208, 276; 91st Regiment funds, transfer, 691; Middletown, payment of village bonds, VII, 131; extending jail limits, 234; drainage, 508; county roads, amending act, IX, 862; justices of peace, legalizing acts, X, 62; fishing in, amending Game Law, 319, 320; special county judge and surrogate, term of office, 701; close season for game, 954; hares and rabbits, close season, 954.

ORANGE COUNTY MUTUAL INSURANCE COMPANY. Relative to, veto, VII, 412.

ORANGE COUNTY REFERENCE LAW LIBRARY. Appropriation for, veto, VII, 1025.

ORANGE AND SUSSEX CANAL. Transportation of coal on, III, 204.

ORANGE AND SUSSEX CANAL COMPANY. Incorporated, III, 167; location of proposed canal, 167.

ORANGETOWN. Union free school district, date of annual meeting, veto, VIII, 334.

ORDER GERMANIA. Charter, veto, VII, 508.

ORDINANCE. By first Constitutional Convention, II, 6; relative to Secretary of Congress, 245; of Congress, establishing government under Constitution, 290, 299.

VETOES. New York, Code of, X, 580; relative to buildings, violations, 702.

ORDINANCE OF 1787. Effect of, IV, 567; purpose of, V, 300.

ORDNANCE. See also CANNON. Crown furnishes for colony, I, 41, 48; King furnishes for colonial defense, 295; before using, necessary to repair Fort George, 305; expense of transporting to frontier, 305; for Oswego and other frontier garrisons, 315, 316; distribution in New York, 322; sent to Boston, 332; store, repair of, II, 262; purchase of, 569, 608, 619, 629; on Staten Island, sale to United States, 940, 941; settlement of claims, III, 309, 386; statement of, 385, 868; purchase of, Civil War, V, 418.

OREGON. American and British claims to, IV, 285; presidential election of 1876, action by Electoral Commission, VII, 33.

ORIENTAL LODGE NO. 267, INDEPENDENT ORDER OF GOOD TEMPLARS. Charter, veto, VI, 578. ·

ORIENT HARBOR. Protection of shellfish in, veto, VII, 415.

ORISKANY. Indian land grants, claimed to be fraudulent, I, 601, 606, 611; battle of, III, 228.

ORISKANY CREEK. Relation to Chenango canal, III, 419.

ORLEANS. VETOES. Aid to Utica and Black River Railroad Company, amending act, VI, 92; railroad bonds, VII, 412.

ORLEANS COUNTY. Agricultural society in, III, 945; disbandment of separate military company, VII, 826; exempted from Town Auditor's Act, VIII, 49; average excise license fees, 1889, 687; unpaid taxes, sales under special act, 749; highways, cost of labor system, 1892, IX, 200; insane, care of, county and State systems compared, 228.

VETOES. Lock-up at Medina, VI, 273; Barre, town meetings by election districts, 674, 690; Carlton, First Methodist Episcopal burial grounds, prohibiting interments in, 1035; VII, 120; board of supervisors, poor expenses, 328; support of poor, 367; auditing claims for construction of poorhouse, 1046; supervisors, fixing compensation, 1115; VIII, 129; county clerk, recording and indexing notices of pendency, 70; State ditch, Murray, removing obstructions, 539.

ORONDAX INDIANS. Threaten frontier, I, 355.

ORPHAN ASYLUMS. In New York, III, 83; aid from auction duties, 246; act relative to, 265; good work of, 291; incorporated, to share in common school fund, IV, 476; instruction in, veto, VI, 518; transfer of children from almhouses, 528; Susquehanna Valley, Binghamton, appropriation, veto, VII, 90.

ORPHAN ASYLUM OF THE SOCIETY OF REFORMED CHURCHES, BROOKLYN. Changing name, veto, X, 253.

ORPHANS. Act relative to, I, 11.

ORR, ALEXANDER F. Member of Canal Investigating Commission, 1875, VI, 928.

ORR, ISAAC. Communication from, instruction of deaf and dumb, III, 97.

ORTHOPEDIC HOSPITAL. Pavilion for contagious diseases, veto, X, 294.

ORVILLE FEEDER. DeWitt, repairs, veto, X, 426, 645.

OSBORN, SIR DANVERS. Appointed Governor, assumes office, I, 526; instruction relative to forms and methods of legislation, 523, 532; Lords of Trade suggest colonial union, 577; extract from commission, II, 498; death of, I, 526; official service, I, pref. x.

OSBORN, WILLIAM CHURCH. Nominated as State commissioner in lunacy, X, 42; Governor Roosevelt sends papers to Senate, 42.

OSEETAH LAKE. Cleaning and removing timber from, veto, X, 792.

OSGOOD, ANN. Cancellation of taxes, veto, X, 701.

OSGOOD, J. R. & COMPANY. Publishers of "New York Public Service," VII, 920.

OSSEY, FRANCIS. Petition from, report on, II, 307.

OSSINING. Act to incorporate, two-thirds bill, IV, 193; fire department, veto, X, 443; revising charter, extending boundaries, veto, 812.

OSTRANDER, WILLIAM L. Claim, cancellation of taxes, veto, X, 446, 588.

O'SULLIVAN, DENIS. Stenographer, New York Municipal Court, compensation, veto, X, 310.

OSWALD, ELEAZER. Suit against State, II, 330, 335, 351.

OSWEGATCHIE. VETOES. Assessment-rolls, VI, 88, 288; town meeting, legalizing proceedings, VIII, 885.

OSWEGATCHIE INDIANS. Parent stock of Onondagas and Cayugas, II, 552; claim of, 553; British build houses for, 553.

OSWEGATCHIE RIVER. Source in Adirondack region, IX, 147; act to prevent pollution of, 385.

VETOES. Repairing State works on, VI, 94; breakwater, 331; improving navigation, VIII, 848; repair of highway, Fowler, X, 791.

OSWEGO (Colony). Governor of Canada demands abandonment of, I, 225; trading-house at, 226, 227, 228, 232, 243, 251, 257, 260, 264, 518, 520, 529, 537; estimated expense of garrison at, 228; Governor Burnet's accounts of expenses, 231; importance of, 236, 239, 299, 304, 315, 319; act for maintaining troops at, 237, 239; Assembly memorial relative to, 237; French encroachments in vicinity, 241; support of garrison at, 243, 251, 290, 308, 389, 416, 421, 440, 459, 473, 477, 503, 518, 566; new commissary at, 245; petition for appointment of Kerr as surgeon at, 258; danger of French acquisition of Tierondequat, 272; victuallers at, not paid, 283; strengthening trading-house at, 296, 299; doubling garrison, 304, 305, 537; ordnance for, 305; cannon and gunpowder for, 315, 316, 318; act for support of, 318; re-enforcements for, 318, 546; interpreter for, 318; Indians in service at, 319; improving fortifications at, 323; trading-house to be used for strengthening fort, 323; Indian traders, retreat from, 326; French designs on, 328; defense of, 334, 338, 369, 540, 680; Indians complain of lack of hospitality at, 357; guard for transporting provisions to, 410; smith for, 460, 462; more re-enforcements for, 568; Governor Burnet's claim for supplies at, 592; captured by French, 602; troops for protection of, 677.

OSWEGO (State). Indian lands near, not in jurisdiction of State, II, 273; sale of lots in, 456; militia in service at, 736, 743, 746; arms supplied to Sterling, 774; advantages derived from internal improvements, III, 815; cession of land under water, IV, 591; training school at, V, 448; fixing value of certain lots, VI, 215; canal repairs, 857; number of excise licenses, 1887, VIII, 359; creating office of city chamberlain, reducing number of aldermen, 427; excise license fees, 1889, 686.

VETOES. Taxes, extending time for collection, V, 116; restoring channel of Oswego river, VI, 96; armory, addition, VII, 482; armory, repairing street and sidewalk, 927; water supply, 1100; VIII, 98; police department, amending act, 469; revising charter, non-partisan boards, 624; method of letting contracts, 1158; law library, IX, 130; electoral college for appointment of officers, 360, 432; armory, indoor rifle range, 604; amending charter, X, 59; recorder, 806.

OSWEGO CANAL. Appropriation for construction of, III, 70; debt, 304, 334, 736; IV, 252; receipts, III, 335, 370; deficiency, 410, 506, 710; completion of, 465; expense exceeds income, 549, 553; should not be abandoned, 799; length of, 811; appropriation for, charged on canal fund, IV, 199; enlargement, 588, 692, 743; V, 68; appropriation for, IV, 678, 743; tolls, V, 65, 153, 257, 361; proposed new locks, 502, 787; comparative financial statement,

OSWEGO CANAL — (*Continued*).

VI, 746; various repairs, 857; financial statement, 930; VII, 5, 145; deepening, general appropriation, VI, 994; tonnage, 1893, IX, 301; Enlargement Act of 1895, 305; X, 141; enlargement, survey for, 1900, X, 141, 215; improvement, State Engineer's special report, 1901, 244; Improvement Act of 1903, 252, 363, 496; Syracuse, bridge, North Salina street, act of 1906, 929.

VETOES. Syracuse,— swing-bridge, Salina street, VI, 1005; — lift-bridge, Salina and Bridge streets, VII, 95, 232, 363, 456; dam on Oswego river, 365; improving State ditch, VIII, 377; improvement, IX, 110; Phœnix, bridge, Bridge street, 216; new blue line maps, X, 297, 423; Syracuse, bridge, North Salina street, 327; dredging Baldwinsville branch, 426; Syracuse, filling side cuts, 569.

OSWEGO COUNTY. Appropriation for agricultural purposes, II, 1089; communication from inhabitants urging issue of more bank bills, IV, 48; exempted from Town Auditor's Act, VIII, 49; jail, changing site, 429; average excise license fees, 1889, 687; unpaid taxes, sales under special act, 749; decrease in population, IX, 3; highways, cost of labor system, 1892, 200; insane, care of, county and State systems compared, 228.

VETOES. Taxes, extending time for collection, IV, 116; Oneida River road, VI, 211; Mexico, rebuilding town hall, VII, 71; amending County Treasurer's Act, 266; Game Law, releasing certain waters from operation of, 442; Ox creek improvement, VIII, 292; inspection of steamboats, 469; unpaid taxes, sales for assignments of land, IX, 796; exemption from act relating to rebate of taxes for wide tire wagons, X, 393; Fort Brewster, acquiring site of, 435; special county judge and surrogate, term of office, 701; Old Home Week, proposed use of battle flags, 919.

OSWEGO COUNTY AGRICULTURAL SOCIETY. Mortgage for indebtedness, veto, VIII, 341.

OSWEGO DAM. Claims for damages, Court of Claims, veto, X, 311.

OSWEGO DRY DOCK AND MARINE RAILWAY COMPANY. Charter, veto, IV, 525.

OSWEGO FALLS. Amending village charter, veto, VII, 861.

OSWEGO FIRE DEPARTMENT. Amending charter, veto, VIII, 1040.

OSWEGO AND MIDLAND RAILROAD COMPANY. Aid to, memorandum of approval, V, 813; exempting construction bonds from taxation, 813; asks State aid, 866.

OSWEGO PIER AND DOCK COMPANY. Charter, veto, VI, 84.

OSWEGO RIVER. Improvement of, II, 1010, 1011; lighthouse at mouth of, 1055; improvement for canal navigation, III, 26; land below low-water mark, cession to Oswego, IV, 591.

    VETOES. Restoring channel at Oswego, VI, 96; bridge at Phoenix, 147; bridge over, 212; fishway at State dam, VII, 61; canal dam, 365; improvement, VIII, 292; fishways in, 888.

OSWEGO TRAINING SCHOOL. Established, V, 448; appropriation increased, 604; number of pupils, 695; instruction of kindergarten teachers, veto, VII, 792; industrial department, appropriation, veto, VIII, 865.

OSWEGO WATERWORKS COMPANY. Alleged interest in Oswego water supply bill, VIII, 98; supposed relation to bill reducing number of aldermen in Oswego, 428.

OTISCO LAKE. Bridge over inlet, veto, IX, 777.

OTISVILLE AND WURTSBORO TURNPIKE COMPANY. Rates of toll, veto, VI, 216.

O'TOOLE, LUKE. Commissioner of deeds, legalizing acts, veto, X, 948.

OTSEGO COUNTY. Connecticut land claims in, II, 370; court of oyer and terminer, Arnold murder case, 575; agricultural effort in, 957; convicts to be sent to Sing Sing prison, III, 316; agricultural society in, 945; silk culture in, 945; petition, Aylesworth pardon case, IV, 294; Clark patent, 332; Banyer leases, 334; refunding illegal taxes, VI, 278; exempted from Town Auditor's Act, VIII, 49; average excise license fees, 1889, 687; Cooperstown, Hurford and Barnett escheat, veto, 882; highways, cost of labor system, 1892, IX, 200; insane, care of, county and State asylums compared, 228.

OTSEGO COUNTY AGRICULTURAL SOCIETY. Mortgaging property, veto, VIII, 388.

OTSEQUETTE, ANTHONY. Act for relief of, II, 1080.

OTSEQUETTE, PETER. Act for relief of, II, 1030, 1080.

OTT, LOUIS. Relief, veto, VII, 601.

OTTENDORFER, OSWALD. Resigns as Regent, VI, 566; member of Tilden Municipal Reform Commission, 1875, IX, 417.

OTTER LAKE. Removing obstructions in outlet, veto, VIII, 613.

OURS HOSE COMPANY NO. 4, ELMIRA. Charter, veto, VI, 56.

OUTREY, MAXIME. French Minister to United States, chief of delegation to Yorktown Centennial Celebration, VII, 738; acknowledges courtesies of New York Commission, 742.

OUTSCOUTS. See also SCOUTS. Enlistment of, recommended, I, 130; for service toward Crown Point, 325; employment of, 346, 353; blockhouses for, 357; for Kinderhook, 394; for frontier, 462; offer of, from Connecticut, 468.

OVERINGS, MR. Leasehold estate, IV, 333.

OVERSEERS OF HIGHWAYS. To maintain roads, I, 129; act providing for, II, 385; annual report, amending Highway Law, veto, IX, 301; appointment, amending Highway Law, veto, X, 594.

OVERSEERS OF THE POOR. To provide for care of insane, II, 650.

VETOES. Ontario county, compensation in certain towns, VIII, 696; Long Island City, amending charter, 886; Cortland, salaries for, IX, 722; Jamestown, salary, X, 717.

OVID. State Agricultural College at, V, 177, see that title; Willard Asylum at, 583.

OWASCO. Justice of the peace to appoint special officers, veto, IX, 623.

OWASCO LAKE. VETOES. Trout, prohibition against taking, VII, 69; protection of highway along outlet, IX, 141, 239; highway on west shore, protection of, 239; X, 646.

OWEGO. Removal of postmaster, II, 1072; railroad in certain streets, VI, 330.

VETOES. Village, amending charter, VI, 79; VII, 935; school district No. 35, establishing cemetery, VI, 697; consolidating school districts, VII, 935; electric light, VIII, 129.

OX CREEK. Improvement, veto, VIII, 292.

OXFORD. Postmaster at, removal of, II, 1070, 1071; indications of coal at, III, 168; amending village charter, veto, IV, 684; election of police justice, 684.

OXFORD UNIVERSITY. Extension movement, IX, 17.

OYER AND TERMINER. See COURT OF OYER AND TERMINER.

OYSTER BAY. Smuggling at, efforts to prevent, I, 83; partition of lands in, act approved, 292.

VETOES. School moneys, VII, 807; Bethpage cemetery, sale of lots, improvement fund, 1122; Brunn escheat bill, VIII, 723; school district No. 5, new schoolhouse, 977, general act passed; legalizing town election, 1897, IX, 818.

OYSTER ISLAND. See also ELLIS ISLAND. Fortifications on, II, 360, 636.

OYSTER PROTECTORY. Cost of, 1891, IX, 11.

OYSTERS. Shells not to be burned in New York, I, 103; right of fishing, New York and Newark bays, IV, 564; culture, encouragement of, IX, 193; leases of land for beds, 194.

P.

PACIFIC TELEGRAPH. Completion of, V, 388.

PACKARD, GAVIT & COMPANY. Engravers, map and illustrations, geological survey, III, 994, 998; failure of, 994.

PADDOCK, STEPHEN. Affidavit by, anti-rent trouble, III, 829.

PADDON, JAMES B. Oneida county clerk, expenses, notaries public, veto, VII, 83.

PAINE, EPHRAIM. Commissioner to Hartford Convention on Taxation, II, 190.

PAINTED POST. Act for protection of persons and property, X, 632.

PALAEONTOLOGIST. Appointment of, III, 642, 681; Timothy A. Conrad appointed, 681; report, 682; IX, 575.

PALAEONTOLOGY. Publication of, veto, VIII, 553; IX, 402.

PALATINE BRIDGE. Village, amending charter, qualifications of voters, veto, VI, 195.

PALATINES. See also GERMANS. Proposed settlement in colony, I, 146; to engage in production of naval stores, 146; location of, 146, 147; mortality among, 147; proposed naturalization of, 146, 147; enlistments among, 156; number in military service, 156.

PALISADES. Commission on Preservation of, 1895, IX, 670; general note, 735; cession to United States, 735; description of park, 736; X, 124; report of commission, IX, 754; report of commission, 1900, summary of, X, 127; purchase of land in reservation, 215; proposed inclusion of Hook mountain, veto, 451; extending park, Hook mountain, 940.

PALISADES INTERSTATE PARK COMMISSION. Created, 1900, IX, 735; X, 124; powers extended, 1901, 216; appropriation for, 216; extending jurisdiction, veto, 451.

PALLADINO, JOSEPH. Claim against New York, relief, veto, X, 324, 581.

PALENVILLE. Fish hatchery, veto, VII, 902.

PALMER, ABIAH W. Senate, bill, organization of savings banks, VI, 352; New York charter, 499.

PALMER, A. EMERSON. New York, relief, veto, X, 582.

PALMER, ERASTUS. Member of Commission on Statues, VI, 435; contract for statues, 435.

PALMER, GEORGE M. Assembly, member of Prince Henry reception committee, X, 479; escorts Admiral von Tirpitz at reception, 480.

PALMER, GEORGE W. Colonel, conference with Washington authorities as to quotas of volunteers, V, 625; Commissary-General of ordnance, report, VI, 44.

PALMER, SAMUEL. Survivor of Remington & Palmer, Court of Claims, veto, X, 449.

PALMER, SAMUEL J. Contests seat of Assemblyman Matthews, Kings county, 1905, X, 795.

PALMERSTON, LORD. English Foreign Secretary, applied to, for leave to transcribe colonial documents, IV, 168.

PALMERTOWN. Blockhouse at, II, 113.

PALMYRA. VETOES. Lift-bridge, VI, 1005; canal bridge, Earle and Kent streets, VII, 116; permitting supervisor to hold school office, VIII, 47; union school, additional building, X, 752.

PAMELIA. Town, aid to Utica and Black River Railroad Company, amending act, veto, VI, 92.

PANAMA CANAL. Beginning of construction, proposed International Isthmian Exposition in honor of, X, 866.

PANAMA RAILROAD COMPANY. Refunding taxes erroneously paid, veto, IX, 605.

PAN-AMERICAN EXPOSITION. Provision for New York's represenation at, X, 124; proposed department of social economy, 125; various acts relating to, 1901, 228; report, printing and distribution, veto, 571.

PANIC (Financial). 1834, causes of, III, 483, 494; abatement of, 496; effects of, 521; 1837, Governor Marcy's comments on, 656; 1857, Governor King's comments on, V, 42; Governor Morgan on, 75; expected, Governor Fenton's comment, 876; of 1869, VI, 134.

PAPER. Used in legal proceedings, proposed tax on, I, 248; in legal proceedings, substituted for parchment, II, 409; stamped, Federal tax on, 789.

PARADES. Sons of Veterans, with firearms, veto, IX, 398.

PARAGUAY. Participation in Cotton States Exposition, IX, 581.

PARCHMENT. In legal proceedings, paper substituted for, II, 409.

PARDONING POWER. Under first Constitution, II, 68; limitations on, 599; difficulties incident to exercise of, 982; IV, 725; under Constitutions, III, 1, 284; V, 93, 116, 266, 758; VII, 707; effect of inconsiderate clemency, III, 861; proposed constitutional amendment, 863; Friends, penalty for refusal to perform military service, 880; modification needed if capital punishment abolished, 940; procedure, IV, 405, 435, 480, 788, 845; duty and responsibility of Governor, 610; proposed review by Supreme Court of convictions in capital cases, 610, 652; should be cautiously exercised, V, 93, 266; appropriation for Governor's expenses, 172; proposed bureau of pardons, 758; proper scope of, VII, 707.

PARDONS (General). Of offenses against New York, Vermont controversy, II, 164; large number of applications due to overcrowded prison, 874; on condition that convict leave State, 913; life prisoners, effect of restricted, 1108; principles applied in granting, III, 130; Governor's report, IV, 405, 427, 480, 564, 624, 681, 779; V, 115, 137, 171, 305, 564, 793; VI, 143, 268, 426, 554, 661, 977; VII, 42, 178, 315, 536, 994; VIII, 43, 195, 399, 534, 789, 980, 1107; IX, 49, 218, 343, 570, 688, 852; X, 32, 142, 229, 371; does not affect validity of judgment of conviction, IX, 250.

PARDONS (Governor). See also PARDONS, LEGISLATURE. Two for arson, II, 855; resulting from classification of convicts, III, 22; William Kirby, conditional, 32; Lieutenant-Governor Throop's observations on, 284; number of, 340, 384, 402, 862; IV, 480, 609; V, 170, 267,

Pardons (Governor) — (*Continued*).

371; VI, 110, 234, 268, 427; VII, 994; Marcus Aylesworth, IV, 294; reports, special message of Governor Morgan, V, 115; mistakes in granting, 169; applications for, expense of witnesses and sheriff's fees, veto, VIII, 861; John Roberts' case, IX, 250.

Pardons (Legislature). Amy Augur, II, 68; Jonah Wood, 78; Thomas Cummings, 82; John Pastano, 454; Benjamin Holmes, pardon refused, 454; George Peters, pardon refused, 514, 515; " Stiff-Armed " George, 531; William Conklin, 541; Stephen Arnold, sentence commuted to life imprisonment, 577; David Williams, sentence commuted to life imprisonment, 578; Francisco Son, Legislature declines to act, 588; John Williams, sentence commuted to imprisonment for five years, 621; Rufus Hill, 635, 636; John Bowman, sentence commuted to imprisonment for life, 738; Mary Cool, 749; Joseph Moser, 790; Michael Dwyer, 805; Thomas Burke, 856; Daniel Northrup, 874; Diana Sillick, sentence commuted to imprisonment for life, 894; Abraham Kesler, Legislature directs execution of sentence, 921; David Linus, John Denny, Roswell T. Pratt, John Harris and James O'Brien, 923; Jack Hodges and David Conklin, 997; James Teed and David Dunning, Legislature refuses to act, 997; Thomas Burke, 998; Soo-non-gize (Tommy Jemmy), 1120.

Parent and Child. Death of child resulting from chastisement, II, 577; rights of aliens, III, 845; adoption, effect of, VI, 817.

Vetoes. Child, legitimizing birth, Ehlers case, VII, 633; illegitimate children, right of inheritance, 1126; legitimizing illegitimate child, Barker case, X, 770.

Paris, France. Royal Library, colonial documents in, IV, 188; Universal Exhibition, report of commissioner, 865; New York commissioner of deeds in, V, 213; exposition at, report of New York commissioner, 791, 862.

Paris, New York. Election of railroad commissioners, veto, VI, 194.

Paris Green. Sale of, preventing fraud, veto, IX, 815; X, 318.

Parish, Jasper. Purchase of Cayuga land, II, 478; compensation as Indian interpreter, 605, 607; purchase of Squaw island, 857; communication from, Seneca Indians, 1076; Indian agent, communication from, missionaries to Senecas, III, 35.

Parishville. Vetoes. Townhouse, VIII, 516; lock-up, 1039.

Park, Roswell. Claim against Niagara county, reconsideration by board of supervisors, veto, X, 268.

Parker, Amasa J. Supreme Court justice, presides at O'Connor and Van Steenburgh murder trials, Steele case, IV, 319; communication from, vagrants, trial jurors, 505; member of Statutory Revision Commission, 1870, VI, 238.

PARKER, D. N. Commissioner, repairing bridges Cattaraugus reservation, VII, 383.

PARKER, JAMES. New Jersey commissioner on New York boundary, VI, 779.

PARKER, JOEL. Governor of New Jersey, communication from, boundary, VI, 775; quarantine jurisdiction, 777.

PARKER, JOSEPH. Relief of minor daughter, claim, New York fire department, veto, X, 818.

PARKER & COMPANY, CHARLES F. Court of Claims, veto, X, 703, 944.

PARKER'S POND. VETOES. Removing obstructions in outlet, VIII, 613; Canton, cleaning obstructions from outlet, X, 810.

PARKHURST, CHARLES H. Approves Harvey claim against New York city, VIII, 1162.

PARKHURST, JONATHAN. Major, arms and supplies delivered to, II, 774.

PARKS, ABIAL. VETOES. Relief, State lands, IX, 721; Board of Claims, 797.

PARKS. See STATE PARKS, ADIRONDACK PARK and FOREST PRESERVE. At Niagara Falls, VII, 300; New York, extending jurisdiction of commissioners, VIII, 430; New York, department, extending jurisdiction, 714; Bensonhurst, Kings county, amending act to establish, 1157; Chickamauga and Chattanooga National Military park, dedication, IX, 575; John Brown farm transferred to State, 669.

VETOES. Private, northern wilderness, protection of, VII, 264; in forests, 412; Riverside, New York, improvement, 655; Prospect, Brooklyn, 804; Richford public square, 807; New York, keepers, 934, 1086; New York, Washington park, prohibiting tunnel under, 999; New York, park department, government of, 1075, 1118; Cedar, New York, discontinuing proceedings relative to, VIII, 129; Brooklyn, protection of, 131; New York, department, jurisdiction, 293; High Bridge, New York, 294; New York, 23d and 24th wards, altering map, 350; Central park, New York, zoological collections, accommodations, 449; Central, New York, parade ground, 467; Brooklyn, park department, 468; police, New York, 638; New York, bi-partisan Park Commission, 757, 758; board of commissioners, Utica, 880; Long Island City, parks and parade grounds, 888; New York, Van Courtland, vaults and burial plats in, 889; Brooklyn, acquiring land for, 1036; Tonawanda, establishment of, 1115; New York,—West End avenue, IX, 262; — compensation of laborers and employees, 393; — appointment of commissioners, 434; — protection of, 517; Brooklyn,— duplicate bill, 434; — 31st ward, 632; — general act relating to, 720; Troy, park commission, 633; Rochester, 724, 727; Long Island City, 726; New York,

PARKS, VETOES — (*Continued*).

   protection of, 727; Rochester, park boulevards, 731; Brooklyn —
   park police pension fund, 733; — improvement, 779; — parkway and driveway, amending act, 782; Auburn, establishing,
   783; New York — acquiring site, 806; — East river, legalizing
   laying out, refunding assessments, 808; — park, 4th ward, X,
   60; — Hamilton park, 60, 473; — St. Nicholas park, 60; —
   Jerome park reservoir, bridge over, 176, 326; — 12th ward,
   176; — relative to, 178; — park commissioners, powers, 179;
   Ausable Chasm, acquiring for, 317; New York park department,
   jurisdiction over certain streets and places, 323; Prospect,
   Brooklyn, zoological garden in, 476; Brooklyn park department, 477; New York,— additional, 582; — street and park
   openings, fund for, 635; Buffalo, land for, 11th ward, 712;
   New York, St. Nicholas, proceedings, rehearing by Supreme
   Court, 713; Silver lake, Richmond county, 715; East River,
   New York, refunding assessments, 715, 806.

PARLIAMENT. Model for colonial Legislature, I, 10; Ireland, continuance
   under succeeding Governors, 196; British, premium on exportation
   of manufactures, 198; frequent election of members of, 207;
   financial methods, imitation of, recommended by colony, 283; royal
   recommendation a prerequisite to provision for service, 489, 506;
   proposed act for colonial union, 579; appropriation to aid colonies,
   598; approves conduct of New York Assembly, 607; requested to
   provide for expense of Canadian expedition, 620, 634, 643, 654,
   663; appropriation for colonies, 645; Sugar Act, mischiefs of, 684;
   petition from New York Assembly, 687, 696, 698, 703, 768, 771,
   775, 776; act for quartering troops in colonies, 702, 716, 721;
   alleged encroachment on colonial rights, 702; colonists owe obedience
   to acts of, 704; no power to grant colonial estates to Crown, 705;
   Stamp Act repealed, 706, 710; described as " grand Legislature of
   the nation," 710, 772; declares extent of authority in colonies, 712;
   prohibits legislation in New York until supplies for troops granted,
   721, 730, 773; difference with American colonies, 765; New York
   Assembly declares its attitude toward home government, 769; small
   number of laws enacted, V, 849; notice of application for private
   and local law, cost of enactment, X, 21.

PARLIAMENTARY LIBRARY. Canada, destroyed by fire, New York gives
   books for, IV, 573.

PARMA. Town Insurance Company, veto, VI, 592.

PARSONS, ELI. Arrest authorized, II, 269.

PARSONS, FRANK G. Canal Department, appropriation for services,
   veto, IX, 716.

PARSONS, JOHN E. Opinion, voter's freedom of selection of candidate cannot be restricted by form of ballot, IX, 395, 479.

PARSONS, SAMUEL. Protest against corporal punishment in prisons and public employment of prisoners, II, 996.

PARTIES (Political). See also BI-PARTISAN BOARDS. In colony, Bellomont urges reconciliation of, I, 77, 82, 85; natural offspring of republican government, II, 1019; Governor Clinton on malignant party spirit, III, 198; relations to government, 274; causes of party division, 425; under free governments, VI, 462; act through caucuses, 462; representation in election boards, VII, 203, 233; representation in fire and police commissions, 318; representation in local boards, 330; representation in State Civil Service Commission, 838; political assessments prohibited, 838; political contributions by health officer of New York, 968; new capitol, political tests in employment prohibited, 982; bi-partisan representation in Troy police board, VIII, 86; representation in constitutional conventions, 310; partisan influence in excise legislation, 364; Republican State Convention, 1887, favors tax reform, 478; nominations, limiting rights of voters, 568; political committees, statement of election expenses, 918, 971, 1079; IX, 197, 310, 555; Legislature of 1892 in political accord with Governor, IX, 2; change of control in executive and legislative departments, 1895, 536; emblems on ballots, 554; bi-partisan boards, limiting selection to particular political parties, 589; management of schools, political considerations should be excluded, X, 151; political enrollment in towns, 417; judges not to make political contributions, 516; Republican party committed to repeal of tax on surplus of savings banks, 767; Republican party, effect of Mortgage Tax Law, 803; political contributions by corporations prohibited, 842, 847; direct nominations, 847; duty of citizens to participate in making nominations, 847; reports of committees, 847; restricting campaign expenses, 847.

VETOES. Libel, candidates for office, II, 551; official newspapers, Albany, increasing number, VII, 1121; new capitol employees, political selection of, VIII, 215; Monroe county, enrollment at primaries, X, 257; enrollment lists in towns, filing with county clerk, 705.

PARTIES TO ACTION. Required to take oath of allegiance, II, 171; jurisdiction of court, consent does not give, III, 362.

PARTITION. Relative to, I, 285; lands in Oyster Bay, act approved, 292. VETOES. Bill relating to, I, 231; — Jansen estate, II, 663; — lands held by husband and wife, VII, 416; — actions, VIII, 1039.

PARTNERSHIPS. VETOES. Fictitious firm names, preventing use of, VIII, 131; limited, amending Revised Statutes, IX, 718; pleadings, denying allegations of, X, 309; amending general law, 585.

PASSENGERS. Steamboat, tax on, II, 902, 1010; on foreign vessels, tax on, IV, 75, 77; masters refuse to pay tax, 76; Tax Act, unconstitutional, 273; bond from masters of vessels, 441; from foreign ports, tax on unconstitutional, 441, 485.

PASSES. To Canada, Assembly recommends restriction of, I, 200.

PASTANO, JOHN. Convicted of murder, pardon of, II, 454.

PATENT AND COPYRIGHT PROTECTIVE ASSOCIATION, NEW YORK. Amending charter, veto, X, 312.

PATENTS (Inventions). Legislature cannot interfere with, VII, 571, 591; Savage magazine rifle, IX, 637; Patent and Copyright Protective Association, New York, amending charter, veto, X, 312; electrocution apparatus, purchase of rights, veto, 567.

PATENTS (Land). Settlements in, compared with townships, I, 552; certain grants of Indian lands claimed to be fraudulent, 601, 606, 611, 685; Assembly memorial relative to Indian lands, 686; of bounty lands, relative to, veto, II, 309; Massachusetts boundary, exchange of lands occasioned by, 351; act relating to, veto, 354; on condition of settlement, inquiry concerning, 432; source of title to lands in military tract, 664; of land in military tract, 991; Freemasons, land in, relating to, veto, III, 15; to John Morin Scott, Schoharie county, IV, 331; Blenheim, 331; Kortright, 332; Hardenburg, 333; royal, not void because containing manorial privileges, 413; Dongan, 1685, confirmed, 413; land under water of lakes, VI, 156; defective, remedy, 215.

PATENT RIGHTS. VETOES. Frauds in sale of, VI, 334, 502; manufacturing corporations, powers of, VII, 621.

PATHOLOGIST. Authorized at Utica Lunatic Asylum, VI, 115.

PATRICK, ALBERT T. Trial for murder, right to appeal from order denying motion for a new trial, amending Code, veto, X, 928.

PATRIOTIC TRACT SOCIETY. Charter, veto, VIII, 131.

PATRIOTISM. Encouragement of, veto, VIII, 1040.

PATRIOTISM, MANUAL OF. Publication of, veto, X, 297.

PATTERSON, CHARLES E. Speaker of Assembly, 1881, VII, 676.

PATTERSON, DANIEL T. Commodore, commanding American fleet at New Orleans, thanked by Legislature, II, 858; letter from Governor Tompkins, reply, 861.

PATTERSON, JULIA C. Release of land to, owned by New York city in Putnam county, veto, IX, 806.

PATTON, JOHN K. Assembly, member of joint legislative committee on services in memory of former Governor Higgins, X, 963.

PATTON, JOHN M., Lieutenant-Governor of Virginia, communication from, Curry extradition case, III, 915.

PAULIST FATHERS. Spalding Literary Union, New York, exempted from taxation, veto, IX, 810.

PAUNCEFOTE, LORD. British Ambassador, correspondence relative to Cayuga Indian claim, X, 128.

PAUPERISM. Increase of, III, 176; causes of, 292; rapid increase of, V, 192; report on, 274, 376; inquiry concerning, VI, 724; relative to, 949.

PAWLING AND BEEKMAN TURNPIKE COMPANY. Surrender of part of road, veto, VI, 215.

PAWNBROKERS. VETOES. Regulation of, VII, 803; amending Penal Code, VIII, 889.

PAX, JOHN. Escheat, veto, VII, 805.

PAYMASTER. Of militia, appointment of, II, 764, 767; department recommended, 796; gives bond, 809; statement of killed and wounded, 872; compensation of, 953; report, X, 486.

PAYMASTER-GENERAL. Deputy Mortier to draw for Amherst loan, I, 637; Mr. Pierce attends Legislature, II, 133; report, funds for bounties exhausted, V, 571; communication relative to bounties, 578; payments under Bounty Law, 689; report, 718, 862; Civil War, enlistments, expenditures, veto, VII, 478.

PAYNE, ROBERT. Court of Claims, veto, X, 591.

PAY-ROLLS. Of militia, II, 57.

PEABODY MUTUAL BENEFIT COMPANY, NEW YORK. Charter, veto, VI, 171.

PEACH TREES. VETOES. Preventing spread of yellows, VII, 416; VIII, 376; new bill passed, 376; yellows and black knot, examinations, compensation of agent, IX, 354.

PEACOCK, WILLIAM. Commissioner, report on Buffalo Creek harbor, II, 991.

PEALE, REMBRANDT. Paints portrait of Washington, III, 143.

PEARS. Size of barrels, veto, X, 317.

PEARL ASHES. Inspection of, II, 471, 1093; exportation of, 1091; communication from inspector, 1113.

PEARSALL, THOMAS. Lands of, II, 289.

PEARSE, L. Expenses, removal of Montgomery's remains, II, 1001.

PEARSON, J. H. Canal Department, appropriation for services, veto, IX, 716.

PEARTREE, WILLIAM. Colonel, commands expedition against French privateer, I, 128.

PEASE, R. H. Contract for printing and engraving plates, geological survey, IV, 464.

PEAT. Discovery of, II, 1094; accumulations of, III, 1036.

PECK, CHARLES H. State Botanist, expenses, veto, VII, 582, 779.

PECK, JEDEDIAH. Associate judge, Arnold case, II, 578; member of Commission on Common School System, 707.

PECK, JOHN. Residence, terminus of special highway, Fulton county, veto, VI, 598.

PECK, RUFUS T. Election of Senators, 1891, rejection of certain irregular ballots, VIII, 670.

PECK, WILLIAM BURKE. Bond for return of arms, II, 772.

PECK, SYLVESTER F. Act authorizing use of waters of Onondaga creek, III, 36.

PECK & COMPANY, LINUS JONES. Board of Claims, veto, IX, 600; new act, 1895, 369, 600.

PECKHAM, WHEELER H. Opinion, voter's freedom of selection of candidate cannot be restricted by form of ballot, IX, 395, 479.

PECONIC RIVER. Completing channel, veto, VIII, 846.

PEDDLERS. Petition of New York grand jury against, I, 170; license, act of 1870 sustained, VI, 120.

   VETOES. License, board of supervisors, IX, 372; license to veterans, 811; license to volunteer firemen, 866; license, X, 163.

PEEKSKILL. Camp of instruction at, VII, 826; VIII, 14.

   VETOES. Additional water bonds, X, 443; — building commissioner, creating office, 961.

PEEKSKILL ACADEMY. Amending charter, veto, VI, 1030.

PEINPACK. Memorial from, requesting protection, II, 55.

PELET, BARON. Director-general of archives, French War Department, aid to Mr. Brodhead in examining records, IV, 187.

PELHAM. Part of, merged in Greater New York, IX, 300.

   VETOES. Town, relative to, VII, 807; town meeting, restricting powers, VIII, 721; bridge, purchase of, amending act, 889.

PELL, FERRIS. Commissioner on claims against United States, report, II, 999, 1038, 1080.

PELTRY. Trading in, I, 193; amount received from Five Nations, 212; in trade with Far Indians, 214.

PEMAQUID. Representation in First Assembly, I, 9; French attack on, 69.

PENAL CODE. Revision of, II, 336, 349, 363, 399, 983; punishment for escape, 426; proposed, submission to Legislature, V, 596; VI, 29; enacted, V, 597; report of commission, VI, 29; adopted in Territories, 29; submitted to Statutory Revision Commission, enacted, 118; provisions relating to conspiracies, 122; established, VII, 663, 722; postponing time of taking effect, 723; superseded acts repealed, VIII, 37; revision and promulga-

PENAL CODE—(*Continued*).

tion of, 38; should include all crimes, 633; general amendments, 1892, IX, 135; amendments, 1895, poolselling, bookmaking and gambling, 548.

VETOES. Printing, VII, 416; enactment, 417; Senate committee on, printing for, 493; imprisonment, hard labor, 805; disturbance of religious meeting, 1043; obscene literature, VIII, 293; false labels, 632; trade-marks, 632; public officers, 889; pawnbrokers, 889; malicious destruction of property, 890; insolvent banks, receiving deposits, 890; gilded ware, preventing deception in manufacture and sale of, IX, 47; false pretenses, evidence, 259; general amendments, 282; gunpowder, keeping, unauthorized use, 289; State lands, trespasses, procedure, 530; autopsies in State hospitals, 534; loan on personal credit, 534; lotteries, 534; trades and mechanical employments on Sunday, 623; houses of refuge, 718; cruelty, 793; prohibiting sale of horse-flesh as food, 793; steamboats, frauds on owners and managers, 793; servile labor, 793; sales on prescription, 860; larceny by false pretense, 860; flag, national or State, improper use of, 860; badges or buttons, relative to, X, 62; public health, 63; crimes against elective franchise, 162; trials for keeping slot machines, 162; executors, accounting proceedings, Surrogate's Court, 282; electric meters and wires, unlawful interference with, 311; corporations, director, definition, 311; quarantine, entering grounds or vessels without leave, 317; sale of drugs and medicine, offenses connected with, 592; kidnapping, punishment of, 699; building ordinances, violations, 702; stamping articles made of gold, 705; commitments to New York and Rochester houses of refuge, 705; crimes against public peace, 807; unauthorized wearing of badges, 807; sentences to Elmira Reformatory, 917.

PENATAQUIT CREEK. Improving navigation, veto, VIII, 848.

PENDERS, THOMAS. Claim, work and materials, board of education, Long Island City, veto, X, 322.

PENITENTIARIES. Federal prisoners admitted to, III, 163; in Albany, IV, 74, see ALBANY PENITENTIARY; inspection by Prison Association, V, 526, 601; in certain districts, women sent to, 599; State penitentiary recommended, VI, 57; commission to select site, 58, see ELMIRA REFORMATORY; International Congress, report of commissioners, 554; investigation commission created, VII, 287, 432, 528; proposed supervision by Superintendent of Prisons, VIII, 12; freedom of worship in, 23, 178, 302, 479; use of machinery abolished, 658.

PENITENTIARIES — (*Continued*).

   VETOES. Onondaga county, V, 336; Kings county, sentences, VI,
      512; Onondaga county, maintenance of convicts, 587; confine-
      ment of convicts, 711; commutations for good behavior, 899;
      convicts, maintenance in penitentiaries, deficiency appropriation,
      VII, 462, 584, 792; VIII, 118; Onondaga county, sale of, 945;
      manufactures in, branding and marking, IX, 138; medical treat-
      ment of persons convicted of intoxication, 252; furnishing
      cheese for inmates, 287; manufacture of certain articles pro-
      hibited in, 464; Kings county, removal, X, 177; transfers to,
      amending State Charities Law, 312; Erie county, commitments
      from Olean, 806.

PENN, JOHN. Lieutenant-Governor of Pennsylvania, communication
   from, relative to New York boundary, I, 761.

PENNSYLVANIA (Colony). Benjamin Fletcher appointed Governor of,
   I, 25, 37, 45; meeting of Assembly in, 46; letter from Governor
   relative to importation of salt, 219; Millington Library, clergy to
   use, 234; Weiser, Indian interpreter, journal of, 355; joins in
   Indian conference, 359; troops from, in expedition against Canada,
   373; papers from, relative to enemy's privateers, 467; letter from
   Governor Hamilton relative to Indian affairs, 508; resists French
   encroachments on Ohio frontier, 536; French forts on Ohio frontier
   probably in territory of, 543; New York grants aid in dispossessing
   French, 547, 552; provisions for Crown Point expedition, 571; Lords
   of Trade recommend colonial union, 578; represented in Albany
   Convention, 578; historical records, Albany plan of union, 579;
   Indian incursions in northern part of, 587; proposed joint expedition against Indians, 593; troops for Crown Point expedition,
   596; remits to New York overpayment of French War grant, 713;
   communication from Governor relative to New York boundary, 761.

PENNSYLVANIA (State). Letter from Executive Council, II, 69; Olmstead case, 665; constitutional amendment, tribunal for determining
   questions between Federal and State governments, 667; disapproves
   Massachusetts and Connecticut resolutions (see page 827), 830;
   act relative to canal connecting Tioga river with Seneca lake, 902;
   communication from Governor, canal connection between Seneca
   lake and Susquehanna river, 918, 965; constitutional amendment,
   prohibiting national banking corporations, except in District of
   Columbia, 1024; Federal officers not eligible to certain State offices,
   1063; report of commissioners on canal between Tioga river and
   Seneca lake, III, 98; anthracite coal from, 127, 203, 204; internal
   improvements, 171; sustains tariff of 1828, 315; resolutions,— Constitution binding on every citizen, acts of Congress cannot be nulli-

PENNSYLVANIA (State) — (*Continued*).

fied, no State can withdraw from Union, President bound to execute laws, Congress may impose tariff duties, pledges support to national government, 432, 433; recommends abolition of lotteries, 481; tax for internal improvements, 507; resolution on distribution of proceeds of public lands, 590; proposition to connect North Branch canal with Chemung canal, 759; favors distribution of proceeds of public lands and increase of tariff, 908; method of bank supervision, 1004; resolutions, navy yard on lake frontier, IV, 625; action relative to independence monument, 682; V, 122; resolutions on secession movement, V, 321; military to be subordinate to civil power, 470; Governor calls on Governor Seymour for assistance to repel Lee's invasion, 544; appropriation for Antietam cemetery, 840; communication from Governor, Centennial Celebration, VI, 303; committee appointed, 303; tax exemptions, 371; cumulative voting, 544; removing anti-commercial restrictions, 553; resolutions protesting against Federal interference in Louisiana, 785; protests against New York wharfage tax, 981; excise taxes used for local purposes, VIII, 439; university extension movement, IX, 18; provision for agricultural instruction, 178; large deposits of anthracite coal in, 183; retail liquor licenses, 1892, 666; State prisons, use of foot or hand power machinery, X, 167.

PENNSYLVANIA BOUNDARY. Negotiations relative to, I, 761; line between Delaware and Susquehanna rivers, 761; act to establish, II, 225; letter from Governor, boundary, 225; proceedings relating to, 265; report of Surveyor-General, 272; effect on Indian titles, 273; line established, 282; Regents authorized to establish, VII, 720.

PENNSYLVANIA RAILROAD COMPANY. Terminal facilities in New York, X, 396.

PENROSE, CHARLES B. Pennsylvania, member of committee on canal connecting North Branch canal with Chemung canal, III, 759.

PENN YAN. VETOES. New armory at, VIII, 886; changing boundary, IX, 63; amending charter, 249; Bellis, police justice, legalizing acts, 258; water supply, 411.

PENSIONS. Principles on which they should be granted, III, 721.

PENSIONS (Civil). For judges, II, 362; police, V, 181; towns authorized to establish fund for teachers, IX, 564.

VETOES. Retirement of teachers, New York and Brooklyn, VII, 606; teachers, New York, 804, 931; X, 477; police, New York, VII, 937; VIII, 891, 1129; X, 580; New York fire department, Nunn and Wilson, VII, 1088; Brooklyn fire department, VIII, 131; Brooklyn police, VII, 413; VIII, 523; Brooklyn, Abraham Dalley, 638; Rochester paid fire department pension fund, IX,

Pensions (Civil), Vetoes — (Continued).

249; act passed, 1894, 249; teachers, conditional compensation after twenty-five years' service in towns, 463; Albany police pension fund, amending act, 632; New York fire department, Hudson claim, 728; New York police pension fund, 728; X, 60, 474; New York fire department, Mahoney claim, hearing, IX, 732; Brooklyn park police, 733; Brooklyn police pensions, time of payment, 781; Rochester, teachers' retirement fund, 788; Syracuse police pension fund, amending act, 790; Utica police pensions, 790; health department, New York, 804; New York fire department pension-roll, claims of chiefs of battalions to be placed thereon, 808; Buffalo police, X, 276, 958; New York firemen, Bowen case, 321; Jamestown police, 322; New Rochelle teachers, tax for, 435; Utica firemen's pension fund, 476; New York fire department, 582; Rochester — fire department, 713, 714; — police pension fund, 714; New York — firemen, 717; — Mahon, 807; — Murphy, fire department, 816; Buffalo, police, Dowd case, 875; for retiring veterans, 924.

Pensions (Military). In colonial service, I, 598; temporary for returning troops, 671; relief of families of men who fell in battle under General Herkimer, II, 25; for members of militia, 92; act for, 187; for Revolutionary soldiers, 259, 1027; III, 179, 214, 352, 388; War of 1812, II, 738, 748, 760, 794; IV, 524; for members of national army, 381; Mexican War, 524; provision for Civil War, V, 420; importance of, 462; national system commended, 683; Federal law applicable to organized State militia, X, 16.

People. Claim right to share in colonial government, I, 1; choose Eight Men, 2; petition for representative government, 2; prohibited from leaving colony without Leisler's consent, 16; absentees required to return to colony, 16, 17; proclamation recalling absentees, 22; Bellomont urges reconciliation of parties, 77, 82, 85; Assembly asserts rights of, as English subjects, 110; right to know proceedings of Assembly, 447; duty to government, 528; of colonies, character of, 691; gifts to government, 705; of colony, have all rights of British subjects, 772, 775; constitutional liberties of, 776; sovereign in a free State, II, 1; source of authority under Constitution, 27; entitled to be secure in their property, 62; right of appeal to courts, 173; orderly conduct at close of Revolutionary War, 196; rights of, as results of war, 215; danger from too many corporations, 230; all should share in representative government, 237; government needs confidence and good will of, 290, 293; duty of defending independence, 423; entitled to protection of government, 452; right of

PEOPLE —(*Continued*).

petition, 508; freedom of business, 614; lack of power in despotic governments, 718; right to keep and bear arms, 1016; IV, 726; V, 281; power as to constitutional amendments, II, 1043; right to determine question as to holding constitutional convention, 1055; sit in judgment on form of government, 1088; source of power, III, 41, 54; right to choose presidential electors, 42; approve district plan of choosing presidential electors, 52; can be trusted with control of political affairs, 427; owe allegiance to government, 435; perpetuity of republican institutions, 803; right to require record of legislative proceedings, 976; to elect canal commissioners, IV, 61; approval of State debt, 104, 227, 371, 546, 670; VI, 178; when may not approve law, IV, 475; VI, 437, 484, 503; will of majority, acquiescence in, IV, 581; acquiescence in results of elections, V, 34, 468; approve canal loan, 70; respect for laws and rulers, 460; right to assemble and petition, 483; VI, 375; VIII, 578; approve act for Civil War bounties, V, 610; own street railroad grants, VI, 64; dangers from special judicial tribunals, 492; large sums paid in taxes, 766, 827; dangers from unlawful military violations, 772; delegation of powers to municipalities, 831; progress of local self-government, 832; effect of non-participation in local government, 837; should remedy evils of local government, VII, 31; approve abolition of prison contract labor, 828; Binghamton judgment, payment of, submitting question to, veto, 1017; legislative power vested in, VIII, 143; approve proposition for constitutional convention, 1886, VIII, 178; majority live in cities and villages, IX, 29.

PEOPLE'S COLLEGE. Incorporated, IV, 648; located at Havana, V, 178; erection of buildings, 290; appropriation for, 376.

PEOPLE'S MUTUAL BENEFIT ASSOCIATION. Charter, veto, VI, 326.

PEOPLE'S SAVINGS BANK, NEW YORK. Financial condition of, VII, 66.

PEOPLE'S WATER TRANSIT COMPANY. Amending charter, veto, VI, 703.

PEPPERELL, SIR WILLIAM. General, letter from, raising troops for Louisburg, I, 369; two companies from his regiment ordered to Oswego, 563.

PERJURY. Act to prevent, I, 10; punishment of, II, 451; extending definition of, veto, VII, 413; presumption outside contradictory statements, X, 905.

PERKINS, BISHOP. Assembly, member of select committee on anti-rent troubles, IV, 328.

PERLEY, FRANK E. Secretary to Governor Higgins, communication to Speaker relative to executive office hours, X, 748.

PERNAMBUCO. Vessels from, detained for observation, yellow fever, VI, 533.

PERRY. VETOES. First Presbyterian church, sale of property, VI, 45; cemeteries, reinterments, VII, 870; railroad aid, using funds for general town purposes, VIII, 1105, new bill passed.

PERRY, FRANK. Canal Department, appropriation for services, veto, IX, 716.

PERRY, ISAAC G. Capitol commissioner, requests appropriation for continuing work, VIII, 93; bill abolishing office, veto, 213; duties under act of 1888, 610; member of New Capitol Commission, 1888, 650; appointed new capitol commissioner, 1019; communication to Governor Flower relative to sanitary condition of capitol, IX, 358.

PERRY, OLIVER H. Commodore, victory on Lake Erie, thanked by New York Senate, II, 799; letter from Governor Tompkins, 799; reply, 800.

PERSONAL PROPERTY. First Tax Law, II, 9; includes mortgages held by non-residents, III, 440; taxation of, IV, 436, 480, 564, 598; V, 176, 369; taxable valuation of, 453; defective methods of assessment, 691, 751, 825; VIII, 1063; statement by owner of property, V, 691; assessments in several States, 825; VIII, 307; returns by owners as basis of assessment, V, 826; exemption from taxation, VI, 373, 411; VIII, 152; reduction in assessments, VII, 514, 942; taxation, deduction of debts, VIII, 153; New York, small ratio of taxation, 308; escapes taxation, 1066; X, 80; taxation, restricting deduction of debts, IX, 93, 158; assessments for taxation, X, 620.

VETOES. Assessment, Newtown, VI, 450; title, relative to, VII, 508; McLoughlin escheat, 748; Meyer escheat, 749; household furniture and sewing machines, sale on installment plan, 758; illegitimate children, right to inherit, 1126; conditional sales, amending act, IX, 287; licensing itinerant vendors of goods, 465; corporations to make loans on, general act, 534; in town of Hempstead, relative to, 817; sale to satisfy lien, 865; Queens county, apportionment under Nassau County Act, X, 62; mortgages, where to be filed, 63; held by State, Kinneally claim, escheat, Court of Claims, 310; loan associations, amending act, 317; undertakings on discharge of attachments, 441; Personal Property Loan Company, charter, 594, 708; taxation of non-residents, 876, new bill passed; transfers of goods in bulk, 929.

PERSONAL PROPERTY LOAN COMPANY. Charter, veto, X, 594, 708.

PERTH. Dairymen's Manufacturing Association, charter, veto, VI, 501.

PESTHOUSE. Erection of, recommended, I, 592; Schenectady, veto, X, 806.

PETER, CZAR. Establishes capital at Petersburg, II, 1124.

PETER (Oneida Indian). Alleged fraud on transfer of land, II, 223.

PETERBOROUGH. Relief of distressed families at, II, 112.

PETERS, GEORGE. Brothertown Indian, convicted of murder, Legislature declines to pardon, II, 514, 515.

PETERS, WILLIAM. Entertainment of French commissioners, I, 510.

PETERS, WILLIAM R. Escheat, veto, IX, 816; grant of land by State, extending time to fulfill certain conditions, veto, X, 266, 376.

PETERSBURG (Russia). Establishment and growth, II, 1124.

PETITION. By Secretary Livingston for payment of salary, I, 200; from Albany — for dissolution of Assembly, 252; — for appointment of Charles Kerr as surgeon at Oswego, 258; — for removal of Fort Hunter garrison to Carrying Place, 258; from settlers north of Albany, 343; from Schenectady garrisons for blockhouses, 368; from Kinderhook for men for garrison and outscouts, 394; de Joncourt, claim for translating documents, 507; of traders at Oswego, 518; from Goshen for protection against Indians, 589; Ulster county regiment for pay, 613, 627; by Assembly to King, Lords and Commons, 687, 729, 768, 771, 775, 776; Assembly asserts right of, 730; for aid to New York Hospital, 743; Richard Morris, compensation as court clerk, 750; for new roads, 753; of Continental Congress presented to Lord Dartmouth, 770; from Coxsackie, in behalf of John Cumming, II, 20; from Tryon county committee, 25; from Tryon and Ulster counties, defense of frontier, 70; from Westchester county, relative to outrages in, 80; from Nicholas Richter and John Oekerman, for relief, 81; from James Huey and others, requesting grant of land, 82; from Saratoga, supply of salt, 82; from soldiers, relative to wives serving as nurses, 95; from Catherine Snell and others, relief, 117; from Tryon county, defense of frontier, 117; from Bellinger and another, appointment of surgeon, 117; from Moulton, for grant of lands, 117; from Ketchum and another, exportation of provisions, 127; from inhabitants of Vermont territory, 166; from inhabitants of Tryon county for relief, 168; from Francis Ossey, 307; from Stockbridge Indians, 373; from Columbia College, 393; town of Livingston, disorders in, 411; St. Regis Indians, purchase of land, 472; abuse of right of, 508; from Regents, 518; for pardon of Roswell Pratt, 929; St. Regis Indians, trustees, 938; Hopkinton Cavalry Company, use of arms, III, 180; Morgan abduction case, 185; in Albro case, 262; New York Orphan Asylum, 265; for repeal of act abolishing imprisonment for debt, 446; for Western House of Refuge, 748; Sally Ann Niles, sale of Niles' Register, 978; Frederick Colquhoun, IV, 84; Otsego county, restoring Aylesworth to citizenship, 294; right of, 712; V, 483; Millard Fillmore and others, canals, 506; from canal forwarders and boatmen, VI, 788; for removal of Judge Sanford, VII, 542.

PETRI, WILLIAM. Petition for appointment of, as surgeon, II, 117.

PETROLEUM. Refining, nuisance, report of State Board of Health, VII, 547.

PETTIBONE, RUFUS. Grant of Oneida lands, II, 894.

PETTIT, CHARLES. Assistant Quartermaster-general, letter from, II, 54.

PETTIE, MICAJAH. Brigadier-general, commands troops at Plattsburgh, II, 746.

PFEIFFER, ALMA V., CLARENCE AND PETER. Court of Claims, veto, X, 701.

PHARMACISTS AND DRUGGISTS. Clerks, regulating hours, act of 1900, X, 56, 96; sales of liquor by, amending Liquor Tax Law, 542. VETOES. New York, regulating prescriptions, etc., IX, 871; — regulating hours, X, 56.

PHARMACY. Amending Public Health Law, veto, X, 956.

PHELPS. Town meeting, legalizing, veto, VIII, 887.

PHELPS, CHARLES H. Clerk in State Treasurer's office, defalcation of, VI, 632.

PHELPS, GEORGE W. Relief, veto, VI, 306.

PHELPS, OLIVER. Purchase of Bayard's reservation, II, 1030.

PHELPS, DR. W. C. Surgical services, Thomas Orphan Asylum, appropriation, veto, X, 798.

PHELPS, W. L. M. Preparing railroad report, 1881, appropriation, veto, VII, 778.

PHILADELPHIA, NEW YORK. VETOES. Aid to Utica and Black River Railroad Company, amending act, VI, 92; relief from railroad burdens, VII, 847, new bill passed.

PHILADELPHIA, PENNSYLVANIA. Meeting of Congress in, I, 766; British evacuate, II, 50; convention at, for regulating prices, 84; Federal Constitutional Convention meets at, 271, 282; infectious disease at, 336; exports, comparison with New York, 596; population of, 596; Athenæum, distribution of statutes to, 994; Holland Land Company's office at, close of, III, 755; proposed monument to commemorate national independence, IV, 624, 681; V, 121; Centennial Celebration, 1876, VI, 302; relation of taxation to population and property, 412; benefits derived from Centennial Exposition, VII, 718; exportation of grain, IX, 557.

PHILBROOK, DANIEL. Extradition of, III, 748.

PHILIP. Indian King, war mentioned, I, 204.

PHILIPPINE ISLANDS. Acknowledgment of instruments executed in, X, 63; proposed illustration of social conditions at Pan-American Exposition, 125.

PHILIPS, AMBROSE. Colonial agent, thanks from, I, 181; communications from, 183.

PHILIPS, SILAS. Bond for return of arms, II, 772.

PHILIPS, WILLIAM. Estate, relief, veto, II, 688.

PHILIPSE, ADOLPH. Speaker, suggests resolutions against Court of Chancery, I, 229.

PHILIPSTOWN. VETOES. Opening highway, VI, 326; town business, 674; MacGuire dock, 705; ferry at, 813.

PHILLIPS, CHARLES A. Coroner's clerk, New York, claim, veto, X, 951.

PHILLIPS, JESSE S. Assembly, member of joint legislative committee on services in memory of former Governor Higgins, X, 963.

PHILOMATHIAN SOCIETY FOR MUTUAL IMPROVEMENT, SHERBURNE. Charter, veto, V, 129.

PHINNEY, E. Foreman of grand jury, Arnold case, II, 578.

PHIPPS, SIR WILLIAM. Governor of Boston, letter from, I, 49.

PHIPS, SPENCER. Acting Governor of Massachusetts, letter from, requesting aid in defending Louisburg, I, 358; urging union of colonies, 365, 366; Crown Point expedition, 572, 574.

PHOENIX. VETOES. Village, protection of bridge at, VI, 147; amending charter, VIII, 1123; canal bridge, IX, 216.

PHOENIX TRUST COMPANY, NEW YORK. Charter, veto, VI, 342.

PHYSICIANS. In military service, pay of, II, 134; and surgeons, college of, 317, 904; educational requirements, 905.

   VETOES. Evidence, amending Code, VIII, 639; evidence, confidential communications, IX, 44, new bill passed; civil service, exemption from examinations for municipal appointments, 230.

PICKERING, TIMOTHY. Colonel, Quartermaster-General, letter from, forage, II, 151; Indian treaty, 328; speech of Onondaga chiefs, 328; Secretary of State, letter from, treaty with Northwest Indians, 367.

PIEDMONT DRIVING CLUB, GEORGIA. New York buildings at Cotton States Exposition transferred to, IX, 582, 673.

PIERCE, BENJAMIN K. Lieutenant-colonel, correspondence relative to disturbance in northeastern part of State, III, 760.

PIERCE, CAROLINE E. Escheat, veto, VIII, 630.

PIERCE, FRANKLIN. President, approves views of Jefferson and Jackson, IV, 748; views on presidential election of 1856, V, 29.

PIERCE, JAIRUS. Court of Claims, veto, X, 442.

PIERCE, JOHN. Paymaster-General, attends Legislature, II, 133.

PIERCEFIELD. Highways, repairs, appropriation, veto, X, 428, 645.

PIERMONT. Macadamizing highways, veto, VII, 509.

PIERMONT CREEK. Northern boundary of Palisades Park, IX, 736.

PIERSON, CATHERINE D. Widow of William W. Pierson, Senate journal clerk, appropriation for residue of salary, veto, VII, 917, 1082; VIII, 109.

PIERSON, HENRY R. Chancellor of university, report on Clinton Papers, VII, 809.

PIERSON, WILLIAM W. Senate journal clerk, death of, appropriation for widow, veto, VII, 917, 1052; VIII, 109.

PIGEONS. VETOES. Homing and fancy, protection of, VIII, 633; Antwerp or homing, interference with, amending Game Law, X, 309.

PIKE. Sale of portion of schoolhouse site, veto, VII, 111.

PILLORY. Abolition of, recommended, II, 336.

PILON, ELIZABETH W. Board of Claims, veto, VIII, 889.

PILOTAGE. Act relating to, I, 623, 631; Hell Gate, Maine protests against, VI, 561; New York, veto, 911; Hell Gate, Connecticut's protest, VII, 47; complaint against laws, 436; protest from Connecticut, new act passed, 441.

PILOTS. Act relating to, I, 623, 631; New York, fees of, II, 888; fees, British vessels at New York, 918; licenses, III, 637; bill returned without action, 1032; New York, memorial from, IV, 156; act of Congress, 1837, 157; State law, 159; competition with New Jersey pilots, 160; Federal system recommended, 162; Hell Gate, Maine protests against fees exacted by, VI, 561; Hell Gate, reducing fees, veto, VII, 568; reduction of fees, 970; Hell Gate, relative to, veto, IX, 728; X, 316.

PILSBURY, AMOS. Appointed commissioner to investigate State prison affairs, V, 372; instructions to, 424, 430; report on Clinton prison, 425; report on Sing Sing prison, 431; member of Elmira Reformatory Commission, VI, 233.

PINCKNEY, CHARLES C. Draft of Federal Constitution, Congress determining questions relating to election of members, VIII, 985.

PINCKNEY, DANIEL. Commissioner, bridge over Onondaga creek, veto, VII, 476.

PINCKNEY, JOSEPH C. Colonel 6th Regiment, supplies from Union Defense Committee, VII, 500.

PINE. In Mohawk and Hudson valley, I, 146, 147.

PINE HILLS TUNNEL COMPANY. Appropriation for construction, veto, VI, 172.

PINE LAKE POSTOFFICE. Terminus of special highway, Fulton county, veto, VI, 598.

PINHORNE, WILLIAM. Speaker of Second Assembly, I, 12.

PINKLEY, JOHN W. New York policeman, relief, veto, X, 581, 817.

PINS. Corporations for manufacture of, II, 855.

PIPE LINES. General act, VII, 241. VETOES. Lease, Allegany reservation, VII, 73;—charters, 133;—taxes, apportionment between school districts, X, 439.

PIRACY. Practice of, in colony, I, 79.

PIRATES. Governor Fletcher recommends act relative to, act passed, I, 29; New York, charged with being receptacle of, 75.

PISER, ISAAC. Relief, veto, VII, 509, 1089.

PITCH. How made, I, 146; communication from Lords of Trade relative to, 188.

PITCHER, NATHANIEL. State road commissioner, III, 124; Lieutenant-Governor, becomes acting Governor on death of Governor Clinton, 197, 220; I, pref. xii; Georgia resolutions, III, 221; Ohio resolutions, 222; Morgan abduction matter, 222; maps from other States, 225; official service, I, pref. xii; autograph, III, 221.

PITSHKE, WILLIAM F. Justice, New York City Court, illness, suspension from office, VIII, 935; death of, 935.

PITT, WILLIAM. Secretary of State, urges large enlistments in colonies, I, 619; preparations for campaign against French, 632; completing reduction of Canada, 642; prosecution of war, 653.

PITTS, EDMUND L. Senate, member of insane asylum investigating committee, IX, 312.

PITTSBURGH. Prison at, solitary cells in, II, 1051.

PITTSBURGH, LACKAWANNA AND NORTHEASTERN RAILROAD COMPANY. VETOES. Changing name to "Central New York and Southwestern Railroad Company," VIII, 327; railroad aid, relief of certain towns, 371.

PITTSFIELD. Manufacture of arms at, II, 668, 681.

PITTSFORD. Payment for canal damages, VI, 861; rebuilding canal wall, 862.

PIUS IX. Pope, gift of engravings, etc., to State, IV, 455, 487.

PLAINS OF ABRAHAM. English victory on, I, 640.

PLANKROAD COMPANIES. General law for incorporation, IV, 379.

VETOES. Additional tolls, V, 656; White's Corners and Buffalo Plankroad Company, extending charter, VI, 161; Webster Plankroad Company, extending charter, 163; Albany county, tolls, 209; repealing certain acts, 596; Clyde and Rose, abandonment of road, VII, 267; amending act, 267; inspectors, exempting Ulster county, 414; Salisbury and Manheim Plankroad Company, renewing charter, 1106; Salina and Central Square Plankroad Company, amending charter, IX, 795; counties to acquire title, amending act, X, 952.

PLANT, MRS. HENRY B. Member of Cotton States Exposition Commission, 1895, IX, 582.

PLANTAGENET, THE. British vessel, engagement with American vessel at Fayal, II, 859.

PLANTERS. Benefits derived from flourishing trade, I, 259.

PLATE GLASS INSURANCE COMPANIES. Deposit of securities, veto, VII, 55, new act passed; statistics, 825.

PLATT, JONAS. Supreme Court, communication from, Burk case, II, 856; communication from, case of David Linus and others, 922; opinion, leasehold estates, IV, 360.

PLATT, THOMAS C. Resignation as United States Senator, VII, 555, 568; protests against appointment of William H. Robertson as collector, 557.

PLATT, ZEPHANIAH. Regent, death of, II, 629.

PLATTERS. For King's troops, Assembly declines to furnish, I, 282.

PLATTSBURGH. Deposit of arms, II, 682; militia in service, 736, 746, 822; deposit of military stores, 755, 769, 771; defeat of British, 803, 808; General Eddy's brigade at, 807; purchase of land by United States, 825; extending wharf, III, 822; normal school, V, 695.

    VETOES. Amending village charter, IV, 592; fire department, charter, VII, 64; taxes, collection of, 130, 265; stone crusher for highways, IX, 433; street improvement, borrowing money for, 723; elections, 819; taxes, sales and redemptions, applying General Village Law, 819; bonds for public improvements, X, 440; free public library, charter, 713, 717.

PLATTSBURGH NORMAL SCHOOL. Established, V, 695; reducing number of managers, veto, IX, 433.

PLEISSEN, VON. General, accompanies Prince Henry to Assembly chamber at his reception, X, 480.

PLEURO-PNEUMONIA. Resolutions relative to, VII, 537; expenditures, 698; repeal of appropriation acts, 990; Federal legislation requested, 990.

PLUMBAGO. Discovery of, III, 1036.

PLUMBERS. VETOES. Registration, New York and Brooklyn, VII, 933; registration and supervision, amending act, IX, 631, 729, 810.

PNEUMATIC RAILWAY AND EXPRESS COMPANY. Charter, veto, V, 670.

PNEUMATIC TUBES. Beach Pneumatic Transit Company, VI, 291; Engineer Tracy's report, 292, 299; act of 1868, noted, VII, 1031.

    VETOES. Amending act, VI, 289; supplemental act, 485; corporation using, franchise tax, IX, 794.

POINSETT, JOEL R. Secretary of War, correspondence with, militia claims, III, 691; communication from, wharf at Plattsburgh, 822.

POINT A'FERE. Conduct of British garrison at, II, 318.

POINT CHAUTAUQUA ASSOCIATION. Powers, defining and extending, veto, VIII, 294.

POISON. Attempt to, punishment of, III, 285; coloring matter in food products prohibited, X, 30.

POISON —(*Continued*).

VETOES. Regulating sale, VI, 710; sale in Kings county, VII, 936; liquid, preparation and sale of, IX, 447; applied to fruit trees while in blossom, prevention of, 811; sales on prescription, 860; paris green, preventing fraud in sale of, 318.

POLAND. Partition of, II, 138; sympathy for, III, 366.

POLLARD, CAPTAIN. Seneca chief, joins in address to Governor, II, 943.

POLICE. Increasing efficiency of, III, 941; reform in New York, V, 26, 53; metropolitan police district created, 27, 89; efficiency in New York, 181, 282; pensions, 181; at elections, 182; number in proportion to population, 283; New York, proposed reorganization, VI, 384; bi-partisan boards, 445; Troy, act relative to, VIII, 84; New York, enforcement of tenement-house ordinances, 317; Gravesend, police department, authorizing increased expenditures for, 1111; matrons in cities, act of 1891, 1147; patrolmen, pay in certain cities, act relative to, IX, 498; West Troy, act relative to, 539; better system needed, X, 208; system reorganized, 1901, 211; New York, department, reform needed, 505; proper functions of, 505; New York, police commission, decisions should not be subject to judicial review, 506.

VETOES. Richmond county, VI, 511; VII, 130; New York, board of, granting new trials, VI, 848; Troy, police commissioners, VII, 132; Buffalo, amending act, 266; district telegraph companies, 268, 416; pension fund, Brooklyn, 413; VIII, 523; false impersonation of, VII, 573; Binghamton, amending act, 752, 806; matrons, relative to, 804; VIII, 890; commissioners, New Lots, VII, 804; Yonkers, VII, 807; New York, salaries, 935; pensions, New York, 937; New York, additional patrolmen, 1087; reducing fares, Watervliet, 1101; captains, New York, increasing salary, VIII, 211; Ithaca, police department, 256; Saratoga Springs, establishing department, 292; Brooklyn, police station, fourteenth precinct, 294; police constables, Herkimer, 330; appointment of, agricultural and horticultural societies, 378; Rome, extending jurisdiction of fire commissioners over, 390; Oswego, police department, 469; New York, sergeants and detective sergeants, salaries, 524; Vienna, police regulations, 534, 1131; New York, park police, 638; IX, 52, 630; Buffalo department, VIII, 886; Brooklyn, patrolmen, 887; Utica, commissioners, 889; New York, patrolmen acting as precinct detectives, salaries, 889; New York pension fund, 891, 1129; IX, 728; X, 60, 474; Brooklyn bridge, compensation, VIII, 992; Brooklyn, amending charter, 1036; IX, 151, 152; department, amending act, VIII, 1038; Flatbush,—increasing policemen and

POLICE, VETOES — (*Continued*).

salaries of officers, 1110; — increasing salaries, IX, 107, 117; Brooklyn, police department, engineer, qualifications, 119; Rochester, vacations, 120; patrolmen, Long Island City, salaries, 141; New York Senate investigation, 1894, expense of committee, 484; departments, Albany, Troy, New York and Richmond county, reorganization, 489; Albany, pension fund, 632; New York, police department, 632; X, 176, 325; surgeons and doormen, New York, compensation, IX, 632; Brooklyn, police department, 633; New York, uniforms, 732; Brooklyn, park police pension fund, 733; Brooklyn, pension fund, time of payment, 781; Mount Vernon, police department, 787; Syracuse, police pension fund, 790; Utica, pensions, 790; Chautauqua county, charter, 795; New York,— reinstatements, X, 53, 713; — Wilson, relief, 61; — appointment of Cohen, policeman, 176; — patrolmen, qualifications, 176, 476, 580, 581; Buffalo, pensions, 276; Jamestown, pensions, 322; Medina, police department, 440; clerk to chief, second-class cities, 444; Rochester, police department, reorganization, 469; Jamestown, police, 472; New York,— promotions for bravery, 580; — police pensions, 580; — Bradley, Linehan, Cohen, Taylor, Pinkley and Barrett, relief, 581; Buffalo, amending charter, 583; New York, qualifications, 713; Buffalo, police department, 713, 805, 958; Rochester, police pension fund, 714; Rensselaer, members and compensation, 715; New York,— Duggan and Campbell, patrolmen, 806; — patrolmen, appointment, 806; — police clerks, 807; — McGee, policeman, 807; — appointment of Pinkley, 817; — Dillon, rehearing charges, 817; — Carrigan, patrolman, reinstatement, 949; — Hughes, patrolman, reinstatement, 950; — Devlin, roundsman, reinstatement, 951; Buffalo, police pension, Dowd case, 875.

POLICE COURTS. Second-class cities, amending act, veto, X, 586.

POLICE JUSTICE. Lansingburgh, how chosen, Governor's objections, V, 137; in villages, VI, 244; New York, extravagant salaries, 543; New York,— number increased, VIII, 794;— power of removal, IX, 579; — office abolished, 580; — city magistrate substituted for, 580.

VETOES. Oxford, election of, IV, 684; Geneva, appointment, VI, 216; New York, 397; Watervliet, 1032; Greene county, repealing act, 1035; Carthage, extending powers, VII, 78; villages, election of, 131; Wolcott, 389; Tonawanda, repealing act, 415; Northville, 932; Wellsville, legalizing acts, VIII, 132; Herkimer,

POLICE JUSTICE, VETOES — (*Continued*).

330; police courts, Brooklyn, 1036; Watervliet, amending act, IX, 87; Bellis, Penn Yan, legalizing acts, 258; Dansville, creating office, 471; Brooklyn, appointments, 502; Syracuse, bonds, fines and warrants, 790; Waterford, amending act, 867; second-class cities, jurisdiction, X, 593; acting, Jamestown, 717.

POLICE MATRONS. In cities, act for, VIII, 1147. VETOES. Relative to, VII, 804; — amending act, VIII, 890; — compulsory appointment, 1034, 1147.

POLICE POWER. Regulation, exhibiting pictures of suspected or convicted persons, veto, X, 585.

POLICY OF 1842. Description and purpose of, III, 1008, 1044; IV, 15, 58, 111, 208, 665; objections to, III, 1046; proposed amendment to confirm, IV, 60, 104; expectations not realized, 93; immediate effect of, 101, 225; Governor Wright's review of, 198; Assembly report, basis of act, 205, 209; statements relating to canal debt, 255; canal damages resulting from, 437.

POLITICAL CODE. Proposed, submission to Legislature, V, 596; report of commission, VI, 29; submitted to Statutory Revision Commission, 118.

POLITICAL DIVISIONS. General act, veto, IX, 272.

POLITICAL ECONOMY. Books on, school district libraries, III, 878.

POLITICAL PARTIES. See PARTIES; BI-PARTISAN BOARDS.

POLITICAL YEAR. When it begins, III, 1.

POLK, JAMES K. President, vetoes river and harbor bill, IV, 392; vetoes bill for public improvements in Wisconsin, 393.

POLL CLERKS. VETOES. Bi-partisan, election of, VII, 333; Queens county, compensation, VIII, 340; Cohoes, amending charter, IX, 64; New York, amending charter, 151; compensation in certain counties, 722.

POLL LIST. How disposed of, II, 35.

POLL TAX. In villages, action to recover, veto, IX, 62.

POLOCK, CORNELIUS. Claim, bridge tender, Watervliet, Court of Claims, veto, X, 593.

POLOPELS ISLAND. Proposed statue of Hendrick Hudson, veto, IX, 222.

POLYTECHNIC INSTITUTE, BROOKLYN. Charter, veto, VIII, 708.

POLYTECHNIC SCHOOL, CHITTENANGO. Established, III, 298; instruction in forms of government, 299.

POMEROY, MR. Manufacture of arms at Pittsfield, II, 681.

POMEROY, L. Director Western Railroad Company, communication from, III, 750.

POMEROY, THEODORE M. Appointed commissioner of State survey, fails to qualify, VIII, 255.

POMFRET. Establishing union free school district, veto, VIII, 82.

POMPELLY, CHARLES. Paymaster of militia, II, 764; funds received by, 765, 766.

POOLE, CHARLES D. W. Canal Department, appropriation for services, veto, IX, 716.

POOLE, THEODORE L. Commander G. A. R., opposes repeal of law exempting from taxation property purchased with pension money, IX, 115.

POOLS. Prohibited, VII, 32.

POOL-SELLING. Act relating to, VIII, 434; amending act, exempting certain association, veto, 631; tax, see POOL TAX; prohibited, constitutional provision, IX, 548, 602; act of 1895, 601.

POOL TAX. Receipts from, VIII, 663, 934, 1082; IX, 9.

POOR. Taxation for support of, I, 10; support of local, duty, II, 365; emigrants, support by State, 365; emigrants, bond to indemnify against expense of, 384; England source of poor laws, 914; unfortunate results of prodigal benevolence, 915; Poor Debtors Act, communication from New York grand jury, 923; care of, III, 176, 346; foreign, aid from auction duties, 246; revision of laws, 294; sale of liquor to paupers prohibited, 516; statistics, V, 192; number of insane, 583; results of Civil War, 581; insane, care of, VI, 114, 235; children, inquiry concerning, 235, 356, 528; expensive accommodations for, 873; State, number in almshouses, VII, 704, 829; aliens returned to their homes, 705, 830; orphan children, care of, VIII, 465; State should not furnish palaces for, IX, 831.

VETOES. Tax for support of, II, 95; employment of paupers, New York, VI, 982; Clinton, Niagara and Orleans, support of, VII, 367; children, exempting certain counties from act relative to, 413; State paupers, deficiency appropriation, 471; statutes, revision and consolidation, 505; freedom of worship in institutions for care of, 596; compilation of laws, 1124; Fulton county, relief, amending act, VIII, 130; overseers, compensation, 130; appeals from superintendent, 199; Kings county farm,—amending act, 292;—changing supervision, 594; officers giving orders on places where liquors are sold, 633; Greenbush, relief, 699; adult blind, New York, appropriation, amending act, 889; adult blind, New York, relief, 1036; relief and support, amending Revised Statutes, 1040; Jefferson county, amending act, 1121; Union Mission Chapel Association, Brooklyn, trusts, legacies and donations, 1127; indigent children, Westchester county, care of, 1159; non-residents, care of, IX, 68; sick, Long Island

POOR, VETOES — (*Continued*).
>   City, medical and surgical aid, 253; Newburgh, St. Luke's Home and Hospital, support in, payments for, 723; Lockport, poor fund, maintenance of provident woodyard, 785; Indian poor, support of, 802; soldiers, relief from Union Veteran Legion, 803; support, amending general law, X, 61; Westchester county, outdoor relief, 272; Jamestown, care of indigent sick, 472; soldiers and sailors, relief, 808, 809, 947.

POORHOUSE. System commended, III, 346, 378, 453; instruction of paupers in, 346; farms for, 409; number of inmates, 409; raising mulberry trees on farm, 514; insane inmates, investigation, V, 583; care of insane, VI, 235; limiting commitment of children to, 724; bad condition of, VII, 431, 528, 706.

>   VETOES. Keepers, Sullivan county, exemption, VII, 508; freedom of worship in, 596; Orleans, construction of, auditing claims, 1046.

POPE'S DAM. Purchase of, veto, IX, 80.

POPISH EMISSARIES. Alleged practices of, in colony, I, 400.

POPISH PRETENDER. Favored by French, I, 314, 318.

POPPENHUSEN, CONRAD. Institution at College Point, relative to taxation of, veto, X, 700.

POPPENHUSEN INSTITUTION AT COLLEGE POINT. Relative to taxation of, veto, X, 700.

POPPLE, ALURED. Secretary to Lords of Trade, communication as to Governor's relation to Legislature, I, 253; suggestion as to prorogation adopted, 258.

POPULAR SCIENCE MONTHLY. Quoted, university extension, government aid, IX, 20.

POPULATION. Of New York in 1771, I, 743; increase of, 750; census of white inhabitants, II, 164; basis of apportionment of Federal expenses, 184, 276; of New York and Philadelphia, 1807, 596; under Federal census, 1810, 704; Indians, 1819, 976; west of Genesee river, estimated, 1820, 1032; rapid increase in State, III, 303; ratio of colored to white, 717; average number per square mile varies according to commercial advantages, 814; census of 1840, IV, 42; State, 1845, 247; distribution of, 247; number of Indians, 249; colored in New York diminishing, 620; State census, 1855, 856; V, 9; statement of increase, 9; nativity, 10; required for new county, 225; eighth Federal census, 1860, 296; of United States in 1900, estimated, 753; in 1865, 775; one-half in cities, VI, 31; census of 1875, 950; of cities, certificate to be filed after each enumeration, IX, 678; requisite for incorporation of villages, veto, 866.

PORK. Frauds in, I, 530; inspection, 617, 749; II, 436, 439, 457, 513, 529; reports of inspection, 1113; improved inspection, III, 99; reduction of tolls, 505.

PORT BYRON. Erie canal, rebuilding wall, VI, 857. VETOES. Cemetery, VI, 1035; free school district, relief, VII, 265; State dam, enlargement, VIII, 452.

PORT BYRON AND CONQUEST TURNPIKE ROAD AND BRIDGE COMPANY. Amending charter, veto, V, 146; bill returned to Governor and approved, 148.

PORT CHESTER. VETOES. Amending village charter, VIII, 621; legalizing sewer bonds, 942; harbor master, creating office, X, 590.

PORT CHESTER FIRE DEPARTMENT. Charter amended, V, 574.

PORT CHESTER SAVINGS BANK. Amending charter, veto, VI, 441.

PORTER, DAVID. Captain, naval successes, II, 802.

PORTER, DAVID D. Commodore, communication from, defense of New York harbor, V, 567.

PORTER, ELBERT BALL. Escheat, veto, VII, 549.

PORTER, EUGENE D. Escheat, veto, VII, 549.

PORTER, PETER B. General, success in Niagara campaign, II, 802; thanked by Legislature and presented with sword, 832; letter from Governor Tompkins, reply, 839.

PORT GIBSON. Canal repairs at, VI, 860.

PORT JERVIS. Police justice in, VI, 277; number of excise licenses, 1887, VIII, 360; public building, veto, IX, 371; city charter, 1907, 679; dykes along Delaware river, veto, X, 946.

PORT JERVIS AND MONTICELLO RAILROAD COMPANY. Asks State aid, VI, 70.

PORTLAND. Special highway, veto, VIII, 879.

PORT MORRIS LAND AND IMPROVEMENT COMPANY. Amending charter, veto, VI, 593.

PORT MORRIS WAREHOUSE AND ELEVATOR COMPANY. Charter, veto, VI, 328.

PORTO RICO. Acknowledgment of instruments executed in, veto, X, 63; proposed illustration of social conditions at Pan-American Exposition, 125.

PORTRAITS AND ILLUSTRATIONS. Governors: Black, IX, 738; Bouck, IV, 1; Clark, 780; Cleveland, VII, 815; Clinton, De Witt, II, 897; Clinton, George, 1; Cornell, VII, 418; Dix, VI, 522; Fenton, V, 582; Fish, IV, 421; Flower, IX, 1; Higgins, X, 718; Hill, VIII, 1; Hoffman, VI, 1; Hunt, IV, 538; Jay, II, 358; King, V, 1; Lewis, II, 545; Marcy, III, 399; Morgan, V, 64; Morton, IX, 536; Odell, X, 180; Robinson, VII, 1; Roosevelt, X, 1; Seward, III, 706; Seymour, IV, 640; Tayler, II, 887; Throop, III,

PORTRAITS AND ILLUSTRATIONS—(*Continued*).

 269; Tilden, VI, 719; Tompkins, II, 616; Van Buren, III, 230; Wright, IV, 87; Yates, III, 1; Young, IV, 363.

 George Washington, II, 461; Lafayette, III, 110; Abraham Lincoln, V, 676; old and new capitol, VII, 268.

PORT RICHMOND. Village, road to New Springville, veto, VI, 330.

" PORTSMOUTH, THE." Used in cholera epidemic, V, 765.

PORTSMOUTH, VIRGINIA. Epidemic in, IV, 852.

PORTVILLE. Bridge over canal and Allegany river, veto, VI, 709.

PORT WARDENS. New York, fees of, II, 888; act relative to, V, 53, 95, 381; work of, 187; compensation a tax on commerce, VII, 163; status, legislation needed, 531, 714; board, cost of, 1891, IX, 11.

 VETOES. Expenses, appropriation, IX, 68; office expenses, appropriation, 83; services, assisting board of alienists, appropriation, X, 793.

" POSSE COMITATUS." Summoned, anti-rent troubles, III, 827, 830; described, IV, 145; proper use of, 245; in Delaware county, 246, 301; statutory provisions, 706, 728; suggested use in labor strikes, VIII, 1074.

POST. Between Albany and Boston, I, 136.

POST, DR. WRIGHT. Memorial of, anatomical museum for Columbia College, II, 389.

POSTAGE. Reduction of letter, IV, 45, 84.

POSTMASTERS. Number in State, 1821, II, 1068; at Manlius and Sandy Hill, removal of, 1068; Caldwell, Hartford and Poughkeepsie, removal of, 1069; Herkimer and Bath, suggested removal of, 1070; Little Falls and Oxford, removal of, 1070; Owego, removal of, 1072.

POSTOFFICE. Established, I, 34; memorial from Andrew Hamilton relative to, 42; new law passed, 129; revival of, recommended, 144; recommended by Washington, III, 803; appropriation for, Georgia opposes, 977; abolishing franking privilege, IV, 45, 84; reducing letter postage, 45, 84; Alabama proposes continuance of postal arrangements, V, 318; Albany, cession for, veto, VI, 449.

POST ROADS. Recommended by Washington, III, 803; State's relation to, 969.

POTASH. Inspection of, II, 457, 1093; exportation of, 1091; communication from inspector, 1113; adulteration, III, 391.

POTATOES. Sweet, cultivation of, III, 386; weights and measures, amending act, veto, VII, 414; size of barrels, veto, X, 317.

POTOMAC RIVER. Canal connection with Ohio river, III, 171.

POTSDAM. Normal school at, V, 695, 780; McCormick, justice of the peace, legalizing acts, veto, X, 813.

POTSDAM NORMAL SCHOOL. Established, V, 695, 780, 852; insurance, veto, VIII, 864; repairs and improvements, veto, 864.

POTSDAM AND WATERTOWN RAILROAD. Discharging judgment against, veto, IV, 693.

POTTER, REV. HORATIO. Memorial sermon on President Harrison, III, 914.

POTTER, PARACLETE. Prepares system of military tactics, II, 951, 953, 995, 998.

POUCHER, WILLIAM A. Member of Forest Investigating Commission, 1884, VIII, 23.

POUGHKEEPSIE. Legislature meets at, II, 17, 43, 50, 105, 132, 146, 163, 281, 348; IX, 688; Council of Safety and convention meet at, II, 17; convention on Federal constitution meets at, 283; removal of postmaster, 1069; charter of, V, 338; qualifications of voters on tax questions, 339; Hudson River Asylum for Insane located at, 763; authorized to borrow money for insane asylum site, 763; number of excise licenses, 1887, VIII, 359; Hudson River bridge, extending time for completion, 443; centennial anniversary of New York's ratification of Federal Constitution, 505; excise license fees, 1889, 686.

VETOES. Purchase of steam fire-engine, V, 338; First Congregational church, changing name, VI, 433; street railroads, discontinuing service during winter months, VII, 73; armory, erection, 481; bonding commissioners, transferring duties, 509; street railroads, changing motive power, VIII, 729; employees, term of service, amending charter, 751; amending charter, IX, 633, 634, 788.

POUGHKEEPSIE ASSOCIATED FIRE DEPARTMENT. Exempting property from taxation, veto, VIII, 878, 972.

POUGHKEEPSIE SILK COMPANY. Incorporated, III, 387.

POUND, CUTHBERT W. Senate, 1894, speech on New York Park Commission bill, IX, 435.

POWDER. Magazine at Fort Anne, I, 156; in New York recommended, 199; house for, at Schenectady recommended, 202; French furnish to Indians, 248; for King's troops, Assembly declines to furnish, 282; colony to furnish, 295, 310; supply for magazines, 314; to be stored in Fort George magazine, 352; royal instruction relative to powder duty, 357, 744; magazine supply exhausted, II, 149; loaned to Western Inland Lock Navigation Company, 365; manufacture of, 681; for artillery practice, 954; purchase of, Civil War, V, 414.

POWDER-HOUSE. At Schenectady recommended, I, 202; keeper of, appointment of counsel for, 532.

POWDER MAGAZINE. At Fort Anne, protection of, I, 156; in New York, recommended, 199; in New York, act relating to, II, 601, 618, 620, 636, 643, 649, 680; act for, near Albany, 683.

POWELL, ABNER. Board of Claims, veto, IX, 119.

POWELL, FRANK. Board of Claims, veto, IX, 119.

POWELL, JEREMIAH. President, Massachusetts General Assembly, letter from, scarcity of wheat and flour, II, 69.

POWELL, LENA AND MARIA. Board of Claims, veto, IX, 119.

POWELL, ORVILLE. Board of Claims, veto, IX, 119.

POWELL, PETER. Service of process on, Van Rensselaer rent, III, 825.

POWELL, SAMUEL S. Mayor of Brooklyn, communication on truant officers, V, 108.

POWER, CATHERINE LOUISA. Will, execution of certain provisions, veto, X, 391.

POWER, JOHN SCOTT. Escheat, veto, X, 958.

POWER, MARGARET J. Estate, escheat, veto, X, 958.

POWERS, GERSHOM. State agent, expenses of, military tract investigation, II, 991.

POWERS, JOHN R. New York dockmaster, claim, veto, X, 321.

POWERS, TIMOTHY. Bond for return of arms, II, 774.

POWNALL, THOMAS. Governor of Massachusetts, letter from, fire in Boston, I, 646.

PRATT, BENJAMIN. Appointed chief justice, I, 662.

PRATT, CALVIN E. Supreme Court, Roberts pardon case, IX, 251.

PRATT, DANIEL. Attorney-General, commissioner on quarantine, jurisdiction, report, VI, 778.

PRATT, GEORGE N. Bookkeeper, Mechanics and Traders' Savings Institution, statement by, VII, 56.

PRATT, ROSWELL T. Convicted of murder, pardoned, II, 923; petition for pardon of, 929.

PRATTSBURGH. Village, relative to, veto, VII, 806.

PRECEDENTS. Not binding on Legislature, III, 194.

PRECINCT. Committee of, power to continue denied, II, 28; revision of statutes relating to, 219.

PREFERENCE OF DEBTS. Restriction suggested, II, 986.

PREMIUM. See also BOUNTIES, COMMERCIAL. For service of privateers, I, 333; for domestic woolen cloth, II, 702; on canal loans, 1097; to encourage agriculture, III, 422; on sale of bank franchises, 471; on State loan, IV, 422, 474; on canal certificates, 598; on canal enlargement loan, 783, 834; proposed for best international decimal system of weights and measures and currency, V, 324; on interest on State debt if paid in coin, 491, 579; on coin for payment of general fund debt, VI, 167; on gold, reduction of, 249; improving manufacture of butter and cheese, and cultivation of hops, veto, VII, 1078; life insurance, Tax Law construed, X, 720.

PRENTICE, EZRA P. Assembly, member of insurance investigating committee, 1905, X, 825.

PREROGATIVE. Of Queen, threat to assert in colony, I, 166; fixing number and compensation of officers, 221; Governor Montgomerie commanded to sustain, 231; King expects submission to, 249; prorogation or dissolution of Assembly, 254; interfered with by triennial Assembly bill, 279; to appoint revenue officers, 293, 299; Assembly's limitation of, 204, 455, 456, 661; making peace and war, relations with foreign nation, 426; in military affairs, 428; as to appropriations, 489; power to confirm or repeal colonial laws, 506; Assembly disclaims intention to encroach on, 559; colony cannot limit, 661; limited as to colonial Legislature, 730; of Governor, prorogation of Legislature, II, 708.

PRESBYTERIAN SOCIETY OF STEPHENTOWN. Charter, veto, IV, 633.

PRESENTS TO GOVERNOR. Dongan, I, 11; Fletcher vetoes act for, 56; Queen Anne prohibits, 106, 148; Hunter protests against, 143, 145; prohibited, 530; salary voted for, declined, 738, 745.

PRESENTS TO INDIANS. I, 25, 44, 45, 46, 65, 82, 95, 128, 130, 132, 161, 173, 194, 196, 200, 257, 304, 310, 312, 319, 341, 346, 354, 376, 391, 406, 416, 417, 419, 421, 424, 434, 466, 505, 510, 513, 517, 526, 531, 537, 540, 568; II, 273, 342, 352, 377.

"PRESIDENT, THE." Frigate, British attack on, II, 690.

PRESIDENT OF CONGRESS. Letters from, II, 78, 83, 211; relative to provisions for Rhode Island, 69; assessment of States, 85; State quotas, 93; system of finance, 97; confederation of United States, 112; Vermont controversy, 178; representation in Congress, 190, 210; from Washington, accompanying Constitution, 298.

PRESIDENT OF THE COUNCIL. William Smith claims right to executive power after Bellomont's death, I, 90, 91; when, becomes acting Governor, 94; Peter Schuyler, government transferred to, 190; communication from Secretary Craggs relative to prorogation, 192; Rip Van Dam assumes executive authority, 238; George Clarke assumes executive authority, 254; Council's address to, 257; Cadwallader Colden assumes executive authority, 647.

PRESIDENT OF THE SENATE. When President of Council of Appointment, II, 3; powers in Council of Safety, 16; oath of, 22; when assumes executive office, I, pref. ix; member of Commission on Purchase of Executive Residence, VII, 178; member of New Capitol Advisory Board, VIII, 31; member of Board of Capitol Construction, veto, 213; member of New Capitol Commission, 1888, 610; first, Pierre Van Cortlandt, 1777, IX, 688.

PRESIDENT OF THE UNITED STATES. Election of, II, 297, 299, 322; George Washington chosen, 300; proposed erection of house for, in New York, 305; convenes Congress in extraordinary session, 398; powers under Militia Act, 398; proposed amendment as to eligibility

PRESIDENT OF THE UNITED STATES —(*Continued*).

of, 425; qualifications of, 433; expenditures under Fortifications Act, 440; reply to New York Legislature's address on relations with France, 446; power of appointment, 500; message, letter from, militia system, 532; election of, Twelfth Amendment, 537, 546, 608; Jefferson declines third term, 626; announces revocation of French decrees relative to commerce, 672; calls for troops, War of 1812, 742; proclaims treaty of peace, War of 1812, 824; ineligibility to re-election, proposed amendment, 828; III, 199, 786, 907, 908, 909, 929, 972; VIII, 691; Governor Clinton's comment on method of choosing, II, 1040; action relative to British act regulating commercial intercourse between Canada and United States, III, 23; congressional nomination of, Tennessee protests against, 31; proposed election by popular vote, 137, 184; proposed amendment, House of Representatives not to determine election of, 182, 199, 589, 591; election of, Governor Van Buren's comment on, 258; Louisiana proposition extending term to six years without re-election, 281; vetoes Lexington and Maysville road bill, 319, 391, 464; to see that laws and treaties are faithfully executed, 365; suggests revision of militia system, 405, 569; proposed amendment limiting power of appointment, 747, 786; correspondence with Governor Seward on disturbances in northeastern part of State, 760; qualifications of, 883; first death in office (William Henry Harrison), 914; assists in procuring examination of colonial documents in England, 935, 1016; IV, 175; action in McLeod case, III, 942; uniform date for election of, 972, 988; veto power, approved by Georgia, 977; opposes protective tariff, 1041; vetoes river and harbor bill, IV, 392; vetoes bill for public improvements in Wisconsin, 393; treaty power, 417; Secretary of Agriculture, member of cabinet, 505; death of Zachary Taylor, 572; election of 1860, effect of, V, 302, 394; Arkansas proposes alternate choice from slaveholding and non-slaveholding States, 354; calls out State militia, 356; calls for 300,000 men, 453; power to declare martial law, 465, 468; proclamation of emancipation, 473; memorial to, Federal use of New York canals, 506; message to Congress, New York canals, 506, 507; receives thanks of New York Chamber of Commerce, 507; title to office should be clear, 509; assumes extraordinary powers, 551; death of President Lincoln, 677; power to establish new governments in seceding States, 857; communication from, reciprocity with Canada in use of canals, VI, 363; requests States to furnish statues for statuary hall, 434; action relative to Louisiana disturbances, 771; election of 1876, action by Electoral Commission, VII, 33; statute relating to counting votes, 33; action on New York appointments,

PRESIDENT OF THE UNITED STATES—(*Continued*).

1881, 556; James A. Garfield assassinated, 678; attends with cabinet Yorktown Centennial Celebration, 736; presidential election, 1888, Governor Hill's comment on, VIII, 664, 896; provision for ex-Presidents, 691; term of office of President, Vice-President, six years, proposed amendment, 691; ex-Presidents, proposition to make them members of Senate, 692; when may call out State militia, X, 15; elections, amending Primary Elections Law, X, 149; assassination of President McKinley, 340.

PRESIDENTIAL ELECTORS. Method of choosing, II, 293, 294; III, 30, 38, 50, 56, 1020; functions of, II, 297; first election and meeting of, 299; proceedings by Legislature on election of, 299; chosen by Legislature, 322, 323, 633; election by districts, 471, 513, 750, 919, 924, 990; III, 156; Twelfth Amendment adopted, II, 537; electors chosen, 545; filling vacancies, 545; changing method of choosing, 1039; III, 30, 38, 50; Senators and Representatives not eligible as, II, 1062; to be chosen by districts, III, 51, 57, 1001; proposed election by popular vote, 184; variety of methods of choosing, 198; to be chosen at annual elections on general ticket, 248; uniform day for choosing, 908, 929; are State officers, VII, 33; how appointed, 35.

PRESS. Assembly asserts liberty of, I, 447; Governor Clinton's comments on, 450; free, secured by Constitution, III, 589, 645; V, 483; anti-slavery agitation, III, 589; restricting freedom of, X, 340.

PREVILLE, OLIVER. Claim, relative to, veto, VII, 805.

PREVOST, JOHN B. Member of Commission on Astor Claim, II, 867.

PRICE, JOHN H. Canal Department, appropriation for services, veto, IX, 716.

PRICE, RODMAN M. Governor of New Jersey, complains of New York violation of quarantine agreement, V, 35; member of New Jersey commission to procure Constitutional Convention, 325.

PRICES. Regulated by law, II, 25; New Haven Convention plan not accepted by all States, 46; joint committee of Legislature recommends further regulation of, 77; acts and proceedings relative to limitation of, 83, 84, 87; of labor, advance in, 349; of provisions, advance in, 349; relation of currency to, VI, 754, 759; principles applicable to regulation of, 969; influence of legal tenders, 970.

PRIMARY ELECTIONS. Act relative to, VII, 839, 978; general act, VIII, 386; act of 1898, IX, 852; act amended, presidential elections, X, 149; enrollment in towns, 417; transfer of voters from one district to another, 507; regulations, amendments of 1903, 508; more legislation needed, 612; judicial review authorized, 613; direct nominations, 847; in second-class cities, 895.

PRIMARY ELECTIONS — (*Continued*).

VETOES. Elmira, regulating, .VIII, 386; amending act, 890; oaths, town clerk to administer, X, 161; Monroe county, enrollment, 257; general amendments, 420, 442; enrollment books, publishing list of electors, 700; ballots, written consent of citizens to use of name, 709.

PRIME, ALANSON J. Commissioner of deeds, Yonkers, legalizing acts, veto, IX, 368.

PRIMOGENITURE. Abolished, IV, 712.

PRINCESS OF SAXE-GOTHA. See SAXE-GOTHA.

PRINCE HENRY. See HENRY, PRINCE.

PRINCE OF WALES. See WALES, PRINCE OF.

PRINCE, GARVIS. Trustee, Binghamton Insane Asylum, charges against, not removed, VII, 443.

PRINCES BAY. Cession of land for lighthouse at, III, 178.

PRINCIPAL AND AGENT. Factors, III, 89; breaches of trust, V, 190, 294, 387.

PRINDLE, HORACE G. Chenango county judge, charges against, VI, 440.

PRINDLE, JOSEPH. Bond for return of arms, II, 774.

PRINTING. Reducing expense of, V, 92; legislative, legalizing Bloomingdale Asylum investigation, act relative to, VIII, 793.

VETOES. Public or legislative, defining, VII, 1120; Governor's message, printing in German, VIII, 251; legislative, continuing appropriation of 1885, 252; legislative, 1886, appropriation, 255; report, State Dairymen's Association, extra copies, 860; colonial history, volume 15, deficiency, 866; Sheridan memorial, 875; legislative, amending act, 891, 1037; civil list, appropriation, 1038; New York House of Refuge, establishing plant, IX, 771; legalizing legislative resolutions, 814; Albany, paying debts for, 869; report, Louisiana Purchase Exposition, appropriation, X, 796; report, birds of New York, appropriation, 797; nature study and extension bulletins, 797; Forest, Fish and Game Commission, seventh report, appendix, 797.

PRIOR, JOHN. Colonel, commands militia at Plattsburgh, II, 822.

PRISON ASSOCIATION, NEW YORK. Memorial from, V, 486; required to inspect penal institutions, 526; appropriation for, 527; report, 601, 757; VI, 143; general purposes of, V, 697; authorized to appoint prison investigating commission, 698; VI, 18; communication from prison discipline committee of, 261; compilation of criminal statistics, veto, VIII, 122.

PRISON DISCIPLINE SOCIETY. Payments for prison chaplains, III, 977.

PRISONERS (General). Providing for custody of, II, 14; inquiry concerning, 20; exemption from military service, 43; United States, to be received in jails, 304.

PRISONERS (General)—(*Continued*).

   VETOES. Civil, maintenance in certain counties, VI, 596, 706; Albany county, commitments, etc., IX, 730; Hardy, escape, claim for capture, X, 62; regulating exhibition of pictures, 585; Chinese, Essex county, 701, 708; United States, boarding in Cattaraugus county jail, 706.

PRISONERS (Military, Colony). French, maintenance of, I, 166, 327, 328, 375, 388, 445; Spanish, allowance to, 328; to be sent out of colony, 329, 330, 624; sent to St. Domingo, 334; Assembly neglects to provide for, 344; English, exchange of, 409; Colonel Johnson's certificate as to French, 441; exchange of, 467, 470, 474, 476, 486, 489, 492, 500, 507, 510, 519; claims for subsistence, 478, 508, 608; Mohawks deliver, to Johnson, 486.

PRISONERS (Military, State). Regulations concerning treatment of, II, 25; exchange of, 33; accounts relating to, where presented, 33; exemptions from service, 43; New York officers in custody of British, 101; in New York and on Long Island, relief of, 116; retaliation in treatment, 116; American, compensation for losses, recommended, 168; Francis claim for support of, 259; William Gray, War of 1812, death of, 938; Civil War, New York men, V, 405.

PRISON INVESTIGATING COMMISSION. Appointed, 1824, III, 22; appointed, 1854, IV, 723, 777, 786; Prison Association authorized to appoint, V, 698; new commission created, 1876, VI, 942; VII, 9; report, 9.

PRISON LABOR. See also CONVICT LABOR. Regulations concerning, II, 364; investigation of contracts, V, 425; injuriously affected by Civil War, 524; objections to contract system, 757; State system, 842; employment should be on State account, VI, 18, 109; commission on, 109, 234; contract system prohibited in Elmira Reformatory, 110; reform commission created, VIII, 168; general act, 1888, 477; prohibited, act of 1892, IX, 138; constitutional provisions, 181, 549, 559, 653; manufacturing clothing, etc., for institutions, 181; on highways, 181, 329, 740; goods manufactured in and imported from other States, branding required, act unconstitutional, 329; X, 9; license to sell foreign prison-made goods, IX, 329; by contract prohibited, employment of prisoners provided for, 656; Governor Black's comment on, 1897, 739; new system successful, 831; importation into State of prison-made goods from other States should be regulated by Congress, X, 111.

   VETOES. Prohibiting manufacture of certain articles in penal institutions, IX, 464; on highways near Sing Sing prison, 775; convict-made goods, sales and license fees, 813; convict-made goods, labeling, repealing certain acts, 813.

PRISON LABOR REFORM COMMISSION. Created, VIII, 168; report not acted on, 478.

PRISONS. See also STATE PRISONS. Unsatisfactory condition of, II, 981; schools in, III, 289; benefits of system, 400; system highly commended, 446; better classification of offenses and offenders needed, IV, 785; criminal statistics, compilation, veto, VIII, 122; International Prison Congress, delegate to, 127; number of inmates, 1889, 821; United States has none, IX, 655; commission on prison buildings, X, 863; commission on probation system, 863.

PRIVATEER. French near New York, expedition against, I, 117, 119, 128, 131.

PRIVATEERS. Governor Fletcher recommends act relative to, act passed, I, 29; premiums to, in French War, 333; infesting American coast, 467.

PRIVATE LAWS. See STATUTES. Instruction relative to, I, 210; notice of application for, 210, 782; IX, 676; X, 21; bills for, interested party should be heard, II, 191, 544, 782, 1081, 1112; excessive number of, 449, 574; V, 252, 613; VI, 45, 117, 153, 277, 550, 640; VII, 535, 939; VIII, 342; IX, 676, 848; X, 21, 33, 503, 626; comparative statement, 1894 to 1900, 504; persons interested should bear expense of, 865.

PRIVATE PURPOSE. Question as to meaning. of, IV, 56.

PRIVILEGES. Exclusive, power of Legislature to grant, II, 466, 476, 783; VIII, 411, 880; granted to Robert Fulton, III, 151; auction sales, 246.

VETOES. Ithaca, School Act, VII, 1105; Lake Champlain ferry, VIII, 411, 463; ferry between Tarrytown and Nyack, 880.

PRIVILEGES AND IMMUNITIES. Equal, granted by Leisler's Assembly, I, 16; recommended by Congress for French subjects, II, 91; insurance by non-residents, 613; steamboat franchise, 1026; State Constitutions, slavery, 1041; bankrupt laws, III, 844; interstate commerce, 981; not to be affected by slavery, V, 308, 325; Fourteenth Amendment, 790.

PRIVY COUNCIL. Recommends approval of New York act relative to Connecticut boundary, I, 208; objections to bills prohibiting sale of Indian goods to French, 237; supervision of colonial affairs, IV, 178; scarcity of New York documents, 182.

PROBASCO, SAMUEL. See Mesereau claim, veto, VII, 774.

PROBATES, COURT OF. See COURT OF PROBATE.

PROBATES, JUDGE OF. Powers of, II, 257.

PROBATE AND SUCCESSION TAX. Recommended by Governor Hill, VIII, 1067.

PROCEDURE. Act relative to, in certain cases, I, 11; arrest on civil process, 11; habeas corpus, II, 943; judicial, commission to

PROCEDURE—(*Continued*).

revise, III, 611; reform in, 773; commission under third Constitution, IV, 366, 654; V, 596; VI, 29; VII, 182; in pardon
cases, IV, 405, 435, 788, 845; Code of 1848, 414; affirmance
of judgment, 533; further revision needed, 655; limiting issue
of injunctions, V, 57; proceedings for removal of judges, 723;
injunctions against corporations, VI, 122; Governor Robinson's
discussion of, VII, 168; legislative, commission on, 1895, IX,
676; commission on, 1895, 680; divorce, decision and entry of
judgment, X, 224; admission of inmates to insane asylums,
reform needed, 331; appeals, delay in capital cases, 344; prompt
argument of appeals in capital cases, 345; reforms suggested
by Commission on Law's Delay, 516; legislative, trial of Justice
Hooker, 827.

VETOES. Preference of certain actions, IV, 510; Code of Remedial
Justice, amendments, VII, 134; habeas corpus, certiorari, 197;
summary proceedings, New York, 413; removal of officers, New
York, 413; justices' courts, verification of pleadings, 506; judgment on attachment, 1093; trial, exceptions, IX, 625; demurrer,
amendments after decision, 791; trials, postponement, 791; preferred causes, X, 159, 173; undertaking given by Indian, prosecution of, 169; pleadings, copartnership, denying allegations
of, 309; review of assessments for local improvements, 316;
condemnation, proceedings necessary, 442; compulsory accountings in equity actions, 443; orders of publication, papers for,
443; judgment, notice of application, 444; rapid transit, condemnation proceedings, 446; attachment, undertaking on discharge, 534; foreign wills and letters of administration, certification, 585; trials, requests to find, 587; appeal, decision on,
587; possession of property on giving security, 590; trial in certain counties, 709; substituted service, publication, 952.

PROCESSIONS. Governor Hoffman's discussion of, VI, 374; act regulating, 377; amending act, veto, VII, 335.

PROCLAMATION. Governor Sloughter, recalling absentees, I, 22; acting
Governor Ingoldesby, fast day, 24; Governor Fletcher,— dissolving
First Assembly, 31; — adjourning Assembly, 64; Council,— an-
nouncing death of Governor Bellomont, 91; — convoking Assembly,
91; Lieutenant-Governor Nanfan, dissolving Seventh Assembly, 93;
Governor Cornbury,— convening Assembly in extraordinary session,
119; — at Burlington, New Jersey, dissolving New York Assembly,
126; Governor Hunter, at Burlington, New Jersey, proroguing New
York Assembly, 149; Governor Burnet,— requiring return of New
York residents in Canada, 202; — dissolving Seventeenth Assembly,

PROCLAMATION —(*Continued*).

220; Governor Montgomerie, for arrest of horse thief, 238; Governor Hardy, inviting River Indians into settlements, 607; Lieutenant-Governor Delancey, adjourning Assembly, 618; Governor Moore, for conviction of New York rioters, 726; Governor Clinton, convening Legislature in New York, 780; Council of Safety, convening Legislature, II, 7; Governor Clinton,— convening Legislature at Poughkeepsie, 17, 43, 50, 105, 132, 146, 163, 182; — convening Legislature at Kingston, 75, 96, 186; — against plundering inhabitants of Long Island, 80; — convening Legislature at Albany, 87, 114, 289, 301; by Governor Trumbull, announcing repeal of Connecticut embargo laws, 110; Congress,— appointing thanksgiving day, 152; — appointing fast day, 170; Governor Chittenden, asserting authority of Vermont, 178; Governor Clinton, convening Legislature at New York, 195, 217, 251; British court, on West India trade, 197; Congress, announcing ratification of treaty of peace, 206; Governor Jay, convening Legislature at Albany, 420; President, revocation of French commercial decrees, 672; Governor Tompkins, extraordinary session, 800; President Madison,— War of 1812, 824; — appointing thanksgiving day, 824; Governor Tompkins, appointing thanksgiving day, 824; Governor Yates, extraordinary session, III, 38; Governor Throop, extraordinary session, 392; Governor Seward,— offering reward for conviction of participants in disturbances in northeastern part of State, 760; — anti-rent troubles, 775, 835; Governor Wright,— declaring Delaware county in State of insurrection, IV, 236, 246, 297; — revoking insurrection proclamation, 238, 326; Governor Fish, public health, Asiatic cholera, 468; Governor Hunt, extraordinary session, 578; Governor Seymour, extraordinary session, 694; Governor of Massachusetts, ceding Boston Corners to New York, 817; Governor King, Staten Island quarantine, V, 99, 103; Governor Morgan,— calling out militia, 400, 403; — offering war bounties, 454; President Lincoln, emancipating slaves, 473; Governor Seymour, draft riots, 546; Governor Fenton,— fall of Richmond, 676; — announcing death of President Lincoln, 677; Governor Robinson,— convening Senate in extraordinary session, Ellis case, VII, 122; — obstructing railroads, 153; Governor Hill,— convening Legislature in extraordinary session, census, VIII, 132; — extraordinary session, July, 1888, 643; Governor Flower, extraordinary session, April, 1892, IX, 84; Governor Black, extraordinary session, July, 1898, 876; Governor Roosevelt,— extraordinary session, May, 1899, X, 64; — Dewey reception days to be public holidays, 1899, 72; Governor Higgins, calling extraordinary session, Hooker case, 819; Governor of Florida, proposed International Isthmian Exposition, 866.

PROCTOR, HENRY A. General, defeated by Americans, II, 786.

PRODUCTS. Statistics of, II, 1048.

PROGRESS HEALTH INSURANCE COMPANY, NEW YORK. Charter, veto, VI, 332.

PROHIBITION. Bill providing for, veto, IV, 753; recommended by Governor Clark, 800; act passed, unconstitutional, 802, 858; V, 19; violations of law, IV, 859; high license a possible substitute for, VIII, 362; Governor Hill on, 1890, 920; amendment, 1890, adopted by Legislature but not submitted to people, 923, 1060.

PROPERTY. Act to regulate transportation of, I, 16; security of, II, 62; destruction of, by enemy, inquiry concerning, 162; public, regulating purchases from soldiers, 189; ascertaining value of taxable, 219; taken for public use, 329, 330, 522, 585, 646, 663; III, 73; IV, 347, 496, 694; V, 517, 652, 880; VI, 90, 97, 217, 605, 642; VII, 241, 775, 866, 1015, 1108; VIII, 730, 874; IX, 513; X, 761, 800; private, when cannot be taken without consent, II, 633, 714; private, cannot be taken for private use, 663; VI, 605; VII, 243; foreign control, dangers of, II, 1032; heirs, vested rights, Legislature cannot interfere with, 1036; statistics of, 1048; mortgages held by non-residents to be deemed personalty, III, 440; slaves, status of, 921, 1030; personal, assessment, IV, 64; ownership of, not required to hold office, 109, 137; right of, cannot be destroyed by legislation, 761; census statistics, 1855, V, 10; preventing free use of, VI, 95; amount held by certain companies, 119; land under water of lakes, 156; intoxicating liquors, when may not be confiscated or destroyed, VIII, 361, 367; burial grounds, Legislature cannot authorize control of, by other cemetery association without consent, 712.

VETOES. Private, protection of, VII, 640; malicious destruction of, VIII, 890; where to be assessed, IX, 626; State, appraisal and inventory, 775; attachment, claim, how tried, X, 807.

PROROGATION OF LEGISLATURE. Power of, vested in colonial Governor, I, 7, 18; Assembly prorogued, 147, 153; Assembly not to be dissolved for want of, 192; adjournment not same as, 254; practice of proroguing instead of adjourning adopted, 258; followed by adjournment without quorum, effect considered, 263; by Governor Clinton, II, 7; Governor Clinton threatens if Assembly adopts certain resolutions, 144; Governor Tompkins, 708; III, 1005; Governor Hoffman suggests revival of executive power, VI, 401.

PROTECTION (Industrial). To American manufacturers, II, 525, 572; manufacture of powder, 681; domestic manufactures, 702; III, 23; manufactures as basis of national independence, II, 855; encourage-

PROTECTION (Industrial)—(*Continued*).

ment of, 899, 1091; III, 420; New York favors, 24, 1041; South Carolina against, 218; Georgia protests against encouragement of domestic manufactures, 221; Connecticut favors, 906, 972; Alabama against, 907; Mississippi against, 913; Massachusetts favors, 929; New Jersey favors, 988; President opposes, 1041; tariff of 1846, ill effects of, IV, 570, 616; lack of, causes depression in manufacturing business, 812; special, at war with general sentiment, VI, 247; a false system, 248; presidential election, 1888, Governor Hill's comment, VIII, 664.

PROTECTION HOSE COMPANY NO. 3, BINGHAMTON. Charter, veto, VI, 179.

PROTECTIVES NO. 1, ROCHESTER. Amending charter, veto, VI, 329.

PROTEST. Against parliamentary encroachments on colonial rights, I, 703, 730.

PROTESTANT EPISCOPAL CHURCH. VETOES. Incorporation of churches connected with, amending act, VIII, 618; vestrymen and church wardens, annual election of, 618.

PROTESTANT EPISCOPAL CHURCH FUND FOR AGED AND INFIRM CLERGYMEN. Incorporating trustees, veto, IV, 637.

PROTESTANT REFORMED DUTCH CHURCH, DUANESBURGH. Changing name, veto, V, 125.

PROTESTANTS. Principal settlers in New York, I, 688, 698.

PROUDFIT, ALEXANDER. Trust fund, charter, veto, II, 717.

PROVIDENCE. Convention at, New York not to be represented, II, 108.

PROVIDENCE PLANTATIONS. Resolution of Congress, supplies for, II, 69.

PROVIDENT INDUSTRIAL INSURANCE COMPANY. Charter, veto, VIII, 414.

PROVINCIAL CONGRESS. First, meeting of, I, 778; Second, meeting of, 778; Third, meeting of, 778; Fourth, meeting of, 778; ratifies Declaration of Independence, 778; name changed, 778; temporary expedients, II, 27; bills of credit issued by, defaced, to be canceled, 77; journals and records to be transcribed, 542, 543; III, 935, 1035; journals of, copies transmitted to M. Vattemare, IV, 385.

PROVISIONS. Scarcity of, in Indian country, I, 300; for expedition against West Indies, 301; possible market for, 302; for militia at Oswego, 339, 369, 389, 410, 440, 459, 566; for militia on frontier, 362, 440; for Indians in Canadian expedition, 376; supplying transportation of, for army, 386; reported abuses relative to supply of, 388; for Canadian expedition, 391, 620; for Albany rangers, 402; fusileers at Albany, 409; transporting provisions to Albany, 410, 436; for Saratoga, 413; exportation of, restricted, 564, 596, 600; for militia and Indians, 607; captured at Fort Frontenac, 625; for troops in Indian war, 677; certain persons refuse to sell, II, 34;

PROVISIONS—(*Continued*).

embargo on, 46; export of, 68, 72; scarcity of, in Rhode Island, 69; scarcity of, in Massachusetts, 69, 72; production of, limited by the war, 73; clandestine exportation of, 73; impressment of, 99, 134; plentiful supply of, 106; Washington states scarcity of, 122; dangers resulting from scarcity of, 123; act supplying enemy with, veto, 129; for Indians visiting Albany, 273, 342; advance in price of, 349; inspection of, 436, 439, 457.

PROVOOST, DAVID. Dispute with DePeyster, I, 156; carries copies of instructions to Assembly, 203.

PROVOST MARSHAL-GENERAL. Communication to Governor of Minnesota, relative to quotas, V, 619; information relative to New York quotas, 621.

PRUSSIA. Partition of Poland, II, 138; interest in education, III, 455.

PRYOR, ROGER A. Counsel, Senate investigation of trusts, 1888, VIII, 843.

PUBLIC ACCOUNTANTS. VETOES. Exemption from examinations, X, 239; New York, Feely claim, 690.

PUBLIC ACCOUNTS. Statement of, I, 63, 66, 73, 202; commissioners of, 89, 96, 100, 103; relative to Receiver-General's accounts, 164; examination of, 199; Governor presents abstract of, 252; bills of credit, deficiency in sinking fund, 269; expenses of Canadian expedition to be sent to Duke of Newcastle, 441; how verified, 478; appropriations for Indian presents, 518; tax for, settlement of, II, 124, 125, 147; settlement of, veto, 172, 288; commissioner of, 172, 184; commissioners, report, V, 486.

PUBLIC ADMINISTRATOR. In New York, complaint relative to, III, 216; powers limited as to effects of deceased sailors, 216.

VETOES. New York, amending Revised Statutes, VI, 583; regulating bureau of, 584; Kings county, IX, 792; New York, execution of certain provisions in Power will, X, 391.

PUBLIC BUILDINGS. See also CAPITOL and NEW CAPITOL. For State officers to be erected in Albany, II, 397; repair of, 515, 516; Governor Clinton's message relative to, 934; deposit of maps and plans of, III, 934; uniform supervision needed, VI, 650; title to site should be undisputed, VII, 541; trustees, office created, 837, 982; cost of, 1891, IX, 11; expenditures, 1900, X, 182; new building for State Library and Department of Education, 741; plumbing, heating and lighting, 741.

VETOES. New York and Brooklyn, exemption from taxation, VII, 267; foreign flags not to be displayed on, IX, 527; act passed, 1895, 527; general repairs and improvements, 768; employees and furniture, appropriation, X, 573; New York, commissioners,

PUBLIC BUILDINGS, VETOES — (*Continued*).

    costs, 582; New York, court buildings and jail, 582; State, control of repairs, additions and alterations, 586; Genesee, authorizing erection of, 960.

PUBLIC CREDIT. Restoration of, recommended, I, 77, 97, 142, 149; II, 254; act to preserve, mem., III, 1008; exhaustion of, canal policy, IV, 100; effect of act of 1842, IV, 101; should be scrupulously maintained, V, 492.

PUBLIC DEBT. Acting Governor Ingoldesby urges provision for, I, 28; act for payment of, 32, 34, 81, 172, 504, 623, 646, 681; amount of, 1692, 34; Governor urges payment of, 63, 116, 155, 553; excise money appropriated for, 171; *caveat* against, 175; procuring royal assent to bill for payment of, 180; payment of, bills of credit authorized, 264; Colonel Johnson's claim, 473; payment of, urged, 492, 515; Governor Burnet's claim against colony, 592; Amherst, loan for war purposes, 637; partial payment of, 639; payment of Amherst loan, 646; funding, plans for, II, 158; United States, contribution for, 186; provision for payment of, 199; national, arrears of interest, 218; United States, duties exclusively devoted to payment of, 276; act for relief of creditors, 312; amount of, 1822, 1098; 1823, III, 29; beginning of, reign of Henry VI, III, 324; must not be repudiated, 1047; IV, 40, 46, 48, 86.

PUBLIC EXCHANGE. Amending charter, veto, VI, 593.

PUBLIC FUNDS. Oneida county, reimbursing collector for losses, unconstitutional, VII, 753; X, 275; bank failure, deposit of public funds, Legislature cannot direct reimbursement of officers, VI, 334.

    VETOES. Schaub, relief, failure of bank, VI, 334, 591; New Hartford, reimbursing collector, 701; Canandaigua, local tax, reimbursement for loss of property, VII, 569; Sangerfield, refunding surety for payment on supervisors' bond, 753; Binghamton, judgment against superintendent of streets, proposed payment by city, 1018; Chatfield, loss of public funds, Elbridge, relief, X, 275.

PUBLIC HEALTH. See also INFECTIOUS DISEASES; HEALTH OFFICER. Distillation of rum and burning of oyster shells in New York prohibited, I, 103; smallpox in colony, 240, 242, 280; smallpox in West Indies, 315; infectious diseases, Governor urges prevention of, 316; II, 336, 344; lazaretto on Governor's island, 382; New York, sanitary powers, 433, 451, 571; communications relating to, 520; local sanitary regulations, 537, 542, 1018; III, 395; fever hospital, 12; receipts by commissioners, 100;

PUBLIC HEALTH — (*Continued*).

act relating to, 395, 400; cholera epidemic of 1832, 399, 401; 1849, IV, 468; act of 1832 revived, 468; general act, 470; communication from Secretary of State, United States, 704; investigating condition of emigrant vessels and passengers, 720; New York, too many officials, V, 81; floating hospital, New York, 184, 278, 378; vaccination of school children, 189; New York, scientific sanitary regulations needed, 294, 386; quarantine diseases, what included in, 418; in metropolitan district, 701; metropolitan sanitary district established, 702; metropolitan board of health established, 702; New York, department established, VI, 129; act relating to Brooklyn, 129; New York, board reorganized, 627; State Board of Health established, VII, 14, 529; Brooklyn, amending charter, health department, 455; abandoned canals cause malaria, 517; nuisance, New York and Brooklyn, report of State board, 547; abandoned Chemung canal, nuisance, 575; local boards needed, 710; Ogdensburg, amending charter, sewers, VIII, 97; State board reorganized, 175; New York, act relative to, 430; animals as sources of disease, IX, 179; should be a subject of State jurisdiction, 207; duty of Federal officers at foreign ports, 208; New York, water supply, sanitary protection, 225; sanitary inspection of steamboats, railroad stations and cars; State sanitary commissioner, 234; effect of cemeteries, Newtown, 255; preventing pollution of Oswegatchie river, 385; New York, Garbage Disposal Act, 1900, X, 57; revision of quarantine laws, 1900, 119; communication from State commissioner of health relative to pollution of waters of New York bay, 523; investigation as to infectious and contagious diseases, 624; inspecting sources of water supply, 743.

VETOES. Brooklyn, extending jurisdiction of board, VI, 517; Kings county, act to establish board, 518; milk, adulteration of, 710; Brooklyn, department, relative to, 415; extending village limits for health purposes, 416; special agent, provision for, 582; reclaiming overflowed lands, Jefferson and St. Lawrence counties, 934; board of health, Saratoga Springs, appointment of health physician, 1098; New York, service of summons in actions for penalties, 1117; State board, sanitary work, appropriation, VIII, 254; improvement of State ditch, Onondaga county, 377; cities and villages, amending act, IX, 151; vital statistics, registration of, 238; Seneca Falls School of Anatomy, dissections, 264; restricting rules of State board, 367; depositing refuse matters in waters about New York, repeal, 384; penalties, collection, 504; pharmacy, practice of, 532; Corning, waters of Chemung

PUBLIC HEALTH, VETOES — (*Continued*).

river, 719; local boards, amending general act, 720; medicine, practice of, admission to examinations, 803; dentists, displaying professional signs, 803; medicine, license to practice, 803; New York, health department, pension fund, 804; Brooklyn, offensive trades, X, 57; amending Penal Code, 63; New York anti-toxin accountant, compensation, 160; New York, removal of garbage and night soil, 177; adulteration of drugs, chemicals, etc., 447.

PUBLIC HEALTH LAW. Vital statistics, V, 863; enacted, 1893, IX, 206.

PUBLIC INSTRUCTION. Department established, IV, 716; department, rooms in new capitol, VII, 694; increasing salary of deputy superintendent, VIII, 565.

VETOES. Amending Consolidation Act of 1864, VII, 442; department, printing bulletins, 494; amending general act, 507; VIII, 293; department, deputy superintendent's salary, 72, new bill passed.

PUBLIC LAND (United States). Maryland proposition as to proceeds of, II, 1079; New York Assembly committee report on, 1079; distribution, 1862, for agricultural colleges, 1080; Ohio resolutions, 1117; Massachusetts resolutions, 1119; III, 929; Tennessee resolutions, 391; distribution of, President's veto, 482; Arkansas resolutions, 705; Governor Seward's views on, 707, 895; Connecticut resolutions, relative to, 747, 907; North Carolina and New Jersey resolutions, 752; Missouri resolutions, 758; quantity of, 1840, 816; Governor Seward protests against using proceeds of, by Federal government, 818; New York resolutions, 747, 819, 903, 974; Vermont resolutions, 821; Maine resolutions, 821, 1020; Kentucky resolutions, 851; Pennsylvania and Delaware resolutions, 908; Rhode Island and Indiana resolutions, 909; restoration to State, 966; application of future receipts from, 971; Alabama resolutions relative to, 974; act of Congress for distribution of proceeds, 974; Georgia resolutions, 977; South Carolina refuses to receive proceeds of, 984; acquisition of, 985; New York's share of proceeds, 1040; Connecticut resolutions against, IV, 45; communication from Treasury Department relative to, 49, 162; amount received, application of, 117; Assembly resolutions, Governor Wright's reply, 162; distribution considered by Governor Seymour, 749; donation to States, New York's share, V, 596.

PUBLIC MONEY. To be paid out only on warrant, I, 8; not to be drawn from treasury except by warrant, 164, 168, 534.

PUBLIC OFFICERS. Compensation of, II, 199; revision of laws relating to, III, 255; deposit of funds, bank failure, VI, 334; improper

PUBLIC OFFICERS —(*Continued*).

conduct, severe punishment should be inflicted, 638; frauds and malversations, 727; actions against, for misappropriation of public funds, 727, 829; embezzlements by, 727; attachments for misappropriation of public funds, 730; actions by Attorney-General, 732; accountability, 734, 804, 829, 836; trustees for people, 836.

VETOES. Staying suits against, II, 170, 173; payment of salaries, 249; New York civil list, furnishing copies of, VII, 493; security of bonds, 508; amending Penal Code, VIII, 889.

PUBLIC OFFICERS' LAW. Enacted, 1892, IX, 28; proceedings for removal, V, 717.

PUBLIC PEACE. Act to restore and establish, I, 19.

PUBLIC PRINTING. Statutes and legislative proceedings, IV, 31; act relating to, 32; contracts by general State officers, 32; excessive cost of, statement, 1896, IX, 674; unbalanced bids, protest against, 675; revision of law, 1893, 676; State Printing Law, 1901, 676; X, 123, 196, 269; reform needed, IX, 846; X, 269; expenditures, 1900, 182, 195; contracts by McCarthy and Williams, 270; legislative, cost for ten years, 270; department, cost for five years, 271; comparative statement of appropriations, 1893–4; 1901–2, 464; unauthorized bulletins by departments, 617.

VETOES. Relative to, III, 1021; defining, VII, 1120; office, and superintendent, relative to, IX, 70; legislative, 1899, settlement of balance, X, 315; Brandow Printing Company, claim, Court of Claims, 315; Water Storage Commission report, publication and distribution, 651; legislative, reappropriation unexpended balance not specified, 933; messages and reports, 952.

PUBLIC PURPOSE. Legislative declaration not conclusive, V, 442, 653; village, aiding private academy, VI, 78; soldiers' monuments, VII, 847; Bartholdi statue fund, veto, 1088; erection of courthouse by Hornellsville for Steuben county, VIII, 880; World's Fair, expenditures by New York, 996.

PUBLIC SCHOOLS. Grammar free school established, I, 100.

PUBLIC SCHOOL SOCIETY OF NEW YORK. Succeeds Free School Society, III, 115; instruction of teachers, 159; supervision of schools, 455, 948; needed revision of powers, 949.

PUBLIC SERVICE COMMISSIONS. Created, X, 855; supersede inspector of gas meters, VI, 284; X, 855; powers of Gas and Electricity Commission transferred to, VIII, 244, 312; IX, 761; X, 221, 855; powers of Railroad and Rapid Transit Commissions transferred to, IX, 761; X, 855; regulating railroad rates, 364.

PUBLIC USE. Property taken for, canals, II, 329, 330; III, 73; making streams highways, II, 522; Newburgh water supply, 585; free road, damages, how ascertained, 592; streets in New York, 646; lands overflowed by mill dam, 663; lands taken for, compensation, IV, 347; V, 880; VI, 90, 97, 217; VII, 775, 1108; X, 761, 800; railroads, IV, 496; railroads in New York, V, 517; second taking, 802; VI, 206; VII, 1101; Mill brook, running logs in, VI, 97; waterworks companies, 285; land for cemeteries, 605; scope of provision, 642; defined, VII, 243; villages, damages, how ascertained, 775; electric-light poles and wires, 866; owner entitled to notice, VIII, 874; New York Rapid Transit Railroad, IX, 513.

VETOES. Property taken for, ascertaining damages, IV, 694; Susquehanna River dam, V, 653; local appointment of freeholders as commissioners, VI, 217; Amsterdam charter, VII, 1014; snow drifts, obstructing highway, ascertaining damages, 1108; Poughkeepsie street railroads, changing motive power, VIII, 729.

PUBLIC UTILITIES. State should control, X, 85; taxation of, 198, 489; municipal ownership, 219; Public Service Commissions created, 1907, 221, see that title; regulation needed, 854.

PUBLIC WORKS. Supervision of, proposed board of internal improvements, III, 712; advantages of concentrated capital in construction of, 809; deposit of maps and plans of, 934; opposition to internal improvements, 801, 955; estimated cost, 965; combinations to procure, IV, 105.

PULASKI. Fire limits, veto, VII, 806.

PULTNEY. Excepting from Highway Act as to orchards and vineyards, veto, VII, 1098.

PULTNEYVILLE. Arms and supplies for, II, 775; guard at, 822.

PUNISHMENT. See also CRUEL AND UNUSUAL PUNISHMENTS and CAPITAL PUNISHMENT. Limitation of State's power, II, 61; should produce beneficial results, 401; for escape, 426, 478; of perjury, 451; lack of uniformity in, 549; for assault on prison officers by convicts, 589; discriminations criticised, 590; of extraterritorial offenses, 623, 624; whipping for petit larceny, 633; substituting imprisonment for death penalty, 634; commutation for good behavior, 875; IV, 723, 787, 844; V, 374, .525, 842; VI, 18, 899; VII, 147, 708; whipping for violation of prison discipline, II, 983; corporal in prisons, protest against, 996; infliction of, more discrimination needed, 1109; III, 129, 173, 383; IV, 609, 724, 845; V, 59, 93, 171, 266, 386; VII, 147; sentence of death, conditional pardon, imprisonment for life, III, 33; too severe for first offenses, IV, 406, 434; cruel and un-

PUNISHMENT — (*Continued*).

usual, II, 61, 65, 85, 131, 284; V, 268; intoxication, 285; in State prison, VI, 109, 233; unjustifiable discrimination in favor of prominent offenders, 637, 728; indeterminate sentences, see that title; unreasonable delay in inflicting after conviction, VIII, 80, 180; indeterminate sentences, transfers from Elmira Reformatory to State prisons, IX, 331, 389; of attempts to commit murder, enlarging term of imprisonment, X, 342.

VETOES. At discretion of court-martial, II, 131; imprisonment hard labor, VII, 805; vagrants, hard labor in jail, VIII, 132; sentences to Elmira Reformatory, X, 917.

PURCELL COMPANY, C. J. Changing name, veto, IX, 794.

PURVIANCE, WILLIAM. Pennsylvania committee on canal connecting North Branch canal with Chemung canal, III, 759.

PUTNAM COUNTY. Astor claim, II, 867, 940, 986, 990; III, 132, 146; settlement of claim, 174, 389; survey of Dutchess boundary, 389; average excise license fees, 1889, VIII, 687; unpaid taxes, sales under special act, 749; highways, cost of labor system, 1892, IX, 200; insane, care of, county and State systems compared, 228; included in ninth judicial district, 547; X, 850.

VETOES. Town business, Phillipstown and Carmel, VI, 674; notaries public, relative to, 1036; excepting from provisions of County Treasurer's Act, VII, 265; water for New York, 593; clerk, sheriff and treasurer, appointment of New York water inspectors, 594; land owned by New York in, release to Julia C. Patterson, IX, 806; town meetings, 862; institutions, purchase of supplies for, X, 700.

PUTNAM, JOHN R. Board of Claims, veto, VIII, 889; IX, 269, 353.

PYTHIAN ASSOCIATION, AMSTERDAM. Exemption from taxation, veto, IX, 449.

Q.

QUAKERS. Affirmation of allegiance, II, 38; exemption from militia service, III, 85, 880; IV, 39.

QUARANTINE. Establishment on Staten Island, II, 990; IV, 75; exemption of vessels from certain ports, III, 87; hospital erected, 164; new buildings at, 343; against cholera, 395; against convicts, 401; aid from mariners' fund, IV, 272; excitement in Richmond county, 438; hospital indicted as a nuisance, 438; change of buildings, 439; repair of buildings needed, 852, 866; act relative to, 853; large deficiency in receipts from commutation tax, 866; new hospital provided for, V, 23; removal from Staten Island, 28, 54, 79, 185; New Jersey complains of violation of agreement, 35; report of commissioners on removal,

QUARANTINE —(*Continued*).

63, 80, 99, 109, 198, 307; destruction of buildings by mob, 79, 100, 279; VI, 783; proposed change of site, V, 80; temporary establishment on Staten Island, 81; reimbursement of Governor King for expenses, 89; at Sandy Hook, land ceded by United States, 101; regulations interfere with commerce, 185; floating hospital, 184, 278, 378; revision of laws, 279; damages resulting from destruction of station on Staten Island, 279; quarantine diseases, what included in, 418; board of commissioners, repeal of law recommended, 419; general act, 450; new hospital buildings, 599; general references, 699; VI, 25, 116, 236, 358, 532, 625, 943; VII, 433, 530, 833, 966; separate warehouses suggested in lower and upper bay, V, 639; jurisdiction over lower bay, 640; negotiations with New Jersey concerning regulations, 640; corporation for erecting warehouse and docks, 641; precautions against cholera, 700, 765; new establishment at West Bank, 701; Legislature asks aid of Federal government, 701, 767; report of commissioners on warehouses, 719; temporary establishment on Barren island, 767; establishment on Coney island, 767; Commission on Sale of Property, report, 791; number of vessels under, 844; boarding station at West Bank, VI, 27; boarding station for arrivals from non-infected ports, 534; report of commissioners on new boarding station, 776; communication from Governor of New Jersey, 777; coasting vessels, New Jersey complaint relative to, 778; sketch of yellow fever epidemics, 782; coasting vessels, history of regulations, 783; Commission on Harbor Encroachments, 776; New York methods approved by national board of health, VII, 433; New York, approved by foreign visitors, 531; regulation of fees, congressional action requested, 968; New York establishment, report on condition of, VIII, 527; general act, amendment of 1888, 557; Commission on Purchase for Repairs, etc., report, 717; IX, 37; cholera epidemic, 1892, 204; purchase of part of Fire island, 204; duty of Federal officers at foreign ports, 208; appropriations, 292; revision of statutes, 1900, X, 119; maintenance account, deficiencies in salaries, appropriation, 568.

VETOES. Commissioners of, completing contract for Southfield land, VII, 385, 929; repairs of buildings, 473; Hoffman island, repairs and improvements, 588; warehouse company, revival, 588, 1085; IX, 405; various repairs and improvements, VII, 791, 1084; VIII, 425; X, 294, 549; Kirkham claim, repairs to hospital ships, VII, 792, 929; Appleton contract, Southfield land, appropriation, 929; care of establishment, appropriation, VIII,

QUARANTINE, VETOES — (Continued).

  252; commissioners, method of appointment, 555; general improvements, IX, 83; artesian wells on Swinburne and Hoffman islands, 292; painting buildings, Swinburne and Hoffman islands, 292; Hoffman island, enlargement, 292; Swinburne island, buildings on, 777; entering grounds or vessels without leave, 317; hospital, Buffalo, purchasing land for, 475; Swinburne island, general repairs and completing dock, 549; health officer, landing at Clifton Station, 567; Swinburne and Hoffman islands, repairs, appropriation, 792; health officers, repairs to steamers, 792; — plumbing, 792; — mason work, 792; — heating apparatus, 792; — gas apparatus, 792.

QUARRY. Rights reserved, cession at Black Rock, IV, 46.

QUARTERING SOLDIERS. By Governor Lovelace, I, 133; provision for, recommended, 565, 673; act for, 589, 604, 671, 725, 732, 735, 737, 741, 746, 748, 755; act of Parliament relating to, 702, 716, 721; General Gage's claim for, 744.

QUARTERMASTER. For provincial regiment, I, 572; of militia gives bond, II, 809; department, appropriation for, 831.

QUARTERMASTER-GENERAL. Deputy, letter from, obstructions in Hudson river, II, 19; letter from assistant, 54, 56; suggested inquiry as to conduct of department, 66; letters from,— army supplies, 90; — various matters, 108; — public contracts, 208; report, V, 444, 486, 564, 623, 718, 793; VI, 44; transportation of returning soldiers, V, 685; report, relief of soldiers, 724; revision of claims against United States, 754.

QUARTER-SALES. In Rensselaerwyck leases, III, 665; abolished IV, 653.

QUEBEC. Sachems visit to negotiate with French, I, 271, 272; taken by England, 640; commercial relations with, 773; act for government of, protest against, 773; General Montgomery's remains removed from, II, 986.

QUEBEC BOUNDARY. Fixed by royal proclamation, I, 715; survey of, recommended, 715; proceedings to establish, 739, 744, 747, 750, 755, 756, 757, 764; alleged error in, II, 606.

QUEEN ANNE. See ANNE, QUEEN.

QUEEN CAROLINE. See CAROLINE, QUEEN.

QUEENS BOROUGH. Tunnel connection with Manhattan, X, 396.

  VETOES. Public schools, X, 60; volunteer firemen, relative to, 60; taxation, 177; taxes, equalizing, 322; veteran volunteer firemen associations, exemptions, 323; sewer in, 474; fire department, deputy chief, 818; street railroads, fares in, 882; claim of Brown & Fleming Contracting Company, highway department, materials, 950; Kelly, coroner's clerk, compensation, 956.

QUEENS BOROUGH ELECTRIC LIGHT AND POWER COMPANY. New York, payment for lighting, veto, X, 308.

QUEENSBURGH. See KAYADEROSSERAS.

QUEENSBURY. Quitrents in, II, 1079.

QUEEN CITY GASLIGHT COMPANY, BUFFALO. Supplying city with gas, repeal, veto, IX, 723.

QUEENS COUNTY. Act for support of ministers in, I, 39; burning of woods in, prohibited, 143; sheriff of, account for subsistence of prisoners, 388, 478; militia ordered to Fort Edward, 614; Zebulon Seaman, Assembly, favors colonial union, 767; act for completing courthouse and jail, II, 417; nomination of sheriff, proceedings in Council of Appointment, 474, 491; cessions of land in, how made, 825; bridge over East river to New York, VI, 582; Lloyd's Neck annexed to Suffolk county, VIII, 289; average excise license fees, 1889, 687; deputy county treasurer, act providing for, 998; increase in population, IX, 3; highways, cost of labor system, 1892, 200; insane, care of, county and State systems compared, 228; included in metropolitan elections district, IX, 885; transfer tax assistant, X, 108; court attendants, act of 1900, 151.

VETOES. New indices of deeds and mortgages, VI, 310; Newtown,— opening highway, 330; — local government, 449, 558; Middle Village, Lutheran cemetery, 595; notaries public, relative to, 1036; VII, 131; repealing Metropolitan Sanitary District Act, VII, 113; excepting from County Treasurer's Act, 265; unpaid taxes, sales of land, 415; Winfield, Gooderson Fire Engine Company No. 2, changing name, 748; Sea Cliff, village charter, 936; Newtown, free school district No. 12, charter, VIII, 338; inspectors of elections, poll clerks, compensation, 340; cession of lands to United States, 1113; highway labor, 1154; justices' courts, laymen not to practice in, IX, 373; tunnel under Newtown creek, 474; Woodbine street, opening, 778; Thompson avenue, Long Island City, making part of county highway system, 786; unpaid taxes, arrearages, settlement, 796; unpaid taxes, county treasurer's list and notice of sale, 796; digging worms on shores of, 799; county judge and surrogate, compensation, 800; taxes, sales, 862; personal property, apportionment under Nassau County Act, X, 62; railroads on macadamized roads, 145; taxation, 177; street railroads, 316, 431; supervisors, powers under Game Law, 441; county judge and surrogate, salary, 584; street railroads, exempting certain highways, 587; surrogate, salary, 711; court attendants, compensation, 711; volunteer firemen, New York, relative to, 715.

QUEENSTOWN. Ferry at, II, 526; attack on, 737, 775.

QUIA EMPTORES. Statute of, IV, 358.

QUINCES. Size of barrels, veto, X, 317.

QUINCY, JOSIAH, JR. Director of Western Railroad Company, communication from, III, 750.

QUINCY RURAL CEMETERY ASSOCIATION, RIPLEY. VETOES. Charter, VI, 501; acquiring additional land, 501.

QUINN, CHRISTOPHER C. Relief, veto, X, 178.

QUINTILIAN. Quoted, qualifications of teachers, II, 726.

QUIRK, EDWARD J. Relief, veto, VI, 595.

QUITRENTS. Used for Receiver-General's salary, I, 293; royal repeal of two acts relating to, 361; reform in method of collecting, 554; military bounty lands, exempted from, 598; commutations for, in New Hampshire grants, II, 49; relief from, 399; appropriated to educational purposes, 968; commutation authorized, 1079.

QUOTA. Among colonies for Crown Point expedition, I, 570.

R.

RACKA, BERTHA. Brooklyn, escheat, veto, VIII, 722.

RACING ASSOCIATIONS. VETOES. Examination of books, compensation of experts, IX, 856; examiner, furnishing office, and rent of office for, X, 422; annual tax on gross receipts, 891.

RACKET RIVER. Improving navigation, veto, VI, 348, 599; improvement of, 576; improving navigation, VIII, 561.

RADCLIFF, JACOB. Judge, correspondence with Governor Jay, Council of Appointment, II, 483.

RADII, THE. Newspaper for deaf and dumb, III, 715.

RAILROAD AID (Local). Exempting bonds from taxation, V, 813; Olean, Buffalo and Washington Railroad Company, VI, 91; Utica and Black River Railroad Company, consent of taxpayers, 92; general act, 1869, 95, 190; consent of taxpayers necessary, 178; act extended, 369; bonds, investments by savings banks, 441; heavy local indebtedness, VII, 298, 437; Hancock, compromising railroad indebtedness, VIII, 128; exempting town bonds from taxation, 128; constitutional restriction on grants of, 239.

    VETOES. In certain counties, VI, 95; Greenwich, Union Village and Johnsonville Railroad Company, 164; Hector, part of town, 187; amending act, 190; VIII, 459; Paris, election of railroad commissioners, VI, 194; by municipal corporations, 214; Wilna, Diana and Edwards, Black River and St. Lawrence Railway Company, 348; Morristown, legalizing town bonding proceedings, 583; county commissioners, 911; Vienna and Constantia

RAILROAD AID (Local), VETOES — (*Continued*).

bonds, VII, 267; Orleans, bonds, 412; Midland Railroad bonds, postponement, 415; town commissioners, abolition of office, 509; town taxes for, 847; municipal bonds, payment of, 937; relief of certain towns, VIII, 371; Auburn, payment of bonds, 504; town bonds in certain counties, 639; Perry, using funds for general town purposes, 1105; Berlin, railroad commissioner, abolishing office, IX, 232; Mamakating, bonds to retire outstanding bonds, X, 235; municipal claims, Court of Claims, amending act, 315; counties, railroad aid bonds, Court of Claims, 945.

RAILROAD COMMISSION. Reports, additional copies, VII, 921; usefulness of department, 971; accidents, fatalities and injuries, 972; freight rates, 973; purpose of its creation, VIII, 105; nomination of Edward A. Durant, no action, 373; nomination of James Arkell, withdrawn, 373; nomination of William A. Armstrong, withdrawn, 374; nomination of James A. Buckbee, withdrawn, William E. Rogers and Isaac V. Baker, Jr., 374; cost of, 1891, IX, 11; number of commissioners, increasing from three to five, 761; abolished, 1907, succeeded by Public Service Commissions, 761; X, 855; self-supporting, 119; should have supervision of gas and electric light companies, 220; removal of grade crossings, 227.

VETOES. Clerk, preparing index, maps and report, VII, 921; maps from State Engineer's office, 921; defining duties of commissioners, 1096; agreement with Brooklyn Elevated Railroad Company, annulment, VIII, 293; increasing number of commissioners, IX, 761; grade crossings, reappropriation, X, 647, 653.

RAILROAD COMMISSIONERS. See BOARD OF RAILROAD COMMISSIONERS.

RAILROAD COMPETITION. With canals, III, 375; IV, 674, 739, 820; V, 208, 365, 709; VI, 789; effect on canal revenues, IV, 820; V, 593; causes reduction of tolls, 156; through traffic chiefly affected, 157; canals keep down transportation rates, VI, 104; temporary reduction of rates, effect on railroad traffic, 239; diversion of trade from canals, VII, 5; Governor Cornell's comment, 685; effect of high railroad rates in 1893, IX, 302; five great trunk lines, 1895, 556.

RAILROADS. From Otsego to Ithaca, III, 204; Otsego lake to Erie canal, 204; projected by Delaware and Hudson Canal Company, 237; beneficent effects of, 327; established in England, 327; between Albany and Schenectady, 328; several charters granted, 328; probable usefulness of, 374; competition with canal, see RAILROAD COMPETITION; tolls from, 376, 787; Assembly report on, general note, 396; first mention of, 396; motive power, 396;

Railroads — (*Continued*).

speed of trains, 397; charters granted reserving State's right to
buy road, 398; projected from New York and Lake Erie through
southern tier, 509; advantage over canals, 509; New York and
Erie Railroad, 510, 999; crossing highways, 511; projected from
Williamsport, Pennsylvania, to Elmira, 527; three lines suggested, 730; compared with canals, 732; from Boston to Albany,
750; new lines constructed, 786; may be constructed by State,
800; loans to, 810; IV, 10, 62, 386, 831; V, 3; summary of
railroad construction, III, 812, 1041; IV, 495; results derived
from construction of, 813; between Hudson river and Lake Erie,
866; from Ogdensburg to Lake Champlain, survey, 866, 964,
983; companies in default on State loan, 952; IV, 10, 92;
connecting Boston and the west, III, 953; governmental management of, 961; probable success of, 962; supervision of, 963;
connecting New York with interior of State, 964; survey in
Essex county, 984; outside connections, 1042; incorporation,
State should reserve control of, IV, 12; number of companies,
495; accidents, 495, 612; general act of 1850, 496; no real conflict with canals, 590; duty of State in regulating use of, 613;
reports to be filed with State Engineer, 659; V, 76; total mileage, IV, 659, 835; extravagant bonding of, 805; board of
railroad commissioners, 805, see that title; increase in construction, 864; increasing transportation charges, V, 47; large indebtedness of companies, 76; more needed in New York city,
189, 238, 294; legislation needed, 192; unsafe condition of road-
beds, 192, 294; increased tonnage of, 207; objections against
powers in perpetuity, 240; reducing passenger charges, 239;
continental railway, 295; furnish free transportation to rejected
volunteers, 417; estimated commerce on, 452, 532, 594; Indiana
memorial relative to use of, 493; diversion of business from
canals, 594; bonds in aid of construction, exempting from taxation, 813; elevated, see Elevated Railroads; improved supervision and facilities, VI, 636; New York, cheap trains for laboring people, 658; importance in distribution of commerce, 748;
uniform reports, VII, 28; riots, 1877, 151; obstructions, new
act, Governor's proclamation, 153; constitutional prohibition
against special acts, intent of provision, 396; report of legislative committee, 434; transportation problem, 433, 525, 700;
VIII, 39; discriminations in freight rates, VII, 700; Spuyten
Duyvil accident, 730; prevention of accidents, 731; Railroad
Commission created, 1882, 732; safety appliances required, 732;
cars, heating, stoves and furnaces prohibited, 732; New York,

RAILROADS — (*Continued*).

percentage of income payable by West Side and Yonkers Patent Railway Company, 852; usefulness of Railroad Commission, 971; accidents, fatalities and injuries, 972; grade crossings, 972, see that title; freight rates, 973; more supervision needed, 974; Hancock, compromising railroad indebtedness, VIII, 128; protection from fires caused by operation of, 323, 481; general law, 1890, 1027; IX, 26, 135; monthly payment of wages, VIII, 1079; in New York annexed district, act relative to, IX, 99; limiting hours of service on, act relative to, 145; switchmen's strike, Buffalo, 1892, 159; grade crossings, general act, 1897, 744; employees, actions for personal injuries, X, 97; alleged discrimination against New York, 131, 136, 364; taxation, statutes amended, 198; proposed prohibition in forest preserve, 340; receivers, limiting expense of administration, 352; regulating rates, 364; settling negligence cases, 372; Pennsylvania Railroad, terminal facilities in New York, 396; heavy payments for taxes, 528; incorporation and powers, amending general act, 799; New York, terminating use of steam railroads in certain streets, 897; English rule as to liability for injuries to employees, 925.

VETOES. Transportation of mail, III, 592; transportation of liquor, IV, 768; in certain streets in New York, V, 238, 517; Pneumatic Railway and Express Company, 670; freight, regulating transportation, 803; aiding construction, 814; VI, 91; aid in certain counties, 95; highway crossings in Great Valley, encroachments, 160; between Long Wharf and Matteawan, 211; municipal aid, 214; aiding unfinished, 345; consolidation of certain companies, 814, new act passed; county commissioners, 911; amending act of 1869, VII, 266; town sinking funds, 268; soliciting patronage for, 415; cars and engines, preventing intrusions on, 417; Assembly investigating committee, 1879, expenses, deficiency, 463; town commissioners, abolition of office, 509; laying down tracks, constitutional prohibition, 593, 1063; preparing annual report, 1881, 778; amending general act, 806, 1096; IX, 803, 865; Erie and New York Company, extending time for completion, VII, 807; assessment in Jefferson and St. Lawrence counties, 807; taking lands of Soldiers and Sailors' Home, 808; Jefferson and St. Lawrence counties, stocks, relief from existing burdens, 847; elevated, New York, fares, 850; regulating speed of trains, Sandy Hill, 936; in certain parts of New York prohibited, 999; school taxes, exempting Cattaraugus county, 1095; corporations in foreign countries, 1097; in Geneva, 1105;

RAILROADS, VETOES — (*Continued*).

 extending time for completion, VIII, 237; mountain, rates of fare, 291; mountain, operation of, 293; amending County Act, 470; White Plains and Connecticut line, 615; commission to ascertain damages, amending general act, 619; passenger cars, lighting, 889; elevated, construction outside New York, 889; using tracks of other companies, 889; cable, New York, 1035; grade crossings, 1037; extortion, prevention of, 1128; Rome, Watertown and Ogdensburg Railroad Company, purchasing bridge company stock, 1130; reviewing assessments, 132; sanitary inspection of stations and cars, 234; State engaging in business, transportation facilities at Elmira Reformatory, 244; electric light and power companies becoming railroad companies, 246; construction and operation, action for damages caused by, limitation, 260; local authorities, definition, 462; receipts from freight, 472; street surface and elevated, hours of labor, 626; in first-class cities, right of way, use of, in certain cases, 791; highway labor assessments, 801; tunnel roads, 803; taxes, apportionment between school districts, X, 439; New York and Harlem Railroad, motive power and terminal facilities, 466; terminal facilities, first-class cities, 466; Buffalo, grade crossings, damages, 474; grade crossings, appropriation, 568; consents for construction, 574; grade crossings, relative to, 591; reports, 699; condemnation, right of, 710; railroads, inspection of locomotive boilers, 772; Buffalo Union Railroad Commission, 777; injuries to employees, 924; freight transportation, 926; in hands of receivers, limiting time for construction, 959.

RAILROAD TOLLS. For protection of canals, III, 376; amount of, IV, 373; abolition of, 670, 820; V, 161, 661; VI, 737; reimposition recommended, IV, 823; V, 47, 163, 205, 259; early diversity of statutes, 161; report of canal auditor, 209; total amount of, 212; by Utica and Schenectady Railroad Company, 660; Governor Fenton's comment on, 803.

RAINES, JOHN. Temporary President of Senate, resolutions on death of former Governor Higgins, X, 962.

RAINES, THOMAS. State Treasurer, payment to Timothy J. Sullivan, VII, 499, 790.

RAMAPO. Normal school at, veto, IX, 711.

RAMAPO WATER COMPANY. Act of 1895 repealed, X, 212, 694.

RAMSEY, JOSEPH H. Senate, committee on alleged interference in speakership contest; V, 485.

RAMSEY, MARY G. Relief, veto, VI, 692.

RAMSPERGER, SAMUEL J. Senate, member of Prince Henry reception committee, X, 479; member of joint legislative committee on services in memory of former Governor Higgins, 963.

RANDALL, NELSON. Major-general, commands militia on frontier, V, 550.

RANDALL, ROBERT R. Gift for Sailors' Snug Harbor, II, 566.

RANDALL, SAMUEL S. Commissioner to prepare common school code, IV, 603.

RANDALL'S ISLAND. House of refuge removed to, IV, 789, 846, see NEW YORK HOUSE OF REFUGE; channel between it and Ward's island, protest against filling, VII, 46; proposed removal of house of refuge from, X, 611.

RANDOLPH, BEVERLY. Lieutenant-Governor of Virginia, letter from, constitutional amendments, II, 294.

RANDOLPH, EDMUND. Letter from, proposed commercial convention, II, 260.

RANDOLPH, EDMUND. Governor of Virginia, letter from, II, 286.

RANDOLPH, JOSEPH F. Member of New Jersey commission to procure Constitutional Convention, V, 325.

RANGERS. For Albany county, I, 377, 393, 394, 395, 439; difficulties of service, 395; provisions for, 402; at Kinderhook, 439; at Schenectady, 439; Schoharie, 439; Canajoharie, 439; Mohawk's country, 439; Orange and Ulster counties, 588, 595, 616; to serve with King's troops, 599; Orange county, expenses of, II, 43; in Ulster county, request for, 55; for defense of frontier, 117.

RAPALLO, CHARLES A. Court of Appeals, quoted, exclusive franchise, VIII, 411.

RAPE. Punishment of, III, 285; punishment, proposed commutation for good behavior, veto, VI, 899.

RAPIDE-PLAT ISLANDS. Conflicting claims of title to, II, 554.

RAPID TRANSIT. New York, importance of, V, 669, 810; VI, 244; Central Underground Railroad Company, VI, 207; Governor Hoffman's discussion of, 244; New York Railway Company, 245; on canals, 537; IX, 168, 457; Husted bill approved, VI, 905; general act, 1875, VII, 397; needed in New York, 857; VIII, 930, 1070; how affected by General Street Railroad Act of 1884, 1070; Harvey experiments, act relative to, VIII, 125; unconstitutional, 127; Brooklyn Elevated Railroad, 129; New York Arcade Railway Company, act relative to, 261; Governor Hill's special message, 1889, 759; New York Subway Act of 1891, 761, 1071, 1142; New York, amending act of 1891, IX, 90; act of 1894, 504; commission abolished, 1907, 761; X, 855; Governor Roosevelt's special message, 1899, X, 43; act amended,

Rapid Transit —(Continued).

 1902, 394, 467; act amended, tunnel roads, 395; tunnel roads, communication from mayor of New York, 396; amendments, 1904, 630; Syracuse Rapid Transit Railway Company, contribution to expense of canal bridge, 929.

Vetoes. Arcade Railway, New York, VI, 197; pneumatic tubes, amending act, 289, 485; New York Rapid Transit Company, charter, 585, 694; Brooklyn Elevated Silent Safety Railway Company, charter, 595; New York Elevated Railroad, extending road, 715; cities to provide for, 905; Brooklyn, Atlantic avenue, VII, 394; Broadway Underground Railway Company, extending rights, powers and duties, 1031; New York Arcade Railway Company, extending powers, VIII, 102; New York, relative to, X, 60; condemnation procedure, 446; New York commissioners, costs, 582; presentation of claims, 806.

Raquette Pond. Removing dead and floating timber from, veto, X, 428.

Raritan Bay. Vessels in, alleged to carry infectious diseases, V, 35; cession to New Jersey, 640; jurisdiction of New Jersey over, VI, 780; depositing refuse matters in waters of, repeal, veto, IX, 384.

Raritan Canal. Transportation of coal on, III, 204.

Rate Bill. Support of common schools, IV, 66, 378, 396, 428, 476; V, 523, 603, 778, 851; abrogated and re-established, IV, 551; objections to, 796, 842; abolished, V, 780; good effect of abolition, 852.

Rate of Exchange. Between continental money and specie, II, 94; between national and State bills of credit, 97; on French loan, 155.

Rathbun, Stephen P. Farm canal bridge for, veto, VI, 689.

Ratification. See Legalizing Acts.

Rations. Allowance for, II, 43.

Ray, Chester. Board of Claims, veto, VIII, 626.

Raynor, George H. Member of Adirondack Park Commission, 1872, VII, 722.

Read, John Meredith. Appointed commissioner of deeds, Paris, V, 215.

Real Estate and Progress Board, Buffalo. Charter, veto, VIII, 293.

Real Property. Confirming titles to, I, 11; act to prevent fraud in conveyances of, 11; adults authorized to convey, 11; certain actions relating to, regulated, 11; justices may try title to, 60; military bounties, 598; first Tax Law, II, 9; ascertaining taxable, 184; facilitating sales of, 986; sale of, to pay assessments, III, 1029; number of acres assessed, IV, 24, 64; changing leases to tenures, 240, 307; agricultural leases, limiting term of, 244; when

REAL PROPERTY —(*Continued*).

State may not bring action for, 345; feudal tenures abolished, 409; sales for unpaid taxes, 436; inequality of assessment, 564; must be assessed at full value, 597; disproportionate taxation of, V, 369; VII, 942; VIII, 152, 1063; X, 80; taxable valuation of, V, 370, 453; aliens, case of Venezuela minister, 617; taxation of buildings, plan of Tax Commission, VI, 372; right to hold, status of American citizens in foreign countries, 551; taxation, increasing burden of, VII, 514; taxation, deduction of debts, VIII, 153; unincorporated associations not to take, 877.

VETOES. Debeavois estate, II, 222; deeds of, curing defects in, 245; creating corporation to deal in, IV, 592; persons dying seized of, relative to, VII, 413; decedents, sale of, 414; sold for taxes, conveying State's interest, 656; right of aliens to hold, 662; IX, 725; illegitimate children, right to inherit, VII, 1126; judgment levy after ten years, VIII, 468; sale on execution, effect of, 470; sale on judgment, appointment of referee, 632; McNamara, Amsterdam, sale, 1090; New York, 23d and 24th wards, recording documents, IX, 460; liens, vacating attachments, 474; maps, division of lots, abandonment, 623; action to recover, 791, 792; penalty for using long forms of covenants, repeal, 803; divided by tax district line, assessment, 803; devised by Michael Flood, relative to, 811; sale to guardians in socage, X, 62; franchise tax, 63; acquisition by electric light companies, 159; eminent domain, incomplete proceedings, restoring land to owner, 260; Munn case, land conveyed to trustee, sale of, 312; exempt from taxation, report on, 439; acknowledgment of conveyances, 444; life estates, sale to unknown remaindermen, 592.

REAR-ADMIRAL. Governor Hardy appointed, I, 613.

RECEIVER OF CONTINENTAL TAXES. Alexander Hamilton appointed for New York, II, 185.

RECEIVER-GENERAL. Accounts of, I, 48, 96, 176; quarterly account by, proposed, 164; functions of, 293; collection of quitrents, 554.

RECEIVERS. Of moneyed institutions, compensation of, memorandum, III, 973; regulating appointment of, VI, 122; of corporations, payment of wages to employees, VIII, 36; of banks, action for dissolution, IX, 741; corporations, limiting expense of administration, X, 352; relation to judicial system, 677; restricting compensation, regulating fees of counsel, 845.

VETOES. Lands conveyed to, VI, 562; of taxes, VII, 62; moneyed corporations, 416; of insolvent corporations, transfer of property to State Treasurer, 798; Best, National Trust Company,

Receivers, Vetoes — (Continued).

Senate investigation, counsel fees, 906; bankrupt corporations, VIII, 129; of taxes in cities, proceedings by, X, 272; corporations, relative to certain actions, 309; taxes, Rye, bond and deputy, 443; commissions, bonds, 589; of taxes, Saratoga Springs, surety, 591; railroads in hands of, limiting time for construction, 959; corporations, commissions, compensation of counsel, 960.

Reciprocity. Commercial, with British provinces, IV, 656.

Recognizance. Of Van Schaick discharged, I, 214.

Recorder. New York, petition of, relative to French prisoners, I, 166; Albany and New York to be commissioners of excise, 529; in New York, administration of, III, 1011.

Vetoes. Utica, increasing salary, VI, 427; Cohoes, chamber powers of Supreme Court justices vested in, VII, 327; Norwich, creating office, IX, 75; New York, fixing compensation, X, 321; Watervliet, appointment of, 434; Oswego, amending charter, 806.

Recruits. See Volunteers and Troops.

Red Cross Society. Organization and service, X, 16.

Redding, Thomas. Conviction of, claim against State, hearing, veto, VIII, 888.

Redfield, Heman. Resigns as canal commissioner, III, 570.

Red Hook. Proposed battery at, I, 295, 324.

Red House. State road, Allegany reservation, improvement, veto, VIII, 847.

Red House Driving Park Agricultural Society. Charter, veto, VII, 506.

Red Men. Improved Order of, Delaware Tribe No. 44, Eldred, charter, veto, VIII, 877; taking and holding property, veto, 877.

Redington, Jacob S. Extradition of, II, 1104.

Red Jacket. Seneca chief, joins in address to Governor, II, 943; communication from, 1076; method of election noted, IV, 504.

Redknap, Captain. Colonial engineer, I, 125; visits Albany, 130.

Reed, Alexander. Board of Claims, veto, VIII, 1166.

Reed, Amos. Bond for return of arms, II, 774.

Reed, John R. Manager, Jamaica normal school, Waters case, X, 561.

Reed, Julius C. Claim against Livonia, audit of, veto, VIII, 889.

Reed, Samuel C. Assembly, resolution requesting information from Harbor Defense Commission, V, 564; resolution requesting information as to quotas, 624.

Reed, Seth. Claim of, Indian lands, II, 307.

Reed, Thomas B. Speaker, House of Representatives, article on contested elections, VIII, 1075.

Reed, W. F. Communication on Boston truant officers, V, 108.

Reeve, Henry. Librarian of archives, Privy Council, examination of colonial documents, IV, 182.

Reevs, Gabriel. Commissioner of deeds, Yonkers, legalizing acts, veto, VIII, 518.

Referees. Compelling submission to, II, 205; standing, probably unconstitutional, IV, 414; provision for, 414; to investigate cause of fall of New York arsenal, V, 175; examination of, alleged abuses, VI, 365; relation to judicial system, X, 677; historical sketch, 681.

Vetoes. Investigating charges against attorneys, compensation, VII, 266; fees in highway proceedings, VIII, 470; sales of real property, appointment of, 632; appointment in first judicial department, X, 318; Walts' fees, Armour case, 648.

Reformatories. Investigating commission created, VII, 287, 432; fiscal year established, 297; employment of children by contract prohibited, 957; proposed supervision by Superintendent of Prisons, VIII, 12; freedom of worship in, 23, 178, 302, 479; use of machinery abolished, 658; for women, additional, established, IX, 144; removal of superintendents, 332, 387; monthly estimates of expenses, 436; temperance instruction, 616; at Bedford, completion of, X, 106; institutions included, 1902, 334; comparative expense *per capita*, 334; transfer of inmates, 740.

Vetoes. Employment of children by contract, VII, 764; for women, bill to establish, VIII, 819; manufactures in, branding and marking, IX, 138; eastern, Wawarsing, relative to, 245; furnishing cheese for inmates, 287; manufacture of certain articles prohibited, 464; Elmira, sentences to, X, 917.

Reformed Church of Helderberg. Sale of property, veto, VI, 209.

Reformed Dutch Church of German Flats. Relief, veto, II, 671.

Reformed Dutch Church of New Utrecht. Sale of land, veto, II, 645.

Reformed Low Dutch Church of Harlem. Appropriation for, veto, II, 1111.

Reformed Low Dutch Church, Taghkanick. Changing name, veto, VII, 807.

Reformed Protestant Dutch Church of Cattsbane. Changing name, veto, IX, 37.

Refugees. From South Carolina, exempted from duties, I, 177; from Nova Scotia, land grants to, II, 308; from St. Domingo, aid to, 353, see St. Domingo Refugees; from Canada, relief of, 787.

REFUGEE TRACT. Land in, cession to United States, II, 878, 879, 890.

REGENTS. See also UNIVERSITY OF NEW YORK. Of University, board created, II, 200; resignation of John Jay, 308; authorized to establish College of Physicians and Surgeons, 317; communication from, Columbia College, 375; resignation of John Mc-Donald, 375; lands ceded to, resumption of, 376, 377; report of, anatomical museum for Columbia College, 389; annual report of, 392, 413, 438, 459, 476, 520, 534, 543, 565, 610; V, 448, 605, 781; report of, Columbia College, II, 393; petition from, 518; proposed powers of, relative to common schools, 557; proposed limitation of power to grant charters, III, 62; management of literature fund, 232; report on instruction of teachers, 499; extending powers of supervision, 617; report sent to Netherlands, 1051; supervision of Albany normal school, IV, 67, 265; to make exchanges of laws, journals and documents, 466, 508; books for Canadian Parliamentary Library, 573; teachers' classes in academies, 647; dissolution of academies, VI, 336; may grant college charters, 339, 671; VIII, 708; purchase of Clinton manuscripts, VII, 688; authorized to establish New Jersey and Pennsylvania boundaries, 720; chartering medical colleges, VIII, 101; organization of board, 168; Governor Hill recommends abolition of, 171, 301, 479, 680, 792; board perpetuated by Constitution, 1894, 171; X, 113; statutes revised, 1889, VIII, 680; teachers' classes, transfer to Department of Public Instruction, 791; supervision of university extension, IX, 18, 21; board reorganized, 1904, X, 115, 604; resignation of St. Clair McKelway, withdrawal and re-election, 518; secretary, office abolished, 605.

VETOES. Practice of medicine, degrees, VI, 337, 339; purchase of revolutionary letters, VII, 409; purchase of objects of natural history, 410; appropriation for Secretary Woolworth, 467; examinations in academies and academic departments, deficiency appropriation, 467; manual, 1880, printing and binding, 494; purchase of Tompkins papers, 922; secretary's salary, VIII, 71, new bill passed; assistant secretary's salary, 72, new bill passed; public accountants, exemption from examinations, X, 239; co-operation with Scenic and Historic Society, 241; evening examinations, 432.

REGISTER. Removal of, III, 133; New York, bill relative to, returned for amendment, VII, 1028, 1072; New York, act relative to, 1072; New York, office not self-supporting, VIII, 1024; New York, made a salaried officer, report of Fassett investigating committee, IX, 414; Kings county, salaried office, X, 25, 208, 290.

REGISTER —(*Continued*).

VETOES. New York, closing office on holiday, VI, 287; Kings county, closing office on holiday, 287; New York, duties and compensation of, VII, 412; Kings county,— relative to, VIII, 124;— salaried office, X, 179; — salaries of clerks, 449; — employees, 592;— salary, 594;— transcribing records, compensation, 710; — management of office, 711; — additional subordinates, appointment and salaries, 770; New York,— compensation of copyists, 712;— additional deputy, 956.

" REGISTER " (Niles). Proposed sale to State, III, 978.

REGISTRATION OF VOTERS. Suggested, III, 158; V, 53; in New York, act for, III, 771, 851 (memorandum), 881, 988 (memorandum); general, suggested, 881; constitutional provision, IV, 825; V, 92, 195, 605; VII, 306; VIII, 566, 580; IX, 309, 555; general act, V, 92, 195; importance of, 293; new general act, 606; laws should be uniform, VI, 125; laws repealed, 125, 225; does not prevent election frauds, 389; in certain cities and towns, act for, VII, 435; publication of registry, New York, 579; naturalized citizens, production of papers, VIII, 20; Brooklyn, defects in law, 182; limitations on legislative power, 567; general law needed, 719, 720, 962; act of 1890, 719, 904; Australian plan, 898; Governor Flower recommends personal registration throughout State, IX, 34, 180, 309; general personal registration bill passed by Assembly, 1893, 180; publication of registry lists recommended in cities, 310; additional regulations needed to prevent fraud, X, 508, 728; judicial review, 612; additional information required, 729.

VETOES. Albany, providing for, VII, 263; New Lots, 413; requiring personal appearance of voter, VIII, 415; Cities Act, extending to Fishkill, 719; consolidating registry books with enrollment books, X, 279; forms of, amending Election Law, 808.

REHOBOTH. Conference of Governors at, I, 140.

REHWINKE, HENRY. VETOES. Relief, X, 53; New York fireman, charges against, hearing, 63.

REID, GEORGE W. Bank examiner, charges against Superintendent Ellis, VII, 66.

REID, FRANK W. Justice of the peace, Johnstown, legalizing acts, veto, IX, 725.

REID, SAMUEL C. Commander of frigate General Armstrong, thanked by Legislature for services at Fayal, II, 859; letter from Governor Tompkins, 862; reply, 863.

REIDSVILLE. Resistance to process, Van Rensselaer rent, III, 826, 828, 832, 835.

REILLY, JAMES P. New York fireman, reinstatement, veto, IX, 727, 804.

REILLY, MARY ROSE. Escheat bill, veto, IX, 467.

"RELATIONS." Published by French, plans of conquest, I, 550.

RELIGION. See also RELIGIOUS TOLERATION. Support of ministers, I, 19, 32, 35, 38, 39, 42, 115; Protestant in colony, 40, 77, 98; irreligion and immorality in colony, 80; instruction of Indians in, 86; progress among Indians, 291; Indian church at Canajoharie, 554; Protestant situation in Europe, 622; George II carrying on war to maintain, 635; resolution by Continental Congress for encouragement of, II, 56; gospel and school lots, 291; languishing state of, 715; bible in public schools, 727; religious instruction in State prisons, appropriation, veto, VII, 784.

RELIGIOUS CORPORATIONS. Act relating to, II, 467, 468; IV, 634; expenses of, assessment of members recommended, II, 467; property, sale of, 645; property exempt from taxation, IX, 232. VETOES. In Harlæm, appropriations for, II, 1111; changing names, V, 125, 127; VI, 270, 433; VII, 133, 807; VIII, 205, 617, 1096; IX, 37, 348; X, 700; authorizing sale of property, V, 150; VI, 45, 209, 437; supplemental act, 583, 684; amending general acts, VII, 132; extinct churches, 265; devises to, limiting amount of, 266; First Wesleyan Methodist church, Chazy, confirming organization, 357; appointment of constables, 508; First Congregational and First Baptist church, Kendall, sale and division of property, 881; grounds, buildings and property, powers of trustees, 931; Ebenezer Baptist church, exemption from assessments, 931; burial plats, taking in trust, 935; St. Paul's Methodist Episcopal church, Onondaga Valley, legalizing title to land, 1100; Kings county, relief of, VIII, 468; Protestant Episcopal Church,—incorporation of churches connected with, amending act, 618;—vestrymen and church wardens, annual election of, 618; African Methodist Episcopal churches, special provisions, 1095; New York Conference of the African Methodist Episcopal Church, charter, 1101; devise to, limiting effect of, IX, 623; trusts for, 725; First Universalist Society, Mount Vernon, relief from assessment, X, 254; Ninth Baptist church, Syracuse, changing name, 377; New York, exemption from assessments, 583; Methodist Episcopal church, transfers and conveyances, 704; St. Paul's Reformed Episcopal church, Bronx borough, relative to, 806; Congregational churches, extinct or disbanded, relative to property of, 813.

RELIGIOUS MEETINGS. VETOES. Disturbance of, VII, 1043; disturbing camp meetings, prevention of, IX, 811; X, 170.

RELIGIOUS TOLERATION. See also RELIGION. Shakers, II, 921, 948; in common schools, III, 768; sectarian instruction prohibited in schools, 951; indispensable in free government, IV, 711; secured by Constitution, V, 472; VII, 597; VIII, 23, 178, 302, 479; freedom of worship, institutions for care of poor, veto, VII, 596; additional instruction for convicts in State prisons, veto, 919; freedom of worship in public institutions, VIII, 23, 178, 302, 479.

RELYEA, PETER, JR. Colonel, affidavit by, anti-rent troubles, III, 829.

REMINGTON AND PALMER. Court of Claims, veto, X, 449.

REMINGTON RIFLES. Altering sights, appropriation, veto, VII, 478.

REMONSTRANCE. By London merchants against colonial tariff, I, 198; Assembly sends to Governor, 422, 432; publication of, 446; against repeal of act abolishing imprisonment for debt, III, 446; from District of Columbia, power of Congress, 906; Senecas, against act confirming new government, IV, 503; Canada, against interruption of navigation between Missisquoi bay and Richelieu river, 574; New York Chamber of Commerce against incorporation of Hell Gate Navigation Company, 824; Albany, street improvement bill, V, 655.

REMOVAL. Of disaffected persons, II, 34.

REMOVAL OF CAUSES. In Federal courts, II, 404, 415; under act to suppress immorality, 416; foreign insurance companies, prevention of, veto, VII, 265, 573.

REMOVAL OF OFFICERS. Under first Constitution, II, 500; Federal judges, proposed amendment, 627, 630; United States Senator, by State Legislatures, proposed amendment, 631; Ulster county courthouse commissioners, 944; Van Ness case, 1031; by Governor, III, 133; Inglis case, 906; judges, principles applicable to, 929; power not legislative but executive, 1021; judicial, amendment relative to, IV, 55, 109, 137; Governor's power should be extended, V, 190, 294, 387; suspension should be authorized, 387; in general, principles applicable to, 716; commissioners to take testimony, 716; judges, constitutional provision, 723; VI, 833; VII, 533; VIII, 935; X, 828; justices of the peace, VI, 49; health officer, Governor cannot remove, 361; Judge Prindle, charges against, 440; Judge McCunn, charges against, removed, 497; Judge Curtis, charges against, 498; State Treasurer, 633; local constitutional provision, 734; general constitutional provision, 806, 833; separating from power of appointment, 833; sheriff, 833; procedure in nature of a summary trial, 833; charges against Superintendent of Banks Ellis, VII, 56, 65; charges against Superintendent of Insurance Smyth, 180; charges against trustees of Binghamton Insane Asylum, 443; disabled judges, 533; Senate's exclusive power in certain cases, VIII, 487; case of Justice Pitshke, New

Removal of Officers — *(Continued).*

    York City Court, 935; superintendents of reformatories, IX, 332, 387; power essential to good government, 387; Governor may remove district attorney, 410; New York, power of removal bill, 1895, 420, 552; New York, police justices, 579; Governor's power as to New York city, X, 209, 230; New York, city employees, regulations concerning removal, 211; county officers, Governor's power of removal, 230; Governor may remove Fiscal Supervisor and superintendents of charitable institutions, 336; judges, what constitutes cause, 829.

    Vetoes. Relative to, IV, 772; New York, procedure, VII, 413; New York, park keepers, 1086; investigations by Governor, expenses, appropriation, IX, 75; New York, department heads, removal by mayor, 415.

Remsen, Henry. Claim of, lands in Montgomery county, II, 261.

Rendezvous. For expedition against West Indies, I, 287, 288; at Albany, Crown Point expedition, 419; at Niagara for Indian War, 676; places of, Civil War, V, 400.

Rensselaer. Police, members, compensation, veto, X, 715.

Rensselaer County. Repair of courthouse and jail, II, 417; act for powder magazine, 683; militia brigade called out, 807; militia ordered into service, anti-rent troubles, III, 834; riots in, 941; agricultural society in, 945; anti-rent troubles in, IV, 147; tenants represented before Assembly committee on anti-rent troubles, 328; Van Rensselaer leases, description of, 329; memorial on anti-rent troubles, V, 792; exempted from Town Auditor's Act, VIII, 49; average excise license fees, 1889, 687; highways, cost of labor system, 1892, IX, 200; surrogate, increasing salary, act relative to, 224; insane, care of, county and State systems compared, 228; Berlin, railroad commissioner, abolishing office, 232.

    Vetoes. Cullers of staves and heading, III, 438; street railroads, fares on, V, 653; treasurer, increasing fees, VI, 333; support of poor, 339; house of industry, board of governors for, care of poor, 1032; publication of session laws, VII, 267; contested election, Derrick, Assembly, expenses, 917; sheriff, fixing compensation, 1115; coroner, compensation and proceedings, VIII, 62; Greenbush, relief of poor, 699; county judge and surrogate, increasing compensation, IX, 107; surrogate, increasing compensation, 108, 225; contracting board, bill to create, X, 63; county treasurer, relative to, 583.

Rensselaer School, Troy. Offers use of school for instruction of teachers, III, 219.

RENSSELAERVILLE. Proceedings for collection of Van Rensselaer rent, III, 823; Van Rensselaer leases, description of, IV, 329.

RENSSELAERWYCK. Representation in first Assembly, I, 9; Abraham Ten Broeck, Assembly, favors colonial union, 767; manor, description of leases, III, 775; commission appointed to examine conditions in, 776, 863; represented before Assembly committee on anti-rent troubles, IV, 328; description of, 328; claim of tenants, 338.

RENT. Distress for, abolished, IV, 241, 242, 338, 653; reserved, taxation, 242, 338, 653; taxation, report of Assembly committee, 338, 357.

REPLEVIN. VETOES. Proposed Code substitute for, VII, 188; possession of property on giving security, X, 590.

REPORTER. Supreme Court, provided for, III, 5; VI, 261; IX, 546; X, 679; — furnishing papers to, veto, IX, 791; miscellaneous, appropriation for expenses, veto, X, 555.

REPRESENTATIVES IN CONGRESS. Election of, 324, 705; IV, 5; bill for election of, veto, II, 325; letter and papers from, 386; proposed amendment as to eligibility, 426; qualifications, 433, 434, 439; III, 883; election by districts, II, 471, 750, 919, 924, 990; III, 939, 1033; apportionment, II, 324, 546, 705; III, 387, 392, 939; IV, 85; VIII, 135; amendment, prohibiting increase of salary during term, II, 919, 930; ineligibility to certain offices, 1062; proposed amendment making ineligible to civil appointment by President, III, 137; State's power to determine election, 820; how apportioned, Fourteenth Amendment, V, 790; disqualified by participation in rebellion, 790; election, constitutional provision, IV, 5; VI, 38; election, supervision, congressional action, 255; VII, 306; qualifications of voters, 306.

REPRIEVE. Of Jacob Leisler and Jacob Milborne suggested, not granted, I, 21; by Legislature, Wood case, II, 78; by Governor,— Arnold case, 576; — Williams case, 621; — Burk case, 856; Northrup case, 874.

REPUBLIC LIFE INSURANCE AND TRUST COMPANY, NEW YORK. Charter, veto, VI, 336.

REPUBLICAN FORM OF GOVERNMENT. Rhode Island denies power of Congress to inquire concerning, in State, IV, 86; guaranteed to each State, V, 616; proposed guarantee to cities not adopted, VII, 728.

REPUDIATION. Of State debts, suggestion condemned, III, 1047; IV, 40; Georgia opposes, 46, 86; New Jersey and Alabama oppose, 48; partial, by payment of interest in currency instead of coin, V, 580.

RESCUE HOOK AND LADDER COMPANY, No. 1, BATH. Charter, veto, VI, 55.

RESCUE HOOK AND LADDER COMPANY, TONAWANDA. Charter, veto, VI, 825.

RESERVOIR. VETOES. New York, Jerome park, bridge over, X, 176, 326; State, Woodhull, Herkimer, cleaning, 320; Madison, repair of bridge over, 645.

RESIDENT. Suggested legislative definition for election purposes, III, 772.

RESTLESS, THE. United States steamship, repairing and equipping, veto, X, 299.

RETAIL GROCERS' UNION, NEW YORK. Charter, veto, VIII, 197; protests against liquor bill, 1888, 543.

RETALIATION. In treatment of prisoners, II, 116; sale of forfeited estates, 203; of Virginia against New York for refusal to surrender alleged fugitive from justice, III, 910, 925, 936, 980, 1028, 1037; by South Carolina, sympathizing with Virginia in same matter, 980, 1028; on insurance legislation, condemned, VII, 574; foreign insurance companies, act of 1896, IX, 691.

RETROSPECTIVE LAWS. Proceedings of Council of Safety, II, 30; crimes not to be created by, 38; rights of citizens as result of war, 215; reversions and remainders, 240; curing defects in deeds, 245; widows of attainted persons, 582, 784; Van Rensselaer leases, IV, 241; second appeal from judgment, 532; objectionable character of, 536; Syracuse penitentiary, veto, VI, 587; Western House of Refuge, veto, 599.

REVENUE. Support of government, 1, 10, 11, 15, 16, 20, 33, 40, 81, 132, 148, 173, 176, 184, 188, 191, 206, 208, 216, 230, 243, 264, 277, 291, 307, 312, 470, 505, 515, 520, 584, 616, 641, 649, 660, 670, 681, 701, 715, 737, 741, 755, 759; provided for, I, 10, 81; act explained, 11; act passed by Leisler Assembly, 15, 16; by first General Assembly, 20; memorial from collector of port relative to, 22; payment of public debt, 32; from New York weighhouse, Crown to receive, 36, 38; perpetual for Crown proposed, 36; refused, 40, 42; act for, limited to six years, 81, 191; act for, to be in force two years, 95; Governor Cornbury urges consideration of, 108, 112, 127; received from Crown, no control by Assembly, 109; recommended, 142; act passed, 168; Crown rejects act imposing tariff on European imports, 198, 211; new act for three years, 217; discussion relative to, 221; act for five years passed, 230, 243; Governor presents abstract of accounts, 252; deficiency in, 255, 259, 264; new bills of credit authorized, 264; difference between Assembly and Lieutenant-Governor as to, 273; officers, King's right to appoint, 293, 299; Assembly insists on right to appoint officers, 294; lottery for raising public funds, 345, 363; for Canadian expedition, 374; laws to be indefinite in duration, 533; proposed indirect taxes, 574; Assembly suggestions concerning, 586; duties on colonies, protest against, 730; indirect methods of raising, II, 199; inquiry recommended, 219; Federal system, 264; 275; estimate of, 573; expected from canals, 1098; Federal, distribution among States, III, 154, 186, 307, 330,

REVENUE—(*Continued*).

373, 438, 898; under Federal constitution, control of, 331, 898; IV, 616; Federal, increasing, III, 368; new system necessary, 413; product of Liquor Tax Law, 1896, X, 30; derived wholly from indirect taxation, 1906, 923.

REVENUE BILLS. Terms of, prescribed, I, 8.

REVISED LAWS. Distribution of, II, 953.

REVISED STATUTES. Enacted, III, 129; IV, 713; included crimes, III, 129, 174; proof and recording of deeds, 176; vacancies in office, 176; care of poor, 177; Governor Clinton's comment on, 210; standard of weights and measures, 215; Governor Van Buren's comment on, 231; publication of, 253; repeal of certain bank provisions, 311; Governor Throop's comment on, 312; increase of State prison offenses, 383; murder, commission of another felony, IV, 309; unreasonable searches and seizures, 755; taxation of corporations, 775; religious corporations, sale of property, V, 150; VI, 45; expenditures for highways, 47; expenses in criminal cases, 143; special district attorney, 144; fast driving on bridges, 147, 151; grants of land under waters, 156, 690, 705; establishing highways, 182; defective patents, 215; bridges, 311; public administrator, 583; width of highways, 670; proof of wills, 684; dissolution of manufacturing corporations, VII, 59; definition of ballot, VIII, 913.

VETOES. Drainage, VI, 190; VIII, 130; X, 812; highways, amending act, 695; trusts, 709; assessment and collection of taxes, VII, 110; notices of elections, 129; inspectors of election, 130, 203; appointment of collectors of canal tolls, 131; habeas corpus and certiorari, 197; discontinuing highway, 201; taxation of corporations, 502; defining land, 506; officers chosen at certain elections, 506; amending, three bills, 805; comptroller's warrants, publishing statement of, VIII, 129; uses and trusts, 131; comptroller's report, 208; county treasurers, 291; sheep killed by dogs, 469; property liable to taxation, 890; assessments, 1038; poor, relief and support, 1040; executors and administrators, IX, 272; clerk of prisons, 428; limited partnerships, 718; exempting property of clergymen from taxation, 722; taxes, collection of, 722; ninth edition, appropriation for distribution, 767; State prisons, 814, 816; State prisons, manufacture of school furniture, X, 165; Birdseye's edition, purchase and distribution, 430; parole of prisoners, 585.

REVOLUTION, AMERICAN. Beginning of, I, 765; martial law in New York, 765, 779.

REVOLUTION, ENGLISH. Mentioned, I, 194.

REVOLUTIONARY WAR. See WAR OF THE REVOLUTION.

REWARDS. For scalps, I, 389, 460, 468; by Massachusetts for scalps, 595; King offers land for military service, 598; for conviction of New York rioters, 726; New York riot, arrest of instigators, II, 246; for recapture of escaped prisoner, 393, 427; for destruction of animals, 1107; suggested for inventions, III, 65; in Morgan abduction case, 185; offered for conviction of participants in disturbance in northeastern part of State, 760; should not be frequently offered in criminal cases, IV, 706, 728; conviction of incendiaries, burning of quarantine buildings, V, 102; free navigation of Mississippi, 327, 341; for apprehension of criminals, 698; received by public officers, VI, 37; convictions for obstructing railroads, VII, 153; appropriation for, 153.

REYNOLDS, ANDREW. Estate, relief, II, 582.

REYNOLDS, MARY. Relief of, II, 582.

REYNOLDS, RICHARD S. Assignee of patent of Savage magazine rifle, IX, 637.

REYNOLDS, THOMAS. Act legalizing contract with town of Galen, VIII, 1148.

REYNOLDS, VALENTINE. Relief, veto, VI, 185.

RHINEBECK. Contraband goods landed at, II, 58; committee of, relief, 167.

RHODES, J. HARSEN. President State Association of Savings Bank, opinion on taxation of mortgages, X, 801.

RHODE ISLAND. Lieutenant-Governor Ingoldesby's proposed visit to, I, 139; colonial union, 366; represented in Albany Convention, 578; financial aid from Crown, 599, 604; troops for Canadian expedition, 620, 634, 644, 654; conference on paper currency, II, 11; letter from Governor Green, scarcity of bread, 68; resolution of Congress, supplies for, 69; delegates in Congress, letter from, alleged improper publication by Francis Childs, 274; disapproves Georgia proposition to reduce senatorial term, 830; disapproves North Carolina and Massachusetts propositions relative to representatives in Congress and presidential electors, 866; favors distribution of proceeds of public lands, establishment of national bank, III, 909; favors uniform election of President and Vice-President, 988; usurpation of government in, 1037; recommends refunding fine imposed on General Jackson, IV, 45; denies power of Congress to inquire into form of State government, 86; Massachusetts boundary, application to New York for record of, 456, 507; record presented by New York, 457, 507; resolutions,— slavery, 507; — national bureau of agriculture, 510; — Dorr treason case, 817; — French spoliation claims, 865; action on independence monument, V, 122; appropriation for Antietam cemetery, 840; usury laws repealed, VI, 552; information as to vital statistics, X, 870.

RICE, MRS. GERTRUDE S. Communication to Governor, relative to appointment of William Church Osborn as commissioner in lunacy, X, 42.

RICE, VICTOR M. Superintendent of Public Instruction, work commended, V, 694.

RICE, WILLIAM A. Member of New Capitol Commission, VI, 229.

RICE, WILLIAM M. Alleged murder of, X, 928.

RICHARDS, PAUL. Service in exchange of prisoners, I, 489.

RICHARDSON, A. P. Justice of peace, Chesterfield, legalizing acts, veto, X, 63.

RICHARDSON, JOHN. Indian claims, II, 514.

RICHARDSON, JOHN P. Governor of South Carolina, letter from Governor Seward, III, 982.

RICHELIEU RIVER. Water connection with Missisquoi bay, alleged interruption of, IV, 574.

RICHFORD. Public square, veto, VII, 807.

RICHMOND, THE. Transporting General Montgomery's remains, expense of, II, 1001.

RICHMOND BOROUGH. VETOES. Public schools, X, 60; volunteer firemen, 60; veteran volunteer firemen associations, exemptions, 323; high school, changing site, erecting buildings, 447; Edgewater fire department, charter, 473; Memorial Day celebration, appropriation, 762; unpaid taxes, sales, 806.

RICHMOND COUNTY. Act for support of ministers in, I, 39; fortifications at Narrows, II, 750; arsenal in, 751, 753; cessions of land in, how made, 825; convict labor in, 875; yellow fever epidemic in, IV, 438; question as to oyster fishing in New York and Newark bays, 564; included in metropolitan police district, V, 27; VI, 30; declared to be in a state of insurrection, V, 79; liable for destruction of quarantine buildings, 105, 280; VI, 783; amount of damages awarded, V, 280; completing indices of records, VI, 167; average excise license fees, 1889, VIII, 687; highways, cost of labor system, 1892, IX, 200; insane, care of, county and State systems compared, 228; merged in Greater New York, 300; included in metropolitan elections district, 885.

VETOES. Laying out Central park, VI, 191; construction of certain avenues, 196; Castleton school district No. 4, borrowing money, 262; recording notices of pendency of actions and discharges of mortgages, 323, 331; highway labor, 336; Rossville road extension, 340; survey, water supply, 503; police force, 511; VII, 130; New Brighton, use of dock, VI, 907; notaries public, relative to, 1036; VII, 131; Northfield, macadamizing certain roads, 132; changing site of courthouse and clerk's office, 250; clerk's office, recording certain papers, 497, 506; Middletown,

RICHMOND COUNTY, VETOES — (*Continued*).
        separate road district, 497, 507; judicial sales of land, VII, 933; assessors, establishing board, 1114; Northfield, board of education, amending act, VIII, 1039; taxes, facilitating collection, abolishing town collectors, IX, 399; police department, reorganization, 490; election of police commissioner, 494; common schools, 718; commissioner of jurors, creating office, 796; courts, where to be held, amending Laws 1897, chapter 541, 868; stenographer, Surrogate and County Courts, compensation, X, 259; Silver Lake park, relative to, 715; volunteer firemen, New York, relative to, 715; park commissioners, secretary and watchman, compensation, 959; deputy sheriff, attending court, compensation, 961.

RICHMOND COUNTY STORAGE AND BUSINESS COMPANY. Increasing capital stock, veto, VI, 815.

RICHMOND HILL. Volunteer Firemen's Benevolent Association, charter, veto, X, 472.

RICHMOND, VAN RENSSELAER. State Engineer and Surveyor, Buck case, VI, 682.

RICHMOND, VIRGINIA. Fall of, V, 676.

RICHTER, NICHOLAS. Petition from, distresses of, II, 81.

RICKARD, MICHAEL. Nominated as railroad commissioner, withdrawn, VIII, 373.

RIDDER, THOMAS B. Affidavit by, anti-rent trouble, III, 829.

RIDER, LEWIS. Board of Audit, veto, VII, 936.

RIDERS. On New York tax bill, V, 869; Governor Robinson protests against, VII, 26, 159; constitutional limitation of, 26, 159; IX, 403; supply bill, quarantine warehouse company, VII, 588, 1085; board of claims, awards, 1889, veto, VIII, 885; 1893, veto, IX, 275; appropriation bill, 1894, appointments by Attorney-General, veto, 403, 488; executive protests against, VII, 26, 158, 588; IX, 404; protest by President Hayes, 406.

RIFLE MEN. For frontier service, II, 13; organization of, 339.

RIFLE RANGES. For first and second divisions, VI, 358; inspector of rifle practice, 621.
        VETOES. Creedmoor, repairs, IX, 76; Bath-on-Hudson, additional land, 244; indoor, Oswego Armory, 604; Creedmoor, additional land, X, 319.

RIKER'S ISLAND. Soldiers' hospital on, V, 488.

RILEY, ELLA. Widow of James Riley, escheat, veto, X, 446.

RILEY, JOHN. Relief, veto, VI, 213.

RILEY, JOHN. Troy school janitor, claim, veto, X, 634.

RINDERPEST. Board of commissioners, report, V, 791, 861; VI, 260; commission should be continued, 246.

RINGGOLD. Battle, monument to New York troops, VIII, 1077; IX, 324, 577.

RIO GRANDE RIVER. Operations on, war with Mexico, IV, 416.

RIO JANEIRO. Vessels from, detained for observation, yellow fever, VI, 626.

RIORDAN, DANIEL J. Senate, member of insurance investigating committee, 1905, X, 825.

RIOT. In Livingston manor, I, 610; in New York, 707, 711, 725; II, 245; III, 524, 527; payment of losses suffered by, I, 713; in Albany and Dutchess counties, 717; in Cumberland county, 764; in Rensselaer and Schenectady counties, III, 941; at election in New York, 1034; resulting from draft, in New York, V, 545; railroads, 1877, VII, 151.

RIPLEY. VETOES. Quincy Rural Cemetery Association,— charter VI, 501; — acquiring additional land, 501.

RIPLEY, ELEAZER W. General, success in Niagara campaign, II, 802; thanked by Legislature and presented with sword, 832; letter from Governor Tompkins, 837; reply, 838.

RISLEY, EDWIN H. Attorney for State dairy commissioner, Senate investigation, appropriation, veto, VIII, 840; Board of Claims, veto, 1038; X, 709; assignee of patent of Savage magazine rifle, IX, 637.

RITTENHOUSE, DAVID. Survey of boundary between New York and Pennsylvania, I, 761; II, 225.

RIVER IMPROVEMENT COMMISSION. VETOES. Appropriation, X, 793; assessment of property benefited, 955.

RIVER INDIANS. Come into settlement on Governor's proclamation, I, 607; removed to Mohawk castles, 607.

RIVERS. Act to prevent casting ballast in, I, 11; improvement of, IV, 391; legislative resolutions, 393; improvement, benefits to canal commerce, 738; appropriations for improvement, observations by Governor Dix, VI, 576; effect of declaring them to be public highways, VIII, 381, 407, 454; public highways, condemnation proceedings, act of 1902, X, 457; Federal expenditures on, 730.

VETOES. Floating timber, logs and lumber, VII, 415, 506; IX, 815; Independence, relative to, VIII, 507; tidal, bridges and highways over, 640; free flow of, amending Highway Law, IX, 801; Improvement Commission, appropriation, X, 793.

RIVES, GEORGE L. Former corporation counsel, New York, opinion, East River Gas Company, bill, X, 660.

RIVES, WILLIAM C. Delegate from Virginia to Washington Peace Convention, V, 311.

ROADS. See also HIGHWAYS AND STATE ROADS. Between New York and Hartford, proposed improvement of, I, 757; from Walton to Great Shandaken, II, 312; State roads, lottery for, 385; construction of free, veto, 591; between Albany and St. Lawrence river, report of commission on, 756, 795; improvement of, through interior of State, 853; III, 80; encouraging improvement of, II, 971, 1012; III, 374; Roman, description of, 374; in France and Holland, 374; Carthage to Lake Champlain, veto, VI, 315; through State lands at Clinton prison, veto, VII, 920; improvement of, VIII, 923; IX, 198; county, act to establish, VIII, 1041; good roads act of 1906, 1043; macadam roads, estimated cost, IX, 201; market roads recommended, 203; National Good Roads Conference, Atlanta, 1895, 667; good roads, State should aid in construction of, X, 214; total mileage in State, 1904, 618; private, amending Highway Law, veto, 809.

ROANOKE, THE. Transferred from New York harbor to Hampton Roads, V, 549.

ROANOKE ISLAND. Success of Union Army at, V, 439.

ROBBERIES. Diminution of, II, 76; punishment of, III, 285.

ROBERTS, ABNER L. Board of Claims, veto, VIII, 1040.

ROBERTS, JAMES A. Comptroller, opinion, sale of State bonds, X, 802.

ROBERTS, JOHN. Colonel, letter from, I, 385; goes to Boston to confer with Governor Shirley, 391, 398.

ROBERTS, JOHN. Board of Claims, damages for imprisonment on alleged improper conviction of burglary, veto, IX, 250; act passed, 1895, 250.

ROBERTS, JOHN H. Claim against New York, veto, VIII, 884.

ROBERTSON, E. Dock on Oneida lake, veto, VI, 156.

ROBERTSON, JAMES. Appointed Governor, I, 779; jurisdiction and functions of, limited, 779; seeks to re-establish civil government, 779; leaves New York, 780; official service, pref. x.

ROBERTSON, JAMES. Dock on Oneida lake, veto, VI, 156.

ROBERTSON, JOHN. Appointed by Virginia commissioner to visit seceding States, V, 312.

ROBERTSON, WILLIAM H. Senate, member of committee on arrangements, opening of new capitol, VII, 270; appointed collector of New York, 556; delegate to National Republican Convention, 1880, 562.

ROBINSON, C. Governor-elect of Kansas, communication from, expected invasion from Missouri, VI, 864; letter from, V, 345.

ROBINSON, DAVID C. Governor's private secretary, proclamation convening Senate in extraordinary session, VII, 123.

ROBINSON, HAMILTON W. New York, Superior Court, opinion, vacancies in office, VI, 990.

ROBINSON, JEREMIAH P. Authorized to build and maintain bulkhead, 12th ward, veto, IX, 873.

ROBINSON, LUCIUS. Comptroller, communication from, interest on State debt, V, 490; financial operations, bounty debt, VI, 1014; Governor, portrait, VII, 1.

1877. Annual message, VII, 1; finances, 2; debt, 3; bounty debt, 4; general fund debt sinking fund, 4; canals, 5; diversion of trade from canals, 5; high or low tolls, 6; boatmen partners of State, 7; reduction of tolls, 7; lateral canals, 8; State prisons, 8; State Prison Investigating Commission, 9; Elmira Reformatory, 10; age limit of prisoners, Elmira Reformatory, 11; constitutional amendments, Superintendent of Prisons, Superintendent of Public Works, 11; public buildings, 12; protest against new capitol, 12; State Board of Health, 13; commissioners of emigration, 14; Indemnity Bond Act, unconstitutional, 14; savings banks, 16; method of ascertaining value of surplus held by savings banks, 16; deposits with ordinary banks or trust companies, 16; limiting individual deposits, 17; deposits of money paid into court, 17; dividends, 18; savings bank reserves, 18; common school statistics, 19; need of education, 20; opposes taxation for higher education, 21, 156; are normal schools worth what they cost?, 21; changes in school text books, 21; colleges and academies, 22; State Library, and Museum of Natural History, 23; National Guard, 23; reduction of taxes, 24; increased valuations, 24; taxation, exempting churches, schools and hospitals, 25; taxing surplus of banks, 25; legislation in appropriation bills, 26; State survey, 26; currency, 27; railroad reports, 28; insecurity of places of public resort, 29; municipal reform, 30; people should remedy evils of local government, 31; corrupt use of money in elections, 31; betting upon elections, 32; national affairs, 32; presidential electors, 35; Louisiana returning board, 37; Florida, Board of State Canvassers, 37; South Carolina, Board of State Canvassers, 38; usurpation of power, election of 1876, 39; various reports, 42; imperfect condition of bills, 42; communication from Governor of Michigan, lighthouse at Stannard Rock, 46; protest against bill authorizing filling of channel between Ward's and Randall's islands, 46; communication from Secretary of State of Connecticut, Hell Gate pilotage, 47; communication from commissioners of emigration, affairs and resources, 55; communication from director-general of United States Centennial Commission, awards, 55; charges against Superintendent of Banks Dewitt C. Ellis, 56; communication from Governor of Michigan, refuge harbor at Grand Marais harbor, Lake

Robinson, Lucius, 1877 — (*Continued*).

    Superior, 60; additional charges against Bank Superin-
tendent Ellis, 65; report on exterior pier and bulkhead
lines, 71; comments on new capitol, 92; home rule in New
York, 101; proclamation convening Senate in extraordinary
session, Ellis case, 122.

Memorandum of Approval. Appropriations, new capitol and
insane asylums, VIII, 123.

Vetoes. Guion, justice of peace, Seneca Falls, legalizing acts,
VII, 44; Binghamton, amending charter, 46; New York
District Court clerks, 47; superintendent of public works,
49; notaries public, additional number, 54; VIII, 44; plate
glass insurance companies, deposit of securities, VII, 55;
manufacturing corporations, Herkimer county, facilitating
dissolution, 59; Seneca Falls board of education, appointment of assessor, 60; fishways, State dams, Oswego, Oneida
and Seneca rivers, 61; taxes, collectors and receivers, 62;
Kings county, New Lots, Bushwick avenue, 63; Plattsburgh
fire department, 64; Watervliet, election of town officers,
64; Andes fire department, 65; Sag harbor, fire apparatus
and water supply, 68; Owasco lake, prohibition against
taking trout, 69; highways, system of repairs, 69; Mexico,
rebuilding town hall, 71; county treasurers, Monroe and
Seneca, 71; Poughkeepsie, street railroads, 73; Seneca
Indians, oil pipe line, Allegany reservation, 73; villages,
amending general law, Niagara city, 75; Baptist church
and Society, Hoosick, removing dead from burying ground,
76; women, election as school officers, 76; Carthage, amending village charter, 78; Dunkirk, amending village charter,
79; Surrogate's Court, proceedings in, 79; married women,
insuring husbands' lives, 80; items in supply bill, 81;
Brooklyn Library Building Fund Association, eastern district, amending charter, 96; Clyde and Rose Plank Road
Company, repealing charter, 97; Skaneateles engine-house,
97; villages, amending general act, Niagara Falls, 98;
Harpersville Cemetery Association, granting certain powers,
98; New York charter, supplemental act, 99; common
schools, apportionment of moneys, 109; taxes, assessment
and collection, 110; Pike, sale of portion of schoolhouse
site, 111; New York harbor, pier and bulkhead lines, Newtown creek, 111; Erie county Surrogate's Court, 113; metropolitan sanitary district, repeal as to Queens county, 113;

ROBINSON, LUCIUS, 1877, VETOES — (*Continued*).

items in canal administration bill, 114; item in Canal Awards Act, 119; Rockton, amending village charter, 120; First Methodist Episcopal Church, Carlton, burial ground, preventing interments in, 120; First Methodist Episcopal Society, Watkins, 121; Saratoga Springs, Nelson Street cemetery, removing dead, 121; Albany harbormaster, 121; New York, securing better administration, 125; Brooklyn, government of, 126; Insurance Department, amending act, 126; New York public instruction, 127; omnibus veto, 128; general note on MUNICIPAL REFORM, VII, 134.

1878. Annual message, VII, 137; finances, 137; debt, 138; taxation, 139; too many town officers, 140; congratulates people on payment of bounty debt, V, 610; VII, 141; payment of general fund debt, 141; canal debt, 142; business and revenues of canal, 142; lateral canals, 145; State prisons, 145; commutation of punishments for good behavior, 147; more discrimination in inflicting punishments needed, 147; State reformatory at Elmira, 147; unemployed labor, 148; inflation of currency, 149; resumption of specie payments, 150; railroad riots of July, 151; calls out National Guard, 152; proclamation, interference with railroads, 153; National Guard, 154; separate companies of National Guard in counties, 154; common schools, 155; taxation for education, 156; colleges and academies, 157; constitutional amendments, 157; general legislation in appropriation bills, 159; village charter amendments, 159; New York city affairs, 160; new charter needed, 162; harbormasters and port wardens, 163; excise laws, 163; reapportionment, 164; life insurance companies and savings banks, 165; extravagant administration condemned, 167; failure of adequate supervision, 167; code of procedure, 168; commissioners to revise statutes, 168; repeal of Code of Civil Procedure, 169; specie payments, 170; Connecticut boundary, through Long Island sound, 172; Antietam National cemetery ceded to United States, 172; slow progress of work on new capitol, 173; completion of Assembly chamber, 174; other public buildings, 175; various annual reports, 178; report of Commission on Purchase of Executive Residence, 178; member of commission, 178; charges against Insurance Superintendent John F. Smyth, 180; Connecticut resolu-

ROBINSON, LUCIUS, 1878 — (*Continued*).

    tions, appointing commissioners on boundary, 200; unable to attend ceremonies at opening of Assembly chamber, new capitol, 271; Legislature occupies new capitol, 271.

  MEMORANDUMS OF APPROVAL. Pipe line companies, general act, VII, 241; State survey, 248, 875; Albany Burgess Corps, arms for, 248.

  VETOES. Commissioners of excise, Bath, legalizing acts of, VII, 178; Code of Civil Procedure, supplemental act, 182; habeas corpus and certiorari, amending Revised Statutes, 197; taxes, Hudson, extending time for collection, 199; Westchester county, keeping open certain offices, 201; highways, discontinuance, amending Revised Statutes, 201; American Jersey Cattle Club, charter, 202; elections, inspectors, method of appointment, 203; Fort Edward board of education, contract with Fort Edward Collegiate Institute, 205; New York commissioners of deeds, additional number, 206; Saratoga county, clerk hire, authorizing oyer and terminer to direct payment of, 207; New York Central and Hudson River Railroad Company, taxes in Mentz, 207; Monroe county, sale of property for unpaid taxes, 208; New York, payment of debt, 209; villages, amending general act, 1870, Northville, 214; German Flats, board of alms, 215; Genesee Valley canal, extending time for sale, 216; Scio, appointment of constables, 218; items in supply bill, 218; Tornado Hook and Ladder Company No. 1, Union, charter, 233; Orange county jail limits, 234; fish, Esopus creek, protection, 234; canals, general act, 234; Grand Council of Royal Templars of Temperance, charter, 240; Auburn City Hospital, charter, 241; item in canal administration bill, 249; town insurance companies, general act, 249; citizens, claims against other States, 250; Richmond county, changing site of courthouse and clerk's office, 250; New York, commissioner of jurors, 251; New York, public administration, 252; Supreme Court, third judicial district, justices' salaries, 257; Code of Civil Procedure, general amendments, 262; Albany elections, registration, 262; Game Law, special game constables, 263; omnibus veto, 264.

  1879. Annual message, VII, 271; finances, 273; general fund, bounty and floating debts paid, 273; debt, 275; taxation, 276; unappropriated balance in treasury, 277; canals, 278;

ROBINSON, LUCIUS, 1879 — (*Continued*).

reduction of tolls, 280; State prisons, 280; prisons over-crowded, 282; proposed enlargement of Clinton prison, 282; asylums for insane, 282; county jails and poorhouses, 286; inebriate asylum abolished, insane asylum established, 287; Soldiers and Sailors' Home, 288; protest against new capitol, 289; urges discontinuance of appropriations for new capitol, 292; National Guard, 293; children entitled to common school education, 295; opposed to taxation for higher education, 295; criticism on normal schools, 296; common school statistics, 296; reports of charitable institutions, 297; local debt and taxation, 298; evils of debt, 299; protection of Niagara Falls, 299; park at Niagara Falls, 300; game laws, 301; repeal of provision giving supervisors power to enact game laws, 302; suggests repeal of Code of Civil Procedure, 302; legislative apportionment, 303; insurance and savings banks, 303; recommends abolition of Insurance Department, 304; public guardianship of savings banks not needed, 305; Federal interference at elections, 306; new charter for New York city, 307; port wardens and harbormasters, 309; commissioners of emigration, 309; excise laws, 310; resumption of specie payments, 310; unemployed labor, revival of business, 312; agriculture underlies all other industries, 312; pardon report, 315; use of old Assembly chamber granted to ladies of Albany, 315; Tennessee resolutions, expressing thanks for aid in yellow fever epidemic, 316; transmitting communication from Secretary of Navy, 319; charges against Superintendent of Insurance Smyth, 319; New Jersey resolutions, commercial relations between United States and other countries, 321; announces death of former Governor Dix, 328; report of Federal commissioners on New York harbor pier and bulkhead lines, 353; recommends discontinuance of State and Adirondack surveys, 373; Cold Harbor lighthouse, 393.

MEMORANDUMS OF APPROVAL. New capitol, liability of commissioners, liquidation, VII, 399; apportionment act, 401; new capitol appropriation, 403; interest, reducing rate of, 404.

VETOES. Buffalo city hall and jail, construction and custody of, VII, 316; Syracuse police and fire commissioners, 317; Hamilton county highway, Johnsburgh to Long lake, 320;

ROBINSON, LUCIUS, 1879, VETOES — (Continued).

Brooklyn, amending charter, 321; fire insurance, false and
deceptive statements, 322; Lansingburgh, amending charter,
323; Erie canal, Rochester, bridge, Brown and Smith
streets, 324; Oneida Lake canal, completing reconstruction,
325; highway labor, 325; New York District Court janitors,
326; Cohoes, amending charter, powers of recorder, 327;
Gouverneur Fire Company charter, 327; Niagara and Orleans counties, boards of supervisors, poor expenses, 328;
Rockton, amending charter, 330; married women, contracts,
331; fire insurance, construction of policies, 332; elections,
poll clerks, 333; Corning, payment of bonds, 334; Five
Points House of Industry, New York, powers of, 334; processions and parades, cities, regulation of, 335; Troy Public Library, charter, 336; Le Roy, additional powers of
trustees, 337; Code of Civil Procedure, supplemental act,
337; Civil Code, 348; medical science, amending act, 353;
Long Island City, Steinway avenue improvement, 353; Erie
county and Buffalo, public buildings and grounds, 354;
United States Trade-Mark Association, charter, 355;
Buffalo, county taxes, collection of, 356; Erie county,
Supreme Court clerk, 356; First Wesleyan Methodist
Church, Chazy, confirming reorganization, 357; Jefferson
county, Black creek public highway, 358; items in canal
administration bill, 358; poor, Clinton, Niagara and Orleans
counties, support, 367; highways, laying out and altering,
367, 372; Long Island City,— Flushing avenue improvement, 368;—Astoria, certain streets and avenues, 369;
Brooklyn, elections, counting ballots and facilitating trial
of actions, 370; items in supply bill, 372; salt springs, lots,
Onondaga, 385; town insurance companies, general act, 387;
town meeting, time of transacting business, 387; merchandise, fraud in sale or exchange of, 388; board of supervisors, election districts, 388; police justices, Wolcott, 389;
Erie county, publication of legal notices in German newspaper, 390; Milton, school bonds, payment of, 391; Saratoga Springs, cemeteries, confirming purchase of land for,
391; New Rochelle, drainage, 392; salt springs, sale of lots,
purchase of other lands, 393; Brooklyn, Atlantic Avenue
Railroad, 394; Cayuga lake outlet, removal of obstructions,
405; United States, jurisdiction of Harlem river, Spuyten

ROBINSON, LUCIUS, 1879, VETOES — (*Continued*).

Duyvil creek, 406; taxes, Revision Commission, 407; Secretary of State, collection of labor statistics, 409; Regents, purchase of revolutionary letters, 409; Washington's headquarters, Tappan, purchase of, 410; Regents, objects of natural history, purchase of, 410; revision of militia laws, 411; omnibus veto, 412.

Quoted: Governor and Legislature, restriction on power to appropriate public funds, VIII, 118; — legislative violation of constitutional duty, effect on people, 158; — canals and prisons, improved administration resulting from change of system, 173; — State Board of Health, 174; — neglect of Legislature to enact Apportionment Law, 495; — need of excise revision, 512, 513, 1058; — protest against riders in appropriation bills, IX, 404; approves Poughkeepsie bridge extension bill, VIII, 444; pardon of John Roberts, 250; death of, 1094; legislative action thereon, 1095; official service, I, pref. xiii.

ROBINSON, LUCIUS J. C. New Jersey commissioner on New York boundary, VI, 779.

ROBINSON, PETER. Legal representatives, relief, veto, VI, 334.

ROBINSON, SIR THOMAS. Secretary of State, letter from, I, 555; colonial defense, 561, 565.

ROBINSON, WILLIAM C., and BOYDEN. Redemption from tax sale, Hamilton county, veto, X, 953.

ROCHESTER, MONROE COUNTY. Colored children to constitute separate school, III, 378; school for mechanical instruction, 381; market, act relating to, 531; public inconvenience resulting from unfinished canal bridges, IV, 16; State Fair at, 80; Western House of Refuge, 408; armory at, V, 175, 642; large number of special acts, VIII, 346; number of excise licenses, 1887, 359; excise license fees, 1889, 686; law library, IX, 46; wards, increasing number, 85; armory proposed at, 573; a city of the second class, 1898, 678; first-class city, 1908, 678; public schools, erection of new buildings, X, 34; streets and water pipes, 540.

VETOES. Protectives No. 1, amending charter, VI, 329; Safe Deposit Company, amending charter, 503; amending charter, 587; VII, 134; VIII, 468; X, 583, 635, 705; swing-bridge, Buffalo street, VI, 852; canal bridge, Averill and Munger streets, 859; approach to canal bridge, Averill street, 1008; VII, 117; law library, 220; Genesee river feeder, stop-gate, 233, 362; bound-

Rochester, Monroe County, Vetoes — (*Continued*).

aries, 267; erecting bridge over Erie canal, 324; canal bridge, Lyell street, 362, 589; ferry, Genesee river, 417; Rochester Electro-Medical Institute, charter, 416, 506; arsenal, local assessments, 927; house of refuge, local assessments, 927; exemption from damages for injuries by defective sidewalks, VIII, 629; Court of Appeals law library, appropriation, 856; salaries for members of board of education, 882; Erie canal bridge, Monroe avenue, IX, 59; police vacations, 120; claims, Board of Claims, 154, 290, 797; streets, restricting right to lay out, repeal, 217; paid fire department pension fund, 249; new act, 1894, 249; Children's Aid Society, charter, 450; claim against city, amending Submission Act, 719, 797; indorsement of ballots, shade trees, repeal, amending charter, 723; parks, 724, 727; city hall, remodeling, 731; waterworks bonds, 731; free academy, redemption of bonds, 731; park boulevards, 731; teachers' retirement fund, 788; arsenal, acquiring site, 788; Lutheran League, changing name, 793; State property, assessment, appropriation, X, 321; police department, reorganization, 469; armory, 586; assessments on State property, 640; assessments on State hospital, 697; fire department pension fund, 713, 714; police pension fund, 714; Brighton, enrollments, 806; Erie canal bridge, Lyell avenue, 929; Court of Appeals library, librarian, 952.

Rochester, Ulster County. Line of blockhouses from, I, 590; murder by Indians near, 626; petition, defense of frontier, II, 70.

Rochester, William B. Suggested appointment as postmaster at Bath, II, 1070.

Rochester Atheneum. Amending charter, veto, VI, 671; changing name and number of directors, VIII, 1162.

Rochester and Charlotte Turnpike Road Company. Changing name, veto, VII, 938.

Rochester Electro-Medical Institute. Charter, veto, VII, 416, 506.

Rochester Homeopathic Hospital. Exempting property from taxation, veto, IX, 235.

Rochester Institute of Practical Education. Incorporated, III, 378.

Rochester, Lockport and Niagara Falls Railroad Company. Consolidation with other companies authorized, V, 803.

Rochester and Olean Canal. See Genesee Valley Canal.

Rochester and Pine Creek Railway Company. Changing name, veto, VI, 1034.

Rochester and Syracuse Railroad Company. Consolidation with other companies authorized, V, 803.

Rochester State Hospital. Local assessment, veto, X, 697.

Rochester University. Aid recommended, IV, 603.

Rockaway. Beacon at, I, 151, 607; watchhouse at, 607; blockhouse, sea fencibles in, II, 810.

"Rocket, The." Locomotive engine, speed of, III, 397.

Rockland County. Average excise license fees, 1889, VIII, 687; highways, cost of labor system, 1892, IX, 200; insane, care of, county and State systems compared, 228; included in ninth judicial district, 547; X, 850.

    Vetoes. Dogs running at large, VI, 92; taxes, sales for nonpayment, 1035; notaries public, relative to, 1036; VII, 131; House of Good Shepherd, exempting property from taxation, 266; Monsey, Brewer Fire Company, charter, 268; Tappan, Washington's headquarters, purchase of, 410; county judge, compensation, 507; Orangetown union school district No. 1, changing date of annual meeting, VIII, 334; taxes, collection, 878; Penny bridge over Minisecongo creek, declaring jurisdiction of, IX, 264; taxes, bill to enforce collection, 282; justice of the peace, legalizing acts, X, 62; taking game in, 444.

Rockland Lake. Highway improvement, veto, VI, 338.

Rockton. Vetoes. Fire department, VII, 120; bi-partisan commission of public grounds, 330.

Rocky Rift Feeder. Dam, appropriation for completion, VI, 853; farm bridge, veto, 854.

Rodger & Co. Loss of public funds, relief of official depositor, veto, X, 275.

Rodgers, John, Dr. Regent, death of, II, 707.

Rodman, Charles. Canal award, veto, VII, 774.

Roebling, Washington A. Requests approval of Harvey rapid transit bill, VIII, 125.

Roebuck, Joseph. Estate, escheat, veto, X, 953.

Rogers, James T. Assembly, member of insurance investigating committee, 1905, X, 825; member of joint legislative committee on services in memory of former Governor Higgins, 963.

Rogers, William E. Nominated as railroad commissioner, VIII, 374.

Rogers Construction Company. Claim for construction of Tonawanda armory, veto, X, 383.

Roman Catholic Benevolent Society, New York. Relative to, veto, II, 1036, new bill passed.

Roman Catholic Orphan Asylum, New York. Reappropriation, veto, VI, 587.

Romans. Privileges of citizens not accorded to colonists, I, 491; knowledge of agriculture and art, II, 956; rights of creditors over debtors, III, 344; construction of roads, 374.

Rome, Italy. Imprisonment for debt, III, 344.

Rome, New York. Deposit of arms at, II, 682; deposit of military stores at, 755; arms for Mexico, 774; number of excise licenses, 1887, VIII, 359; excise license fees, 1889, 686.

     Vetoes. Increasing salaries, VI, 503; amending charter, VII, 265; retaining wall, Whitesboro street, 586; board of education, VIII, 130; canal bridge, George street, 294; IX, 628; fire commissioners, extending jurisdiction over police department, 390; defining boundary, 408; borrowing money for school buildings, 874; Erie canal wall, reappropriation, 890; sewer system, refunding assessments, 788; highways outside of tax district, X, 438, 446; city officers, powers and duties, 472; included in Highway Improvement Act of 1898, 522.

Rome Custodial Asylum. Repairs and improvements, veto, X, 295, 549; how classified, 334; increased accommodations, 610; general improvements, veto, 656; additional accommodations provided, 726.

Rome Street Railroad Company. Charter, veto, VII, 806.

Rome, Watertown & Ogdensburg Railroad Company. Purchasing bridge company stock, veto, VIII, 1130.

Rondout and Oswego Railroad Company. Asks State aid, V, 866; VI, 71.

Rood, Abijah. Claim, service of warrant, I, 762.

Roosevelt, Isaac. Member of Council of Appointment, II, 314.

Roosevelt, Theodore. Assembly, 1882, introduced bill prescribing method of electing New York aldermen, VIII, 281; 1884, second bill, 281; transmits report of Canal Investigating Commission of 1898, IX, 850; Governor, portrait, X, 1.

     1899. Annual message, X, 1; Spanish War, 1; condition of State affairs, 2; taxation, 2; revision of tax system needed, 2; canals and commerce, 3; decrease of commerce at New York, 3; extension of time of Commerce Commission, 3; condition of canals, 3; work of Canal Investigating Commission, 4; labor interests, 5; additional factory inspectors, 7; sweat shop system, 7; license of buildings for manufacturing purposes, 8; enforcement of Eight Hour Law, 9; unconstitutionality of act requiring marking of prison-made goods, 9; National Guard, 11; service of National Guard in Spanish War, 12; United States army should be increased, 13; major-general head of National Guard, act of 1898, 13; arms for National Guard, 13; arms of National Guard should be uniform with those of Federal Army, 14; defects of Springfield muskets, 14; regimental hospital, 16; good work of Red Cross Society, 16; Naval Militia, 17;

ROOSEVELT, THEODORE, 1899 — (*Continued*).

civil service, uniform system needed, 18; overlegislation, biennial sessions, 21; extending woman suffrage, 21; good roads, 21; forest preserve, 22; economy in State expense, 22; special counsel for State hospitals should be abolished, 22; University of the State of New York, 23; efficiency of State Library, 24; rapid transit, New York, 24; economy in New York's municipal government, 24; special commissioner of jurors, New York, 24; New York and Kings county clerk, sheriff and register should be salaried officers, 24; judges of Municipal Courts should be required to sit every day, 25; second and third-class cities, 25; uniform system of accounting, 25; number of corporation papers filed in Secretary of State's office, 26; Comptroller's report, 26; receipts from indirect taxation, 26; balance in State treasury, 27; Attorney-General's report, 27; school statistics, 27; revision of School Law, 27; banks, 28; condition of prisons, 28; grade crossings, 28; Department of Agriculture, 29; Excise Law, 30; various annual reports, 31, 32; claim of Canadian branch of Cayuga Indians, 31; pardon report, 32; returning Sullivan escheat bill, 33; certificates of necessity of immediate passage of bills, 33, 42, 44, 45, 47, 72, 73; report of Canal Investigating Commission, 34; condition of Rochester public schools, 34; report of commissioners to Trans-Mississippi International Exposition, 34; revision of tax laws, special message, 35; injustice in light taxation of corporations, 35; municipal ownership of corporations, 36; joint committee to investigate proper scheme of taxation, 37; communication from Fox and MacFarlane, canal counsel, 39; transmitting to Senate papers relative to nomination of William Church Osborn as commissioner in lunacy, 42; rapid transit, New York city, special message, 43.

MEMORANDUM OF APPROVAL. Regulating hours of labor, X, 48.

VETOES. Attorneys wearing gowns, X, 37; tenement-houses, licenses to manufacture in, 37; commissioner of jurors, Albany county, 44; New York Legislative Department, 46; new capitol Senate chamber, rearranging lighting system, 51; theater tickets, regulating sale, 51; labor, employees, safety appliances, 52; Albany Railway Company, bridge over Hudson river, 52; New York firemen and police, reinstatements, nineteen bills, 53; Niagara river, power ex-

ROOSEVELT, THEODORE, 1899, VETOES — (*Continued*).
periments, 54; adulteration of beer, 55; pharmacists and
druggists, regulating hours, 56; Brooklyn, offensive trades,
57; omnibus veto, 59.

Proclamation convening Legislature in extraordinary session,
May, 1899, X, 64; message, taxation of franchises, 64; reception to Admiral Dewey, 72; payment of fees into State
treasury, 73; appropriation for expenses of extraordinary
session, 73; announces death of former Governor Flower,
IX, 534; presides at Flower memorial services, 1900, 535.

1900. Annual message, X, 74; canals, 74; new Canal Commission,
1899, 75; complaints against former canal management, 76;
appointment of special counsel to assist Attorney-General,
77; Canal Board, 79; proceedings for termination of contracts under Nine-Million-Dollar Act, 79; problem of taxation, 80; taxation of foreign capital, 82; franchise tax, 83;
increase of salaries of State Tax Commission, 84; State
should control public utilities, 85; modern industrial conditions, 86; trusts, 88; protection of employees, 91; State's
right to prevent monopolies, 93; labor, 94; strikes for increase of wages, 94; license of employment bureaus, 95;
unsalaried inspectors, proposed appointment, 96; reform in
laws governing tenement-houses, 96; Tenement-House Commission, 96; hours of labor of drug clerks, 96; liability of
employers, 97; National Guard and Naval Militia, 97; State
camp, 98; rifle practice, 99; Fisheries, Forest and Game
Commission, 100; game wardens, 100; Adirondack and
Catskill forests should be public parks, 100; forest fires
should be prevented, 101; birds should not be killed to
obtain ornaments, 102; uniform open season, 102; building
and loan associations, 102; repeal of Horton Boxing Law,
104; amendment of Vagrancy Law, 105; completion of Bedford Reformatory, 106; completion of revision of statutes,
106; finances, 108; too many transfer tax assistants, 108;
fees of local officers under transfer tax, 109; alphabetical
list of corporations in office of Secretary of State, 110;
uniform time for laws to take effect, 111; excellent working of principle of indeterminate sentences, 111; separate
prison for confinement and execution of condemned
prisoners, 111; importation into State of prison-made goods
from other States should be regulated by Congress, 111;

ROOSEVELT, THEODORE, 1900 — (*Continued*).

consolidation of State land survey with State Engineer and Surveyor's office, 112; public instruction, 112; pedagogical department, Cornell University, 113; unification of educational system, 113; Unification Commission, 1899, 114; recommends department of education, 114; Excise Department, 115; Commission in Lunacy, 116; decrease in number of insane in State hospitals, 116; State charitable institutions, 116; repeal of act permitting courts to send female felons of mature age to houses of refuge, 117; commissioners of land office, leases with power of renewal for riparian lands, 117; Civil Service Commission, increased salaries, 117; grade crossings, appropriation, 118; health officer and quarantine, 119; self-supporting offices, 119; Department of Agriculture, 119; preventing adulteration of food, 120; property of State Agricultural Society transferred to State, 120; control of State Fair, 120; good work of farmers' institutes, 121; increase in engineering force of State Architect's office, 121; Superintendent of Public Buildings, 121; New York City Charter Commission, 122; memorandum on appointment of commissioners, 122; political assessments and the judiciary, 123; good roads, 123; State Printing Bureau, 123; Palisades, 123; Pan-American Exposition, 124; overlegislation, 126; blanket appropriation for bridges and repairs of canals, 126; report of Palisades Commission, 126; correspondence between Department of State at Washinton and British embassy, claim of Canadian branch of Cayuga Indians, 127; transmits report of Commission on Unification of Educational System, 128; certificates of necessity of immediate passage of bills, 130, 144, 145, 148, 149, 150; various annual reports, 130, 142; transmitting report of New York Commerce Commission, 130; discrimination of railroads against New York city, 131; report of canal investigating committee, 134; canals should be enlarged, 137; ship canal not practicable as State undertaking, 137; barge canal, 138; unlimited capital of canal transportation companies, 140; mechanical motive power on canals, 141; civil service should be applied to canals, 141; revision of laws for letting public contracts and advertising, 141; pardon report, 142; cession of Iona island to United States, 143; Tenement-house Commission in first-class cities, 146.

ROOSEVELT, THEODORE, 1900 — (Continued).

MEMORANDUMS OF APPROVAL. Queens County Court attendants, X, 151; stenographers, first judicial department, salaries, 152; teachers' salaries, 154; Brooklyn, Bedford and Remsen avenues, improvement, 155; Soldiers and Sailors' Home, 156; Kings county interpreter's compensation, 158.

VETOES. Street railroads, villages in Nassau county, X, 145; actions, settlement without consent of attorneys, 150; Troy, commissioner of education, 151; electric light companies in towns and villages, acquiring real estate, 159; New York Consolidation Act, summary proceedings, 159; trials, preferred causes, two bills, 159; New York, health department, anti-toxin accountant, compensation, 160; Game Law, fishing in Ouleout creek, 161; Watkins water supply, 161; Game Law, forest fires, services at, 161; primary elections, oaths, town clerk to administer, 161; suffrage, right of, crimes against, 162; slot machines, trials for keeping, 162; sale of liquor on election days, 162; villages, peddler's license, 163; justices of the peace, legalizing acts, 163; Keenan, monument to, 163; Indian reservation, felonies committed on, expenses of trials and proceedings, 164; second-class cities, charter amendment, duplicate, 164; Court of Claims, various claim bills, 165; State prisons, labor in, manufacture of school furniture, 165; New York Municipal Court attendants, claims, 168; Game Law, fishing in certain waters in Seneca county, 168; veterinary medicine, regulating practice, 169; Indians, undertaking given by, prosecution of, 169; New York, Garvey claim, 169; Court of Claims, Considine, 170; religious meetings, preventing disturbance of, 170; county clerk, authentication by, 171; franchise tax, amending act of 1899, 171; fees of tax collectors, 171; usury on personal credit security, 171; New York teachers, supply of, 172; midwifery, New York, regulating practice, 172; New York finance department, city magistrate's court, claims, 172; Court of Claims, canals, damages under Nine Million Dollar Act, 1895, 172; National Guard, Hollingworth service medal, 173; county detective, amending act, 173; Jamestown schools, designating special holidays, 173; fishing in Canandaigua and Honeoye lakes, 173; preference of actions, 173; Waterloo, amending village charter, 174; fishing in Chautauqua lake, 174; dentists, relief of certain students, 174; fishing in

RCOSEVELT, THEODORE, 1900, VETOES — (*Continued*).
Skaneateles lake, 174; Schiff, Regent's certificate, clerk of Court of Appeals to file *nunc pro tunc*, 174; St. Lawrence county purchasing committee, 175; Tidal Waterway Company, amending charter, 175; omnibus veto, 175.
QUOTED. Criticism on system of taxation, X, 835; official service as Governor, I, pref. xiii.

ROOT (Town). Leasehold estates in, IV, 331.

ROOT, ELIHU. Opinion, voter's freedom of selection of candidate cannot be restricted by form of ballot, IX, 395, 479.

ROOT, ERASTUS. Resigns as Niagara courthouse commissioner, II, 1117; chosen Lieutenant-Governor, III, 1; appointed Statutory Revision Commissioner, 18.

ROOT, JOSHUA. Claim, service of warrant, I, 762.

ROPES, RIPLEY, State charities commissioner, protests against Kings county farm bill, VIII, 595.

ROSE. Grand Army of the Republic, Sherman Post, use of room in town hall, veto, VIII, 528.

ROSEBOOM, ROBERT. Council of Appointment, communication from, II, 490, 491.

ROSENBURG, THOMAS. Commissioner, Allegany reservation, Red House bridge, veto, VII, 587.

ROSIN. How made, I, 146.

ROSS, ERASTUS. Trustee, Binghamton Insane Asylum, charges against, not removed, VII, 443.

ROSS, JOSIAH. Captain, sued by deserters for pay, I, 469.

ROSS AND SANFORD. Board of Claims, veto, IX, 237, 721.

ROSSVILLE ROAD. Richmond county, extension, veto, VI, 340.

"ROTA, THE." British vessel, engagement with American vessel at Fayal, II, 859.

ROTH, GEORGE W. Court of Claims, veto, X, 944.

ROTTERDAM. VETOES. Taxes, extending time for collection, V, 116; assessors, fixing compensation, 439.

ROUND LAKE ASSOCIATION. Water supply, right to condemn property, veto, IX, 794.

ROUSES POINT. Fortifications at, II, 877; island, cession to United States, 878, 890, 919; burning of, III, 760.

ROUSSEAU, JEAN JACQUES. Quoted, status of teachers, II, 725.

ROWLEY, FRANCIS E. Suit against, counsel fees, appropriation, veto, VII, 905.

ROYAL ARCANUM, GRAND COUNCIL. Charter, veto, VII, 507.

ROYAL LIBRARY. Paris, colonial documents in, IV, 188.

ROYAL TEMPLARS OF TEMPERANCE, GRAND COUNCIL. Charter, veto, VII, 417.

ROYAL TEMPLARS OF TEMPERANCE, NEW YORK. Grand council, charter, veto, VII, 240.

ROYALTON. VETOES. Eighteen Mile creek, improvement, VII, 364, 456; Erie canal, vertical wall, VIII, 887; IX, 48; drainage of flooded lands, X, 437.

"RUBY, THE." Relative to convoying to Cape Breton, I, 371.

RUGER, WILLIAM C. Chief judge, Court of Appeals, death of, IX, 36.

RUGGLES, SAMUEL B. Commissioner to present to Federal government plan for use of New York canal for military operations, V, 367; report, 368, 501, 503.

RUM. Distillation in New York prohibited, I, 103; proposed duty on, 115; proposed prohibition on sale of, to Mohawks, 170; reported deficiency of, for army, 387; not to be sold to Indians, 466, 549, 569; offered by Congress, New York declines to purchase, II, 84.

RUNYON, LEWIS. Ferry on Seneca lake, amending act, veto, VI, 1033.

RUSH. State industrial school established in, X, 502.

RUSH, JOHN. Conviction of, II, 250.

RUSH, ROSINA. Relief, veto, II, 250.

RUSO, JAMES M. Board of Claims, veto, IX, 623.

RUSS, JOHN D. Corresponding secretary, Prison Association, communication from, vagrants, trial jurors, IV, 505.

RUSSEL. Deposit of military stores at, II, 755; arms and supplies for, 772; town bridge over Grass river, veto, VII, 474.

RUSSELL, ARCHIMEDES. Examination of Assembly ceiling and staircase, appropriation, veto, VIII, 839.

RUSSELL, EBENEZER. Regent, resignation of, II, 753, 755.

RUSSELL, HORACE. Member of Yorktown Centennial Commission, VII, 734.

RUSSELL, JAMES A. Claim against New York for services, veto, X, 476, 690, 817.

RUSSELL, LESLIE W. Attorney-General, recommends single architect to supervise construction of new capitol, VIII, 222, 1018; quoted, constitutionality of statutes authorizing women to vote at school meetings, IX, 94.

RUSSELL, ROLLIN. Residence, Johnsburgh, terminus of special highway, veto, VI, 443.

RUSSELL, SAMUEL. Member of Commission on Common School System, II, 707.

RUSSIA. Partition of Poland, II, 138; Emperor offers mediation between United States and Great Britain, 785, 801; colonies of, American contact with, 909; early railroads in, III, 396; canal development should keep pace with railroads, X, 135.

RUSSIA (Herkimer County). Arms and supplies for, II, 774.

RUTGERS, HARMANUS. Assembly meets at house of, I, 239.

RUTGERS, HENRY. Elected regent, II, 517; resigns, III, 142.

RUTGER'S WHARF, NORTH RIVER. Locating battery at, I, 322.

RUTHERFORD, ALLEN. Supplies for 9th Regiment, appropriation, veto, VII, 500.

RUTHERFORD, JOHN. Lieutenant-Governor of Virginia, communication relative to extradition case of Johnson and others, III, 932.

RUTLAND, NEW YORK. Aid to Utica and Black River Railroad Company, veto, VI, 92.

RYAN, JOHN. New York, relief, veto, X, 582.

RYAN, PHILIP. Relief, veto, X, 53.

RYCKMAN, PETER. Claim of, Indian lands, II, 307.

RYE. To be used for subsistence of troops, II, 169.

RYE (Town). Letter from Governor Treat relative to, I, 73; defection of, 73; grist mills in, act for erection of, II, 485; receiver of taxes, bond and deputy, veto, X, 442.

RYER, JOHN. Conviction of, expense of guarding, II, 345.

S.

SABBATH. Act to prevent breaking, I, 12; proper observance of, recommended, 32; II, 400; act relative to, I, 59; closing canal locks on, IV, 81.

SACANDAGA BRANCH. Proposed canal route connecting with Erie and Champlain canals, III, 733.

SACANDAGA RIVER. VETOES. Bridge, VII, 474; public highway, VIII, 621.

SACHEMS. Visit Quebec to negotiate with French, I, 271, 272; Mohawk representations as to chapel, 290; Senecas request armorer and smith, 323; visit from, 418; speech of, at New York, 421; present to, 421; number in French interest, 425; Mohawk, speech of, 524.

SACHS, JOHN J. New York, relief, veto, X, 176.

SACKETT, WILLIAM A. Relief, veto, VI, 344.

SACKETT'S HARBOR. Militia in service at, II, 736, 743, 823; troops stationed at, 745, 746; care of arms after discharge of militia, 773; defense of, 786; orders for defense of, 806; fortifications at, IV, 294; cession of land at, 381.

SACRED HEART ACADEMY. Changing name to Clason Point Military Academy, veto, X, 813.

SADLER, ABIGAIL. Board of Claims, veto, IX, 721.

SAFE DEPOSIT COMPANY, ROCHESTER. Amending charter, veto, VI, 503.

SAFE DEPOSIT AND TRUST COMPANY, BUFFALO. Charter, veto, VI, 503.

SAFETY ELEVATOR INSURANCE COMPANY, NEW YORK. Charter, veto, VII, 1113.

SAFETY FUND BANKS. Act passed, III, 245; operation described, 260,
475; IV, 33; opposition to, III, 311; contributions to fund, 502;
amount of fund, 545, 619, 673, 711, 764, 860; IV, 375, 837; results of, III, 654; due from general fund, 707; due from Lockport
Bank, 711; proposed use of fund, 782; replenishing, 938; not liable
for private deposits, 938; insolvent banks, liabilities of, IV, 69, 215,
271; banks reorganized, 836; circulation issued to banks, V, 586.

SAFETY FUND MUTUAL INSURANCE COMPANY. Amending charter, veto,
VII, 1121.

SAGE, ALBERT G. Relief, veto, VI, 591.

SAGE, ORRIN W. Action against canal auditor, appropriation, veto, VII,
· 582, 905.

SAG HARBOR. Acquisition of land for fortifications, II, 752; arsenal at,
supplies for, 768; militia at, 822; fire apparatus, water supply, veto,
VII, 68.

SAGUA LA GRANDE. Vessels from, detained for observation, yellow fever,
VI, 626.

SAILORS' SNUG HARBOR. Gift to establish, II, 566; incorporated, 567;
report of, 1076; III, 103; IV, 452; V, 219, 444, 507, 577, 643, 725;
VI, 60, 434, 788, 981; VII, 199, 321, 441, 547, 746, 864, 1006; VIII,
205, 340, 528, 721, 969, 1094; IX, 53, 218, 366, 581, 756, 852; X, 37,
145.

ST. ANN'S CHURCH, BROOKLYN. Sale of property, veto, II, 561, passed
over veto.

ST. ANN'S TOTAL ABSTINENCE AND BENEVOLENT SOCIETY, HORNELLSVILLE.
Charter, veto, VI, 672.

ST. CECELIA ROMAN CATHOLIC CHURCH, NEW YORK. Canceling assessment on opening portion of Lexington avenue, veto, IX, 809.

ST. CHRISTOPHER'S ISLAND. Devastation on, I, 120.

ST. CLAIR, ARTHUR. General, campaign by, pensions for service in, II,
760.

ST. CLAIR FLATS. Improvement of, Michigan resolutions, V, 115.

ST. CLAIR FLATS CANAL. Reciprocity in use of, VI, 363.

ST. CROIX, JOSHUA T. D. Deed by, II, 289.

ST. DOMINGO. French prisoners sent to, I, 334; refugees, aid to, 353,
364, 369, 383, 384, 405, 413.

ST. GEORGE'S METHODIST EPISCOPAL CHURCH, NORTH HAVERSTRAW.
Changing name, veto, VIII, 617.

ST. JAMES' MERCY HOSPITAL. Hornellsville, payment of excise money to,
veto, IX, 723.

ST. JOHN, ALEXANDER. Bond for return of arms, II, 772.

ST. JOHN, HECTOR. French consul in New York, letter from, indignity
to French flag by British seamen, II, 245.

ST. JOHN, MILTON H. Relief, veto, VI, 591.

ST. JOHNLAND. Kings county farm at, changing supervision of, veto, VIII, 594.

ST. JOHNS. Tariff regulations at, I, 773.

ST. JOHN'S ARMENIAN APOSTOLIC CHURCH. Exempting property from taxation, veto, X, 326.

ST. JOHN'S COLLEGE, BROOKLYN. Charter, veto, VI, 339.

ST. JOHN'S ISLAND. Reduction of, I, 624; regained from French, 669.

ST. JOSEPH'S ASYLUM. VETOES. Exemption from taxation, X, 176, 179; New York assessments, release, 473; exemption from taxation, 176.

ST. JOSEPH'S COLLEGE, BUFFALO. Charter, veto, VI, 691.

ST. JOSEPH'S INSTITUTION FOR THE IMPROVED INSTRUCTION OF DEAF-MUTES. VETOES. Deficiency appropriation, VII, 470; relative to, 806.

ST. JOSEPH'S ORPHAN ASYLUM, CORNING. Payment of excise moneys to, veto, VIII, 465.

ST. JOSEPH'S SEMINARY, NEW YORK. Relative to real estate, veto, IX, 808.

ST. LAWRENCE CANAL. Reciprocity in use of, VI, 363; enlargement, steam power on, 538; proposed enlargement of, 635; disadvantages of St. Lawrence route, 635.

ST. LAWRENCE COUNTY. Deposit of arms in, II, 682; militia from, 1812, 743; defense of, 744; arms and supplies for, 772; Kirby murder case, III, 32; agricultural society in, 945; arsenal and equipments to be sold, IV, 495; increase in population, VI, 578; Morristown, legalizing town bonding proceedings, 583; land in, State park, 629; timbered lands, acquisition by State, VII, 722; average excise license fees, 1889, VIII, 687; decrease in population, IX, 3; highways, cost of labor system, 1892, 200; insane, care of, county and State systems compared, 228.

VETOES. Soldier's monument, VI, 162; breakwater on Oswegatchie river, 331; Norwood burial ground, removal of bodies, 1035; Canton, law library, VII, 82; county clerk, expenses, notaries public, appropriation, 83; Gouverneur Fire Company, charter, 327; assessments for railroad purposes, 807; relieving certain towns from railroad burdens, 847, new bill passed; commissioner to manage forest lands, 933; reclaiming overflowed lands, 934, 1115; Young Men's Christian Association, Ogdensburg, charter, VIII, 379; Parishville townhouse, 516; Oswegatchie river improvement, 848; Parishville lock-up, 1039; sales for non-payment of taxes, IX, 804; taking bass in, X, 61; board of supervisors, appointment of purchasing committee, 175; changing boundaries,

ST. LAWRENCE COUNTY, VETOES — (*Continued*).
320; highway repairs in certain towns, appropriation, 428; highway improvement, 439; special county judge and surrogate, term of office, 701.

ST. LAWRENCE RESERVATION. Repairing docks, pavilions, etc., veto, X, 934.

ST. LAWRENCE RIVER. King requested to send naval force to, I, 420, 457; western terminus of Quebec boundary, 747; Oswegatchie Indian lands on, II, 553; road to Albany, report of commission, 756, 795; improvement of, 965; III, 510; canal connection with Lake Champlain, II, 1011; III, 68, 69, 166; British commercial regulations, 23, 68; canal connection with Black river, 166; colonial documents relative to, 1019; granting authority to United States to purchase islands in, IV, 294, 381; diverts only small part of commerce from New York canals, V, 595; ship canal connecting with Lake Champlain, VI, 539. ·

VETOES. Preservation of fish in, VI, 911; stocking with black bass and California trout, VIII, 75; Wolf Island Bridge Company, charter, IX, 248.

ST. LAWRENCE STATE HOSPITAL. Excessive cost *per capita*, X, 410; number of visits of local managers, 415.

VETOES. Building for employees, IX, 294; roads and grading, 294; bridge over Tibbett's Brook ravine, X, 432.

ST. LAWRENCE UNIVERSITY AND THEOLOGICAL SEMINARY. Amending charter, veto, VIII, 703.

ST. LOUIS. Suggested selection as site of World's Fair, 1892, VIII, 931; Louisiana Purchase Exposition, X, 350.

ST. LUKE'S CHURCH, NEW YORK. Relief from certain assessments, veto, IX, 809.

ST. LUKE'S HOME, UTICA. Changing name, veto, VIII, 326.

ST. LUKE'S HOME AND HOSPITAL, NEWBURGH. Support of poor in, payments for, veto, IX, 723.

ST. MARIE FALLS. Proposed ship canal around, congressional aid requested, III, 907.

ST. PATRICK'S BENEVOLENT SOCIETY, DANSVILLE. Charter, veto, VI, 592.

ST. PATRICK'S CATHEDRAL, NEW YORK. Devise to, act concerning, II, 1036.

ST. PAUL'S CHURCH, NEW YORK. Monument to General Montgomery, II, 1000.

ST. PAUL'S METHODIST EPISCOPAL CHURCH, ONONDAGA VALLEY. Legalizing title to land, veto, VII, 1100.

ST. PAUL'S REFORMED EPISCOPAL CHURCH, BRONX BOROUGH. Relative to, veto, X, 806.

St. Peter's Church, Cortland. Westchester county, regulating interments, veto, X, 593.

St. Peter's Church, New York. Devise to, act concerning, II, 1036.

St. Peter's Episcopal Church, Albany. Memorial services for President Harrison·at, III, 914; choir furnishes music at Higgins memorial services, X, 964.

St. Regis Indians. Representing Seven Villages, claim of, II, 343, 345; conference with, 351; acquiring lands of, 352; treaty with, 364, 368, 381; Grey claim, 391; survey of lands, 435; map of lands, 454; settlement with, authorized, 457; purchase of land from, 472, 513; purchase of Mile Square tract, 520; III, 36; request right to establish ferry, II, 520; school, church and flags for, 520; conflicting claims to title to lands, 553; land purchased from, 866; destruction of corn, advance from annuities, 882; communication from Loran Torbell, 932; appointment of trustees, 938; treaty with, purchase of land, 941; number of, 1819, 976; laying out village, 986; attorney for, 1076; Green Bay treaty, 1107; contested elections among, III, 135.

Vetoes. Relief, VII, 414; Franklin county, removing intruders, VIII, 115; regulating occupation of land, 1120; amending Indian Law, IX, 801.

St. Regis Reservation. Number of Indians on, 1819, II, 976. Vetoes. Highway on, VII, 91, 475, 909; highway repairs, VIII, 850; X, 427.

St. Regis River. Ferry on, II, 520. Vetoes. Improvement of east and west branches, VI, 579; improvement of west branch, Stony brook, VIII, 115; improvement of west branch, 423; preventing obstruction of, 619.

St. Vincent's Retreat for the Insane. Exempting property from taxation, veto, IX, 253.

Salamanca. Vetoes. Village charter, VI, 704; State road, Allegany reservation, improvement, VIII, 847.

Salaries. Of King's officers in colonial service, I, 459; Governor urges increase of, 606; of judges, 670, 750; compensation of Attorney-General, 672; Governor declines salary, 738, 745; of chancellor and judges, II, 362; act relating to, 249, 460; Representatives in Congress, proposed amendment prohibiting increase during term, 919, 930; reduction of, 1013; of bank commissioners, paid by banks, III, 1007; of judges, continuing after removal for disability, VII, 533; allowance not included in, 550; when successful contestant not entitled to salary, 661; Monroe county clerk, fixing salary, VIII, 260; uniform, in State hospitals, IX, 652; State tax commissioners, increased, 1900, X, 84; excessive, in New York, 344.

SALARIES — (*Continued*).

    VETOES. Aldermen, Long Island City, VII, 641; Onondaga, super-
visors, 806; Greene county judge, repealing Salary Law, 807;
county treasurers, regulating, 807; Judge Mullin, retired, appropriation of residue of salary for widow, 916; Senate journal
clerk, death of, appropriation for widow, 917; State Assessor,
death of, appropriation for widow, 917; Justice Balcom, payment of salary, 931; increase, several items, VIII, 71, 72; court
officers, New York, 132; Justice Westbrook, death of, unearned
salary, appropriation for widow, 250; Justice Stemmler, New
York, district court, 294; secretary normal school board, proposed, 407; New York, police sergeants and detective sergeants,
524; Rochester, board of education, 882; New York, borough
presidents, X, 580; loans on, 700; several bills involving questions relating to, 710; commission on classification of, allowance
for expenses, 792.

SALEM. VETOES. Excise commissioners, legalizing acts, VIII, 354; electric light plant, IX, 819.

SALINA. Salt springs in, II, 456; III, 856; lateral canal at, II, 1007;
prosperity resulting from manufacture of salt, III, 708; canal repairs, VI, 857; State ditch, removing obstructions, veto, VIII, 857;
IX, 150; bridge over Seneca river, veto, X, 697.

SALINA AND CENTRAL SQUARE PLANK ROAD COMPANY. Rates of toll,
statement of receipts and disbursements, veto, IX, 795.

SALISBURY. Including portion in Adirondack park, veto, X, 379.

SALISBURY AND MANHEIM PLANK ROAD COMPANY. Renewing charter,
veto, VII, 1106.

SALMON RIVER. St. Regis lands on, II, 454; declared a public highway,
VIII, 380; improvement, 560.

    VETOES. Bridge over, VI, 46, 212; preservation of fish in, VII,
807; protection of banks, VIII, 380; public highway, repealing
act, IX, 121.

SALMON RIVER IMPROVEMENT COMPANY. Incorporated, object of, VIII,
380.

SALT. General references, V, 529; VI, 16, 110, 230, 350, 527, 616, 943;
importation of, recommended, I, 219, 233; scarcity of, II, 78; act
to aid in procuring, 79; petition from Saratoga, relative to supply
of, 82; letter from Commissary-General of Purchases, relative to
supply of, 84, 109; act relating to manufacture of, 384; tax on,
902, 1010; probable adequate supply of, 1009; domestic
supply sufficient, 1092; improved quality of, III, 29; IV, 25;
increasing supply of, III, 81; IV, 68; manufacture at Salina,
relative to, veto, III, 147; duties on, reduction, amendment

SALT — (*Continued*).

of 1833, 330, 384, 414, 477, 505, 544, 619; income from, 305, 334, 708, 763, 855, 951, 1040; IV, 23, 853; V, 20, 72; VI, 110; VII, 697; smuggling, III, 346; business embarrassed by competition, 348; duties restored to general fund, amendment, 1835, 414, 505, 544, 552, 619; IV, 53; extending market for, III, 477; at Kenhawa springs, 477; source of public wealth and municipal prosperity, 708; gravel pump for use in manufacture of, 709; transportation facilitated by canals, 815; reduction of tolls, negotiations with Ohio, 871; improving process of manufacture, 951; reduction of duties, 951; V, 277; market for, III, 953; business affected by Federal revenue system, 1040; canal tolls on, IV, 18; bounties for, 68; wide distribution of product, 68; V, 20; condition of industry, IV, 853; decline in production, 48; VI, 867; production, V, 83, 176, 276, 377, 529; VI, 17, 110, 230, 350, 527, 616, 943; VII, 697; coal for fuel, V, 176; large exports of, 277; reducing duty on, veto, VII, 930.

SALT LANDS. Disposing of certain lots, II, 1010.

SALTONSTALL, GURDON. Governor of Connecticut, letter from, relative to boundary, I, 176; transmits act relative to, 206.

SALT SPRINGS. Reservation of, in Onondaga treaty, II, 329; preservation of, 384; defects in act relating to, 456; lease of, recommended, 509; general act relating to management, 695; III, 478; office of superintendent created, 82; not to be sold, 148; VI, 822; VII, 386; duties of officers, III, 149; gravel pump for use at, 709; quality of, 856; increasing revenue from, 871; abundance of, 1036; general act, sale prohibited, V, 83; legislative investigating committee, VI, 943; sale of, prohibition abrogated, 1894, IX, 274, 550; disposal authorized, act of 1897, 550.

VETOES. Lots, Onondaga, VII, 385; sale of lots, purchase of other lands, 393, 935; experimental well, 787, 907; donation of land to Onondaga Historical Association, 932; sale and exchange of lots, VI, 822; repairs and improvements, 866; current expenses, 1002; amending act, VIII, 886; renewing leases, IX, 274.

SALT SPRINGS LAW. Enacted, 1892, IX, 28.

SAMMIS, DAVID S. S. Ferry, Babylon to Fire Island beach, amending act, veto, VII, 936.

SANDERS, JOHN. Council of Appointment, action on nominations, II, 475.

SAND'S POINT. See WATCH POINT.

SANDUSKY. Defense at, War of 1812, II, 786.

SANDY HILL. Postmaster at, removal of, II, 1068. VETOES. Regulating speed of railroad trains, VII, 936; — trustees, borrowing money, legalizing proceedings, X, 960.

SANDY HOOK. Lighthouse at, I, 655; ceded to United States, II, 304; pilots, licenses of, III, 637; New Jersey objects to location of quarantine buildings at, V, 70; land at, ceded by United States to New York for quarantine, 101.

SANFORD, CHARLES W. Major-general, letter to, calling for artillery, anti-rent troubles, III, 831; commands militia on Staten Island, quarantine disturbance, V, 88, 103; services in draft riot, 548.

SANFORD. Monument, veto, VII, 806.

SANFORD, CHARLES F. Judge, New York Superior Court, proposed removal for disability, VII, 533, 542; death of, 533.

SANFORD, JONAH. Member of Commission on St. Regis River Improvement, VIII, 115.

SANFORD, NATHAN. Appointed chancellor, III, 85; resigns on election as Senator, 85, 132; elected Senator, 132.

SAN FRANCISCO. Western terminus of Pacific telegraph, V, 388; International Exposition, 1894, IX, 317; earthquake and fire, New York sends relief, X, 890.

SANGERFIELD. Supervisor's bond, refunding surety for payment on, veto, VII, 753.

SANITARIUM FOR HEBREW CHILDREN. VETOES. Exemption from taxation, VIII, 1036; exempting certain property from taxation, IX, 152.

SANITARY COMMISSION. Aid to soldiers, V, 685.

SANTEN, LUCAS. Member of first legislative council, I, 9.

SARANAC LAKE. Village charter, veto, IX, 258.

SARANAC LAKE. Cleaning and removing timber from, veto, X, 792.

SARANAC RIVER. Land on, purchased by United States, II, 825.

VETOES. Removing obstructions, VII, 382; improvement, IX, 62; protection of, 816; dredging, X, 427; cleaning, between Lake Flower and State dam, 570.

" SARATOGA, THE." Used in cholera epidemic, V, 765.

SARATOGA. French in vicinity of, I, 241; proposed settlements north of, 278; soldiers sent to, 318; destruction of, 361, 363; rebuilding fort, 364, 366, 377; occupying fort, 397, 428; distance from Albany, 407; transporting provisions to, 410; supplies for, 413; garrison at, 421; II, 151; removing cannon to Albany, I, 460; petition from, supply of salt, II, 82; farm bridge, Champlain canal, veto, VI, 504; National Conference on Uniform Legislation at, VIII, 930.

SARATOGA AGRICULTURAL SOCIETY. Improvement of grounds, veto, VI, 181.

SARATOGA COUNTY. Militia called out, II, 807; Northrup murder case, 874; memorial, improvement of upper Hudson, III, 748; agricultural society in, 945; refunding illegal taxes, VI, 278; exempted from Town Auditor's Act, VIII, 49; average excise

SARATOGA COUNTY — (Continued).
　　license fees, 1889, 637; highways, cost of labor system, 1892, IX, 200; insane, care of, county and State systems compared, 228.

VETOES. Removal of insane from State asylums to poorhouse, VI, 182; revolutionary monument, appropriation, VII, 84; clerk hire, authorizing oyer and terminer to direct payment of, 207; highways, damage by Champlain canal, VIII, 453; county auditor, creating office, X, 450.

SARATOGA COUNTY MUTUAL FIRE INSURANCE COMPANY. Reducing number of directors, veto, VI, 197.

SARATOGA MONUMENT ASSOCIATION. Schuylerville battlefield monument, veto, VIII, 253.

SARATOGA SPRINGS. Number of excise licenses, 1887, VIII, 360; law library, IX, 46.

VETOES. Union school, consolidation of districts, VI, 182; bonds for waterworks, 271; regulating burials, 591; Nelson Street cemetery, removing dead, VII, 121; floating debt, 130; cemeteries, confirming purchase of land, 391; fire department, 413; street improvements, 930; VIII, 873; board of health, VII, 1098; fire department, hose, 1102; sewage, 1102; hack stands, 1112; armory, VIII, 291; clerk to fire commissioners, 292; Congress street, grading, 292; police department, 292; sewers in Church street, 331; normal school at, 888; sewage, disposal of, IX, 819; receiver of taxes, surety, X, 591; sewer, water and street commissioners, 811.

SARGENT, CHARLES S. Member of Forest Investigating Commission, 1884, VIII, 23.

SARLE, CHARLES H. Canal Department, appropriation for services, veto, IX, 716.

SATURDAY. Closing certain offices on, New York and Kings counties, veto, VII, 757.

SAUGERTIES. Number of excise licenses, 1887, VIII, 360. VETOES. Toll-bridge at, II, 1081; certain town officers, compensation, VII, 130; harbor and creek improvement, VIII, 249, 293; town clerk and highway commissioner, salaries, X, 810.

SAUTHIER, CLAUDE J. Claim, surveying Quebec boundary, I, 757.

SAVAGE, ARTHUR W. Inventor of Savage gun, affidavit as to place of birth, IX, 637; question as to citizenship, 637.

SAVAGE, CHARLES E. Patrolman, New York, rehearing charges, veto, X, 817, 950.

SAVAGE, JOHN. Member of Commission on Astor Claim, II, 867; Comptroller, report on taxation, IV, 340.

Savage Military Magazine Rifle. Recommended for National Guard, IX, 635.

Savannah, Georgia. Success of Union Army at, V, 439.

Savannah, New York. Engine house and fire department, veto, VIII, 410.

Savings Banks. New York Bank for Savings, incorporated, II, 981, 1016; deposits by minors, 1016; unclaimed dividends and deposits, III, 566; depositing funds with trust companies, IV, 731; amount of deposits, V, 823; number, VI, 20, 112, 231, 351, 529, 623, 952; VII, 427, 520, 689, 822, 948; examination, VI, 112, 232; special charters not to be granted, 119, 725; VIII, 232; general act, VI, 186; restricting investments, 308, 310, 322, 580; VII, 167; organization of, certificate of trustees, VI, 352; limiting individual deposits, 353, 530, 623; VII, 17, 167; investments in railroad aid bonds, VI, 441, 530; suggested limitation of interest, 623; uniform charters, 725; method of ascertaining value of surplus, VII, 16; interest reduced, reserve increased, 18; large number of failures, 166; failure of adequate supervision, 167; legislative administration not expedient, 304; public guardianship not needed, 305; proceedings on closing and dissolution of, 305; condition of, 521; tax on surplus, 571; X, 199; increase of surplus, VII, 689; examination, 823, 949; not to be associated in business with discount banks, IX, 563; large increase in deposits, 1896, 740; Franchise Tax Act, 1901, X, 200; resources, 221, 733; loans on real estate securities, maximum per cent. of value increased, 357; reducing rate of interest, 358; investments, Los Angeles bonds, act of 1902, 454; tax, New York's contribution to, 1902, 483; amount invested in mortgages, 1903, 531; investments, Buffalo Creek Railroad Company, act of 1903, 576; tax on surplus, repeal of law recommended, 721, 766; periodical examinations required, 735; investments, general provisions, 1905, 735.

Vetoes. Investments in railroad aid bonds, VI, 190; investment in municipal bonds of other States, 211; receivers, VII, 416; insolvent, settlement of affairs, 797; enlarging scope of investments, 893; insolvent, reducing deposits, 934; Ithaca Savings Bank, exclusive privilege, 1105; Hope Savings Bank, Albany, dissolution, VIII, 469; publishing statements of deposits, IX, 425; taxation, X, 451.

Savings and Loan Associations. Defects of system, X, 221; reorganization needed, 222; annual expenses limited, 222.

Sawmill Creek. Water supply for New York city, II, 1017.

Sawquoit Creek. Route of Chenango canal, III, 234, 419.

SAWYER'S CREEK. Palatine settlements on, I, 147; deepening and improving channel, veto, X, 300, 427.

SAXE-GOTHA, PRINCESS OF. Marriage to Prince of Wales, I, 258.

SAXTON, CHARLES T. Senate, resolution on death of General Sherman, VIII, 1088.

SCAJAQUADA CREEK. Removal of State dam, VI, 861; Buffalo, dredging, veto, X, 319.

SCALPS. Reward for, I, 389, 460, 468; Colonel Johnson's certificate as to, 441; Massachusetts offers bounties for, 595.

SCANNELL, CHARLES. Court of Claims, veto, X, 165.

SCARSDALE. Highway improvement, veto, VI, 328.

SCATCHERD, JOHN N. Member of Canal Investigating Commission, 1899, X, 75.

SCHACKOCK INDIANS. Governor Cornbury recommends presents to, I, 129.

SCHATAKOOK. See SCHAGHTICOKE.

SCHAGHTICOKE. Bridge at Mechanicville, veto, VI, 333.

SCHAUB, JACOB. VETOES. Relief, failure of bank, VI, 334; relief, 591.

SCHENCK, MARTIN. Estate of, purchase of land for naval hospital, III, 181.

SCHENECTADY. Representation in First Assembly, I, 9; re-enforced by Major Ingoldesby, 26; fort to be built at, 33, 93; garrison at, 52, 108, 131; defense of, 99, 166, 548; destruction of guardhouse and firewood, 125; repair of fort at, 143, 144, 147, 157, 202; condition at, 154; stockades at, 196; powder-house recommended, 202; fort, 247, 249; ordnance for, 305; cannon and military stores for, 316; garrisons for blockhouses at, 368; troops at, 397; distance from Albany, 407; rangers at, 439; plan of fortifications, 572; Colonel Gage at, 591; barracks at, 602; church lands, boundary question with Half Moon, II, 117; railroad to Albany, III, 328; public inconveniences resulting from unfinished canal bridges, IV, 16; number of excise licenses, 1887, VIII, 359; excise license fees, 1889, 686; armory proposed at, IX, 573; second-class city, 1905, 678; State aid in removing grade crossings, X, 619.

VETOES. Police, amending act, VI, 698; lease of armory to Union University, 709; additional policemen, protection of Union College, 1032; fence on berme bank of canal, VII, 364; Mill creek, 804; sewers, 806; Mill creek, filling up, damages from, 937; Erie canal bridge, Church street, VIII, 890; Elizabeth Smith, escheat, IX, 403; street on canal land, 788, 789; sewer bonds, 789; assessments, amending charter, X, 262; pesthouse, 806; diverting Fourth of July appropriation to San Francisco relief, 908.

SCHENECTADY COUNTY. Riots in, III, 941; tenants represented before Assembly committee on anti-rent troubles, IV, 328; includes Duanesburg tract, 331; exempted from Town Auditor's Act, VIII, 49; average excise license fees, 1889, 687; highways, cost of labor system, 1892, IX, 200; insane, care of, county and State systems compared, 228.

    VETOES. Farmers and Mechanics' Savings Bank, charter, VI, 214; Superintendent of the Poor Clute, legalizing election, 424; Glenville,—highway assessment, 701;—school district fire department, 1035; Rotterdam, assessors, fixing compensation, X, 439.

SCHENECTADY FREE DISPENSARY. Changing name, veto, VIII, 617.

SCHENECTADY AND TROY RAILROAD COMPANY. State aid to, IV, 10, 831; consolidation with other companies authorized, V, 803.

SCHERER, JACOB. Escheat, veto, VIII, 882.

SCHIFF, BENJAMIN. Regent's certificate, clerk of Court of Appeals to file *nunc pro tunc*, veto, X, 174.

SCHIMMELPENNICK, BARON. Minister of Interior, Netherlands, grants leave to transcribe colonial documents, IV, 170.

SCHLAEFER, WALTER J. Court of Claims, veto, X, 442.

SCHLOSSER. Troops at, 1812, II, 746; seizure of Caroline at, III, 678, 687; murder at, McLeod case, 941.

SCHMIDT, MARGARETHA. Straack escheat bill, veto, VIII, 734.

SCHNEIDER, WILLIAM. Assembly, member of Prince Henry reception committee, X, 479; escorts Admiral von Seckendorff at reception, 480.

SCHOELLKOPF, JACOB F. Canal award, veto, VII, 1072.

SCHOHARIE. Palatine settlements in, I, 147; rangers at, 439; armory at, V, 175.

SCHOHARIE CENTRAL BRIDGE COMPANY. Extending charter, veto, IV, 513, 637; V, 147.

SCHOHARIE COUNTY. Act for building courthouse and jail, II, 417; nomination of sheriff, proceedings of Council of Appointment, 475, 493; militia called out, 807; oyer and terminer, conviction of Abraham Kesler, 921; anti-rent troubles in, IV, 234; tenants represented before Assembly committee on anti-rent troubles, 328; Scott patent, description of, 331; Clark patent, 332; excepting from act relative to county treasurer's fees, veto, VI, 151; exempted from Town Auditor's Act, VIII, 49; average excise license fees, 1889, 687; highways, cost of labor system, 1892, IX, 200; insane, care of, county and State systems compared, 228.

SCHOHARIE CREEK. Constructing embankment, Fort Hunter, veto, VIII, 886.

SCHOHARIE TURNPIKE ROAD. Amending charter, veto, II, 776.

SCHOHARIE VALLEY RAILROAD COMPANY. Extending road, veto, VI, 90.

SCHOLES, WILLIAM C. Relief, veto, X, 178.

SCHOOL BOOKS. Proper selection of, II, 726; lack of, suitable for common schools, III, 337; Brooklyn, free books and supplies, veto, VII, 626.

SCHOOL COMMISSIONER. Consent needed to change schoolhouse site, III, 338; office created, IV, 843; V, 14; women voting for, act unconstitutional, VII, 77; IX, 94; districts, how established under general act of 1894, VIII, 713.

VETOES. Steuben county, increasing number of districts, VIII, 402; districts,— amending act, 470, 639; — Cattaraugus county, increasing number, 713; — formation in certain counties, IX, 365; — amending general act, 625; rights, powers and duties, 800; Cattaraugus county, Ashford, transfer from third to first school commissioner district, X, 948.

SCHOOLCRAFT, HENRY R. Agent to take census of Indians, IV, 289.

SCHOOL DISTRICTS. Creation of, suggested, II, 557, 721; number of, III, 295, 336, 377, 407, 456, 499, 538, 616, 653, 740, 857; IV, 22, 66, 112, 264, 427, 475, 549, 645, 795, 839; V, 13, 51, 82, 174, 523, 603, 779, 851; VI, 23, 528, 617, 946; VII, 19, 155, 296, 424, 513, 687; to receive Hall's Lectures on Schoolkeeping, III, 378; libraries in, 499, 538, 743; libraries, United States deposit fund, 613; Onondaga Indian land a separate district, 887; dissensions from property tax, IV, 550; consolidation of, VI, 86; tax for instruction of children in other districts, IX, 663; Kingston, consolidation of, X, 437; board of education, election in certain districts, 439; railroad, telephone, telegraph and pipe-line companies, apportionment of taxes, 439; comparative statement, 1905, 736.

VETOES. Election of officers in certain, VII, 508, 664; Mentz, amending act, 938; officers, election, VIII, 129; Fort Covington, annual meeting, 130; Lenox, extending boundaries, 130; payment of teachers' wages, 240; distribution of Code of Public Instruction, 422; Mount Morris, consolidation, IX, 73, 817; Mentz, consolidating, 252; alteration, 800; Half Moon and Stillwater district No. 10, regulating elections in, 817; Smithtown, No. 5, relief, X, 449; bonded indebtedness, alteration in case of, 812; Albion, amending charter, 948; North Hempstead, No. 2, refunding bonds, 961.

SCHOOLHOUSES. Memorial for, I, 181; proposed general plan relating to, II, 557, 724; commissioner must consent to change of site, III, 338; should not be mortgaged, VI, 262; national flag to be displayed on, IX, 564.

VETOES. New, burned before completion, relief of contractor, VI, 337; Huntington, sale of, 506; Onondaga reservation, VII, 909; Allegany reservation, 909; condemnation of, IX, 800.

School Lots. See Gospel and School Lots.

Schoolmaster. Provided for, in New York, I, 100; to be member of militia reserves, 549.

Schools. See also Public Schools; Education and Common Schools. Grammar free school established in New York, I, 100; memorial for a schoolhouse and master's dwelling, 181; proposed establishment of seminary, 521, 522; act to establish King's College, 523; Governor Clinton urges establishment of, II, 183; gospel and school lots, 291; College of Physicians and Surgeons, 317; common, established, 350; for St. Regis Indians, 520; New York Free School Society incorporated, 551; Lancastrian, 725, 903, see Lancastrian Schools; appropriation of national public land for, 1080; in Great Britain for infants, III, 114, 213; Rensselaer school offered for instruction of teachers, 219; in prisons, 289; infant schools, see that title; agricultural, 298; polytechnic, Chittenango, 298; for mechanical instruction, 381; for Onondaga Indians, 887; for colored children, 887; IV, 476, 795; private and unincorporated, 428, 476; free, act for, submission unconstitutional, 475, 551; Common School Code, 603, 693; union, 647; town board of education recommended, 840; high schools, 840, see that title; school commissioner, 843, see that title; not seriously affected by Civil War, V, 602; public, when academies are not, VI, 95; New York, additional evening high school, VIII, 261; industrial training, general act, 483; cities, instruction in music, IX, 116; temperance instruction, 613; Legislature may prescribe courses of study, 616; New York, Governor Morton's special message, 1896, 686; national military, instruction of State militia officers in, X, 16; management, political considerations should be excluded, 151; certain charitable institutions classed as educational, 334; collector's notice to taxpayers, 439; Boys' Training School established, 683; comparative statement, 1905, 738.

Vetoes. Public, preventing nuisances near, VI, 95; truant reform school, Brooklyn, VII, 133; for truants, Brooklyn, VIII, 293; Buffalo, amending charter, 639; State Truant School, 1889, 818; nautical school, establishing, IX, 256; military instruction in, 628; Syracuse, new high school, 731; Jamestown, maintenance and government, 858; — designating special holidays, X, 173; New York, — amending charter, 177; — janitors, 319; Auburn, grammar and high school buildings, 717; good roads school, 793.

Schoonmaker, Augustus, Jr. Attorney-General, opinion, bill extending time for sale of Genesee Valley canal, VII, 217; opinion, pipe-line companies, eminent domain, 242; opinion, Danolds case, 377.

SCHROEDER, ROBERT. VETOES. Escheat, VII, 1116; conveyance of land in Franklin county, veto, VIII, 131.

SCHROEPPEL. Oneida river road, veto, VI, 211.

SCHROON. Fish hatchery at, veto, IX, 777.

SCHUH, PHILIP. Relief, veto, VIII, 630.

SCHULTZ, JOHN. Estate, relief, II, 714.

SCHURMAN, JACOB G. President, Cornell University, communication to Governor, College of Forestry, X, 628; delivers memorial address on former Governor Higgins, 964.

SCHURZ, C. Communication to Governor relative to appointment of William Church Osborn as State Commissioner in Lunacy, X, 43.

SCHUYLER, ABRAHAM. Agent among Five Nations, letter from, I, 219.

SCHUYLER, CAMPBELL V. Escheat, veto, X, 252.

SCHUYLER, DAVID. Appropriation for, I, 134.

SCHUYLER, JOHN. Expenses in maintaining troops at Oswego, I, 251.

SCHUYLER, LOUISA LEE. Communication to Governor relative to appointment of William Church Osborn as State commissioner in lunacy, X, 43.

SCHUYLER, PETER. Expedition to Canada, I, 24; information from, relative to Indians, 46; commands fusileers, 57; service at Albany, 70; absence from Council meeting noted, 91; visits Onondagas, 124; expense of entertaining Indians, 131; letter from, relative to Canadian expedition, 155; claim for expenses in Indian service, payment of, 167; President of Council, government of colony transferred to, 190; adjourns Assembly, 190; communication from Secretary Craggs relative to prorogation, 192; letter from Governor of Canada, 196; member of Council of Appointment, II, 314; official service, I, pref., ix.

SCHUYLER, PETER, JR. Letter from, I, 200.

SCHUYLER, PHILIP. Memorial from, relative to service at Schenectady, I, 202; to be sent with smith to Senecas, 249; to defend frontier against Canada Indians, 353; recommends detachments for frontier, 366; letter from, relative to frontiers, 379; Assembly, resolution, correspondence relative to colonial affairs, 768; letter from, Indian affairs, II, 26; letters from, 41; elected delegate to Congress, 83; letter from, operations on northern frontier, 99; commissioner to Hartford Convention, 107; Senate, resolution relative to method of choosing presidential electors, 300; chosen Senator in Congress, 301; status as member of Council of Appointment, 310; seat in Senate declared vacant, 310; Indian claims, 514; letter from Walter Butler noted, Cherry Valley massacre, VII, 812.

SCHUYLER, HARTLEY AND GRAHAM. Contract for purchase of arms, V, 414.

SCHUYLER COUNTY. Erection of, V, 229, 230; borrowing money, county buildings, veto, VII, 859; average excise license fees, 1889, VIII, 687; highways, cost of labor system, 1892, IX, 200; insane, care of, county and State systems compared, 228; special tax for benefit of State, veto, 796.

SCHUYLERVILLE. Battlefield monument, veto, VIII, 253.

SCHWARTZ, HENRY L. Assignee of Brock and Wiener, National Guard uniforms, claim, veto, IX, 237.

SCHWARZWAELDER, ARTHUR. Colonel, 5th Regiment, supplies from Union defense committee, VII, 500.

SCIO. VETOES. Constables, appointment of, VII, 218; monument to Maj. Peter Keenan, X, 163.

SCOTLAND. Rebellion in, I, 401; unhappy conditions in, IV, 398; illiteracy as compared with New York, X, 859.

SCOTT, DRED. Case of, slavery, Missouri Compromise, IV, 813; V, 31; New York protests against Supreme Court decision, 34.

SCOTT, HUGH. Service of process on, Van Rensselaer rent, III, 824; communication from, 826.

SCOTT, JOHN MORIN. Commissioner on Massachusetts boundary, I, 721; member of Council of Appointment, II, 14; Senate, communicates resolutions to Governor, II, 57; delegate to Continental Congress, letters from, 100; patentee of land in Schoharie county, IV, 331.

SCOTT, L. A. Clerk of Council of Appointment, letter from Aaron Burr, II, 328.

SCOTT, WINFIELD. General, success in Niagara campaign, II, 802; thanked by Legislature and presented with sword, 832; letter from Governor Tompkins, 835; reply, 836; conduct approved by Minnesota, V, 327.

"SCOTT'S EXERCISE." Cited, II, 951; purchase for use of militia, 995.

SCOTT PATENT. Schoharie county, description of, IV, 331.

SCOUTS. See also OUTSCOUTS. Provided for, I, 99, 105; services, 124; for service at Albany, 125, 130; Indians employed as, 318, 325, 439; sent to Sacrament lake, 396.

SCRIBA. Old Burt cemetery, removal of remains, veto, VIII, 1118.

SEA-BATHING PLACES. Protection of persons and property, veto, VII, 130.

SEA CLIFF. Village charter, veto, VII, 936.

SEA FENCIBLES. Organization of, II, 808, 810, 811; pay of, 816.

SEAL. State,— keeper of, II, 361; — repair of, 404, 952; great, Secretary of State custodian of, VII, 439; privy, Governor custodian of, 439; historical note, 726; act of 1882, 726.

SEAMAN, HENRY J. Private secretary, correspondence relative to quarantine affairs, V, 99.

SEAMAN, ZEBULON. Assembly, favors colonial union, I, 767.

SEAMEN. In foreign service, powers of magistrates as to, veto, II, 459; tax on, III, 343; IV, 30, 77; relief of sick and disabled, 30.

SEAMEN'S FRIEND SOCIETY. Mortgage to mariner's fund, IV, 272.

SEAMEN'S RETREAT. Provided for, III, 343; hospital, general improvements, appropriation, veto, VII, 490, 585.

SEARCH WARRANT. In excise cases, IV, 754; changing name to warrant, veto, VII, 1092.

SECESSION. Right of, denied, III, 429, 432; movement in southern States, V, 298; Washington Peace Convention, 311; action by different States, 314, 315, 319, 320, 321, 324, 326, 328, 396; Georgia ordinance, 318; President Jackson denies right of, 322; Louisiana secession ordinance, 341; fruit of nullification, 394; South Carolina ordinance, 396; President Buchanan's special message, 397.

SECKENDORFF, VON. Admiral, accompanies Prince Henry to Assembly chamber at his reception, X, 480.

SECOND AVENUE RAILROAD COMPANY. Extension of tracks, veto, V, 667.

SECOND BAPTIST CHURCH, HARLEM. Relief from assessment for street improvement, veto, VI, 710.

SECOND-CLASS CITIES. Commission on General Laws, 1895, IX, 677; general act, 1898, 678; list of, 678; new general act, 1906, 678; proposed uniform system of accounting, X, 25; act of 1899, 46; amendments of 1902, 375; tabulation of accounts and expenses, 764; revised charter, 1906, 892; primary elections in, 895; elections to be held in odd-numbered years, 911.

VETOES. General charter, 1897, IX, 791; charter amendment, duplicate, X, 164; clerk to chief of police, 444; amending general act, 447, 448, 450; police courts, 586; designation of official newspapers, 589; jurisdiction of police justices, 593; reports of financial conditions, amending act, 816.

SECOND JUDICIAL DEPARTMENT. How constituted, IX, 546; X, 850.

SECOND JUDICIAL DISTRICT. Additional justices for, VII, 837; X, 850, 936; constitutes second judicial department, IX, 546; division of, creation of ninth district, 547; X, 850; Commission on Law's Delay, 515, 516.

VETOES. Stenographers,— deficiency appropriation, VII, 583; — Kings county, appointment and removal, 769; — excepting Kings county, deficiency appropriation, 780; justices, additional compensation, 780; Supreme Court library, Newburgh, appropriation, VIII, 856; law library, Newburgh, appropriation, IX, 769; court interpreter, classification of, 812; expense of justices outside of Kings county, 815.

SECRET SOCIETIES. Lieutenant-Governor Throop's comment, III, 278.

SECRETARY (Colony). House of, destroyed by fire, I, 297; rebuilt, 298;
    new office proposed, 745; repairs on office, 763.
SECRETARY OF AGRICULTURE. Office created, member of cabinet, IV, 505;
    department, communication from, VII, 178.
SECRETARY OF BOARD OF REGENTS. Publication of natural history, V,
    855.
SECRETARY OF FOREIGN AFFAIRS. Papers from, II, 165; letter from,
    supplies, 165.
SECRETARY TO THE GOVERNOR. Opening speech sent by, I, 186; attests
    proclamation calling extraordinary session, III, 40; communication
    from, relative to executive office hours, X, 747.
SECRETARY OF INDIAN AFFAIRS. . Philip Livingston, petition for payment
    of salary, I, 200.
SECRETARY OF INTERIOR. Communication from,— census, IV, 577; —
    sale of Seneca land for taxes, V, 36; — congressional apportion-
    ment, 388.
SECRETARY OF NAVY. Communications from,— cession of land for naval
    hospital, III, 181; — cession of land at Sackett's Harbor, IV, 331,
    332; — land for Brooklyn navy yard, 465, 506, 512, 573; V, 728,
    794, 862; aids New York in preventing cholera epidemic, 765; com-
    munication from, VII, 319; requests cession of Iona island, X, 143.
SECRETARY OF STATE (English). Letters from,— expedition to Canada,
    I, 147; — military stores, 160; — relative to continuance of
    Assembly, 192, 196; letters from, 200, 555; memorial from Kennedy,
    supplies for troops, 202; letters from,— board of ordnance, 202;
    letter to Governor relative to supplies for troops, 202; communi-
    cations from,— relative to Captain Holland's claim, 202; — Gov-
    ernor's relation to Legislature, 253; — Tonnage Act, 271; — recruits
    for expedition against West Indies, 299; — expected invasion of
    colony, 531; — appointment of Earl of Loudoun commander-in-
    chief, 597; — subsistence of French prisoners, 603; urges large en-
    listments in colonies, 619, 632, 642, 653, 663; letter from, relative
    to King's veto of colonial act for support of troops, 716; papers
    sent to Superintendent of Indian Affairs, 727.
SECRETARY OF STATE (New York). Duties under Election Law, II, 36;
    ex officio clerk of Council of Revision, 369; letters from, 377,
    605; office to be kept in Albany, 397; letter from, Indian affairs,
    416; revolutionary records to be deposited with, 543; letter
    from, standard of measures, 640; member of commission to
    make cessions to United States, 825; member of Canal Board,
    901; communication from, occupancy of rooms in capitol, 936;
    forgery of records, 952; becomes superintendent of common
    schools, 1050; communication from, weights and measures, III,

SECRETARY OF STATE (New York)—(*Continued*).

142; communication from, militia commissions, 189; plan for geological survey, 567; proposed special deputy for school purposes, 615; Holland Land Company papers deposited with, 756; consultation with, anti-rent trouble, 829, 833; how chosen, 1004; communication from, distribution of geological survey, IV, 384; Rhode Island boundary record, copied and presented to that State, 457; transmits books to Canadian Parliamentary Library, 573; supervision of common schools transferred to Department of Public Instruction, 716; report on pauperism and criminal statistics, V, 274, 376; member of Commission to Organize Militia, 281, 400; member of Commission to Care for Recruits and Returning Volunteers, 563; member of Commission on Normal Schools, 695; communication from Governor, action on bills after adjournment, 814; publication of natural history, 855; proposed appointment by Governor, VI, 396; member of Commission on Statues, 435; duties under census acts, 723; communication to Governor, imperfect condition of bills, VII, 42; member of Connecticut Boundary Commission, 172; custodian of great seal, 439; requests Attorney-General's opinion as to banker's bill, vetoed, 667; communication from Governor Cornell, veto of ten-day bills, 671; rooms in new capitol, 694; office, State arms to be hung on walls of, 727; purchase of Clinton papers, 808; Court of Appeals reports, contract for publication, 892; suggests change of time for completion of State census, VIII, 42; *ex officio* Regent of University, 169; report, publication of colonial history, 425; recommends omission of statistics from enumeration, 493; enumeration, certificate of population of each city to be filed with, IX, 678; alphabetical list of corporations, X, 110; office self-supporting, 119; member of State Printing Board, 196.

VETOES. Collection of labor statistics, VII, 409; carpets and office furniture, 463; compilation and publication of records of Sullivan's Indian campaign, 1084; honorably discharged soldiers and sailors' certificates, 1110; compilation of poor laws, 1124; expense of preparing for census, 1885, VIII, 111; disposing of certain papers, IX, 811; office expenses, temporary services, reappropriation, X, 557; gallery and book cases in corporation department, 557, 639; allowance for expenses, 637; first deputy, allowance for expenses, 639.

SECRETARY OF STATE (United States). John Jay appointed, II, 237; Timothy Pickering, letter from, 367; communication from, distribution of Federal statutes, 409; correspondence with, relative to New York fortifications, 419; communications from,— amendment, titles

SECRETARY OF STATE (United States)—(*Continued*).

of nobility, 761; pilot fees on British vessels, New York, 918; — New York statutes for Federal departments, 1026; — public administrator, New York, III, 216; Governor Van Buren's appointment, 266; communications from,— public health, IV, 704; — International Educational Exhibition, London, 752; — statues for hall of House of Representatives, V, 635; transmits Fifteenth Amendment, VI, 50; communication, Netherlands Exposition, 50.

SECRETARY OF THE TREASURY (United States). Communication from, lighthouse at Staten Island, III, 178, 180; Federal statutes received from, 226; letter from, monument to General Herkimer, 989; communication from, national loan, V, 330; statement of national debt, 553; communication relative to acquisition of property in New York for custom-house, 641; designation of commissioners on quarantine warehouses, 719; report on extinction of national debt, 752; payments on New York claims, 754; furnishes revenue cutter to aid quarantine authorities, 765; contraction of legal tenders by Secretary McCulloch, VI, 253.

SECRETARY OF WAR. Communications from: Indian claims, II, 351; claim of Seven Nations, 376; treaty with Seven Nations, 390; requesting loan of cannon, 416; New York fortifications, 419; military post at Black Rock, 512; defense of New York, 628; militia for northern frontier, 1812, 742; pensions, 1812, 760; acquisition of land, 777; adjusting military accounts with State, 868; Staten Island fortifications, 1081; acquisition of land at New Utrecht Point, III, 46, 48, 137; military academy at West Point, 140, 141; cession of land for Watervliet arsenal, 264; railroad from Williamsport to Elmira, 527; militia claims, Canadian disturbance, 691; wharf at Plattsburgh, 822; requests cession of land at Black Rock, IV, 46; land for fortifications on northeastern frontier, 293; enrollment of State militia, 415; expected attack on northern frontier, V, 550; relative to military situation at Elmira, 562; Brooklyn pier and bulkhead lines, VI, 452; land at West Point, 553; Antietam National cemetery, VII, 172; cession of land for Cypress Hills National cemetery, VI, 558; VII, 998; dedication of Chickamauga and Chattanooga national military park, IX, 575.

Demands return of borrowed arms, II, 609; correspondence with Governor Seward on disturbances in northeastern part of State, III, 760; land at Oswego, IV, 591; purchase of arms, V, 416; calls on Governor Seymour to repel Lee's invasion, 544; action on New York quotas, 628; allows use of the " Illinois " in cholera epidemic, 718; aids New York in preventing cholera epidemic, 765; action relative to Louisiana disturbances, VI, 771.

SECTARIAN APPROPRIATIONS. Opposed by Governor Dix, VI, 525; Roman Catholic Orphan Asylum, veto, 587; proposed prohibition of, 945; Catholic Protectory, veto, VII, 914; payments to charitable institutions, prevention of, IX, 568.

SECTARIAN INSTRUCTION. Prohibited in schools, III, 951; in charitable institutions, VI, 468; proposed prohibition of, 945.

SECURITY BANK, BROOKLYN. Charter, veto, VI, 210; financial condition, VII, 66.

SEDDON, JAMES A. Delegate from Virginia to Washington Peace Convention, V, 311.

SEEDS. Distribution of, by Agricultural Society, II, 970.

SEELEY, SIDNEY. Canal claim, settlement, veto, VI, 592, 696.

SEGUINES POINT. Selected for new quarantine station, V, 101.

SELDEN, HENRY R. Joins in instructions to Captain Benham, quarantine affairs, V, 100; Court of Appeals, opinion, voter, when statement for whom he votes immaterial, VIII, 587.

SELECT KNIGHTS OF THE AMERICAN ORDER OF UNITED WORKMEN, GRAND LEGION. Charter, veto, VII, 546.

SELIGMAN, EDWIN R. A. Professor, Columbia College, opinion, taxation of mortgages, X, 802.

SEMINARIES. Proposed establishment of, I, 521, 522; Governor Clinton urges establishment of, II, 183, 200; flourishing condition of, 321; Governor Lewis urges aid to, 551; Wesleyan Seminary, New York, incorporated, 972; female seminary at Catskill, 1018; instruction of teachers, III, 159; Jewish Theological Seminary, New York, relative to, veto, X, 60.

SENATE (State). Successor to colonial council, II, I; Council of Appointment chosen from, 3; members of, when chosen, 10; papers from Tryon county committee relative to a member of, 12; sudden adjournment of, 15; address to Governor, 14, 15, 292; asserts freedom of legislation notwithstanding veto power of Council of Revision, 21; observations on Federal Constitution, 292; address to Governor, relations with France, 442; number of members, 468; alleged improper attempt to influence vote of member, 710; approves Tennessee amendment reducing senatorial term from six years to four years, 795; address on resignation of Governor Tompkins, 886; appoints committee to investigate alleged forgery in secretary's office, 952; requests information as to Federal interference in elections, 1054, 1059; criticises Governor Clinton, 1059; official term under second Constitution, III, 1; power to confirm executive nominations, 2; action as to method of choosing presidential electors, 39; publication of executive journals, 55, 107; disapproves Tennessee

SENATE (State)—(*Continued*).

proposition for election of President and Vice-President by popular vote, 137; extraordinary session, June, 1827, 195; action on presidential elections and eligibility of President, 199; action on suggestion to fix definite annual period of canal navigation, 203; recommends discontinuance of Central Asylum for Deaf and Dumb, 409; proposed amendment, not to determine election of Vice-President, 589, 591; refuses to receive memorandum of approval of bill, 974; refuses to receive communication from Governor Seward, 975; removal of judicial officers, procedure on, IV, 55, 109, 137; first election under Constitution of 1846, 363; twelve members resign, 577; special election to fill vacancies, 580; favors taxation of railroads for benefit of canals, V, 103; requests information as to military supplies, 417; delegation visits Washington on matters relating to quotas, 632; vacancies, how filled, VI, 242, 366; judiciary committee, 1847, quoted State not an insurer of canal boats, 312; object and composition of (Hoffman), 401; charges against Judge Prindle, 440; charges against Judge McCunn, 497; charges against Judge Curtis, 498; extraordinary session, trial of Bank Superintendent Ellis, VII, 58, 122; charges against Superintendent of Insurance Smyth, 182; occupies room in new capitol, 269; charges against trustees of Binghamton Insane Asylum, 443; Governor Hoffman suggests removal of Judge Sanford for disability, no action, 533; occupies chamber in new capitol, ceremonies, 539; inquiry concerning arms of State, 725; death of Senator Wagner, 730; confirmation of nomination of emigration commissioner, 888; health officer of New York, department investigated, 966; requests facts as to harbor masters and captain of the port, Governor Cleveland declines to furnish, 996, 998; tax revision, investigation by committee, VIII, 155; action on death of former Governor Seymour, 196; confirmation of appointments, 235, 373, 426, 490, 520; nomination of railroad commissioners, 373; confirming power, abolition recommended except as required by Constitution, 487, 680, 1080; power of removal, Governor Hill's comment, 487; members, *viva voce* voting under first Constitution, 913; deadlock, resolution for canal investigation, 1891, 1117; IX, 26; committee to investigate condition of insane asylums, 1882, 312; Fassett investigating committee, 1890, opinion, powers of mayor of New York, 417; under early Constitutions, 644; increased to fifty members, Constitution, 1894, 644; Pierre Van Cortland, first president of, 688; receives from Governor Roosevelt papers

SENATE (State)—(*Continued*).

relative to appointment of William Church Osborn as State commissioner in lunacy, X, 42; members of joint committee to investigate life insurance companies, 1905, 825; Apportionment Act of 1906 unconstitutional, 852; new act passed, 1907, 852; status of members elected under unconstitutional act of 1906, 852; right to determine election of members, 852; receives papers in Kilburn matter, 872; returns papers to Governor, 878; members of joint committee on Higgins memorial services, 963.

REPORTS. Financial situation, II, 980; congressional nomination of President and Vice-President, III, 31; Hudson river improvement, 48; publication of executive proceedings, 107; banks, 245; distribution of Federal revenues, 331; taxation, 439; agricultural instruction, 458; canal enlargement, 461; excise report, committee on general laws, VIII, 640; investigating committee, New York register's office, IX, 414.

RESOLUTIONS. Scarcity of provisions, II, 54; use of flags of truce, 57; Vermont controversy, 142; no discrimination in distribution of public lands, 256; Council of Appointment, 490, 502; requesting information as to war expenditures, 750; thanking Commodore Perry for victory on Lake Erie, 799; requesting information as to movement of troops, 815; declaring extraordinary session indiscreetly called, III, 51; resignation of Governor Van Buren, 268; speakership contest, V, 485; expenditure of appropriation for soldiers and their families, 487; vacancies in New York marine court, VI, 985; Bankers' Life Insurance and Trust Company bill, status under ten-day rule, VII, 667; on Ulster and Delaware plankroad bill, status under ten-day rule, 671; as to practicability of placing telegraph and electric light wires under ground, 865; on death of General Sherman, VIII, 1088; and committee on reception of Prince Henry, X, 478; investigation of Bank Department, 872; death of former Governor Higgins, 962.

VETOES. Reconstructing districts, II, 651, 688; apportionment, 849; employees and investigating committees, VII, 133; index to documents, 225, 461; index to record, Ellis trial, 226, 461; index to record, Smyth trial, 226, 461; journals, relative to, 264; Martinus, messenger, appropriation, 459; clerk, additional clerical service, 462; New York investigating committee, 1875, expenses, 462; committee to revise statutes, printing and material for, 493; committee on Code revision, printing for, 493; judiciary committee, printing for, 494; clerk, deficiency

SENATE (State), VETOES — (*Continued*).

appropriation, 581; removal of library to new capitol, appropriation, 581; death of Chauncey O. Abbott, committee clerk, expenses of committee attending funeral, 586; stenographers, special railroad committee, 1882, compensation, 780; messenger to finance committee, compensation, 782; health office investigating committee, clerk, compensation, 783; insurance investigating committee, clerk, compensation, 783; cartage of documents, 901; VIII, 106, 851; cities committee, investigation of New York public works department, counsel fees, VII, 905; Gravesend investigation, counsel fees, 905; insurance committee, investigation of Receiver Best, counsel fees, 906; library, arrangement and classification, 906; journal clerk, substitute for, compensation, 907; Pierson, journal clerk, death of, appropriation for widow, 917, 1082; VIII, 109; compensation of certain officers after adjournment, VII, 1078; VIII, 106; library, purchase of standard geographic time globe for, 108; printing Clerk's Manual, 118; gas investigating committee, printing testimony, 119; telephone renewal, 245; gas investigating committee, printing testimony, 251; library, stairs and book cases, 422; library, removing and rearranging books, 422; committee on taxation and retrenchment, services of counsel and stenographers, appropriation, 439; committee on privileges and elections, stenographer, appropriation, 547; committee on taxation and retrenchment, counsel, appropriation, 548, 842; committee on public health, counsel fees, appropriation, 841; clerk's room, furniture for, appropriation, 841; committee on general laws, investigation of trusts, appropriation for attorney, 843; stenographer, committee on taxation and retrenchment, appropriation, Bloomingdale Asylum investigation, 844; stenographers, 1889, preparing record for publication, 854; clerk, advances to, purchase of file boards, 857; furnishing various books for library, 859; superintendent of wrapping department, compensation, 1889, 859; indexing legislative documents, appropriation, 860; clerk, services to committee on general laws, 860; electrical investigation, printing testimony, 1038; investigation of cities, 1890, services of committee, appropriation, 1140; sergeant-at-arms, compensation, 1141; Thornton, stenographer, 1141; X, 570, 647; library, promoting usefulness of, IX, 153; committee to investigate State Board of Health, counsel fees, 401; investigating committee, New York police department, expenses, 484; investigation of election frauds, 1894, counsel fees, 533; library, books and binding, 773.

SENATE (United States). Resolution relating to first meeting of, II, 297; member of, cannot hold seat in Legislature, 310; proposed organization of, 366; ratifies treaty with Seven Nations, 390; power of confirmation, 500; ratifies treaty of peace with Great Britain, 824; proposed tribunal to settle controversies between State and national governments, III, 79; special session called, 1825, 104; publication of executive proceedings, 109, 110; treaty power, IV, 417; V, 480; President, alleged usurpation of power, election of 1876, VII, 39; proposition to make ex-Presidents members of, VIII, 692.

SENATE CHAMBER. New capitol, completion of, VII, 175, 430, 523; first occupancy by Senate, 539; State arms to be hung on walls of, 727; rearranging lighting system, veto, X, 51.

SENATE DISTRICTS. Delegates to Constitutional Convention of 1867, V, 748; proposed increase of size, VI, 401; criticism of apportionment of 1879, VII, 402.

SENATORS (State). When chosen, II, 10; official term, beginning of, 10; abolishing property qualifications, IV, 137; chosen by single districts, 363; elected under unconstitutional act of 1906, status of, X, 852.

SENATORS (United States). First election of, II, 301; bill for election of, veto, 303; proposed amendment as to eligibility, 426; as to qualifications of, 433, 434, 439; proposed removal by State Legislature, 631; amendment reducing term from six years to four years, 795, 827; ineligible to certain offices, 1062; qualifications, III, 883; disqualified by participation in rebellion, V, 790; proposed election by people, VI, 377; resignations of Senators Conkling and Platt, VII, 555, 568; duties and responsibilities, 563.

SENECA. Overseers of the poor, compensation, veto, VIII, 696.

SENECA COUNTY. Militia from, 1812, II, 743; election of clerk confirmed, III, 217; agricultural society in, 945; purchase of farm for State Agricultural College, V, 16; average excise license fees, 1889, VIII, 687; highways, cost of labor system, 1892, IX, 200; insane, care of, county and State systems compared, 228; estimated contribution to cost of barge canal, X, 602.

VETOES. Subjecting to Railroad Aid Act, VI, 214; county treasurer, amending act, VII, 71; State school moneys, 412; judge and surrogate, compensation, 549; county clerk, transcribing certain records, IX, 39; fishing in certain waters, X, 168; draining Gorman swamp, cleaning Black brook, 651; draining Gorman swamp, 698, 797.

SENECA FALLS. Number of excise licenses, 1887, VIII, 360.

VETOES. Guion, justice of the peace, legalizing acts, VII, 44; board of education, appointment of assessor, 60; revising charter, 935; bonds for bridge and cemetery addition, X, 278; gas, regulating price of, 907.

SENECA FALLS SCHOOL OF ANATOMY. Dissections, veto, IX, 264.

SENECA INDIANS. Protest against sale of liquor to Indians, I, 157; trading-house, Lake Cadaracqui, 201; agents to reside among, 212, 217; persons to reside among, 222, 277; French in vicinity of, 241; smith for, 249, 323, 389, 419, 548, 570; smith and presents for, 257; grant leave to Frenchman to build house at Tierondequat, 262, 265; interpreter and smith for, 265; payment of persons serving among, 270, 306; sachems visit Quebec to negotiate with French, 272; condition of Fort Hunter, 277; acquiring land from, for fort, 277, 548; French presents to, 310; posting party of men with, 316; armorer for, 323; proposed new fort for protection of, 324; report relating to, 521; fort in country, 548; making war on whites, 676; at Albany, negotiations with, II, 273; sale of land at Niagara, 477; land for military post at Black Rock, 513; claim of, 514; treaty with, 523; George murder case, 531; privileges at Black Rock ferry, 605; sale of islands in Niagara river, 677, 857, 866; destruction of corn, advance from annuities, 882; address from chiefs, 941; number of, 1819, 976; conference with, on various subjects, 1029; communication from, oppression of whites, 1076; attorney for, 1076; IV, 291; Green Bay treaty, 1107; assume jurisdiction to punish crimes, 1119; communication from, relative to missionaries, III, 35; communication from, 142; memorial, diversion of Tonawanda creek for canal purposes, 182; negotiations with, Senate chairman of committee on Indian affairs to attend, 939; treaties with United States, Massachusetts claim, IV, 290; Cattaraugus and Allegany reservations, report concerning, 290; Tonawanda reservation, treaties relative to, 295; sachems, power to make treaties, 295; new form of government, 457; remonstrance by certain chiefs against new form of government, 503, 505, 506; method of choosing chiefs, 504; protest against repeal of Confirming Act, 507; sale of land for taxes, V, 36; Tonawanda band, communication from, 199; bribery of officers, act to prevent, VII, 436.

VETOES. Leases, ratification, VI, 336; amending act, 910; oil pipeline, Allegany reservation, VII, 73; Tonawanda band, annuity, payment for bridge, 477; monument to William Tall-Chief, VIII, 110.

SENECA LAKE. Canal connection with Hudson river, II, 321; canal connection with Chenango and Tioga rivers, 902, 903; canal connection with Susquehanna river, 918, 1011; III, 70; canal connection with other lakes and Erie canal, 70; canal to Tioga river, report of Pennsylvania commissioners, 98; connection with Chemung canal, 865.

SENECA LAKE —(Continued).

VETOES. Ferry at Lodi Landing, VI, 1033; ferry, extending Goodwin franchise, IX, 372; assessment, local improvement, Geneva, X, 648; breakwater, repairs, 798.

SENECA LAKE CANAL. Provision for construction of, II, 902.

SENECA RIVER. A public highway, bridges over, V, 148. VETOES. Fishway at State dam, VII, 61; canal bridge, 116; removing obstructions, 405; fishways in, VIII, 888; bridge, Salina and Lysander, X, 697.

SENECA RIVER TOWING PATH. Tolls, V, 66, 154, 258, 362; financial statement, 1875, VI, 930.

SENNETT AND AUBURN PLANKROAD COMPANY. Assessing stockholders and making gravel road, V, 119, 233.

SEQUESTRATION. VETOES. Power of commissioners, II, 191; indemnification by commissioners, 233.

SERGEANT, JOHN, JR. Letter from, removal of Stockbridge Indians, II, 987; receives conveyance of Indian land, 989, 992.

SERGEANT-AT-ARMS. Of Assembly, appointed, I, 101; to be appointed, 266.

SERVANTS. Act to punish fugitives, I, 11; act relating to, 11; importation of white, recommended, 161, 248, 618; impressment of, 374; enlistment of apprentices, reimbursing masters for, 599; frequenting tippling-houses, 660; slaves, abandonment to State, II, 508; exportation prohibited, 978.

SETH N. HEDGES POST No. 216, G. A. R., DANSVILLE. Charter, veto, VIII, 462.

SEVEN NATIONS OF CANADA. Treaty with, II, 368, 380, 381, 386, 390; claim of, 376; Grey claim, 391.

SEVENTEENTH WARD SAVINGS BANK, NEW YORK. Charter, veto, VI, 342.

SEVENTH JUDICIAL DISTRICT. Law library, Rochester, veto, VII, 220; additional justices for, 837; included in fourth judicial department, IX, 546.

SEVEN VILLAGES (Canada Indians). Claim of, II, 328, 343.

SEWALL, —. Prisoner at Clinton, murders Keeper Wright, V, 429.

SEWARD, FREDERICK W. Acting Secretary of State, United States, communication relative to statues for hall of House of Representatives, V, 635; member of Yorktown Centennial Commission, VII, 734.

SEWARD, WILLIAM H. Governor, portrait, III, 706.
1839. Annual message, III, 706; finances, 707; proceeds of public lands, 707; auction and salt duties, 708; salt manufacture, 708; canal finances, 709; school and bank finances, 711; limiting term of canal commissioners, 711; board of internal improvements,

Seward, William H., 1839 — (*Continued*).

712; militia, 713; State lunatic asylum, 713; deaf and dumb, 715; blind, 715; House of Refuge, 716; State prisons, 716; judicial reform, 718; restricting appointing power to Court of Common Pleas, 719; fees of court officers, 720; reduction of number of inspection officers, 722; foreclosure of mortgages, 722; circulation of small bills, 723; financial affairs, 723; banks, 724; circulation of foreign bills, 725; conduct of elections, 726; relation of education to prosperity, 727; immigration adds labor as a source of wealth, 728; immigration should be encouraged, 729; instruction of immigrants, 729; Erie canal enlargement, 729; railroads, 730; Hudson river improvement, 733; internal improvements, 734; Assembly report on canals, 735; indebtedness of State, 736; improvement of highways, 739; colleges, 739; academies, 740; common schools, 740; normal schools, 743; school district libraries, 743; importance of visitation of schools, 743; department of education proposed, 744; agriculture, 744; board of agriculture proposed, 745; monument to DeWitt Clinton, 746; Connecticut resolutions, 747; Georgia resolutions, 748; communication from Charity Hospital, New Orleans, 748; memorial relative to Hudson river improvement, 748; Stockbridge Indians, 748; petition for House of Refuge in western part of State, 748; American Antiquarian Society applies for laws and judicial decisions, 749; depositions taken in this State to be used in other States, 749; Albany and West Stockbridge Railroad Company, 750; announces death of Stephen Van Rensselaer, 750; publication of colonial documents, 751; North Carolina and New Jersey resolutions, 752; geological survey, report, 752; Holland Land Company papers, 755; Indiana resolutions, 756; northeastern boundary controversy, 756; Missouri resolutions, 758; proposed canal connection with North Branch canal of Pennsylvania, 759; disturbances in northeastern part of State, 759; correspondence relative to disturbance, 760; proclamation offering reward for conviction of participants in disturbance, 760; Ohio resolutions, 761; Masonville Turnpike Road Company, charter, veto, 758.

1340. Annual message, III, 762; finances, 763; State prisons, 764; complaints against prison management, 765; county jails, 765; house of refuge, 765; blind, deaf and dumb, 766; State lunatic asylum, 766; colleges, 766; school district libraries, 767; extending benefits of common schools, 767; geological survey, 768; militia, 769; restricting appointing power to county judges, 770; imprisonment of non-resident debtors, 770; rights of aliens,

SEWARD, WILLIAM H., 1840 — (*Continued*).

771; elections, 771; meaning of "resident," 772; judicial reform, 772; collection of debts, mortgage foreclosure, 773; reform in procedure, 773; fees of attorneys and solicitors, 774; anti-rent troubles, 774, 822; Virginia extradition case, 777; promotion of commerce, 779; mixed currency, 780; use of bank fund, 782; revision of Banking Law, 783; election of United States Senator, 784; national affairs, 784, 818; limiting tenure of President to one term, 786; railroads, 786; railroad tolls, 787; Erie canal enlargement, 787; statement of canal debt, 791; State. debt, 793; probable increase of canal tolls, 794; new financial policy needed, 796; board of internal improvement, 797; lateral canals should not be abandoned, 799; railroads may be constructed by State, 800; opposition to internal improvements, 801; quotes Washington and Jefferson in favor of internal improvements, 805; action of Convention of 1821 on canals, 807; policy of constructing internal improvements, 808; loaning credit of State, 809; quotes Governor Van Buren on internal improvements, 810; summary of internal improvements, 811; principles applicable to internal improvements, 812; financial results of policy, 813; wide area of commerce, 814; advantages derived from internal improvements, 815; quantity of public lands, 816; New Jersey resolutions, 820; Vermont resolutions, 821; authentication of instruments executed abroad, 821; Missouri and Maine resolutions, 821; communication from Kentucky relative to cultivation of silk and beet sugar, 821; South Carolina resolutions, 822; wharf at Plattsburgh, 822; report on anti-rent troubles, 822; national Bankrupt Law, 841; protection of minors, veto, 845; conveyance of land to United States for fortifications, 850; Kentucky resolutions, 851; memorandum, New York, elections bill, 851; Maine resolutions, 851; Indiana resolutions, 852; extradition of Johnson and others, 852.

1841. Annual message, III, 853; general legislative powers, 853; New York's great future, 854; condition of State, 855; salt springs, 856; colleges, 857; academies, grammar and common schools, 857; school district libraries, 858; deaf and dumb, blind, 859; State Lunatic Asylum, 859; geological survey, 859; redemption of bank notes, 860; State prisons, 860; pardoning power, 861; capital punishment, 863; report on conditions in manor of Rensselaerwyck, 863; canals, 863; railroads, 866; State debt, 867; number of militia, 868; Virginia extradition case, 869, 915; United States deposit fund, 869; increasing rev-

Seward, William H., 1841 — (*Continued*).

enue from salt springs, 871; judicial reform, 871; reform in legal proceedings, 872; charitable institutions, 874; penitentiaries, 874; retreat for women convicts, 875; houses of refuge, 876; imprisonment of non-resident debtors, 876; national Bankrupt Law, 876; banks, 876; agriculture, 877; militia reform, 879; exemptions from military service, 880; elections, 881; bribery, 882; naturalization, 882; number of white illiterates, 884; education, 884; internal improvements, 887; canal policy contrasted with previous administration, 889; public lands, 896; distribution of Federal revenues, 898; national affairs, 903; tribute to President Harrison, 904, 914; tribute to DeWitt Clinton, 905; complaint against Judge William Inglis, 906; remonstrance from District of Columbia, 906; Connecticut resolutions, 906; Vermont resolutions, 907; proceedings by Georgetown requesting retrocession to Maryland, 907; Michigan resolutions, 907; Alabama resolutions, 907, 908; Indiana resolutions, 908, 909; Pennsylvania resolutions, 908; Delaware resolutions, 908, 909; Burchard claim, attorney for Oneida Indians, 909; Kentucky and Rhode Island resolutions, 909; transmits resignation of Representative Francis Granger, 909; Maryland resolutions, 909, 929; Curry extradition case, 910, 915; Virginia attempts to restrict commerce with New York, 910; Mississippi resolutions, 913; announces death of President Harrison, 914; correspondence with Lieutenant-Governor of Virginia, Curry extradition case, 915; charges against Madison county judges, 928; Massachusetts resolutions, 929; memorial on convict labor, 930; McLeod case, 932, 941.

1842. Annual message, III, 934; new State Hall completed, 934; deposit of maps and plans, 934; asylum for insane, 935; geological survey, 935; journals of Provincial Congress, 935; publication of colonial documents, 935; constitutional amendments, judiciary, 936; Virginia extradition case, 936, 972, 982; Georgia extradition case, Greenman, 937; banks, 938; Indian affairs, 939; congressional apportionment, 939; prison affairs, 940; convict labor, 940; capital punishment, 940; county jails, 941; difficulties in administering justice, 941; British naval armament on border lakes, 945; militia system, 945; agricultural societies, 945; silk manufacture, 945; education and education funds, 946; schools for foreigners, 947; New York city, school system, 948; condition of treasury, 951; salt manufacture, 951; canal tolls, 952; railroad companies in default in payment of interest on

SEWARD, WILLIAM H., 1842 — (Continued).

State loan, 952; railroads and canals, 953; importance of internal improvements, 954; Erie canal enlargement, 955; new financial policy needed, 957; purpose of Erie canal, 958; direct tax revived, 959; New York and Erie Railroad, 959, 999; governmental management of railroads, 961; lateral canals, 963; estimated cost of all public works, 965; restoration of public lands to State, 966; rate of interest on loans, 967; State's relation to post roads, 969; application of future receipts from public lands, 971; transmits resignation of Secretary of State Spencer, 972; repair to arsenals, 972; Connecticut, Maine, Delaware and Vermont resolutions, 972; memorandum, receivers of moneyed institutions, expunged by Senate, 973; Governor's relation to legislation, 973; works of, quoted, 974, 977; Alabama resolutions, 974, 975; Senate refuses to receive communication from, 975; Georgia resolutions, 977; Prison Discipline Society, 977; Kentucky resolutions, 978, 979; Niles' Register, proposed purchase of, 978; claims against United States, War of 1812, 978; retrocession of Alexandria to Virginia, 980; South Carolina law for search of New York vessels, 980; correspondence with Governor Richardson of South Carolina, Virginia extradition case, 982; railroad between St. Lawrence river and Lake Champlain, 983; South Carolina resolutions, public lands, 984; New Jersey resolutions, 988; Herkimer monument, 989; geological survey, 990, 1036; publication of colonial history, 1008, 1013; resolutions from other States, 1020; Fort Plain bill returned for amendment, 1028; act to provide jury trial for fugitive slaves deemed unconstitutional, 1028; suggests amendment to bill relating to sale of real estate, 1029; suggests amendment to bill relating to village of Black Rock, 1029; suggests amendment to bill relating to city of Albany, 1029; message on Legislature's action on Virginia extradition case, 1031; declines to transmit legislative resolutions to Virginia, 1031; returns tax bill without action, 1032; returns New York pilot-bill without action, 1032; congressional apportionment, 1033; Genesee Wesleyan Seminary destroyed by fire, 1033; reform in judiciary, 1034; State prisons, 1034; convict labor in mines, 1034; election riot in New York, 1034; Croton aqueduct, 1034; journals of Provincial Congresses, 1035; volumes of colonial history, 1035; coal not found in State, 1036; Virginia's retaliatory law, 1037; trial by jury, fugitive slaves, 1037; Rhode Island extradition case, 1037; northern boundary treaty with Great Britain, 1038;

Seward, William H., 1842 — (Continued).

  international extradition, 1038; foreign imprisonment of American citizens, 1039; immigration, 1039; finances, 1039; manufacture of salt, 1040; distribution of proceeds of public lands, 1040; protective tariff, 1041; internal improvements, 1041; policy of 1842, 1044; sends Regents' reports to Netherlands, 1051; Mississippi resolutions, 1051; official service, I, pref. xii.

Secretary of State, United States, communication from, official residence of Venezuelan Minister, V, 617; murderous assault on, 649; legislative resolutions, 649.

Seward's Works. Quoted, memorandum of approval of receivers' bill, III, 974, 977.

Sewing Machines. Sale on installment plan, veto, VII, 758.

Seybert's Statistics. Noted, II, 994.

Seymore, Catherine. Relief, veto, VI, 673.

Seymour, Henry. Commissioner on New Jersey boundary, VI, 779.

Seymour, Henry J. Relief, veto, VI, 185.

Seymour, Horatio. Governor, portrait, IV, 640.

  1853. Annual message, IV, 640; general conditions, 640; epidemic, 640; charitable institutions, 641; recommends another lunatic asylum, 642; State asylum for idiots, 642; deaf and dumb and blind, 643; emigration, 644; school statistics, 645; instruction of teachers, 647; union free schools, 647; colleges and academies, 647; State Agricultural College, 648; houses of refuge, 650; State prisons, 650; iron manufacture, Clinton prison, 651; survey of State, 652; manorial titles, 652; Commission on Procedure, 654; further revision of procedure needed, 655; militia, 655; reciprocal commerce with British provinces, 656; World's Fair, 656, 708; banks, 657; railroads, 658; finances and public works, 660; canals, 662; defective canal policy, 663; policy of 1842, 664; canal tolls, 666; Canal Act of 1851, 668; railroad tolls, 670; completion of canals, 670; tonnage of boats, 671; water for canals, 672; canal boats, 673, 686; purpose of canal system, 674; railroad competition, 674; amount necessary to complete canals, 676; unsatisfactory financial condition, 678; national affairs, 680; pardon report, 681; monument to commemorate Declaration of Independence, 681; appropriations for improvement of Erie and Oswego canals, 686; description of canal boats, 687; improvements needed in Erie canal, 690; report on revision of public school system, 693.

SEYMOUR, HORATIO, 1853 — *(Continued)*.

VETOES. Oxford, amending charter, IV, 684; James and William Knox, releasing interest in securities, 693; discharging judgment against Potsdam and Watertown Railroad, 693; McCaughel escheat bill, 693; Franklin Bridge Company, charter, 694.

Convenes Legislature in extraordinary session, IV, 694; New York tax bill, 695; charges against Canal Commissioner Mather, 695; interest on canal debt, 696; canal appropriations, 696; returns for amendment canal loan bill, 700; authorizing business of banking, amending act, veto, 700; amount of stock debt, 702; number and capital of banks, 703; city stocks not suitable for bank securities, 704, 731; encroachments on New York harbor, 704; Lawrence assault case, 705, 727; invited to attend opening of World's Fair, 708.

1854. Annual message, IV, 709; general duties of Legislature, 709; condition of State, 710; all nations of Europe represented in New York State, 711; sources of State's prosperity, 711; New York's part in Revolutionary struggle, 712; high character of first Constitution, 712; New York's leadership in internal improvements, 713; common school statistics, 714; common school education, 715; separation of office of superintendent from that of Secretary of State, 716; State scholarships, 716; asylums for training idiots, 717; lunatic asylums, 718; asylum for the blind, 718; removal of asylum for instruction of deaf and dumb, 718; emigration, 719; cholera on emigrant ships, 719; houses of refuge, 720; State prisons, 721; appointments to penal and charitable institutions should not be subject to political influence, 722; commutation for good behavior, 723; condition of jails, 723; good condition of Albany penitentiary, 724; term of imprisonment, modification of, 724; difficulties in exercising pardoning power, 725; militia, 726; manorial titles, 727; resistance to legal process, Albany county, 727; *posse comitatus*, 728; banks, 729; restricting power of municipal corporations to create debt, 730; State stock available for bank securities, 731; modification of usury laws, 731; encroachments on New York harbor, 732, 751; relief of canal contractors, 733; improvements needed in canals, 734; appropriations for canals, 735; canal constitutional amendment, 735; commerce diverted from canals, 736;

SEYMOUR, HORATIO, 1854 — (*Continued*).

    number and tonnage of boats, 737; railroad competition
with canals, 739; sketch of canal policy, 740; condition of
general fund, 743; State debt exceeds constitutional limit,
744; prohibiting expenditures in excess of available appropriations, 744; bribery at elections, 744; intemperance,
745; excise laws inadequate, 745; Code of Procedure, 745;
national affairs, 746; distribution of public lands, 749;
amendments to United States Constitution proposed by New
York, 750; recall of bills for amendment, general note,
751; International Educational Exhibition, London, 752;
too many commissions, 778; pardon report, 779.

  VETOES. Suppression of intemperance, IV, 752; Canandaigua
highway bill, 771; vacancies in office, amending Revised
Statutes, 772; New York, amending Croton Water Act, 773;
taxation of corporations, amending Revised Statutes, 775;
special county judge and surrogate, Washington county,
776; State prisons, Investigating Commission, 777.

1863. Annual message, V, 445; official oath, 445; number of New
York troops in national service, 445; New York soldiers
commended, 446; military appointments, 446; prosperous
condition of State, 446; charitable institutions, 447; commissioner of lunacy, 447, 521; schools, 448; colleges and
academies, 448; houses of refuge, 448; State prisons, 448;
bank statistics, 449; Insurance Department, 450; emigration, 450; quarantine, 450; excise licenses, 450; State debt
paid in coin, 450; funded debt, 451; canal fund, 451; tonnage of canals, 452; Hudson river improvement, 453; valuations of real and personal property, 453; State tax, 453;
President calls for troops, 453; Civil War bounties, 454;
number of men of military age, 1860, 455; inequality and
injustice of draft laws, 455; exemption from military service, 456; adjustment of quotas, 457; amounts due soldiers,
War of 1812, 457; national affairs, 458; causes of the war,
459; respect for laws and rulers, 460; war should have been
averted, 461; economy and integrity, 461; importance of
pensions, 462; limitations of power, 463; State rights, 464;
arbitrary arrests, 465; abduction of citizens for alleged
political offenses, 466; issues in State election of 1862, 468;
martial law, 468; constitutional protests against martial law,
470; President's proclamation of emancipation, 473; central and western States, 474; unhappy effect of war on

SEYMOUR, HORATIO, 1863 — (*Continued*).

center and western States, 475; border State policy, 475; extremes will not prevail, 477; adjustment of interests, 478; commercial importance of free navigation of Mississippi river, 478; political interests, 479; national debt, 481; Union must be restored, 482, 484; lessons derived from war, 484; election of Speaker, 485; declines to interfere in election of Speaker, 485; various annual reports, 486, 487; memorial from Prison Association of New York, 486; report of quarantine commissioners, 487; appropriation for sick and wounded soldiers, how expended, 487; interest on State debt, 490; public credit should be maintained, 492; Indiana memorial relative to use of New York canals and railroads, 493; Kentucky resolutions relative to Federal affairs, 499; report of Samuel B. Ruggles on canals, 501; soldiers' vote, 508; returning for amendment bill incorporating Harlaem Savings Bank, 512; returning for amendment bill in relation to draining low lands situate in certain towns in Orange county, 512.

VETOES. Hamilton county, publication of legal notices, V, 508; Amsterdam, revising village charter, 512; soldier vote bill, 513; railroads in certain streets in New York, 517.

1864. Annual message, V, 520; reports of State charitable institutions, 520; staff reports on military affairs, 521; Bureau of Military Statistics, 521; veterans of 1812, 522; education, 522; common school statistics, 522; recommends increase in teachers' wages, 524; houses of refuge, 524; prison labor affected by Civil War, 524; improvements needed at Sing Sing prison, 525; State prison statistics, 525; commutation for good behavior, 525; Prison Association of New York, inspection of penal institutions, 526; State banks, 527; national banks, 528; salt springs, 529; finances, 529; State tax, 530; canal fund, 531; internal carrying trade, 532; canals, 532; abolition of tolls on western products, 533; enlarging canals, 533; Chenango canal extension, 533; obstructions in Hudson river, 534; foreign commerce, 534; immigration, 535; constitutional amendment, commission of appeals, 535; Constitutional Convention, 536; enrollment and draft, 536; Commission on Readjustment of Quotas, 537; failure of draft, 539; depreciation in currency reduces pay of soldiers, 539; bounties, 540; large number of troops called for, 540, 553; militia should be armed and equipped, 541; militia, 543; unprotected condition of New York city, 543; invasion of Pennsyl-

SEYMOUR, HORATIO, 1864 — (*Continued*).

vania, 544; militia ordered to Harrisburgh, 544; Commission on Harbor and Frontier Defense, 545; riot in New York resulting from draft, 545; proclamation on draft riots, 546; declares New York in state of insurrection, 547; asylum for colored children, New York, destroyed, 547; number killed and wounded in riots, 548; defenseless condition of New York, 549; expected attack on northern frontier, 550; martial law, 551; number of men in national service, 553; national debt, 553; plans for termination of war, 554; reorganization of southern States as result of war, 556; only way to save Union, 560; soldiers returning from war, 561; crowded condition of places of rendezvous, 562; Commission on Care of Recruits and Returning Volunteers, 563; various reports, 563, 564, 570, 571, 577, 578; West Virginia resolutions, 564; report of Commission on Harbor Defense, 564; adjustment of standard of weights and measures, 570; lack of funds for bounties, 571; authorized to borrow money for bounties, 571; inequality of enrollment, 571; adjustment of quotas, 574, 575; returns for correction bill to amend charter of Sing Sing Savings Bank and bill amending Port Chester fire department charter, 574; proper method of amending statutes, 575; transcribing military records, 576; alphabetical list of volunteers, 577; report of auditing board, troops, 577; report of New York State soldiers' depot, 577; discrimination in payment of State debt, 578; urges payment of interest in coin, 579; member of Adirondack Park Commission, 1872, VII, 722; requests approval of Harvey rapid transit bill, VIII, 125; death of, 195; legislative memorial services, 196; report on pardons, V, 116; quoted, — commutation of sentences for good behavior, IV, 787; — opinion on excise legislation, VIII, 363, 364; — temperance habits, 683; official service as Governor, I, pref. xiii.

SEYMOUR, JOHN F. Member of Tax Revision Commission, 1881, VII, 538.

SEYMOUR, WILLIAM. Justice of the peace, legalizing acts of, veto, VI, 479.

SHAATS, RINIER. Appointed doorkeeper to Council of Revision, II, 369.

SHAFFER, JOHN H. Member of National Guard, blindness incurred in State's service, claim for damages, veto, X, 592.

SHAKERS. Joining of, ground for divorce, II, 920, 946; right to enjoy peculiar religious belief, 921, 947.

SHALER, ALEXANDER. Major-general, reviews first division, National Guard, Yorktown Celebration, VII, 739.

SHALER, NATHANIEL. Relief of, II, 563.

SHARPE, GEORGE H. Speaker, remarks on opening of new Senate Chamber, VII, 540.

SHARPE, ICHABOD B. Death from fall of canal bridge, VII, 88.

SHARPE, MARILA I. Widow of Rev. Ichabod 'B. Sharpe, damages for husband's death, veto, VII, 88; extending time to file claim, veto, 773.

SHAVER, JOHAN JOST. Service of process on, Van Rensselaer rent, III, 825.

SHAVER, JOHN. Service of process on, Van Rensselaer rent, III, 825.

SHAW, ALBERT D. Member of board of examiners of arms for National Guard, IX, 635.

SHAW, JAMES. Legislative employee, compensation, veto, VII, 372.

SHAWANESE INDIANS. Movement against, I, 676.

SHAWANGUNK. Legalizing resolution fixing place of town meeting, veto, VI, 581.

SHAYS, DANIEL. Arrest authorized, II, 269.

SHAYS' REBELLION (Massachusetts). Papers and resolutions relating to, II, 269; insurgents flee into New York, 271.

SHEEDY, EDMUND. Troy school janitor, claim, veto, X, 634.

SHEEP. Breed introduced, quality of cloth from, II, 658; prevention of infectious diseases among, VI, 28; killed by dogs, amending Revised Statutes, veto, VIII, 469; killed by dogs, fund for damages, 824.

SHEFFIELD, JAMES R. Assembly, 1894, introduces blanket ballot bill, IX, 396.

SHELBURNE, LORD. Secretary of State, letter from, relative to King's veto of colonial act for support of troops, I, 716.

SHELDON, ALEXANDER. Chosen Regent, II, 629.

SHELDON, RAYMOND. Bond for return of arms, II, 774.

SHELDON, WILLIAM. Letter to Governor Tompkins on behalf of Alfred Davis, II, 847.

SHELDON'S LIGHT DRAGOONS. Stationed near Westchester county line, II, 113.

SHENANDOAH, CHRISTINE. Indian land claim, veto, VI, 184.

SHEPARD, EDWARD M. Member of Forest Investigating Commission, 1884, VIII, 23.

SHEPHERD, ABRAHAM. Speaker, Ohio Senate, communication from, Erie canal, II, 891.

SHERBURNE. VETOES. Philomathian Society, V, 129; raising money for new bridge, VIII, 336.

SHERIDAN, PHILIP H. Lieutenant-general, report on disturbance in Louisiana, VI, 769; memorial, printing and distributing, veto, VIII, 875.

SHERIDAN, THOMAS J. Contested election, Assembly, Kings county, expenses, veto, VII, 918.

SHERIFF. Taking unlawful fees, II, 22; removal of, III, 133; appointments to fill vacancies, 176; when under-sheriff to execute office, 176; Albany county, resistance to process, 774, 822; summons power of county, 827; IV, 147; when may summon power of county, 145, 706, 728; offering rewards in criminal cases, V, 698; method of selection and removal, VI, 833; New York, compensation changed from fees to salary, VIII, 1023, 1103; Erie, office becomes salaried, 1103; several offices become salaried, IX, 124; Erie county asks military aid in Buffalo railroad strike, 1892, 160; New York, salaried officer, act for, 413, 459; Kings, salaried office, X, 25, 208, 290; New York, large compensation received by, 207.

VETOES. Increasing fees, V, 875; New York, exclusive right of sale in foreclosure judgment, 877; office, closing on holidays, VI, 287; anomalous appointing power, Kings county board of charities, 1019; jury, New York, VII, 595; Rensselaer, fixing compensation, 1115; Albany, compensation, 1121; coroner acting as, VIII, 292; fees, amending Code, IX, 150; New York, deputies, appointment and compensation, 459; Tamsen, New York, charges against, expenses of investigation, 777; office hours, 801, 863; Erie, relative to, X, 61; Kings county, salaried office, 179; Nassau, reimbursement for services and expenses after expiration of term, 242; Essex, making office salaried in part, 316; Erie, compensation of deputies, 318; New York, allowance for expenses after expiration of term, 321, 594, 716; Erie, additional subordinates, purchase of supplies, 380; Kings, Guden case, appropriation for counsel, 559; New York, amending act, 581, 706; Essex, Chinese prisoners, 701, 708; Cattaraugus county, boarding United States prisoners, 706; Kings, assistant deputies, 710, 711; New York, salaries, 711, 773, 948; Kings, additional subordinates, 770; Livingston, compensation of under-sheriffs, jailer and attendants, 811; Dutchess legalizing audit of accounts, 956; New York, amending title to act, also amending act, 960; Richmond, deputy, attending court, compensation, 961.

SHERMAN, JEFFERSON. Justice of the peace, Marion, legalizing acts, veto, IX, 346.

SHERMAN, WILLIAM T. General, delivers address at celebration of battle of Newtown, VII, 1084; death of, VIII, 1087; flags at half staff, 1087; Assembly, McMahon memorial and resolutions, 1088; Senate, Saxton resolution, 1088.

SHERMAN POST, G. A. R., ROSE. Use of room in town hall, veto, VIII, 528.

SHERRILL, JAMES D. Dam across Hudson river, North Creek, veto, X, 705.

SHEW, GODFREY. Bond for return of arms, II, 772.

SHEW, JACOB. Bond for return of arms, II, 772.

SHILL, HENRY H. Claim against New York, audit, veto, IX, 807.

SHINNECOCK BAY. VETOES. Dredging channel connecting with Moriches bay, X, 645; dredging channel between, and Great South bay, 786.

SHINNECOCK BAY AND GREAT SOUTH BAY CANAL. Reappropriation for, veto, X, 302.

SHINNECOCK AND PECONIC BAYS CANAL. Ross and Sanford construction claim, veto, IX, 237, 721.

SHIP BUILDING. Proposition to encourage, I, 246; neglected in colony, 255, 280; encouragement of, recommended, 260, 618; proposed subsidy for, 281; scarcity of wood for, II, 1094; a lost art, VI, 247.

SHIP CANAL. Proposed between Greenbush and New Baltimore, III, 124, 465; suggested from Hudson river to Lake Ontario, 509; around Niagara falls, 509, 816, 959; IV, 817; V, 533; proposed around St. Marie falls, III, 907; canal connecting St. Lawrence river and Lake Champlain, VI, 539; between Lake Erie and Hudson river, 636; not deemed practicable, X, 137.

SHIP FEVER. Classed as a quarantine disease, V, 418; quarantine against, VI, 237, 359; in immigrant vessels, 532, 626.

SHIRES. Erection and description of, I, 10.

SHIRLEY, WILLIAM. Governor of Massachusetts, letter from, relative to union of colonies, I, 330; asks New York aid against French, 331; letter from, relative to Six Nations, 341, 355; expedition against Louisburg, 347; letter from, relative to Cape Breton expedition, 350, 355; relative to murders by French Indians, 355; letter from, relative to expedition against Canada, 373, 375, 381, 404; employment of land forces in Canadian expedition, 383; Colonel Roberts conference with, relative to frontier defense, 391, 398; forts at northern Carrying Place, 392; exchange of English prisoners, 409; dispatches from Duke of Newcastle, 410; retaining forces at Albany, 418; joins in movement against French, 464, 466; letter from Governor of Canada relative to exchange of prisoners, 467; letter from, 538; communication from, relative to New York boundary, 541; letter from Secretary Robinson to, 555; letter from, colonial defense, union of colonies, 565; plan of defense approved, 566; papers from, 572; letter from, relative to Colonel Dunbar's forces, 574; letter from, expedition against Ticonderoga, 589, 590; holds council of war in New York, 591; letter from, troops for Crown Point expedition, 594.

Shoes. For troops, I, 639; manufactured at Clinton prison, V, 426.

Shore Inspector. Increasing number, veto, VII, 1124.

Shot. See Ball.

Shriver, Thomas. Heirs, escheat, veto, VII, 805.

Shuckburgh, Dr. Richard. Claim for medical services, I, 518.

Shute, Samuel. Governor of Massachusetts, letter from, demanding assistance from New York, I, 203.

Sickles, Jacob. President, General Synod of Reformed Church, communication from, fast day, II, 716.

Sidepaths. Vetoes. Amending act, X, 594; establishing,— Niagara county, IX, 629; — Oneida county, 726; — Chemung county, 729; — Monroe county, 731.

Sidewalks. Vetoes. Rochester, defective, damages for injuries, VIII, 629; Watertown, amending charter, 1041; Waterford, injuries from defects, notice, IX, 54; New York, removal of snow and ice from, X, 60; White Plains, compelling lotowners to repair, 61; Cortland, relative to, amending charter, 593; Fulton, amending charter, 715.

Sidney Plains. Separate road district, veto, VI, 684.

Signal Hill. Erecting redoubt on, II, 778.

Silk. Manufacture of, III, 298, 387; manufacture of, in prisons, 514, 541, 931, 945; communication from Kentucky relative to, 821; large exportations from Italy, 878; bounty for, 879, 945.

Sillick, Diana. Convicted of murder, sentence commuted to imprisonment for life, II, 894.

Silver. See also Gold; Money and Currency. Exportation of coin prohibited, I, 133; act relative to rates of foreign coin, 134; continental bills of credit, interest to be paid in gold or silver, II, 97; coin, counterfeiting prohibited, 224; duties payable in, 277; encouraging circulation of, III, 517; production and coinage, VI, 645; Bland bill, legislative protest against, VII, 150.

Silver Creek. Straightening Walnut creek, veto, VIII, 129.

Silversmith's Company. Board of Claims, veto, IX, 627, 717.

Simon, Charles. Assembly, contested election, appropriation, veto, VI, 866.

Simon, Nelson B. Commissioner of deeds, legalizing acts, veto, X, 958.

Simpson, Joseph P. New York, sealer of weights and measures, communication from, III, 101.

Simson, John. Canal award, veto, VII, 1072.

Sinclair, Sir John. England, aids in establishing National Board of Agriculture, II, 956.

Sing Sing. Prison at, III, 129; armory at, veto, IX, 625.

Sing Sing Branch of the American Society for the Prevention of Cruelty to Animals. Charter, veto, VII, 744.

SING SING PRISON. Erection, III, 129; convict labor on, 129; to receive convicts from certain counties, 316; additional cells for, 317, 382; number of convicts, 339, 382; IV, 609, 650, 721, 844; V, 77, 163, 271, 374, 525; VI, 941; VII, 8, 146, 828, 954; female convicts kept in New York almshouse, III, 379; water for, IV, 482; self-supporting, 607; VII, 281; new buildings, V, 78; sale of part of farm, 166; fires at, 272; alleged severity of punishment, investigation of, 423; Superintendent Pilsbury's report, 431; methods of punishment, 434; improvements needed, 525; removal of certain female convicts, 599; statistics, VI, 616; VII, 425, 519, 701, 827, 954; IX, 25; assault on Keeper Brandow by convict, VII, 464; prisoners idle as result of abolition of contract system, VIII, 645; built in 1825, X, 28; unsanitary condition of, 204; dangerous condition, 342; commission on new site, 863, 895.

VETOES. Marble quarry, Bloomer claim, VI, 589; removal of, 600; various repairs and improvements, VII, 483; Hamilton contract for materials, appropriation, 485; dock at, appropriation, 784; sidewalk and gutters in front of, 920; additional cells, 937; prison labor on highways near, IX, 775; McDough claim for injuries, Court of Claims, X, 699.

SING SING SAVINGS BANK. Charter amended, V, 574.

SINKBAICK. See SINKHAICK.

SINKHAICK. French Indians attack, I, 553.

SINKING FUND. Bills of credit, deficiency in, I, 269; for redemption of bills of credit, 716; for payment of canal debt, IV, 207, 221; how sustained, 219; constitutional provision, 227; canals, third Constitution, 371, 473; V, 159, 590; VI, 10, 914; VII, 818; general fund, IV, 371, 661, 679; V, 3, 368, 590; VI, 10, 914; loan for, IV, 473, 782; amendment of 1874, VI, 540; should not be pledged for other purposes, 541, 629; proposed constitutional amendment, 541; Comptroller's report, 658; revision needed, 916; recommended for local municipal purposes, VII, 299; comparative statement, 421; for barge canal bonds, 1906, X, 833; annual contributions, act of 1906, 849.

VETOES. Canals, tax for, VI, 1010; towns, railroads, VII, 268; New York, improving condition of, 1087; VIII, 99, 161, 183, 189; Mount Vernon, sinking fund commission, establishing, IX, 787.

SINNOTT, JAMES P. Appointed judge of New York marine court, VI, 986.

SISTERHOOD OF GREY NUNS. Gratuities, granting teachers' certificates to, VI, 948.

SISTERS OF MERCY, BROOKLYN BOROUGH. Relief from assessments, veto, X, 716.

SIX NATIONS OF INDIANS. Providing for persons to reside among, I, 215; Governor's conference with, 222, 224, 232; treaty with, 233; fidelity of, importance of Oswego in relation to, 236, 239, 299, 304, 315, 319; need smiths, 248; renewal of covenant chain, 251, 262; Governor to meet, 262, 265; danger of French acquisitions at Tierondequat, 272; proposed acquisition of land for fort at Tierondequat, 277, 548; proposed conference with, 278, 286, 296, 319, 353, 359, 376, 392, 466, 512, 537; services of, at Oswego, 290, 296; growth of Christian faith among, 291; presents to, 304; smith for three tribes, 306; danger of defection of, if Oswego lost, 308; friendship of, important to British interests, 312, 320, 458, 462; two from each nation employed at Oswego, 319; reluctant to engage in war with French, 319; complain against rates of trade, 327; expected benefits of new forts, 333; alleged negotiations with French, 341; danger of seduction by French, 342, 504; preserving friendship of, 346; neutrality treaty broken by Canada Indians, 352, 356, 358; uneasiness among, 353, 355; visit Governor of Canada, 353, 355; Chonondado and Attowas invited to join conference, 354; invited by Governor of Canada to join in war against English, 355, 356; complain of lack of hospitality at Oswego, 357; result of conference with, 359; new treaty with, 359; agree to join in war against French, 359, 362; French intrigues with, 366, 381, 464; refuse to engage in war, 368; subsistence of, in Canadian expedition, 376; agree to join in Canadian War, 382; rewards for scalps, 389; fidelity of, secured, 391, 395, 411, 511; message from Governor of Canada, 400; loyal to English, 405, 415; Governor declines longer to maintain fidelity of, without aid from colony, 409; enlistments in Crown Point expedition, 419; condition of, 421; sent against Canada, 425; Colonel Johnson's influence over, 425; receive belts from Governor of Canada, 425; families to be protected while warriors are in service, 421, 426; smith for each, 439; smith for Oswego, 460, 461; Colonel Johnson's negotiations with, for Crown Point expedition, 466; restricting trade with, 466, 549; exchange of prisoners, 467, 492, 495, 507, 519; Canadian Governor's designs to alienate, 486, 515; uneasiness among, owing to French influence, 508; conference with, relative to Mohawks, 524; Colonel Johnson appointed to confer with, 526; alarmed at French encroachments, 536; good disposition toward British, 548; pernicious effects of use of rum, 549; invited to meeting at Montreal, 570; effect of Braddock's defeat, 573; securing fidelity of, 592; certain land grants claimed to be fraudulent, 601, 606, 611; exposed by French capture of Oswego,

SIX NATIONS OF INDIANS — (*Continued*).

602; long friendly intercourse with, 678; chastise Delawares,, 680; conciliation of, II, 273; friendly relations with, 342; granted free use of ferry on Niagara river, 1029; relations with, III, 939; Sullivan's expedition against, publication of records, veto, VII, 934, 1084.

SIXPENNY SAVINGS BANK, ALBANY. Charter, veto, VI, 342.

SIXTH AVENUE RAILROAD, NEW YORK. Statement of receipts, VI, 66.

SIXTH JUDICIAL DISTRICT. Tribunal of conciliation established in, IV, 444; additional justice for, VII, 837; included in third judicial department, IX, 546.

VETOES. Law library,— Delhi, VII, 219; — Binghamton, 220; — use of books, 807; — Elmira, IX, 45; established, 1895, 45; — Elmira, appropriation, 769; — Elmira, books and rebinding, appropriation, X, 556; — Delhi, books and rebinding, 556; — Follett, appropriation, 784; justices' clerks, IX, 816; additional justice, X, 947.

SKANEATELES. VETOES. Engine-house, VII, 97; revising charter, 933, 1008.

SKANEATELES FEEDER. Repairs, veto, X, 314.

SKANEATELES LAKE. Water from, Syracuse, act of 1890, VIII, 1015; steam and naphtha vessels on, veto, 1121.

SKINNER, CHARLES R. Superintendent of Public Instruction, expenses in defending Waters case, appropriation, veto, X, 561.

SKINNER, ROGER. Member of Commission on Common School System, II, 707; action in removal of postmaster, 1068, 1069.

SKINNER, ST. JOHN B. L. Major-general, correspondence relative to disturbance in northeastern part of State, III, 760.

SLANDER. Action for, costs, III, 219.

SLAVERY. See also SLAVES. Deliverance of colony from, I, 77; bill to abolish, veto, II, 237; in New York, abolition of, 692, 881; III, 572; IV, 446, 493; V, 30; Assembly report on, II, 692, 693; Governor Clinton opposes extension of, 1022, 1041; Missouri Compromise, 1023; gradual abolition of, and foreign colonization of colored persons, III, 34, 99; Georgia report on, 94; abolition of. Governor Marcy's views on, 571, 603, 605; proceedings of abolitionists, 573; agitation may result in war, 574; each State entitled to control the subject, 578, 590; New York resolutions on abolition movement, 582; in District of Columbia, South Carolina protests against abolition of, 582; protests against anti-slavery agitation, 582, 588, 589, 590, 591, 756, 821; in District of Columbia, Congress has power to abolish, 645; discussion resulting from extradition case, 916, 921; in territory acquired from Mexico, IV, 382, 497;

SLAVERY —(*Continued*).

abolished by Mexico, 445; New York resolutions relative to District of Columbia, 448, 502; Wilmot proviso, 466; Missouri resolutions, 466; in original States, 499; prohibited in northwest territory, 499; Vermont resolutions on, 504, 507; Connecticut resolutions, 506; Rhode Island and Virginia resolutions, 507; Georgia resolutions, 507; Mississippi resolutions, 512; in District of Columbia, Maryland resolutions, 513; Texas resolutions, 526; ordinance of 1787, 567; V, 300; existence in other nations, IV, 619; probable slow disappearance of, 620; Lemmon case, 809, 860; V, 61; Dred Scott case, IV, 813; in Arkansas, 814; recognized by national government, 815; Arkansas resolutions, 824; New York resolutions, 1855, 827; struggle in Kansas, 861; V, 60; Vermont resolutions relative to Kansas, IV, 865; New York opposed to extension of slavery, V, 28, 96; attitude of free States, 29; status in Territories, power of Congress to determine, 29, 198; controversy over extension of, 196; invasion of Virginia, 197; acquiescence of free States, 303; Crittenden resolutions, 312, 324, 328; Tennessee propositions for perpetuation of, 315; proposed amendment securing perpetuity of, 349, 398; Arkansas recites grievance of slaveholding States, 353; in Territories, Arkansas proposition, 354; President's proclamation of emancipation, 473; border State policy, 475; abolition of, expected by peaceful methods, 614; prohibited, Thirteenth Amendment, 616, 623; succeeded by free labor system, 713; good results of emancipation, 855; terminated forever, VI, 768.

SLAVES. See also SLAVERY; FUGITIVE SLAVES. Act relating to, I, 11; act to prevent them from running away, 116; better regulation of, proposed, 161; act to prevent conspiracies, 166; duty on, veto, 171; importation of, should be discouraged, 248; learning trades, artificers complain against, 260; poll tax on, suggested, 574, 606, 618; frequenting tippling-houses, 660; three-fifths of, basis of apportionment of public expense, II, 184; emancipated, denied right of suffrage, 237; sale and manumission of, 239; abandonment to State, 508; included in basis of representation in Congress, 546; importation of, from West Indies,— North Carolina resolution, 552; — Massachusetts resolution, 562; — Vermont resolutions, 586; importation of,— Tennessee resolutions, 589; — Maryland resolutions, 605; act to prevent voting by, 686; emancipation of, considered, 693; transportation of, Governor protests against, 693; in New York, emancipated, 882; exportation prohibited, 978; importation into State without its consent, III, 34; gradual emancipation proposed, 34, 99; debtors under Roman law, 344; return of, 572; indications of insurrection, 575; Atticus, alleged abduction of, 748; status as

SLAVES — (*Continued*).

property, 921; stealing, right to extradition, 937, 938, 1030; IV, 8; proposition to exclude from basis of apportionment, IV, 85; right of owner to carry from one State to another, 526; slave trade condemned, 619; brought to New York, Lemmon case, 809, 860; slave trade, restriction of, V, 30, 98; in transit, right of owners, 355; emancipation of, 473; emancipation, owners have no claim against Federal or State government, 791; average value in 1860, 825; beneficent effects of emancipation, 855.

SLOAN, GEORGE B. Assembly, member of committee on arrangements, opening of new capitol, VII, 270.

SLOCUM, JOSEPH. Bond for return of arms, II, 772.

SLOOPS. On Hudson river to carry stones to Albany for fort, I, 35; for Hudson river service, 153.

SLOT MACHINES. Trials for keeping, veto, X, 162.

SLOUGHTER, HENRY. Appointed Governor, I, 17; arrives in New York, 18; new Assembly, 18, pref. vi.

OPENING SPEECH, I, 19; judicial system, ministers, quieting recent troubles, garrison at Albany, revenue, 19, 20; militia, 20; reward to Captain Kidd, 21; communications to Assembly relative to Leisler, 21; judicial salaries, 22; tradesmen and laborers, 22; memorial from collector of port. 22; death of, 23; official service, pref. ix.

SLUNG SHOT. Preventing use of, veto, VI, 507.

SMALLPOX. Compels Assembly to change place of meeting, I, 240; Assembly adjourns because of, 242, 280; in West India Islands, 315; at Greenwich and Jamaica, 367; at New York, 367, 522, 616; inoculation for, veto, II, 225; vaccination of school children, V, 189; classed as quarantine disease, 418; quarantine against, VI, 237, 359; brought to New York in immigrant vessels, 532, 625; prevalence among immigrants, VII, 713; in Long Island City, 1893, IX, 253; investigations by State Department of Health, appropriation, veto, X, 787.

SMALLWOOD, SAMUEL M. Mayor of Washington, lottery memorial, II, 1126.

SMITH, MR. Postmaster at Little Falls, removal of, II, 1070, 1071.

SMITH, ANNIE M. Claim for damages, State Industrial School, X, 443.

SMITH, ARTHUR. Letter from, Staten Island fortifications, II, 1037.

SMITH, ARTHUR J. Assistant law librarian, acknowledgments to, I, pref. xv.

SMITH, CHARLES. Relief, veto, VI, 185; X, 176.

SMITH, CHARLES C. Relief, veto, VI, 185.

SMITH, CHAUNCEY. Member of Commission on Readjustment of Quotas, V, 537, 572.

Smith, David. Service of process on, Van Rensselaer rent, III, 825.

Smith, David T. Board of Claims, veto, VIII, 1040, 1129.

Smith, Edward. Extradition, III, 852, 869, 920, 932, 937, 982; IV, 47; legislative action on, III, 1030.

Smith, Elisha. Communication from, relative to Oneida land, VI, 665.

Smith, Elizabeth. Escheat, veto, IX, 403.

Smith, Elizabeth M. Assistant in State Library, acknowledgments to, I, pref. xv.

Smith, F. C. Canal contractor, return of certificate of deposit, veto, VII, 545.

Smith, George W. Oneida county judge, charges against, V, 723; exonerated, 723.

Smith, Jacob. Extradition, of, II, 1104.

Smith, J. Elliott. New York, legal services, settlement of claim, veto, IX, 806.

Smith, James C. Delegate to Washington Peace Convention, V, 310.

Smith, John. Chosen United States Senator, II, 537.

Smith, John L. Bath excise commissioner, legalizing acts of, veto, VII, 178.

Smith, John T. Court of Claims, veto, X, 701.

Smith, Nathan. Contract with Chatfield, II, 580; chosen Regent, 644.

Smith, Owen and Thomas. Estate of, escheat, veto, IX, 467.

Smith, Samuel. Conveyance to, II, 581.

Smith, Thomas H. Court of Claims, veto, 445.

Smith, William. Conveyance to, II, 581.

Smith, William. President of Council, I, 90.

Smith, William. Estate, escheat, veto, X, 952.

Smith, William, Jr. Commissioner on Massachusetts boundary, I, 721; chief justice, favors re-establishing civil government, 779.

Smith, William S. Trustee, Binghamton Insane Asylum, charges against, not removed, VII, 443.

Smith, Zilpha. Conveyance by, veto, II, 580.

Smith and Parmelee Gold Company. Issuing preferred stock, veto, VI, 96.

Smith's Commentaries on Statute and Constitutional Law. Quoted, constitutional interpretation, common usage of words, VIII, 779.

Smith's History of New York. Cited, II, 498; continuation published, III, 162.

Smiths. For Indian country, I, 145, 201; needed by Six Nations, 248, 511; one for Senecas, 249, 265, 323, 548, 570; for certain Indian nations, 419, 516; for each Indian nation, 439; for Oswego, 460, 562; for Onondagas, 306, 389, 419, 548; at Niagara and Detroit, 733.

SMITHTOWN. Relief of, IX, 703; relief of school district No. 5, veto, X, 449.

SMUGGLING. At Oyster Bay, efforts to prevent, I, 83.

SMYTH, JOHN F. Superintendent of Insurance, charges against, VII, 180; trial, not removed, 182; index to record of trial, veto, 226, 461; second charges, 319; not removed, 319.

SNEDEKER, THEODORE. Legacies payable to, veto, II, 283.

SNELL, CATHERINE. Petition for relief, II, 117.

SNOOK, CLARK. Relief, veto, VI, 183.

SNOW. Prevents meeting of Legislature, II, 87; removal from highways, act of 1904, X, 632.

VETOES. Drifting, obstructing highways, damages, VII, 1108; New York,—removal from streets, IX, 459; — removal from sidewalks, X, 60; removal from highways, 594, 707.

SNOW, JOHN. Seneca chief, joins in address to Governor, II, 943.

SNOW, ROBERT. Communication from, inspection of pot and pearl ashes, II, 1113.

SNYDER, ALBERT. Court of Claims, veto, X, 707.

SNYDER, WILLIAM L. Member of Commission on Uniform Laws, VIII, 1068.

SOAP. Manufacture, license for, II, 382.

SOCIAL CLUBS. Amending act, veto, VI, 501; VIII, 889.

SOCIETIES AND CLUBS. VETOES. Amending act, VII, 664; VIII, 625, 890; maximum amount of property, 1119.

SOCIETY OF ARTS, MANUFACTURES AND COMMERCE. London, proposed International Educational Exhibition, IV, 752.

SOCIETY OF THE HOSPITAL IN THE CITY OF NEW YORK IN AMERICA. See also NEW YORK HOSPITAL. Charter of, I, 743.

SOCIETY FOR THE PREVENTION OF CRUELTY TO ANIMALS. Act relating to, VII, 744; Sing Sing branch, charter, veto, 744.

SOCIETY FOR THE PROMOTION OF USEFUL ARTS. Assignment of room in capitol, II, 937.

SOCIETY FOR THE PROPAGATION OF THE GOSPEL IN FOREIGN PARTS. Communication from secretary relative to library, I, 234; library, sources of American history, III, 162.

SOCIETY FOR THE PROTECTION OF DESTITUTE ROMAN CATHOLIC CHILDREN. Name changed to New York Catholic Protectory, see that title. VETOES. Charter, VII, 415; act relative to, 505.

SOCIETY FOR THE RELIEF OF ORPHAN AND DESTITUTE CHILDREN, ALBANY. Changing name, increasing property limit, veto, IX, 56.

SOCIETY FOR THE REFORMATION OF JUVENILE DELINQUENTS. See also NEW YORK HOUSE OF REFUGE. Incorporated, III, 82; high character of, 130, 291; authorized to receive children from any

SOCIETY FOR THE REFORMATION OF JUVENILE DELINQUENTS —(*Continued*).
part of State, 131; work of, 162; appropriation for, 252; aid
from passenger tax, IV, 75; number of children cared for, V,
85; report, 383, 448; VII, 537; IX, 37; removal from Randall's
island, X, 611; should be subject to Civil Service Law, 742.

VETOES. Relative to, IV, 518; relief fund, V, 219; repairing wall
and restocking greenhouse, X, 298; cottage for florist and
gardener, additional window sash and casings, 545.

SOCIETY OF ST. VINCENT DE PAUL, YONKERS. Charter, veto, VII, 805.

SOCIETY OF THE WAR OF 1812. Amending charter, veto, X, 947.

SODUS. Election districts, veto, VI, 58.

SODUS POINT AND SOUTHERN RAILROAD COMPANY. VETOES. Docks, VI,
690; rebuilding canal wall at Newark, 860.

SOLDIERS. In Civil War, aiding sick and disabled, V, 383, 585; families
of, provision for, 408; pensions for, care of families, 420; appropriation for sick and wounded, how expended, 488; home
for, 489, 490, 684, 774, 834; local boards of relief, 490; absent,
right to vote, 508, 512, 606; alleged interference with exercise of
political opinions, 511; sick and wounded, appropriation, 530,
585; effect of depreciation of currency, 539; returning, transportation and subsistence, 561; recruits and returning volunteers, care of, 563; State depot established, report, 577; agent
for care of sick, wounded, furloughed and discharged, 577,
578, 681; cemeteries at Gettysburg and Antietam, 636; relief
of, 681, 755; national asylum, transfer of inmates from Soldiers'
Home, 684; aid from various sources, 685; deceased, children
of, free tuition in common schools, 696, see MILITARY AGENCIES;
buried in Antietam cemetery, list of, 870; aliens, naturalization,
VI, 40; absent, voting, IX, 877.

VETOES. Absent, right to vote, V, 513; monument, St. Lawrence
county, VI, 162; honorably discharged, certificates of service,
VII, 1110; and sailors, relief, amending act, VIII, 626, 872;
arch or monument, New York, 1029; memorial arch, New York,
1160; memorial arch, Brooklyn, legalizing act, IX, 211; relief
from Union Veteran Legion, 803; authorizing incorporation of
associations for erection of monuments, X, 63; relief, G. A. R.,
809; monument corporations, relative to, 810.

SOLDIERS' HOME. Incorporated, V, 489; G. A. R. Home at Bath, 490;
Albany, transfer of inmates, 684; temporary use of, 774, 835;
number of inmates, 836; Albany, appropriation for, 837; VI, 61, 62.

SOLDIERS' NATIONAL CEMETERY ASSOCIATION. Communication from, relative to cemeteries at Gettysburg and Antietam, V, 636.

SOLDIERS AND SAILORS. Relief, amending Poor Law, veto, X, 808, 947.

SOLDIERS AND SAILORS' HOME. Established at Bath, VII, 289; appropriation for, 289; overcoats for inmates, 289; nomination of Charles J. Fox as trustee, VIII, 236; right of inmates to vote in Bath, 497; use of prison-made clothing, 659; supervision of State Board of Charities, act of 1900, X, 156; additional building provided, X, 345.

VETOES. Hospital, VII, 478; improvements, 478; chapel, 478; lands of, taking for railroad purposes, 808; exempting from general excise act of 1892, IX, 625; officers, local rank of, 815; cement walks, X, 293; claim for damages and extra work, Court of Claims, 377; repairs and improvements, 546.

SOLDIERS AND SAILORS' LIBRARY COMMITTEE. Library for Soldiers' Depot, V, 685.

SOLICITOR-GENERAL (English). Opinion as to Governor's relation to Legislature, I, 253.

SOLICITORS. Fees of, III, 774.

SOMERSET. Canal drainage, deepening Golden Hill creek, etc., veto, X, 645.

SON, FRANCISCO. Convicted of murder, Legislature declines to act, II, 588.

SONS OF LIBERTY. Grand Lodge, charter, veto, VIII, 737.

SONS OF VETERANS. VETOES. Issuing arms to, X, 61; use of armories, 385; parading with fire-arms, amending Military Code, IX, 398.

SONYEA. Craig Colony for Epileptics established at, IX, 240.

SOO-NON-GIZE. Convicted of murder, pardoned, II, 1120.

SOREL RIVER. St. John's, tariff regulations at, I, 773.

SOULT, MARSHAL. Duke of Dalmatia, French Minister of War, grants permission to examine colonial documents, IV, 187.

SOUTH AMERICA. British dominions in, expected French attack on, I, 340; efforts to establish republican government, III, 18.

SOUTH AMERICAN REPUBLICS. Afford opportunities for commerce, II, 1093; difficulty in establishing government, III, 320.

SOUTHAMPTON. Discontinuing road, veto, VI, 333; compulsory voting in, VIII, 676.

SOUTHARD, SAMUEL L. Communication from, cession of land for Brooklyn navy yard, III, 181.

SOUTH BROOKLYN LOAN AND TRUST COMPANY. Charter, veto, VI, 342.

SOUTH CAROLINA. Indian war, refugees exempted from payment of duties, I, 177; not represented in Albany Convention, 578; agent, how appointed, 732; laws of, received, II, 530; encouraging internal communications, 1011; disapproves North Carolina proposition relative to method of choosing presidential electors, 1024; legislative action as to revolutionary pensions, 1027; Constitution, procedure

SOUTH CAROLINA — (*Continued*).

to amend, 1057; disapproves Pennsylvania proposition as to banks, III, 13; resolutions on tariff, internal improvements and colonization, 218; protests against Tariff Act of 1828, 263; nullification proceedings, 427, 429, 441; recommends convention to consider question of power between the nation and the States, 431; resolutions on proceedings of abolitionists, 582; protests against Maine's refusal to surrender alleged abductors of Atticus, 822; law for search of New York vessels, 980, 1028; refuses to receive proceeds of public lands, 984; opposes Federal assumption of State debts, favors annexation of Texas, IV, 84; resolutions, Wilmot proviso, 466; makes war on nation, V, 306; secession ordinance, 396; military to be subordinate to civil authority, 470; assessment of personal property, 825; presidential election, 1876, action by Electoral Commission, VII, 33; State Canvassing Board, alleged usurpation of power, 38.

SOUTHERN CENTRAL RAILROAD COMPANY. Aid to, memorandum of approval, V, 813; exempting construction bonds from taxation, 813; asks State aid, 866; VI, 71.

VETOES. School tax, Hartford, distribution, VI, 1035; Auburn, payment of bonds, VIII, 504.

SOUTHERN TIER SAVINGS BANK, ELMIRA. Amending charter, veto, VI, 324.

SOUTHERN CONFEDERACY. Movement to establish, V, 299; Tennessee resolutions, 317; not practicable, Governor Seymour's comment on, 479; States composing, civil government destroyed, 856; Governor Fenton denies President's power to establish new governments, 857; new State Constitutions, 860; States composing, slow financial restoration, VI, 767; reconstructed States, misgovernment of, 961.

SOUTHFIELD. Land for quarantine, completing contract, veto, VII, 385, 929.

SOUTH HILL WATERWORKS COMPANY, ITHACA. Charter, veto, VI, 320.

SOUTH INLET. Cleaning and clearing shore, veto, X, 320.

SOUTHOLD. Deposit of military stores in, II, 769.

SOUTHPORT. Chemung river bridge, bonding for, veto, VII, 578.

SOUTH RIVER. Colony on, IV, 174.

SOUTH SANDY CREEK. Public highway, veto, X, 444.

SOUTH SIDE SPORTSMEN'S CLUB, LONG ISLAND. Amending charter, veto, IX, 217.

SOUTH VALLEY. VETOES. State road, Allegany reservation, improvement, VIII, 847; division of, legalizing action of board of supervisors, 1089, new bill passed.

SOUTHWICK, DR. A. P. Member of Commission on Method of Inflicting Death Penalty, VIII, 484.

SOUTHWICK, SOLOMON. Chosen Regent, II, 707.

SPAFFORD, HORATIO G. Opinion, common school fund, II, 722.

SPAIN. See also SPANISH. War against, I, 187; attempt against Ireland, 187; fleet of, battle with English in Mediterranean, 314; allowance to prisoners of war, 328; England declares war against, 666; Havana taken by English, 669; seizure of Fort Egmont, 737; John Jay appointed Minister to, II, 83; engaged in American war, 153; small loans from, 154; conduct of intendant at New Orleans, 522; Spanish America, possible complications with, II, 910; war with United States, 1898, I, 288.

SPANISH. See also SPAIN. Seizes mayor's sloop and cargo, I, 186.

SPANISH PRISONERS. Claims for subsistence of, I, 478.

SPALDING LITERARY UNION, NEW YORK. Exempting property from taxation, veto, IX, 810.

SPAULDING, ALEXANDER. New York marine court, death of, VI, 986.

SPAULDING, LOYAL W. Ferry from Barber's Point across Lake Champlain, veto, VIII, 410.

SPAULDING, W. M. Counsel, Assembly committee on privileges and elections, 1903, appropriation, veto, X, 571.

SPEAKER (Colony). Mathias Nicolls, first Dongan Assembly, I, 9, 11; William Pinhorne, second Dongan Assembly, 12; John Spratt Leisler Assembly, 15; James Graham, first General Assembly, 20; Abraham Gouverneur chosen, 84; Governor Burnet approves choice of, 214; Philipse, suggests resolutions against Court of Chancery, 229; receives letters from Governor Clinton, 309; Governor refuses to receive Assembly communication except from, 445, 449; access to Governor, 479; presents communication relative to petition of Continental Congress, 770; to correspond with other Speakers relative to colonial grievances, 777.

SPEAKER (State). Letter from, State Treasurer, II, 458; when may become Governor, IV, 433; contest over election of, 830; V, 42, 445; election of 1863, alleged interference by mob, 485; Governor Seymour declines to interfere in election of, 485; member of Centennial Celebration committee, VI, 302; member of Commission on Purchase of Executive Residence, VII, 178; contest over election, 1881, 676; ex-officio, trustee of public buildings, 837; member of New Capitol Advisory Board, VIII, 31; member of Board of Capitol Construction, veto, 213; member of New Capitol Commission, 1888, 610; first, Walter Livingston, 1777, IX, 688; Gulian Verplanck, 1797, 689; S. Frederick Nixon, address at reception of Prince Henry, X, 480.

SPEAR, AMOS C. Executor, Howard estate, restitution of collateral inheritance tax, veto, VIII, 1139.

SPECIAL CITY LAWS. Constitutional provision, IX, 339, 547, 617, 677;
X, 624, 683; Manhattan State Hospital, veto, IX, 617; not acted
on by city, 1895, IX, 628; 1896, 734; 1899, X, 59; 1900, 179, 322;
not returned in time, 1895, IX, 629; 1896, 734; 1901, X, 327; 1902,
472, 478; 1904, 685; not accepted by city, 1895, IX, 629; 1896, 725;
1898, 869; 1899, X, 59, 60; 1900, 151, 175, 179; 1901, 280; 1902,
472; 1903, 580; 1904, 712; 1905, 805; 1906, 910; large number, 1895,
IX, 677; Liquor Tax Law, 1896, not a special law, 696; defined, 696;
Greater New York bill, 1896, 709; Albany and Bath-on-the-Hudson
Bridge Company, charter, 715; scope of constitutional requirement,
X, 151, 152, 153, 159, 208, 291; veto power vested in mayors, 504;
railroad, relative to consents for construction, veto, 574; East River
Gas Company, veto, 657; Boys' Training School, 683.
SPECIAL PROCEEDINGS. Procedure in, revision needed, IV, 655.
SPECIAL TERM. Supreme Court, extraordinary, VI, 492.
SPECIALTIES. Act relating to assignment of, I, 11.
SPECIE. See also GOLD and CURRENCY. Small returns from commerce,
I, 694; ratio with continental money, II, 94; continental bills of
credit, interest to be paid in gold or silver, 97; tax to be paid in,
98, 134, 186; required from States, 116; exchanging for United
States drafts, 189; Federal requisition to be paid in, 264; duties
payable in, 277; congressional requisitions to be paid in, 291; funded
debt of United States, value in, 438; excessive amount of bank paper,
696; banks discontinue payment of, 871; dangers from excessive
circulation of bank notes, 917; small quantity in circulation, 979,
981; exportation of, 980; III, 658; circulation of gold and silver
should be encouraged, 517; unusual quantity of new, 519; suspension
of specie payments, 659; resumption of specie payments, 667, 694;
IV, 34; supply from California, 479; payments suspended by New
York banks, V, 43; payments resumed, 44; payment of interest on
State debt, 491, 579; payments, contraction of legal tender currency
not necessary, VI, 135; payments, suspension of, unfortunate consequences, 645.
SPECIE PAYMENTS. Return to, contraction of legal tenders not necessary,
VI, 135; England returns to, 135; resumption, 250, 763; VII, 150;
hindered by legal tender notes, VI, 253; resumption, elements of
problem, 763; resumption without convulsion, 974; legislative
resolutions on, 975; VII, 150; New York statute requiring, 170;
resumption date fixed, 170; resumption accomplished, 310; conse-
quent readjustment of public expenditures, 437.
SPENCER, AMBROSE. Council of Appointment, communications from,
II, 490, 491; chief justice, Supreme Court, communication from,
criminal jurisdiction over Indian land, 1119; sale of leasehold estate, IV, 361.

SPENCER, CHARLES. Canal damages, proceedings relative to, IX, 428.

SPENCER, DAVID. Bond for return of arms, II, 774.

SPENCER, JOHN C. Appoints counsel in Morgan matter, III, 264; report, 314; resignation, 351; Secretary of State, correspondence relative to disturbance on northeastern frontier, 761, 762; resigns as Secretary of State, 972; member of Codification Commission, resignation of, IV, 488.

SPENCER, JOSHUA A. Senate report, liability of State for loss of canal boats, VI, 314.

SPENCERPORT. VETOES. Nuisance, VII, 805; canal waste gates, 1100.

SPICER, HENRY. VETOES. Escheat, VIII, 882; escheat, amending act, 1036.

SPIER, JACOB. Bond for return of arms, II, 772.

SPIES. Employing Indians as, I, 296; testimony in certain cases, veto, VII, 624.

SPINOLA, FRANCIS B. Assembly, member of committee, first occupation of new Senate chamber, VII, 540.

SPOFFORD, A. R. Article on ballot, Lalor's Cyclopedia, VIII, 584.

SPRAGGE, JOHN. Clerk of First Assembly, 9; member of First Legislative Council, 9.

SPRAGUE, G. Bond for return of arms, II, 772.

SPRATT, JOHN. Speaker of Leisler Assembly, I, 15.

SPRINGFIELD (Massachusetts). Conference on paper currency, I, 11; manufacture of arms at, V, 415.

SPRINGFIELD CENTER. Separate road district, veto, VIII, 1039.

SPRINGFIELD RIFLES. Manufacture of, V, 415; use of, 769.

SPRING SUPPLY WATER COMPANY, ONEIDA. Changing name to Warner Waterworks Company, veto, VII, 1000.

SPUYTEN DUYVIL. Railroad accident at, VII, 730.

SPUYTEN DUYVIL CREEK. Granting to United States jurisdiction over, veto, VII, 406.

SPUYTEN DUYVIL ROAD. New York, special act, veto, VII, 629.

SQUADRON. For expedition against West Indies, I, 287.

SQUAW ISLAND. Sold to Jasper Parish, II, 857; terminus of proposed sewerage system under Erie canal, Buffalo, veto, VII, 365.

S. R. SMITH INFIRMARY. Exempting property from taxation, veto, VIII, 538, 733.

STAATS, BARENT. Receives grant of Oneida land, VI, 666.

STAATS, ISAAC. Captain, service in French war, I, 396.

STABLES. At Fort George recommended, I, 306, 339, 460; completion of, 511.

STAGE COMPANIES. Incorporation of, veto, VII, 807.

STAMFORD. Leasehold estates in, IV, 332; Wakeman escheat, veto, VII, 935.

STAMP ACT. Effect of, I, 704; opposition in New York, stamped paper destroyed, 706; repeal of, 706, 710; general note, 710.

STAMPS. See also STAMP ACT. Duty suggested, I, 574; act passed, 606, 617; revision of act suggested, 641; stamped paper, Federal tax on, II, 789.

STANCHFIELD, JOHN B. Delivers memorial address on former Governor Flower, IX, 535; counsel for Assemblyman Vacheron, appropriation, veto, 775; counsel for Justice Hooker, X, 829.

STANCTIFT, JACOB I. Bond for return of arms, II, 774.

STANNARD'S ROCK. Lake Superior, proposed lighthouse on, VII, 46.

STANTON, EDWIN M. Secretary of War, communication to, rendezvous at Elmira, V, 562.

STANWIX, JOHN. Brigadier, marches to Mohawk river, I, 625; builds fort at Oneida station, 626.

"STAR OF THE WEST." Fired on by Confederates, V, 399.

STARCH. Manufacture of, license for, II, 382.

STARK, JOHN. Brigadier-general, letter from, situation at Saratoga, II, 151.

STATE AGENT. Acts relating to, II, 109; difficulties of administering office, 134; report of, army supplies, 150; authorized to sell wheat, 161; forage in Westchester county, 165; collection of forage, 169; authorized to settle Trimble claim for impressment of flour, 186.

STATE AGENT FOR DISCHARGED CONVICTS. Office created, VII, 10; amending act, veto, 264; Governor Hill recommends abolition of office, VIII, 324, 481; bill to abolish office, veto, 870; office abolished, 1895, 325, 870.

STATE AGRICULTURAL COLLEGE. Recommended, IV, 432, 552, 603; established, loan from United States deposit fund, 853; V, 16; purchase of farm in Seneca county, 16; erection of buildings, 118, 177; located at Ovid, 177, 290; authorized to borrow money, 178; annual report, 199, 307; closed for want of means, 596.

STATE AGRICULTURAL COLLEGE, CORNELL UNIVERSITY. Established, X, 627. VETOES. Good roads school, 793; free winter courses for farmers' sons and daughters, appropriation, 935.

STATE AGRICULTURAL EXPERIMENT STATION, GENEVA. Established, located near Geneva, VII, 697; VIII, 33; appropriation for purchase of farm, VII, 698; general appropriation for, VIII, 33; cost of, 1891, IX, 11; new building for dairy investigations, etc., 745; report, X, 371; general repairs and improvements, veto, 546.

STATE AGRICULTURAL AND INDUSTRIAL SCHOOL. Succeeds State Industrial School, X, 502.

STATE AGRICULTURAL SCHOOL. Incorporated, IV, 30.

STATE AGRICULTURAL SOCIETY. Recommended, II, 957; incorporated, III, 386; county societies formed under auspices of, 945; room for, in old State hall, IV, 37; work of, 80; report of, 138; State Fair, see that title; resolutions on pleuro-pneumonia, VII, 537.

STATE AGRICULTURAL SOCIETY. Transfers property to State, X, 120; liquidation of debts, 120.

STATE AID TO PRIVATE ENTERPRISE. Western Inland Lock Navigation Company, III, 321, 335, 511; Northern Inland Lock Navigation Company, 321, 335; Delaware and Hudson Canal Company, 70, 167, 237, 308, 348, 810; IV, 10; New York and Erie Railroad Company, III, 551, 620, 731, 866; IV, 10, 661; railroads, III, 731; IV, 10, 62, 386, 831; opposition to, III, 809; railroad companies in default, 952; IV, 10; general corporations, 10; proposed abrogation of power, 55; claims, enforcement of, 262; contingent liability on loan of credit, 422; V, 3; Albany and Susquehanna Railroad, 531; requested by many companies, 866; VI, 71; questions should be submitted to people, VI, 178; constitutional provision, V, 138, 245, 443; VI, 178, 346; VII, 90.

VETOES. Albany and Susquehanna Railroad, V, 138, 245, 350, 443, 737; Whitehall and Plattsburgh Railroad, 737, 864; VI, 68; railroads, General Aid Act, V, 814; appropriations to several companies, VI, 172; aiding unfinished railroads, 345; Susquehanna Valley Orphans' Home, Binghamton, VII, 90; promotion of agriculture, 90; State Fair, reconstructing buildings destroyed by fire, 90; Catholic Protectory, appropriation, 915; donation of salt lands to Onondaga Historical Association, 932; Gettysburg Battlefield Memorial Association, appropriation for battlefield monuments, 1084; Schuylerville battlefield monument, VIII, 253; Gettysburg battlefield monument, 253; escheat Beattie, 405; drainage, Conewango valley, IX, 107.

STATE ARCHITECT. Office suggested, VI, 652; office created, 653; VII, 837; successor to capitol commissioner, 837; additional experts, appropriation for, X, 121; additional inspectors needed, 740.

VETOES. Office salaries, reappropriation, X, 424; engineer's stenographer and office expenses, appropriation, 552; office expenses, deficiency appropriation, 561; stenographers' salaries, deficiency appropriation, 561; consulting experts, reappropriation, 561.

STATE ASSESSORS. Office created, IV, 25; V, 91; report, 370; approves taxation of collateral inheritances, VIII, 102.

VETOES. Increasing number, VI, 332; additional powers, VII, 133; report, printing, 495; James H. Weatherwax, death of, appropriation for widow, 917.

State Asylum for Idiots. Established, superintendent appointed, IV, 605; State pupils at, 605, 643; V, 177; report, IV, 642; new buildings, 643; removed to Syracuse, 791, 849; appropriation for, 792; number of inmates, 849; V, 177, 288, 521; Superintendent of Public Instruction *ex officio* trustee, V, 88; new methods of instruction and management, 288; additional land for, 288; good condition of, 447; various appropriations, veto, VII, 913; plumbing and furniture, veto, VIII, 853.

State Asylum for Insane Criminals, Matteawan. Established, VIII, 822; acquiring land for sewer, veto, IX, 74; supplies and improvements, veto, 77.

State Auditor. Powers under State Law, II, 172; report of, 318; succeeded by Comptroller, 383.

State Bank. Discount advances, removal of Montgomery's remains, II, 1001.

State Bank of Sackett's Harbor. Failure of, V, 8.

State Bar Association. Recommends printed instead of engrossed bills, VII, 43; recommends change in divorce proceedings, X, 365; receives complaint from Jamestown Bar Association against Justice Hooker, 826; represented by counsel at Hooker trial, 829; report on designation of Appellate Division justices from other departments, 938.

State Board of Agriculture. Established, II, 970, 1005.

State Board of Arbitration. Established, VIII, 36, 165, 321, 476; powers, 165; how functions invoked, 1072; cost of, 1891, IX, 11; powers should be extended, 742; service should be efficient, X, 10; good work of, 94; salaries and office expenses, 1900, 188; abolished, 1901, 189; special boards recommended, 365; amending Labor Law, veto, 439.

State Board of Audit. Governor Robinson's comment on work of, VII, 381; abolished, 821, 978.

  Vetoes. Appeals from, VII, 412; awards, veto of items, 498; defining powers, 509; medical services, Auburn prison, 666; certain claims of contractors, 666; submission of Cayuga county claim, Auburn prison, 801; Moore claim, 849; Rider claim, 936; Lawlor and quarantine improvement claims, 938; applications for legislation, VIII, 470.

State Board of Canvassers. How constituted, II, 10.

State Board of Charities. Created, V, 761; VI, 24; VIII, 171; constitutional provisions, V, 761; X, 157; appointment of commissioners, V, 839; visitations by, VI, 24; VII, 959; chronic insane, care of, VI, 235; number of insane, VII, 283; uniformity of time in reports from institutions, 297; State paupers, deficiency appropriation, veto, 471; current expenses, deficiency appropriation, 471; report, 828; powers

STATE BOARD OF CHARITIES —(*Continued*).

should be extended, 960; president, member of Commission on Administration of Charitable Institutions, 964; Governor Hill recommends abolition of, VIII, 171, 301, 479, 680, 931, 1081; perpetuated by Constitution of 1894, 173; X, 157; investigation of Elmira Reformatory, 1893, 387; reorganized, 1895, 550; powers under Constitution, 1894, 568; regulations as to placing out, veto, 812; supervision of Soldiers' Home limited, act of 1900, X, 156; visitation and inspection, defined, 157; salaries and office expenses, 1900, 190; abolition recommended, one commissioner to be substituted for, 191; Governor Odell's comment on supervision by, 503; power to transfer inmates from one institution to another, 728.

STATE BOARD OF EDUCATION. Suggested, III, 744.

STATE BOARD OF EMBALMERS. Established, 1898, IX, 265; reports, X, 142; authorizing receipt of application of Burke for license, veto, 818.

STATE BOARD OF EQUALIZATION. Created, IV, 25; V, 9; work of, 175, 280.

STATE BOARD OF HEALTH. See also PUBLIC HEALTH. Established, VII, 14, 529; probable usefulness of, 529; report, 536, 859; VIII, 197, 326, 505, 711, 941, 1091; IX, 38, 216, 575, 685, 754, 852; X, 32, 142; report on nuisances, New York and Brooklyn, VII, 547; report on abandoned Chemung canal nuisance, 575; occupies rooms in new capitol, 694; good work of, 710, 990; to supervise test of illuminating oils and fluids, 751; how composed, VIII, 173; Governor Hill recommends abolition of, 174, 301, 479, 680, 931, 1081; new act, 1893, composition of board, 175; reorganized, 1901, 175, 931; statement of alcoholic beverages, 353; cost of, 1891, IX, 11; general duties, 206; preventive measures against cholera, 1893, 327; report on samples of food colors, X, 148; appropriation for office expenses, 1900, 192; reorganized, succeeded by State commissioner of health, 192; supervision of tuberculosis and glanders in cattle transferred to Department of Agriculture, 192.

VETOES. Adulteration of food and drugs, VII, 924; sanitary inspectors, deficiency appropriation, VIII, 111; printing mortality bulletins, 111; office supplies, 112; sanitary work, appropriation, 254; deficiency appropriation, 856; rules and regulations, IX, 367.

STATE BOARD OF LAW EXAMINERS. Established, VIII, 1100.

STATE BOARD OF MEDICAL EXAMINERS. Deficiency appropriation, veto, IX, 76.

STATE BOARD OF PHARMACY. Annual report, IX, 339, 570, 754, 851; X, 31, 130. VETOES. Amending act, VIII, 622; pharmacy, regulating practice of, IX, 532.

STATE BOARD OF UNDERTAKERS. Establishing, veto, IX, 265.

STATE BOTANIST. Expenses, appropriation, veto, VII, 582, 779.

STATE CENTENNIAL BOARD. Created, VI, 725, 951.

STATE CHARITIES AID ASSOCIATION. Communication to Governor relative to appointment of William Church Osborn as State commissioner in lunacy, X, 42.

STATE CHARITIES LAW. Enacted, V, 761; amended, 1902, office of Fiscal Supervisor created, IX, 436; transfers to penitentiaries and reformatories, veto, X, 312.

STATE CIVIL SERVICE COMMISSION. See also CIVIL SERVICE. Created, VII, 838; report, 996; VIII, 43, 195, 326, 509, 714, 935, 1085; IX, 52, 216, 343, 570, 685, 852; X, 34, 144, 628; cost of, 1891, IX, 11; additional powers and opportunities, 843; salaries of commissioners increased, X, 118; general office expenses, deficiency appropriation, veto, 562.

STATE CLOTHIER. Office created, II, 76; letter from, clothing for State troops, 91.

STATE COLLEGE OF FORESTRY. See also FOREST PRESERVE. Established, IX, 837; report, X, 32, 142, 628; appropriation, veto, 555, 605; Governor Odell's comment on operations of, 605.

STATE COMMISSION ON GAS AND ELECTRICITY. Established, VIII, 244, 312; X, 764; abolished, 1907, superseded by Public Service Commissions, 855.

STATE COMMISSION IN LUNACY. Created, VI, 629; VIII, 485, 867; IX, 191; required by Constitution of 1894, VIII, 173, 485; IX, 191; report, VIII, 938; cost of, 1891, IX, 11; hospitals, monthly estimates of expenses, 229, 314; central board recommended, 1879, 1882, 312; legislative investigation, administration approved, 1895, 652; nomination of William Church Osborn, Governor sends papers to Senate, X, 42; powers of State hospital managers vested in, 332, 496; should have supervision of insane criminals, 342; modified powers, 405; extending powers, veto, 538; office expenses, reappropriation, veto, 565.

STATE COMMISSION OF PRISONS. Established, 1895, IX, 551, 654; constitutional provision, 654; X, 191; appropriation, 1900, 191; reducing number of commissioners, 191; commission reorganized, 1907, 191.

STATE COMMISSIONER OF EXCISE. See also EXCISE and LIQUOR TAX LAW. Office created, I, 529; IX, 666; to be party to actions under Liquor Tax Law, X, 201; secretary, allowance for expenses, veto, 424.

STATE COMMISSIONER OF HEALTH. See also STATE BOARD OF HEALTH and PUBLIC HEALTH. Office created, VIII, 175; X, 192, 461; communication from, pollution of waters of New York bay, 523; increasing facilities for preservation of records, 624.

STATE COMPTROLLER. Office created, II, 383; office to be kept in Albany, 397; authorized to repair State seal, 404; to pay expense of fortifications and New York's proportion of public debt, 438; communication from, repair of public buildings, 515; investment of State funds, 526; investments for educational purposes, 528; act creating office revived, 565; report on common school fund, 722; member of Canal Board, 901; communication from, relative to capitol, 936; communication from, State prison guard, 952; letter from, literature fund lottery, 990, 1027; report, removal of General Montgomery's remains, 999; report on claims against United States, III, 15, 180; to arrange claims against United States, 309; to borrow funds and loan to banks and citizens, 481; to make general loan, 505; how chosen, 1004; militia expense in anti-rent troubles, IV, 236; report on taxation of reserved rent, 243; Savage report on taxation, 340; investment of bank funds, 479; banks, supervision transferred to new department, 564; appointment of Prison Investigating Commission, 777, 786; correspondence with Governor King, quarantine affairs, V, 99, 105; member of Commission to Organize Militia, 281, 400; to pay New York's share of direct tax, 390; communication from, interest on State debt, 490; member of Commission on Harbor and Frontier Defense, 545; member of Commission to Care for Recruits and Returning Volunteers, 563; authorized to borrow money for bounties, 571; fixing price of Cornell land scrip, 694; member of Commission on Normal Schools, 695; report, powers of canal commissioners, VI, 344; proposed appointment by Governor, 397; increasing tax levy to cover deficiencies, 525; report on sinking funds, 658; action on Buck case, 682; communication to Governor, appropriation bills, 1875, 908; charges against Insurance Superintendent Smyth, VII, 180; to examine Swift claim, 374: charges against trustees of Binghamton Insane Asylum 443; member of Commission on State's Property Rights, War of 1812, 601; Court of Appeals reports, contract for publication, 892; member of Commission on Administration of Charitable Institutions, 964; appoints Forest Investigating Commission, VIII, 22; recommends abolition of common school fund, 147; audit of claims for witness fees before investigating committees, 727; monthly estimates of expenses in certain charitable institutions and reformatories, IX, 436; quoted 1895, obstacles to low tax rate, 683; duties under

State Comptroller — (*Continued*).

    Transfer Tax Law, X, 183; member of State Printing Board, 196; James A. Roberts, sale of State bonds, 802.

    Vetoes. Non-resident highway taxes, Essex and Hamilton, VI, 338; expenses incurred by legislative committees and officers of State government, appropriation, VII, 586; expenses of legislative committees, reception of Massachusetts delegates, 779; expenses of legislative committees, compensation of witnesses, 779; settlement of claims against sureties of First National Bank, Buffalo, 874; sale of Horton judgment, 878; canal auditor's case, counsel fees, 904; Rowley case, counsel fees, 905; New York, public works department, Senate investigation, counsel fees, 905; Gravesend investigation, counsel fees, 905; investigation of Receiver Best, counsel fees, 906; Henry Gallien, deputy, salary appropriation for widow, 1081; VIII, 109; to adjust accounts of legislative stenographers, 107; clerical services on tax sales, deficiency appropriation, 110; expenses of agent, examination of auctioneers' accounts, 114; public statement of warrants, 129; annual report, amending Revised Statutes, 208; appraisal and inventory of State property, appropriation, IX, 775; Mittnacht claim for cancellation of tax, 815; examination of public institutions, X, 295; Transfer Tax and Land Bureaus, furniture, 296; expenses of examinations of public institutions, 422; Corporation Tax Bureau, New York office, temporary clerks and stenographers, appropriation, 557; special counsel, deficiency appropriation, 557; accountant, examination of county treasurers' accounts, compensation, 558; office expenses, reappropriation, 558; repayment to Hamilton county, 558; Ennis, confidential inspector Bureau of Charitable Institutions, Comptroller's office, compensation, 558.

State Contracts. Public notice of, veto, VIII, 1040.

State Dairy Commission. Office created, VIII, 34; attorney for, Senate investigation, appropriation, veto, 840; cost of, 1891, IX, 11; object of, 171.

State Dairymen's Association. Vice-president, expenditure of appropriation for extending dairy knowledge, VIII, 34.

    Vetoes. Extending dairy knowledge, appropriation, VII, 907; VIII, 246; report, printing extra copies, 860; report, expenses of annual meeting, appropriation, IX, 772.

State Dam. Vetoes. Genesee river, Mount Morris, appropriation, VII, 908; Port Byron, enlargement, VIII, 452; Black river, waste gates, IX, 244; Genesee river, 609; Grasse river, repairs, X, 789; Erie county, drainage of land overflowed by, 790; Mamakating, cleaning, 791.

STATE DEBT. Includes only canal expenses, III, 300, 309; a mortgage on private property, 325; objections to, 415; statistics, 736, 793, 867, 952, 965; IV, 19, 62, 252, 371, 386, 422, 470, 540, 595; V, 3, 64, 151, 360, 589, 691, 750, 819; VI, 6, 99, 229, 348, 526, 614, 720, 914; VII, 3, 138, 275, 420, 512, 680, 815, 940; VIII, 4, 303, 496, 663, 934, 1082; IX, 7; X, 180; interest should not exceed surplus revenues, III, 797, 892, 970; act for payment of, mem., 1008; amount held by foreigners, IV, 20; power to create, limiting term of credit, 55, 104, 227, 371, 545, 546, 549, 587, 631, 660, 668, 670, 677, 744, 833; V, 68, 153, 253, 360, 590, 705, 783, 817, 828; VI, 11, 72, 178, 346, 349, 384, 890; VII, 399, 430; VIII, 926; X, 600; extending term of credit, IV, 56, 833; V, 7; extravagant increase of, IV, 58; when for a single object only, 105, 227; objection to preferred stock, 110; loans for casual deficits, 473, 589, 660; V, 152, 253, 360, 590, 705; VI, 890, 923; VII, 399; when people must approve, IV, 546, 670; V, 708; VI, 72, 107, 178, 346; exceeds constitutional limit, IV, 744; canal loan approved by people, V, 70, 152, 159, 256; payment of, 450; VIII, 145; interest, payment of, V, 490, 578; for Civil War bounties, people approve act, 610; amount caused by Civil War, 752; should be paid in coin, VI, 100, 166, 349, 526; plan of funding, 540; floating, payment of, VII, 273; paid, 420; IX, 9; highways, constitutional amendment, 1905, VIII, 1043; X, 214, 732; paid in full, 1893, IX, 296; funded debt,— 1896, 738; — 1897, 821; — 1901, X, 327; — 1902, 485; — 1904, 595; — 1905, 718; — 1906, 832; extending term of credit, amendment of 1905, X, 214, 496, 577, 731; public defense, 327, 832; payments from general fund, amendment of 1905, 577, 601, 731, 848, 923; probable increase, 1906, 833.

STATE DENTAL SOCIETY. Disapproves students' relief bill, 1900, X, 174.

STATE DEPARTMENT OF AGRICULTURE. Established, 1893, IX, 175, 318; expert instruction in agriculture, 321; supervision of tuberculosis and glanders in cattle transferred to, X, 192.

STATE DEPARTMENT OF EDUCATION. Proposed by Unification Commission of 1899, X, 129; new building for, 741.

STATE DEPARTMENT OF EXCISE. Established, I, 529; IX, 666; expenses, 1900, X, 182.

STATE DEPARTMENT OF HEALTH. See also STATE BOARD OF HEALTH and STATE COMMISSIONER OF HEALTH. Office established, X, 192, 461; special equipment, expenses, veto, X, 787; epidemics and contagious diseases, appropriation, 787; general functions of, 860.

STATE DEPARTMENT OF LABOR. Established, 1901, X, 189, 365, 461; expert examiner of machinery, compensation, veto, 787.

STATE DITCH. Tonawanda, bridges over, VI, 1007; VII, 95, 96; North Tonawanda, bridges over, 363.

VETOES. Cleaning, VII, 456; Onondaga county improvement, VIII, 377, new bill passed; Mentz, bill relative to, 413; Murray, Orleans county, removing obstructions, 539; Salina, removing obstructions, 867; IX, 150; Douglass, reimbursement of Lenox for bridge over, 817; Douglass, reimbursement of Sullivan for bridge over, 818; Erie and Champlain canals, cleaning, X, 569; 569; Erie county, cleaning, 790.

STATE DOCK. Babylon, repairs, veto, X, 935.

STATE ENGINEER AND SURVEYOR. Railroad reports to be filed with, IV, 659; McAlpine, estimate, Erie canal enlargement, 689; member of Board of Railroad Commissioners, 805, 836; should examine railroads, V, 192; report on canals and railroads, 276; member of Commission to Organize Militia, 281, 400; report on canal improvements, VI, 15, 107; proposed appointment by Governor, 397; action on Buck case, 682; member of Commission to Consider Disposal of Lateral Canals, 750; report on lateral canals, 933; report on lift-bridges, 1005; member of Connecticut Boundary Commission, 172; to examine Swift claim, 374; should have charge of State survey, 988; constitutional office, VIII, 74, 175; IX, 425; ex officio member State Board of Health, VIII, 175; should have charge of all State surveys, 176; duties under county road system, 1043; New Capitol Commission, 1895, IX, 545; member of Greater New York Charter Commission, 553; communication from State Engineer Adams recommending canal investigation, 850; special report on canal improvement, 1901, X, 244; estimated speed of canal boats, 248; supervision of improved highways, 340.

VETOES. Carpet, oilcloth and letterhead die, VII, 463; maps for Railroad Commission, 921; clerk, preparing railroad report, 922; Assembly chamber ceiling investigation, appropriation, VIII, 547; inspection of bridges, IX, 801; new blue line maps, Erie, Oswego and Champlain canals, X, 297, 423; furniture and repairs, 299; engineer's compensation, 550; expenses, monuments on State boundaries, 559, 786; chief bridge designer and assistants, compensation, 560; balconies in office, 560; surveys for Forest Commission and forest preserve, appropriation, 560; highway improvement, appropriation, 572; engineers, salaries and expenses, 637; survey of canal from Hempstead bay to Jamaica bay, 649; United States geological survey, appropria-

STATE ENGINEER AND SURVEYOR—(*Continued*).

tion, 785; United States geological survey, hydrographic work, water supply, 785; Breed claim, Phoenix dam investigation, appropriation, 786; dredging channel between Great South bay and Shinnecock bay, 786.

STATE ENTOMOLOGIST. Office expenses, veto, VII, 778, 906.

STATE EXPERIMENT STATION. Report, X, 142. VETOES. Building on State Fair grounds, IX, 291; — buildings for chief chemist and others, 291.

STATE FAIR. At Rochester, IV, 80; commended, 138; Utica, 283; Buffalo, 431; Syracuse, 478; reconstruction of buildings at Elmira, veto, VII, 90; building for State experiment station, veto, IX, 291; act to establish, X, 120, 145; property of State Agricultural Society transferred to, 120; success of project, 216; appropriation for, 216; time of holding, 216; repairs on poultry building and changing railroad track, veto, 544; plans for improvement, 861.

STATE FAIR COMMISSION. Established, X, 120; investigations to be made by, 861.

STATE FINANCE LAW. Act of 1897, IX, 436; receipts and expenditures, amending act, veto, X, 812.

STATE FLAG. Act prescribing, description of arms, VII, 727; amending act relative to, veto, IX, 622.

STATE GAS COMMISSION. Recommended, VIII, 244, 311, 431, 481, 680, 930, 1021, 1078; established, 244; X, 220; powers transferred to Public Service Commissions, VIII, 244; abolished, 1907, succeeded by Public Service Commissions, IX, 761; X, 221.

STATE GEOLOGIST. Report, IX, 343, 575, 756, 852; printing and distributing paleontology, volume 8, part 2, veto, 402.

STATE HALL. Marble for, III, 764; IV, 28; rooms for State museum, III, 769, 860; new, transfer of offices to, 859, 934; old, room for State Agricultural Society, IV, 37; old, proposed establishment of museum of mechanic arts, 47.

STATE HISTORIAN. Office created, VII, 814; translation of ecclesiastical documents, veto, X, 298, 563.

STATE HOSPITALS. See also particular hospitals. Investments in, 1891, IX, 32; inmates, 1891, 32; 1892, 191; manufacture of articles for, in prisons, 181; preparation for use under State Care Act, 188; monthly estimates of expenses, 190, 229, 314, 651; Long Island, established, 541, 575; Manhattan, established, 541; new method of apportioning appropriations recommended, 566; large appropriations requested, 574; uniform salaries and wages, 652; special counsel should be abolished, X, 22; decrease in number of patients, 116; expenditures, 1900, 182; attorneys

STATE HOSPITALS — (*Continued*).

for, act amended, 1901, 187; inmates, 1900, 224; extravagance in buildings and equipments, 225; boards of managers abolished, 226, 332, 404, 496; boards of visitation established, 332, 496; comparative statement of expenses, 414; visits by members of local boards, comparative statement, 415; temporary commitments pending examinations, 499; proposed new hospital in northeastern part of State, 500, 724, 794; establishment of tuberculosis departments in, 500; appropriations, 1903, 539; emergency hospitals proposed, 609; number of, 1905, 723; boards of managers restored, 724; reception hospital in New York, 724; hospitals for acute insane, 724; hospital for chronic insane, 724; Kings Park State Hospital, see that title.

VETOES. Letters by or to inmates, regulations concerning, IX, 118; autopsies, 534; general maintenance, appropriation, X, 425; changing methods of supervision and administration, 538; Matteawan, reception and maintenance of patients, 591; treasurers' clerical assistants, appropriation, 641; general maintenance, deficiency appropriation, 642; employees, additional compensation, 650; Rochester, local assessment, 697; Central Islip State Hospital, relative to, 704.

STATE HOUSE. Illuminated in honor of Union victories, V, 439.

STATE INDUSTRIAL SCHOOL. Classed as a reformatory, X, 334; new site, 502, 611, 726; report of commission, 502; name changed to State Agricultural and Industrial School, 502.

· VETOES. Act to establish, VII, 631; repairs and improvements, VIII, 853; appropriation, X, 319; Smith claim for damages, 443; commitments, amending Penal Code, 705; claim of chaplain, 707; Cleever claim, inmate, 707.

STATE INEBRIATE ASYLUM. At Binghamton, established, V, 86, 180; appropriation from excise money, 87, 180; memorial from secretary, 107; plan of institution, 238; authorized to borrow money for buildings, 289; progress of construction, 383; good work of, 447; opened, 521; legislative investigation of, 761; property transferred to State, 761, 839; VI, 24; finishing basement and first story, veto, VII, 229; abolished, property transferred to Binghamton Insane Asylum, 286, 287, 431.

STATE INSPECTOR OF GAS METERS. Report, X, 371; office expenses and seals, veto, 934.

STATE INSTITUTIONS. Printing reports, veto, VIII, 129.

STATE LANDS. Unappropriated, bounties of, II, 115, 148, 187, 305, 308; unpatented, petition for grant of, 117; sale of, 199; settlement of, 199; claims of absentees and aliens, 218; no discrimination in distribution of, 256; Remsen claim, Montgomery

STATE LANDS —(*Continued*).

county, 261; military tract, 286; intrusions on waste and unappropriated, 302, 370, 527; income from sale of, 320; claimed by Connecticut, intrusions on, 370; ceded to Regents, resumption of, 377; grant to Union College, 453; forfeited and unappropriated, provisions relating to, 538; unappropriated, number of acres, 556, 1099; proposed disposition for educational purposes, 556; appropriation for common school fund, 560; IV, 112; in New York, sale of, 642, 679; confiscated, claims against, 695; assessment for local improvements, 680; gift to Commodore Macdonough, 832, 833; refugee tract, land in, cession to United States, 878, 879; investigation of Clark title, 883; value equal to State debt, 908; received from Holland Land Company, 994; Grand Island, sale for canal purposes, III, 26; belonging to general fund, 300; quantity unsold, IV, 263; proposed survey and sale of, 558, 615; John Brown tract, V, 24; retention for State park, VI, 629; State survey, act for, VII, 248; in Adirondack region should not be sold, 722; sale of, non-payment of taxes, 984; purchased by State for non-payment of taxes, 984; acquisitions in forest preserve, cancellation of tax sales, IX, 187; leases for oyster beds, 194; Smithtown, taxation of, act authorizing, 703; timber on, not to be cut, 835; leases of riparian lands, X, 117; in forest preserve, taxation of, 607.

VETOES. Sale of waste and unappropriated, II, 213; appropriated for bounties, bill relating to, 309; forfeited and unappropriated, 603; military tract, survey of, 664; sale of, authorized, V, 235; road at Clinton prison, repairs, VII, 920; under water, Yonkers, conveyance of, VIII, 53; Franklin county, conveyance to Robert Schroeder, 131; Genesee Valley canal, release to adjoining owners, 463; under water, Tonawanda, conveyance to Munch, IX, 284; trespasses, procedure, 530; deed, effect on rights of others, 623; Parks, relief, 721; taxation, Morehouse, relief, X, 274; taxation of, in Dannemora and Altona, 953.

STATE LAW. Enacted, 1892, IX, 28; description of arms, VII, 727.

STATE LIBRARY. Manuscript records relative to Morgan matter, III, 185; gift from English government, 751; engravings, medals, etc., received from Pope, IV, 453, 487; new buildings needed, 453, 486; number of volumes, 486, 844; VI, 619; VII, 23; new building provided for, IV, 487, 563, 613; receives copies of French publications, 524; donations from foreign government, 793; appropriation for deficiency, 794; good condition of, VI, 22; growth of, 619, 945; location in new capitol, VII,

STATE LIBRARY —(*Continued*).
696, 836, 947; Clinton papers, arranging and indexing, 808; report on Clinton papers, 808; old building removed, 980; under supervision of Regents, VIII, 169; completion of rooms, 650; greatness and efficiency of, IX, 829; X, 24; new building, 741.

VETOES. Frame for portrait of Abraham Lincoln, appropriation, VII, 86; purchase of "Public Service of New York," 920; trustees, proposed purchase of Tompkins papers, 922; purchase of standard geographic time globe for, VIII, 108; additional assistant librarian, VIII, 113; Clinton papers, arrangement of, appropriation, 247; transfer to new rooms, expenses, 861; books, binding, etc., 862; temporary services, appropriation, X, 551.

STATE LOAN AND TRUST COMPANY, NEW YORK. Charter, veto, VII, 1096.

STATE LUNATIC ASYLUM, UTICA. Established, III, 379, 452, 516, 543, 617, 676, 713; plan of construction, 713; IV, 43; appropriation for, III, 715, 766, 859; IV, 43, 78, 280; report of commissioners, III, 766; board of trustees, 859, 930, 935; communication from Commissioner Foxton, 930; expense of, IV, 43; superintendent appointed, 43; number of inmates, 77, 125, 279, 429, 554, 604, 641, 718, 790; V, 86, 176, 520, 838, 958; additional building at, IV, 78, 279; good work of, 125; poor and insufficient water, 281; prosperous condition of, 483, 554; V, 447; fire at, 54, 86; new buildings, 55, 86; insane convicts removed to Auburn Asylum, 272; transfer of insane female convicts to State prison, 583; special pathologist authorized, VI, 115; expense of construction, VII, 283; neglect to report, 706.

VETOES. Land for, appropriation, VII, 89; various appropriations, 786, 787; appropriation of surplus, 912; repairs, deficiency appropriation, VIII, 851; purchase of additional lands, 852; repairs, IX, 294.

STATE MEDICAL LIBRARY. Books and binding, appropriation, veto, IX, 69, 84.

STATE MEDICAL SOCIETY. Beneficial operation of, II, 62; recommends registration of births, marriages and deaths, V, 863; recommends legislation regulating child labor, VIII, 163.

STATE MUSEUM. Rooms in State hall, III, 769, 860; usefulness of, VI, 619; under supervision of Regents, VIII, 169; to have accommodations in new State Library building, X, 741.

VETOES. Printing and binding for, VII, 494, 1082; purchase of Hurst collection of zoological specimens, VIII, 108; geological map, publication of, 113; publication of paleontology, 553; expenses, appropriation, X, 552.

"STATE OF NEW YORK," THE. Tug, new boiler, veto, IX, 292.

STATEN ISLAND. Representation in First Assembly, I, 9; jurisdiction over adjacent waters in New York harbor, II, 540; beacon on, 586, 589; acquisition of lands for fortifications, 642; erection of Fort Richmond on, 658; batteries on, 659; fortifications at, 676; III, 309; cession of land for military academy, II, 676, 677; troops stationed on, 1812, 746; General Swartwout's brigade at, 809; accommodations for cadets, 814; completion of fortifications, 831; fortifications on, improvement of, 864; Governor authorized to sell fortifications to Federal government, 865, 940, 999; report on quarantine establishment, 990; fortifications, communications relative to, 1037, 1081; inspectors of customs, alleged improper conduct at elections, 1066; sale of fortifications, III, 178, 309; IV, 72, 154, 288; lighthouse at Prince's bay, III, 173; sale of land on, to United States for fortifications, 570, 972; change of quarantine buildings, IV, 439; Marine Hospital, patients in, 644; removal of quarantine establishment, V, 28, 54, 378; service of militia, quarantine disturbance, 88; Seguine's Point, quarantine at, 101.

VETOES. Water supply, VI, 503; Seamen's Retreat Hospital, appropriations, VII, 490, 585; bulkhead lines, New York harbor, VIII, 1037.

STATEN ISLAND BRIDGE COMPANY. Charter, veto, VI, 91.

STATEN ISLAND AND ELIZABETHPORT FERRY COMPANY. Extending time, veto, VI, 595.

STATEN ISLAND NORTH SIDE RAILROAD COMPANY. Charter, veto, VI, 323.

STATE OFFICERS. Reducing salaries of, II, 1013; how chosen, III, 1004; contracts for public printing, IV, 32; should be appointed by Governor, VI, 396; attend ceremonies on first occupation of new capitol, VII, 270; legislative bill file boards for, veto, 493; Governor Hill's acknowledgment to, VIII, 1085; investigation of, appropriation, veto, IX, 712; attend Higgins memorial services, X, 963.

STATE PAPER. Publications in, IV, 31; publishing notices of canal contracts, V, 365.

STATE PAPER OFFICE, ENGLAND. American colonial records in, III, 1015; IV, 168, 176; part of Royal Library, 177; arrangement of papers, 181.

STATE PARKS. Report of commission, VI, 629.

STATE PAUPERS. Statistics, VII, 959.

STATE PRINTER. Gratuity to, I, 500; official term, III, 1021; bill to remove, 1021; Thurlow Weed appointed, 1023; duties of, IV, 31; act providing for, 32; superintendent of State printing, creating office, veto, IX, 70.

State Printing. See Public Printing.

State Printing Board. Established, X, 196.

State Prisons. Erection of two, recommended, II, 336; act for erection of, 364, 387; sentences to, 451; punishment for escape, 478; management of, 508; guards for, 508; in New York, partially destroyed by fire, 547; repair of, 548; deficit in accounts of, 612; at Auburn established, 855; Governor Clinton's comment on system, 911; manufacturing operations unprofitable, 912; solitary confinement recommended, 913; guard, accommodations for, 952; violation of discipline, whipping for, 983; separate dormitories proposed, 984, 1015; at New York, removal of, 993, 1016; discipline, communication from Thomas Eddy, 995; corporal punishment in, protest against, 996; needed reform in administration, 1051; transfers between Auburn and New York, 1108; solitary confinement, 1109; III, 9; pardons resulting from classification of convicts, 22; investigating commission appointed, 22, see Prison Investigating Commission; insane convicts to be received, 33; new prison to be established in place of New York prison, 82; commissioners appointed to locate new prison, 82; at Sing Sing, 129; Federal prisoners admitted to, 163; for female convicts, 207, 208, 403, 448, 515, 716; short terms predominate, 285; chaplains for, 289, 977; improved plan of construction, 288; legislative committee 'to visit, 290; transfer of young convicts to House of Refuge, 292; general statistics, 339, 617, 674; IV, 27, 121, 482, 844; V, 163, 269, 449, 525, 599, 696, 756, 841; VI, 17, 109, 233; 355, 616, 941; VII, 8, 146, 281, 425, 519, 701, 827, 954; IX, 25; X, 204; Assembly committee to visit, report of, III, 401; self-supporting, 446, 512; IV, 273; report of Convict Labor Commission, III, 514; limiting instruction in mechanical trades, 514; silk manufacture in, 514, 931, 945; convicts, ratio of colored to white, 717; complaints against management of, 765; Sunday schools in, 861; reformation of convicts, 874; results of Convict Labor Act of 1842, IV, 48; good discipline in, 556; overcrowded, 608; VI, 57; VII, 282; appointments should not be subject to political influence, IV, 722; wardens, short term of service, 722; investigating commission created, 723, 777, 786; inspectors, 777, see that title; aggregate liabilities, 786; report of investigating commission, 786; agents, duties of, 786; payments to discharged convicts, 845; revision of statutes, V, 78; change of administration recommended, 78; Superintendent of Prisons, 78, 373; separate reports for male and female prisons, 166; Kingsland claim, 167, 272; severe punishments in, 268; new, recom-

STATE PRISONS — (*Continued*).

mended, 271; improved conditions in, 272; appointment of commissioner to investigate, 372, 424; discipline defective, 372, 427, 434; new system of administration, 373; inspection by Prison Association, 526, 601; sending insane female convicts to, 583; management should be free from partisan influence, 697, 757; VI, 18; Prison Association authorized to appoint investigating commission, V, 698; estimated value of property, 757; new prison recommended, VI, 57; mutinies in, 109; punishments in, 109, 233; concentration of management needed, 355; proposed board of managers, 355; Superintendent of State Prisons, office created, 398, 942; should be self-supporting, 942; investigating commission created, 1876, 942; VII, 9; report of investigating commission of 1876, 9; administration, no appointments on grounds of political partisanship, 9; offenses committed in, State liable for expense of trial, 87; good results of change of method of administration, 146, 519, 963; self-sustaining,— 1881, 701; — 1882, 827, 963; — 1885, VIII, 167; abolition of contract labor approved by people, VII, 828; transfers from Elmira Reformatory, 955; freedom of worship in, VIII, 23, 178, 302, 479; employment of prisoners on State account, 165; Labor Act of 1888, 296; use of machinery abolished, 658; Revision Act of 1889, 814; execution of death penalty, proposed central building for, IX, 23; X, 111; additional instruction, IX, 80; contract labor prohibited, 181, 549; X, 166; manufacturing articles for public institutions, IX, 181; employment of prisoners on highways, 181, 239; aiding prisoners to acquire new homes after discharge, 182; prison-made goods manufactured in and imported from other States, branding required, act unconstitutional, 329; X, 9; license to sell foreign prison-made goods, IX, 329; transfer of prisoners from Elmira Reformatory, 330, 389; commission established, act of 1895, 551, 654; prisoners from other States, 655; contract labor prohibited, employment of prisoners provided for, 656; number of prisoners employed in various industries, 1895, 658; new system of labor successful, 831; cells should be reconstructed, X, 28; capital fund not payable into State treasury, 73; expenditures, 1900, 182; Bertillon system of measurement, 205; new buildings needed, 342, 614; comparative statement of appropriation, 1893–4; 1901–2, 464; transfers from Elmira Reformatory, 501; good results of administration, 514; inequalities of administration, 614; separate prison for condemned prisoners, 614; new system of appropriations, 615; Commission on New Site for Sing Sing Prison, 863.

State Prisons —(*Continued*).

　　Vetoes. Assaults on officers by convicts, punishment for, II, 589; repealing part of act, VI, 334; accounts of purchases and sales, 507; reducing force, 507; amending acts, 582; new, removal from Sing Sing, 600; Gilson claim, 703; commutations for good behavior, 399; Sing Sing, various appropriations, VII, 483; Auburn, various appropriations, 484; Clinton, various appropriations, 484; Superintendent, various appropriations, 485; Asylum for Insane Convicts, repairs and improvements, 485; religious instruction, appropriation, 784, 919; dock at Sing Sing, 784; confinement of convicts, 937; Convict Labor Investigating Commission, extending time, 1001; manufactures in, branding and marking, IX, 138; furnishing cheese for inmates, 237; clerk of prisons, 428; manufacture of certain articles prohibited in, 464; authorizing double chloride of gold treatment, 622; convict-made goods, sales and license fees, 813; convict-made goods, labeling, repealing certain acts, 813; amending Revised Statutes, 814, 816; labor in, manufacture of school furniture, X, 165; plant for publication of literature for blind, 293; commutations, insane criminals, 309; electrocution apparatus, purchase of patent rights, 567; parole of prisoners, 585, 812; appropriations for, 655; Bertillon method of identifying criminals, amending act, 707.

State Property. Vetoes. Appraisal and inventory, IX, 775; Buffalo, local assessment, 784.

State Racing Commission. Created, 1895, IX, 601.

State Reporter. Reports, Court of Appeals, contract for publication, VII, 892.

State Reservoir. Woodhull, Herkimer county, cleaning, veto, X, 320.

State Roads. Lottery for, II, 385; between Albany and St. Lawrence river, report of commission, 756, 795; proposed, from Hudson river to Cayuga lake, III, 80; from Hudson river to Lake Erie through southern tier of counties, 81, 170, 200, 233; commission on, provided for, 81, 124; in northern counties, 125; Oneida and Herkimer counties, repairs, VIII, 560; two in each county suggested, 925, 1068; State debt for, 926; X, 214; Governor Odell's suggestions, 1901, 214; progress of construction, 1902, 340; comparative statement of appropriations, 1893-4, 1901-2, 464; number of miles constructed with State aid, 618; improvement bonds, 1906, 834.

　　Vetoes. Repair of road through State lands at Clinton prison, VII, 920; Allegany reservation, improvement of, VIII, 847; Forestport to Woodhull, 850, 1138; Piercefield, repairs, X, 645.

STATES. To supply accoutrements, II, 43; disapproval of recommendations of New Haven Convention, 46; recommended to encourage
religion and good morals, 56; apportionment of Federal expenses,
65, 116; restricting inland trade between, 81; proposed convention
for regulating prices, 84; assessments in aid of national government,
85; seperate support of troops, 88; quotas of troops for Continental
Army, 93; apportionment of army supplies, 98; abound with provisions, 106; imports of foreign merchandise, 120; all, ratify
Articles of Confederation, 127; thanksgiving day recommended by
Congress, 152; bound to provide for public creditors, 158; New
York protests against uniform scale of depreciation, 167; pay of
militia called from one State to another, 167; fast day recommended
by Congress, 170; not deprived of territory by United States, 179;
proposed convention to revise system of government, 194; restitution of, 206, 207; each to have three delegates in Congress, 213;
Virginia proposes commercial convention, 259, 270; convention to
revise Articles of Confederation, 270; no power to construe or
limit national treaty, 274; Constitution submitted to, 282; Federal
government established, general note, 296; suability of, 334; actions
between, removal of, 404, 415; proceedings against non-residents
under highway laws, 593; insurance by non-residents, 613; punishment of extraterritorial offenses, 623, 624; III, 598; invited to aid
canal enterprise, 675; Federal direct tax, 788; admission of new,
proposed limitation of power, 827; government of, should be preserved, 1042; elections, alleged interference of Federal officers, 1042,
1054, 1059, 1060; national bank business in, power to tax, 1077;
power to tax national bank, 1078; one State should not hold land
in another without the latter's consent, 1118; rights of, Federal
encroachments on, III, 78; jurisdiction over land ceded to United
States, 139; distribution of Federal revenues among, 155, 186, 307,
330, 373, 438, 898; South Carolina resolutions, reciprocal rights of,
218; reserved powers of, 234, 582, 590; Virginia claims for itself
the right to construe the national Constitution, 280; controversies
between, jurisdiction of Federal courts, 312, 357, 359; Federal power
to change boundaries, 390; South Carolina nullification proceedings, 427; a community of republics, 570; power to punish residents
for interference in affairs of other States, 581; power as to fugitives
from justice, 597; a State has no foreign relations, 689; cede territory to United States, 896; right to regulate election of Representatives, 940; relation to post roads, 969; measure of sovereignty reserved to, 985; VI, 831; claim to territory, 985; should guard against
Federal encroachments, IV, 4; status of slavery in, 499; western,
growth of, 590; reserved rights and powers, 618, 750; no tax on ex-

STATES — (*Continued*).

    ports from, 667; may determine status of persons in their juris-
diction, 811; V, 61; free, attitude toward slavery, 29; new, power
of Congress to admit, 30; secession movement, 298; right of secession denied, 300; Tennessee propositions relative to status of slavery,
315; proposed liability for refusing to surrender fugitive slaves,
316; compulsory power of national government, 343; holding slaves,
Arkansas recites grievances of, 353; procedure under Federal Direct
Tax Act, 389; limitations of power, 463; rights must be respected,
464; constitutional protests against martial law, 470; antagonistic
opinions concerning slavery, 474; reorganization as result of Civil
War, 556; western, benefited by New York canals, 595; donation
of public lands to, 596; republican form of government, 616; reconstruction following Civil War, 714, 743; cannot pay claims for
property or slaves lost by participants in rebellion, 791; Southern
Confederacy, civil government destroyed, 856; seceding, new Constitutions in, 860; seceding, slow progress of reconstruction, VI, 41;
Georgia, alleged subjection to military power, 131; obligation only
equitable, 893; cannot impose tonnage duty, VII, 121; no suit by
citizens of another State, 250; right to determine questions of
suffrage, 306; may change policy as to public works, liability to
contractors, 375, 376; participate in Yorktown Centennial Celebration, 736; not to keep troops in time of peace without consent of
Congress, 763; proposed convention for consideration of uniform
laws, VIII, 930; should retain jurisdiction of matters relating to
public health, IX, 207; biennial sessions of Legislature, 847.

STATES-GENERAL OF HOLLAND. Supervision of colonial affairs, I, 1;
    records of, IV, 171.

STATE SANITARY COMMISSION. Bill to establish, veto, IX, 234.

STATE STOCK. Form of certificate, IV, 204; amount of debt, 212, 702;
    United States deposit fund, 270; due in 1848, 387; used for re-
demption of bank notes, 395; received by canal contractors on
claims, 665; available for banking purposes, 731; under amendment of 1854, 784; V, 5; character of certificates, V, 245; may be
held by banks, 376; as bank securities, 449; resolution against
discrimination as between domestic and foreign holders, 578; redemption of, VI, 167; redemption, new loan, 615.

STATE SUPERINTENDENT OF ELECTIONS. Metropolitan elections district,
    appointment of John McCullough, IX, 886; report, X, 31, 142.

STATE SURVEY. Recommended, IV. 652; protest against, VII, 26; act
        providing for, 248, 875; discontinuance recommended, 373; be-
ginning of legislation, 987; continuing appropriations, 988;
commissioners, extending official existence, 988; proposed trans-

STATE SURVEY—(*Continued*).

fer to State Engineer's office, 988; methods and expenditures disapproved, VIII, 176; completion ordered, 177; nomination of commissioners, 255; topographic, joint State and Federal survey, IX, 323, 424, 670; continued, 1895, 425, 669; office of superintendent abolished, X, 112.

VETOES. Continuance, VII, 372; VIII, 452; deficient appropriation, VII, 464; commissioners, 806; appropriation, 1077; topographical map, VIII, 73; expense of completion, 423; publishing and distributing report, 551; appropriation, 1894, IX, 423; superintendent, bill to create office, 423; oil and gas regions, 774; boundary between Lewis and Herkimer counties, appropriation, 856.

STATE TAX COMMISSIONERS. To appraise corporate franchises, X, 71; salaries, increased, 1900, 84; duties under Franchise Tax Act of 1899, 196; suggested power to review local assessments, 343; experts, appropriation, veto, 554; expense under Mortgage Tax Law, veto, 798; counsel in review proceedings, designation and compensation, 845.

STATE TRAINING SCHOOL FOR BOYS. Provision for, succeeding New York House of Refuge, X, 726; acts amended, selection of lands and time of making report, 893.

STATE TRAINING SCHOOL FOR GIRLS. Established at Hudson, X, 726.

STATE TREASURER. Appointed, II, 9; payments to United States, 9; to exchange old continental money for new, 147; to pay Gov. George Clinton's claim, 161; payment to Superintendent of Finance, 186; to pay requisition of Congress, 264; payment on certain purchases, 288; report of, 318; office to be kept in Albany, 397; oath and bond, 459; office for, 516; member of Canal Board, 901; how chosen, III, 1004; member of Commission to Organize Militia, V, 281, 400; distribution of funds for soldiers' families, 408; member of Commission on Normal Schools, 695; proposed election by Legislature, VI, 398; defalcation of clerk, 632, 720; removal of, constitutional provision, 633; tax to cover defalcation, 634; payment to Timothy J. Sullivan, new capitol, VII, 499; taxes, when payable to, IX, 542.

VETOES. Receivers of insolvent corporations, VII, 798; settlement of claims against sureties of First National Bank, Buffalo, 874; removing books and records to new capitol, VIII, 249; office expenses, deficiency appropriation, 861; additional clerk hire, appropriation, 891; deposit of funds, IX, 57.

STATE TRUANT SCHOOL. Bill to establish, 1889, veto, VIII, 818.

STATE TUBERCULOSIS HOSPITAL. Established, X, 149.

STATE UNIVERSITY. See UNIVERSITY OF NEW YORK.

STATE WATER SUPPLY COMMISSION. Established, 1905, X, 744; act amended, approval of maps, etc., 855.

STATE WOMEN'S HOSPITAL. Amending charter, veto, VIII, 458.

STATE WORKINGMEN'S ASSEMBLY. Recommends legislation regulating child labor, VIII, 163.

STATION SHIP. At New York, I, 320; absent in West Indies, 332.

STATUARY. Marble group, "Struggle for Liberty," proposed purchase of, veto, IX, 812.

STATUES. For hall of House of Representatives, V, 635; VI, 434, 435, 555.

VETOES. Robert R. Livingston, appropriation, VII, 382, 469; Hendrick Hudson, IX, 222; Baron Steuben, 427; Alexander Hamilton, X, 586.

STATUTES. Examination of, proposed, I, 204, 211, 219; royal instruction relative to private, 210; importance of following English precedents, 279, 293; how long to be in force, 484; instruction as to titles and contents, 493, 494, 506; King's power over colonial, 506; enactments of Council of Safety have effect of, II, 29; retrospective, 30, 38, 215, 240, 245; revision of, recommended, I, 521; II, 52, 200, 219, 255, 660; expired, cannot be continued without revival, 81; private, interested parties should be heard, 191, 544, 782, 1081, 1112; Revision Commission appointed, 255; of Congress, distribution of, 302, 322, 409, 459, 530, 567; III, 226; Criminal Code, revision of, II, 334, see CRIMINAL CODE; exchange with Virginia, 371; Massachusetts proposes interchange of, 514; should be known and understood, 526; received from several States, 530; interchange with States and Federal government, 543; publication in newspapers, 555; IV, 31; colonial continued, II, 610; have no extra-territorial effect, 624; III, 598; Apportionment Act cannot be amended, II, 651, 849; revision provided for, 675, 692; III, 11, 18; Revised Laws, distribution of, II, 953; distribution to societies, 994; distribution to Federal departments, 1026; requested for Congressional Library, 1116; should contain but one subject, III, 90; protest against log-rolling, 91; Legislature responsible for enactment, 973; when entitled to be read in evidence, IV, 32; American Athenæum requests copies of, 46; tendency to excessive enactments, 50; general laws, 379, see that title; local powers of boards of supervisors, 434; international exchange of, 466, 508; colonial, publication of, 488; confusion, need of revision, 560, 615; creation of State debt, 677; title should state subject, 776; quarantine, revision of, V, 279; proper method of amending, 575; legalizing acts, see that title; hasty legislation, 849; existing

STATUTES — (*Continued*).

laws not applicable by reference, constitutional provision, VI, 90; IX, 431; revision, appointment and work of various commissions, VI, 118; sketch of revisions, 123; purity of legislation, 391; excessive number of, 399; effect of later statute on same subject, VII, 1053; superseded by Penal and Criminal Codes, VIII, 37; list of revisions, 38; general revision needed, 38; Legislature may interpret, 264; large number, comparative statement, 343; should reflect public sentiment and have fair trial, 535; uniform, commission on, 929, 1068; IX, 188; uniform Negotiable Instruments Law, 930; publication in newspapers of opposite politics, 944; large number relating to cities, 1895, IX, 677; over-legislation, evils of, X, 21; revision, general results, 1900, 106; uniform time of taking effect, 111; Assembly select committee on revision, 1901, 223; special committee on revision appointed by Governor, 1902, 224; Board of Consolidation established, 224; general and special, comparative statement, 1894–1900, 504; constitutional provisions as to continuance, 681; summary of important legislation, 1906, 931.

VETOES. Expired, reviving by reference, VI, 193; repealing act, VII, 129; publication of, Rensselaer county, 267; Hough's Abstract, purchase of, 469; Senate Committee on Revision, printing and material for, 493; poor, revision and consolidation, 505; enforcement of, 807; publication in newspapers, amending act, VIII, 130; chronological table, 293; general laws, correcting manifest errors, IX, 447; index, 1886–1897, purchasing, 774; purchase and distribution of, 776; publication, designation of newspapers, 813; publication of, X, 704.

STATUTORY CONSTRUCTION LAW. Enacted, 1892, IX, 28; amendments, veto, X, 319.

STATUTORY REVISION COMMISSION. Compilation of colonial laws, I, 11; IV, 488; IX, 681; appointed, II, 255, 675; III, 11, 18; 1870, powers of, VI, 118, 225; VII, 168, 184; Commissions of 1889 and 1904, VI, 118; sketch of revisions, 123; 1870, members of commission, 238; report, 261, 318, 415; recommends printing legislative bills in final form, VII, 43; appropriation for printing, veto, 231; taxes creation of commission, 407; revision of militia laws, veto, 411; 1889, duty as legislative counsel, VIII, 26, 478; IX, 210; 1889, created, VIII, 39, 348; IX, 26, 679; X, 222; prepares escheat bill, 1890, VIII, 1015; first series of bills passed, 1890, corporations, towns and highways, 1027; plan of revision, IX, 26; bills reported in 1891, 27; general laws passed, 1892, 28, 135; judicial construction, 137; commission discontinued, 1900, 210; X, 107, 148, 223; succeeded

STATUTORY REVISION COMMISSION —(*Continued*).
by bill drafting department, IX, 210; bills passed in 1896, 680; appointed code commissioners, 680; prepares revised Education Law, X, 27; work of, summary of results, 106; special Assembly committee on revision bills, 107; joint committee appointed, 107, 222; bills presented in 1900, 222.

STAVES AND HEADING. Inspection of, II, 477, 518; III, 183; cullers of, Rensselaer county, veto, 438.

STEAM. Motive power on canals, V, 786; VI, 107, 242, 537, 744; on Canadian canals, 538; application to navigation, Centennial Celebration, X, 874.

     VETOES. Boilers, insurance, VII, 507; motive power, Champlain canal, 508; vessels on certain lakes, inspection, VIII, 1121.

STEAMBOAT. Use of, privileges relating to, II, 415; tax on passengers, 902; tax suspended, 1010; privileges, equal rights in, 1025; needed inspection of, III, 46; rules of navigation applicable to, 135; sketch of Fulton's experiments, 150; first launched in New York, IV, 713.

     VETOES. Soliciting patronage for, VII, 415; inspection in certain counties, VIII, 469; sanitary inspection of, IX, 234; frauds on owners and managers, amending Penal Code, 793; inspectors, traveling expenses, X, 465; excursion boats and barges, fire protection, 805; ferry and excursion boats, life saving crews, 807.

STEAM BOILERS. Inspector's report, VI, 43; inspection by metropolitan police, veto, 96; inspection, X, 771.

STEAMSHIP COMPANIES. Emigration tax, Inspection Act unconstitutional, VII, 712; carriers of emigrants, contract with, unconstitutional, 712.

STECHE, ERNEST. Escheat, veto, VII, 805.

STEELE, HERBERT G. Justice of peace, legalizing official acts, veto, X, 62.

STEELE, OSMAN N. Deputy sheriff, Delaware county, murder of, IV, 235, 300; convictions for murder of, 237; history of crime, 309; number of persons convicted, 323.

STEELE'S CREEK. Cleaning channel, veto, X, 301.

STEMMLER, BABETTE. Relief, veto, VII, 508, 661.

STEMMLER, JOHN A. Justice, district court, New York, salary, veto, VIII, 294, 884.

STENOGRAPHERS. In Surrogates' Courts, general, VI, 318; Supreme Court, third judicial district, salaries, VIII, 699; first judicial department, salaries, X, 152.

     VETOES. Appointment, amending Code, VI, 209; Surrogates' Courts, second and third districts, 317; Onondaga County Court, 326;

STENOGRAPHERS — (*Continued*).

New York, oyer and terminer, notes, 330; New York, coroners, 910; second judicial district, deficiency appropriation, VII, 583; New York, general sessions, compensation, 768; second judicial district, Kings county, appointment and removal, 769; for a judge of the Court of Appeals to be paid by Kings county, 770; second judicial district (excepting Kings county), deficiency appropriation, 780; Senate special railroad committee, compensation, 780; services, 808; Surrogates' Court, New York, increasing salary, VIII, 82; legislative, accounts to be adjusted by Comptroller, 107; Buffalo, Superior Court, 291; Senate Committee on Taxation and Retrenchment, services, 439; grand jury's, compensation, 468; Senate Committee on Privileges and Elections, appropriation, 547; fees, investigation of New York commissioners of excise, 551; Code of Civil Procedure, compensation, 639; Lee, Assembly committees, 1889, appropriation, 839; Assembly Committee to Prepare Rules, appropriation, 844; Senate Committee on Taxation and Retrenchment, Bloomingdale Asylum investigation, appropriation, 844; Senate and Assembly, preparing records for publication, 854; Kings county, coroners, 890; amending Code of Criminal Procedure, duties, 890; Thornton, Senate Committee on Cities, investigation, 1890, appropriation, 1141; X, 570, 647; Surrogates' Courts, transcribing notes, IX, 115; eighth judicial district, additional, 286; grand jury's, amending act, 725, 811; New York, thirteenth civil district court, legalizing appointment, 309; New York, Municipal Court, X, 168; New York Municipal Court, O'Sullivan, compensation, 310; grand jury, Westchester county, 387; Forest, Fish and Game Commission, salary, 421; for State Architect, appropriation, 552, 561; transfer tax, appointment, 586; amending Code, 587; Supreme Court, trial terms, 699; New York, City Court, additional, 805, 816; Kings County Court, 808; Moynahan, New York, services Supreme Court, criminal term, 950.

STEPHENS, BENJAMIN. Contract with Chatfield, II, 580.

STEPHENS, JOHN L. Urges publication of colonial documents, IV, 167.

STEPHENS, ZENA. Contract with Chatfield, II, 580.

STEPHENSON, GEORGE. Locomotive engine, Rocket, speed of, III, 397.

STEPHENSON, JAMES. Seneca chief, joins in address to Governor, II, 943.

STEPHENTOWN. Presbyterian Society, charter, veto, IV, 633.

STERLING. Arms and supplies for, II, 774; land in, presented to Commodore Macdonough, 831.

STERLING. See STIRLING.

STIRLING, LORD (William Alexander). Major-general, situation at Saratoga, II, 151.

STIRLING IRON WORKS. Employment of, Hudson river obstructions, II, 19.

STERNE, SIMON. Member of Tilden Municipal Reform Commission, 1875, IX, 417.

STETSON, FRANCIS L. Opinion, voter's freedom of selection of candidate cannot be restricted by form of ballot, IX, 395, 479.

STEUBEN, FREDERICK WILLIAM. Baron, letter from, recruiting continental battalions, II, 82; need of supplies for New York troops, 88; courtesies to family, Yorktown Centennial Celebration, VII, 741; manuscripts, Yorktown campaign, New York Historical Society, 742; statue, veto, IX, 427.

STEUBEN COUNTY. Certain streams in, declared public highways, II, 521; defense of, 713; militia from, 1812, 743; arms and supplies for, 775; infantry company applies for arms from arsenals, 1120; local custody of United States deposit fund, VIII, 429; average excise license fees, 1889, 687; county clerk; salaried office, 1102; highways, cost of labor system, 1892, IX, 200; insane, care of, county and State systems compared, 228.

VETOES. Third Assembly district, proposed erection of Canisteo county from, V, 223; proposed erection of Conhocton county, 249; protection of fish, Loon lake, VII, 446; unpaid taxes, sales for, 506; Hornellsville, extending time for collection of taxes, 878; increasing school commissioner districts, VIII, 402; jury districts and courthouse in Hornellsville, 880; Redding trial, claim against State, 888; Greenwood fire district waterworks bonds, X, 704.

STEVENS, AARON (Arent). Indian interpreter, I, 459; service in exchange of prisoners, 510.

STEVENS, EBENEZER. Colonel, plan of New York fortifications, II, 418, 419; compensation, 434; major-general, number of troops under his command, 809.

STEVENS, FRANK W. Counsel for Jamestown Bar Association at trial of Justice Hooker, X, 829.

STEVENS, JOHN AUSTIN. Member of Yorktown Centennial Commission, VII, 734; secretary of commission, 743.

STEVENSON, JONATHAN D. Colonel, 7th Regiment, sent to California, IV, 415.

STEVENSON, ROBERT. American Minister to Great Britain, interviews with Mr. Brodhead, publication of colonial documents, IV, 168, 169.

STEVENSON'S SYSTEM OF CANAL TOWAGE. Testing, veto, VII; 266.

STEWART, ALEXANDER T. Manufacturing establishment at Glenham, decline of, X, 693.

STEWART, BERTRAM E. Canal Department, appropriation for services, veto, IX, 716.

STEWART, DANIEL. Escheat, veto, VII, 619.

STEWART, WILLIAM RHINELANDER. Member of Yorktown Centennial Commission, VII, 734.

STIER, JOSEPH F. Notary public, legalizing acts, veto, VIII, 387.

STIERLE, FRANCISKA. Formerly Franciska Braun, escheat, veto, X, 273.

STILES, JOHN W. Colonel 9th Regiment, supplies from Union Defense Committee, VII, 500.

STILLS. Federal tax on, II, 789.

STILLWATER. VETOES. Amending charter, VIII, 889; school district No. 10, regulating elections in, IX, 817.

STOCKADES. At Albany and Schenectady, I, 196; at Crown Point, 241; at Albany, repair of, 553.

STOCKBRIDGE. French and Indians reported near, I, 363.

STOCKBRIDGE INDIANS. Petition from, II, 373; address from, 379; agreement with, 394; number of, 1819, 976; removal to White river, Indiana, 987; land purchased from, 989, 1119; III, 13; attorney for, II, 1076; Green Bay treaty, 1107; treaty with, III, 34; purchase of residue of land, 96; payment of annuities, 183; communication from, payments to, 748; school and gospel fund, IV, 831; V, 159; claim title to land, IV, 857; Wisconsin memorial, claim of title to land, VI, 415; claim, Court of Claims, veto, X, 703.

STOCKBRIDGE RESERVATION. Number of Indians on, 1819, II, 976.

STOCK CORPORATIONS. General law, 1890, VIII, 1027; IX, 26; increasing or reducing number of directors, act of 1891, VIII, 1144; revised, 1892, IX, 28, 135; monopolies prohibited, 136; reports, liability of directors for failure to file, X, 185.

VETOES. Foreign, licensing, IX, 529; amending general act, IX, 625, 627; issue and transfer of stock, X, 62; issue of debenture bond stock, 321; increasing or reducing capital stock, 446; mortgages, consents of stockholders, 590; reducing capital stock, 590; borrowing money and mortgaging property, 810.

STOCK EXCHANGE, NEW YORK. Charter, veto, VI, 221.

STOCKINGS. For troops, I, 639.

STOCKJOBBING. A species of gambling, III, 565.

STOCKPORT. Legalizing settlement of Hanes claim, veto, X, 814.

STOCKS. Gambling in, IV, 807; banks speculating in, 838; transfer, tax on, VII, 571; VIII, 305; X, 490; certificates, advance not subject to usury laws, VII, 719; bucket shops, business prohibited, 1090; certificates should not be issued for less than

STOCKS—(*Continued*).

 par value, VIII, 180, 303, 480; New York sinking fund, 190; capital employed in State, defined, X, 720, 722; transfers, taxation of, act of 1905, 769, 836.

 VETOES. Bucket shops, business prohibited, VII, 1090; increasing or reducing capital, X, 446; New York and London Trust Company, authorizing purchase of, 586; corporations, reducing, 590.

STOCKTON, ROBERT F. Member of New Jersey Commission to Procure Constitutional Convention, V, 325.

STOCK TRANSFER TAX. Act of 1905, X, 769, 836; amending act, veto, 958.

STONE, ANDREW. Secretary to Lords Justices, letters from, military preparations, I, 314.

STONE, WILLIAM L. Urges publication of colonial documents, IV, 167.

STONEHOUSE, JOHN B. Assistant Adjutant-General, communication to Secretary of War relative to military depot at Elmira, V, 562; conference with Washington authorities as to quota of volunteers, 625, 632; agent to settle claims against United States, VI, 357; VII, 501.

STONY BROOK. Improvement, veto, VIII, 115.

STOREN, MICHAEL. Relief, veto, VI, 135.

STORM. Injures Fort George and Copsey battery, I, 529; prevents meeting of Legislature, II, 87; on Staten Island, effect on fortifications, 1038; effect on canal construction, 1096; damages Fort Richmond, III, 35; interference with operation of *posse* in anti-rent troubles, 832, 839; of March, 1888, VIII, 507.

STORMS, ELLIS W. Administrator Cora Storms, Court of Claims, veto, X, 445.

STORY, JOSEPH. United States Supreme Court, opinion, obligation of contracts, IV, 349; Commentaries on Constitution, quoted, secrecy of ballot, VIII, 585.

STOUDT, CASPER. Claim of, manufacture of sulphur and copperas, II, 92.

STOWELL, R. R. Canal Department, appropriation for services, veto, IX, 716.

STRAACK, GOTTFRIED. Estate, escheat, veto, VIII, 734.

STRAACK, JOHANN HEINRICH. Escheat bill, veto, VIII, 734.

STRAIT, JAMES W. Canal Department, appropriation for services, veto, IX, 716.

STRANAHAN, NEVADA N. Senate, member of joint committee on taxation, 1899, X, 801.

STRANG, JOHN. Deputy judge-advocate, claim, settlement of, II, 150.

STRATFORD. Arms and supplies for, II, 772; including portion in Adirondack park, veto, X, 379.

STRAUSS, WILLIAM. Relief, veto, X, 178.

STREET RAILROADS. Grants belong to people, VI, 64; New York, Wall Street ferry to North river, 601; exempting from taxation, act of 1880, Governor Cornell's protest against, VII, 454; consent of local authorities, 896, 1040, 1064; consent of adjoining owners, constitutional provision, 1037, 1064; operation and extension, act relative to, 1063; percentage of receipts, payment to local treasurer, 1068; cities and villages, act relative to, VIII, 200; Broadway Surface Railroad Company, charter annulled, corporation dissolved, 205; Cantor act, sale of franchise, IX, 41; Yonkers Railroad Company, completing road, 270; taxation, statutes amended, X, 198; proposed prohibition in forest preserve, 340; use of canal bridges, act relative to, 363; heavy payments for taxes, 528.

VETOES. Mohawk and Ilion Railroad Company, using bank of canal, VI, 581; Brooklyn, Flatbush, 597; fares in certain counties, V, 653; New York Rapid Transit Company, eminent domain, VI, 694; Poughkeepsie, discontinuing service during winter months, VII, 73; Brooklyn, Atlantic avenue, change of motive power, 394; maintenance and operation in cities, towns and villages, 793, 894, 1065; Rome Street Railroad Company, charter, 806; cities, regulating hours of drivers and conductors of horse cars, 1109; Poughkeepsie, changing motive power, VIII, 729; consents and percentages, 887; percentages payable by, 1037, 1124; consents, 1037; West Side Street Railway Company, Buffalo, relief, 1117; Eleventh Avenue Railroad Company, relief, 1119; Fulton, Wall and Cortland Street Ferry Railroad Company, relief, 1119; Niagara Street Railroad Company, changing route, 1132; hours of labor, IX, 144, 626; rate of fare, 150; hours of labor in certain cities, 266; abandoning part of road, 443; Brooklyn,— Hooper street, IX, 778; — Hall street and St. James place, 778; —Bedford avenue, 779, 780; — Prospect place, 780; — East Eighteenth street, 780; — Twelfth street and others, 780; — Throop avenue and other places, 781; — Cumberland street and others, 781; — Cropsey avenue, 781; X, 322; — Enfield street, IX, 781; — St. Mark's place, etc., 782; — Second avenue, etc., 782; — Penn street, etc., 782; Buffalo, Louisiana street, 783; fare, rates in villages and third-class cities on certain grades, 866; Brooklyn,— East Eighteenth street, 874; — East Nineteenth street, 874; — East Fourteenth street, 874; — Atlantic avenue, X, 175;— Ashland place, 176,324; villages in Nassau county, 175; acquisition of property, 310; Queens and Nassau counties, 316, 431; amending general act, 448; Queens and Nassau counties, exempting certain highways, 587; fares in Brooklyn and Queens boroughs, 882.

Stride Town. Seneca chief, joins in address to Governor, II, 943.

Striebel, Charles. Relief, veto, X, 178.

Stringer, Gertrude. Legitimizing illegitimate child, veto, X, 770.

Strohm, Michael. Board of Claims, veto, IX, 149.

Strom, Fred E. Claim against New York, Brooklyn maps, settlement, veto, IX, 874.

Strong, Caleb. Governor of Massachusetts, interchange of maps and statutes, II, 514.

Strong, Chapman S. Keeper Auburn prison, injuries, appropriation, veto, VII, 465.

Strong, N. T. Attorney, Seneca Indians, communication from, new form of government, IV, 506.

Strong, Samuel. General, commands Vermont militia at battle of Plattsburgh, II, 803; thanked by Legislature and presented with sword, 832; letter from Governor Tompkins, 843; reply, 844.

Strong, William. Judge Pennsylvania court, opinion, qualification of voters, IX, 95.

Stryker, Thomas J. Member of New Jersey Commission to Procure Constitutional Convention, V, 325.

Stryker, William. Canal Department, appropriation for services, veto, IX, 716.

Stuart, Alexander H. McI. Court of Claims, veto, X, 442.

Stuyvesant, Peter. Governor, Nine Men associated with, I, 2.

Subsidy. For ship building proposed, I, 281.

Subway. New York Rapid Transit Act, 1891, VIII, 1071; Syracuse, wires underground, municipal ownership, veto, IX, 789; relation to Pennsylvania Railroad Company's project concerning terminal facilities in New York, X, 401.

Suffolk County. Burning of woods in, prohibited, I, 143; inhabitants refuse to volunteer for Crown Point expedition, 570; William Nicoll and Nathaniel Woodhull, Assembly, favor colonial union, 767; defense of, II, 745; cessions of land in, how made, 825; agricultural society in, III, 945; silk culture in, 945; exempted from Town Auditor's Act, VIII, 49; annexation of Lloyd's Neck, 289; average excise license fees, 1889, 687; highways, cost of labor system, 1892, IX, 200; insane, care of, county and State systems compared, 228; Smithtown, relief of, taxation of State land, 703; transfer tax assistant, X, 108; not subject to New York city water statutes, 692.

Vetoes. Smallpox, inoculation for, II, 225; Southampton, discontinuing road, VI, 333; notaries public, relative to, 1036; Sag Harbor fire apparatus and water supply, VII, 68; taxes, collection, 807; Peconic river improvement, VIII, 846; Penataquit

SUFFOLK COUNTY—(*Continued*).
creek, improving navigation, 848; county judge and surrogate, salaries, IX, 369; digging worms on shores of, amending Game Law, 799; taxes, collector's notice, X, 310, 441; supervisors, powers under Game Law, 441; poll tax, 955.

SUFFRAGE, RIGHT OF. Denied to emancipated slaves, II, 237; restrictions on, 637; under second Constitution, III, 9; proposed limitation to free white male citizens in election of President and presidential electors, 217; danger of corruption, 158, 249, 525; equal distribution of power, 882; enlarged in Rhode Island, 1038; possessed by Indian women, IV, 504; illegal voting, bill to prevent, veto, 825; negroes not to enjoy, V, 355; protection needed, 605; conferred on negroes, 856; under United States Constitution, VI, 38; protection guaranteed, Fifteenth Amendment, 50; who may be excluded, 264; VIII, 566; exclusion of persons convicted of bribery, VI, 725; women not included, VII, 78; subject to State control, 306; in Australia and England, Governor Hill's comment on, VIII, 897; exclusion on conviction of bribery, 1002; by women, extension of, X, 21; crimes against, veto, 162.

SUGAR. Mischiefs of act, I, 684; offered by Congress, New York declines to purchase, II, 84; maple, manufacture, 313; manufacture in southern States, III, 386; beet, cultivation of, 821, see BEET SUGAR; fraud in manufacture and sale, veto, VII, 648; bounty for, veto, IX, 725; beet, bounties for, 745; X, 216.

SUGAR COLONIES. Parliamentary act to encourage, protest against, I, 240; result of, 243; inadequate market for British wares, 692.

SUICIDE. Defense by life insurance companies, veto, VII, 1098.

SUINE. Preventing sale of, VII, 700.

SULLIVAN, JAMES. Connecticut commissioner to settle claim against New York, II, 407.

SULLIVAN, JOHN. Major-general, expedition against Six Nations, publication of records, veto, VII, 934, 1084.

SULLIVAN, MARGARET and MICHAEL. Escheats, veto, IX, 370; recall of escheat bill, X, 33.

SULLIVAN, THOMAS. Claim for capture of Hardy, an escaped convict, veto, X, 62.

SULLIVAN, TIMOTHY J. Work on new capitol, appropriation, veto, VII, 498, 788; paid, 789.

SULLIVAN, TIMOTHY P. Admission to examination of attorney, veto, X, 63.

SULLIVAN COUNTY. Livingston leases in, IV, 332; Desbrosses leases in, 332; Hunter and Overings leases, 333; forest lands included in forest preserve, VIII, 23; average excise license fees, 1889, 687;

SULLIVAN COUNTY—(*Continued*).

unpaid taxes, sales for, repeal of Special Act, 749; fish hatchery, act of 1893, IX, 192; highways, cost of labor system, 1892, 200; insane, care of, county and State systems compared, 228; extending forest preserve in, X, 22.

VETOES. Highland, appropriation of certain moneys, VI, 592; excepting from provisions of County Treasurer's Act, VII, 265; town officers, compensation, repealing act, 507, 540; poorhouse keeper, exempting from act, 508; Beattie escheat, VIII, 405; Eldred, Improved Order of Red Men, Delaware Tribe, No. 44, charter, 877; fish hatchery, IX, 38; map of forest preserve in, 776; lands in, Parks claim, 797; fire wardens and assistants, compensation, 799; justice of the peace, legalizing acts, X, 62; extending forest preserve, 291; Game Law, hunting and fishing on Sunday, 589.

SULLIVAN LECTURES. Cited, IV, 358.

SULLIVAN (Town). Reimbursement for bridge over Douglass State ditch, veto, IX, 818.

SULPHUR. Manufacture of, claim relating to, II, 92.

SUMMARY PROCEEDINGS. VETOES. New York, relative to, VII, 413, 417; X, 159, 175; rents and taxes, amending Code, VII, 1094; restitution on appeal, VIII, 469; petition, amending Code, X, 450; New York, service of precept, 714, 717, 805, 806.

SUMMERS, GEORGE W. Delegate from Virginia to Washington Peace Convention, V, 311.

SUNDAY. Sale of liquor on, prohibited, II, 400; observance of, V, 220; VI, 127; proper observance of, benefits of Saturday half-holiday, VIII, 537; Columbian Exposition, New York's exhibit not to be opened on, 933; sale of liquor on, should not be permitted, X, 356.

VETOES. Observance, Game Law, VI, 505; processions and parades, music, VII, 335; trades and mechanical employments on, IX, 623; barbering on, 804; sale and delivery of uncooked flesh foods, X, 280, 292; hunting and fishing in Sullivan county, 589.

SUNDAY MERCURY. Act for relief of, VIII, 128.

SUNDAY SCHOOLS. Established, III, 33; mentioned, 160, 292; in State prisons, 861.

SUNDERLAND, LORD. Letters from, I, 140.

SUPERINTENDENT OF BANKS. Office created, IV, 564; report, V, 449, 527; VI, 112; examination of savings banks, 232; supervision of trust companies, 622; IX, 561; charges against Superintendent Ellis, VII, 56, 65; should control and regulate authorization of trust companies, VIII, 6; supervision of individual bankers, 7; department

SUPERINTENDENT OF BANKS — (*Continued*).

    self-supporting, X, 119; second deputy, office created, 369; supervision of building, loan and kindred associations, 369; incidental expenses, appropriations, veto, 552; charges against Mr. Kilburn, 872.

SUPERINTENDENT OF BROTHERTOWN INDIANS. Report, intrusions, II, 929; annual report, 991, 1027, 1060, 1115; III, 96, 182, 218.

SUPERINTENDENT OF CANALS. Proposed appointment by Governor, VI, 397.

SUPERINTENDENT OF CANAL REPAIRS. Abolishing office, veto, VI, 344.

SUPERINTENDENT OF COAST SURVEY. Member of board on Brooklyn pier and bulkhead lines, VI, 452; communication from, protection of signals and stations, 991.

SUPERINTENDENT OF COMMON SCHOOLS. Office created, II, 967; office abolished, 1050; Secretary of State to act as, 1050; unable to visit schools, III, 117; supervision of New York Institution for the Instruction of the Deaf and Dumb, 292, 874; to furnish Hall's Lectures on School Keeping to school districts, 378; supervision of New York Institution for the Blind, 716; supervision of school district libraries, 746; supervision of Albany normal school, IV, 67, 265; pupils in New York Institution for Instruction of Deaf and Dumb, IV, 643; requested to join in International Education Exhibition, London, 752; office abolished, 716.

SUPERINTENDENT OF FINANCE. Communication from, II, 146, 167; Robert Morris, letter from, 152, 180; papers from, 190.

SUPERINTENDENT OF HIGHWAYS. Office created, II, 385; communication from, Westchester county, 410.

SUPERINTENDENT OF INDIAN AFFAIRS. Sir William Johnson, papers sent to, I, 727; Jasper Parish, compensation of, II, 607.

SUPERINTENDENT OF INSURANCE. Office created, V, 75; report, 275, 376, 450; charges against Superintendent Smyth, VII, 180, 319; department self-supporting, X, 119.

SUPERINTENDENT OF NEW STOCKBRIDGE INDIANS. Report, intrusions, II, 939; report, 991, 1027, 1060, 1115; III, 96, 182, 218.

SUPERINTENDENT OF THE POOR. Reports by, III, 294; instruction of paupers, 346; vacancy in office, how filled, 516; method of appointment, 719, 770, 872; supervisor not eligible, VI, 424; Legislature cannot appoint, 425.

    VETOES. Schenectady county, Clute, legalizing election, VI, 424; Albany county, 504; Erie county, transfer of powers, VII, 441; Westchester county, relative to, 508; Columbia county, relative to, 508; Fulton county, election, 930; appeals, VIII, 130, 199; Lewis county, reducing number, 461; Clinton county, keeper of poorhouse, 537; election, amending act, 1038.

SUPERINTENDENT OF PUBLIC BUILDINGS. Office created, VII, 837; duties
   of, 982; authorizing purchase of marble group "Struggle for Liberty," veto, IX, 812; efficient work of, X, 121.
SUPERINTENDENT OF PUBLIC INSTRUCTION. Office created, IV, 716; work
   commended, V, 83; *ex officio* trustee of State asylum for idiots,
   88; report, 448, 522, 602; supervision of Oswego training school,
   448; member of Commission on Normal Schools, 695; how
   chosen, VI, 398; teachers' certificates, 948; rooms in new capitol,
   VII, 694; *ex officio* Regent of University, VIII, 169; licensing
   teachers throughout State, 448; deputy, act increasing salary,
   565; teachers' classes, transfer from Regents, 791; should possess
   general jurisdiction to license teachers, IX, 600; relations with
   University, 1901, X, 227; apportionment of appropriation for
   high school tuition, 515; office abolished, 115, 605.
   VETOES. Establishing department for instruction of teachers in
      anatomy and kindred subjects, VII, 923; salary of deputy, VIII,
      72, new act passed; law books, 246; uniform examination of
      teachers, deficiency appropriation, 865; State certificates, ex-
      amination, deficiency appropriation, 865; clerk hire, deficiency,
      866; furniture, books and office expenses, deficiency, 866; Man-
      ual of Patriotism, publication and distribution, X, 297; legal
      expenses, Waters case, 561; chief of statistical bureau, salary,
      561; inspector of various schools, compensation, 637; inspector,
      traveling expenses, 637; six inspectors, compensation, 637; con-
      tract with American Museum of Natural History, appropriation,
      638.
SUPERINTENDENT OF PUBLIC WORKS. Office created, VI, 397, 934; VII,
   11, 50, 143, 235, 358, 423; act fixing salary and bond, 12; statement of powers, 235, 358, 365; general legislation, 1882, 423;
   Canal Department, Civil Service Act of 1883 not applicable, 838;
   appointment of bridge tenders, 1024; appointment, confirmation
   by Senate, VIII, 487; should be permitted to exercise his own
   discretion as to doing work by contract or otherwise, 521; quoted,
   recommends general appropriations for canal repairs, 516;
   appointment of inspectors of vessels, 1121; canal towage experiments authorized, IX, 169; member of New Capitol Commission, 1895, 545; department, effect of civil service provision of
   Constitution of 1894, 549, 663; to complete capitol, 746; communication from Superintendent Aldridge, recommending canal
   investigation, 1898, 850.

SUPERINTENDENT OF PUBLIC WORKS — (*Continued*).

VETOES. Act relative to, VII, 49; authorizing return of certain certificates of deposit, 545; preventing damages from filling up Mill creek, Schenectady, 937; canal bridge, Genesee street, Utica, VIII, 206; dredging Catskill creek, 248; Saugerties harbor and creek, improvement, 249; clerks, expenses of collectors and inspectors, X, 422.

SUPERINTENDENT OF SALT SPRINGS. Office created, III, 82; duties of, 149; prohibited from engaging in inconsistent business, IV, 26; report, V, 20, 699; VI, 16.

SUPERINTENDENT OF STATE LAND SURVEY. Bill to create office, 1894, veto, IX, 423; survey of boundary between Lewis and Herkimer counties, veto, 856; office abolished, X, 112.

SUPERINTENDENT OF STATE PRINTING. Creating office, veto, IX, 70.

SUPERINTENDENT OF STATE PRISONS. Office created, V, 78, 373; VI, 109, 233, 355, 398, 942, 984; VII, 11, 424, 519, 963; proposed appointment by Governor, VI, 397; salary fixed, VII, 9; transfer of female convicts, 10; various appropriations, veto, 485, 784; contract labor prohibited, 957; proposed supervision of reformatories and penitentiaries, VIII, 12; employs prisoners on State account, 165, 477; prison labor, authorized to use piece price plan, 168; appointment, confirmation by Senate, 487; communication from, employment of convicts, 644; department, effect of civil service provision, Constitution of 1894, IX, 549, 663; electrocution apparatus, purchase of patent rights, veto, X, 567; Bertillon method of identifying criminals, amending acts, veto, 707.

SUPERINTENDENT OF WEIGHTS AND MEASURES. Report, V, 377; communication, readjustment of standards, 570; salary, veto, VII, 907; removal of standards to new capitol, reappropriation, veto, VIII, 246; Governor Odell recommends abolition of office, X, 194.

SUPERVISOR-AT-LARGE. Kings county, powers and duties, IX, 584.

SUPERVISORS. See also BOARD OF SUPERVISORS. Legislature cannot delegate assessors' power to, II, 41; powers under Tax Law, 235; Delaware county, join anti-rent associations, IV, 302; to disburse school moneys, 843; not apportioned according to population, VI, 80; laws should be uniform, 165; ineligible to office of superintendent of poor, 424; Brooklyn, filling vacancies, act relative to, IX, 223.

VETOES. Albany county, VI, 165; compensation, amending general act, VII, 131; Erie county, relative to, 206; preservation of records, 268; Foley, New York, salary, 643, 933; bond, Sangerfield, refunding surety for payment on, 753; Onondaga county, salaries, 806; compensation, exempting Monroe county, 883; Monroe, Orleans and Broome counties, fixing compensation,

SUPERVISORS — (*Continued*).
1115; Palmyra, exempting from prohibition against holding school office, VIII, 47; Monroe and Orleans counties, compensation, 129.

SUPPLEMENTARY PROCEEDINGS. VETOES. New section, amending Code, IX, 792; for collection of taxes, X, 592.

SUPPLY BILL. Purpose of, V, 263; improper use of, VI, 641; after 1874, action on, VI, 866, 921, 1001; VII, 81, 218, 372, 458, 581, 777, 901, 1078; VIII, 106, 245, 418, 546, 839, 1135; IX, 75, 290, 401, 712, 767; X, 51, 293, 295, 422, 555, 639, 784, 933; supplemental, action on, IX, 533, 605, 713, 774; X, 430, 571, 648, 795.

SUPREME COURT. See COURT, SUPREME.

SUPREME COURT COMMISSIONERS. Proposition to establish, X, 516; bill to establish, veto, 662; historical sketch of office, 669; powers under early statutes, 670; office abolished in 1846, 670; adding new section to Code providing for cases of appointment of, veto, 709.

SUPREME GRANGE LIFE ASSOCIATION. Exemption from payment before commencing business, veto, IX, 802.

SURGEON-GENERAL. Report, V, 412, 486, 571, 641, 724.

SURGEON. Petition for appointment of Kerr at Oswego, I, 258; petition for appointment of Petrie at Forts Herkimer and Dayton, II, 117; in military service, pay of, 134; and physicians, college of, 317, 904; educational requirements, 905; evidence, confidential communications, veto, IX, 44.

SURGERY. Act to regulate practice of, I, 11.

SURROGATE. Not to be appointed in New York, II, 258; regulating method of appointment, III, 7; Chenango county, charges against Judge Prindle, VI, 440; method of removal, 833; when separate, may be chosen, VII, 615; New York, bill relative to, returned for amendment, 1028, 1072; New York, additional, act for, IX, 122; constitutional provision, 1894, 122; salary, how fixed, 124; Rensselaer county, increasing salary, 224; special, constitutional provision, X, 675.

VETOES. Special, Washington county, IV, 776; VII, 551; increasing compensation, Monroe county, 414; Seneca county, compensation, 549; Clinton county, powers of county judge conferred on, 614; clerk, compensation, 649; New York, official term, expenses of proceedings relative to, 804; Niagara county, compensation, VIII, 1038; Oneida county, new seal, 1096; Rensselaer county, increasing compensation, IX, 107, 108; transfer tax clerk, fees, 273; Suffolk county, salary, 369; Albany county, fixing salary, 624; Queens county, compensation, 800; X, 584; special, term of office in certain counties, 700; Queens county, salary, 711.

SURROGATE'S COURT. See COURT, SURROGATE.

SURVEY. State, need of, IV, 652; New York harbor, V, 21.

SURVEYOR OF CUSTOMS. At Oyster Bay, appointment of, I, 83.

SURVEYOR-GENERAL. To ascertain taxable real property, II, 184; act relating to, 224; difficulties of administering office, 256; advances to, 262; letter from, 270, 322, 351, 369, 387; report of, Pennsylvania boundary, 272; map of military tract, 286; letter from, ascertaining Massachusetts boundary line, 306; report, 330; to ascertain Massachusetts boundary line, 351; authorized to repair State seal, 404; survey of Niagara lands, 411; letter from, survey of patented lands, 432; letter from, map of St. Regis lands, 454; to execute deeds of salt lands, 456; office for, 516; treaty with Oneidas, 519; authorized to lease Black Rock ferry, 605; member of Commission to make Cessions to United States, 825; to dispose of Colonie arsenal, 829; member of Canal Board, 901; sale of Oneida land for church, 930; to lay out St. Regis village, 986; communication from, land in Fish Creek reservation, 999; communication from, Konkapot claim, 1120; death of Simeon De Witt, III, 526; how chosen, 1004.

SURVEYOR OF THE PORT, NEW YORK. Supervision of customs officers, II, 1066.

SUSPENSION BRIDGE. Immigrant passengers, protection of, IV, 793; Niagara University incorporated at, VII, 947.

SUSQUEHANNA RIVER. New York and Pennsylvania boundary on, I, 761; canal connection with Seneca lake, II, 918, 965, 1011; improvement of, 965; canal connection with Genesee and Allegany rivers, III, 70; canal connection with Erie canal, 70, 165; canal connection with Seneca lake, 70; dam, amending act relative to, veto, V, 652, 659; veto message withdrawn, bill signed, 659; Binghamton, supervision of bridges, VI, 150.

SUSQUEHANNA TURNPIKE COMPANY. Abandoning part of road, veto, VIII, 539.

SUSQUEHANNA VALLEY ORPHANS' HOME, BINGHAMTON. Improvements, appropriation, veto, VII, 90.

SUTHERLAND, JACOB. District attorney, conduct of elections, II, 1068.

SWAN, GEORGE. Affidavit by, I, 328.

SWARTWOUT, BERNARDUS. See Fitzpatrick relief bill, VI, 159.

SWARTWOUT, JACOBUS. Major, communication from, relative to expected invasion by French and Indians, I, 366.

SWARTWOUT, JOHN. Brigadier-general, commands brigade on Staten Island, II, 809.

SWARTWOUT, PHILIP. House burned and family murdered by Indians, I, 593.

SWARTWOUT, ROBERT. Lieutenant-colonel, commands troops at Narrows, II, 746.

SWEARING. Act to prevent profane, I, 12.

SWEDEN. Illiteracy as compared with New York, X, 859.

SWEDEN, NEW YORK. Soldiers and sailors' monument, veto, X, 703.

SWEENEY, ROBERT J. New York fire department, reappointment, veto, X, 818.

SWEET, S. H. Requests approval of Harvey rapid transit bill, VIII, 125.

SWIFT, ASA R. Son of Gen. John Swift, presented with sword by Legislature, letter from Governor Tompkins, II, 845; reply, 846.

SWIFT, FRANCIS. Contractor, quarantine buildings, appropriation, veto, VII, 373; claim rejected by Court of Appeals, 373.

SWIFT, JOHN. Brigadier-general, killed at Fort George, son presented with sword by Legislature, II, 832.

SWIFT, MRS. JOHN. Widow of Gen. John Swift, letter from Governor Tompkins transmitting resolutions of Legislature, II, 845.

SWIFT, JOSEPH G. Brigadier-general, engineer, Rouse's Point fortifications, II, 878; surveyor of the port, New York, alleged improper conduct at elections, 1066.

SWIFT, PHILETUS. Colonel, service on Niagara frontier, 1812, II, 746; regiment supplied with State arms, 775.

SWIKEHARD, JULIA C. Commissioner of deeds, legalizing acts, veto, IX, 150.

SWINBURNE ISLAND. Improvements, appropriation, 1892, IX, 205; repairs and improvements, 1893, 292.

    VETOES. Artesian wells, IX, 292; painting buildings, 292; quarantine buildings on, 777; general repairs, dock, X, 549; quarantine repairs, 792.

SWINE. Act to prevent running at large, I, 10; act authorizing local ordinances concerning, 12; prevention of infectious diseases among, VI, 28.

SWITZERLAND. Illiteracy as compared with New York, X, 859.

SYLVAN BEACH. Village charter, veto, VIII, 1131; note on acts relating to, 1131.

SYLVESTER, PETER. Regent, death of, II, 644.

SYMONS, THOMAS W. Major, United States army, member of Canal Investigating Commission, 1899, X, 75; member of Canal Advisory Board, 629.

SYNOD OF ASSOCIATE REFORMED CHURCHES IN AMERICA. Joins in movement for fast day, II, 715.

SYPHONS. Used in connection with certain drinks, veto, IX, 267.

SYRACUSE. Prosperity resulting from manufacture of salt, III, 708; salt spring in, 856; State Fair at, IV, 478; idiot asylum located near, 555, 791; armory at, V, 175, 642; bi-partisan police com-

SYRACUSE —(*Continued*).

    missioners, VI, 445; riots of 1877, VII, 152; water department established, VIII, 258; number of excise licenses, 1887, 359; jail limits include city, 632; excise license fees, 1889, 686; increasing salaries, 828; Water Act, 1890, 1015; law library, IX, 46; a city of the second class, 678; claims against, audit, X, 288; department of assessment and taxation, supplemental act, 1906, 876; Oswego canal bridge, North Salina street, act of 1906, 929.

    VETOES. Relief of, VI, 185; canal bridge, 324; penitentiary, maintenance of convicts, 587; rebuilding canal walls, 855; canal footbridge, Franklin street, 857; canal raceway wall, 868; armory, replacing property destroyed by fire, 875; Oswego canal swingbridge, Salina street, 1005; assessment on State property, VII, 86, 228, 472, 585, 928; Oswego canal, lift-bridge, Salina and Bridge streets, 95, 232, 366, 456; police and fire commissioners, 317; bridge, Catherine street, 364; fire department, 1098; IX, 789, 790; Marvin escheat, VII, 1107; waterworks company, purchase of property, VIII, 469; State law library, appropriation, 856; canal bridge, Crouse avenue, 855; canal bridge, Clinton street, 886; canal bridge, Crouse avenue or Beach street, IX, 245; exempting bonds from taxation, 450; amending charter, VII, 267; IX, 628, 631, 633, 727, 789, 790; culvert under Harbor brook, 731; high school, new site and building, 731; Onondaga creek and Harbor brook, 734; subways, municipal ownership, 789; police justice, warrants, bonds and fines, amending Police Pension Act, 790; officers, relative to, 790; bridge, Onondaga creek, West Water street, 790; Bridge street canal bridge, 870; Westcott street canal bridge, 870; light and heat supply, investigation of sources, X, 59; electric light plant, 327, 474; canal bridge, North Salina street, 327; Municipal Court, practice and fees of jurors, 441; filling mill race and side cuts, 569, 643; legalizing local assessment, 634, 705; assessments for local improvements, 815; department of assessment and taxation, supplemental act, 815; repealing certain acts, 960.

SYRACUSE AND AUBURN RAILROAD. Completion of, III, 786; State aid to, IV, 10.

SYRACUSE, CHENANGO AND NEW YORK RAILROAD COMPANY. Using Chenango canal towing path, veto, VII, 268.

SYRACUSE INSTITUTION FOR FEEBLE-MINDED CHILDREN. Successor to State Asylum for Idiots, IV, 556; electric light plant, veto, VIII, 1138; laundry machinery and sidewalks, veto, X, 294; how classified, 334.

SYRACUSE AND NORTHERN RAILROAD. Railroad aid, relief of certain towns, veto, VIII, 371.

SYRACUSE RAPID TRANSIT RAILWAY COMPANY. Contribution to expense of constructing canal bridge, X, 929.

SYRACUSE AND UTICA RAILROAD COMPANY. Consolidation with other companies authorized, V, 803.

SYRACUSE WATER COMPANY. VETOES. Supplying adjacent villages, VII, 1100; contract with Danforth, 1105; sale of property, VIII, 469.

SYRUPS. Fraud in manufacture and sale, veto, VII, 648.

T.

TABER, AZOR. Letter from, anti-rent troubles, III, 837.

TABOR, CHARLES F. Attorney-General, quoted, constitutionality of statutes authorizing women to vote at school meetings, IX, 95.

TAGHKANICK. Reformed Low Dutch church, changing name, veto, VII, 807.

TALL CHIEF, WILLIAM. Seneca Indian chief, monument for, veto, VIII, 110.

TALCOTT, W. H. Member of board of engineers, New York harbor defense, V, 568.

TALLMADGE, BENJAMIN. Major, letter from, conditions in Westchester county, II, 113.

TALLMADGE, NATHANIEL P. Chosen United States Senator, III, 784; resignation, IV, 154.

TAMSEN, EDWARD J. H. Sheriff, New York, charges against, expenses of investigation, appropriation, veto, IX, 777.

TANEY, ROGER B. Chief justice, United States Supreme Court, opinion, obligation of contracts, IV, 349.

TANNER, HUDSON C. Board of Claims, veto, VIII, 292.

TAPPAN. Washington's headquarters, purchase of, veto, VII, 410.

TAPPAN, CHRISTOPHER. Governor Clinton receives Senate's address at house of, II, 14.

TAR. Proposed manufacture of, I, 146; communication from Lords of Trade relative to, 188.

TARBELL, JONATHAN. Member of Connecticut Boundary Commission, V, 112.

TARBELL, PETER. Appointed trustee of St. Regis Indians, II, 938.

TARBUSH, PETER. . Service of process on, Van Rensselaer rent, III, 825.

TARIFF. Imports from other colonies, I, 115; on European imports, 198, 211; proposed revision of, 247; exempting vessels and stores intended for Canadian expedition, 420; on importations from England, protest against, 773; general note on, II, 275; under control of national government, 899; protective, recommended by Legislature,

TARIFF —(*Continued*).

III, 24, 1041; South Carolina resolutions protesting against, 218, 263; Georgia protests against increase of duties, 221; Virginia opposes, 280; Pennsylvania sustains, 315; Delaware and Ohio sustain, 318; Louisiana sustains, 354; Maine urges revision of, 387; power of Congress, 432; proposed convention to reconsider, 433; proposed modification of, 436; permanency desired, 459; Connecticut sustains, 482, 972; reduction of, 486; Alabama against, 907; Mississippi against, 913; Massachusetts favors, 929; New Jersey favors, 988; of 1846 causes suspension of industries, IV, 570, 616; railroad bars, Alabama recommends temporary suspension of, 864; on wool, Maine urges increase, V, 423; Governor Hoffman protests against, VI, 131, 247; favors special interests, 132.

TARRYTOWN. VETOES. Construction of sewers, VIII, 462; ferry to Nyack, continuance, 880.

TATE, HENRY M. Accountant, service to Senate Committee on Cities, appropriation, veto, VIII, 1140.

TAU CHAPTER OF THE DELTA KAPPA EPSILON FRATERNITY, CLINTON. Charter, veto, VI, 592.

TAVERN. Justices' courts usually held in, II, 170; license of, IV, 753.

TAX. General statistics, VI, 6, 101, 228, 349, 527, 616, 722, 878, 917, 1012; VII, 24, 139, 276, 421, 513, 681, 816, 941; VIII, 4, 497, 663, 934, 1082; IX, 820; proposed, on paper used in legal proceedings, I, 248; bills of credit proposed, pending collection of, 370; for Canadian expedition, 374; for war purposes, 446; excise, collection of, 529; poll tax on slaves suggested, 574, 606, 618; excise on tea, 574, 606, 617; stamp tax, 574, 606, 617; equality of, II, 40, 60; in aid of national government, 77; to be paid in specie, 97; for support of national government, 186; vestrymen authorized to impose, 212; preferable to loan, 423; direct, imposed by United States, 788, 906; on salt, 902, 1010; on steamboat passengers, 902, 1010; on auction sales, 902; reduction of, 907; III, 58; special, on territory contiguous to canals, II, 1012; Federal power to impose on Bank of United States for business in particular State, 1077; State, discontinued, III, 232, 322, 412, 503, 543; on seamen, 343; direct, should be resumed, 503; direct, under Federal Constitution, 622; direct, revived, 959, 1008; IV, 17; bill for collection of taxes returned without action, III, 1032; passengers on foreign vessels, IV, 75; vote for, on State loan, 107; proposed on suits in Supreme Court, 368; revision of laws, 435, 480; unpaid, sales for, 436; reducing rate, 598; none on exports from State, 667; creation of State debt, 677; rate increased, 680; sale of

TAX —(*Continued*).

Seneca land for, release of, V, 36; for canal debt, 50; State, summary of, 73; extending time for collection, V, 91, 117, 119, 215, 263, 343, 370; assessment-roll, assessor's oath, 175; increased for war purposes, 369; direct, by Federal government, 1861, 388; annulment for invalidity, 736; law must state object of, 817; VI, 584; VII, 220, 772; IX, 60; proposed Code, commission of 1870, VI, 428; levy, increase by Comptroller to cover deficiencies, 525; when to be paid by county, 630; to cover defalcation in State Treasurer's office, 634; appropriations, reenactment after two years, 864; rate of, 878; comparative statement, 879, 1012; VII, 273; VIII, 146; reimbursing collectors for losses, Oneida county, unconstitutional, VII, 753; amount limited in certain counties and cities, constitutional provision, VIII, 188; corporations, organization, 305; on notaries public, 305; on sales of liquor, 436; poll tax, see that title; on dogs, 823; rate,— 1890, 1026; — 1891, 1164; — 1892, IX, 122; — 1895, 588, 647; direct, United States, amount refunded to New York, VIII, 1107; owner of property entitled to notice of assessment, IX, 60; separate act for State care of insane, 189, 226, 568; sales, cancellation of, 219, 300, 377; on foreign insurance companies for benefit of volunteer firemen, 249; on traffic in intoxicating liquors, 666; on mortgages, X, 81, 197, 200, 524, 763, 800, 836, 885; proposed on bank stock, 81, 199; corporations, statutes noted, 198; proposed on capital of trust companies, 199; on premiums of insurance companies, 200; franchise on trust companies, 200; franchise of savings banks, 200; direct, discontinued, IX, 296; X, 459, 532, 577, 595, 633, 922; franchise tax on transfer of stocks, 490; commission created, 1906, 837; mortgages, recording tax, 1906, 885, 920.

VETOES. First State act, II, 9, 39; general bill, 52, 59, 172; new bill passed, support of poor, 95; act imposing, suspension of, 128; payable in specie, 134; general bill, 213; amending Croton Water Act, IV, 773; New York city, V, 221; assessment-rolls, Oswegatchie, VI, 88; Columbia county, equalizing assessments, 95; State, equalizing among counties, 332; non-resident, highways, Essex and Hamilton, 338; highways, Hamilton and Warren counties, 442; Morrisania and West Farms, collection of, 589; Harlem, Second Baptist church, relief from assessment, 710; Church of the Resurrection, relief from assessments, 711; Auburn, assessments on State property, refunding, 869; for canal sinking fund, 1010; assessment on State property at Syracuse, VII, 86, 585; corporations, amending act, 807, 1096;

TAX — (*Continued*).

on manufacturers, Albany, VIII, 468; franchise, equalizing, 640; on beverages, 1889, 688, 797; on dogs, Tonawanda Indian reservation, IX, 725; franchise on corporation using pneumatic tubes, 794; Schuyler county, special, for benefit of State, 796; cancellation, Mittnacht claim, Comptroller to hear, 815; Greenburgh, assessment, when made, compensation of assessors, 817; Missionary Society of the Most Holy Redeemer, release from existing assessments, 868; White Plains, for fire protection, X, 592; on mortgages, 809, 885; poll tax, — exempting Westchester county, 952; — Suffolk and Westchester counties, 955; — in towns under money system, 956; stock transfers, amending act, 958.

TAXATION (Colony). Municipal, support of poor, I, 10; by Governor and Council, 13; for public purposes, 15, 16, 20, 33, 40; for payment of public debt, 32; heavy, in colony, 37; complaint of inequality in Westchester, 42; imports from other colonies, 115; for general purposes, 216; of intoxicating liquors, 529; poll tax on slaves suggested, 574, 606, 618; excise on tea, 574, 606, 617; stamp duty, 574, 606, 617; only by consent, 683, 688, 769, 772; Assembly petition relative to, 688; without representation, Assembly denies right of, 683, 696, 704, 705, 729, 772; II, 95; one part of dominion not to tax another part, I, 699; colony should impose its own burdens, 700; stamp acts, effect of, 704.

TAXATION (State). See also INDIRECT TAXATION. Arbitrary assessments on certain kinds of business, II, 59; delegation of power, 61, 95; revision of system, 183, 187, 383, 507; ascertaining taxable real property, 184; Federal system, convention to prepare, 190; III, 433; of imports, II, 199; ascertaining value of taxable property, 219; by municipal corporations, 315; equality, 400, 402; general act passed, 423, 465; of Mississippi river commerce, protest against, 606; of State property for local purposes, 680, 895, 953, 999, 1115; of bank stock, 700; exemption of certain manufacturing establishments, 876; of territory immediately contiguous to canals, 1012; State tax discontinued, III, 232, 322, 412, 503, 543; in England, to meet heavy loans, 325; advantages of indirect, 332; indiscriminate, dangers of, 333; direct, should be resumed, 413; direct preferable to indirect, 439; of non-resident creditors, 440; not favored for internal improvements, 796; direct tax revived, 959, 1008; IV, 17; principles applicable to internal improvements, IV, 10; number of acres assessed, 24, 64; local, rate of, 24; equalizing assessments between counties, 25; State Board of Equalization created,

TAXATION (State)—(*Continued*).

25; assessment of personal property, 64; passengers on foreign vessels, 75; reserved rents, 242, 338, 357, 653; double, subject considered, 340; revision of laws, 435, 480; V, 281, 369; personal property, IV, 436, 480; local assessments, 437; for sinking funds, 473; Tuscarora Indians, protest against, 507; for schools, inequality of, 550; inequality of assessments, 564; large increase in assessments, 597; State Board of Equalization created, V, 91, 175; oath of assessors, 175; of Indian lands, 200; real estate bears undue share of, 369; to meet Federal direct tax, 391; assessment, notice of hearing, 512; general statement, 690; defective methods of assessing personal property, 691; statement by owner of property, 691; powers of municipal corporations, 735; exemption of railroad aid bonds, 813; burdens, by whom borne, 821; personal property, wide difference in assessments in various States, 825; in cities, right of local supervision, VI, 33; village, aiding educational institution, 78; by corporations, cemeteries, 184; laws amended, 226; Revision Commission, 238, 269, 370; bank capital, 280; powers of boards of supervisors should not be transferred to Comptroller, 316; New York not sufficiently liberal in exemptions, 371; buildings, plan of Tax Commission, 372; relation to population and property, 412; real and personal estate, inequality of assessment, 553; VII, 942; of Indian lands prohibited, VI, 704; for canals, comparative statement, 791; comparative statement, 1875, 882; farm divided by town line, 1033; increased valuations, VII, 24; exempting churches, 25; bank surplus, 25; education, when proper object of, 156; revision needed, 421, 514, 681, 816; VIII, 152, 298, 478, 680, 926, 1062; X, 2, 80; joint legislative investigating committee appointed, VII, 422, 538; corporations, act of 1880, 454, 682; reduction in assessment of personal property, 514; banks and moneyed institutions, 515; savings banks, surplus, 571; sales of liquor, 571; transfer tax, 571; trust companies, surplus, 571; mortgages, 571; transfers of stock, 571; State property should not be assessed for local purposes, VI, 869; VII, 86, 228, 472, 585; abolishing deduction for debts, 943; collateral inheritance, act relative to, VIII, 102; deducting debts, 153, 1065; Senate investigation, 1886, 155; amount limited in certain counties and cities, constitutional provision, 188; failure to make assessment, new authorized, Milo, 257; inefficient administration of laws, 307; imposed by license fees, 357; of occupations should be uniform, 447; equalizing burdens recommended by Repub-

TAXATION (State)—(*Continued*).

lican State Convention, 1887, 478; corporations, evidences of debt, 480; IX, 10; New York Historical Society, changing site, exemption continued, VIII, 824; historical societies, property exempt from, 824; New York Hospital, changing site, exemption continued, 824; hospitals, property exempt from, 824; exemption, fire companies, 878, 972; new Tax Law, 1896, 929; exemption laws should be uniform, 973; probation and succession tax, 1067; exemption, New York and Brooklyn bridge, IX, 91; restricting deduction of debts, act for, 93; revision plans, 1892, 158; forest preserve lands, 187; exemption, special laws prohibited, 232; direct, field should be enlarged, 539; of State land in Smithtown, 703; State Revision Commission created, 1898, 846; joint legislative committee, 1899, X, 3, 37; report, 81; revision, Governor Roosevelt's special message, 1899, 35; franchise, general act, 1899, 46; " power of taxation is power of destruction," 67; real property bears undue burdens, 80; of foreign capital, 82; foreign corporations, 367; bank stock, 368; trust companies, 368; franchise, earning capacity as basis of tax, 487; lands in forest preserve, 607; personal property assessments, 620; life insurance premiums, new rule, 722; transfers of stock, 769, 836; joint legislative committee, 1899, report, 801, 886.

VETOES. First State act, II, 9, 39; general bill, 52, 59, new bill passed; assessment of corporate stock, 777; corporations, IV, 775; aiding manufacturing establishment, VI, 180; extending relief act, 278; protection of taxpayers, 429, new act passed; powers of assessors, Newtown, 450; delegation of power of, to private corporation, 850; foreign capital, VII, 445; assessment of corporations, amending Revised Statutes, 502; corporations in New York, 777; telegraph, telephone and electric light lines, 934; banks, amending act, 936; assessments, regulating and equalizing, 1109; assessments for local improvements, New York, VIII, 293; bucket shops, 445; illegal assessments, review of, costs, 466; Erie county, equalizing real estate, 752; property liable to, 890; assessments, amending Revised Statutes, 1038; Brooklyn, stocks and bonds, IX, 148; real property divided by tax district line, 803; amending general law, 803; franchise, taxing as real property, X, 63; Queens and Nassau counties, 177; Queens borough, 177; State should be deemed a unit for purpose of equalizing assessments, Schenectady bill, 262; State lands, Morehouse, relief bill, 274; New York, reservoirs, 308; assessment of State property, Rochester, appropriation, 321:

TAXATION (State), VETOES — (*Continued*).

real property, report on exemptions, 439; savings banks, 451; foreign life insurance companies, 590; Poppenhusen Institution at College Point, relative to, 700; personal property of non-residents, 876, new bill passed; State lands in Dannemora and Altona, 953.

VETOES — EXEMPTIONS. Railroad receiving local aid, VI, 164; hotel property, 215; property of Industrial Exhibition Company, 331, 482; New York Hospital, 703; Rockland County House of Good Shepherd, VII, 266; public buildings, New York and Brooklyn, 267; International Fair Association, 413; library company, 845; Ebenezer Baptist church, 931; West Side German Dispensary, New York, VIII, 294; Young Women's Association, Troy, 332; German American School Society, 460; Masonic Hall Association, Buffalo, 464; Methodist Episcopal Hospital, Brooklyn, 464; S. R. Smith Infirmary, 538; agricultural and horticultural societies, 619; Gallaudet Home, 623; Catholic Union, Albany, 623; Sanitarium for Hebrew Children, 1036; IX, 152; property purchased with pension money, repeal, IX, 113; Ladies' Deborah Nursery and Child's Protectory, 232; Rochester Homeopathic Hospital, 235; St. Vincent's Retreat for Insane, 253; Larchmont Manor Park Society, 431; Oneida, refunding bonds, 432; Pythian Association, Amsterdam, 449; Syracuse, bonds, 450; Grand Army of the Republic posts, 470; property of clergymen, 722; exempt property, assessments for local improvements, X, 595; colleges and universities, 947.

TAXES. Act for more efficient collection, I, 67; statement of arrears, 73; involuntary, free State should be exempted from, 699; payment in certificates of purchasing officers, II, 100; assessments on wheat, 114; returns by county treasurers, 147; continental, appointment of receiver, 185; large payments by people, VI, 766, 827; for common schools, comparative statement, 946; Federal, comparative statement, 957; to be paid in gold or equivalent, VII, 170, 310; unpaid, Brooklyn, act relative to, 502; large sales in Adirondack region, 657; non-payment on lands purchased from State, 984; unpaid, sales for, list of counties under special act, VIII, 749; cancellation of sales, reform needed, IX, 187; when State should not refund to corporations, 281; when to be paid into State treasury, 542; corporations, credit on resettlement, may assign claim to other corporations, 715.

VETOES. Collection of, II, 234; sales for non-payment, Rockland and Delaware counties, VI, 1035; Monroe county, collection of, 1035; Cohoes, State and county, legalizing, 1035; VII, 133; Hart-

TAXES, VETOES — (Continued).

ford, Southern Central Railroad Company, school, distribution, VI, 1035; collectors and receivers, VII, 62; assessment and collection, amending Revised Statutes, 110; Plattsburgh, collection of, 130, 265; Hudson, extending time for collection, 199; Mentz, New York Central and Hudson River Railroad Company, application of, 207; Monroe county, unpaid, sale of property for, 208; Long Island City, unpaid, collection of, 265; Thurman, highway, non-resident, 268; Erie county, assessments in Buffalo, collection, 356; Revision Commission, appointment, 407; Binghamton, extending time for collection, 412; Albany, annexed territory, 412; Flushing, correcting assessment maps, 413; redemption from sale of 1877, 414; bonds, Midland Railroad, postponement, 415; unpaid, Queens county, sales of land, 415; unpaid, Hempstead, 415; common schools, delinquent, payment of, 442; Steuben county, sales for unpaid, 506; land sold for, conveying State's interest, 656; Herkimer and Lewis counties, rejected, reassessment, 664; equalizing assessments, 666; Buffalo, unpaid, 804; Jefferson county, enforcement of, 805; Suffolk county, collection, 807; Richmond county, extending time for collection, 866; Hornellsville, extending time for collection, 878; Albany county, filing certificates of sale with assessors, 888; canals, 1881, reappropriation, 930; Erie county, unpaid, 937; railroads for school purposes, excepting Cattaraugus county, 1095; unpaid, Long Island City, VIII, 120; recovery by action against non-residents, 121; Binghamton, sale for unpaid, 392; Madison county, sale for unpaid, 411; corporations, evasions by, expense of inquiry, 418; New York, sales for, notice to unknown owners, 467; New York, 12th ward, discharge of, 638; Jefferson county, collection, 706, 1039; Niagara county, board of equalization, act creating, 737; delinquent, statements by county treasurers, 749; Wayne county, collection, 754; Rockland county, collection, 878; special act, Chautauqua and Cattaraugus counties, amending, 967; New York, 120th street, settlement, 1036; receipts by collectors, 1040; Oneida county, redemption, 1126; York, confirming and levying, IX, 59; villages, poll tax, action to recover, 62; Cohoes, bonds for, 120; review, railroad and telegraph companies, 132; Monroe county, collection, 148; New York, McCaddin property, settlement of, 238; corporations, illegal claims for, 278; Rockland county, collection, 282; Clinton, collection, 282; non-residents, sales for non-payment, 282; Richmond county, collection, 399; unpaid, Mount Vernon, bonds for, 450; villages, non-resident, report to county

TAXES —(*Continued*).

treasurer, 523; Union College, adjustment of, 534; Panama Railroad Company, refunding, 605; in fire districts, 622; property assessments, where made, 626; equalization of, 627; German Looking Glass Plate Company, refunding, 713; General Electric Company, refunding, 713; collection, amending Revised Statutes, 722; Elmwood, collection, 723; assessments, reassessments for illegal, 724; Long Island, unpaid, 726; Buffalo, amending charter, 784; Masonic Association, Utica, exemption, 791; University Settlement Society, New York, and Educational Alliance, exemption, 794; Union Methodist Episcopal church, New York, releasing from taxes, 1894, 794; Oswego county, unpaid, sales for, assignment of land, 796; Queens county, settlement of arrearages, 796; Queens county, unpaid, county treasurer's list and notice of sale, 796; schools, payment of unpaid, 800; unpaid in certain counties, sales for non-payment, 804; Beth Israel Hospital Association, exemption, 806, 810; Spalding Literary Union, exemption, 810; Gilmour, application for cancellation, Flatbush, Comptroller to hear, 810; Flushing, bonds for arrears, 819; villages, sales and redemptions, application to Plattsburgh, 819; Queens county, sales, amending act, 862; sales, amending general act, 865; House of Good Shepherd, exemption, 868; Young Men's Hebrew Association, exemption, 869; X, 179; New York, Westchester annexed district, cancellation, IX, 870; New York, unpaid, Long Island City, Jamaica, Flushing and Hempstead, X, 62; collectors' fees, 171; Missionary Society of the Most Holy Redeemer, New York, exemption, 176; New York University, exemption, 179; St. Joseph's Asylum, New York, exemption, 176; New York, foreign insurance companies, 177; cancellation, Cozine case, 263; cities, receivers of, proceedings by, 272; Morehouse, relief, 274; Suffolk county, collector's notices, 310, 441; sale, cancellation, Leech and Lord claim, 317; Queens borough, equalizing, 1898, 1899, 322; New York, Greenfield, cancellation, 325; St. John's Armenian Apostolic church, exemption, 326; collector's notice to non-residents, 386; highways, rebate for wide tire wagons, exempting certain counties, 393; corporations, State fees and taxes, 433; Cohoes, collection of arrears, 435; school districts, railroad, telephone, telegraph and pipe line companies, apportionment, 439; unpaid, sales, Clinton county, 440; Rye, receiver, bond and deputy, 442; statement and payment of, 445; cancellation,— Ostrander case, 446, 588; — Wheeler case, 447; Oneida county, collection, 447; cancellation, Warren, 448; First

TAXES, VETOES — (*Continued*).

National Bank, Ballston Spa, refund, 452; Mount Vernon, assessment and collection, 1902, 471; New York, levy and collection, 472; Buffalo, collectors of unpaid, 476; corporations acquiring property without State, exemption, 521; cancellation, Walker case, 589; assessments, when to be made in certain towns, 590; cancellation, Moriarity case, 590; Saratoga Springs, receiver, surety, 591; supplementary proceedings for collection, 592; cancellation, Doherty case, 592; unpaid, Clinton county, sales for, 595; cancellation, Osgood, 701; reimbursement, Wostergron Company, 784; Utica, legalizing, 806, 819; unpaid, sales, Richmond borough, 806; Hamilton county, redemption, Robinson, 953; cancellation, Dreyer case, 953; poll tax, Suffolk and Westchester counties, 955; cancellation, Jones, 960.

TAX LAW. Corporations, taxing franchise, VII, 454; interpretation, 454; notice of assessment and grievance day, X, 809.

TAXPAYERS. Protection of, veto, VI, 429, new act passed; appeal from town audit, 436; actions against public officers, 727, 829; actions against public officers, veto, IX, 364.

TAX RATE. 1890, VIII, 1026; 1891, 1164; 1892, IX, 122; 1895, 588, 647; 1897, 820; 1899, X, 108; 1900, 181; 1902, 459; 1903, 577; 1904, 683; low rate impracticable, Comptroller's opinion, 1895, IX, 683; comparative statement, X, 464.

TAYLER, JOHN. Senate, negotiates purchase of Cayuga land, II, 605; negotiates purchase of Oneida land, 607.

Lieutenant-Governor, becomes acting-Governor on resignation of Governor Tompkins, 887; I, pref. xii; portrait, II, 887; again elected Lieutenant-Governor, 887; purchase of Onondaga lands, 887, 888; fees of New York pilots, 888; fortifications at Rouse's Point, 890; Ohio offers aid in constructing Erie canal, 891; Sillick murder case, 894; exchange of lands with Second Christian Party of Oneida Indians, 894; street improvements about New York arsenal, 895; succeeded by Gov. De Witt Clinton, 897; letter from J. Sergeant, Jr., removal of Stockbridge Indians, 987; official service, I, pref. xii.

TAYLOR, ENOCH, 2D. Commissioner, repairing highway, Cattaraugus reservation, veto, VII, 221.

TAYLOR, JOHN. Indian negotiations, payment of expenses, II, 339; report on Indian lands, 518.

TAYLOR, RICHARD. Claim against New York, veto, X, 806.

TAYLOR, RICHARD E. New York, relief, veto, X, 581.

TAYLOR, STEPHEN. Damages, new capitol, veto, VII, 911.

TAYLOR, WILLIAM A. New York policeman, relief, veto, X, 581.

TAYLOR, WILLIAM B. Member of Adirondack Park Commission, 1872, VII, 722.

TAYLOR, ZACHARY. Invited to visit New York, IV, 420; letter declining invitation, 420; President, death of, 572.

TEA. Excise on, I, 574, 606, 617.

TEACHERS. In academies, scarcity of, II, 557; qualifications of, common schools, 725; for Lancastrian schools, 905, 972; instruction of, 904, 972, 1049; III, 61, 116, 159, 212, 337, 408, 499; IV, 115, 647; needed qualifications of, III, 116; instruction in academies, 159, 454, 499, 538, 613, 653; IV, 552, 647; proposed monitorial high schools, III, 212; offer of Rensselaer school, 219; Hall's Lectures on School Keeping to be furnished to school districts, 378; sources of supply, 652; normal schools, 652, 743; institutes, formation of, IV, 269; classes in academies, 647; V, 523, 695; number of, V, 13, 174, 448, 523, 603, 779, 851; VI, 23, 356, 528, 617, 946; VII, 19, 155, 296, 424, 518, 687, 821, 946; IX, 748; compensation too small, V, 13, 524, 604; Oswego training school, see that title; professional instruction of, 781; New York, proposed exclusion by new charter, VI, 470; State certificates, 948; Sisterhood of Grey Nuns, graduates, teachers' certificates, 948; classes in academic departments, VII, 947; New York, retirement fund, act for, IX, 411; professional training, act of 1895, 484, 564; pension fund in towns, 564; qualifications required in certain cities, 564; Mount Vernon, licenses, 598; temperance instruction, 613; proposed pedagogical department in Cornell University, X, 113; New York, salaries, act of 1900, 144, 154; training schools, act of 1894, 349; comparative statement, 1905, 736.

VETOES. Examination by school trustees, VI, 337; Clarence, employment fund, 484; common schools, instruction of, 1035; instruction of, appropriation, VII, 495; retirement, New York and Brooklyn, 606; kindergarten instruction, Oswego training school, 792; pensions, New York, 804, 931; department for instruction in anatomy and kindred subjects, 923; Cortland normal school, removed and restored, salaries, 927; wages, payment of, VIII, 240; Teachers' Mutual Benefit Association, New York, charter, 336; licenses, 448; uniform examinations, deficiency appropriation, 865; State certificate examinations, deficiency appropriation, 865; professional training, promotion of, 1037; IX, 482; instruction by American Museum of Natural History, New York, 84; conditional compensation in towns after twenty-five years' service, 463; examinations, 622; retirement fund, Rochester, 788; New York salary bill, 854; salaries, Greater New

TEACHERS —(*Continued*).

York, 859; New York, supply of, X, 172; New Rochelle, teachers' pensions, tax for, 435; New York teachers' pensions, 477; New Rochelle, retirement, 478.

TEACHERS' INSTITUTES. Formation of, IV, 269; attendance, V, 523, 604, 695, 779, 852; instruction in music, IX, 116.

VETOES. Time spent at, VIII, 291; deficiency appropriation, 1391, 1141; instruction by American Museum of Natural History, IX, 84; closing schools for, 800.

TEACHERS' MUTUAL BENEFIT ASSOCIATION, NEW YORK. Charter, veto, VIII, 336.

TEED, JAMES. Convicted of murder, not pardoned, II, 997.

TEEPLE, GEORGE. Estate of, veto, II, 708.

TELEGRAPH. Pacific, completion of, V, 388; New York, public use of, veto, VI, 706; wires, placing under ground, resolution of inquiry, VII, 865.

TELEGRAPH COMPANIES. Supervising commission recommended, VIII, 1078.

VETOES. Relative to, VII, 507; assessment, 934; review of assessments, IX, 132; Gamewell Fire Alarm Telegraph Company, claim against Far Rockaway, X, 324; taxes, apportionment between school districts, 439.

TELEGRAPH STAGE COMPANY, NEW YORK. Sale of rights and franchise, Dry Dock, East Broadway and Battery Railroad Company, veto, V, 646.

TELEPHONE COMPANIES. Supervising commission recommended, VIII, 1078. VETOES. Assessment of, VII, 934; — taxes, apportionment between school districts, X, 439.

TEMPERANCE. Instruction in schools, IX, 612.

TEMPERANCE SOCIETIES. General act for, V, 655; Grand Council of Royal Templars of Temperance, VII, 417.

TEMPLE ADAS JESHURUN SOCIETY. Holding land for cemetery purposes, veto, VI, 588.

TEMPORARY LAWS. Provision relating to, I, 8.

TENANT. Right to vote, III, 9.

TENANTS IN TAIL. Bill relating to, veto, II, 779.

TEN BROECK, ABRAHAM. Assembly, favors colonial union, I, 767; motion to consider proceedings of Continental Congress, 767.

TENBROOK, CAPTAIN. Company sent to Kinderhook, I, 463.

TEN-DAY PERIOD. Veto of bills, general note, VII, 667; constitutional provision, VIII, 434.

TENEMENT-HOUSE COMMISSION. Created for first-class cities, 1900, X, 96, 146, 206; report, 96, 206, 237; letter from Chairman de Forest, 287.

TENEMENT-HOUSES. Construction and sanitary conditions should be regulated by law, VII, 711; VIII, 317; New York police supervision, 317; New York, act relative to, 430; restricting manufactures of clothing in, IX, 164, 325; X, 7; sweat shops condemned, 8, 37; frequent revision of laws needed, 96; Commission of 1900, 96, 146, 206, 237; sweat shops, inspection and license, 189; act of 1901, 206, 286; judicial construction, 206; large number in New York, 237; amendments, 1901, 281; act amended, 1902, 395; amendments of 1903, 511; fire proof buildings, act of 1904, 632; successful operation of new statutes, 746; fire escapes, 746.

VETOES. New York,— amending Consolidation Act, VIII, 886; — changing definition, IX, 67; — improvement of, 868; license to manufacture certain articles in, X, 37.

TEN EYCK, FRANCIS J. Court of Claims, veto, X, 165.

TENIS, MARY. Petition for relief, act passed, II, 109.

TENNESSEE. Constitutional amendments,— importation of slaves, II, 589; — reducing senatorial term from six years to four years, 795; — prohibiting increase of salary of Representatives during term, 930; — election of President and Vice-President by popular vote, III, 137; — to perpetuate slavery, V, 315; Constitution, procedure to amend, II, 1058; protest against congressional nominations of President and Vice-President, III, 31; protests against distribution of Federal revenues for local internal improvements; approves President's veto of Lexington and Maysville turnpike road bill, recommends sale of public lands and appropriation of proceeds for education, 391; annexation of Texas, 1020; Governor and Legislature invited to visit Albany, V, 203; protests against New York's offer of aid to Federal government, 314; secession ordinance, 396; resolutions, expressing thanks for aid from other States in yellow fever epidemic, VII, 316; cedes to United States jurisdiction over roads on Missionary Ridge and Lookout Mountain, VIII, 1076; Centennial Exposition, 1897, negro department, report of commission to, IX, 852; Centennial Exposition, report of commission, 852.

" TENNESSEE, THE." American flag-ship salutes French vessels bringing delegates to Yorktown Centennial Celebration, VII, 738.

TENNEY, A. W. President Garfield withdraws appointment of, VII, 559.

TENTS. King to furnish, for Canadian expedition, I, 620, 634, 644, 654, 663; for army chaplain, 623; for Indian War, 677; New York's claim against Connecticut for, II, 101.

TENURES. Changing leases to, anti-rent troubles, IV, 240, 307, 359; leasehold, effect on agriculture, 334; act of 1788, 345, 359; military, abolished, 712.

TERRITORIES. Power of Congress to determine status of slavery in, IV, 506, 507, 508, 512; V, 29, 198; New Mexico, IV, 565; Utah, 565; Kansas and Nebraska, 827; organization, constitutional provision, 828; V, 29, 32; Arkansas proposition relative to slavery in, 354.

TERRY, GEORGE E. Canal Department, appropriation for services, veto, IX, 716.

TERWILLIGER, JAMES. Senate clerk, resolutions on speakership contest, V, 485; resolutions on military expenditures, 487.

TEUTONIA SINGING SOCIETY, WINFIELD. Charter, veto, VI, 341.

TEXAS. Annexation of, III, 683, 691, 975, 1020, 1051; IV, 84, 85, 416; protest against acquisition by foreign power, 85; becomes part of Union, 416 ; new States from territory of, 499; resolutions, slavery, 526; boundary settled, 565; denies compulsory power of nation against State, V, 343; secession ordinance, 396; uniform liquor tax, VIII, 437; resolutions, constitutional amendment, tenure of office, 1091.

TEXT-BOOKS. For academies, IV, 552; schools, regulating changes of, VII, 21; IX, 615; for temperance instruction, 615.

THACHER, JOHN BOYD. Mayor of Albany, chairman Capital Centenary Commission, 1897, IX, 689; letter from, relative to capital centennial, 690.

THANKSGIVING DAY. Congress appoints, II, 152; President and Governor designate after peace, following War of 1812, 824; proposed, to celebrate fall of Richmond, V, 676; a public holiday, VI, 679.

THAYER, ADIN. Canal commissioner, rejection of bids, VI, 800.

THEATERS. VETOES. Brooklyn, exits, VII, 804; regulating sale of tickets, X, 51.

THEATRICAL ENTERTAINMENTS. Suppression of, recommended by Congress, II, 56; act to prevent, veto, 85.

THEBAUD, EDOUARD. Escheat, veto, VIII, 731.

THEBAUD, EMILE. Escheat, veto, VIII, 731.

THEISS, FREDERICK. Escheat, veto, VIII, 890.

THERESA. VETOES. Aid to Utica and Black River Railroad Company, amending act, VI, 92; relief from railroad burdens, VII, 847, new bill passed; fish hatchery, State co-operating with United States, IX, 81.

THIRD AVENUE RAILROAD COMPANY. Extension of tracks, veto, V, 667.

THIRD AVENUE SAVINGS BANK. Financial condition of, VII, 67.

THIRD-CLASS CITIES. Commission on general laws, 1895, IX, 677; outline of proposed general law, 678; number of, 679; proposed uniform system of accounting, X, 25; right to vote at special elections, proposed extension to women, 730; tabulation of accounts and expenses, 764.

THIRD CLASS CITIES — (*Continued*).

VETOES. Street railroads, rates of fares on certain grades, IX, 866; contracts for lighting streets, 869; special elections, sale of liquor on days of, X, 162; reports of financial condition, amending act, 816.

THIRD JUDICIAL DEPARTMENT. How constituted, IX, 546.

THIRD JUDICIAL DISTRICT. Additional justice for, VII, 837; included in third judicial department, IX, 546.

VETOES. Supreme Court justices, salaries, VII, 257; stenographers, salaries, VIII, 699; law library, Kingston, rebinding books, X, 556; additional justices, 947.

THIRTY-DAY PERIOD. Established, VI, 642, 852; action on bills, 852, 1004; VII, 123, 249, 404, 454, 663, 774, 891; VIII, 93, 273, 436, 561, 797, 1017, 1152; IX, 230, 413, 604, 705, 756, 854; X, 48, 150, 290, 418, 542, 633, 770, 907; first application of, VI, 884; large number of bills for executive consideration, IX, 848; number in 1905, X, 865.

THISTLE BENEVOLENT ASSOCIATION OF NEW YORK. Charter, veto, IV, 531.

THOMAS, EDWARD. Ferry on Conesus lake, veto, VIII, 1098.

THOMAS, EDWIN. Auburn prison convict, crime committed by, trial, reimbursing Cayuga county, veto, VII, 87, 227, 471, 781.

THOMAS, GEORGE. Governor of Pennsylvania, letter from relative to Mohawk Indian lands, I, 355; declines to join in expense of furnishing provisions to Indians, 378.

THOMAS, HENRY. Insane convict, Sing Sing, assault on keeper, VII, 464.

THOMAS, JOHN. Assembly, favors colonial union, I, 767; Assembly, rejects motion to choose delegates to Continental Congress, 769.

THOMAS, JOHN R. Architect Eastern New York Reformatory, claim for services, veto, X, 296.

THOMAS, LORENZO. Adjutant-General, United States, order dismissing officer, V, 515.

THOMAS ASYLUM FOR ORPHAN AND DESTITUTE INDIAN CHILDREN. Communication requesting increase of appropriation, IX, 339; classed as an educational institution, X, 334.

VETOES. Repairs and improvements, VII, 489; X, 295; boiler-house and heating apparatus, VIII, 853; power-house and electric-light plant, X, 544; laundry and apparatus, 544; Phelps claim for surgical services, appropriation, 798.

THOMPSON, CHARLES. Secretary of Congress, letter to Gov. George Clinton noted, VII, 812.

THOMPSON, EUGENE. New York, relief, veto, X, 176.

THOMPSON, SILAS. Communication from, Kesler case, II, 921.

THOMPSON, SMITH. Chosen Regent, II, 753; resigns as Regent, 993; justice Supreme Court, United States, communication from, Astor case, III, 355.

THORNE, STEPHEN. Lieutenant-colonel, artillery, service on Champlain frontier, 1812, II, 744; loans cannon, 770.

THORNTON, GEORGE H. Stenographer, Senate Committee on Cities Investigation, appropriation, veto, VIII, 1141; X, 570, 647.

THORPE, HARVEY. Auburn prison convict, crime committed by, trial, reimbursing Cayuga county, veto, VII, 227, 471, 781.

THOUSAND ISLANDS. Waters of, taking sturgeon in, veto, IX, 798, 863.

THREE-FIFTHS BILLS. Roads in Coeymans, IV, 513; effect of resignation of Senators, 578; constitutional provision, IX, 618.

THROOP, ENOS T. Judge, decision as to salt lots, III, 148.

1829. Lieutenant-Governor becomes acting Governor on resignation of Governor Van Buren, III, 269; I, pref. xii; portrait, III, 269; address on assuming office, 269; education, 272; banks, 272; roads and canals, 272; finances, 273; relation of parties to government, 274; party affiliations, 275; Morgan abduction, 278; Virginia resolutions, 280, Louisiana resolutions, 281; returns for correction bill incorporating New York Sacred Music Society, 281.

1830. Annual message, III, 282; general condition of State, 282; national administration approved, 283; national debt, 283; pardons, 284; revision of Criminal Code, 284; county jails, 286; State prisons, 288; school in prisons, 289; legislative committee to visit State prisons, 290; charitable institutions, 290; infant schools, 290; New York Orphan Asylum, 291; New York House of Refuge, 291; instruction of deaf and dumb, 292; care of insane, 292; recommends hospital for indigent insane, 293; poor laws, 294; education, 294; colleges, 296; agriculture and manufactures, 297; agricultural schools, 298; finances, 299; State capable of sustaining 8,000,000 of inhabitants, 303; canal finances, 304; distribution of Federal surplus revenues, 307, 330, 898, 986; additional lateral canals, 308; aid to Delaware and Hudson Canal Company, 308; claims against United States, 308; fortifying New York harbor, 309; purchase of Oneida Indian lands, 310; banks, 310; New Jersey boundary, 311, 349; Astor claim, 312, 318, 349; corrupt practices at elections, 313; disapproves of lobby, 313; Watervliet arsenal cession, 314; counsel's report in Morgan matter, 314; Georgia resolutions, 314; Vermont resolutions, 315, 318; Pennsylvania resolutions, 315; condition of penitentiaries, 316; Delaware and Ohio resolutions, 318.

THROOP, ENOS T.—(*Continued*).

1831.   Annual message, III, 318; national affairs, 319; finances, 321; means of supplying revenue, 323; internal improvements, 327; railroads, 327; canals, 329; canal debt, 333; common schools, 336; medical colleges, 338; State prisons, 339; pardons, 340; commutations, 341; classification of murder, 341; criminal statistics, 341; county prisons, 342; New York House of Refuge, 342; quarantine establishment, 343; imprisonment for debt, 343; militia, 345; insane poor, 345; poorhouse system, 346; frauds at salt springs, 346; manufacture of salt, 347; Delaware and Hudson canal, 348; claims against United States, 349; removal of Oneida Indians to Green Bay, 349; Morgan abduction matter, 350, 354, 365; revolutionary pensions, 352; manufactures, 352; Connecticut resolutions, 353; Vermont, Mississippi and Louisiana resolutions, 354; water from Erie canal for Watervliet arsenal, 355; Ohio resolutions, 356; New Jersey suit over boundary, 356; Massachusetts resolutions, 364.

1832.   Annual message, III, 366; benign character of American institutions, 366; national prosperity, 368; early payment of national debt, 369; finances, 369; education, 372; canals, 372; special fund for internal improvements, 373; roads, 374; railroads, 374; highways, 376; common schools, 377; county poorhouse system, 378; insane poor, 378; penitentiary for females, 379; county jails, 380; infant schools, 381; industrial education, 381; State prisons, 381; Criminal Code, 383; criminal statistics, 383; pardons and commutations, 384; imprisonment for debt, 384; duty on salt, 384; militia, 385; agriculture, 386; fairs, 386; cotton and sugar, 386; silk, 387; congressional apportionment, 387; resolutions from various States, 387; revolutionary pensions, 388; Astor suits, 389; Massachusetts resolutions on northeastern boundary, 389; Tennessee resolutions, 391; Indiana resolutions, 391; adulteration of potash, 391; distribution of map, 391.

Proclamation convening extraordinary session, III, 392; Asiatic cholera, 394; report on railroads, general note, 396; appointment of Jacob S. Bogert, commissary-general, 430; official service, I, pref. xii.

THROOP, MONTGOMERY H.   Member of Statutory Revision Commission, 1870, VI, 238.

THURMAN.   Arms and supplies for, II, 771; non-resident highway taxes, veto, VII, 268.

THURMAN, ALLEN G.   Arbitrator of labor disputes in Ohio, VIII, 165.

THURSTON, ROBERT H.   Member of board of examiners of arms for National Guard, IX, 635.

TIBBITS, GEORGE. Member of Prison Investigating Commission, III, 22.

TIBBITT, WILLIAM H. Justice of peace, Fabius, legalizing acts, veto, X, 948.

TICONDEROGA. Expedition against, I, 589, 590; English defeat at, 624; French driven from, 640; investigation as to surrender of, II, 15; lands at, ceded to Regents, resumption of, 376.

TIDAL WATERWAY COMPANY. Amending charter, veto, X, 175.

TIEBOUT. See TYEBOUT.

TIERONDEQUAT (Irondequoit). Senecas grant leave to Frenchman to build house at, I, 262; Indians propose transfer of, to French, 271, 272; Lieutenant-Governor Clarke urges acquisition of, by New York, 272; land for fort at, 277; new fort at, 324.

TILDEN, SAMUEL J. Assembly, chairman select committee on anti-rent troubles, IV, 328; 1872, approves veto of cumulative voting bill, VIII, 286; Governor, portrait, VI, 719.

1875. Annual message, VI, 719; New York's influence in other States, 719; receipts and expenditures, 720; State debt, 720; taxes, 722; other departments of State, 722; State census, 723; pauperism, 724; commission to investigate management and relief of poor, 724; centennial exhibition, 724; constitutional amendments, 725; excluding persons convicted of bribery from right of suffrage, 725; uniform charters for savings banks, 725; general laws, 726; frauds and malversation by public officers, 727; imperfection of criminal laws, 727; fraudulent audit of claims, New York city, 728; civil remedies, 729; attachments against public officers for misappropriation of funds, 729; remedy for malversations in local government, 730; actions by Attorney-General against public officers to recover misappropriated funds, 732; local self-government, 733; official accountability a condition of municipal independence, 734; municipal problem, 735; Erie canal and transportation problem, 735; the natural pass of commerce, 736; the Northwest, 736; New York's liberal policy, the Erie Canal trust, 737; Erie canal not to be abandoned, 738; duty of the State, 738; lake and canal navigation cannot be assimilated, 738; lake boats unfit as canal boats, 739; enlarged locks and unenlarged waterway, 740; economy from the best group of adaptations, 740; perfecting canal the wise policy, 741; its capacity — its economy, 741; capacity ample, 741; economy per ton per mile, 742; to be increased by perfecting waterway, 742; future inventions and economies, 744; income and outgo, 744; tolls, 744; no rash innovations, 745; financial results of last three

TILDEN, SAMUEL J., 1875 — (Continued).

years, 745; paying canals, 747; non-paying canals, 747; increase income before discarding income, 747; New York the
trustee for the interests of all, 748; chief function of canal
system, New York city, 748; disposition of non-paying
canals, 749; use as feeders, 749; Commission on Disposal
of Lateral Canals, 750; New York's interest in financial
policy of United States, 750; can more currency revive prosperity, 751; currency but a part of circulating credits, 752;
bank notes and checks the same in effect, 753; relation of
currency to prices, 754; experience of England, 755; why
and how convertible currency depreciates, 756; legal tender
financing, 756; distress from falling values and lacking
capital, 760; how distress cannot be cured, 761; increase of
currency cannot cure distress, 761; changing forms and
varying volume of circulatory credits, 762; easy conditions
of resuming specie payments, 763; resumption less costly
than present impolicy, 764; results during ten years of
peace, 765; misused powers of Federal government, 765;
governments too costly, 766; taxation too burdensome, the
prostration of the South, 767; final acceptance of amendments to Federal Constitution, 767; people must tend to
public affairs, 768; disturbance in Louisiana, 769; cession
of land at Willet's Point to United States, 774; New Jersey
boundary, 775; Virginia resolutions protesting against
Federal interference in Louisiana, 776; communication from
Governor of New Jersey, quarantine jurisdiction, 776; report of commissioners on quarantine jurisdiction, 778;
Ohio, Missouri, Georgia and Pennsylvania resolutions protesting against Federal interference in Louisiana, 785; communication from director-general of Centennial Celebration,
785; West Virginia and Delaware resolutions, Federal
interference in Louisiana, 787; land ceded to United States
at West Point, 788; special message on canals, 788; probable income of canals, 790; taxation for canal purposes,
791; character of expenditures, 793; appropriations for
ordinary expenses and repairs, 796; lateral canals should
be sold, 796; appropriations for extraordinary repairs, 797;
Erie canal capacity, 797; canal lettings, 799; unbalanced
bids, 800; engineer's estimates, 803; biddings, 804; official
accountability, 804; canal commissioners, 805; inspector of
public works, 806; removal of officers, 806; regulation of

TILDEN, SAMUEL J., 1875 — (*Continued*).

canal estimates, 807; memorial, New York Historical Society, preparation of memorial volume for centennial exhibition, 809; municipal reform, 825; municipal taxation, 826; large sums paid in taxes, 827; consequences, 828; judicial remedies, 829; actions against public officers, 829; additional measures, 830; duty of State, 831; delegation of power to municipalities, 831; progress of local self-government, 832; principles, 834; conditions, 835; public officers trustees for people, 836; experience of metropolis, 836; charter of 1830, 837; interference with local government, 838; abuses of power follow power, 838; charter of 1870, 839; charter of 1873, 840; early method of preparing city charters, 841; Commission on Municipal Reform, 844; action on canal appropriation bill, 852; general considerations on reappropriation bill for extraordinary work and repairs on canals, 863; general considerations in respect to supply bill, 877; appropriation for new capitol, 877; reduction in taxation, 878; reduction in appropriations, 880; charges on canal revenue, 880; future reduction of taxation, 882; action on General Canal Act, 884; unnecessary as to ordinary repairs, 885; unconstitutional as extraordinary repairs, 887; obstacles to reform, 889; taxation and appropriation for payment of principal and interest of canal debt, 891; tax to pay floating canal debt, 891; canal awards and certificates of indebtedness, 891; reappropriation bill, 894; appropriations for expenses, collection, superintendents, and ordinary repairs, 894; appropriations for extraordinary repairs of canals, 895; history of marine court, 897.

VETOES. Black River Insurance Company, Watertown, changing name, VI, 813; ferry, Hudson river, Phillipstown, 813; consolidation of certain railroad companies, 814; Richmond County Storage and Business Company, increasing capital stock, 815; adoption of minors, 816; married women, release of dower rights, 820; Onondaga county clerk's office, records and indexes, 821; salt springs, sale and exchange of lots, 822; Canajoharie, revising village charter, 824; Rescue Hook and Ladder Company, Tonawanda, charter, 825; New York, coroners' inquests, expenses, 844; Elmira, common council, legalizing acts of, 845; New York board of police, granting new trials, 848; felony, trial, second

TILDEN, SAMUEL J., 1875, VETOES— (*Continued*).

         offense, 849; Chautauqua Lake Camp Meeting Association, taxing power, 850; Buffalo, Fillmore avenue extension, 851; items in supply bill, 866; canals, general act, 884; New York police justices, 897; State prisons and penitentiaries, commutations for good behavior, 899; women, imputing unchastity to, 901; militia, certificates of service, 1812, 902; adulteration of milk, 904; rapid transit, general act, 905; various fish and game laws, 906; New Brighton, regulating use of dock, 907; benevolent and charitable corporations, amending act, 907; Hudson river and Catskill creek, improving navigation, 908; omnibus veto, 909.

1876.   Annual message, VI, 912; general condition of State, 912; advantages of location of State, 913; debts of State, 914; sinking funds, 914; bounty debt, 915; canal debt, 916; total amount of debt, 916; constitutional restriction on public debts, 916; large indebtedness of cities, 917; taxes for State purposes, 917; reduction, 918; appropriations of 1875, 918; reduction of appropriations for canal revenues or funds, 919; items of reduction of taxes, 919; reduction of State taxes for 1876 to one-half the taxes of 1874, 921; permanent result, 923; Governor's accountability for appropriations, 925; Erie canal policy, 925; situation at last session, 927; Canal Investigating Commission, 928; income and expenses of canals, 929; comparative statement, 1874–75, 931; future measures, 933; disposition of lateral canals, 933; change in canal administration, 934; reduction of tolls, 934; new capitol, 936; insane asylums and reformatory, 938; State prisons, 941; State prisons should be self-supporting, 942; Prison Investigating Commission, 942; Superintendent of State Prisons, 942; salt springs, 943; quarantine, 943; National Guard, 944; colleges and academies, higher education, 945; common school statistics, 945; State taxes in aid of common schools, 946; method of appropriation, 947; State teachers' certificates, 948; pauperism, 949; methods of dealing with tramps, 950; revision of poor laws, 950; State census, 950; municipal government, 951; centennial exhibition, 951; banks, 951; savings banks, 952; trust, loan and indemnity companies, 953; insurance companies, 954; depression in business, 955; causes, 956; waste of national capital by excessive governmental consumption, 956; present scale of governmental

TILDEN, SAMUEL J., 1876 — (*Continued*).

expenditure, 957; aggregate taxation of eleven years, 958; relation to national savings, 958; incidental evils, 959; sacrifice caused by unskillful modes of taxation, 959; governmental class of tax consumers, 960; waste larger than national debt, 961; misgovernment in South, 961; injury to our own prosperity, 962; excessive speculation, 962; New York's interest in these questions, 964; action of Federal government the ultimate cause, 964; bank notes an insignificant part of credit machinery, 966; other instruments of credit preferred, 967; bank notes slow and difficult of increase, 968; law of depreciation of inconvertible currency, 969; how issues of legal tenders inflated prices, 970; influence of opinion and imagination, 970; causes of present reaction, 971; sound finance demanded, 974; resumption of specie payments without convulsion, 974; example of France, 976; various reports, 977; special message on Canal Investigating Commission, 978; Pennsylvania resolution, New York wharfage tax, 981; vacancy in New York marine court, 985; protection of signals and stations, coast survey, 991; extraordinary repairs, statement of canal contracts, 991; closing existing contracts for extraordinary repairs, 993; improvement of Champlain canal, 994; conferring judicial functions on Canal Board, 996; ample appropriations for defense of fraudulent canal contracts, 996; law requiring bond from parties bringing emigrants unconstitutional, 997; comparative statement of emigration, 999; importance of immigration in national development, 1000; taxes for 1874, 1876, 1012; debts paid in 1874 and 1876, 1012; sources of economies causing reduction of taxes, 1014; canal expenditures, 1015; general expenses, 1015; ordinary canal repairs, 1016; Commission on Municipal Government, 1025.

VETOES. New York convicts and paupers, employment of, VI, 982; items in supply bill, 1001; items in bill relating to canal contracts and extraordinary repairs, 1004; canal sinking fund, tax for, 1010; Kings county board of charities, 1018; item in canal awards bill, 1027; New York volunteer fire department, benevolent fund, 1028; New York district court clerks, 1029; New York local government, 1029; Ontario town meeting, legalizing proceedings, 1031; Albany, street repairs, 1031; Schenectady, additional police in,

TILDEN, SAMUEL J., 1876, VETOES — (*Continued*).

   Union College, 1032; Watervliet police justice, 1032; Rensselaer County House of Industry, board of governors, 1032;
   Vienna. real estate assessments, 1033; Seneca lake, ferry to
   Lodi Landing, 1033; Alden town meeting, legalizing election of highway commissioner, 1034; Rochester and Pine
   Creek Railway Company, changing name, 1034; omnibus
   veto, 1876, 1035.

  Electoral vote for President in 1876, VII, 33; approves limiting State census to enumeration of inhabitants, VIII, 138;
   election as Governor, platform favored uniform excise
   laws, 356; quoted,— exclusive ferry franchise, 411; —
   official accountability, 596; official service as Governor, I,
   pref. xiii.

TILDEN, PATTERSON & COMPANY. Manufacturers of powder, II, 681;
  explosion at mill, inquiry concerning, 681, 682.

TILLARY, JAMES. Resident physician, letter from, II, 520.

TILLOTSON, ROBERT. District attorney, conduct of elections, II, 1068.

TILLOTSON, THOMAS. Member of Council of Appointment, II, 314.

TIMBER. Preservation of, I, 555; permission to cut, granted to certain
  persons in Tryon county, II, 168; rapid destruction of, 1094; finds
  market in New York, III, 815; floating on streams, veto, VII, 415;
  VIII, 1041; IX, 815; in forest preserve, not to be cut, 835.

TIME. Uniform standard, corporations for securing, amending Manufacturing Corporations Act, veto, VII, 1027.

TIOGA COAL, IRON MINING AND MANUFACTURING COMPANY. State aid
  to, IV, 10, 831.

TIOGA COUNTY (New York). Connecticut land claims in, II, 370; agricultural society, III, 945; silk culture, 945; distribution of supervisors, VI, 79; average excise license fees, 1889, VIII, 687; highways, cost of labor system, 1892, IX, 200; insane, care of, county
  and State systems compared, 228; railroad strike, expenses of
  National Guard, appropriation, 594; special county judge and surrogate, term of office, X, 701.

TIOGA COUNTY (Pennsylvania). Coal in, III, 204.

TIOGA RIVER. Canal connection with Seneca lake, II, 903; III, 98; coal
  on headwaters of, 71.

TIOUGHNIOGA RIVER. Bridge over, veto, VI, 78.

TIPPLING-HOUSES. Unlicensed, suppression recommended, I, 78; excessive number of, 660; II, 427.

TIRPITZ, ALFRED P. VON. Admiral, accompanies Prince Henry to
  Assembly chamber at his reception, X, 480.

TITLE GUARANTY COMPANIES. Securities, veto, X, 955.

TITLES OF NOBILITY. See NOBILITY, TITLES OF.

TOBACCO. Cultivation of, recommended, III, 206; inspector of, 207; leaf, regulating sale in New York, veto, VI, 480; cigarettes, preventing sale to children, veto, VII, 1108; VIII, 131, 633.

TOCQUEVILLE, ALEXIS C. H., COUNT DE. Quoted, America's commercial supremacy, VII, 992.

TOLL-BRIDGE. Across Mohawk river, II, 641; across Esopus creek, veto, 1081; New Windsor, making free, veto, IX, 818; abolition of, veto, X, 813.

TOLL ROADS. Abolition of, veto, X, 813.

TOLLS. See CANAL TOLLS.

TOMMY JEMMY. See SOO-NON-GIZE.

TOMPKINS. Bridge over Delaware river, veto, X, 873.

TOMPKINS, DANIEL D. Governor, portrait, II, 616.

    1808, JANUARY. Opening speech, II, 616; British impressment of American seamen, 616; embargo by Federal government, 617; defense of New York, 618, 628; northern and western frontiers, 618; militia organization under act of Congress, 619; extending powers of cession commissioners, 620; powder magazine in New York, 620; Williams murder case, 621, 627; New Jersey boundary, 621, 629; compensation of judges, 621; agriculture, manufactures and commerce, 622; crimes, veto, 623; correspondence with President Jefferson, 624; Vermont resolution, 627; transmits his father's resignation as Regent, 629; purchase of ordnance and ammunition, 629; gunhouses, 630; Delaware resolutions, 630; Virginia resolutions, 631; reform in Court of Chancery, 631.

    1808, NOVEMBER. Opening speech, II, 632; foreign relations, 632; embargo, 632; presidential election, 633; punishment of petit larceny, 633; death penalty, 633; whipping should be abolished, 634; Hill murder case, 635, 639; distribution of arms and ammunition, 636; New York arsenal, 636; acquisition of land for fortifications, 636; powder magazine, 636, 643, 649; defense of New York, 636; European affairs, 637; Canajoharie and Palatine Bridge Company, charter, veto, 638; Donnelly stage route along Hudson river, veto, 638; Kosciusko's treatise on horse artillery, 639; standard of measures, 640; acquisition of Ellis island, 641; Watch Point, 641; fortifications, 642; sale of two gores of land in New York, 642; announcing Regent Sylvester's death, 644; purchase of Oneida Indian land, 644, 651; Reformed Dutch church of New Utrecht, sale of lands, veto, 645; New York, Canal street, veto, 646; purchase of rifles, 647; military

TOMPKINS, DANIEL D., 1808 — (*Continued*).

accounts, 648, 654; Maryland resolution, 649; care of lunatics, 650; procedure in Court of Chancery, 650; Massachusetts resolution, 650; Senate districts, veto, 651.

1810, JANUARY. Opening speech, II, 655; European war, 655; British impressment of seamen, 656; efforts toward conciliation with England, 657; agriculture and manufactures, 658; fortifying New York, 658; Fort Richmond battery, 658; defense of New York harbor, 659; revision of statutes, 660; education, 660; Massachusetts and Vermont resolutions, 665; Pennsylvania resolutions, Olmstead case, 665; claims against United States for fortifications, 667; manufacture of small arms, 667; reply to Senate and Assembly addresses, 668; sustains national administration, 669; Federal finances, 670; purchase of land for Christian party of Oneida Indians, 670.

VETOES. New York city surveys, II, 661; Devoe, relief, 662; Hardenburgh and others, relief, 663; military tract, survey of, 664; New York and Brooklyn, relief, 665; Reformed Dutch church of German Flats, relief, 671.

1811, JANUARY. Opening speech, II, 671; foreign relations, 672; revocation of French Commercial Decrees, 672; British orders in council, 672; manufactures, 673; announces death of Lieutenant-Governor Broome, 674; revision of statutes, 675; military expenses, 675; canals, 675; common schools and common school fund, 675; fortifications at Staten Island, 676; military academy, 676; purchase of Seneca Indian land, 677; purchase of Oneida Indian land, 678; Union College lottery, 678; titles of nobility, 678; sale of State lands in New York, 679; purchase of arms, 680; manufacture of arms, 680; manufacture of powder, 681; deposits of arms, 682; powder magazines near Albany, 683; Onondaga Indian agent, 684.

VETOES. Jones estate, relief, II, 685; elections, authorizing minors to vote for members of Assembly, 685; elections, colored voters, 686; Philips estate, relief, 688; Ford relief bill, 688.

1812, JANUARY. Opening speech, II, 689; foreign relations, 690; British aggressions, 690; national administration commended, 691; military preparations, 691; militia, 692; military schools, 692; court-martial, 692; revision of laws, 692; abolition of slavery, 692; Indian affairs, 694; salt

TOMPKINS, DANIEL D., 1812 — (*Continued*).

springs, 695; claims against confiscated State lands, 695; banks, 696; Court of Chancery, revision of fee system, 702; common schools, 702, 707, 717; domestic manufactures, 702; capital punishment, 702, 729; Federal census, 1810, 704; Union Bank, 705; apportionment of Representatives in Congress, 705; Ohio resolutions relative to canals, 706; canals, 706; election of Regents, 707; report of Commission on Common School System, 707, 717; prorogues Legislature, 708; III, 1005; banking capital, 1812, II, 710; battery on North river, 712; defense of frontiers, 713; Greenbush magazine, 714; fast day, 715; common school system permanently established, 729.

VETOES. Estates of married women, II, 703; Teeple estate, 708; Hart and others, estate of, 713; Schultz estate, relief, 714; Marvin estate, 716; Fairchild, relief, 716; Proudfit trust fund, charter, 717.

1812, NOVEMBER. Opening speech, II, 735; war with Great Britain, 735; military preparations, 736; attack on Queenstown, 737; various military movements, 737; pensions, 738, 748, 760, 794; Bowman murder case, 738; exemptions from military duty, 739; statement of military movements, 742, 747; Cool murder case, 748; North Carolina resolutions, 750; statement of expenditures for fortifying New York harbor, 750; communication from commissioner of fortifications, 751; acquiring land for United States, 752, 777; purchase of Indian lands, 753, 754; transcribing minutes of Court of Chancery, 754; deposit of United States military stores in Colonie arsenal, 755; proposed sale of Watervliet arsenal to United States, 755; road between Albany and St. Lawrence river, 756; statement of military expenditures, 757; organizing reserve force of troops, 758, 759; communication from Secretary of United States, amendment, titles of nobility, 761; arms loaned by United States, 762; statement of funds furnished by United States, 763; appoints paymaster of militia, 764; militia in Federal service same pay and supplies as regular army, 767; statement of distribution of military stores, 768; fortifications at Hendrick's Reef, 777; Signal Hill redoubt, 778; Legislature thanks naval officers, 780.

VETOES. Supreme Court judges, II, 740; Supreme Court clerks, 756; Schoharie turnpike road, 776; joint tenants, tenants

Tompkins, Daniel D., 1812, Vetoes — (*Continued*).

in tail, abolishing entails, 779; bigamy, 780; Harlem Bridge Company, amending charter, 782; forfeited estates, limitation of actions, 783.

1814, January. Opening speech, II, 784; negotiations for peace, 785; notes various military successes, 786; engagement at Black Rock, 787; British invasion of western frontier, 787; volunteers, 787, 791; Federal direct tax, 788; Moser murder case, 790; invasion of Niagara frontier, 791; Tennessee resolution, 795; Albany and St. Lawrence road, 795; pay of militia in case of invasion, 795; fortifications and military stores, 797; compensation of officers of commissary's department, 798; arms received from United States, 798; Perry's victory on Lake Erie, 799; convenes Legislature by proclamation, 800.

1814, September. Opening speech, II, 800; progress of war, 801; Washington burned by British, 802; American successes on Niagara frontier, 802; British defeat at Baltimore, 802; defeat of British at Plattsburgh, 803, 808; Macdonough's victory on Lake Champlain, 803, 808; unequal operation of militia system, 803; troops furnished by State, 804; proposed session of Legislature in New York, 805; Dwyer murder case, 805; statement of measures of defense, 806; sea fencibles for New York, 808; gratuitous service of aides, 810; reorganization of militia, 811; military schools, 812; cannon foundry on Hudson, 813, 814; military stores, 814, 821; various military expenses, 814, 816; volunteers for service on Niagara frontier, 815; reimbursement for expenses, 817; military secretary, 818; no hope of immediate peace, 818; vessels at New York, veto, 819; deserters, arrest of, veto, 819; distribution of militia, 822; treaty of peace, 824; appoints thanksgiving day, 824; purchase of land by United States, 825; protest against terms of peace proposed by Great Britain, 826; Massachusetts, Georgia and Connecticut resolutions, 827; sale of arsenal at Albany, 828; Commissary-General to reside at Albany, 829; Maryland resolutions, 829; Rhode Island and Pennsylvania resolutions, 830; urges completion of fortifications, 830; support of military departments, 831; correspondence with army and navy officers complimented by Legislature, 832, 859; Appropriation Act, including Senate apportionment, veto, 849.

1816, January. Opening speech, II, 850; some results of the war, 850; elevation of American character, 851; war with Algiers, 852; militia, 853; improvement of roads, 853; supervision of

TOMPKINS, DANIEL D., 1816 — (*Continued*).

    turnpike companies, 853; canals, 854; manufactures, 854; pardons for arson, 855; new State prison at Auburn, 855; Burke murder case, 856; purchase of Niagara islands from Senecas, 857, 866; announces death of Andrew King, Regent, 857; North Carolina, Massachusetts and Vermont resolutions, 864; improvement of fortifications on Staten Island, 864; guard at Fort Richmond, 865; military academy, 865; Rhode Island resolutions, 866; purchase of land at French Mills from St. Regis Indians, 866; Commission on Astor Claim, 867; claims against United States, 867; III, 15; militia accounts with United States, II, 868; report of killed and wounded, 869, 872; Ohio resolutions, 870; sale of perishable military stores, 870; arsenal at Albany to be leased, 871; Bank of Niagara, veto, 871.

    1816, NOVEMBER. Opening speech, II, 872; general peace, 873; Northrup murder case, 874; condition of New York prison, 874; convict labor, 875; domestic manufactures, 876; education, 876, 877; fortifications at Rouse's Point, 877; lands ceded to United States, 878; condition of Albany arsenal, 878; abolition of slavery, 881; North Carolina resolution, 882; advances to aid Indians, 882; Clark land claim, 883; appoints commissioners to investigate condition of Montauk Indians, 931; resigns to become Vice-President, 883; I, pref. xii; Assembly's address, II, 884; Senate's address, 886.

    Vice-President, candidate for Governor, II, 1065; signs cession to United States, III, 140; major-general in War of 1812, 177; cited, separating power of appointment from power of removal, VI, 833; papers, proposed purchase, veto, VII, 922; official service as Governor, I, pref. xii.

TOMPKINS, G. W. B. Colonel, 2d Regiment, supplies from Union Defense Committee, VII, 500.

TOMPKINS, JONATHAN G. Resigns as Regent, II, 628.

TOMPKINS COUNTY. Lumber from, finds market in New York, III, 815; agricultural society in, 945; silk culture, 945; inspection of steamboats, veto, VIII, 469; average excise license fees, 1889, 687; Groton Cemetery Association, changing name, veto, 974; highways, cost of labor system, 1892, IX, 200; insane, care of, county and State systems compared, 228.

TOMPKINS COUNTY NEW YORK PATRONS' MUTUAL FIRE RELIEF ASSOCIATION. Charter, veto, VII, 133.

TOMPKINSVILLE. Methodist Episcopal church, changing name, veto, VI, 270.

TONAWANDA. VETOES. Relief of Christian church, VI, 185; Rescue Hook and Ladder Company, charter, 825; canal bridges, 1007; State ditch, three bridges, 1007; VII, 95, 96; foot-bridge, Kohler street, 232; bridge, Maine and Delaware streets, 233, 361, 577; Tonawanda creek, drainage of leakage, 363; fence on berme bank of canal, 364; police justice, repealing act, 415; cleaning State ditches, 456; canal bridge, 505, 665; amending charter, 805; sewers, VIII, 876; public parks and places, improvement, 1115; lands under water, release of, IX, 284; village taxes, collection, 718; armory site, unexpended balance raised for, refunding to Erie county, 795; Delaware road, refunding indebtedness, X, 63; canal bridge, North Niagara street, 314, 435; moving canal bridge, 319; armory, relief of contractors on construction, 383, 587; armory, settlement of claims, 703.

TONAWANDA BAND (Seneca Indians). Communication from, treaties of 1838 and 1842, V, 199; relinquish Kansas lands, 200.

TONAWANDA CREEK. Diversion for canal purposes, III, 182; improvement of, 763.

    VETOES. Bridge over, VI, 696; VII, 477, 805; canal bridge over, VI, 859; fishing in, 906; Tonawanda leakage, VII, 363; breakwater at Wendellville, VIII, 888; bridge over, IX, 348, new act passed.

TONAWANDA FEEDER. Improvement, veto, VII, 358, 457.

TONAWANDA GAS COMPANY. Charter, veto, VII, 807.

TONAWANDA INDIAN RESERVATION. Number of Indians on, 1819, II, 976; memorial from, Indian treaties, IV, 295; Seneca Indians on, communication from, V, 199; location and acreage, 199; part of, sold for taxes, 201; tax title extinguished, 202.

    VETOES. Manual labor school, VII, 132; bridge over Tonawanda creek, 477; IX, 348, new bill passed; dog tax, 725; repair of highways, appropriation, X, 429.

TONAWANDA INDIANS. Manual labor school, veto, VII, 477.

TONAWANDA RAILROAD COMPANY. State aid to, IV, 10, 831.

TONNAGE. Exempting transports for Canadian expedition, I, 153; duty on, veto, 171; bill objected to by Lords of Trade, 185; proposed, on foreign vessels, 246, 618; act of 1734, danger of rejection, 270, 271; Federal, on Erie canal, proposed, III, 27, 50, 76, 154; State, no power to impose, VII, 121.

TOPOGRAPHIC SURVEY. See STATE SURVEY.

TORBELL, LORAN. Trustee, St. Regis Indians, communication from, II, 938.

TORNADO HOOK AND LADDER COMPANY No. 1, UNION. Charter, veto, VII, 233.

TORRY, JOHN. Geological survey, botanical branch, III, 638, 753, 991; report, 644, 761, 993; IV, 81.

TORTURE. Abolished, II, 364.

TOTTEN, JOSEPH G. Engineer, letter from, fortifications at Rouse's Point, II, 877, 878; second letter, 890; survey of New York harbor, V, 21; location of quarantine station, 104.

TOTTEN AND CROSSFIELD'S PURCHASE. Exempting townships from highway taxes, veto, VI, 701.

TOWER, REGINALD. British chargé d'affaires at Washington, correspondence relative to Cayuga Indian claim, X, 128.

TOWN AUDITORS. Several counties exempted, VIII, 49; general act repealed, 1883, 50.

VETOES. Raising money for roads and bridges, VI, 329; Lenox, 435; separate boards in towns, 437, 675; Moravia, applying act, VII, 413; exempting Chemung and Greene counties, 554, 622; VIII, 49; exempting Coeymans, VII, 622; Westchester county, — repealing act, 806; — relative to, 807; Hornellsville, creating board, VIII, 48; Wappinger, 616; amending act, 872, 1039.

TOWNHOUSE. New York, I, 83; Albany, 89.

VETOES. Fort Covington, VI, 910; Harrietstown, VIII, 508; Hopkinton, tax for, VI, 309; Long Lake, VIII, 1041; Mexico, rebuilding, VII, 71; Parishville, VIII, 516; Rose, town hall, use of room for G. A. R., 528.

TOWN INSURANCE COMPANIES. General act passed, VII, 387; laws amended, 692.

VETOES. Amending act, VI, 153, 509; VIII, 131; Parma, authorizing company, VI, 592; authorizing formation of, VII, 130, 249, 387; Venice, changing location of business office, 1013; amending repealed act, 1098; co-operative, classification of risks, VIII, 293; extending powers, 881; co-operative insurance companies, IX, 152.

TOWN LAW. General, 1890, VIII, 1027; IX, 26; compensation of officers, veto, 147; clerk and collector, official term, veto, 149.

TOWN MEETING. Making appropriations for highways, III, 377; character and scope of, VI, 59, 675; Myers' automatic ballot cabinet, use authorized, IX, 34; legalizing action of boards of supervisors changing time, X, 236.

VETOES. Shawangunk, legalizing resolution fixing place of, VI, 581; Ontario, legalizing proceedings, 1031; Alden, legalizing election of highway commissioner, 1034; time for transacting business, VII, 387; voting by ballot on money propositions, 807; Hector, fixing time of, 842; voting on tax propositions, 1106; tax proposition, voting by ballot, VIII, 470; Batavia, place of holding,

Town Meeting, Vetoes — (*Continued*).

698; Pelham, restricting powers, 721; Oswegatchie, legalizing proceedings, 885; North Collins, election districts, 886; Phelps, legalizing, 887; Johnstown, voting by ballot on bridge appropriation, 1087; Bath, time and place of holding, IX, 117; continuance and adjournment of, repeal, 392; Davis voting machine, authorizing use of, 626; Albany and Onondaga counties, fixing time, 718; Goshen, biennial, on general election day, 816; Hancock, voting in three places, 817; Putnam county, 862; amending general law, X, 62; Montgomery county, 449.

Towns. Regulating financial affairs of, II, 464, 465; number of justices, III, 17; local courthouses proposed, 58; commissioner of deeds, office abolished, 770; boards of education recommended, IV, 840; division of, V, 126; filling vacancies in office, 218; when authorized to erect bridges, 346, 385; VI, 53; board of relief for soldiers, V, 490; right of local government, VI, 29; borrowing money for roads and bridges, 55, 98, 319; election districts, 58, 193; VII, 388; alteration or erection of, VI, 60; fire companies, 119; special laws should be repealed, 120; boards of excise, 127; laws should be uniform, 165, 402, 437, 449; cannot be divided for purposes of railroad aid, 187; notice of special legislation, 585; large expenses for official fees, VII, 140; heavy debt and taxation, 298, 437; registration of voters, 435; depopulation and depreciation of property resulting from extravagant railroad aid, 437; refunding bonded indebtedness, 437; street railroads, operation and extension, act relative to, 1063; audit of accounts, historical sketch, VIII, 48; highway commissioners, when residents may not vote for, VIII, 55; Milo, failure to make assessment, new authorized, 257; general law, 1890, 1027; highways, State aid, 1042; with large population, should receive municipal charter, 1098, 1110, 1111; Governor Flower recommends personal registration in, IX, 180; payments to charitable institutions, 551; teachers' pension fund, 564; use of Davis voting machine authorized, 665; responsible for maintenance of highways, 768; political enrollment in, X, 417.

Vetoes. Bounties, legalizing, V, 673; Hamburg, fixing bail of overseer of highways, VI, 91; Deer Park, additional justices, 208; Hopkinton, town hall, tax for, 309; Verona, additional justices of the peace, 326; reducing expenses, 329; town auditors, raising money for roads and bridges, 329; town auditors, Lenox, 435; Newtown, local government, 449, 558; local option, 568; Shawangunk, legalizing resolution fixing place of town meeting, 581; water supply, 591; Phillipstown and Carmel, business, 674; New

TOWNS, VETOES — (*Continued*).

Hartford, reimbursing collector, 701; Fort Covington, townhouse, 910; Vienna, real estate assessments, 1033; collectors and receivers of taxes, taking county orders, VII, 62; Watervliet, election of officers, 64; Mexico, rebuilding hall, 71; Saugerties, compensation of certain town officers, 130; Northfield, macadamizing certain roads, 132; Mentz, overseers of highways, special act, 208; German Flats, creating board of alms, 215; Scio constables, appointment of, 218; constables, jurisdiction in villages, 265; Newtown, amending Metropolitan Sanitary District Act, 267; railroad sinking funds, 268; Newtown Lutheran cemetery, relief, 268; highway labor, 325; Corning bonds, payment of, 334; town meetings, time for transacting business, 387; Moravia town auditors, 413; Sullivan county, pay of certain, repeal, 507; railroad commissioners, abolition of office, 509; Canandaigua, reimbursement for loss of property, 569; Sangerfield, supervisor's bond, refunding surety for payment on, 753; defective highways, liability for damages, 767; street railroads, maintenance and operation, 793, 894; Brutus, fixing northern boundary, 806; Pelham, relative to, 807; Richford public square, 807; taxation in aid of railroads, 847; Perry cemeteries, reinterments, 870; Hornellsville, extending time for collection of taxes, 878; Easton highway commissioner, election, 932; New Lots, annexing to Brooklyn, 936; Venice Town Insurance Company, changing location of office, 1013; Westchester, borrowing money for highway improvement, 1023; Glenville, purchasing bridge, 1102; Denmark, conveyance of certain land, 1105; tax propositions, voting on, 1106; Flatbush, licensing public hacks, etc., 1111; Westmoreland, cemetery association, reducing number of trustees, VIII, 52; Greenburgh, election of highway commissioners, 54; Lenox, extending school district boundaries, 130; Colton lock-up, 229; Westchester highway bonds, 292; railroad aid, relief, 371; Cairo, bridge over Catskill creek, 383; number of highway commissioners, 461; Eastchester, number of highway commissioners, 461; Newtown, road improvement, 469; excise moneys, 469; Harrietstown, town hall, 508; Parishville, townhouse, 516; Rose, town hall, use of room for G. A. R., 528; Vienna, police regulations, 534; reimbursing Lyonsdale for bridge over Moose river, 552; New Utrecht, special highway, 615; overseers of the poor, Ontario county, compensation, 696; Flatbush fire company, amending charter, 728; officers, reducing number, 887; divided by navigable tidal stream, highways between, 888; Livonia, auditing claim of Reed and others, 889; Flatlands, public hacks and

TOWNS, VETOES — (*Continued*).

amusements, licenses, 975; Parishville lock-up, 1039; Long Lake, townhouse, 1041; Johnstown officers, method of voting for, 1041; division of South Valley, legalizing act, 1089; Flatlands fire department, charter, 1097; Perry, railroad aid, using funds for general town purposes, 1105; compensation of officers, IX, 147; clerk and collector, official term, 149; New Utrecht highway improvement, 264; highway bridges broken by heavy loads, when town not liable, 274; division ditches, 286, 522; Brighton assessors, compensation, 371; division fences, compelling erection of, 401; balloting outside incorporated villages, 439; highway commissioner, compensation, 462; local authorities under Railroad Law, definition, 462; teachers, conditional compensation after twenty-five years' service, 463; Davis voting machine, authorizing use of, 626; Cortland, reducing town expenses, salaries for justices and overseers of poor, 722; Washington county, expense of convictions for crimes less than felony, 796; amending general law, 804; money for observance of Memorial Day, 813; lighting district, amending act, 814; Lenox, reimbursement for bridge over Douglass State ditch, 817; Manlius, soldiers' monument, changing location of, 817; Oyster Bay, legalizing town election, 1897, 818; Olive, Bushkill creek improvement, bonds for, 818; Sullivan, reimbursement for bridge over Douglass State ditch, 818; West Turin, legalizing division into election districts, 818; elections, places of registry and voting, 863; Frankfort, better administration of justice, 867; electric-light companies, acquiring real estate, X, 159; Dewitt, special highway system, 234; Mamakating railroad aid bonds, retiring outstanding bonds, 235; Nassau county, preservation of records, 243; compensation of officers, 309; railroad aid claims, Court of Claims, 315; highways in, two or more in same county, 316; Catskill, purchasing stone crusher, 380; division fences, 440; Nassau county, officers, compensation, 533; renting rooms for G. A. R., 535; highways, State aid, 585; commissioners of highways in certain, 590; Colonie, relative to eastern boundary, 702; primary elections, enrollment lists, 705; Saugerties, town clerk and highway commissioner, salary, 810; West Seneca, collection of assessments for local improvements, 811; New Hartford, legalizing aid to Bridgewater turnpike, 811; Stockport, legalizing Hanes claim, 814; Frankfort, payment of certain indebtedness, 815; Tompkins, bridge over Delaware river, 873; Indian Lake, services of fire wardens, claim bill, 946; Westchester, lighting highways, public places, etc., 948; highways, State aid, 952; poll-tax in towns under money system, 956.

TOWNSEND, MRS. A. HOWARD. Member of Cotton States Exposition Commission, 1895, IX, 582.

TOWNSEND, CORNELIA. Relief, veto, VI, 438, new act passed.

TOWNSEND, FRANKLIN. Affidavit by, anti-rent trouble, III, 829; Adjutant-General, quoted, efficiency of National Guard, VI, 531; agent to settle claims against United States, VII, 501.

TOWNSEND, FREDERICK. Major, enlistment of volunteers, V, 538; superintendent of volunteer recruiting service, 561.

TOWNSEND, HENRY A. Arms and supplies delivered to, II, 775.

TOWNSEND, JOHN. Appointed surveyor and searcher of customs at Oyster Bay, resigns, I, 83.

TOWNSHIPS. Bill confirming division of, veto, I, 231; settlements in, compared with patents, 552; settlements in, recommended, 613; division of Indian lands into, II, 291.

TOWN SUPERINTENDENTS OF SCHOOLS. Office established, IV, 23, 66; abolished, 797, 843.

TRACY, EDWARD H. Member of board of engineers, New York harbor defense, V, 568; New York, chief engineer of public works, report on pneumatic tubes, VI, 292, 299, 486.

TRACY, MARGARET. Widow of Dennis Tracy, escheat, veto, X, 954.

TRADE. Act to encourage, I, 11; Governor Fletcher recommends remedy for decay of, 28; disadvantages of, in colony, 58; restrictions by Crown, 79; adverse effect of certain regulations, 86, 90; with France, prohibited, 117; act relating to, 184; Indians with French prohibited, 193; with Indians, 198; clandestine, with French prohibited, 200; with Far Indians, 206, 207, 214, 225, 315; with Indians, appropriation to promote, 208; restricting, with Canada, 209, 212, 600; merchants oppose Canadian trade regulations, 212; with Indians increasing, 212; recent laws not well executed, 217; on Onondaga river, 217, 223; Indian, at Albany and westward, 223; King vetoes bills prohibiting sale of Indian goods to French, 236; memorial against parliamentary aid to sugar colonies, 240, 243; French attempt to interfere with, at Oswego, 241; with Indians regulated, 243; conditions of, considered, 246; relief of, proposed, 259; fur, at Oswego, possible interception by French, 262; fur, act regulating, 265; danger of French acquisition of Tierondequat, 262; secured by guardship, 276; prevention of illicit, 291; expected benefits from conquest of Cuba, 302; retreat of traders from Oswego, 326; proposed exclusion of French Indians from privileges of, 356; with Indians restricted, 466; danger from French privateers, 467; on Great lakes, French attempts to destroy, 486; to be encouraged, 506; in Albany county, duties on goods, 514; French interference with, among Indians, 515, 535; frauds in various commodities, 530; with Louisburg, French profit by, 564; limitations on, to be avoided, 585; ruinous condition of,

TRADE —(*Continued*).

692; with West Indies, 692; with sugar colonies, 692; lumber and Irish linen, 693; extension of, 701; with Indians, colony to regulate, 723, 735, 738; with England, should be free, 773; with Indians, affected by Quebec trade regulations, 773; inland, between States, restriction of, II, 81; illicit, with British, act to prevent, 164, 184; West India, British attempt to monopolize, 197; act imposing duties on imports, 220, 236; with India, encouragement of, 254; Virginia proposes commercial convention, 259; benefits of internal, 1006; with South American republics, 1093; internal, should be encouraged, III, 298; foreign, number of houses engaged in, IV, 42; capital invested in foreign, 42; conspiracies against, VI, 121; regulating sale of leaf tobacco in New York, veto, 480; origin and development of, 752; on Sunday, veto, IX, 623.

TRADE-MARKS. Protection of, VII, 355; amending Penal Code, veto, VIII, 632.

TRADERS. Income tax on, II, 39.

TRADERS' SAVINGS BANK. Financial condition of, VII, 66.

TRADESMEN. Governor Sloughter recommends legislation to prevent extravagance of, I, 22; proposition to encourage, 246; artificers complain against slaves learning trades, 260; incorporating, veto, II, 228.

TRADE-UNIONS. General law recommended, VIII, 35, 163, 303.

TRADING-HOUSES. French on frontier, I, 192; at Niagara, 193, 222, 227; on Lake Cadaracqui, 201; at Oswego, 225, 226, 227, 228, 232, 243, 251, 257, 260, 264, 296, 299, 318, 518, 520, 529, 537; at Oswego to be used for strengthening fort, 323.

TRADING STAMPS. Licenses for, Lockport, veto, X, 636.

TRAFFARN, M. Canal Department, appropriation for services, veto, IX, 716.

TRAMPS. Method of dealing with, VI, 950; punishment of, veto, VII, 413; IX, 867; Columbia county, regulating commitment and discharge of, veto, VIII, 891.

TRANSFER TAX. See also COLLATERAL INHERITANCE TAX. Imposed on gifts, legacies and inheritances, VII, 571; act of 1885, VIII, 102; family exemption, 928; income from, IX, 538, 648; X, 26, 108, 181; surrogates, district attorneys, assistants in several counties, X, 108; fees of local officers, 109; statement of receipts and expenses, 1900, 182; appraisers, appointment and compensation, 183; act amended, appointment of appraisers, stenographers, etc., 394; New York's contribution, 1902, 483.

VETOES. Experts, appointment, X, 550; amending general act, 586; appraisers and stenographers, 586; appraisers and surrogates' assistants, 770.

Transportation. Of slaves, protest against, II, 693; commodities, expected reduction of cost by canals, 964; problems, Governor Tilden's discussion of, VI, 735; elements of machinery, 740.

Transportation Corporations. General law, 1890, VIII, 1027; canal navigation, unlimited capital, X, 132, 140, 204.

Transports. Exempted from tonnage duty in Canadian expedition, I, 153; for expedition against West Indies, 287, 298, 301; from Virginia for Cape Breton, 371.

Travelers. Protection, powers of conductors, veto, VII, 414.

Tread-Mill. Authorized at Albany jail, III, 10.

Treason. Indictment of William Dyer, I, 4; Jacob Leisler convicted of, execution, 17, 21, 22; Jacob Milborne convicted of, execution, 21, 22; Assembly protests against sending accused to England for trial, 770, 772; act of Congress to prevent, II, 20; removal of disaffected persons, 34; disloyal person disqualified as voter, 37; post mortem declaration of, 70; pardon of Thomas Cummings, 82; misprision of, 216; subject to death penalty, 363, 731; V, 172; pardon, proposed constitutional amendment, III, 863; Dorr case, judgment annulled by Rhode Island Legislature, IV, 817; alleged to exist in southern States, V, 306, 319.

Treasurer (Colony). Assembly authorized to appoint, I, 123, 168, 298; protests against Assembly's appointment of, 166; royal, only entitled to general funds, 168; Abraham De Peyster, Jr., appointed, 197; papers relating to, 200; authority of, 293, 298; receives funds granted by Parliament, 604; Abraham Lott, appointment approved, 722.

Treasurer, State. See State Treasurer.

Treasury, United States. Act to organize, II, 65; sub-treasury system, Rhode Island opposes, III, 909; Georgia condemns repeal of Sub-Treasury Law, 977; statistics of coin, VI, 251.

Treat, Malachi. Doctor, letter from, relative to hospital nurses, II, 95.

Treat, Robert. Deputy Governor of Boston, letter from, I, 73.

Treaty. With Five Nations for conveyance of land, I, 94; with Waganhas, 134, 136; between Great Britain and France, trade provisions, 209; Six Nations, 233; neutrality with Six Nations broken by Canada Indians, 352, 356, 358; new, with Six Nations, 359, 548; with Indians for Crown Point expedition, 466; of peace, Aix-la-Chapelle, 471, 481; of Utrecht, status of Five Nations, 542; Indians at Fort Stanwix, 727; of peace with Great Britain, 730; II, 191; between United States and France, 44, 67; privileges and immunities of French subjects, 91; between United States and Netherlands, 188; of peace, 191, 192, 195; contradicted by alien bill, 204; contradicted by bill relating to debts due persons within enemy's lines, 205; of

TREATY — (*Continued*).

 peace, ratified, 206; contradicted by Freedom and Independence Act, 216; of commerce between United States and Great Britain, 236; of peace, repugnant State provisions should be repealed, 274; with Oneidas and Onondagas, 291; Cayugas, 296; Indians at Chemung Point, 328; Onondagas, salt springs, 329; of peace, violated by British occupancy of western posts, 253, 334; St. Regis Indians, 352, 364, 368, 941; III, 36, 47; national approval of, II, 366; with northwest Indians, 367; with Seven Nations of Canada, 368, 380, 381, 386, 390; purchase of St. Regis lands, 472, 520, 866; with Senecas and Oneidas, 523; of peace, rights of widows of attainted persons, 582; with Cayugas and Senecas, 605; with Oneidas, 519, 607, 644, 651, 671; III, 47, 143, 310; of peace with Great Britain, II, 824; with Senecas, 857; with Onondagas, 887, 888, 1118; III, 13; commercial, with Great Britain, II, 888, 1104; with Oneidas, second Christian party, 894; between Delawares and United States, 987; with Stockbridge Indians, 989, 1119; III, 13, 34; Indian tribes, land at Green Bay, II, 1107; with Creek Indians, III, 183; of Ghent, northeastern boundary question, 389; with Great Britain, northern boundary, 1038; between United States and Seneca Indians, IV, 290, 295; power to make, 417; V, 480; between United States and Great Britain, reciprocity in use of canals, VI, 363.

TREES. In highways, ownership of, II, 331, 385; shade trees along highways, planting recommended, X, 851.

VETOES. Shade, encouraging planting of, VII, 266; on Lake George islands, preservation of, 655; fruit, to prevent poisoning while in blossom, IX, 811; New York, cultivation of, X, 60, 178; Buffalo, Department of Forestry, 713; fruit, preventing disease, 809.

TRENTON. Arms and supplies for, II, 774.

TRESPASS. On Indian lands, see INTRUSIONS.

TRIAL BY JURY. In general, I, 693, 704, 769, 772; under Election Law, II, 37; unlawfully acquiring riches, 61, 64; forfeiture of estates, 70; justice's court, 85; increasing opportunities for, 171; referees, 205; disorderly persons, 223, 284; collection of taxes, 235; Legislature exercising judicial powers, 249, 250; settlement of decedents' estates, 268, 269; collection of debts due State, 757; in Court of Chancery, III, 649, 720; fugitive slaves, 778, 911, 925, 936, 981, 1028, 1037; IV, 7; V, 301; Fugitive Slave Act unconstitutional, IV, 7; V, 301; challenges in criminal cases, IV, 490; capital cases, giving defense right to make closing address, veto, VII, 754; in probate cases, veto, X, 318.

TRIBUNALS OF CONCILIATION. Constitutional provision, IV, 443, 480, 856; established, act repealed, 444.

TRICYCLES. See CYCLES.

TRIMBLE, GEORGE. Letter from, army supplies, II, 90; suit against, in Connecticut for impressment of flour, claim settled, II, 186.

TRISBE, PHILIP. Memorial from, II, 54.

TROIS RIVERS. Letter from Governor of, I, 225.

TROOPS (Colony). Crown furnishes for colony, I, 36, 49, 95; appropriation for King's, 57; quartering, 133; 565, 589, 604, 671, 673, 725, 732, 735, 737, 741, 746, 748, 755; for Canadian expedition, 151, 620, 633, 643, 645; for frontier defense, 155; Canadian expedition, disbanded, 156; pay of British officers, 157; memorial relative to supplies for, 202; Assembly's action on quotas of, 203; to be maintained at Oswego, 237; English in colony, 276; for Spanish War, 287, 289; desertions from, 290; for expedition against West Indies, 301, 304, 306; transportation of, 305, 306, 363, 379, 460; supplies for, 306; for Oswego and Saratoga, 318; for service at Oswego, 329; King's, for Oswego, 334; for Albany, 372, 416, 436; at northern carrying place, 396; should be stationed at Albany, 409; enlistments under union agreement, 419; enlisted for Canadian expedition to be discharged, 441; from Connecticut to assist New York, 463; for frontier service, 468; discharge of, 470; two companies sent to aid Virginia against French, 535, 546; at Albany, bedding for, 555; apportionment among colonies, 566; for Crown Point expedition, 570, 575, 588, 591, 594; King's, for service in Crown Point campaign, 598; to be recruited by volunteers, 598; colonial, not to serve outside North America, 598; subsistence in winter quarters, 608; sent from England, 609; desertions at Fort Edward, 614; Earl of Loudoun arrives in New York, 615; King's, immoderate use of liquor by, 617; from New York at various places, 627; hardships of campaign, 628; extent of military service, 628; continuing in service, 638, 651; additional, for Canadian service, 651, 653; for frontier service, 657, 670; for general service, 663; King's, recruits for, 664; relief of, returning from service, 671; for Indian War, 675, 676; organization of, 676; act of Parliament relating to quartering, 702, 716, 721; return of, for New York, 708; King's requisition for support of, 708, 709, 710, 716; supplies for, 719; Assembly's statement relative to expense, 719.

TROOPS (State). For service in Tryon county, II, 13; New York regiments in national service, 18; act providing for, veto, 32, 41; continental battalion, 33, 57, 82, 108; allowance for rations, 43; accoutrements for, 43; clothing for, 53, 80, 88, 91, 100, 110; reinforcements for Federal army, 77; separate support by States, 88; State quotas, 93; compensation for depreciation in currency, 110; returns of, 132; completing New York regiments, 133, 163; new levies, bounties for, 115, 148; pay of, 148, 169; number of New York levies, 180; settle-

Troops (State)—(*Continued*).

     ment of accounts, 187; subsistence furnished by frontier residents, 189; orderly conduct after disbandment, 197; arrears, settlement of, 197; for defense of northwestern frontier, 245; act of Congress for augmenting, 264; organization under act of Congress, 619; War of 1812, 735; New York's quota, 742; number and location of, 1812, 746, 809; organizing reserve force, 758, 759; furnished by New York, War of 1812, 804; proposed organization of cadets, 812; statement of killed and wounded, 869, 872; New York in Civil War, V, 359; clothing for, Civil War, 401; number furnished by New York, 402, 404, 445, 454, 607; losses in battle and otherwise, 404; commended by Governor Morgan, 405; appointment of officers, Governor Seymour's rule, 446; large number called for, 540, 553; report of auditing board, 577; quotas under calls in 1864, 607, 618, 621, 634; enlistments for two years, 610; Commission on War Claims against United States, 756; States not to keep, in time of peace without consent of Congress, VII, 763; First New York Volunteers, relative to, veto, 804; 1st Regiment, Mexican Volunteers, relief, veto, 882; New York organizations in battle of Lookout Mountain and Missionary Ridge, veto, VIII, 1076; number of New York regiments in battle of Antietam, IX, 341; New York, at battle of Chattanooga, 576.

Trotter, Matthew. Relief, veto, II, 343.

Troup, Robert. Counsel to examine dower cases, II, 374.

Troy. Rensselaer school offered for instruction of teachers, III, 219; immigrant passengers, protection of, IV, 793; Militia Act, V, 53; northern terminus of proposed Hudson river improvement, 453; amending charter, increasing salaries, VII, 776; new armory, 1883, 953; bi-partisan board of police, VIII, 84; Young Women's Association, exempting property from taxation, 332; number of excise licenses, 1887, 359; sewer expenses, how assessed, 399; excise license fees, 1889, 686; a city of the second class, IX, 678.

Vetoes. Village, powers of, II, 402; board of school commissioners, VI, 508; ferry to West Troy, 705; police commissioners, VII, 132; Troy Public Library, charter, 336; armory, 776; Jacob and North Third streets, assessment for improvements, 1022; police, appointment of chief detective, 1041; excise violations, 1101; amending charter, IX, 149; inspectors of election, 343; police department, reorganization, 489; street improvement, 629; inferior local courts, 630; parks and park commission, 633; commissioner of education, X, 151; Young Men's Association, changing name, 235; waterworks, 583; disposition of lands, 583; claims of Riley and others, school janitors, 634.

TROY CITY GUARDS. Called into service, anti-rent troubles, III, 834.

TROY CITIZENS' CORPS. Called into service, anti-rent troubles, III, 834.

TROY AND COLONIE BRIDGE COMPANY. Charter, veto, X, 585.

TROY FEMALE SEMINARY. Trustees, increasing number, method of appointment, veto, IX, 373, new bill passed.

TROY AND GREEN ISLAND BRIDGE COMPANY. Charter, veto, IX, 153.

TROY INDEPENDENT ARTILLERY COMPANY. Called into service, anti-rent trouble, III, 834.

TROY AND POESTENKILL PLANK ROAD COMPANY. Property transferred to Webster Plank Road Company, VI, 163.

TROY PUBLIC LIBRARY. Charter, veto, VII, 336.

TROY YOUNG MEN'S ASSOCIATION. Changing name to Troy Public Library, veto, X, 235.

TRUANT OFFICERS. Communication from mayor of Brooklyn, V, 108; Boston, report of, 108; proposed appointment of, 190.

TRUANT REFORM SCHOOL. Brooklyn, establishing, veto, VII, 133.

TRUANTS. State school for, veto, VIII, 818; laws difficult of enforcement, X, 515.

TRUMBULL, JONATHAN. Governor of Connecticut, proclamation announcing repeal of inland embargo laws, II, 110; letter from, army supplies, 111; letter from, 127.

TRUMBULL, JOSEPH. Commissary-General, claim of, II, 79.

TRUST COMPANIES. May receive deposits from savings banks, IV, 731; regulations needed, VI, 621; subject to supervision of Bank Department, 622; IX, 561; general statistics, VI, 953; VII, 428, 521, 690, 823; VIII, 6; X, 733; tax on surplus, VII, 571; examinations, 949; authorization to conduct business should be derived from Bank Department, VIII, 6; first charter, limitation of powers, 232; general act, 234, 296, 376, 463, 476; proposed tax on stock, X, 81, 199; franchise tax, 200; resources, 1900, 221; taxation of, 368; tax, New York's contribution, 1902, 483; periodical examinations required, 735.

VETOES. Special charter, VI, 337; receivers, VII, 416; insolvent, settlement of affairs, 797; State Loan and Trust Company, New York, charter, 1097; relative to, 1097; Ulster County Company, VIII, 230; Nassau Trust Company, charter, 291; Grocers' Trust Company, New York, charter, 292; Merchants' Trust Company, charter, 292; Manhattan Loan and Trust Company, charter, 293; Westchester Trust Company, charter, 469; organization in villages, 507; Franklin Loan and Trust Company, New York, amending charter, 630, 890; American Mortgage and Trust Company, New York, amending charter, 630; New York Finance Company, charter, IX, 256; extending powers to certain

TRUST CORPORATIONS, VETOES — (*Continued*).

moneyed corporations, 366; American Title Insurance and Trust Company, charter, 718; powers in certain counties, amending act, X, 318, 320; directors' quorum, 586; New York and London Trust Company, purchase of stocks and issue of debentures, 586; amending general act, 810.

TRUSTEE. VETOES. Relief of sureties, VII, 508; appointment by justices of Supreme Court, X, 450; commissions and bonds, 589.

TRUSTEE OF PUBLIC BUILDINGS. Office created, VII, 837, 982; communications from capitol architects, VIII, 501; to select site for new State Library building, X, 741.

TRUSTS. Executed, effect of, II, 354; infant's real estate, 485; for libraries, act of 1892, IX, 21; alleged coal combination, 183; for supply of commodities of articles of common use prohibited, 183; Governor Roosevelt's definition and discussion of, X, 88.

VETOES. Amending Revised Statutes, VI, 708; VIII, 131; for charitable purposes, VII, 868; provisions in Lyons charter, 879; burial plats, holding by religious corporations, 935; Senate investigation, 1833, attorney for committee, appropriation, VIII, 843; funds, investment, 1040; establishing for humane, charitable and religious purposes, IX, 725.

TRUXTON. Not liable to aid in erection of certain bridge, VI, 78.

TRYON, WILLIAM. Appointed Governor, I, 739; previous incumbency in North Carolina, 739, 742; Assembly continued, 740.

OPENING SPEECH. Thirty-first Assembly, fourth session, I, 740; reviews recent conditions in North Carolina, 740; Militia Act, 741; fortifications in New York, 741; quartering King's troops, 741, 746, 748, 755; support of government, 741, 748, 755; New York hospital, 742; population of New York city, 1771, 743; instruction relative to powder duty, 744; claim of General Gage, 744; Metcalf claim, 744; Quebec boundary, 744, 747, 750, 755, 756, 757; declines salary from colony, 745; secretary's office, 745.

OPENING SPEECH. Thirty-first Assembly, fifth session, I, 746; Massachusetts boundary, 747, 752; New Jersey boundary, 747; Mansion House, 748; battery at Fort George, 748; inspection of beef, flour and pork, 749; counterfeiting bills of credit, 749; Hardenbrook claim, 750, 756; increasing judicial salaries, 750; purchase of cannon and gunpowder, 751, 758; settlement of Mohawk claims, 751.

OPENING SPEECH. Thirty-first Assembly, sixth session, I, 753; fire in New York city, 753, 756; losses by fire, 754; Massachusetts

TRYON, WILLIAM — (*Continued*).

boundary, agreement by commissioners, 754; New Hampshire grants, 756, 765; conference with Governor Hutchinson, 756; Yates claim, survey of Hudson river, 757; road to Hartford, improvement, 757; claims for survey, Quebec boundary, 757; petitions for new roads, 758; Ludlow, reimbursed for fire losses, 758; goes to England, 756, 758, 765; returns to New York, 765; succeeded by Governor Robertson. 779; official service, I, pref. x.

TRYON COUNTY. Gallant conduct of militia, II, 8; papers from committee of, 12, 13, 25; disorders in, 13; prisoners from, 14; Indian ravages on western frontier, 50; persons driven from home in, 81; contingent expenses, veto, 95; relief of distressed families in, 109, 112, 116, 117, 168.

TUBBS, J. NELSON. Canal resident engineer, report, Smith contract, VII, 546.

TUBERCULOSIS. See also CATTLE. In cattle, preventive measures, 1893, IX, 327; commission created, 327; in cattle, examinations for, veto, 773; animals, report of special investigating committee, 1900, X, 120; hospital established, 149, 351; hospital, New York, veto, 178; in cattle, supervision transferred to Department of Agriculture, 192, 217; large number affected with, 351; departments for treatment in State hospitals, 500.

TUBERCULOSIS HOSPITAL. Established, X, 149, 351; regulating admission of inmates, 352; expense of maintenance a local charge, 352; act of 1903, 575.

TUCKER, WILLIS G. Analyst, State Board of Health, statement of alcoholic beverages, VIII, 353.

TULLY, WILLIAM J. Senate, member of insurance investigating committee, 1905, X, 825; member of joint legislative committee on services in memory of former Governor Higgins, 963.

TUNNEL. New, East river, authorized, 1895, VIII. 1135; new, North and East rivers, Pennsylvania Railroad, X, 396.

VETOES. New York, under Washington park prohibited, VII, 999; New York and Brooklyn Tunnel Company, charter, VIII, 883, 1135; under Newtown creek, IX, 474; tunnel railroads, 803; New York railroads, franchise, X, 471.

TURF. See PEAT.

TURIN. Arms and supplies for, II, 775.

TURNPIKE COMPANIES. Restricting powers of, II, 511; supervision of, 527, 528, 854; general act for, 574; inspectors, act relating to, 593; bad condition of roads, 900; improper assessments by, 972; general law for incorporation of, IV, 379.

TURNPIKE COMPANIES — (*Continued*).

    VETOES. East Hamburgh Turnpike Road Company, extending charter, VI, 162; Pawling and Beekman Turnpike Company, surrender of part of road, 215; Otisville and Wurtsboro Turnpike Company, rates of toll, 216; Guilderland Center Turnpike Company, 339; New Baltimore and Rensselaerville Turnpike Road Company, authorizing sale of road, VII, 132; Middletown and Wurtsboro turnpike, extending charter, 265; amending act, 267; Rochester and Charlotte Turnpike Company, changing name, 938; Susquehanna Turnpike Company, abandoning part of road, VIII, 539; Highland and Modena Turnpike Road Company, tolls chargeable by, 1112; Newburg and Cochecton turnpike road, relative to, IX, 793; New Hartford, legalizing aid to Bridgewater turnpike, X, 811; counties to acquire title of, 952.

TURNER, BENTON. Escheat, veto, VIII, 1040.

TURNER, JENNIE. Stenographer Senate Committee on Taxation and Retrenchment, Bloomingdale Asylum investigation, appropriation, veto, VIII, 844; Board of Claims, veto, 1041.

TURNER, JOHN A. Claim against New York finance department, veto, X, 310; relief, veto, 581.

TURPENTINE. Proposed manufacture of, I, 146.

TURZKOWSKA, FRANCES. Court of Claims, injuries received at Niagara reservation, veto, X, 707.

TUSCARORA INDIAN RESERVATION. Number of Indians on, 1819, II, 976.

TUSCARORA INDIANS. Proposed alliance with Five Nations, I, 170; smith for, 306; address from, II, 379; chiefs visit Governor and President, 410; sufferers by British invasion, relief, veto, 787; protest against citizenship and taxation, IV, 507.

TUSTEN. Beattie escheat, veto, VIII, 405.

TUTTLE, SALMON. Board of Claims, veto, VIII, 886.

TWELVE MEN. Powers of, I, 1.

TWENTY CANOES. Seneca Chief, joins in address to Governor, II, 943.

TWICE IN JEOPARDY. Constitutional provision, VII, 755.

TWO-THIRDS BILLS. Appropriating public property for private use, III, 15, 36, 37; IV, 56; public money, defined, VII, 49; creating corporations, III, 531; amending railroad company charter, carrying mail on, 592; incorporating banks, 655; incorporating town of Ossining, IV, 193; effect of resignation of Senators, 578; escheats, 694; X, 778; aiding railroad company, V, 139, 245, 351, 442; constitutional provision, IX, 618; X, 778.

    VETOES. Bridge over Great Sodus bay, VI, 212; Oswegatchie river breakwater, 331; Jay, separate road district, 332; St. Regis

TWO-THIRDS BILLS, VETOES — (*Continued*).

river improvement, 579; Edymoin case, habeas corpus, 678; Allegany Indian reservation, highways and bridges, 690; Faenger escheat, 692; Allegany reservation, Vandalia bridge, 707; New York, payment of court clerks illegally appointed, VII, 48; Military Code, 1882, 797; Salmon river improvement, VIII, 381; Genesee Valley canal, release to adjoining owners, 463.

TYEBOUT, ALBARTUS. Captain, service in French War, I, 396.

TYPHOID FEVER. Large number of cases, 1903, X, 623.

TYLER, JOHN. Ex-President, delegate from Virginia to Washington Peace Convention, V, 311; appointed by Virginia to confer with President, 312.

TYRIAN HALL ASSOCIATION OF EAST NEW YORK, NEW LOTS. Charter, veto, VI, 590.

TYRON, NORMAN. Court of Claims, veto, X, 61.

TYRONE. Union free school district, relative to, veto, VII, 265.

TYRRELL, JOHN and JAMES. Loss of canal boat, veto, VII, 599, 805.

U.

ULRICH, JOHN F. New York Municipal Court, attendant, claim, veto, X, 168.

ULSTER (Village). Amending charter, duplicate bill, veto, IX, 432.

ULSTER COUNTY. Persons prohibited from leaving, without Leisler's consent, I, 16; militia sent against Indians at Minisink, 587; blockhouses proposed for, 590, 616; Indians destroy Swartwout house and family, 593; Indian incursions in, 594, 616, 626, 675; rangers in, 588, 595; militia engaged in frontier defense, 597; defense of frontier, 607; 2d Regiment, asks for pay, 613, 627, 679; militia ordered into service, 614; expense of Indian raids, 631; uneasiness among Indians, 657, 658; line between it and Albany county, survey recommended, 672; regiments present accounts for frontier service, 679; George Clinton and Charles De Witt, Assembly, favor colonial union, 767; Council of Safety meets at several places in, II, 17; committee, relief of indigent persons and of soldiers' families, 21; Indian ravages on western frontier, 50; Peinpack, memorial from, 55; Hopewell congregation request grant of land, 82; oyer and terminer, communication from, Cummings case, 82; oyer and terminer, Cool murder case, 748; courthouse commissioners, appointment, 944; Livingston leases in, IV, 332; Shawangunk, legalizing resolution fixing place of town meeting, VI, 581; forest lands included in forest preserve, VIII, 23; average excise license fees, 1889, 687; unpaid taxes, sales for, special act repealed, 749;

ULSTER COUNTY —(*Continued*).

decrease in population, IX, 3; highways, cost of labor system, 1892, 200; insane, care of, county and State systems compared, 228; extending forest preserve in, X, 22; transfer tax assistant, 108.

VETOES. Indemnifying sheriff for escapes, II, 84; contingent expenses, 95; highways, relative to, 348; county treasurer's fees, VI, 508; bridge over Rondout creek, Marbletown, 585; Hurley, town meetings by election districts, 674, 690; compensation of certain town officers, VII, 130; protection of trout in certain waters, 131; Esopus creek, protection of fish in, 234; extending jail limits, 265; plank road inspectors, exemptions, 414; Wawarsing, establishing union school district boundary, 806; bonds to pay former bonds, 994; insane asylum, purchase by State, IX, 243; map of forest preserve in, 776; Marbletown, free bridge, contributing to expense of, 817; extending forest preserve, X, 291; Ulster and Delaware road repairs, 696.

ULSTER COUNTY LOAN AND TRUST COMPANY, KINGSTON. Charter, veto, VIII, 230.

ULSTER AND DELAWARE FIRST BRANCH TURNPIKE COMPANY. Suspending powers of, veto, II, 1081.

ULSTER AND DELAWARE PLANK ROAD COMPANY. Extending charter, veto, VII, 565; veto not transmitted within ten-day period, 667, 671.

ULSTER FEMALE SEMINARY. Amending charter, veto, VI, 693.

UNADILLA. Village sidewalks, veto, VI, 195.

UNADILLA BRIDGE COMPANY. Extending charter, veto, IV, 636.

UNDERTAKERS. State board, bill to establish, veto, IX, 265; to be licensed, 265.

UNDERWOOD, NATHAN. Remission of interest on mortgage, veto, III, 15.

UNIFORMS. Civil War, supply of, V, 406.

UNIFORMED VETERANS, TWENTY-THIRD REGIMENT, NATIONAL GUARD. Charter, veto, VII, 1108.

UNION. Village, Tornado Hook and Ladder Company No. 1, charter, veto, VII, 233.

UNION. See also COLONIES. Of colonies, importance of, I, 320; negotiations for, 320; should join in frontier defense, 324, 336, 337, 364; Governor Clinton urges negotiations for, 335; joining in Cape Breton expedition, 332, 340, 346, 349, 351; for mutual protection, 366, 368, 465; Massachusetts appoints commissioners to negotiate for, 370; in expedition against Canada, 373, 376, 392, 404, 413; estimated expense of attack on Crown Point, 393; new war measures, estimated expense of, 404; agreement for colonial union, 419, 457, 461, 462; Crown Point expedition, 419, 440; of colonies in Indian treaty, 514;

UNION —(Continued).

Crown urges colonies to join in opposing invasion, 531, 539, 565; meeting of commissioners at Albany, 541; general plan of, formed at Albany, 550, 577; plan of, reported by Lords of Trade, 582; Albany plan not approved, 582; agreement as to northern garrisons, 584; expense of northern garrisons, 585; common fund recommended, 599; with Great Britain, importance of, 729; Indian trade regulations, 735, 739; Congress meets in Philadelphia, 766.

UNION ASSOCIATION OF AGRICULTURAL SOCIETIES. Three members of State Fair Commission to be chosen from, X, 120.

UNION BANK. Charter dependent on New Jersey statute, II, 705.

UNION COLLEGE. See also UNION UNIVERSITY. Aid to, II, 453, 551, 973; lottery, payment of prizes, 678; flourishing condition of, III, 296, 540, 739, 766, 857; appointment of policemen for, Schenectady, veto, VI, 1032; adjustment of taxes, veto, IX, 534.

UNION DEFENSE COMMITTEE. Supplies for militia regiments, VII, 500.

UNION FREE SCHOOL DISTRICT No. 4, ORANGETOWN. Amending charter, date of annual meeting, veto, VIII, 334; act amended, 334.

UNION FREE SCHOOLS. Act providing for, IV, 647; VI, 86; successful operation of, IV, 799; academical departments, 619; VII, 947; borrowing money, general act, VII, 1013; instruction in music, IX, 116; Warwick, legalizing district bonds, X, 283.

VETOES. Academic departments, Regents' examinations, deficiency, VII, 467; instruction of teachers, appropriation, 495; Wawarsing, establishing school district boundary, 806; Weedsport, amending act, 933; VIII, 717; Hoosick, board of education, additional powers, VII, 934; Baldwinsville, borrowing money, 1013; Lysander and Van Buren, school district, 1106; Pomfret, establishing school district, VIII, 82; Carthage, new school building, appropriation, 117; Fort Covington, annual meeting, 130; Lenox, extending district boundaries, 130; Orangetown, union free school district No. 4, changing date of annual meeting, 334; Newtown, free school district No. 12, charter, 338; Lyons district No. 6, additional accommodations, 702; Cortland, amending act, 888; districts, powers except in cities and villages, 889; academic departments, use of academies, IX, 361; new act passed; Lyons, clerk of trustees, 431; Ontario, district No. 6, bonds for new schoolhouse site and building, 470; Walton, refunding bonds, 812; Cortland district No. 7, establishing boundary, 816; Jamestown, special holidays, X, 173; Palmyra, additional building, 752; union school district No. 1, Luzerne and Hadley, legalizing proceedings relative to new site and school building, 811; free school fund, apportionment to certain districts, 1906, 949.

UNION LEAGUE CLUB. Aid to soldiers, V, 685; quoted, opposes new Croton aqueduct, VII, 639; urges electoral reform, VIII, 788.

UNION LITERARY SOCIETY, ELLISBURGH. Vetoes, changing name, VIII, 980; changing name, enlarging income limit, IX, 56.

UNION METHODIST EPISCOPAL CHURCH, NEW YORK. Taxes, 1894, release of, veto, IX, 794.

UNION MISSION CHAPEL ASSOCIATION, BROOKLYN. Trusts, legacies and donations, veto, VIII, 1127.

UNION UNIVERSITY. See also UNION COLLEGE. Lease of Schenectady armory, veto, VI, 709.

UNION VETERAN LEGION. Relief of soldiers. veto, IX, 803.

UNION VETERAN PROTECTIVE ASSOCIATION. Annual meetings, veto, IX, 793.

UNION VILLAGE AND JOHNSONVILLE RAILROAD COMPANY. Aid from Greenwich, veto, VI, 164.

UNITED LIFE AND ACCIDENT INSURANCE ASSOCIATION. Changing name, act relative to, VIII, 1144.

UNITED PRESBYTERIAN CHURCH, NORTH HAMDEN. Changing name, veto, VIII, 1096.

UNITED STATES. See also CESSIONS TO UNITED STATES. War with Spain, I, 288; claims against State, payment of, II, 9, 570; collecting debts due to, 32, 65; treaty with France, 44, 67; New York's claims against, 52; treasury organized, 65; New York Tax Law in aid of, 77; preservation and protection of property, 79; John Jay appointed Minister to Spain, 83; General Hospital, nurses in, 95; Congress adopts system of finance, 97; Connecticut's claim for cannon and ball, 101; object of union, 103; defects in Continental Congress, 107; confederation of, 112; imports on foreign merchandise, 120, 121; union established, Articles of Confederation ratified, 127; accounts with New York for supplies, 134; too much reliance on European powers, 153; independence not acknowledged in Europe, except by France, 153; estimated annual cost of Revolutionary War, 157; cannot deprive State of territory, 179; limitation of power of Congress to admit Territory into Union, 179; British designs to separate from French, 184; treaty with Netherlands, 188; treaty of peace with Great Britain, 191, 192, 195; Federal affairs, general note, 192; proposed convention to revise system of government, 194; British attempt to monopolize West India trade, 197; public debt, arrears of interest, 218; proposed treaty of commerce with Great Britain, 236; intrusions on land of, 245; claims against New York, 253, 437, 438; statement of expenditures, 256; Virginia proposes commercial convention, 259; requisition on New York, 263; convention to frame Constitution, 270; national treaty binding on States, 274; Federal

UNITED STATES — (*Continued*).

revenue system, general note, 275; duties exclusively devoted to payment of public debt, 276; Constitution submitted to States, 282; New York suggests convention for consideration of constitutional amendments, 290, 293; Virginia proposes amendments to Constitution, 294; Federal government established, general note, 296; election of President, 297, 299; use of jails for confinement of prisoners, 304; Sandy Hook lighthouse, 304; relation to war in Europe, 333; suability of States, 334; prosperous condition of, 359; judges to be ineligible to other office, 366; commissioner of, treaty with Indians, 368; treaty with Seven Nations, 368, 380, 381, 386, 390; borrows cannon from New York, 416; relations with France, 420, 423, 442, general note; French depredations on commerce, 445; development of national idea, 447; sole power as to seamen in foreign service, 459; appointment of officers, 500; Spanish aggressions at New Orleans, 522; militia system, 532; Louisiana purchased from France, 535; presidential elections, Twelfth Amendment, 537; loans arms to New York, 609; invited to aid canal enterprise, 675; British reparations in Chesapeake case,. 690; a Christian country, 729; declares war against Great Britain, 735; acquiring land, struck jury in proceedings for, 752, 753, 777, 878; deposit of military stores in Colonie arsenal, 755; proposed purchase of arsenal, 755; arms furnished by, 1812, 762, 798; funds furnished by, 1812, 763; Emperor of Russia offers mediation with Great Britain, 785, 801; direct tax on States, War of 1812, 788, 906; deserters from army and navy, bill relating to, veto, 819; treaty of peace with Great Britain, War of 1812, 824; purchase of land at Plattsburgh, 825; admission of new States, proposed limitation of power, 827; some results of the war, 850; War with Algiers, 852; organization of militia, 853; purchase of Staten Island fortifications, 865, 940; Commercial Convention with Great Britain, complaint relative to New York pilot fees, 888; frequent wars, 909; effect of dismemberment, 966; character of republican government, 1023; relation to States, 1042, 1072; officers of, alleged interference in State elections, 1042, 1054, 1059, 1060; power to tax Bank of United States, State business, 1077; public land, Maryland proposition as to proceeds of, 1079; appropriation of public land for schools, 1080, 1101, see PUBLIC LANDS; should aid construction of western canals, 1096; commercial treaty with Great Britain, 1104; British act regulating commercial intercourse with Canada, III, 23; jurisdiction over State canals, 49, 76, 78, 154; jurisdiction over land ceded by State, 139; distribution of public revenue among States, 155, 186, 307, 330, 373, 433, 612, 624; convicts admitted to State prisons and penitentiaries, 163; election of 1828, general effects of, 258; payment of national debt, 283; New

UNITED STATES —(Continued).

York denies jurisdiction of Federal court in New Jersey boundary controversy, 312, 357, 422; beautiful structure of government, 360; supreme law, what constitutes, 364; judicial power, 364; early payment of national debt, 369; northeastern boundary question, 389; cannot change boundaries of a State without its consent, 390; South Carolina nullification proceedings, 427; public debt extinguished, 493; improving navigation of Hudson river, 511; mail, transportation of, veto, 592; funds deposited with States, 612; power to coin money, 630; franking privilege, proposed extension, 637; exclusive jurisdiction of foreign relations, 689; liable to State for military expenses incurred in its defense, 692; regulation of currency, 780; measure of sovereignty reserved to States, 985; jurisdiction of courts, 1026; northern boundary, British treaty, 1038; possible encroachments on rights of States, IV, 4, 6; Michigan requests additional river and harbor improvements, 46; Massachusetts denies power to acquire independent foreign State, 85; claims to Oregon, 285; northern boundary, difference with Great Britain, 286; improvement of rivers and harbors, 392; War with Mexico, State militia called out, 415; annexation of Texas, 416; acquisition of territory by Mexican War, 445; recognizes Seneca Indian Constitution, 459; northwest territory, slavery prohibited in, 499; acquisitions of territory, 500; ordinance of 1787, status of slavery, 567; limiting spirit of conquest, 568; sectional differences should be discouraged, 617; independence, proposed monument to commemorate, 624; commercial reciprocity with British provinces, 656; amount of stock debt, 702; New York city the financial center, 732; relation to slavery, 815; cession to New York of land at Sandy Hook for quarantine, V, 101; embassy from Japan, 297; visit of Prince of Wales, 297; property seized by secessionists, 306; loan based on deposit fund, 330; Texas denies compulsory power against State, 343; proposed liability for loss of fugitive slave, 355; use of New York canals for military purposes, 367, 502; stock may be held by banks, 376; direct tax on States, 1861, 388; disloyal persons visit foreign countries, 409; limitations of power, 463; emancipation of slaves, 473; duty to provide for defense of New York, 570; donation of public lands to States, 596; slavery prohibited, Thirteenth Amendment, 616; acquiring property in New York for custom-house, 642; large army disbanded at close of war, 680; asked to aid in preventing cholera, 701; general beneficial results of Civil War, 715; admiralty laws applicable to Erie canal, 720; estimated population in 1900, 753; validity of public debt confirmed, Fourteenth Amendment, 791; cannot pay for property or slaves lost by participants in rebellion, 791; revenue, New York's contribution, 820; legal tenders, fractional currency and bank notes,

UNITED STATES —(*Continued*).

822; taxes should be revised and reduced, 824; control of New York canals, Governor Hoffman's protest against, VI, 16, 239; redemption of legal tender notes, 134; coin should be restored to its proper place, 137; decline of ship building, 247; Centennial Celebration at Philadelphia, 1876, 302; public buildings at Albany, veto, 449; Virginia resolutions, Federal assumption of State debts, 563; convicts in Albany penitentiary, 712; New York's interest in financial policy, 750; should furnish currency sufficient for business, 762; taxes, comparative statement, 957; payments to foreign creditors, 958; tax consumers, 960; excessive speculation, 962; importance of immigration in national development, 1000; acquires title and assumes jurisdiction of Antietam National cemetery, VII, 172; acquiring jurisdiction over Harlem river and Spuyten Duyvil creek, veto, 406; cession of land in Brooklyn, veto, 932; commercial supremacy, opinion of De Tocqueville, 992; sea-coast defenses, VIII, 182; direct tax, amount refunded to New York, 1107; jurisdiction over land ceded by States, 1115; cession of land in Queens county, veto, 1113; cessions to, general act, 1896, 1113; topographic survey of New York, IX, 323; Cullum legacy, release of transfer tax, veto, 349; relation to question between Great Britain and Venezuela, concerning boundary, 646; has no prisons, convicts in State prisons, 655; Palisades Military and National park, 735; regular army should be increased, X, 13; militia, definition, act of Congress, 1903, 15; furnishes arms, equipments and accoutrements for State militia, 16; boarding prisoners in Cattaraugus county jail, veto, 706; expenditures for rivers and harbors, X, 730; policy as to forest preservation, 755.

UNITED STATES COMMISSION AND STORAGE COMPANY. Charter, veto, VI, 325.

UNITED STATES DEPOSIT FUND. See also COMMON SCHOOL FUND and LITERATURE FUND. Established, III, 612, 622; income, appropriation of, 612, 613, 650; IV, 65, 89; V, 2; loan of, commissioners provided for, III, 613; total amount of, 622; IV, 22, 64, 118, 270, 377, 395, 426, 475, 551, 602, 645, 782, 831; V, 2, 74; benefit to agricultural interest, III, 624; loan of, 673; IV, 120; investment in canal stock, III, 674; IV, 120; fourth installment withheld, III, 764, 869; collection postponed, IV, 47; distribution of, 270; not to be diverted, 782; IX, 69; loan to State Agricultural College, IV, 853; V, 16; State pledges amount equal to, 330; returning fund to State treasury, VIII, 402; Steuben county, local custody of fund, 429; reducing rate of interest, act relative to, 1149; origin of, X, 622; proposed investment in municipal and local bonds, 623; method of investment, 745; losses on loans, 745.

UNITED STATES DEPOSIT FUND —(*Continued*).

VETOES. Jefferson county, VI, 511; Delaware county, Horton judgment, sale of, VII, 877; mortgage on Ward's island property, payment of interest, VIII, 112; loan commissioners, Ontario county, transferring funds to, 401; loan commissioners, increasing fees, IX, 115.

UNITED STATES HARVEY WAY AND CONSTRUCTION COMPANY. Relative to, veto, VIII, 639.

UNITED STATES MILITARY PHILOSOPHICAL SOCIETY. President of, translates Kosciusko's treatise on Horse Artillery, II, 639.

UNITED STATES MORTGAGE COMPANY. Amending charter, veto, VI, 580.

UNITED STATES MUTUAL BENEFIT COMPANY OF NEW YORK. Charter, veto, VI, 167.

UNITED STATES TRADE-MARK ASSOCIATION. Charter, veto, VII, 355.

" UNTIL." How construed in statutes, VII, 1006.

UNIVERSAL EXPOSITION, PARIS. Report of commissioners, V, 791, 862.

UNIVERSITIES. Educational operation only partial, II, 719; liberal endowments, VII, 688; legalizing certain charters, veto, 937; new charters, 947; St. Lawrence University and Theological Seminary, amending charter, veto, VIII, 703; amount of property which may be held by, general act, 1889, 728; exemption from taxation, veto, X, 947.

UNIVERSITY OF ALBANY. Organization of, IV, 603.

UNIVERSITY OF BUFFALO. Cancer investigation, appropriation, veto, IX, 772; appropriations for cancer investigation, 1899, 1900, 772; report of New York Pathological Laboratory, X, 142.

UNIVERSITY OF THE CITY OF NEW YORK. Mentioned, III, 501; plan of, 540; aid from United States deposit fund, 613, 711; grammar school, 766; condition of, 766, 857; State debt against, canceled, 767.

UNIVERSITY EXTENSION. Scope and purpose of, IX, 17; Regents given supervision of, 18; disapproved by Governor Flower, 18; R. G. Moulton's views on, 19; University Act of 1892, 21; provision relative to extension, 21; appropriation, veto, 82; investigating relations between capital and labor, 742.

UNIVERSITY LAW. Amending, veto, IX, 804.

UNIVERSITY OF NEW YORK. See also REGENTS. Established, II, 200; supplemental act, 220; original plan of, VIII, 168; revision of laws, included in Constitution of 1894, 171; X, 112; consolidated with Department of Public Instruction, VIII, 171; X, 27, 114, 115, 537, 604, 628, 736; statutes revised, 1889, VIII, 680; revised act of 1892, provision relative to university extension, IX, 21; Governor's comment on, 1898, 828; — 1899, X, 23; supervision of local libraries, X, 829; Unification Commission, 1899, X,

UNIVERSITY OF NEW YORK —(*Continued.*)
114, 128; State Department of Education, 129; relations with Department of Public Instruction, 1901, 227; apportionment of appropriation for high school tuition, 515.

VETOES. Amending charter, VII, 266; convocation, 1876, printing and binding report, 494; Regents' manual, 1880, printing and binding, 494; convocation, 1884, printing proceedings, VIII, 119; general appropriation, X, 551; State Library, temporary services, 551; State Museum, appropriation, 552.

UNIVERSITY OF PENNSYLVANIA. Extension movements, IX, 18.

UNIVERSITY SETTLEMENT. Proposed application to labor questions, IX, 833.

UNIVERSITY SETTLEMENT SOCIETY, NEW YORK. Exempting from taxation, veto, IX, 794.

UNREASONABLE SEARCHES AND SEIZURES. Constitutional provision, IV, 755; V, 471.

UPJOHN, RICHARD W. Examination of Assembly stone arch vault, appropriation, veto, VIII, 840.

UPPER MOHAWK. See CANAJOHARIE.

USES AND TRUSTS. Amending Revised Statutes, veto, VIII, 131.

USURY. Violation of laws relating to, II, 400; policy of law, III, 630; revision of law, IV, 731, 802; corporations not to plead, 805; Corn Exchange Warehouse Company, charter, veto, VI, 215; exempting Stock Exchange, veto, 221; laws should be repealed, 551; report of New York grand jury, 564; modification of laws recommended, VII, 719; advance on various commercial transactions authorized, 719; on personal credit security, veto, X, 171.

UTAH. Territorial organization of, IV, 565.

UTICA. Deposit of arms and ammunition at, II, 636; canal construction begun at, 902; northern terminus of Chenango canal, III, 234; State Lunatic Asylum, 452, 516, 543, 617, 676, 713; advantages derived from internal improvements, 815; State Fair at, IV, 283; bi-partisan police boards, VI, 445; number of excise licenses, 1887, VIII, 359; excise license fees, 1889, 686; additional enginehouse, 1003; river improvements, act relative to, 1145; law library, IX, 46; second-class city, 1905, 678; legalizing Central Advance school bonds and Mary street school bonds, X, 285; courthouse, expense of construction, increasing amount, 768.

VETOES. Recorder's court, increasing salary, VI, 427; canal bridge, Genesee street, 854; VII, 506; VIII, 206; creating board of assessors, VII, 131; assessment on State property, 229; assessment on State property, sewers, 472; Erie canal, pipe under, 938; water supply, 1101; St. Luke's Home, changing name,

UTICA, VETOES — (Continued).

VIII, 326; sewer, Andes avenue, 454; sewer under Erie canal, 710, new bill passed; board of park commissioners, 880; police and fire commissioners, amending act, 889; culvert under Erie canal, 1132; amending charter, IX, 732; bridge over Erie canal, Genesee street, removal, 732; police pensions, 790; Masonic Association, exempting from taxation, 791; firemen's pension fund, X, 476; law library, librarian, increasing compensation, 519; town expense, 686; drainage, extending system, 717; taxes, legalizing, 806, 819; extending Hickory street through State hospital land, 957.

UTICA AND BLACK RIVER RAILROAD COMPANY. Asks State aid, V, 866; consolidation with Black River and Morristown Railroad Company, VII, 847.

UTICA, CHENANGO AND CORTLAND RAILROAD. Extension, veto, VI, 433, new act passed.

UTICA CORN HILL BENEFIT ASSOCIATION. Charter, veto, X, 320.

UTICA ICE COMPANY, LIMITED. Extending time for payment of stock, veto, VII, 869.

UTICA AND SCHENECTADY RAILROAD COMPANY. Right of transportation of freight limited, V, 660; consolidation with other companies authorized, 803.

UTICA STATE HOSPITAL. See also STATE LUNATIC ASYLUM. Extravagant cost of improvements, X, 412; number of visits by local managers, 415.

VETOES. Purchase of farm lands, VIII, 1137; repairs, IX, 194; printing press and equipments, 294; barn at Graycroft and silos, X, 934; extending Hickory street through lands of, 957.

UTICA AND SYRACUSE RAILROAD. Completion of, III, 786.

UTRECHT. Proposed exposition at, VI, 50.

UTRECHT, TREATY OF. Status of Five Nations, I, 542.

UVALDE ASPHALT PAVING COMPANY. Labor and materials, Brooklyn, veto, X, 951.

V.

VACANCIES. Act relating to, II, 511; presidential electors, 545; Lieutenant-Governor, act relating to, 674, 887; Governor, election to fill, 887; Ulster county courthouse commissioners, 944; in militia offices, 992; in Assembly, how filled, III, 133; Governor's power to fill, 176; superintendent of the poor, 516; in office of Governor and Lieutenant-Governor, IV, 433; acts of 1849, 433; in Senate, special elections to fill, 580; in office of town collector, V, 218; filling, constitutional provision, VI, 75, 989; VII, 44; IX, 224;

VACANCIES — (*Continued*).

    justices of sessions, how filled, VI, 121; Senate and Assembly, how filled, 242, 366; New York marine court, 986; New York Superior Court, 988; effect of failure to file bond, VIII, 355.

VETOES. Relative to, IV, 772; justice of the peace, Lowville, VI, 48; justice of peace, amending general act, 74; judicial officers, amending act, VII, 415.

VACCINATION. Of children in public schools, V, 189.

VACHERON, EUGENE F. Proceedings against, appropriation for counsel fees, veto, IX, 775.

VAGRANTS. Disguised persons deemed, IV, 150; new definition needed, 490; special message on, 505; statute amended, 1900; X, 106.

VETOES. Relating to, II, 222; V, 384; New York, amending act, VI, 330; commitment, VII, 932; X, 312; arrest without process, Amsterdam charter, VII, 1016; sentences, hard labor in jail, VIII, 132; Columbia county, regulating commitment and discharge, 891.

VALATIE. Public hall, borrowing money for, veto, VII, 265.

VAN ALEN, J. TRUMBULL. Colonel, Governor's aide, letter to General Taylor, IV, 420.

VAN ARNAM, ABRAHAM. Bond for return of arms, II, 772.

VAN ARNUM, LEWIS S. Board of Claims, veto, IX, 430.

VAN ARVEN, JOSEPH. Bond for return of arms, II, 772.

VAN BENTHUYSEN, ABRAHAM B. Deposition, Buck case, VI, 683.

VAN BENTHUYSEN, ANDREW. Caveat, Buck case, VI, 681.

VAN BENTHUYSEN, BARRET. Caveat, Buck case, VI, 681.

VAN BENTHUYSEN AND SONS. Printing various reports, veto, VII, 490, 491.

VAN BEUREN, BEEKMAN M. Commands troops, 1812, II, 747.

VAN BRUNT STREET AND ERIE BASIN RAILROAD COMPANY. Relief, veto, VI, 518.

VAN BUREN. VETOES. Union school district, VII, 1106; improvement of Dead creek, VIII, 452.

VAN BUREN, JOHN D. Attorney-General, opinion, required population for new county, V, 229.

VAN BUREN, JOHN D., JR. Member of Canal Investigating Commission, 1875, VI, 928; declines appointment as commissioner of State survey, VIII, 255.

VAN BUREN, MARTIN. Chosen Regent, II, 857; Attorney-General, communication from, intrusions on Grand Island, 995; chosen Senator in Congress, 1040; letter from, removal of postmaster, 1070; only Senator from New York, III, 85; Governor, portrait, 230.

VAN BUREN, MARTIN —(*Continued*).

     1829. Annual message, III, 230; condition of State, 230; completion of Revised Statutes, 231; finances, 232; canals, 233; extension of canal system, 235; Delaware and Hudson canal, 237; education, 238; banks, 238; Safety Fund Act, 245; auction duties, 245; elections, 247; bribery at elections, 249; Morgan abduction matter, 250, 264; Society for the Reformation of Juvenile Delinquents, 251; hemp cultivation, 253; publication of Revised Statutes, 253; resigns as Senator in Congress, 253; revision of laws relating to public officers, 255; salaries of judicial officers, 255; Federal relations, 256; renewal of bank charters, 259; Georgia resolutions, 261; Albro relief bill, veto, 262; South Carolina resolutions, 263; cession for Watervliet arsenal, 264; vice-chancellor, 264; New York orphan asylum, 265; resigns as Regent, 267; resigns to become Secretary of State, 266, 269; I, pref. xii; legislative action on resignation, III, 268; official service as Governor, I, pref. xii; chosen President, III, 608; North Carolina condemns financial policy, 752; quoted on internal improvements, 810; as life Senator, possible length of service, VIII, 694.

VAN CORTLANDT, PIERRE. Assembly, favors colonial union, I, 767; first President of Senate, Lieutenant-Governor, 1777, IX, 688.

VAN CORTLANDT, PIERRE, JR. Brigadier-general, orders out Westchester brigade, II, 796.

VAN CORTLANDT, STEPHEN. Member of First Legislative Council, I, 9; account of revenue and taxes, 63, 66, 73, 96.

VAN CORTLANDT, WILLIAM R. Vesting estate in trustees, veto, II, 248.

VAN COTT, JOSHUA M. Member of Tax Revision Commission, 1881, VII, 538.

VAN COURTLAND, STEPHEN. Member of First Legislative Council, I, 9. See VAN CORTLANDT.

VANCOUVER'S ISLAND. Relation to boundary controversy with Great Britain, IV, 286.

VANDALIA. Allegany reservation, bridge at, veto, VI, 707.

"VANDALIA, THE." Conveys French delegates to West Point, VII, 740.

VAN DAM, ISAAC. Subsistence of French prisoners, I, 445; entertainment of French commissioners, 510.

VAN DAM, RIP. President of Council, assumes executive authority, I, 238.

     OPENING SPEECH. Twentieth Assembly, fourth session, I, 239; maintenance of Oswego, 239; blockhouses at Albany, 239; excise, 240; transmits various papers, 240; Assembly changes place of meeting, 240; memorial against aid to sugar colonies,

VAN DAM, RIP — (*Continued*).

240; Massachusetts boundary, 241; French at Crown Point, 241; requested to communicate with neighboring colonies relative to French encroachments, 242; charges against Governor Cosby, 253; official service, pref. ix.

VANDENBERG, PETER. Dock on Oneida lake, veto, VI, 156.

VANDENBERGH, GYSBERT. Account for war expenses, I, 394.

VAN DEN BROEK, J. W. United States Consul at Amsterdam, IV, 173.

VANDERBILT, CORNELIUS. Member of Yorktown Centennial Commission, VII, 734.

VANDERHEUF, FRANCIS ADRIAN. Appointed to translate Dutch records, II, 1115.

VANDERHYDEN, DAVID. Services on mission to Canada, I, 518; report, Indian attack on Brimmer family, 571.

VANDERKEMP. See KEMP, FRANÇOIS ADRIAN VANDER.

VANDERKEMP, JOHN J. Agent, Holland Land Company, communication from, III, 755.

VANDERLOCHT, WILLIAM. Relief of creditors of, veto, II, 287.

VANDERVOORT, SOPHIA G. Claim against New York, veto, IX, 451, 727; new act passed, 1895, 451; act unconstitutional, 451.

VAN DEUSEN, GEORGE. Canal Department, appropriation for services, veto, IX, 716.

VAN DE WATER, MARY A. Relief, veto, VII, 507.

VAN DYCK, HENRY H. Superintendent of Public Instruction, work commended, V, 83.

VAN GORDER, MORGAN. Court of Claims, veto, X, 165.

VAN HOESEN, JOHN. Dock on Oneida lake, veto, VI, 156.

VAN HORNE, CORNELIUS. Service in exchange of prisoners, I, 489.

VAN LAER, ARNOLD J. F. Archivist, State Library, acknowledgments to, I, pref. xv.

VANN, IRVING J. Court of Appeals, historical sketch of judicial system, X, 671; quoted, power of Supreme Court justices to exercise administrative functions, 679.

VAN NESS, JACOB. Clerk, Dutchess county, removal of, II, 1069; appointed postmaster at Poughkeepsie, 1069.

VAN NESS, WILLIAM W. Justice of Supreme Court, letter from, Williams' case, II, 627; communication from, Hodges murder case, 997; inquiry concerning conduct of, 1031; exonerated, 1031.

VAN NESS AND WOODWORTH. Revision of statutes noted, VIII, 38.

VAN ORDEN, PETER S. Brigadier-general, commands brigade at Great Barn island, II, 810.

VAN PEYMA, CHARLOTTE. Assistant in State Library, acknowledgments to, I, pref. xv.

VAN RENSSELAER, HENRY I. Affidavit of, disorders, II, 244.

VAN RENSSELAER, JOHN I. Tract, Columbia county, description of leases, IV, 330.

VAN RENSSELAER, PHILIP S. Mayor of Albany, resolution of common council relative to capitol, II, 936.

VAN RENSSELAER, SOLOMON. Payment of expenses incurred in removing General Montgomery's remains, II, 987, 1000, 1002.

VAN RENSSELAER, STEPHEN. Major-general, commands troops on Niagara frontier, 1812, II, 746, 764, 766; funds received by, 765.

Chosen Regent, II, 993; aids geological survey, III, 591; death of, 750; action of Legislature, 751; proceedings by executors for collection of rent, 823; unwillingness to collect rents, IV, 337; claim of tenants, 338; Lieutenant-Governor, 1797, IX, 689.

VAN RENSSELAER, STEPHEN, JR. Executor of Stephen Van Rensselaer, proceedings to collect rent, III, 823; rents building for idiot asylum, IV, 555.

VAN RENSSELAER, WILLIAM BAYARD. Member of Capital Centenary Commission, IX, 689.

VAN SCHAICK, GOOSE. Recognizance discharged, relief of widow, 1, 214.

VAN SCHAICK, SYBRANT G. Recorder of Albany, sent on mission to Indians, I, 570.

VAN SCHOLOZER, HERR. German minister, accompanies German delegates to Yorktown Celebration, VII, 741.

VAN SLYCK, EDWARD D. Relief, veto, VI, 697; trustee Binghamton Insane Asylum, charges against, not removed, VII, 443.

VAN SLYKE, JAMES W. Court of Claims, veto, IX, 858; X, 449.

VAN STEENBURGH, JOHN. Convicted of murder of Deputy Sheriff Steele, IV, 309; personal description of, 315; jury asks for commutation of sentence, 316.

VANUXEM (Vannuxem) LARDNER. Geological survey, geologist fourth district, III, 640, 991; report, 644, 683, 754; IV, 81; transferred to third district, III, 681, 754.

VAN WYCK, JOHN. Queens county sheriff, claim for subsistence of prisoners, I, 478.

VAN WYCK, ROBERT ANDERSON. Objects to New York teachers' salary bill, X, 154.

VAN ZANDT, JACOBUS. Claim for labor, Fort George, I, 511.

VARICK, RICHARD. Commissioner to revise statutes, II, 255; expenses, removal of Montgomery's remains, 1001; communication from, condition of Merchants' Bank, 1029.

VARNEY, EDMOND. Bond for return of arms, II, 774.

VARNUM, JAMES M. Member of Yorktown Centennial Commission, VII, 734.

VASSAR COLLEGE. Right to hold additional property, veto, VIII, 728.

VATTEL. Quoted, subjects of one State interfering in affairs of another, III, 594, 599.

VATTEMARE, ALEXANDRE. Documents from, international exchanges, IV, 384; deposits Pope's gift in State Library, 453; presents report from France, 465; report on international exchanges, 508; presents French publications, 524; report as commissioner to Universal Exposition, Paris, 865.

VEDDER, COMMODORE P. Senate, bill taxing beverages, VIII, 797.

VENDUES. See also AUCTION. Petition of New York grand jury against, I, 170; tax on sales at, II, 199.

VENEZUELA. Minister from, requests permission to acquire and hold real estate in New York, V, 617; participation in Cotton States Exposition, IX, 581; question with Great Britain relative to boundary, 646.

VENICE TOWN INSURANCE COMPANY. Changing location of business office, veto, VII, 1013.

VENUE. Change of, in Federal courts, II, 404, 415.

VERIFICATION. Of accounts, I, 478.

VERMONT. State government organized, II, 67, 176; demands New York's relinquishment of claim to disputed territory, 135; exertions against British, 138; New Hampshire boundary, 140; territorial claims of, 145, 177; alleged treasonable conduct of leaders, 163, 166; proclamation asserting authority as independent State, 178; alleged usurpations of, 180; New York consents to erection of, 307; letter from Governor soliciting aid to establish university, 330; resolution, Federal constitutional amendment, 449; proposed amendment, importation of slaves, 586; communication from, relative to Canadian boundary, 606; constitutional amendment, removal of Federal judges, 627; disapproves Massachusetts embargo amendment, 665; disapproves Pennsylvania resolution as to special tribunal, 667; militia at battle of Plattsburgh, 803; disapproves Massachusetts amendment (see page 827), 864; disapproves Kentucky resolutions relative to salary of Representatives, and also Massachusetts resolution relative to election of representatives and presidential electors, 937; constitutional amendment, election of Representatives and presidential electors by districts, 990; disapproves Pennsylvania proposition as to national banks, 1075; approves Ohio proposition relative to abolition of slavery, III, 136; disapproves Tennessee proposition to elect President and Vice-President by popular vote and making Congressmen ineligible to civil appointments, 181; disapproves Maine proposition relative to distribution of Federal revenue, 217; disapproves Georgia proposition relative to election of President and Vice-President by popular vote and limiting power of House of Representatives to

VERMONT —(*Continued*).

determine election of President, 217; disapproves Ohio proposition limiting right of suffrage to free white male persons, 217; resolutions on presidential elections, 315; disapproves resolutions by southern States denying to Congress the constitutional power to regulate the tariff and to make appropriations for internal improvements, 315; resolutions recommending fortifications on northern frontier, 318; disapproves Georgia proposition as to election of President and jurisdiction of House of Representatives to determine an election; also Louisiana proposition extending presidential term, 354; resolutions on anti-slavery agitation, 645; marauders supposed to be from, 759; resolutions on public lands, 821; constitutional amendment, ineligibility of President to second term, 907; uniform date for presidential elections, 972; approves abolition of franking privilege and reduction of letter postage, IV, 45; resolutions on slavery, 504, 507; resolutions,— national bureau of agriculture, 505; — Fugitive Slave Law, extension of slavery, 865; act relative to fishing in Lake Champlain, V, 719; appropriation for Antietam cemetery, 840; tax exemptions, VI, 371.

VERMONT CONTROVERSY. Origin of, I, 756, 758, 765; disturbance in territory, 764; II, 51, 76; plans for independent government, 24; general note, 47, 102, 135; legislative action on, 47, 51; organizing new government, 67; act of Congress relative to, 82; matter submitted to Congress, 102, 144, 174; hearing before Congress, 105; Vermont demands New York's relinquishment of claim to disputed territory, 135; Governor Chittenden's letter to Congress, 136; Senate resolutions relative to, 142; papers relating to, 148; alleged treasonable conduct of Vermont leaders, 163, 166; pardon of offenses against New York, 164; petitions from inhabitants of disputed territory requesting pardon, 166; New York resolutions, historical statement, 174; disturbance in Cumberland county, 188, 210; settlement of, 307.

VERONA. VETOES. Additional justice of the peace, VI, 326; canal wall, IX, 469.

VERPLANCK, GULIAN. Speaker of Assembly, 1797, IX, 689; chosen Regent of University, II, 308; leasehold estates, IV, 333.

VERPLANCK, GULIAN C. Chairman Assembly committee on colleges, academies and common schools, report on national public lands, II, 1079; appointed Regent, III, 142.

VERPLANCK, PHILIP. Commissioner on colonial union, I, 370; plan of frontier fortifications, 572.

VERPLANCK, SAMUEL. Leasehold estates, IV, 333.

VERSAILLES, COURT OF. Insincerity in negotiations, I, 662.

VESSELS. Powder duty on, recommended, I, 357, 744; intended for Canadian expedition, exempt from duty, 420; for service on

VESSELS — (*Continued*).

    lake, 567; foreign, tonnage on, proposed, 618; exceeding fifty tons, embargo on, 622; French destroyed at Cadaraqui, 625, 627; impressment of, II, 99; British alone to be used in West India trade, 197; in New York harbor, Governor to direct disposition of, 246; at New York, act relating to, 819; British, pilot fees at New York, 918; from certain ports, exempt from quarantine, III, 87; New York, inspection proposed by Virginia, 910, 925, 936, 980, 1028; New York, South Carolina act for search of, 980, 1028; masters, tax on, IV, 77; seamen, tax on, 77; master's bond against passengers becoming paupers, 441; number surveyed at New York, V, 187; arrivals at New York, 380; tonnage and value at port of New York, 410; quarantine, detained for observation, VI, 533, 626; coasting, quarantine regulations, New Jersey complaint, 778; coasting, relieved from pilotage on entering port of New York by Hell Gate, VII, 441.

VETOES. Steam and naphtha on certain lakes, inspection of, VIII, 1121; demands against, collection of, IX, 813; ferry and excursion boats, life saving crews, X, 807.

VESTED RIGHTS. Proceeds of Harlaem common lands, II, 1112; under judgment, IV, 532; under railroad franchise, V, 874; highway damages, VI, 158, 489; highways, Westchester county, 512; married women, insuring husbands' lives, rights of children, VII, 80; New York, Putnam county water supply, 595; property in intoxicating liquors, VIII, 361.

VESTRYMEN. Have power to call dissenting minister, I, 55; authorized to impose tax, II, 212.

VETCH, COLONEL. Letter from, noted, II, 136; instructions from Crown 139.

VETERAN ASSOCIATION CORCORAN IRISH LEGION. Charter, veto, VI, 341.

VETERAN ASSOCIATION. Seventy-first Regiment, National Guard, charter, veto, VII, 1108; VIII, 404.

VETERAN RESERVE OF THE NATIONAL GUARD. Charter, veto, VII, 1111.

VETERANS. See also CIVIL SERVICE. Preference in civil service, VII, 977; VIII, 19, 151; IX, 560; X, 20; preference as orderlies and watchmen in new capitol, VIII, 20; preference as workmen on new capitol, 226; rights, more legislation needed, 483; Soldiers' Home, review of Silvey case, 498; survivors of New York troops at Gettysburg, IX, 324; preference according to compensation, act of 1895 unconstitutional, 561; civil service, protection of, act of 1896, 664; rights, act of 1901, X, 279; preferences, removals, amending Civil Service Law, 410.

VETOES. Exempting from taxation property purchased with pension money, repeal, IX, 113; see act of 1897, 113; Union Veteran

VETERANS, VETOES — (*Continued*).

    Legion, relief of soldiers, 803; peddlers' licenses to, 811; sons, issuing arms to, X, 61; associations, use of armories, 385; sons of, use of armories, 385; amending Civil Service Act, 592, 710, 714, 805; pensions for retiring, 924.

VETERINARY MEDICINE AND SURGERY. VETOES. Regulating practice, IX, 153; X, 169; practitioners, legalizing acts, IX, 376; admission to examinations, X, 317; practicing without license, penalty, 438; Regents' examinations, appropriation, 551.

VETOES. See various persons and subjects; by Crown, XI, 55; by Colonial Governors, 55; Council of Revision, 55; by Governors of State, 58; by President, 163.

VETO POWER. By Colonial Governor, I, 7, 18; Governor has absolute negative on all bills, 254; Governor no power as to separate provisions in appropriation bills, 489; Council of Revision, II, 4; passage of bills over veto, 4; first veto by Council of Revision, 21; effect on powers of Legislature, 21; separate items in appropriation bills, 460; V, 263; VI, 369, 403, 642, 852, 864, 924; IX, 404; X, 794, 799, 935; cannot be evaded by adopting concurrent resolution instead of passing bill, II, 740; Assembly committee suggests change of, 1021; vested in Governor, III, 2; IV, 769; passing bill over veto, vote required, III, 531, 1003; IV, 252; occasions for exercise of, III, 973; President, 977; IX, 406; boards of supervisors, proposition to vest veto power in county judge, V, 385; omnibus veto, see that title; executive accountability for appropriations, VI, 925; ten-day bills, general note, VII, 667; interference with legislative discretion, VIII, 85, 89; X, 921; Governor Odell's rule relative to, 228; vested in mayors by constitutional provision relative to special city laws, 504.

VICE-CHANCELLOR. Office created, III, 264; additional, recommended, 610; for eighth circuit, 720; assistant for first circuit, 720; powers of, vested in justices of the Supreme Court, IV, 443.

VICE-PRESIDENT. Election of, II, 322; proposed amendment as to eligibility, 425; as to qualifications of, 433, 434; letter from, resignation of Senator Watson, 459; Governor Tompkins resigns executive office to become, 883; Governor Clinton's comment on method of choosing, 1040; congressional nomination of, Tennessee protest against, III, 31; proposed election by popular vote, 137; proposed amendment, Senate not to determine election of, 589, 591; Millard Fillmore succeeds to presidency on death of Zachary Taylor, IV, 572; Arkansas propositions, alternative choice between slave-holding and non-slaveholding States, V, 354; Chester A. Arthur becomes President on death of President Garfield, VII, 678.

VICTORIA UNIVERSITY. Extension movement, IX, 17.

VICTUALLERS. At Oswego, non-payment of, I, 233.

VICTUALLING HOUSES. Quartering soldiers in, I, 604.

VIELE, EGBERT L. Requests approval of Harvey rapid transit bill, VIII, 125.

VIENNA. Sylvan Beach, municipal regulations, note, VIII, 1131.

VETOES. Real estate assessments, VI, 1033; railroad bonds, VII, 267; police regulations, VIII, 534, 1131.

VIGO. English victory at, I, 104.

VILLAGES. St. Regis, laying out, II, 986; general law for incorporation, IV, 379; dissolution, 380; officers, how chosen, 684; judicial officers, how chosen, V, 138; too many special charters, 191, 294, 387; bounties for volunteers, 455; restricting financial operations of, IV, 701, 730; V, 849; VI, 825; VII, 31, 637; right of local government, VI, 30; fire, hook and ladder and hose companies, 55, 181, 277; property qualifications of voters, 77; lands for public improvements, trustees cannot appoint commissioners to ascertain damages, 90, 120; general act of 1870, 120, 226; special charters prohibited, amendment of 1874, 120, 683; general act of 1897, 120; sidewalks, act sustained, 120; boards of excise, 127; special message recommending general law, 145; special, reincorporating under general act, 188; appointment of police justices, 216; clerk cannot appoint commissioners to ascertain damages, 217; police justices, 244; water supply, interference by private corporation, 272; eminent domain, waterworks, 285; laws should be uniform, 402; amending act, Akron, 502; what constitutes a village, 704; on Allegany and Cattaraugus reservations, survey under act of Congress, 704; separate companies of National Guard, VII, 155; charter amendments, Governor Robinson's protest against, 159; heavy debt and taxation, 298; officers, property qualifications, 324; number in 1881, 645; proposed constitutional amendment, 1882, not adopted, 728; property for public use, assessors cannot appraise damages, 775; charters granted before 1874, may be amended, 775, 878; should be compelled to reorganize under general law, 881; general act should be made applicable to villages incorporated by special act, 1009; street railroads, operation and extension, act relative to, 1063; when residents may not vote for highway commissioner, VIII, 55; street railroads, act relative to, 200; incorporated under general law, not entitled to special legislation, 330; general registration law recommended by Governor Cornell, 721; included in county road system, 1042; Sylvan Beach, special municipal regulations, 1131; large number of people living in,

VILLAGES —(*Continued*).

IX, 29; Governor Flower recommends personal registration in, 180; payments to charitable institutions, 551; when registration of voters required, 555; civil service applicable to, 663; East Aurora, legalizing bonds, X, 284; Brockport, legalizing special election for establishment of sewer system, 518; Highway Improvement Act of 1898 not applicable to, 523; tabulation of accounts and expenses, 764; Cobleskill, legalizing election for public improvements, 892.

VETOES. Plattsburgh, amending charter, IV, 592; Oxford, amending charter, 684; Canandaigua, highway bill, 771; Gouverneur, declaring street a public highway, VI, 76; Chateaugay, village charter, 76; Owego, increasing number of supervisors, 79; Jamaica, amending charter, 90; New Hartford, charter, 183; De Ruyter, extending boundaries, 189; sidewalks, Unadilla, 195; charter elections, non-resident voters, 195; Goshen, powers of street commissioner, 213; amending general act, 341; VII, 130, 131; VIII, 640; Memphis, special charter, VI, 341; Hart's Falls, changing name, 341; water supply, 591; Canajoharie, revising charter, 683, 824; amending general act, Corning, 693; Dansville, extending boundaries, 702; Matteawan, lighting street, 704; Salamanca, charter, 704; Clyde, borrowing money, amending charter, 706; West Troy, board of fire commissioners, 911; Bath-on-Hudson, amending charter, 1035; Camden, amending charter, 1036; Plattsburgh fire department, VII, 64; Andes fire department, 65; Sag Harbor fire apparatus, water supply, 68; Niagara city, amending general act, 75; Carthage, amending charter, 78; Dunkirk, amending charter, 79; Skaneateles engine-house, 97; Niagara Falls, amending general act, 98; Rockton fire department, 120; Saratoga Springs, floating debt, 130; amending general act of 1847, 131; police justices, 131; Middletown, payment of bonds, 131; trustees, confirming election and allotting terms, 132; Fort Edward board of education, contract with Collegiate Institute, 205; amending general act of 1870, Northville, 214; White Plains, bonded indebtedness, 265; Valatie public hall, borrowing money for, 265; amending general act, jurisdiction of town constables, 265; bonds, investments by insurance companies, 266; Lansingburgh, eligibility to office, 323; Le Roy, trustees, additional powers, 337; police justice, Wolcott, 389; Baldwinsville, relative to, 415; Little Falls, amending charter, 416; Lancaster, amending charter, 416; extending limits for health purposes, 416; Middleburgh, separate road district, 414, 440; Warwick, Excelsior Hose Company, charter,

VILLAGES, VETOES — (*Continued*).

507; incorporation, relative to, 509; Piermont, macadamizing highways, 509; amending general act, Dresden, 644; amending act of 1847, Clayton, 664; street railroads, maintenance and operation, 793, 894; Greenport, relative to, 805; Tonawanda, amending charter, 805; Mount Vernon, relative to, 806; Pulaski fire limits, 806; Geddes, relative to, 806; waterworks companies, 807; Albion, relative to, 807; Fayetteville, purchasing fire apparatus, 848; Mechanicville, purchasing fire apparatus, 849; Perry cemeteries, reinterments, 870; Lyons, revising charter, 878; Gravesend investigation, counsel fees, 905; Saratoga Springs, street improvements, 930; White Plains, repealing charter, as to town of Greenburgh, 931; Northville police justices, 932; general act, 933; Skaneateles, revising charter, 933, 1008; Montezuma, amending charter, 934, 1104; Hornellsville, amending charter, 935; Seneca Falls, revising charter, 935; Owego, amending charter, 935; Sea Cliff, incorporating, 936; Mount Vernon, amending charter, 936; Middletown, Orange county, village hall, 1042; VIII, 61; Carthage, excise licenses, VII, 1047; Saratoga Springs,— fire department, 1102; — sewage, 1102; Geneva railroads, 1105; Danforth, contract with Syracuse Water Company, 1105; Amsterdam waterworks, claims for work, 1107; hack stands, Saratoga Springs, 1112; Newark, revising charter, 1123; Phœnix, amending charter, 1123; Owego, electric-lights, VIII, 129; Silver Creek, straightening Walnut creek, 129; Fort Covington, annual school meeting, 130; water supply, 130; police justice, Wellsville, legalizing acts, 132; Ithaca police department, 256; Oneonta, prohibiting new cemeteries, 327; Herkimer police justice and police constables, 330; Saratoga Springs, sewers in Church street, 331; Sherburne, raising money for new bridge, 336; Canandaigua, sewers and drains, 348; West Troy, contract with water company, water for sewers, 382; Mohawk cemetery, revising act, 391; taxation for water, qualifications of voters on proposition, 406; Gloversville fire department, term of service, 409; Savannah engine-house and fire department, 410; Tarrytown and North Tarrytown, sewers, 462; Chatham, amending charter, 469; organization of trust companies, 507; Westfield, establishing water department, 518; New Brighton fire department, 532; Edgewater fire department, charter, 616; Bath-on-Hudson, amending charter, 620; Weedsport, amending village charter, 620; Port Chester, amending village charter, 621; Mechanicville fire commissioners, creating board, 621; Lima, amending charter, 621; Horseheads, regulating sales

VILLAGES, VETOES — (*Continued*).

of goods, 622; Edgewater, changing boundaries, 639; superintendent of buildings, amending general act, 639; Flushing, street improvements, 724; unincorporated, fire districts in, 872; Saratoga Springs, street improvements, 873; Tonawanda sewers, 876; local improvements, assessments, 888; Stillwater, amending charter, 889; amending general act, Mount Vernon, 891; amending general act, New Rochelle, 942; Port Chester, legalizing sewer bonds, 942; Lansingburgh, new wards and sidewalk repairs, 991; water supply commissioners, 1040; Haverstraw, amending charter, 1040; oath of office, amending general act, 1041; Tonawanda public parks and places, 1115; West Troy, electric light commission, 1117; Clifton Springs, legalizing election of officers, 1122; Olean, amending village charter, 1133; North Tonawanda, highway improvement, 1155; poll-tax, action to recover, IX, 62; Penn Yan, changing boundary, 63; electric-light companies, contracts with, 126; ordinary expenditures, amending act of 1870, 131; Ilion, amending charter, 148; public health, nuisance, 151; Myers' automatic ballot machine, authorizing use of, 247; crosswalks, assessment on property benefited, 252; Saranac Lake, special village charter, 258; Norwich, revised charter, 289; licensing temporary or transient business, 350; balloting in towns outside of villages, 439; taxes, non-resident, report to county treasurer, 523; streets, opening or altering, damages, 622; contracts with electric-light companies, 623; water rates, amending act, 627; College Point, amending charter, 628; Tonawanda, collection of taxes, 718; Warsaw, amending charter, 718; Waterville, open air concerts, 718; Cohocton, water commissioners, abolishing board, 722; Elmwood, enforcement of taxes, 723; Plattsburgh, street improvement, borrowing money for, 723; water supply, contracts with water companies, 810; extending water system outside corporate limits, 813; contracts with lighting companies, amending act, 814; Catskill, amending charter, fixing boundaries, 818; College Point,—school taxes, amending act, 818; — conveying real estate to school district, Flushing, 819; Flushing,— surplus on certain bonds, authorizing use for other purposes, 819; — bonds for arrears of taxes, 819; Plattsburgh,— amending charter, elections, 819; — taxes, sales and redemptions, applying General Village Law, 819; Salem, electric-light plant, 819; Saratoga Springs, disposal of sewage, 819; White Plains, amending charter, 819; Whitesborough, fixing village boundaries, 862; water, furnishing to other municipalities, 866; incorporate, requisite population, 866; street railroads, rates of fare on certain grades, 866;

VILLAGES, VETOES — (*Continued*).

Croton-on-the-Hudson, highway tax in, town to pay to, 867; White Plains, sidewalks and curbs, compelling lot owners to repair, X, 61; Watkins, amending charter, 61; election notices, publication of, 62; Ardsley, relief of, 62; Nassau county, street railroads in, 145; electric-light companies, acquiring real estate, 159; Watkins, water supply, amending act, 161; peddlers' licenses, 163; Goshen water supply, 232; Hastings-on-Hudson, changing boundaries, 233; Seneca Falls, bonds for bridge and cemetery addition, 278; East Aurora, legalizing bonds, 284; relief of certain, 309; railroad aid, claims, Court of Claims, amending act, 315; Far Rockaway, claim of Gamewell Fire Alarm Telegraph Company, 324; Plattsburgh, bonds for public improvements, 440; Medina, police department, 440; in two or more towns, withdrawal of part, 441; changing boundaries, 449, 523; changing boundaries, 523, new bill passed; lease of buildings to G. A. R. posts, 585; incorporation, requisite territory and population, 591; Newark Valley, legalizing water bonds, 702; Camden, legalizing proceedings for electric-light system, 708; fence viewers in, 812; Ossining, revising charter, extending boundaries, 812; Kenmore, frontage tax for water purposes, 812; borrowing money, 814; Albion, schools and school districts, 948; Sandy Hill, trustees, borrowing money, legalizing acts, 960; Geneseo public building, 960; Peekskill, building commissioner, creating office, 961.

VILLEMAN, ABEL FRANÇOIS. French Minister of Public Instruction, grants permission to examine documents in Royal Library, IV, 188.

VINCENT, PAUL H. Service of process on, Van Rensselaer rent, III, 824.

VINEGAR. Composition of, VIII, 354; defects in statutes, X, 627.

VETOES. Adulterated, preventing sale, VII, 507; adulteration, 572; sales, deception in, IX, 148; cider, relative to, 863.

VINEYARDS. Opening roads through, exempting certain towns, veto, VII, 806.

VIRGIL. Opening highway, extending time, veto, VIII, 1086.

VIRGINIA. Safety of, dependent on security of Albany, I, 30; Robert Hunter, Governor of, 141; transports from, for Cape Breton, 371; troops from, in expedition against Canada, 373; presents to Indians, 417; invitation to join in Crown Point expedition, 420; act for revision of statutes, 521; requests aid in resisting French encroachment on Ohio frontier, 535, 538; aid granted, 547, 552, 555, 629; arrival of General Braddock with troops, 565; Lords of Trade recommend colonial union, 578; not represented in Albany Convention, 578; agent of, how appointed, 732; commissioners on Indian trade, 739; New York troops march to, II, 149; Yorktown, surrender

VIRGINIA —(*Continued*).

of Lord Cornwallis, 150; letter from Governor of, 209; resolutions from, 256; proposes commercial convention, 259, 270; proposes amendments to Federal Constitution, 294; suability of State, 334; constitutional amendments, approval of treaty, court of impeachments, reorganizing Federal Senate, United States judge ineligible to other office, 366; letter from Governor, exchange of laws, 371; resolutions, Federal Constitution a compact, 429; condemns alien and sedition acts, 430; eligibility to office, qualifications of Senators, Representatives, judicial and executive officers, 439; laws of, received, 530; manufactures arms for militia, 572; constitutional amendment, removal of Senator, 631, 649, 650; encouraging internal communications, 1011; who not eligible to Legislature, 1062; cession of territory for District of Columbia, III, 138; exchanges maps with New York, 225; approves South Carolina and Georgia resolutions on tariff and relations of State to nation, 280; protests against South Carolina nullification proceedings, requests modification of tariff laws, 436; resolutions relative to anti-slavery agitation, 589; demand on Governor Seward for surrender of fugitives from justice, 777; Governor's views on right of extradition, 777; communication from Governor and Lieutenant-Governor, Johnson and others extradition case, 852, 869, 920, 932, 972, 981, 982, 1028; IV, 47; attempts to restrict commerce with New York, III, 910, 925, 936, 980, 1028; refuses to surrender Curry, a fugitive from justice, 910; Curry surrendered, 915; retrocession of Alexandria from District of Columbia, 980; colonial documents relative to, 1019; protests against Massachusetts apportionment propositions, IV, 85; protests against slavery proviso in Mexican War Act, 382; resolutions,— fugitive slaves, 466; — slavery, 507; action relative to independence monument, 683; Lemmon case, Governor criticises New York's decision, 809; John Brown's invasion of, V, 197; recommends convention to adjust national difficulties, 308, 311; returns New York resolutions offering aid to Federal government, 314; secession ordinance, 396; Federal assumption of State debts, VI, 563; protests against Federal interference in Louisiana, 776; resolutions, support of common schools, VII, 744.

"VIRGINIA, THE." Arrives in New York, cholera on, V, 766.

VITAL STATISTICS. Registration of, V, 863; registration, amending general act, veto, IX, 238; increased facilities for preservation of records, X, 624; information included in census of 1905, 870.

VOGEL, GEORGE. Relief, veto, VIII, 638.

VOGEL, JAMES A. Claim against New York, veto, VIII, 884.

VOLCKENS, WILLIAM. Judgment against people for costs, payment, veto, VII, 926.

VOLK, JOHN J. Assembly, member of joint legislative committee on services in memory of former Governor Higgins, X, 963.

VOLUNTEER FIREMEN'S BENEVOLENT ASSOCIATION, RICHMOND HILL. Charter, veto, X, 472.

VOLUNTEER LIFE SAVING CORPS. Report, IX, 682, 754, 851; X, 31, 130.

VOLUNTEERS. For expedition against West Indies, I, 288, 289, 300, 304, 306; transportation of, 305, 306; supplies for, 306, 393; bounties for, 374, 664, 668; enlistment under union agreement, 419; independent companies on frontiers, 440; for frontier service, 468; outscouts from Connecticut, 468; application to Connecticut for, 567; request granted, 575; to recruit King's troops, 598; enlistments to aid King's troops, 609, 612; large enlistments urged for campaign, 619; for Canadian expedition, 620, 633, 643, 645; continuing in service, 638, 651; additional, for Canadian service, 651, 653; for frontier service, 657, 670; for general service, 663; for King's regiments, 664; relief of, returning from service, 671; for Indian war, 675, 676; War of 1812, II, 743; for reserve regiments, 758, 759; organization of, recommended, 787, 794; two regiments of colored men authorized, 811; for service on Niagara frontier, 815; New York troops for Civil War, V, 402, 403; allotments of pay for families, 407; discharged on inspection, pay of, 417, 421; rejected, railroads furnish free transportation home, 417; bounties for, 454; superintendents of recruiting service, 561; adjustment of quotas, 575; records in Adjutant-General's office, transcription recommended, 576; alphabetical list of, 577; enlistment for two years, 610; large number wounded or disabled, 775.

VON GERICHTUN, CHARLES B. Relief, veto, X, 53.

VON UTASSY, GEORGE. Charges against Superintendent of Banks Kilburn, X, 872.

VOSBURGH, MARTIN. Caveat, Buck case, VI, 681.

VOSBURGH, WILLIAM F. Commissioner, repairing highway, Cattaraugus reservation, veto, VII, 221.

VOTERS. Method of voting, II, 10; for member of Assembly, 35; disloyal person disqualified, 37; qualifications under Convention Act, 283; restrictions on rights of, 686; qualifications of, constitutional convention suggested to consider, 1021; qualifications, III, 9, 772; IV, 133, 825; V, 509, 605, 749; VI, 389, 460; VIII, 566, 580, 910, 955, 1008; IX, 95; X, 421; tenant paying taxes, III, 9; extending qualifications of, 58, 135, 158; IV, 52; colored, property qualifications, III, 59; registration, 158, see REGISTRATION OF VOTERS; entertainment of, prohibited, 250; resident, suggested legislative definition of term, 772; secret ballot, IV, 129; proposed disfranchisement for betting, 132; number of

Voters — (*Continued*).

voters in State, 248; when qualifications may be abridged, 825; number, 1885, 856; colored, abolishing property qualifications; V, 54, 99, 193; General Registry Act, 92, 195; should be compelled to vote, 196; qualifications on tax questions, 839; negroes not to be, Arkansas proposition, 355; absent soldiers and sailors, 508, 512, 513 (veto), 606; increase in number during Civil War, 602; protection needed, 605; limiting right to vote for delegates to Constitutional Convention, 748; oath of loyalty on election of delegates to Constitutional Convention, act unconstitutional, 749; Legislature cannot add to constitutional qualifications, 749; VI, 389; VIII, 910; number, 1865, V, 776; rights of, should be equal under the law, VI, 37; qualifications, United States Constitution, 38; VII, 306; property qualifications, VI, 77; minority representation, 460; challenges, 725; bribery, exclusion of persons convicted of, 725; women not included, VII, 78; at school meetings, qualifications of, 518; publication of registry, New York, 579; naturalized citizens, registration, production of papers, VIII, 20, 296; Soldiers' Home, right of inmates to vote in Bath, 497; voting residence, constitutional provision, 499; refusing to vote unless paid, 675; booths at elections, 763, 898, 900, 916, 962, 1010; illiterate, right to vote cannot be abridged, 911, 955; right to vote for all officers, 959, 1117; election of officers, property qualifications cannot be imposed, 1117; women authorized to vote for school commissioners, IX, 94, act unconstitutional; right to vote for any candidate of his choice cannot be abridged, 395; term of citizenship required, constitutional provision, 555; soldiers away from home, right to vote, act of 1898, 877; alleged colonization in hotels, X, 202; primary elections, transfer from one district to another, 502; registration, additional information, 729; women, at special elections in third-class cities, 730.

Vetoes. Authorizing minors to vote for members of Assembly, II, 685; charter elections, non-residents, VI, 195; cumulative voting, New York, VIII, 278, 283; villages, qualifications on proposition for water debt, 406; registration, requiring personal appearance, 418; independence, bill to secure, 566; ballot reform bill, 1899, 762.

Votes of Assembly. Printing of, I, 55.

Voting. Method of, II, 10.

Voting Machines. General act authorizing use of, IX, 247; Davis voting machine, authorizing use of, in towns and cities, veto, 626; use of Davis voting machine authorized in cities and towns, 665.

VROOM, PETER D. Member of New Jersey Commission to Procure Constitutional Convention, V, 325.

VROOMAN, JOHN W. Smyth case, preparing journal and index, veto, VII, 461; Senate clerk, resolutions, Yorktown Centennial, 734.

VROOMAN, PETER L. Nominated sheriff of Schoharie, proceedings of Council of Appointment, II, 493.

W.

WABASH RIVER. Campaign on, pensions for service in, II, 760.

WABASH AND ERIE CANAL. Description of, III, 902; completion of, IV, 61.

WADSWORTH, JAMES. Connecticut commissioner to settle claim against New York, II, 407.

WADSWORTH, JAMES S. Delegate to Washington Peace Convention, V, 310.

WADSWORTH, JEREMIAH. Commissary-General, letter from, II, 78; supply of salt, 84.

WADSWORTH, WILLIAM. Brigadier-general, service on Niagara frontier, 1812, II, 746; member of Commission to Distribute Appropriation for Niagara Frontier Sufferers, 787.

WAGES. Of mechanics and laborers, II, 25, 46; efforts to increase, when not conspiracy, VI, 122; payment to employees, VIII, 36; laborers, preference in collection of, 318; weekly payment by corporations, 680, 930; monthly payment by railroad companies, 1079; uniform in State hospitals, IX, 652; women should receive same as men for same work, 742; prevailing rate, act of 1899 unconstitutional, X, 7; prevailing rate, act of 1906, 914.

VETOES. Women, judgments for, VIII, 293; State laborers, regulating pay of, 1041; judgments for, amending Code, IX, 246; laborers, Brooklyn, fixing rate of, 448; amount and preferences, Lockport, 719; actions for, amending Code, 726; Brooklyn, public works, employees, 733; prevailing rate, how determined, 864.

WAGHANA INDIANS (Waganhas, Waganna). Expected attack on Five Nations, I, 114; treaty with Five Nations, 134, 136.

WAGNER, JOSEPH. Senate, member of Prince Henry reception committee, X, 479.

WAGNER, WEBSTER. Senator, death of, VII, 730; memorial, preparation, veto, 777, 928.

WAGNER PALACE CAR COMPANY. Appropriation for expense of legislative committee, Atlanta Exposition and Chickamauga Park dedication, IX, 582.

WAINWRIGHT, J. MAYHEW. Assembly, member of joint legislative committee on services in memory of former Governor Higgins, X, 963.

Waistcoat. For troops, I, 639.

Waite, J. Harvey. Contests seat of Assemblyman Dodd, Kings county, 1905, X, 795.

Wakefield. Claims against, settlement, veto, IX, 732.

Wakeman, Catherine S. Claimant, Stewart escheat, veto, VII, 620, 935.

Waldron, Richard. Will of, II, 288.

Wales, Prince of. Marriage of, address on, I, 258; death of, 512; birth of child to George III, 669; visits United States, 1860, V, 297.

Wales, Thomas B. Director of Western Railroad Company, communication from, III, 750.

Walker, Charles C. B. Member of Elmira Reformatory Commission, VI, 233.

Walker, Everett R. Taxes, cancellation, veto, X, 589.

Walker, James. Painting, repulse of Longstreet at Gettysburg, purchase of, veto, IX, 291.

Walker, Truman. Bond for return of arms, II, 774.

Wallabout Improvement. Brooklyn, veto, VI, 579.

Wallace, Hugh. Attainder of, widow's rights, II, 374.

Wallace, Margaret J. Court of Claims, veto, X, 943.

Wallace, Sarah. Suit for dower, II, 374.

Wallace, William A. Speaker of Senate, Pennsylvania, member of Centennial Celebration committee, VI, 303.

Waller, John, Jr. Relief, veto, VII, 267.

Wallkill. Number of excise licenses, 1887, VIII, 360.

Wallkill River. Taking fish from, veto, VII, 506.

Wallkill Valley Railroad Company. Asks State aid, VI, 71.

Walls, William. Court of Claims, veto, X, 165.

Walnut Creek. Straightening, veto, VIII, 129.

Walpole, Horatio. Auditor-General, statement as to expenses of government, I, 202.

Walsh, George H. Relief, veto, X, 53.

Walsh, John F. New York, relief, veto, X, 582.

Walters, —. Leisler's Assembly meets at his house, I, 15.

Walton. Road from, to Great Shandaken, II, 312; new armory proposed at, IX, 573; armory, repairs and improvements, veto, 245; union free school district, refunding bonds, veto, 812.

Walts, Charles H. Referee's fees, Armour case, veto, X, 648.

Walworth, Reuben H. Chancellor, communication from, Albro case, III, 263; opinion, sale of leasehold estate, IV, 361; Code commissioner, VII, 183.

Wampum. Five Nations return belt in Flathead matter, I, 170.

Wapingo Indians. Presents to, I, 341.

WAPPINGER. Board of town auditors, veto, VIII, 616.

WAPPINGER'S CREEK. Drake's draw-bridge, maintenance, operation and repair, veto, IX, 712.

WAR. Against Spain, I, 187, 286; against Eastern Indians, 203; King Philip's war mentioned, 204; between United States and Spain, 1898, 288; employing Indians as spies, 296; declared by French against England, 316; French Indians declare, against English, 355, 356; apportionment among colonies of expense of French War, 392, 406; French, conclusion of, 471, 481; among Indian tribes, encouragement of, by French, 504; preparations for, with French, 565; council of war at Carrying Place, 575; council of, on Crown Point expedition, 591; England declares, against French, 602; Amherst loan to raise money for expense of, 637; England declares, against Spain, 666; Havana taken by English, 669; with western Indians, 674, 678; Revolutionary, 765; board of, II, 33; in Europe, 332, 365, 655; with Great Britain, 735; power to declare, limitation of, proposed amendment, 827; with Algiers, 852; United States often engaged in, 909; Civil, possible result of slavery agitation, III, 574; with Mexico, IV, 415; Congress has power to declare, 417; financial conditions resulting from, V, 739.

WAR OF THE REVOLUTION. British movements, II, 7; defeat of British on northern frontier, 8; battle of Bennington, 8; military movements, 8, 18; movements on frontier, 13; inquiry as to surrender of Ticonderoga and Mount Independence, 15; campaign in Highlands, 15, 16; Hudson river obstructions, 19, 31; relief of soldiers' families, 25; treatment of prisoners, 25; defense of Hudson river, 31, 34; recruiting continental battalions, 33; exchange of prisoners, 33; removal of disaffected persons, 33, 34; exemption of deserters and prisoners from military service, 43; establishment of continental army, 44; treaty with France, 44, 67; embargo on provisions, 46; progress of war, 50; Indian ravages on western frontier, 50; clothing and supplies for troops, 53, 55; army supplies, 54, 57, 66; obtaining goods from enemy under flags of truce, 57; defense of western frontier, 70; British invasion of Westchester county, 75; recruits and clothing, 76; New York renders financial aid to national government, 77; Long Island, proclamation to prevent plundering inhabitants of, 80; difficulty in obtaining proper subsistence for troops, 88; British losses, 89; privileges and immunities of French subjects, 91; quotas of troops, 93; relief of northern frontier, 99; relief of New York prisoners of war, 101; defense of western settlements, 106; supplies for French fleet and army, 108, 111; relief of prisoners of war, 116; aid from France, 148, 154; too much reliance on European powers, 153; difficulty in obtaining foreign loans,

WAR OF THE REVOLUTION —(*Continued*).

154; French loan, 155, 159; estimated annual cost of, 157; New York, proportion of, expenses, Congress to settle, 184; British designs to separate United States and France, 184; negotiations for peace, 188; provisional treaty, 191, 192, 195; definitive treaty signed, 191, 195; treaty ratified, 200; restitution of estates, 206, 207; claims resulting from, 539, 1027; ascertaining survivors of army, III, 979; documents relating to, English archives, 1019; battle of Saratoga, monument, appropriation, veto, VII, 84; Yorktown Centennial Celebration, 733; prison-ship martyrs, monument to, New York, veto, IX, 874.

WAR OF 1812. British impressment of American seamen, II, 616, 656; embargo, 617; preparations for defense, 618, 658, 675, 742; British attack American vessel, 616, 656; efforts toward conciliation with England, 657; report of engineer and commissioners of fortifications, 667; British Orders in Council, 672, 690; British reparation in Chesapeake case, 690; British vessel, Little Belt, attacks American frigate President, 690; declaration of war against Great Britain, 735; various military movements, 736; President's call for troops, New York's quota, 742; fortifications, 750, 757; general expenses, 757; funds furnished to State by United States, statement of, 763; capture of militia at French Mills, 770; British invasion of Ogdensburg, 773; attack on Queenstown, 737, 775; American naval successes, 780; Emperor of Russia offers mediation with Great Britain, 785, 801; various military successes noted, 786; British invasion on Niagara frontier, 791; battle at Black Rock, 793; Perry's victory on Lake Erie, 799; British movement against northern frontier, 801; Washington burned by British, 802; British defeat at Baltimore, 802; battle of Plattsburgh, 803; troops furnished by State, 804; American successes at Fort Erie, 806; treaty of peace, 824; New York resolutions on proposed terms of peace, 826; Legislature adopts resolutions of thanks and presents swords to several officers, 832; New Orleans under martial law, General Jackson fined, IV, 44, 45; pensions, 524; Commission on Services of Militia, V, 175; claims against United States, II, 757, 789, 817, 867, 919, 986, 999, 1105, 1122; III, 14, 36, 106, 145, 177, 308, 349, 386, 978; V, 175, 457, 522; redemption of militia certificates, VI, 113, 654, 903; militia certificates of service, veto, 902; State's property rights, commission created, VII, 601; Canadian branch of Cayuga Indians assist Great Britain, X, 32; documents relative to, compiling and arranging, veto, X, 572; preparation of papers, Mather claim, veto, 784; Society of, amending charter, veto, 947.

WAR WITH MEXICO. Militia called out, IV, 415; expenses connected with, 418; soldiers' cemeteries, 419; termination of, 444; pensions, 524; First Regiment, New York Volunteers, relief, veto, VII, 882.

WAR OF THE REBELLION. Secession movement, V, 298, 299; Washington Peace Convention, 311; Georgia secession ordinance, 318; Louisiana secession ordinance, 341; action by different States, 314, 315, 319, 320, 321, 324, 326, 328, 396; seizure of national forts and property, 306, 314; attack on Fort Sumter, 306; Fort Pulaski seized by Georgia authority, 315; Arkansas proposes radical slavery amendments, 354; President Lincoln calls for militia, 356, 400; Governor Morgan's comment, message of 1862, 358; use of New York canals, 367; aiding sick and disabled soldiers, 383; Federal direct tax, 1861, 388; bombardment and capture of Fort Sumter, 399; defense of Washington, 400; battle of Bull Run, 402; purchase of arms, 413; pensions, 420; campaign in Mississippi valley and on Atlantic coast, 439; defense of New York, 444; President calls for 300,000 men, 453; draft for 300,000 ordered, 454; causes discussed by Governor Seymour, 459; effect of riots of citizens, 466; martial law, 468; emancipation of slaves, 473; unhappy effect on central and western States, 475, 478; lessons derived from, 484, 822; hospital accommodations, 488; Bureau of Military Statistics, 521; injury to commerce, 534; large number of troops called for, 540; Lee's invasion of Pennsylvania, 544; draft riots in New York, 545; plan for termination of, 554; only way to save Union, Governor Seymour's views, 559; New York's increase of commerce, 593; State bounties, 610; fall of Richmond, 676; Lee's surrender, 676; death of President Lincoln, 677; termination of, 680; soldiers' claims, 683; pensions, 683; military agencies, 684; reconstruction of seceding States, 714, 743, 857; increase of State debt resulting from, 752; Commission on Claims against United States, 756, 832; no claim for property or slaves lost as result of, Fourteenth Amendment, 791; slow progress of reconstruction, VI, 41; severe test of Constitution, 457; results accepted, 768; inflation of currency, 756; VII, 149; enlistments, expenditures, veto, 478; roster of volunteers, printing, appropriation, veto, 491; veterans, preference in civil service, 977.

WAR WITH SPAIN. Absent soldiers and sailors, right to vote, V, 606; Governor Black's special message recommending appropriation, 1898, IX, 852; appropriation for military expenses, 853, 877; high character of New York troops, 878; Governor Roosevelt's comment, 1899, X, 1; service of National Guard, 12; certain employees to receive compensation while absent in Federal service, 13, 264, 314; New York troops not properly armed, 14; State employees in military or naval service, compensation while absent, appropriation, veto, 314.

WARD, HAMILTON, Attorney-General, opinion, Bankers' bill, ten-day period, VII, 667, 671.

WARD, MARY E. Survivor of Ward & Company, claim against New York, settlement, veto, IX, 873.

WARD, SAMUEL B. Nominated as commissioner of State survey, VIII, 255.

WARD, WILLARD AND PRENTICE. Labor contracts, Clinton prison, V, 425.

WARDENS. See PORT WARDENS.

WAR DEPARTMENT. Order dismissing officer from Federal service, V, 515; communication from, cession of land at Willet's Point, VI, 774.

WARD'S ISLAND. Immigrant refuge hospital, patients in, IV, 644, 793; V, 85, 530, 965; patients from marine hospital removed to, V, 184; immigrant hospital, 844; improvement of immigrant accommodations, VI, 28; ship fever patients, 237; immigration, property on, 534; channel separating from Randall's island, protest against filling, VII, 46; repairs on property, 965; mortgage on State property, payment of interest, veto, VIII, 112; acquisition of water rights, veto, X, 176.

WARD'S ISLAND BRIDGE COMPANY. Charter, veto, IX, 725, 793.

WAREHOUSES. At quarantine, suggestions concerning, V, 639, 641; corporation for erection of, 641; VII, 588; report of commissioners, V, 719; needed for quarantine purposes, 845; location in New York bay, 846; regulating business relative to, veto, X, 319.

WAREHOUSE RECEIPTS. Advances on, not subject to usury laws, VII, 719.

WARNER, ANDREW. Recording secretary, New York Historical Society, memorial on centennial volume, VI, 813; memorial, centennial anniversary of New York's ratification of Federal Constitution, VIII, 506.

WARNER, CLEMENT. Dock on Oneida lake, veto, VI, 156.

WARRANTS (Criminal). By certain military officers, power to issue, suggested, I, 123; justices, arrest in other counties, II, 210; when necessary on arrest, 820; in excise cases, IV, 754; general, English case, 756.

WARRANTS (Treasury). To be issued by Governor and Council, I, 164; 168, 483, 534, 556; for expenses in Indian service, 228.

WARREN, DORMAN T. Taxes, cancellation, veto, X, 448.

WARNER, JAMES. Colonel, commands cavalry squadron, II, 810.

WARREN, PETER. Commodore, commands British naval forces in North America, I, 340, 347, 366; Governor required to furnish aid to, 343, 347, 350, 351, 356; letter from, relative to expedition against Louisburg, 351, 355, 358; admiral, letter from, 366; raising troops for Louisburg, 369, 371; letter from, Canadian expedition, 381; employment of land forces in Canadian expedition, 383.

WARREN, WILLIAM E. Accountant, examines State Treasurer's books, VI, 632; report, 658.

WARREN COUNTY. Militia brigade called out, II, 807; memorial, improvement of upper Hudson, III, 748; three towns excepted from repeal of Town Auditor's Act, VIII, 50; average excise license fees, 1889, 687; highways, cost of labor system, 1892, IX, 200; insane, care of, county and State systems compared, 228.

   VETOES. Opening road, VI, 93; State loan to, 194; separate road district taxes, 442; Brant lake, black bass, close season, VIII, 975; dam across Hudson river, X, 446; tax sale, cancellation, Moriarity case, 590; dam across Hudson river, North Creek, 705.

WARREN COUNTY ELECTRIC LIGHT, HEAT AND POWER COMPANY. Dam across Hudson river, veto, X, 446, 453.

WARRINGTON. Naval successes, II, 802.

WARSAW. VETOES. Wyoming County Agricultural Society, escheat, VI, 708; amending charter, IX, 718.

WARWICK. Excelsior Hose Company, charter, veto, VII, 507; union free school district, legalizing bonds, X, 283.

WASHBURN'S REAL PROPERTY. Cited, franchises considered real property, X, 68.

WASHINGTON, BUSHROD. United States Supreme Court, opinion, obligation of contracts, IV, 349.

WASHINGTON, GEORGE. Colonel, commanding British troops, defeated by French and Indians, I, 546, 549; general, enters New York, 780; vigilance of, II, 8; letter from, New York regiments, 18; successes against British, 50; letter from, scarcity of forage, 54, 56; recommended to institute inquiry as to purchases of wheat and flour, 54; grants flag of truce to Samuel Hake, 58; letter from, recruits and clothing, 76; letters from, 78, 83, 99, 133, 163, 167; letter from, need of army supplies, 89, 107; orders reinforcements for western frontier, 106; letter from, scarcity of clothing, 115; conditions on frontier, 121; letters from, relative to enlistments, 133; surrender of Lord Cornwallis, 150; forage for army, 185; exchanging drafts for specie, 189; circular letter from, at close of war, 196; president, National Constitutional Convention, 297; letter from, accompanying Constitution, 298; chosen first President of United States, 300; circular letter from, relative to acts of Congress, 302; quoted, happy condition of public affairs, 358; retires from public life, 380; President Adams on, 447; construction of Federal Constitution as to State militia, 749; engages in agriculture, 958; recommends post-offices and post roads, III, 803; visits Mohawk valley, opinion on internal improvements, 804, 818; president of a canal company, 809; letters to

WASHINGTON, GEORGE —(*Continued*).
Gov. George Clinton noted, VII, 813; as life Senator, possible length of service, VIII, 693; centennial anniversary of inauguration, 694; death of, II, 448, 461 (general note); proposed monument for, at Washington, 462; portrait, II, 461; III, 143; headquarters at Newburgh acquired by State, IV, 502; service in establishing nation, IV, 618; did not declare martial law, V, 469; quoted,— national dependence on virtue, II, 728; — divine guidance in national affairs, 881; — revolutionary pensions, 1028; — value of national union, IV, 502; — combinations to obstruct government, 829; — departments of government not to encroach on each other, V, 463.

WASHINGTON, HENRY.   Elmira, escheat, veto, VIII, 755.

WASHINGTON'S BIRTHDAY.   First observance of, II, 462; a public holiday, VI, 679.

WASHINGTON, D. C.   Becomes national capital, II, 469; British attack on, 802; lottery memorial, 1123; rapid growth of, 1124; agricultural society in, III, 945; convention to adjust national difficulties, V, 309; unprotected condition of, 400; New York military agency at, 684; suggested selection as site of World's Fair, 1892, VIII, 931.

WASHINGTON COUNTY.   Divided on erection of Clinton county, II, 272; militia from, 1812, 744, 807; average excise license fees, 1889, VIII, 687; decrease in population, IX, 3; highways, cost of labor system, 1892, 200; insane, care of, county and State systems compared, 228.

VETOES.   Highways in, II, 348; clerk of, practicing as attorney, 395; special county judge and surrogate, IV, 776; VII, 551; assistant district attorney, VI, 143; exemption from act relative to pauper children, VII, 413; highway near Fort Miller bridge, 805, 886; Easton, highway commissioner, election, 932; Salem, excise commissioners, legalizing acts, VIII, 354; highways, damage by Champlain canal repairs, 453; superintendent of the poor to be keeper of poorhouse, 537; convictions for crimes less than felony, charging expense on towns, IX, 796; fishing through ice, X, 309, 313.

WASHINGTON'S FAREWELL ADDRESS.   Noted, II, 380.

WASHINGTON'S HEADQUARTERS.   Newburgh,— acquired by State, IV, 502.   VETOES.   Care of, VI, 581; — purchase of additional land, VIII, 855; Tappan, purchase of, veto, VII, 410.

WASHINGTON HEIGHTS.   New York Institution for Instruction of Deaf and Dumb located on, V, 287.

WASHINGTON HOOK AND LADDER COMPANY No. 1, LAWRENCE AND CEDARHURST.   Changing name and additional powers, veto, X, 261.

WASHINGTON MARKET COMPANY.   Lease of market, preference, veto, VI, 594.

WASHINGTON PARK ASSOCIATION. Charter, veto, VI, 501.

WASHINGTON PEACE CONVENTION. Virginia recommends, V, 309, 311; New York delegates to, 310, 398; Kentucky delegates to, 329; Indiana approves, 331; Illinois delegates to, 342.

WASHINGTON RIFLES, NEW YORK. Charter, veto, VII, 412.

WASHINGTON SAVINGS BANK, BROOKLYN. Charter, veto, VI, 342.

WASSERMAN, ADOLPH S. Relief, veto, X, 53, 175.

WASSON, WILLIAM. Canal appraiser, appropriation for, VI, 421.

WATCHERS. Militia exempts to serve as, I, 297.

WATCHERS AT ELECTIONS. Provided for, VII, 435.

WATCHHOUSES. At Narrows and Rockaway, I, 607.

WATCH POINT. Lighthouse at, II, 636, 641.

WATER. For cities, II, 1017; III, 87; for New York, 1034; IV, 773; for Mount Pleasant prison, 125, 276; for Utica State Lunatic Asylum, 281; for Sing Sing prison, 482; supply for canals insufficient, 542; rent of surplus, of canals, V, 154; municipal indebtedness, constitutional provision, VI, 917; New York, increasing supply, VII, 900; VIII, 270; maintaining supply, importance of forests, VII, 983; bonds for, not included in constitutional limitation of municipal indebtedness, VIII, 185; Syracuse department established, 258; Syracuse Act, 1890, 1015; Baldwinsville, legalizing water bonds, 1026; 1,500 square miles in State, IX, 192; New York water supply, sanitary protection, 225; Penn Yan supply, act for, 411; Albany filtration plant, acts of 1897 and 1905, 420; New York water supply, charter amendments, 1901, X, 212; Lockport supply, 418; Dutchess county water rights, 691; New York rights, extent of, 691; sources of supply should be inspected by public health department, 743; Water Storage Commission, 1904, 743; State Water Supply Commission, 1905, 744; New York, additional supply, 748, 759; New York, using for generation of electricity, 804; State commission, approval of maps, etc., 855.

VETOES. Town and villages to furnish, VI, 591; New York, 23d and 24th wards, VII, 129; blind asylum, Batavia, 229; Deer river, supply, 505; New York, 1881, 593, 635; Brooklyn, construction of storage reservoir, 617; for new capitol, 903; Oswego, supply, 1100; VIII, 98; Syracuse Water Company, supplying adjacent villages, VII, 1100; Utica, supply, 1101; Amsterdam waterworks, claims for labor, 1107; Cohoes supply, 1124; New York, 1885, amending Aqueduct Act, VIII, 45; village supply, 130; for villages, taxation, qualifications of voters on proposition, 406; Westfield water department and supply, 518; New York, extending and improving aqueduct system, 636; Yonkers

WATER, VETOES — (*Continued*).

    water supply, amending act, 887; villages, supply, commissioners, 1040; commissioners, Buffalo, increasing salaries, 1106; New Utrecht, supply, IX, 151; surface, obstructing flow of, 247, 473; Albany, water supply and water commissioners, 420; rates in villages, amending act, 627; Long Island City, additional supply, 726; Albany, supply, 729; Dunkirk, supply, 730, 785; Rochester waterworks bonds, 731; Mount Vernon, supply, 734; Buffalo waterworks, 784; Jamestown, supply, 785; Round Lake Association, supply, right to condemn property, 794; free flow in rivers and streams, amending Highway Law, 801; supply, New York charitable institutions, amending act, 805; exempting Beth Israel Hospital Association from payment of water rents, 806, 810; villages, contracts with waterworks companies, 810; village system, extending outside corporate limits, 814; Jamestown, supply, acquiring property, 858; villages, furnishing to other municipalities, 866; Yonkers, rents, X, 60; Watkins water supply, amending act, 161; Goshen, supply, 232; New York reservoirs, assessment and taxation, 308; Clinton prison waterworks, sale to Dannemora, 440; Peekskill, additional bonds, 443; New York, rents, apportionment, 475; Hudson, 583; Troy, relative to, 583; White Plains, fire protection tax, 592; investigating sources of supply and systems of sewerage, 650; Storage Commission report, publication and distribution, 651; supply, Custodial Asylum for Women at Newark, 653; Greenwood fire district water supply, 704; United States geological survey, hydrographic work, 785; Kenmore, frontage tax for water purposes, 812; Niagara river, limiting use of, 918.

WATERBURY, NELSON J. Member of Statutory Revision Commission, 1870, VI, 238; unconstitutionality of ballot bill, 1888, VIII, 574, 580; counsel fees, claim against New York, retaxation, veto, 1035; X, 807.

WATERFORD. Female academy at, II, 972, 1018; north side water commissioners, sprinkling streets, X, 593.

    VETOES. Champlain canal bridge, VII, 116, 361; sidewalks, injuries from defects, notice, IX, 54; police justice, amending act, 867.

WATERLOO. Centennial celebration of Sullivan's campaign, VII, 1084.

    VETOES. Sewer under canal, VI, 339; Cayuga and Seneca canal bridge, VII, 115; amending charter, 775; X, 174; sewer under Cayuga and Seneca canal, VIII, 413; regulating price of gas, X, 907.

WATERS, JAMES E. Mandamus proceedings, Jamaica normal school case, X, 561.

WATERS OF THE STATE. Protection of life and property in certain cases, veto, IX, 720.

WATERTOWN. Deposit of arms at, II, 682; deposit of military stores at, 755; arsenal, report on, 818; arsenal, seizure of arms at, III, 683; number of excise licenses, 1887, VIII, 359; excise license fees, 1889, 686.

VETOES. Aid to Utica and Black River Railroad Company, amending act, VI, 92; Frontier Gaslight Company, charter, 215; amending charter, 509, 581; IX, 870; Black River Insurance Company, changing name, VI, 183; sidewalks, amending charter, VIII, 1041; legalizing local assessments, duplicate bill, IX, 451; amending charter, election inspectors, 458; armory, repairs, X, 319; commissioners of education, 713.

WATERVILLE. Open air concerts, veto, IX, 718.

WATERVLIET. Van Rensselaer leases, description of, IV, 329; canal bridge, appropriation for completion, VI, 854; police justice, amending act, IX, 87; fire commissioners, act of 1901, X, 281.

VETOES. Police justice, VI, 1032; election of town officers, VII, 64; part annexed to Albany, taxes, 412; public peace, relative to, 1101; annexing territory to Green Island, X, 179; restoring territory to Green Island, 179; amending charter, appointment of recorder, X, 434; retaining wall, Erie canal, 646.

WATERVLIET ARSENAL. Erection of, II, 436, 437, 458; manufacture of arms at, 437, 458, 477; completed, 477; deposit of powder in, 683; deposit in, of military stores by Federal government, 755; proposed sale of, to United States, 755; cession of land for, III, 264, 314; supply of water from Erie canal, 355.

WATERWORKS COMPANIES. General act, VI, 580. VETOES. Eminent domain, VI, 285; cities and villages, VII, 807; relative to, VIII, 640; Malone Waterworks Company, amending charter, sale of water, 941, new bill passed; Brooklyn, city to acquire property of, IX, 779; formation of, amending Transportation Corporations Law, 804; contracts with villages, 810; Woodside Water Company, New York, relief, X, 175, 326.

WATKINS. VETOES. First M. E. Society, relative to, VII, 121; normal school at, VIII, 888; Glen creek, improvement of, 1123; X, 314, 435; amending charter, X, 61; water supply, amending act, 161.

WATKINS CREEK. Fish hatchery on, veto, IX, 221.

WATKINS GLEN. Acquisition of, X, 940.

WATSON. Aid to Utica and Black River Railroad Company, amending act, veto, VI, 92.

WATSON, JAMES. Elected United States Senator in place of Hobart, resigned, II, 424; claim of United States against State, 437; resignation of, 460.

Watson, William. Brooklyn police justice, expiration of term, 1905, IX, 503.

Watt, John T. Member of board of education, Ogdensburg, communication favoring school bill, X, 912.

Watters, Michael and Mary. Escheat, veto, X, 958.

Watts, James W. Court of Claims, veto, X, 709.

Wauhatchie. Battle of, monuments to New York troops, VIII, 1077; monuments for New York soldiers, IX, 324, 577.

Waverly. Railroad strike, 1892, IX, 594.

Wawarsing. Vetoes. Union school district, boundary, VII, 806; Eastern New York Reformatory, relative to, IX, 245.

Wayne. Union free school district, relative to, veto, VII, 265.

Wayne, Anthony. General, campaign by, pensions for service in, II, 761.

Wayne County. Agricultural society in, III, 945; average excise license fees, 1889, VII, 687; county clerk, salaried office, 1103; legalizing contracts, county agricultural society and town of Galen, 1148; decrease in population, IX, 3; highways, cost of labor system, 1892, 200; insane, care of, county and State systems compared, 228.

　　Vetoes. Bridge over Great Sodus bay, VI, 212; highways and bridges, 332; Newark canal repairs, 861; Ontario town meeting, legalizing proceedings, 1031; extending charter of Clyde and Rose Plank Road Company, VII, 97; police justice, Wolcott, 389; contested election, Hotchkiss, Assembly, expenses, 917; unpaid taxes, sales for, special act, VIII, 750, 754.

Wayne County Agricultural Society. Legalizing Borck contract, VIII, 1148.

Wayne County Bank. Injunction against, III, 860.

Wealth. Accumulation of, danger of encouraging, II, 701; III, 325; increase due to immigrant labor, 728; State's relation to, X, 86.

Weather. Severity of, prevents meeting of Assembly, I, 630; inclement, prevents meeting of Assembly, II, 87; effect on canal navigation, III, 202, 203; New York meteorological observatory records, evidence, veto, X, 955.

Weather Bureau. Established, IX, 179.

Weatherwax, Delia. Widow of James H. Weatherwax, State Assessor, appropriation for residue of salary, veto, VII, 917.

Weatherwax, James H. State Assessor, death of, appropriation for widow, veto, VII, 917.

Webb, Daniel. General, commands force on northern frontier, I, 614.

Webb, James H. Speaker of House, Pennsylvania, member of Centennial Celebration Committee, VI, 303.

WEBB, WILLIAM HENRY. Proposed gift of Webb's Academy and Home for Ship Builders, VIII, 623.

WEBB'S ACADEMY AND HOME FOR SHIP BUILDERS. Charter, veto, VIII, 623.

WEBSTER, ALEXANDER. Member of Council of Appointment, II, 14, 314.

WEBSTER, DANIEL. Death of, IV, 641.

WEBSTER, EPHRAIM. Onondaga agent, suggested appointment in place of, II, 995; death of, III, 105.

WEBSTER'S DICTIONARY. Quoted, meaning of "extra," VII, 261.

WEBSTER PLANK ROAD COMPANY. Extending charter, veto, VI, 163; acquires property of Troy and Poestenkill Plank Road Company, 163.

WEED, SMITH M. Sale of land to State, Clinton prison, V, 882; Assembly, alleged assault on, VII, 81.

WEED, THURLOW. Appointed State printer, III, 1023; appointed delegate to Washington Peace Convention, declines appointment, V, 311, 333.

WEED, PARSONS & CO. VETOES. Printing for Statutory Revision Commissioners, VII, 231; various appropriations, 492; Board of Claims, VIII, 1167.

WEEDSPORT. Canal repairs at, VI, 856; union school, amending act, veto, VII, 933; VIII, 717; amending village charter, veto, 620.

WEIGHHOUSE. In New York, Crown to receive revenue from, I, 36, 38.

WEIGHTMAN, U. Washington committee, lottery memorial, II, 1120.

WEIGHMASTER. Deputy Heath, matter of, I, 195; in New York, limiting powers of, veto, III, 528; canals, office abolished, VII, 819.

WEIGHTS AND MEASURES. Standard of, act to define, II, 640, 641; alleged to be inaccurate, III, 98, 101; destroyed by fire, 142; new standards to be purchased, 142; included in Revised Statutes, 215; proposed international decimal system, V, 323; new standards furnished, 377; report of superintendent, readjustment of standards, 570; inspectors of, office abolished, VI, 282; VII, 659, 751.

VETOES. Amending act, VI, 912; amending act, potatoes, VII, 414; New York, appointment of inspectors, VIII, 131; reappropriation, 246; sealers of, New York, salaries, X, 308.

WEISE, WILLIAM H. New York fireman, reinstatement, veto, X, 950.

WEISHEM, MARGARET. Court of Claims, veto, X, 946.

WELCH, JAMES. Commissioner, repairing highway, Cattaraugus reservation, veto, VII, 475.

WELLAND CANAL. Reciprocity in use of, VI, 363; enlargement, steam power on, 538.

WELLER, A. S. Justice of the peace, legalizing acts, veto, VII, 413.

WELLS. Arms and supplies for, II, 772.

WELLS, A. Bond for return of arms, II, 772.

WELLS, DAVID A. Member of Tax Revision Commission, VI, 238, 269, 370; correspondence with Governor Hoffman, 404, 405.

WELLS, GIDEON. Secretary of the Navy, communication from, additional land for Brooklyn navy yard, V, 728.

WELLS, JAMES N, JR. Notary public, legalizing acts, veto, VIII, 291.

WELLS, WILLIAM. Bond for return of arms, II, 772.

WELLSVILLE. Tax for bridge, veto, VI, 311; police justice, legalizing acts, veto, VIII, 132.

WEMPLE, JOHN. Claim of, II, 346.

WEMPLE, WILLIAM W. Assembly, member of insurance investigating committee, 1905, X, 725.

WENDELLVILLE. Breakwater, Tonawanda creek, veto, VIII, 888.

WINNEBAGO INDIANS. Green Bay treaty, II, 1107.

WENTWORTH, THOMAS. General, commands expedition against West Indies, I, 300; applies for troops, 301, 306.

WERDEN, SIR JOHN. Duke's secretary, letter to Anthony Brockholls, I, 4.

WERNBERG, ANDREW P. Claim against New York finance department, veto, X, 817.

WESLEYAN SEMINARY. In New York, incorporated, II, 972.

WEST, FRANK A. Member of commission, Onondaga reservation highways, VIII, 116.

WEST, MARVIN J. Refunding money to, as surety on supervisor's bond. Sangerfield, veto, VII, 753.

WEST BANK. Quarantine establishment at, V, 701; VI, 26; appropriation for, V, 767; VI, 27, 238; hospital at, V, 845; progress of construction, VI, 26; boarding station, 27, 116; hospital completed, 116; communication from commission, 145; yellow fever patients, 237, 532; patients with contagious diseases, 360; additional buildings, 360.

WESTBROOK, JULIA A. Widow of Justice Westbrook, appropriation for his salary, veto, VIII, 250.

WESTBROOK, THEODORIC R. Justice of Supreme Court, investigation, counsel fees, veto, VII, 924; death of, unearned salary, appropriation for widow, veto, VIII, 250.

WESTCHESTER. Merged in Greater New York, IX, 300.

    VETOES. Highway in, VI, 158; avenue in, 505; borrowing money for highway improvement, VII, 1023; bonds for highway purposes, VIII, 292; claims against, settlement, IX, 732.

WESTCHESTER, BOROUGH OF. Proposed meeting of Assembly in, I, 367.

WESTCHESTER COUNTY. Delegates of, to Hempstead Convention, I, 2; act relating to court of sessions in, 11; act for support of ministers in, 39; complain of inequality of taxation in, 42; members of Assembly from, absent themselves, 69; defection of Rye and

WESTCHESTER COUNTY —(*Continued*).

Bedford, 73; sheriff, claim for subsistence of prisoners, 478; levies in, 570; militia ordered to Fort Edward, 614; John Thomas, Assembly, favors colonial union, 767; protecting inhabitants, II, 8; prisoners from, 14; British invasion of, 75; petition from, outrages in, 80; inhabitants supply enemy with cattle, 90; relief of distressed families in, 109; conditions in, 113; forage in, 151, 165; suits in justice's court, special privileges granted, 171; claim of sheriff, Ryer case, 345; superintendent of highways, communication from, 410; grist-mills in, act for erection of, 485; militia brigade ordered out, 796; removal of New York prison to, 1016; included in metropolitan police district, V, 27; VI, 30; laying out highways in, 118; Morrisania, West Farms and Kings Bridge, annexed to New York, 712; VII, 629; VIII, 350, 795; average excise license fees, 1889, VIII, 687; unpaid taxes, sales under special act, 749; increase in population, IX, 3; highways, cost of labor system, 1892, 200; insane, care of, county and State systems compared, 228; included in ninth judicial district, 547; X, 850; included in metropolitan elections district, IX, 885; transfer tax assistant, X, 108.

VETOES. Contingent expenses, II, 95; highways in, 348, 592; extending act to relieve from illegal taxes, VI, 278; Scarsdale and Greenburgh, highway improvement, 328; Mount Pleasant, opening highway, 330; highway labor, 336; Mamaroneck avenue, repayment of money, 488; Fordham and Pelham avenues, 158, 505; highways in Yonkers and Eastchester, 512; Morrisania, 167th street, 566; Morrisania and West Farms, collection of taxes, 589; North Castle, Bedford and Lewisborough, public roads in, 589; Morrisania, changing grade of certain streets, 590; maintenance of civil prisoners, 596; banks, amending general act, 599; Mount Pleasant, town meetings by election districts, 674; Annexation Act, amendment, 911; notaries public, relative to, 1036; VII, 131; White Plains, county jail, addition to, 130; Eastchester, highways, 130; keeping open certain offices, 201, 412; New Rochelle drainage, 392; exemption from act relative to pauper children, 413; superintendent of poor, relative to, 508; town auditors, repealing act, 806; town auditors, relative to, 807; designation of constables to attend court, 1092; Greenburgh, election of highway commissioners, VIII, 61; recording and indexing notices of pendency, 70; Westchester highway bonds, 292; Eastchester, number of highway commissioners, 461, 616; indigent children, care of, 1159; territory annexed to New York, recording in New York documents relating to real estate,

Westchester County, Vetoes — (*Continued*).

IX, 460; special highway, 722; historical society, books and records to be delivered to, 862; indexing records, 862; poor, outdoor relief, X, 272; payments to Westchester County Society for the Prevention of Cruelty to Children, 311; stenographer for grand jury, 387; Bronx River Sewer Commission, 713; lighting highways, public places, etc., in towns, 948; exemption · from poll-tax, 952; poll-tax, 955.

Westchester County Society for the Prevention of Cruelty to Children. Payments by Westchester county, veto, X, 311.

Westchester Trust Company. Charter, veto, VIII, 469.

Westenhook. Boundary question with Massachusetts, I, 226.

Westerlo. Proceedings for collection of Van Rensselaer rent, III, 823; Van Rensselaer leases, description of, IV, 329; Chesterville, separate road district, veto, VIII, 615.

Western House of Refuge. See also State Industrial School. Petition for, III, 748; recommended by Governor Seward, 765, 876; located at Rochester, IV, 408; appropriation for, 408; V, 180; completion of, IV, 481; territorial jurisdiction, 482; good work of, 556, 650, 789; V, 18; number of inmates, IV, 606, 720, 789, 846; V, 18, 85, 179, 289; to receive children sentenced by United States courts, IV, 650; supervision, 720; report, V, 383, 448; illiteracy, earnings, VII, 765; violation of rules, abuse of inmates, 961, 1082.

Vetoes. Amending act, VI, 599; establishing female department, 875; various appropriations, VII, 489; steam heating apparatus, 916; local assessments, 927; establishing school of technology, 1082; compensation for loss of earnings, 1082.

Western House of Refuge for Women, Albion. Classed as a reformatory, X, 334.

Vetoes. Farm buildings, IX, 293; additional accommodations, 293; commitments, 525; horses and carriages, electrical plant, X, 547; chapel, assembly hall and gymnasium, 655.

Western Indians. Negotiations with, I, 391, 426; attack on western frontier, 674; submission of, 680, 682.

Western Railroad Company, Massachusetts. Communication from, relative to connection with Albany, III, 750.

West Indies. Advice from, concerning proposed French attempt on colony, I, 119; expedition against, 287, 300, 301, 304, 306; smallpox in, 315; New York's trade with, 692; agent of, how appointed, 732; British losses in, II, 89; trade with, British attempt to monopolize, 197; importation of slaves from, 552, 562; probable source of controversy, 909; closed against American products, 1091; suggested negro colonization in, IV, 623.

WESTERN INLAND LOCK NAVIGATION COMPANY. Incorporated, II, 321; State aid to, 321, 355, 511; money and powder loaned to, 365; proposition to purchase interests of, 675, 706; provision for acquiring property of, 902, 1010; III, 25.

WESTERN MORTGAGE DEBENTURE COMPANY. Charter, veto, X, 439.

WESTERN NEW YORK AGRICULTURAL SOCIETY. Sale of real estate, veto, VI, 1036; regulating voting, veto, 1036.

WESTERN UNION TELEGRAPH COMPANY. Claim for overpayment of taxes, veto, IX, 278.

WEST FARMS. Annexed to New York, VI, 712.
    VETOES. Highway in, VI, 158; avenue in, 505; collection of taxes, 589; relief of board of education, 718; Annexation Act, amendment, 911; VII, 417; exempt firemen, VIII, 1036.

WESTFIELD, CHAUTAUQUA COUNTY. Establishing water department, veto, VIII, 518.

WESTFIELD. Post to Albany and Boston, I, 136.

WESTFIELD, RICHMOND COUNTY. District No. 7, school supplies, claims for, veto, X, 320.

WESTFIELD ACADEMY. Donation of certain fossils to, veto, VII, 417.

WESTMORELAND. Lowell Cemetery Association, reducing number of trustees, veto, VIII, 52.

WEST POINT. Security of posts at, II, 165; military academy established at, 677; proposed instruction of State cadets at, 814; cession of land at, III, 141; academy, propositions to abolish, IV, 45, 46, 83; military academy, additional land for, VI, 558, 788; visit of French delegates to Yorktown celebration, VII, 740; Cullum Memorial Hall, legacy for, IX, 349.

WEST SENECA. Assessments for local improvements, collection of, veto, X, 811, 952.

WEST SIDE ELEVATED RAILROAD COMPANY. Claims certain franchise, VI, 715; property sold, 716.

WEST SIDE GERMAN DISPENSARY, NEW YORK. VETOES. Exempting from taxation, VIII, 294; amending charter, IX, 534.

WEST SIDE STREET RAILWAY COMPANY, BUFFALO. Relief from certain obligations, veto, VIII, 1117.

WEST SIDE AND YONKERS PATENT RAILWAY COMPANY. Succeeded by New York Elevated Railway Company, VII, 851; statutes regulating fare, 851; percentage of net income payable to State, 852.

WEST STOCKBRIDGE. Western terminus of railroad from Boston, III, 750.

WEST TROY. Police, act relative to, IX, 589.
    VETOES. Ferry to Troy, VI, 705; board of fire commissioners, 911; lift-bridge, Genesee street, 1005; fire commissioners, VII, 805; contract with West Troy Waterworks Company, water for sewers VIII, 382; electric light commission, 1117.

WEST TROY WATERWORKS COMPANY. Contract with village of West Troy, water for sewers, veto, VIII, 382.

WEST TURIN. VETOES. Bagg, justice of the peace, legalizing acts, IX, 725; legalizing division into election districts, repeal, 818; X, 441.

WEST VIRGINIA. Adheres to Union, V, 476; urges measures to improve navigation of Ohio river, 564; appropriation for Antietam cemetery, 840; resolutions protesting against Federal interference in Louisiana, VI, 787.

WETHY, PORTER P. Mentz, overseer of highways, appointment, veto, VII, 208.

WEYBURN, WILLIAM. Heirs, relief of, veto, III, 37.

WHALE FISHERIES. Act to encourage whaling, I, 507.

WHARF. Petition for, in New York, I, 96; Burnett's Key, tax for use of, 247; on East river, New York, regulating use of, IX, 873; New York, amending charter, veto, X, 175.

WHARFAGE. New York harbor, Pennsylvania protests against, VI, 981.

WHEAT. Scarcity of, II, 54; scarcity in Massachusetts, 69; army consumption of, 73; Legislature declines to permit exportation of, 74; exportation of, permitted in exchange for salt, 79; embargo on, 114, 120; collection of assessment on, 114; sale of, authorized, 161; to be used for subsistence of troops, 169; ravages by insects, 266; reduction of tolls on, III, 505; market for, advantage of canals, 815; transported on Erie canal, 893; New York, consumption far exceeds product, VI, 240; canal freight, 1881, VII, 683; adulterated, preventing sale of, veto, VIII, 887.

WHEATON, HENRY G. Letter from, anti-rent troubles, III, 837.

WHEELBARROW. Seneca chief, joins in address to Governor, II, 943.

WHEELER, ADAM. Arrest authorized, II, 269.

WHEELER, EVERETT R. Claim, cancellation of tax sale, veto, X, 447.

WHEELER, GEORGE S. J. New York, relief, veto, X, 178.

WHEELER, WILLIAM A. Vice-President, received majority of electoral votes, 1876, VII, 33; member of Adirondack Park Commission, 1872, 722.

WHEELOCK, GEORGE G. Communication to Governor relative to appointment of William Church Osborn as commissioner in lunacy, X, 43.

WHEELOCK, WILLIAM F. Canal Department, appropriation for services, veto, IX, 716.

WHILEY, R. Communication from, arms for State, II, 1113.

WHIPPING. Abolition of, recommended, II, 336; abolished in criminal cases, 364; bill to provide for, veto, 584, 591, 602, 624; for petit larceny, 633, 634; violation of prison discipline, 983.

WHISH, GEORGE A., JR. Court of Claims, veto, X, 165.

WHITE, AARON. Relief of, veto, VI, 185.

WHITE, EVE. Suit for dower, II, 374.

WHITE, GEORGE B. Commander of "Kearsarge," visit of French delegates to West Point, VII, 740.

WHITE, GEORGE R. Damages and extra work, Soldiers and Sailors' Home, Court of Claims, veto, X, 377.

WHITE, GERSHOME. Bond for return of arms, II, 774.

WHITE, HENRY. Attainder of, widow's rights, II, 374.

WHITE, HORACE. Senate, member of Prince Henry reception committee, X, 479; chairman of joint legislative committee on services in memory of former Governor Higgins, 963.

WHITE, JOHN J. Dockmaster, claim against New York, veto, X, 308.

WHITE, STANFORD. Examination of Assembly ceiling and staircase, appropriation, veto, VIII, 839.

WHITEHALL. Northern terminus of Champlain canal, II, 962; bridge over Champlain canal, veto, VI, 154, 689, 1007; IX, 139; armory proposed at, 573; armory, veto, 575; provided for, 1898, 575; Williams and Manogue claim, armory, veto, X, 650.

WHITEHALL (New York). Battery at, I, 247, 249; examination of, 338, 339.

WHITEHALL AND PLATTSBURGH RAILROAD COMPANY. Facilitating construction of road, veto, V, 737, 864; VI, 68, 172; aid to, 1867, V, 864; asks State aid, VI, 70.

WHITE PLAINS. Army at, consumption of wheat, II, 73.

VETOES. Consolidation of school districts, VI, 183; county jail, addition to, VII, 130; bonded indebtedness, 265; repealing acts as to part of village in Greenburgh, 931; railroad to Connecticut line, VIII, 615; normal school at, 888; State memorial hall, IX, 221; amending charter, 248, 819; sidewalks and curbs, compelling lot owners to repair, X, 61; water system, fire protection tax, 592; monument commemorating battle of, 698.

WHITE RIVER, INDIANA. Proposed removal of Stockbridge Indians to, II, 987; lands ceded to United States, 987.

WHITES. More, needed in colony, I, 266; more white servants needed, 618; census of, II, 164; number of, as basis of apportionment of public expense, 184; number of illiterates, III, 884.

WHITESBORO. VETOES. Normal school at, VIII, 888; fixing village boundaries, IX, 862.

WHITES' CORNERS AND BUFFALO PLANK ROAD COMPANY. Extending charter, veto, VI, 161.

WHITESTOWN. Culvert enlargement, veto, VIII, 453.

WHITING, BOWEN. District attorney, Ontario county, appointed special counsel, Morgan matter, III, 351; compensation of, 352.

WHITNEY, ELI. Manufacturer of arms, II, 680, 769.

WHITNEY, FRANKLIN C. Notary public, legalizing acts, veto, VII, 507.

WHITNEY, HENRY G. Court of Claims, veto, X, 443.

WHITNEY, WILLIAM. Superintendent of streets, Binghamton, judgment against, payment, submitting question to people, VII, 1017.

WICKLIFFE, CHARLES A. Delegate from Kentucky to Washington Peace Convention, V, 329.

WIDOW. When entitled to husband's bounty land, I, 598; dower in lands of persons attainted, II, 374, 507.

WIDRIG, GEORGE. Major-general, detaches militia for service on northern frontier, II, 743.

WIENER, MAGNUS. See BROCK AND WIENER.

WIESER, COENRADT. Indian interpreter, Pennsylvania, Journal of, I, 355.

WILBER, DR. H. B. Superintendent of State Asylum for Idiots, IV, 605; V, 88.

WILBOR, JOHN B., JR. Appointed commissioner of deeds, Paris, V, 215.

WILCOX, JESSE. Bond for return of arms, II, 775.

WILDMAN, THOMAS. Letter from, I, 200.

WILKINSON, JAMES. Clothier General, letter from, II, 80.

WILKINSON, ROBERT. Relief, veto, VIII, 630.

WILKINSON, ROBERT F. Member of Education Unification Commission, 1899, X, 114.

WILLARD, JOHN. Justice of Supreme Court, communication from, vagrants, trial jurors, IV, 505.

WILLARD, DR. S. D. Report on insane poor, V, 583.

WILLARD ASYLUM FOR CHRONIC INSANE. Established at Ovid, V, 584, 762; appropriation for, 584, 838; erection of buildings, 837; chronic insane, transfers from poorhouses, VI, 235; expense of construction, VII, 283; advantages of, 285; number of inmates, 958.

VETOES. Additional buildings, VI, 870; new buildings, appropriation, VII, 88; various repairs and improvements, 486; new building, 583; prohibiting sale of liquors within half a mile of, VIII, 340.

WILLARD STATE HOSPITAL. Purchase of farm from member of board, alleged extravagant price, X, 412; number of visits by local managers, 415; repairs and improvements, veto, IX, 294; clergymen for, appropriation, X, 565, 783.

WILLENKS, WILLIAM (and others). Holland Land Company, purchasing property of, II, 1031.

WILLERS, DIEDRICH, JR. Secretary of State, supervises enumeration of 1875, VIII, 138.

WILLET, ISAAC. Westchester county sheriff, claim for subsistence of prisoners, I, 478.

WILLET'S POINT. Cession of land at, VI, 774.

WILLETT, COLONEL. Claim of, II, 239.

WILLIAM III. See also WILLIAM AND MARY. King of England, revolution begun by, I, 194; instructions relative to colonial union, 337; paper currency in New York, 694; policy as to public loans, III, 324; supervision of colonial affairs, IV, 178, 185; death of, I, 98.

WILLIAM AND MARY. See also WILLIAM III. Become sovereigns of England, 1, 14; effect of accession, 18; address to, by First Assembly, 22; second address, 29.

WILLIAMS, CHARLES F. Contract for department printing, X, 270.

WILLIAMS, DAVID. Convicted of murder, sentence commuted to life imprisonment, II, 578.

WILLIAMS, REV. ELEAZER. Grant of Oneida lands, II, 894.

WILLIAMS, GEORGE. Relief, veto, VI, 185.

WILLIAMS, H. A. Administrator of May Williams, Court of Claims, veto, X, 445.

WILLIAMS, JOHN. Convicted of murder, sentence commuted to imprisonment for five years, II, 621, 627.

WILLIAMS, JONATHAN. Colonel, letters from, II, 41; letter from, cession of land to United States, 628; chief engineer of the United States, services in erecting fortifications, 637, 642.

WILLIAMS, NATHAN. District attorney, letter to, Indian affairs, II, 518.

WILLIAMS, PARDON C. Supreme Court, opinion, fishing nets not public nuisance, VIII, 627.

WILLIAMS, ROBERT G. Proceedings for extradition of, III, 583, 594; not in Alabama when alleged offense was committed, 596.

WILLIAMS, SAMUEL. Justice of the peace, legalizing acts, veto, VII, 507.

WILLIAMS, THOMAS, JR. Service in exchange of prisoners, I, 476.

WILLIAMS, W. K. Canal Department, appropriation for services, veto, IX, 716.

WILLIAMS AND MANOGUE. Claim, Whitehall armory, veto, X, 650.

WILLIAMSBRIDGE. Claims against, settlement, veto, IX, 732.

WILLIAMSBURGH. Firemen, charter, veto, IV, 531.

WILLIAMSBURGH VOLUNTEER FIREMEN'S ASSOCIATION. Headquarters for, veto, X, 175.

WILLIAMSON, BENJAMIN. Member of New Jersey Commission to Procure Constitutional Convention, V, 325.

WILLIAMSON, JOHN M. Assignee of Jamaica Electric Light Company, claims against New York, veto, X, 316.

WILLIAMSPORT, PENNSYLVANIA. Railroad to Elmira, III, 527.

WILLIAMSVILLE. Main street road improvement, amending act, veto, IX, 356, 795.

WILLIAMSVILLE ACADEMY. Sale of property, veto, VI, 336.

WILLINGTON, A. A. Canal Department, appropriation for services, veto, IX, 716.

WILLS. Act relating to, II, 465, 466; legislative alteration of, 567; probate and record of, 986; modifying limitations of legislative power, 1036; revision of statutes relative to, III, 89; aiding creditors pending probate, IV, 615.

    VETOES. Relative to, II, 257, 267; amending act, VI, 505; proof of, 684; devises and bequests, preventing lapse, VII, 266; foreign, relative to, 665; probate, effect of, IX, 131; devises to charitable and religious corporations, limiting effect of, 623; construction of, X, 316; revocation of probate, jury trial, 318; Catherine L. Power, execution of certain provisions, 391; John H. Hoff, Brooklyn borough, 584; foreign certification, 585; Cunningham estate, relative to, 585.

WILLS, DAVID. President, Soldiers' National Cemetery Association, communication relative to appropriations, V, 636.

WILLSEE, JACOB. Bond for return of arms, II, 774.

WILLSEY, ISAAC. Service of process on, Van Rensselaer rent, III, 824.

WILMINGTON. Highway to North Elba, repairs, VII, 1099.

WILMOT PROVISO. South Carolina resolutions on, IV, 466; Georgia protests against, 508; Mississippi protests against, 512.

WILNA. Justices of the peace in, VII, 78. VETOES. Aid to Utica and Black River Railroad, amending act, VI, 92; aid to Black River and St. Lawrence Railroad Company, 348; excise licenses in Carthage, VII, 1047; Carthage, new union schoolhouse, appropriation, VIII, 117.

WILSON, PETER. Memorial, protests against repeal of act confirming Seneca government, IV, 507.

WILSON, THOMAS P. Relief, veto, X, 53, 61, 177.

WILSON, WILLIAM. Relief, veto, VI, 698.

WILSON, WILLIAM. New York Municipal Court attendant, claim, veto, X, 168.

WILSON, WILLIAM H. Relief, veto, VII, 803; New York fire department, pensions, veto, 1088.

WINDHOLZ, LOUIS. Court of Claims, veto, X, 946.

WINDOM, WILLIAM. United States Senator, approves appointment of Edwin A. Merritt as collector of New York, VII, 560.

WINFIELD. Teutonia Singing Society, charter, veto, VI, 341.

WINE. Manufacture of, III, 298; adulteration and sale, act relative to, VIII, 320.

WINES, E. C. Member of Prison Labor Commission, VI, 234.

WINNE, ISAAC. Albany, deputy sheriff, service of process, Van Rensselaer rent, III, 827.

WINSHIP, HOWARD. Escheat, veto, IX, 285.

WINSLOW, JOHN. General, memorial relative to pay, I, 613.

WINNEY'S BAR. Pier at, II, 562.

WISCONSIN. Flour from, transported on Erie canal, III, 893; bill for public improvements in, veto, IV, 393; tenders aid to Federal government, V, 319; pledges support to President Lincoln's administration, 348; appropriation for Antietam cemetery, 840; National Soldiers' Home, VI, 61; booths for voters, VIII, 902; provision for agricultural instruction, IX, 178.

WISCONSIN RIVER. Improvement for canal purposes, VI, 104.

WISE, DR. PETER M. Communication to Governor, relative to appointment of William Church Osborn as State commissioner in lunacy, X, 42.

WISNER, HENRY. Delegate to Continental Congress, I, 768.

WITBECK, MR. Interference in service of process, Van Rensselaer rent, III, 826.

WITHERBEE, FRANK S. Member of Canal Investigating Commission, 1899, X, 75; report on European canals, 135.

WITNESSES. In court-martial, compelling attendance of, II, 87; fined without hearing, 171; husband and wife, when incompetent, 704; accomplice turning State's evidence, 997; taking testimony in Court of Chancery, III, 649, 720; against himself, constitutional provision, IV, 310, 764; detention of, 787; V, 19, 243, 366; house of detention for, V, 181; in proceedings for removal of officers, 716; against himself, in bribery cases, VI, 37; conviction of infamous crime, effect of, VII, 197; testimony of convicts, 345; not to be unreasonably detained, 611; before legislative investigating committee, Comptroller may audit fees, VIII, 727.

    VETOES. Commission to examine, II, 227; perpetuation of testimony, 1083; attachments against, power of corporation, VI, 586; agents, informers and spies, testimony, VII, 624; testimony in action against deceased party, VIII, 292; in criminal cases, VIII, 468; fees, IX, 446, 860; conditional examination, 718.

WOLCOTT. Arms and supplies for, II, 775; police justice, veto, VII, 389.

WOLCOTT, ALEXANDER. Connecticut commissioner to settle claim against New York, II, 407.

WOLCOTT, CHARLES D. Natural history collection, purchase of, veto, VII, 467.

WOLFE, JAMES. General, conquest of Quebec, I, 640.

WOLF ISLAND BRIDGE COMPANY. Charter, veto, IX, 248.

WOLVES. Act for destruction of, I, 10; in Franklin county, rewards for destruction of, II, 1107.

WOMEN'S RELIEF CORPS HOME. Report, IX, 851; X, 31.

    VETOES. Construction, equipment and repairs, IX, 772; additional buildings, 777; electric light and power machinery, vegetable cellar, X, 545; electric light unit, 654.

WOMEN. See also MARRIED WOMEN. Disorderly, exclusion from colony, I, 116; prison for, III, 207, 208, 339, 379, 403, 443, 515, 618, 675, 716, 861, 874; V, 165; convicts, proposed retreat for, III, 875; Indian, right of suffrage, IV, 504; convicts, sending to penitentiary instead of prison, V, 293, 386; convicts, place of imprisonment, 599; American, marrying foreigners, status of children, VI, 365; convicts, where to be imprisoned, VII, 10; reformatories for, 528; eligible to school offices, 76, 423, 518, 761; Hudson House of Refuge, 529; employment in manufacturing establishments, act regulating, VIII, 163; members of boards of managers, Columbian Exposition, 933; members of World's Fair Commission, IX, 24; authorized to vote for school commissioners, 94, act unconstitutional; regulating employment in manufacturing establishments, 163; separate prison for, Auburn, 182; members of Cotton States Exposition Commission, 582; should receive same compensation as men for same work, 742; not to be employed in certain manufactories, X, 7; extending right of suffrage, 21; crimes against, needed reform in punishment, 106; commitments to houses of refuge, 117; commitments, amending New York charter, 709; voting at special elections in third-class cities, proposed grant of right, 730.

    VETOES. Imputing unchastity to, VI, 901; school officers, VII, 76; trustees or managers of charitable institutions, 761; judgments for wages, VIII, 293; reformatory for, 819; employment in manufacturing establishments, 837; IX, 477; Hudson House of Refuge, nursery cottage, VIII, 1137; Brooklyn, female delinquents, commitment to Wayside Home, IX, 733; lectures for working, amending act, 807.

WOOD. Scarcity of, II, 1094.

WOOD, ANSON S. Commissioner to examine Oneida Indian claims, report, VI, 663.

WOOD, HIRAM. Court of Claims, veto, X, 945.

WOOD, JONAH. Convicted of murder, execution suspended, Legislature grants three reprieves, II, 78; pardoned, 78.

WOOD, THADDEUS M. Onondagas request appointment as agent, II, 995.

WOODCOCK, D. P. Fowler, breakwater on lands of, VI, 331.

WOOD CREEK (Lake Champlain). Camp at, I, 137, 138; Assembly recommends discontinuance of fort at, 139; French encroachments at, 271; fort proposed at, 272; canal from, to Hudson river, II, 312, 320.

WOOD CREEK (Mohawk). Canal from, to Fort Stanwix, II, 312, 320.

WOODFORD, STEWART L. President Garfield withdraws appointment of, VII, 559.

WOODHULL. State road to Forestport, repairs, veto, VIII, 850, 1138.

WOODHULL, JESSE. Member of Council of Appointment, II, 14.

WOODHULL, NATHANIEL. Assembly, favors colonial union, I, 767; resolution thanking delegates to Congress, 768; proposed monument to, III, 214, 226; sketch of, 226.

WOODIN, WILLIAM B. Senate, remarks on opening new Senate chamber, VII, 540; member of insane asylum investigating committee, IX, 312.

WOODRUFF, ISAAC C. Colonel, United States Engineer, communication from, cession for lighthouse-keeper's dwelling, Clinton county, VI, 414.

WOODRUFF, TIMOTHY L. Lieutenant-Governor, address on reception of Prince Henry, X, 479.

WOODS. Burning of, prohibited, I, 143.

WOODS, ARTHUR. Claim against Buffalo, settlement, veto, IX, 869.

WOODSIDE WATER COMPANY, NEW YORK. VETOES. Relief, X, 175; claim against Long Island City, 326.

WOODWARD, HENRY L. Prepares index to statutes, 1886-1897, IX, 774.

WOODWORTH, G. Bond for return of arms, II, 772.

WOODWORTH, JOHN. Chosen Regent, II, 753.

WOODWORTH, SELAH. Bond for return of arms, II, 772.

WOODWORTH, WILLIAM G. Bond for return of arms, II, 772.

WOOL. Palatines not to manufacture woolen goods, I, 146; carding and spinning, II, 534; bounty for hemp production, 702; increasing price of, 1092; cultivation of, III, 126; production of, IV, 42; Maine urges increase of tariff on, V, 423.

WOOL, JOHN E. Brigadier-general, commanding northern frontier, letter to, on seizure of arms, III, 684; anxiety concerning defense of New York, V, 544; defense of New York, 545; letter from, defenseless condition of New York, 549.

WOOL, JOHN W. Major-general, delegate to Washington Peace Convention, V, 310.

WOOLEN. Manufacture exempt from taxation, II, 876; abundance of raw material, 899; statistics of manufacture, IV, 42.

WOOLWORTH, SAMUEL B. Honorary secretary, Board of Regents, compensation, veto, VII, 467.

WOOSTER, B. W. & Co. Furniture for clerk's rooms, Legislature, veto, VIII, 841.

WORCESTER. VETOES. Separate road district, VI, 196; Congregational Society, removing remains from cemetery, IX, 57.

WORCESTER'S ENGLISH DICTIONARY. Quoted, definition of "ballot," VIII, 584.

WORDEN, ALVAH. Code commissioner, VII, 183; member of Codification Commission, resignation of, IV, 488.

WORDEN, SIR JOHN. Secretary to Duke of York, letters from Governor Andros missing, IV, 184. See also WERDEN.

WORKINGMEN'S FRIENDLY SOCIETY OF AMERICA. Charter, veto, VI, 326.

WORLD'S COLUMBIAN EXPOSITION. Established in Chicago, VIII, 953, 1077; New York board of managers, 933; Governor Hill's special message, 1890, 938; act providing for fair, New York, 996; dedication of New York building, IX, 170; appropriations, 1893, 170; report of commission of 1893, 210; Governor Flower's report on New York exhibit, 317; report of general managers, 1894, 383.

WORLD'S FAIR. See also INTERNATIONAL EXPOSITION. London, 1851, IV, 509, 572; agent's report, 625; in New York, 656, 708; Paris, report of commissioner, 865; Universal Exposition, Paris, report of commissioners, V, 791; proposed exposition at Utrecht, VI, 50; Centennial Celebration, Philadelphia, 1876, 302; to commemorate discovery of America, VIII, 931; act of 1890, 933, 996.

WORLD'S FAIR COMMISSION. Created, VIII, 1077; IX, 24; New York, naval review, 1893, 24; report, 1893, 210.

WORLD'S INDUSTRIAL AND COTTON CENTENNIAL EXPOSITION. Established, objects of, VIII, 31; appropriation, 32.

WORTH, WILLIAM J. Colonel, correspondence relative to disturbance on northeastern frontier, III, 760, 762.

WORTHINGTON, GEORGE. Claim against State, Attorney-General's opinion, VII, 377; claim, veto, 381, 788; paid, 381, 788.

WOSTERGRON COMPANY (M. F.). Taxes, reimbursement, veto, X, 784.

WRIGHT, —. Keeper at Clinton prison, murder of, V, 429.

WRIGHT, ANSEL E. Canal Department, appropriation for services, veto, IX, 716.

WRIGHT, B. Appraisal of Oneida land, VI, 665.

WRIGHT, BENJAMIN. Engineer, report on Chenango canal, III, 233; surveys route for New York and Erie Railroad, 510.

WRIGHT, GEORGE. Colonel, commandant, Fort Ontario, communication from, land in front of fort, IV, 591.

WRIGHT, JACOB. Service of process on, Van Rensselaer rent, III, 824.

WRIGHT, LUTHER. Relief, veto, VI, 185, 343.

WRIGHT, PETER P. Landlord's agent, Delaware county, anti-rent troubles, IV, 300, 317.

WRIGHT, SILAS, JR. Chosen United States Senator, III, 429; resigns, IV, 154; Governor, portrait, 87.

WRIGHT, SILAS, JR.—(*Continued*).

1845. Annual message, IV, 87; finances, 87; debt against general fund, 92; policy of 1842, 93, 198; canal debt sinking fund, 95; canals constructed on credit, 96; canal debt, 96; discussion of canal policy, 99; immediate effect of policy of 1842, 101; constitutional amendments, 103; proposed amendment to confirm act of 1842, 104; limiting power to create State debts, 104; payment of canal debt, 107; Constitutional Convention, 109; State debt, objection to preferred stock, 110; common school fund, 112; instruction of common school teachers, 115; Albany normal school, 115; literature fund, 117; United States deposit fund, 118; colleges and academies, 118; loan of United States deposit fund, 120; penitentiary system, 121; prison labor, 123; Clinton prison, 124; State lunatic asylums, 125; deaf and dumb institutions, 127; New York Institution for the Blind, 128; election reform, 129; judiciary amendments, 135; removal of officers, 137; abolition of property qualifications, 137; agriculture, 138; anti-rent trouble, 139; orders out militia, anti-rent troubles, 148; punishment of disguised persons, 150, 233; loan of arms for local purposes, 150, 155; recent presidential election, 151; foreign relations, 152; election of United States Senators, 153; resignation of Nathaniel Tallmadge, United States Senator, 154; New York arsenal and Staten Island fortifications, 154; New York pilots, 156; contract for printing and binding geological survey, 162; proceeds of public lands, 162; report of agent on colonial history, 164; returns Ossining bill for two-thirds vote, 192; veto, canals, 194.

1846. Annual message, IV, 230; dignity of Legislature, 231; anti-rent trouble, 232; disturbance in Delaware county, 234; murder of Osman N. Steele, deputy sheriff, Delaware county, 235; proclamation declaring Delaware county in state of insurrection, 236, 297; commutation of persons convicted of murder of Deputy Sheriff Steele, 237, 309; proclamation declaring Delaware county in state of insurrection revoked, 238, 326; changing leasehold estates to fee-simple estates, 240; distress for rent, 241; taxation of reserved rents, 242; limiting term of agricultural leases, 244; relief of Delaware county, 246; census, 247; Indian census, 248; Constitutional Convention, 249; legislative apportionment, 250; financial condition, 251; canal debt, 252; canal tolls, 259; general fund, 260; common school statistics, 263; Albany normal school, 265; teachers' institutes, 269; literature fund, 269; United States deposit fund, 270; safety fund, 271; mariners' fund, 272; State prisons, 273; epidemic at Mount Pleasant prison, 275; Clinton prison, 276;

WRIGHT, SILAS, JR., 1846 —(*Continued*).

lunatic asylums, 278; New York Institution for the Blind, 281; Institution for the Deaf and Dumb, 282; militia, 283; State Agricultural Society, 283; general prosperity, 284; national affairs, 284; relations with Mexico, 284; Oregon controversy, 285; Commissary-General's report, 287; geological survey, 289; Indian affairs, 289, 295; land for fortifications on northwestern frontier, United States, 293; Aylesworth pardon case, 294; letter to sheriff of Delaware county, 309; death of, 383; official service, I, pref. xii.

WRIGHT ON TENANTS. Cited, IV, 358.

WRITS OF ELECTION (Assembly). Issued by Governor Dongan, I, 9, 12; by Leisler, 14, 15, 16; form of, 15; by Governor Sloughter, 18; Governor Fletcher, 31, 39, 43; by Governor Bellomont, 75; by Governor Cornbury, 98, 126; by Governor Lovelace, 132; by Governor Hunter, 174; by Governor Burnet, 220, 225, 229; by Lieutenant-Governor Clarke, 275; by Governor Clinton, 345, 457, 520; by President Colden, 650; by Governor Moore, 723, 731; by Council of Safety, II, 6.

WYDLER, ADOLPH S. Reinstatement in New York water supply department, veto, X, 815.

WYLIE, DANIEL D. Brigadier-General, Commissary-General's report, VII, 200, 316.

WYMAN, ROBERT H. Rear-admiral, on flagship Tennessee, salutes French vessel bringing delegates to Yorktown Celebration, VII, 738; escorts delegates to West Point, 740.

WYNN, JAMES C. New York, relief, veto, IX, 809.

WYNN, WILLIAM S. New York, relief, veto, IX, 809.

WYOMING COUNTY. Silk culture in, III, 945; disbandment of separate military company, VII, 826; average excise license fees, 1889, VIII, 687; highways, cost of labor system, 1892, IX, 200; insane, care of, county and State systems compared, 228.

VETOES. Aiding railroads, VI, 95; refunding moneys paid to State, 867; fishing in Tonawanda creek, 906; Pike, sale of portion of schoolhouse site, VII, 111; Boughton, coroner, legalizing acts, X, 813.

WYOMING COUNTY AGRICULTURAL SOCIETY. Escheat, veto, VI, 708.

Y.

YALE COLLEGE. Law school graduates, relative to, veto, VII, 416.

"YANKEE," THE. Warship, Spanish War, manned largely from New York naval militia, X, 17.

YARD, WESLEY S. Relief, veto, VII, 1089.

YATES, ABRAHAM. Member of Council of Appointment, II, 14.

YATES, JOHN B. Colonel, Governor's aide, sent to Niagara frontier, II, 806.

YATES, JOSEPH C. Chosen Regent, II, 707; Supreme Court, communication from, Kesler case, 921; chosen Governor, portrait, III, 1.

1823. Annual message, III, 2; tribute to framers of first Constitution, 3; judiciary, 5; militia, 7; appointment of officers, 7; common school fund, 8; suffrage, 8; Criminal Code, 9; prison discipline, 9; canals, 10; finances, 10; New Jersey boundary, 11; revision of statutes, 11; epidemic in New York, 12; fever hospital in New York, 12; prosperous condition of State, 13; purchase of Indian lands, 13; Massachusetts, South Carolina and North Carolina resolutions, 13; Georgia resolutions, 14; claims against United States, 14; Underwood relief, veto, 15.

1824. Annual message, III, 16; new judiciary system successfully established, 16; special district attorneys, 17; justices of the peace, 17; auctioneers, 18; revision of statutes, 18; South American affairs, 18; American sympathy for Greek patriots, 19; militia, 19; election of militia officers, 20; arms received from United States, 21; condition of prisons, 21; transfer of prisoners, 22; commercial intercourse with Canada, 23; agriculture, 23; domestic manufacture should be encouraged, 23; canals, historical sketch, 24; Hudson river improvement, 26; New York harbor, 28; finances, 28; salt, 29; method of choosing presidential electors, 30, 38; Tennessee resolution, protest against congressional nominations of President and Vice-President, 31; Kirby murder case, 32; lottery institutions, 33; Sunday schools, 33; treaty with Stockbridge Indians, 34; Georgia and Ohio resolutions, 34; Maine resolutions, 35; repairs at Fort Richmond, 35; Seneca Indians, missionaries, 35; settlement of State claims against United States, 36; Ohio resolutions, 36; purchase of mile-square tract, St. Regis Indians, 36. VETOES. Peck relief, III, 36; Weyburn and Jewell relief bills, 37.

Extraordinary session, III, 38; rights of people, 41; inspection of steamboats, 46; visit of Lafayette, 46; land ceded to United States at New Utrecht Point, 47, 48; treaty with St. Regis and Oneida Indians, 47; death of, legislative proceedings on, 645; official service, I, pref. xii.

YATES, DR. Establishes Chittenango Polytechnic School, III, 298.

YATES, PETER. Colonel, letter from, northern frontier, II, 101.

YATES, ROBERT. Survey of Hudson river, matter of Massachusetts boundary, I, 757.

YATES, ROBERT. Supreme Court, member of Council of Revision, II, 21; delegate to Federal Constitutional Convention, 271.

YATES COUNTY. Agricultural society in, III, 945; silk culture in, 945; exempted from Town Auditor's Act, VIII, 49; Milo, failure to make assessment, new authorized, 257; average excise license fees, 1889, 687; highways, cost of labor system, 1892, IX, 200; insane, care of, county and State systems compared, 228.

    VETOES. Altering Assembly district, V, 126; subjecting to Railroad Aid Act, VI, 214; Benton, taxes for schoolhouse, 337; Hoenig-Porter escheat, VII, 550; Dresden, amending General Village Law, 644; highways, improvement, X, 703.

YATES COUNTY AGRICULTURAL SOCIETY. Selling part of real estate, veto, VII, 1103.

YELLOW FEVER. Epidemic in Richmond county, IV, 438; hospital for patients, V, 183; patients in floating hospital, 278; danger from infected cargoes, 378; classed as quarantine disease, 418; large number of vessels from ports infected with, 844; VI, 237, 532, 625; VII, 433, 530; precautions against, VI, 236, 358; sketch of precautions against, 782; epidemic in Tennessee, VII, 316.

YELVERTON, ABIJAH, JR. Paymaster at Oswego, II, 764; funds received by, 765.

YONKERS. Number of excise licenses, 1887, VIII, 359; excise license fees, 1889, 686; tax, 1893, IX, 61; second-class city, 1905, 678.

    VETOES. Immaculate Conception Total Abstinence Society, VI, 325; completion of highways, 512; amending charter, 683; VII, 509; IX, 858; creating school commissioner districts, VI, 708; bonded debt, consolidation of, 712; ward bill, VII, 664; Society of St. Vincent de Paul, charter, 805; police, 807; land under water, conveyance, VIII, 53; Reevs, commissioner of deeds, legalizing acts, 518; water supply, amending act, 887; bonds for election purposes, IX, 61; Prime, commissioner of deeds, legalizing acts, 368; amending charter, election inspectors, also legislating certain persons out of office, 458; City Court, 791; board of police to borrow money, 870; water rents, X, 60; revising charter, 62; electric light wires and appurtenances, supervision and inspection, 433; commissioner of deeds, additional number, 437; City Court, supplementary proceedings, 522; City Court, removal of causes to Supreme Court, repeal, 819.

YONKERS RAILROAD COMPANY. Completion of road, act authorizing, IX, 270.

YORK. Capture of, II, 786; Howe, justice of the peace, legalizing acts, veto, VIII, 943; taxes, confirming and levying, veto, IX, 59.

YORK, DUKE OF. Becomes proprietor of New York, I, 2; Duke's Laws promulgated, 2; rejects propositions for Assembly, 3; receives petition for Assembly, 4; secretary's letter to Brockholls relative to Assembly, 4; letter to Brockholls promising Assembly, 5; grants Assembly, 5; proprietary powers of, 6; approves, but afterward rejects Charter of Liberties, 10; becomes James II of England, 12, 14; instructions and reports, III, 1018; documents relating to government of, IV, 180, 184; grant from, question as to New Jersey boundary, VI, 775.

YORK, HARRY. Indian interpreter, Seneca address, II, 943.

YORKSHIRE. Additional justice of the peace, veto, VIII, 338.

YORKSHIRE RURAL CEMETERY ASSOCIATION. Charter, veto, VI, 596.

YORKTOWN. Surrender of British at, I, 779; II, 150; Centennial Celebration, reception of French delegates, VII, 733; Federal appropriation for monument, 735.

YORKTOWN CENTENNIAL CELEBRATION. Reception of French delegates, VII, 733; Federal appropriation for monument, 735; French delegates visit West Point and Niagara Falls, 740; reception of German delegates, 741.

YOUNG, C. H. Judge-Advocate-General, member of auditing board of enlistments, V, 870.

YOUNG, JOHN. Governor, portrait, IV, 363.

1847. Annual message, IV, 363; new Constitution, 364; popular elections, 364; court for correction of errors, 365; review of decisions, 365; judicial districts, 365; Judiciary Act, 365; Commission on Procedure, 366; proceedings in law and equity, 366; compensation of judicial officers, 368; canals, 369; Erie canal enlargement, 369; limiting power to create State debt, 371; amount of State debt, 371; sinking funds, 371; canal revenues 373; small canal contracts desirable, 376; education, 377; appropriations for literary and charitable institutions, 378; militia, 378; corporations, 379; registry of bills and notes, 380; Missouri resolutions, 381; cession of land at Sackett's Harbor, 381; Clinton prison, appropriation for, 381; Virginia resolutions, 382; communication from Onondaga Indian chiefs, 382; Niagara county assembly districts, 383; announces death of Silas Wright, 383; distribution of geological survey to France, 384.

1848. Annual message, IV, 385; indebtedness of State, 386; enlargement of Erie canal, 388; suspension of canal construction a mistake, 389; lake harbors, 391; value of lake commerce, 391; improvement of rivers and harbors, 392; redemption of bank notes, 394; banking institutions, 394; education, 395; Albany normal school, 395; colleges and academies, 396; literature fund, 397; agriculture, 398; benefit of manufactures, 399; manufactur-

Young, John, 1848 — (*Continued*).

    ing corporations, 400; dues from corporations, 401; personal liability of corporations, 402; liability of bank stockholders, 403; agricultural schools, 404; reprieves, commutations and pardons, 405; procedure in pardon cases, 405; reducing severity of punishment, 406; State prison statistics, 406; Western House of Refuge, 408; manor excitement, 408; ejectment to test validity of Van Rensselaer titles, 412; judiciary, 414; referees in equity cases, 414; equity Special Term, 414; war with Mexico, 415; Zachary Taylor invited to visit New York, 420; cited, action to test validity of manorial title, 654; official service, I, pref. xii.

Young, John C. Damages, new capitol, veto, VII, 911.

Young, King. Seneca chief, joins in address to Governor, II, 943.

Young, Samuel. Member of Commission on Astor Claim, II, 867; appointed Secretary of State, III, 972.

Youngs, John. Member of First Legislative Council, I, 9.

Youngs, William J. Secretary to Governor Roosevelt, correspondence relative to Cayuga Indian claim, X, 128.

Youngstown. Regulating ferry at, veto, VI, 593.

Young Men's Association, Buffalo. Membership, exemption from collateral inheritance tax, veto, VIII, 732.

Young Men's Catholic Association, Rochester. Amending charter, veto, VI, 683.

Young Men's Christian Associations. General act, VIII, 379; amending general act, veto, 974.

Young Men's Christian Association, Mount Vernon. Relief, veto, X, 806.

Young Men's Christian Association, Ogdensburg. Charter, veto, VIII, 379.

Young Men's Father Mathew Total Abstinence Benefit Society, No. 1. Charter, veto, V, 654.

Young Men's Hebrew Association. Exemption from taxation and water rates, veto, IX, 869; X, 179.

Young Men's Association, Troy. Exempting property from taxation, veto, VIII, 332, 538, 733.

Young Women's Christian Associations. State executive committee, charter, IX, 86.

Youth. Selected, educated at public expense, II, 1049; III, 116, 213; Indian, instruction in normal schools, VII, 709.

Youth's Companion. Quoted, provision for ex-Presidents, VIII, 694.

Z.

Zeiser, Andrew. Kessel case, Kings county, VII, 651.

Zinc. Deposits in New York, III, 1036.

Zinke, Louis. Brooklyn, estate of, escheat, veto, VIII, 722.